D0204286

CISSP®

Certification

Second Edition

EXAM GUIDE

ALL·IN·ONE

CISSP®
Certification

Second Edition

EXAM GUIDE

Shon Harris

McGraw-Hill/Osborne

New York • Chicago • San Francisco • Lisbon
London • Madrid • Mexico City • Milan • New Delhi
San Juan • Seoul • Singapore • Sydney • Toronto

The McGraw-Hill Companies

McGraw-Hill/Osborne
2100 Powell Street, 10th Floor
Emeryville, CA 94608
U.S.A.

To arrange bulk purchase discounts for sales promotions, premiums, or fund-raisers, please contact **McGraw-Hill**/Osborne at the above address. For information on translations or book distributors outside the U.S.A., please see the International Contact Information page immediately following the index of this book.

CISSP® Certification All-in-One Exam Guide, Second Edition

67890 DOC DOC 01987654

Book p/n 0-07-222967-5 and CD p/n 0-07-222968-3
parts of
ISBN 0-07-222966-7

Publisher
Brandon A. Nordin

Vice President & Associate Publisher
Scott Rogers

Editorial Director
Gareth Hancock

Project Editor
Jody McKenzie

Acquisitions Coordinator
Jessica Wilson

Copy Editors
Lunaea Weatherstone
Jan Jue
Lisa Theobald

Proofreaders
Laurie Stewart
Karen Mead

Indexer
Valerie Perry

Computer Designers
Carie Abrew
George Toma Charbak
Lucie Ericksen

Illustrators
Lyssa Wald
Kathleen Fay Edwards

Series Designer
Peter F. Hancik

This book was composed with Corel VENTURA™ Publisher.

May more people in this world have the integrity and the gentle loving strength of **George Fairbairn**, my Grandpa.

ABOUT THE AUTHOR

Shon Harris, MCSE, CISSP, is a security consultant who provides security assessments and analysis, vulnerability testing, and solutions to a wide range of different businesses. She is an engineer in the Air Force's Information Warfare unit, which performs military base assessments and "red-teaming" activities during aggressor exercises.

Shon is a contributing writer to *Information Security Magazine* and *Windows 2000* magazine, a contributing author to *Hacker's Challenge: Test Your Incident Response Skills Using 20 Scenarios*, by Mike Schiffman (McGraw-Hill/Osborne, 2001), and author for *Mike Meyers' CISSP Certification Passport* (McGraw-Hill/Osborne, 2002). She also teaches network security and CISSP classes around the nation.

CONTENTS AT A GLANCE

Chapter 1 Reasons to Become a CISSP 1

Chapter 2 Security Trends 17

Chapter 3 Security Management Practices 49

Chapter 4 Access Control 107

Chapter 5 Security Models and Architecture 185

Chapter 6 Physical Security 253

Chapter 7 Telecommunications and Networking Security 311

Chapter 8 Cryptography 457

Chapter 9 Business Continuity Planning 549

Chapter 10 Law, Investigation, and Ethics 595

Chapter 11 Application and System Development 657

Chapter 12 Operations Security 753

Appendix A Security Policies 793

Appendix B British Standard 7799 799

Appendix C Who's Who? 801

Appendix D Gramm-Leach-Bliley Act 805

Appendix E Various Networking Components 809

Appendix F Wireless Technologies 813

Appendix G HIPAA 823

Appendix H About the CD-ROM 863

Glossary 867

Index 887

CONTENTS

Foreword xxv
Acknowledgments xxvii
Introduction xxix

Chapter 1 Reasons to Become a CISSP 1

Why Become a CISSP? 1
The CISSP Exam 2
CISSP: A Brief History 6
How Do You Become a CISSP? 7
Recertification Requirements 7
    Further Explanation of CPE Activities and Associated Credits 8
What Does this Book Cover? 8
Tips for Taking the CISSP Exam 9
    On the Day of the Exam 10
How to Use this Book 10
    References 11
    Questions 11
    Answers 15

Chapter 2 Security Trends 17

Security Trends 17
Areas of Security 20
Information Warfare 21
    Evidence of the Evolution of Hacking 21
    How Are Nations Affected? 23
    How Are Companies Affected? 25
    The U.S. Government's Actions 26
    So What Does This Mean to Us? 27
Hacking and Attacking 28
Management 30
Internet and Web Activities 31
    Two-Tier Architecture 33
    Database Roles 36
A Layered Approach 39
    Security at Different Layers 39
An Architectural View 40
    A Layer Missed 42
    Bringing the Layers Together 43
Politics and Laws 44

Education	46
Summary	46

Chapter 3 Security Management Practices **49**

Security Management	49
Security Management Responsibilities	50
Security Administration and Supporting Controls	51
Fundamental Principles of Security	53
Availability	54
Integrity	55
Confidentiality	55
Security Definitions	56
References	58
The Top-Down Approach	58
Organizational Security Model	59
Business Requirements: Private Industry versus Military Organizations	61
Risk Management	61
Risk Analysis	62
Risk Analysis Team	63
Value of Information and Assets	63
Costs that Make Up the Value	64
Identifying Threats	65
Quantitative Approach	66
Analysis Inputs and Data Gathering	67
Automated Risk Analysis Methods	67
Steps of a Risk Analysis	68
Results of a Risk Analysis	71
Qualitative Risk Analysis	72
Quantitative versus Qualitative	73
Protection Mechanisms	74
Putting It Together	77
Total Risk versus Residual Risk	77
Handling Risk	78
References	78
Policies, Procedures, Standards, Baselines, and Guidelines	79
Security Policy	79
Standards	80
Baselines	81
Guidelines	82
Procedures	82
Implementation	84
References	85
Information Classification	85
Private Business versus Military Classifications	86
Reference	89

Layers of Responsibility 89

    Personnel 91

    Structure 92

Hiring Practices 92

    Operations 93

    Termination 93

Security Awareness 94

    Different Types of Security Training 94

    References 95

Summary 95

Quick Tips 96

    Questions 99

    Answers 104

Chapter 4 Access Control 107

Access Control 107

Security Principles 108

    Availability 108

    Integrity 109

    Confidentiality 110

Identification, Authentication, Authorization, and Accountability 110

    Identification and Authentication 112

    References 116

    References 121

    Reference 123

    Authorization 123

    Single Sign-On 126

    References 128

    References 133

    References 133

Access Control Models 135

    Discretionary 135

    Reference 136

    Mandatory 136

    Reference 136

    Reference 137

    Role-Based 137

Access Control Techniques and Technologies 140

    Rule-Based Access Control 140

    Constrained User Interfaces 140

    Access Control Matrix 141

    Capability Tables 141

    Access Control Lists 142

    Content-Dependent Access Control 142

Access Control Administration 143

    Centralized 144

Decentralized 146
Hybrid 146
Access Control Methods 147
Access Control Layers 148
Administrative Controls 149
Physical Controls 151
Technical Controls 153
Access Control Types 156
Accountability 161
References 164
Access Control Practices 165
Unauthorized Disclosure of Information 165
Access Control Monitoring 168
Intrusion Detection 168
References 170
References 171
A Few Threats to Access Control 172
Dictionary Attack 173
Brute Force Attack 173
Spoofing at Logon 174
Reference 175
Penetration Testing 175
Summary 176
Quick Tips 176
Questions 178
Answers 182

Chapter 5 Security Models and Architecture 185

Security Models and Architecture 186
Computer Architecture 187
Central Processing Unit 187
Memory 189
References 189
CPU Modes and Protection Rings 193
Process Activity 195
Input/Output Device Management 198
Tying It Together 199
System Architecture 200
Defined Subset of Subjects and Objects 202
Trusted Computing Base 202
Security Perimeter 203
Reference Monitor and Security Kernel 204
References 206
Domains 206
Resource Isolation 208
Security Policy 208

Least Privilege 209

References 209

Layering, Data Hiding, and Abstraction 210

Security Models 210

State Machine Models 211

Bell-LaPadula Model 212

Biba Model 214

Clark-Wilson Model 216

Information Flow Model 217

Noninterference Model 217

Brewer and Nash Model 218

Graham-Denning and Harrison-Ruzzo-Ullman Models 218

References 220

Security Modes of Operation 220

Dedicated Security Mode 220

System-High Security Mode 220

Compartmented Security Mode 220

Multilevel Security Mode 221

References 221

Trust and Assurance 221

Systems Evaluation Methods 222

The Orange Book 222

Division D: Minimal Protection 224

Division C: Discretionary Protection 224

Division B: Mandatory Protection 225

Division A: Verified Protection 226

References 227

Rainbow Series 227

References 228

Red Book 228

Information Technology Security Evaluation Criteria 229

References 230

Common Criteria 231

Different Components of the Common Criteria 233

References 234

Certification versus Accreditation 234

Certification 234

Accreditation 234

7799 Standards 235

Open versus Closed Systems 236

Open Systems 236

Closed Systems 236

A Few Threats to Security Models and Architectures 236

Covert Channels 237

Backdoors 238

	Asynchronous Attack		239
	Buffer Overflows		240
	Summary		240
	Quick Tips		241
	Questions		245
	Answers		250
Chapter 6	Physical Security		**253**
	Physical Security		253
	Planning Process		255
	Facilities Management		255
	Physical Attributes of the Facility		257
	Construction		259
	Facility Components		261
	Computer and Equipment Rooms		262
	Physical Security Risks		264
	Physical Security Component Selection Process		265
	Security Musts		265
	Security Shoulds		265
	Backups		266
	Environmental Issues		273
	Ventilation		276
	Fire Prevention, Detection, and Suppression		276
	Types of Fire Detection		277
	Fire Suppression		281
	Administrative Controls		284
	Emergency Response and Reactions		285
	Perimeter Security		286
	Facility Access Control		286
	Personnel Access Controls		290
	External Boundary Protection Mechanisms		292
	Intrusion Detection Systems		296
	Summary		298
	References		298
	Quick Tips		299
	Questions		302
	Answers		306
Chapter 7	Telecommunications and Networking Security		**311**
	Telecommunications and Network Security		312
	Open System Interconnect Model		313
	Application Layer		316
	Presentation Layer		317
	Session Layer		318
	Transport Layer		318

Network Layer 320
Data Link Layer 320
Physical Layer 322
Tying the Layers Together 324
References 325
TCP/IP 325
TCP 326
TCP Handshake 329
Data Structures 330
IP Addressing 331
Types of Transmission 332
Analog and Digital 332
Asynchronous and Synchronous 333
Broadband and Baseband 334
Networking 334
References 335
Network Topology 335
Ring Topology 336
Bus Topology 336
Star Topology 337
Mesh Topology 337
LAN Media Access Technologies 337
References 339
References 342
References 343
References 344
Cabling 346
Cabling Problems 348
LAN Transmission Methods 350
Reference 351
LAN Media Access Technologies 352
Token Passing 352
CSMA 353
Reference 353
Collision Domains 354
Reference 355
Polling 355
Protocols 355
Address Resolution Protocol 356
References 357
Reverse Address Resolution Protocol 357
Internet Control Message Protocol 358
References 358
Networking Devices 358
Repeaters 358

Bridges 359
Forwarding Tables 360
References 361
Routers 361
Routing 363
References 365
Switches 365
References 367
VLAN 367
Gateways 368
PBX 370
Firewalls 371
Network Segregation and Isolation 388
Networking Services 388
Network Operating Systems 389
References 390
DNS 390
Internet DNS and Domains 391
Directory Services 393
References 394
Intranets and Extranets 395
References 396
Network Address Translation 396
References 397
Metropolitan Area Network 397
References 398
Wide Area Network 398
Telecommunications Evolution 399
Dedicated Links 402
T-Carriers 402
References 403
S/WAN 403
References 404
WAN Technologies 404
Reference 407
References 409
Reference 410
References 412
Multiservice Access Technologies 412
References 415
Remote Access 416
Dial-Up and RAS 416
ISDN 417
DSL 418
References 419

Cable Modems 419
Reference 420
VPN 420
Tunneling Protocols 421
References 427
References 428
Network and Resource Availability 429
Single Points of Failure 429
RAID 430
Reference 431
Clustering 431
Backups 432
Wireless Technologies 432
Wireless Communications 433
References 434
References 439
References 441
References 443
Summary 444
Quick Tips 444
Questions 448
Answers 453

Chapter 8 Cryptography 457
Cryptography 457
History of Cryptography 458
References 461
Cryptography Definitions 462
Strength of the Cryptosystem 464
Goals of Cryptosystems 465
Types of Ciphers 466
Substitution Cipher 466
Transposition Cipher 467
Running and Concealment Ciphers 468
References 468
Steganography 469
References 469
The Government's Involvement with Cryptography 470
Clipper Chip 470
References 472
References 474
Methods of Encryption 474
Symmetric versus Asymmetric Algorithms 474
References 476
References 480

Stream and Block Ciphers 480
Types of Symmetric Systems 483
References 486
Asymmetric Encryption Algorithms 489
References 491
Hybrid Encryption Methods 491
Public Key Infrastructure (PKI) 496
Certificate Authorities 497
Certificates 498
Registration Authority 498
PKI Steps 498
References 500
Message Integrity 501
One-Way Hash 501
Digital Signatures 504
Digital Signature Standard (DSS) 506
Various Hashing Algorithms 506
References 509
Attacks Against One-Way Hash Functions 509
Reference 510
One-Time Pad 510
Key Management 511
Key Management Principles 513
References 514
Link versus End-to-End Encryption 514
Reference 516
Hardware versus Software Cryptography Systems 516
E-mail Standards 517
MIME 517
Privacy-Enhanced Mail 518
Message Security Protocol 519
References 519
Pretty Good Privacy (PGP) 519
References 520
Internet Security 521
Start with the Basics 521
References 524
References 527
References 531
Attacks 531
Ciphertext-Only Attack 531
Known-Plaintext Attack 531
Chosen-Plaintext Attack 532
Chosen-Ciphertext Attack 532
Man-in-the-Middle Attack 533
Dictionary Attacks 534

Replay Attack 534
Side Channel Attacks 535
Summary 536
Quick Tips 536
Questions 540
Answers 545

Chapter 9 Business Continuity Planning 549
Business Continuity and Disaster Recovery 550
Make It Part of the Security Policy and Program 552
Business Impact Analysis 553
Interdependencies 557
Reference 558
Business Continuity Planning Requirements 558
Developing Goals for the Plans 560
Developing the Team 562
Enterprise-Wide 563
Plan Development 565
References 566
Identifying Business Critical Functions 566
Identifying the Resources and Systems that Support
the Critical Functions 566
Estimating Potential Disasters 566
Selecting Planning Strategies 566
Implementing Strategies 567
Testing and Revising the Plan 567
References 567
End-User Environment 567
Backup Alternatives 568
Hardware Backup 568
Software Backup 573
Choosing a Software Backup Facility 577
Documentation 577
Human Resources 578
Recovery and Restoration 578
Testing and Drills 579
Checklist Test 580
Structured Walk-Through Test 580
Simulation Test 581
Parallel Test 581
Full-Interruption Test 581
Other Types of Training 581
Emergency Response 582
Reference 583
Summary 584

Quick Tips 584
    Questions 586
    Answers 591

Chapter 10   Law, Investigation, and Ethics 595

The Many Facets of Cyberlaw 596
Ethics 596
    Computer Ethics Institute 598
    Internet Architecture Board 598
    Generally Accepted System Security Principles (GASSP) 599
    References 600
    Motive, Opportunity, and Means 600
Hackers and Crackers 601
    Operations Security 602
    References 607
Well-Known Computer Crimes 608
    The Cuckoo's Egg 609
    Kevin Mitnick 609
    Chaos Computer Club 610
    Cult of the Dead Cow 610
    Phone Phreakers 610
    References 612
Identification, Protection, and Prosecution 612
Liability and Its Ramifications 614
    Personal Information 617
    Hacker Intrusion 618
Types of Laws 618
    Intellectual Property Laws 620
    References 622
Discarding Equipment and Software Issues 624
Computer Crime Investigations 625
    A Different Approach 625
    Incident Handling 629
    References 630
    What Is Admissible in Court? 630
    Surveillance, Search, and Seizure 633
    Interviewing and Interrogating 635
Import and Export Laws 636
    Transborder Information Flow 636
    References 637
Privacy 637
Laws, Directives, and Regulations 639
    Health Insurance Portability and Accountability Act (HIPAA) ... 640
    Gramm-Leach-Bliley Act of 1999 640

Computer Fraud and Abuse Act 641
Federal Privacy Act of 1974 641
European Union Principles on Privacy 642
Computer Security Act of 1987 643
Security and Freedom Through Encryption Act 643
Federal Sentencing Guidelines 643
Economic Espionage Act of 1996 644
International Cooperation Efforts 644
G8 644
Interpol 645
European Commission 645
References 645
Summary 645
Quick Tips 646
Questions 648
Answers 653

Chapter 11 Application and System Development **657**

Software's Importance 657
Device versus Software Security 658
Different Environments Demand Different Security 660
E-Commerce 661
Client/Server Model 661
Environment versus Application Controls 661
Complexity of Functionality 662
Data Types, Format, and Length 663
Implementation and Default Issues 663
Implementation 664
Failure States 665
Database Management 665
Database Management Software 667
Database Models 668
Database Interface Languages 670
Relational Database Components 670
Data Dictionary 671
Integrity 673
Reference 675
Database Security Issues 675
Data Warehousing and Data Mining 680
System Development 682
Management of Development 682
Life Cycle Phases 683
Software Development Methods 697
References 698

	Change Control		698
	Capability Maturity Model		700
	Software Escrow		701
	Application Development Methodology		701
	Object-Oriented Concepts		702
	Data Modeling		709
	Software Architecture		709
	Data Structures		711
	ORBs and CORBAs		712
	Computer-Aided Software Engineering (CASE)		714
	Prototyping		715
	COM and DCOM		716
	Open Database Connectivity (ODBC)		716
	Object Linking and Embedding (OLE)		717
	Dynamic Data Exchange		718
	Distributed Computing Environment		718
	Enterprise Java Bean		719
	Expert Systems and Knowledge-Based Systems		719
	Artificial Neural Networks		722
	Java		724
	ActiveX		726
	Malicious Software (Malware)		727
	Attacks		731
	Summary		739
	Quick Tips		740
	Questions		744
	Answers		748
Chapter 12	**Operations Security**		**753**
	Operational Security		754
	Administrative Management		754
	Accountability		756
	Security Operations and Product Evaluation		757
	Input and Output Controls		763
	Electronic Mail Security		763
	References		767
	Facsimile Security		767
	References		770
	Hack and Attack Methods		770
	Operations Department		781
	Summary		782
	Quick Tips		783
	Questions		784
	Answers		789

Appendix A Security Policies **793**

    Types of Security Policies 793

        Information Protection Policy 793

        Remote Access Policy 794

        Extranet and Business Partner Policy 794

    Policy Samples 795

        Information Protection Policy 795

        Remote Access Policy 796

    Writing Security Policies 797

        References 797

Appendix B British Standard 7799 . . . . **799**

    Section Overview 799

        References 800

Appendix C Who's Who? **801**

    NSA 801

        References 801

    NIST 802

        Reference 802

    NCSC 803

        Reference 803

    ISO 803

        Reference 804

    ANSI 804

        Reference 804

    IEEE 804

        References 804

Appendix D Gramm-Leach-Bliley Act **805**

    Security Program Components 806

        Responsibility 806

        Risk Management 806

        Training 806

        Test Security Measures 806

        Service Provider 807

        Disclosing Procedures 807

        Responding to Incidents 807

    Summary 807

        References 807

Appendix E Various Networking Components **809**

    Ethernet 809

        Ethernet 10 Mbps 809

Fast Ethernet 100 Mbps—IEEE 802.3u 810
Gigabit Ethernet 1000 Mbps 810
Ethernet Frames 812

Appendix F Wireless Technologies **813**

The New Wireless Standard 813
What Is Wrong with the Current Implementations? 814

Appendix G HIPAA **823**

Are You HIPAA Compliant? 823
Oh, How It's Changed 824
What Do I Have to Do? 824
Establish Security Policies, Procedures, Standards,
and Guidelines 826
Assess the Security Architecture 826
Develop a Security Awareness Program 827
Cultural Issues 827
How Do We Implement Our Changes? 827
What Is This All For? 828
HIPAA Regulation Expectations 829
Administrative Procedures to Guard Data Integrity,
Confidentiality, and Availability 829
Physical Safeguards to Guard Data Integrity,
Confidentiality, and Availability 833
Technical Security Services to Guard Data Integrity,
Confidentiality, and Availability 835
Technical Security Mechanisms to Guard Against
Unauthorized Access to Data That Is Transmitted
over a Communications Network 836
HIPAA Security Requirements Matrix 837
IEEE Standards 860
References 862

Appendix H About the CD-ROM **863**

Running the QuickTime Cryptography Video Sample 863
Troubleshooting 864
Technical Support 864
Installing Total Seminars' Test Software 864
Navigation 864
Minimum System Requirements for Total Seminars' Software ... 865
Technical Support 865

Glossary **867**

Index **887**

FOREWORD

Information security, in today's world, is somewhat of an oxymoron. As applications and systems hit the market at a rapid-fire pace, there is less time to assess them for security. We are quickly learning from experiences like *CodeRed* and *Slammer* that we need to look deeper, but where do we start? This is a good question with a multitude of answers, all of which lead back to educating our IT force in security awareness.

In 1999, McClure, Scambray, and Kurtz introduced the IT industry to the mind of a hacker with the book *Hacking Exposed* (McGraw-Hill/Osborne). They identified a trend that was overtaking the world and provided the first published bible of defense. The Computer Emergency Response Team (CERT) formed in 1988 and dealt with six reported incidents involving information security their first year; in the first three quarters of 2001, there were 85,334 incidents. We must act on that unbelievable statistic. Complacency is not an option; efficiency in education is the key. The IT industry is growing much faster than we can educate our people to maintain it. This leaves less time for the average IT specialist and security professional to "discover" new security practices and procedures and more time for hackers to learn how to get around them. We must provide our IT specialists with the tools required to maintain a secure information system without putting their company in debt with incident recovery costs and professional consultation fees. The only way we can do that is through documentation and education.

Only a handful of books exclusively outline good practices for network security. Of those books, none of them give a practical snapshot of how systems should be set up in order to efficiently and predictably balance risk with service. In the CERT's first 11 years of existence, no one provided a complete doctrine on how to design, implement, and maintain secure information systems. The lack of standardization for security professionals inspired the formation of the International Information Systems Security Certifications Consortium, Inc. (ISC)^2, home of the Certified Information Systems Security Professional (CISSP) certification. This is the first nonvendor-specific security certification introduced to the IT industry and security world.

The need for standard guidelines on information security formed by many is much like teamwork versus individual effort. We can produce more results collectively than we can independently. We need to build a wall between our information and those who want to exploit it. Standardization combined with collaboration is the key to success. Without it, we are an unorganized force of chaos desperately grasping at our data as it flies by us into the wrong hands.

This *CISSP Certification All-in-One Exam Guide* you are about to read will bring you intimately close to information and network security. The author writes this book based on her broad range of experience in network and application security resulting from her work with the international banking industry and as a network aggressor for the Information Warfare group in the military. She has immeasurable passion for this industry. She will entertain you with her wit and beguile you with her knowledge. If your goal is to avoid becoming a CERT statistic, you have come to the right place.

Joseph Kowtko
Information Security Specialist—
Network Engineering Infrastructure Manager for
the Financial Solutions Group Logistics Getronics

ACKNOWLEDGMENTS

I would like to thank Sam Tomaino for attempting to explain to me many, many years ago how computers work. Dan Ferguson for never complaining about the bombardment of questions I continually fling his way and for fostering my never ceasing curiosity and quest for knowledge. And Joe Kowtko for the insight into the computing world and life in general that he continually provides me. Each one of these people has helped me write this book in more ways than they will ever know.

And most especially, I would like to thank my husband, **David Harris,** for his continual support and love. Without his steadfast confidence in me, I would not be able to accomplish half the things I have taken on in this lifetime.

INTRODUCTION

Computer, information, and physical security are becoming more important at an exponential rate since the tragedies of September 11, 2001. Over the last few years, the necessity for computer and information security has slowly been realized as Web sites are being defaced, denial-of-service attacks increase, credit card information is stolen, hacking tools that are openly available to the public are increasing in sophistication, and today's viruses and worms are causing more damage than ever before.

Companies have had to spend millions of dollars to clean up the effects of these issues and millions of more dollars to secure their perimeter and internal networks with equipment, software, consultants, and education. But after September 11, 2001, the necessity and urgency for this type of security has taken on a new paradigm. It is slowly becoming apparent that governments, nations, and societies are vulnerable to many different types of attacks that can happen over the network wire and air waves. These societies depend heavily on all types of computing power and functionality that is mostly provided by the public and private sectors. This means that although governments are responsible for protecting their citizens, it is slowly becoming apparent that the citizens and their businesses must become more secure to protect the nation as a whole.

This type of protection can really only *begin* through proper education and understanding, and it must continue with a dedicated execution of this knowledge. This book is written to provide a foundation to the many different areas that make up effective security. We are all in a different time and place after September 11, for better or worse, and we need to understand *all* of the threats and dangers we are vulnerable to and the steps that need to be taken to mitigate these vulnerabilities.

Reasons to Become a CISSP

In this chapter, you will learn the following information:

- The reasons to become a CISSP
- What the CISSP exam entails
- What the Common Body of Knowledge contains
- The history of (ISC)^2 and the CISSP exam
- Recertification requirements
- You will also be able to take a preassessment test to gauge your current computer and information security knowledge

To properly study for the Certified Information Systems Security Professional (CISSP) exam, you must read a stack of books to ensure that you have studied all the necessary areas this test covers. You are required to have at least three years of experience and a college degree or four years experience in one of the domains within the Common Body of Knowledge (CBK). This book is intended to combine the information from a large number of resources necessary for passing the CISSP exam into one resource. The exam covers ten domains, and each domain is a full field of study that has several books and papers written on just that subject. This book attempts to extract the necessary information out of many different types of sources for each domain that is required to pass the CISSP exam. It also serves as a reference that can be used long after you achieve the CISSP certification.

This book is also intended to welcome you to the exciting world of security and start you on a new path toward obtaining your CISSP certification!

Why Become a CISSP?

Security is a hot issue in not only the security and technology fields, but also in any organization that has computers hooked up to a network. Computer and information security used to be an obscure term known only by a few. The demand for security expertise was not high because risks were low and hacking was not a common event. Today, however, most corporations and organizations are desperately searching for talented and experienced security professionals to help them protect the resources that keep their companies

1

alive and competitive. The CISSP certification identifies you as a security professional who has successfully met a predefined standard of knowledge and experience. Keeping this certificate current shows that you are interested in keeping abreast of security technologies and events relevant to practicing information security.

There are many reasons to achieve a CISSP certification:

- To meet a growing demand and thrive in an exploding field
- To expand your current knowledge of security concepts and practices
- To bring security expertise to your current occupation
- To become more marketable in a competitive workforce
- To show a dedication to the security discipline
- To increase your salary and be eligible for more employment opportunities

The CISSP certification helps companies identify individuals who have the technical ability, knowledge, and experience to implement solid security practices, perform risk analysis, identify necessary countermeasures, and help the organization as a whole protect its facility, network, systems, and information. The CISSP certification also provides security professionals with the credential that acknowledges the skill set they want to offer to employers. Today, a greater demand is put on security as an integral part of corporate success. This, in turn, increases the demand for highly skilled security professionals. The CISSP certification shows that a formalized organization recognizes an individual's technical and theoretical security expertise and distinguishes that individual from the rest.

Security is an essential part of being a good network administrator, programmer, or engineer. Job descriptions that are not specifically targeting security professionals often require a potential candidate to understand security concepts and be able to implement them. Many organizations cannot afford a network staff and a security staff, but they understand that security has an important place in many aspects of technology. Therefore, combining security knowledge with other technical knowledge can put you ahead of other individuals who do not possess this type of insight.

The CISSP Exam

The CISSP exam covers ten domains that make up the CBK. This exam is commonly described as an inch deep and a mile wide, meaning that the questions are not necessarily very detailed in nature and do not require you to be an expert in each and every subject. However, the questions do require you to be familiar with many different subjects within the security arena.

The CISSP exam is made up of 250 multiple-choice questions, and you are given up to six hours to complete it. These questions are chosen from a large question bank to ensure that the exams are as unique as possible for each person. The exam bank is constantly changing and evolving in order to reflect the real world of security. Exam questions are rotated and replaced in the bank as the need arises. Each question has four choices with only one correct answer. Only 225 questions are scored; the remaining 25 questions are for research purposes only. These 25 questions are not distinguished from the questions that will be scored, so you will not know which questions are counted toward your overall grade. To pass the exam you must obtain a raw score of 700 points. Each question is weighted based on how well it has tested in the past, and not all questions are worth the same amount of points. The exam is not product- or vendor-oriented. Therefore, you will not have specific Windows NT or Unix questions asked of you, but you will be asked about the security models and methodologies used by these types of systems. As of this writing, the exam fee is $450.

To qualify to take the CISSP exam, you must have three years of direct work experience in one or more of the ten domains that make up the CBK, supplemented by a college degree or four years work experience in one of the ten domains. You are asked to supply the information that proves you indeed have this type of experience when you register for the exam. After you have passed the exam, you may be asked to have a sponsor sign a document vouching for your security experience. You may also need to submit a résumé demonstrating your information security experience. This helps ensure that someone who achieves the certification has real-world experience to offer companies. There is nothing like a paper certification to bring down the value of the certification for everyone. Book knowledge is extremely important for theory, concepts, and understanding standards and regulations, but it will never take the place of real, hands-on experience.

What makes this exam challenging is that most individuals who work in the security field are not familiar with all ten domains. If a security professional is considered an expert in vulnerability testing or application security, she may not be familiar with physical security, cryptography, or security practices. Studying for this exam will stretch your boundaries of knowledge within the security field.

The exam questions address the security domains that make up the CBK. These are shown in Table 1-1.

The International Information Systems Security Certification Consortium, or $(ISC)^2$, attempts to keep up with the changes in technology and methodologies brought to the security field by adding a large number of new questions to the test question bank each year. These questions are based on current technologies, practices, approaches, and standards. For example, the CISSP exam given in 1998 did not have wireless security questions, but present and future exams may contain wireless security topics because of its evolution and most recent importance to the technology industry.

Although the test is given only in English at this time, this does not mean it is exclusive to certain countries or regions. The test is based on internationally accepted information security standards and practices, and the same English language version is given throughout the world. If you look at the $(ISC)^2$ Web site for test dates and locations, you will find that this Tuesday a test may be offered in California and next Wednesday the same test may be offered in Saudi Arabia.

If you do not pass the exam, you can retake it as soon as you would like. $(ISC)^2$ used to restrict individuals to a waiting period before attempting the exam again, but this rule has been removed. Of course, it is better to take the time to properly study and go over the areas that you were weak in, but if you would like to give $(ISC)^2$ another $450 for the very next testing date, I am sure they will happily accept it.

Domain	Description
Access Control Systems and Methodology	This domain examines mechanisms and methods used to enable administrators and managers to control what subjects can access, the extent of their capabilities after authentication and authorization, and the auditing and monitoring of these activities. Some of the topics covered include: –Access control security models –Identification and authentication technologies and techniques –Access control administration –Data ownership –Attack methods
Telecommunications and Network Security	This domain examines internal, external, public, and private communication systems; networking structures; devices; protocols; and remote access and administration. Some of the topics covered include: –OSI model and layers –Local area network (LAN), metropolitan area network (MAN), and wide area network (WAN) technologies –Internet, intranet, and extranet issues –Virtual private networks (VPNs), firewalls, routers, bridges, and repeaters –Network topologies and cabling –Attack methods
Security Management Practices	This domain examines the identification of company assets, the proper way to determine the necessary level of protection required, and what type of budget to develop for security implementations with the goal of reducing threats and monetary loss. Some of the topics covered include: –Data classification –Policies, procedures, standards, and guidelines –Risk assessment and management –Personnel security, training, and awareness
Application and Systems Development Security	This domain examines the security components within operating systems and applications and how to best develop and measure their effectiveness. This domain looks at software life cycles, change control, and application security. Some of the other topics covered include: –Data warehousing and data mining –Various development practices and their risks –System storage and processing components –Malicious code

Table 1-1 Security Domains that Make Up the CBK

Domain	Description
Cryptography	This domain examines methods and techniques for disguising data for protection purposes. This involves cryptography techniques, approaches, and technologies. Some of the topics covered include: –Symmetric versus asymmetric algorithms and uses –Public key infrastructure (PKI) and hashing functions –Encryption protocols and implementation –Attack methods
Security Architecture and Models	This domain examines concepts, principles, and standards for designing and implementing secure applications, operating systems, and systems. This covers international security measurement standards and their meaning for different types of platforms. Some of the topics covered include: –Operating states, kernel functions, and memory mapping –Security models, architectures, and evaluations –Evaluation criteria—Trusted Computer Security Evaluation –Criteria (TCSEC), Information Technology Security Evaluation –Criteria (ITSEC), and Common Criteria –Common flaws in applications and systems
Operations Security	This domain examines controls over personnel, hardware, systems, and auditing and monitoring techniques. This also covers possible abuse channels and how to recognize and address them. Some of the topics covered include: –Administrative responsibilities pertaining to personnel and job functions –Maintenance concepts of antivirus, training, auditing, and resource protection activities –Preventive, dete, corrective, and recovery controls –Standards comctivepliance and due care concepts
Business Continuity Planning and Disaster Recovery Planning	This domain examines the preservation of business activities when faced with disruptions or disasters. This involves the identification of real risks, proper risk assessment, and countermeasure implementation. Some of the topics covered include: –Business resource identification and value assignment –Business impact analysis and prediction of possible losses –Unit priorities and crisis management –Plan development, implementation, and maintenance

Table 1-1 Security Domains that Make Up the CBK (continued)

6

Domain	Description
Laws, Investigations, and Ethics	This domain examines computer crimes, laws, and regulations. This includes techniques in investigating a crime, evidence gathering, and handling procedures. It also covers how to develop and implement an incident-handling program. Some of the topics covered include: –Laws, regulations, and crimes –Licensing and software piracy –Export and import laws and issues –Evidence types and admissibility into court –Incident handling
Physical Security	This domain examines threats, risks, and countermeasures to protect facilities, hardware, data, media, and personnel. This involves facility selection, authorized entry methods, and environmental and safety procedures. Some of the topics covered include: –Restricted areas, authorization methods, and controls –Motion detectors, sensors, and alarms –Intrusion detection –Fire detection, prevention, and suppression –Fencing, security guards, and security badge types

Table 1-1   Security Domains that Make Up the CBK *(continued)*

CISSP: A Brief History

Computer security has suffered a history of confused perception and ill-defined professional objectives and purposes instead of a structured and disciplined profession.

In the mid-1980s, it was recognized that a certification program was needed to bring structure to the information security profession and provide ways of demonstrating competence and providing evidence of qualifications. This effort would help the credibility of the computer security profession as a whole and the individuals who make up the profession.

In November 1988, the Special Interest Group for Computer Security (SIG-CS) of the Data Processing Management Association (DPMA) brought together several organizations that were interested in forming a security certification program. The organizations included the Information Systems Security Association (ISSA), the Canadian Information Processing Society (CIPS), the Computer Security Institute (CSI), Idaho State University, and several U.S. and Canadian government agencies. As a voluntary joint effort, these organizations developed the necessary components needed to offer a full-fledged security certification for interested professionals. The (ISC)^2 was formed in mid-1989 as a nonprofit corporation to develop a security certification program for information systems security practitioners. The certification was envisioned to measure professional competence and help companies in their selection of security professionals and personnel. The (ISC)^2 was established in North America, but has quickly gained international acceptance and offers training and testing capabilities all over the world.

Because security is a broad subject and can cover many different areas within the technology and business worlds, the group decided upon an information systems security CBK, which is made up of ten domains pertaining to every part of computer, network, business, and information security. In addition, because technology continues at a fast pace of change and evolution, staying current on security trends, technology, and business developments is a requirement to maintain the CISSP certification. The group developed a Code of Ethics, test specifications, a draft study guide, an eight-day training seminar, and the exam itself.

How Do You Become a CISSP?

To become a CISSP, you must register for the exam at **www.isc2.org**. There you will find an exam registration form that you need to fill out and send to (ISC)^2. You will be asked to provide your security work history to ensure that you have a college degree and at least three years of experience in one of the ten domains that the test covers (or four years work experience without the college degree). You will also be asked to agree to read the (ISC)^2 Code of Ethics and sign a form indicating that you understand these requirements and promise to abide by them. You then provide payment along with the registration form, where you will also indicate your preference of exam location. The numerous testing sites and dates are listed at **www.isc2.org**.

Although three or four years of related experience is required, it can be experience that was accrued over time; thus, you do not need to have performed related security tasks for three or four years in a row.

Some people feel as though they do not have the necessary experience to take this exam, but it is best to contact (ISC)^2 to see if you are actually qualified before throwing this chance away. Remember that it is experience in *one* of the domains, which could be physical security, networking, security management practices, or operations.

Recertification Requirements

Once you are successful in passing the CISSP exam, the certification is valid for three years. In order to recertify for an additional three years, you will not be required to retake exams, like Microsoft and Cisco require, but you do need to earn continuing professional education (CPE) credits. Maintaining a CISSP certification requires earning 120 CPE credits over a three-year recertification period. If you are not interested in earning the 120 credits, you can retake and pass the exam every three years to maintain your certification.

There are many types of activities that can qualify for CPE credits, and they are broken down into two main sections: activities directly related to information security, and educational activities that enhance a security professional's skill and knowledge.

Further Explanation of CPE Activities and Associated Credits

The following items can count as CPEs to keep your CISSP certification current:

- Vendor training course
- Security conference
- University or college security course
- Publishing a security article or book
- Providing security training
- Serving on a board of a professional security organization
- Self-study
- Reading a security book
- Volunteer work

Other activities may be counted as CPE credits. Contact (ISC)^2 if you have questions on other items for which you would like to obtain credit.

CISSPs have up to 120 days after the end of the certificate holder's three-year re-certification cycle to complete the necessary requirements. Any CPEs exceeding the amount required that were achieved during the last six months of the recertification cycle are carried forward for credit toward the next cycle.

Along with providing the necessary level of CPEs, CISSPs are required to pay an annual maintenance fee, due each year on the anniversary of their successful CISSP certification.

There is substantial information regarding recertification on the (ISC)^2 Web site, **www.isc2.org**.

What Does this Book Cover?

This book covers everything you need to know to become an (ISC)^2-certified CISSP. It teaches you how and why corporations develop and implement policies, procedures, guidelines, and standards. It goes over network, application, and system vulnerabilities, what exploits them, and how to counter these exploits. The book explains physical security, operational security, and why systems implement the security mechanisms that they do. It also reviews U.S. and international security criteria and evaluations that are performed on systems for assurance ratings, what these criteria mean, and why they are used. This book also explains the legal and liability issues that surround computer systems and the data they hold, security crimes, forensics, and what should be done to properly prepare computer evidence for court.

This book is meant to be a study guide for the CISSP exam, but it can also be used as a reference guide after you achieve your certification.

Tips for Taking the CISSP Exam

The test is 250 questions and you are given up to six hours to take it. Depending on the facility that hosts the test, you may or may not be allowed to bring in food or drink, so plan ahead and eat a good breakfast full of protein for brainpower. Restroom breaks are usually limited to allowing only one person to leave at a time, so drinking 15 cups of coffee right before the exam might not be the best idea.

The questions are not long, which is good because the test has so many questions, but this also means you get less information about what they are really asking for. Make sure to read the question and the answers thoroughly instead of reading a few words and assuming you know what they are asking right off the bat. Some of the answers can be subtly different from the others, so give yourself the time and patience to read through the question more than once. Like most tests, it is best to go through the questions and answer the ones that you know and come back to the ones that are causing you more difficulty. The CISSP exam is not computerized, so you will have a piece of paper with bubbles to fill in. I know you haven't seen those since the SAT, but they are back. The reason I bring this up is because if you scribble outside the lines, the machine that reads your answers may count a correct answer as wrong. So I suggest that you go through each question and mark the right answer in the booklet with the questions, if the host allows this, and then go through the questions again and fill in the bubble only when you are sure of the answer. This causes less erasing and potential problems for the scoring machine.

When you are finished, take an extra couple of minutes to make sure you answered each question and that you did not accidentally fill in two bubbles for one question. Unfortunately, you will not receive the results of your test right away. They tell you that it can take up to six weeks, but the average is two to three weeks to receive your results in the mail or through e-mail. It can be a frustrating ordeal if you don't pass, but know that some very smart and talented security professionals did not pass on their first try, mainly because the test covers so many broad topics.

If you passed the exam, the results sent to you will not contain your score; you will only know that you successfully passed. If you did not pass the exam, the results will have a breakdown of each domain, showing you where your weak areas are.

One of the most commonly heard complaints about this exam is the exam itself. The questions are not long-winded, like many Microsoft tests, but at times it is difficult to decipher between two answers that seem to say the same thing. It has also been said that the test seems to be a bit subjective. For example, it might be easy to answer a technical question that asks for the exact mechanism used in Secure Sockets Layer (SSL) that protects against man-in-the-middle attacks. It's not quite as easy to answer a question that asks if an eight-foot perimeter fence provides low, medium, or high security. I don't say this to criticize the (ISC)² and the people who write the test, I only say it to help you better prepare for the test. This book covers all the necessary material for the test, as well as many questions and self-practice tests. Many of these questions are formatted in a way to better prepare you for what you will see on the test. So make sure to read all the material in the book, and pay close attention to the questions and their formats. Even if you know the subject quite well, you can still get some answers wrong—it is part of learning how to take tests in general.

Familiarize yourself with industry standards and expand your technical knowledge and methodology outside the boundaries of what you use today. I cannot stress enough that just because you are the top dog in your particular field, it does not ensure that you are properly prepared for each and every domain this exam covers. Run through the assessment test in this chapter to gauge where you stand and be ready to read a lot of material you have not read before.

On the Day of the Exam

Some key things to remember about exam day are the following:

- Pay attention to your time—at the three-hour mark you should have completed at least 50 percent of the exam (125 questions).

- Use all of the time you have.

- Read each question at least twice.

- There are no absolutes on what will work best for each candidate taking the exam. Some candidates prefer to answer all the "easy" questions first and then do the "hard" questions. Some like to highlight those they are unsure of and go back again to those questions, others just persevere slowly through each question, finish, close the book and turn it in. Whatever is your most comfortable mode for taking the exam, follow it—just keep your time restrictions in account.

- Bring something to snack on. Most exam times begin in the morning and continue through the lunch hour into the afternoon. If you think you will need sugar to get through, bring a candy bar; if you will need something more healthy to keep your energy level high, bring a snack such as fruit or a protien bar.

- Take a stretch break—it may help more oxygen flow to the brain. Most exam proctors will allow you to take a stretch break at the back of the room.

- Do not plan anything for after the exam except rest and relaxation.

How to Use this Book

A lot of effort has gone into putting all the necessary information into this book; now it is up to you to put the effort into truly understanding this material and the necessary concepts. To best benefit from this book, you might want to use the following study method:

1. Study each chapter carefully and make sure you understand each concept presented. There are many concepts you need to fully understand, and glossing over a couple here and there could be detrimental in the end.

2. Make sure to study and answer all of the questions at the end of the chapter and on the CD included with the book. If any of the questions confuse you, go back and study those sections again. Remember, some of the questions on the actual exam are a bit confusing because they do not seem straightforward. I have attempted to do the same on several questions to prepare you for this. So do not ignore the confusing questions thinking they're not worded well, but pay even closer attention to them because they are there for a very distinct purpose.

3. If you are not familiar with specific topics, such as firewalls, laws, physical security, or protocol functionality, use other sources of information (books, articles, and so on) to get more in-depth understanding of those subjects. Don't just rely on what you think you need to know to pass the CISSP exam.

4. After reading this book, study the questions and answers, and take the practice tests. Then review the (ISC)^2 study guide and make sure you are comfortable with each bullet item presented. If there are some items you are not comfortable with, revisit those chapters.

5. If you have taken other certification exams, such as Cisco, Novell, or Microsoft, you might be used to having to memorize details and configuration parameters. But remember, the CISSP test is an inch deep and a mile wide, so make sure you understand the concepts of each of the subjects *before* trying to memorize the small, specific details.

References

(ISC)^2: **www.isc2.org**

CSI ("Should You Take the CISSP Exam?"): **www.gocsi.com/cissp.htm**

CISSP.com Web Portal: **www.cissps.com**

CISSP and SSCP Open Study Guides: **www.cccure.org**

Questions

To get a better feel for your level of expertise and your current level of readiness for the CISSP exam, run through the following questions:

1. What is derived from a passphrase?

   A. Personal password

   B. Virtual password

   C. User ID

   D. Valid password

2. Which access control method is user-directed?

   A. Non-discretionary

   B. Mandatory

C. Identity-based

D. Discretionary

3. Which item is not part of a Kerberos authentication implementation?

A. Message authentication code

B. Ticket-granting ticket

C. Authentication service

D. Users, programs, and services

4. If a company has a high turnover rate, which access control structure is best?

A. Role-based

B. Decentralized

C. Rule-based

D. Discretionary

5. In discretionary access control, who/what has delegation authority to grant access to data?

A. User

B. Security officer

C. Security policy

D. Owner

6. Remote access security using a one-time password scheme is an example of which of the following?

A. Something you have

B. Something you know

C. Something you are

D. Two-factor authentication

7. What is a crossover error rate (CER)?

A. Rating used to rank a biometric system

B. The number of Type I errors

C. The number of Type II errors

D. The number reached when Type I errors exceed the number of Type II errors

8. What does a retina scan biometric system do?

A. Examines the pattern, color, and shading of the area around the cornea

B. Examines the patterns and records the similarities between an individual's eyes

C. Examines the pattern of blood vessels at the back of the eye

D. Examines the geometry of the eyeball

9. If you are using a synchronous token device, what does this mean?

  A. The device synchronizes with the authentication service by using internal time or events.

  B. The device synchronizes with the user's workstation to ensure that the credentials it sends to the authentication service are correct.

  C. The device synchronizes with the token to ensure that the timestamp is valid and correct.

  D. The device synchronizes by using a challenge-response method with the authentication service.

10. What is a clipping level?

  A. Threshold for an activity

  B. Size of control zone

  C. Explicit rules of authorization

  D. Physical security mechanism

11. Which intrusion detection system would monitor user and network behavior?

  A. Statistical

  B. Signature-based

  C. Static IDS

  D. Host-based

12. When should a Class C fire extinguisher be used instead of Class A?

  A. When electrical equipment is on fire

  B. When wood and paper is on fire

  C. When a combustible liquid is on fire

  D. When the fire is in an open area

13. How does Halon suppress fires?

  A. It reduces the fire's fuel intake.

  B. It reduces the temperature of the area.

  C. It disrupts the chemical reactions of a fire.

  D. It reduces the oxygen in the area.

14. What is the problem with high humidity in a data processing environment?

  A. Corrosion

  B. Fault tolerance

  C. Static electricity

  D. Contaminants

15. What is the definition of a power fault?

    A. Prolonged loss of power

    B. Momentary low voltage

    C. Prolonged high voltage

    D. Momentary power outage

16. Who has the primary responsibility of determining the classification level for information?

    A. Functional manager

    B. Middle management

    C. Owner

    D. User

17. Which best describes the purpose of the ALE calculation?

    A. Quantifies the security level of the environment

    B. Estimates the loss potential from a threat

    C. Quantifies the cost/benefit result

    D. Estimates the loss potential from a threat in a year span

18. How do you calculate residual risk?

    A. Threats × risks × asset value

    B. (Threats × asset value × vulnerability) × risks

    C. SLE × frequency = ALE

    D. (Threats × vulnerability × asset value) × control gap

19. What is the Delphi method?

    A. A way of calculating the cost/benefit ratio for safeguards

    B. A way of allowing individuals to express their opinions anonymously

    C. A way of allowing groups to discuss and collaborate on the best security approaches

    D. A way of performing a quantitative risk analysis

20. What are the necessary components of a smurf attack?

    A. Web server, attacker, and fragment offset

    B. Fragment offset, amplifying network, and victim

    C. Victim, amplifying network, and attacker

    D. DNS server, attacker, and Web server

21. In phone freaking, what is a red box?

    A. Voltage manipulation

    B. Replaying the noise coins make when dropping into a pay phone

C. Using a handheld device attached to a live phone wire to intercept calls

D. Tone manipulation

22. What do the reference monitor and security kernel do in an operating system?

A. Intercepts and mediates subjects attempting to access objects

B. Points virtual memory addresses to real memory addresses

C. Houses and protects the security kernel

D. Monitors privileged memory usage by applications

Answers

1. B.
2. D.
3. A.
4. A.
5. D.
6. A.
7. A.
8. C.
9. A.
10. A.
11. A.
12. A.
13. C.
14. A.
15. D.
16. C.
17. D.
18. D.
19. B.
20. C.
21. B.
22. A.

Security Trends

In this chapter, you will learn about the following items:
- Evolution of computing and how it relates to security
- Different areas that fall under the security umbrella
- Information warfare
- Security exploits
- A layered approach to security
- Politics that affect security

Security is a fascinating topic because it covers so many different areas (physical, network, platform, application, and so on), each with its own risks, threats, and solutions. When information security is discussed, it is usually about hackers and operating system vulnerabilities. Although these are big parts of security, they are only two components within a large sea of security issues. Hacking is thought about most because that is what is in the headlines and usually what fascinates the media. Hacking is flashy and newsworthy, while not much coverage is given to what is going on behind the scenes with corporations' global security issues and the Internet as a whole.

Security Trends

It is interesting to pick up various computer books and see that there is usually a history section that sets the stage for where society is today pertaining to computing and data processing. Unlike histories that tell of times long past, the history of computing usually starts as recently as the 1960s. A lot has happened in a short period of time, and computer security is just starting to reach its time in the limelight.

Twenty years ago, the only computers were mainframes. They were few and far between and used for specialized tasks, usually running large batch jobs and complex computations. If users were connected to the mainframes, it was through dumb terminals that had limited functionality and were totally dependent on the mainframe for their operations and processing environment. This was a *closed environment* with little risk of security breaches or vulnerabilities being exploited. This does not mean that things were perfect, that security vulnerabilities did not exist, and that people were in a computing utopia. Instead, it meant there were a handful of people working in a "glass house" who knew how to operate the computer. They decided who could access the mainframe and when. This provided a much more secure environment, because of its simplicity, than what we see in today's distributed world.

In the days of mainframes, Web sites describing the steps of how to break into a specific application or operating system did not exist. The network stacks and protocols being used were not as fully understood by such a vast amount of people as they are today. Point-and-click utilities that could overwhelm buffers or interrogate ports were nonexistent. This was a truly closed environment that only a select few understood.

If networks were connected, it was done in a crude fashion for specific tasks, and corporations did not totally depend on data processing as they do today. The operating systems of that time had problems, software bugs, and vulnerabilities, but not many people were interested in taking advantage of them. Computer operators were at the command line and if they encountered a software problem, they usually just went in and manually changed the programming code. All this was not that long ago, considering where we are today.

As companies became more dependent on the computing power of mainframes, the functionality of the systems grew and various applications were developed. It was clear that only giving employees small time slices of access to the mainframes was not as productive as it could be. Processing and computing power was brought closer to the employees, enabling them to run small jobs on their desk computers while the big jobs still took place within the "glass house." This trend continued and individual computers became more independent and autonomous, only needing to access the mainframe for specific functionality.

As individual personal computers became more efficient, they continually took on more tasks and responsibilities. It was shown that several users accessing a mainframe was inefficient and that some major components needed to be more readily available so users could perform their tasks in an efficient and effective way. This thinking brought along the birth of the client/server model. Although many individual personal computers had the processing power to compute their own calculations and perform their own logic operations, it did not make sense that each computer held information that was needed by all other computers. Programs and data were centralized on servers with individual computers accessing them when necessary and accessing the mainframes less frequently, as shown in Figure 2-1.

As computing and processing was brought closer to the people, the individuals who used computers learned more about using the technology and getting the most out of it. However, the good things in life often have a darker side. Bringing technology down from the pedestal of the mainframe and into so many individuals' hands brought a lot of issues that never had to be dealt with in the mainframe days. Now there were thousands of people not versed and experienced in computing who had much more access to important data and processes. Barriers and protection mechanisms were not in place to protect employees and systems from mistakes, so important data got corrupted accidentally, and individual mistakes affected many other systems instead of just their own.

Because so many more people were using systems, the software had to become more idiot-proof so that a larger audience could use the same platform. Computer operators in the mainframe days understood what the systems expected, knew how to format input, and properly read output. When this power was put into individuals' desktops, all imaginable and unimaginable inputs were used, which corrupted information and mangled operating systems.

Figure 2-1   This figure shows the relationship among a mainframe, servers, and workstations.

Companies soon realized that employees had to be protected from themselves and the data had to be protected from mishaps and mistakes. The employees needed layers of software between them and the operating system components and data they could destroy. These layers not only brought safety by taking individuals away from the core of the operating systems and files, but functionality continued to be inserted to make computers more useful to businesses and individuals.

As the computing world evolved, symbiotic relationships grew among the technological advances of hardware, circuitry, processing power, and software. Once a breakthrough was made that enabled a computer to contain more memory and hard drive space, new software was right on its heels to use it and demand more. When software hit a wall because it was not supplied with the necessary registers and control units, the hardware industry was Johnny-on-the-spot to develop and engineer the missing pieces to the equations. As the hardware end grew to provide a stable and rich platform for software, programmers developed software that provided functionality and possibilities not even conceived of a few years earlier. It has been a wonderful game of leapfrog that does not seem to have any end in sight.

Lovely story, but what does it mean to security?

In the beginning, the issues associated with bringing computing closer to individuals brought along many mistakes, technological hurdles, and operational issues not encountered in the workforce before. Computers are tools; just as a knife can be a useful tool to cut meat and vegetables, it can also be a dangerous tool if it is in the hands of someone with malicious intent. The vast capabilities and functionality that computers have brought to society have also brought complex and troubling methods of destruction, fraud, abuse, and insecurity.

Because computers are built on layers (hardware platform, chips, operating systems, network stacks, services, and applications), these complex issues have been interwoven throughout the stratum of computing environments. Plugging the holes, writing better software, and providing better perimeter security is often easier said than done because of the density of functionality within an infrastructure, interoperability issues, and the availability of the necessary functionality.

Over a short period of time, people and businesses have come to depend greatly upon computer technology in many different aspects of their lives. Computers run public utilities, military defense systems, financial institutions, and medical equipment, and are heavily used in every possible business sector. Almost every company relies on data processing for one reason or another. This level of dependence and the extent of integration that technology has attained in our lives have made security a much more necessary and essential discipline.

Computer security is a marathon to be run at a consistent and continual pace. It is not a short sprint, and it is not for those who lack dedication or discipline.

Areas of Security

Security has a wide base that touches on several different areas of life. The developers of the CISSP exam had the vision to understand this and demand that an individual who claims to be a security expert and wants to achieve this certification must also show that his expertise does not just lie in one area of security. There are many areas of security that affect each other. Physical security is interrelated with information security, database security lies on top of operating system security, operations security affects how computer systems are used, disaster recovery deals with systems in emergency situations, and almost every instance has some type of legal or liability issue tied to it. Technology, hardware, people, and procedures are woven together as a security fabric, as illustrated in Figure 2-2.

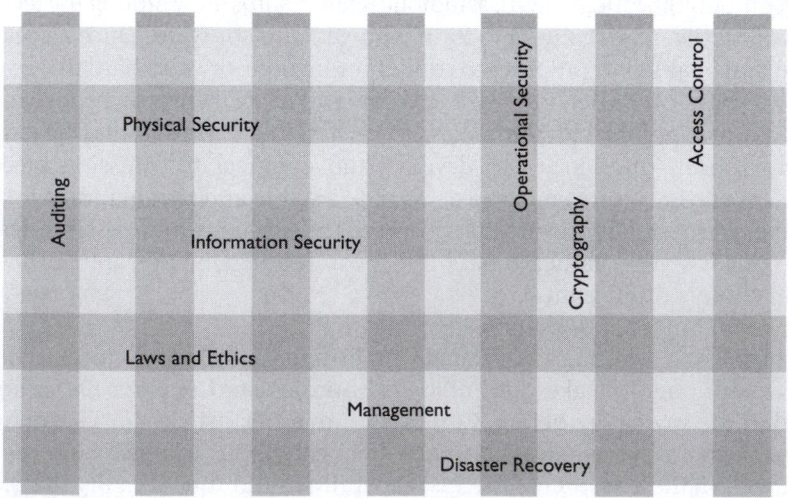

Figure 2-2 Technology, hardware, people, and procedures are woven together as a security fabric.

When it is time to chase down a specific problem, several layers of unraveling may need to take place and the pieces of the puzzle need to be understood so the best and most effective solution can be provided. The more stones that get lifted seem to find layers of possibilities that can be used for good or, in some cases, evil.

The next sections address some specific issues in security as it pertains to computers, information, and organizations. This is not an attempt to cover all relevant subjects, but to show specific instances to get an idea of the vastness of areas that security can touch. The information in these sections is provided to set the stage for the deeper levels of coverage that will be addressed in the following chapters.

Information Warfare

Computers and networks touch every facet of modern life. We are increasingly dependent on computer/network technology for communication, funds transfers, utility management, government services, military action, and maintaining confidential information. We use technology to provide energy, water supplies, emergency services, defense systems, electronic banking, and public health services. At the same time, this technology is being used in a form to disrupt communications and perform a variety of illegal activities. This technology is used to steal credit card numbers, perform fraudulent use of the telephone systems, illegally transmit trade secrets and intellectual property, deface Web sites for political reasons, disrupt communications, reveal critical national secrets and strategies, and even commit extortion.

The term "information warfare" covers many different activities that pertain to individuals, organizations, and nations. Governments have used information warfare tactics to gather tactical information for years. Organizations have stolen trade secrets and plans of the competition's new products before they were released. Individuals have also used computers to steal money, gain personal financial information, and steal individual identity, deface Web sites, and cause destruction to draw attention to a particular cause.

Many of the hacking activities, viruses, and malware incidents that have been seen so far have been relatively benign. Most were carried out just to prove to the attacker that he is indeed clever enough to disrupt some businesses here and there, but not inflict the type of damage that is actually possible. Even though one of the worms released, called "The Naked Wife," actually deletes operating system files, it is only a lightweight. It is only a small step away from the more devastating destruction possible with worms and viruses. The developer of this worm is only getting self-satisfaction from the endeavor—the developer receives no money, trade secrets, political statements, or crucial military information. But the trend of joyride hacking is showing evidence of evolving into profit-driven activities. As the old saying goes, "Why did the thief rob the bank? Because that is where the money was kept." Why are thieves attacking computers? Because that is where financial information and critical data are kept today.

Evidence of the Evolution of Hacking

Several incidents indicate that not only is hacking activity on the rise, but that the sophistication of the attacks is advancing rapidly. Alarmingly, a majority of attacks are using methods that have been understood for quite some time and for which fixes have been readily available. This proves that not enough network maintainers have kept up to date on security changes and installed the necessary patches or configurations.

It was discovered that a group of European hackers has been exploiting various computer vulnerabilities to steal millions of credit card numbers from U.S. computer systems associated with e-commerce and online banking, as shown in Figure 2-3. The FBI and Secret Service have been working with the National Infrastructure Protection Center (NIPC) to investigate this series of hacker attacks. The attackers actually contact the financial institutions and use extortion to increase the bounty from their misdeeds. They offer a "security service" to patch the systems and if the institutions do not agree to pay, the attackers threaten more damage such as posting customers' credit card numbers on Web sites available to the public. Many times this credit card information is sold to other organized crime groups.

The public only hears about the viruses, worms, and hacks that make the news. Many other types of attacks are underway, and they will only become more prevalent. The main reason the public was being continually informed of the European hackers is because they are affecting so many financial institutions and customers. The FBI and Secret Service need the public to be aware and take the necessary steps to help stop this type of activity.

There are many other financially motivated attacks. One involved a hacker who claimed to be 19 years old and from Russia. After he stole up to 300,000 card numbers from CD Universe customers in December 1999, he contacted the company, explained his actions, and then asked for a $100,000 ransom. When this money was not paid to him, he released thousands of the credit card numbers on the Internet. Another Russian hacker stole more than 55,000 credit cards from CreditCards.com. Again, a $100,000 ransom was requested and after being ignored, 25,000 card numbers were posted on a Web site.

Bibliofind, an online bookseller service, realized attackers had been accessing customer credit card information every month between October 2000 and February 2001. The credit card information of more than 98,000 customers was compromised.

Two hackers published a program that breaks the encryption mechanisms on older versions of IBM's e-commerce software. Using this tool and taking advantage of a server software flaw pertaining to address formatting, anyone can get the usernames and passwords of each and every account on a site using IBM's Net.Commerce and WebSphere

Figure 2-3   Attackers have been able to access critical information through Web servers.

Commerce Suite software. The hackers reported that they knew of more than 330 Web sites vulnerable to this type of attack.

Egghead.com in California had reports from some customers that their credit card numbers were stolen, and one person reported having a debit charge to a Web site in Russia.

In September 2000, Western Union shut down its Web site for five days after hackers stole more than 15,000 customer credit card numbers. Microsoft itself was attacked and the source code of a new product could have easily been manipulated or stolen.

It has been reported that many financial institutions and brokerage firms have paid "hush money" to hackers who have then carried out extortion acts. In October 29, 2002, a seminar sponsored by Cable & Wireless Internet Services, addressed a 127-page study that details these issues along with others. The goal was to open others' eyes to the dependency of these types of institutions on public telecommunications systems, outsourcing services, and the growth of wireless technologies that open the door to these types of compromises.

In April 2001 a large credit card company experienced a $20 million extortion attempt. In April 2002 the Bank of the State of California found out that 265,000 state employees had had their personal information stolen by a hacker. In August of 2002 Daewoo Securities found out that $21.7 million in stock was illegally sold.

These examples represent only a small percentage of all the hacking activity that is going on. These attacks were identified and reported, but most are not. Many organizations do not report hacking activity because they are afraid of hurting their reputation, losing the faith of their customer base, and adversely affecting their shareholders and stock prices. Other attacks are not even realized or identified, and thus not reported. Computers and networks are great tools that have brought society much advancement, but like many other tools, they are also used for sinister gains.

How Are Nations Affected?

The art of war requires soldiers to outmaneuver the enemy and strike them down if necessary. In past wars, the enemy was usually easily detected. They were driving a tank, bombing from an airplane, attacking from a submarine, or shooting intercontinental missiles. Today the enemy is harder to find, some attacks are harder to track, and the objectives of the attacker are at times more nebulous. Many governments' military intelligence have had to develop new methods of collecting information on potential foreign enemy movement, surveillance techniques, and proving guilt of criminal activities.

Although militaries still train most soldiers how to shoot, fight in combat, and practice evasive maneuvers, a new soldier is being taught and molded. Because a majority of the military vehicles, weapons systems, and communication systems are controlled by technology, new soldiers need to know how to use these technological tools to achieve the same goal of the soldier of the past—to win in war. Not only do today's soldiers need to know how to operate the new technology-driven weapon systems, but they also need to know how to defend these systems from attacks and possibly attack the enemy's defense systems. Figure 2-4 shows how attacks can come from many different sides.

Disrupting communication has always been an important tactic in war because it impedes proper planning and warnings of imminent attacks. Knocking out communication lines is one of the first steps in the recipe of a successful attack. Today, the military's

Figure 2-4 Information warfare tactics come in many forms from many origins.

communication is handled through computer-based systems, and the tools to disrupt communication of the enemy have changed.

For example, the CIA reported to a U.S. congressional committee that foreign nations include information warfare in their military arsenal and provide defensive and offensive attack methods. These nations are devising documentation, strategic plans, and tools to carry out information warfare on other nations.

During the Gulf War in 1990, it was reported that hackers from the Netherlands penetrated 34 American military sites that supported Operation Desert Storm activities. They extracted information about the exact location of military troops, weapon details, and movement of American warships. It could have been a different war if Saddam Hussein had actually bought this information when it was offered to him, but he did not—he thought it was a trick.

In another example, it was reported that the Irish Republican Army stole telephone bills to determine the addresses of potential targets in their political attacks. Authorities seized a batch of computer disks in Belfast and were able to decrypt the information after months of effort. This information was most likely gained by successfully hacking into the telephone company's database.

A report declassified in May 1995 stated that prior to the August 1991 coup attempt in Russia, the KGB had been writing and developing viruses to disrupt computer systems during times of war. Another report by the U.S. Defense Intelligence Agency indicated that Cuba had developed viruses to infect and damage U.S. civilian computers. There is no written proof that these viruses were released and actually caused damage, but there is no proof that they weren't either. It has also been reported that during the 1998 Kosovo air campaign, false messages were injected into Yugoslavia's computer-integrated air defense systems to point the weapons at false targets. It is clear that military use of computer-based tools and attacks is growing in sophistication and utilization.

Almost every task in an individual's day interrelates with a technology that is controlled or monitored by a computer-based system. Turning on the lights, paying a gas bill, flying on a plane for a business trip, talking on the telephone, and receiving medical treatments are all events that depend on large computer systems monitoring and providing the flow of service. Even sophisticated military defense systems rely on commercial power, communication, transportation, and monitoring capabilities, which are computer based. A country's strength relies on its privately owned critical infrastructures and industries. These private sector infrastructures have already been victimized by computer attacks. A concerted attack on any of these key economic sectors or governmental services could have widespread ramifications. Most governments have recognized this vulnerability and have started taking steps to evade these types of attacks and provide the necessary mechanisms to enable a quick and efficient recovery after an attack.

Enemy bullets used to come only from guns. Now different types of bullets come from laptops and personal computers. The next war could target a country's infrastructure with the new weapons—computer-generated attacks. Several factions of militaries are developing more robust and skilled information warfare units to act defensively and offensively in the best interest of their nation. There is a good reason. Future wars and power struggles may take place over computer lines instead of the more traditional battlefield.

How Are Companies Affected?

Many companies fail to understand how security implementations will help their bottom line: the gross margin. After all, business is done to make profit and if there is not a direct correlation for an item that ties in neatly to the linear cost and profit concept, that item is often pushed to the back of the bus. However, today many companies are finding out how security affects their bottom line in ways they never expected.

If a company suffers a security breach, it will have to deal with a wide range of issues that it most likely is not prepared for. Several companies recently had their databases attacked and their customers' information compromised. Once customers find out that a company is not protecting their confidential and financial information properly, they will often take their business elsewhere. If the number of customers affected is in the range we have seen over the last year (10,000 to 300,000 credit cards stolen at a time), and if the company loses this many customers at one time, many businesses would go out of business. Of course, these events also affect the reputation of the company, their shareholders, and their stock prices. In addition, the customers can sue the company, which could incur punitive damages and court fees. This would definitely impact the bottom line.

Organizations have had trade secrets and intellectual property stolen by employees who left to work for a competitor. In these instances, unless the original company took the proper steps to protect this data and inform their employees that this action is wrong, the company has no legal leg to stand on. The company has to practice due care to protect its intellectual property from competitors inside and outside its walls.

We are seeing more and more cases of employees being fired for improper use of computer systems. However, if companies do not take the proper steps by having a comprehensive security policy in place and providing security awareness to the employees, they are often successfully sued for unfairly ending employment.

Another way a company can lose money and time is by its readiness to react to a situation. If a network does not have properly configured security mechanisms, the company's IT staff usually spends unnecessary time and resources putting out fires. In addition, when they are racing in a chaotic manner to find a solution, they may be creating more open doors into the network without realizing it. Without proper security planning, a lot of money, staff productivity, and time are wasted that could be used for other tasks.

Many companies are covered by insurance in case of a natural disaster or a major security breach. However, to get a good insurance rate, companies must provide the necessary responsible and secure foundation and prove that they are doing all that they can to protect their own investments. In some cases, insurance providers refused to pay for a company's loss because the correct security measures were not in place. In a recent case, a company indeed did not provide a security policy, proper security mechanisms, and an updated disaster plan. The insurance company won the case in court and the company lost a lot more than just a court case.

Every business market is full of competition. If a company endures a security compromise that makes the press—which has been happening almost every month over the last year—they will have an even harder time attracting new business. A company wants to be in a position where all the customers come to it when another company suffers a security compromise, not the other way around.

The U.S. Government's Actions

One of the U.S. government's responsibilities is to protect American resources, people, and their way of life. One complex task the government has been faced with recently is protecting several critical infrastructures from computer-based attacks. Because computer technology is relatively young and changing rapidly, and because security has only come into real focus over the last few years, all these core structures contain their own vulnerabilities. If attackers disrupt these structures, the ramifications can be far reaching. For example, if attackers could bring down electrical grids forcing the government to concentrate on that crisis, they could then perform military action attacks from another side. This might sound like a John Grisham novel, but scenarios like this need to be thought through, and defensive plans must be devised. One of the biggest threats we face is that terrorists or a hostile nation will attempt to inflict economic damage, disrupt business or productivity, and degrade our defense response by attacking the critical infrastructures.

On July 15, 1996, President Clinton approved the establishment of the President's Commission on Critical Infrastructure Protection (PCCIP). The responsibility of this commission was to investigate the types of attacks that were happening, extrapolate how attacks could evolve in the future, determine how they could affect the nation's computer infrastructures, and assess how vulnerable these structures were to such attacks at that time.

The returned report card was very sobering. The PCCIP published its report "Critical Foundations: Protecting America's Infrastructures" in 1997. The report outlined the current vulnerability level of critical U.S. infrastructures pertaining to criminal activity, natural disasters, international terrorists, hackers, national intelligence, and information warfare. Long-standing security weaknesses were identified and reported, placing federal operations at serious risk. In response to this report, President Clinton signed two orders, Presidential Decision Directives (PDD) 62 and 63, to improve the nation's defenses against terrorism, other computer-based attacks, and information warfare activities. The focus of these directives was to address cyberattacks at a national level.

The report recognized that many of the nation's critical infrastructures were privately owned and operated. This meant that there needed to be a marriage between these private organizations and government services to protect all of America's interests pertaining to these vulnerabilities.

It was obvious that the government and the private sector had to work together to properly and successfully fight this battle. There would be little benefit if the government services tried to provide this protection all by themselves. In fact, it was recognized that these government departments could not provide this level of protection without the help and sharing of information with the public sector. A new National Coordinator within the Executive Office of the President was appointed to facilitate a partnership between the government and the private sector. The goal was for the government and the private sector to work together to strengthen the nation's defenses against cyberterrorism, theft, fraud, and other criminal activity. This produced the Critical Infrastructure Assurance Office (CIAO) under the Department of Commerce, Information Sharing and Analysis Centers (ISACs), and the NIPC under the sponsorship of the FBI.

ISAC provides a mechanism that enables information sharing among members of a particular industry sector. The information comes from public sector organizations and government agencies, and is shared by both. Sources of information can be authenticated or anonymous, and the information can pertain to vulnerabilities, incidents, threats, and solutions. Submitted information is directed to the appropriate team members, who then investigate each submittal, quantify the seriousness of the vulnerability, and perform a trend analysis to identify the steps that might thwart this type of attack. The outcome is to enhance the security of individual organizations and the entire nation one industry sector at a time.

In 2002 President Bush created the Office of Homeland Security in response to the attack on the United States on September 11, 2001. Information technology and cybersecurity were included, and specific committees and roles were developed to protect against attacks that could negatively affect the nation's infrastructure. The bill was signed November 25, 2002, and allocated $2.12 billion for technology and cybersecurity.

These are just some of the changes that have been taking place, which shows the elevation of the importance of computer, business, architecture, personnel, and infrastructure security.

So What Does This Mean to Us?

Evidence and trend analysis show that people, businesses, and countries are becoming increasingly dependent on computer/network technology for communication, funds transfers, utility management, government services, military action, and maintaining confidential information. If any of these experienced a major disruption, millions of people could be affected. As our dependence grows, so should our protective measures.

Currently, the majority of computer attacks, hacks, and cracks are done for thrills and to measure one's skills, and only a small percentage of attacks are motivated by financial gain. It seems likely that this ratio will reverse in the future, and a majority of computer compromises and attacks will be for theft and fraud. At the same time, the laws will increase in severity so that computer joyriding will not be so joyful when one is caught snooping around or releasing a virus.

Militaries are quietly growing their information warfare units. This growth is a response to the computer-related military actions that have already occurred and reflect an awareness of the need to plan for the future. Computer networks, communication systems, and resources are prime targets to reconfigure or destroy in the time of war or crisis, and good tools to use to watch other nations' movements and intentions during peacetime.

The antes are being raised, security issues are becoming more serious, and the effects are more detrimental. Take the necessary steps to protect yourself, your company, and your country.

Hacking and Attacking

There has been a definite and distinct evolution of hacking, cracking, and attacking. At one time, it was a compliment to be called a hacker because it meant the person took the time to learn things about computers that many others did not know and had the discipline and desire to find out what makes a computer tick. These people did not perform malicious acts, but were the ones called upon when really tough problems left everyone else scratching their heads.

As computers became widespread tools used in many environments, this definition started to change. The new hackers took on a profile of geeky young men who would rather spend their time pinging computers all over the Internet instead of looking for dates. Even this profile has evolved. Girls and women have joined this once all-boy club and are just as knowledgeable and dangerous as the guys. Hacking and attacks are on the rise, and the profile of an attacker is changing. However, the real change in the profile is that the serious attackers are out for specific purposes with certain types of damage or fraud in mind.

Hacking and attacking is on the rise and the profile of an attacker is changing.

The dangerous attacker is the one who is willing to do his homework. He will build a profile about the victim, find all the necessary information, and uncover many possible ways of getting into an environment before actually attempting it. The more an attacker knows about the environment, the more tools he has at his disposal. Attacks and hacks have involved information warfare, stealing money and credit cards, and defacing Web sites for political reasons. These are usually groups of determined and knowledgeable individuals that are hard to stop.

Another dangerous evolution pattern is the tools that are available to hackers these days. It used to take a certain skill set to be able to enter a computer through a port, reconfigure system files, find the hidden data, and get out without being noticed. Today there are many tools with graphical user interface (GUI) front ends that only require a person to enter an IP address or range, and click the Start button. Some of these tools provide a quiet mode, which means the interrogations and exploit attempts will use methods and protocols that may not show up on intrusion detection systems or cause the user of that computer to recognize that something is going on. These tools allow for sophisticated attacks to be carried out by people who do not understand the tool or maybe even the attack itself.

Security exploits and attacks are getting easier for the novice computer user.

The proliferation of tools on the Internet, the ease of use of these tools, Web sites, and books describing exactly how to exploit vulnerabilities have greatly increased the hacker population. So some attacks that may require in-depth knowledge of protocol behaviors or skillful programming skills are now available to a wide range of people who have not necessarily ever heard of Transmission Control Protocol/Internet Protocol (TCP/IP).

As more vulnerabilities are uncovered every week, many more people are interested in trying out the exploits. Some just want to satisfy their curiosity, some want bragging rights with other hackers, and others have distinct destructive goals to accomplish.

There is another aspect of hacking and attacking, though. While it can be looked at as doom and gloom, or in terms of good versus evil, hacking can also be looked at as the computing society continually challenging itself to come up with better products, practices, and procedures. If hackers were not continually trying to break products, the products would not necessarily continue to evolve in the way that they have. Sure, products would continue to grow in functionality, but not necessarily in security.

So maybe instead of looking at hackers and attackers as selfish individuals out to cause harm and destruction, they can be looked at as the thorn in the side of the computing society that keeps it on its toes and ensures that the next product will provide great functionality, but in a secure manner.

Management

Changes in management and security can be painful for many companies. Management usually feels it is the IT department's responsibility to choose the correct technologies, install and maintain them, and keep them secure. Management has never really been pulled inside the realm of computers and the issues that surround them. This distance and mentality hurts many companies when it comes to dealing with security effectively.

Management has been responsible for hitting their numbers—whether it be profit margins, sales goals, productivity marks—and for managing people and projects. They have not had to think much about firewalls, hackers, and security breaches. However, this trend is fading, and the new trend demands that management be much more involved in security and how it affects the company as a whole.

It is management's responsibility to set the tone for what type of role security will play in an organization. It is their responsibility to state what data is valuable and needs to be protected, who is responsible for protecting it and to what extent, what the acceptable actions are for employees, and what the consequences are for noncompliance. However, as of this writing, few corporations see these issues in this light and instead bounce security back into the laps of the IT staff. It is usually not that management is trying to dodge a bullet or skirt some type of responsibility. Instead, it is usually a lack of understanding of what computer and information security entails. Many organizations incorrectly assume that information security is a technical issue. It is not. Information security is a management issue that may require technical solutions. This is why information security professionals are so important. They must not only understand the goals and objectives of the organization, but also the technical issues involved in securing those assets that are most important.

Good security does not begin and end with erecting a firewall and installing antivirus software. Good security is planned, designed, implemented, maintained, and is able to evolve. For security to be a good fit for a company, it has to be in line with the company's business goals and objectives. Management needs to understand security issues and how security affects the company and its customers, so that proper resources, time, and funding can be provided. In other words, information security should be applied in a top-down approach. Unfortunately, many times security is kept within the IT department, which can be overwhelmed with daily tasks and dealing with weekly disasters. In these cases, security is done in a reactionary, bottom-up approach, which drastically reduces its effectiveness. In addition, when the IT department requests funds for security purposes, it often falls on deaf ears.

It is too much responsibility to put the full brunt of the security of a whole company on the IT department. It needs to be understood, supported, and funded from the top down. Management does not need to know the security mechanisms used, protocols in place, or configurations of components, but they do need to set the stage for everyone else to follow. Management should provide the framework and delegate who is to fill in the rest.

When a company is hacked and thousands of customers' credit cards are stolen, intellectual property is taken, confidential information is leaked, or the organization's reputation is damaged, it is the management staff that will be called to the carpet. They are the ones who will have to explain why due diligence and due care were not practiced in protecting the company and its resources. These explanations may be given to corporate offices, shareholders, judges, and to customers. So it should be management who truly understands how security works within the organization and should be calling the shots from the beginning.

Internet and Web Activities

The Internet started so that universities and government organizations could communicate in a more instantaneous manner and share information easily. It not only provided a different communication path, it opened the door to the possibility of mass communication, as well as a new and exciting mechanism that could provide layers of functionality and potential for individuals and businesses all around the world.

Communication on the Internet was mainly made up of nongraphical e-mail, news groups, and File Transfer Protocol (FTP) sites to exchange files. When Hypertext Markup Language (HTML) came to life, people were able to make graphical representations of their concepts and ideas. These sites provided static pages with a small amount of capability to accept information from Internet users through forms and scripts. When it was realized that money could be made and the Internet was a new forum for advertising, sites became more abundant, Web pages more complex, and more products and services were offered. Companies started integrating this new communication mechanism into their business model.

Another game of leapfrog began between telecommunication capabilities, Internet protocols, hardware platforms, and supporting applications. As HTML became more dynamic, Web server applications were developed to manage these pages and the back-end processes. This increased the need for more hard drive space, processing power, and memory accessible to the applications. Protocols evolved and matured to create more of a stable and meaningful experience on the Internet. These protocols enabled confidential information to stay secret and provided the necessary level of integrity for data being transmitted. Web servers became more powerful in processing as they offered more functionality to the users. As more sites connected to each other, the Internet brought along the World Wide Web.

The Web is actually a layer that operates on top of the Internet. The Internet provides the hardware, platforms, and communication mechanisms, whereas the Web provides the abundant software capabilities and functionality. Figure 2-5 illustrates this difference.

As companies brought their networks to the Internet and brought their services to the Web, they connected to the world in a different fashion. It is a great thing for a business to enable thousands or millions of people to view their product line, understand their business objectives, and learn about services offered. However, this also opens the doors to others who are interested in taking a peek under the covers, finding out more about the company's network topology and applications being used, accessing confidential information, and maybe causing some mayhem here and there in the process.

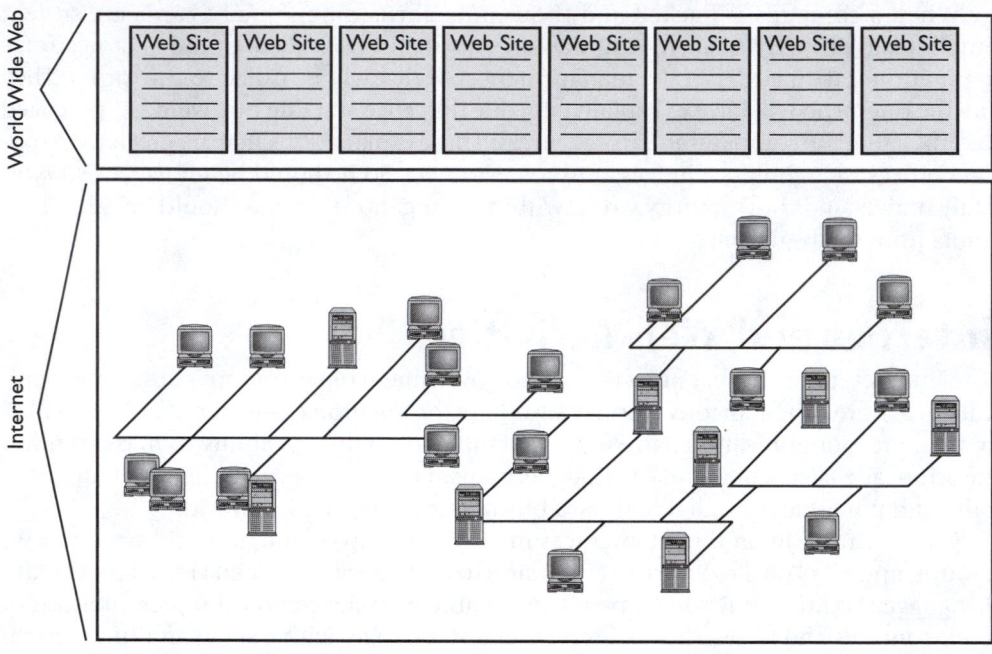

Figure 2-5 There is a difference between the Internet and the World Wide Web. The Web is a layer that exists on top of the Internet.

Offering services through the Internet is not the same as offering just another service to a customer base. It can be a powerful and useful move for a company, but if done haphazardly or in a manner that is not clearly thought out, implemented, and maintained, it could end up hurting a company or destroying it.

The software being used to present a presence on the Web, the hardware configurations, and security measures that should be taken depend on the company, its infrastructure, and the type of data it needs to protect. In the beginning, a Web server was just another server on the Internet with a connection outside of the network. Static pages were used, and no real information came from the Internet to the company through this channel. As forms and Common Gateway Interface (CGI) scripts were developed to accept customer information and the Internet as a whole became more used and well known, Web servers were slowly moved to demilitarized zones (DMZs) or the perimeter networks (Figure 2-6). (Sadly, however, many Web servers today still live inside of networks, providing a lot of vulnerabilities to companies.)

As the Web servers and applications evolved from just showing customers a home page and basic services to providing complete catalogs of products and accepting orders via the Internet, databases had to be brought into the picture. Web servers and databases lived on the same system, or two systems within the DMZ, and provided information to (and accepted information from) the world. This setup worked until more customers

Figure 2-6   Web servers were eventually moved from the internal network to the DMZ.

were able to access back-end data (within the database) and corrupt it accidentally or intentionally. It was shown that there were not enough layers and protection mechanisms between the users on the Internet and the data that was important to the company at hand.

This quickly brings us to where we are today. More and more companies are coming online and connecting their once closed (or semiclosed) environments to the Internet, which brings along threats, vulnerabilities, and problems not dealt with before. If a company has static Web pages, their Web servers and back-end needs are not half as complicated as the companies that accept payments and offer services or hold confidential customer information via the Web. The companies that take credit card numbers, allow customers to view their bank account information, and offer products and services can work in a two-tier (see Figure 2-7) or three-tier configuration.

Two-Tier Architecture

A two-tier architecture includes a line of Web servers that provide customers with a Web-based interface and a back-end line of servers or databases that hold data and process the requests. The two tiers are either within a DMZ or the back-end database is protected by another firewall. Figure 2-8 shows a two-tier architecture.

This architecture is fine for some environments, but for companies that hold bank and/or credit card, or other sensitive information, a three-tier architecture is usually more appropriate. In the three-tier architecture, the first line is made up of a server farm that presents Web pages to customers and accepts requests. The farm is usually clustered and redundant to be able to handle a heavy load of connections and to be able to balance that load between servers.

The back-end tier is basically the same as in the two-tier setup, which has database(s) or host systems. This is where sensitive customer information is held and maintained. The middle tier is new and provides the most interesting functionality. In many cases,

Figure 2-7   Attackers have easy access if databases are directly connected to Web servers with no protection mechanisms.

this is where the business logic lives and the actual processing of data and requests happen. Figure 2-9 shows the three-tier architecture.

The middle tier is made up of application servers running some type of middleware, which communicates with the Web (presentation tier) and can be customized for proprietary purposes and needs, or acts basically as another layer of server farms with off-the-shelf products. This layer takes the heavy processing tasks off the front-line servers and provides a layer of protection between the users on the Internet and the sensitive data held in the databases. The middleware is usually made up of components built with object-oriented languages. The objects are the entities that work as binary black boxes by taking in a request, retrieving the necessary information from the back-end servers, processing the data, and presenting it back to the requesting entity. Figure 2-10 illustrates how a component works as a black box.

Figure 2-8   A two-tier architecture consists of a server farm and back-end databases.

Figure 2-9   A three-tier architecture is made up of a front server farm, middle servers running middleware software, and back-end databases.

There are a lot of advantages to this architecture other than the previously mentioned issues. Security can be supplied in a more granular fashion if it is applied at different places in the tiers. The first firewall supports a particular security policy and provides the first line of defense. The first tier of Web servers only accepts specific requests, can authorize individuals before accepting certain types of requests, and can dictate who gets to make requests to the next tiers. The middle tier can provide security at the component level, which can be very detail-oriented and specific in nature. No requests should be made from the Internet directly to the back-end databases. Several middlemen should have to pass the request, each looking out for a specific security vulnerability and threat.

Figure 2-10   Components take requests, pass them on, and process the answer.

The back-end databases are then acted upon by the components in the middle tier, not the users themselves.

The second firewall should support a different security policy. If an attacker gets through the first firewall, it makes no sense for the second firewall to have the same configurations and settings that were just defeated. This firewall should have different settings that are more restrictive to attempt to stop a successful intruder at that particular stage.

Database Roles

Many times databases will only accept requests from predefined roles to ensure that if an intruder made it all the way through the middleware and to the place that holds the goods, it can only make a request if it is a member of the right group. This is shown in Figure 2-11.

All access attempts are first checked to make sure the requester is a member of a predefined and acceptable group. This means that individuals cannot make direct requests of the database, and it is highly unlikely that an attacker would know the necessary group she needs to be a member of and have the capability to add herself to this group. This is an example of another possible layer of protection available in a tiered approach of Web-based operations.

These are architectural issues, which look at a broad view of things and how large components interact. However, security vulnerabilities usually take advantage of smaller components and issues that are easier to overlook. A great three-tier architecture can be set up with firewalls in the right places, Web servers, and databases providing their layers of functionality and security, but an attack can still take place at the protocol,

Figure 2-11   This database only accepts requests from members of the operators, accounting, and administrators roles.

component, or service level of an operating system or application. The types of attacks cover a wide range from denial-of-service (DoS) attacks, spoofing, or masquerading, to buffer overflows and using an application's own functionality against itself. We will take a quick look at only one type of attack that has been used to steal millions of credit card numbers over the Internet.

Microsoft Data Access Components

Many companies use Microsoft Internet Information Services (IIS) for their Web server software. There are some specific vulnerabilities that can give attackers access to data on the back-end servers in a privileged mode, which enables them to capture or modify information. These vulnerabilities have been known for quite a while, but financial institutions are still falling victim to them because the IT staff is not properly installing the necessary security patches and making the corresponding configuration changes.

Microsoft Data Access Components (MDACs), which are used in IIS and Windows platforms, have many functions and services. One of the services, Remote Data Service, enables Web-based clients to issue structured query language (SQL) queries to remote resources using the Hypertext Transfer Protocol (HTTP). When Internet users make requests to the IIS server, the user executes the command at her browser, and the msadcs.dll on the IIS server facilitates this request and employs the Data Factory Object. The Data Factory Object enables requests to be sent and received to the back-end database.

The problem lies in Microsoft's database engine, which enables embedded arguments to be passed within SQL query strings, as shown in Figure 2-12. This means attackers can embed commands within a request made to the database, which in turn can execute shell commands, tunnel Open Database Connectivity (ODBC) requests to the back-end database, and access secured, nonpublished files. What makes this even more devastating is that IIS lets these ODBC commands run with system_local privileges.

In other words, the company could do a good job in setting up the right infrastructure, configure the necessary firewalls, disable unnecessary ports and services, and have the intrusion detection systems running, and still lose control of thousands or millions of credit card numbers to attackers. This is because there are several pieces to security. They all have their place, their importance, and their problems.

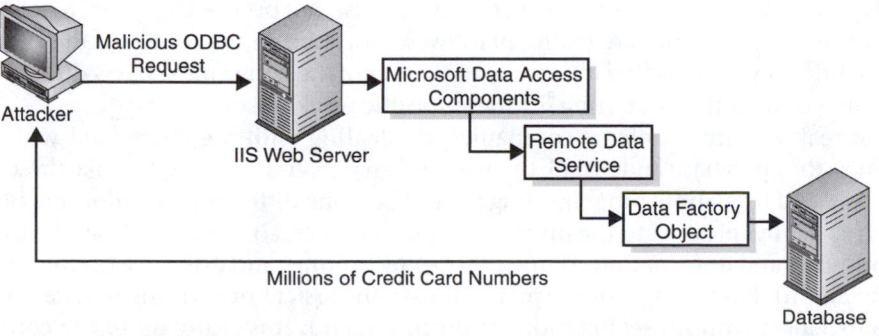

Figure 2-12   Weaknesses in the components of IIS running on Windows enable attackers to access confidential information in back-end databases.

This example shows that vulnerabilities can lie at a code level that many network administrators and security professionals are not necessarily aware of. There are usually two main camps in the computer world: infrastructure individuals and programmers. Security vulnerabilities lie in each camp and affect each other, so it's wise to have a full understanding of an environment and how security breaches can take place through infrastructure and code-based means.

So where do the vulnerabilities lie in Web-based activities?

- Incorrect configurations at the firewall
- Web servers that are not hardened or locked down and are open to attacks to the operating system or applications
- Middle-tier servers that do not provide the right combination and detailed security necessary to access back-end databases in a controlled manner
- Databases and back-end servers that accept requests from any source
- Databases and back-end servers that are not protected by another layer of firewalls
- Not running intrusion detection to watch for suspicious activity
- Routers that forward packets instead of routing them properly
- Enabling unnecessary protocols and services on computers
- Not keeping the computers patched and up to date

The list is endless, but one last item is important to touch on that is not approached as much as it should be in security: application and programming security. Security is usually thought of in terms of firewalls, intrusion detection systems, and port scanners. However, the vulnerabilities that are exploited are within the code of the operating systems and applications. If these problems did not exist in the programming code in the first place, there would be nothing to exploit and no real reason to have firewalls and intrusion detection systems.

Programming has usually only been looked at in the light of providing more functionality to the user, not protecting the system it is installed upon or the data that it holds and processes. The security point of view has also not been as important as it is today. Attacks and exploits that are taking place were not even in the minds of the programmers while they were coding it a couple of years ago; thus, they most likely did not think of coding differently and testing for these specific weaknesses.

The real security problems companies are dealing with are embedded within the products they purchase and install. Only recently have vendors started to take these issues seriously and think how programming should be done differently. Vendors are often in a rush to get the product to the market and patch it later, so this may always be the crux of computer and information security. Proper techniques and extensive testing add a lot of expense to developing a product, and most vendors are not willing to take on those extra expenses without seeing more profit in the end. It is really up to the consumer market to demand more secure products and pay for the products that have the necessary embedded protection mechanisms and methods. Until then, administrators will spend their days patching systems and applications and adjusting firewall and router configurations to thwart new vulnerabilities. They will need to continually update intrusion detection signatures, and the rat race of trying to outrun hackers will continue.

A Layered Approach

Networks have advanced in possibilities, functionality, and complexity. Because vulnerabilities can take place at different layers of an infrastructure, it has been necessary for vendors, developers, administrators, and security professionals to understand these layers and how each should be protected.

Many times we hear about a layered approach to security. We are supposed to implement different layers of protection to protect networks from different types of attacks. But what does a layered approach really mean? How do we know if we are applying a layered approach?

These are excellent questions that should be explored in depth if you are serious about protecting your interior and exterior networks from all of the possible security compromises and breaches. To protect an environment, you must truly understand the environment, the fixes that are to be applied, the differences between the numerous vendor applications and hardware variations, and how attacks are actually performed. The road to a secure environment is a winding one, with some bumps, sharp turns, and attacks that lunge out from the dark. However, the most important thing about this road to security is to understand the facets of the adventure and that the road never ends.

Security at Different Layers

A layered approach to security can be an abstract and nebulous topic because theory has to be represented and implemented in reality. Many times a layered approach means to implement solutions at different spectrums of the network. The spectrums can reach from the programming code, the protocols that are being used, the operating system, and application configurations, through user activity and the security program that is supposed to govern all of these issues. A layered approach presents layers of barriers an attacker must go through and compromise before getting to the sought-after resource. Running antivirus software only on workstations is not a layered approach in battling viruses. Running antivirus software on each workstation, file server, mail server, and applying content filtering via a proxy server is considered a layered approach toward combating viruses. This is just one example of what has to take place.

How is file access protection provided in a layered approach? If an administrator puts all users in specific groups and dictates what those groups can and cannot do with the company's files, this is only one step in the layer. To properly protect file access, file and registry access control lists need to be configured to provide more granularity to users' and groups' file permissions. The system default user rights (in a Windows environment) need to be properly configured to give certain types of users certain types of rights. Physical security of the environment and of the computers needs to be considered and restraints applied where required. Users need to be placed into groups that have implicit permissions necessary to perform their duties and no more. A strict logon credential policy needs to be drafted and enforced, so not all users are logging on as the same user. Monitoring and auditing of file access and actions need to be in place to identify any suspicious activity.

Sound like overkill? Not really. If an administrator made all users log in using different accounts, applied file and registry access lists, configured groups, and monitored audit logs without thinking about physical security, a user could use a floppy disk with a simple program to get around all other security barriers. All of these components must work in a synergistic manner, provide a blanket of security that individual security mechanisms could not fulfill on their own, and fill in all the gaps—even the smallest ones.

An Architectural View

Once we look at different types of vulnerabilities, attacks, and threats, we find that they exist at different layers within a network. This layered approach digs into more of the technology of an environment and the complexity of each of these technologies at each layer. This applies to the various protocols, applications, hardware, and security mechanisms that work at one or more of the seven layers in the OSI model. (The OSI model is fully described in Chapter 7.) IP spoofing is an attack at the network layer, dictionary attacks happen at the application layer, traffic sniffing is at the data link and physical layers, and viruses enter through the application layer. If an organization just employs strict password rules and a firewall, this leaves many layers vulnerable to other types of attacks.

Many times organizations put too much faith in their new shiny firewalls, intrusion detection systems, or antivirus software. Once one or more of these solutions are implemented, there can be a false sense of security within the IT staff that travels up to management. It is more important to look at the flow of data in and out of a network and how the applications and devices work together. This is an architectural view versus a device or application view.

In an architectural view, you must look at the data flow in and out of the environment, how this data is being authorized and monitored at different points, and how all the security solutions speak to each other in different situations. The firewall, for instance, is only part of the overall architecture. It is the architecture itself that needs to have an adequate level of security, not just the firewall. A network could either perform as a well-tuned orchestra or as several pieces that play wonderfully all by themselves but give you a headache when they are all brought into the same room. Each individual security component could be doing its job by protecting its piece of the network, but when it is time to interrelate or to communicate its findings or status to another security component, the security ball may be dropped in the process.

Each environment is dissimilar because of the installed hardware, software, technologies, and configurations. However, the main differences between environments are the goals each is trying to achieve. A local area network (LAN) provides authentication, resources to its users, and an overall controlled inner atmosphere. A wide area network (WAN) provides connections between users and remote sites, protocol tunneling, and access control. An e-commerce arrangement provides a Web interface to Internet users, connection to data held on back-end servers, access control, and a different type of authentication than LANs and WANs. These diverse goals require different architectures, but can use the same basic security concepts.

Because there are particular levels within an environment, as shown in Figure 2-13, different types of attacks can happen at these levels. The following is a small list of countermeasures, the layers they work at, and vulnerabilities to protect against:

- The firewall has packet filtering configured, which provides protection at the network layer. This combats a range of attacks including denial of service and fragmentation.

- Proxy software configurations protect at the application layer. This combats a range of attacks including unauthorized access and packet spoofing.

- Network address translation (NAT) works at the network layer. This hides LAN IP addresses and topology.

- Shielded twisted pair (STP) wiring works at the physical layer. This helps protect against network eavesdropping and signal interference.

- Network intrusion detection sensor monitors network traffic at the network level for known attack signatures. This identifies known attacks and resets TCP connections if necessary.

Figure 2-13   This shows a graphical representation of devices and protocols and where they appear within the OSI model.

- The perimeter domain name server contains resource records. This protection is at the application layer. It protects private domain name server records, network mapping, and individual computer information.

- IPSec, which works at the network layer, is configured for virtual private network (VPN) connections into the perimeter network. This protects against masquerading, data manipulating, and confidential information via encryption.

- Web server configuration protects at the application layer by using different sites for public versus confidential information. This protects from directory hopping and unauthorized access.

- Only necessary services and ports are enabled on all perimeter devices, which work at the network layer. This reduces entry points into the network and denial-of-service attacks.

- Mail server uses a store-and-forward method of messaging and runs antivirus software at the application layer. This protects against viruses and denial-of-service attacks.

- Secure Sockets Layer (SSL), which works at the transport layer, is configured at the Web sites when customers need to access personal confidential information. This provides confidentiality, data integrity, and protects against masquerading.

- Network scanner runs a weekly probe on all perimeter network server ports at the data link and network layers to identify new vulnerabilities. This protects from new vulnerabilities resulting from configuration changes or additional technology added.

- A Web server, working at the application layer, uses embedded cryptography within Extensible Markup Language (XML) code and Distributed Component Object Model (DCOM) security. This provides confidentiality of information and restricts components from performing risky actions.

- Web servers, working at the application and presentation layers, require valid digital signatures from each other for proper communication. These protect against session hijacking and masquerading.

This list shows a small percentage of the activity that happens at different points of the OSI model. If one or more of the devices or software had incorrect configurations or if the environment were missing one of these components, this could leave an open portal for an attacker into a network.

A Layer Missed

Many environments do not contain all the devices and components in the previous list of security vulnerabilities and solutions. The following example shows how employing several security mechanisms can seem to provide a fully secured environment, but can leave a small doorway of opportunity available for the clever attacker to take advantage of.

A firewall with packet filtering, a proxy server with content filtering, public and private DNS records clearly separated, SSL for Internet users, IPSec for VPN connections, public key infrastructure (PKI), and restricted service and port configuration may seem like a fortified environment, and a network administrator most likely implemented these mechanisms with the best intentions. However, one problem is that it is fortified only for a moment in time. Without a scanning device that probes the environment on a scheduled basis or an intrusion detection system that looks out for suspicious activity, the environment could be vulnerable even after the company has spent thousands of dollars to protect it. Technology continually changes, and so do networks and environments. The new application configurations, patches applied, or device installation brings change to the environment that could have unpredictable consequences—not to mention the new ways hackers have found to circumvent the original security mechanisms.

Bringing the Layers Together

It is not always necessary to purchase the newest security solutions on the market or pay top dollar for the hardware solution versus the software solution. It *is* necessary to be aware of where risks can develop and take steps to make sure all the bases are covered. That's what is meant by a layered approach.

In the computer and network world, the complexity of the levels can be a bit overwhelming at times. But the most important first step is to understand the environment that needs to be protected. Many times IT members come into an environment that was established years ago by another group of people. The environment is continually added on to; it is never stagnant. Usually, there is not an up-to-date network diagram because the daily tasks are time consuming, there is a lack of useful documentation, and no one person understands how the entire network works. This means when something goes wrong, 80 percent of the effort and time is spent in a chaotic scramble for a solution. It does not need to work this way, and there would be fewer security compromises if this scene were not so familiar.

Instead of looking at updating that old network diagram (or creating a first one) as a boring task, it could be approached as a fact-finding mission of crucial information. Instead of putting down the IT staff after a successful hacker attack, a change of attitude and practices can be employed. New software, patches, and devices should be clearly tested prior to implementation for any unforeseen events. An intrusion detection system should be established in potentially vulnerable segments of the network, if not all segments. Scheduled security scans should take place to seek out new vulnerabilities, not just when an audit is around the corner. In addition, security should be at the forefront of every network administrator's mind by keeping up to date on the recent security compromises, being aware of how changes to the network could open a door to clever attackers, and keeping those intrusion detection and antivirus signatures current.

Keeping up to date on network, software, configurations, and education can be overwhelming, but most of us in this line of work love to learn. Being effective in managing security means we will never stop learning.

Politics and Laws

The U.S. President appointed a cybersecurity czar for the first time. This is a strong message indicating that this government realizes the importance of security, both in the government and the private sectors. Governments all over the world have started to look at computers, and the security issues that surround them, more seriously over the last few years. Continual scuffle goes on about transborder issues pertaining to cryptography, what can be encrypted, at what strength, and by whom. There are also broader issues that come into play when an attack comes from another country that does not see that activity as illegal behavior. The legal system is meeting many unprecedented challenges when it comes to computer security.

As the Internet brings the world closer, it requires governments to come to the table and agree upon matters pertaining to computers, security, boundaries, and acceptable behavior. One sign of countries attempting to get in step with each other is the acceptance of the Common Criteria. (Common Criteria is discussed at length in Chapter 5.) Most countries have their own way of evaluating and testing the security of a system or device. For instance, the United States has the Trusted Computer System Evaluation Criteria (TCSEC), which is referred to as the Orange Book. The Canadians have the Canadian Trusted Computer Product Evaluation Criteria (CTCPEC), the Europeans have the Information Technology Security Evaluation Criteria (ITSEC), and other countries have developed their own criteria on how to determine the amount of trust and security in products and systems. The Common Criteria is an attempt to take the best of all of these methods and provide the world with one way of determining a product's security and protection level. In other words, it is an attempt to harmonize and standardize using one common tool to measure trust in security-related products, services, and systems.

Other than different countries viewing computer security differently, another barrier to proper security is how investigators deal with computer crimes. The courts have been running a continual game of catch up. The legal system cannot keep ahead of (or even in step with) technology, which is important if it is to regulate it and determine who is guilty or innocent. It is hard for a judge or jury to declare who is guilty in a computer crime because the playing field has changed. Investigators have a hard time collecting usable evidence to present in court, and defense lawyers cannot fall back on precedent cases where similar acts took place.

In addition, these difficulties start with law enforcement who have a lack of personnel skilled in computer technology and computer forensics. If a person is accused of a cybercrime, law officers must search for evidence. But what do they search for? Some law enforcement individuals do not necessarily know how to dump data from memory into a file, find remnants of data after the criminal formatted the drive, or understand how computer crimes take place so they can look for the right clues. Law enforcement has to know how to remove evidence from computer systems and drives in a way that does not corrupt the data and is admissible in court. They must gain much more computer knowledge and skills to be able to deal with computer crimes.

Law enforcement has to know how to remove evidence from computer systems and drives in a way that does not corrupt the data and is usable in court.

Computers are used in many types of crimes and provide many types of barriers that law enforcement and the courts are not used to dealing with. Data and communication may be encrypted, and there are jurisdiction issues if a crime took place in Europe but originated in North America. Also, much of the communication is spoofed, so law enforcement must know how to track down criminals through binary, hexadecimal, and packet header means.

These barriers and issues help criminals who are computer savvy. If they do get caught, many of them are not prosecuted to the extent they would be if they had committed a crime that the courts were used to dealing with.

Tougher penalties need to be developed and enforced when it comes to computer crimes.

Even though law enforcement has been lagging behind with the problem of cybercrime, there are initiatives at many levels to try to deal with the problem. There are many international organizations such as the G8, the United Nations, and the European Union that are trying to promote cooperation and harmonization in dealing with global computer crime.

These are tough issues for local police forces, Interpol, the FBI, the CIA, other organizations, and international judicial systems. However, with change comes growth. Laws are quickly being made and procedures being developed to effectively deal with computer crimes. Personnel is being increased to include people with technology skills, and computer security training is a must in many parts of these organizations.

Education

Generally, if a person is considered a security specialist, he has to have the interest and discipline to teach himself security issues, go to seminars and conferences all over the world, read stacks of books, and have a wide range of experience in different environments. There has not been a uniform standardized way of teaching security in vocational schools or universities. Some educational institutions offer security classes in their CIS or MIS programs, and there are some schools that offer master's degrees or doctorates in computer security. However, they are few and far between.

Networking, programming, operating systems, and engineering are widely taught. Security may be sprinkled in as an elective or not even offered. This is because there has not been a high demand or need for this type of knowledge in the job market. However, computer and information security is gaining in importance, need, and demand. This has caused a handful of schools to offer security classes and programs, and they will probably become more available as the job market demands more individuals with this skill set.

In addition to security courses and programs being offered, it's important that networking, programming, and engineering classes have security integrated into them. Security should not be looked upon as an extra component or an option to be added on later. It should be interwoven into the code as a program is being developed. It should be an important piece of architecture and engineering. And it should be understood and practiced when networks are being built, added upon, and maintained.

Education is something that most governments have recognized as an important step to protect any country's critical infrastructure. Countries have set up criteria for schools to follow, which will, in turn, receive government grants and subsidiaries. If countries want to protect themselves and their resources from computer and cyberattacks, they must teach their people how to do this through education.

Summary

This chapter has touched on only a few of the exciting things that are happening within computer security and showed evidence of growth, evolution, and the inevitable change. It has been recognized for quite some time that computers, data processing capabilities, and the Internet are extremely important tools for a vast array of reasons. It is only recently that securing these items has also been recognized as an important task.

This chapter was written to prepare you for the chapters that follow. Some chapters, or sections within chapters, might seem more interesting than others, but the CISSP certification was developed to ensure that you broaden your horizon when looking at and dealing with security issues. Information security would not be as effective if it was not provided with strong physical security; thus, it is important to know how each part works, and how they overlap and integrate. No part of security would be totally effective if it was not enforced by regulations, laws, and liability responsibilities. The courts and law enforcement are having a larger involvement in many parts of computer security, and understanding these pieces can help you determine what is acceptable and what is illegal, and how to deal with the issues that fall in between.

Each chapter ends with a section called "Quick Tips." This section provides a clear-cut bulleted list of items that outlines what is important in the chapter for the CISSP exam. The same is true for the questions at the end of the chapter and on the accompanying CD-ROM. As stated before, these questions are presented in a way to prepare you for the exam. Each type of exam has its own way of asking questions. Novell and Microsoft give simulations and long-winded, scenario-based questions. Cisco gives shorter questions that get right to the point. $(ISC)^2$ asks short, cognitive questions. Knowing how the exam is structured will help you achieve the CISSP certification.

Security Management Practices

In this chapter, you will learn about the following items:

- Security management responsibilities
- Three main security principles
- Difference among administrative, technical, and physical controls
- Risk management and risk analysis
- Information classification
- Security policies
- Security awareness training

We hear about viruses causing millions of dollars in damages, hackers from other countries capturing credit card information from financial institutions, large corporation Web sites being defaced for political reasons, and clever hackers being caught and sent to jail. These are the more exciting aspects of computer security, but realistically these activities are not what the average corporation or security professional usually has to deal with when it comes to daily or monthly security tasks. Although viruses and hacking get all the headlines, security management is the core of a company's computer and information security structure.

Security Management

Security management includes risk management, information security policies, procedures, standards, guidelines, baselines, information classification, security organization, and security education. These core components serve as the foundation of a corporation's security program. The crux of security, and a security program, is to protect the company's assets. A risk analysis will identify these assets, discover the threats that put them at risk, and estimate the possible damage and potential loss a company could endure if any of these threats become real. The results of the risk analysis help management construct a budget with the necessary funds to protect the recognized assets from their identified threats and develop applicable security policies that provide direction for security activities. Security education takes this information to each and every employee within the company so that everyone is properly informed and can more easily work toward the same security goals.

Security management has changed over the years because networked environments, computers, and the applications that hold information have changed. Information used to be held in mainframes, which is a more centralized network structure. The mainframe and management consoles used to access and configure the mainframe were placed in a centralized area instead of the distributed approach we see today. Only certain people were allowed access and only a small set of people knew how the mainframe worked, which drastically reduced security risks. Users were able to access information on the mainframe through dumb terminals (they were called this because they had little or no logic built into them). This also drastically reduced the need for strict security controls to be put into place. However, the computing society did not stay in this type of architecture. Now most networks are filled with personal computers that have advanced logic and processing power, users know enough about the systems to be dangerous, and the information is not centralized within one "glass house." Instead, the information lives on servers, workstations, and other networks. Information passes over wires and airways at a rate that was not even conceived of 10 to 15 years ago.

The Internet, extranets (business partner networks), and intranets not only make security much more complex, they make security even more critical. The core network architecture has changed from being a stand-alone computing environment to a distributed computing environment that has increased exponentially with complexity. Although connecting a network to the Internet adds more functionality and services for the users and gives more visibility of the company to the Internet world, it opens the floodgates to potential security risks.

Today, a majority of organizations could not function if they lost their computers and computing capabilities. Computers have been integrated into the business and individual daily fabric and would cause great pain and disruption if they were suddenly unavailable. As networks and environments have changed, so has the need for security. Security is more than just a firewall and a router with an access list; these systems have to be managed, and a big part of security is the actions of users and the procedures they follow. This brings us to security management practices, which focus on the continual protection of company assets.

Security Management Responsibilities

Okay, who is in charge and why?

In the world of security, management's functions involve determining objectives, scope, policies, priorities, standards, and strategies. A clear scope needs to be defined, and actual goals that are expected to be accomplished from a security program need to be determined before 100 people run off in different directions trying to secure the environment. Business objectives, security risks, user productivity, and functionality requirements and objectives need to be evaluated. Steps need to be drawn up to ensure that all of these issues are accounted for and properly addressed. Many companies only look at the business and productivity elements of the equation and figure that information and computer security fall within the IT administrator's responsibilities. In these situations, management is not taking computer and information security seriously and it will most likely remain underdeveloped, unsupported, under-funded, and unsuccessful. Security needs to be addressed at the highest levels of management. The IT administrator can consult on the subject, but the security of a company should not be laid in her lap.

Security management relies on the proper identification of a company's assets, assigning values to these assets, developing, and documenting. Then, implementation of security policies, procedures, standards, and guidelines provide integrity, confidentiality, and availability for these assets. Various management tools are used to classify data and perform risk analysis and assessments. These tools identify threats and exposure rates and rank the severity of identified vulnerabilities so that effective countermeasures can be implemented to mitigate risk overall. Management's responsibility is to provide protection for the resources it is responsible for and the company it relies upon. These resources come in human, capital, hardware, and informational forms. Management must concern itself with recognizing the risks that can affect these resources and be assured that the necessary protective measures are put into effect.

The necessary resources, funding, and strategic representatives need to be available and ready to participate in the security program. Management must assign responsibility and the roles necessary to get the security program off the ground and keep it thriving and evolving as the environment changes. Management must also integrate the program into the current business environment and monitor its accomplishments. Management's support is one of the most important pieces of a security program. A simple nod and a wink will not provide the amount of support required.

Security Administration and Supporting Controls

If there is not a current security administration, one should be established by management, which is directly responsible for monitoring a majority of the facets of a security program. Depending on the organization, security needs, and size of the environment, the security administration can consist of one person or a group of individuals who work in a central or decentralized manner. A clear reporting structure, understanding of responsibilities, and monitoring are important to make sure that compromises do not slip in because of a lack of communication or comprehension.

Information owners should dictate who can access resources and how much capacity users can possess pertaining to those resources. The security administration's job is to make sure that these objectives are implemented. Administrative, physical, and technical controls should be utilized to achieve the management's security directives. *Administrative controls* include the development and publication of policies, standards, procedures, and guidelines, the screening of personnel, security awareness training, and change control procedures. *Technical controls* (also called *logical controls*) consist of access control mechanisms, password and resource management, identification and authentication methods, security devices, and configuration of the infrastructure. *Physical controls* entail controlling individual access into the facility and different departments, locking systems and removing unnecessary floppy or CD-ROM drives, protecting the perimeter of the facility, monitoring for intrusion, and environmental controls. Figure 3-1 illustrates how the administrative, technical, and physical controls work together to provide the necessary level of protection.

The *information owner* is usually a senior executive within the management group of the company. The information owner has the final corporate responsibility for data and resource protection and would be the one held liable for any negligence when it comes to protecting the company's assets. The person who holds this role is responsible for assigning classifications to information and dictating how the data should be protected. If the information owner does not lay out the foundation of data protection and ensure that the directives are being enforced, this would violate the due care concept. (The due care concept is explained later in the chapter in the section "Implementation.")

Security administration brings a focal point to security and a hierarchical structure of responsibility. The security administration's job is to ensure that management's directives are fulfilled when it comes to security, not to construct those directives in the first place. There should be a clear communication path between the security administration and senior management to ensure that the security program receives the proper support and that management makes the decisions. Too many times senior management is extremely disconnected from security issues and when a serious security breach takes place, they are the ones who have to explain the reasons to their business partners, shareholders,

Figure 3-1
Administrative, technical, and physical controls should work in a synergistic manner to protect a company's assets.

Example of Security Management

Anyone who has been involved with a security initiative understands the conflicts between securing an environment and still allowing the necessary level of functionality so productivity is not affected. Many security projects start with proactive individuals who know the end result they are wanting to achieve and have lofty ideas of how quick and efficient their security rollout will be, only to hear all the users go up in arms when they find out what restrictions will be placed upon them. The users then express how they will not be able to fulfill certain parts of their job if this actually takes place. This usually causes the project to screech to a halt. *Then* the proper assessments, evaluations, and planning are initialized to see how the environment can be slowly secured and how to ease users and tasks delicately into new restrictions or ways of doing business. This causes a lot of heartache and wastes time and money. Individuals who are responsible for security management activities should see that the understanding of the environment and proper planning happen *before* trying to kick off an implementation phase of a security program.

and the public. After this, they can become too involved. A healthy relationship between the security administration and senior management should be developed from the beginning and communication should easily flow in both directions.

Inadequate management can undermine the entire security effort in a company. This can happen because management does not fully understand the necessity of security, security is in competition with other management goals, it is viewed as expensive and unnecessary, or management applies lip service but no real action. Powerful and useful technologies, devices, software packages, procedures, and methodologies are available to provide the exact level of security required, but without proper security management and management support, it doesn't really matter.

Fundamental Principles of Security

Now, what are we trying to accomplish again?

There are several small and large objectives of a security program, but the main three principles in all programs are availability, integrity, and confidentiality. These are referred to as the *AIC triad*. The level of security required to accomplish these principles differs per company because their security goals and requirements may be different. All security controls, mechanisms, and safeguards are implemented to provide one or more of these principles and all risks, threats, and vulnerabilities are measured in their potential capability to compromise one or all of the AIC principles. Figure 3-2 illustrates the AIC triad.

Figure 3-2
The AIC triad

Availability

The systems and networks should provide adequate capacity in order to perform in a predictable manner with an acceptable level of performance. It should be able to recover from disruptions in a secure and quick manner so productivity will not be negatively affected. Single points of failure should be avoided, backup measures should be taken, redundancy mechanisms should be in place when necessary, and the negative effects from environmental components should be prevented. Necessary protection mechanisms need to be in place to protect against inside and outside threats that could affect the availability and productivity of the network, systems, and information. *Availability* ensures reliability and timely access to data and resources to authorized individuals.

System availability can be affected by device or software failure. Backup devices should be used and available to quickly replace critical systems, or employees should be skilled and available to make the necessary adjustments to bring the system back online. Environmental issues like heat, cold, humidity, static electricity, and contaminants can also affect system availability. These issues are addressed in detail in Chapter 6. Systems should be protected from these elements, properly grounded electrically, and closely monitored.

Denial-of-service (DoS) attacks are popular methods for hackers to disrupt a company's system availability and productivity. These attacks are mounted to reduce the ability of users to access system resources and information. To protect against these attacks, only the necessary services and ports should be available on systems, and intrusion detection should monitor the network traffic and host activities. Certain firewall and router configuration can also reduce the threat of DoS attacks and possibly stop them from occurring.

Integrity

Integrity is upheld when the assurance of accuracy and reliability of information and systems is provided, and unauthorized modification of data is prevented. Hardware, software, and communication mechanisms must work in a concerted manner to maintain and process data correctly and move data to intended destinations without unexpected alteration. The systems and network should be protected from outside interference and contamination.

Environments that enforce and provide this attribute of security ensure that attackers or mistakes by users do not compromise the integrity of systems or data. When an attacker inserts a virus, logic bomb, or back door into a system, the system's integrity is compromised. This can, in turn, negatively affect the integrity of information held on the system by corruption, malicious modification, or replacing the data with incorrect data. Strict access controls, intrusion detection, and hashing can combat these attempts.

Users usually affect a system or its data's integrity by mistake, although internal users can also be up to malicious deeds. Users may accidentally delete configuration files because their hard drives are full and they don't remember ever using a boot.ini file. Or they can insert incorrect values into a data processing application that ends up charging a customer $300 instead of $3,000,000. Incorrectly modifying data kept in databases is another popular way of corrupting data by users that can have lasting effects.

Security should streamline the users' abilities and give them only certain choices and functionality so errors become less common and less devastating. System-critical files should be restricted from the users' view and access. Applications should provide mechanisms that check for valid and reasonable input values. Databases should let only authorized individuals modify data, and data in transit should be protected by encryption or other mechanisms.

Confidentiality

Confidentiality provides the ability to ensure that the necessary level of secrecy is enforced at each junction of data processing and prevention of unauthorized disclosure. This level of confidentiality should prevail while data resides on systems and devices within the network, as it is transmitted, and once it reaches its destination.

Attackers can thwart confidentiality mechanisms by network monitoring, shoulder surfing, stealing password files, and social engineering. These topics will be addressed in more depth in later chapters, but briefly, *shoulder surfing* is when a person looks over another person's shoulder and watches keystrokes or views data as it appears on a computer screen. *Social engineering* is tricking another person into sharing confidential information by posing as someone authorized to have that information.

Users can intentionally or accidentally disclose sensitive information by not encrypting it before sending it to another person, falling prey to a social engineering attack, sharing a company's trade secrets, or not providing the extra care of protection of confidential information when processing it.

Confidentiality can be provided by encrypting data as it is stored and transmitted, network traffic padding, strict access control, data classification, and training personnel on the proper procedures.

Availability, integrity, and confidentiality are critical principles of security. Understanding their meaning, how they are provided by different mechanisms, and how their absence can negatively affect an environment should be understood to best identify problems and provide proper solutions.

Security Definitions

Many times the words "threat," "vulnerability," "exposure," and "risk" are used to represent the same thing even though they have different meanings and relationships to each other. It is important to understand each word's definition, but more importantly, you should understand its relationship to the other concepts.

A *vulnerability* is a software, hardware, or procedural weakness that may provide an attacker the open door he is looking for to enter a computer or network and have unauthorized access to resources within the environment. A vulnerability characterizes the absence or weakness of a safeguard that could be exploited. This vulnerability can be a service running on a server, unrestricted modem dial-in access, an open port on a firewall, lax physical security that allows anyone to enter a server room, or non-enforced password management on servers and workstations.

A *threat* is any potential danger to information or systems. The threat is that someone, or something, will identify a specific vulnerability and use it against the company or individual. The entity that takes advantage of a vulnerability is referred to as a threat agent. A threat agent could be an intruder accessing the network through a port on the firewall, a process accessing data in a way that violates the security policy, a tornado wiping out a facility, or an employee making an unintentional mistake that could expose confidential information or destroy a file's integrity.

A *risk* is the likelihood of a threat agent taking advantage of a vulnerability. A risk is the possibility and probability that a threat agent will exploit a vulnerability. If a firewall has several ports open, there is a higher risk that an intruder will use one to access the network in an unauthorized method. If users are not educated on processes and procedures, there is a higher risk that an employee will make an intentional or unintentional mistake that may destroy data. If an intrusion detection system is not implemented on a network, there is a higher risk that an attack will go unnoticed until it is too late. Reducing the vulnerabilities or the threat reduces the risk.

An *exposure* is an instance of being exposed to losses from a threat agent. A vulnerability can cause an organization to be exposed to possible damages. If password management is lax and password rules are not enforced, the company can be exposed to the

Critical Security Services

Availability prevents disruption of service and productivity.
Integrity prevents unauthorized modification of systems and information.
Confidentiality prevents unauthorized disclosure of sensitive information.

possibility of having users' passwords captured and used in an unauthorized manner. If a company does not have its wiring inspected and does not put proactive fire prevention steps into place, it can expose itself to potentially devastating fires.

A *countermeasure*, or safeguard, mitigates the potential risk. A countermeasure is a software configuration, hardware, or procedure that eliminates a vulnerability or reduces the risk of a threat agent from being able to exploit a vulnerability. Countermeasures can be strong password management, a security guard, access control mechanisms within an operating system, the implementation of basic input/output system (BIOS) passwords, and security awareness training.

If a company has antivirus software and the virus signatures are not kept up-to-date, this is a vulnerability. The company is vulnerable to virus attacks. The threat is a virus showing up in the environment and disrupting productivity. The likelihood of a virus showing up in the environment and causing damage is the risk. If a virus infiltrates the company's environment, then it has an *exposure*. The countermeasures in this situation are to update the signatures and install the antivirus software on all computers. The relationships among risks, vulnerabilities, threats, and countermeasures are shown in Figure 3-3.

Applying the right countermeasure can eliminate the vulnerability and exposure and reduce the risk. The company cannot eliminate the threat agent, but it can protect itself and prevent this threat agent from exploiting vulnerabilities within the environment.

Figure 3-3
The relationships among the different security components

> ## Order of Concepts
> The test looks at these issues in this order: threat, exposure, vulnerability, counter-measures, and finally, risk. It makes sense to talk about them in that order because, logically, that is how they relate to each other. For example, you start with a threat, but unless you are exposed to it, it is not really a vulnerability. If you have a vulner-ability, you then apply countermeasures to mitigate the risk, which you can never really reduce to zero; therefore, that leaves you with "residual risk."

References

NIST Computer Security Resource Center: **csrc.ncsl.nist.gov**

SANS Institute: **www.sans.org**

CISSP and SSCP Open Study Guides: **www.cccure.org**

CISSP.com: **www.cissps.com**

The Top-Down Approach

When a house is built, the workers start with a blueprint of the structure, the foundation is poured, and the frame is erected. As the building of the house continues, the workers know what the end result is supposed to be, so they add the right materials, insert doors and win-dows in logical places, erect support beams, provide sturdy ceilings and floors, and add the plaster and carpet and smaller details until the house is complete. Then inspectors come in to ensure that the structure of the house and the components that were used to make it are acceptable. If this process did not start with a blueprint and a realized goal, the house could end up with an unstable foundation or with doors and windows that don't seem to shut properly. This house would not pass inspection; thus, a lot of time and money would have been wasted. Figure 3-4 illustrates this point.

The building of a house analogy can be applied to the building of a security program. When designing and/or implementing a security program, the functionality and end re-sult expected need to be determined and realized. Many times companies just start lock-ing down computers and installing firewalls without taking the time to understand the overall security requirements, goals, and assurance levels they expect from security as a whole within their environment. This process should start from the top with very broad ideas and terms (blueprint) and work its way down to detailed configuration settings and system parameters (windows and carpets). At each step, the overall security goals need to be kept in mind so that each added piece is sure to add more granularity to the intended goal and not splinter the main objectives by running in 15 different directions at once.

The security policy works as a blueprint for a company's security program and pro-vides the necessary foundation to build upon. This policy needs to be taken seriously from the beginning and developed with the idea that it will continually be reviewed to

Figure 3-4
Without a solid blueprint (policy) and organized procedures, a security program could end up looking like this house.

ensure that all security components stay in step and work to accomplish the same objectives. The next step is to develop and implement procedures, standards, and guidelines that support the security policy and identify the security countermeasures and methods that need to be put into place. Once these items are developed, the process increases with granularity by developing standards and configurations for the chosen security controls and methods.

If security starts with a solid foundation and develops over time with understood goals and objectives, a company does not need to make drastic changes midstream. The process can be methodical, requiring less time, funds, and resources, and provide a proper balance between functionality and protection. This is not the norm, but with your insight, maybe you can help companies approach security in a more controlled manner. You could provide the necessary vision and understanding of how security should be thought out, properly implemented, and should evolve in an organized manner instead of resulting in a giant heap of security products that are disjointed and full of flaws.

A security program should use a ***top-down approach***, meaning that the initiation, support, and direction come from top management and work their way through middle management and then to staff members. In contrast, a ***bottom-up approach*** would be if the IT department tried to develop a security program without getting proper management support and direction. A bottom-up approach is usually less effective, not broad enough, and doomed to fail. A top-down approach makes sure that the people actually responsible for protecting the company's assets (senior management) are driving the program.

Organizational Security Model

My security model is shaped like a pile of oatmeal. Response: Lovely.

An organizational security model is a framework made up of many entities, protection mechanisms, logical and physical components, procedures, and configurations that all work together in a synergistic way to provide a security level for an environment. Each model is different, but all models work in layers: one layer providing support for the layer above it and protection for the layer below it. The goal of a security model is assurance, which is the sum total of all security components within an environment that provide a level of confidence. Because a security model is a framework, companies are free to plug in different types of technologies, methods, and procedures to accomplish the necessary security assurance level for their environment. Figure 3-5 illustrates the pieces that can make up a security model.

Figure 3-5
A comprehensive and effective security model has many integrated pieces.

Effective security requires a balanced approach and application of all security components and procedures. Some security components are technical (access control lists and encryption) and some are non-technical (physical and administrative, such as developing a security policy and enforcement of compliance), but each has an important place within the framework and if one is missing or incomplete, the whole framework can be affected.

A security model has various layers, but it also has different types of goals to accomplish in different time frames. You might have a goal for yourself today to brush your teeth, run three miles, finish the project you have been working on, and spend time with your kids. These are daily goals or *operational goals*. You might have mid-term goals to complete your master's degree, write a book, and get promoted. These take more time and effort and are referred to as *tactical goals*. Your long-term goals may be to retire at age 55, save enough money to live comfortably, and to live on a houseboat. These goals are *strategic goals* because they look farther into the future.

The same thing happens in security planning. Daily goals, or operational goals, focus on productivity and task-oriented activities to ensure that the company's functionality happens in a smooth and predictable manner. Mid-term goals, or tactical goals, could be to integrate all workstations and resources into one domain so more central control can be achieved. A long-term goal, or strategic goal, may involve moving all the branches from dedicated communication lines to frame relay, implementing IPSec virtual private networks (VPNs) for all remote users instead of dial-up entry, and integrating wireless technology with the necessary security measures into the environment.

This approach to planning is called the *planning horizon*. A company cannot usually implement all changes at once, and some changes are larger than others. Many times certain changes cannot happen until other changes take place. If a company wants to implement its own certificate authority and wants to implement a full public key infrastructure (PKI) enterprise-wide, this cannot happen in a week if the company currently works in decentralized workgroups with no domain structure. So the operational goals are to keep production running smoothly and make small steps toward readying the environment for a domain structure. The tactical goal would be to put all workstations and resources into a domain structure, and centralize access control and authentication. The strategic goal is to have all workstations, servers, and devices within the enterprise use the PKI to provide authentication, encryption, and more secure communication channels.

Security works best if its operational, tactical, and strategic goals are defined and work to support each other, which can be much harder than it sounds.

Business Requirements: Private Industry versus Military Organizations

The security model an organization chooses depends on its critical missions and business requirements. The private industry usually has much different missions and requirements than that of the military. The private industry thrives by beating the competition, which is done through marketing and sales, solid management decisions, understanding the target audience, and understanding the flow and ebb of the market. A private sector business is successful if its data is readily available, so processing order requests and fulfilling service orders can happen quickly and painlessly for the customer. The data also needs to be accurate to satisfy the customers' needs. Out of the three security services (availability, integrity, and confidentiality), data integrity and availability usually rank higher than confidentiality to most private sector businesses.

The military also thrives by beating their competition (other countries or its enemies), which requires proper training, readiness, intelligence, and deployment. Although the private industry does need a degree of secrecy and ensured confidentiality, it does not play as important of a role as it does with a military organization. The military has more critical information that must not fall into the wrong hands; therefore, out of the three main security services, confidentiality is the most important to the military sector. In turn, this would cause a military installation to implement a more strict security model that emphasizes confidentiality more than a private sector organization.

Risk Management

Life is full of risk.

Risk is the possibility of damage happening. **Risk management** is the process of identifying, assessing, and reducing this risk to an acceptable level and implementing the right mechanisms to maintain that level of risk. There is no such thing as a 100 percent secure environment. Every environment has vulnerabilities and risks to certain degrees. The skill is in identifying these risks, assessing the probability of them actually occurring and the damage they could cause, and then taking the right steps to reduce the overall level of risk in the environment to what the organization identifies as acceptable.

Risks come in different forms to a company, and they are not all computer related. When a company purchases another company, they are taking on a lot of risk with the hope that this move will increase their market base, productivity, and profitability. If a company increases its product line, this can add overhead, increase the need for personnel and storage facilities, require more funding for different materials, and maybe increase insurance premiums and marketing campaigns. The risk is that this added overhead might not be matched in sales; thus, profitability will be reduced or not accomplished.

When we look at information security, there are several types of risk a corporation needs to be aware of and address properly. The following items touch on the major categories:

- **Physical damage**   Fire, water, vandalism, power loss, and natural disasters
- **Human error**   Accidental or intentional action or inaction that can disrupt productivity
- **Equipment malfunction**   Failure of systems and peripheral devices
- **Inside and outside attacks**   Hacking, cracking, and attacking
- **Misuse of data**   Sharing trade secrets, fraud, espionage, and theft
- **Loss of data**   Intentional or unintentional loss of information through destructive means
- **Application error**   Computation errors, input errors, and buffer overflows

The threats need to be identified, classified by category, and the actual magnitude of potential loss needs to be calculated. Real risk is hard to measure, but making priorities of the potential risks is attainable.

Risk Analysis

I have determined that our greatest risk is this paperclip. Response: Nice work.

Risk analysis, which is really a tool for risk management, is a method of identifying risks and assessing the possible damage in order to justify security safeguards. It is used to ensure that security is cost-effective, relevant, timely, and responsive to threats. Security can be quite complex, even for well-versed security professionals, and it is easy to apply too much security, not enough security, or the wrong security components, and spend too much money in the process without attaining the necessary objectives. Risk analysis helps companies prioritize their risks and shows them the amount of money that could be applied to protecting against those risks in a sensible manner.

A risk analysis has four main goals: identify assets and their threats, quantify the business impact of these potential threats, calculate the risk, and provide an economic balance between the impact of the risk and the cost of the countermeasure. Risk analysis provides a *cost/benefit comparison* where the annualized cost of safeguards to protect against threats is compared with the expected cost of loss. A safeguard, in most cases, should not be implemented unless the annualized cost of loss exceeds the annualized cost of the safeguard itself. This means that if a facility is worth $100,000, it does not make sense to spend $150,000 trying to protect it.

A risk analysis helps integrate the security program objectives with the company's business objectives and requirements. The more the business and security objectives are in alignment, the more successful the two will be. The analysis also helps the company draft a proper budget for a security program and the security components that make up that program. Once a company knows how much their assets are worth and the possible threats they are exposed to, they can make intelligent decisions on how much money to spend on protecting those assets.

A risk analysis needs to be supported and directed by senior management if it is going to be successful. Management needs to define the purpose and scope of the analysis, a team needs to be appointed to carry out the assessment, and the necessary time and funds need to be available to conduct the analysis. It is essential for senior management to review the outcome of the risk assessment and analysis and act on its findings. What good is it to go through all the trouble of a risk assessment and not react to its findings? Surprisingly, this does happen.

Risk Analysis Team

Each organization has different departments. Each department has its own functionality, resources, tasks, and quirks. For the most effective risk analysis, a team needs to be built that includes individuals from many or all of the departments to ensure that all of the risks are identified and addressed. The team members can be management, application programmers, IT staff, systems integrators, and operational managers— indeed, any key personnel from key areas of the organization.

This is necessary because if the risk analysis team is only made up of individuals from the IT department, they may not understand the types of risks the accounting department faces with data integrity issues, or if their data files were wiped out in an accidental or intentional act, what this would mean to the company as a whole. The IT staff may not understand all the risks the employees in the warehouse would face if a natural disaster hit, what it would mean to their productivity and how it would affect the organization overall. Many times the risk analysis team is made up of members from various departments, and if that is not possible, the team should make sure to interview people in each department so all risks are fully understood and quantified. The risk analysis teams also need to be made up of people who understand the processes that are part of their individual departments. It is therefore important to make sure that risk analysis teams are made up of individuals at the right levels of each department. This is a difficult task, since managers will tend to delegate any sort of risk analysis task to lower levels within the department. However, these lower levels may not have the adequate level of knowledge and understanding of the processes that the risk analysis team may need to deal with.

Value of Information and Assets

If information does not have any value, then who cares about protecting it?

The value placed on information is relative to the parties involved, what work it took to develop this information, how much it costs to maintain it, what loss it would cause if it was lost or destroyed, and what benefit would be gained if another party obtained this information. If a company does not know the value of the information and the other assets they are trying to protect, they do not know how much money and time should be spent on protecting them. If you were in charge of making sure Russia does not know the encryption algorithms used when transmitting information to and from U.S. spy satellites, you might use more extreme (and expensive) security measures than if you were going to protect your peanut butter and banana sandwich recipe from your next door neighbor. The value of the information supports security measure decisions.

Many of the following examples refer to assessing the value of *data* and protecting it, but this logic applies toward an organization's facility, systems, and resources. The value of the company's facility needs to be assessed, along with all printers, workstations, servers, peripheral devices, supplies, and employees. You do not know how much is in danger of being lost if you don't know what you have and what it is worth in the first place.

Costs that Make Up the Value

An asset can have a quantitative and qualitative measure assigned to it, but this measurement needs to be derived. The actual value of an asset is determined by the cost it takes to acquire, develop, and maintain it. The value is determined by the importance it has to the owners, authorized users, and unauthorized users. Some information is important enough to a company to go through the steps of making it a trade secret or the company may choose to protect specific logos and trademarks.

The value of an asset should reflect all identifiable costs that would arise if there were an actual impairment of the asset. If a server cost $4,000, this value should not be inputted as the value of the asset in a risk assessment. If the server went down, the cost of replacing it or repairing it, the loss of productivity, and the value of any data that may be corrupted or lost need to be accounted for to properly capture the amount the company would lose if the server were to fail for one reason or another.

The following issues should be considered when assigning values to assets:

- Cost to acquire or develop the asset
- Cost to maintain and protect the asset
- Value of the asset to owners and users
- Value of the asset to adversaries
- Value of intellectual property
- Price others are willing to pay for the asset
- Cost to replace the asset if lost
- Operational and production activities that are affected if the asset is unavailable
- Liability issues if the asset is compromised
- Usefulness of the asset

Understanding the value of an asset is the first step to understanding what security mechanisms should be put in place and what funds should go toward protecting it. A very important question is how much it could cost the company to not protect the data.

Determining the value of an asset can fulfill several different types of requirements a company may be facing, including the following:

- The value of each asset is necessary to perform effective cost/benefit analysis.

- An asset's value supports the selection of specific countermeasures and helps in the safeguard selection decision-making process.

- The value of each asset is often required for insurance purposes.

- The value of each asset is necessary to understand what exactly is at risk.

- The value of each asset may be required to prevent negligence, conform to due care, and comply with legal and regulatory standards.

Identifying Threats

Okay, what should we be afraid of?

Earlier it was stated that the definition of a risk is the probability of a threat agent exploiting a vulnerability to cause harm to a computer, network, or company. There are many types of threat agents that can take advantage of several types of vulnerabilities that can result in specific threats. Table 3-1 shows the relationship among some of these. The list is in no way meant to be complete, it only shows a sampling of the risks that many organizations would have to take care of in their risk management programs.

There are other types of threats that can happen within a computerized environment that are much harder to identify than those listed in Table 3-1. These have to do with application and user errors. If an application uses several complex equations to produce

Threat Agent	Can Exploit this Vulnerability	Resulting in this Threat
Virus	Lack of antivirus software	Virus infection
Hacker	Powerful services running on a server	Unauthorized access to confidential information
Users	Misconfigured parameter in the operating system	System malfunction
Fire	Lack of fire extinguishers	Facility and computer damage, and possibly loss of life
Employee	Lax access control mechanisms	Damaging mission-critical information
Contractor	Lax access control mechanisms	Stealing trade secrets
Attacker	Poorly written application	Conducting a buffer overflow
Intruder	Lack of security guard	Breaking windows and stealing computers and devices
Employee	Lack of auditing	Altering data inputs and outputs from data processing applications
Attacker	Lack of stringent firewall settings	Conducting a denial-of-service attack

Table 3-1 Relationship of Threats and Vulnerabilities

results, it can be difficult to discover and isolate if these equations are incorrect or if the application is using inputted data incorrectly. This can result in *illogical processing* and *cascading errors* as invalid results are passed on to another process. These types of problems can lie within applications' code and are very hard to identify.

User errors, intentional or accidental, are easier to identify through the monitoring and auditing of user activities. Audits and reviews need to be conducted to uncover if employees are inputting values incorrectly into programs, misusing technology, or modifying data in an inappropriate manner.

Risks have *loss potential*, meaning what the company would lose if a threat agent actually exploits a vulnerability. The loss can be corrupted data, destruction to systems and/or the facility, unauthorized disclosure of confidential information, and a reduction in employee productivity. When performing a risk analysis, the team also needs to look at *delayed loss* when assessing the damages that can occur. Delayed loss has negative effects on a company after a vulnerability is initially exploited. The time period can be anywhere from 15 minutes after the exploitation to years. Delayed loss issues can be reduced productivity over a period of time, reduced income to the company, accrued late penalties, extra expense to get the environment back to proper working conditions, and delayed collection of funds from customers.

For example, if a company's Web servers are attacked and brought offline, the immediate damage could be data corruption, the man-hours necessary to bring the servers back online, and the replacement of any code or components that may be required. The company could lose productivity if it usually accepts orders and payments via its Web sites. If it takes a full day to get the Web servers fixed and back online, the company could lose a lot more sales and profits. If it takes a full week to get the Web servers fixed and back online, the company could lose enough sales and profits to not be able to pay other bills and expenses. This would be a delayed loss. If the company's customers lost confidence in them because of this activity, they could lose business for months or years. This is a more extreme case of delayed loss.

These types of issues bring complexity to being able to properly quantify losses that specific threats could cause, but they need to be taken into consideration to ensure that reality is represented in this type of analysis.

So up to now, we have management's support of the risk analysis, we constructed our team so that it represents different departments in the company, we placed a value on each of the company's assets, and identified all the possible threats that could affect the assets. We have also taken into consideration all potential and delayed losses the company may endure per asset per threat. The next step is to use qualitative or quantitative methods to calculate the actual risk the company faces.

Quantitative Approach

There are two types of approaches to risk analysis: quantitative and qualitative. *Quantitative risk analysis* attempts to assign real and meaningful numbers to all elements of the risk analysis process. These elements may include safeguard costs, asset value, impact, threat frequency, safeguard effectiveness, probabilities, and so on. When all of these are quantified, the process is said to be quantitative. Quantitative also provides concrete probability percentages when determining the likelihood of threats and risks. Each element within the analysis (asset value, threat frequency, severity of vulnerability, impact damage, safeguard costs, safeguard effectiveness, uncertainty, and probability items) is quantified and entered into equations to determine total and residual risks. *Purely quantitative risk analysis is not possible, because the method is attempting to quantify qualitative items and there are always uncertainties in quantitative values.* If a severity level is high and a threat frequency is low, it is hard to assign corresponding numbers to these ratings and come up with a useful outcome.

Quantitative and qualitative approaches have their own pros and cons, and each applies more appropriately to some situations than others. The company, risk analysis team, and the tools they decide to use will determine which approach is best.

Analysis Inputs and Data Gathering

So where do we start?

After identifying the scope, goals, and team of a risk analysis, the next step is to gather the necessary data. This is the most time-consuming piece of an analysis and can prove to be the most difficult.

The necessary input for a quantitative analysis differs from a qualitative analysis because it deals with real numbers and percentages. The first step is to identify the following components that will make up the analysis:

- The assets that are to be protected should have values estimated and assigned.
- Each threat and corresponding risk needs to be identified.
- The loss potential of each threat needs to be estimated.
- An estimation of the possible frequency of the threat needs to be calculated.
- Remedial measures need to be recognized and recommended.

Once the data is gathered, it can be used in manual or automated methods to calculate the identified risks, their potential damages, and the amount of money that can be reasonably designated for the necessary countermeasures.

Automated Risk Analysis Methods

Collecting all the necessary data that needs to be plugged into risk analysis equations and properly interpreting the results can be overwhelming if done manually. There are several automated risk analysis tools on the market that can make this task much less painful and hopefully more accurate. The gathered data can be reused, greatly reducing the time required to perform subsequent analysis. They can also print out reports and comprehensive graphs to be presented to the management.

The objective of these tools is to reduce the manual effort of these tasks, perform calculations quickly, estimate future expected losses, and determine the effectiveness and benefits of the security countermeasures chosen. Most automatic risk analysis products port information into a database and are run several times with different parameters used to give a panoramic view of what the outcome will be if different risks come to bear. For example, after the tool has all the necessary information inputted, it can compute the potential outcome if a large fire took place, then rerun with different parameters to find out the potential losses if a virus damaged 40 percent of the data on the main file server, then rerun to find out how much the company would lose if an attacker stole all the customer credit card information held in three databases, and so on. Running through the different risk possibilities will give companies a more detailed understanding of which risks are more critical than others, and thus which ones to address first. Figure 3-6 shows a simple example of this process.

Steps of a Risk Analysis

There are many methods and equations that could be used when performing a quantitative risk analysis and many different variables that can be inserted into the process. We are going to go over the some of the main steps that should take place in every risk analysis and assessment.

1. Assign value to information and assets.

   a. What is the value of this asset to the company?

   b. How much does it cost to maintain it?

   c. How much does it make in profits for the company?

   d. How much would it be worth to the competition?

   e. How much would it cost to recreate or recover?

   f. How much did it cost to acquire or develop?

2. Estimate potential loss per risk.

   a. What physical damage can take place and how much would that cost?

   b. How much productivity can be lost and how much would that cost?

   c. What is the value lost if confidential information is disclosed?

Figure 3-6
A simplistic example showing the severity of current threats versus the probability of them occurring

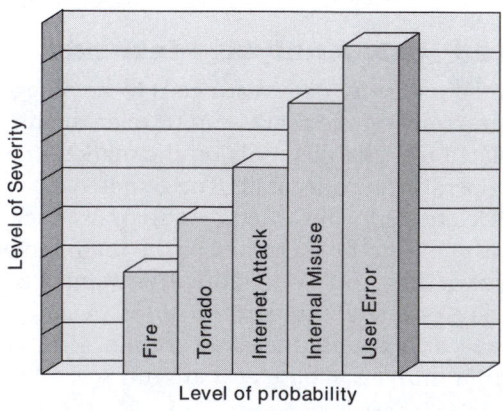

    d. What is the cost of recovering from a virus attack?

    e. What is the cost of recovering from a hacker attack?

    f. How much would it cost if critical devices failed?

    g. Calculate the single loss expectancy (SLE) for each risk.

3. Perform a threat analysis.

    a. Gather information about the likelihood of each risk taking place from people in each department, past records, and official security resources that provide this type of data.

    b. Calculate the probability of occurrence for each threat identified.

    c. Calculate the annualized rate of occurrence (ARO), which is how many times each threat could happen in a year.

4. Derive the overall loss potential per threat.

    a. Combine potential loss and probability.

    b. Calculate the annualized loss expectancy (ALE) per threat by using the information calculated in the first three steps.

    c. Choose remedial measures to counteract each threat.

5. Reduce, assign, or accept the risk.

    a. Risk reduction methods.

        i. Install security controls and components.

        ii. Improve procedures.

        iii. Alter environment.

        iv. Provide early detection methods to catch the threat as it's happening and reduce the possible damage it can cause.

        v. Produce a contingency plan of how business can continue if a specific threat takes place, reducing extending damages of the threat.

        vi. Erect barriers to the threat.

    b. Risk assignment.

        i. Buy insurance to transfer some or all of the risk.

    c. Risk acceptance.

        i. Live with the risks and spend no money toward protection.

Because we are stepping through a quantitative risk analysis, real numbers are used and calculations are necessary. *Single loss expectancy (SLE)* and *annualized loss expectancy (ALE)* were mentioned in the previous analysis steps. The SLE is a dollar amount that is assigned to a single event that represents the company's potential loss amount if a specific threat took place.

    asset value × exposure factor (EF) = SLE

The *exposure factor* represents the percentage of loss a realized threat could have on a certain asset. So if a data warehouse has the asset value of $150,000 and if a fire took place, it is estimated that 25 percent of the warehouse would be damaged and the SLE would be $37,500. This figure is derived to be inserted into the ALE equation.

SLE × annualized rate of occurrence (ARO) = ALE

The *annualized rate of occurrence (ARO)* is the value that represents the estimated frequency of a specific threat taking place within a one-year time frame. The range can be from 0.0 (never) to 1.0 (always) and anywhere in between. For example, if the probability of a flood taking place in Mesa, Arizona is once in 1,000 years, the ARO value is 0.001.

So if a fire taking place within a company's data warehouse facility can cause $37,500 in damages and the frequency, or ARO, of a fire taking place has an ARO value of 0.1 (indicating once in ten years), then the ALE value is $3,750 ($37,500 × 0.1 = $3,750).

The ALE value tells the company that if they want to put in controls or safeguards to protect the asset from this threat, they can sensibly spend $3,750 or less per year to provide the necessary level of protection. It is important to know the real possibility of a risk and how much damage, in monetary terms, that the threat can cause to know how much can be spent to try and protect from that threat in the first place. It would not make good business sense for the company to spend more than $3,750 per year to protect itself from this threat.

Now that we have all these numbers, what do we do with them? Let's look at the example shown in Table 3-2.

Table 3-2 shows the outcome of a risk analysis. With this data, the company can make intelligent decisions on what risks need to be addressed first because of the severity of the risk, the likelihood of it happening, and how much could be lost if the risk did become real. The company now also knows how much money can be spent to protect against each threat, which will result in good business decisions instead of just buying protection here and there without a clear understanding of the big picture. Because the company has a risk of losing up to $5,200 if data is corrupted by virus infiltration, up to this amount of funds can be earmarked to go toward providing antivirus software and methods to ensure that a virus attack will not happen.

Risk Analysis Definitions

Exposure factor (EF)   Percentage of asset loss caused by identified threat
Single loss expectancy (SLE)   Asset value × exposure factor
Annualized rate of occurrence (ARO)   Estimated frequency a threat will occur within a year
Annualized loss expectancy (ALE)   Single loss expectancy × annualized rate of occurrence

Asset	Threat	Asset Value	Single Loss Expectancy (SLE)	Annualized Frequency	Annual Loss Expectancy (ALE)
Facility	Fire	$560,000	$230,000	.25	$57,500
Trade secret	Stolen	$43,500	$40,000	.75	$30,000
File server	Failed	$11,500	$11,500	.5	$5,750
Data	Virus	$8,900	$6,500	.8	$5,200
Customer credit card info	Stolen	$323,500	$300,000	.65	$195,000

Table 3-2   Breaking Down How SLE and ALE Values Are Used

We have just explored the ways of performing risk analysis through quantitative means. This method tries to measure the loss in monetary values and assign numeric sums of each component within the analysis. A pure quantitative analysis is not achievable because it is impossible to assign the exact figures to each component and loss values. Although we can look at past events, do our best to assess the value of the assets, and contact agencies that provide frequency estimates of disasters happening in our area, we still cannot say for a fact that we have a 25 percent chance of a fire happening in a year and that it will cause exactly $57,500 in damage. In quantitative risk analysis, we do our best to provide all the correct information to the best of our knowledge and we will come close to the risk values, but we cannot predict the future and how much the future will cost us or the company.

Results of a Risk Analysis

The risk analysis team should have clearly defined goals and results that they are seeking. The following is a short list of what generally is expected from the results of a risk analysis.

- Assigned monetary values assigned to assets
- Comprehensive list of all possible and significant threats
- Probability of the occurrence rate of each threat
- Loss potential the company can endure per threat in a 12-month time span
- Recommended safeguards, countermeasures, and actions

Although this list looks small, there is usually an incredible amount of detail under each bullet item. This report will be presented and given to the senior management. They will be concerned with possible monetary losses and the necessary costs to mitigate these risks. Although the reports should be as detailed as possible, there should be executive abstracts for the senior management to quickly understand the overall findings of the analysis.

Qualitative Risk Analysis

Another method of risk analysis is *qualitative*, which does not assign numbers and monetary values to components and losses. Instead, qualitative methods walk through different scenarios of risk possibilities and rank the seriousness of the threats and the validity of the different possible countermeasures. Qualitative analysis techniques include judgment, intuition, and experience. Examples of qualitative techniques are Delphi, brainstorming, storyboarding, focus groups, surveys, questionnaires, checklists, one-on-one meetings, and interviews. The risk analysis team will determine the best technique for the threats that need to be assessed and the culture of the company and individuals involved with the analysis.

The team that is performing the risk analysis gathers personnel who have experience and education on the threats being evaluated. When this group is presented with a scenario that describes threats and loss potential, they will respond with their gut feeling on the likelihood of the threat and the extent of damage that may result.

A scenario approximately one page in length is written for each major threat. The functional manager who is most familiar with this type of threat should review the scenario to ensure that it reflects how an actual threat would be carried out. Safeguards that would diminish the damage of this threat are then evaluated, and the scenario is played out for each safeguard. The exposure possibility and loss possibility can be ranked as high, medium, or low on a scale of 1 to 5 or 1 to 10. Once the selected personnel rank the possibility of a threat happening, the loss potential, and the advantages of each safeguard, this information is compiled into a report and presented to management to help them make better decisions on how best to implement safeguards into the environment. The benefits of this type of analysis are the communication that has to happen among the team members to rank the risks, the identification of safeguard strengths and weaknesses, and the people who know these subjects the best providing their opinions to management.

Let's look at a *simple* example of a qualitative risk analysis.

The risk analysis team writes a one-page scenario explaining the threat of a hacker accessing confidential information held on the five file servers within the company. They distribute it to a team of five people (the IT manager, database administrator, application programmer, system operator, and operational manager). The team is given the sheet to rank the threat's severity, loss potential, and each safeguard's effectiveness with a rating of 1 to 5, 1 being the least severe, effective, or probable. Table 3-3 shows the results.

This data is complied and inserted into a report and presented to management. When management is presented with this information, they will see that their staff feels that purchasing a firewall will protect the company from this threat more than purchasing an intrusion detection system, or setting up a honeypot system.

This is the result of looking at only one threat, and the management will view the severity, probability, and loss potential of each threat so that they know which threats cause the greatest risk and should be addressed first.

Threat = Hacker Accessing Confidential Information	Severity of Threat	Probability of Threat Taking Place	Potential Loss to the Company	Effective-ness of Firewall	Effective-ness of Intrusion Detection System	Effective-ness of Honeypot
IT manager	4	2	4	4	3	2
Database administrator	4	4	4	3	4	I
Application programmer	2	3	3	4	2	I
System operator	3	4	3	4	2	I
Operational manager	5	4	4	4	4	2
Results	3.6	3.4	3.6	3.8	3	1.4

Table 3-3   Example of a Qualitative Analysis

Delphi Technique

The Delphi technique is a group decision method used to ensure that each member gives an honest opinion of what he or she thinks the result to a particular threat will be. This avoids a group of individuals feeling pressured to go along with others' thought processes and enables them to participate in an independent and anonymous way. Each member of the group writes down his or her opinion of a certain risk on a piece of paper and turns it into the team that is performing the analysis. The results are compiled and distributed to the group members who then write down their comments anonymously and return them back to the analysis group. The comments are compiled and redistributed for more comments until a consensus is formed. This method is used to obtain an agreement on cost, loss values, and probabilities of occurrence without individuals having to agree verbally.

Quantitative versus Qualitative

So which method should we use?

Each method has its advantages and disadvantages, and Table 3-4 is a list of some of the differences between the two methods.

The risk analysis team, management, risk analysis tools, and culture of the company will dictate which approach, quantitative or qualitative, will be used. Management may feel very comfortable with their staff's opinion and just want the data gathered and presented. Another company with a different management might demand real numbers to be able to use with other business profit gain and loss numbers, expense forecasts, and market trends.

The goal of either method is to estimate a company's real risk and rank the severity of the risks so the correct countermeasures can be put into place using a practical budget.

Attribute	Quantitative	Qualitative
Requires more complex calculations	x	
Degree of guesswork that is involved		x
Is easily automated	x	
Provides a cost/benefit analysis	x	
Uses independent and objective metrics	x	
Provides the opinions of the staff that knows the processes best		x
Shows clear-cut losses that can be accrued within one year's time	x	

Table 3-4   Quantitative versus Qualitative Characteristics

Protection Mechanisms

Okay, so we know we are at risk, we know the probability of it happening, now what do we do?

The next step is to identify the current security mechanisms and evaluate their effectiveness.

Because a company has such a wide range of threats and not just computer viruses and attackers, each threat type needs to be addressed and planned for individually. Site location, fire protection, site construction, power loss, and equipment malfunctions are examined in detail in Chapter 6. Software malfunctions and applications considerations are covered in Chapter 5. Telecommunication and networking issues are analyzed and presented in Chapter 7. Disaster recovery and business continuity are addressed in Chapter 9. All of these subjects have their own associated risks and planning requirements. The following section addresses identifying and choosing the right countermeasures for computer systems and gives the best attributes to look for and all the different cost scenarios that must be investigated when comparing different types of software countermeasures. The end product of the analysis of alternatives is to demonstrate why the selected alternative is the most advantageous to the company.

Countermeasure Selection

A security countermeasure, sometimes called a safeguard, must make good business sense. Good business sense means that it is cost-effective and that its benefit outweighs its cost. This requires another type of analysis: a *cost/benefit analysis*.

A commonly used cost/benefit calculation for a given safeguard is:

(ALE before implementing safeguard) – (ALE after implementing safeguard) – (annual cost of safeguard) = value of safeguard to the company

For example, if the ALE of the threat of a hacker bringing down a Web server is $12,000 and after the suggested safeguard is implemented the ALE is now $3,000 and the annual cost of maintenance and operation of the safeguard is $650, then the value of this safeguard to the company is $8,350 each year.

The cost of a countermeasure is more than just the amount that is filled out on the purchase order. The following items need to be considered and evaluated when deriving the full cost of a countermeasure:

- Product costs
- Design/planning costs
- Implementation costs
- Environment modifications
- Compatibility with other countermeasures
- Maintenance requirements
- Testing requirements
- Repair, replace, or update costs
- Operating/support costs
- Effects on productivity

A company can decide that to protect many of their resources, an intrusion detection system (IDS) is warranted. So the company pays $5,500 for the software. Is that the total cost? Nope. This software should be tested in an environment that is segmented from production to uncover any unexpected activity. After this testing is complete and the IT group feels it is safe to insert into their production environment, they must install the monitor management software, the sensors, and properly direct the communication paths from the sensors to the manager console. Routers may need to be reconfigured to redirect traffic flow, and it needs to be ensured that users cannot access the IDS manager console. A database needs to be configured to hold all attack signatures, and simulations need to be run.

Anyone who has worked in an IT group knows that some adverse reaction almost always takes place in this type of scenario. The network performance can take an unacceptable hit after installing this product. Users may no longer be able to access the Unix server for some mysterious reason. The IDS vendor may not have explained that two more service patches are necessary for the whole thing to work correctly. Staff time will need to be allocated to respond to all of the correct and incorrect alerts the new IDS sends out.

So the cost of this countermeasure is $5,500 for the product, $3,400 for the lab and testing time, $2,600 for the loss in user productivity once the product was introduced into production, $4,000 in labor for router reconfiguration, product installation, troubleshooting, and installation of the two service patches. The real cost of this countermeasure is $15,500. If our total potential loss was calculated at $9,000, we went over budget when applying this countermeasure for the identified risk. Some of these costs may be hard or impossible to identify before they are acquired, but an experienced risk analyst would account for these possibilities.

Functionality and Effectiveness of Countermeasures

The countermeasure doesn't work, but it's pretty. Response: Good enough.

Once you have a handle on the cost of the safeguard, you will then need to evaluate its functionality and effectiveness. When selecting a safeguard, some attributes are more favorable than others. Table 3-5 provides a list of attributes that should be considered *before* purchasing and committing to a security protection mechanism.

Safeguards provide deterrence attributes if they are highly visible. This tells potential evildoers that adequate protection is in place and that they should move on to an easier

Characteristic	Description
Modular in nature	It can be installed or removed from an environment without adversely affecting other mechanisms.
Provides uniform protection	A security level is applied to all mechanisms it is designed to protect in a standardized method.
Provides override functionality	An administrator can override the restriction if necessary.
Defaults to least privilege	When installed, it defaults to a lack of permissions and rights instead of installing with everyone having full control.
Independence of safeguard and the asset it is protecting	The safeguard can be used to protect different assets and different assets can be protected by different safeguards.
Flexibility and functionality	The more functionality the safeguard provides, the better. This functionality should come with flexibility, which enables you to choose different functions instead of all or none.
Clear distinction between user and administrator	A user should have fewer permissions when it comes to configuring or disabling the protection mechanism.
Minimum human intervention	When humans have to configure or modify controls, this opens the door to errors. The safeguard should be able to set itself up, pull the necessary information from the environment, and require the least amount of input from humans as possible.
Easily upgraded	Software continues to evolve, and updates should be able to happen painlessly.
Auditing functionality	There should be a mechanism that is part of the safeguard that provides minimum or verbose auditing.
Minimizes dependence on other components	The safeguard should be flexible and not have strict requirements about the environment into which it will be installed.
Easily useable, acceptable, and tolerated by personnel	If the safeguards provide barriers to productivity or add extra steps to simple tasks, users will not tolerate it.
Must produce output in usable and understandable format	Important information should be presented in a format easy for humans to understand and use for other tasks.

Table 3-5   Characteristics to Look for When Obtaining Safeguards

Characteristic	Description
Must be able to reset safeguard	The mechanism should be able to be reset and return to original configurations and settings without affecting the system or asset it is protecting.
Testable	The safeguard should be able to be tested in different environments under different situations.
Does not introduce other compromises	The safeguard should not provide any covert channels or back doors.
System and user performance	System and user performance should not be greatly affected.
Proper alerting	A threshold should be able to be set as to when to alert personnel of a security breach, and this type of alert should be acceptable.
Does not affect asset	The assets in the environment should not be adversely affected by safeguard.

Table 3-5 Characteristics to Look for When Obtaining Safeguards *(continued)*

target. Although the safeguard should be highly visible, the way that it works should not be attainable so the evildoers cannot attempt to modify the safeguard or know how to get around the reaches of the protection mechanism.

Putting It Together

To perform a risk analysis, a company first decides what assets need to be protected and to what extent. It also indicates the amount of money that should go toward protecting specific assets. Next, the functionality of the available safeguards needs to be evaluated and which ones would be most beneficial for the environment needs to be determined. Finally, the costs of the safeguards are appraised and compared. These steps and the resulting information enable management to make the most intelligent and informed decisions about selecting and purchasing countermeasures. Figure 3-7 illustrates these steps.

Total Risk versus Residual Risk

The reason that a company implements countermeasures is to reduce their overall risk to an acceptable level. As stated earlier, no system or environment is 100 percent secure, which means there is always some risk left over to deal with. This is called *residual risk*.

Residual risk is different than *total risk*, which is when a company chooses not to implement any type of safeguard. The reason that this type of scenario takes place is because of the cost/benefit analysis results. If there is a small likelihood that a company's Web servers can be compromised and the necessary safeguards to provide a higher level of protection cost more than the potential loss in the first place, the company will choose not to implement the safeguard and is left with the total risk.

Figure 3-7
The main three
steps in risk
analysis

There is an important difference between total risk and residual risk and which type of risk a company is willing to accept.

threats × vulnerability × asset value = total risk

(threats × vulnerability × asset value) × controls gap = residual risk

During a risk assessment, the threats and vulnerabilities are identified. The possibility of these taking place is multiplied by the value of the assets that are at risk, which results in the total risk. Once the controls gap (protection the control cannot provide) is factored in, the result is the residual risk. Implementing countermeasures is a way of mitigating risks. Because no company can remove all threats, there will always be some type of risk left over. The question is what level of risk the company is willing to accept.

Handling Risk

Now that we know about the risk, what do we do with it?

Once a company knows the amount of total and residual risk they are faced with, they must decide how to handle it. There are four basic ways of dealing with risk: transferring, rejecting, reducing, or accepting the risk.

There are many types of insurance available to companies when it comes to protecting its assets. If a company decides that the total or residual risk is too high to gamble with, they can purchase insurance, and this would *transfer the risk* to the insurance company.

If the company implements countermeasures, this will *reduce the risk*. If a company is in denial about its risk or ignores it, this is *rejecting the risk*, which can be very dangerous and is unadvisable. The last approach is to *accept the risk*, which means the company understands the level of risk they are faced with and the cost of damage that is possible and they decide to just live with it. Many companies will accept risk when the cost/benefit ratio indicates that the cost of the countermeasure outweighs the potential loss value. So the company will not implement the countermeasure and accept the risk.

References

Risk Associates: **www.securityauditor.net**

Strategic Security and Intelligence resources: **www.all.net/journal/netsec/ 9703.html**

Policies, Procedures, Standards, Baselines, and Guidelines

The risk assessment is done. Let's call it a day. Response: Nope, there's more.

Computers and the information that is processed on them usually have a direct relationship with a company's critical missions and objectives. Because of this level of importance, senior management should make protecting these items a high priority and provide the necessary support, funds, time, and resources to ensure that systems, networks, and information are protected in the most logical and cost-effective manner possible. A comprehensive management approach needs to be developed to accomplish these goals successfully.

For security to be ultimately successful in a business, it needs to start at the top level and be useful and functional at every single level within the organization. The senior management needs to define the scope of security, what needs to be protected, and to what extent. Management must understand the regulations, laws, and liability issues that they are responsible for complying with when it comes to security and ensuring that the company as a whole fulfills the obligations of each of these. Senior management also needs to determine what is to be expected from employees and what the consequences of noncompliance will be. These decisions should be made by the individuals who will be held ultimately responsible if something goes wrong.

A security program contains all the pieces necessary to provide overall protection to a corporation and a long-term security strategy. A security program should have security policies, procedures, standards, guidelines, baselines, security awareness training, incident handling, and a compliance program. Human resources and the legal department need to be involved in the development and enforcement of some of these issues.

The language, level of detail, formality of the policy, and supporting mechanisms should be examined. Security policies, standards, guidelines, and procedures must be developed in a realistic view to be most effective. Highly structured organizations will usually follow guidelines in a more uniform way. Less structured organizations may need more explanation and emphasis to promote compliance. The more detailed the rules are, the easier it is to know when one has been violated. However, overly detailed documentation and rules can prove to be more of a burden than helpful. On the other hand, many times the more formal the rules, the easier they are to enforce. The business type, its culture, and goals need to be evaluated to make sure the right type of language is used when writing security documentation.

Security Policy

A *security policy* is a general statement produced by senior management (or a selected policy board or committee) to dictate what type of role security plays within the organization. A security policy can be an organizational policy, issue-specific policy, or system-specific policy. In an *organizational security policy*, management establishes how a security program will be set up, lays out the program's goals, assigns responsibilities, shows the strategic and tactical value of security, and outlines how enforcement should be carried out. This policy must address relative laws, regulations, and liability issues and how they are to be satisfied. The organizational security policy provides scope and direction for all future security activities within the organization. It also describes the amount of risk senior management is willing to accept.

Issue-specific policies, also called functional implementing policies, address specific security issues that management feels need more detailed explanation and attention to make sure a comprehensive structure is built and all employees understand how they are to comply to these security issues. Organizations may choose to have an e-mail security policy that outlines what management can and cannot do with employees' e-mail messages for monitoring purposes and how employees can or cannot use different e-mail functionality and address specific privacy issues. As an example, an e-mail policy might state that management can read any employee's e-mail messages that reside on the mail server, but not when they reside on the user's workstation. It might also state that employees cannot use e-mail to share confidential information or use it to pass inappropriate material, and may be subject to monitoring of these actions. The employees should be made aware of these issues by signing a document, clicking Yes in a dialog box that explains these issues before they use their e-mail clients, or it can be presented as a banner when the users sign on to their computers. The policy provides direction and structure for the staff indicating what they can and cannot do. It informs the users of the expectations of their actions, and it provides liability protection in case an employee cries "foul" for any reason dealing with e-mail use.

A *system-specific policy* presents the management's decisions that are closer to the actual computers, networks, applications, and data. This type of policy can provide an approved software list, which contains a list of applications that can be installed on individual workstations. This policy can describe how databases are to be protected, how computers are to be locked down, and how firewalls, intrusion detection systems, and scanners are to be employed.

Policies are written in broad overview terms to cover many subjects in a general fashion. Much more granularity is needed to actually support the policy, and this happens with the use of procedures, standards, and guidelines. The policy provides the foundation. The procedures, standards, and guidelines provide the security framework. And the necessary security components, implementations, and mechanisms are used to fill in the framework to provide a full security program and secure infrastructure.

Further information and sample policies are in the appendices.

Standards

Some things you just gotta do.

Organizational security *standards* specify how hardware and software products are to be used. They can also be used to indicate expected user behavior. They provide a means to ensure that specific technologies, applications, parameters, and procedures are carried out in a uniform way across the organization. It may be an organizational standard that requires all employees to have their company identification badges on their person at all times, or that unknown individuals are to be challenged about their identity and purpose for being in a specific area, or that confidential information has to be encrypted.

Types of Policies

Policies can fall into one of the following categories:

- **Regulatory**   This policy is written to ensure that the organization is following standards set by a specific industry and is regulated by law. The policy type is detailed in nature and specific to a type of industry. This is used in financial institutions, health care facilities, and public utilities.

- **Advisory**   This policy is written to strongly suggest certain types of behaviors and activities that should take place within the organization. It also outlines possible ramifications if employees do not comply with the established behaviors and activities. This can be used for handling medical information, financial transactions, and processing confidential information.

- **Informative**   This policy is written to inform employees of certain topics. It is not an enforceable policy, but one to teach individuals about specific issues relevant to the company. It could explain how the company interacts with partners, the company's goals and mission, and a general reporting structure in different situations.

These rules are usually compulsory within a company, and if they are going to be successful, they need to be enforced.

As stated in an earlier section, there is a difference between tactical and strategic goals. A strategic goal can be viewed as the ultimate end point; the tactical goals are the steps to achieve it. As shown in Figure 3-8, standards, guidelines, and procedures are the tactical goals used to achieve and support the directives in the security policy, which is considered the strategic goal.

Baselines

Baselines provide the minimum level of security necessary throughout the organization. A consistent baseline needs to be established before the security architecture can be properly developed. When standards are implemented and followed properly, they provide a baseline of security. In this sense baselines can be considered the abstraction of standards.

Most of the time, baselines are platform-unique security implementations that are necessary to provide the required level of protection. For example, a company may require all workstations in the company to have at least a C2 assurance rating. The baseline security level would be C2 and supporting procedures would provide step-by-step instructions on how the operating system and components have to be installed to achieve this specific security level.

Figure 3-8
Policy establishes the strategic plans, and the lower elements provide the tactical support.

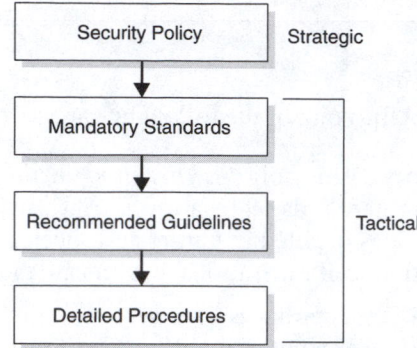

The baseline is a *minimum* level of security and other business requirements may require specific systems to contain mechanisms that provide an even higher level of protection.

Guidelines

Guidelines are recommended actions and operational guides to users, IT staff, operations staff, and others when a specific standard does not apply. They can deal with the methodologies of securing computers and their software. There are always gray areas in life, and guidelines can be used as a reference during those times. Whereas standards are specific mandatory rules, guidelines are general approaches that provide the necessary flexibility for unforeseen circumstances.

A policy might state that access to confidential data must be audited. A supporting guideline could further explain that audits should contain sufficient information to allow for reconciliation with prior reviews. Supporting procedures would outline the necessary steps to configure, implement, and maintain this type of auditing.

Procedures

Procedures are detailed step-by-step tasks that should be performed to achieve a certain goal. The steps can apply to users, IT staff, operations staff, security members, and others who may need to carry out specific tasks. Many organizations have written procedures on how operating systems are to be installed, how security mechanisms are to be configured, implementing access control lists, setting up new user accounts, assigning computer privileges, audit activities, material destruction, incident reporting, and much more.

Procedures are looked at as the lowest level in the policy chain because they are closest to the computers and users and provide detailed steps for configuration and installation issues.

Procedures spell out how the policy, standards, and guidelines will actually be implemented in an operating environment. If a policy states that all individuals who access confidential information must be properly authenticated, the supporting procedures will explain the steps for this to happen by defining the access criteria for authorization,

Modular Elements

Standards, guidelines, and baselines should not be in one large document. Each has a specific purpose and a different audience. A document describing how to be in compliance with a specific regulation may go to the management staff, whereas a detailed procedure on how to properly secure a specific operating system is directed toward an IT member.

Being separate and modular in nature helps for proper distribution and updating when it is necessary.

how access control mechanisms are implemented and configured, and how access activities are audited. If a standard states that backups should be performed, then the procedures will define the detailed steps necessary to perform the backup, timelines of backups, storage of backup media, and so on. Procedures should be detailed enough to be able to be understood and used by a diverse group of individuals.

Security procedures, standards, measures, practices, and policies cover a number of different subject areas. Table 3-6 describes some of the subject areas affected.

To tie these items together, let's walk through an example.

A corporation's security policy indicates that confidential information should be properly protected. It states the issue in very broad and vague terms. A supporting standard

Subject Area	Examples
Accountability controls	Audit trails, reviewing audit logs, automation of auditing and necessary configurations, and storage of audit information
Physical and environmental controls	Intrusion detection system installation, configuration, and monitoring; cooling system maintenance, and monitoring
Administration controls	Separation of duties, performing background checks, supervision, and rotation of duties
Access controls	Identification and authentication mechanisms; biometric installation, configuration, and calibration; smart card creation, use, and destruction
Cryptography	When to use it, which encryption technology to use, installation, and configurations
Business continuity planning (BCP) controls	Who is on the BCP team, when drills take place, what is to be documented, and what off-site facility is to be used
Computer operations	How operating systems are to be installed and configured, how applications are to be installed, how to secure workstations, and how to replace hard drives
Incident handling	What defines a security incident, who the report should go to, what should be in the report, and what is done with a report once it is turned in

Table 3-6   Areas Covered by Policies, Standards, Guidelines, and Procedures

mandates that all customer information held in databases must be encrypted with the Data Encryption System (DES) algorithm while it is stored and only transmitted over the Internet using IPSec encryption technologies. The standard indicates what type of protection is required and another level of granularity and explanation is provided. The supporting procedures explain exactly how to implement the DES and IPSec technologies, and guidelines could cover how to handle cases when data is accidentally decrypted, corrupted, or compromised during transmission. As shown in Figure 3-9, all of these work together to provide a company with a security structure.

Implementation

Unfortunately, many times security policies, standards, procedures, baselines, and guidelines are written because an auditor instructed a company to document these items, but they live at the bottom of a file cabinet and are not shared, explained, or used. To be useful, they need to be put to use. No one is going to follow the rules if people don't know that the rules exist. Security policies and the items that support them not only have to be developed, they also have to be implemented.

To be effective, employees need to know about security issues within these documents; therefore, the policies and their supporting counterparts need visibility. Awareness training, manuals, presentations, newsletters, and legal banners can achieve this visibility. It needs to be clear that the directives came from senior management and the full management staff supports these policies. Employees need to understand what is expected of them in their actions, behavior, accountability, and performance.

Implementing security policies and the items that support them shows due care by the company and its management staff. Informing employees of what is expected of them and the consequences of noncompliance can come down to a liability issue. If a company fires an employee because he was downloading pornographic material to the company's computer, the employee can take the company to court and win if the employee

Figure 3-9
Security policies, procedures, standards, and guidelines work together.

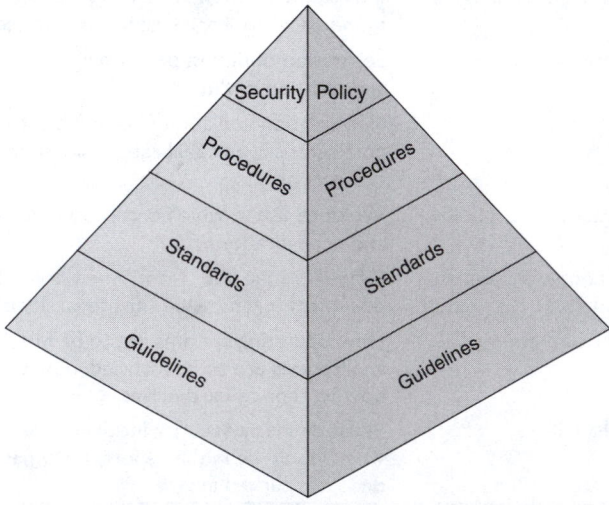

Due Care and Due Diligence

Due care and due diligence are terms that are used throughout this book. *Due diligence* is the act of investigating and understanding the risks the company faces. A company practices *due care* by developing security policies, procedures, and standards. Due care shows that a company has taken responsibility for the activities that take place within the corporation and has taken the necessary steps to help protect the company, its resources, and employees from possible risks. So due diligence is understanding the current threats and risks and due care is implementing countermeasures to provide protection from those threats. If a company does not practice due care and due diligence pertaining to the security of its assets, it can be legally charged with negligence and held accountable for any ramifications of that negligence.

can prove that he was not properly informed of what was considered acceptable and unacceptable use of company property and what the consequences were. Security awareness and training are covered in later sections, but understand that companies that do not supply these to their employees are not practicing due care and can be held negligent and liable in the eyes of the law.

References

NCSA Security Policies and Procedures: **www.ncsa.uiuc.edu/People/ncsairst/Policy.html**

Security Policies and Baseline Standards: **www.security.kirion.net/securitypolicy**

SANS Institute Security Policy Project: **www.sans.org/resources/policies**

Information Security Policy World: **www.information-security-policies-and-standards.com**

Information Classification

My love letter to my dog is top secret. Response: As it should be.

Earlier in this chapter, the importance of recognizing what information is critical to a company and assigning a value to it was touched upon. The rationale behind assigning a value to data is to be able to gauge the amount of funds and resources that should go toward protecting it because not all data has the same value to a company. After the exercise of identifying important information, it should then be properly classified. A company has a lot of information that is created and maintained. The reason to classify data is to organize it according to its sensitivity to loss or disclosure. Once data is segmented according to its sensitivity level, the company can decide what security controls are necessary to protect different types of data. This ensures that information assets receive the appropriate level of protection and classifications indicate the priority of that security protection. The primary purpose of data classification is to indicate the level of confidentiality, integrity, and availability that is required for each type of information.

Data classification helps ensure that the data is protected in the most cost-effective manner. There are costs in protecting and maintaining data, and it is important to endure these costs for the information that actually requires this type of protection. Going back to our very sophisticated example of spies and the peanut butter and banana sandwich recipe, if a company was in charge of protecting spy files, it would classify this data as top secret and apply complex and highly technical security controls and procedures to ensure that it is not accessed in an unauthorized method and disclosed. On the other hand, the sandwich recipe would have a lower classification, and you might protect it by not talking about it.

Each sensitivity classification should have separate handling requirements and procedures pertaining to how that data is accessed, used, and destroyed. For example, in a corporation, confidential information may be only accessed by senior management and a select few throughout the company. To access the information, it may require two or more people to enter their access codes. Auditing could be very detailed and monitored daily, and paper copies of the information may be kept in a vault. To properly erase this data from the media, degaussing or zeroization may be required. Other information in this company may be classified as sensitive and a slightly larger group of people can view it. Access control on the information classified as sensitive may require only one set of credentials. Auditing happens but is only reviewed weekly, paper copies are kept in locked file cabinets, and the data can be deleted using regular measures when it is time to do so. Then the rest of the information is marked public. All employees can access it, and no special auditing or destruction methods are required.

Private Business versus Military Classifications

Earlier we touched on how organizations choose different security models. It depends upon the type of organization, its goals, and objectives. Military organizations are more concerned about not disclosing confidential information when compared to most private sector businesses. Private sector businesses are usually more concerned with the integrity and availability of data. These different perspectives affect data classification also.

To properly implement data classifications, a company must first decide upon the sensitivity scheme they are going to use. One company may choose to use only confidential and public, while another company may choose to use top secret, secret, confidential, sensitive, and unclassified. Table 3-7 explains the types of classifications available. Note that some classifications are used for commercial businesses, whereas others are military classifications.

The following shows the levels of sensitivity from the highest to the lowest for commercial business:

- Confidential
- Private
- Sensitive
- Public

Classification	Definition	Examples	Organization that Would Use This
Sensitive	–Requires special precautions to ensure the integrity of the data by protecting it from unauthorized modification or deletion. –Requires higher than normal assurance of accuracy and completeness.	–Financial information –Details of projects –Profit earnings and forecasts	Commercial business
Confidential	–For use within the company only. –Data that is exempt from disclosure under the Freedom of Information Act or other laws and regulations. –Unauthorized disclosure could seriously affect a company.	–Trade secrets –Health care information –Programming code –Information that keeps a company competitive	Commercial business and military
Private	–Personal information for use within a company. –Unauthorized disclosure could adversely affect personnel.	–Work history –Human resource information –Medical information	Commercial business
Proprietary	–If disclosed, it could reduce competitive edge.	–Recipe to soft drink or other trade secret –Technical specifications of a product	Commercial business
Public	–All data that does not fit into previous classes. –Disclosure is not welcome, but it would not cause an adverse impact to company or personnel.	–How many people are working on a specific project –Upcoming projects	Commercial business
Secret	–If disclosed, it could cause serious damage to national security.	–Deployment plans for troops –Nuclear bomb placement	Military
Top secret	–If disclosed, it could cause grave damage to national security.	–Blueprints of new wartime weapons –Spy satellite information –Espionage data	Military

Table 3-7 Commercial Business and Military Data Classifications

Classification	Definition	Examples	Organization that Would Use This
Sensitive but unclassified (SBU)	–Minor secret. –If disclosed, it could cause serious damage.	–Medical data –Answers to test scores	Military
Unclassified	–Data is not sensitive or classified.	–Computer manual and warranty information –Recruiting information	Military

Table 3-7 Commercial Business and Military Data Classifications *(continued)*

The following shows the levels of sensitivity from the highest to the lowest for the military:

- Top secret
- Secret
- Confidential
- Sensitive but unclassified
- Unclassified

Once the scheme is decided upon, the company needs to develop the criteria they are going to use to decide what information goes into which classification. The following list shows some criteria parameters that an organization may use to determine the sensitivity of data:

- Usefulness of data
- Value of data
- Age of data
- The level of damage that could be caused if the data was disclosed
- The level of damage that could be caused if the data was modified or corrupted
- Laws, regulations, or liability responsibility about protecting the data
- Effects the data has on national security
- Who should be accessing this data
- Who should be maintaining this data
- Where this data should be kept
- Who should be able to reproduce this data
- What data would require labels and special marking

Data Classification Procedures

The following outlines the necessary steps for a proper classification program:

1. Identify data custodian who will be responsible for maintaining data and its security level.

2. Specify the criteria that will determine how data is classified.

3. The data owner must indicate the classification of the data she is responsible for.

4. Indicate the security controls that are required for each classification level.

5. Document any exceptions to the previous classification issues.

6. Indicate the methods that can be used to transfer custody of the information to a different data owner.

7. Indicate termination procedures for declassifying the data.

8. Integrate these issues into the security awareness program so that all employees understand how to handle data at different classification levels.

Now that we have the sensitivity scheme chosen and all data is classified, which was determined by the criteria it met, the next step is to specify how each classification should be dealt with. Provisions for access control, identification, and labeling need to be specified along with how data in specific classifications is stored, maintained, transmitted, and destroyed. Auditing, monitoring, and compliance issues need to be ironed out also. Each classification requires a different degree of security and therefore different requirements from each of the mentioned items.

Reference

Data Classification: **www.sans.org/infosecFAQ/securitybasics/class.htm**

Layers of Responsibility

Senior management and other levels of management understand the vision of the company, the business goals, and objectives. The next layer down is the functional management, who understand how their individual departments work, what roles individuals play within the company, and how security affects their department directly. The next layers are operational managers and staff. These layers are closer to the actual operations of the company. They know detailed information about the technical and procedural requirements, the systems, and how they are used. These layers understand how security mechanisms integrate into systems, how to configure them, and how they affect daily productivity. Each layer has a different insight into what type of role security plays within an organization. Each layer should have input into the best security practices, procedures, and chosen controls to ensure that the security level that is agreed upon provides the necessary level of protection without negatively affecting the company's productivity.

Although each layer is important to the overall security of an organization, there are specific roles that must be clearly defined. These roles are the data owner, data custodian, and user.

Data Owner   The *data owner* is usually a member of senior management and is ultimately responsible for the protection and use of a specific subset of information. The data owner falls within the bounds of due care responsibilities and will be held responsible for any negligent acts that result in the corruption or disclosure of the data. He decides upon the classification of the data he is responsible for and alters these classifications if the business needs arise. The data owner will delegate the responsibility of the day-to-day maintenance of the data, which is the responsibility of the data custodian.

Data Custodian   The *data custodian* is given the responsibility of the maintenance and protection of the data. This role is usually filled by the system administrator, and the duties include performing regular backups of the data, implementing security mechanisms, periodically validating the integrity of the data, restoring data from backup media, and fulfilling the requirements specified in the company's security policy, standards, and guidelines that pertain to information security and data protection.

 NOTE   A system administrator has the responsibility of individual computers and devices while a network administrator is more concerned with how the computers and devices are connected and work together within a network. In smaller environments, they are usually one in the same.

User   The *user* is considered any individual who routinely uses the data for work-related tasks. The user must have the necessary level of access to the data to perform the duties within her position and is responsible for following operational security procedures to ensure the data's confidentiality, integrity, and availability to others.

Poor security management causes a majority of security problems. Different levels of management have different layers of security responsibility. A senior-level committee should be established to ensure that security issues receive appropriate and proper attention by senior officials. A chief information officer (CIO) or security officer should work with senior management to define strategic security procedures and support business managers in defining their information and security needs. Business managers have the primary responsibility for determining the level of protection needed for information system resources, therefore, they should be intimately involved with the selection of security safeguards. A security administrator's tasks are many, and include creating new system user accounts, implementing new security software, testing security patches and components, and issuing new passwords. They should not have to actually *approve* of new system user accounts; this is a responsibility of the business managers.

Security Roles Within an Organization

The following are security roles found in an organization:

- **Senior manager** Ultimately responsible for security of the organization and the protection of its assets

- **Security professional** Functionally responsible for security and carrying out senior manager's directives

- **Data owner** Determines data classification of information within the organization

- **Data custodian** Maintains data in ways to preserve and protect its confidentiality, integrity, and availability

- **User** Uses data for data-processing tasks

- **Auditor** Examines security practices and mechanisms within the organization

A decision maker is not the proper role for the information security specialists or system administrator in protecting system resources. They may have the technical knowledge of how security mechanisms should be implemented and configured, but they should not be put into a position of deciding how the company approaches security and what security measures should be implemented. Too many times companies handle security at the security administrator level. In these situations, security is not viewed in broad enough terms. Proper risk analysis is usually not performed. Senior management is not fully aware of the risks the company faces. Not enough funds are available for security, and when a security breach takes place, there is not an efficient way of dealing with it. As stated previously, security should work in a top-down fashion to be ultimately successful.

A company's security is not only tied to the type of firewall installed and the timeliness of security patches being applied. A company is an environment filled with various resources, activities, people, and practices. The security of the environment needs to be approached in a holistic way with each part of security addressed in a serious and responsible manner. The following sections describe compartments of security not usually considered when one thinks about securing a company's environment.

Personnel

There are many facets of personnel responsibilities that fall under management's umbrella, and several of these have a direct correlation to the overall security of the environment.

Although society has evolved to be extremely dependent upon technology in the work area, people are still the key ingredient to a successful company. Within security, people are often the weakest link. Either accidentally through mistakes or lack of training or intentionally through fraud and malicious intent, personnel cause more security issues than hacker attacks, outside espionage, or equipment failure. Although the future actions of individuals cannot be predicted, it is possible to minimize the risks by providing preventive measures. These include hiring the most qualified individuals, performing background checks, employing detailed job descriptions, providing necessary training, enforcing strict access control, and terminating individuals in a way that protects all parties involved.

Structure

If a company wants to have effective employee safety, a certain structure needs to be put into place by management and actually followed. This structure includes job descriptions, clear definitions of responsibilities, lines of authority, and acceptable reprimands for specific activities. A clear-cut structure takes the mystery out of who does what and how things are handled in different situations.

There are several items that can be put into place to reduce the possibilities of fraud, sabotage, misuse of information, theft, and other security compromises. *Separation of duties* makes sure that one individual cannot complete a critical task by herself. In the movies when a submarine captain launches a nuclear torpedo, which is necessary to blow up the enemy and save civilization as we know it, it usually requires three codes to be entered into the launching mechanism by three different senior crewmembers. This is an example of separation of duties, and it makes sure that the captain cannot complete such an important and terrifying task all by himself.

In an organization that practices separation of duties, collusion is required to take place for different types of security compromises. *Collusion* means that at least two people would need to work together to cause some type of destruction or fraud, and this drastically reduces its probability.

In a software development environment, there should be clear distinctions between programmers, test beds, libraries, operations, and production. Programmers should be able to work on their code and test it as needed. Once the programmer is finished with her tasks, she turns the code over to quality assurance who run their own tests in another environment that mirrors the production environment. Once the code passes all the necessary tests, it should be stored in a software library. When it is necessary for the code to go into production, it moves from the library to the production environment. Code should not go from the programmer directly to production without testing and checking it into the library. The test environment should be clearly differentiated from the production environment to ensure that untested code does not accidentally go into production. And the programmer should not tinker with the software once it is in production. These clear-cut methods make sure that no steps are skipped in the phases of software development and that changes are not made in unstructured and dangerous ways.

Hiring Practices

I like your hat. You're hired!

Depending on the position that needs to be filled, a level of screening should be practiced to ensure that the company hires the right individual for the right job. Skills should be tested and evaluated, and the caliber and character of the individual should be examined. Joe might be the best programmer in the state, but if someone looked into his past and found out that he hacked up his wife with a knife, the hiring manager might not be so eager to bring Joe into the organization.

Nondisclosure agreements need to be developed and signed by new employees to protect the company and its sensitive information. Any conflicts of interests need to be addressed, and there should be different agreements and precautions taken with temporary and contract employees.

References should be checked, military records reviewed, education verified, and if necessary, a drug test should be administered. Many times, important personal behaviors can be concealed, and that is why hiring practices now include scenario questions, personality tests, and observations of the individual versus just looking at a person's work history. When a person is hired, he is bringing in his business skills and whatever other baggage he carries. A company can reduce its heartache pertaining to personnel by first conducting useful and carefully carried out hiring practices.

Operations

A management structure must be in place to make sure everyone has someone to report to and the responsibility for another person's actions is spread equally and intelligently. Consequences for noncompliance or unacceptable behavior must be communicated before an event takes place. Proper supervisory skills need to be acquired and used to ensure that operations go smoothly and any out-of-the-ordinary activities can be taken care of before they get out of control.

Job rotation is an important part of keeping operations a healthy and productive part of the company. No one person should stay in one position for a long period of time because it can end up giving too much control of a segment of the business to this individual. Such total control could result in fraud, data modification, and misuse of information. Employees in sensitive areas should be forced to take their vacations. This would require other individuals to fulfill their positions and any fraudulent errors or activities can be detected.

Job rotation can be used to teach others specific tasks of a particular role within the company. Once these other individuals understand the necessary tasks of the role, they may be able to detect when someone fulfilling that role is carrying out fraudulent activity.

Termination

Because terminations can happen for a variety of different reasons and people will have different reactions, companies should have a specific set of procedures that happen with each and every termination. The employee must leave the facility immediately under the supervision of a manager or security guard. The employee must surrender any identification badges or keys, complete an exit interview, and return company supplies. That user's accounts and passwords should be disabled or changed immediately. It seems harsh and cold when this actually takes place, but too many companies have been hurt by vengeful employees who have lashed out at the company when their positions were revoked for one reason or another. If an employee is disgruntled in any way or the termination is unfriendly, that employee's accounts should be disabled right away and all passwords on specific systems changed.

Security Awareness

The management's directives pertaining to security is captured in the security policy, and the standards, procedures, and guidelines are developed to support these directives. However, this will not be effective if no one knows about these items and how the company expects them to be implemented. For security to be successful and effective, senior management on down to the rest of the staff need to be fully aware of the importance of computer and information security. All employees should understand the underlying significance of security and the specific security-related requirements expected of them.

The controls and procedures of a security program should reflect the nature of the data being processed. A company that sells baseball cards would not need the level of structured controls and security procedures that may be required of a company that develops heat-seeking missiles. These different types of companies would also have very different cultures. For a security awareness program to be effective these considerations must be understood. The program should be developed in a fashion that makes sense for that environment.

For an organization to achieve the desired results of their security program, they must communicate the what, how, and why of security to their employees. It should be comprehensive, tailored for specific groups, and organization-wide. The goal is that each employee understands the importance of security to the company as a whole and to each individual. Expected responsibilities and acceptable behaviors need to be clarified, and noncompliance repercussions that could range from a warning to dismissal need to be explained before being invoked.

Different Types of Security Training

I want my training to have a lot of pictures and pop-up books.

There are usually at least three audiences for a security awareness program: management, staff, and technical employees. Each type of awareness training needs to be geared toward the individual audience to ensure that each group understands its particular responsibilities, liabilities, and expectations. If a technical security training were given to senior management, their eyes would glaze over as soon as protocols and firewalls were mentioned. On the flip side, if legal ramifications, company liability issues pertaining to protecting data, and shareholder's expectations were discussed with the IT group, they would quickly start a game of hangman or tic-tac-toe with their neighbor.

Management would benefit the most from a short, focused security awareness orientation that discusses corporate assets and financial gains and losses pertaining to security. They need to know how stock prices can be negatively affected by compromises, possible threats and their outcomes, and an explanation of how it needs to be integrated into the environment in the same way as other business policies. The management group must lead the rest of the company in support for security; thus, they must gain the right mind-set about its importance.

Mid-management would benefit from more detailed explanations of the policies, procedures, standards, and guidelines and how they map to individual departments that this level of management is responsible for. They should be shown how critical their support is for their specific departments and their level of responsibility for ensuring that employees practice safe computing activities. They should also be shown how the consequences of noncompliance by individuals who report to them can affect the company as a whole and how they, as managers, may have to answer for such indiscretions.

The technical departments must receive a different presentation that aligns more to their daily tasks. They should receive a more in-depth training to discuss technical configurations, incident handling, and indications of different types of security compromises so they can be properly recognized.

Each group needs to know whom it should report suspicious activity to and how they are expected to handle these situations. Employees should not try to combat an attacker or address fraudulent activities by themselves. Each employee should be told to report these issues to upper management, and upper management should determine how the situation is to be handled.

Staff members need to understand why security is important to the company and important to them individually. The more that it can be shown how individuals can be negatively affected by insecure activities, the more they will be willing to participate. This presentation should have many examples of acceptable and unacceptable activities. Examples of these activities can include questioning an unknown individual in a restricted portion of the facility, proper Internet use, expected use of e-mail capabilities, not removing company-owned material, and intellectual property issues. The employees should fully understand what is expected of them and what could happen if they do not follow these guidelines. It is usually best to have each employee sign a document indicating that he has heard and understands all the security topics discussed and he understands the ramifications of noncompliance. This reinforces the importance to the employee and also provides evidence down the road if the employee claims that he was never told about these expectations.

Security training should happen periodically and continually. We learn mostly by repetition, and this training should take place at least once a year. The goal is to not only get individuals to understand how security works in their environment, but to also get individuals to understand *why*. The main reason to perform security awareness training is to modify employees' behavior and attitude toward security.

References

CISSP.com: **www.cissps.com**

CISSP and SSCP Open Study Guides: **www.cccure.org**

Summary

Security management embodies the administrative and procedural activities necessary to support and protect information and company assets throughout the enterprise. It includes

Figure 3-10
Necessary pieces that fit together to form effective and efficient security

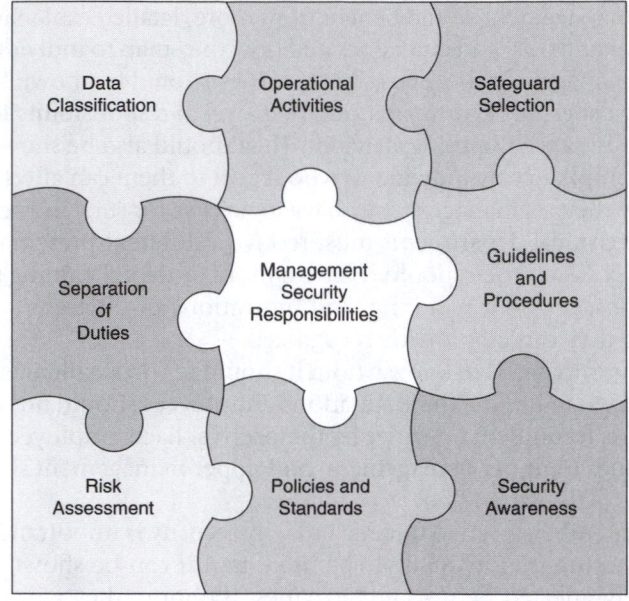

development and enforcement of security policies and their supporting mechanisms: procedures, standards, baselines, and guidelines. It encompasses risk management, security awareness training, and proper countermeasure selection and implementation. Personnel (hiring, terminating, training, and management structure) and operational (job rotation and separation of duties) activities must also be conducted properly to ensure a secure environment. The management must understand the legal and ethical responsibilities it is required to respect and uphold. Figure 3-10 illustrates some of the necessary pieces for an effective and efficient security program.

Security is a business issue and should be treated as such. It needs to be properly integrated into the company's overall business goals and objectives because security issues can negatively affect the resources the company depends upon. More and more corporations are finding out the price that has to be paid when security is not given the proper attention, support, and funds. This is a wonderful world to live in, but bad things can happen. The ones who realize this notion not only survive, but they also thrive.

Quick Tips

- A vulnerability is the absence of a safeguard or a weakness that could be exploited.
- A threat is the possibility that someone would exploit a vulnerability.
- A risk is the probability of a threat agent exploiting a vulnerability and the loss potential from that action.
- Reducing vulnerabilities and/or threats reduces the risk.
- An exposure is an instance of being exposed to losses from a threat.

- A countermeasure, also called a safeguard, mitigates the risk.
- A countermeasure can be an application, software configuration, hardware, or procedure.
- Security management has become more important over the years because networks have evolved from centralized environments to distributed environments.
- The objectives of security are to provide availability, integrity, and confidentiality of data and resources.
- Strategic planning is long term, tactical planning is mid-term, and operational planning is day to day. They make up a planning horizon.
- Security components can be technical (firewalls, encryption, and access control lists) or non-technical (security policy, procedures, and compliance enforcement).
- Assurance is a degree of confidence that a certain security level is being provided.
- Security management should work from the top down, from senior management down to the staff.
- The security model a company chooses depends on the type of business, its critical missions, and objectives.
- Risk management is the process of reducing risk to an acceptable level and maintaining that level.
- Risk can be transferred, rejected, reduced, or accepted.
- An example of risk transference is when a company buys insurance.
- A way of reducing risk is to improve security procedures and/or implementing safeguards.
- If a company is rejecting risk, it is choosing to ignore it, which can be dangerous.
- Threats × vulnerability × asset value = total risk
- (Threats × vulnerability × asset value) × controls gap = residual risk
- The main goals of risk analysis are the following: identify risks, quantify the impact of potential threats, and provide an economic balance between the impact of the risk and the cost of the safeguards.
- A risk analysis is a tool used to identify the degree of risk a company is under and estimate the proper budget that should be formed to reduce and mitigate this risk.
- A quantitative risk analysis attempts to assign monetary values to components within the analysis.
- A purely quantitative risk analysis is not possible because it is trying to quantify qualitative items.
- When determining the value of information, the following issues need to be considered: the cost to acquire and develop data; the cost to maintain and

protect data; the value of the data to owners, users, and adversaries; the cost of replacement if lost; the price others are willing to pay for the data; and the usefulness of the data.

- There are automated risk analysis tools that reduce the amount of manual work involved. They estimate future expected losses and calculate the benefits of different security measures.

- Single loss expectancy is the amount that could be lost if a specific threat agent exploited a vulnerability.

- Single loss expectancy × frequency per year = annualized loss expectancy (SLE × ARO = ALE)

- Qualitative risk analysis uses judgment and intuition instead of numbers.

- Qualitative risk analysis uses scenarios that walk through risks and have the people with the experience and education on such matters rate the probability, potential loss, and severity of each risk.

- The Delphi technique is a group decision method where each member can vote anonymously.

- When choosing the right safeguard to reduce a specific risk, the cost, functionality, and effectiveness need to be evaluated and a cost/benefit analysis needs to be performed.

- Safeguards should be highly visible, but their mechanisms should be hidden.

- A security policy is a statement by management dictating the role security plays in the organization.

- Procedures are detailed, step-by-step actions that should be followed to achieve a certain task.

- A standard specifies how hardware and software are to be used. Standards are compulsory.

- Baselines provide a minimum level of security acceptable for an environment.

- Guidelines are recommendations and general approaches that provide advice and flexibility.

- Data is classified to assign priorities to data and ensure that the appropriate level of protection is provided.

- The military is more concerned about confidentiality of data, whereas commercial businesses are usually more concerned with data integrity and availability.

- Data owners specify the classification of data.

- The objective of every loss prevention program is to reduce losses to a predefined level of tolerance.

- Security has functional requirements, which define the expected behavior from a product or system, and assurance requirements, which establish confidence in the implemented products or systems overall.

- Risk management mitigates risks by defining and controlling threats and vulnerabilities.

- The security program should be integrated with current business objectives and goals.

- Management needs to define the scope and purpose of security management, provide support, appoint a security team, delegate responsibility, and review the team's findings.

- The security team should be individuals from different departments within the organization and not just technical personnel.

- A risk analysis can take a lot of time from different people within the company. The process of a risk analysis needs to be understood prior to starting the analysis.

- A risk can have delayed loss and/or delayed damages, meaning that losses can be experienced over a period of time or damages can be experienced at a later date.

- A qualitative rating would be expressed in high, medium, or low, or on a scale of 1 to 5 or 1 to 10. A quantitative result would be expressed in dollar amounts and percentages.

- Safeguards should default to least privilege, have fail-safe defaults, and override capabilities.

- Safeguards should be imposed uniformly so everyone has the same restrictions and functionality.

- For security purposes, information should be categorized on the basis of availability, integrity, and confidentiality.

- A key element during the initial security planning process is to define reporting relationships.

Questions

Please remember that these questions are formatted and asked in a certain way for a reason. You must remember that the CISSP exam is asking questions at a conceptual level. Questions may not always have the perfect answer, and the candidate is advised against always looking for the perfect answer. The candidate should look for the best answer in the list.

1. Who has the primary responsibility of determining the classification level for information?

    A. Functional manager

    B. Senior management

    C. Owner

    D. User

2. Which group causes the most risk of fraud and computer compromises?

    A. Employees

    B. Hackers

C. Attackers

D. Contractors

3. If different user groups with different security access levels need to access the same information, which of the following actions should management take?

A. Decrease the security level on the information to ensure accessibility and usability of the information.

B. Require specific written approval each time an individual needs to access the information.

C. Increase the security controls on the information.

D. Increase the classification label on the information.

4. What does management need to consider the most when classifying data?

A. Type of employees, contractors, and customers who will be accessing the data.

B. Availability, integrity, and confidentiality.

C. First assess the risk level and disable countermeasures.

D. The access controls that will be protecting the data.

5. Who is ultimately responsible for making sure data is classified and protected?

A. Data owners

B. Users

C. Administrators

D. Management

6. What is a procedure?

A. Rules on how software and hardware must be used within the environment

B. Step-by-step directions on how to accomplish a task

C. Guidelines on how to approach security situations that are not covered by standards

D. Compulsory actions

7. Which factor is the most important item when it comes to ensuring that security is successful in an organization?

A. Senior management support

B. Effective controls and implementation methods

C. Updated and relevant security policies and procedures

D. Security awareness by all employees

8. When is it acceptable to not take action on an identified risk?

A. Never. Good security addresses and reduces all risks.

B. When political issues prevent this type of risk from being addressed.

    C. When the necessary countermeasure is complex.

    D. When the cost of the countermeasure outweighs the value of the asset and potential loss.

9. What are security policies?

    A. Step-by-step directions on how to accomplish security tasks

    B. General guidelines used to accomplish a specific security level

    C. Broad, high-level statements from the management

    D. Detailed documents explaining how security incidents should be handled

10. Which is the most valuable technique when determining if a specific security control should be implemented?

    A. Risk analysis

    B. Cost/benefit analysis

    C. ALE results

    D. Identifying the vulnerabilities and threats causing the risk

11. Which best describes the purpose of the ALE calculation?

    A. Quantifies the security level of the environment

    B. Estimates the loss possible for a countermeasure

    C. Quantifies the cost/benefit result

    D. Estimates the loss potential of a threat in a year span

12. Tactical planning is:

    A. Mid-term

    B. Long-term

    C. Day-to-day

    D. Six months

13. What is the definition of a security exposure?

    A. An instance of being exposed to losses from a threat

    B. Any potential danger to information or systems

    C. An information security absence or weakness

    D. A loss potential of a threat

14. An effective security program requires a balanced application of:

    A. Technical and non-technical methods

    B. Countermeasures and safeguards

    C. Physical security and technical controls

    D. Procedural security and encryption

15. The security functionality defines the expected activities of a security mechanism, and assurance defines:

   A. The controls the security mechanism will enforce

   B. The data classification after the security mechanism has been implemented

   C. The confidence of the security the mechanism is providing

   D. Cost/benefit relationship

16. Which statement is true when looking at security objectives in the private business sector versus the military sector?

   A. Only the military has true security.

   B. Businesses usually care more about data integrity and availability, whereas the military is more concerned with confidentiality.

   C. The military requires higher levels of security because the risks are so much higher.

   D. The business sector usually cares most about data availability and confidentiality, whereas the military is most concerned about integrity.

17. How do you calculate residual risk?

   A. Threats × risks × asset value

   B. (Threats × asset value × vulnerability) × risks

   C. SLE × frequency = ALE

   D. (Threats × vulnerability × asset value) × controls gap

18. Which of the following is not a purpose of doing a risk analysis?

   A. Delegate responsibility

   B. Quantify impact of potential threats

   C. Identify risks

   D. Define the balance between the impact of a risk and the cost of the necessary countermeasure

19. How does a risk analysis show management how much money to spend per security measure?

   A. It shows management how much could be lost if the security measure is not implemented.

   B. It calculates the frequency of the risk times the cost/benefit ratio of the ALE.

   C. It shows management how much money could be saved if the security program was implemented.

   D. It provides the qualitative severity of the security measure.

20. Which of the following is not a management role in the process of implementing and maintaining security?

    A. Support

    B. Perform risk analysis

    C. Define purpose and scope

    D. Delegate responsibility

21. Why should the team that is going to perform and review the risk analysis information be made up of people in different departments?

    A. To make sure the process is fair and that no one is left out.

    B. They shouldn't. It should be a small group brought in from outside the organization because otherwise the analysis is biased and unusable.

    C. Because people in different departments understand the risks of their department and it ensures that the data going into the analysis is as close to reality as possible.

    D. Because the people in the different departments are the ones causing the risks, so they should be the ones held accountable.

22. Which best describes quantitative risk analysis?

    A. Scenario-based analysis to research different security threats

    B. A method used to apply severity levels to potential loss, probability of loss, and risks

    C. A method that assigns monetary values to components in the risk assessment

    D. A method that is based on gut feelings and opinions

23. Why is a truly quantitative risk analysis not possible to achieve?

    A. It is possible, which is why it is used.

    B. It assigns severity levels. Thus, it is hard to translate into monetary values.

    C. It is dealing with purely quantitative elements.

    D. Quantitative measures must be applied to qualitative elements.

24. If there are automated tools for risk analysis, why does it take so much time to complete?

    A. A lot of data has to be gathered to be inputted into the automated tool.

    B. Management has to approve it and then a team has to be built.

    C. Risk analysis cannot be automated because of the nature of the assessment.

    D. Many people have to agree on the same data.

25. Which of the following is a legal term that pertains to a company or individual taking reasonable actions and is used to determine liability?

   A. Standards

   B. Due process

   C. Due care

   D. Downstream liabilities

Answers

1. **C.** A company can have one specific data owner or different data owners who have been delegated the responsibility of protecting specific sets of data. One of the responsibilities that goes into protecting this information is properly classifying it.

2. **A.** It is commonly stated that internal threats comprise 70–80 percent of the overall threat to a company. This is because employees already have privileged access to a wide range of company assets. The outsider who wants to cause damage must obtain this level of access before she can carry out the type of damage that internal personnel can carry out. A lot of the damages that are caused by internal employees are brought about by mistakes and system misconfigurations.

3. **C.** If data is going to be available to a wide range of people, more security should be implemented to ensure that only the necessary people access the data and the operations they carry out are controlled. The security implemented can come in the form of authentication and authorization technologies, encryption, and specific access control mechanisms.

4. **B.** The best answer to this question is B because to properly classify data the data owner needs to evaluate the availability, integrity, and confidentiality requirements of the data. Once this is done this will dictate what employees, contractors, and users can access the data, which is expressed in answer A. This assessment will also help determine the controls that should be put into place.

5. **D.** The key to this question is the use of the word "ultimately." Management is ultimately responsible for everything that takes place within a company. They need to make sure data and resources are being properly protected on an ongoing basis. They can delegate tasks to others, but they are ultimately responsible.

6. **B.** Standards are rules that must be followed, thus they are compulsory. Guidelines are recommendations. Procedures are step-by-step instructions.

7. **A.** Without senior management's support a security program will not receive the necessary attention, funds, resources, and enforcement capabilities.

8. **D.** Companies may decide to live with specific risks they are faced with because it would cost more to try and protect themselves than they have a potential of

losing if the threat became real. Countermeasures are usually complex to a degree, and there are almost always political issues surrounding different risks, but these are not reasons to not implement a countermeasure.

9. **C.** A security policy captures senior management's perspectives and directives on what role security should play within the company. They are usually vague and use broad terms so they can cover a wide range of items.

10. **B.** Although the other answers may seem correct, B is the best answer here. This is because a risk analysis is performed to identify risks and come up with suggested countermeasures. The ALE tells the company how much it could lose if a specific threat became real. The ALE value will go into the cost/benefit analysis, but the ALE does not address the cost of the countermeasure and the benefit of a countermeasure. All the data captured in answers A, C, and D are inserted into a cost/benefit analysis.

11. **D.** The ALE calculation estimates the potential loss that can affect one asset from a specific threat within a one-year time span. This value is used to figure out the amount of money that should be earmarked to protect this asset from this threat.

12. **A.** There are three types of goals that make up the planning horizon: operational, tactical, and strategic. The tactical goals are mid-term goals that must be accomplished before the overall strategic goal is accomplished.

13. **A.** An exposure means that a vulnerability has been exploited by a threat agent. Examples are: a hacker accesses a database through an open port on the firewall, an employee shares confidential information via e-mail, or a virus infects a computer.

14. **A.** Security is not defined by a firewall, an access control mechanism, a security policy, company procedures, employee conduct, or authentication technologies. It is defined by all of these and how they integrate together within an environment. Security is not purely technical and it is not purely procedural, but rather, a mix of the two.

15. **C.** The functionality describes how a mechanism will work and behave. This may have nothing to do with the actual protection it provides. Assurance is the level of confidence in the protection level a mechanism will provide. When systems and mechanisms are evaluated, their functionality and assurance should be examined and tested individually.

16. **B.** Although answer C may seem correct to you, it is a subjective answer. Businesses will see their threats and risks as being more important than another organization's threats and risks. The military has a rich history of having to keep their secrets secret. This is usually not as important in the commercial sector relative to the military.

17. **D.** The equation is more conceptual than it is practical. It is hard to assign a number to a vulnerability and a threat individually. What this equation is saying is look at the potential loss of a specific asset and look at the controls

gap, which means what the specific countermeasure cannot protect against. What is left is the residual risk. Residual risk is what is left over after a countermeasure is implemented.

18. **A.** The other three answers are the main reasons to carry out a risk analysis. An analysis is not carried out to delegate responsibilities. Management will take on this responsibility once the results of the analysis are reported to them and they understand what actually needs to be carried out.

19. **A.** The crux of carrying out a risk analysis is to calculate risk and estimate how much specific threats could cost the company. From these numbers senior management can make a decision on the best security mechanisms and how much should be spent on them.

20. **B.** The number one ingredient management needs to provide when it comes to security is support. They need to define the role of security, the scope of security, and the different assessments that will be carried out. They will also delegate who does what pertaining to security. They will not carry out the analysis, but are responsible for making sure one is done and that they act on the results it provides.

21. **C.** An analysis is only as good as the data that goes into it. Data pertaining to risks the company faces should be extracted from the people who understand the business functions and environment of the company the best. Each department understands their own threats and resources, and may have possible solutions to specific risks that affect their part of the company.

22. **C.** A quantitative risk analysis assigns monetary values and percentages to the different components within the assessment. A qualitative analysis uses opinions of individuals and a rating system to gauge the severity level of different threats and the benefits of specific countermeasures.

23. **D.** During a risk analysis the team is trying to properly predict the future and all the risks that future may bring. It is somewhat of a subjective exercise and educated guessing must take place. It is very hard to properly predict that a flood will take place once in ten years and cost a company up to $40,000 in damages, but this is what a quantitative analysis tries to accomplish.

24. **A.** An analysis usually takes a long time to complete because of all the data that must be properly gathered. There are usually a lot of different sources for this type of data and properly extracting it is extremely time consuming. In most situations it involves setting up meetings with specific personnel and going through a question-and-answer process.

25. **C.** A company's or individual's actions can be judged by the "Prudent Person Rule," which looks at how a prudent or reasonable person would react in similar situations. Due care means to take these necessary actions to protect the company, its assets, customers, and employees. Computer security has many aspects pertaining to practicing due care. If management does not ensure that these things are in place, they can be found negligent.

Access Control

In this chapter, you will learn about the following items:
- Identification methods and technologies
- Authentication methods, models, and technologies
- Discretionary, mandatory, and nondiscretionary access control
- Accountability, monitoring, and auditing practices
- Emanation security and technologies
- Possible threats to access control practices and technologies

A cornerstone in the foundation of information security is controlling how resources are accessed so they can be protected from unauthorized modification or disclosure. The controls that enforce access control can be technical, physical, or administrative in nature.

Access Control

Access controls are security features that control how users and systems communicate and interact with other systems and resources. They protect the systems and resources from unauthorized access and can be a component that participates in determining the level of authorization after an authentication procedure has successfully completed. Although we usually think of a user as the entity that requires access to a network resource or information, there are many other types of entities that require access to other network entities and resources that are subject to access control. It is important to understand the definition of a subject and an object when working in the context of access control.

Access is the flow of information between a subject and an object. A *subject* is an active entity that requests access to an object or the data within an object. A subject can be a user, program, or process that accesses an object to accomplish a task. When a program accesses a file, the program is the subject and the file is the object. An *object* is a passive entity that contains information. An object can be a computer, database, file, computer program, directory, or field contained in a table within a database. When you look up information in a database, you are the active subject and the database is the passive object. Figure 4-1 illustrates subjects and objects.

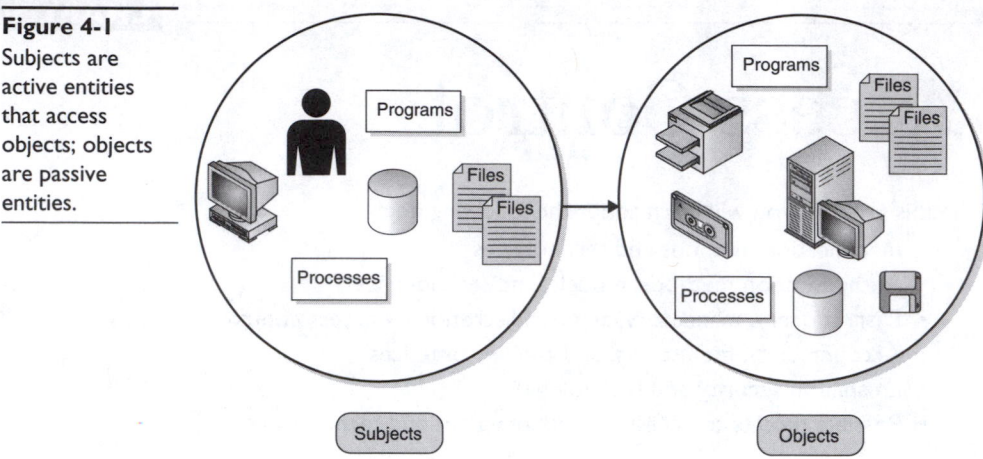

Figure 4-1
Subjects are active entities that access objects; objects are passive entities.

Access control is a broad term that covers several different types of mechanisms that enforce access control features on computer systems, networks, and information. It is extremely important because it is one of the first lines of defense used to fight against unauthorized access to systems and network resources. When a user is prompted for a username and password to be able to use a computer, this is access control. Once the user logs in and later attempts to access a file, that file can have a list of users and groups that have the right to access it. If the user is not on this list, the user is denied. This is another form of access control. The users' permissions and rights are based on the identity, clearance, and/or group membership. Access controls give organizations the ability to control, restrict, monitor, and protect resource availability, integrity, and confidentiality.

Security Principles

The three main security principles for any type of security control are availability, integrity, and confidentiality. Figure 4-2 shows these three attributes. These issues were touched upon in Chapter 3 and will be a running theme throughout this book because each core subject of each chapter approaches these principles in a unique way. In Chapter 3, security management procedures include identifying threats that can negatively affect the availability, integrity, and confidentiality of the company's assets and finding cost-effective countermeasures that will protect them. This chapter looks at the ways that the three principles can be affected and protected through access control methodologies and technologies.

Availability

Hey, I'm available. Response: But no one wants you.

Information, systems, and resources need to be available to users in a timely manner so productivity will not be affected. Most information needs to be accessible and available

Figure 4-2
The three main attributes of security are availability, integrity, and confidentiality.

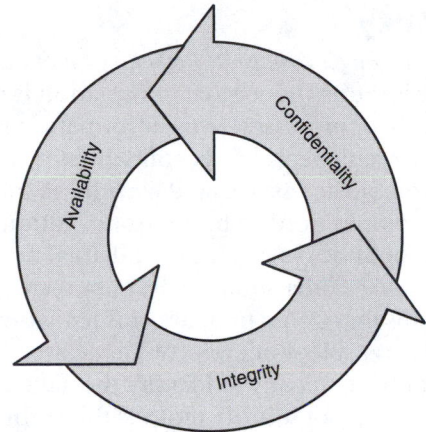

for users when it is requested so they can carry out tasks and fulfill their responsibilities. Accessing information does not seem that important until it is inaccessible. Administrators experience this when a file server goes offline or a highly used database is out of service for one reason or another. Fault tolerance and recovery mechanisms are put into place to ensure the continuity of the *availability* of resources. User productivity can be greatly affected if requested data is not readily available.

Information has various attributes such as accuracy, relevance, timeliness, and privacy. It may be extremely important for a stockbroker to have information that is accurate and timely, so he can buy and sell stocks at the right times at the right prices. The stockbroker does not necessarily care about the privacy of this information, only that it is readily available. A soft drink company that depends on its soda pop recipe would care about the privacy of this trade secret, and the security mechanisms in place need to ensure this secrecy.

Integrity

Information must be accurate, complete, and protected from unauthorized or unexpected modification. When a security mechanism provides *integrity*, it will protect data from being altered in an unauthorized fashion. If some type of illegitimate modification does occur, the security mechanism must alert the user or discard the message altogether. One example is when a user sends a request to her online bank account to pay her $24.56 water utility bill. This user needs to be sure that the integrity of that transaction was not altered during transmission, so the user does not end up paying the utility company $240.56 instead. Integrity of data is very important. What if a confidential e-mail was sent from the Secretary of State to the President of the United States and was intercepted and altered without a security mechanism in place that disallows this or alerts the President that this message has been altered? Instead of receiving a message reading, "We would love for you and your wife to stop by for drinks tonight," the message could be altered to say, "We have just bombed Libya." Big difference.

Confidentiality

This is my secret and you can't have it. Response: I don't want it.

Confidentiality is the assurance that information is not disclosed to unauthorized individuals, programs, or processes. Some information is more sensitive than other information and requires a higher level of confidentiality. Control mechanisms need to be in place to dictate who can access data and what the subject can do with it once it has been accessed. These activities need to be controlled, audited, and monitored. Examples of information that could be considered confidential are health records, financial account information, criminal records, source code, trade secrets, and military tactical plans. Some security mechanisms that would provide confidentiality are encryption, logical and physical access controls, transmission protocols, database views, and controlled traffic flow.

It is important for a company to identify the data that needs to be classified so it can ensure that a top priority of security protects this information and keeps it confidential. If this information is not singled out, too much time and money can be spent on implementing the same amount of security levels for critical and mundane information. It may be necessary to configure virtual private networks (VPNs) between organizations with the IPSec encryption protocol to encrypt all messages passed when communicating about trade secrets, sharing customer information, or making financial transactions. This takes a certain amount of hardware, man-hours, funds, and overhead. The same security precautions are not necessary when communicating that today's special in the cafeteria is liver and onions with a roll on the side. So the first step in protecting data's confidentiality is identifying which information is sensitive, to what degree, and then implementing security mechanisms to protect it properly.

Different security mechanisms can supply different degrees of availability, integrity, and confidentiality. The environment, the classification of the data that is to be protected, and the security goals need to be evaluated to ensure that the proper security mechanisms are bought and put into place. Many corporations have wasted a lot of time and money not following these steps and instead buying the new "gee whiz" product that recently hit the market.

Identification, Authentication, Authorization, and Accountability

For a user to be able to access a resource, it must be determined if this individual is who he claims to be, if he has the necessary credentials, and if he has been given the necessary rights or privileges to perform the actions he is requesting. Once these steps are completed successfully, the user can access and use network resources; however, it is necessary to track the user's activities and enforce accountability for his actions. *Identification* describes a method of ensuring that a subject (user, program, or process) is the entity it claims to be. Identification can be provided with the use of a username or account number. To be properly *authenticated*, the subject is usually required to provide a second piece to the credential set. This piece could be a password, passphrase, cryptographic key, personal identification number (PIN), anatomical attribute, or token. These two credential items are compared to what information has been previously stored for this subject. If these credentials match the stored information, the subject is authenticated. But we are not done yet. Once the subject provides its credentials and is properly identified, the system it is trying to access needs to determine if this subject has been given the necessary rights and privileges to carry out the requested actions. The system will look at some type of access control matrix or compare security labels to verify that this subject can indeed access the requested resource and perform the actions he is attempting. If the subject can access the resource, the subject has just been *authorized*. Although identification, authentication, and authorization have close and complementary definitions, they each have distinct functions that fulfill a specific requirement in the process of access control. A user may be properly identified and authenticated to the network, but he may not have the authorization to access the files on the file server. On the other hand, a user may be authorized to access the files on the file server, but until she is properly identified and authenticated, those resources are out of reach. Figure 4-3 illustrates the three steps that must happen for a subject to access an object.

The subject needs to be held accountable for the actions taken within a system or domain. The only way to ensure accountability is if the subject is uniquely identified and the subject's actions are recorded.

Logical access controls are tools used for identification, authentication, authorization, and accountability. They are software components that enforce access control measures for systems, programs, processes, and information. The logical access controls can be embedded within operating systems, applications, add-on security packages, or within database and telecommunication management systems. It can be challenging to get all access controls synchronized without producing overlaps of functionality and ensuring that all vulnerabilities are covered; however, if it were easy, security professionals would not be getting the big bucks!

 NOTE The words "logical" and "technical" can be used interchangeably in this context. It is conceivable that the CISSP exam would refer to logical and technical controls interchangeably.

Figure 4-3
There are three steps that must happen for a subject to access an object: identification, authentication, and authorization.

1. Identification

2. Authentication

3. Authorization

Resource

If resources are valuable, they need to be protected and made accessible to only authorized individuals.

An individual's identity needs to be verified during the authentication process. Authentication usually contains a two-step process: entering public information (a username, employee number, account number, or department ID) and then entering private information (a static password, smart token, cognitive password, one-time password, PIN, or digital signature). Entering public information is the identification step and entering private information is the authentication step of the two-step process. Each technique used for identification and authentication has its pros and cons. Each should be properly evaluated to determine the right mechanism for the correct environment.

Identification and Authentication

Now, who are you again?

Once a person has been identified, through the user ID or a similar value, she must be authenticated, which means she must prove she is who she says she is. There are three general factors that can be used for authentication: something a person knows, something a person has, and something a person is. Something a person knows can be a password, PIN, mother's maiden name, or a combination to a lock. Authenticating a person by something that she knows is usually the least expensive to implement. The downside to this method is that another person may gain this knowledge and gain unauthorized access to a system or facility. Something a person has can be a key, swipe card, access card, or badge. This method is mainly common for accessing facilities, but could also be the use of a memory or smart card. A downside to this method is that the item can be lost or stolen, which could result in unauthorized access. Something a person is becomes a bit more interesting, which is biometrics. *Strong authentication* contains two out of these three methods; something a person knows, has, or is. Using a biometric system by itself does not provide strong authentication because it is only providing one out of the three methods. Biometrics supplies what a person is, not what a person knows or has. For a strong authentication process to be in place, a biometric system needs to be coupled with a mechanism that checks for one of these other two methods. Many times a PIN number is typed into a keypad before the biometric scan is performed. This satisfies the "what the person knows" category. Conversely, the person could be required to swipe a magnetic card through a reader prior to the biometric scan. This would satisfy the "what the person has" category. Whatever identification system is used, for strong authentication to be in process, it must include two out of the three categories. This is also referred to as two-factor authentication.

The following sections explain the various types of authentication methods commonly used today.

Biometrics

I would like to prove who I am. Please look at the blood vessels at the back of my eyeball. Response: Gross.

Biometrics verifies an individual's identity by a unique personal attribute, which is one of the most effective and accurate methods of verifying identification. Biometrics is a very sophisticated technology; thus, it is much more expensive and complex than the other types of identity verification processes. A system scans an attribute of a person and compares it to a record that was created in an earlier enrollment process. Because this system inspects the grooves of a person's fingerprint, the pattern of someone's retina, or pitches of someone's voice, it has to be extremely sensitive. The system must perform accurate and repeatable measurements of anatomical or physiological characteristics. This type of sensitivity can easily cause false positives or false negatives. The system must be calibrated so these false positives and false negatives have a low occurrence, and the results are as accurate as possible.

Biometrics can use several different types of physiological attributes of a person.

When a biometric system rejects an authorized individual, it is called a **Type I error.** When the system accepts impostors who should be rejected, it is called a **Type II error.** The goal is to obtain low numbers for each type of error. When comparing different biometric systems, many different variables are used, but one of the most important variables is the *crossover error rate (CER)*. This rating is stated in a percentage and represents the point at which the false rejection rate equals the false acceptance rate. This rating is the most important measurement when determining the system's accuracy. A biometric system that delivers a CER of 3 will be more accurate than a system that delivers a CER of 4.

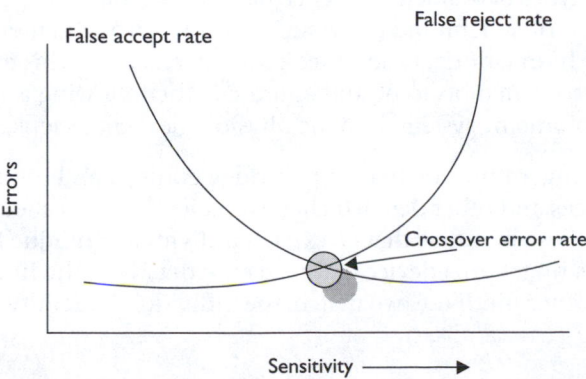

What is the purpose of this CER value anyway? If you are going to buy a biometric system, you need a way to compare the accuracy between different systems. You can just go by the different vendors' marketing material (they all say they are the best), or you can compare the different CER values of the products to see which one really is more accurate than the others. It is also a way to keep the vendors honest. One vendor may tell you, "We have absolutely no Type II errors." This would mean that their product would not allow any imposters to be improperly authenticated. But what if you asked how many Type I errors their product had and the salesman sheepishly replied, "We average around ninety percent of Type I errors." That would mean that 90 percent of the authentication attempts would be rejected, which would negatively affect your employees' productivity. So you can ask about their CER value, which represents when the Type I and Type II errors are equal, to give you a better understanding of the product's overall accuracy.

Individual environments have specific security levels, which will dictate how many Type I and Type II errors are acceptable. For example, a military institution that is very concerned about confidentiality would be prepared to accept a certain amount of Type I errors, but would absolutely not accept any false accepts (Type II errors). Because all biometric systems can be calibrated, if you lower the Type II error rate, it will result in an increase in Type I errors. The military institution would obviously calibrate the biometric system to lower the Type II errors to zero, but that would mean that they would have to accept a higher rate of Type I errors.

Biometrics is the most expensive method of verifying a person's identity, and it faces other barriers to becoming widely acceptable. These include user acceptance, enrollment time frame, and throughput. Many times people are reluctant to let a machine read the pattern of their retina or scan the geometry of their hand. This lack of enthusiasm has slowed down the widespread use of biometric systems within our society. The enrollment phase requires an action to be performed several times to capture a clear and indistinguishable reference record. People are not particularly fond of expending this time and energy when they are used to just picking a password instead and quickly typing it into their console. When a person attempts to be authenticated by a biometric system, sometimes the system will request an action to be completed several times. If the system was unable to get a clear reading of an iris scan or could not capture a full voice verification print, the individual may have to repeat the action. This causes low throughput, stretches the individual's patience, and reduces acceptability.

There are many types of biometric systems that examine different personal characteristics. With each type of system, the individual must go through an enrollment process, which captures the biometric data and stores it in a reference file. This reference file is used later when the person attempts to be authenticated. The following is an overview of the different types of biometric systems and the physiological characteristics they examine.

Fingerprint   Fingerprints are made up of ridge endings and bifurcations exhibited by the friction ridges and other detailed characteristics that are called *minutiae*. It is the distinctiveness of these minutiae that gives each individual a unique fingerprint. An individual places his finger on a device that reads the details of the fingerprint and compares this to a reference file. If the two match, the individual's identity has been verified.

NOTE Fingerprint systems store the full fingerprint, which is actually a lot of information that takes up hard drive space and resources. The finger-scan technology extracts specific features from the fingerprint and stores just that information, which takes up less hard drive space and allows for quicker database lookups and comparisons.

Palm Scan The palm holds a wealth of information, and has many aspects that are used to identify an individual. The palm has creases, ridges, and grooves throughout it that are unique to a specific person. The palm scan also includes the fingerprints of each finger. An individual places his hand on the biometric device, which scans and captures this information. This information is compared to a reference file and the identity is either verified or rejected.

Hand Geometry The shape of a person's hand (the length and width of the hand and fingers) defines hand geometry. This trait differs significantly between people and is used in some biometric systems to verify identity. A person places her hand on a device that has grooves for each finger. The system compares the geometry of each finger, and the hand as a whole, to the information in a reference file to verify that person's identity.

Retina Scan A system that reads a person's retina scans the blood-vessel pattern of the retina on the backside of the eyeball. This pattern has shown to be extremely unique between different people. A camera is used to project a beam inside the eye and capture the pattern and compare it to a reference file recorded previously.

Iris Scan The iris is the colored portion of the eye that surrounds the pupil. The iris has unique patterns, rifts, colors, rings, coronas, and furrows. The uniqueness of each of these characteristics within the iris is captured by a camera and compared with the information gathered during the enrollment phase.

 NOTE When using an iris pattern biometric system, the optical unit must be positioned so that the sun does not shine into the aperture, so when implemented it must be properly placed in a building.

Signature Dynamics When a person signs a signature, usually it is done in the same manner and speed each time. Signing a signature produces electrical signals that can be captured by a biometric system. The physical motions performed when someone is signing a document create these electrical signals. The signals provide unique characteristics that can be used to distinguish one individual from another. There is more information within signature dynamics versus a static signature, so there are more variables to verify when confirming an individual's identity and more assurance that this person is who he claims to be.

Signature dynamics is different from a digitized signature. A digitized signature is just an electronic copy of someone's signature and is not a biometric system that captures the speed of signing, the way the person holds the pen, and the pressure the signer exerts to generate the signature.

Keyboard Dynamics   Signature dynamics is a method that captures the electrical signals when a person signs a name, and keyboard dynamics capture electrical signals when a person types a certain phrase. As a person types a specified phrase, the biometric system captures the speed and motions of this action. Each individual has a certain style and speed, which translate into unique signals. This type of authentication is more effective than typing in a password because a password is easily obtainable. It is much harder to repeat a person's typing style than it is to acquire a password.

Voice Print   There are many subtle distinguishing differences in people's speech sounds and patterns. A biometric system that is programmed to capture a voice print and compare it to the information captured in a reference file can differentiate one individual from another. During the enrollment process, an individual is asked to say several different words. Later when this individual needs to be authenticated, the biometric system jumbles these words and presents them to the individual. The individual then repeats the sequence of words given. This is used as a deterrent so others will not attempt to record the session and play it back in hopes of obtaining unauthorized access.

Facial Scan   A system that scans a person's face takes many attributes and characteristics into account. People have different bone structures, nose ridges, eye widths, forehead sizes, and chin shapes. These are all captured during a facial scan and compared to an earlier captured scan held within a reference record. If the information is a match, the person is positively identified.

Hand Topology   Hand geometry looks at the size and width of an individual's hand and fingers. During a hand topology scan, a side-view picture of the hand is captured. Hand topology looks at the different peaks and valleys of the hand, along with its overall shape and curvature. When an individual wants to be authenticated, a hand is placed on the system, and a camera is off to one side of it. The camera snaps a picture of the hand from a different view and angle than that of systems that target hand geometry, and thus captures different data.

References

Biometrics Research: **biometrics.cse.msu.edu**

The Biometric Digest: **www.biodigest.com**

National Biometric Test Center: **www.engr.sjsu.edu/biometrics**

Passwords

User identification coupled with a reusable password is the most common form of system identification and authorization mechanisms. A password is a protected string of characters that is used to authenticate an individual. As stated previously, authentication factors are based on what a person knows, has, or is. A password is something the user knows.

Password Management   *What is my password to get to my most sacred, top secret, important information? Answer: Password.* Although passwords are the most commonly used authentication mechanisms, they are also considered one of the weakest security mechanisms available. Why? Users usually choose passwords that are easily guessed (spouse's name, birth date, or dog's name), tell others their passwords, and many times write the passwords down on a sticky note and leave it under the keyboard. To most users, security is usually not the most important or interesting part of using their computers—except when someone hacks into their computer and steals confidential information. Then security is all the rage.

This is where password management steps in. If passwords are properly generated, updated, and kept secret, they can provide effective security. Password generators can be used to create passwords for users. This ensures that a user will not be using "Bob" or "Spot" for a password, but if the generator spits out "kdjasijew284802h," the user will surely scribble it down on a piece of paper and safely stick it to the monitor, which defeats the whole purpose. If a password generator is going to be used, the tools should create pronounceable non-dictionary words to help users remember them and not be too complicated to cause the user to write them down.

If the users can choose their own passwords, the operating system should enforce certain password requirements. The operating system can require that a password contain a certain number of characters, unrelated to the user ID, include special characters, include upper- and lowercase letters, and is not easily guessed. The operating system can keep track of the passwords a specific user generates to ensure that no passwords are reused. The users should also be forced to change their passwords periodically. All of these factors make it harder for an attacker to guess or obtain passwords within the environment.

If an attacker is after a password, there are a few techniques she can try, such as electronic monitoring, accessing the password file, brute force attacks, dictionary attacks, and social engineering. *Electronic monitoring* is an activity of listening to network traffic and can capture information, especially when a user is sending her password to an authentication server. The password can be copied and reused by the attacker at another time. Accessing the password file is usually done on the authentication server. The password file contains many users' passwords, and if compromised, can cause a lot of damage. This file should be protected with access control mechanisms and one-way encryption. Brute force attacks are performed with tools that cycle through many possible character, number, and symbol combinations to uncover a password. Dictionary attacks have files of thousands of words that are used to compare to the user's password until a match is found.

There are techniques that can be implemented to provide another layer of security for passwords and their use. After each successful logon, a message can be presented to a user indicating the date and time of the last successful logon, the location of this logon, and if there were any unsuccessful logon attempts. This alerts the user if suspicious activity has been going on, and if anyone has attempted to log on using his credentials. An administrator can set operating parameters that allow a certain number of failed logon attempts to be accepted before a user is locked out; this is also referred to as a *clipping level*. The user can be locked out for five minutes or a full day after the threshold (or clipping level) has been exceeded. It depends on how the administrator configures this mechanism. An audit trail can also be used to track password usage, and successful and unsuccessful logon attempts. This audit information should include the date, time, user ID, and workstation the user logged on from.

A password's lifetime should be short but practical. The shorter the lifetime of a password, the more assurance that the password will not be guessed by an intruder. If the lifetime is too short, however, it causes unnecessary management overhead and users may forget which password is active. A balance between protection and practicality needs to be decided upon and enforced.

As with many things in life, education is the key. Password requirements, protection, and generation should be addressed in security awareness programs so users understand what is expected of them, why they should protect their passwords, and how passwords can be stolen. Users should be an extension to a security team, not the opposition.

Password Checkers   Several organizations test user-chosen passwords using tools that perform a dictionary attack to detect the weak passwords. This helps make the environment as a whole less susceptible to dictionary and exhaustive attacks that are used to discover users' passwords. Many times the same tools used to attempt to crack a password are used by a network administrator to make sure the password is strong enough and by the attacker in an attempt to discover a user's password. Most security tools have this dual nature. They are used by security professionals and IT staff to test for vulnerabilities within their environment in the hope of uncovering them and fixing them before an attacker finds the vulnerabilities. An attacker uses the same tools to uncover vulnerabilities to exploit before the security professional can fix them. It is the never-ending cat-and-mouse race.

If a tool is called a password checker, it is a tool used by a security professional to test the strength of a password. If a tool is called a password cracker, it is usually used by a hacker; however, most of the time, these tools are one and the same.

Password Aging   Many systems enable administrators to set expiration dates for passwords, forcing users to change them at regular intervals. The system may also keep a list of the last five to ten passwords and not let the users revert back to previously used passwords.

Limit Logon Attempts   A threshold can be set to allow only a certain number of unsuccessful logon attempts. After the threshold is met, the user's account can be locked for a period of time or indefinitely, which requires an administrator to manually unlock the account. This protects against dictionary and exhaustive attacks that continually apply credentials until the right combination of username and password is discovered.

Cognitive Passwords

What is your mother's name? Answer: Shucks, I don't remember. I have it written down somewhere.

Cognitive passwords are fact- or opinion-based information used to verify an individual's identity. A user is enrolled by answering several questions based on her life experiences. Passwords can be hard for people to remember, but that same person will not likely forget her mother's maiden name, favorite color, dog's name, or the school she graduated from. After the enrollment process, the user can answer the questions asked of her to be authenticated instead of having to remember a password. This authentication process is best for a service the user does not use on a daily basis because it takes longer than other authentication mechanisms. This can work well for help-desk services. The user can be authenticated via cognitive means. This way the person at the help desk can be sure he is talking to the right person, and the user in need of help does not need to remember a password that may be used once every three months.

One-time Passwords

How many times is a one-time password good for? Answer: One, brainiac.

A *one-time password* is also called a dynamic password. It is used when a user needs to authenticate himself. It is only good once. After the password is used, it is no longer valid; thus, if a hacker obtained this password, it could not be reused. This type of authentication mechanism is used in environments that require a higher level of security than static passwords provide. There are two general types of one-time passwords token generators: synchronous and asynchronous. The token device generates the one-time password for the user to submit to an authentication server. The following sections explain these concepts.

Token Device

The *token device*, or password generator, is usually a handheld device that has an LCD display and keypad. This hardware is separate from the computer the user is attempting to access. The token device and authentication service need to be synchronized in some manner to be able to authenticate a user. The token device presents the user with a list of characters to be entered as a password when logging onto a computer. Only the token device and authentication service knows the meaning of these characters. Because the two are synchronized, the token device will present the exact password the authentication service is expecting. This is a one-time password, also called a token, and is no longer valid after initial use.

Synchronous   A *synchronous token device* synchronizes with the authentication service by using time or an event as the core piece of the authentication process. If the synchronization is *time based*, the token device and the authentication service must hold the exact same time within their internal clocks. The time value on the token device is encrypted with a secret key and displayed to the user. The user enters this value and a user ID into the computer, which then passes it to the server running the authentication service. The authentication service decrypts this value and compares it to the value that it expected. If the two match, the user is authenticated and allowed to use the computer and resources.

If the token device and authentication service use *event-synchronization*, the user may need to initiate the logon sequence on the computer and push a button on the token device. This causes the token device and the authentication service to advance to the next authentication value. This value is encrypted by the token device and displayed to the user. The user enters this value along with a user ID to be authenticated. In either time- or event-based synchronization, the token device and authentication service must share the same secret key used for encryption and decryption.

Asynchronous   A token device that is using an *asynchronous token*-generating method uses a challenge/response scheme to authenticate the user. In this situation, the computer the user is attempting to log onto displays a challenge value to the user that it received from the authentication service. The user types this value into the handheld token device. The token device encrypts this value and presents the new value to the user, who then types it and an ID into the computer. The authentication service will be expecting a particular value and if the user types in this value, she is authenticated, as shown in Figure 4-4. As with the synchronous systems, this type of asynchronous method creates a one-time password, which is sometimes called a token.

NOTE   The actual implementation and process that these devices follow can differ between different vendors. What is important to know is that asynchronous is based on challenge/response mechanisms and synchronous is based on time- or event-driven mechanisms.

Both token systems can fall prey to masquerading if a user shares his identification information (ID or username) that is entered along with the one-time password and the token device is shared or stolen. The token device can also have battery failure or other malfunctions that would stand in the way of a successful authentication. However, this type of system is not vulnerable to electronic eavesdropping, sniffing, or password guessing.

If the user has to enter a password or PIN into the token device before it provides a one-time password, then strong authentication is in effect because it is using two factors—something the user knows (PIN) and something the user has (the token device).

Figure 4-4
Authentication using a token device includes a workstation, token device, and authentication service.

1. Challenge value displayed on workstation.
2. User enters challenge value and PIN into token device.
3. Token device presents a different value to the user.
4. User enters new value into the workstation.
5. Value sent to authentication service on server.
6. Authentication service is expecting a specific value.
7. User is authenticated and allowed access to workstation.

References

RSA SecurID: **www.rsasecurity.com/products/securid**

Token-based authentication: **www.networkcomputing.com/1018/1018f1.html**

Cryptographic Keys

Another way to prove one's identity is to use a private key or generate a digital signature. A private key or digital signature could be used in place of using a password. Passwords are the weakest form of authentication and can be easily sniffed as they travel over a network. Private keys and digital signatures are forms of authentication used in environments that require higher security protection than what is provided by passwords.

A private key is a secret value that should be in the possession of one person, and one person only. It should never be disclosed to an outside party. A digital signature is a technology that uses a private key to encrypt a hash value (message digest). The act of encrypting this hash value with a private key is called *digitally signing* a message. A digital signature attached to a message proves that the message originated from a specific source, and that the message itself was not changed while in transit.

A public key can be available to anyone; this is why it is called a public key. We explore private keys, public keys, digital signatures, and public key infrastructure (PKI) in Chapter 8, but for now, understand that a private key and digital signatures are other mechanisms that can be used to authenticate an individual.

Passphrase

A *passphrase* is another method used for authentication and in some cases takes the place of a password during an authentication process. The passphrase is a sequence of characters that is longer than a password, and thus is called a phrase. The user enters this phrase into an application and the application transforms the value into a *virtual password*. If a user wants to authenticate to an application, such as Pretty Good Privacy (PGP), he types in a passphrase, let's say "StickWithMeKidAndYouWillWearDiamonds." The application converts this phrase into a virtual password that is used for the actual authentication. The user usually generates the passphrase just like when a user creates a password the first time he logs onto a computer. A passphrase is more secure than a password because it is longer, and thus harder to obtain by an attacker. In many cases the user is more likely to remember a passphrase than a password. The drawback, however, is that the passphrase takes longer to enter into the system during the authentication process.

Memory Cards

The main difference between memory cards and smart cards is the processing power. A *memory card* holds information, but does not process information. A *smart card* has the necessary hardware and logic to actually process information. A memory card can hold a user's authentication information, so this user only needs to type in a user ID or PIN, present the memory card, and if the two match and are approved by an authentication service, the user is successfully authenticated. In most cases, identification data is pulled from the memory card. It travels with the PIN to a backend authentication server. An example of a memory card is a swipe card that must be used for an individual to be able to enter a building. The user enters a PIN and swipes the memory card through a card reader. If this is the correct combination, the reader flashes green and the individual can open the door and enter the building. Another example is an ATM card. If Buffy wants to withdraw $40 from her checking account, she needs to enter the correct PIN and slide the ATM card (or memory card) through the reader.

Memory cards can be used with computers, but they require a reader to process the information. The reader adds cost to the process, especially when one is needed per computer, and card generation adds additional cost and effort to the whole authentication process. A memory card provides a more secure authentication method than using a password because the attacker would need to obtain the card and know the correct PIN. Administrators and management need to weigh the costs and benefits of a memory token-based card implementation to determine if it is the right authentication mechanism for their environment.

Smart Card

My smart card is smarter than your memory card.

A smart card has the capability of processing information because it has a microprocessor and integrated circuits incorporated into the card itself. Memory cards do not have this type of hardware and lack this type of functionality. The only function they can perform is simple storage. A smart card, which adds the capability to process information that is stored on it, can also provide a two-factor authentication method because the user may have to enter a PIN to unlock the smart card. This means the user must provide something she knows (PIN) and something she has (smart card).

To authenticate using a smart card, the user inserts the card into the card reader and enters a PIN. The reader performs a one-way transformation on the PIN and stores it in the memory of the card reader. The reader then performs the same one-way transformation on the information on the smart card and compares the two values. If the values match, the reader authenticates the user to the computer she is attempting to access. The authentication to the computer can be in the form of a one-time password, use of a challenge/response value, or by providing the user's private key if it is used within a PKI environment.

Memory and smart cards can be used to authenticate users.

The information held within the memory of a smart card is not readable until the correct PIN is entered. This fact and the complexity of the smart token make these cards resistant to reverse-engineering and tampering methods. If George loses the smart card he uses to authenticate to the domain at work, the person who finds the card would need to know his PIN to be able to do any real damage. The smart card can also be programmed to store information in an encrypted fashion, as well as detect any tampering of the card itself. In the event that tampering is detected, the information stored on the smart card can be automatically wiped.

The downfalls to using a smart card is the extra cost of the readers and the overhead of card generation, as with memory cards, although this cost is decreasing. The smart cards themselves are more expensive than memory cards because of the extra integrated circuits and microprocessor.

Reference

JavaWorld, "Smart Cards: A Primer": **www.javaworld.com/javaworld/ jw-12-1997/jw-12-javadev.html**

Authorization

Now that I know who you are, let's see if I will let you do what you want.

The difference between authentication and authorization can be a little confusing at first. Although these two concepts are quite different, they require a synergic relationship to accomplish the task of allowing a user to access a resource. Authentication is the process of proving that an individual holds the identity that he claims to hold. A system may know who you are, but will it allow you to carry out the actions you are requesting? That piece is authorization, specifying the privileges allowed with the resource that is being protected.

Authorization is a core component of every operating system, but applications, security add-on packages, and resources themselves can also provide this functionality. Once Marge is authenticated through the authentication server, she requests to view a spreadsheet that resides on a file server. When she finds this spreadsheet and double-clicks on the icon, she sees an hourglass instead of a mouse pointer. At this stage, the file server is seeing if Marge has the rights and permissions to view the requested spreadsheet. It also checks to see if Marge can modify, delete, move, or copy the file. Once the file server searches through an access matrix and finds that Marge does indeed have the necessary rights to view this file, the file opens up on Marge's desktop. The decision of whether to allow Marge to see this file or not was based on an access criteria. Access criteria is the crux of authentication.

Access Criteria

You can perform that action only because we like you, and you wear a funny hat.

We have gone over the basics when it comes to access control. This subject can get very granular in its level of detail when it comes to dictating what a subject can or cannot do to an object or resource. This is a good thing because network administrators and security professionals want to have as much control as possible over the resources they have been put in charge of protecting, and a fine level of detail enables them to give out just the precise level of access to individuals. It would be frustrating if access control permissions were based only on full control or no access. These choices are very limiting, and an administrator would end up giving everyone full control, which would provide no protection. Instead, there are different ways of limiting access to resources and, if they are understood and used properly, they can give just the right level of access desired.

Granting access rights to subjects should be based on the level of trust a company has in a subject and the subject's need to know. Just because a company completely trusts Joyce with its files and resources does not mean she fulfills the need-to-know criteria to access the company's tax returns and profit margins. If Maynard fulfills the need-to-know criteria to access employees' work histories, it does not mean that the company trusts him to access all of the company's other files. These issues need to be identified and integrated into the access criteria. The different access criteria can be broken up into roles, groups, location, time, and transaction types.

Roles can be an efficient way to assign rights to a type of user who performs a certain task. This role is based on a job assignment or function. If there is a position within a company for a person to audit transactions and audit logs, that role would only need a read function to those types of files. This role would not need full control, modify, or delete privileges.

Groups are another effective way of assigning access control rights. If several users require the same type of access to information and resources, it is easier to manage if they are all put into a group and then rights and permissions are assigned to that group instead of to each and every individual within the group. If a specific printer is only available to the accounting group, when a user attempts to print to it, the group membership of the user will be checked to see if she is indeed in the accounting group. This is one way that access control is enforced through a logical access control mechanism.

Physical or logical location can also be used to restrict access to resources. Some files may only be available to users who can log on interactively to a computer. This means the user must be physically at the computer and enter the credentials locally versus logging on remotely from another computer. This restriction is implemented on several server configurations to restrict unauthorized individuals from being able to get in and reconfigure the server remotely.

Logical location restrictions are usually done through network address restrictions. If a network administrator wants to ensure that status requests of an intrusion detection management console are only accepted from a certain section of the network, this can be configured within the software and any requests originating outside of this section would be rejected. An administrator who configures a domain name server to only allow zone transfers to a specific IP address is another example of a logical location access control restriction.

Time of day or temporal isolation, is another access control mechanism that can be used. If a security professional wants to ensure that no one is accessing payroll files between the hours of 8:00 P.M. and 4:00 A.M., this is a configuration that can be implemented to ensure that access at these times are restricted. If the same security professional wants to ensure that no bank account transactions happen during days that the bank is not open, she can indicate in the logical access control mechanism that this type of action is prohibited on Sundays.

Transaction type restrictions can be used to control what data is accessed during certain types of functions and what commands are carried out on the data. An online banking program may allow a customer to view his account balance, but may not allow the customer to transfer money until he has a certain security level or access right. A bank teller may be able to cash checks up to $2,000, but would need a supervisor's access code to retrieve more funds for a customer. A database administrator may be able to build a database for the human resource department, but may not be able to read certain confidential files within that database. These are all examples of transaction-type restrictions to control access to data and resources.

Default to No Access
If you're unsure, just say no.

Access control mechanisms should default to no access to provide the necessary level of security and ensure that no security holes go unnoticed. There is a wide range of access levels that are available to assign to individuals and groups, depending on the application and/or operating system. A user can have read, change, delete, full control, or no access permissions. When it is said that security mechanisms should default to no access, it means that if nothing has been specifically configured for an individual or the group she belongs to, that user should not be able to access that resource. If access is not explicitly allowed, it should be implicitly denied. Security is all about being safe, and this is the safest approach to practice when we are dealing with access control methods and mechanisms. In other words, all access controls should be based on the concept of starting with zero access, and building on top of that. Instead of giving everything, and then taking away based on need-to-know, the better approach is to start with nothing, and adding privileges based on need-to-know.

This is how most access control lists (ACLs) work on routers and packet-filtering firewalls. Figure 4-5 shows that traffic from subnet A is allowed to access subnet B, traffic from subnet D is not allowed to access subnet A, and subnet B is allowed to talk to subnet A. All other traffic not listed here is not allowed by default. If subnet D wants to talk to subnet B, this will not happen because it is not explicitly indicated in the router's ACL.

Need to Know
If you need to know, I will tell you. If you don't have a need to know, leave me alone.

The **need-to-know** principle is similar to the least-privilege principle. It is based on the concept that individuals should only be given access to the information that they absolutely require in order to perform their job duties. Giving any more rights to a user just asks for headaches and the possibility of that user abusing the permissions assigned to him. An administrator wants to give a user the least amount of privileges she can, but just enough for that user to be productive when carrying out tasks. The management will decide what a user needs to know, or what access rights are necessary, and the administrator will configure the access control mechanisms to allow this user to have that level of access and no more, and thus least privileged.

Figure 4-5
What is not explicitly allowed should be disallowed.

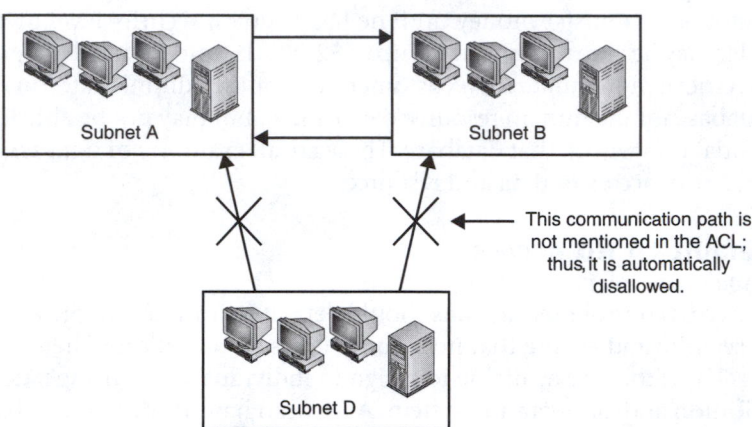

For example, if management has decided that Dan the copy boy needs to know where the files are that he needs to copy and how to print them, this fulfills Dan's need-to- know criteria. Now, an administrator can give Dan full control of all the files he needs to copy, but that would not be practicing the least-privilege principle. The administrator should restrict Dan's rights and permissions to only allow him to read and print the necessary files, and no more. Besides, if Dan accidentally deletes all the files on the whole file server, whom do you think management will hold ultimately responsible? Yep, the administrator.

It is important to understand that it is the management's job to determine the security requirements of individuals and how access is authorized. The administrator and IT staff configure the access control, and the security officer configures the security mechanisms to fulfill these requirements, but it is not their job to determine security requirements of users. Those should be left to the owners. If there is a security breach, management will ultimately be held responsible, so they should be the ones making these decisions in the first place.

Single Sign-On

I only want to have to remember one username and one password for everything!

Many times employees need to access many different computers and resources in the course of a day to complete their tasks. This requires the employees to remember multiple user IDs and passwords for these different computers. In a utopia, a user would only need to enter one user ID and one password to be able to access all resources in all the networks this user is working in. In the real world, this is hard to implement and hard to control.

Because of the proliferation of client/server technologies, networks have migrated from centrally controlled networks to heterogeneous, distributed environments. The propagation of open systems and the increased diversity of applications, platforms, and operating systems have caused the end user to have to remember several user IDs and passwords just to be able to access and use the different resources within his own network. Although the different IDs and passwords are supposed to provide a greater level of security, they often end up compromising security and causing more effort and overhead for the staff that manages and maintains the network.

As any network staff member or administrator can attest to, too much time is devoted to resetting passwords for users who have forgotten them. More than one employee's productivity is affected when forgotten passwords have to be reassigned. The network staff member who has to reset the password could be working on other tasks, and the user who forgot the password cannot complete his task until the network staff member is finished resetting the password. Many help-desk employees report that a majority of their time is spent on users forgetting their passwords. System administrators have to manage multiple user accounts on different platforms, which all need to be coordinated in a manner that maintains the integrity of the security policy. At times the complexity can be overwhelming, which results in poor access control management and the generation of many security vulnerabilities because the user IDs and passwords are usually written down and posted on the side of the monitor or underneath the user's keyboard. This fact defeats the purpose of using passwords in the first place. A lot of time is spent on multiple passwords, and in the end, they do not provide us with more security.

The increased cost of managing a diverse environment, security concerns, and user habits, coupled with the users' overwhelming desire to remember one set of credentials, has brought about the idea of *single sign-on* capabilities. These capabilities would allow a user to enter credentials one time and be able to access all resources in primary and secondary network domains. The idea of single sign-on would also allow users to access, through the one set of credentials, all other resources that they have access to, including legacy and other application systems. This reduces the amount of time users spend authenticating to resources and it gives the administrator the ability to streamline user accounts and have better control over access rights. It improves security by reducing the probability of users writing down passwords and reduces the administrator's time spent on adding and removing user accounts and modifying access permissions. In the event that an administrator needs to disable or suspend a specific account, it can be done uniformly instead of having to alter configurations on each and every platform.

So that is our utopia: log on once and you are good to go. What bursts this bubble? Mainly interoperability issues. For single sign-on to actually work, every platform, application, and resource needs to accept the same type of credentials, in the same format, and interpret their meanings the same. When Steve logs onto his NT 4.0 workstation and gets authenticated by a mixed-mode Windows 2000 domain controller, it needs to authenticate him to the resources he needs to access on the Apple computer, the Unix server running VisionFS, the mainframe host server, the MICR print server, and the Windows 98 computer in the secondary domain that has the plotter connected to it. Nice idea, until reality hits.

Single sign-on technology enables a user to enter credentials one time to be able to access all resources within the domain

There is also a security issue to consider in a single sign-on environment. Once an individual is in, he is in. If an attacker was able to break into the network by hijacking or creating an account, he would have access to every resource within the environment.

There are different types of single sign-on technologies. Each has its own advantages and disadvantages, shortcomings, and quality features. It is rare to see a real single sign-on environment, but instead, you will see a cluster of computers and resources that accept the same credentials, whereas other resources still require more work on the administrator or the user side to access the systems. The most popular single sign-on technologies that may be addressed in the CISSP exam are described in the next sections.

References

Single Sign-On Deployment Guide: **developer.netscape.com/docs/manuals/ security/SSO**

The Open Group, "Single Sign-On": **www.opengroup.org/security/sso**

Scripting

The more simplistic single sign-on systems are written with batch files and scripts that contain each user's ID, password, and logon commands necessary for each platform. When a user requests access to a resource, a script will run in the background and perform the same commands and tasks that the user would have to perform to properly authenticate to this resource. The scripts can use a macro language that replays user keystrokes or provide commands that work within a shell. Although this is easier on the user, it demands much more work on the administrator and his staff. The scripts have to be written, and if a user changes his user ID or password, the script needs to be updated also. Because these scripts contain credentials, they must be stored in a protected area and the transmission of the scripts must be dealt with carefully. As platforms are upgraded and changed, this requires the scripts to follow the same suit to ensure the proper interface between the user's computer, script, and resource.

Kerberos

Sam, there is a three-headed dog in front of the server!

Kerberos is the name of a three-headed dog that guards the entrance to the underworld in Greek mythology. This is a great name for a security system that provides authentication and message protection. Kerberos is an authentication protocol and was designed in the mid-1980s as part of MIT's Project Athena. Products supporting Kerberos are becoming more frequent, so this one might be a keeper.

Three-headed dog Kerberos (from Greek mythology) protects the gates of the underworld.

Kerberos is an example of a single sign-on system for distributed environments, and is a de facto standard for heterogeneous networks. Kerberos incorporates a wide range of security technologies, which gives companies much more flexibility and scalability when needing to provide an encompassing security architecture. However, this open architecture also invites interoperability issues. When a vendor has a lot of freedom to customize a product, it usually means that no two vendors will customize it in the same fashion. This brings interoperability and incompatibility issues.

Kerberos uses symmetric key cryptography and provides end-to-end security, meaning that information being passed between a user and a service is protected without the need of an intermediate component. Although it allows the use of passwords for authentication, it was designed specifically to eliminate the need for transmitting passwords over the network. Most Kerberos implementations work with cryptography keys and shared secret keys.

Main Components in Kerberos   The *Key Distribution Center (KDC)* is the most important component within a Kerberos environment. The KDC holds all users' and services' cryptographic keys. It provides authentication services, as well as key distribution functionality. The clients and services trust the integrity of the KDC, and this trust is the foundation of Kerberos security.

The KDC provides security services to entities referred to as *principals*. These principals can be users, applications, or services. The KDC and each principal share a secret key. (A secret key is a cryptographic key used to encrypt and decrypt data.) When the KDC and a principal share a secret key, this means the KDC uses the secret key to encrypt data, sends it to the principal, and the principal uses the secret key to decrypt and process the data. Because the KDC and the principal are the only ones sharing this specific secret key, their communication is protected from eavesdropping or network sniffing. The KDC has a database that contains identity information on all principals within its realm and a secret key it shares with each and every principal.

A *ticket* is generated by the KDC and given to a principal when that principal, let's say a user, needs to authenticate to another principal, let's say a print server. The ticket enables one principal to authenticate to another principal. If Emily needs to use the print server, she needs to prove to the print server she is who she claims to be and that she is authorized to use the printing service. So Emily requests a ticket from the KDC. The KDC gives Emily the ticket, and in turn, Emily passes this ticket on to the print server. If the printer server approves of this ticket, Emily is allowed to use the print service.

A KDC provides security services for a set of principals. This set is called a *realm* in Kerberos. The KDC is the trusted authentication server for all users, applications, and services within a realm. One KDC can be responsible for one realm or several realms. Realms are used to allow an administrator to logically group resources and users.

So far we have principals (users and services) that authenticate to a KDC. The KDC has a database filled with information about each and every principal within its realm. The KDC holds and delivers cryptographic keys and tickets. Tickets are used for principals to authenticate to each other. So how does this work?

Kerberos Authentication Process   The user and the KDC share a secret key; the service and the KDC share a different secret key. The user and the service do not share a secret key in the beginning. The user trusts the KDC because they share a secret key. They can encrypt and decrypt data they pass between each other, and thus have a protected communication path. The same is true for the service and the KDC. Once the user authenticates to the service, they too will share a secret key (session key) that will enable them to encrypt and decrypt the information they need to pass to each other. This is how Kerberos provides data transmission protection.

What are the exact steps, you ask? Hold on to your hat, here we go!

1. Emily needs to print a very important "Happy Birthday" sign for her cousin Katie.

2. The Kerberos client software on Emily's computer prompts her for a user ID. Emily enters her user ID, and the client software sends the ID to the KDC along with the name of the print service Emily has requested.

3. The ticket granting service, which is part of the KDC, receives this request and verifies that Emily and the print service are in its database. If both are in the database, the KDC provides a session key for Emily and the print service to use. One instance of the session key is encrypted with the service's secret key, and the other instance of the session key is encrypted with Emily's secret key. This

ensures that this session key came from the KDC, because only the KDC shares the secret key with a principal.

4. The KDC generates a service ticket that holds both instances of the session key, and it is sent back to the client software on Emily's computer. The client software prompts Emily for a password. Once she types the password in, the client converts it into the key that is necessary to decrypt the session key within the ticket. If Emily did not type in the right password, the client could not generate the correct key to decrypt the ticket, which means Emily could not authenticate and use the print service. However, Emily is a bright lass, and she remembers her password.

5. The client software on Emily's computer decrypts her portion of the ticket, which gives her a copy of the session key and sends the ticket on to the print service to authenticate Emily. The print service has the necessary secret key to decrypt the ticket, so the print service now also has a copy of the session key.

6. The client software decrypted a session key for Emily and the print service decrypted the ticket and has a copy of the same session key. Emily is now authenticated to the print service and they can use this session key to encrypt and decrypt messages they send to each other.

7. Emily can now print Katie's birthday banner, and *you* can sit back and have a glass of water.

The user, Emily, asks the KDC to give her a ticket to present to the print service. This ticket will authenticate her to the print service and enables her to use this service. The KDC verifies that it knows about Emily and the print service, and sends Emily the ticket. Emily then sends the ticket to the print service, and she is now allowed to print to her heart's desire. Figure 4-6 provides a simplistic view of this process.

The authentication service (AS) is the part of the KDC that authenticates a principal, and the ticket granting service (TGS) is the part of the KDC that makes the tickets and hands them out to the principals. Be sure you understand that a session key is different from a secret key. A secret key is shared between the KDC and a principal and is static in nature. A session key is shared between two principals and is generated when needed and destroyed after the session is completed. This is a very basic view of how Kerberos works. There are types of security technologies that can be plugged into a Kerberos framework, with many different parameters and configurations.

If a Kerberos implementation is configured to use an *authenticator*, the user will send the printer server her identification information and a time stamp encrypted with the session key they share. The printer server will decrypt this information and compare it with the identification data the KDC sent to it about this requesting user. If the data is the same, the printer server allows the user to send print jobs. The time stamp is used to help fight against replay attacks. The printer server will compare the sent time stamp with its own internal time. This will help determine if the ticket had been sniffed and copied by an attacker and submitted at a later time in hope of impersonating the legitimate user and gain unauthorized access.

I. User authenticates to AS.
2. AS sends initial ticket to user.
3. User requests to access file server.
4. TGS creates new ticket with session keys.
5. User extracts one session key and sends ticket to file server.

Figure 4-6   The user needs to receive a ticket from the KDC before being able to use the requested resource.

So why are we talking about Kerberos? Because it is one example of a single sign-on system. The user enters a user ID and password one time and one time only. The tickets have time limits on them that administrators can configure. Many times the lifetime of a ticket is eight hours, so when the user comes in the next day, he will have to present his credentials again.

Weaknesses of Kerberos   Kerberos provides confidentiality of data by the use of its cryptographic keys and encryption processes and provides access control to resources. It does not protect a computer's or service's availability, which is another security service. The following lists some of the potential weaknesses of Kerberos:

- The KDC is a single point of failure. If the KDC goes down, no one can access needed resources, so in many instances users cannot work.
- The KDC must be able to handle the number of requests it receives in a timely manner.
- Secret keys are temporarily stored on the users' workstations, which means it is possible for an intruder to obtain this cryptographic key.
- Session keys are decrypted and reside on the users' workstations, either in a cache or in a key table. Again, an intruder can capture this key.
- Kerberos is vulnerable to password guessing. The KDC does not know if a dictionary attack is taking place.
- Network traffic is not protected by Kerberos if encryption is not enabled.
- When a user changes his password, it changes the secret key and the KDC database needs to be updated.

References

Kerberos FAQ: **www.nrl.navy.mil/CCS/people/kenh/kerberos-faq.html**

Kerberos papers and documentation: **www.mit.edu/afs/athena.mit.edu/astaff/ project/kerberos/www/papers.html**

SESAME   The *Secure European System for Applications in a Multi-vendor Environment (SESAME)* project is a single sign-on technology that was developed to extend Kerberos functionality and improves upon its weaknesses. SESAME uses symmetric and asymmetric cryptographic techniques to protect exchanges of data and to authenticate subjects to network resources. (Kerberos is a strictly symmetric key-based technology, and SESAME is based on both asymmetric and symmetric key cryptography.)

Kerberos uses tickets for authenticating subjects to objects and SESAME uses Privileged Attribute Certificates (PACs), which contain the subject's identity, access capabilities for the object, access time period, and lifetime of the PAC. The PAC is digitally signed so that the object can validate that it came from the trusted authentication server, which is referred to as the Privileged Attribute Server (PAS). The PAS holds a similar role as the KDC within Kerberos. After a user successfully authenticates to the authentication service (AS), he is presented with a token to give to the PAS. The PAS then creates a PAC for the user to present to the resource he is trying to access. (See Figure 4-7.)

References

SESAME in a Nutshell: **www.cosic.esat.kuleuven.ac.be/sesame/html/ sesame_what.html**

SESAME links: **www.cosic.esat.kuleuven.ac.be/sesame/html/ sesame_links.html**

Thin Clients   Diskless computers, sometimes called dumb terminals or thin clients, cannot store information because of their lack of an operating system and necessary resources. This type of technology forces users to log onto the network just to be able to use the computer. When the user starts the computer, it runs a short list of instructions and then points itself to a server that will actually download the operating system to the terminal. This enforces a strict type of access control because the computer cannot do anything on its own until it authenticates to the server, and then the server gives the computer its operating system, profile, and functionality. Thin client technology provides another type of single sign-on access for users because the user only has to authenticate to the central server or mainframe, and she accesses all necessary resources through this centralized system.

Directory Services   A network service is a mechanism that identifies resources (printers, file servers, domain controllers, peripheral devices) on a network and provides a way to make them available to users and programs. A network directory service

Figure 4-7 SESAME is very similar to Kerberos conceptually.

contains information about these different resources and provides a naming scheme. It also provides a hierarchical database that outlines the resources' characteristics, such as name, logical and physical location, subjects that can access them, and the operations that can be carried out on the resources.

Network directory services provide users access to network resources transparently without needing to know their exact location and the steps required to access them. These issues are taken care of for the user in the background. Some examples of directory services are Lightweight Directory Access Protocol (LDAP), Novell's NetWare Directory Service (NDS), and Microsoft's Active Directory.

Examples of Single Sign-On Methods

- **Scripts** Files containing user credentials for different resource types
- **Kerberos** Authentication protocol that uses a centralized authentication server, the KDC, and symmetric key cryptography
- **SESAME** An access control technology developed in Europe and based on public key cryptography
- **Thin clients** Dumb terminals authenticating to a server or mainframe
- **Directory services** Network aware services that control access to resources

Access Control Models

An *access control model* is a framework that dictates how subjects access objects. It uses access control technologies and security mechanisms to enforce the rules and objectives of the model. There are three main types of access control models: discretionary, mandatory, and nondiscretionary (also called role-based). Each model type uses different methods to control how subjects access objects, and each has its own merits and limitations. The business and security goals of an organization will help prescribe what access control model should be used, along with the culture of the company and the habits of conducting business. Some models are used exclusively, and sometimes they are combined to be able to accomplish the necessary level of security an environment requires.

These models are built into the core or the kernel of the different operating systems and possibly their supporting applications. The following sections explain these models, their supporting technologies, and when they should be implemented.

Discretionary

It is up to me to allow you to access my files. Response: Mother, may I?

If a user creates a file, he is the owner of that file. An identifier for this user is placed in the file header. Ownership might also be granted to a specific individual. For example, a manager for a certain department might be made the owner of the files and resources within her domain. A system that uses *discretionary access control (DAC)* enables the owner of the resource to specify which subjects can access specific resources. This model is called discretionary because the control of access is based on the discretion of the owner.

In a DAC model, access is restricted based on the authorization granted to the users. This means that users are allowed to specify what type of access can occur to the objects they own. If an organization is using a DAC model, the network administrator can allow resource owners to control who has access to their files. The most common implementation of DAC is through ACLs, which are dictated and set by the owners and enforced by the operating system. This does not lend itself to a centrally controlled environment and can make a user's ability to access information dynamic versus the more static role of mandatory access control (MAC).

Most of the operating systems we are used to dealing with are based on DAC models, such as all Windows and Macintosh systems and most flavors of Unix. When you look at the properties of a file or directory and you see the choices that allow you to choose what users can have access to this resource and to what degree, this is an instance of ACLs enforcing a DAC model.

It is through the discretionary model that Sam can share his D: drive with David, so David can copy all of Sam's MP3s. Sam can also block access to his D: drive from his manager so his manager does not know that Sam is wasting valuable time and resources by downloading MP3s and sharing them with friends.

Reference

Guide to Understanding DAC in Trusted Systems: **http://security.tsu.ru/info/ rainbow/tg03.htm**

Mandatory

In a *mandatory access control (MAC)* model, data owners do not have as much freedom to determine who can access their files. The operating system makes the final decision and can override the data owner's wishes. This model is much more structured and strict and is based on a security label system. Users are given a security clearance (secret, top secret, confidential, and so on), and data is classified in the same way. The classification is stored in the security labels of the resources. The classification label specifies the level of trust a user must have to be able to access the file. When the system makes a decision about fulfilling a request to access an object, it is based on the clearance of the subject and the classification of the object. The rules for how subjects access data are made by management, configured by the administrator, enforced by the operating system, and supported by security technologies.

Security labels are attached to all objects; thus, every file, directory, and device has its own security label with its classification information.

A user may have a security clearance of secret, and the data that he requests may have a security label of top secret. In this case, the user will be denied because his clearance is not equivalent or superior to the classification of the object.

This type of model is used in environments where information classification and confidentiality is of utmost importance, such as a military institution. Special types of Unix systems are developed to include the MAC model. It is not like a company can choose to turn on either DAC or MAC. They have to purchase an operating system that has been specifically designed to enforce MAC rules. DAC systems do not understand security labels, classifications, or clearances, thus cannot be used in institutions that require this type of structure for access control. The most recently released MAC system is SE Linux developed by the NSA and Secure Computing.

Reference

Determining MAC Access: **http://csrc.nist.gov/publications/nistpubs/800-7/ node36.html**

Sensitivity Labels

I am very sensitive. Can I have a label? Answer: Nope.

When MAC is being used, every subject and object must have a sensitivity label, also called a security label. It contains a classification and different categories. The classification indicates the sensitivity level, and the categories enforce need-to-know rules. Figure 4-8 illustrates a sensitivity label.

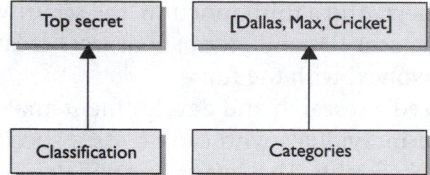

Figure 4-8
A sensitivity label is made up of a classification and categories.

The classifications follow a hierarchical structure, one level being more trusted than another. However, the categories do not follow a hierarchical scheme, because they represent different areas of information within a system. The categories can correspond to departments (UN, Information Warfare, Treasury), projects (CRM, AirportSecurity, 2003Budget), or management levels. In a military environment, the classifications could be top secret, secret, confidential, and unclassified. Each classification is more trusted than the one below it. A commercial organization might use confidential, proprietary, corporate, and sensitive. The definition of the classification is up to the organization and should make sense for the environment they are used in.

The categories portion of the label enforces need-to-know rules. Just because someone has a top secret clearance does not mean that she now has access to all top-secret information. She must also have a need-to-know. As shown in Figure 4-8, if Cheryl has a top secret clearance, but she does not have a need-to-know to access any of the listed categories (Dallas, Max, Cricket) she cannot look at this object.

NOTE In MAC implementations, the system makes access decisions by comparing the subject's clearance and need-to-know level to that of the security label. In DAC, the system compares the subject's security token (permissions and rights) to the ACL on the resource.

Reference

Determining MAC Access: **csrc.nist.gov/publications/nistpubs/800-7/node37.html**

Role-Based

I am in charge of chalk, thus I need full control of all servers! Response: Good try.

A *role-based access control (RBAC)* model, also called *nondiscretionary access control*, uses a centrally administered set of controls to determine how subjects and objects interact. This type of model allows access to resources based on the role the user holds within the company.

Administrators should never assign rights and permissions without involving the owners of the system or of the information. By following the concept of "separation of duties," the process should work as follows. The owners decide what privileges to assign to the roles. The owners also decide which users to assign to those roles. The administrators create the roles and functions within the systems that they are maintaining on behalf of the owners. And a third function, the security administrator, actually adds the privileges to those user IDs and groups that were created by the administrators. Everyone should be involved with the fun.

Let's say we need a research and development analyst role. This role is developed to create a subset of individuals who can access a specific compartment of information with a certain level of rights. The data owner will decide who should access this information, thus determining who should be put into this role and with what rights and permissions. The actual act of creating the role is done by the data custodian (network or system administrator). The security administrator assigns the rights and permissions that the data owner has decided upon.

NOTE Introducing roles also introduces the difference between rights being assigned explicitly and implicitly. If rights and permissions are assigned explicitly, it indicates that they are assigned to a specific individual. If they are assigned implicitly, it indicates that they are assigned to a role or group and the user inherits those attributes.

Roles and groups are different, although they serve a similar purpose. They both work as containers for users to be put into. A company may have an auditors group, which contains several different users. These users can be part of other groups and usually have their own individual rights and permissions assigned to them also. If Diane is part of the auditors group, she can access files and resources assigned to this group, but as a user, she also has permissions that give her certain other access rights. If a company uses roles, any user assigned to that role only has the rights of that role. This provides tighter control. For example, if John is assigned to the contractor role, he can only access resources that are granted to this role; he will not usually have any of his own individual rights or permissions. Figure 4-9 shows the concept of roles.

A RBAC model is the best system for companies that have high employee turnovers. If John, who is mapped to the contractor role, leaves the company, then Chrissy can be easily mapped to this role. This way the administrator does not need to continually change the individual's permissions that fulfill a specific role in the company. He only needs to create a role (contractor), assign permissions to this role, and map the new user to this role.

Access Control Models

- **DAC** Data owners decide who has access to resources.
- **MAC** Access decisions are based on security labels.
- **RBAC** Access decisions are based on subject's role.

Figure 4-9
Individuals
assigned to roles
usually only have
the permissions
of that role.

 NOTE   RBAC is considered discretionary in nature because the data owner
will make the determination if specific roles and groups can access the
information he is responsible for.

Organizations usually set up a hierarchical structure of groups and roles and assign
each employee to the corresponding container. If Stacy is in charge of ordering brooms,
she is the BroomMaster, and this is the account she uses to access information within
the network. When she moves on to bigger and better things, the next person who is in
charge of ordering brooms uses this same account. The RBAC model can use *role-based
access* (determined by the role the user has within the company), *task-based access* (determined by the task assigned to this user), or a *lattice-based access* (determined by the
sensitivity level assigned to the role).

Lattice-based access control is a variation of nondiscretionary access control and provides an upper bound and lower bound of access capabilities for every subject and object relationship. When using the lattice-based model, subjects have the least upper
bound and the greatest lower bound of access to labeled objects based on their clearances, or assigned lattice position.

For example, when a user who is mapped to a specific role wants to carry out an operation on an object, the system will look at the clearance and need-to-know of that role,
look at the operation that is being requested, and compare this to the object's classification and access restrictions. All of this information is combined to generate a class or a
relationship between that subject and that object, which dictates what the subject can or
cannot do with it. The upper and lower bounds of access are illustrated in Figure 4-10.

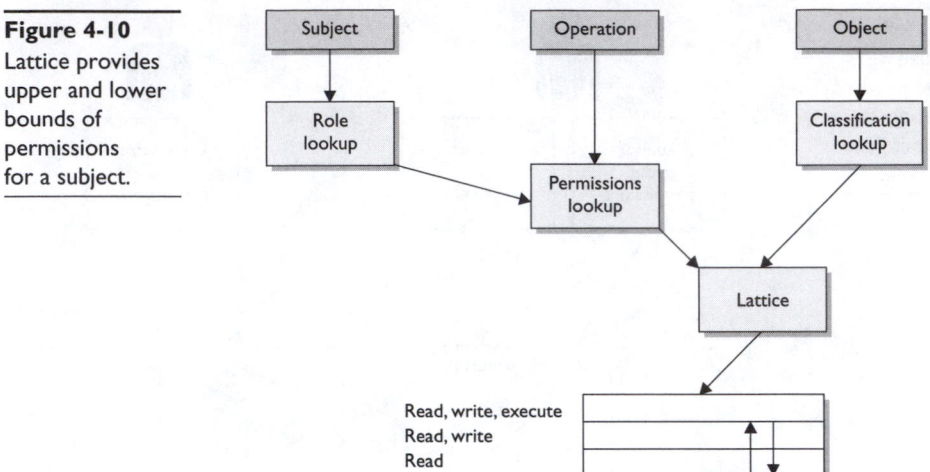

Figure 4-10
Lattice provides upper and lower bounds of permissions for a subject.

Access Control Techniques and Technologies

Once an organization determines what type of access control model is going to be used, the technologies and techniques need to be identified and refined to support the model. The following sections describe the different access controls and technologies available to support different access control models.

Rule-Based Access Control

Everyone will adhere to my rules. Response: Who are you again?

   Rule-based access control is based on specific rules that indicate what can and cannot happen to an object. Many routers and firewalls use rules to determine which types of packets are allowed into a network and which ones are rejected. Rule-based access control is a type of compulsory control because the administrator sets the rules and the users cannot modify these controls. A rule-based control means that everyone is restricted by it no matter what his identity is. For example, an administrator can configure a mail server to not allow attachments over a certain size to be accepted or that all user mailboxes will be 10 Mb.

Constrained User Interfaces

Constrained user interfaces restrict users' access abilities by not allowing them to request certain functions or information, or have access to specific system resources. There are three major types of restricted interfaces: menus and shells, database views, and physically constrained interfaces.

   When menu and shell restrictions are used, the users are only given the options of the commands they can execute. If an administrator only wants users to be able to run and execute one program, these are the only choices that would be available on the menu. This limits the user's functionality. A shell is a type of virtual environment within a system; it is the user's interface to the operating system and works as a command interpreter. If restricted shells were used, the shell would contain only the commands the administrator wants the users to be able to execute.

Many times a database administrator will configure a database so users cannot see fields that he wants to keep secret. *Database views* are mechanisms used for restricting user access to data that is contained in databases. If the database administrator wants managers to be able to view their employees' work records, but not their salary information, then the salary fields would not be available to these types of users. Similarly, when payroll employees look at the same database, they will be able to view the salary information, but not the work history information. This example is illustrated in Figure 4-11.

Physically constraining a user interface can be implemented by only providing certain keys on a keypad or touch buttons on a screen. We see this when we get money from an ATM machine. This device has a type of operating system that can accept all kinds of commands and configuration changes, but we are physically constrained from being able to carry out these functions. We are presented with buttons that only enable us to withdrawal, view our balance, or deposit funds. Period.

Access Control Matrix

An *access control matrix* is a table of subjects and objects indicating what actions individual subjects can take upon individual objects. Matrices are data structures that programmers implement as table lookups that will be used and enforced by the operating system. Table 4-1 provides an example of an access control matrix.

This type of access control is usually an attribute of DAC models. The access rights can be assigned directly to the subjects (capabilities) or to the objects (ACLs).

Capability Tables

A *capability table* specifies the access rights a certain subject possesses pertaining to specific objects. A capability table is different from an ACL because the subject is bound to the capability table, whereas the object is bound to the ACL.

The capability corresponds to the subject's row in the access control matrix. In Table 4-1, Diane's capabilities are File1: read and execute; File2: read and write; File3: no access. This outlines what Diane is capable of doing to each resource. An example of a capability-based

Figure 4-11
Different
database views

Harris, D	$45,000	8am-5pm
Torkelson, T	$60,000	6pm-2am
Kowtko, J	$45,000	8am-5pm
Swenson, J	$65,000	6pm-2am

Harris, D	Work history	8am-5pm
Torkelson, T	Work history	6pm-2am
Kowtko, J	Work history	8am-5pm
Swenson, J	Work history	6pm-2am

Payroll database view   Manager database view

Table 4-1	User	File1	File2	File3
Access Control Matrix	Diane	Read and execute	Read and write	No access
	Katie	Read and write	Write and execute	No access
	Chrissy	Read, write, and execute	Read	Read
	John	Read and execute	Read	Read, write, and execute

system is Kerberos. In this environment, the user is given a ticket, which is his capability table. This ticket is bound to the user and dictates what objects that user can access and to what extent. The access control is based on this ticket, or capability table, not on an ACL bound to the object, although ACLs and capability tables can be used together. Figure 4-12 shows the difference between a capability table and an ACL.

Access Control Lists

Access control lists (ACLs) are used in several operating systems, applications, and router configurations. They are lists of subjects that are authorized to access a specific object and they define what level of authorization is granted. Authorization can be specified to an individual, role, or group.

ACLs map values from the access control matrix to the object. Whereas a capability corresponds to a row in the access control matrix, the ACL corresponds to a column of the matrix. The ACL for File1 in Table 4-1 is shown in Table 4-2.

Content-Dependent Access Control

Just like the name sounds, with *content-dependent access control* access to objects is determined by the content within the object. This is used many times in databases and the type of Web-based material a firewall allows. Our earlier example pertaining to database views showed how content-dependent access control can work. The content of the database fields dictates which users can see specific information within the database tables.

Figure 4-12
A capability table is bound to a subject, whereas an access control list is bound to an object.

Capabilities Table

```
Plotter—Print
Printer1—Print
Printer2—No access
Accountng.xls—Full control
Accounting.doc—Read, write
Payroll.xls—No access
Clipart—Full control
```

Access Control Lists

```
Tom Harris—Print
Joni Swenson—Full control
Maynard Harris—No access
Evelyn Seaton—Print
Iqqi Hammond—Full control
David Arnold—Print
```

Table 4-2	User	
The ACL for File1	Diane	Read and execute
	Katie	Read and write
	Chrissy	Read, write, and execute
	John	Read and execute

Let's say we give department managers access to the payroll database. But specific managers would only be given access to the records that display those employees who actually work for the specific managers. That would require the access control system to look at the contents of the data in order to decide whether to give access or not. Therefore, that would be considered content-dependent access control.

Access Control Administration

Once an organization develops a security policy, supporting procedures, standards, and guidelines (described in Chapter 3), the decision of the type of access control model must be decided upon: DAC, MAC, or role-based models. Once the model is chosen, the different access control technologies and techniques need to be selected and implemented. Access control matrices, restricted interface, content-dependent, and rule-based controls are just a few of the choices.

Access Control Techniques

Access control techniques are used to support the access control models.

- **Rule-based** All subjects are restricted by specific rules and the authentication service does not take their identity into account.

- **Restricted interfaces** Limit the user's environment within the system, thus limiting access to objects.

- **Access control matrix** Table of subjects and objects outlining their access relationships.

- **Capability table** Bound to a subject and indicates what objects that subject can access.

- **ACL** Bound to an object and indicates what subjects can access it.

- **Content-based access** Access decision based on the sensitivity of the data, not solely on subject identity.

If the environment does not require a high level of security, the choices are usually discretionary and role-based. The discretionary model gives data owners the ability to allow other users to access their resources, so that choice should be made with full knowledge of what it entails. If the organization has a high turnover rate, the role-based model is more appropriate. If the environment requires a higher security level and it is desired that only the administrator grants access control, then a MAC model is the best choice.

What is left to work out is how the access control model will be administered. Access control administration comes in three basic flavors: centralized, decentralized, and a hybrid of the two. Each should be understood so that the proper method is chosen and implemented to achieve the level of protection required.

Centralized

I control who accesses what. Response: So what.

A *centralized access control administration* method is basically what it sounds like. One entity (department or individual) is responsible for granting all users access to resources. The management determines how users and resources should interact. This entity configures the mechanisms that enforce access control, processes any changes that are needed to a user's access control profile, disables access when necessary, and completely removes these rights when a user is terminated, leaves the company, or moves to a different position. This type of administration provides a consistent and uniform method of controlling users' access rights. It can supply strict control over data because only one entity (department or individual) has the necessary rights to change access control profiles and permissions. Although this provides for a more consistent and reliable environment, it can be a slow one because all changes must be processed by one entity.

The following sections show some examples of centralized access control technologies.

RADIUS

Remote Authentication Dial-in User Service (RADIUS) is an authentication protocol that authenticates and authorizes users, usually dial-in users. A network may have a modem pool dedicated for remote users to dial into, which is connected to access servers. The access server requests the remote user's logon credentials and passes them back to a RADIUS server, which houses a database of usernames and passwords or other authenticating information. The remote user is a client to the access server, and the access server is a client to the RADIUS server.

The access server may be at the same location as the requested network or it may be at the Internet service provider (ISP) that the remote user connects to obtain Internet access. Figure 4-13 shows how RADIUS implementations can be configured.

TACACS

Terminal Access Controller Access Control System (TACACS) has a very funny name. Not funny ha-ha, but funny "huh?" TACACS has been through three generations: TACACS, Extended TACACS (XTACACS), and TACACS+. TACACS combines its authentication and au-

Figure 4-13
RADIUS is
one way of
administrating
access control
centrally.

thorization processes, XTACACS separates authentication, authorization, and accounting processes, and TACACS+ is XTACACS with extended two-factor user authentication.

TACACS is a client/server protocol that provides the same type of functionality as RADIUS. A remote user can dial into a location that has a TACACS client, most likely an ISP. The client (or access server) prompts the user for credentials, and the client passes these credentials on to the TACACS server. The TACACS server verifies the credentials and authenticates the user to now be able to use resources within the network. TACACS+ enables credentials to take the form of username and passwords, Kerberos tickets, or dynamic passwords through security tokens.

TACACS+ and RADIUS provide the same functionality, but RADIUS is an actual Internet standard and TACACS+ is a Cisco proprietary protocol. Figure 4-14 shows how RADIUS and TACACS work.

Figure 4-14
The RADIUS or
TACACS client
could reside at
an ISP.

1. User initiates PPP authentication with ISP.
2. RADIUS client prompts user for credentials.
3. User supplies credentials.
4. RADIUS client sends credentials to RADIUS server.
5. RADIUS server responds with Accept, Reject, or Challenge.
6. If authentication is successful, RADIUS client allows access to network.

Diameter

Diameter is an authentication protocol that has the capability of authenticating many types of devices over different types of connections. RADIUS is restricted to only working over PPP and SLIP connections and can only authenticate computers and laptops that use modems and regular authentication protocols, as in PAP, CHAP, and EAP. Today companies have many different types of wireless devices that do not use these protocols and mechanisms, thus these companies cannot authenticate them using the RADIUS protocol.

Companies that need this extra flexibility can look at implementing Diameter instead of RADIUS or TACACS+. Diameter was developed to be able to work with IPSec if network layer security and encryption are required.

Decentralized

A *decentralized access control administration* method gives control of access to the people closer to the resources—the people who better understand who should and should not have access to certain files, data, and resources. Many times it is the functional manager who assigns access control rights to employees. An organization would use a decentralized model because managers usually have better judgment of which users should be able to access different resources, and there is no business requirement that dictates that strict control through a centralized body is necessary.

Changes can happen faster through this type of administration because not just one entity is making changes for the whole organization. However, there is a possibility that conflicts of interest could arise that may not benefit the organization. Because there is no single entity controlling access as a whole, different managers and departments can practice security and access control in different ways. This does not provide uniformity and fairness across the organization. One manager could be too busy with daily tasks and decide that it is easier to let everyone have full control over all the systems in the department. Another department may practice a more strict and detail-oriented method of control by only giving employees the level of permissions needed to fulfill their tasks.

Also, certain controls can overlap; thus, actions are not properly proscribed or restricted. If Mike is part of the accounting group and has been recently under suspicion for altering personnel account information, the accounting manager may restrict his access to these files to read. However, the accounting manager does not realize that Mike still has full control access under the network group he is also a member of. This type of administration does not provide methods for consistent control like a centralized method would. Another issue that comes up with decentralized administration is proper consistency pertaining to the company's protection. For example, when Sean is fired for looking at girly pictures on his computer, all the groups Sean is a member of may not disable his account once he is fired. So the company could still give access to Sean once he is terminated, which could cause the company heartache if Sean is vindictive.

Hybrid

A *hybrid access control administration* is a combination of the centralized and decentralized access control administration methods, but I bet you already guessed that. Many times when an organization employs this type of control, the central administration is used for the sensitive types of access (domain logon, system file access, and database access) and the users can determine who can access the individual files and directories they have created. Many times users are required to log onto a network domain so that they can access network resources. This type of access is controlled centrally by the network administrator. When users create files and share them, they can dictate who can and cannot access them, which is a type of decentralized access control. This gives the users more control and functionality, but it does not provide a strictly secure and controlled environment.

Figure 4-15 shows a hybrid model where the administrator can control which subjects can access specific objects within the environment and data owners can control which subjects can access the resources they are responsible for.

Access Control Methods

Access controls can be implemented at various layers of a network and individual systems. Some controls are core components of operating systems or embedded into applications and devices, and some security controls require third-party add-on packages. Although different controls provide different functionality, they all work together to keep the bad guys out and the good guys in, and to provide the necessary quality of protection.

Most companies do not want people to be able to walk arbitrarily into their building, sit down at an employee's computer, and access network resources. Companies also

Figure 4-15
Hybrid access control administration

Administrator controls access to database, printer, intellectual information, host computer, and fax.

File

File

File

File

File

File

File

File

File

Data owners control access to their files and resources.

don't want every employee to be able to access all information within the company, as in human resource records, payroll information, and trade secrets. Companies want to have some assurance that employees who can access confidential information will have some restrictions put upon them so a disgruntled employee does not have the ability to delete financial statements, tax information, and top secret data that would put the company at risk. There are several types of access controls that prevent these things from happening.

Access Control Layers

There are three broad categories of access control: administrative, technical, and physical. Each category has different access control mechanisms that can be carried out manually or through automated means. All of these access control mechanisms should work in concert with each other to protect an infrastructure and its data.

Each category of access control has several components that fall within it. The following list shows these components and the category they belong to:

Administrative

- Policy and procedures
- Personnel controls
- Supervisory structure
- Security awareness training
- Testing

Physical Controls

- Network segregation
- Perimeter security
- Computer controls
- Work area separation
- Data backups
- Cabling

Technical Controls

- System access
- Network architecture
- Network access
- Encryption and protocols
- Auditing

The following sections quickly explain each of these components and how they relate to access control.

Administrative Controls

Senior management must decide how security will play a role in their organization. They must determine the security goals and objectives within the organization. These directives will dictate how all the supporting mechanisms will fall into place. Basically, senior management provides the skeleton of a security infrastructure and then appoints the proper entities to fill in the rest.

The first piece to building a security foundation within an organization is a security policy. It is management's responsibility to construct a security policy and delegate the development of the supporting procedures, standards, and guidelines, indicate which personnel controls should be used, and how testing should be carried out to ensure that all pieces fulfill the company's security goals. These items are described as *administrative controls* and work at the top layer of a hierarchical access control model. (Administrative controls are examined in detail in Chapter 3, but are shown here briefly to show the relationship to logical and physical controls pertaining to access control.)

Policy and Procedures

Now, what's our overall plan?

A *security policy* is a high-level plan stating management's intent pertaining to how security should be practiced within an organization, what actions are acceptable, and what level of risk the company is willing to accept. This policy is derived from the laws, regulations, and business objectives that shape and restrict the company. The security policy provides direction for each employee and department pertaining to how security should be implemented and followed, and the repercussions for noncompliance. Procedures, guidelines, and standards provide the details that support and enforce the company's security policy.

Personnel Controls

Personnel controls indicate how employees are expected to interact with security mechanisms and noncompliance issues pertaining to these expectations. These controls indicate what security actions should be taken when an employee is hired, terminated, suspended, moved into another department, or promoted. Specific procedures need to be developed for each situation, and many times the human resource and legal departments are involved with making these decisions.

The separation of duties and rotation of duties are also personnel controls that need to be dictated by management. The *separation of duties* should be enforced so no one individual can carry out a critical task alone that could prove to be detrimental to the company. A bank teller who needed to get supervisory approval to cash checks over $2,000 would be an example of separation of duties. For a security breach to occur, it would require *collusion*, which means that more than one person would need to commit fraud and this effort would need to happen in a concerted effort. This drastically reduces the probability of security breaches and fraud.

Rotation of duties means that people know how to fulfill the obligations of more than one position. In many companies, there is just that one person who knows how to work the big important machine that keeps the company in business. If this person gets hit by a bus or finds a better job, the company's productivity can drop while it is frantically training the new person. If there were a practice of rotation of duties within this company, so much would not be riding on just one individual.

If an individual attempts to commit fraud within his position, it would be easier to detect by another individual who knows what tasks should be performed in that position and how they should be performed. The rotation of duties acts as a safeguard against fraud and it provides cross-training and supplies trained backup personnel.

Supervisory Structure

Management must construct a management and supervisory structure. Each employee has a superior to report to, and that superior is responsible for that employee's actions. This forces management staff members to be responsible for employees and take a vested interest in their activities. If an employee is caught hacking into a server that holds customer credit card information, that employee and her supervisor will be called on the carpet. This is an administrative control that aids in fighting fraud and enforcing proper access control.

Security Awareness Training

How do you know they know what they are supposed to know?

In many organizations, management has a hard time spending money and allocating resources to items that do not seem to affect their bottom line: profitability. This is why training is usually pushed to the back of the bus, but as computer security becomes more and more of an issue to companies, security awareness training is not viewed as a waste of time.

A company's security depends upon technology and people, and people are usually the weakest link and cause the most security breaches and compromises. If users understand how to properly access resources, why access controls are in place, and the ramifications for not using these access controls properly, a company can reduce many of the types of security incidents that take place.

Testing

All security controls, mechanisms, and procedures need to be tested on a periodic basis to ensure they properly support the security policy, goals, and objectives set for them. This testing can be a drill to test reactions to a physical attack or disruption of the network, a penetration test of the firewalls and perimeter network to uncover vulnerabilities, a query to employees to gauge their knowledge, or a review of the procedures and standards to make sure they still align to business and/or technologies changes that have been implemented. Because change is constant and environments continually evolve, security procedures and practices should be continually tested to ensure that they align with the management's expectations and stay up to date with each addition to the infrastructure. It is management's responsibility to make sure these tests take place.

Physical Controls

We will go much further into physical security in Chapter 6, but it is important to understand that there are physical controls that must support and work with administrative and logical controls to supply the right degree of access control. Physical controls range from verifying individuals' identities prior to entering a facility, erecting fences around the exterior of the facility, making sure server rooms and wiring closets are locked and protected from environmental elements (humidity, heat, and cold), and allowing only certain individuals to access work areas that contain confidential information. The following items explain some physical controls, but these and more physical mechanisms are explored in Chapter 6.

Network Segregation

Network segregation can be carried out through physical and logical means. A network might be physically designed to have all AS400 computers and databases in a certain area. This area can have doors with security swipe cards that allow only individuals who have a specific clearance to access this section and these computers. Another section of the network can contain Web servers, routers, and switches, and yet another network portion have employee workstations. Each area would have the necessary physical controls to ensure that only the right individuals would have access into and out of those sections. A simple example of network segregation is shown in Figure 4-16.

Perimeter Security

How perimeter security is implemented depends upon the company and the security requirements of that environment. One environment may require employees to be authorized by a security guard by showing a security badge that contains picture identification before being allowed to enter a section. Another environment may require no authentication process and let anyone and everyone into different sections. Perimeter security can also encompass closed-circuit TVs that scan the parking lots and waiting areas, fences surrounding a building, lighting of walkways and parking areas, motion detectors, sensors, alarms, and the location and visual appearance of a building. These are examples of perimeter security mechanisms that provide physical access control by providing protection for individuals, facilities, and the components within facilities.

Computer Controls

Each computer can have physical controls installed and configured. These types of controls could be locks on the cover so the internal parts of a computer cannot be stolen, the removal of the floppy and CD-ROM drives to prevent copying of confidential information, or implementing a protection device that reduces the electrical emissions to thwart attempts of gathering information through airwaves.

Work Area Separation

Some environments might dictate that only particular individuals can access certain sections of the facility. Research companies might not want office personnel to be able to enter laboratories in fear of disrupting experiments or having access to test data. Most

Figure 4-16
Network segmentation allows the network administrator to better control the environment.

Router

network administrators only allow network staff in the server rooms and wiring closets to reduce the possibilities of errors or sabotage attempts. In financial institutions, only certain employees can enter the vaults or other restricted areas. These are examples of work area separation and they are physical controls that are used to support access control and the overall security policy of the company.

Data Backups

Backing up data is a physical control to ensure access to information in case of an emergency or a disruption of the network or a system. When a network administrator of a bank backs up that day's transaction records, account histories, and financial information, it is stored on a type of physical media (tape, drive, or CD-ROM) and usually kept in a fireproof safe or copied and transported to an off-site facility. This provides physical protection of this data and a way to recover this information in case the original data is lost.

Cabling

There are different types of cabling that can be used to carry information throughout a network. Some cable types have sheaths that protect the data from being affected by electrical interference of other devices that emit electrical signals. Some types of cable have protection material around each individual wire to ensure that there is no cross- talk between the different wires. All cables need to be routed throughout the facility in a manner that is not in people's way or that could be exposed to any danger of being cut, burnt, crimped, or eavesdropped upon. (Please refer to Chapter 6 for more in-depth information.)

Technical Controls

Technical controls, also called logical controls, are the software tools used to restrict subjects' access to objects. They are core components of operating systems, add-on security packages, applications, network hardware devices, protocols, and access control matrixes. These controls work at different layers within a network or system and need to maintain a synergistic relationship to ensure that there is no unauthorized access to resources and that the resources' availability, integrity, and confidentiality are guaranteed. Technical controls protect the integrity and availability of resources by limiting the number of subjects that can access them and protect the confidentiality by preventing disclosure to unauthorized subjects. The following sections explain how some technical controls work and where they are implemented within an environment.

System Access

Different types of controls and security mechanisms control how a computer is accessed. If an organization is using a MAC architecture, the clearance of a user is identified and compared to the resource's classification level to verify that this user can access the requested object. If an organization is using a DAC architecture, the operating system checks to see if a user has been granted permission to access this resource. The sensitivity of data, clearance level of users, and users' rights and permissions are used as logical controls to control access to a resource.

There are many types of technical controls that enable a user to access a system and the resources within that system. This can be a username and password combination, Kerberos implementation, biometrics, public key infrastructure (PKI), RADIUS, TACACS, or being authenticated using a smart card through a reader connected to a system. These technologies verify that the user is who he says he is by different types of authentication methods. Once a user is properly authenticated, he can be authorized and allowed access to network resources. These technologies are addressed in further detail in future chapters, but for now understand that system access is a type of technical control that can enforce access control objectives.

Network Architecture

The architecture of a network can be constructed and enforced through several logical controls to provide segregation and protection of an environment. Networks can be segregated by physical walls and location, which are types of physical segregation. There is also a way of segregating a network logically. This consists of IP address ranges, subnets, and controlling the communication flow between the segments. Many times it is important to control how one segment of a network communicates with another segment.

Figure 4-17 is an example of how an organization may segregate its network and determine how network segments can communicate. This example shows how the organization does not want the internal network and the demilitarized zone (DMZ) to have open and unrestricted communication paths. There is usually no reason for internal users to have direct access to the systems in the DMZ, and cutting off this type of communication reduces the possibilities of internal attacks on those systems. Also, if an attack came from the Internet and successfully compromised a system on the DMZ, it is important that the attacker could not easily access the internal network, which this type of logical segregation protects against.

This example also shows how the management segment can communicate with all other network segments, but those segments cannot communicate in return. This is because the management consoles that control the firewalls and intrusion systems reside in the management segment and there is no reason for users, other than the administrator, to have access to these computers.

A network can be segregated physically and logically. This type of segregation and restriction is accomplished through logical controls.

Figure 4-17   Technical network segmentation controls how different network segments communicate.

Network Access

Systems have logical controls that dictate who can and cannot access them and what those individuals can do once they are authenticated. This is also true for networks. Routers, switches, firewalls, and bridges all work as technical controls to enforce access restriction into and out of a network, and access to the different segments within the network. If an attacker from the Internet wants to get to a specific computer, chances are that she will have to hack through a firewall, router, and a switch just to be able to start an attack on a specific computer that resides within the internal network. Each device has its own logical controls that make decisions about what entities can access them and what type of actions they can carry out.

Access to different network segments should be granular in nature. Routers and firewalls can be used to ensure that only certain types of traffic get through to each segment.

Encryption and Protocols

Encryption and protocols work as technical controls to protect information as it passes throughout a network and resides on computers. They ensure that the information is received by the correct entity, and that it is not modified during transmission. These logical controls can preserve the confidentiality and integrity of data and enforce specific paths for communication to take place. (Chapter 8 is totally dedicated to cryptography and encryption mechanisms.)

Control Zone

I will ensure that no signal escapes this room by using my incredible mental abilities. Response: How about a control zone instead?

A *control zone* is a combination of technical and physical controls. It is a specific area that surrounds and protects network devices that emit electrical signals. These electrical signals can travel a certain distance and can be contained by a specially made material, which is used to construct the control zone. Some companies use this material in their walls of the building to zone off areas that have computers that deal with top-secret information. It is used to resist penetration attempts and disallow sensitive information to "escape" through the airwaves. We will address how information can be captured from emitted electrical waves in the "Emanation Security" section of this chapter, but for now understand that a control zone is used as a technical and physical control to ensure that confidential information is contained and to hinder intruders for accessing information through the airwaves. Figure 4-18 depicts a control zone. Companies that have very sensitive information would likely protect that information by creating control zones around the systems processing that information.

Auditing

Auditing tools are technical controls that track activity within a network, on a network device, or on a specific computer. Even though auditing is not an activity that will deny an entity access to a network or computer, it will track activities so a network administrator can understand the types of access that took place, identify a security breach, or warn the administrator of suspicious activity. This information can be used

Figure 4-18 Companies can implement control zones, which control the amount of electrical signals that are emitted from sections of the facility.

to point out weaknesses of other technical controls and help the administrator understand where changes need to be made to preserve the necessary security level within the environment.

NOTE Many of the subjects touched on in these sections will be fully addressed and explained in later chapters. What is important to understand is that there are administrative, technical, and physical controls that work toward providing access control, and you should know several examples of each for the exam.

Access Control Types

Previously, it was stated that access control types (administrative, physical, and technical) work at different levels, but different levels of what? They work together at different levels within their own categories. A security guard is a type of control used to scare off evildoers and ensure that only authorized personnel enter a building. If an intruder gets around the security guard in some manner, he could be faced with motion detectors, locks on doors, and alarms. These layers are depicted in Figure 4-19.

Each control works at a different level of granularity, but they can also perform different functionalities. The different functionalities of access controls are *preventive, detective, corrective, deterrent, recovery,* and *compensating.* When looking at a security structure of an environment, it is most productive to use a preventive model and then use detective, recovery, and corrective mechanisms to help support this model. Basically, you want to stop any trouble before it starts, but you need to be able to quickly react and combat trouble if it does find you. All security controls should be built on the concept of preventive

Figure 4-19
Security should
be implemented
in layers, which
provides several
barriers to
attackers.

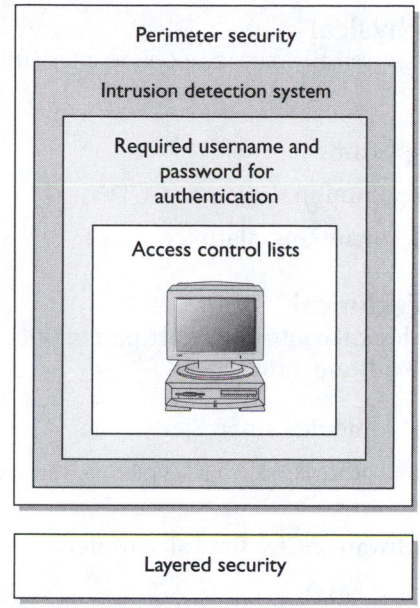

security. However, it is not feasible to prevent everything, therefore, what you cannot prevent, you should be able to quickly detect. That's why preventive and detective controls should always be implemented together and should complement each other. To take this concept further, what you can't prevent, you should be able to detect, and if you detect something, it means that you weren't able to prevent it, therefore you should take corrective action to make sure that it is indeed prevented the next time around. This means that you now take corrective action to prevent it from happening again. Therefore, all three types work together, preventive, detective, and corrective.

The following control types (administrative, physical, technical) are preventive in nature. These are important to understand when developing a security access control model and for the CISSP exam.

Preventive—Administrative

The following are the *soft* mechanisms that are put into place to enforce access control and protection for the company as a whole:

- Policies and procedures
- Effective hiring practices
- Pre-employment background checks
- Controlled termination processes
- Data classification and labeling
- Security awareness

Preventive—Physical

The following can physically restrict access to a facility, specific work areas, or computer systems:

- Badges, swipe cards
- Guards, dogs, motion detectors, CCTV
- Fences, locks, mantraps, alarms

Preventive—Technical

The following are logical controls that are part of operating systems, third-party application add-ons, or hardware units:

- Passwords, biometrics, smart cards
- Encryption, protocols, call-back systems, database views, constrained user interfaces
- Antivirus software, ACLs, firewalls, routers, clipping levels

Table 4-3 shows how these categories of access control mechanisms perform different types of functionality. The table is used to show how different controls can provide one or more security attributes, but does not necessarily cover all the possibilities. For example, a fence can provide preventive and deterrent measures by making it harder for intruders to access a facility, but it could also be a compensating control. If a company cannot afford a security guard, it might erect a fence to act as the compensating physical control. There are good arguments for each control being able to meet more requirements than what is listed in the table. Table 4-3 is only an example to show the relationship among the different controls and the security attributes they could provide.

 NOTE Locks are usually considered delay mechanisms because they will only delay a determined intruder. The goal is to delay access enough to allow law enforcement or the security guard to respond to the situation.

There are several types of security mechanisms, and they all need to work together. The complexity of the controls and of the environment they are in can cause the controls to contradict each other or leave gaps in security. This can introduce unforeseen holes in the company's protection that are not fully understood by the implementers. Very strict technical access controls can be in place and all the necessary administrative controls up to snuff, but if any person is allowed to physically access each and every system in the facility, then there are clear security dangers present within the environment. Together these controls should work in harmony to provide a healthy, safe, and productive environment.

Type of Control	Preventive	Detective	Corrective	Deterrent	Recovery	Compensation
	Controls used to deter and avoid undesirable events from taking place	Controls used to identify undesirable events that have occurred	Controls used to correct undesirable events that have occurred	Controls used to discourage security violations	Controls used to restore resources and capabilities	Controls used to provide alternatives to other controls
Category of Control						
Physical						
Fences	X			X		
Locks	X			X		
Badge system	X			X		
Security guard	X	X		X		
Biometric system	X					
Mantrap doors	X			X		
Lighting	X					
Motion detectors		X				
Closed-circuit TVs		X		X		
Alarms	X	X		X		
Backups					X	
Administrative						
Security policy	X					
Monitoring and supervising	X	X		X		X
Separation of duties	X			X		
Job rotation	X	X				
Information classification	X					
Personnel procedures	X			X		X
Investigations		X				

Table 4-3   Services that Security Controls Provide

2

Type of Control	Preventive	Detective	Corrective	Deterrent	Recovery	Compensation
	Controls used to deter and avoid undesirable events from taking place	Controls used to identify undesirable events that have occurred	Controls used to correct undesirable events that have occurred	Controls used to discourage security violations	Controls used to restore resources and capabilities	Controls used to provide alternatives to other controls
Category of Control						
Administrative						
Testing	x					
Security awareness training	x			x		
Technical						
ACLs	x					
Routers	x					
Encryption	x			x		
Audit logs		x				
IDS		x	x			
Antivirus software	x	x	x		x	
Firewalls	x	x		x		
Smart cards	x					
Dial-up call-back systems	x					
Alarms and alerts		x				

Table 4-3   Services that Security Controls Provide *(continued)*

Accountability

Auditing capabilities ensure that users are accountable for their actions, verify that the security policies are enforced, and are used as investigation tools. There are several reasons why network administrators and security professionals want to make sure accountability mechanisms are in place and configured properly: to be able to track bad deeds back to individuals, detect intrusions, reconstruct events and system conditions, provide legal recourse material, and produce problem reports. Audit documentation and log files hold a mountain of information—the trick is usually deciphering it and presenting it in a useful and understandable format.

Accountability is tracked through recording user, system, and application activities. This recording is done through auditing functions and mechanisms within an operating system or security application. Audit trails contain information about operating system activities, application events, and user actions. They can be used to verify the health of a system by checking out performance information or certain types of errors and conditions. After a system crashes, many times a network administrator will review audit logs to try and piece together the status of the system and attempt to understand what events could have attributed to the disruption.

An administrator configures what actions and events are to be audited and logged. If it were a high-security environment, the administrator would configure more activities to be captured and the threshold of those activities to be more sensitive. The events can be reviewed to identify where breaches of security occurred and if the security policy had been violated. If the environment does not require such level of security, the events analyzed would be fewer with less demanding thresholds.

Items and actions to be audited can become an endless list. A security professional should be able to assess an environment and its security goals, know what actions should be audited and what is to be done with that information after it is captured, without wasting too much disk space, CPU power, and staff time. The following gives a broad overview of the items and actions that can be audited and logged:

System-level Events

- Monitor system performance
- Logon attempts (successful and unsuccessful)
- Logon ID
- Date and time of each logon attempt
- Lockouts of users and terminals
- Use of administration utilities
- Devices used
- Functions performed
- Requests to alter configuration files

Application-level Events

- Error messages
- Files opened and closed
- Modifications of files
- Security violations within application

User-level Events

- Identification and authentication attempts
- Files, services, and resources used
- Commands initiated
- Capture security violations

The threshold (clipping level) and parameters for each of these items needs to be configured. For example, an administrator can audit each logon attempt or just each failed logon attempt. System performance can look only at the amount of memory used within an eight-hour period, or the memory, CPU, and hard drive space used within an hour.

Intrusion detection systems (IDSs) continually scan audit logs for suspicious activity, and if an intrusion or harmful event takes place, audit logs are usually kept to be used later to prove guilt and prosecute if necessary. If severe security events take place, many times the IDS will alert the administrator or staff member so proper actions can take place to end the destructive activity. If a dangerous virus is identified, administrators may take the mail server offline. If an attacker is accessing confidential information within the database, this computer may be temporarily disconnected from the network or Internet. If an attack is in progress, the administrator may want to watch the actions taking place so she can track down the intruder. IDSs can watch for this type of activity during real time and/or scan audit logs and watch for specific patterns or behaviors.

Review of Audit Information
It does no good to collect it if you don't look at it.

Audit trails can be reviewed manually or through an automated means—either way, they must be reviewed and interpreted. If an organization reviews audit trails manually, there needs to be a rhyme and reason to how they are viewed, when, and why. Usually audit logs are very popular items right after a security breach, unexplained system action, or system disruption. An administrator or staff member rapidly tries to piece together the activities that led up to the event. This type of audit review is event-oriented. Audit trails can also be viewed periodically to watch for unusual behavior of users or systems, and to help understand the baseline and health of a system. Then there is a real-time audit analysis, or near real-time, that can use an automated tool to review audit information as it is created. Administrators should have a scheduled task of reviewing audit data. The audit material usually needs to be parsed and saved to another location for a certain time period. This information should be stated in the company's security policy and procedures.

Reviewing audit information manually can be overwhelming. There are applications and audit trail analysis tools that reduce the volume of audit logs to review and improve the efficiency of manual review procedures. A majority of the time, audit logs contain information that is unnecessary, so these tools parse out specific events and present them in a useful format. There are three main types of audit trail analysis tools: audit reduction, variance-detection, and attack signature-detection.

An *audit reduction* does just what it sounds like—reduces the amount of information within an audit log. This tool discards mundane task information and records system performance, security, and user functionality information that can be useful to a security professional or administrator. A *variance-detection* tool can monitor computer and resource usage trends and detect variations. If an employee works from 8:00 A.M. to 5:00 P.M., which is the normal time his computer is used and resources are accessed, and recently this computer has been used at 2:00 A.M. and on the weekend, the analysis tool can capture this information and alert the administrator of unusual activity. If an *attack signature-detection* tool is used, the application will have a database of information that has been known to indicate specific attacks. This type of tool will parse audit logs in search of certain patterns. If a pattern matches a pattern or signature held within its database, the tool indicates that an attack has taken place or is in progress.

Keystroke Monitoring

Oh, you typed an L, let me write that down. Oh, and a P, and a T, and an S…hey, slow down!

Keystroke monitoring is a type of auditing that can review and record keystrokes entered by a user during an active session. The person using this type of monitoring can either view the characters as they are typed, or have the characters written to an audit log to be reviewed at a later time. This type of auditing is usually done only for special cases and only for a specific amount of time, because the amount of information captured can be overwhelming. If a security professional or administrator is suspicious of an individual and his activities, this type of monitoring may be invoked.

Keystroke monitoring captures every keystroke.

A hacker can also use this type of monitoring. If an attacker can successfully install a Trojan horse on a computer, it can install an application that will capture data as it is typed into the keyboard. Most of the time these programs are most interested in user credentials and can alert the attacker when credentials have been successfully captured.

There are privacy issues with this type of monitoring, and administrators could be subject to criminal and civil liabilities if it is done without proper notification and authorization. As of this writing, there have been no known court cases pertaining to keystroke monitoring and thus no legal precedent has been set. If a company wants to be able to use this type of auditing, it should be stated in the security policy, addressed in security awareness training, and a banner notice should be presented to the user warning that the activities at that computer may be monitored in this fashion. These steps should be taken to protect the company from violating an individual's privacy, and it should inform the users where their privacy boundaries start and stop pertaining to computer use.

Protecting Audit Data and Log Information

If an intruder breaks into your house, he will do his best to cover his tracks, not leave fingerprints or any other clues that can be used to tie him to the criminal activity. The same is true in computer fraud and illegal activity. The intruder will work to cover his tracks. Many times attackers delete audit logs that hold this incriminating information. (Deleting specific incriminating data within audit logs is called *scrubbing*.) Deleting this information can cause the administrator to not be alerted or aware of the security breach, and can destroy valuable data. Therefore, audit logs and information should be protected by strict access control.

Only certain individuals (the administrator and security personnel) should be able to view, modify, and delete audit trail information. No other individuals should be able to view this data, much less modify or delete it. The integrity of the data can be ensured with the use of digital signatures, message digest tools, and strong access controls. Its confidentiality can be protected with encryption and access controls, if necessary, and the information can be stored on *write-once media* (CD-ROM) to prevent losing or modification of the data. Unauthorized access attempts to audit logs should be captured and reported.

Audit logs may be used in a trial to prove an individual's guilt, demonstrate how an attack was carried out, or corroborate a story. The integrity and confidentiality of these logs will be under scrutiny. Proper steps need to be taken to ensure that the confidentiality and integrity of the audit information is not compromised in any way.

References

Authentication, Authorization, and Accounting Charter: **www.ietf.org/html.charters/aaa-charter.html**

Google authentication categories: **directory.google.com/Top/Computers/Security/Authentication**

Security in Open Systems: **csrc.nist.gov/publications/nistpubs/800-7/node2.html**

Access Control Practices

Least amount of doors open allows the least amount of flies in.

We have gone over how users are identified, authenticated, and authorized, and how their actions are audited. These are necessary parts of a healthy and safe network environment. You also want to take steps to ensure there are no unnecessary open doors and that the environment stays at the same security level you have worked so hard to achieve. This means you need to implement good access control practices. Not keeping up with daily or monthly tasks usually causes the most vulnerabilities in an environment. It is hard to put out all the network fires, fight the political battles, fulfill all the users' needs, and still keep up with small maintenance tasks. However, many companies have found that not doing these small tasks caused them the greatest heartache of all.

The following is a list of tasks that need to be accomplished on a regular basis to ensure that security stays at a satisfactory level:

- Deny access to systems by undefined users or anonymous accounts.
- Limit and monitor the usage of administrator and other powerful accounts.
- Suspend or delay access capability after a specific number of unsuccessful logon attempts.
- Remove obsolete user accounts as soon as the user leaves the company.
- Suspend inactive accounts after 30 to 60 days.
- Enforce strict access criteria.
- Enforce the need-to-know and least-privilege practices.
- Disable unneeded system features, services, and ports.
- Replace default password settings on accounts.
- Limit and monitor global access rules.
- Logon IDs need to be nondescriptive of job function.
- Remove redundant resource rules from accounts and group memberships.
- Remove redundant user IDs, accounts, and role-based accounts from resource access lists.
- Enforce password rotation.
- Enforce password requirements (length, contents, lifetime, distribution, storage, and transmission).
- Audit system and user events and actions and review reports periodically.
- Protect audit logs.

Unauthorized Disclosure of Information

There are several ways that information can become available to others for whom it was not intended, which can bring about unfavorable results. Sometimes this is done intentionally, but it can be done unintentionally also. Information can be disclosed unintentionally when one falls prey to attacks that specialize in this. These attacks are social engineering, covert channels, malicious code, and electrical airwave sniffing. Information can be disclosed accidentally through object reuse methods, which are explained in the next section.

Object Reuse

Can I borrow this floppy? Answer: Let me destroy it first.

Object reuse issues pertain to reassigning media to a subject that contained one or more objects. Huh? This means before someone uses a hard drive, floppy disk, or tape it should be cleared of any residual information that was on it previously. This concept also applies to objects that are reused by computer processes, such as memory locations, variables, and registers. The sensitive information that may be left by a process should be securely cleared before allowing another process the opportunity to access the object. This ensures that information not intended for this individual or any other subject is not disclosed to that particular subject. Many times floppy disks are exchanged without much thought in a work environment. What if a supervisor lent a floppy to an employee without erasing it and it contained confidential employee performance reports and salary raises forecasted for the next year? This could prove to be a bad decision and maybe turn into a morale issue if the information was passed around. Formatting a disk or deleting files only removes the pointers to the files; it does not remove the actual files. This information will still be on the disk and available until the operating system needs that space and overwrites those files. So for media that holds confidential information, more extreme methods should be taken to ensure the files are actually gone, not just their pointers.

Sensitive data should be classified (secret, top secret, confidential, unclassified, and so on). The flow of this data should be understood and tracked, and how it is stored and accessed should also be strictly controlled and audited. However, it does not end there; before allowing one subject to use media that was previously used, the media should be erased, degaussed, or formatted. If media holds sensitive information and cannot be purged, there should be steps on how to properly destroy it so that there is no way for others to obtain this information. The most effective way of ensuring that confidential information is not disclosed in an unauthorized manner is to physically destroy the media.

 NOTE Sometimes evildoers will actually configure a sector on a hard drive so that it is marked as bad and unusable to an operating system, but this sector is actually fine and may hold malicious data. The operating system will not write information to this sector because it thinks it is corrupted. This is a form of *data hiding*.

Emanation Security

Quick, cover your computer and your head in tinfoil!

All electronic devices emit electrical radiation, as shown in Figure 4-20. This radiation can hold important information, and if an attacker bought the right equipment and positioned himself in the right place, the attacker could capture this information from the airwaves and access data transmissions as if he had a tap directly on the network wire.

Figure 4-20
All electrical
devices emit
electrical signals.

There have been several incidents of intruders purchasing inexpensive equipment and intercepting electrical emissions as they radiated from a computer. This equipment can reproduce data streams and display the data on the intruder's monitor. This can enable intruders to learn of covert operations, find out military strategies, and uncover and exploit confidential information. This is not just stuff found in spy novels, it really happens, so the proper countermeasures have been devised.

Tempest

Tempest is the study and control of spurious electrical signals that are emitted by electrical equipment. There is special shielding that equipment uses to suppress or mask the signals as they are radiated from devices. Tempest equipment is implemented to prevent intruders from picking up information through the airwaves with listening devices. There are specific standards that this type of equipment must meet to be rated as providing Tempest shielding protection. Tempest refers to standardized technology that suppresses signal emanations with shielding material. It is an actual standard, and vendors who manufacture this type of equipment must be certified to this standard.

The devices (monitors, computers, printers, and so on) have an outer metal coating referred to as a Faraday cage. It is a type of metal and materials with the necessary depth to ensure that only a certain amount of radiation is released. In devices that are Tempest rated, other components are modified, especially the power supply, to help reduce the amount of electricity that is used.

There are allowable limits of levels of emissions that can radiate and still be considered safe. The approved products must ensure that only this level of emissions is allowed to escape the area. This type of protection is usually only needed in military institutions, although other highly secured environments do utilize this type of safeguard.

Many military organizations are concerned with stray radio frequencies emitted by computers and other electronic equipment because an attacker may be able to pick them up, reconstruct them, and give away some secrets that were meant to stay secret.

Tempest technology is complex, cumbersome, and expensive, and therefore only used in highly sensitive areas that really need this high level of protection.

Two alternatives to Tempest are using white noise or a control zone concept, explained next.

NOTE Tempest is the name of a program, and now a standard, that was developed in the late 1950s by the U.S. and British governments. It was developed to deal with electrical and electromagnetic radiation emitted from electrical equipment, mainly computers. This type of equipment is usually used by intelligence, military, government, and law enforcement agencies and the selling of this type of equipment is under constant scrutiny.

White Noise

Some implementations used to combat intruders from extracting information from electrical transmissions use white noise. *White noise* is a uniform spectrum of random electrical signals. It is distributed over the full spectrum so that the bandwidth is constant and an intruder is not able to decipher real information from random noise or random information.

Zones

Another alternative to using Tempest equipment is to use the zone concept, which was addressed earlier in this chapter. Some environments use material in their facility walls to contain electrical signals to prevent intruders from being able to access information that is emitted via electrical signals from network devices. This control zone creates a type of security perimeter and is constructed to protect against unauthorized access to data or compromise of sensitive information.

Access Control Monitoring

Access control monitoring is a method of keeping track of who attempts to access specific network resources. It is an important detective mechanism, and there are different technologies that can fulfill this need.

Intrusion Detection

Intrusion detection systems (IDSs) are used to monitor a network or individual computers. There are two main types of IDS: *network-based*, which monitors a network or a segment of the network, and *host-based*, which monitors a particular system.

IDSs can be configured to watch for attacks, parse audit logs, alert an administrator as attacks are happening, protect system files, expose a hacker's techniques, illustrate which vulnerabilities need to be addressed, and possibly help track down individual hackers.

Host-based IDSs can be installed on individual workstations and/or servers and watch for inappropriate or anomalous activity and insider attacks. Host-based IDSs are usually used to make sure users do not accidentally delete system files, reconfigure important settings, or put the system at risk any other way. Network-based IDSs monitor network traffic and uncover possible attacks or suspicious activities. This is usually done by anomaly detection and pattern detection.

Knowledge- or Signature-Based Intrusion Detection

Knowledge is accumulated about specific attacks and how they are carried out. Models of how the attacks are carried out are developed and called *signatures*. Each identified attack has a signature, which is used to detect an attack in progress or determine if one has occurred within the network. Any action that is not recognized as an attack is considered acceptable. The effectiveness of this type of protection depends on the regularity of updating the software with new signatures or known attacks. This type of IDS is weak against new types of attacks because it can only recognize the ones that have been previously identified.

Behavior-Based or Statistical Intrusion Detection

My host IDS says I have been very bad. Response: We will beat you later.

This type of software observes and detects deviation from expected behavior of users and systems. A reference model of normal behavior is compiled and future activities are compared against it. This type of IDS can use *expert system* technology, which attempts to think like a human expert and provide the same type of reasoning. It can detect real-time anomalies by detecting deviations from sequential rules, and it can review audit log files to detect suspicious activity that has already taken place.

For an IDS to be able to perform real-time anomaly detection, it uses a **time-based induction machine (TIM)**. This is a virtual machine that tracks and builds behavior profiles for system usage, network traffic, and user activities. The profile is made up of sequences of events to be used to try and determine when something out of the ordinary happens.

The behavior-based, or statistical, IDS can detect new, unforeseen vulnerabilities, but it can also cause many false alarms.

Once an attack is discovered, there are several things that can take place, and this is up to the capabilities of the IDS and the policy that has been assigned to it. The IDS can send an alert to a console to tell the right individuals that an attack is being carried out. It can send an e-mail or page to the individual who has been delegated to respond to such activities. It can kill the connection of the detected attack, or it can reconfigure a router or firewall to try and stop any further similar attacks.

IDS Sensors

Network-based IDSs use sensors for monitoring purposes. A sensor is placed on the network segment it is responsible for monitoring. This sensor works as an agent and sends data back to a monitoring console for further analysis. The monitoring console monitors all sensors and supplies the network staff with an overview of the activities of all of the sensors in the network.

These are the components that enable network-based intrusion-detection to actually work. Sensor placement is a critical part of configuring an effective IDS. An organization can place a sensor outside of the firewall to detect attacks and inside the firewall (in the perimeter network) to detect actual intrusions. Sensors should also be placed in highly sensitive areas, on networks with many transient employees, and on extranets. Figure 4-21 shows the sensors reporting their findings to the central console.

There are five basic components of intrusion detection:

- **Sensors**   Detects events and sends this data to the monitoring software.
- **Central monitoring software**   Accepts data from all sensors on the network and analyzes it.
- **Analysis of event reports**   Might offer a recommendation for counteracting the event.
- **Database components**   Determines if an IP address or an attack has been seen before. This is trend analysis.
- **Response boxes**   Can take information for the previous components and respond to the event.

Figure 4-21 Sensors need to be placed in each network segment that is to be monitored by the IDS.

Network Traffic

If the network traffic volume exceeds the IDS system's threshold, attacks can go unnoticed. Each vendor's IDS system product has its own threshold, and that should be known and understood before it is purchased and implemented.

In very high-traffic environments, multiple sensors should be in place so that no packet can pass without being investigated. If it is necessary for optimizing network bandwidth and speed, different sensors can be set up to analyze each packet for different signatures. This way the analysis load can be broken up over different points.

Note that IDS systems will not be able to detect attacks within encrypted traffic.

References

Network Intrusion Detection Systems FAQ: **www.robertgraham.com/pubs/ network-intrusion-detection.html**

CSI Intrusion Detection System Resource: **www.gocsi.com/intrusion.htm**

Intrusion Detection FAQ: **www.sans.org/resources/idfaq**

Honeypot

Hey, curious, ill-willed, and destructive attackers, look at this shiny new vulnerable computer.

A *honeypot* is a computer set up as a sacrificial lamb on the network. The system is not locked down and has open ports and services enabled. This is to entice a would-be attacker to this computer instead of attacking authentic computers on a network. The honeypot contains no real company information, and thus will not be at risk if and when it is attacked.

This enables the administrator to know when certain types of attacks are happening so he can fortify the environment and perhaps track down the attacker. The longer the hacker stays at the honeypot, the more will be disclosed about her techniques.

It is important to draw a line between *enticement* and *entrapment* when implementing a honeypot system. There are legal and liability issues around each. If the system only had open ports and services an attacker might want to take advantage of, this would be an example of enticement. If the system had a Web page indicating that the user can download files, and once the user does this the administrator charges this user with hacking, it would be entrapment. Entrapment is where the intruder is induced to commit a crime that they weren't originally contemplating. Entrapment is illegal and cannot be used when charging an individual with hacking or unauthorized activity.

References

The Honeynet Project: **project.honeynet.org**

What Is a Honeypot?: **www.sans.org/resources/idfaq/honeypot3.php**

Network Sniffers

I think I smell a packet! Response: Nope. It's my feet.

A packet or network *sniffer* is a type of wiretap device that plugs into a network for the purpose of eavesdropping on network traffic. The traffic that is being transferred over a network medium is in binary (actually electrical signals that represent binary code), so the sniffer has to have a protocol analysis capability to recognize the different protocols passing over the network.

The sniffer has a network adapter that works in promiscuous mode and a driver that captures the data. This data can be overwhelming, so it must be properly filtered. The filtered data is stored in a buffer and this information is displayed. Many sniffers allow the data to be modified and retransmitted over the network. This is how some types of spoofing and man-in-the-middle attacks are carried out. Figure 4-22 illustrates a sniffer connected to a network.

Network sniffers are used by the people in the white hats (administrators and security professionals) usually to try and track down a recent problem with the network. But the guys in the black hats (attackers and evildoers) can use them to learn about what type of data is passed over a specific network segment and to modify data in an unauthorized manner.

NOTE Sniffers are dangerous because they are very hard to detect and their activities cannot be audited.

Figure 4-22 Sniffers are used to capture data as it travels throughout the network.

Network sniffers are great tools, but like most tools, they can be used for good and evil agendas.

A Few Threats to Access Control

A majority of security professionals know that there is more risk and higher probability of an attacker causing mayhem from within an organization than outside the organization. However, many people within organizations do not know this because they only hear stories about the attackers who defaced a Web server or circumvented a firewall to access confidential information.

An attacker from the outside can come in through remote dial-in entry points, through firewalls and Web servers, physically break in, or exploit a partner communication path (extranet, vendor connection, and so on). An insider has legitimate reasons for using the system and resources, but can misuse his privileges and launch an actual attack. The danger of insiders is that they have already been given a wide range of access that a hacker would have to work to obtain, and the insider probably has intimate knowledge of the environment. We have discussed many different types of access control mechanisms that work to keep the outsiders outside and restrict the insiders' abilities to a minimum and audit their actions.

Dictionary Attack

There are several programs that enable an attacker (or proactive administrators) to identify user credentials. The program is fed lists (dictionaries) of commonly used words or combinations of characters, and the program compares these values to capture passwords. In other words, the program will hash the dictionary words and compare the resulting message digest with the system password file that also stores its passwords in one-way hashed format. If the hashed values match, it means that the word from the dictionary that was hashed is the correct word used as the password. Once the right combination is identified, the attacker can authenticate herself as a legitimate user. Because many systems have thresholds that dictate how many logon attempts are acceptable, the same type of activity can happen to a captured password file. The program encrypts the combination of characters and compares them to the encrypted entries in the password file. If a match is found, the program has uncovered a password.

The dictionaries come with the programs and extra dictionaries can be found on several sites on the Internet.

Countermeasures

To properly protect an environment against dictionary and other password attacks, the following practices should be followed:

- Do not allow passwords to be sent in clear text.
- Encrypt the passwords with encryption algorithms or hashing functions.
- Employ one-time password tokens.
- Use hard-to-guess passwords.
- Rotate passwords frequently.
- Employ IDS to detect this type of suspicious behavior.
- Use dictionary attacks to find weak passwords chosen by users.
- Use special characters, numbers, and upper- and lowercase letters within the password.
- Protect password files.

Brute Force Attack

I will try over and over until you are defeated. Response: Okay, wake me when you are done.

There are several types of ***brute force attack***, but overall it is an attack that continually tries different inputs to achieve a predefined goal. Brute force is defined as "trying every possible combination until the correct one is identified." In password guessing, an attacker will try different variations of characters to try and derive the correct combination. If a dictionary tool has found that a user's password starts with Dallas, then the brute force tool will try Dallas1, Dallas01, Dallasa1, and so on until a successful logon credential is uncovered.

These attacks are also used in *wardialing* efforts. A long list of phone numbers are inserted into a wardialing program in hopes of finding a modem that can be exploited to gain unauthorized access. A program is used to go through many phone numbers and weed out the numbers that are used for voice calls and fax machine services. The attacker usually ends up with a handful of numbers he can now try to exploit and gain access into a system or network.

So a brute force attack perpetuates a specific activity with different input parameters until the goal is achieved.

Countermeasures

For phone brute force attacks, auditing and monitoring of this type of activity should be in place to uncover patterns that could indicate a wardialing attack.

- Perform brute force attacks to find weaknesses.
- Make sure only necessary phone numbers are made public.
- Provide stringent access control methods that would make brute force attacks less successful.
- Monitor and audit for such activity.
- Employ an IDS to watch for suspicious activity.
- Set lockout thresholds.

Spoofing at Logon

So, what are your credentials again?

A program that presents a fake logon screen can be presented by an attacker, which tricks the user to attempt to log on. The user is asked for a username and password, which is stored for the attacker to access at a later time. The user does not know this is not his usual logon screen because they look exactly the same. A fake error message can appear, indicating that the user mistyped his credentials. At this point, the fake logon program exits and hands control over to the operating system, which prompts the user for a username and password. The user assumes he mistyped his information and doesn't give it a second thought, but an attacker now knows the user's credentials.

Countermeasures

The system can be configured to display the number of failed logon attempts that could indicate to the user what just happened. If the first logon attempt seemed to have failed, but was really the attacker's program, and it was not reported at the second attempt and the user could get suspicious as to what just took place.

A guaranteed *trusted path* can be provided. A trusted path tells the user that he is communicating directly to the operating system instead of a fake, spoofing program. Windows NT uses a sequence of CTRL-ALT-DEL to invoke the operating system's logon screen. (However, some sneaking fake programs can set themselves to be called by this combination of keys also.)

Reference

Articles on hacking and hackers: **www.sans.org/rr/hackers/**

Penetration Testing

Excuse me. Could you please attack me?

Penetration testing is the process of simulating attacks on a network and the systems that make it up at the request of the owner, usually senior management. The goal of penetration testing is to identify vulnerabilities, estimate the true protection the security mechanisms within the environment are providing, and see how suspicious activity is reported.

The penetration team must have signed consent from the owner of the environment outlining what is to be accomplished in the test and to what degree the vulnerabilities should be tested. The team then goes through a process made up of five steps:

1. **Discovery**   Footprinting and gathering information about the target

2. **Enumeration**   Performing port scans and resource identification methods

3. **Vulnerability mapping**   Identifying vulnerabilities in identified systems and resources

4. **Exploitation**   Attempting to gain unauthorized access by exploiting vulnerabilities

5. **Report to management**   Documentation of findings of test goes to management along with suggested countermeasures

The team can have varying degrees of understanding of the target before the tests are actually carried out:

- **Zero knowledge**   Team does not have much knowledge of target and must start from ground zero.

- **Partial knowledge**   Team has some information about target.

- **Full knowledge**   The team has intimate knowledge of target.

It is important that the team start off with only basic user-level access to properly simulate different attacks. The team needs to utilize a variety of different tools and attack methods, and look at all possible vulnerabilities, because this is how actual attackers will function. It is also extremely important that the team gets written permission from the right level of management before proceeding with any of these types of activities.

Summary

Access controls are security features that are usually considered the first lines of protection. They are used to dictate how subjects access objects and resources, and their main goal is to protect the resources from unauthorized access. These controls can be administrative, physical, or technical in nature and can supply preventive, detective, deterrent, recovery, compensative, and corrective services.

Access control defines how users and subjects should be identified, authenticated, and authorized. These issues are carried out differently in different access control models and technologies, and it is up to the organization to determine which best fits their business and security needs.

Quick Tips

- Access is a flow of information between a subject and an object.
- A subject is an active entity that requests access to an object, which is a passive entity.
- A subject can be a user, program, or process.
- Confidentiality is the assurance that information is not disclosed to unauthorized subjects.
- Some security mechanisms that provide confidentiality are encryption, logical and physical access control, transmission protocols, database views, and controlled traffic flow.
- There are three main access control models: discretionary, mandatory, and nondiscretionary.
- Discretionary access control (DAC) enables data owners to dictate what subjects have access to the files and resources they own.
- Mandatory access control (MAC) uses a security label system. Users have clearances and resources have security labels that contain data classifications. MAC compares these two attributes to determine access control capabilities.
- Nondiscretionary access control uses a role-based method to determine access rights and permissions.
- Lattice-based access provides an upper and lower bound of access control rights.
- Role-based access control is based on the user's role and responsibilities within the company.
- There are three main types of restricted interface measurements: menus and shells, database views, and physically constrained interfaces.
- Access control lists are bound to objects and indicate what subjects can use them.
- A capability table is bound to a subject and lists what objects it can access.

- There are three main ways of administrating access control: centralized, decentralized, and a hybrid of both.

- Centralized administration examples are RADIUS, TACACS+, and Diameter.

- A decentralized administration example is a peer-to-peer working group.

- There are three main categories of access control: administrative, technical, and physical.

- Examples of administrative controls are security policy, personnel controls, supervisory structure, security awareness training, and testing.

- Examples of physical controls are network segregation, perimeter security, computer controls, work area separation, data backups, and cable.

- Examples of technical controls are system access, architecture of a network, network access, encryption and protocols, and auditing.

- Access control mechanisms provide one or more of the following functionalities: preventive, detective, corrective, deterrent, recovery, or compensating.

- For a subject to be able to access a resource, it must be identified, authenticated, authorized, and should be held accountable for its actions.

- Authentication can be accomplished by biometrics, a password, passphrase, cognitive password, one-time password, or token.

- A Type I error in biometrics means the system rejected an authorized individual and a Type II error means an imposter was authenticated.

- A memory card cannot process information, but a smart card can.

- Access controls should default to no access.

- Least-privilege and need-to-know principles limit users' rights to only what is needed to perform tasks of their job.

- Single sign-on only requires a user to be authenticated to the network one time.

- Single sign-on can be accomplished through scripting, Kerberos, SESAME, and thin clients.

- In Kerberos, a user receives a ticket from the KDC to be able to authenticate to a service.

- Thin clients or dumb terminals must receive their operating systems from another source.

- Types of access control attacks include denial of service, spoofing, dictionary, brute force, and wardialing.

- Accountability is usually performed through audits.

- Audits can track user activities, application events, and system events.

- Keystroke monitoring is a type of auditing that tracks each keystroke made by a user.

- Audit logs should be protected and reviewed.
- Object reuse can unintentionally disclose information.
- Just removing pointers to files is not always enough protection for proper object reuse.
- Information can be obtained via electrical signals in airwaves. The ways to combat this type of intrusion are Tempest, white noise, and control zones.
- User authentication is accomplished by what someone knows, is, or has.
- One-time passwords token device generators can use synchronous or asynchronous methods.
- Strong authentication requires two of the three user authentication attributes (what someone knows, is, or has).
- Kerberos does not protect computers or servers; it authenticates principals and provides a secure communication channel to be established.
- Kerberos addresses privacy and integrity but not availability.
- The following are weaknesses of Kerberos: KDC is a single point of failure, it is susceptible to password guessing, session keys can be vulnerable, KDC needs to always be available, secret keys are on workstations temporarily, and there must be management of secret keys.
- Users must be authorized explicitly or implicitly.
- Access control monitoring happens through intrusion detection systems (IDSs).
- IDSs can be statistical (monitors behavior), signature-based (watches for known attacks).
- Degaussing is a safeguard against disclosure of confidential information because it returns media back to its original state.

Questions

Please remember that these questions are formatted and asked in a certain way for a reason. You must remember that the CISSP exam is asking questions at a conceptual level. Questions may not always have the perfect answer, and the candidate is advised against always looking for the perfect answer. The candidate should look for the best answer in the list.

1. Which of the following statements correctly describes biometric methods?

   A. They are the least expensive and provide the most protection.

   B. They are the most expensive and provide the least protection.

   C. They are the least expensive and provide the least protection

   D. They are the most expensive and provide the most protection.

2. What is derived from a passphrase?

   A. Personal password

   B. Virtual password

   C. User ID

   D. Valid password

3. Which of the following statements correctly describes passwords?

   A. They are the least expensive and most secure.

   B. They are the most expensive and least secure.

   C. They are the least expensive and least secure.

   D. They are the most expensive and most secure.

4. What is the reason for enforcing the separation of duties?

   A. No one person can complete all the steps of a critical activity.

   B. It induces an atmosphere for collusion.

   C. It increases dependence on individuals.

   D. It makes critical tasks easier to accomplish.

5. Which of the following is not a logical access control?

   A. Encryption

   B. Network architecture

   C. ID badge

   D. Access control matrix

6. An access control model should be applied in a _____ manner.

   A. Detective

   B. Recovery

   C. Corrective

   D. Preventive

7. Which access control policy is enforced when an environment uses groups?

   A. Rule-based

   B. Role-based

   C. Identity-based

   D. Mandatory

8. How is a challenge/response protocol utilized with token device implementations?

   A. This protocol is not used; cryptography is used.

   B. An authentication service generates a challenge, and the smart token generates a response based on the challenge.

   C. The token challenges the user for a username and password.

   D. The token challenges the user's password against a database of stored credentials.

9. Which access control method is user-directed?

   A. Nondiscretionary

   B. Mandatory

   C. Identity-based

   D. Discretionary

10. Which provides the best authentication?

   A. What a person knows

   B. What a person is

   C. What a person has

   D. What a person has and knows

11. Which item is not part of a Kerberos authentication implementation?

   A. Message authentication code

   B. Ticket granting service

   C. Authentication service

   D. Users, programs, and services

12. Which model implements access control matrices to control how subjects interact with objects?

   A. Mandatory

   B. Centralized

   C. Decentralized

   D. Discretionary

13. What does authentication mean?

   A. Registering a user

   B. Identifying a user

   C. Validating a user

   D. Authorizing a user

14. If a company has a high turnover rate, which access control structure is best?

   A. Role-based

   B. Decentralized

   C. Rule-based

   D. Discretionary

15. A password is mainly used for what function?

   A. Identity

   B. Registration

    C. Authentication

    D. Authorization

16. The process of mutual authentication involves _____.

    A. A user authenticating to a system and the system authenticating to the user

    B. A user authenticating to two systems at the same time

    C. A user authenticating to a server and then to a process

    D. A user authenticating, receiving a ticket, and then authenticating to a service

17. Reviewing audit logs is an example of which security function?

    A. Preventive

    B. Detective

    C. Deterrence

    D. Corrective

18. In discretionary access control security, who has delegation authority to grant access to data?

    A. User

    B. Security office

    C. Security policy

    D. Owner

19. Which could be considered a single point of failure within a single sign-on implementation?

    A. Authentication server

    B. User's workstation

    C. Logon credentials

    D. RADIUS

20. What role does biometrics play in access control?

    A. Authorization

    B. Authenticity

    C. Authentication

    D. Accountability

21. What determines if an organization is going to operate under a discretionary, mandatory, or a nondiscretionary access control model?

    A. Administrator

    B. Security policy

    C. Culture

    D. Security levels

22. What type of attack attempts all possible solutions?

    A. Dictionary

    B. Brute force

    C. Man-in-the-middle

    D. Spoofing

23. Spoofing can be described as which of the following?

    A. Eavesdropping on a communication link

    B. Working through a list of words

    C. Session hijacking

    D. Pretending to be someone or something else

24. Which of the following is not an advantage of a centralized access control administration?

    A. Flexibility

    B. Standardization

    C. Higher level of security

    D. No need for different interpretations of a necessary security level

25. Which of the following best describes what role-based access control offers companies in reducing administrative burdens?

    A. It allows entities closer to the resources to make decisions about who can and cannot access resources.

    B. It provides a centralized approached for access control, which frees up department managers.

    C. User membership in roles can be easily revoked and new ones established as job assignments dictate.

    D. It enforces an enterprise-wide security policy, standards, and guidelines.

Answers

1. **D.** Compared to the other available authentication mechanisms, biometric provides the highest level of protection and is the most expensive.

2. **B.** Most systems do not use the actual passphrase or password the user enters. Instead, they put this value through some time of encryption or hashing function to come up with another format of that value, referred to as a virtual password.

3. **C.** Passwords provide the least amount of protection, but are the cheapest because they do not require extra readers (as with smart and memory cards), they do not require devices (as do biometrics), and they do not require a lot

of overhead in processing (as in cryptography). Passwords are the most common type of authentication method used today.

4. **A.** Separation of duties is put into place to ensure that one entity cannot carry out a task that could be damaging or risky to the company. It requires two or more people to come together to do their individual tasks to accomplish the overall task. If a person wanted to commit fraud and this was in place, they would need to participate in collusion.

5. **C.** A logical control is the same thing as a technical control. All of the answers were logical in nature except an ID badge. Badges are used for physical security and are considered physical controls.

6. **D.** The best approach to security is to try and prevent bad things from taking place by putting the necessary controls and mechanisms in place. Detective controls should also be put in place, but a security model should not work from a purely detective approach.

7. **B.** Groups and roles work as containers for users. The administrator or security professional creates the roles or groups and assigns rights to them and then assigns users to the container. The users then inherit the permissions and rights from the containers (roles and groups), which is how implicit permissions are obtained.

8. **B.** An asynchronous token device is based on challenge/response mechanisms. The authentication service sends the user a challenge value and the user enters this into the token. The token encrypts or hashes this value and the user uses this as her one-time password.

9. **D.** The DAC model allows users, or data owners, the discretion of allowing other users access to their resources. DAC is implemented by ACLs, which the user can configure.

10. **D.** This is considered a strong authentication approach because it is two-factor—it uses two out of the possible three authentication techniques (something a person knows, is, or has).

11. **A.** Message Authentication Code (MAC) is a cryptographic function and is not a key component of Kerberos. Kerberos is made up of a KDC, a realm of principals (users, services, applications, devices), an authentication service, tickets, and a ticket granting service.

12. **D.** DAC is implemented and enforced through the use of access control lists (ACLs), which are held in a matrix. MAC is implemented and enforced through the use of security labels.

13. **C.** Authentication means to validate the identity of a user. In most systems the user must submit some type of public information (username, account number) and a second credential is needed to prove that this identity is really bound to this person. The second piece of the credential set is private and should not be shared.

14. **A.** It is easier on the administrator if she only has to create one role, assign all of the necessary rights and permissions to that role, and plug a user into that role when needed. Otherwise she would need to assign and extract permissions and rights as each individual came and left the company.

15. **C.** As stated in a previous question, passwords are the most common authentication mechanism used today. They are used to validate a user's identity.

16. **A.** Mutual authentication means that it is happening in both directions. Instead of just the user having to authenticate to server, the server also has to authenticate to the user.

17. **B.** Reviewing audit logs takes place after the fact, after some type of incident happens. It is detective in nature because the security professional is trying to figure out what exactly happened, how to correct it, and possibly who is responsible.

18. **D.** This question may seem a little confusing if you were stuck between user and owner. Only the data owner can decide who can access the resources she owns. She may be a user and she may not. A user is not necessarily the owner of the resource. Only the actual owner of the resource can dictate what subjects can actually access the resource.

19. **A.** In a single sign-on technology all users are authenticating to one source. If that source goes down, authentication requests cannot be processed.

20. **C.** Biometrics is a technology that validates an individual's identity by reading a physical attribute.

21. **B.** The security policy will set the tone for the whole security program. It will dictate the level of risk the management and company is willing to accept. This will in turn dictate the type of controls and mechanisms that are to be put into place to ensure that this level of risk is not exceeded.

22. **B.** A brute force attack tries a combination of characters in an attempt to discover the correct sequence that represents the captured password or whatever the goal of the task is. It is an exhaustive attack, meaning the attacker will try over and over again until she is successful.

23. **D.** Spoofing is the process of pretending to be another person or process with the goal of obtaining unauthorized access. Spoofing is usually done by using a bogus IP address, but it could be using someone else's authentication credentials.

24. **A.** A centralized approach does not provide as much flexibility as a decentralized access control administration because one entity is making all the decisions instead of several entities that are closer to the resources. A centralized approach is more structured in nature, which means that there is less flexibility.

25. **C.** An administrator does not need to revoke and reassign permissions to individual users as they change jobs. Instead, the administrator assigns permissions and rights to a role, and users are plugged into those roles.

Security Models and Architecture

In this chapter, you will learn about the following topics:

- Computer architecture and the items that fall within it
- Trusted computing base and security mechanisms
- Components within an operating system
- Various security models
- Security criteria and ratings
- Certification and accreditation processes

Computer and information security covers many areas within an enterprise. Each area has security vulnerabilities and, hopefully, some corresponding countermeasures that raise the security level and provide better protection. Not understanding the different areas and security levels of network devices, operating systems, hardware, protocols, and applications can cause security vulnerabilities that can affect the environment as a whole.

Two fundamental concepts in computer and information security are the security model, which outlines how security is to be implemented—in other words, providing a "blueprint"—and the architecture of a computer system, which fulfills this blueprint.

A security policy outlines how data is accessed, what level of security is required, and what actions should be taken when these requirements are not met. The policy outlines the expectations of a computer system or device. A *security model* is a statement that outlines the requirements necessary to properly support and implement a certain security policy. If a security policy dictates that all users must be identified, authenticated, and authorized before accessing network resources, the security model might lay out an access control matrix that should be constructed so that it fulfills the requirements of the security policy. If a security policy states that no one from a lower security level should be able to view or modify information at a higher security level, the supporting security model will outline the necessary logic and rules that need to be implemented to ensure that under no circumstances can a lower-level subject access a higher-level object in an unauthorized manner. A security model provides a deeper explanation of how a computer operating system should be developed to properly support a specific security policy.

NOTE Individual systems and devices can have their own security policies. We are not talking about organizational security policies that contain management's directives. The systems' security policies and models they use should enforce the higher-level organizational security policy that is in place.

Security Models and Architecture

Computer security can be a slippery term because it means different things to different people. There are many aspects of a system that can be secured, and security can happen at various levels and to varying degrees. We have stated in previous chapters that information security is made up of the following main attributes:

- **Availability**   Prevention of loss of access to resources and data
- **Integrity**   Prevention of unauthorized modification of data
- **Confidentiality**   Prevention of unauthorized disclosure of data

From here these main attributes branch off into more granular security attributes such as authenticity, accountability, non-repudiation, and dependability. How does a company know which of these it needs, to what degree they are needed, and if the operating systems and applications they use actually provide these features and protection? These questions get much more complex as one looks deeper into the questions and systems themselves. Companies are not just concerned about e-mail messages being encrypted as they pass through the Internet. They are also concerned about the confidential data stored in their databases, the security of their Web farms that are connected directly to the Internet, the integrity of data entry values going into applications that process business-oriented information, the internal users sharing trade secrets, the external attackers bringing down servers and affecting productivity, viruses spreading, the internal consistency of data warehouses, and much more. These issues not only affect productivity and profitability, but also raise legal and liability issues with securing data. Companies, and the management that runs them, can be held accountable if many of the previously mentioned issues go wrong. So it is, or at least it should be, very important for companies to know what security they need and how to be properly assured that the protection is actually being provided by the products they purchase.

Many of these security issues must be thought through before and during the design and architectural phase for a product. Security is best if it is designed and built into the foundation of operating systems and applications and not added on as an afterthought. Once security is integrated as an important part of the design, it has to be engineered, implemented, tested, audited, evaluated, certified, and accredited. The security that a product provides has to be rated on the availability, integrity, and confidentiality it claims. Consumers then use these ratings to determine if specific products provide the level of security they require. This is a long road, with many entities involved with different responsibilities. This chapter takes you from the steps necessary before actually developing an operating system to how these systems are evaluated and rated by governments and other agencies, and what these ratings actually mean.

However, before we dive into these concepts, it is important to understand how the basic elements of a computer system work. These elements are the pieces that make up any computer's architecture.

Computer Architecture

Put the processor over there by the plant, the memory by the window, and the secondary storage upstairs.

Computer architecture encompasses all the parts of a computer system necessary for it to function, including the operating system, memory chips, circuits, hard drive, security components, buses, and networking components. The interrelationships and internal working of all of these parts can be quite complex, and making them work together in a secure fashion is comprised of complicated methods and mechanisms. Thank goodness for the smart people who figured this stuff out! Now it is up to us to learn how they did it and why.

The more you understand how these different pieces work and process data, the more you will understand how vulnerabilities actually occur and how countermeasures work to impede and hinder vulnerabilities from being introduced, found, and exploited.

Central Processing Unit

Hey, when is it my turn to use the CPU? Answer: When the control unit says it's your turn.

The *central processing unit (CPU)* is a microprocessor that contains a control unit, an *arithmetic logic unit (ALU)*, and registers, which are holding places for data and instructions. The *control unit* manages and synchronizes the system while different applications' code and operating system instructions are being executed. It determines what application instructions get processed and in what priority and time slice. It controls when instructions are executed and this execution enables applications to process data. The control unit does not actually process the data; it is like the traffic cop telling traffic when to stop and start again, as shown in Figure 5-1.

The chips within the CPU cover only a couple of square inches, but contain over a million transistors. All operations within the CPU are performed by electrical signals at different voltages in different combinations, and each transistor holds this voltage, which represents 0s and 1s to the computer. The CPU contains registers that point to memory locations that contain the next instructions to be executed and enable the CPU to keep status information of the data that needs to be processed. The ALU performs mathematical functions and logical operations on data. The ALU can be thought of as the brain of the CPU and the CPU as the brain of the computer.

Software holds its instructions and data in memory. When action needs to take place on the data, the instructions and data are passed to the CPU portion of the system, as shown in Figure 5-2. The CPU components handle the flow of instructions from the operating system and applications. The data that needs to be processed is passed into the instruction registers. When the control unit indicates that the CPU can process them, they are passed to the CPU for actual processing, number crunching, and data manipulation. The results are sent back to the computer's memory so the application can use this processed data to continue its tasks.

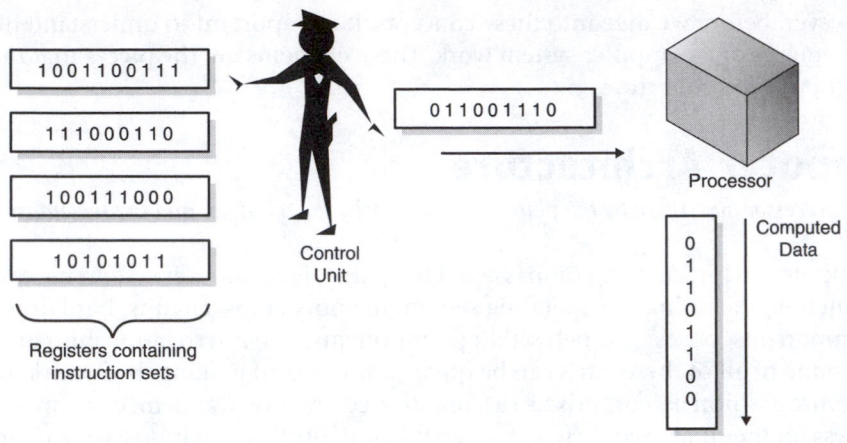

Figure 5-1 The control unit works as a traffic cop, indicating when instructions are sent to the processor.

Instructions and data are held in registers until needed by the CPU. The software instructions are first ported into the CPU because these instructions indicate what actually needs to happen to the data. The registers are not permanent storage areas, but a temporary memory area to hold instructions that are to be interpreted by the CPU and used for data processing.

The data being processed is entered into the CPU in blocks at a time. If the software instructions do not properly set the boundaries for how much data can come in as a block (for example, 64 bits at a time), extra data can slip in and be executed. This is how *buffer overflows* work. If a buffer overflow takes place, it is due to the operating system or

Figure 5-2 Instructions and data are passed to the CPU for processing.

application software instructions that are processing the data, not the computer system itself. If extra data slips in, it can be executed in a privileged mode and cause disruption and lead to unauthorized access or different degrees of damage. This can result in the computer system freezing, rebooting, or allowing data corruption. Buffer overflows can be corrected by well-written programs that verify how much data is being accepted and sent to the CPU at any given point in time.

A CPU's time and processing power has to be shared between many tasks. Software and system interrupts are used to make sure that all data is processed in a timely manner and priorities are used to ensure that critical tasks are performed before less important tasks.

Memory

The operating system instructions, applications, and data are held in memory, but so are the basic input/output system (BIOS), device controller instructions, and firmware. They do not all reside in the same memory location or even the same type of memory. The different types of memory, what they are used for, and how each is accessed can get a bit confusing because the CPU deals with several different types for different reasons.

The following paragraphs quickly outline the different types of memory within a computer system.

Random access memory (RAM) is a type of temporary storage facility where data can be held and altered. It is used for read/write activities by the operating system and applications. It is described as *volatile* because if the computer's power supply is terminated, then all information within this type of memory is lost. There are different types of RAM, but the most well-known types are dynamic and static RAM. *Static RAM* lives up to its name, because when it stores data, it stays there without the need of being continually refreshed. *Dynamic RAM*, on the other hand, requires that the data held within it be periodically refreshed because the data can dissipate and decay.

Read-only memory (ROM) is a *nonvolatile* storage facility, meaning that when a computer's power is turned off, the data is still held within the memory chips. For the most part, when data is inserted into ROM memory chips, it cannot be altered. The software that is stored within ROM is called *firmware*.

Erasable and programmable read-only memory (EPROM) can be modified, deleted, or upgraded. EPROM holds data that can be electrically erased or written to.

References

How RAM Works: **www.howstuffworks.com/ram.htm**

Unix/Linux Internals Course and Links: **www.softpanorama.org/Internals**

Cache Memory

I am going to need this later, so I will just stick it into cache for now.

Cache memory is a type of memory that is used for high-speed writing and reading activities. It holds instructions and data from primary storage and is accessed when application instructions and data are being executed. When the system assumes that it will need to access specific information many times throughout its processing activities, it will store it in cache memory so that it is easily and quickly accessible. Data being retrieved from cache can be accessed much more quickly than if it was stored in real memory; thus, it affects the overall speed of the computer system. Therefore, any information needed by the CPU very quickly, and very often, is often stored in cache memory.

An analogy is how the brain stores information that is used often. If one of Marge's primary functions at her job is ordering parts and telling vendors the company's address, this information is held within a portion of her brain that is easily and quickly accessible for Marge when she needs it. This information is held in a type of cache. If Marge was asked to recall her third grade teacher's name, this information would not necessarily be held in cache memory, but in a more long-term storage facility within her noggin. The long-term storage within her brain is comparable to a system's hard drive. It takes more time to track down and return information from a hard drive than specialized cache memory.

Memory Mapping

Okay, here is your memory, here is my memory, and here is Bob's memory. No one use each other's memory!

Because there are different types of memory holding different types of data, a computer system does not want to let every user, process, and application access all types of memory anytime they want to. Access to memory needs to be controlled to ensure that data does not get corrupted. This type of control takes place through memory mapping and addressing.

The CPU is one of the most trusted components within a system, and therefore it can access memory directly. It uses physical addresses instead of pointers to memory segments. The CPU has physical wires connecting it to the memory chips within the computer. Because there are physical wires connecting the two types of components, physical addresses are used to represent the intersection between the wires and the transistors on a memory chip. Software does not use physical addresses; instead, it uses virtual or logical memory. Accessing memory indirectly provides an access control layer between the software and the memory, which is done for protection and efficiency. Figure 5-3 illustrates how the CPU can access memory directly using physical addresses and how software must use memory indirectly through a memory mapper.

Let's look at an analogy. You would like to talk to Mr. Marshall about possibly buying some acreage in Iowa. You don't know Mr. Marshall personally, and you do not want to give out your physical address and have him show up at your doorstep. Instead, you would like to use a more abstract and controlled way of communicating, so you give Mr. Marshall your phone number so you can talk about the land and you can make a determination if you want to meet Mr. Marshall in person. The same type of thing happens in computers. When a computer runs software, it does not want to expose itself unnecessarily to software written by good and bad programmers. Computers enable software to use memory indirectly using index tables and pointers, instead of giving them the right to access the memory directly. Only the system itself can access memory directly and programs can access the memory indirectly, but it is the same memory storage. This is one way the computer system protects itself.

When a program attempts to access memory, its access rights are verified and then instructions and commands are carried out in a way to ensure that badly written code does not affect other programs or the system itself. Applications, and their processes, can only

Figure 5-3 The CPU and applications access memory differently.

access the memory allocated to them, as shown in Figure 5-4. This type of memory architecture provides protection and efficiency.

If programs accessed data held in memory directly, each program would have to wait until the prior program is done before it could access and process data. Mapped memory enables different programs to access the data and perform their own separate functions on it in a more economical and resourceful manner.

Secondary storage is considered nonvolatile storage media, which can be the computer's hard drive, floppy disks, or CD-ROM.

When RAM and secondary storage are combined, the result is *virtual storage*. The system uses hard drive space to extend RAM memory space capability. The hard drive space that is used to extend the RAM memory capabilities is incremented in pages. When a system fills up its volatile memory space, it will write data from memory onto the hard drive. When a program or user requests access to this data, it is brought from the hard drive back into memory. This process is called *paging*. Accessing data that is kept in pages on the hard drive takes more time than accessing data kept in memory because actual disk access has to take place; however, the payoff is that it seems as

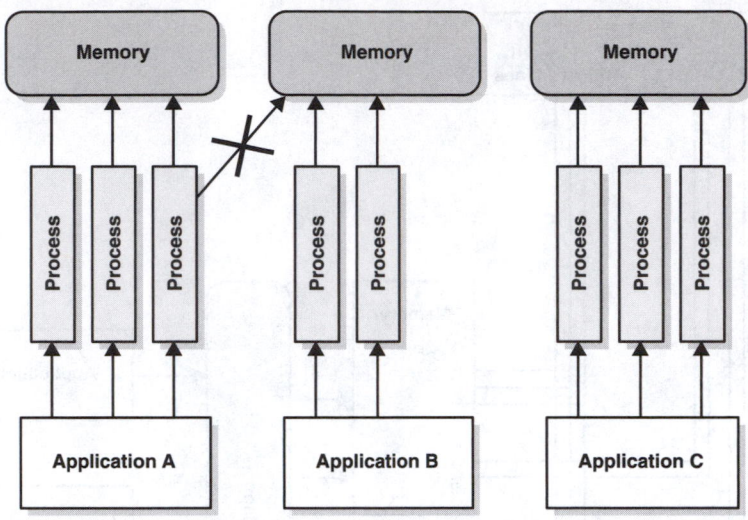

Figure 5-4   Applications, and the processes they use, only access their own memory segments.

though the system can hold an incredible amount of information in memory, as shown in Figure 5-5.

The different types of memory we looked at are summed up here:

- **Primary storage**   Main memory directly accessed by the CPU and indirectly accessed by applications, considered volatile memory

- **Secondary storage**   Nonvolatile storage (floppy disk, CD-ROM disk, hard drive, and so on)

- **Virtual storage**   RAM and secondary storage used together

- **RAM**   Random access memory, where instructions and data are placed when being executed

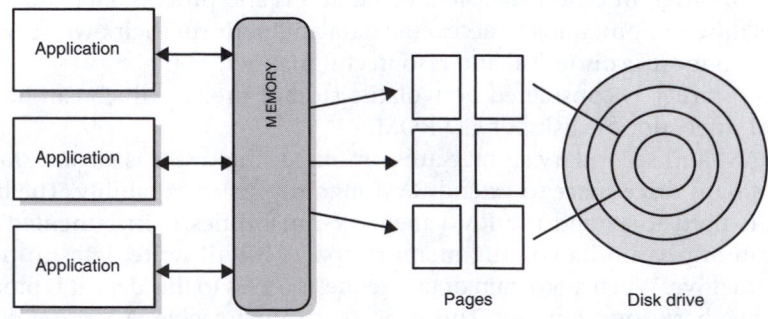

Figure 5-5   Systems send data from memory to the hard drive in units of pages to enable memory to reach gigabyte sizes.

CPU Modes and Protection Rings

If I am corrupted, very bad things can happen. Response: Then you need to go into ring 0.

If an operating system is going to be stable, it must be able to protect itself from its users and their applications. This requires the capability to distinguish between operations performed on behalf of the operating system itself and operations performed on behalf of the users or applications. This can be complex because the operating system software can be accessing memory segments, sending instructions to the CPU for processing, and accessing secondary storage devices. Each user application (e-mail client, antivirus, Web browser, word processor, personal firewall, and so on) can be attempting the same types of activities at the same time. The operating system must keep track of all of these events and ensure that none of them violates the security policy.

The operating system has several protection mechanisms to ensure that processes do not negatively affect each other or the critical components of the system itself. One has already been mentioned: memory segments. Another security mechanism that the system uses is *protection rings*. These rings provide strict boundaries and definitions for what the processes that work within each ring can access and what operations they can successfully execute. The processes that operate within the inner rings have more privileges than the processes operating in the outer rings. This is because the inner rings only permit the most trusted components and processes to operate within them. Although operating systems can vary in the number of protection rings, processes that execute within the inner rings are usually referred to as existing in a *privileged*, or supervisor, mode. The processes working in the outer rings are said to execute in a *user mode*.

 NOTE The actual ring architecture that is being used by a system is dictated by the processor and the operating system. The hardware chip (processor) is constructed to work with a certain number of rings, and the operating system must be developed to also work in this ring structure. This is one reason why one operating system platform may work with an Intel chip, but not an Alpha chip. They have different architectures and ways to interpret instruction sets.

Operating system components operate in a ring that gives them the most access to memory locations, peripheral devices, system drivers, and sensitive configuration parameters. Because this ring provides much more dangerous access to critical resources, it is the most protected. Applications usually operate in ring 3, which limits the type of memory, peripheral device, and driver access activity, and is controlled through the operating system functions or system calls. The different rings are illustrated in Figure 5-6. The type of commands and instructions that are sent to the CPU from applications in the outer rings are more restrictive in nature. If an application tries to send instructions to the CPU that fall outside of its permission level, the CPU treats this violation as an exception and may show a general protection fault, panic, or exception error and attempt to shut down the offending application.

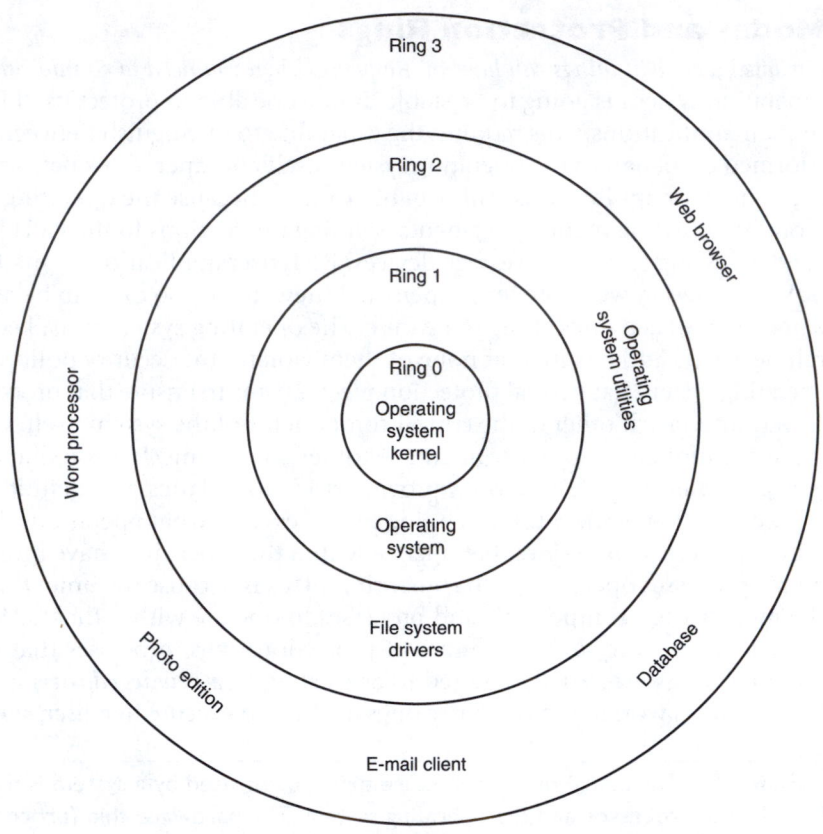

Figure 5-6　More trusted processes operate within lower-numbered rings.

Protection rings support the availability, integrity, and confidentiality requirements of multitasking operating systems. Many systems use four protection rings:

- **Ring 0**　Operating system kernel
- **Ring 1**　Remaining parts of the operating system
- **Ring 2**　I/O drivers and utilities
- **Ring 3**　Applications and programs

These protection rings provide an intermediate layer between subjects and objects, and are used for access control when a subject tries to access an object. The ring determines the access level to sensitive system resources. The lower the number, the greater the amount of privilege that is given to the process that runs within that ring. Each subject and object is logically assigned a number (0 through 3) depending upon the level of trust the operating system assigns it. A subject in ring 3 cannot directly access an object in ring 1, but subjects in ring 1 can directly access an object in ring 3. Entities can only access objects within their own ring and outer rings, as shown in Figure 5-7. When an application needs access to components in rings that it is not allowed to directly access, it makes a request of the operating system to perform the necessary tasks. This is handled through system calls, where the operating system executes instructions not allowed in user mode. The request is passed off to an operating system service, which works at a higher privilege level and can carry out the necessary task.

When the operating system executes instructions for processes in rings 0 and 1, it operates in system mode or privileged mode. When the operating system executes instructions for applications and processes in ring 3, it operates in user mode. User mode provides a much more restrictive environment for the application to work in, which in turn protects the system from misbehaving programs.

Process Activity

Computers can run different applications and programs at the same time. They have to share resources and play nice with each other to ensure a stable and safe computing environment that maintains its integrity. Some memory, data files, and variables are actually shared between different applications. It is critical that more than one process does not attempt to read and write to these items at the same time. The operating system is the master program that prevents this type of action from taking place and ensures that programs do not corrupt each other's data held in memory. The operating system works with the CPU to provide time slicing and interrupts to ensure that processes are provided with adequate access to the CPU. This also ensures that critical system functions are not negatively affected by rogue applications.

Figure 5-7
Processes in inner rings can directly access processes in outer modes but not vice versa.

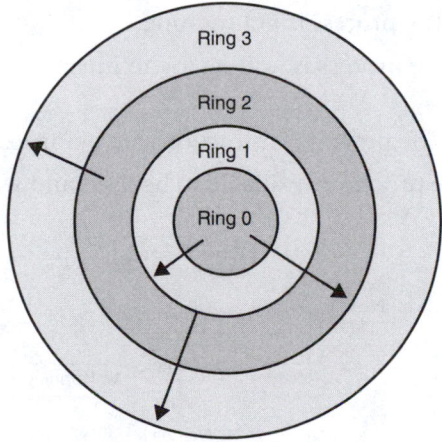

Ring 0—Operating system kernel
Ring 1—Remaining parts of the operating system
Ring 2—I/O drivers and utilities
Ring 3—Applications and programs

Process versus Thread

A *process* is a program in execution that works in its own address space and can only communicate with other processes in a controlled manner. A *thread* represents a piece of code that is executed within a process, as shown here. A process can have one or more threads running at one time, depending upon the tasks it needs to carry out.

PROCESS

Threads of Code

Operating States

I am in a problem state. Is that bad? Answer: Nope, the CPU is just carrying out your request.

The operating system itself can be in one of two modes at any given point in time. The operating system can operate in privileged (supervisor state) or user mode (problem state) depending on what process made a request to execute instructions, but there are also different *operating states* in which the different processes can work within. The following outlines the four possible states a process can operate in:

- **Stopped** The process is not running.

- **Waiting** The process is waiting for an interrupt to be able to be interact with the CPU.

- **Running** The process's instructions are being executed by the CPU.

- **Ready** The process is available to be used and waiting for an instruction.

These protection rings, operational modes, and operating states work together to ensure a secure and predictable operating environment. They enable the system to protect itself and work to protect the availability, integrity, and confidentiality of the system, the information that is being processed, and the applications installed.

When an application runs on a computer, it thinks it is the only program running. It does not necessarily know that it is sharing resources with several other types of programs, the operating system, and other processes. This simplifies the issues that programmers need to be concerned about when writing an application. Because the application thinks it is the only one executing, it needs to be presented with an environment that reflects this type of reality. This can be done through virtual machines and virtual memory. The operating system creates a virtual environment (virtual machine) for the application to work in and allots it a segment of virtual memory, as shown in Figure 5-8. Another application could have its own virtual machine and virtual address segment, and the two would not know that each other even existed. This way the two applications do not interact with each other's data in memory or step on each other's toes while being executed by the CPU. It is a very orchestrated, controlled, and timed event-oriented atmosphere. An analogy is two people with two different offices. George has his office, computer, file cabinet, closet, and window. Marge has an office with the same materials. If George and Marge had to use the same computer, file cabinet, and closet, they could easily move each other's items around, accidentally delete each other's files, or wear each other's coat home. However, because they each have their own office and components, these events will not take place.

The granularity of this type of separation and protection becomes very detailed within a computer system. A process is used to request resource access and carry out data manipulation activities, and is the mechanism used to enable applications and the operating system to communicate. A process is like a phone call. If an application wants to print a form, it calls (or communicates via a process) the operating system, which calls the printer driver, and the printer driver calls the printer. These processes can only communicate in a way that has been previously approved by the operating system and outlined in the security model. The application cannot make a direct call to the printer driver because it does not operate in a privileged ring; thus, it does not have the necessary type of authority. The security architecture of the operating system dictates this type of communication authority.

Figure 5-8   Virtual machines only access their allotted memory segments.

One application can make several calls at one time. It can ask to print a form, accept a fax, display data to the monitor, and ask for an address from the address book. These different calls use different threads and are an example of *multithreading*. A system that can process more than one request at a time is capable of multithreading. If the CPU can process more than one process, or task, at one time, it is considered a *multitasking* system. If a computer has more than one CPU (also called processor), it can use them in parallel to execute instructions; this activity is called *multiprocessing*. *Multiprogramming* is the interleaved execution of two or more programs by a CPU. The system can run more than one application, but not necessarily perform multithreading or multitasking. Older operating systems used multiprogramming instead of multitasking, but this was not an effective practice because a process could commit a resource and no other processes could use that resource until it was properly released by the first process. This approach to operating system operations gives the processes too much control. Newer operating systems gave this control to the operating system instead of the individual processes.

An operating system has to protect its integrity and ensure that users do not accidentally or intentionally access someone else's data. Multitasking systems interleave the execution of processes belonging to different users, which adds complexity to protecting itself and users' data. The operating system uses logical separation between users' data, which takes place in file and memory management.

Input/Output Device Management

When a user chooses to print a document, or a word processor displays a file previously stored, or if a user saves files to a zip drive, these requests are going from the application the user is working in, through the operating system, and to the device requested. The operating system uses a device driver to communicate to a device controller, which is an electrical component with its own software used to provide a communication path that enables the device and operating system to exchange data. The operating system sends commands to the device controller's registers and the controller then writes data to the peripheral device or extracts data to be processed by the CPU, depending on the given commands. This communication happens through specific communication channels dedicated just for these types of functions. Once the device controller retrieves the requested information, it is stored in main memory for the operating system, application, and CPU to perform their necessary functions.

It is important that the devices and computer resources are properly accessed and released. Different operating systems handle accessing devices and resources differently. For example, Windows NT is considered a more stable and safer data processing environment than Windows 9x because applications cannot make direct requests to hardware devices. Windows NT and Windows 2000 have a much more controlled method of accessing devices than Windows 9x. This helps to protect the system from badly written code that does not properly request and release resources. This level of protection helps to ensure the resources' integrity and availability.

Proper input/output management is a core component of operating systems. When a request for a resource (memory allocation, printer, secondary storage devices, disk space) is made, certain data structures are built and processes are dedicated for this action to take place. Once the action takes place (a document is printed, a file is saved, or data is retrieved from the drive), the program, or operating system, needs to tear down these built structures and release the resources back into a pool to be available for other programs and processes. If this does not happen properly, a *deadlock* situation can occur or a computer may not have enough resources to process other requests (result of a denial-of-service attack). A deadlock situation can happen with peripheral devices, memory, database, or file access. If Sean accesses a database and his process never properly releases the necessary resources back to the system, when Debbie attempts to perform the same action, a deadlock situation can occur and Sean, Debbie, and the system that contains the database can be negatively affected. This has a direct correlation to a main security principle: availability. The database software should apply a software lock when Sean accesses information in the database, which will ensure that no one else, including Debbie, can access and modify the same data until Sean is done.

Another common deadlock situation is when process A commits resource 1 and needs to use resource 2 to properly complete its task. But process B has committed resource 2 and needs resource 1 to finish its job. So both processes are "hung" because they do not have the resources they need to finish the function they are to carry out. This activity does not take place as much as it used to because better programming is usually performed. Also the environment (operating system, database software, application) now has the intelligence to detect this activity and will either release committed resources or control how resources are going to be properly shared between processes.

Operating systems have different methods of dealing with resource requests and releases and solving deadlock situations. In some systems, if a requested process is unavailable for a certain period of time, some operating systems will kill that process. This action releases the process from the application that had committed it, releases the supporting system resources necessary to commit this resource, and restarts the process so it is "clean" and available to be used by other applications. Other operating systems might require a program to request all of the resources it needs *before* it actually starts executing instructions or requires a program to release its currently committed resources before being able to acquire more. Input/output management is a core responsibility of the operating system, along with memory management, CPU tasks, and file system management.

Tying It Together

Each of the topics discussed in earlier sections have complete books written on them because of their complexity and importance to the computing world. Each topic also relates in some way to a part of security. An operating system is a complex beast that performs many complicated tasks in order to provide a useful and secure work environment for a user. It must recognize each process and program that is running, make access decisions, support system calls, protect memory segments, validate requested commands, properly process instructions, and ensure that none of these activities introduce vulnerabilities that can violate the security policy of the system. It does this by enforcing protection rings, mapping memory, implementing virtual machines, working in different states, and assigning trust levels to each and every process. These are integral parts of the security model for the operating system.

System Architecture

Designing a system from the ground up is a complicated task and has many intricate and abstract goals that have to be achieved through mathematics, logic, design, programming code, and implementation. There are fundamental design decisions that need to be made when constructing a system. Security is only one of the goals of a system, but it is the goal security professionals are most concerned about.

Availability, integrity, and confidentiality can be enforced at different places within an enterprise. For example, a company may store customer credit card information in a database that many users can access. This information, obviously, requires protection to ensure that it is not accessed or modified in an unauthorized manner. We start with general questions and gradually drill down into the details. Where should this protection be placed? Should there be access controls that screen users when they log in and assign them their rights at that point dictating what data they can and cannot access? Should the data files holding the credit card information be protected at the file system level? Should protection be provided by restricting users' operations and activities? Or should there be a combination of all of these? The first and most general question is "Where should the protection take place: at the user's end, where the data is stored, or by restricting user activities within the environment?" This is illustrated in Figure 5-9.

Once these general questions have been answered, the placement of the mechanisms needs to be addressed. Security mechanisms can be placed at the hardware, kernel, operating system, services, or program layers. At which layer(s) should security mechanisms be implemented? If protection is implemented at the hardware layer, the protection mechanisms will be more simplistic and provide broad and general protection. As we ascend up the layers, more complexity is added, and functionality becomes more specific and granular. The top layer holds the most complexity because it is directed toward providing the user with a vast amount of functionality and options. Functionality and complexity of security increases as it approaches the layers that are closer to the user. The increased complexity lowers the assurance levels of the security mechanisms. This is shown in Figure 5-10.

The more complex a security mechanism becomes, the less assurance it provides. This is because the complexity of the mechanism demands more technical understanding from the individuals who install, test, maintain, and use it. The more complex the tools, the more chances there are for errors, and therefore increased chances for security compromises. The more complex the security mechanism, the harder it is to fully test it under

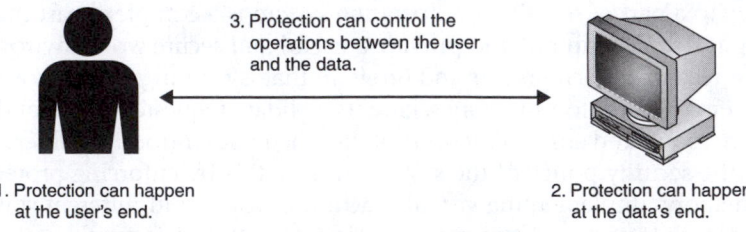

3. Protection can control the
operations between the user
and the data.

1. Protection can happen
at the user's end.

2. Protection can happen
at the data's end.

Figure 5-9   Security can take place at three main areas.

Figure 5-10
As functionality
increases,
complexity
increases and
the assurance of
security decreases.

As functionality increases and security increases in complexity.

Functionality decreases and security decreases in complexity.

Applications

Services

Operating System

Kernel

Hardware Layer

Assurance of security mechanisms decrease as complexity increases.

all possible conditions. On the other hand, simplistic mechanisms cannot provide the desired richness of functionality and options, although they are easier to install, maintain, use, and test. So the tradeoffs between functionality and assurance need to be fully understood to make the right security mechanism choices when designing a system.

Once the designers have an idea of what the security mechanisms should focus on (users, operations, or data), what layer(s) the mechanisms should be placed at (hardware, kernel, operating system, services, or program), and the complexity of each mechanism, the mechanisms need to be built and integrated in a way to have a proper relationship with other parts of the system.

The first step is to decide what system mechanisms need to be trusted and specify how these entities can interact in a secure manner. Although it might seem that you would want to trust all the components within the system, this would cause too much overhead, complexity, and performance bottlenecks. For a mechanism to be trusted, it means that it protects itself and the data it is processing, it performs in predictable and secure manners, and it does not adversely affect other trusted or untrusted mechanisms. In return, these trusted components have access to more privileged services, have direct access to memory, usually have higher priority when requesting CPU processing time, and have more control over system resources. So the trusted subjects and objects need to be identified and distinguished from the untrusted ones and placed into defined subsets.

Defined Subset of Subjects and Objects

I totally trust you. You can do whatever you want. Response: I want to leave.

As stated previously, not all components need to be trusted and therefore do not fall within the ***trusted computing base (TCB)***. The TCB is defined as the total combination of protection mechanisms within a computer system. The TCB includes hardware, software, and firmware. These are part of the TCB because the system is sure that these components will enforce the security policy and not violate it.

The components that do fall under the TCB need to be identified and their accepted capabilities defined. For example, a system that has a lower trust level rating may permit all authenticated users to access and modify all files on the computer. This subset of subjects and objects is large and the relationship between them is loose and relaxed. A system with a much higher trust level rating may permit only two subjects to access all files on a computer system, and only one of those subjects can actually modify all the files. This subset is much smaller and the rules being enforced are more stringent and detailed.

Again, it depends upon what type of system the developers are aiming at building. If developers want to develop a system that achieves an Orange Book security rating of D (very low), then what makes up the TCB or not is not much of an issue because the system will not be expected to provide a very high level of security. However, if the developers want to develop a system with an Orange Book rating of B2 or B1 (much higher than rating D), they will need to specify what makes up the TCB. They need to enforce strict rules that dictate how subjects and objects interact. The developers also need to ensure that these items are identified, authenticated, and audited because these are the components that will be scrutinized, tested, and evaluated before a rating of B2 or B1 can be given. (The Orange Book and its ratings are addressed in the section "The Orange Book" later in the chapter.)

Trusted Computing Base

The term "trusted computing base" originated from the Orange Book and does not address the level of security a system provides, but the level of trust, albeit from a security sense. This is done because no computer system can be totally secure. The types of attacks and vulnerabilities change and evolve over time, and with enough time and resources, most attacks can become successful. However, if a system meets a certain criteria, it is looked upon as providing a certain level of trust, again, from a security perspective.

The TCB does not just address operating systems, because a computer system is not made up of only an operating system. The TCB addresses hardware, software components, and firmware. Each can affect the computer's environment in a negative and positive manner, and each has a responsibility to support and enforce the security policy of that particular system. Some components and mechanisms have direct responsibilities in supporting the security policy, such as firmware that will not let a user boot a computer from a floppy disk or the memory manager that will not let users overwrite other users' data. Then there are components that do not enforce the security policy, but must behave properly and not violate the trust of a system. The types of violations a component could cause against the system's security policy could be an application that attempts to make a direct call to a piece of hardware instead of using the proper calls through the operating system, a program that attempts to read data outside of its approved memory space, or a piece of software that does not properly release resources after use.

Not every part of a system needs to be trusted. Part of evaluating the trust level of a system is to identify the architecture, security services, and assurance mechanisms that make up the TCB. It must be shown how the TCB is protected from accidental or intentional tampering and compromising activity. For systems to achieve a higher trust level, they must meet well-defined TCB requirements, and the details of their operational states, developing stages, testing procedures, and documentation will be reviewed with more granularity than systems that are attempting to achieve a lower trust rating.

By using specific security criteria, trust can be built into a system, evaluated, and certified. This approach can provide a measurement system for customers to use when comparing one system to another. It also gives vendors guidelines on what expectations are put upon their systems and provides a common security rating so when one group talks about a C2 rating, everyone else is on the same page and understands what these terms mean.

The Orange Book defines a trusted system as hardware and software that utilize measures to protect the integrity of unclassified or classified data for a range of users without violating access rights and the security policy. It looks at all protection mechanisms within a system to enforce the security policy and provide an environment that will behave in a manner expected of it. This means that each layer of the system must trust the underlying layer to perform the expected functions, provide the expected functionality, and operate in an expected manner under many different situations. When the operating system makes calls to hardware, it is anticipating data to be returned in a specific data format and to behave in a consistent and predictable manner. Applications that run on top of the operating system expect to be able to make certain system calls and receive the required data in return and to be able to operate in a reliable and dependable environment. Users expect the hardware, operating system, and applications to perform in particular fashions and provide a certain level of functionality. For all of these actions to behave in such predicable manners, the requirements of a system must be addressed in the planning stages of development, not afterwards.

Security Perimeter

Now, whom do we trust? Answer: Anyone inside the security perimeter.

As stated previously, not every component and resource falls within the TCB, so some resources fall outside of this imaginary boundary referred to as the *security perimeter*. A perimeter is a boundary that divides the trusted from the untrusted. For the system to stay in a secure and trusted state when a component within the TCB needs to communicate with a component outside of the TCB, precise communication standards must be developed to ensure that this type of communication cannot bring on unexpected security compromises. This type of communication is handled and controlled through interfaces.

For example, a resource that is within the boundary of the TCB, or security perimeter, must not pass confidential information to resources outside the TCB. The resource within the TCB must also be careful about the commands and information it accepts from less-trusted resources. These limitations and restrictions are built into the interfaces that permit this type of communication to take place and are the mechanisms that enforce the security perimeter, as shown in Figure 5-11. Communication between trusted components and untrusted components needs to be controlled to ensure that confidential information does not flow in an unintended way.

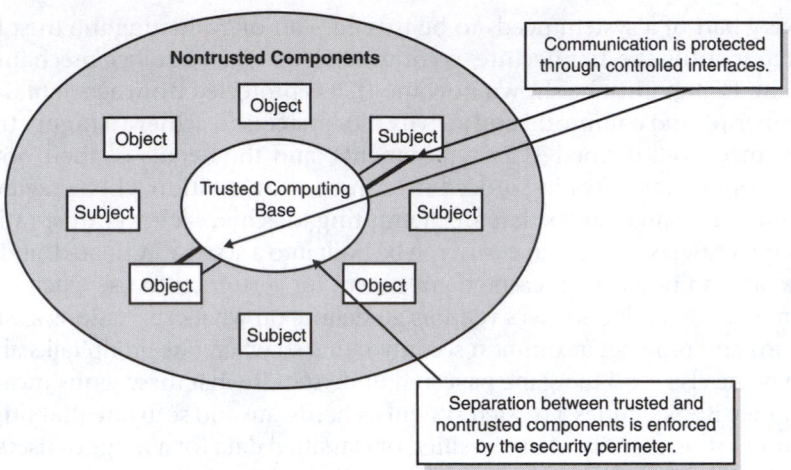

Figure 5-11   Interfaces control the communication between trusted and untrusted processes.

 NOTE   The TCB and security perimeter are not physical entities, but conceptual constructs used by the operating system to delineate between trusted and untrusted components. They are illustrated here to show the relationship of the TCB, security perimeter, and different components.

Reference Monitor and Security Kernel

Up to now, our computer system architecture developers have accomplished many things in developing their system. They have defined where the security mechanisms will be located (hardware, kernel, operating system, services, or program), they have defined the objects that are within the TCB and how those components will interact with each other. The security perimeter that separates the trusted components and the untrusted components has been constructed. They have developed proper interfaces for these entities to communicate securely. Now they need to develop and implement a mechanism that ensures that the subjects that access objects have been given the necessary permissions to do so. This means the developers need to develop and implement a reference monitor and security kernel.

The *reference monitor* is an abstract machine, which mediates all access subjects have to objects to ensure that the subjects have the necessary access rights and to protect the objects from unauthorized access and destructive modification. For a system to achieve a higher level of trust, it must enforce subjects (programs, users, or processes) to be fully authorized prior to accessing an object (file, program, or resource). It must be made certain that the subject has been granted access privileges prior to letting the subject use the requested object. The reference monitor is an access control concept, not an actual physical component, and that is why it is normally referred to as the "reference monitor concept."

The *security kernel* is made up of mechanisms that fall within the TCB and implements and enforces the reference monitor concept. The security kernel is made up of hardware, firmware, and software components that mediate all access and functions between subjects and objects. The security kernel is the core of the TCB and is the most commonly used approach to building trusted computing systems. There are four main requirements of the security kernel:

- It must provide isolation for the processes carrying out the reference monitor concept and they must be tamperproof.

- The reference monitor must be invoked for every access attempt and must be impossible to circumvent. Thus, the reference monitor must be implemented in a complete and foolproof way.

- The reference monitor must be verifiable as being correct. This means that all decisions made by the reference monitor should be written to an audit log, and verified as being correct.

- It must be small enough to be able to be tested and verified in a complete and comprehensive manner.

These are the requirements of the reference monitor; therefore, they are the requirements of the components that provide and enforce the reference monitor concept—the security kernel.

These issues work in the abstract, but are implemented in the physical world of hardware devices and software code. The assurance that the components are enforcing the abstract idea of the reference monitor is proved through testing and functionality.

 NOTE The reference monitor is a concept where an abstract machine mediates all accesses to objects by subjects. The security kernel is the hardware, firmware, and software of a TCB that implements this concept. The TCB is the totality of protection mechanisms within a computer system that work together to enforce a security policy. The TCB contains the security kernel and all other security protection mechanisms.

Figure 5-12 provides a quick analogy to show you the relationship between the components that make up the kernel, the kernel itself, and the reference monitor concept. Individuals make up a society. The individuals can represent the components and the society can represent the kernel. For a society to have a certain standard of living, it needs to react in specific ways, which is why we have laws. The laws represent the reference monitor, which enforces proper activity. Each individual is expected to stay within the bounds of the laws and act in specific ways so society as a whole is not adversely affected and the standard of living is not threatened. The components within a system must stay within the bounds of the reference monitor's laws so that they will not adversely affect other components and threaten the security of the system.

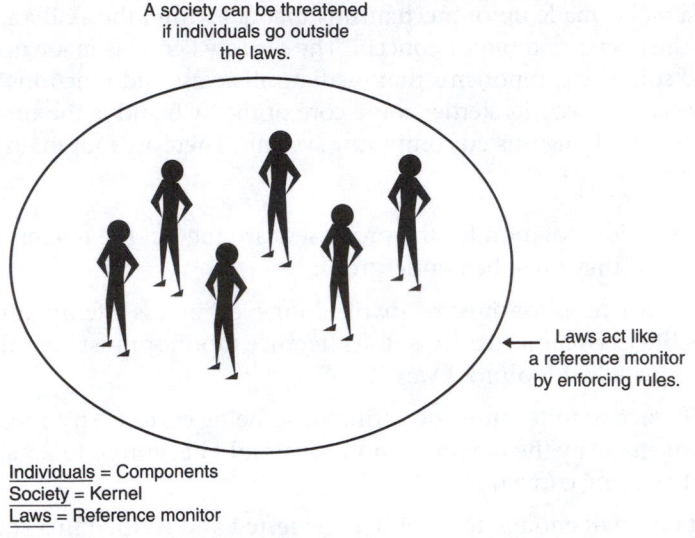

A society can be threatened
if individuals go outside
the laws.

Laws act like
a reference monitor
by enforcing rules.

Individuals = Components
Society = Kernel
Laws = Reference monitor

Figure 5-12   Components, like people, need to say inside the bounds of the rules.

References

Rationale Behind the Evaluation Classes: **www.kernel.org/pub/linux/libs/ security/Orange-Linux/refs/Orange/OrangeI-II-6.html**

The Reference Monitor Concept: **citeseer.nj.nec.com/299300.html**

Implementing Complete Mediation: **www.cs.cornell.edu/html/cs513-sp99/ NL05.html**

Domains

Okay, here are all the marbles you can play with. We will call that your domain of resources.

A *domain* is defined as a set of objects that a subject is able to access. This domain can be all the resources a user can access, all the files available to a program, the memory segments available to a process, or the services and processes available to an application. A subject needs to be able to access and use objects (resources) to perform tasks, and the domain defines which objects are available to the subject and which objects are untouchable and therefore unusable by the subject.

These domains have to be identified, separated, and strictly enforced. An operating system may work in a privileged mode and a user mode. The reason to even use these two different modes is to define two different domains. The privileged mode has a much larger domain to work with (or more resources to access); thus, it can provide much more functionality. When an operating system works in privileged mode, it can physically access memory modules, transfer data from an unprotected domain to a protected domain, and directly access and communicate with hardware devices. An application that functions in user mode cannot access memory directly and has a more limited amount of resources available to it. Only a certain segment of memory is available to this application and it must be accessed in an indirect and controlled fashion. The application can copy files only within its own domain and cannot access hardware directly.

A program that resides in a privileged domain needs to be able to execute its instructions and process its data with the assurance that programs in a different domain cannot negatively affect its environment. This is referred to as an *execution domain*. Because programs in a privileged domain have access to sensitive resources, the environment needs to be protected from rogue program code or unexpected activities resulting from programs in other domains. Some systems may only have distinct user and privilege areas, whereas other systems may have complex architectures that contain up to ten security domains.

A security domain has a direct correlation to the protection ring that a subject or object is assigned to. The lower the protection ring number, the higher the privilege and the larger the security domain. This concept is depicted in Figure 5-13.

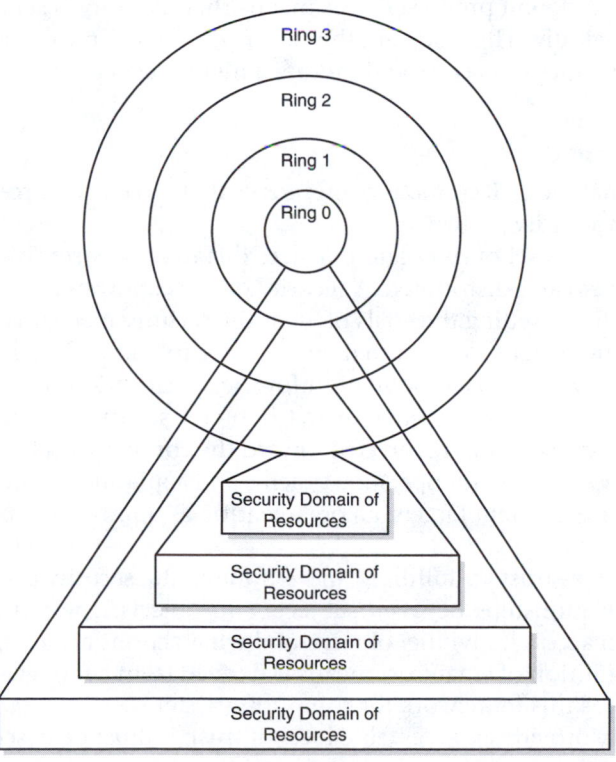

Figure 5-13   The higher the level of trust, the larger the number of available resources.

Resource Isolation

You, go into this room and play all by yourself.

To properly enforce access control, auditing, and determining what subjects and objects reside in specific domains, each resource has to be clearly separated from one another. This modularity requirement enables each subject and object to be identified uniquely, permissions and rights to be assigned independently, accountability to be enforceable, and intricate activities to be tracked precisely. The subjects, objects, and protection controls need to be clearly isolated from each other, and the isolation methods and enforcement are a requirement of the architecture of a system and its security model.

Processes are also resources that need to be isolated and this is usually done through distinct address allocation. Virtual memory (explained in the section "Process Activity" earlier in the chapter) techniques are used to make sure different processes have their own memory addresses to use and do not access each other's memory. If a process has a particular memory range allocated to it, it does not know there is other memory in the system. The process works happily in the memory allocated and does not stomp on another process's data in another segment of memory.

Systems of a higher trust level may need to implement *hardware segmentation* of the memory used by different processes. This means that memory is separated physically instead of just logically. This adds another layer of protection to ensure that a lower-privileged process does not access and modify a higher-level process's memory space.

Security Policy

We have stated that the TCB contains components that directly enforce the security policy, but what is a security policy?

A *security policy* is a set of rules and practices dictating how sensitive information is managed, protected, and distributed. A security policy expresses exactly what the security level should be by setting the goals of what the security mechanisms are to accomplish. This is an important element that has a major role in defining the design of the system. The security policy is a foundation for the specifications of a system and provides the baseline for evaluating a system. In Chapter 3, security policies were examined in depth, but those policies were directed toward the company itself. The security policies being addressed here are for operating systems and applications. The different policies are similar but have different targets: an organization as opposed to an individual computer system.

A system provides trust by fulfilling and enforcing the security policy and typically deals with the relationships between subjects and objects. The policy must indicate what subjects can access individual objects, and what actions are acceptable and unacceptable. The definition of what trust means is derived from a framework and the security policy works as this framework for computing systems.

For a system to provide an acceptable level of trust, it must be based on an architecture that provides the capabilities to protect itself from untrusted processes, intentional or accidental compromises, and attacks at different layers of the system. A majority of the trust ratings require a defined subset of subjects and objects, explicit domains, and the isolation of resources so their access can be controlled and activities performed on them can be audited.

Let's regroup. We know that a system's trust is defined by a set of criteria. When a system is tested against this set of criteria, a rating is assigned to the system and this rating is used by customers, vendors, and the computing society as a whole. The criteria will determine if the security policy is being properly supported and enforced. The security policy lays out the rules and practices pertaining to how a system will manage, protect, and distribute sensitive information. The reference monitor is a concept that says all subjects must have proper authority to access objects and is implemented by the security kernel. The security kernel is made of all the resources that supervise system activity in accordance with the system's security policy and is part of the operating system that controls access to system resources. For this to work correctly the individual resources need to be isolated from each other and domains need to be defined to dictate what objects are available to what subjects.

Security policies that prevent information from flowing from a high security level to a lower security level are called *multilevel security policies*. These types of policies permit a subject to access an object only if the subject's security level is higher than or equal to the object's classification.

As we said, these are abstract ideas that will be manifested into physical hardware components, firmware, software code, and activities through designing, building, and implementing a system. These ideas are like abstract goals and dreams we would like to accomplish, which are accomplished by our physical hard work and items that we produce.

Least Privilege

Once resources and processes are isolated properly, *least privilege* needs to be enforced. This means that a process has no more privileges than necessary to be able to fulfill its functions. Only processes that *need* to carry out critical system functions should be allowed to, and other less-privileged processes should call upon the more privileged processes to carry out these types of activities when necessary. This type of indirect activity protects the system from poorly written or misbehaving code. Processes should possess a level of privilege only as long as they really need it. If a process needs to have its status elevated so it can interact directly with sensitive information, as soon as its tasks are complete, the process's status should be dropped to a lower privilege to ensure that another mechanism cannot use it to adversely affect the system. Only processes needing complete system privileges are located in the kernel; other less-privileged processes call upon them to process sensitive or delicate operations.

References

Access Control Policies and Mechanisms: **www.cs.cornell.edu/html/cs513-sp99/NL03.html**

Information Warfare Site: **www.iwar.org.uk/comsec/resources/standards/rainbow/NCSC-TG-028.htm**

Discretionary Protection: **www.kernel.org/pub/linux/libs/security/Orange-Linux/refs/Orange/OrangeI-II-2.html**

Layering, Data Hiding, and Abstraction

You can't see me, you don't know that I exist, so you can't talk to me. Response: Fine by me.

Systems that meet certain trust levels must supply mechanisms that force processes to work in layers, which means certain functionality takes place in different layers of a system. This requires a structured and hierarchical architecture that has the basic functionality taking place at lower layers and more complex, sensitive functions at the higher layers. *Layering* further separates processes and resources and adds modularity to the system. The layers can communicate, but only through detailed interfaces that uphold the security integrity of the system. In some instances, it is required that processes in different layers do not communicate; therefore, they are not supplied with interfaces to interact with each other. This process is called *data hiding* in that the data in one layer is hidden because the subjects in another layer do not even know that the data exists. If a subject in one layer has no interface to be able to communicate with data at another layer, this data is hidden from that subject.

Objects can be grouped into sets called classes. When a class of objects is assigned specific permissions and acceptable activities are defined, it is called *abstraction*. This makes management of different objects easier because classes can be dealt with instead of each and every individual object. When a class is defined, all the objects within that class are assigned an abstract data type, which is a precise definition of the format the object will accept data and the format it will present its processed data to other objects and subjects. This provides a predictable way of communicating and helps prevent authorized entities from modifying the data within an object in an inappropriate way. For example, when one object passes a registry value to another object, it is done in a predefined manner and the receiving object will not accept values outside of these predefined boundaries. If the receiving object is expecting a binary value, it will not accept a hexadecimal value in its place. This type of restriction is defined in the object's abstract data type.

Layering, data hiding, and abstraction are all methods to protect subjects, objects, and the data within the objects. These concepts are foundational pieces to a security model.

Security Models

An important concept in the design and analysis of secure systems is the security model, because it incorporates the security policy that should be enforced in the system. A model is a symbolic representation of a policy. It maps the desires of the policy makers into a set of rules that are to be followed by a computer system.

We have continually mentioned the security policy and its importance, but it is an abstract term that represents the objectives and goals a system must meet and accomplish to be deemed secure and acceptable. How do we get from an abstract security policy to an administrator being able to uncheck a box on the graphical user interface (GUI) to disallow David from accessing configuration files on his system? There are many complex steps in between that take place during the system's design and development.

A security model maps the abstract goals of the policy to information system terms by specifying explicit data structures and techniques necessary to enforce the security policy. A security model is usually represented in mathematics and analytical ideas, which are then mapped to system specifications, and then developed by programmers through

Analogy of the Relationship Between a Security Policy and a Security Model

If someone tells you to live a healthy and responsible life, this is a very broad, vague, and abstract notion. So when you ask this person how this is accomplished, they outline the things you should and should not do (do not harm others, do not lie, eat your vegetables, and brush your teeth). The security policy provides the abstract goals, and the security model provides the dos and don'ts necessary to fulfill these goals.

programming code. So we have a policy that encompasses security goals like "each subject must be authorized to access each object." The security model takes this requirement and provides the necessary mathematical formulas, relationships, and structure to be followed to accomplish this goal. From here, specifications are developed per operating system type (Unix, Windows, or Macintosh), and individual vendors can decide how they are going to implement mechanisms that meet these necessary specifications.

So in a very general and simplistic example, if a security policy states that subjects need to be authorized to access objects, the security model would provide the mathematical relationships and formulas explaining how x can access y only through outlined specific methods. Specifications are then developed to provide a bridge to what this means in a computing environment and how it maps to components and mechanisms that need to be coded and developed. The developers then write the program code to produce the mechanisms that provide a way for a system to use access control lists and give administrators some degree of control. This mechanism presents the network administrator with a GUI representation, like check boxes, to choose which subjects can access what objects, to be able to set this configuration within the operating system. This is a rudimentary example because security models can be very complex, but it is used to demonstrate the relationship between the security policy and the security model.

Some security models enforce rules to protect confidentiality, such as the Bell- LaPadula model. Other models enforce rules to protect integrity, such as the Biba model. Formal security models, such as Bell-LaPadula and Biba, are used to provide high assurance in security. Informal models, such as Clark-Wilson, are used more as a framework to describe how security policies should be expressed and executed.

A security policy outlines goals with no idea of how they would be accomplished. A model is a framework that gives the policy form and solves security problems for particular situations. Several security models have been developed to enforce security policies, and the following sections provide overviews of each model.

State Machine Models

No matter what state I am in, I am always trustworthy.

In *state machine models*, to verify the security of a system, the state is used, which means all current permissions and all current instances of subjects accessing objects must be captured. Maintaining the state of a system deals with each subject's association with objects. If the subjects can only access objects by means that are concurrent with the security policy, the system is secure. State machines have provided a basis for important security models. A state of a system is a snapshot of a system in one moment of time. There are many activities that can alter this state, which is referred to as a *state transition*. The developers of an operating system that will implement the state machine model need to look at all of the different state transitions that are possible and assess if a system starts up in a secure state, can any of these events put the system into an insecure state? If all of the activities that are allowed to happen in the system do not compromise the system and put it into an insecure state, then the system executes a secure state machine model.

So a system that has employed a state machine model will be in a secure state in each and every instance of its existence. It will boot up into a secure state, execute commands and transactions securely, allow subjects to access resources only in secure states, and shut down and fail in a secure state. Failing in a secure state is extremely important. It is imperative that if anything unsafe takes place that the system can "save itself" and not make itself vulnerable. When a user sees error messages, or a system reboots or freezes, these are all safety measures. The operating system has experienced something that is deemed illegal and it cannot take care of the situation itself, so to make sure it does not enter an insecure state it reacts in one of these fashions. So if an application or system freezes on you, know that it is the system just trying to protect itself and your data.

Bell-LaPadula Model

I don't want anyone to know my secrets. Response: We need Mr. Bell and Mr. LaPadula in here then.

In the 1970s, the U.S. military used time-sharing mainframe systems and was concerned about the security of these systems and leakage of classified information. The *Bell-LaPadula model* was developed to address these concerns. It was the first mathematical model of a multilevel security policy used to define the concept of a secure state machine and modes of access and outline rules of access. Its development was funded by the U.S. government to provide a framework for computer systems that would be used to store and process sensitive information. The model's main goal is to prevent secret information from being accessed in an unauthorized manner.

A system that employs the Bell-LaPadula model is called a multilevel security system because users with different clearances use the systems, and the systems process data with different classifications. The level at which information is classified determines the handling procedures that should be used. These access rights together form a *lattice*, which is an upper bound and lower bound of authorized access. A subject that has top secret clearance can access top-secret, secret, and unclassified data. Top secret is the upper bound and unclassified is the lower bound. Mandatory access control is based on a lattice of security labels.

The Bell-LaPadula model is a state machine model enforcing the confidentiality aspects of access control. A matrix and security levels are used to determine if subjects can access different objects. The subject's clearance is compared to the object's classification;

if the clearance is higher or equal to the object's classification, the subject can access the object without violating the security policy.

The model uses subjects, objects, access operations (read, write, and read/write), and security levels. Subjects and objects can reside at different security levels and have relationships and rules dictating the acceptable activities between them. If properly implemented and enforced, this model has been mathematically proven to prevent data from a higher security level from flowing to a lower security level. It is an *information flow security model* also, which means that information does not flow in an insecure manner.

The Bell-LaPadula model is a subject-to-object model. An example would be how you could take an element from a specific database and write it into another database. The Bell-LaPadula has a focus of ensuring that subjects are properly authenticated, by having the necessary security clearance and need-to-know, before accessing an object.

There are three main rules used and enforced in the Bell-LaPadula model: the simple security rule, the *-property rule, and the strong star property rule. The *simple security rule* states that a subject at a given security level cannot *read* data that resides at a higher security level. The **-property* rule states that a subject in a given security level cannot *write* information to a lower security level. The simple security rule is referred to as the "no read up" rule, and the *-property rule is referred to the as the "no write down" rule, as shown in Figure 5-14. The third rule, the *strong star property rule*, states that a subject that has read and write capabilities can only perform those functions at the same security level, nothing higher and nothing lower. The simple security and *-property rules, and the strong star property rule, indicate what states the system can go into.

The state of a system changes as different operations take place. The Bell-LaPadula model defines a secure state, meaning a secure computing environment and the allowed actions, which are security-preserving operations. This means that the model provides a secure state and only permits operations that will keep the system within a secure state and not let it enter into an insecure state. So if 100 people access 2,000 objects in a day using this one system, this system is put through a lot of work and several complex activities have to take place. However, at the end of the day, the system is just as secure as it

Figure 5-14   In the Bell-LaPadula model, each subject has a lattice of rights.

was in the beginning of the day. This is the definition of the Basic Security Theorem used in computer science.

 NOTE The definition of the Basic Security Theorem is that if a system initializes in a secure state and all state transitions are secure, then every subsequent state will be secure no matter what inputs occur.

An important thing to note is that the Bell-LaPadula model was developed to make sure secrets stay secret; thus, it provides and addresses confidentiality only. This model does not address integrity of the data the system maintains—only who can and cannot access the data.

So What Does This Mean and Why?

Subjects and objects are assigned labels. The subject's label is a clearance label (top secret, secret, confidential, and so on) and the object's label is a classification label (top secret, secret, confidential, and so on). When a subject attempts to access an object, the system compares the subject's clearance label and the object's classification label and looks at a matrix to see if this is a legal and secure activity. So let's say it is a perfectly fine activity, and the subject is given access to the object. Now if the subject's clearance label is top secret and the object's classification label is secret, the subject cannot write to this object, because of the *-property rule. This makes sure that subjects cannot accidentally or intentionally share confidential information by writing to an object at a lower security level. Let's say a busy and clumsy general in the army opens up a briefing letter that will go to all clerks at all bases all around the world. He attempts to write that the United States is attacking Cuba. The Bell-LaPadula model will come into action and not permit this general to write this information to this type of file because his clearance is higher than that of the memo.

Likewise, if a nosey clerk tried to read a memo that was available only to generals and above, the Bell-LaPadula model would stop this activity also. The clerk's clearance is lower than that of the object, the memo, and this violates the simple security rule of the model. It is all about keeping secrets secret.

The following lists some criticisms of the Bell-LaPadula model:

- It deals only with confidentiality and does not address integrity.
- It does not address management of access control, because there is no mechanism to modify access rights.
- The model does not prevent or address covert channels.
- The model does not address file sharing used in more modern systems.

Biba Model

The *Biba model* was developed after the Bell-LaPadula model. It uses a state machine model and is very similar to the Bell-LaPadula model. Biba addresses the integrity of data being threatened when subjects at lower integrity levels are able to write to objects at higher integrity levels and when subjects can read data at lower levels. If implemented and enforced properly, the Biba model prevents data from any *integrity* level from flowing to a higher integrity level. Biba has two main rules to provide this type of protection. The first rule, referred to as "no write up," states that a subject cannot write data to an object at a higher *integrity* level. The second rule, referred to as "no read down," states that a subject cannot read data from a lower integrity level. This second rule might sound a little goofy, but it is protecting the subject and data at a higher integrity level from being corrupted by data in a lower integrity level. An analogy would be if you were writing an article for the *New York Times* about the security trends over the last year, the amount of money businesses lost, and the cost/benefit ratio of implementing firewalls, intrusion detection systems, and vulnerability scanners. You do not want to get your data and numbers from any old Web site without knowing how those figures were calculated and the sources of the information. Your article (data at a higher integrity level) can be compromised if mixed with unfounded information from a bad source (data at a lower integrity level).

When first learning about the Bell-LaPadula and Biba models, they seem very similar, and the reasons for their differences may bring about some confusion. The Bell-LaPadula model was written for the U.S. government, and the government is very paranoid about the leakage of their secret information. In their model, a user cannot write to a lower level because that user might let out some secrets. Similarly, a user at a lower level cannot read anything at a higher level because that user might learn some secrets. However, not everyone is so worried about confidentiality and has such big, important secrets to protect. The commercial industry is more concerned about the integrity of its data. An accounting firm is more worried about keeping their numbers straight and making sure decimal points are not dropped or extra zeros are not added in a process carried out by an application. The accounting firm is more concerned about the integrity of this data and is usually under little threat of someone trying to steal these numbers, so they would employ the Biba model. Of course, the accounting firm does not look for the name Biba on the back of a product or make sure it is in the design of their application. It is something that was decided upon and implemented when the application was being developed. The security ratings are what consumers use to determine if a system is right for them. So even if the accountants are using a system using the Biba model, they would not know (and we're not going to tell them).

Bell-LaPadula versus Biba

The Bell-LaPadula model is used to provide confidentiality. The Biba model is used to provide integrity. The Bell-LaPadula and Biba models are informational flow models because they are most concerned about data flowing from one level to another. Bell-LaPadula uses security levels and Biba uses integrity levels.

> ## Confusion of the Different Rules
>
> It is important for CISSP test takers to know the rules of Biba and Bell-LaPadula. Their rules sound very similar, simple and *-rules—one writing one way and one reading another way. A tip to remember them is that if the word "simple" is used, the rule is talking about reading. If the rule uses * or "star", it is talking about writing. So now you just need to remember reading and writing in which direction for the different models.

Clark-Wilson Model

The *Clark-Wilson model* was developed after Biba and takes some different approaches to protecting the integrity of information by focusing on preventing authorized users from making unauthorized modification of data, or commit fraud and errors within commercial applications.

As stated earlier, military institutions are usually more concerned about confidentiality, and the commercial sector is usually more concerned with the integrity of the data they process. In the Clark-Wilson model, users cannot access and manipulate objects directly, but must access the object through a program. This provides another layer of protection between the subject and the object and further restricts the type of actions that can take place on that object, thus protecting the integrity of the object.

Let's say Emily is a user of an application that has been built using the Clark-Wilson model. She cannot access files directly, but must open and manipulate files through the program built upon the Clark-Wilson model. The programs have their own set of restrictions dictating what actions the users can and cannot perform on objects. This streamlines the way objects are protected and reduces the methods that could cause the data to be corrupted or changed in an undesirable manner.

NOTE Ensuring that subjects can only access objects through the use of an application is referred to as *access triple*. A subject has to go through an application to access an object: subject – application – object.

This model also enforces *separation of duties*, which divides an operation into different parts and requires different users or rules to perform each part. This ensures that a critical task cannot be carried out by one entity. Auditing is also required in this model to track the information coming in from the outside of the system.

So the Clark-Wilson model prevents authorized users from making modifications by requiring them to go through programs to modify objects. It also prevents authorized users from making improper modifications by enforcing separation of duties, and maintains an audit log for external transactions.

Goals of Integrity

There are three main goals of integrity:

- Prevent unauthorized users from making modifications
- Prevent authorized users from making improper modifications
- Maintain internal and external consistency

Clark-Wilson addresses each of these goals in its model. Biba only addresses the first goal.

Information Flow Model

Now, which way is the information flowing in this system? Answer: Not to you.

The Bell-LaPadula model is concerned about information that can flow from a high security level to a low security level. The Biba model is concerned about information that can flow from a high integrity level to a low integrity level. Both of these were built upon the *information flow model*. Information flow models can deal with any kind of information flow, not only the direction of the flow. This type of model looks at insecure informational flow that can happen at the same level and between objects along with the flow between different levels. When the information flow model is used, a system is secure if there is no illegal information flow permitted.

Basically, information can flow from one security level to another or from one object to another in the same security level until a restricted operation is attempted. In most systems, once a restricted operation is attempted, the system looks at an access control matrix to see if this action has been specifically permitted for this specific subject or object.

Noninterference Model

Stop touching me. Stop touching me. You are interfering with me!

Multilevel security properties can be expressed in other ways, one being *noninterference*. This concept is implemented to ensure that any actions that take place at a higher security level do not affect, or interfere, with actions that take place at a lower level. This type of model does not concern itself with the flow of data, but with what a subject knows about the state of the system. So if an entity at a higher security level performs an action, it cannot change the state for the entity at the lower level.

If a lower-level entity was aware of a certain activity that took place by an entity at a higher level and the state of system changed for this lower-level entity, the entity might be able to deduce too much information about the activities of the higher state, which in turn is a way of leaking information.

Users at a lower security level should not be aware of the commands executed by users at a higher level and should not be affected by those commands in any way.

Brewer and Nash Model

The *Brewer and Nash model*, also called the Chinese Wall model, was created to provide access controls that can change dynamically depending upon a user's previous actions. The main goal of the model is to protect against users accessing data that could be seen as conflicts of interest. For example, if a large marketing company provided marketing promotions and materials for several banks, one individual working on a project for Bank A should not be looking at information the marketing company has for Bank B. So this marketing company could implement a product that tracked the different marketing representatives' access activities and disallow certain access requests that would present a conflict of interest. In Figure 5-15, we see that when a representative accesses Bank A's information the system automatically makes Bank B's information off limits. If the representative accessed Bank B's data, Bank A's information would be off limits. These access controls change dynamically depending upon the user's activities and previous access requests.

Graham-Denning and Harrison-Ruzzo-Ullman Models

Remember that these are all models, thus they are not very specific in nature. Each individual vendor must decide upon how it is going to actually meet the rules outlined in the chosen model. Bell-LaPadula and Biba don't define how the security and integrity ratings are defined and modified, nor do they provide a way to delegate or transfer access rights. The *Graham-Denning model* addresses these issues and defines a set of basic rights in terms of commands that a specific subject can execute on an object. The *Harrison-Ruzzo-Ullman model* outlines how access rights can be changed and how subjects and objects should be created and deleted.

These newer models provide more granularity and direction for vendors on how to actually meet the goals outlined in the earlier models.

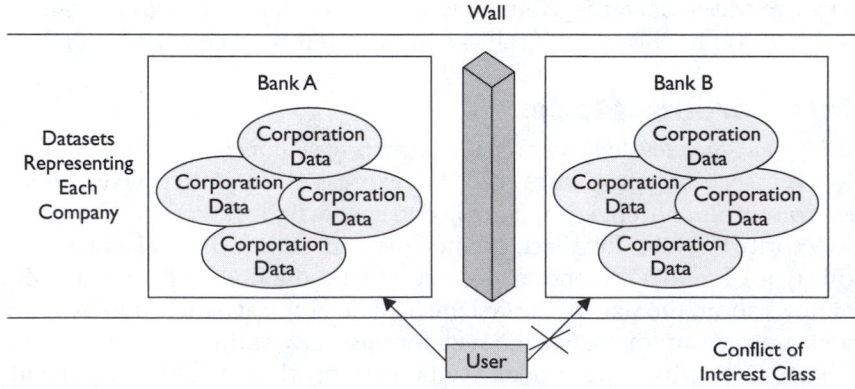

Figure 5-15   The Chinese Wall model provides dynamic access controls.

Security Models

- **Bell-LaPadula model**   A model that protects the confidentiality of the information within a system.

  - **Simple security rule**   A subject cannot read data at a higher security level (no read up).

  - ***-property rule**   A subject cannot write data to an object at a lower security level (no write down).

  - **Strong star property rule**   A subject that has read and write capabilities can only perform those functions at the same security level.

- **Biba model**   A model that protects the integrity of the information within a system.

  - **Simple integrity axiom**   A subject cannot read data at a lower integrity level (no read down).

  - ***-integrity axiom**   A subject cannot modify an object in a higher integrity level (no write up).

- **Clark-Wilson model**   An integrity model implemented to protect the integrity of data and to ensure that properly formatted transactions take place.

  - Subjects can only access objects through authorized programs (access triple).

  - Separation of duties is enforced.

  - Auditing is required.

- **Information flow model**   Information is restricted in its flow to only go to and from entities in a way that does not negate the security policy.

- **Noninterference model**   Commands and activities performed at one security level should not be seen or affect subjects or objects at a different security level.

- **Brewer and Nash model**   A model that allows for dynamically changing access controls that protect against conflicts of interest

- **Graham-Denning model**   A model that creates rights for subjects, which correlate to the operations that can be execute on objects.

- **Harrison-Ruzzo-Ullman model**   A model that allows for access rights to be changed and specifies how subjects and objects should be created and deleted.

References

Access Control Models: **www.cccure.org/Documents/HISM/087-089.html**

Models of OS Protection: **all.net/books/ip/Chap3-3.html**

Computer Security Models: **infoeng.ee.ic.ac.uk/~malikz/surprise2001/ spc99e/article1**

Database Security: **www.wi-inf.uni-essen.de/~ifs/summerschool**

Security Modes of Operation

A system can operate at different types of modes depending on the sensitivity of the data being processed, the clearance level of the users, and what those users are authorized to do. The mode of operation describes the security conditions under which the system actually functions. There are four modes of operations a system can function under and the following sections describe each one.

Dedicated Security Mode

A system is operating in a *dedicated security mode* if all users have the clearance and formal need-to-know to *all* data processed within the system. All users have been given formal access approval for *all* information on the system and have signed nondisclosure agreements pertaining to this information. The system can handle a single classification level of information.

Many military systems have been designed to handle only one level of security, which works in dedicated security mode. This requires everyone who uses the system to have the highest level of clearance required by any and all data on the system. If a system held top-secret data, only users with this clearance could use the system. Other military systems work with multiple security levels, which is done by compartmentalizing the data. These types of systems can support users with high and low clearances simultaneously.

System-High Security Mode

A system is operating in *system-high security mode* when all users have a security clearance or authorization to access the information but not necessarily a need-to-know for all the information processed on the system. So the difference between the dedicated security mode and the system-high security mode is that in the dedicated security mode, all users have a need-to-know pertaining to *all* data on the system; in system-high security mode, all users have a need-to-know pertaining to *some* of the data.

This mode also requires all users to have the highest level of clearance required by any and all data on the system. However, just because a user has the necessary security level to access an object, the user could be restricted because they do not have a need-to-know pertaining to that specific object.

Compartmented Security Mode

A system is operating in *compartmented security mode* when all users have the clearance to access all the information processed by the system, but might not have the need-to-know and formal access approval. In compartmented security mode, users are restricted from being able to access some information because they do not need to access it to perform the functions of their jobs and they have not been given formal approval to access this data. In this mode, users can access a segment, or compartment, of data only.

The objective is to ensure that the minimum possible number of people learn of information at each level. Compartments are categories of data with limited number of subjects cleared to access data at each level. *Compartmented mode workstations (CMWs)* enable users to process multiple compartments of data at the same time, if they have the necessary clearance.

Multilevel Security Mode

A system is operating in *multilevel security mode* when it permits two or more classification levels of information to be processed at the same time when all the users do not have the clearance or formal approval to access all the information being processed by the system.

The Bell-LaPadula model is an example of a multilevel security model because it handles multiple information classifications at a number of different security levels within one system.

References

Data Protection Measures: **www.tpub.com/ans/51.htm**

Personal Computer Security: **www.cs.nps.navy.mil/curricula/tracks/security/notes/chap02_17.html**

Physical Model of Operations: **chacs.nrl.navy.mil/publications/CHACS/1997/jifi_web/node24.html**

Defense Security Service, NISPOM Chapter 8: **www.dss.mil/isec/ch8nispom/toc.htm**

Trust and Assurance

I trust that you will act properly, thus I have a high level of assurance in you.

We discussed the TCB concept in the section "Trusted Computing Base" and explained that no system is really secure because with enough resources almost any system can be compromised in one way or another; however, systems can provide levels of trust. The trust level tells the customer how much he can expect out of this system, what level of security it will provide, and the *assurance* that the system will act in a correct and predictable manner in each and every computing situation.

The TCB is made up of all the protection mechanisms within a system (software, hardware, firmware). All of these mechanisms need to work in an orchestrated way to enforce all the requirements of a security policy. When evaluated, these mechanisms are tested, their designs are inspected, and the supporting documentation is reviewed and evaluated. How the system is developed, maintained, and even delivered to the customer are all under review when the trust for a system is being gauged. All of these different evaluation components are put through an evaluation process to assign the correct level of trust and assurance. Customers then use this assignment, or rating, to determine which system best fits their security needs.

Assurance and trust are similar in nature, but slightly different when we are looking at rating computer systems. A trusted system means that all protection mechanisms work together to process sensitive data for many types of uses and still keeps the same secure computing environment. Assurance looks at the same issues but with more depth and detail. Systems that provide higher levels of assurance means that their designs were thoroughly inspected, the development stages were reviewed, the technical specifications and test plans were evaluated, and the system was tested extensively. You can buy a car and you can trust it, but you have a much deeper sense of assurance of that trust if you know how it was built, what it was built with, who built it, what tests it was put through, and how it performed in many different situations.

In the Trusted Computer Security Evaluation Criteria, commonly known as the Orange Book, which we will address shortly, the lower security level ratings look at a system's performance and testing results to produce a security rating, but the higher security level ratings look more at the system design, specifications, development procedures, supporting documentation, and the testing results. The protection mechanisms in the higher security level systems may not necessarily be much different from those in the lower security level systems, but the way they were designed and built is under much more scrutiny. With this extra scrutiny comes higher levels of assurance of the trust that can be put into a system.

Systems Evaluation Methods

A *security evaluation* examines the security-relevant parts of a system, meaning the TCB, access control mechanisms, reference monitor, kernel, and protection mechanisms. The relationship and interaction between these components are also evaluated. There are different methods of evaluating and assigning assurance and trust levels to systems. The reason that there is more than one type of security evaluation process is that the methods and ideologies have evolved over time and because various parts of the world look at computer security differently and rate some aspects of security differently than others. Each method will be explained and then at the end of the section they will be compared to each other to show the differences and strengths, and look at where security evaluation methods are heading.

The Orange Book

The U.S. Department of Defense developed the *Trusted Computer System Evaluation Criteria (TCSEC)*, which is used to evaluate operating systems, applications, and different products. This evaluation criteria is published in a book with an orange cover, which is called appropriately the *Orange Book*. (We like to keep things simple in security!) Customers use the security rating that the criteria presents so they have a metric to use when comparing different systems. It also provides direction for manufactures so they know what specifications to build to, and provides a one-stop evaluation process so customers do not need to have individual components within the systems evaluated.

The Orange Book evaluates products to assess if they contain the security properties they claim and evaluate if the product is appropriate for a specific application or function.

The Orange Book looks at the functionality, effectiveness, and assurance of a system during its evaluation, and it uses classes that were devised to address typical patterns of security requirements.

TCSEC provides a graded classification of systems that is divided into hierarchical divisions of security levels:

A   Verified protection

B   Mandatory protection

C   Discretionary protection

D   Minimal security

The classification A represents the highest level of security and D represents the lowest level of security.

Each division can have one or more numbered classes and each has a corresponding set of requirements that must be met for a system to achieve that particular rating. The classes with higher numbers indicate a greater degree of trust and assurance. So B2 would offer more trust than B1, and C2 would offer more trust than C1.

The criteria includes four main topics: security policy, accountability, assurance, and documentation, but these actually break down into seven different areas:

- **Security policy**   The policy must be explicit and well defined and enforced by the mechanisms within the system.

- **Identification**   Individual subjects must be uniquely identified.

- **Labels**   Access control labels must be associated properly with objects.

- **Documentation**   This includes the test, design, specification documents, user guides, and manuals.

- **Accountability**   Audit data must be captured and protected to enforce accountability.

- **Life cycle assurance**   Software, hardware, and firmware must be able to be tested individually to ensure that each enforces the security policy in an effective manner throughout their lifetimes.

- **Continuous protection**   The security mechanisms and the system as a whole must perform predictably and acceptably in different situations continuously.

These categories are evaluated independently, but the rating that is assigned at the end does not specify these different objectives individually. The rating is a sum total of these items.

Each division and class incorporates the requirements of the ones below it. This means that C2 must meet its criteria requirements and all of C1 requirements, and B3 has its requirements to fulfill along with those of C1, C2, B1, and B2. Each division or class ups the ante on security requirements and is expected to fulfill the requirements of all the classes and divisions below it.

When a vendor submits a product for evaluation, the product is submitted to the National Computer Security Center (NCSC). The process of evaluation is called the Trusted Products Evaluation Program (TPEP). Successfully evaluated products are placed on the Evaluated Product List (EPL) with their corresponding rating. When consumers are interested in certain products and systems, they can check the EPLs to find out the security level that are assigned to these products.

Division D: Minimal Protection

There is only one class in this division. It is reserved for systems that have been evaluated but fail to meet the criteria and requirements of the higher divisions.

Division C: Discretionary Protection

The C rating category has two individual assurance ratings within it; these ratings are described below. The higher the number of the assurance rating, the more protection that is provided.

C1: Discretionary Security Protection

Discretionary access control is based on individuals and/or groups. It requires a separation of users and information, and identification and authentication of individual entities. Some type of access control is necessary so users can ensure that their data will not be accessed and corrupted by others. The system architecture must supply a protected execution domain so privileged system processes are not adversely affected by lower-privileged processes. There must be specific ways of validating the system's operational integrity. The documentation requirements include design documentation, which shows the way the system was built to include protection mechanisms, test documentation (test plan and results), a facility manual so companies know how to install and configure the system's correctly, and user manuals.

The environment that would require this rating would be where users are processing information at the same sensitivity level; thus, strict access control and auditing measures are not required. It would be a trusted environment with low security concerns.

C2: Controlled Access Protection

Users need to be identified individually to provide more precise access control and auditing functionality. Logical access control mechanisms are used to enforce authentication and the uniqueness of each individual's identification. Security-relevant events are audited and these records must be protected from unauthorized modification. The architecture must provide resource, or object, isolation so proper protection can be applied to the resource and that actions taken upon it can be properly audited. The *object reuse* concept must also be invoked, meaning that any medium holding data must not contain any remnants of information after it is released for another subject to use. If a subject uses a segment of memory, that memory space must not hold any information after the subject is done using it. The same is true for storage media, objects being populated, temporary files being created—all data must be efficiently erased once the subject is done with that medium.

This class requires a more granular method of providing access control. The system must enforce strict logon procedures and provide decision-making capabilities when subjects request access to objects. A C2 system cannot guarantee that it will not be compromised, but it supplies a level of protection that would make compromising attempts harder to accomplish.

The environment that would require systems with a C2 rating would be one that contains users that are trusted, but a certain level of accountability is required. C2, overall, is regarded to be the most reasonable class for commercial applications, but the level of protection is still relatively weak.

Division B: Mandatory Protection

Mandatory access control is enforced by the use of security labels. The architecture is based on the Bell-LaPadula security model and evidence of reference monitor enforcement must be available.

B1: Labeled Security

Each data object must contain a classification label and each subject must have a clearance label. When a subject attempts to access an object, the system must compare the subject and object's security labels to ensure the requested actions are acceptable. Data leaving the system must also contain an accurate security label. The security policy is based on an informal statement and the design specifications are reviewed and verified.

It is intended for environments that require systems to handle classified data.

 NOTE   Security labels are not required until security rating B; thus, C2 does not require security labels but B1 does.

B2: Structured Protection

The security policy is clearly defined and documented, and the system design and implementation are subjected to more thorough review and testing procedures. This class requires more stringent authentication mechanisms and well-defined interfaces among layers. Subjects and devices require labels, and the system must not allow covert channels. A trusted path for logon and authentication processes must be in place, which means there are no trapdoors. A trusted path means that the subject is communicating directly with the application or operating system. There is no way to circumvent or compromise this communication channel. There is a separation of operator and administration functions within the system to provide more trusted and protected operational functionality. Distinct address spaces must be provided to isolate processes, and a covert channel analysis is conducted. This class adds assurance by adding requirements to the design of the system.

The environment that would require B2 systems could process sensitive data that requires a higher degree of security. This environment would require systems that are relatively resistant to penetration and compromise.

(A trusted path means that the user can be sure that he is talking to a genuine copy of the operating system.)

B3: Security Domains

In this class, more granularity is provided in each protection mechanism, and the programming code that is not necessary to support the security policy is excluded. The design and implementation should not provide too much complexity because as the complexity of a system increases, the ability of the individuals who need to test, maintain, and configure it reduces; thus, the overall security can be threatened. The reference monitor components must be small enough to test properly and be tamperproof. The security administrator role is clearly defined, and the system must be able to recover from failures without its security level being compromised. When the system starts up and loads its operating system and components, it must be done in an initial secure state to ensure that any weakness of the system cannot be taken advantage of in this slice of time.

An environment that requires B3 systems is a highly secured environment that processes very sensitive information. It requires systems that are highly resistant to penetration.

Division A: Verified Protection

Formal methods are used to ensure all subjects and objects are controlled with the necessary discretionary and mandatory access controls. The design, development, implementation, and documentation are looked at in a formal and detailed way. The security mechanisms between B3 and A1 are not very different, but the way that the system was designed and developed is evaluated in a much more structured and stringent procedure.

A1: Verified Design

The architecture and protection features are not much different from systems that achieve a B3 rating, but the assurance of an A1 system is higher than a B3 system because the formality in the way the system was designed, the way the specifications were developed, and the level of detail in the verification techniques. Formal techniques are used to prove the equivalence between the TCB specifications and the security policy model. More stringent change configuration is put in place with the development of an A1 system, and the overall design can be verified. In many cases, even the way that the system is delivered to the customer is under scrutiny to ensure that there is no way of compromising the system before it reaches its destination.

An environment that would require A1 systems is the most secure of secured environments. This environment deals with top-secret information and cannot adequately trust anyone using the systems without strict authentication, restrictions, and auditing.

 NOTE TCSEC addresses confidentiality, but not integrity. Functionality of the security mechanisms and the assurance of those mechanisms are not evaluated separately, but combined and rated as a whole.

References

Trusted Computer System Evaluation Criteria: **www.boran.com/security/ tcsec.html**

Trusted Computer Systems: **williamstallings.com/Extras/Security-Notes/ lectures/trusted.html**

Rainbow Series

Why are there so many colors in the rainbow? Answer: Because there are so many security topics in the computing world that needed names.

The Orange Book mainly addresses government and military requirements and expectations from their computer systems. Many people within the security field have pointed out several deficiencies of the Orange Book, particularly when it is being applied to systems that are to be used in commercial areas instead of government organizations. The following summarizes a majority of the troubling issues security practitioners have expressed about the use of the Orange Book:

- The Orange Book looks specifically at the operating system and not other issues like networking, databases, and so on.

- The Orange Book focuses mainly on one attribute of security, confidentiality, and not at integrity, availability, and authenticity.

- The Orange Book works with government classifications and not the protection classifications that commercial industries use.

- The Orange Book has a relatively small number of ratings, which means many different aspects of security are not evaluated and rated independently.

The Orange Book places great emphasis on controlling which users can access a system and virtually ignores controlling what those users do with the information once they are authorized. Authorized users can, and usually do, cause more damage to data than outside attackers. Commercial organizations have expressed more concern about the integrity of their data while the military organizations stress that their top concern is confidentiality. Because of these different goals, the Orange Book is a better evaluation tool for government and military systems.

Because the Orange Book focuses on the operating system, many other areas of security were left out. The Orange Book provides a broad framework for building and evaluating trusted systems, but it leaves many questions about topics other than just an operating system unanswered. So more books were written to extend the coverage of the Orange Book into other areas of security. These books provide detailed information and interpretations of certain Orange Book requirements and describe the evaluation processes. These books are collectively called the *Rainbow Series* because each book has a different color cover.

For an explanation of each book and its usage, please refer to the following references.

References

Rainbow Series Library: **www.radium.ncsc.mil/tpep/library/rainbow**

Rainbow Series: **csrc.ncsl.nist.gov/secpubs/rainbow**

Rainbow Series and Related Documents: **www.fas.org/irp/nsa/rainbow.htm**

Red Book

The Orange Book addresses single-system security, but networks are a combination of systems and the network needs to be secure without having to fully trust each and every system connected to it. The *Trusted Network Interpretation (TNI)*, also called the *Red Book* because of the color of its cover, addresses security evaluation topics for networks and network components. It addresses isolated local area networks and wide area internetwork systems.

Like the Orange Book, the Red Book does not supply specific details about how to implement security mechanisms; instead, it provides a framework for securing different types of networks. A network has a security policy, architecture, and design, as does an operating system. Subjects accessing objects on the network need to be controlled, monitored, and audited. In a network, the subject could be a workstation and an object could be a network service on a server.

The Red Book rates confidentiality and integrity of data and operations that happen within a network and the network products. Data and labels need to be protected from unauthorized modification, and the integrity of information as it is transferred needs to be ensured. The source and destination mechanisms used for messages are evaluated and tested to ensure that modification is not allowed.

Encryption and protocols are components that provide a lot of the security within a network, and the Red Book measures their functionality, strength, and assurance.

The following is a brief overview of the security items addressed in the Red Book:

- Communication integrity:

  - **Authentication**   Protects against masquerading and playback attacks. Mechanisms include digital signatures, encryption, timestamp, and passwords.

  - **Message integrity**   Protects protocol header, routing information, and the packet payload from being modified. Mechanisms include message authentication and encryption.

  - **Nonrepudiation**   Ensures that a sender cannot deny sending a message. Mechanisms include encryption, digital signatures, and notary.

- Denial-of-service prevention:

  - **Continuity of operations**   Ensures that network is available even if attacked. Mechanisms include fault tolerant and redundant systems and the capability to reconfigure network parameters in case of an emergency.

  - **Network management**   Monitors network performance and identifies attacks and failures. Mechanisms include components that enable network administrators to monitor and restrict resource access.

- Compromise protection:
  - **Data confidentiality**   Protects data from being accessed in an unauthorized method during transmission. Mechanisms include access controls, encryption, and physical protection of cables.
  - **Traffic flow confidentiality**   Ensures that unauthorized entities are not aware of routing information or frequency of communication via traffic analysis. Mechanisms include padding messages, sending noise, or false messages.
  - **Selective routing**   Routes messages in a way to avoid specific threats. Mechanisms include network configuration and routing tables.

Assurance is derived from a theory of how things should work and then compared to how they actually perform. Assurance is also derived by testing configurations in many different scenarios, evaluating engineering practices, and validating and verifying security claims. The Red Book ratings available are the following:

- **None**
- **C1**   Minimum
- **C2**   Fair
- **B2**   Good

TCSEC was introduced in 1985 and retired in December 2000. It was the first methodical and logical set of standards developed to secure computer systems. It was greatly influential to several countries who based their evaluation standards on the TCSEC guidelines. TCSEC was finally replaced with the Common Criteria.

Information Technology Security Evaluation Criteria

The *Information Technology Security Evaluation Criteria (ITSEC)* was the first attempt at establishing a single standard for evaluating security attributes of computer systems by many European countries. ITSEC is only used in Europe. The United States looked to the Orange Book and Rainbow Series, and Europe employed the ITSEC to evaluate and rate computer systems. (Actually, today everyone is migrating to the Common Criteria, explained in the next section.)

There are two main attributes of a system when it is evaluated under ITSEC: functionality and assurance. When the functionality of a system is being evaluated, the services that are provided to the users (access control mechanisms, auditing, authentication, and so on) are examined and measured. System functionality can be very diverse in nature because systems are developed differently just to provide different functionality to users. Nonetheless, when functionality is evaluated, it is tested to see if the system delivers what it says it delivers. Assurance, on the other hand, is more abstract and harder to test. Assurance is the degree of confidence in a security component, and its effectiveness and capability to perform consistently. Assurance is generally tested by examining development practices, documentation, configuration management, and testing mechanisms.

It is possible for two systems that provide the same functionality to have very different assurance levels. This is because of the underlying mechanisms providing the functionality, and the way it was developed, engineered, and implemented. ITSEC actually separates these two attributes and rates them separately, whereas TCSEC clumps them together and assigns them one rating (D through A1).

When we look back at our example of two systems that provide the same functionality but have very different assurance levels, using the TCSEC approach will make this individual factor hard to distinguish. Under the ITSEC approach, the functionality is rated separately from the assurance. In the ITSEC criteria, classes F1 to F10 rate the functionality of the system, whereas E0 to E6 rate the assurance of a system.

So the fundamental difference between ITSEC and TCSEC is that TCSEC bundles functionality and assurance, whereas ITSEC evaluates these two attributes separately.

The following is a general mapping of the two evaluation schemes to show you their relationship to each other:

ITSEC		TCSEC
E0	=	D
F1 + E1	=	C1
F2 + E2	=	C2
F3 + E3	=	B1
F4 + E4	=	B2
F5 + E5	=	B3
F5 + E6	=	A1
F6	=	Systems the provide high integrity
F7	=	Systems that provide high availability
F8	=	Systems that provide data integrity during communication
F9	=	Systems that provide high confidentiality (like cryptographic devices)
F10	=	Networks with high demands on confidentiality and integrity

As you can see, a majority of the ITSEC ratings can be mapped to the Orange Book ratings, but then ITSEC took a step farther and added F6 through F10 for specific needs consumers might have that the Orange Book does not address.

ITSEC is a criteria for operating systems and other products and refers to them as the target of evaluation (TOE). So if you are reading literature discussing the ITSEC rating of a product and it states that the TOE has a rating of F1 and E5, you know that the TOE is the product that was evaluated and that it has a low functionality rating and a high assurance rating.

References

Criteria and Methods of Evaluations of Information Systems: **www.cordis.lu/infosec/src/crit.htm**

ITSEC: **www.iwar.org.uk/comsec/resources/standards/itsec.htm**

Common Criteria

"The TCSEC is too hard, the ITSEC is too soft, but the Common Criteria is just right," said the baby bear.

The Orange and Red Books provided evaluation schemes that were too rigid. ITSEC attempted to provide a more flexible approach by separating the functionality and assurance attributes and considering the evaluation of entire systems. However, this flexibility added complexity because evaluators could mix and match functionality and assurance ratings, which ended up in too many classifications to keep straight. Because we are a species that continues to try to get it right, the next attempt for an effective and usable evaluation criteria was the *Common Criteria*.

In 1990, the International Organization for Standardization (ISO) identified the need of international standard evaluation criteria to be used globally. The Common Criteria project started in 1993 when several organizations came together to combine and align existing and emerging evaluation criteria (TCSEC, ITSEC, Canadian Trusted Computer Product Evaluation Criteria [CTCPEC], and the Federal Criteria). It was developed through a collaboration among national security standards organizations within the United States, Canada, France, Germany, the United Kingdom, and the Netherlands.

The benefit of having a worldwide recognized and accepted criteria helps consumers by reducing the complexity of the ratings and eliminating the need to understand the definition and meaning of different ratings within various evaluation schemes. This also helps manufacturers because now they can build to one specific set of requirements if they want to sell their products internationally, instead of having to meet several different ratings with varying rules and requirements.

The Orange Book evaluated all systems by how they compared to the Bell-LaPadula model. The Common Criteria provides more flexibility by evaluating a product against a protection profile, which is structured to address specific security problems. So while the Orange Book said, "Everyone march this direction in this form using this path," the Common Criteria says, "Okay, what are the threats we are facing today and what are the best ways of battling them?"

An evaluation is carried out on a product and is assigned an *evaluation assurance level (EAL)*. The thoroughness and stringent testing increases in detailed-oriented tasks as the levels increase. The Common Criteria has seven assurance levels. The ranges go from EAL1, where functionality testing takes place, to EAL7, where thorough testing is performed and the system design is verified. The different EAL packages are listed here:

- **EAL 1**   Functionally tested
- **EAL 2**   Structurally tested
- **EAL 3**   Methodically tested and checked
- **EAL 4**   Methodically designed, tested, and reviewed
- **EAL 5**   Semiformally designed and tested
- **EAL 6**   Semiformally verified design and tested
- **EAL 7**   Formally verified design and tested

The Common Criteria uses **protection profiles** to evaluate products. The protection profile contains the set of security requirements, their meaning and reasoning, and the corresponding EAL rating that the intended product will require. The profile describes the environmental assumptions, the objectives, and functional and assurance level expectations. Each relevant threat is listed along with how it is to be controlled by specific objectives. It also justifies the assurance level and requirements for the strength of each protection mechanism.

The protection profile provides a means for a consumer, or others, to identify specific security needs; this is the security problem that is to be conquered. If someone identifies a security need that is not currently being addressed by any current product, this person can write a profile of the product that would be a solution for this real-world problem. The profile goes on to provide the necessary goals and protection mechanisms to achieve the necessary level of security and a list of the things that can go wrong during this type of system development. This list is used by the engineers who develop the system and the same list is used by the evaluators to make sure the engineers dotted every i and crossed every t.

The Common Criteria was developed to stick to evaluation classes but also to retain some degree of flexibility. Protection profiles were developed to describe the functionality, assurance, description, and rationale of its findings.

Like other evaluation criteria before it, Common Criteria works to answer two basic and general questions about products being evaluated: what does it do (functionality), and how sure are you of that (assurance)? This system sets up a framework for consumers to be able to clearly specify their security issues and problems; developers to specify their security solution to those problems; evaluators to unequivocally determine what the product actually accomplishes.

A protection profile contains the following five sections:

- **Descriptive elements**   Name of profile and a description of the security problem that is to be solved.

- **Rationale**   Justification of the profile and a more detailed description of the real-world problem to be solved. The environment, usage assumptions, and threats are illustrated along with guidance on the security policies that can be supported by products and systems that conform to this profile.

- **Functional requirements**   A protection boundary is established, meaning the threats or compromises that are within this boundary to be countered. The product or system must enforce the boundary established in this section.

- **Development assurance requirements**   The development phases from design to implementation have specific requirements established that the product or system must meet.

- **Evaluation assurance requirements**   Establishes the type and intensity of the evaluation.

The evaluation process is just one leg of determining the functionality and assurance of a product. Once a product achieves a specific rating, it only applies to that particular version and only to certain configurations of that product. So if a company buys a firewall product because it has a high assurance rating, it doesn't mean the next version of that software automatically inherits that rating. The next version will need to go though its own evaluation review. If this same company buys the firewall product and installs it with configurations not recommended, the level of security they were hoping to achieve can easily go down the drain. So all of this rating stuff is a formalized method of a system being evaluated in a lab. When the product is implemented into a real environment, other factors than just its rating need to be addressed and assessed to ensure that it is properly protecting resources and the environment.

Different Components of the Common Criteria

The different components of the Common Criteria are shown in Figure 5-16 and described here:

- **Protection profile** Description of needed security solution.
- **Target of evaluation** Product proposed to provide needed security solution.
- **Security target** Written by vendor explaining security functionality and assurance mechanisms that meet the needed security solution. In other words, "This is what our product does and how it does it."
- **Packages—evaluation assurance levels (EALs)** Functional and assurance requirements are bundled into packages for reuse. This component describes what must be met to achieve specific EAL ratings.

Figure 5-16   Relationship of the different components

References

CSRC, Common Criteria: **csrc.nist.gov/cc**

Common Criteria, The Standard for Information Security: **www.commoncriteria.org**

Common Criteria overview: **www.rycombe.com/cc.htm**

Certification versus Accreditation

We have gone through the different types of evaluation criteria a system can be appraised against to receive a specific rating. This is a very formalized process, and the evaluated system or product will then be placed on an EPL indicating what rating it achieved. Consumers can check this listing and compare the different products and systems to see how they rank against each other in the property of security. However, once a consumer buys this product and sets it up in his environment, it does not guarantee security. Security is made up of system administration, physical security, installation, and configuration mechanisms within the environment, and other security issues. To fairly say a system is secure, all of these items need to be taken into account. The rating is just one piece in the puzzle of security.

Certification

How did you certify this product? Answer: It came in a very pretty box.

Certification is the comprehensive technical evaluation of the security components and their compliance for the purpose of accreditation. A certification process can use safeguard evaluation, risk analysis, verification, testing, and auditing techniques to assess the appropriateness of a specific system, which processes a certain classification level of information within a particular environment. For example, if Dan were the security officer for a company that just purchased new systems to be used to process their confidential data, he would like to know if these systems are appropriate for these tasks and if they are going to provide the necessary level of protection. He could pay a company that specializes in these matters to perform the necessary procedures to certify the systems. The company will perform tests on the software configurations, hardware, firmware, design, implementation, system procedures, and the physical and communication controls. The certification will indicate the good, bad, and the ugly about the security protection level and the mechanisms that support it within these systems and how they work within the given environment. If the outcome of this process looks good to Dan, he will take it to his management to start the accreditation process.

Accreditation

Accreditation is the formal acceptance of the adequacy of a system's overall security and functionality by management. The certification information is presented to management, or the responsible body, and it is up to the management to ask questions, review the reports and findings, and decide upon the acceptance of the safeguards and if any corrective action needs to take place. Once satisfied with the system's overall security as it is presented, management makes a formal accreditation statement. By doing this, management is stating that it understands the level of protection the system will provide in its current environment and understands the security risks associated with installing this system.

To summarize, certification is a technical review that assesses the security mechanisms and controls and evaluates their effectiveness. Accreditation is management's official acceptance of the information in the certification process findings.

Because software, systems, and environments continually change and evolve, the certification and accreditation should also continue to take place. Any major addition of software, change to the system, or modification of the environment should initiate a new certification and accreditation cycle.

7799 Standards

The *British Standard 7799* is a risk-based method for assessing, evaluating, and managing risks. It takes a holistic approach to security, instead of just focusing on the technical issues. It is a standard and a framework for developing a security program. This can provide guidelines for organizations all around the world on how to develop and implement a security program and how to improve currently deployed programs. Companies can be certified against these standards, which evaluate and "grade" their overall security posture.

The British Standard is divided into ten sections:

- Security policy
- Security organization
- Assets classification and control
- Personnel security
- Physical and environmental security
- Computer and network management
- System access control
- System development and maintenance
- Business continuity planning
- Compliance

The British Standard 7799 was developed in England (who would of thought) and became a de facto standard. A de facto standard just means that the industry basically stated, "Hey, that's a good idea. Let's all do that." A de facto standard is not dictated by a standards board. Then a standards board did get into the act. The International Organization for Standardization (ISO), which develops standards for 145 countries, formalized the approach a bit and gave it a more international name, ISO I7799, which is also referred to as the Code of Practice for Information Security Management.

Open versus Closed Systems

Computer systems can be developed to integrate easily with other systems and products (open systems) or can be developed to be more proprietary in nature and work with only a subset of other systems and products (closed systems). The following sections describe the difference between these approaches.

Open Systems

I want to be able to work and play well with others.

Systems that are described as *open* are built upon standards, protocols, and interfaces that have published specifications, which enable third-party vendors to develop add-on components and devices. This type of architecture provides interoperability between products by different vendors of different operating systems, applications, and hardware devices. This interoperability is provided by all the vendors involved who follow specific standards and provide interfaces that enable each system to easily communicate with other systems and allow add-ons to hook into the system easily.

A majority of the systems in use today are open systems. The reason that an administrator can have Windows NT 4.0, Windows 2000, Macintosh, and Unix computers on the same network communicating easily is because these platforms are open. If a software vendor creates a closed system, they are restricting their sales to proprietary environments instead of to the whole world.

Closed Systems

I only want to work and play with you and him.

Systems that are referred to as *closed* use an architecture that does not follow industry standards. Interoperability and standard interfaces are not employed to enable easy communication between different types of systems and add-on features. Closed systems are proprietary, meaning that the system can only communicate with like systems.

A closed architecture can provide more security to the system because it does not have as many doorways in, and it operates in a more secluded environment than open environments. Because a closed system is proprietary, there are not as many tools to thwart the security mechanisms and not as many people who understand its design, language, and security weaknesses to exploit. However, more security brings less functionality. A majority of the systems today are built with open architecture to enable them to work with other types of systems, easily share information, and take advantage of the functionality that third-party add-ons bring. However, this opens the doors to more hacks, cracks, and attacks. You can't have your cake and eat it too.

A Few Threats to Security Models and Architectures

Now that we have talked about how everything is supposed to work, let's take a quick look at some of the things that can go wrong when designing a system.

Software almost always has bugs and vulnerabilities. The rich functionality demanded by users brings about deep complexity, which usually opens the doors to problems in the computer world. Also, vulnerabilities are always around because attackers continually find ways of using system operations and functionality in a negative and destructive way. Just like there will always be cops and robbers, there will always be attackers and security professionals. It is a game of trying to outwit each other and seeing who will put the necessary effort into winning the game.

Covert Channels

A *covert channel* is a way for an entity to receive information in an unauthorized manner. It is an information flow that is not controlled by a security mechanism or the mechanism has been successfully compromised. This type of information path is usually not used for communication; thus, the system does not properly protect this path because the developers never envisioned information being passed this way. For an entity to receive information in this manner violates the security policy of the system.

There are two types of covert channels: timing and storage. In a *covert timing channel*, one process relays information to another by modulating its use of system resources. The modulation of system resources can be accessing the hard drive, using excessive CPU cycles, or head placement on a hard drive track. For example, if one process wrote to the hard drive 30 times within 30 seconds this could mean something to another process that is programmed to look for this type of activity. The second process watches out for this "signal" and once it receives it, the second process carries out whatever evil activity it is programmed to do. You can think of it as a type of Morse code, but with the use of some type of system resource.

A *covert storage channel* is when a process writes data to a storage location and another process directly, or indirectly, reads it. The problem occurs when the processes are at different security levels, and therefore not supposed to be sharing sensitive data. Maybe an attacker figures out that two processes with different trust levels can view the pagefile.sys file. Process 1 writes some type of confidential information to the pagefile.sys file, and process 2 reads it. This would go against the information flow of the system and directly negate the security policy.

The most common covert channel in use today is the Loki attack. This attack uses the ICMP protocol for communication purposes. This protocol was not developed to be used in this manner, it is only supposed to send status and error messages. But someone developed a tool (Loki) that will allow an attacker to write data right behind the ICMP header. This allows the attacker to communicate to another system through a covert channel. It is usually very successful because most firewalls are configured to allow ICMP traffic in and out of their environments. This is a covert channel because it is using something for communication purposes that was not developed for this type of communication functionality.

 NOTE An overt channel is a channel of communication that was developed specifically for communication purposes. Processes should be communicating through overt channels, not covert channels.

Countermeasures

Because all operating systems have some type of covert channels, it is not always feasible to attempt to get rid of them all. The number of acceptable covert channels usually depends on the security rating of a system. A system that has a B2 rating has fewer convert channels than a C1 system. There is not much a user can do to countermeasure these channels; instead, they are addressed when constructing and developing a system.

In the Orange Book, covert channels in operating systems are not addressed until the security level B2 and above because these are the systems that would be holding data sensitive enough for others to go through all the necessary trouble to access data in this fashion.

Detecting a covert channel is very difficult to do; the following are some points about countermeasures:

- It is unlikely that intrusion detection systems will detect this type of attack within an operating system, but it's always worth a try.

- A network and host intrusion detection system can be more successful in identifying covert channels within the network.

- Auditing should be enabled to try and detect a covert channel use pattern, although it can be hard to detect within an operating system or product. Auditing for covert channel violations within the network could be much more successful.

Backdoors

In the programming world, *backdoors* are also called *maintenance hooks*. They are instructions within software that only the developer knows about and can invoke. They are placed in the software for easy access. They also allow the developer to view and edit the code without having to go through regular access controls. During the development phase of the software, these can be very useful, but if they are not removed before going into production, they can cause major security issues.

The backdoor is usually initiated by a random sequence of keystrokes that provides access into the software without having to go through normal access control and security checks and mechanisms.

An application that has a maintenance hook enables the developer to execute specific commands by using a specific sequence of keystrokes. Once this is done successfully, the developer is inside the application looking directly at the code. She might do this to watch problem areas within the code, check variable population, export more code into the program, or fix problems that she sees that are taking place. Although this sounds nice and healthy, if an attacker finds out about this maintenance hook, more sinister actions may be taken. So all backdoors need to be removed from software before it goes into production.

Countermeasures

Because backdoors are usually inserted by programmers, they are the ones who usually have to take them out before the programs and systems go into production. Code reviews and unit and integration testing should always be looking out for backdoors in case the programmer overlooked extracting them. Because backdoors are within the code of an application or system, there is not much a user can do to prevent their presence, but when a vendor finds out that a backdoor exists in their product, they usually develop and release a patch to reduce this vulnerability. Because most vendors sell their software without selling the associated source code with it, it may be very difficult for companies who have purchased software to identify backdoors. The following lists some preventative measures against backdoors:

- A host intrusion detection system can be used to watch for an attacker using a backdoor into the system.
- File system permissions can be set to try and protect configuration files and sensitive information from being modified.
- Strict access control can be added to prevent access to the system in the first place.
- File system encryption can be used to protect sensitive information.
- Auditing should be in place to detect any type of backdoor use.

Asynchronous Attack

Specific attacks can take place on a system that take advantage of the way a system processes requests and performs tasks. An *asynchronous attack* deals with the sequences of steps a system uses to complete a task. For example, if a system uses an autoexec.bat file, the system first goes through a boot process and checks to see if an autoexec.bat file exists on the system. If one does not exist, it will continue with its bootup procedures, but if it does exist, it will open the file and process it line by line. There is a timing difference of when the system checks to see if an autoexec.bat file exists and actually executing the contents of the file. There are actually two different and distinct steps here. A *time-of-check versus time-of-use (TOC/TOU)* attack could replace the autoexec.bat with a different autoexec.bat that compromises the system before the system actually initiates it.

A similar but different issue is called a *race condition*. When two different processes need to carry out their tasks on a resource, they need to follow the correct sequence. Process 1 needs to carry out its work before process 2 accesses the same resource and carries out its tasks. If process 2 goes before process 1, the outcome could be very different. If an attacker could manipulate the processes so that process 2 did its thing first, she is controlling the outcome of the processing procedure.

Countermeasures

It would take a dedicated attacker with great precision to perform these types of attacks, but it is possible and has been done. The following can be used to protect against this type of attack:

- A host intrusion detection system can be used to watch for this type of suspicious behavior.
- File system permissions and encryption can be set to protect sensitive files.

- Strict access control measures can be used to prevent an intruder from accessing the system in the first place.

- Auditing should be in place to catch patterns or indications of TOC/TOU attacks.

 NOTE This attack would be extremely hard to detect because it deals with the sequence of steps processes take when carrying out their tasks. There are few, if any, protection tools that look at these issues to this level of granularity. It is best addressed during the development of the product.

Buffer Overflows

Buffer overflows happen when programs do not check the length of data that is inputted into a program. The programmer can set the value of a required input to be 80 characters, but does not ensure that only up to 80 are actually inputted from a user or another program. If more than 80 characters are entered, this extra data overflows its allotted memory segment and is executed by the CPU. The extra data can launch another program or be a set of code that was devised to perform disruptive behavior in the system. This is sometimes referred to as "smashing the stack." A buffer overflow is usually aimed at systems that let the extra code be executed with privileged rights, meaning the software executes in a more privileged mode and has access to more critical resources.

Countermeasures

The first and best countermeasure to buffer overflows is proper programming and good coding practices. There are also several types of tools available to help prevent buffer overflows. Some tools monitor dynamic link library (DLL) usage, and other tools provide a wrapper around the kernel that monitors calls and watches for known buffer overflow attacks.

There is not much a user can do to prevent buffer overflows, because they are part of the program code. But when vendors discover these issues, they develop and distribute patches to reduce this type of vulnerability. The following can be used to protect against buffer overflows:

- A host intrusion detection system can be used to watch for this type of suspicious behavior.

- File system permissions and encryption can be set to protect sensitive files.

- Strict access control measures can be used to prevent an intruder from accessing the system in the first place.

- Auditing should be in place to catch patterns or indications of buffer overflow attacks.

Summary

The architecture of a computer system is very important and covers many topics. The system has to make sure that memory is properly segregated and protected, ensure that only authorized subjects access objects, ensure that untrusted processes cannot perform activities that would put other processes at risk, control the flow of information, and define a domain of resources for each subject. It also must ensure that if the computer experiences any type of disruption, it will not result in an insecure state. Many of these issues are dealt with in the system's security policy, and the security model is built to support the requirements of this policy.

Once the security policy, architecture, and model have been developed, the computer operating system, or product, must be built, tested, evaluated, and rated. An evaluation is done by comparing the system to a predefined criteria. The rating that is assigned to the system depends upon how it fulfills the requirements in the criteria. Customers use this rating to understand what they are really buying and how much they can trust this new product. Once the customer buys the product, it must be tested within their own environment to make sure it meets their company's needs, which takes place through certification and accreditation processes.

Quick Tips

- A system can have the exact same hardware, software components, and applications, but provide different levels of protection because of the different security policies and security models that the systems were built upon.

- A CPU contains a control unit, which controls the timing of the execution of instructions and data, and an ALU, which performs mathematical functions and logical operations.

- Most systems use protection rings. The more privileged processes run in the lower ring numbers and have access to all or most of the system resources. Applications run in higher-numbered rings and have access to a smaller amount of resources.

- Operating system processes are executed in privileged or supervisory mode, and applications are executed in user mode, also known as "problem" state.

- Secondary storage is nonvolatile and can be a hard drive, CD-ROM, floppy drive, tape backup, or a zip drive.

- Virtual storage combines RAM and secondary storage so the system seems to have a larger bank of memory.

- A deadlock situation occurs when two processes are trying to access the same resource at the same time or when a process commits a resource and does not release it.

- Security mechanisms can focus on different issues, work at different layers, and vary in complexity.

- The more complex a security mechanism is, the less amount of assurance it can provide.

- Not all system components fall under the TCB, only those that enforce the security policy directly and protect the system. These components are within the security perimeter.

- Components that make up the TCB are hardware, software, and firmware that provides some type of security protection.

- A security perimeter is an imaginary boundary that has trusted components within it (those that make up the TCB) and untrusted components on the outside of the boundary.

- The reference monitor concept is an abstract machine that ensures that all subjects have the necessary access rights before accessing objects. Therefore, it mediates all accesses to objects by subjects.

- The security kernel is the mechanism that actually enforces the rules of the reference monitor concept.

- The security kernel must isolate processes carrying out the reference monitor concept, must be tamperproof, must invoke the reference monitor for each access attempt, and must be small enough to be properly tested.

- A security domain is all the objects available to a subject.

- Processes need to be isolated, which can be done through segmented memory addressing.

- A security policy is a set of rules that dictate how sensitive data is to be managed, protected, and distributed. It provides the security goals that the system must accomplish.

- The level of security a system provides depends upon how well it enforces the security policy.

- A multilevel security system processes data at different classifications (security levels), and users with different clearances (security levels) can use the system.

- Processes should be assigned least privilege so that they have just enough system privileges to fulfill their tasks and no more.

- Some systems provide functionality at different layers of the system, which is called layering. This separates the processes and provides more protection for them individually.

- Data hiding is when the processes at different layers do not know about each other, and therefore do not have a way to communicate to each other. This provides more protection for the data.

- When a class of objects is assigned permissions, it is called abstraction.

- A security model maps the abstract goals of a security policy to computer system terms and concepts. It gives the security policy structure and provides a framework for the system.

- The Bell-LaPadula model deals only with confidentiality, and the Biba and Clark-Wilson models deal with integrity.

- A state machine model deals with the different states a system can enter. If a system starts in a secure state, all state transitions take place securely, and the system shuts down and fails securely, the system will never end up in an insecure state.

- A lattice provides an upper bound and a lower bound of authorized access.

- An information flow security model does not permit data to flow to an object in an insecure manner.

- The Bell-LaPadula model has a simple security rule, which means that a subject cannot read data from a higher level (no read up). The *-property rule means that a subject cannot write to an object at a lower level (no write down). The strong star property rule dictates that a subject can only perform an operation at the exact same classification level, nothing higher, and nothing lower.

- The Biba model does not let subjects write to objects at a higher integrity level (no write up), and it does not let subjects read data at a lower integrity level (no read down). This is done to protect the integrity of the data.

- The Bell-LaPadula model is used mainly in military systems. The Biba and Clark-Wilson models are used in the commercial sector.

- The Clark-Wilson model dictates that subjects can only access objects through applications, that separation of duties is enforced, and auditing is in place.

- If a system is working in a dedicated security mode, it only deals with one level of data classification and all users must have this level of clearance to be able to use the system.

- Compartmented and multilevel security modes enable the system to process data classified at different classification levels.

- Trust means that a system uses all of its protection mechanisms properly to process sensitive data for many types of users. Assurance is the level of confidence you have in this trust and that the protection mechanisms behave properly in all circumstances predictably.

- The lower ratings in the evaluation criteria review the performance of a system and its testing results. The higher ratings look at this information and the system design, development procedures, and documentation.

- The Orange Book, also called Trusted Computer System Evaluation Criteria (TCSEC), was developed to evaluate systems built to be used mainly by the military.

- In the Orange Book, D classification means a system provides minimal security and is used for systems that were evaluated but failed to meet the criteria of higher divisions.

- In the Orange Book, the C division deals with discretionary protection and division B deals with mandatory protection (security labels).

- In the Orange Book, the A division means the system's design and level of protection is verifiable and provides the highest level of assurance and trust.

- In the Orange Book, C2 requires object reuse protection and auditing.

- In the Orange Book, B1 is the first rating that requires security labels.

- In the Orange Book, B2 requires all subjects and devices to have security labels, there must be a trusted path and covert channel analysis, and separate administrator functionality is provided.

- In the Orange Book, B3 requires that a security administrator role is defined, trusted recovery takes place, and the system monitors events and notifies security personnel.

- In the Orange Book, C1 outlines access control to be based on individuals and/ or groups. It requires a separation of users and information, and identification and authentication of individual entities.

- The Orange Book deals mainly with stand-alone systems, so a range of books were written to cover many other topics in security. These books are called the Rainbow Series.

- The Red Book, or Trusted Network Interpretation (TNI), provides guidelines for networks and network components.

- The Information Technology Security Evaluation Criteria (ITSEC) was an attempt by European countries to develop and use one set of evaluation criteria instead of several.

- The ITSEC evaluates the assurance and functionality of a system separately, whereas the TCSEC combines the two into one rating.

- The Common Criteria was developed to provide a globally recognized evaluation criteria and is in use today. It combines sections of the TCSEC, ITSEC, CTCPEC, and the Federal Criteria.

- The Common Criteria uses protection profiles and ratings from EAL1 to EAL7.

- Certification is the technical evaluation of a system and its security components. Accreditation is management's formal approval and acceptance of the security provided by a system.

- An open system provides better interoperability with other systems and products. A closed system works within a proprietary environment, which lowers its interoperability and functionality possibilities.

- A covert channel is an unintended communication path that transfers data in a way that violates the security policy. There are two types: timing and storage covert channels.

- A covert timing channel enables a process to relay information to another process by modulating its use of system resources.

- A covert storage channel enables a process to write data to a storage medium so another process can read it.

- A maintenance hook is developed to let a programmer into the application quickly for maintenance or adding functionality. This should be removed before the application goes into production or it can cause a serious security risk.

- An execution domain is where instructions are executed by the CPU. The operating system's instructions are executed in a privileged mode, and applications' instructions are executed in user mode.

- Process isolation ensures that multiple processes can run concurrently and the processes will not interfere with each other or affect each other's memory segments.

- The only processes that need complete system privileges are located in the system's kernel.

- A single state machine processes data of a single security level. A multistate machine processes data at two or more security levels without risk of compromising the system's security.

- Strong typing indicates that there is strong enforcement of abstract data types.

- TOC/TOU stands for time-of-check versus time-of-use. This is a class of asynchronous attacks.

- The Biba model is based on a hierarchical lattice of integrity levels.

- The Biba model addresses the first goal of integrity, which is to prevent unauthorized users from making modifications.

- The Clark-Wilson model addresses all three integrity goals: prevent unauthorized users from making modifications, prevent authorized users from making improper modifications, and maintain internal and external consistency.

- In the Clark-Wilson model, users can only access and manipulate objects through programs. It uses access triple, which is subject-program-object.

- ITSEC was developed for European countries. It was not an international evaluation criterion.

Questions

Please remember that these questions are formatted and asked in a certain way for a reason. You must remember that the CISSP exam is asking questions at a conceptual level. Questions may not always have the perfect answer, and the candidate is advised against always looking for the perfect answer. The candidate should look for the best answer in the list.

1. What flaw creates buffer overflows?

    A. Application executing in privileged mode

    B. Inadequate memory segmentation

    C. Inadequate protection ring use

    D. Insufficient parameter checking

2. The operating system performs all except which of the following tasks?

    A. Memory allocation

    B. Input and output tasks

   C. Resource allocation

   D. User access to database views

3. If an operating system allows sequential use of an object without refreshing it, what security issue can arise?

   A. Disclosure of residual data

   B. Unauthorized access to privileged processes

   C. Data leakage through covert channels

   D. Compromising the execution domain

4. What is the final step in authorizing a system for use in an environment?

   A. Certification

   B. Security evaluation and rating

   C. Accreditation

   D. Verification

5. What feature enables code to be executed without the usual security checks?

   A. Antivirus software

   B. Maintenance hook

   C. Timing channel

   D. Ready state

6. If a component fails, a system should be designed to do which of the following?

   A. Change to a protected execution domain

   B. Change to a problem state

   C. Change to a more secure state

   D. Release all data held in volatile memory

7. What security advantage does firmware have over software?

   A. It is difficult to modify without physical access.

   B. It requires a smaller memory segment.

   C. It does not need to enforce the security policy.

   D. It is easier to reprogram.

8. Which is the first level of the Orange Book that requires classification labeling of data?

   A. B3

   B. B2

   C. B1

   D. C2

9. Which of the following best describes the reference monitor concept?

    A. A software component that monitors activity and writes security events to an audit log

    B. A software component that determines if a user is authorized to perform a requested operation

    C. A software component that isolates processes and separates privilege and user modes

    D. A software component that works in the center protection ring and provides interfaces between trusted and untrusted objects

10. The Information Technology Security Evaluation Criteria was developed for which of the following?

    A. International use

    B. U.S. use

    C. European use

    D. Global use

11. A security kernel contains which of the following?

    A. Software, hardware, and firmware

    B. Software, hardware, and system design

    C. Security policy, protection mechanisms, and software

    D. Security policy, protection mechanisms, and system design

12. What characteristic of a trusted process does not allow users unrestricted access to sensitive data?

    A. Process isolation enforcement

    B. Security domain enforcement

    C. Need-to-know enforcement

    D. TCB enforcement

13. The Orange Book states that a system should uniquely identify each user for accountability purposes and _____.

    A. Require the user to perform object reuse operations

    B. Associate this identity with all auditable actions taken by that individual

    C. Associate this identity with all processes the user initiates

    D. Require that only that user have access to his specific audit information

14. The trusted computing base (TCB) controls which of the following?

    A. All trusted processes and software components

    B. All trusted security policies and implementation mechanisms

C. All trusted software and design mechanisms

D. All trusted software and hardware components

15. What is the imaginary boundary that separates components that maintain security from components that are not security related?

A. Reference monitor

B. Security kernel

C. Security perimeter

D. Security policy

16. Which model deals only with confidentiality?

A. Bell-LaPadula

B. Clark-Wilson

C. Biba

D. Reference monitor

17. What is the best description of a security kernel from a security point of view?

A. Reference monitor

B. Resource manager

C. Memory mapper

D. Security perimeter

18. When is security of a system most effective and economical?

A. If it is designed and implemented from the beginning of the development of the system

B. If it is designed and implemented as a secure and trusted front end

C. If it is customized to fight specific types of attacks

D. If the system is optimized before security is added

19. In secure computing systems, why is there a logical form of separation used between processes?

A. Processes are contained within their own security domains so that each does not make unauthorized accesses to other objects or their resources.

B. Processes are contained within their own security perimeter so that they can only access protection levels above them.

C. Processes are contained within their own security perimeter so that they can only access protection levels equal to them.

D. The separation is hardware and not logical in nature.

20. What type of attack is taking place when a higher level subject writes data to a storage area and a lower level subject reads it?

    A. TOC/TOU

    B. Covert storage attack

    C. Covert timing attack

    D. Buffer overflow

21. What type of rating does the Common Criteria give to products?

    A. PP

    B. EPL

    C. EAL

    D. A–D

22. Which best describes the *-integrity axiom?

    A. No write up in the Biba model

    B. No read down in the Biba model

    C. No write down in the Bell-LaPadula model

    D. No read up in the Bell-LaPadula model

23. Which best describes the simple security rule?

    A. No write up in the Biba model

    B. No read down in the Biba model

    C. No write down in the Bell-LaPadula model

    D. No read up in the Bell-LaPadula model

24. Which of the following was the first mathematical model of a multilevel security policy used to define the concept of a security state, modes of access, and outlines rules of access?

    A. Biba

    B. Bell-LaPadula

    C. Clark-Wilson

    D. State machine

25. Which of the following is not a characteristic of the Bell-LaPadula model?

    A. Confidentiality model

    B. Integrity model

    C. Developed and used by the U.S. DoD

    D. First mathematical multilevel security model

Answers

1. **D.** A buffer overflow takes place when too much data is accepted as input. Programmers should implement the correct security controls to ensure that this does not take place. This means they need to perform bounds checking and parameter checking to ensure only the allowed amount of data is actually accepted and processed by the system.

2. **D.** The operating system has a long list of responsibilities, but implementing database views is not one of them. This is the responsibility of the database management software.

3. **A.** If an object has confidential data and this data is not properly erased before another subject can access it, this leftover or residual data can be accessible. This can compromise the data and system's security by disclosing this confidential information.

4. **C.** Certification is a technical review of a product, and accreditation is management's formal approval of the findings of the certification process. This question asked you which step was the final step of authorizing a system before it is to be used in an environment, and that is what accreditation is all about.

5. **B.** Maintenance hooks get around the system's or application's security and access control checks by allowing whoever knows the key sequence to access the application and most likely its code. Maintenance hook should be removed from any code before it gets into production.

6. **C.** The state machine model dictates that a system should start up securely, carry out secure state transitions, and even fail securely. This means that if the system encounters something it deems as unsafe, it should change to a more secure state for self-preservation and protection.

7. **A.** Firmware is a type of software that is held in a ROM or EROM chip. It is usually used to allow the computer to be able to communicate with some type of peripheral device. The system's BIOS instructions are also held in firmware on the motherboard. In most situations firmware cannot be modified unless someone has physical access to the system. This is different from other types of software that may be modified remotely.

8. **C.** These assurance ratings are from the Orange Book. B levels and on up require security labels to be used, but the question asks which is the first level to require this. B1 comes before B2 and B3, thus it is the correct answer.

9. **B.** A reference monitor is the abstract machine that holds all of the rules of access for the system. The security kernel is the active entity that enforces the reference monitor's rules. They control the access attempts of any and all subjects, a user is just one example of a subject.

10. **C.** In ITSEC, the I does not stand for international, it stands for information. This is a criteria that was developed to be used by European countries to evaluate and rate their security products.

11. **A.** The security kernel makes up the main component of the TCB, which is made up of software, hardware, and firmware. The security kernel performs a lot of different activities to protect the system; enforcing the reference monitor's access rules is just one of those activities.

12. **C.** A system that enforces need-to-know does not allow subjects to access objects unless they have been granted the formal approval, which is based on a need-to-know. This question is targeting MAC-based systems that would use security labels, clearances, and classifications also in its access criteria.

13. **B.** Proper security implementations include tracking individuals and their actions. The users need to be identified uniquely to be able to track their individual activities. If all users logged in and authenticated to a system as user001, the system could never be able to distinguish which user actually carried out specific actions.

14. **D.** The TCB contains and controls all protection mechanisms within the system, whether they be software, hardware, or firmware.

15. **C.** The security perimeter is a boundary between items that are within the TCB and the ones that are not part of the TCB. It is just a mark of delineation between these two groups of items.

16. **A.** The Bell-LaPadula model was developed for the U.S. government with the main goal of keeping sensitive data unreachable to those who were not authorized to access and view it. This model was the first mathematical model of a multilevel security policy used to define the concept of a security state, modes of access, and outlines rules of access. The Biba and Clark-Wilson models do not deal with confidentiality, but with integrity instead.

17. **A.** The security kernel is a portion of the operating system's kernel and enforces the rules outlined in the reference monitor. It is the enforcer of the rules and is invoked each time a subject makes a request to access an object. A portion of the kernel is the resource manager, not the security kernel. A memory mapper is a distinct function of the kernel also, and the security perimeter delineates between what is within the TCB and what is not.

18. **A.** It is difficult to add useful and effective security at the end of developing a product or adding security as a front end to an existing product. Adding security at the end of a project is usually more expensive because it will break items and the team will need to go back to the drawing board and redesign and recode portions of the product.

19. **A.** Processes are assigned their own variables, system resources, and memory segments, which makes up their domain. This is done so that they do not corrupt each other's data or processing activities.

20. **B.** A covert channel is being used when something is using a resource for communication purposes and that is not the reason this resource was created. A process can write to some type of shared media or storage place that another process will be able to access. The first process writes to this media and the second process reads it. This action goes against the security policy of the system.

21. **C.** The Common Criteria uses a different assurance rating system than the previously used systems. It has packages of specifications that must be met for a product to obtain the corresponding rating. These ratings and packages are called evaluation assurance levels (EALs). Once a product achieves any type of rating, customers can view this information on an Evaluated Products List (EPL).

22. **A.** The *-integrity axiom (or star integrity axiom) indicates that a subject of a lower integrity level cannot write to an object of a higher integrity level. This rule is put into place to protect the integrity of the data that resides at the higher level.

23. **D.** The simple security rule is implemented to ensure that any subject at a lower security level cannot view data that resides at a higher level. The reason this type of rule is put into place is to protect the confidentiality of the data that resides at the higher level. This rule is used in the Bell-LaPadula model. Remember that if you see "simple" in a rule it pertains to reading, and * or "star" pertains to writing.

24. **B.** This is a formal definition of the Bell-LaPadula model, which was created and implemented to protect government and military confidential information.

25. **B.** The Bell-LaPadula security model was the first mathematical state machine model that provided multilevel security systems. The model was developed because the U.S. DoD had concerns about the systems it was depending upon to keep its military secrets and confidential information. Bell-LaPadula is a confidentiality model and does not address integrity.

Physical Security

In this chapter, you will learn about the following items:

- Administrative, technical, and physical controls pertaining to physical security
- Facility location, construction, and management
- Physical security risks, threats, and countermeasures
- Electrical power issues and countermeasures
- Fire prevention, detection, and suppression
- Authenticating individuals and intrusion detection

Security is very important to companies and their infrastructures, and physical security is no exception. Physical security encompasses a different set of threats, vulnerabilities, and risks than the other types of security that have been addressed so far. Physical security mechanisms include site design and layout, environmental components, emergency response readiness, training, access control, intrusion detection, and power and fire protection. Physical security mechanisms protect people, data, equipment, systems, and the facility itself.

Physical Security

Physical security of computers and their resources in the 1960s and 1970s was not as challenging as it is today, because computers were mostly mainframes locked away in server rooms with a handful of people who knew what to do with them. Today, with a computer on almost every desk in every company, devices and resources are spread throughout the environment, larger companies have several wiring closets and server rooms, and remote and mobile users take computers and resources out of the facility. Properly protecting these computer systems and devices has become an overwhelming burden to many companies.

Internal theft, fraud, sabotage, and accidents are raising costs for many companies because environments are becoming more complex and dynamic. Most companies have had memory or processors stolen from workstations, and some have had computers and laptops taken. The companies may have resorted to security guards, closed-circuit TVs (CCTVs), and mounted cameras, requiring users to sign out materials, and requiring their staff to have a higher awareness of security risks. Contract and temporary workers may have special access badges and may only be allowed in certain areas if they are escorted. Stricter access control may be implemented with individual access badges and motion detectors, and infrared systems may be installed. These are only some of the items that fall within the physical security boundaries. If any one of these does not provide the necessary protection level, then it could be the weak link that causes security breaches.

Physical security needs to be implemented in a layered defense model, which means that physical controls should work together in a tiered architecture. The concept: if one layer fails, other layers will protect the physical asset. Layers would be implemented moving in from the perimeter. For example, you would have a fence, then your facility walls, then card access, then a guard, then intrusion detection, and then locked cases on individual computers. This series of layers will protect your most sensitive assets, which would be placed in the innermost control zone. So if the bad guy were able to climb over your fence and outsmart the security guard, several layers of controls still would have to be circumvented before getting to your precious resources.

Physical security is accomplished through proper facility construction; fire and water damage protection; proper heating, ventilation, and air-conditioning (HVAC) controls; antitheft mechanisms; intrusion detection systems; and security procedures that are adhered to and enforced. The components that achieve this type of security are composed of good physical, technical, and administrative control mechanisms.

Security needs to protect all assets of the organization, including people and hardware. Security should enhance productivity by providing a secure and predictable environment. It enables employees to focus on their tasks at hand, and the evildoers will know to move on to a more vulnerable and easy target. This is the hope, anyway.

Physical security has a different set of vulnerabilities than computer and information security. These vulnerabilities have more to do with physical destruction, intruders, environmental issues, and employees misusing their privileges and causing unexpected damage to data or systems. When security professionals are looking at *computer* security, they are thinking about how someone can enter an environment in an unauthorized manner through a port or modem. When they are looking at *physical* security, they are concerned with how people can physically enter an environment, how environmental issues affect the systems, or what type of intrusion detection system is best for a particular facility. Figure 6-1 illustrates the difference between computer and physical security.

Figure 6-1 Whereas computer security involves attackers, crackers, and hackers, physical security involves intruders, vandals, and thieves.

Each type of security has its own issues to be aware of and countermeasures to implement, but the more a security professional knows about all areas of security, the more beneficial it is because she can understand how all the pieces interrelate.

 NOTE   Electronic access control (EAC) tokens are used in physical security to authenticate subjects. They can be proximity readers, programmable locks, or biometric systems, which identify and authenticate users before allowing them entrance into physically controlled areas.

Planning Process

Okay, so what are we doing?

The environment that must be protected through physical security controls includes all personnel, equipment, data, communication devices, power supplies, and wiring. The necessary level of protection depends on the value of the data, the computer systems, and the company assets within the facility. The value of these items can be determined by a *critical-path* analysis, which lists each piece of the infrastructure and what is necessary to keep those pieces healthy and operational. This analysis also outlines the paths data takes when passing through a network. Data can go from remote users to servers, from servers to workstations, from workstations to mainframes, and from mainframes to other mainframes. It is important to understand these paths and the possible threats that can disrupt them.

The critical-path analysis lists all pieces of an environment and how they interact and are interdependent. Diagrams should be developed to show the devices and their place in and relevance to a facility. This diagram should include power, data, water, and sewer lines. Air conditioners, generators, and storm drains may also be included to provide a full description and understanding. Figure 6-2 shows a simplistic example of this type of diagram.

The critical path is defined as the path that is critical for business functionality. The critical path should be shown in detail with all supporting mechanisms. Redundant paths should be shown, and there should be at least one redundant path for every critical path.

Facilities Management

The physical facility is usually the building that houses employees, equipment, data, network components, and other assets. Facility management responsibilities start before the building is built, by choosing the right location, materials, and supporting systems. Many times in a company, a facilities manager is hired to be totally responsible for all facets of the building, and this individual interfaces with the systems administrator and management staff to ensure that all overlapping issues are agreed upon and properly protected.

Figure 6-2   A diagram showing the power, water and sewer lines and the flow of critical data is a necessary reference.

Physical Security Controls

Several types of controls fall under the physical security umbrella. Here is a list of some of those controls:

- Administrative controls
  - Facility selection or construction
  - Facility management

- • Personnel controls
- • Training
- • Emergency response and procedures
- • Technical controls
  - • Access controls
  - • Intrusion detection
  - • Alarms
  - • Monitoring (CCTV)
  - • Heating, ventilation, and air-conditioning (HVAC)
  - • Power supply
  - • Fire detection and suppression
  - • Backups
- • Physical controls
  - • Fencing
  - • Gates
  - • Bollards
  - • Locks
  - • Lighting
  - • Facility construction materials

Physical Attributes of the Facility

Katie states, "I can't see the building, Dusty." Dusty replies, "That is the whole idea."

When a company decides to erect a building, it considers several factors before pouring the first batch of concrete. Of course, land prices, customer population, and marketing strategies are reviewed, but as security professionals we are more interested in the confidence and protection a specific location can provide. Some organizations that deal with top secret or confidential information make their facilities unnoticeable so they do not attract the attention of would-be attackers. The building can be hard to see from the surrounding roads, the company signs and logos are small and not easily noticed, and the markings on the buildings do not give away any information that pertains to what is going on inside that building. It is a type of urban camouflage that makes it harder for the enemy to seek them out.

Issues with Selecting a Facility Site

When selecting a location for a facility, some of the following items are critical to the decision-making process:

- Visibility
  - Surrounding terrain
  - Building markings and signs
  - Types of neighbors
  - Population of the area
- Surrounding area and external entities
  - Crime rate
  - Proximity to police, medical, and fire stations
  - Possible hazards from surrounding area
- Accessibility
  - Road access
  - Traffic
  - Proximity to airports, train stations, and highways
- Natural disasters
  - Likelihood of floods, tornadoes, earthquakes, or hurricanes
  - Hazardous terrain (mudslides, falling rock from mountains, or excessive snow or rain)

Some buildings are placed in areas surrounded by hills or mountains to help prevent eavesdropping of electrical signals emitted by the facility's equipment. In some cases, the organization itself will build hills or use other landscaping techniques to guard against eavesdropping. Other facilities are built underground or right into the side of a mountain for concealment and disguise in the natural environment, and for protection from radar tools and spying activities.

Location selection also means identifying other types of risks related to specific areas. These issues deal with natural disaster possibilities, crime rates, surrounding neighbors, and proximity to airports and railways. If a company is considering the possibility of building a facility in Kansas, then tornado insurance will certainly have to be built into cost and maintenance equations. If the company is also looking at erecting a building in a low-income area, although the land prices will most likely be cheap, there will be a need for higher physical and perimeter security levels, which bring along costs and overhead.

An inspection of the facility should be done to reveal the vulnerabilities and the extent of those vulnerabilities. In other words, a risk analysis should be done to evaluate those significant risks. The value of property within the facility and the value of the facility itself need to be ascertained to determine the budget that should be allotted for physical security.

Construction

We need a little more than glue, tape, and a stapler.

Physical construction materials and structure composition need to be evaluated for their protective characteristics, their utility, and their costs and benefits. Different building materials provide different levels of fire protection and combustibility, which correlate with their fire ratings. When making structural decisions, the type of construction material used (wood, concrete, or steel) needs to be combined with what the building is going to be used for. If an area is going to be used to store documents and old equipment, it has far different needs and legal requirements than if this area were to be used for employees to work in every day.

The *load* (how much weight that can be held) of a building's walls, floors, and ceilings needs to be estimated and projected to ensure that the building will not collapse in different situations. In some cases, this may be dictated by local building codes. The walls, ceilings, and floors must contain the necessary materials to meet the required fire rating and to protect against water damage. The windows (interior and exterior) may need to provide ultraviolet (UV) protection, may be required to be shatterproof, or may need to be translucent or opaque, depending on the placement of the window and the contents of the building. The doors (exterior and interior) may need to have directional opening, have the same fire rating as the surrounding walls, prohibit forcible entries, display emergency egress markings, and depending on placement, may require monitoring and attached alarms. In most buildings, raised floors are used to hide and protect wires and pipes, but in turn these floors need to be electrically grounded because they are raised.

Building codes may regulate all of these issues, but there are still many options within each category. The right options should accomplish the company's security and functionality needs and still be cost effective.

When designing and building a facility, the following major items need to be addressed from a physical security point of view:

Walls

- Combustibility of material (wood, steel, concrete)
- Fire rating
- Reinforcements for secured areas

Doors

- Combustibility of material (wood, pressed board, aluminum)
- Fire rating
- Resistance to forcible entry
- Emergency marking

- Placement
- Alarms
- Secure hinges
- Directional opening
- Electric door locks that revert to a disabled state for safe evacuation in power outages
- Type of glass—shatterproof or bulletproof glass requirements

Ceilings

- Combustibility of material (wood, steel, concrete)
- Fire rating
- Load and weight bearing rating
- Drop ceiling considerations

Windows

- Translucent or opaque requirements
- Shatterproof
- Alarms
- Placement
- Accessibility to intruders

Flooring

- Load and weight bearing rating
- Combustibility of material (wood, steel, concrete)
- Fire rating
- Raised flooring (electrical grounding)
- Nonconducting surface and material

Heating, Ventilation, and Air-Conditioning

- Positive air pressure
- Protected intake vents
- Dedicated power lines
- Emergency shutoff valves and switches
- Placement

Electrical Power Supplies

- Backup and alternate power supplies
- Clean and steady power source
- Dedicated feeders to required areas
- Placement and access to distribution panels and circuit breakers

Water and Gas Lines

- Shutoff valves
- Positive flow (material flows out of building, not in)
- Placement

Fire Detection and Suppression

- Placement of sensors and detectors
- Placement of sprinklers
- Type of detectors and sprinklers

A security professional may be involved with the planning phase of building a facility, and each of these items comes into play when constructing a secure building and environment. These topics will be explained in further detail throughout this chapter.

Facility Components

Many components that make up a facility must be looked at from a security point of view. *Internal partitions* are used to create barriers between one area and another. These partitions can be used to segment a network, separate work areas, and provide protected areas for sensitive systems and devices. Many buildings have dropped ceilings, meaning the interior partitions may not extend above the ceiling. An intruder can lift a ceiling panel and climb over the partition. This example of intrusion is shown in Figure 6-3. In many situations, this would not require forced entry, specialized tools, or much effort. These types of internal partitions should not be solely relied upon for providing protection for sensitive areas.

Surfaces that can conduct electricity, even static electricity, should be avoided in places where sensitive electrical devices are being used. Carpet may be acceptable in employee work areas, but it should not be used in server rooms or wiring closets.

Because data centers usually hold expensive equipment and the company's critical data, their protection should be thoroughly thought out before implementation. Data centers should not be located on the top floors in case of a fire. By the same token, data centers should not be located in basements, so that flooding does not become a problem. Data centers should be located at the core of a building to provide protection from natural disasters or bombs and to provide easier access to emergency crews if necessary. They

Figure 6-3 An intruder can lift ceiling panels and enter a secured area with little effort.

should be in semi-secluded areas to limit their accessibility and not right next to the cafeteria or other areas where employees gather.

External entities may need to be considered also. A company should evaluate how close the facility would be to a police station, fire station, and medical facilities. Many times, the proximity of these entities raises the real estate value of properties, but for good reason. If a chemical company that manufactures highly explosive materials needs to build a new facility, it may make good business sense to put it near a fire station. If another company that builds and sells expensive electronic devices is expanding and needs to move operations into another facility, police reaction time may be looked at when choosing one area over another. Each of these issues—police station, fire station, and medical facility proximity—can also reduce insurance rates and must be looked at carefully. Remember that the ultimate goal of physical security is to ensure the safety of personnel. Always keep that in mind when implementing any sort of physical security control. Protect your fellow man, be your brother's keeper, and *then* run.

Computer and Equipment Rooms

It used to be necessary to have personnel within the computer rooms for proper maintenance and operations. Today most servers, routers, bridges, mainframes, and other equipment that are housed in computer rooms are controlled remotely. This enables computers to live in rooms that have fewer people milling around and spilling coffee. Because the computer rooms no longer have personnel sitting and working in them for long periods, the rooms can be constructed in a manner efficient for equipment instead of people.

Computer rooms do not usually need to provide comfort and operational needs for people; they have become smaller, and expensive fire suppression systems may no longer be required. In the past, Halon fire suppression was the most popular way of protecting personnel who worked inside computer rooms. These systems are expensive to install and maintain. Fire suppression systems are still necessary, but different types can be used if human life is not a major factor within these areas of the facility.

Smaller systems can be stacked vertically to save space. They should be mounted on racks or placed inside equipment cabinets. The wiring should be close to the equipment to save on cable costs and to reduce confusion.

The location of these areas should be in the core areas of a facility, near wiring distribution centers. Only one access door should be necessary, and through-access to other unsecured areas should be impossible. There should be no access to these areas from public areas like stairways, corridors, and restrooms. This helps ensure that the people who are by the doors to secured areas have a specific purpose there versus being on their way to the restroom or standing around in a common area talking with others. Figure 6-4 illustrates only one entryway into a secured area.

 NOTE Depending upon the type of room, fire codes may dictate that in any area, at least two doors are required, so that if one door is blocked, people have a way to escape. In that case, secured rooms should have no more than two entry points. One entry point should only be used for emergencies and should sound an alarm if opened.

Only one way in and out to the secured area and no other entries available.

Figure 6-4   A secured area should have one entry that is properly controlled.

Physical Security Risks

Okay, so what are we supposed to be afraid of?

The main threats that physical security components combat are theft, interruptions to services, physical damage, compromised system integrity, and unauthorized disclosure of information.

Physical theft usually results in stolen computer equipment or other devices. Real loss is determined by the cost to replace the stolen items plus the cost to restore the lost data. Many times companies will just perform an inventory of their hardware and provide value estimates that are plugged into risk analysis to determine what the cost to the company would be if the equipment were stolen or destroyed. However, the information held within the equipment can be much more valuable than the equipment itself, and proper recovery mechanisms and procedures also need to be plugged into the risk assessment for a more realistic and fair assessment.

Interruptions of services can be the loss of computer services, power resources, water supply, and telecommunication services. These scenarios have to be evaluated and recovery plans developed. This was painfully obvious to many companies in California that experienced brownouts and blackouts when the state was running low on power. These factors bring up issues that need to be addressed in business continuity and disaster recovery planning, but they also bring up issues for physical security concerns. If a company loses power supply, it could also lose its electrical security systems and computerized intrusion detection systems. This could provide an intruder with easy access. Thus, a backup generator or backup procedures need to be in place and funds properly allocated before this type of situation arises.

Depending on a company's reliance upon telecommunication services, backup options may need to be put into place to ensure redundancy or communication circuits that can be activated on an as-needed basis. If a company provides a call center for a large software manufacturer, their profitability could be threatened if their telephone connection suddenly were to go down for a time. Stockbrokers need to be in touch with many other entities via their network, the Internet, and through telephone communication lines. If a company of stockbrokers lost communication abilities, their profits and their clients could be severely affected. Other companies may not be so dependent on telecommunication services, but this risk needs to be evaluated, informed decisions need to be made, and backup alternatives need to be available.

The loss of computer services is mainly addressed in Chapter 7 with backup and redundant array of inexpensive disks (RAID) protection mechanisms, and redundancy issues are addressed in Chapter 9 as they pertain to business continuity and disaster recovery. Physical security looks more at providing protection for the computers themselves and the facility they reside in. The magnitude of loss from physical damage depends on the cost of repair or replacement, the cost of replacing data, and the costs arising from service interruptions it causes.

Physical security countermeasures also protect against unauthorized disclosure of information and loss of system integrity and availability. Information can be disclosed to unauthorized individuals in many ways. Network traffic can be sniffed, electrical signals can be extracted from airwaves, and hardware or media can be stolen or modified. Physical security plays a role in each of these types of security vulnerabilities and risks.

Physical Security Component Selection Process

David exclaims, "I spent $30,000 to protect this floppy disk that is worth 50 cents!" Doug replies, "You're not too bright, are ya, son?"

All protection mechanisms must be cost effective to companies, and physical security components are no different. If a company spends $500,000 yearly for protection of an operation that is worth $120,000, it would not be a good example of cost-effective controls. New risk-assessment tools and methods need to be looked at as well as a new operator of those tools. A security mechanism that is cost beneficial means that the reduction in potential loss is significantly greater than the cost of implementing the mechanism in the first place and the cost of its lifetime maintenance. This realization needs to come from precise and detailed fact gathering, risk analysis and assessment, and a proper review of all available mechanisms that can provide the same type of protection—not necessarily the new gee-whiz gadget on the market.

There are some musts in life, like paying taxes, dying, and obeying one's wife. In selecting physical security components, some "musts" and "shoulds" need to be clearly understood so the most informed and intelligent decisions can be made.

Security Musts

Most companies are obliged by law to obey certain safety requirements. A building can contain only a certain number of individuals, must have stairs instead of just elevators, must have properly working fire alarms and smoke detectors, must have exit signs illuminated and easily visible, and must have fire exit doors that are not blocked and that have panic bars on them to enable people to evacuate during emergencies. These options must be implemented and are required by law, no matter how much they cost a company. These controls exist to ensure the safety of personnel, which is, of course, the foremost goal.

These regulations vary depending on the geographic location, the type of business, or if facilities are used for office buildings, storage facilities, or assembly lines. These issues get very detailed with safety codes, federal and state regulations, and building codes. It is out of the scope of this book to go into these issues, but the following items must be looked at very seriously: the costs, overhead, and the inherited vulnerabilities and risks.

Security Shoulds

Procedures should be put into place to help protect the company from devastating activities. Many times these protection procedures use security components that are already part of the environment, and therefore, require no extra expense. These procedures include backing up critical data, configuring security components that are already part of the operating systems and hardware instead of purchasing items that provide the same functionality, watching for suspicious activity of employees, logically and physically segmenting a network, and having the security guard walk around departments instead of staying in just one area. These all add another layer of protection without a lot of extra effort or money.

If there are low-cost security protection mechanisms whose benefit is material, these mechanisms should be implemented. Locks are inexpensive prevention tools, but can protect a facility and its contents from theft and destruction. Providing chains to an outside gate might cause would-be looters to move on to another victim. A guard shack with no real guard could deter individuals who were out to loiter, inflict property damage, or try their hand at graffiti on a building or facility. The cost of upkeep for these security mechanisms is minimal, but the benefits could be significant, so they should be implemented.

Backups

Backing up data seems like a hassle except for the day when the network goes down, data gets lost or corrupted, and users and management are screaming. Then proper backups are better than sliced bread.

Performing continual and consistent backups is done with prevention in mind, because you cannot predict when something is going to go wrong and to what extent. As with many other aspects of security, when the cost of recovery outweighs the cost of the protective mechanism, it always makes good sense to implement the protective mechanism.

Not every piece of data needs to be backed up, so it is important to identify the data that is critical, important, and mundane. This is the process of establishing priorities pertaining to different types of data, applications, and programming code. If you try to save everything, most likely nothing will be saved properly. It is important to establish priorities of what needs to be backed up, and in the case of an emergency, what needs to be restored before other items. The programs that enable different facilities to communicate and access data on host systems, and applications that protect and process business-critical information should be brought online and assurance of their functionality confirmed before worrying about word processors and programs to make birthday cards. Proper prioritizing will provide for realistic scheduling, help assure that critical jobs are done on time, and keep the costs reasonable.

More than just data needs to be backed up and in place in the time of need. Hardware, electrical supplies, and personnel are all necessary pieces to a successful and smooth-running data processing environment.

Hardware

Many companies implement alternate sites to help in the recovery process after a disaster. It is unlikely that two sites will be affected by the same disaster, so the measure seems prudent. The farther the two sites are from each other, the greater the safety factor, but the increase in cost of transporting people, equipment, and data is also greater. If a secondary site must be used, there is an initial cost of getting the site up and running and getting the right people in the right place. However, if operations need to take place at the secondary site for a month and it is over 100 miles away, the cost of providing living areas and travel expenses for employees is a cost that needs to be considered. (Alternate sites will be addressed fully in Chapter 9, but for now understand that it is an example of a type of backup.)

Other than for major disasters, providing redundancy hardware is important for the smaller emergencies. If a particular file server provides critically needed services to the company 24 hours a day, 7 days a week, it is usually mirrored or RAID capabilities are put into place to protect the data. But what about the hardware itself? If there is physical damage to a system, having the necessary files is not useful if there is not a healthy system to install them to. *Service level agreements (SLAs)* with hardware vendors need to be kept up-to-date to ensure that they provide the necessary level of protection. If the vendor promises to repair a product within three days and the business could lose massive profits if the product were down for three hours, then this is not a realistic protection mechanism.

Each device has a *mean time between failure (MTBF)* and a *mean time to repair (MTTR)*. The MTBF estimate is used to determine the expected lifetime of a device or when an element within that device is expected to give out. The MTTR value is used to estimate the time it will take to repair the device and get it back into production. These estimates can be used to calculate the risk of utility failure, and to evaluate other devices that may have better MTBF or MTTR values. If a company depends greatly on a specific cooling device for their server room that contains over 200 servers, they may have one or two backup devices in case the primary one in use fails. Or they may send one of their network staff members to training on how to repair this device to help ensure a lower MTTR value. Figure 6-5 shows an example of MTBF and MTTR values.

Redundant hardware can be an expensive way to provide protection in case of a failure or emergency, but the possible adverse effects and those costs need to be weighed and compared with the cost of having an extra router ready to be put to work if the original router were to fail. A cost analysis of vendor service level agreements, possibly obtaining redundant hardware, the MTTR and MTBF values, and the cost expectancy of critical hardware needs to be done to make the most useful decisions.

Mean-time-between-failure = 652 days
Mean-time-to-repair = 1 day

Mean-time-between-failure = 785 days
Mean-time-to-repair = 6 hours

Mean-time-between-failure = 830 days
Mean-time-to-repair = 2 days

Mean-time-between-failure = 650 days
Mean-time-to-repair = 2 hours

Figure 6-5 When comparing different vendor products, the MTBF and MTTR values should be evaluated.

Power Supply

We don't need no stinkin' power supply. Just rub these two sticks together.

Because computing has become so essential in the corporate world, power failure is a much more devastating event than it was 10 to 15 years ago. The need for good plans to fall back on is more crucial to provide the assurance that a business will not be drastically affected by storms, high winds, hardware failure, lightning, or other causes that can stop or disrupt power supplies.

There are several types of power backup capabilities, and choosing the right one should be done after the total cost of anticipated downtime and its effects are calculated. This information can be gathered from past records and other businesses in the same area on the same power grid. Dividing the annual expenditures by the annual standard hours of use derives the total cost per hour for backup power.

Large and small issues can cause power failure or fluctuations. The effects manifest in variations of voltage that can last a millisecond to days. A company can pay to have two different supplies of power to reduce its risks, but this approach can be extremely costly. Another, less expensive mechanism is to have generators in place. Some generators have sensors to detect power failure and will start automatically. Thresholds can be calibrated to best serve an environment. Depending on the type and size of the generator, it might provide power for hours or days.

Power Protection   There are three main methods of protecting against power problems: uninterrupted power supply (UPS), power line conditioners, and backup sources. UPS uses batteries that range in size and capacity. The UPS can be online or standby. *Online systems* use AC line voltage to charge a bank of batteries. When in use, the UPS has an inverter that changes the DC output from the batteries into the required AC form and regulates the voltage as it powers computer devices. This conversion process is shown in Figure 6-6.

Standby UPS devices stay inactive until a power line fails. The system has sensors that detect a power failure, and the load is switched to the battery bank.

Backup power supplies are necessary when there is a power failure, and the outage will last longer than a UPS can last. Backup supplies can be a line from another electrical substation or from a motor generator and can be used to supply main power or charge the batteries in a UPS system.

Critical systems that need protection from interrupted power supplies need to be identified, and how long secondary power would be needed and how much power is

On-Line UPS

Figure 6-6   A UPS device converts DC current from its batteries to usable AC by using an inverter.

required per device needs to be estimated. Some UPS devices provide just enough power to allow systems to shut down cleanly, whereas others will allow the systems to run for a longer period. It needs to be determined if systems should have enough power supply to be shut down in a proper manner, or if they actually need to be up and running to keep critical operations available.

Just having a generator in the closet should not give a company the warm fuzzy feeling of security. The alternate power source should be tested periodically to make sure it works, and to the extent expected. It is never good to get all the way to an emergency to find out that the generator does not work, or someone forgot to buy the gas necessary to keep the thing running.

Electrical Power Issues   Electric power enables us to be productive and functional in many different ways, but if not installed, monitored, and respected properly, it can do us great harm.

Power needs to be provided in the appropriate levels and with the appropriate quality. There are two main types of power sources: primary and alternate. A *primary power source* is used to provide day-to-day operations, and an *alternate power source* is used in the event of some type of failure of the primary power source. The primary power source has at least one dedicated feeder from a utility station or power grid. An alternate power supply provides backup functionality to a primary power source and can take the form of a UPS, generator, or batteries.

When clean power is being used, it means that the power supply contains no interferences or voltage fluctuation. The types of interference (or *line noise*) possible are from *electromagnetic interference (EMI)* or *radio frequency interference (RFI)* and transient noise, which is disturbance to the flow of electric power while it travels across a power line, as shown in Figure 6-7. EMI can be created by the difference between three wires: hot, neutral, and ground. Lightning and electrical motors can induce EMI. RFI is created by components of an electrical system. Electrical cables and fluorescent lighting usually cause RFI.

Electrical Power Definitions

- **Ground**   The pathway to the earth to enable excessive voltage to dissipate
- **Noise**   Electromagnetic or frequency interference that disrupts the power flow and can cause fluctuations
- **Transient noise**   Short duration of power line disruption
- **Inrush current**   The initial surge of current required when there is an increase in power demand
- **Clean power**   Power that does not fluctuate

Figure 6-7 RMI and EMI can cause line noise on power lines.

Interference interrupts the flow of an electrical current, and fluctuations can actually deliver a different level of voltage than what was expected. Each can be damaging to devices and people. The following explains the different types of voltage fluctuations that are possible with electrical power:

- Power excess:
  - **Spike** Momentary high voltage
  - **Surge** Prolonged high voltage
- Power loss:
  - **Fault** Momentary power out
  - **Blackout** Prolonged loss of power
- Power degradation:
  - **Sag/Dip** Momentary low voltage
  - **Brownout** Prolonged power supply that is below normal voltage

Surge *Yow! That was nice. What was that? Answer: A surge of electricity, you sicko.* Surges can cause a lot of damage very quickly. A *surge* is one of the most common power problems and is controlled with surge protectors. These protectors use a device called a metal oxide varistor, which moves the excess voltage to ground when a surge occurs.

Blackout A *blackout* is when the voltage drops to zero. This can be caused by lightning, a car taking out a power line, storms, or not paying the power bill. It can last for seconds or days. This is when a backup power source is required.

Brownout When power companies are experiencing high demand, they will frequently reduce the voltage in a grid, which is referred to as a *brownout.* Constant-voltage transformers can be used to regulate this fluctuation of power. It can take different ranges of voltage and only release the expected 120 volts to customers.

Noise   *Noise* on a power line takes place when electrical interference is superimposed onto the power line itself. The noise usually results from a local source such as transformers, lightning, fluorescent lighting, and signals from televisions and radios. Frequency ranges overlap, which can affect electrical device operations. Noise suppression circuitry is usually part of other power line conditioners like surge protectors.

Lightning sometimes produces voltage spikes on communication and power lines, which can destroy equipment or alter data that is being transmitted. When generators are switched on because power loads have increased, they too can cause voltage spikes that can be harmful and disruptive. Storms and intense cold or heat can put a heavier load on generators and cause a drop in voltage line. Each of these instances is an example of how normal environmental behaviors can affect power voltage, eventually adversely affecting equipment, communication, or the transmission of data.

Because these and other occurrences are common, there should be mechanisms in place to detect unwanted power fluctuations to protect the integrity of the data processing environment. *Voltage regulators* and *line conditioners* can be used to ensure a clean and smooth distribution of power, and uninterruptible power supplies should always be handy in case of power failure.

Many data centers are constructed to take power-sensitive equipment into consideration. Because surges, sags, brownouts, blackouts, and voltage spikes frequently cause data corruption, the centers are built to provide a high level of protection from these issues. Other types of environments usually are not built with these things in mind and do not provide this level of protection. Offices usually have different types of devices connected and plugged into the same outlets. Outlet strips are plugged into outlet strips, which are connected to extension cords. This causes more line noise and reduction of voltage to each device. Figure 6-8 depicts an environment that can cause line noise, voltage problems, and possibly a fire hazard.

Figure 6-8   This configuration can cause a lot of line noise and a fire hazard.

Offices that experience these types of issues may need voltage regulators and line conditions to maintain a clean and steady power supply. All devices must be grounded properly for safety reasons. Two-prong outlets should be replaced with three-prong outlets to provide proper grounding. Vacuum cleaners and other devices should not be plugged into outlets used by computers and computing devices.

Preventive Measures and Good Practices

Don't stand in a pool of water with a live electrical wire. Response: Hold on, I need to write that one down.

When dealing with electrical power issues, the following items can help protect devices and the environment:

- Every device should have a surge protector to protect from voltage fluctuations.
- Shutting down devices in an orderly fashion helps avoid data loss or damaging devices due to voltage changes.
- Do not have devices or media around powerful magnetic lines, energized conductors, or circuits that could create magnetic fields.
- Power line monitors should be employed to detect frequency and voltage amplitude changes.
- Regulators should be used to keep voltage steady and power clean. Regulators may also filter out line noise.
- Connections need to be grounded from the device to the earth.
- Protection from magnetic induction should be provided through shielded lines.
- UPS or generators should be available for backup power supply.
- Shield long cable runs.
- Avoid fluorescent lights if possible.
- Use three-prong connections and adapters if using two-prong cables.
- Connect all systems to the same power line if possible (this reduces noise and provides a common ground).
- Do not plug outlet strips and extension cords into each other.

Personnel

Sally, you take John's job. John, you take Mike's job. Katie, you take Mitch's job. Dave, could you just leave?

Job rotation has been explained in other chapters, so we will only touch on the subject and show how it pertains to providing a type of backup. A company can have a stack of redundant hardware, more than enough power sources, and offsite facilities, but if the right people are not in place to make these things work, the backup hardware could be a waste of time and money.

Many companies fall into the situation where one individual exists who knows too much. Knowledgeable people are wonderful and necessary, but that knowledge needs to be spread around. Resignations, vacations, illnesses, promotions, or the proverbial "getting hit by a bus" often find a company unprepared to deal with them properly.

It is usually too expensive to have more than one person on payroll to perform a certain job, but cross-training can help when the employees need to take time off or move on. Personnel should also be periodically retrained in manual tasks that have been automated to make sure that if the automated process fails, the company will not take such a big hit.

The following sections list other personnel controls that affect the physical security of an environment.

Pre-employment Screening

- Check references, other employment, and education
- Character evaluation and response to different scenario questions
- Background investigation if needed
- Drug test if needed

Employee Maintenance

- Periodic reviews
- Reevaluating security clearances
- Supervisor updates and recommendations
- Job rotation
- Separation of duties

Post-employment

- Friendly termination
- Exit interview
- Escorted removal from facility
- Locking and removing computer accounts
- Recovering company property
- Changing passwords

These are procedures that should be thought out before hiring or terminating employees and should be practiced for each employee. This will help to ensure that the right individuals are selected, employee actions are always known and reviewed, and that termination processes reduce possible damage to the company and its assets.

Environmental Issues

Improper environmental controls or unsupervised environment utilities can cause damage to services, hardware, and lives. Services can be interrupted that can cause unpredicted and unfortunate results. Power, heating, ventilation, air-conditioning, and air-quality controls can be complex and contain many variables. They all need to be operating properly and be monitored regularly.

During facility construction, make certain that water, steam, and gas lines have proper shutoff valves, shown in Figure 6-9, and *positive drains*, which means their contents flow out instead of in. If there is ever a break in a main water pipe, the water flow must be able to be turned off. In case of a flood, a company wants to ensure that material cannot travel up through the water pipes and into its water supply or facility. In case of fire in a building, gas lines need to be able to be terminated. Facility, operating, and security personnel should know where these shutoff valves are, and there should be strict procedures to follow in these types of emergencies. This will help reduce the possible devastation.

Most electronic equipment must operate in a climate-controlled atmosphere. Although it is important to keep the atmosphere at a good working temperature, it is important to understand that the components within the equipment will suffer the most from overheating. Many times internal computer fans are not cleaned or are blocked, which overheats the internal components of a computer. When devices are overheated, the components can expand and contract, which causes components to change their electronic characteristics, reducing their effectiveness or damaging the system overall.

Figure 6-9   Water, steam, and gas lines should have emergency shutoff valves

Preventive Steps Against Static Electricity

- Use anti-static flooring in data processing areas.
- Ensure proper humidity.
- Have proper grounding of building and outlets.
- Don't have carpeting in data centers, or have static-free carpets if necessary.
- Wear anti-static bands when working inside computer systems.

Maintaining appropriate temperature and humidity is important in any facility, especially facilities with computer systems. Improper levels of both can cause damage to computers and electrical devices, but also remember that the temperature and humidity levels need to be adequate for the personnel working in these areas. High humidity can cause corrosion, and low humidity can cause excessive static electricity. This static electricity can short out devices, cause the loss of information, or provide amusing entertainment for unsuspecting employees. Relative humidity between 45 and 60 percent is acceptable for areas that are processing data.

Lower temperatures can cause mechanisms to slow or stop, and higher temperatures can cause devices to use too much fan power and eventually shut down. The temperature of an area containing computing devices should fall into the range of 70 to 74 degrees Fahrenheit. Table 6-1 lists different components and damaging temperature levels.

In drier climates, or during the winter, the air contains less moisture, which can cause static electricity when two dissimilar objects touch each other. This electricity usually travels through the body and produces a spark from a person's finger that can release several thousand volts. This can be more damaging than you would think. Usually the charge is released on a system casing, but if it were released directly to an internal component, the outcome could be worse. People who work on the internal parts of a computer usually wear anti-static armbands to reduce the chance of this happening.

In more humid climates, or during the summer, more humidity is in the air, which can also affect components. Particles of silver can begin to move away from connectors onto copper circuits, which cement the connectors into their sockets. This can adversely affect the electrical efficiency of the connection. A *hygrometer* is usually used to monitor humidity. It can be manually read, or an automatic alarm can be set up to go off if the humidity passes a set threshold.

Table 6-1	**Material or Component**	**Damaging Temperature**
Components Affected by Specific Temperatures	Computer systems and peripheral devices	175°F
	Magnetic storage devices	100°F
	Paper products	350°F

Ventilation

Can I smoke in the server room? Answer: Security!

Air ventilation has several requirements to aid in providing a safe and comfortable environment. A closed-loop recirculating air-conditioning system should be installed to maintain air quality. "Closed-loop" means that the air within the building is reused after it has been properly filtered, instead of bringing outside air in. Positive pressurization and ventilation should also be implemented to control contamination. ***Positive pressurization*** means that when an employee opens a door, the air goes out, and outside air does not come in. If a facility were on fire, you would want the smoke to go out the doors instead of being pushed back in when people were fleeing. Figure 6-10 illustrates positive pressurization during a fire.

Contaminants need to be understood by how they enter an environment, the damage they could cause, and the steps to ensure that a facility is protected from dangerous substances or high levels of average contaminants. Airborne material and particle concentrations must be monitored for inappropriate levels. Dust can affect a device's functionality by clogging up the fan that is supposed to be cooling the device. Excessive concentrations of certain gases can accelerate corrosion and cause performance issues or failure of electronic devices. Although most disk drives are hermetically sealed, other storage devices can be affected by airborne contaminants. Air quality devices and ventilation systems deal with these issues.

Fire Prevention, Detection, and Suppression

We can either try to prevent fires or have one really expensive weenie-roast.

The subject of physical security would not be complete without a discussion about fire safety. There are national and local standards that must be met pertaining to fire

Figure 6-10   Positive pressurization causes smoke to go out the doors instead of being sucked back into the environment.

prevention, detection, and suppression methods. *Fire prevention* comes from training employees how to react properly when faced with a fire, supplying the right equipment and ensuring that it is in working order, making sure there is an easily reachable fire suppression supply, and storing combustible elements in the proper manner.

Fire detection response systems come in many different forms. There are the red pull boxes we have seen on many walls in many buildings. An example of a red pull box is shown in Figure 6-11. Also, automatic detectors have sensors that react when they detect the presence of a fire. The automatic system can activate a sprinkler system or a Halon discharge system. Automatic sprinkler systems are widely used and highly effective in protecting buildings and their contents. When deciding upon the type of fire suppression systems to install, many factors need to be evaluated, including an estimate of the occurrence rate of a possible fire, the amount of damage that could result, and the types of systems to choose from.

Fire protection consists of early smoke detection and shutting down systems until the source of the heat is eliminated, so combustion does not occur. A warning signal should first sound, and an override button should be available to postpone the shutdown process if the problem is under control and danger has passed.

Types of Fire Detection

Fires present a dangerous security threat because they can damage hardware, data, and risk human life. Smoke, high temperatures, and corrosive gases from a fire can cause devastating results. It is important to evaluate the fire safety measurements of a building and the different sections within it.

A fire begins because something ignited it. Ignition sources can be failure of an electrical device, improper storage of combustible materials, carelessly discarded cigarettes, malfunctioning heating devices, and arson. A fire needs fuel and oxygen to continue to burn and grow; the more fuel per square meter, the more intense the fire will become. A facility should be built, maintained, and operated to minimize the accumulation of fuels that can feed fires.

There are four classes (A, B, C, and D) of fire, which are explained in a later section. It is important to know the difference between the types of fire so you know how to properly extinguish them. Fire extinguishers have markings indicating what type of fire they should be used on. The markings indicate what types of chemicals are within the canisters and what types of fires they have been approved to be used on. Figure 6-12 depicts

Figure 6-11
The red pull box is one example of a fire detection response system.

Figure 6-12   Portable extinguishers are marked indicating what type of fire they should be used on.

a portable extinguisher. Portable extinguishers are filled with a type of suppression substance and should be located within 50 feet of any electrical equipment and located near exits. The extinguishers should be marked clearly, with an unobstructed view. They should be easily reachable and operational by employees, and inspected quarterly.

A lot of systems are made of components that do not support combustion but will melt or char if overheated. Most computer circuits use only two to five volts of direct current, which usually cannot start a fire. Fuses are put into place so that devices will shut down if overheating occurs. If a fire does happen in a computer room, it will most likely be an electrical fire caused by overheating of wire insulation or by overheating components igniting surrounding plastics. Prolonged smoke usually occurs before combustion.

Fire Detectors
There are several types of fire detectors, each working in a different way. The detector can be activated by heat, smoke, flame, or combustion of particles.

Smoke Activated   Smoke-activated detectors are good for early warning devices. They can be used to sound a warning alarm before the water sprinklers turn on. A *photoelectric device,* also referred to as an optical detector, detects the change in the electrical current when there is a variation in light intensity. The detector produces a beam of light across a protected area, and if the beam is obstructed, the alarm assumes it is smoke, and sounds. Figure 6-13 illustrates how a photoelectric device works. Another type of photoelectric device samples the surrounding air by drawing air into a pipe. If the light source is obscured, the alarm will sound.

Figure 6-13   A photoelectric device uses a light emitter and receiver. If there is an obstruction between the emitter and receiver, an alarm will sound.

Heat Activated   Heat-activated detectors can either alarm when a predefined temperature is reached or can detect an increase in temperature that exceeds a predefined rate, or a combination of both. *Rate-of-rise temperature sensors*, shown in Figure 6-14, usually provide a quicker warning than *fixed-temperature sensors* because they are more sensitive, but they can also cause more false alarms. The sensors can either be spaced uniformly throughout a facility, or a line type of installation can be implemented, which is operated by a heat-sensitive cable.

Flame Activated   A flame-activated sensing device either senses the pulsations of a flame or senses the infrared energy that is associated with flames and combustion.

Flame-activated devices are much more expensive than other types of fire detectors and are usually only used in special cases when high-valued equipment needs to be protected. These systems can respond more quickly than other detectors, release an extinguishing agent, and sound an alarm.

Figure 6-14   Once a predefined temperature is reached, this sprinkler head begins to release water into the area.

Automatic Dial-up Alarm   This type of system is configured to call the local fire station, and possibly the police station, to report a detected fire. The system plays a pre-recorded message giving the necessary information so the officials can properly prepare and arrive at the right location. Many times this system is combined with one of the previously mentioned detection systems and adds another layer of functionality.

It is not enough to have these fire and smoke detectors installed in a facility; they must be installed in the right places. Detectors should be on and above suspended ceilings, because smoke usually gathers there first before entering other spaces. Detectors should be installed below raised floors because many types of wires live there that could start an electrical fire. No one would know about the fire until it broke through the floor if a detector were not below the raised floor to protect this area also. Detectors should also be located in enclosures and air ducts because smoke can gather in these areas before entering other spaces. It is important that people are alerted about a fire as quickly as possible so the damage may be reduced, fire suppression activities may start quickly, and lives may be saved. Figure 6-15 illustrates the proper placement of smoke detectors.

Figure 6-15   Smoke detectors should be located above suspended ceilings, below raised floors, and in air vents.

Plenum Area

Wiring and cables are strung through areas called *plenum areas.* These are in the drop-down ceilings, in the walls, and under raised floors. Fire detectors should be in these places, and plenum-rated cabling should be used here. Plenum-rated cabling is made out of material that does not let off hazardous gases if it burns.

Fire Suppression

How about if I just spit on the fire? Answer: I am sure that will work just fine.

It is important to know the types of fires and what should be done to properly suppress them. Each fire type has a rating that indicates what materials are burning. Table 6-2 shows the four types of fire and their suppression methods, which all employees should know.

There are several ways of suppressing a fire, and certain precautions that should be taken. In many buildings, suppression agents located in different areas are designed to initiate after a specific trigger has been set off. Each agent has a zone of coverage, meaning an area that the agent is responsible for. If a fire ignites within a certain zone, it is the responsibility of that suppression agent device to initiate and suppress that fire. There are different types of suppression agents: water, Halon, or CO_2. If an agent uses CO_2, it should have a delay mechanism within it. The delay mechanism would make sure that the agent does not start applying CO_2 to the area until after an audible alarm has sounded and people have been given time to evacuate. CO_2 is a colorless, odorless substance that is potentially lethal because it removes oxygen from the air. Gas masks do not provide protection against CO_2. This type of fire suppression mechanism is best used in unattended facilities and areas.

A fire needs fuel, oxygen, and high temperatures. Table 6-3 shows how different suppression substances interfere with these elements of fire.

Once a smoke detector is activated, an automatic fire suppression system should kick in. Older systems used CO_2, which extinguishes fires but can suffocate people. Halon

Fire Class	Type of Fire	Elements of Fire	Suppression Method
A	Common combustibles	Wood products, paper, and laminates	Water or soda acid
B	Liquid	Petroleum products and coolants	Gas (Halon), CO_2, or soda acid
C	Electrical	Electrical equipment and wires	Gas (Halon) or CO_2
D	Combustible metals	Magnesium, sodium, potassium	Dry powder

Table 6-2 Four Types of Fire and Their Suppression Methods

Combustion Elements	Suppression Methods	How Suppression Works
Fuel	Soda acid	Removes fuel
Oxygen	CO_2	Removes oxygen
Temperature	Water	Reduces temperature
Chemical combustion	Gas—Halon or Halon substitute	Interferes with the chemical reactions between elements

Table 6-3   How Different Substances Interfere with Elements of Fire

was later used, which, in small quantities, is harmless to people, but affects the ozone. Halon has not been manufactured since January 1, 1992, by international agreement. The Montreal Protocol banned Halon in 1987, and countries were given until 1992 to comply with these directives.

Production of Halon has been stopped because it has ozone-depleting substances within it. The most effective replacement for Halon is FM-200, which is similar to Halon, but does not damage the ozone.

Halon

Halon is a gas that was used to suppress fires because it interferes with the chemical combustion of the elements within a fire. It mixes quickly with the air and does not cause harm to computer systems and other data processing devices. It was used mainly in data centers and server rooms.

It was found that Halon has chemicals that deplete the ozone and that concentrations greater than 10 percent were dangerous to people. Halon used on extremely hot fires degraded into toxic chemicals and was even more dangerous to humans.

This caused Halon to be federally restricted, and no companies are allowed to purchase and install new Halon extinguishers. Companies that still have Halon systems have been asked to replace them with nontoxic extinguishers.

The following are EPA-approved replacements for Halon:

- FM-200
- NAF-S-III
- CEA-410
- FE-13
- Water
- Inergen
- Argon
- Argonite

By law companies that have Halon extinguishers do not have to replace them, but the extinguishers cannot be refilled. So companies that have Halon extinguishers do not have to replace them right away, but when the extinguisher's lifetime runs out, FM-200 extinguishers or other EPA-approved chemicals should be used.

Another fire suppression issue is the HVAC (heating, ventilation, and air-conditioning) system. The HVAC system should be connected to the fire alarm and suppression system so that it properly shuts down if a fire is identified. A fire needs oxygen and this type of system can feed oxygen to the fire. Plus, the HVAC can spread deadly smoke into all areas of the building. Many fire systems will configure the HVAC to shut down if a fire alarm is triggered.

Water Sprinklers
I'm hot. Go pull that red thingy on the wall. I need some water.

Water sprinklers can be simpler and less expensive than Halon and FM-200 systems, but can initiate unnecessarily, which can cause water damage. In an electrical fire, the water can increase the intensity of the fire, causing greater damage. A company needs to take great care in deciding which suppression agent and system is best for them.

Sensors should be used to shut down electrical power before water sprinklers activate. Each sprinkler head should activate individually to avoid wide-area damage, and there should be shutoff valves so the water supply can be stopped if necessary.

Four main types of sprinkler systems are available: wet pipe, dry pipe, preaction, and deluge.

Wet Pipe *Wet pipe systems* always contain water in the pipes and are usually discharged by temperature control level sensors. One disadvantage of wet pipe systems is that the water in the pipes may freeze, either breaking the pipes or providing less than acceptable results in a fire. Also, if there is a nozzle or pipe break, it can cause extensive water damage. These types of systems are also called *closed head systems*.

Dry Pipe In *dry pipe systems*, the water is not actually held in the pipes, but is held back by a valve until a specific temperature is reached. There is a delay between the predefined temperature being met and the release of water. This delay can be a good thing because it provides time for someone to shut down the system in case of a false alarm, but it also means it may permit more damage to occur before taking action.

Water is not allowed into the pipes that feed the sprinklers until that actual fire alarm is sounded. First a heat or smoke sensor is activated, then the water fills the pipes leading to the sprinklers, the fire alarm sounds, the electrical power supply is disconnected, and water is then allowed to flow from the sprinklers. These pipes are best used in colder climates because the pipes will not freeze. Figure 6-16 depicts a dry pipe system.

Preaction *I would like the choice of putting out the fire myself and not ruining all of my equipment.* **Preaction systems** can combine the use of wet and dry pipe systems. Water is not held in the pipes and is only released into the pipes once a predefined temperature is

Dry Pipe System

Water Supply

When temperature
meets a predefined value,
the valve opens.

Water Valve Opened   Water Sprinklers

Figure 6-16   Dry pipe systems do not hold water in the pipes, but release it once a specific
temperature is reached.

reached. Once this temperature is met, the pipes are filled with water, but do not release right away. A link has to melt before the water is released from the sprinkler head. The purpose of combining these two techniques is to be able to react faster to false alarms or to small fires that can be handled by other means. If a small fire can be put out by a handheld extinguisher, this would be better than losing a lot of electrical equipment from water damage. These systems are usually chosen for equipment that is costly and when the company wants to prevent water damage.

Deluge   A *deluge system* is the same as a dry pipe system, except the sprinkler head is open. In a dry pipe system the sprinkler head is closed and must open to allow water to escape. In the deluge systems, the heads are open to allow a larger volume of water to be released in a shorter period. Because the water being released is in such large volume, these systems are usually not used in data processing environments.

A dry pipe system is used to protect against unnecessary water damage. In addition, when a facility is in a location where freezing temperatures and broken pipes are an issue, a dry pipe system can be useful because the pipes are not full of water. The pipes are full of air until an alarm is activated, and then water is released into the pipes. In wet pipe systems, the pipes are always full of water and can easily rupture in freezing temperatures.

All sensors and smoke detectors are usually tied to a central security system. The system can cover a specific area, floor, or the entire facility. The system should send a signal to the local fire station alerting them of the emergency, and the air circulation for that area should be shut down.

Administrative Controls

Okay, a disaster hit. Who do we blame?

Ultimately, management is responsible for everything that happens within a company, with little exception. Good management must have the foresight to look into the future and understand that some things may go not go as planned, situations will arise that need special handling, and employees might be faced with emergency situations. It is management's responsibility to practice due diligence and think through many types of scenarios, develop procedures and responses that should take place when these situations arise, and plan for backup and contingency activities to ensure the health of the company and the safety of the people. Disaster recovery and business continuity are covered in Chapter 9. The following sections touch on some of the same issues, but show how they relate to physical security.

Emergency Response and Reactions

You run that way and you run that way. I am going to sit here and cry.

During the development of disaster and business continuity planning, different disaster scenarios are played out, situations are examined, and circumstances are thought through. Physical security issues play a huge role in these exercises and when the real thing occurs. Administrative controls need to be put in place to ensure that when a disaster hits, people are ready to react properly. These administrative controls are evacuation procedures, system shutdown procedures, fire suppression techniques, proper ways of dealing with bomb threats and civil unrest, and what to do if specific utilities fail.

Evacuation plans need to be developed, and procedures of shutting down systems in emergency situations need to be formed. During the development of a business continuity plan, systems that hold important information will be identified. In an emergency, they should be treated differently than regular workstations. Precautions need to be taken to ensure that the systems are shut down as delicately as possible to avoid the loss of data, or to prevent the interruption of some other important service.

Redundant utilities may need to be put in place to provide the necessary coverage and assurance of continued power supply in case of an electronic power failure. The cost of a UPS depends on the electrical load it can support, the length of time it can support this load, and the speed with which it assumes the load when the primary source fails. If long-term power supply is required, an onsite generator may be needed. The type and

Emergency Response and Procedures

- Evacuation procedures
- System shutdown
- Training and drills
- Integration with disaster plans
- Easily accessible documented procedures for different types of emergencies
- Periodic equipment tests

cost of the required generator depends upon the load that would be transferred to it and the size of the onsite fuel supply.

Emergency procedures need to be in place to deal with fires, bomb threats, hurricanes, tornadoes, and civil unrest. The ranking of these risks is done during an exercise discussed in Chapter 9 for disaster and business continuity plan development. When a disaster happens, certain people must take on specific responsibilities and carry out their tasks. These duties are delegated during the business continuity planning phase, periodic training, exercises, and drills, which reinforce the requirements of these duties. It is management's responsibility to ensure that employees are trained on disaster recovery and business continuity procedures. All procedures should be documented, and that documentation should be readily accessible. Periodic inspections should review the documentation, procedures, and the individual's knowledge of what is expected of him. A company and its environment continually change, and therefore so do the threats and vulnerabilities. A recovery plan should be a living document that is continually reviewed, updated, and practiced.

Perimeter Security

Stop! Who goes there?

The first line of defense deals with perimeter control to prevent unauthorized access to the facility. This defense works in two main modes: security practices during operation and security during the time the facility is closed.

When the facility is closed, all doors should be locked with monitoring mechanisms in strategic positions to alert others of suspicious activity. When the facility is in operation, security gets more complicated because authorized individuals need to be distinguished from unauthorized individuals.

Perimeter security deals with access control, surveillance monitoring, intrusion detection, and corrective actions. The following sections describe the elements that make up these categories.

Facility Access Control

Access control needs to be enforced through physical and technical components when it comes to physical security. Access controls protect facilities, computers, and people. In some situations, the objectives of physical access controls and the protection of people's lives may come into conflict. In these situations, a person's life always takes precedence. Many physical security controls make entry into and out of a facility hard, if not impossible. However, special consideration needs to be taken when this could affect lives. A physical security control that is used to ensure that the bad guys do not get in needs to allow the good guys to get out during a fire or similar emergency.

Physical access controls use mechanisms to identify individuals who are attempting to enter a facility, area, or system. They make sure that the right individuals get in and the wrong individuals stay out, and provide an audit trail of these actions. Personnel within sensitive areas can be one of the best security controls a company has because they can personally detect suspicious behavior. However, they need to be trained on what activity is considered suspicious and how reporting of such activities should take place.

Before the proper protection mechanisms can be put into place, a detailed analysis needs to be done on which data is sensitive and needs protection, which individuals should be allowed into what areas, which workspaces and systems are considered critical to the company's mission, and how the data and work flow within the facility. Access control points will be identified and classified as external, main, and secondary entrances. Personnel will be expected to enter and exit through a specific entry, deliveries may be expected to come to a different entry, and sensitive areas will be identified. Figure 6-17 illustrates the different types of access points into a facility. These important first steps help outline what needs to be protected, so the next step is how it is protected.

Locks

Locks and keys are the most inexpensive access control mechanisms. Locks are considered deterrents to semi-serious intruders and delaying devices to serious intruders. The longer it takes to break or pick a lock, the longer a security guard or police officer has to arrive on the scene if the intruder has been detected. Almost any type of a door can be equipped with a lock, but keys can be easily lost and duplicated, and locks can be picked or broken. If a company depends solely on a lock-and-key mechanism for protection, an individual who has the key can come and go as he likes without control and can remove items from the premises without detection. Locks should be used as part of the protection scheme, but not the sole protection scheme.

Locks vary in functionality. Padlocks can be used on chained fences, preset locks are usually used on doors, and programmable locks (requiring a combination to unlock)

Figure 6-17 Access points should be identified, marked, and monitored properly.

are used on doors or vaults. Locks come in all types and sizes. It is important to have the right type of lock so that it provides the correct level of protection.

Preset Locks These locks are usually used on doors. They can be a key-and-knob combination, mortise, or rim locks with latches and deadbolts as needed.

Cipher Locks These locks, also known as programmable locks, use keypads to control access into an area or facility. The lock can require a specific combination to be entered into the keypad and a swipe card. They cost more than traditional locks, but combinations can be changed, specific combinations locked out, and personnel who are in trouble or under duress can enter a specific code that will open the door and initiate a remote alarm at the same time. Thus, cipher locks can provide a much higher level of security and control of who can access a facility than traditional locks.

The following are some options available on many cipher locks that improve the performance of access control and provide for increased security levels:

- **Door delay** If a door is held open for a given time, an alarm will trigger to alert personnel of suspicious activity.

- **Key-override** A specific combination can be programmed to be used in emergency situations to override normal procedures or for supervisory overrides.

- **Master-keying** This option enables supervisory personnel to change access codes and other features of the cipher lock.

- **Hostage alarm** If an individual is under duress and/or held hostage, a combination he enters can communicate this situation to the guard station and/or police station.

  If a door is accompanied by a cipher lock, it should have a corresponding visibility shield so that a bystander cannot see the combination as it is keyed in. Automated cipher locks must have a backup battery system and be set to unlock during a power failure so personnel are not trapped inside during an emergency.

- **Device locks** Unfortunately, hardware has a tendency to walk away from facilities; therefore, device locks are sometimes necessary to thwart these attempts. Cable locks consist of a vinyl-coated steel cable, enabling computers and peripherals to be anchored to desks, chairs, and other stationary components. A cable lock is shown in Figure 6-18, and Figure 6-19 illustrates how to lock

Figure 6-18
FMJ/PAD.LOCK's notebook security cable kit secures a notebook by enabling the user to attach the device to a stationary component within an area.

and secure a computer. A wide range of device locks is available to protect the different types of devices used in an environment.

The following are some of the device locks available and their capabilities:

- **Switch controls**   Covers on/off power switches.
- **Slot locks**   A bracket is mounted in a spare expansion slot, and a steel cable is used to secure the system to a stationary component.
- **Port controls**   Block access to disk drives or unused serial or parallel ports.
- **Peripheral switch controls**   Secure a keyboard by inserting an on/off switch between the system unit and the keyboard input slot.
- **Cable traps**   Prevent the removal of input/output devices by passing their cables through a lockable unit.

Figure 6-19
FMJ/PAD.LOCK's Full Metal Jacket protects a tower computer by providing a "steel cage" for it.

Personnel Access Controls

Proper identification needs to verify if the person attempting to access a facility or area should actually be allowed in. Identification can be verified by matching an anatomical attribute (biometric system), using smart or memory cards (swipe cards), personal recognition by a security guard and presenting a photo ID, using a key, or providing a card and entering a password or PIN.

A common problem with controlling authorized access into a facility or area is called *piggybacking.* This occurs when an individual gains unauthorized access by using someone else's legitimate credentials or access rights. Usually an individual just follows another person closely through a door without providing any credentials. The best preventive measure against this type of problem is a security guard and employee awareness of good security practices.

If a company is employing a card badge reader, there are several types of systems to choose from. The magnetic card can contain a magnetic strip with authorization information, a magnetic dot, or embedded wire (resists tampering). The following sections describe these items in further detail.

Magnetic Cards

Individuals have cards that have embedded magnetic strips that contain access information. The reader can just look for simple access information within the magnetic strip, or it can be connected to a more sophisticated system that scans the information, makes more complex access decisions, and logs badge ID and access time.

If the card is a memory card, then the reader will just pull information from it and make an access decision. If the card is a smart card, the individual may be required to enter a PIN or password, which the reader compares against the information held within the card or in an authentication server. (Memory and smart cards are covered in Chapter 4.)

Wireless Proximity Readers

The two main types of proximity readers are user activated and system sensing.

User Activated   When this type of reader is used, the user swipes a card through the reader. The proximity card transmits a sequence of values to the reader. The reader is expecting a specific sequence, and if what is sent to it matches this preset value, then the individual is given access.

System Sensing   In this type of system, the system-sensing proximity card will recognize the presence of an approaching object within a specific area. A system-sensing access control system is a device that does not require the individual to enter any sequence or perform any action. Figure 6-20 shows how the reader can process the card and send the credentials to an authentication server, which will make the access decision.

Proximity device that accepts a code and transmits the credentials to an authentication system.

AS

Used to gain access into a building.

Figure 6-20 A card communicates with a proximity reader to provide access.

There are three main types of system sensing cards, and the differences among them are based on the way that power is generated.

- **Transponders** The card and reader have a receiver, transmitter, and battery. The reader sends signals to the card to request information. The card sends the reader an access code. These transponder devices contain a radio receiver and transmitter, a storage place for the access code, control logic, and a battery.

- **Passive devices** The card is considered passive because it does not have any power source of its own, but uses power from the reader. If it is a passive device, the card can sense the electromagnetic field, which is transmitted by the reader. When an individual is already in a secure area and is approaching a door to leave the sensitive area to a less sensitive area, the reader will detect the presence of this card and go ahead and unlock the door for the person.

- **Field-powered devices** The card and reader contain a transmitter and active electronics. The card has its own power supply and does not need to rely on the reader's power supply.

External Boundary Protection Mechanisms

Let's build a fort and let only the people who know the secret handshake inside!

Several types of protection mechanisms and controls can be put into place to protect a company's facility. They can deter would-be intruders, detect intruders and unusual activities, and can provide ways of dealing with these issues when they arise. The different mechanisms and controls are examined in the following sections.

Fencing

I just want a little fence to keep out all the little mean people.

Fencing is quite an effective physical barrier because it works as a preventive and deterrent mechanism. Fencing can provide crowd control and helps control access to entrances and access to facilities. However, fencing can be costly and unsightly. Many companies plant bushes or trees in front of the fence that surrounds their buildings for aesthetics and to make the building less noticeable.

Fences come in varying heights, and each height provides a different level of security:

- Fences three to four feet high only deter casual trespassers.

- Fences six to seven feet high are considered too high to climb easily.

- Fences eight feet high with strands of barbed wire at the top mean you are serious about protecting your property. They will deter the more determined intruder.

Critical areas should have fences at least eight feet high to provide the proper level of protection.

Fences work as "first line of defense" mechanisms, but we have a few others that can be used also. Strong and secure gates need to be implemented. It does no good to install a highly fortified and expensive fence and then have an unlocked or weenie gate that allows for easy access.

Bollards can also be used. These usually look like small concrete pillars outside a building. Sometimes companies try and dress them up by putting flowers or lights in them to soften the look of a protected building. They are placed by the sides of buildings that have the most immediate threat of someone driving a vehicle through the exterior wall. They are usually placed between the facility and a parking lot and between the facility and a road that runs close to an exterior wall. Within the United States after

PIDAS Fencing

Perimeter Intrusion Detection and Assessment System (PIDAS) is a type of fencing that has sensors on the wire mesh and at the base of the fence. It is used to detect if someone attempts to cut or climb the fence. It has a passive cable vibration sensor that sets off an alarm if an intrusion is detected. They are very sensitive and can cause many false alarms.

September 11, 2001, many military and government institutions, which did not have bollards, hauled in huge boulders to surround and protect sensitive buildings. These were not overly attractive, but gave you the sense that the government was serious about protecting those facilities.

The last line of defense, before the interior of the building is reached, is the facility walls. They need to be constructed in a manner that provides the necessary level of protection for the company. If the company sells donuts, it will most likely not need to have extra fortified walls in place because it does not have a real threat of someone attempting to bust through the walls with explosives or vehicles, unless the donuts are really good. A bank would need to have stronger walls because it would have a higher risk of robbers trying to enter the bank in this fashion.

Lighting

Lighting should be used to discourage intruders and provide safety for personnel, entrances, parking areas, and critical sections. Lighting is a physical control that provides preventive and deterrent protection. A company practices due care when it supplies the correct type of lighting for areas that could be considered dangerous. For example, if an employee were attacked in the company's parking lot, that employee could sue the company for not providing the proper security measures. If the company did not take the necessary steps to ensure a safe environment for its employees, it could be found negligent and could lose the court case. The National Institute of Standards and Technology (NIST) standard pertaining to perimeter protection states that critical areas should be illuminated eight feet high and use two foot-candles, which is a unit that represents the illumination power of an individual light.

There are several types of lights a company can choose to implement: searchlights, streetlights, floodlights, and fresnel units, which contain small lenses that can be focused.

Surveillance Devices

Usually, installing fences and installing lights does not provide the necessary level of protection a company needs to protect its facility, equipment, and employees. Areas need to be under surveillance so that improper actions are noticed and taken care of before damage occurs. Surveillance can happen through visual detection of problems or through devices that use sophisticated means of detecting abnormal behavior or unwanted conditions. Three main surveillance categories are security guards, dogs, and visual recording devices.

Patrol Force and Guards   *Don't make me put down my donut and come over there!*
One of the best security mechanisms is a security guard and/or a patrol force to monitor a facility's grounds. This type of security control is more flexible than other security mechanisms, provides good response to suspicious activities, and works as a great deterrent. However, it can be a costly endeavor, which requires a salary, benefits, and time off. People can be limited in their reliability. Screening and bonding is an important part of selecting a security guard, but this only provides a certain level of assurance.

Intrusion detection systems and physical protection measures ultimately require human intervention. Security guards can be at a fixed post or can patrol specific areas. Different organizations will have different needs from security guards. They may be required to check individual credentials and enforce filling out a sign-in log. They may be responsible for monitoring intrusion systems and expected to respond to alarms. They may need to issue and recover visitor badges, respond to fire alarms, enforce rules established by the company within the building, and control what materials can come into or go out of the environment. The guard may need to verify that doors, windows, safes, and vaults are secured; report identified safety hazards; enforce restrictions of sensitive areas; and escort individuals throughout facilities.

The security guard should have clear and decisive tasks he is expected to fulfill. The guard should be fully trained on the activities he is expected to perform and on the responses expected from him in different situations. The guard should have a central control point to check in to, two-way radios to ensure proper communication, and necessary access into the areas he is responsible to protect.

The best security has a combination of security mechanisms and does not depend on just one component of security. A security guard should be accompanied by other surveillance and detecting mechanisms.

Dogs   *We could only afford this three-legged Chihuahua. Response: Well it's scaring me. Where's its hair?* Dogs have proven to be highly useful in detecting intruders and other unwanted conditions. Their hearing and sight outperform those of humans, and their intelligence and loyalty can be used for protection.

The best security dogs go through intensive training to respond to a wide range of commands and to perform many tasks. Dogs can be trained to hold an intruder at bay until security personnel arrive or to chase an intruder and attack. Some dogs are trained to recognize smoke so that they can alert others to a fire.

Of course, dogs cannot always know the difference between an authorized person and an unauthorized person, so if someone goes into work after hours, she can have more on her hands than expected. Dogs can provide a good supplementary security mechanism, or a company can ask the security guard to bare his teeth at the sight of an unknown individual instead. Whatever works.

Visual Recording Devices   Because surveillance is based on sensory perception, surveillance devices usually work in conjunction with guards to extend their capabilities and range of perception.

Cameras can be used to take still photographic pictures, which are stored for later viewing, or a company can choose to use *closed-circuit TVs (CCTVs)*. A CCTV enables a guard to monitor many different areas at once from a centralized location.

Critical areas may need another level of protection to ensure that these areas are indeed vacant during off-hours or downtimes. The technical controls used to provide this type of protection are CCTV systems and motion detectors. CCTVs enable one person to view and monitor a large area, but require that person to sit and watch the display. This is a boring task, which puts the night security guard right to sleep. Therefore, a CCTV should be used in combination with another type of intrusion detection system. If this other type of detection system sounds an alarm, then the guard can view the CCTV to assess the situation.

Detecting

Surveillance techniques are used to watch for unusual behaviors, whereas detecting devices are used to sense changes that take place in an environment. Both are monitoring methods, but use different devices and approaches. The following sections address the types of technologies that can be used to detect the presence of an intruder. An example of a perimeter scanning device is shown in Figure 6-21.

Proximity Detection System   A proximity detector, or capacitance detector, emits a measurable magnetic field while in use. The detector monitors this electrical field, and an alarm sounds if the field is disrupted. These devices are usually used to protect specific objects (artwork, cabinets, or a safe) versus protecting a whole room or area.

Photoelectric or Photometric System   This type of system detects the change in the level of light within an area, and thus must be used in windowless rooms. These systems work like photoelectric smoke detectors, which emit a beam, and the beam is expected to hit the receiver. If this beam of light is disrupted, an alarm sounds. The beams emitted by the photoelectric cell are cross-sectional and can be invisible or visible beams. If they are visible, they may be able to be stepped over or gone under, as seen in many suspense movies.

Wave Pattern   Wave-pattern motion detectors range in the frequency of waves that they detect. The different ranges are microwave, ultrasonic, and low frequency. All of these devices generate a wave pattern that is sent over a sensitive area and reflected back to a receiver. If the patterns are returned undisturbed, the device does nothing. If the patterns return altered, then an alarm sounds.

Figure 6-21   Different perimeter scanning devices work by covering a specific area.

Passive Infrared System This type of system identifies the changes of heat waves in an area it is configured to protect. If the particles' temperatures within the air rise, it could be an indication of the presence of an intruder.

Acoustical-Seismic Detection System *Does this detect smelly people? Answer: No, noisy people.* This type of system is sensitive to sounds and vibrations and detects the changes in the noise level of an area it is placed within. These devices do not emit any waves; they only listen for sounds within an area and are considered passive devices.

The type of motion detector, its power capacity, and configurations will dictate the number needed to cover a sensitive area. Also, the size and shape of the room and the items within the room may cause barriers. More detectors would be needed to provide the necessary level of coverage.

Intrusion Detection Systems

Intrusion detection systems, or burglar alarms, are used to detect unauthorized entries and to alert a responsible entity to respond. These systems can monitor entries, doors, windows, devices, or removable coverings of equipment. Many work with magnetic contacts or vibration-detection devices that are sensitive to certain types of changes in the environment. When a change is detected, an alarm is sounded either in the local area, or in both the local area and to a remote police or guard station.

The most popular types of intrusion detection systems in use today are the electromechanical types that detect a change or break in a circuit. The electrical circuits can be strips of foil embedded or connected to windows. If the window breaks, the foil strip breaks, which sounds an alarm. Vibration detectors can detect movement on walls, screens, ceilings, and floors when the fine wires embedded within the structure are broken. Magnetic contact switches can be installed on windows and doors. If the contacts are separated because the window or door is opened, an alarm will sound.

What is the difference among a proximity detector, seismic detector, vibration detector, and intrusion detector? Vibration and seismic detectors both sense vibration or movement, interpret this as a physical attack, and sound an alarm. A proximity detector can sense an object or individual entering a protected area, perceive that as an attack, and sound an alarm. An intrusion detection system is configured to detect an individual or an object crossing a line or entering an area, and then initiates an alarm.

Motion detectors, light beams, and vibration sensors are expensive to install and monitor. If an alarm is sounded, it requires a human response. The devices are prone to activating alarms in situations that do not include intruders or any penetration attempts. These detection devices can be penetrated and are not expected to provide all necessary security for a facility.

Fire, intrusion, and motion detectors do not usually exist separately, but are part of an alarm system. All alarm systems require constant electrical power, and intruders often try to get around the systems by eliminating their electrical source. The system has to be sensitive to tampering and sound an alarm if tampering is detected. The alarms need to have a direct current power source and emergency backup power sources.

Doorways

Entry doors into a facility, or specific areas, should be able to resist forced entry attempts. When determining which type of door to purchase and implement, the level of security required and the level of risk that will be accepted needs to be weighed. Reinforced strike plates and doorframes may be required as well as tamper-resistant hinges, shatterproof vision plates, and alarms that are trigged during forced entry.

If possible, all doors to storage rooms, service areas, equipment rooms, and secured areas should look alike so that the secured areas do not call attention to themselves. Each door should be self-closing and should not contain a hold-open feature. It is preferable to have a sensor built into the doorframe to indicate when a door did not close or has been open for an extended period.

Stationary and revolving doors can be used as physical access control mechanisms. They are used in *mantraps* and *turnstiles* so that unauthorized individuals entering a facility cannot get out if it is activated. A mantrap is a small room with two doors. The first door is locked; a person is identified and authenticated by a security guard, biometric system, smart card reader, or swipe card reader. Once the person is authenticated and access is authorized, the first door opens and allows the person into the mantrap. The first door locks and the person is trapped. The person must be authenticated again before the second door unlocks and allows him into the facility. Figure 6-22 illustrates the function of mantraps. Some mantraps use biometric systems that weigh the person who enters.

Mantrap

People have to go through an area
with two doors so a guard can
check credentials.

Figure 6-22   Mantraps are used in highly secured areas and enable security guards to activate and
restrain an individual in a closed area if necessary.

They are trying to make sure that only one person at a time is trying to enter. This is a control to counter piggybacking.

Doorways with automatic locks can be configured to be fail-secure or fail-safe. A *fail-safe* setting means that if there were a power disruption, which would affect the automated locking system, the doors would default to being unlocked. A *fail-secure* configuration means that a door would default to being locked if there were any problems with the power. A company needs to decide which is best for its needs.

Auditing Physical Access

Physical access control systems can use software and auditing features to produce audit trails pertaining to access attempts. The following information should be logged and reviewed:

- Date and time of access attempt
- Entry point in which access was attempted
- User ID used when access was attempted
- Unsuccessful access attempts, especially if during unauthorized hours

As with audit logs produced by computers, access logs are useless unless someone actually reviews them. A security guard may be required to review these logs, but a security professional or a facility manager should also review these logs periodically. It is important that management knows where entry points into the facility exist and who attempts to use them.

Audit and access logs are detective, not preventive. They are used to piece together a situation after the fact instead of attempting to prevent an access attempt in the first place.

Summary

Our distributed networks have put much more responsibility on the individual user, network personnel, and administrative procedures and controls than in the old mainframe days. Physical security is not carried out just with the night guard who carries around a big flashlight. Now security, if extremely technical, comes in many forms and raises many liability and legal issues. Natural disasters, fires, floods, intruders, vandals, environmental issues, construction materials, and power supplies all need to be planned for and dealt with.

Physical security is not often thought about when people think of security, but real threats and risks need to be addressed and planned for. Who cares if a hacker can get through an open port on the Web server if the building is burning down?

References

Internet/Network Security: **netsecurity.about.com/library/weekly/aa020501a.htm**

Resources Relating to Locks, Safes, and Security: **security.org/dial-80/links.htm**

FIPS Publications Series: **www.itl.nist.gov/fipspubs/0-toc.htm**

Quick Tips

- Physical security is usually the first line of defense against environmental risks and unpredictable human behavior.

- The value of property within the facility and the value of the facility itself need to be ascertained to determine the proper budget for physical security so that security controls can be cost effective.

- Automated environmental controls help minimize the resulting damage and speed the recovery process. Manual controls can be time-consuming, error prone, and require constant attention.

- Physical construction materials and structure composition need to be evaluated for their protective characteristics, their utility, and their costs and benefits.

- Some physical security controls may conflict with the safety of people. These issues need to be addressed; human life is always more important than protecting a facility or the assets it contains.

- When looking at locations for a facility, consider local crime, natural disaster possibilities, and distance to hospitals, police and fire stations, airports, and railroads.

- HVAC should maintain the appropriate temperature and humidity levels, provide closed-loop recirculating air-conditioning, and positive pressurization and ventilation.

- Devices have mean time between failure (MTBF) and mean time to repair (MTTR). These values should be used to determine the total cost of repair and maintenance of the device and of actions necessary to provide uninterrupted service.

- High humidity can cause corrosion, and low humidity can cause static electricity.

- Dust and other air contaminants may adversely affect computer hardware, and should be kept to acceptable levels.

- Administrative controls include drills and exercises of emergency procedures, simulation testing, documentation, inspections and reports, pre-screening of employees, post-employment procedures, delegation of responsibility and rotation of duties, and security awareness training.

- Emergency procedure documentation should be readily available and periodically reviewed and updated.

- Proximity identification devices can be user activated (meaning action needs to be taken by a user) or system sensing (meaning no action needs to be taken by the user).

- A transponder is a proximity identification device that does not require action by the user. The reader transmits signals to the device, and the device responds with an access code.

- Exterior fencing can be costly and unsightly, but can provide crowd control and help control access to the facility.

- Interior partitions may not go all the way up to the ceiling; therefore, an intruder can remove a ceiling tile and climb over the partition into a critical portion of the facility.

- Physical access controls restrict the entry and exit of personnel.

- Intrusion detection devices can be motion detectors, CCTVs, vibration sensors, and/or light beams.

- Intrusion detection devices can be penetrated, are expensive to install and monitor, require human response, and are subject to false alarms.

- CCTV enables one person to monitor a large area, but should be coupled with alerting functions to ensure proper response.

- Security guards are expensive but provide flexibility in response to security breaches and can deter intruders from attempting an attack.

- A cipher lock uses a keypad access control and is programmable.

- Company property should be marked as such, and security guards should be trained how to identify when these items leave the facility in an improper manner.

- Media should be protected from destruction, modification, theft, unauthorized copying, and disclosure.

- Floors, ceilings, and walls need to be able to hold the necessary load and provide the required fire rating.

- Water, steam, and gas lines need to have shutoff valves and positive drains (substance flows out instead of in).

- The threats in physical security are interruption to services, theft, physical damage, unauthorized disclosure, and loss of system integrity.

- Primary power source is what is used in day-to-day operations, and alternate power source is a backup in case the primary source fails.

- Power spike is momentary high voltage, power surge is prolonged high voltage, power fault is a momentary power out, a blackout is a prolonged loss of power, power sag is a momentary low voltage, and a brownout is a prolonged power supply that is below normal voltage.

- Power companies usually plan and implement brownouts when they are experiencing high demand.

- Power noise is a disturbance of power and can be caused by electromagnetic interference (EMI) or radio frequency interference (RFI).

- EMI can be caused by lightning, motors, and the current difference between wires. RFI can be caused by electrical system mechanisms, fluorescent lighting, and electrical cables.

- Power transient noise is the disturbance imposed on a power line, which causes electrical interference.

- Power regulators condition the line to keep voltage steady and clean.

- UPS cost factors are the size of the electrical load it can support, the speed with which it can assume the load when the primary source fails, and the time it can support the load.

- Shielded lines protect from electrical and magnetic induction, which causes interference to the power voltage.

- Perimeter protection is used to deter trespassing and to enable people to enter a facility through a few controlled entrances.

- Fire detectors should be located on and above suspended ceilings, below raised floors, and in air ducts to provide maximum fire detection.

- There are four fire classes: A = common combustibles (suppress with soda acid or water), B = liquids (suppress with Halon, soda acid, or CO_2), C = electrical (suppress with Halon or CO_2), and D = combustible metals (suppress with dry powder).

- A fire needs high temperatures, oxygen, and fuel. To suppress it, one or more of those items needs to be reduced or eliminated.

- Gases, like Halon and FM-200 and other Halon substitutes, interfere with the chemical reaction of a fire.

- HVAC should be turned off before activation of a fire suppressant to ensure that it stays in the needed area and smoke is not distributed to different areas of the facility.

- Portable fire extinguishers should be located within 50 feet of electrical equipment and should be inspected quarterly.

- CO_2 is a colorless, odorless, and potentially lethal substance because it removes the oxygen from the air to suppress fires.

- Piggybacking, when unauthorized access is achieved to a facility via another individual's legitimate access, is a common concern with physical security.

- Halon is no longer available because it depletes the ozone. FM-200 or other similar substances are used instead of Halon.

- Proximity systems (motion detectors, vibration sensors, and light beams) require human response, can cause false alarms, and depend on a constant power supply, so these protection systems should be backed up by other types of security systems.

- Dry pipe systems reduce the accidental discharge of water because the water does not enter the pipes until an automatic fire sensor indicates that there is an actual fire.

- In locations with freezing temperatures where broken pipes cause problems, dry pipes should be used.

- A preaction pipe sounds an alarm and delays water release. A wet pipe releases water at a set temperature and does not delay water release.

Questions

Please remember that these questions are formatted and asked in a certain way for a reason. You must remember that the CISSP exam is asking questions at a conceptual level. Questions may not always have the perfect answer, and the candidate is advised against always looking for the perfect answer. The candidate should look for the best answer in the list.

1. What is the first step that should be done when a fire has been detected?

    A. Turn off the HVAC system and activate fire door releases.

    B. Determine which type of fire it is.

    C. Advise individuals within the building to leave.

    D. Activate fire suppression system.

2. Which of the following items does not provide physical protection?

    A. Smart card

    B. Token

    C. Biometric device

    D. Single sign-on system

3. When should a Class C fire extinguisher be used instead of a Class A?

    A. When electrical equipment is on fire

    B. When wood and paper are on fire

    C. When a combustible liquid is on fire

    D. When the fire is in an open area

4. Which is not a preventive physical security control?

    A. Fences

    B. Locks

    C. Security guard

    D. Access and audit log

5. How does Halon fight fires?

   A. It reduces the fire's fuel intake.

   B. It reduces the temperature of the area and cools the fire out.

   C. It disrupts the chemical reactions of a fire.

   D. It reduces the oxygen in the area.

6. What is a mantrap?

   A. A trusted security domain

   B. A logical access control mechanism

   C. A double-door facility used for physical access control

   D. A fire suppression device

7. What is true about a transponder?

   A. It is a card that can be read without sliding it through a card reader.

   B. It is a passive proximity device.

   C. It is a card that a user swipes through a card reader to gain access to a facility.

   D. It exchanges tokens with an authentication server.

8. When is a security guard the best choice for a physical access control mechanism?

   A. When discriminating judgment is required

   B. When intrusion detection is required

   C. When the security budget is low

   D. When access controls are in place

9. Critical areas should have illumination of _____.

   A. Three foot-candles and eight feet in height

   B. Two foot-candles and eight feet in height

   C. Three foot-candles and six feet in height

   D. Two foot-candles and six feet in height

10. What is a common problem with vibration-detection devices used for perimeter security?

   A. They can be defeated by emitting the right electrical signals in the protected area.

   B. The power source is easily disabled.

   C. They cause false alarms by things that do not threaten the environment.

   D. They interfere with computing devices.

11. What is the optimal temperature for a room that contains systems that perform data processing?

    A. 70 to 74 degrees Fahrenheit

    B. 65 to 70 degrees Fahrenheit

    C. 70 to 75 degrees Fahrenheit

    D. 60 to 65 degrees Fahrenheit

12. What is the relative humidity for an area to conduct safe data processing?

    A. 30 to 40 percent

    B. 50 to 60 percent

    C. 50 to 55 percent

    D. 45 to 60 percent

13. What are the problems from humidity in an area with electrical devices?

    A. High humidity causes excess electricity, and low humidity causes corrosion.

    B. High humidity causes corrosion, and low humidity causes static electricity.

    C. High humidity causes power fluctuations, and low humidity causes static electricity.

    D. High humidity causes corrosion, and low humidity causes power fluctuations.

14. What does positive pressurization pertaining to ventilation mean?

    A. When a door opens, the air comes in.

    B. When a fire takes place, the power supply is disabled.

    C. When a fire takes place, the smoke is diverted to one room.

    D. When a door opens, the air goes out.

15. When deciding on a location to build a facility, which item is not as important as the rest?

    A. Possibility of natural disasters

    B. Crime rate

    C. Proximity to library

    D. Proximity to fire station

16. Which is not an administrative control pertaining to emergency procedures?

    A. Intrusion detection systems

    B. Awareness and training

    C. Drills and inspections

    D. Delegation of duties

17. If an access control has a fail-safe characteristic and not a fail-secure characteristic, what does that mean?

    A. It defaults to no access.

    B. It defaults to being unlocked.

    C. It defaults to being locked.

    D. It defaults to sounding a remote alarm instead of a local alarm.

18. Which of the following is not a type of badge that is processed by a reader?

    A. Voice print

    B. Proximity cards

    C. Cards with embedded wire

    D. Cards with magnetic dots

19. What are the two general types of proximity identification devices?

    A. Biometric devices and access control devices

    B. Swipe card devices and passive devices

    C. Preset code devices and wireless devices

    D. User-activated devices and system sensing devices

20. Which type of device uses radio waves to communicate with an individual's access control badge?

    A. Biometric device

    B. User-activated proximity device

    C. Fail-safe device

    D. Transponder

21. Which item is not an intrusion detection mechanism?

    A. Vibration sensor

    B. CCTV

    C. Fresnel unit

    D. Motion detector

22. Which is not a drawback to installing intrusion detection and monitoring systems?

    A. Expensive to install

    B. Cannot be penetrated

    C. Requires human response

    D. Subject to false alarms

23. What is a cipher lock?

    A. A lock that uses cryptographic keys

    B. A lock that uses a type of key that cannot be reproduced

    C. A lock that uses a token and perimeter reader

    D. A lock that uses a keypad

24. If a cipher lock has a door delay option, what does that mean?

    A. After a door is open for a specific period, the alarm goes off.

    B. It can only be opened during emergency situations.

    C. It has a hostage alarm capability.

    D. It has supervisory override capability.

25. Which of the following has not increased user responsibility pertaining to computer and information security?

    A. We have moved from a central administration model to a distributed network.

    B. Information has decreased in value.

    C. A network can be spread across different facilities, states, or countries, which makes it harder to enforce strict security.

    D. Network devices have taken on a lot of forms, such as handheld computers, personal computers, and remote dial-in devices.

Answers

1. **C.** Human life takes precedence. Although the other answers are important steps in this type of situation, the first step is to warn others to save as many lives as possible.

2. **D.** Each of the other answers contains technologies or devices that can be used for identification and authorization purposes for access control into a facility or sensitive area. Single sign-on technologies are used to logically control users' access to network resources, which does not fall under the physical security umbrella.

3. **A.** A Class C is an electrical fire. Thus, an extinguisher with the proper suppression agent should be used. The following table shows the fire types, their attributes, and suppression methods:

Fire Class	Type of Fire	Elements of Fire	Suppression Method
A	Common combustibles	Wood products, paper, and laminates	Water or soda acid
B	Liquid	Petroleum products and coolants	Gas (Halon), CO_2, or soda acid

Fire Class	Type of Fire	Elements of Fire	Suppression Method
C	Electrical	Electrical equipment and wires	Gas (Halon) or CO_2
D	Combustible Metals	Magnesium, sodium, potassium	Dry powder

4. **D.** Any type of logging or auditing is considered a detective control, because these items are mainly reviewed after something takes place. The other answers contain items that are put into place to prevent some type of security compromise. Logs and audits are not considered components that can be used to prevent a compromise from occurring.

5. **C.** Halon is a type of gas that is used to interfere with the chemical reactions between the elements of a fire. A fire requires fuel, oxygen, high temperatures, and chemical reactions to burn properly. Different suppressant agents have been developed to attack each aspect of a fire: CO_2 displaces the oxygen, water reduces the temperature, and soda acid removes the fuel.

6. **C.** A mantrap is a small room with two doors. The first door is locked; a person is identified and authenticated by a security guard, biometric system, smart card reader, or swipe card reader. Once the person is authenticated and access is authorized, the first door opens and allows the person into the mantrap. The first door locks and the person is trapped. The person must be authenticated again before the second door unlocks and allows him into the facility.

7. **A.** A transponder is a type of physical access control device that does not require the user to slide a card through a reader. The reader and card communicate directly. The card and reader have a receiver, transmitter, and battery. The reader sends signals to the card to request information. The card sends the reader an access code.

8. **A.** Although many effective physical security mechanisms are on the market today, none can look at a situation and make a judgment about it and make a decision on what the next step should be. A security guard is employed when a company needs to have a countermeasure that can think and make decisions in different scenarios.

9. **B.** Critical areas should have proper lighting to protect employees and customers. If the necessary lighting is not in place, the company can be found negligent and successfully sued. The proper lighting is to have lights that provide two foot-candle power and 8 feet in height.

10. **C.** This type of system is sensitive to sounds and vibrations and detects the changes in the noise level of an area it is placed within. This level of sensitivity can cause many false alarms. These devices do not emit any waves; they only listen for sounds within an area and are considered passive devices.

11. **A.** Lower temperatures can cause mechanisms to slow or stop, and higher temperatures can cause devices to use too much fan power and eventually shut down. The temperature of an area containing computing devices should fall into the range of 70 to 74 degrees Fahrenheit.

12. **D.** Relative humidity between 45 and 60 percent is acceptable for areas that are processing data.

13. **B.** High humidity can cause corrosion, and low humidity can cause excessive static electricity. Static electricity can short out devices or cause loss of information.

14. **D.** Positive pressurization means that when someone opens a door, the air goes out and outside air does not come in. If a facility were on fire and the doors were opened, positive pressure would cause the smoke to go out instead of being pushed back into the building.

15. **C.** The following items should be reviewed when deciding upon the proper location of a new facility:

Surrounding area and external entities:

- Crime rate
- Proximity to police, medical, and fire stations
- Possible hazards from surrounding area

Accessibility:

- Road access
- Excessive traffic
- Proximity to airports, train stations, and highways

Natural disasters:

- Likelihood of floods, tornadoes, earthquakes, or hurricanes
- Hazardous terrain (mudslides, falling rock from mountains, or excessive snow or rainfall)

16. **A.** Awareness and training, drills and inspections, and delegation of duties are all items that have a direct correlation to proper emergency procedures. It is management's responsibility that these items are in place, properly tested, and carried out. Intrusion detection systems are technical controls.

17. **B.** A fail-safe setting means that if there were a power disruption that would affect the automated locking system, the doors would default to being unlocked. A fail-secure configuration means that a door would default to being locked if there were any problems with the power.

18. **A.** The other answers contain types of proximity cards that must be put through some type of reader to be read and their information interpreted. All cards require some type of reader to interact with. A voice print biometric system is not a badge reader.

19. **D.** A user activated system requires the user to do something: swipe the card through the reader and/or enter a code. A system sensing device will recognize the presence of the card and communicate with it without the user needing to carry out any activity.

20. **D.** A transponder is a proximity identification device that does not require action by the user. The reader transmits signals to the card, and the card responds with an access code.

21. **C.** The other answers contain technologies that are used to detect intruders. Fresnel units are types of lights that contain small lenses that can be focused.

22. **B.** Monitoring and intrusion detection systems are expensive, they require someone to respond when they set off an alarm, and because of their level of sensitivity can cause several false alarms. Like any other type of technology or device, they have their own vulnerabilities that can be exploited and penetrated.

23. **D.** Cipher locks, also known as programmable locks, use keypads to control access into an area or facility. The lock can require a specific combination to be entered into the keypad and a swipe card.

24. **A.** A security guard would want to be alerted when a door has been open for an extended period. It may be an indication that something other than a person coming in and out of the door is taking place. A security system can have a threshold set so that if the door is open past this period, an alarm sounds.

25. **B.** Security has become a much more complex beast to implement and maintain. This is because of the increased complexity of our computing environments, which have become widely distributed, and the many types of computing devices that are continually added to these environments. Because it is very hard for one person or one department to ensure the overall security of these types of environments, more need for user responsibility has evolved.

Telecommunications and Networking Security

In this chapter, you will learn about the following items:

- OSI model
- TCP/IP and many other protocols
- LAN, WAN, and MAN technologies
- Cabling and data transmission types
- Network devices and services
- Intranets and extranets
- Telecommunication devices
- Remote access methods and technologies
- Resource availability
- Wireless technologies

Telecommunications and networking use various mechanisms, devices, software, and protocols that are interrelated and integrated. Networking is one of the more complex topics in the computer field, mainly because so many things are involved. A network administrator or engineer must know how to configure networking software, protocols and services, and devices; deal with interoperability issues; install, configure, and interface with telecommunication software and devices; and troubleshoot effectively. A security professional must understand these issues and be able to look into and understand these same topics a few levels deeper to understand fully where vulnerabilities can arise within networks. This can be an overwhelming and challenging task. However, if you are someone who enjoys challenges and appreciates the intricacies of technology, then maintaining security and networking infrastructures may be more fun than work.

A security professional cannot advise others on how to secure an environment if he does not fully understand it in the first place. Securing an application that contains a buffer overflow, for example, means that the person understands what a buffer overflow is, what the outcome of exploiting it is, how to identify a buffer overflow properly, and possibly how to write program code to remove this weakness from the program. Securing a network architecture means that the person understands the various networking platforms involved, network devices, and how data flows through a network. This person must know how many protocols work, their purposes, their interactions with other protocols, how the protocols can provide exploitable vulnerabilities, and how to choose and implement the appropriate types of protocols in a given environment. The security professional must also understand the different types of firewalls, routers, switches, and bridges and when one is more appropriate than the other, where they are to be placed, their interactions with other devices, and the degree of security each provides.

The many different types of devices, protocols, and security mechanisms within an environment provide different functionality, but they also provide a layered approach to security. Layers within security are important, so that if an attacker is able to bypass one layer, another layer stands in the way to protect the internal network. Many networks have routers, firewalls, intrusion detection systems (IDSs), antivirus software, and more. Each specializes in a certain piece of security, but they all should work in concert to provide a layered approach to security.

Although networking and telecommunications are complicated topics to understand, it is that complexity that makes it the most fun for those who truly enjoy these fields. However, complexity can be the enemy of security. It is important to understand the components within an environment and their relationships to other components that make up the environment as a whole. This chapter addresses many of the telecommunication and networking aspects that are included in many networks.

Telecommunications and Network Security

Telecommunication is the electrical transmission of data among systems, whether through analog, digital, or wireless transmission types. The data can flow across copper wires, coaxial cable, fiber, or airwaves, which may be a network cable within a company's infrastructure, the telephone company's public-switched telephone network (PSTN), or a service provider's fiber cables, switches, and routers. Definitive lines are drawn between the media used for transmission, technologies, protocols, and whose equipment is being used. However, the definitive lines get blurry when one follows how data that is created on a user's workstation flows through a complex path of Ethernet cables, to a router that divides the company's network and the rest of the world, through the Asynchronous Transfer Mode (ATM) switch provided by the service provider, to the many switches the packets transverse throughout the ATM cloud, on to another company's network, through its router, and to another user's workstation within seconds. Each piece is interesting, but when they all integrate and work together, it is awesome.

Telecommunications usually refers to telephone systems, service providers, and carrier services. Most telecommunication systems are regulated by governments and international organizations. In the United States, telecommunication systems are regulated by the Federal Communications Commission (FCC), which affects voice and data transmissions. Globally, organizations develop policies, recommend standards, and work together to provide standardization and the capability of proper interactions among different technologies.

The main standards organizations are the International Telecommunication Union (ITU) and the International Standards Organization (ISO). Their models and standards have shaped our technology today, and the technological issues governed by these organizations are addressed throughout this chapter.

NOTE Do not get overwhelmed with the size of this chapter and the amount of information within it. This chapter, as well as the others, attempts to teach you the concepts and meanings behind the definitions and answers you will need for the CISSP exam. This book is not intended to give you one-liners to remember for the exam, but it teaches you the meaning behind the answers. The "Quick Tips" section at the end of the chapter and the questions help you zero-in on the most important concepts for the exam itself.

Open System Interconnect Model

I don't understand what all of these protocols are doing. Response: Okay, let's make a model to explain it then.

The Open System Interconnect (OSI) is a worldwide federation that works to provide international standards. In the early 1980s, it worked to develop a protocol set that would be used by all vendors throughout the world to allow the interconnection of network devices. This movement was fueled with the hopes of ensuring that all vendor products and technologies could communicate and interact across country and technical boundaries. The actual protocol set did not catch on as a standard, but the model of this protocol set was adopted and is used as an abstract framework to which most applications and protocols adhere.

Many people think that the OSI model arrived at the beginning of the computing age as we know it and helped shape and provide direction for many if not all technologies. However, this is not true. It was, in fact, developed only in the 1980s and introduced in 1984, and the basics of the Internet had already been developed and implemented and the basic Internet protocols had been in use for many years. The Transmission Control Protocol/Internet Protocol (TCP/IP) protocol suite actually has its own model that is often used today when examining and understanding networking issues. Figure 7-1 shows the differences between the OSI and TCP/IP networking models. In this chapter, we will focus more on the OSI model.

 NOTE The host-to-host layer is sometimes called the transport layer in the TCP/IP model.

Protocol

A network *protocol* is a standard set of rules that determine how systems will communicate across networks. Two different systems can communicate and understand each other because they use the same protocols in spite of their differences. It is the same when two people communicate and can understand each other because they are using the same language.

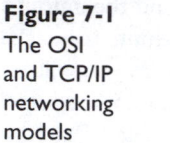

Figure 7-1
The OSI
and TCP/IP
networking
models

The OSI model does provide important guidelines that are used by vendors, engineers, developers, and others. The model segments the networking tasks, protocols, and services into different layers. Each layer has its own responsibilities when it comes to how two computers communicate over a network. Each layer has certain functionalities, and the services and protocols that work within that layer fulfill them.

The OSI model's goal is to help others develop products that will work within an open network architecture. In an *open network* architecture, no one vendor owns it, it is not proprietary, and it can easily integrate various technologies and vendor implementations of those technologies. Vendors have used the OSI as a jumping-off point for developing their own networking frameworks. These vendors used the OSI model as a blueprint and developed their own protocols and interfaces to produce functionality that is different or that overlaps that of other vendors. However, because these vendors use the OSI model as their starting place, integration of other vendor products is an easier task, and the interoperability issues are less burdensome than if the vendors developed their own networking framework from scratch.

Although computers communicate in a physical sense (electronic signals are passed from one computer over a wire to the other computer), they also communicate through logical channels. Each protocol at a specific OSI layer communicates with a protocol that operates at the same OSI layer on another computer. This happens through *encapsulation*. Here's how encapsulation works: A message is constructed at the application layer and then passed down through the protocol's stack. Each layer adds its own information to the message; thus, the message grows in size as it goes down the protocol stack. The message is then sent to the destination computer, and the encapsulation is reversed by taking the message apart through the same steps as the source computer that encapsulated it. At the data link layer, only the information pertaining to the data link layer is extracted, and the message is sent up to the next layer. Then at the network layer, only the network layer data is stripped and processed and the message is again passed up to the next layer. This is how computers communicate logically. Each layer adds its own information to the packet, and then each layer at the destination computer takes only information that pertains to it. The information stripped off at the destination computer informs it how to interpret and process the packet properly. Data encapsulation is shown in Figure 7-2.

Logical Data Movement

Application	→ ←	Application
Presentation		Presentation
Session	→ ←	Session
Transport		Transport
Network	→ ←	Network
Data Link		Data Link
Physical		Physical

Each layer has specific responsibilities and control functions that it performs and data format syntaxes that it expects. The benefit of modularizing these layers, and the functionality within each layer, is that various technologies, protocols, and services can interact with each other and provide the proper interfaces to enable communications. This means that a computer can use an application developed by Adobe, a transport protocol developed by Cisco, and a data link protocol developed by 3COM to construct and send a message over the network. The protocols, technologies, and computers that

Figure 7-2
Each OSI layer adds its own information to the data packet.

Data Encapsulation

operate within the OSI layer are considered *open systems*. Open systems are capable of communicating with other open systems because they implement international standard protocols and interfaces.

OSI Model

Application
Presentation
Session
Transport
Network
Data Link
Physical

Understanding the functionalities that take place at each OSI layer and the corresponding protocols that work at those layers helps you to understand the overall communication process between computers. Once you understand this process, a more detailed look at each protocol will show you the full range of options each protocol provides and the security weaknesses embedded into each of those options.

Application Layer

Hand me your information. I will take it from here.

The *application layer*, layer 7, works closest to the user and provides file transmissions, message exchanges, terminal sessions, and much more. This layer does not include the actual applications but includes the protocols that support the applications. When an application needs to send data over the network, it passes instructions and the data to the protocols that support it at the application layer. This layer processes and properly formats the data and passes it down to the next layer within the OSI model. This happens until the data that the application layer constructed contains the essential information from each layer necessary to transmit data over the network. The data is then put on the network cable and is transmitted until it arrives at the destination computer.

Some examples of the protocols working at this layer are the Simple Mail Transfer Protocol (SMTP), Hypertext Transfer Protocol (HTTP), Line Printer Daemon (LPD), File Transfer Protocol (FTP), Telnet, and Trivial File Transfer Protocol (TFTP). Figure 7-3 shows how applications communicate with the underlying protocols through application program interfaces (APIs). If a user makes a request to send an e-mail through her e-mail client Outlook, the e-mail client sends this information to SMTP. SMTP will add its information to the user's information and pass it down to the presentation layer.

Figure 7-3

Applications
send requests
to an API, which
is the doorway
to the supporting
protocol.

Presentation Layer

You will now be transformed into something that everyone can understand.

The *presentation layer*, layer 6, receives information from the application layer protocols and puts it into a format that all computers following the OSI model can understand. This layer provides a common means of representing data in a structure that can be properly processed by the end system. This means that when a user constructs a Word document and sends it out to several people, it does not matter whether the receiving computer is a Macintosh, Windows 98, Windows NT 3.51, or Unix computer; each of these computers will be able to receive this file and understand and present it to its user as a document. It is the data representation processing that is done at the presentation layer that enables this to take place. For example, when a Windows 98 computer receives a file from another computer system, information within the file's header explains what type of file it is. The Windows 98 operating system has a list of file types it understands and a table describing what program should be used to open and manipulate each of these file types. For example, the sender could create a Word file in Word 2000, while the receiver uses WordStar. The receiver can open this file because the presentation layer on the sender's system converted the file to American Standard Code for Information Interchange (ASCII), and the receiver's computer knows that it opens these types of files with its word processor, WordStar.

The presentation layer is not concerned with the meaning of data, but with the syntax and format of that data. It works as a translator, which translates the format an application is using to a standard format used for passing messages over a network. If a user uses a Corel application to save a graphic, for example, the presentation layer would convert the graphic into a Tagged Image File Format (TIFF), Graphic Interchange Format (GIF), or Joint Photographic Experts Group (JPEG) format. This way, if the user sends this graphic to another user who does not have the Corel application, the user's operating system can still present the graphic because it has been saved into a standard format. Figure 7-4 shows how the presentation layer can convert a file into different standard file types.

This layer also handles data compression and encryption. If a program at the application layer requests a certain file to be compressed and encrypted before being transferred over the network, the presentation layer is the place where this functionality is actually carried out. Instructions are added to the data package that tells the receiving system how to decrypt or decompress the data properly.

Figure 7-4
The presentation layer receives data from the application layer and puts it into a standard format.

Session Layer

When two applications need to communicate, or transfer information, a connection session may need to be set up between them. The *session layer*, layer 5, is responsible for establishing a connection between the two applications, maintaining it during the transferring of data, and controlling the release of this connection. A good analogy for the functionality within this layer is a telephone conversation. When Kandy wants to call a friend, she uses the telephone. The telephone circuitry sets up the connection over the telephone lines and maintains that communication path, and when Kandy hangs up, it releases all the resources it was using to keep that connection open.

Similar to how telephone circuitry works, the session layer works in three phases: connection establishment, data transfer, and connection release. It provides session restart and recovery if necessary and provides the overall maintenance of the session. When the conversation is over, this path is broken down and all parameters are set back to their original settings. This process is known as *dialog management*. Figure 7-5 depicts the three phases of a session. Some protocols that work at this layer are Network File System (NFS), Structured Query Language (SQL), and remote procedure call (RPC).

The session layer protocol can enable communication between two applications to happen in three different modes:

- **Simplex**   Communication takes place in one direction.
- **Half-duplex**   Communication takes place in both directions, but only one application can send information at a time.
- **Full-duplex**   Communication takes place in both directions, and both applications can send information at the same time.

Transport Layer

How do I know if I lose a piece of the message? Answer: The transport layer will fix it for you.

When two computers are going to communicate, they might first agree on how much information each computer will send at a time, how to verify the integrity of the data once it is received, and how to determine whether a packet was lost along the way. The two computers agree on these parameters through a handshaking process at the *transport layer*, layer 4. The agreement on these issues before transferring data helps provide more reliable data transfer, error detection and correction, and flow control, and it optimizes the network ser-

Figure 7-5
The session layer sets up the connection, maintains it, and tears it down once communication is completed.

Session Layer

Connection Establishment

Data Transfer

Connection Release

vices needed to perform these tasks. The transport layer provides end-to-end data transport services and establishes the logical connection between two communicating computers.

The functionality of the session and transport layers may sound similar. They are both setting up some type of session or virtual connection for communication to take place. But the difference is that protocols that work at the session layer are setting up connections between *applications* and protocols that work at the transport layer are setting up connections between *computer systems*. For example, we can have three different applications on computer A communicating to three applications on computer B. The session layer protocols will keep track of these different sessions. You can think of the transport protocol as the bus. It does not know or care what applications are communicating to each other; it just provides the mechanism to get the data from one system to another.

The transport layer receives data from many different applications and assembles the data into a stream so that it can be properly transmitted over the network. If data needs to be multiplexed, it happens at this layer. The protocols that work at this layer are TCP, User Datagram Protocol (UDP), and Sequenced Packet Exchange (SPX). Information is passed down from different entities at higher layers to the transport layer, which must assemble the information into a stream, as shown in Figure 7-6. The stream is made up of the various data segments passed to it. Just like a bus can carry a variety of people, the transport layer protocol can carry a variety of types of application data.

Figure 7-6
TCP formats data from applications into a stream to be prepared for transmission

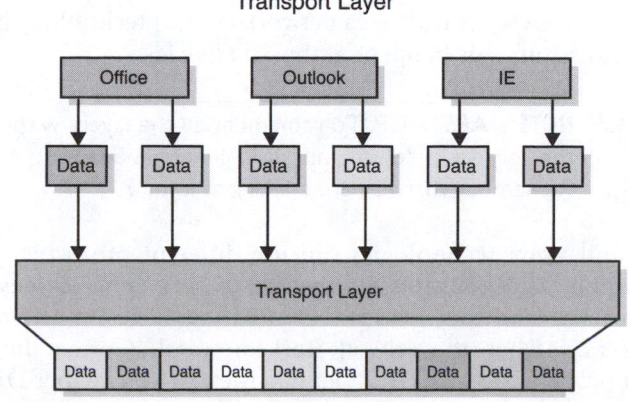

Transport Layer

Office   Outlook   IE

Data Data   Data Data   Data Data

Transport Layer

Data | Data | Data | Data | Data | Data | Data | Data | Data | Data

Assemble Data into a Stream

NOTE Different references can place specific protocols at different layers. For example, many references place the Secure Sockets Layer (SSL) protocol in the session layer, while other documents place it in the transport layer. It is not that one is right or wrong. The OSI model is trying to draw boxes around reality, but some protocols straddle the different layers. SSL is made up of two protocols—one works in the lower portion of the session layer and the other works in the transport layer. For our purposes in the CISSP exam, SSL resides in the transport layer.

Network Layer

Many roads lead to Rome.

The main responsibility of the *network layer*, layer 3, is to insert information into the packet's header so that it can be properly routed. In a network, many routes can lead to one destination. The protocols at the network layer must determine the best path for the packet to take. Routing protocols build and maintain their routing tables at this layer. These tables are maps of the network, and when a packet needs to be sent from computer A to computer M, the protocols check the network table, add the necessary information to the packet's header, and send it on its way.

The protocols that work at this layer do not ensure the delivery of the packets. They depend on the protocols at the transport layer to catch any problems and resend packets if necessary. IP is the main protocol working at the network layer, although other routing and routed protocols work there as well. The other protocols are the Internet Control Message Protocol (ICMP), Routing Information Protocol (RIP), Open Shortest Path First (OSPF), Border Gateway Protocol (BGP), and Internet Group Management Protocol (IGMP). Figure 7-7 shows that a packet can take many routes and that the network layer enters routing information into the header to help the packet arrive at its destination.

Data Link Layer

Can you translate that message into bits for me? That is all I really understand.

As we continue down the protocol stack, we are getting closer to the actual network wire over which all this data will travel. The outer format of the data packet changes slightly at each layer, and it comes to a point where it needs to be translated into local area network (LAN) or wide area network (WAN) technology binary format for proper line transmission. This happens at the *data link layer*.

NOTE APSTNDP: To remember all the layers within the OSI model in the correct order, memorize "All People Seem To Need Data Processing." Remember that you are starting at layer 7.

LAN and WAN technologies can use different protocols, network interface cards (NICs), cables, and transmission methods. These technologies have different data format structures, and they interpret electricity voltages in different ways. The *data link layer*, layer 2, is where the Network Stack knows what format the data frame must be in to transmit properly over Token Ring, Ethernet, ATM, or Fiber Distributed Data Interface

Network Layer

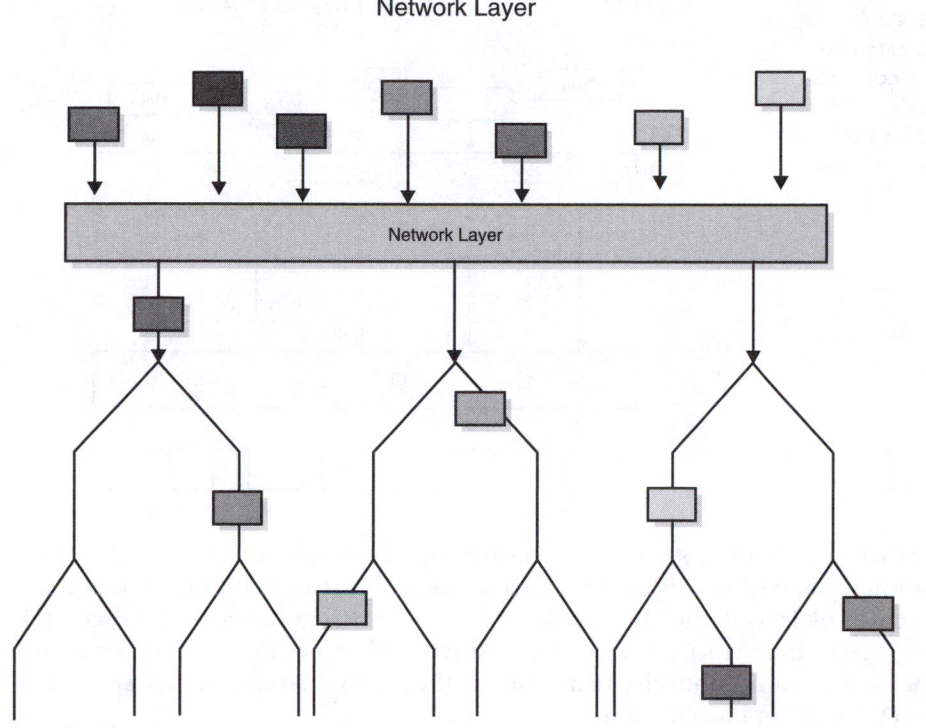

Figure 7-7 The network layer decides on the most efficient path for each packet to take.

(FDDI) networks. If the network is an Ethernet network, for example, all the computers will expect the header to be a certain length, the flags to be positioned in a certain place within the packet, and the trailer information to be in a certain place with specific fields. On a Token Ring network, the computers would expect most of these parameters to be in other specific places and the frames to have particular formats. The data link layer is responsible for proper communication within these technologies and for changing the data into the necessary format for the physical layer.

Some of the protocols that work at this layer are the Serial Line Internet Protocol (SLIP), Point-to-Point Protocol (PPP), Reverse Address Resolution Protocol (RARP), Layer 2 Forwarding (L2F), Layer 2 Tunneling Protocol (L2TP), FDDI, and Integrated Services Digital Network (ISDN). Figure 7-8 shows how the data link layer converts the information into bits and the physical layer converts those bits into electrical signals.

Each network technology (Ethernet, Token Ring, and so on) defines the compatible wire type (coaxial, twisted pair, or fiber) that is required to enable network communication. Each network technology also has defined electronic signaling and bit patterns. This means, for example, that a signal of 0.5 volts may represent a *0* on one technology and a *1* within another technology. The data link protocol specifies the proper bit patterns, and the physical layer translates this information into electrical encoding and

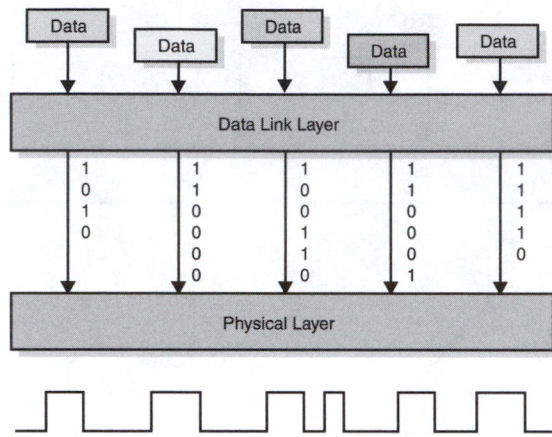

Figure 7-8
The data link
layer converts
the data into
bits for the
physical layer.

Data Link and Physical Layers

electricity state transitions. Network cards bridge the data link and physical layers. Information is passed down through the first six layers and reaches the network card driver at the data link layer. Depending on the network technology being used (Ethernet, Token Ring, FDDI, and so on), the network card driver will encode the bits at the data link layer that are then turned into electricity states at the physical layer, and they are then placed onto the wire for transmission.

Physical Layer

Everything ends up as electrical signals anyway.

The *physical layer*, layer 1, converts bits into voltage for transmission. Signals and voltage schemes have different meanings for different LAN and WAN technologies. If a user sends data through his dial-up software and out his modem onto a telephone line, the data format, electrical signals, and control functionality would be much different than if that user sent data through the NIC and onto a unshielded twisted pair (UTP) wire for LAN communication. The mechanisms that control this data going onto the telephone line, or the UTP wire, work at the physical layer. This layer controls synchronization, data rates, line noise, and medium access.

Functions and Protocols in the OSI Model

You will need to know the functionality that takes place at the different layers of the OSI model, along with specific protocols that work at each layer. Here is a quick overview of each layer and its components.

Application

File transfer, virtual terminals, network management, and fulfilling networking requests of applications.

Here are a few of the protocols that work at this layer:

- File Transfer Protocol (FTP)
- Simple Network Management Protocol (SNMP)
- Simple Mail Transfer Protocol (SMTP)
- Trivial File Transfer Protocol (TFTP)

Presentation

Translation into standard formats, data compression and decompression, data encryption and decryption.

Here are some of the presentation layer standards:

- American Standard Code for Information Interchange (ASCII)
- Extended Binary-Coded Decimal Interchange Mode (EBCDIC)
- Tagged Image File Format (TIFF)
- Joint Photographic Experts Group (JPEG)
- Motion Picture Experts Group (MPEG)
- Musical Instrument Digital Interface (MIDI)

Session

Set up connection between applications; maintain dialog control; negotiate, establish, maintain, and tear down the communication channel.

Here are some of the protocols that work at this layer:

- Network File System (NFS)
- Structured Query Language (SQL)
- Remote procedure call (RPC)

Transport

End-to-end transmission, segmentation into a data stream, integrity checking, multiplexing, flow control, and sequencing.

Here are protocols that work at this layer:

- Transmission Control Protocol (TCP)
- User Datagram Protocol (UDP)
- Sequenced Packet Exchange (SPX)

Network
Internetworking service, routing, addressing.
Here are some of the protocols that work at this layer:

- Internet Protocol (IP)
- Internet Control Message Protocol (ICMP)
- Internet Group Management Protocol (IGMP)
- Routing Information Protocol (RIP)
- Open Shortest Path First (OSPF)

Data Link
Convert into LAN or WAN frames for transmission, convert message into bits, define how a computer accesses a network.
Here are some of the protocols that work at this layer:

- Address Resolution Protocol (ARP)
- Reverse Address Resolution Protocol (RARP)
- Point-to-Point Protocol (PPP)
- Serial Line Internet Protocol (SLIP)

Physical
Convert bits into electrical signals, control physical aspects of the data.
Here are the standard interfaces at this layer:

- High-Speed Serial Interface (HSSI)
- X.21
- EIA/TIA-232 and EIA/TIA-449

Tying the Layers Together

All these layers work together to form the OSI model, which is used as a framework for many products and many types of vendors. Various types of devices and protocols work at different parts of this seven-layer model. Whereas computers can interpret and process data at each of the seven layers, routers can understand information only up to the network layer. This is because a router's main function is to route packets, and it does not need to know about any further information within the packet. A router will peel back the header information until it reaches the network layer data, where the routing information and IP address information is located. The router looks at this information to make its decisions on where the packet should be sent next. Bridges understand only up to the data link layer and repeaters understand data only at the physical layer. Figure 7-9 shows what level of the OSI model each type of device understands.

References

Data communications protocols: **www.protocols.com**

Google listings of protocols: **directory.google.com/Top/Computers/ Internet/Protocols**

TCP/IP

Transmission Control Protocol/Internet Protocol (TCP/IP) is a suite of protocols that governs the way that data travels from one device to another. TCP/IP is made up of two main components, TCP and IP protocols, although other protocols also make up this suite. IP is a network layer protocol and provides datagram routing services. IP's main

Figure 7-9   Each device works at a particular layer within the OSI model.

task is to support internetwork addressing and packet routing. It is a connectionless protocol that envelopes data passed to it from the transport layer. The IP protocol addresses the datagram with the source and destination IP addresses. The protocols within the TCP/IP suite work together to break down the data passed from the application layer into pieces that can be moved along a network. They work with other protocols to transmit the data to the destination computer and then to reassemble the data back into a form that the application layer can understand and process.

Two main protocols work at the transport layer: TCP and UDP. *TCP* is a reliable and *connection-oriented protocol*, which means that it ensures that packets are delivered to the destination computer. If a packet is lost during transmission, TCP has the ability to resend it. TCP also supports packet sequencing (to ensure each and every packet was received), flow and congestion control, and error detection and correction. *UDP*, on the other hand, is a *best-effort* and *connectionless-oriented protocol*. It does not have packet sequencing and flow and congestion control, and the destination does not acknowledge every packet it receives.

TCP

TCP is referred to as a connection-oriented protocol because handshaking takes place between the two systems that want to communicate before any data is actually sent. Once the handshaking completes successfully, a virtual connection is set up between the two systems. The UDP is considered connectionless because it does not go through these steps. Instead, UDP sends out messages without first contacting the destination computer and does not know if the packets were received properly or dropped. Figure 7-10 shows the difference between a connection-oriented and a connectionless protocol.

IP

IP is a connectionless protocol that provides the addressing and routing capabilities for each package of data. It is the mechanism that enables the network to read IP addresses and implement proper routing functions.

The data, IP, and network relationship can be compared to the relationship between a letter and the postal system. The message is the letter, which is enveloped and addressed by IP, and the network and its services enable the message to be sent from its origin to its destination, like the postal system.

Data = Letter

IP = Addressed envelope

Network = Postal system

Figure 7-10
Connection-oriented versus connectionless protocol functionality

Connection-oriented communication performs handshaking, sets up a virtual circuit, and verifies that each packet reaches its destination.

Host A

Host B

Connectionless-oriented communication just puts the packets on the wire.

UDP and TCP sit together on the transport layer, and developers can choose which to use when they are coding applications. Many times, TCP is the transport protocol of choice because it provides reliability and ensures that the packets are delivered. For example, SMTP is used to transmit e-mail messages and uses TCP because it needs to make sure that the data is delivered. TCP provides a full-duplex, reliable communication mechanism, and if any packets are lost or damaged, they are re-sent; however, TCP requires a lot of system overhead. If a programmer knows that data dropped during transmission is not detrimental to the application, he may choose to use UDP because it is faster and requires fewer resources. For example, UDP is a better choice than TCP when a server sends status information to all listening nodes on the network. A node will not be negatively affected if, by some chance, it did not receive this status information, because the information will be re-sent every 30 minutes.

UDP and TCP are transport protocols that applications use to get their data across a network. They both use ports to communicate with upper OSI layers and to keep track of various conversations that take place simultaneously. The ports are also the mechanism used to identify how other computers access services. When a TCP or UDP message is formed, a source and destination port are contained within the header information along with the source and destination address; this makes up a *socket*. This is how packets know where to go—by the address—and how to communicate with the right service or protocol on the other computer—by the port number. The IP address acts as the doorway to a computer, and the port acts as the doorway to the application layer protocol. To communicate properly, the packet needs to know these doors. Figure 7-11 shows how packets communicate with applications and services, through ports.

The difference between TCP and UDP can also be seen in the differences in their message format. Because TCP offers more services than UDP, it must contain much more

Figure 7-11
The packet can communicate with upper layer applications and services through a port.

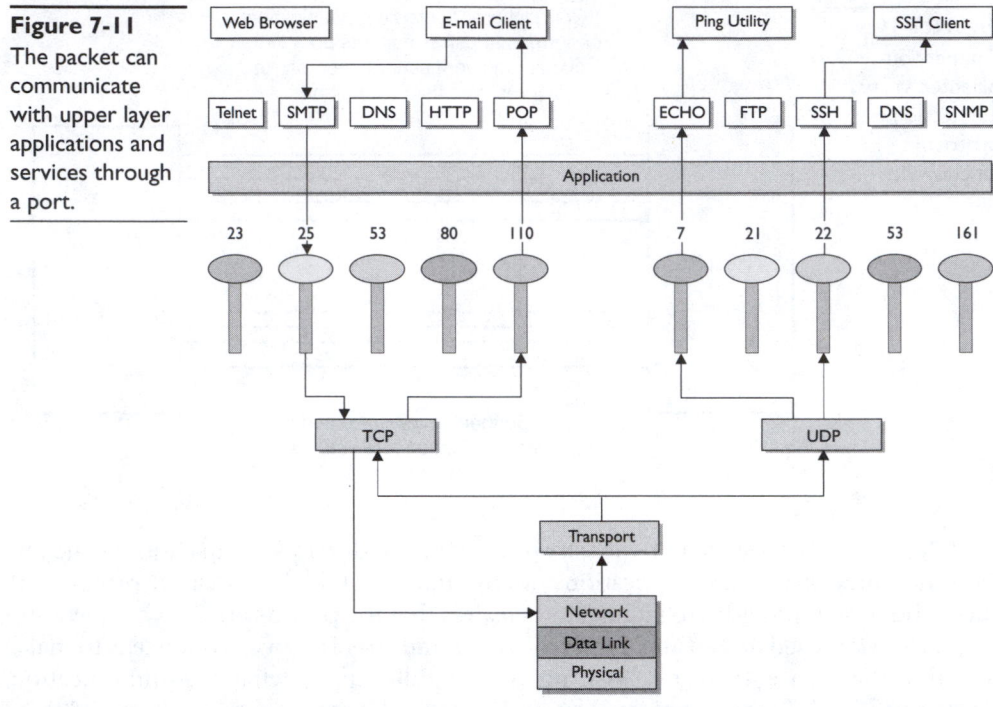

Well-Known Ports

Port numbers up to 1024 are called *well-known ports*, and almost every computer in the world has the exact same protocol mapped to the exact same port number. That is why they are called *well-known*—everyone follows this same standardized approach. This means that on almost every computer, port 25 is mapped to the SMTP protocol, port 21 is mapped to FTP, port 80 is mapped to HTTP, and so on. This mapping between these lower numbered ports to specific protocols is a *de facto standard*, which just means that we all do this and that we do not have a standards body telling us this is how it should be done. Everyone following this approach translates to more interoperability among systems all over the world.

Because this is a de facto standard and not a standard that absolutely has to be followed, administrators can map different protocols to different port numbers if that fits their purpose.

The following shows some of the most commonly used protocols and the ports to which they are usually mapped:

- Telnet port 23
- SMTP port 25

- HTTP port 80
- SNMP port 161 and 162
- FTP port 21 and 20

information within its packet format, as shown in Figure 7-12. Table 7-1 lists the major differences between TCP and UDP.

TCP Handshake

Every proper dialog begins with a polite handshake.

TCP must set up a virtual connection between two hosts before any data is sent. This means that the two hosts must agree on certain parameters, data flow, windowing, error detection, and options. These issues are negotiated during the handshaking phase, as shown in Figure 7-13.

The host that initiates communication sends a synchronous (SYN) packet to the receiver. The receiver acknowledges this request by sending a SYN/ACK packet. This packet translates into "I have received your request and am ready to communicate with you." The sending host acknowledges this with an acknowledgment (ACK) packet, which translates into, "I received your acknowledgment. Let's start transmitting our data."

Service	TCP	UDP
Reliability	Ensures that packets reach their destinations, returns ACKs when a packet is received, and is a reliable protocol	Does not return ACKs and does not guarantee that a packet will reach its destination, and is an unreliable protocol
Connection	Connection-oriented, thus it performs handshaking and develops a virtual connection with destination computer	Connectionless-oriented, thus it does no handshaking and does not set up a virtual connection
Packet sequencing	Uses sequence numbers within headers to make sure that each packet within a transmission is received	Does not use sequence numbers
Congestion controls	The destination computer can tell the source if it is overwhelmed and to slow the transmission rate	The destination computer does not communicate back to the source computer about flow control through UDP
Usage	Used when reliable delivery is required	Used when reliable delivery is not required as in streaming video and status broadcasts
Speed and overhead	Uses a considerable amount of resources and is slower than UDP	Uses fewer resources and is faster than TCP

Table 7-1 Major Differences Between TCP and UDP

Figure 7-12 TCP carries a lot more information within its segment format because it offers more services than UDP.

This completes the handshaking phase, a virtual connection is set up, and actual data can now be passed. The actual connection that has been set up at this point is considered *full-duplex*, which means that transmission in both directions is possible using the same transmission line.

Data Structures

What's in a name?

As stated earlier, the message is usually formed and passed to the application layer from a program and sent down through the protocol stack. Each protocol at each layer adds its own information to the message and passes it down to the next level. This concept is usually referred to as *encapsulation*. As the message is passed down the stack, it goes through a sort of evolution, and each stage has a specific name that indicates what is taking place. When an application formats data to be transmitted over the network, the data is called a *message*. The message is sent to the transport layer, where TCP does its magic on the data. The bundle of data is now a *segment*. The segment is sent to the network layer. The network layer adds routing and addressing, and now the bundle is called a *datagram*. The network layer passes it off to the data link layer, which frames the datagram with a header and a trailer, and now it is a *frame*. Figure 7-14 illustrates these stages.

Figure 7-13
TCP three-way
handshake

Figure 7-14   The data goes through its own evolutionary stages as it passes through the layers within the OSI model.

Sometimes when an author talks about a datagram, he is specifying the stage in which the data is located. If the literature is describing routers, which work at the network layer, he might use the word *datagram* because the data at this level has routing and addressing information attached. If an author is describing network traffic and flow control, she might use the word *frame*, because all data actually ends up in the frame format before it is put on the network wire. However, sometimes an author refers to all data packages as *packets* and calls it a day.

The important thing here is that you understand the various steps a data package goes through when it moves up and down the protocol stack and that just because an author refers to data as a *packet* does not mean that he is necessarily indicating the data structure.

IP Addressing

Take a right at the router and a left at the access server. I live at 10.10.2.3.

Each node on a network must have a unique IP address. Today, **IP version 4 (IPv4)** is the version most in use, compared to **IP version 6 (IPv6)**. IPv6 was created because IPv4 addresses are so high in demand that their supply started running out. (IPv6 also has many security features built into it that are not part of IPv4.)

IPv4 uses 32 bits for its addresses, and IPv6 uses 128 bits; thus, v6 provides more possible addresses to work with. Each address has a host and network portion of the address, and the addresses are grouped into *classes* and then into *subnets*. The subnet mask of the address differentiates the groups of addresses that define the subnets of a network.

Although each node has an IP address, people usually refer to their hostnames instead of IP numbers. Hostnames, like **www.isc2.org**, are easier for humans to remember than *10.13.84.4*. However, the use of these two nomenclatures requires mapping between the hostnames and IP addresses, because the computer understands only the numbering scheme. This process is addressed in the "DNS" (Domain Name Service) section.

Types of Transmission

Data transmission can happen in different ways (analog or digital), can use different controlling schemes (synchronous or asynchronous), and can use only one channel over a wire (baseband) or use several different channels over one wire (broadband). These transmission types and their characteristics are described in the following sections.

Analog and Digital

Analog transmission signals are continuously varying electromagnetic waves that can be carried over air, water, twisted-pair, coaxial, or fiber-optic cable. Through a process of *modulation*, data is combined with a carrier signal of a specific frequency. The modulation of a signal differs in *amplitude* (height of the signal) and *frequency* (number of waves in a defined period of time), as shown in Figure 7-15. This means that data is put on the back of a carrier signal. The carrier signals provide many radio stations, frequency ranges, and communication channels. Each radio station is given a certain carrier signal to use for its transmission. This is how three different country stations can exist on three different radio channels, for example.

Computers use digital signals when moving data from one component to another within the computer itself. When this computer is connected to a telephone line via a dial-up connection, a modem (for *modulate/demodulate*) must transform this digital data into an analog signal, because this is what is expected and used on the telephone lines. The modem actually modulates the digital data onto an analog signal. Once the data reaches the destination computer, it must be transformed back into a digital state so that the destination computer can understand it. *Digital signals* represent binary digits as electrical pulses. Each individual pulse is a signal element and represents either a 1 or a 0. Bandwidth refers to the number of electrical pulses that can be transmitted over a link within a second, and these electrical pulses carry individual *bits* of information.

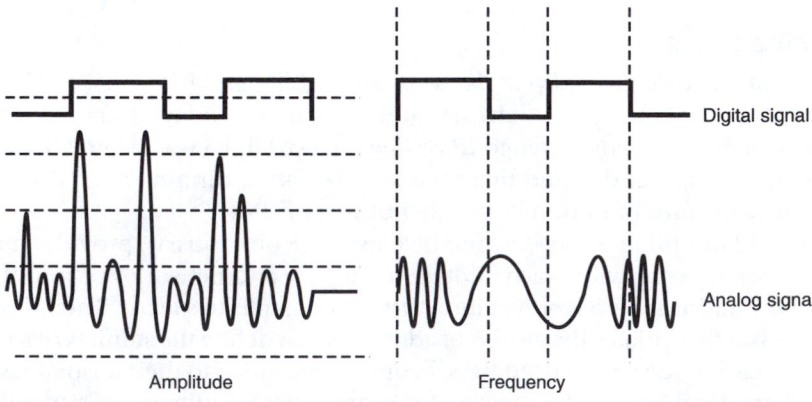

Figure 7-15   Analog signals are measured in amplitude and frequency, whereas digital signals represent binary digits as electrical pulses.

Digital signals are more reliable over a long distance than analog and provide a clear-cut and efficient signaling method because the voltage is either on (1) or not on (0), compared to interpreting the waves of an analog signal. Digital signals can easily be extracted from noise and retransmitted. It is more difficult to extract analog signals from background noise because the amplitudes and frequency slowly lose form. Digital systems are superior to analog systems in that they can transport more calls and data transmissions on the same line at higher quality over longer distances.

Communication used to be transmitted mainly via analog signals over telecommunication links, but today, most communication is digitized. Telephone companies digitize telephone calls, and many corporate telephone systems are digitized. Other than radio waves used by radio stations, ham radios, and the like, the only communication that is still analog is the copper wiring that goes from a residential house or business to the telephone company's central office. This section of the telecommunication network is referred to as the *local loop* or *last mile*.

Asynchronous and Synchronous

It's all in the timing.

Two devices can communicate through asynchronous or synchronous means; it depends on the type of communication and whether the two systems are synchronized in any way.

- *Asynchronous communication* is used when the two devices are not synchronized in any way. The sender can send data at any time and the receiving end must always be ready.

- In contrast, *synchronous communication* takes place between two devices that are synchronized, usually via a clocking mechanism.

Usually, when two devices have a large amount of data to transfer, they will use synchronous transmission; with a small amount of data, they will use asynchronous transmission. This does not mean one device can decide, "Huh, this is a big heap of data. I better send it through my synchronous route instead of asynchronous." Instead, systems that usually transfer large amounts of data will be developed and configured with synchronous communication mechanisms, and systems that transfer smaller amounts of data are developed with asynchronous means.

One example of asynchronous communication takes place between a terminal and a terminal server. If a user is using a system that has terminal emulation software running, she uses the desktop that the terminal server wants her to use. She sees only her desktop on her computer, while all processing actually takes place on the terminal server. This means that every mouse click, keystroke, and command she initiates travels over the networking cable to the terminal server, where the server performs the actions that correspond with these commands. The results are transmitted back to the user's desktop so that it seems to her that her computer did the work—when in fact it was done on the terminal server, which could be on another floor or at another location altogether. This type of technology usually transmits a small amount of data at a time; thus, it uses asynchronous data transmission.

Modems also use asynchronous data transmission. Because the data can travel at any time and be any length, a stop and start delimiter must be used to tell the receiving end when to start processing a request and when to stop. Each character, which is really just a string of 1s and 0s, has a start-of-character bit and a stop bit before and after the character. This produces a lot of overhead and extra bits, but it's necessary in asynchronous communications.

Synchronous communication, on the other hand, transfers data as a stream of bits instead of data framed in start and stop bits. The synchronization can happen between two systems using the same clocking mechanism, or a signal can be encoded into the data stream to let the receiver synchronize with the sender of the message. This synchronization needs to take place before the first message is sent. The sending system can transmit a digital clock pulse to the receiving system, which translates into, "We will start here and work in this type of synchronization scheme."

Broadband and Baseband

How many channels can you shove into this one wire?

Baseband is a transmission method that is accomplished by applying direct current to a cable. The signals, or current, hold binary information. Higher voltage usually represents the binary value of 1, and a lower voltage represents the binary value of 0.

Baseband uses the entire cable for its transmission, whereas *broadband* divides the cable into channels so that different types of data can be transmitted at the same time. Baseband permits only one signal to be transmitted at a time, whereas broadband carries several signals over different channels. For example, a coaxial cable TV (CATV) system is a broadband technology that delivers multiple television channels over the same cable. This system also provides home users with Internet access, but this data is transmitted at a different frequency spectrum than the TV channels. Ethernet is a baseband technology that uses the entire wire for just one channel.

Broadband encompasses many different types of technologies, but one general rule is that it provides data transmissions higher than 56 Kbps, which is what a standard modem dial-up connection line provides. Broadband communications provide channels for data transmission and can be used by many users. The types of broadband communication systems available today are leased lines (T1, T3), ISDN, ATM, Digital Subscriber Line (DSL), broadband wireless, and CATV.

Networking

We really need to connect all these resources together.

The four main reasons to have a network are

- To allow communication between computers
- To share information

- To share resources

- To provide central administration

Most users on a network will need to use the same type of resources, such as information, printers, file servers, plotters, fax machines, Internet connections, and so on. Why not just string all the computers together and have these resources available to all? Great idea, and we shall call it *networking*!

Networking has made amazing advances in just a short period of time. In the beginning of the computer age, mainframes were the name of the game. They were isolated powerhouses, and many had "dumb" terminals hanging off them. However, this was not true networking. In the late 1960s and early 1970s, some technical researchers came up with ways of connecting all the mainframes and Unix systems to enable them to communicate. This marked the Internet's baby steps.

Microcomputers evolved and were used in many offices and work areas. Slowly, dumb terminals got a little smarter and more powerful as users needed to share office resources. *Bam*, Ethernet was developed, which allowed for true networking. There was no turning back after this.

 NOTE Identification and authentication are a large part of networking and are covered extensively in Chapter 4. However, it is important to note that node authentication, by itself, should not be used to establish trustworthiness of a user within the network. Within a distributed network, knowing whom to trust is a major security issue.

References

IEEE Standards Working Groups: **grouper.ieee.org/groups**

Lantronix white papers: **www.lantronix.com/learning/wp/index.html**

Network Topology

Okay, so where is everything?

The physical arrangement of computers and devices is called a ***network topology***. Topology refers to the manner in which a network is physically connected and shows the layout of resources and systems. There is a difference between the physical network topology and the logical topology. A network can be configured as a physical star but work logically as a ring, as in the Token Ring technology.

How nodes are supposed to interact, the protocols used, types of applications that can be available, the reliability, expandability, physical layout of a facility, existing wiring, and the technologies implemented will dictate the best type of topology to install. The wrong topology or combination of topologies can negatively affect the network's performance, productivity, and growth possibilities.

This section describes the basic types of network topologies. Most networks are much more complex and are usually implemented using a combination of topologies.

Ring Topology

A *ring topology* has a series of devices connected by unidirectional transmission links, as shown in Figure 7-16. These links form a closed loop and do not connect to a central system, as in a star topology (discussed a little later). In a physical ring formation, each node is dependent upon the preceding nodes. In simple networks, if one system fails, all other systems could be negatively affected because of this interdependence. Today, most networks have redundancy in place or other mechanisms that will protect a whole network from being affected by just one workstation misbehaving, but one disadvantage of using a ring topology is that this possibility exists.

Bus Topology

In a simple *bus topology*, a single cable runs the entire length of the network. Nodes are attached to the network through drop points on this cable. Data communications transmit the length of the medium, and each packet transmitted has the capability of being looked at by all nodes. Each node decides to accept or ignore the packet, depending upon the packet's destination address.

There are two main types of bus topologies: *linear* and *tree*. The *linear bus topology* has a single cable with nodes attached. A *tree topology* has branches from the single cable, and each branch can contain many nodes.

In simple implementations of a bus topology, if one workstation fails, other systems can be negatively affected because of the degree of interdependence. In addition, because

Figure 7-16

A ring topology forms a closed-loop connection.

all nodes are connected to one main cable, the cable itself becomes a potential single point of failure. Traditionally, Ethernet uses bus topologies.

Star Topology

In a *star topology*, all nodes connect to a central device such as a switch. Each node has a dedicated link to the central device. The central device needs to provide enough throughput so that it does not turn out to be a detrimental bottleneck for the network as a whole. Because a central device is required, it is a potential single point of failure and redundancy may need to be implemented. Switches can be configured in flat or hierarchical implementations so that larger organizations can use them.

When one workstation fails on a star topology, it does not affect other systems, as in the ring or bus topologies. In a star topology, each system is not as dependent on others as it is dependent on the central connection device. This topology generally requires less cabling than other types of topologies; as a result, there is a lower chance of cut cables, and detecting cable problems is an easier task.

Not many networks use true linear bus and ring topologies anymore within LAN environments. A ring topology can be used for a backbone network, but most LANs are constructed in a star topology because it enables the network to be more resilient and not as affected if an individual node experiences a problem. Remember that there is a difference between media access methods and the physical topology. Even though a network is Token Ring or Ethernet, this describes only how each node accesses the media and deals with traffic. Although Token Ring is usually thought of as a ring and Ethernet is considered a bus implementation, this description applies only to how they work logically. They can be easily implemented physically as a star, and they usually are.

Mesh Topology

In a *mesh topology*, all systems and resources are connected to each other in a way that does not follow the uniformity of the previous topologies, as shown in Figure 7-17. This arrangement is usually a network of interconnected routers and switches that provide multiple paths to all the nodes on the network. A full mesh topology has every node is directly connected to every other node, which provides a great degree of redundancy. In a partial mesh topology, every node is not directly connected and each may be used to connect full mesh networks. The Internet is an example of a partial mesh topology.

A summary of the different network topologies and their important characteristics is provided in Table 7-2.

LAN Media Access Technologies

A *LAN* is a network that provides shared communication and resources in a relatively small area. What defines a LAN, as compared to a WAN, depends on the physical medium, encapsulation protocols, and functionality. For example, a LAN could use 10Base-T cabling, IPX/SPX encapsulation, and routing protocols, and it could enable users who are in the same local building to communicate. A WAN, on the other hand, could

Figure 7-17
A mesh topology
has each node
connected to
all other nodes,
which provides
for redundant
paths.

use fiber-optic cabling, the L2TP encapsulation protocol, and could enable users from one building to communicate with other users in another building in another state (or country). A WAN connects LANs over great distances geographically. Most of the differences between these technologies take place at the data link layer.

The definition of *local* in LAN is the limitation of the shared medium, the number of devices and computers that can be connected to it, transmission rates, cable types, and

Topology	Characteristics	Problems	Technologies that Usually Work
Bus	Uses a linear, single cable for all computers attached. All traffic travels the full cable and can be viewed by all other computers.	If one station experiences a problem, it can negatively affect surrounding computers on the same cable.	Ethernet
Ring	All computers are connected by a unidirectional transmission link, and the cable is in a closed loop.	If one station experiences a problem, it can negatively affect surrounding computers on the same ring.	FDDI
Star	All computers are connected to a central device, which provides more resilience for the network.	The central device is a single point of failure.	Logical bus (Ethernet) and ring topologies (Token Ring)
Tree	This is a bus topology that does not have one linear cable, but instead uses branches of cables.		Ethernet
Mesh	Computers are connected to each other, which provides redundancy.	This requires more expense in cabling and extra effort to track down cable faults.	Internet

Table 7-2   Summary of Network Topologies

> ## Question
>
> A LAN is said to cover a relatively small geographical area. When is a LAN no longer a LAN?
>
> **Answer:** When two distinct LANs are connected by a router, the result is an *internetwork*, not a larger LAN. Each distinct LAN has its own addressing scheme, broadcast domain, and communication mechanisms. If two LANs are connected by a different data link layer technology, such as frame relay or X.25, we are looking at a WAN.

devices used. If a network administrator develops a very large LAN that would more appropriately be multiple LANs, too much traffic could result in a big performance hit, or the cabling could be too long, so that *attenuation* (signal loss) becomes a factor. In environments where the network segments are too large, routers, bridges, and switches may be overwhelmed, and administration of this network could get complex, which opens the doors for errors, collisions, and security holes. The network administrator should follow the specifications of the technology he is using, and once he has maxed out these numbers, he should consider implementing two or more LANs instead of one large LAN.

LANs are defined by their physical topologies, data link layer technologies, protocols, and devices used. The following sections cover these topics and how they interrelate.

References

IEEE LAN/MAN Standards Committee: **grouper.ieee.org/groups/802**

Web66 Network Construction Kit: **web66.coled.umn.edu/Construction**

Ethernet

Ethernet is a LAN-sharing technology that enables several devices to communicate on the same network. Ethernet usually uses a bus or star topology. If a linear bus topology is used, all devices connect to one cable. If a star topology is used, each device is connected to a cable that is connected to a centralized device, such as a switch. Ethernet was developed in the 1970s, became commercially available in 1980, and was named the IEEE 802.3 standard.

Ethernet has seen quite an evolution in its short history, from purely coaxial cable installation that worked at 10 Mbps to mostly Category 5 twisted-pair cable that works at 100 Mbps, 1000 Mbps, and Gbps speeds.

Ethernet is defined by the following characteristics:

- Shares media (all devices must take turns using the same media and detect collisions)
- Uses broadcast and collision domains

- Uses carrier sense multiple access (CSMA) access method
- Supports full-duplex on twisted-pair implementations
- Can use coaxial or twisted-pair media
- Is defined by standard IEEE 802.3

Ethernet deals with how computers share a common network, and how they deal with collisions, data integrity, communication mechanisms, and transmission controls. These are the common characteristics of Ethernet, but Ethernet does vary in the type of cabling schemes and transfer rates it can supply. Several types of Ethernet implementations are listed in Appendix E in this book, but the following sections discuss 10Base2, 10Base5, and 10Base-T, which are common implementations.

The different types of Ethernet are shown in Table 7-3.

10Base2   10Base2, ThinNet, is a common Ethernet implementation that uses coaxial cable. It has a maximum cable length of 185 meters, provides 10 Mbps transmission rates, and requires British Naval Connectors (BNCs) to network devices. Figure 7-18 shows a simple 10Base2 Ethernet implementation.

10Base5   10Base5, ThickNet, uses a thicker coaxial cable, which is not as flexible as ThinNet and more difficult to work with. However, ThickNet can have longer cable segments than ThinNet and is often used as network backbones. ThickNet is more resistant to electrical interference than ThinNet and is usually preferred when stringing wire through electrically noisy environments that contain heavy machinery and magnetic fields. ThickNet also requires BNCs because it uses coaxial cables.

10Base-T   10Base-T uses twisted-pair, copper wiring instead of coaxial cabling. Twisted-pair wiring uses one wire for transmitting data and the other for receiving data. 10Base-T is usually implemented in a star topology, which provides easy network configuration. In a star topology, all systems are connected to centralized devices, and these devices can be in a flat or hierarchical configuration.

10Base-T networks have RJ-45 connector faceplates to which the computer connects. The wires usually run behind a wall and connect the faceplate to a punchdown block within a wiring closet. The punchdown block is often connected to a 10Base-T hub that serves as a doorway to the network's backbone cable or to a central switch. This type of configuration is shown in Figure 7-19.

Table 7-3	Ethernet Type	Cabling Type	Speed
Types of Ethernet	10Base2, ThinNet	Coaxial	10 Mbps
	10Base5, ThickNet	Coaxial	10 Mbps
	10Base-T	UTP	10 Mbps
	100Base-TX, Fast Ethernet	UTP	100 Mbps
	1000Base-T, Gigabit Ethernet	UTP	1000 Mbps

Figure 7-18
10Base2 is a coaxial cable Ethernet implementation that provides 10 Mbps transmission.

Fast Ethernet: Ethernet in Overdrive

Not surprisingly, 10 Mbps was heaven-sent when it first arrived to the networking scene, but soon many were demanding more speed and power. The smart people had to gather into small rooms and hit the white boards with ideas, calculations, and new technologies. The result of these meetings, computations, engineering, and testing is Fast Ethernet.

Figure 7-19   Ethernet hosts connect to a punchdown block within the wiring closet, which is connected to the backbone via a hub.

> **Question**
> Why does my NIC have two input connectors that are shaped differently?
>
> **Answer:** Most NICs provide support for 10Base2 and 10Base-T. The round connector is used for 10Base2, which is the BNC used for coaxial wiring. The connector that looks like a phone connector supports 10Base-T, which is twisted-pair wiring. (10Base2, 10Base5, and 10Base-T specifications are explained further in Appendix E.)

Fast Ethernet is regular Ethernet, but it runs at 100 Mbps over twisted-pair wiring instead of at 10 Mbps. Around the same time that Fast Ethernet arrived, another 100 Mbps was developed: 100-VG-AnyLAN. This technology did not use Ethernet's traditional CSMA/CD and did not catch on like Fast Ethernet did.

Fast Ethernet uses the traditional CSMA/CD (explained in the "CSMA" section later in the chapter) and the original frame format of Ethernet. This is why it is used in many enterprise LAN environments today. One environment can run 10- and 100-Mbps network segments that can communicate via 10/100 hubs or switches.

Four main types of Fast Ethernet exist today; their differences pertain to the cabling and transmission distances. For more information on these, refer to Appendix E and the "References" sites presented next.

References

Fast Ethernet Consortium: **www.iol.unh.edu/consortiums/fe**

Links for Fast Ethernet documents: **alumni.caltech.edu/~dank/fe**

Charles Spurgeon's Ethernet Web site: **www.ethermanage.com/ethernet**

Token Ring

Like Ethernet, *Token Ring* is a LAN technology that enables the communication and sharing of networking resources. The Token Ring technology was originally developed by IBM and is now defined by the IEEE 802.5 standard. It uses a *token-passing* technology with a star-configured topology. The *ring* part of the name pertains to how the signals travel, which is in a logical ring. Each computer is connected to a central hub, called a *Multistation Access Unit (MAU)*. Physically the topology can be a star, but the signals and transmissions are passed in a logical ring.

At first, Token Ring technology had the ability to transmit data at 4 Mbps; later it was improved to transmit at 16 Mbps. When a frame is put on the wire, each computer will look at it to see whether the frame is addressed to it. If the frame does not have that specific computer's address, the computer will put the frame back on the wire, properly amplify the message, and pass it to the next computer on the ring.

Token Ring employs a couple of mechanisms to deal with problems that can occur on this type of a network. The *active monitor* mechanism removes frames that are continually circulating on the network. This can occur if a computer locks up or is taken offline for one reason or another and cannot properly receive a token destined to it. Another mechanism this type of network uses is *beaconing*. If a computer detects a problem with the network, it sends a beacon frame. This frame generates a failure domain, which is between the computer that issued the beacon and its neighbor downstream. The computers and devices within this failure domain will attempt to reconfigure certain settings to try and work around the detected fault. Figure 7-20 depicts a Token Ring network in a physical star configuration.

Token Ring networks were popular in the 1980s and 1990s, and although some are still around, Ethernet has become much more popular and has taken over the LAN networking market.

References

Token Ring FAQ: **www.faqs.org/faqs/LANs/token-ring-faq**

Token Ring Technical Summary: **www.techfest.com/networking/lan/token.htm**

Figure 7-20   Token Ring network

> ## Question
>
> Where do the differences between Ethernet, Token Ring, and FDDI lie?
>
> **Answer:** These technologies are data link layer technologies. The data link layer is actually made up of a Media Access Control (MAC) layer and a Logical Link Control (LLC) layer. These technologies live at the MAC layer and have to interface to the LLC layer. These LAN technologies differ in how they communicate to the protocol stack and what type of functionalities they can provide.

FDDI

Fiber Distributed Data Interface (FDDI) technology, developed by the American National Standards Institute (ANSI), is a high-speed token-passing media access technology. FDDI has a data transmission speed of 100 Mbps and is usually used as a backbone network using fiber-optic cabling. FDDI also provides fault tolerance by providing a second counter-rotating fiber ring. The primary ring has data traveling clockwise and is used for regular data transmission. The second ring transmits data in a counterclockwise fashion and is invoked only if the primary ring goes down. Sensors watch the primary ring, and if it goes down, they invoke a ring *wrap* so that the data will be diverted to the second ring. Each node on the FDDI network has relays that are connected to both rings, so if a break in the ring occurs, the two rings can be joined. When FDDI is used as a backbone network, it usually connects several different types of networks, as shown in Figure 7-21.

Before Fast Ethernet and Gigabit Ethernet hit the market, FDDI was used mainly as campus and service provider backbones. Because FDDI can be used for a distance up to 100 kilometers, it was often used in metropolitan area networks (MANs). The benefit of FDDI is that it can work over long distances and at high speeds with minimal interference. It enables several tokens to be present on the ring at the same time, causing more communication to take place simultaneously, and it provides predictable delays that help connected networks and devices to know what to expect and when.

A version of FDDI, Copper Distributed Data Interface (CDDI), can work over UTP cabling. Whereas FDDI would be used more as a MAN, CDDI can be used within a LAN environment to connect network segments.

Table 7-4 sums up the important characteristics of the technologies described in the preceding sections.

References

Consortiums and Testing Services: **www.iol.unh.edu/consortiums**

FDDI FAQ: **www.cicese.mx/~aarmenta/frames/redes/fddi/FDDIFAQ.html**

Figure 7-21   FDDI rings can be used as backbones to connect different LAN networks.

LAN Implementation	IEEE Standard	Characteristics
Ethernet	802.3	–Shared media—all devices must take turns using the same media and detect collisions –Uses broadcast and collision domains –Uses CSMA/CD access method –Can use coaxial or twisted-pair media –Transmission speeds of 10 Mbps–1 Gbps
Token Ring	802.5	–All devices connect to a central MAU –Token-passing media access method –Transmission speeds of 4–16 Mbps –Uses an active monitor and beaconing
FDDI	802.8	–Token-passing media access method –Dual counter-rotating rings for fault tolerance –Transmission speeds of 100 Mbps –Operates over long distance at high speeds and is therefore used as backbones –CDDI works over UTP

Table 7-4   LAN Media Access Methods

Cabling

Why are cables so important? Answer: Without them, our electrons would fall onto the floor.

Network cabling and wiring are important when setting up a network or extending an existing one. Particular types of cables need to be used with specific data link layer technologies. Cable types can have varying speeds, maximum lengths, and connectivity issues with NICs. In the 1970s and 1980s, coaxial cable was the way to go, but in the late 1980s, twisted-pair wiring hit the scene and today it is the most popular networking cable used.

Electrical signals travel as currents through cables and can be negatively affected by many factors within the environment, such as motors, fluorescent lighting, magnetic forces, and other electrical devices. These items can corrupt the data as it travels through the cable. This is why cable standards are used to indicate cable type, shielding, transmission rates, and cable distances.

Cabling has bandwidth and data rate values associated with it. Although these two terms are related, they are indeed different. The **bandwidth** of a cable indicates the highest frequency range that it uses; for instance, 10Base-T uses 10 MHz and 100Base-TX uses 80 MHz. This is different from the actual amount of data that can be pushed through a cable. The **data rate** is the actual data throughput of a cable after compression and encoding have been used. 10Base-T has a data rate of 10 Mbps and 100Base-TX has a data rate of 100 Mbps. The bandwidth can be thought of as the size of the pipe, and the data rate is the actual amount of data that travels through that pipe.

Coaxial Cable

Coaxial cabling has a copper core that is surrounded by a shielding layer and grounding wire, as shown in Figure 7-22. This is all encased within a protective outer jacket. Coaxial cable is more resistant to electromagnetic interference (EMI), provides a higher bandwidth, and longer cable lengths can be used when compared to twisted-pair cabling. So, why is twisted pair more popular? Twisted-pair cabling is cheaper, easier to work with, and the move to switched environments that provide hierarchical wiring schemes has overcome the cable length issue of twisted-pair cables.

The two main types of coaxial cable used within LAN environments are the 50-ohm cable (used for digital signaling) and 75-ohm cable (used for high-speed digital signaling and analog signaling). The coaxial cable types are 10Base2 (ThinNet) and 10Base5 (ThickNet). Coaxial can transmit using a *baseband* method, whereby the cable carries only one channel, or a *broadband* method, whereby the cable carries several channels.

Twisted-Pair Cable

This cable is kind of flimsy. Why do we use it? Answer: It's cheap and easy to work with.

Twisted-pair cabling has insulated copper wires that are surrounded by an outer protective jacket. If the cable has an outer foil shielding, it is referred to as **shielded twisted pair (STP)**, which adds protection from radio frequency interference. Another type of twisted-pair cabling does not have this extra outer shielding and is called **unshielded twisted pair (UTP)**.

The cable contains copper wires that twist around each other, as shown in Figure 7-23. This twisting of the wires protects the signals they carry from radio frequency and elec-

Figure 7-22
Coaxial cable

tromagnetic interference, as well as *crosstalk*. Each wire forms a balanced circuit, because the voltage in each pair uses the same amplitude, just with opposite phases. The tighter the twisting of the wires, the more resistant the cable is to interference and attenuation. UTP has categories of cabling that feature respective characteristics. The difference in the category ratings is based on how tightly wound the cables are.

The twisting of the wires, the type of insulation used, the quality of the conductive material, and the shielding of the wire determine the rate that data can be transmitted. The UTP ratings indicate which of these components were used when the cables were manufactured. Some types are more suitable and effective for specific uses and environments. Table 7-5 lists the cable ratings.

Copper cabling has been around for many years; it is inexpensive and easy to use. A majority of the telephone systems today use copper cabling with the rating of voice grade. Twisted-pair wiring is the preferred network cabling, but it also has its drawbacks. Copper actually resists the flow of electrons, which causes a signal to degrade after it has traveled a certain distance. This is why cable lengths are recommended for copper cables; if these recommendations are not followed, a network could experience signal loss and corruption. Copper also radiates energy, which means that information can be monitored and captured by intruders. UTP is the least secure networking cable compared to coaxial and fiber. If a company requires higher speed, higher security, and cables to have longer runs than what is allowed in copper cabling, fiber-optic may be a better choice.

Fiber-Optic Cabling

Hey, I can't tap into this fiber cable. Response: Exactly.

Twisted-pair and coaxial cabling use copper wires as their data transmission media, but fiber-optic cables use a type of glass that carries light waves, which represent the data

Figure 7-23
Twisted-pair cabling uses copper wires.

UTP Category	Characteristics	Usage
Category 1	Voice-grade telephone cable	Not recommended for network use, but modems can communicate over it
Category 2	Data transmission up to 4 Mbps	Used in mainframe and minicomputer terminal connections, but not recommended for high-speed networking
Category 3	10 Mbps for Ethernet and 4 Mbps for Token Ring	Used in 10Base-T network installations
Category 4	16 Mbps	Used usually in Token Ring networks
Category 5	100 Mbps for 100Base-TX and CDDI networks; has high twisting, and thus low crosstalk	Used in 100Base-TX, CDDI, and ATM installations; most widely used for new network installations
Category 6	155 Mbps	Used in new network installations requiring high-speed transmission
Category 7	1 Gbps	Used in new network installations requiring higher-speed transmission

Table 7-5   UTP Cable Ratings

that is being transmitted. The glass core is surrounded by a protective cladding and is all encased within an outer jacket.

Because it uses glass, fiber-optic cabling has higher transmission speeds that can travel over longer distances, and it is not affected by attenuation and electromagnetic interference (EMI) when compared to cabling that uses copper. It does not radiate signals like UTP cabling and is difficult to tap into; therefore, fiber-optic cabling is much more secure than UTP, STP, or coaxial.

Fiber-optic sounds like the way to go, so you might wonder why you would even bother with UTP, STP, or coaxial? Unfortunately, fiber-optic cabling is extremely expensive and difficult to work with. Fiber-optic cabling is usually used in backbone networks and environments that require high data transfer rates. Most networks use UTP and connect to a backbone that uses fiber.

Cabling Problems

Cables are extremely important within networks, and when they experience problems, the whole network could experience problems. This section addresses some of the more common cabling issues many networks experience.

Noise

Noise on a line is usually caused by surrounding devices or characteristics of the wiring's environment. Noise can be caused by motors, computers, copy machines, florescent lighting, and microwave ovens, to name a few. This background noise can combine with the data being transmitted over the cable and distort the signal, as shown in Figure 7-24. The more noise that interacts with the cable, the more likely that the receiving end will

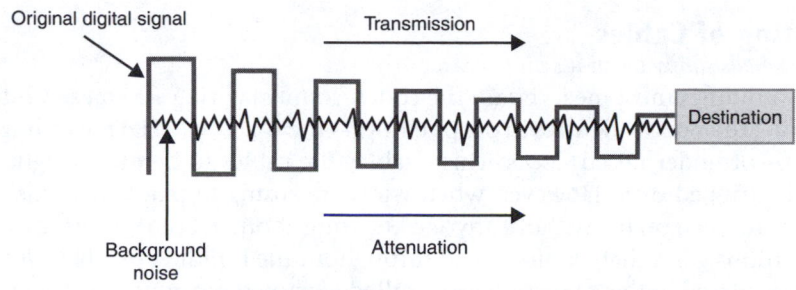

Figure 7-24   Background noise can merge with an electronic signal and alter the signal's integrity.

not receive the data in the form that was originally transmitted. (How these issues affect power lines is discussed in Chapter 6.)

Attenuation

Attenuation is the loss of signal strength as it travels. The longer a cable, the more attenuation will be introduced, and the signal that is carrying data will deteriorate. Suggested cable run lengths are part of standards because once data travels over a certain distance, the resistance of electron flow aggregates and destroys the integrity of the signal.

The effects of attenuation increase with higher frequencies; thus, 100Base-TX at 80 MHz has a higher attenuation rate than 10Base-T at 10 MHz. This means that cables used to transmit data at higher frequencies should have shorter cable runs to ensure that attenuation does not become an issue.

Attenuation can also be caused by cable breaks and malfunctions. This is why cables should be tested. If a cable is suspected of attenuation problems, cable testers can inject signals into the cable and read the results at the end of the cable. The effects of attenuation are illustrated in Figure 7-25.

Crosstalk

Hey, your talking is spilling over into my talking!

UTP is susceptible to *crosstalk*, which occurs when electrical signals of one wire spill over to another wire. When the different electrical signals mix, their integrity degrades and data corruption can occur. UTP is much more vulnerable to this than STP or coaxial because it does not have extra layers of shielding to help protect against it.

As stated earlier, the two-wire pairs within twisted-pair cables form a balanced circuit because they both have the same amplitude, just with different phases. Crosstalk and background noise can throw off this balance, and the wire can actually start to act like an antenna, which means it will be more susceptible to picking up other noises in the environment.

Figure 7-25
Attenuation
weakens a signal.

Fire Rating of Cables

This cable smells funny when it's on fire.

Just as buildings must meet certain fire codes, so must wiring schemes. A lot of companies string their network wires in drop ceilings—the space between the ceiling and the next floor—or under raised floors. This enables the cables to be out of sight and not likely to be tripped over. However, when wires are strung in places like this, they are more likely to catch on fire without anyone knowing about it. Some burning cables produce hazardous gases that would spread throughout the building quickly. Network cabling that is placed in these types of areas, called *plenum space*, must meet a specific fire rating to ensure that it will not produce and release harmful chemicals in case of a fire.

Nonplenum cables usually have a polyvinyl chloride (PVC) jacket covering, whereas plenum-rated cables have jacket covers made of fluoropolymers. When setting up a network or extending an existing network, it is important that you know which wire types are required in which situation.

You must consider the following factors when choosing cabling for a network. The cabling needs to fit the needs of the company and network pertaining to cost, ease of handling, possible signal interference, distance of cable run, necessary speed of transmission, security, and fire rating.

Cables should be installed in unexposed areas so that they are not easily tripped over, damaged, or eavesdropped upon. The cables should be strung behind walls and in the protected spaces between the ceiling and next floor. In some situations, wires are encapsulated within *pressurized conduits*, so that if there is an attempt to access a wire, the pressure of the conduit will change and sound an alarm or send a message to the administrator.

In the cases where heavy machinery or other devices that create electromagnetic fields are used, STP or fiber-optic cabling should be installed. If security is a top priority to a company, fiber-optic cabling should be used.

LAN Transmission Methods

Sometimes a packet needs to go only to one workstation, a set of workstations, or to all workstations on a particular subnet. If a packet needs to go from the source computer to one particular system, a *unicast* transmission method is used. If the packet needs to go to a specific group of systems, the sending system uses the *multicast* method. If a system wants all computers on its subnet to receive a message, it will use the *broadcast* method.

Unicast is pretty simple because it has a source and destination address. The data goes from point A to Z, it is a one-to-one transmission, and everyone is happy. Multicast is a bit different in that it is a one-to-many transmission. Multicasting enables one computer to send data to a selective group of computers. A good example of multicasting is tuning into a radio station on a computer. Some computers have software that enables the user to determine whether she wants to listen to country western, pop, Christian, or head-banging rock, for example. Once the user selects one of these, the software must tell the NIC driver not only to pick up packets addressed to its specific MAC address, but also to pick up packets that contain a specific multicast address.

The difference between broadcast and multicast is that in a broadcast, one-to-all transmission, everyone gets the data, and in multicast, only a few who have chosen to receive the data actually get it. So how does a server three states away multicast to one particular computer on a specific network and no other networks in between? Good question, glad you asked. The user who elects to receive a multicast actually has to tell her local router that she wants to get frames with this particular multicast address passed her way. The local router must tell the router upstream, and this process continues so that each router between the source and destination know where to pass this multicast data. This makes sure that the user can get her head-banging rock music and other networks are not bothered with this extra data. (The user does not actually need to tell her local router anything; the software on her computer will pass along the information and it is passed on and handled through a routing protocol.)

IP multicast protocols use a class D address, which is a special address space designed especially for multicasting. It can be used to send out information, multimedia data, and even real-time video and voice clips.

Reference

IP Multicast: **www.cisco.com/univercd/cc/td/doc/cisintwk/ito_doc/ipmulti.htm**

Transmission Definitions

- *Digital signals* represent binary digits as electrical pulses.

- *Analog signals* are continuous signals that vary by amplification and frequency.

- *Asynchronous communication* transfers data sequentially, uses start and stop bits, and requires that communicating devices communicate at the same speed.

- *Synchronous communication* is high-speed transmission controlled by electronic clock timing signals.

- *Baseband transmission* uses the full bandwidth for only one channel and has a low data transfer rate.

- *Broadband transmission* divides the bandwidth into many channels, enabling different types of data to be transmitted, and it provides a high data transfer rate.

- *Unicast transmission* occurs when a packet is sent from one source computer to one destination computer.

> - *Multicast transmission* occurs when a packet is sent from one source computer to several specific computers.
>
> - *Broadcast transmission* occurs when a packet is sent from one source computer to all computers on a certain network segment.

LAN Media Access Technologies

The physical topology of a network is the lower layer, or foundation, of a network. It determines what type of media will be used and how the media will be connected between different systems. Media access technologies deal with how these systems communicate over this media and are usually represented in protocols and interfaces. LAN access technologies set up the rules of how computers will communicate on a network, how errors are handled, what physical medium is to be used, the maximum transmission unit (MTU) size of frames, and much more. These rules enable all computers and devices to communicate and recover from problems, and they enable users to be productive in accomplishing their networking tasks. Each participating entity needs to know how to communicate properly so that all other systems will understand the transmissions, instructions, and requests. This is taken care of by the LAN media access technology.

 NOTE An MTU is a parameter that indicates how much data a frame can carry on a specific network. Different types of network technologies can require different MTU sizes, which is why frames are fragmented.

Token Passing

All right, who has the magic token? I need to talk!

A *token* is a 24-bit control frame used to control which computers communicate at what intervals. The token is passed from computer to computer, and only the computer that has the token can actually put frames onto the wire. The token grants a computer the right to communicate. The token contains the data to be transmitted and source and destination address information. When a system has data that it needs to transmit, it has to wait to receive the token. The computer then connects its message to the token and puts it on the wire. Each computer checks this message to determine whether it is addressed to it until the destination computer receives the message. The destination computer makes a copy of the message and sets a bit to tell the source computer that it did indeed get its message. Once this gets back to the source computer, it will remove the frames from the network. The designation computer makes a copy of the message, but only the originator of the message can remove the message from the token.

If a computer that receives the token does not have a message to transmit, it sends the token to the next computer on the network. An empty token has a header, data field, and trailer, but a token that has an actual message has a new header, destination address, source address, and a new trailer.

This type of network access method is used by Token Ring and FDDI technologies. Token-passing methods do not cause collisions because only one computer can communicate at a time.

CSMA

Ethernet protocols define how nodes are to communicate, recover from errors, and how they are to access the shared network cable. Ethernet uses CSMA as an access method to the network cable. There are two distinct types of CSMA: CSMA/CD and CSMA/CA.

A transmission is called a *carrier*, so if a computer is transmitting frames, this computer is performing a carrier activity. When computers use the ***carrier sense multiple access with collision detection (CSMA/CD)*** protocols, they monitor the transmission activity, or carrier activity, on the wire so that they can determine when would be the best time to transmit data. Each node monitors the wire continuously and waits until the wire is free before it transmits its data. As an analogy, consider several people gathered in a group talking here and there about this and that. If a person wants to talk, she will usually listen to the current conversation, and then, once it is ended, she can proceed to tell her story. If she does not wait for the first person to stop talking, two people are speaking at the same time and the people around them may not be able to understand fully what each is trying to say.

When using the CSMA/CD access method, computers listen for the absence of a carrier tone on the cable, which indicates that no one else is transmitting data. If two computers sense this absence and transmit data at the same time, contention and a collision can take place. *Contention* means that the nodes have to compete for the same shared medium. A *collision* happens when two or more frames collide, which most likely corrupts both frames. If a computer puts frames on the wire and its frames collide with another computer's frames, it will abort its transmission and alert all other stations that a collision just took place. All stations will execute a random collision timer to force a delay before they attempt to transmit data. This random collision timer is called the ***back-off algorithm***. CSMA/CD is the access method used in the 802.3 Ethernet networking standard. (Contention is usually reduced by dividing a network with bridges or switches.)

When a receiving system receives a message, it will send an acknowledgment indicating that this delivery happened successfully. If the sending system does not receive this acknowledgment, it will assume that the packet did not arrive and will retransmit the data.

Carrier sense multiple access with collision avoidance (CSMA/CA) is an access method in which each computer signals its intent to transmit data before it actually does so. This tells all other computers on the network not to transmit data right now because of a possibility of a collision.

Reference

Media Access Methods: **www.frick-cpa.com/netess/Net_MAC.asp**

Carrier-Sensing and Token-Passing Access Methods

Overall, carrier-sensing access methods are faster than token-passing access methods, but the former do have the problem of collisions. A network segment with many devices can cause too many collisions and slow down the network's performance. Token-passing technologies do not have problems with collisions, but they do not perform at the speed of carrier-sensing technologies.

Collision Domains

As indicated, a collision occurs on Ethernet networks when two computers transmit data at the same time. Other computers on the network detect this collision because the overlapping signals of the collision increases the voltage of the signal above a specific threshold. The more devices on a contention-based network, the more likely collisions will occur, which increases network *latency*. A *collision domain* is a group of computers that are contending, or competing, for the same shared communication medium.

An unacceptable amount of collisions can be caused by a highly populated network, a damaged cable or connector, too many repeaters, or cables that exceed the recommended length. If a cable is longer than what is recommended by the Ethernet specification, two computers on opposite ends of the cable may transmit data at the same time. Because the computers are so far away from each other, they may both transmit data, listen to ensure that a collision did not occur, determine that a collision did not occur, and then go merrily along with their business. If the cable is too long, the computers may not listen long enough for evidence of a collision. If the destination computers received these corrupted frames, they then have to send a request to the source system to retransmit the message, causing even more traffic.

These types of problems are dealt with mainly by implementing collision domains. An Ethernet network can have broadcast and collision domains. One subnet will be on the same broadcast and collision domain if it is not separated by routers or bridges. If the same subnet is divided by bridges, the bridges can enable the broadcast traffic to pass between the different parts of a subnet, but not the collisions, as shown in Figure 7-26. This is how collision domains are formed. Isolating collision domains reduces the amount of collisions that will take place on a network and increases its overall performance.

Another benefit of restricting and controlling broadcast and collision domains is that it makes it more difficult for an intruder to sniff the network and obtain useful information as he transverses the network. A useful tactic for attackers is to install a Trojan horse that sets up a network sniffer on the compromised computer. The sniffer is usually configured to look for a specific type of information, such as usernames and passwords. If broadcast and collision domains are in effect, the compromised system will have access only to the broadcast and collision traffic within its specific subnet or collision domain. The compromised system will not be able to listen to traffic on other broadcast and collision domains, and this can greatly reduce the amount of traffic and information available to an attacker.

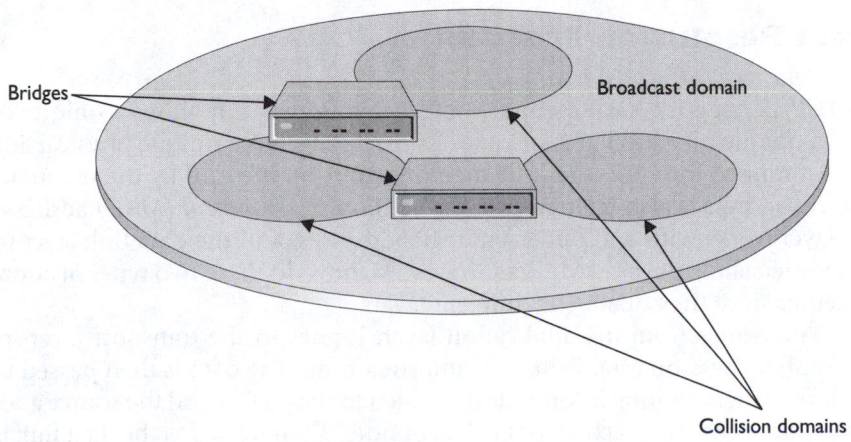

Bridges

Broadcast domain

Collision domains

Figure 7-26   Collision domains within one broadcast domain

Reference

Collision Domains white paper: **www.transition.com/learning/whitepapers/ colldom_wp.htm**

Polling

Hi. Do you have anything you would like to say?

The third type of LAN media access method is polling. In an environment where a *polling* LAN media access method is used, some systems are configured as primary stations and others are secondary stations. At predefined intervals, the primary station will ask the secondary station if it has anything to transmit. This is the only time a secondary station can communicate.

Polling is a method of monitoring multiple devices and controlling network access transmission. If polling is used to monitor devices, the primary device will communicate with each secondary device in an interval to check its status. The primary device will then log the response it receives and move on to the next device. If polling is used for network access, the primary station will ask each device if it has something to communicate to another device. Network access transmission polling is used mainly with mainframe environments.

Protocols

Some protocols, such as UDP, TCP, and IP, have been addressed in earlier sections. Networks are made up of these and many other types of protocols that provide an array of functionality. Several of the most widely used TCP/IP protocols are discussed in the following sections.

Address Resolution Protocol

This IP does me no good! I need a MAC!

On a TCP/IP network, each computer and network device requires a unique IP address and a unique physical hardware address. Each NIC has a unique physical address that is programmed into the read-only memory chips on the card by the manufacture. The physical address is also referred to as the *Media Access Control (MAC)* address. The network layer works with and understands IP addresses, and the data link layer works with and understands physical MAC addresses. So, how do these two types of addresses work together since they operate at different layers?

When data comes from the application layer, it goes to the transport layer for sequence numbers, session establishment, and streaming. The data is then passed to the network layer, where routing information is added to the packet and the source and destination IP addresses are attached to the data bundle. Then it goes to the data link layer, which must find the MAC address and add it to the header portion of the frame. When a frame hits the wire, it only knows what MAC address it is heading toward. At this lower layer of the OSI model, the mechanisms do not even understand IP addresses. So if a computer cannot resolve the IP address passed down from the network layer to the corresponding MAC address, it cannot communicate with that destination computer.

 NOTE A MAC address is unique because the first 24 bits represent the manufacturer code and the last 24 bits represent the unique serial number assigned by the manufacturer.

MAC and IP addresses must be properly mapped so that they can be correctly resolved. This happens through the *Address Resolution Protocol (ARP)*. When the data link layer receives a frame, the network layer has already attached the destination IP address to it, but the data link layer cannot understand the IP address and invokes ARP for help. ARP broadcasts a frame requesting the MAC address that corresponds with the destination IP address. Each computer on the subnet receives this broadcast frame and all but the computer that has the requested IP address ignore it. The computer that has the destination IP address responds with its MAC address. Now ARP knows what hardware address corresponds with that specific IP address. The data link layer takes the frame, adds the hardware address to it, and passes it on to the physical layer, which enables the frame to hit the wire and go to the destination computer. ARP maps the hardware address and associated IP address and stores it in its table for a predefined amount of time. This caching is done so that when another frame destined for the same IP address needs to hit the wire, ARP does not need to broadcast its request again; it just looks in its table for this information.

Sometimes attackers alter a system's ARP table so that it contains incorrect information; this is called ***ARP table poisoning***. The attacker's goal is to receive packets that were intended for another computer. This is a type of ***masquerading*** attack. For example, if computer A has an IP address of 10.19.34.3 and a MAC address of *x* and computer B has this mapping in its ARP table, an attacker can alter the ARP table to indicate that IP address 10.19.34.3 is mapped to MAC address *y* (the attacker's MAC address), so that any packets computer B tries to send to computer A actually go to the attacker's computer.

References

Address Resolution Protocol (ARP): **www.erg.abdn.ac.uk/users/gorry/course/ inet-pages/arp.html**

ARP Protocol Overview: **www.freesoft.org/CIE/Topics/61.htm**

Reverse Address Resolution Protocol

A computer can receive its IP addresses in a few different ways when it first boots up. If it has a statically assigned address, nothing needs to happen. If a computer depends upon a Dynamic Host Configuration Protocol (DHCP) server to assign it the correct IP address, it will boot up and make a request to the DHCP server. The DHCP server will assign the IP address and everyone is happy and healthy. But what if the environment has diskless workstations, meaning they have no operating systems?

Diskless workstations have just enough code to know how to boot up and broadcast for an IP address, and they may have a pointer to the server that holds the operating system. The diskless workstation knows its hardware address, so it broadcasts this information so that a listening server can assign it the correct IP address. As with ARP, ***Reverse Address Resolution Protocol (RARP)*** frames go to all systems on the subnet, but only the RARP server responds. Once the RARP server receives this request, it looks in its table to see which IP address matches the broadcast hardware address. The server then sends a message back to the requesting computer that contains its IP address. The system now has an IP address and can function on the network.

The ***Boot Protocol (BOOTP)*** was created after RARP to enhance the functionality that RARP provides for diskless workstations. The diskless workstation can receive its IP address, the name server address for future name resolutions, and the default gateway address from

The Difference Between ARP and RARP

ARP knows the IP address and broadcasts to find the matching hardware address, the MAC address. RARP knows the hardware address and broadcasts to find the IP address.

the BOOTP server. BOOTP usually provides more functionality to diskless workstations than RARP.

Internet Control Message Protocol

The *Internet Control Message Protocol (ICMP)* is basically IP's "messenger boy." ICMP delivers messages, reports errors, replies to certain requests, reports routing information, and is used to test connectivity and troubleshoot problems on IP networks. ICMP is a protocol within the TCP/IP suite.

The most commonly understood use of ICMP is the *ping* utility. When a person wants to test connectivity to another system, he may ping it, which sends out ICMP ECHO REQUEST frames. The replies on his screen that are returned to the ping utility are called ICMP REPLY frames and are responding to the ECHO REQUEST frames. If a reply is not returned within a predefined time period, the ping utility sends more ECHO REQUEST frames. If there is still no reply, ping indicates that the host is unreachable.

ICMP also indicates when problems occur with a specific route on the network and tells surrounding routers about better routes to take based on the health and congestion of the various pathways. Routers use ICMP to send messages in response to datagrams that could not be delivered. The router selects the proper ICMP response, wraps it into an IP frame, and sends it back to the requesting host, indicating that problems were encountered with the transmission request.

ICMP is used by other connectionless protocols, not just IP. This is because connectionless protocols do not have any way of detecting and reacting to transmission errors as do connection-oriented protocols. In these instances, the connectionless protocol may use ICMP to send error messages back to the sending system to indicate networking problems.

References

ICMP Messages: **www.ee.siue.edu/~rwalden/networking/icmpmess.html**

Routing Sequences for ICMP: **www.ncmag.com/2001_03/ICMP**

Networking Devices

Several types of devices are used in LANs, MANs, and WANs to provide intercommunication between computers and networks. The use of these devices vary according to their functionality, capabilities, intelligence, and network placement.

Repeaters

A *repeater* provides the simplest type of connectivity because it only repeats and amplifies electrical signals between cable segments. A repeater extends a network because it receives data from one cable segment and transmits it onto another segment.

Repeaters work at the physical layer and are add-on devices for extending a network connection over a greater distance. The device amplifies signals because signals attenuate the farther they have to travel.

Repeaters can also work as line conditioners by actually cleaning up the signals. This is more easily accomplished by amplifying digital signals when compared to analog. Because digital signals are discrete units, it is easier for the amplifier to extract background noise from them. If the device is amplifying analog signals, any accompanying noise often will be amplified, which may further distort the signal.

A *hub* is a multiport repeater. A hub is often referred to as a *concentrator* because it is the physical communication device that allows several computers and devices to communicate with each other. A hub does not understand or work with IP or MAC addresses. When one system sends a signal to go to another system that is connected to it, the signal is broadcast to all the ports, thus all the systems connected to the concentrator.

Bridges

A *bridge* is a LAN device used to connect LAN segments. It works at the data link layer and therefore works with MAC addresses. A repeater does not work with addresses; it just forwards on all signals it receives. When a frame comes to a bridge, the bridge will determine whether or not the MAC address is on the local network segment. If the MAC address is not on the local segment, the bridge will forward it on to the necessary network segment.

A bridge is used to divide overburdened networks into smaller segments to ensure better use of bandwidth and traffic control. A bridge amplifies the electrical signal, as does a repeater, but it has more intelligence and is used to extend a LAN and enable the administrator to filter frames so that she can control what frames go where.

One issue that has to be watched carefully with bridges is **broadcast storms**. Because bridges can forward all traffic, they forward all broadcast packets as well. This can overwhelm the network and result in a broadcast storm, which degrades the network bandwidth and performance.

Three main types of bridges are used: local, remote link, and translation. A *local bridge* connects two or more LAN segments within a local area, which is usually a building. A *remote bridge* can connect two or more LAN segments over a WAN by using telecommunications links. A remote bridge is equipped with telecommunication ports, which enable it to connect two or more LANs that are separated by a long distance and can be brought together via telephone lines. A *translation bridge* is needed if the two LANs being connected are different types and use different standards and protocols. A common type of connection would be between a Token Ring network and an Ethernet network. The frames on each network type are different sizes, the fields contain different protocol information, and the two networks transmit at different speeds. If a regular bridge were put into place, Ethernet frames would go to the Token Ring network and vice versa, and neither would be able to understand messages that came from the other network segment. A translation bridge does what its name implies—it translates between the two network types.

The following items outline the functions of a bridge:

- Segments a large network into smaller, more controllable pieces
- Uses filtering based on MAC addresses
- Joins different types of network links while retaining the same broadcast domain
- Isolates collision domains within the same broadcast domain
- Can take place locally within a LAN or remotely to connect two distant LANs
- Can translate between protocol types

 NOTE Routers versus Bridges: Routers work at the network layer and filter packets based on IP addresses. Bridges work at the data link layer and filter frames based on MAC addresses. Routers will *not* usually pass broadcast information. Bridges *will* pass broadcast information.

Forwarding Tables

You go that way. And you—you go this way!

A bridge must know how to get a frame to its destination—that is, it must know to which port the frame must be sent and where the destination host is located. Years ago, network administrators had to type route paths into bridges so that the bridges had static paths indicating where to pass frames that were headed for different destinations. This was a tedious task and prone to errors. Today bridges use *transparent bridging* or *source routing*.

If transparent bridging is used, a bridge starts to learn about the network's environment as soon as it is powered on and as the network changes. It does this by examining frames and making entries into its forwarding tables. When a bridge receives a frame from a new source computer, the bridge will associate this new source address and the port on which it arrived. It does this for all computers that send frames on the network. Eventually, the bridge knows the address of each computer on the various network segments

Question

What is the difference between two LANs connected via bridges versus being connected via routers?

Answer: If two LANs are connected with a bridge, the LANs have been extended because they are both in the same broadcast domain. A router can be configured not to forward broadcast information, so if two LANs are connected with a router, an internetwork results. An *internetwork* is a group of networks connected in a way that enables any node on any network to communicate to any other node. The Internet is an example of an internetwork.

and to which port each is connected. If the bridge gets a request to send a frame onto a destination that is not in its forwarding table, it sends out a query frame on each network segment except for the source segment. The destination host is the only one that replies to this query. The bridge updates its table with this computer address and with which port it is connected and forwards on the frame.

Many bridges use the *Spanning Tree Algorithm (STA)*, which adds more intelligence to the bridge. The STA ensures that frames do not circle networks forever, provides redundant paths in case a bridge goes down, assigns unique identifiers to each bridge, assigns priority values to these bridges, and calculates path costs. This creates much more efficient frame forwarding processes by each bridge. The STA also enables an administrator to indicate whether she wants traffic to travel certain paths instead of others.

If *source routing* is used instead of transparent bridging, the packets contain the necessary information within them to tell the bridge where they should go. The packets hold the forwarding information so that they can find their way to their destination without needing bridges and routers to dictate their paths. If the computer wants to dictate its forwarding information instead of depending on a bridge, how does it know the correct route to the destination computer? The source computer sends out explorer packets that arrive at the destination computer. These packets contain the route information it had to take to get to the destination, including what bridges it had to pass through. The destination computer then sends these packets back to the source computer, and the source computer strips out the routing information, inserts it into the packets, and sends them on to the destination.

 NOTE External devices and border routers should not accept packets with source routing information within their headers. This is because the source routing information will override what is laid out in the forward and route tables configured on the intermediate devices. You want to control how traffic transverses your network; you don't want packets having this type of control and going wherever they want. Source routing can be used by attackers to get around certain bridge and router filtering rules.

References

Bridge MIB Charter: **www.ietf.org/html.charters/bridge-charter.html**

Ethernet Bridges and Switches: **www.erg.abdn.ac.uk/users/gorry/course/lan-pages/bridge.html**

Routers

We are going up the chain of the OSI layers while discussing various networking devices. Repeaters work at the physical layer, bridges work at the data link layer, and routers work at the network layer. As we go up each layer, each corresponding device has more intelligence and functionality. This is because each device can look deeper into the frame. A repeater looks at the electrical signal. The bridge can look at the MAC address within the header. The router can peel back the first header information and look farther into the frame and find out the IP address and other routing information. The farther a device can look into a frame, the more decisions it can make based on the information within the frame. We will see later that gateways can look all the way to the *core* of the frame, which contains the data that the user sent in the first place—not just addresses and routing information.

Routers are layer 3, or network layer, devices that are used to connect similar or different networks. (For example, they can connect two Ethernet LANs or an Ethernet LAN to a Token Ring LAN.) A router is a device that has two or more interfaces and a routing table so that it knows how to get packets to their destination. It can filter traffic based on access control lists (ACLs), and it fragments packets when necessary. Because routers have more network level knowledge, they can perform higher level functions such as calculating the shortest and most economical path between the sending and receiving hosts.

Routers discover information about routes and changes that take place in a network through its routing protocols (RIP, BGP, OSPF, and others). These protocols tell routers if a link has gone down, if a route is congested, and if another route is more economical; they also update router route tables and indicate if a router is having problems or has gone down.

A bridge uses the same network address for all of its ports, but a router assigns a new address per port, which enables it to connect more networks together.

The router may be a stand-alone device or a computer running a networking operating system that is dual homed. When packets arrive at one of the interfaces, the router compares those packets to its ACLs. This list indicates what packets are allowed in and what packets are denied. Access decisions are based on source and destination IP address, protocol type, and source and destination ports. An administrator may block all packets coming from the 10.10.12.0 network, any FTP requests, or any packets headed toward a specific port on a specific host, for example. This type of control is provided by the ACLs, which the administrator must program and update as necessary.

What actually happens inside the router when it receives a packet? Let's follow the steps:

1. A frame is received on one of the interfaces of a router. The router strips off the header information to be able to view the routing data.

2. The router retrieves the destination IP network address from the datagram; it does not care about the host portion of the IP address.

3. The router looks at its routing table to see which port matches the requested destination IP network address.

4. If the router does not have information in its table about the destination address, it sends out an ICMP error message to the sending computer indicating that the message could not reach its destination.

5. If the router does have a route in its routing table for this destination, it decrements the Time to Live (TTL) value and sees whether the MTU is different

for the destination network. If the destination network requires a smaller MTU, the router fragments the datagram.

6. The router changes header information in the frame so the frame can go to the next correct router, or if the destination computer is on a connecting network, the changes made enable the frame to go directly to the destination computer.

7. The router then sends the frame to its output queue for the necessary interface.

Table 7-6 provides a quick review of the differences between routers and bridges.

When is it best to use a repeater, bridge, or router? A repeater is used if an administrator needs to expand a network and amplify signals so that they do not weaken on longer cables. However, a repeater will forward collision and broadcast information because it does not have the intelligence to decipher among different types of traffic. Bridges work at the data link layer and have a bit more intelligence than a repeater. Bridges can do simple filtering, and they separate collision domains, not broadcast domains. A bridge should be used when an administrator wants to divide a network into segments to reduce traffic congestion and excessive collisions. A router splits up a network into collision domains and broadcast domains. A router gives more of a clear-cut division between network segments than repeaters or bridges. A router should be used if an administrator wants to have more defined control of where the traffic goes, because more sophisticated filtering is available in routers, and when used to segment a network, the result is more controllable sections.

A router is used when an administrator wants to divide a network along the lines of departments, workgroups, or other business-oriented divisions. A bridge divides segments based more on the traffic type and load.

Routing

Routing is a packet-forwarding process that takes place on internetworks. When a computer needs to send a packet, the sending computer needs to know if the destination computer is local or on a remote network, which is indicated by the network portion of the destination IP address. If the destination computer is on the same local network segment, the sending computer sends the packet to that computer. If the destination computer is on a remote network, the sending computer must send the packet to its default gateway,

Bridge	Router
Reads header information, but does not alter it	Creates a new header for each frame
Builds forwarding tables based on MAC addresses	Builds routing tables based on IP addresses
Uses the same network address for all ports	Assigns a different network address per port
Filters traffic based on MAC addresses	Filters traffic based on IP addresses
Forwards broadcast packets	Does not forward broadcast packets
Forwards traffic if destination address is unknown to the bridge	Does not forward traffic that contains a destination address unknown to the router

Table 7-6   Main Differences Between Bridges and Routers

usually a router, which will route the packet to the right network. How the router(s) move packets from the source to the destination computer is referred to as *routing*.

Routing is actually performed by protocols and algorithms within the router. The routers use these to determine the next hop that will get the datagram closer to its destination, but the routers are not responsible for knowing and mapping out the complete path to the destination computer. The router just needs to get the packet to the destination computer or to the next router closer to the target network.

Originally, tables were built *statically*, meaning the administrator had to type in each and every route that datagrams could take. Static routing is still used in smaller networks, but the larger the network, the more overwhelming static routing will become. Dynamic routing was developed, in which a dynamic routing protocol discovers routes and makes the necessary changes to the routing tables. If routes go down or become congested, the protocol will update the table with the new information instead of requiring the administrator to alter the table manually.

Routing environments are based on *autonomous systems (ASs)*. An AS is an individual network that is managed by a specific authority and implements its own internal routing. An AS is a routing domain, meaning it uses its own address scheme and internal routing protocols. Figure 7-27 shows two different ASs and how they connect and communicate.

The Internet is a large collection of many different ASs. The lines among these ASs are drawn by the individual service providers and carrier networks, not the individual corporate networks on their own. The ASs are connected to each other through routers and

Figure 7-27   Autonomous systems

routing protocols. Routing takes place within an AS through internal routing protocols such as OSPF and RIP. The ASs communicate to each other through exterior routing protocols such as BGP.

Any traffic that needs to leave an AS heads toward that AS's *border router*. The border router provides a gateway to the world for a specific network. Any data coming into the AS comes to the same border router, and the traffic is routed internally as required. AS networks share routing information so that the Internet works more efficiently.

References

Routing Basics: **www.cisco.com/univercd/cc/td/doc/cisintwk/ito_doc/ routing.htm**

Active IETF Working Groups: **www.ietf.org/html.charters/wg-dir.html**

Google listings for routers and routing: **directory.google.com/Top/Computers/ Internet/Routers_and_Routing**

Switches

I want to talk to you privately. Let's talk through this switch.

Switches combine the functionality of a repeater and the functionality of a bridge. A switch amplifies the electrical signal, like a repeater, and has the built-in circuitry and intelligence of a bridge. It is a multiport connection device that provides connections for individual computers or other hubs and switches. Any device connected to one port can communicate with a device connected to another port with its own virtual private link. How is this different than how devices communicate using a bridge or a hub? When a frame comes to a hub, it sends the frame out through all of its ports. When a frame comes to a bridge, the bridge sends the frame to the port to which the destination network segment is connected. When a frame comes to a switch, the switch sends the frame directly to the destination computer; a reduction of traffic results. Figure 7-28 illustrates a network configuration that has computers directly connected to their corresponding switches.

On Ethernet networks, computers have to compete for the same shared network medium. Each computer must listen for activity on the network and transmit its data when it thinks the coast is clear. This contention and the resulting collisions cause traffic delays and use up precious bandwidth. When switches are used, contention and collisions are not issues, which results in more efficient use of the network's bandwidth and decreased latency. Switches reduce or remove the sharing of the network medium and the problems that come with it.

A switch is a multiport bridging device, and each port provides dedicated bandwidth to the device attached to it. A port is bridged to another port so that the two devices have an end-to-end private link. The switch employs full-duplex communication so that one wire pair is used for sending and another pair is used for receiving. This ensures that the two connected devices do not contend for the connection between them.

Figure 7-28
Switches enable devices to communicate with each other with their own virtual link.

Basic switches work at the data link layer and forward traffic based on MAC addresses. However, today's layer 3, layer 4, and other layer switches have more enhanced functionality than layer 2 switches. These higher level switches offer routing functionality, packet inspection, traffic prioritization, and quality of service (QoS) functionality. These switches are referred to as *multilayered switches* because they combine data link layer, network layer, and other layer functionalities.

Multilayered switches use hardware-based processing power, which enables them to look deeper within the packet, to make more decisions based on the information found within the packet, and then to provide routing and traffic management tasks. Usually this amount of work creates a lot of overhead and traffic delay, but multilayered switches perform these activities within an application-specific integrated circuit (ASIC). This means that most of the functions of the switch are performed at the hardware and chip level versus the software level; this is a much quicker method.

Many enterprises today use a switched network, in which computers are connected to dedicated ports on Ethernet switches, Gigabit Ethernet switches, ATM switches, and more. This evolution of switches, added services, and the capability to incorporate repeater, bridge, and router functionality have made switches an important part of today's networking world.

Because security has to do with controlling who can access specific resources, the more intelligent devices can make more detail-oriented decisions; as a result, they can provide a higher level of protection. When devices can look deeper into the packets, they have more information to make access decisions, which provides more granular access control.

As stated, switching makes it more difficult for intruders to sniff and monitor network traffic because no broadcast and collision information is continually traveling throughout the network. Switches provide a security service that the other devices cannot provide. *Virtual LANs (VLANs)* are also an important part of switching networks because they enable administrators to have more control over their environment and they can isolate users and groups into logical and manageable entities. VLANs are described in the next section.

References

Enterasys White Papers: **www.enterasys.com/products/whitepapers**

Designing Switched LAN Internetworks: **www.cisco.com/univercd/cc/td/doc/ cisintwk/idg4/nd2012.htm**

VLAN

The technology behind switches has introduced the capability to use virtual LANs (VLANS). VLANs enable administrators to separate and group computers logically based on resource requirements, security, or business needs instead of the standard physical location of the systems. When using repeaters, bridges, and routers, systems and resources are grouped in a manner that is dictated by their physical location. Figure 7-29 shows how

These three VLANs span across four different buildings. The computers and users are grouped logically instead of physically.

Building Two

Building One

Building Three

Building Four

Figure 7-29 VLANs enable administrators to put systems into logical networks.

computers that are physically located next to each other can be grouped into different VLANs. Administrators can form these groups based on the users' and company's needs instead of the physical location of systems and resources.

An administrator may want to place all users' computers in the marketing department in the same VLAN network, for example, so that they all receive the same broadcast messages and can access the same types of resources. This arrangement could get tricky if a few of the users are located in another building or on another floor, but VLANs provide the administrator with this type of flexibility. VLANs also enable an administrator to apply particular security policies to respective logical groups. This way, if tighter security is required for the payroll department, for example, the administrator can develop a policy, add all payroll systems to a specific VLAN, and apply the security policy only to the payroll VLAN.

A VLAN exists on top of the physical network, as shown in Figure 7-30. If workstation P1 wants to communicate with workstation D1, the message has to be routed because they are on different logical networks, even though the workstations are physically next to each other.

Gateways

A *gateway* is a general term for software running on a device that connects two different environments and acts as a translator for them or somehow restricts their interactions. Usually a gateway is needed when one environment speaks a different language, meaning

Figure 7-30   VLANs exist on a higher level than the physical network and are not bound to it.

it uses a certain protocol that the other environment does not understand. The gateway can translate Internetwork Packet Exchange (IPX) protocol packets to IP packets, accept mail from one type of mail server, and format it so another type of mail server can accept and understand it, or connect and translate different data link technologies such as FDDI to Ethernet.

Gateways perform much more complex tasks than connection devices, as in routers and bridges. However, some people refer to routers as gateways when they connect two unlike networks (Token Ring and Ethernet) because the router has to translate between the data link technologies. Figure 7-31 shows how a network access server (NAS) functions as a gateway between telecommunication and network connections.

When networks connect to a backbone, a gateway can translate the different technologies and frame formats used on the backbone network versus the connecting LAN. If a bridge was set up between an FDDI backbone and an Ethernet LAN, the computers on the LAN would not understand the FDDI protocols and frame formats. In this case, a LAN gateway would be needed to translate the protocols used between the different networks.

A popular type of a gateway is an *electronic mail* gateway. Several e-mail vendors have their own syntax, message format, and ways of dealing with message transmission. If, for example, David writes an e-mail message and his corporate network uses Sendmail and the message is headed to Dan, whose corporate network uses Microsoft Exchange, a mail gateway is required. The mail gateway will usually convert the message into a standard that all mail servers understand—X.400—and pass it on to Dan's mail server.

Another example of a gateway is a voice and media gateway. Recently, there has been a drive to combine voice and data networks. This provides for a lot of efficiency because the same media can be used for both types of data transfers. However, voice is a streaming

Figure 7-31 Several types of gateways can be used; a NAS is one example.

technology, whereas data is usually transferred in packets. So this shared media eventually has to communicate with two different types of networks: the telephone company's PSTN and routers that will take the packet-based data off to the Internet. This means a gateway must separate the combined voice and data information and put it into a form that each of the following networks can understand.

Table 7-7 shows the devices covered in the last sections and points out their important characteristics.

PBX

Telephone companies use switching technologies for transmitting phone calls to their destinations. The telephone company's central office houses the switches that connect towns, cities, and metropolitan areas through the use of optical fiber rings. So, for example, when Dusty makes a phone call from his house, the call first hits his local central office and the switch within that office decides whether it is a local or long-distance call and where it needs to go from there. A *Private Branch Exchange (PBX)* is a private telephone switch that is located on a company's property. This switch performs some of the same switching tasks that take place at the telephone company's central office. The PBX has a dedicated connection to its local telephone company's central office, where more intelligent switching takes place.

A PBX can interface with several types of devices and provides a number of telephone services. The data is multiplexed onto a dedicated line connected to the telephone company's central office. Figure 7-32 shows how different types of data can be placed on one line at the PBX and sent to the telephone company's switching facility.

PBXs use digital switching devices that can control analog and digital signals. Older PBXs may support only analog devices, but most PBXs have been updated to digital. This move to digital systems and signals has reduced a number of the PBX and telephone security vulnerabilities that used to exist. However, that in no way means that PBX fraud does not take place today. Many companies, for example, have modems

Device	OSI Layer	Functionality
Repeater	Physical layer	Amplifies signal and extends networks
Bridge	Data link layer	Forwards packets and filters based on MAC addresses; forwards broadcast traffic, but not collision traffic
Router	Network layer	Separates and connects LANs creating internetworks; routers filter based on IP addresses
Switch	Data link layer	Provides a private virtual link between communicating devices, allows for VLANs, reduces traffic, and impedes network sniffing
Gateway	Application layer (although different types of gateways can work at other layers)	Connects different types of networks, performs protocol and format translations

Table 7-7 Comparison of the Devices and Their Functionality

Figure 7-32 A PBX combines different types of data on the same lines.

hanging off their PBX to enable the vendor to dial-in and perform maintenance to the system. The modem should be activated only when a problem requires the vendor to dial in, and it should be disabled otherwise.

In addition, many PBX systems have default system manager passwords that are hardly ever changed. These passwords are set by default; therefore, if 100 companies purchased and implemented 100 PBX systems from the PBX vendor ABC and they do not reset the password, a *phreaker* (a phone hacker) who knows this default password now has access to 100 PBX systems. Once a phreaker breaks into a PBX system, she can cause mayhem by rerouting calls, reconfiguring switches, or configuring the system to provide her and her friends with free long-distance calls. This type of fraud happens more often than most companies are aware, because many companies do not closely watch their phone bills.

PBX systems are also vulnerable to brute force and other types of attacks, in which phreakers use scripts and dictionaries to guess the necessary credentials to gain access to the system. In some cases, phreakers have listened to and changed people's voice messages. So when people call to leave Bob a message, for example, they might not hear his usual boring message, but a new message that is screaming obscenities and insults.

Firewalls

Stop! Who goes there?

Firewalls are used to restrict access to one network from another network. Most companies use firewalls to restrict access into their networks from Internet users. They may also use firewalls to restrict one internal network segment from accessing another internal segment. For example, if the network administrator wants to make sure that employees cannot access the Research and Development network, she would place a firewall between this network and all other networks and configure the firewall to allow only the type of traffic she deems acceptable.

A firewall device supports and enforces the company's network security policy. An organizational security policy will provide high-level instructions on acceptable and unacceptable actions as they pertain to security. The firewall has a more defined and granular security policy that dictates what services are allowed to be accessed, what IP addresses and ranges are to be restricted, and what ports can be accessed. The firewall is described as a "choke point" in the network, because all communication should flow through it, and this is where traffic is inspected and restricted.

A firewall is actually a type of gateway that can be a router, server, authentication server, or specialized hardware device. It monitors packets coming into and out of the network it is protecting. It filters out the packets that do not meet the requirements of the security policy. It can discard these packets, repackage them, or redirect them depending upon the firewall configuration and security policy. Packets are filtered based on their source and destination addresses and ports by service, packet type, protocol type, header information, sequence bits, and much more. Vendors can use specific functionality and parameters for identification and access restriction.

Many times, companies set up firewalls to construct a *demilitarized zone (DMZ)*, which is a network segment that is located between the protected and the unprotected networks. The DMZ provides a buffer zone between the dangerous Internet and the goodies within the internal network that the company is trying to protect. As shown in Figure 7-33, two firewalls are usually installed to form the DMZ. The DMZ usually contains Web, mail, and DNS servers, which must be hardened down because they would be the first in line for attacks. Many DMZs also have an IDS sensor that listens for malicious and suspicious behavior.

Many different types of firewalls are available because each environment can have unique requirements and security goals. Firewalls have gone through an evolution of their own and have grown in sophistication and functionality. The following sections describe the various types of firewalls.

Packet Filtering

I don't like this packet. Oh, but I like this packet. I don't like this packet. This other packet is okay.

    Packet filtering is a security method of controlling what data can flow into and out of a network. Packet filtering takes place by using ACLs, which are developed and applied to a device. ACLs are lines of text, called *rules*, that the device will apply them to each packet that it receives. The lines of text provide specific information pertaining to what packets can be accepted and what packets are denied. For instance, an ACL can have one line that states that any packets coming from the IP range 172.168.0.0 must be denied. Another line may indicate that no packets using the Telnet service will be allowed to enter the network, and another line may indicate that no traffic that is headed toward port 443 is to be allowed. Then it can have a line indicating that all traffic on port 80 is acceptable and that it should be routed to a specific IP address, which is the Web server. Each time the device receives a packet, it compares the information in the packet's header to each line in the ACL. If the packet indicates that it is using Telnet or requests to make a con-

Figure 7-33   At least two firewalls are usually used to construct a DMZ.

nection to port 443, it is discarded. If the packet header information indicates that it wants to communicate through port 80 using HTTP over TCP, the packet is accepted and redirected to the Web server.

This filtering is based on network layer information, which means that the device cannot look too far into the packet itself. It can make decisions based on header information only, which is limited. Most routers use ACLs to act as a type of firewall and a router table to carry out routing decisions, but they do not provide the level of protection provided by other types of firewalls, which look deeper into the packet. Because packet filtering looks only at the header information, it is not application-dependent, as many proxy firewalls are. Packet-filtering firewalls also do not keep track of the state of a connection, which takes place in a *stateful* firewall. Packet filtering is the first generation firewall— that is, it is the first type that was created and used, and other types that were developed fall into different generations.

Stateful Inspection

When packet filtering is used, a packet arrives at the router, and the router runs through its ACLs to determine whether this packet should be allowed or denied. If the packet is allowed, it is passed on to the destination host, or to another router, and the router forgets about the packet. This is different from *stateful* filtering, which remembers and keeps track of what packets went where until each particular connection is closed.

Stateful packet filtering is like a nosy neighbor who gets into people's business and conversations. She keeps track of who said what and when. This can be annoying until your house is burglarized. Then you and the cops will want to talk to the nosy neighbor, because she knows everything that is going on in the neighborhood and would be the most likely one to know if something unusual happened. A stateful filtering router is nosier than a regular filtering device, because it keeps track of what computers say to

Pros and Cons of Packet Filtering

Pros

- Scaleable
- Provides high performance
- Application independent

Cons

- Does not look into the packet past the header information
- Low security relative to other options
- Does not keep track of the state of a connection

each other. This requires that the firewall maintain a *state table*, which is like a score sheet of who said what to whom.

Stateful inspection firewalls also make decisions on what packets to allow or disallow, but their functionality goes a step further. For example, a regular packet-filtering device may deny any UDP packets requesting service on port 25, and a stateful packet-filtering device may have the rule to allow only UDP packets through if they are responses to outgoing requests. Basically, the stateful firewall will only allow packets in that its internal hosts requested. So if Mitchell sends a request to a computer on a different network, this request will be logged in the firewall's state table. The table will indicate that Mitchell's computer made a request and that packets should be coming back to Mitchell. When the computer on the Internet responds to Mitchell, these packets will be compared to the data in the state table at the firewall. Because the state table does have information about a previous request for these packets, the firewall allows the packets to pass through. If, on the other hand, Mitchell did not make any requests and packets were coming in from the Internet to him, the firewall will see that no previous request for this information was received and then look at its ACLs to see if these packets should be allowed.

Regular packet filtering compares incoming packets to rules defined in its ACLs. When stateful packet filtering receives a packet, it first looks in its state table to see whether a connection has already been established and whether this data was requested. If there was no previous connection and the state table holds no information about the packet, the packet is compared to the device's ACLs. If the ACL allows this type of traffic, the packet is allowed to access the network. If that type of traffic is not allowed, the packet is dropped.

Although this provides an extra step of protection, it also adds more complexity because this device must now keep a dynamic state table and remember connections.

Stateful Inspection Characteristics

- The firewall maintains a state table that tracks each and every communication channel.

- Frames are analyzed at all communication layers.

- It provides a high degree of security and does not introduce the performance hit that proxy firewalls introduce.

- It is scaleable and transparent to users.

- It provides data for tracking connectionless protocols such as UDP and ICMP.

- The state and context of the data within the packets are stored and updated continuously.

- It is considered a third-generation firewall.

Packet filtering has unfortunately opened the door to many types of denial-of-service (DoS) attacks. Several types of attacks are aimed at flooding the state table with bogus information. The state table is a resource like a system's hard drive space, memory, and CPU. When the state table is stuffed full of bogus information, it can either freeze the device or cause it to reboot. In addition, if this firewall has to be rebooted for some reason, it loses its information on all recent connections; thus, it will deny legitimate packets.

Proxy Firewalls

Meet my proxy. He will be our middleman.

A *proxy* is a middleman. The concept of proxy is to redirect a request to a separate entity. Suppose someone needed to give a box and a message to the president of the United States; this person could not just walk up to the president and hand over these items. Instead, the person would have to go through a middleman, who would accept the box and message and thoroughly go through it to ensure that nothing dangerous was inside. This is what a proxy firewall does—it accepts messages either entering or leaving a network, inspects them for malicious information, and when it decides the messages are okay, it passes the data on to the destination computer. Proxy firewalls are second generation firewalls.

A proxy stands between a trusted and untrusted network and makes the connection, each way, on behalf of the source. So if a user on the Internet requests to send data to a computer on the internal, protected network, the proxy will get this request and look it over for suspicious information. The request does not automatically go to the destination computer—instead, the proxy firewall *impersonates* the internal destination computer and accepts the request on behalf of the computer it is protecting. If the proxy decides the packet is safe, it sends it on to the destination computer. When the destination computer replies, the reply goes back to the proxy server, which repackages the packet to contain the source address of the proxy server, not the host system on the internal network. What is important is that a proxy firewall breaks the communication channel: there is no direct connection to internal computers.

This type of firewall makes a copy of each accepted packet before transmitting it. It repackages the packet to hide the packet's true origin. If an attacker attempts to scan or probe a company's network, he will receive only information that has been intercepted and repackaged by proxy server. The returned packets will have only the IP address of the firewall, and the information released will be sparse; thus the internal network is protected and hidden.

The proxy firewall is the only machine that talks to the outside world. This ensures that no computer has direct access to internal computers. This also means that the proxy server is the only computer that needs a valid IP address. The rest of the computers on the internal network can use private (non-routable IP addresses on the Internet) addresses, because no computers on the outside will see their addresses anyway.

A *dual-homed firewall* has two interfaces: one facing the external network and the other facing the internal network. This is different from a computer that has forwarding enabled, and lets packets pass through its interfaces with no access control enforced. A dual-homed firewall has two NICs and should have packet forwarding and routing turned off for security reasons. If forwarding were enabled, the computer would not apply the necessary ACLs, rules, or other restrictions necessary of a firewall. Instead, a dual-homed firewall requires a higher level of intelligence to tell it what packets should

Pros and Cons of Proxy Firewalls

Pros

- Looks at the information within a packet, possibly all the way up to the application layer
- Provides better security than packet filtering
- Breaks the connection between trusted and untrusted systems

Cons

- Some proxy firewalls are limited to what applications it can support
- Degrades traffic performance
- Application-based proxy firewalls can have scalability issues
- Breaks client/server model, which is good for security but at times bad for functionality

Dual-Homed Host Firewall Characteristics

- Single computer with separate network cards connected to each network.

- Used to divide an internal trusted network from an external untrusted network.

- Must disable computer's forwarding and routing functionality so the two networks are truly segregated.

- Users can easily and accidentally enable packet forwarding, which can cause malicious traffic to enter the internal network.

go where and what types of packets are acceptable. When a packet comes to the external NIC from the untrusted network on a dual-homed firewall, the computer does not know what to do with it, so it passes it up to the firewall software. The software inspects the packet to make sure that it is legitimate. If it is a "safe" packet, the firewall allows it to go to the destination system. When the internal computer replies, the packet goes to the internal interface on the dual-homed firewall and is passed up to the firewall software. The software inspects it and then passes the packet out the external NIC that is connected to the external network.

Many firewalls are multi-homed, meaning they have more than two NICs. This allows the company to create several independent DMZs. One interface is connected to the untrusted network (usually the Internet), one is connected to the trusted network (internal company network), and the other interfaces segment different DMZs. One DMZ may have the company's Web servers, while the other DMZ has the company's public mail and DNS server.

The firewall software is an important part to a dual-homed firewall, and the dual-homed firewall is an important part of a firewall. If the firewall software were on a computer that had packet forwarding enabled, the packets would never be passed up to the firewall software. If the dual-homed firewall did not have firewall software, it would not know what to do with the packets it receives.

Other types of firewalls can reside and work on a dual-homed firewall; proxy firewalls being one of them. These firewall architectures are discussed in the "Firewall Architecture" section, surprisingly enough, later in the chapter.

Two types of firewall proxies can be used—application-level and circuit-level, which are described next.

Application- and Circuit-Level Proxies   Proxies have been described as middlemen between untrusted external hosts and trusted internal hosts. However, there are more issues to understand when looking at the two different types of proxy firewalls available. *Application-level proxies* inspect the entire packet and make access decisions based on the content of the packet. They understand various services and protocols and the commands that are used by them. An application-level proxy can distinguish between an FTP GET command and an FTP PUT command, for example, and it can make access decisions based on this granular level of information; on the other hand, packet-filtering firewalls can allow or deny FTP requests only as a whole, not by the commands used within the FTP protocol.

An application-level proxy works for one service or protocol. A computer can have many types of services and protocols (FTP, NTP, SMTP, Telnet, and so on)—thus, one application-level proxy per service is required.

A *circuit-level proxy* creates a circuit between the client computer and the server. It does not understand or care about the higher level issues that an application-level proxy deals with. It knows the source and destination addresses and makes access decisions based on this type of header information.

Providing application-level proxy services can be a tricky undertaking. The proxy must totally understand how specific protocols work and what commands within that protocol are legitimate. This is a lot to know and look at during the transmission of data. If the application-level proxy firewall does not understand a certain protocol or service, it cannot protect this type of communication. This is when a circuit-level proxy can come into play, because it does not deal with such complex issues. An advantage of a circuit-level proxy is that it can handle a wider variety of protocols and services than an application-level proxy, but the downfall is that the circuit-level proxy cannot provide the degree of granular control that an application-level proxy provides. Life is just full of compromises.

A circuit-level proxy works similar to a packet filter in that it makes access decisions based on address, port, and protocol type. It looks at the data within the packet header versus the data within the payload of the packet. It does not know whether the contents within the packet are safe or unsafe.

Application-Level versus Circuit-Level Proxy Firewall Characteristics

Application-Level Proxy Firewall

- Different proxy required for each service allowed
- Provides more intricate control than circuit-level proxy firewalls
- Reduces network performance

Circuit-Level Proxy Firewall

- Does not require a proxy for each and every service
- Does not provide the detailed access control that an application-level proxy firewall provides
- Provides security for a wider range of protocols

An application-level proxy is dedicated to a particular protocol or service. At least one proxy is used per protocol because one proxy could not properly interpret all the commands of all the protocols coming its way. A circuit-level proxy works at a lower layer of the OSI model and does not require one proxy per protocol because it is not looking at such detailed information.

SOCKS is an example of a circuit-level proxy gateway that provides a secure channel between two computers. When a SOCKS-enabled client sends a request to access a computer on the Internet, this request actually goes to the network's SOCKS proxy server, as shown in Figure 7-34, which inspects the packets for malicious information and checks its policy rules to see whether this type of connection is allowed. If the packet is acceptable and this type of connection is allowed, the SOCKS server sends the message to the destination computer on the Internet. When the computer on the Internet responds, it sends its packets to the SOCKS server, which again inspects the data and then passes it on to the client computer.

The SOCKS server can screen, filter, audit, log, and control data flowing in and out of a protected network. Because of its popularity, many applications and protocols have been configured to work with SOCKS in a manner that takes less configuration on the administrator's part, and various firewall products have integrated SOCKS software to provide circuit-based protection.

If you have ever pointed a browser to a specific proxy server through the browser's configurations, you have most likely already interacted with a SOCKS client. Windows systems have a Winsock client to allow Windows-based systems to communicate with Microsoft's proxy server product. Windows systems also have a SOCKS client, which will allow other types of systems (Macintosh, Unix, and Linux) to communicate with Microsoft's proxy server product.

Figure 7-34   The SOCKS server usually sits behind a router, and each SOCKS client must have SOCKS software installed.

SOCKS Proxy Firewall Characteristics

- Circuit-level proxy firewall
- Requires clients to be SOCKS-ified with SOCKS client software
- Can be resource intensive
- Provides authentication and encryption features similar to other VPN protocols, but is not considered a traditional VPN protocol

Because SOCKS is a circuit-level proxy, it does not provide detailed protocol-specific control. The SOCKS product includes the SOCKS server software, which can run on Unix servers; a SOCKS client library; SOCKS-ified versions of several applications and protocols; and SOCKS wrappers for utilities such as traceroute and ping.

Dynamic Packet Filtering

When an internal system needs to communicate to an entity outside of its trusted network, it has to choose a source port, so the receiving system knows how to respond properly. The receiving system requires an IP address and a port number so that its response can properly find its way to the sender's computer. Ports up to 1024 are called "well known" ports and are reserved for server-side services. The sender must choose a dynamic port higher than 1024 when it sets up a connection with another entity. The dynamic packet filtering firewall will then create an ACL that allows the external entity to communicate to the internal system via this high port. If this was not an available option for your dynamic packet filtering firewall, you would have to allow "punch holes" in your firewalls for all ports above 1024, because the client side chooses these ports dynamically and the firewall would never know exactly on which port to allow or disallow traffic.

An internal system could choose a source port of 11,111 for its message to the outside system. This frame goes to the dynamic packet filtering firewall and builds an ACL, as illustrated in Figure 7-35, that indicates that a response from the destination computer to this internal system's IP address and port 11,111 is to be allowed. When the destination system sends a response, the firewall allows it. These ACLs are dynamic in nature, so once the connection is finished (either a FIN or RST packet is received), the ACL is removed from the list. On connectionless protocols, such as UDP and ICMP, the connection will time out and then the ACL is pulled.

The benefit of a dynamic packet filtering firewall, which is a fourth-generation firewall, is that it gives you the option of allowing any type of traffic outbound and allowing only response traffic inbound.

Kernel Proxy

A *kernel proxy* firewall is considered a fifth-generation firewall. It differs from all of the previous firewall technologies, because it creates dynamic, customized TCP/IP stacks when a packet needs to be evaluated.

Figure 7-35
Dynamic packet
filtering adds
ACLs when
connections
are created.

When a packet arrives at a kernel proxy firewall, a new network stack will be created, which is made up of only the protocol proxies that are necessary to examine this specific packet properly. If it is an FTP packet, only the FTP proxy is loaded in the stack. The packet is scrutinized at every layer of the stack, not just at the data payload. This means the data link header will be evaluated along with the network header, transport header, session layer information, and the application layer data. If anything is deemed unsafe at any one of these layers, the packet is discarded.

Kernel proxy firewalls are faster than application layer firewalls because all of the inspection and processing is taking place in the kernel and does not need to be passed up to a higher software layer in the operating system. It is still a proxy-based system, so the connection between the internal and external entity is broken by the proxy acting as a middleman, and it can perform network address translation by changing the source address, as do the preceding proxy-based firewalls.

Firewall Architecture

Firewalls are great, but where do we put them?

Firewalls can be placed in a number of areas on a network, to meet particular needs. They can protect an internal network from an external network and act as a choke point for all traffic. A firewall can be used to segment network sections and enforce access controls between two or more subnets. Firewalls can also be used to provide a DMZ between an internal network and an external network.

Bastion Host   The *bastion host* can be thought of as the "foundation" for the firewall software. It is a locked down system. A bastion host is usually a highly exposed device because it is the front line in a network's security and its existence is known on the Internet. This means that the device must be extremely secure, no unnecessary services should be running, unused subsystems must be disabled, vulnerabilities must be patched, unused user accounts must be disabled, and ports that are not needed must be closed. These measures are necessary, because if this system is compromised, the network will have lost its main defender. Once the firewall is broken or disabled, little is standing in the way of evildoers on the Internet and the vulnerable systems on the internal network.

A bastion host is not tied to firewall software and activities; it is just a system that is properly locked down. Any system that resides within the DMZ should be installed on a bastion host since it is closer to the Internet and most likely closer to those who would like to do it harm. If firewall software is not installed on a locked down operating system, or bastion host, the firewall is in danger and vulnerable.

Screened Host   A *screened host* is often a firewall that communicates directly with a perimeter router and the internal network. Figure 7-36 shows this type of architecture.

Traffic that is received from the Internet is first filtered via packet filtering on the outer router. The traffic that makes it past this phase is sent to the screened-host firewall, which applies more rules to the traffic and drops the denied packets. Then the traffic moves to the internal destination hosts. The screened host (the firewall) is the only device that receives traffic directly from the router. No traffic goes directly from the Internet, through the router, and to the internal network. The screened host is always part of this equation.

If the firewall is an application-based system, protection is provided at the network layer by the router, and protection is provided at the application level by the proxy. This arrangement offers a high degree of security, because for an attacker to be successful, she would have to compromise two systems.

What does the word *screening* mean in this context? As shown in Figure 7-36, the router is a screening device and the firewall is the screened host. This just means that there is a layer of protection for the firewall. A screened host is different from a screened subnet, which is described next.

Screened Subnet   A *screened-subnet* architecture adds another layer of security to the screened-host architecture. In this environment, the firewall is sandwiched between two routers. The external router is similar to that shown in Figure 7-36. It applies packet

Figure 7-36   A screened host communicates directly with a perimeter router and the internal network.

filtering to data entering the network and ports the traffic to the firewall. However, instead of the firewall then redirecting the traffic to the internal network, an interior router also filters the traffic.

In an environment with only a screened host, if an attacker successfully breaks through the firewall, nothing lies in her way to prevent her from having full access to the internal network. In an environment using a screened subnet, the attacker would have to hack through another router (or firewall) to gain access. In this layered approach to security, the more layers provided, the better the protection. Figure 7-37 shows a simple example of a screened subnet.

The examples shown in the figures are simple in nature. Often, more complex networks and DMZs are implemented in real-world systems. Figures 7-38 and 7-39 show some other possible architectures of screened subnets and their configurations.

The screened-subnet approach provides more protection than a stand-alone firewall or a screened-host firewall because three devices are working together and three devices must be compromised before an attacker can gain access to the internal network. This architecture also sets up a DMZ between the two routers, which functions as a small network isolated among the trusted internal and untrusted external networks. The internal users usually have limited access to the servers within this area. Many times Web, e-mail, and other public servers are placed within the DMZ. Although this solution provides the highest security, it also brings along the most complexity. Configuration and maintenance can prove to be difficult in this setup, and when new services need to be added, three systems may need to be reconfigured instead of just one.

The complexity and configuration of the DMZ, perimeter network, and screened hosts and subnets are dictated by the company security policy. The required level of security, and the services that need to be available to internal and external users, should be clearly outlined in this policy.

Figure 7-37   When using a screened subnet, the firewall is sandwiched between two routers.

Figure 7-38 A screened subnet can have different networks within it and different firewalls that filter for specific vulnerabilities.

NOTE A screened subnet is sandwiched between two screening devices. These devices are usually routers, but they can also be firewalls.

Tables 7-8 and 7-9 list the important concepts and characteristics of the devices and architectures discussed in the previous sections. Although various firewall products can provide a mix of these services and work at different layers of the OSI model, it is important that you understand the basic definitions and functionalities of these firewall types.

Shoulds of Firewalls *Look both ways before crossing a street, and always floss. Response: Wrong rule set.* The default action of any firewall should be to implicitly deny any packets not explicitly allowed. This means that if no rule states that the packet can be accepted,

Figure 7-39 Some architectures have separate screened subnets with different server types in each.

Firewall Type	OSI Layer	Characteristics
Packet filtering	Network layer	Routers using ACLs dictate acceptable access to a network. This looks at destination and source addresses, ports, and services requested.
Application-level proxy	Application layer	This looks deep into packets and makes granular access control decisions. It requires one proxy per service.
Circuit-level proxy	Network layer	This looks only at the header packet information. It protects a wider range of protocols and services than application-level proxies but does not provide the detailed level of control available to application-level proxies.
Stateful	Network layer	This keeps track of each conversation using a state table. It looks at the state and context of packets.

Table 7-8 Differences Among Firewalls

Architecture Type	Characteristics
Dual-homed	Single computer with two or more NICs—one connected to the trusted internal network and another connected to the untrusted external network.
Screened host	Router filters (screens) traffic before it is passed to the firewall.
Screened subnet	External router filters (screens) traffic before it enters the subnet. Traffic headed toward the internal network then goes through the firewall and another router.

Table 7-9　Firewall Architecture Characteristics

that packet should be denied, no questions asked. Any packets entering the network that have a source address of an internal host should be denied. This is a popular attacking trick called *masquerading* or *spoofing*. The attacker modifies a packet header to have the source address of a host inside the network that she wants to attack. This packet is spoofed and illegitimate. There is no reason that a packet coming from the Internet should have an internal source network address, so the firewall should deny it. The same is true for outbound traffic. No traffic should be allowed to leave a network that does not have an internal source address. If this occurs, it means that someone, or some program, on the internal network is spoofing traffic. This is how *zombies* work—the agents used in distributed DoS attacks. If packets are leaving a network with different source addresses, these packets are spoofed and the network is most likely being used as an accomplice in a distributed DoS attack.

When security is a top priority for a company, its firewalls should reassemble fragmented packets before sending them on to their destination. In some types of attacks, the hackers alter the packets and make them seem to be something they are not. When a fragmented packet comes to a firewall, the firewall is seeing only part of the picture. It will make its best guess as to whether this piece of a packet is malicious or not. Because these fragments contain only a part of the full packet, the firewall is making a decision without having all the facts. Once all fragments are allowed through to a host computer, they can be reassembled into malicious packages that can cause a lot of damage. In environments that require higher security, the firewall should accept each fragment, assemble the fragments into a complete packet, and then make an access decision based on the whole packet. The drawback to this, however, is that firewalls that do reassemble packet fragments before allowing them to go on to their destination computer cause traffic delay and more overhead. It is up to the network administrator and company to decide whether this configuration is necessary and whether the added traffic delay is acceptable.

Many companies choose to deny network entrance to packets that contain source routing information. *Source routing* means that the packet decides how it is to get to its destination, not the routers in between the source and destination computer. Source routing moves a packet throughout a network in a predetermined path. The sending computer must know about the topology of the network and know how to route data properly. This is easier for the routers and connection mechanisms in between, because they do not need to make any decisions on how to route the packet—however, it can also pose a security risk. When a router receives a packet that contains source routing information, it figures the packet knows what needs to be done and passes it on. In some cases, not all filters may be applied to the packet and a network administrator may want packets to be routed only through a certain path and not the route that a particular packet dictates. To make sure none of this misrouting happens, many firewalls are configured to check for source routing information within the packet and deny it if it is present.

Unfortunately, once a company erects a firewall, it may have a false sense of security. Firewalls are only one piece of the puzzle, and security has a lot of pieces.

The following list addresses some of the disadvantages of firewalls:

- Security is concentrated in one spot versus a distributed approach that secures many different places within the network.

- Firewalls can present a potential bottleneck to the flow of traffic.

- Firewalls can restrict desirable services that users may want to access. (This is a disadvantage to the users, but an advantage to the security professional.)

- Most firewalls do not protect from viruses being downloaded or passed through e-mail, and hooks to virus-detection techniques are needed.

- Firewalls provide little protection against the inside attacker.

Many firewalls also perform authentication so that the identity of the user or process requesting connections or services can be known. Authenticating users and processes give the firewalls added information to help them make better decisions on allowing or denying specific packets. A network administrator may want to allow remote access to the FTP server only to valid company users, for example. So when remote users request access to the FTP server, the firewall can determine whether the user is authorized to use this functionality. Today, Remote Authentication Dial-in User Service (RADIUS) is a popular way of authenticating users and processes, and it is also used in dial-up network access and by ISPs.

The role of firewalls is becoming more and more complex as they evolve and take on more functionality and responsibility. At times, this complexity works against the network administrator and security professional because there is a lot to understand and properly implement. Without understanding the different types of firewalls and architectures available, many more security holes can be introduced, which lays out the welcome mat for attackers.

Honeypot
Hey! Here is a vulnerable system to attack!

A *honeypot* system is a computer that sits in the screened subnet, or DMZ, with the hopes of luring attackers to it instead of to actual production computers. To make a honeypot system lure attackers, administrators may enable services and ports that are popular to exploit. However, the administrator must be careful to ensure that this box is isolated in a way so that when it is attacked, the hacker is not successful at accessing other computers on the network. Some honeypot systems have services *emulated*, meaning the actual service is not running but software that acts like those services are available. In Chapter 10, honeypot systems are discussed in the context of *enticement versus entrapment*. A legal honeypot can entice attackers to access the computer and attempt to hack into it, but it cannot entrap them. The example given in Chapter 10 shows how having a banner on one system indicating free MP3s to download on the honeypot system is entrapment, because this is setting up the user to access the honeypot for reasons that are different than the intent to harm. If services are running, ports are open, and banners are available for viewing, this will be quite enough to entice, not entrap, attackers.

Some network administrators want to keep the attackers away from their other systems and set up honeypots as decoys. Other administrators want to go after those who hurt them. These administrators would keep detailed logs, enable auditing, and perform different degrees of forensics in the hopes of turning over the attackers to the authorities for prosecution.

Network Segregation and Isolation

Although this topic was covered in Chapter 6, network segregation and isolation is an important piece that interrelates with the topics in this chapter. It is important that you segregate networks and subnets from each other. This usually means implementing routers that do not pass on broadcast and collision domain information and using different address schemes for different segments. Many networks today use Ethernet technology, which continually broadcasts information that can be useful to inside and outside attackers. Because data is so freely broadcast in these environments, it is important that you make sure that networks that house sensitive information are properly segmented from other network sections.

The architecture of a network should be clearly thought out, fully documented, and tested. A network administrator may not want everyone to be able to talk directly to a mainframe that holds critical information, for example. This traffic should be ported through one channel and filtered by a router or firewall. An administrator also may not want everyone on the network to be able to access the administrator's subnet, which holds the management consoles for all the routers, IDS systems, logging servers, and auditing systems. The computers within this subnet need to talk to different systems throughout the network, but there is really no good reason that regular users should be able to access this subnet freely. This subnet needs to be isolated by ACLs enforced by surrounding routers and properly segregated.

Also, it is one thing to document what one thinks the architecture of a network is, but just because it is on paper does not make it true. If the network schematic indicates that no one from subnet A can contact subnet B because of router ACLs, this needs to be tested and penetration attacks should be launched to determine whether this is indeed true.

Networking Services

So far, we have touched on protocols, technologies, topologies, and devices that can be used within a LAN environment. These services are not strictly used in only LAN environments; they are also used in MAN and WAN infrastructures. The purpose of splitting these sections into LAN and WAN segments is to provide a clear-cut explanation of the differences between these networking concepts.

As stated earlier in this chapter, a network is set up to enable users to communicate with each other, create central administration, and share resources. The resources usually come in the form of networking services, and the following sections address many of the most-used services in most LAN environments.

Network Operating Systems

A *network operating system (NOS)* is designed to control network resource access and provide the necessary services to enable a computer to interact with the surrounding network. A NOS is different from a single-user operating system. A NOS is built to work in a client/server model that enables resources, files, and applications to be centralized, while all users access them on servers, rather than having individual copies of those resources stored on each and every workstation.

A NOS also has built-in authentication mechanisms that are necessary for a network environment and auditing functionality. Single-user operating systems do not enforce strong authentication. Anyone who has worked on Windows 95 or 98 knows that you can click the OK button when the OS requests a username and password, even if you don't type in any information. These operating systems do not require authentication. However, anyone who has worked on Windows NT and Windows 2000 systems knows that these systems will not let you access the system if you do not know the correct username and password.

Single-user operating systems can work in a peer-to-peer environment, meaning a type of workgroup, and implement resource and file sharing. However, a peer-to-peer environment does not provide the level of security, centralized management, and access control necessary in most environments. Single-user operating systems also do not have the powerful directory services that NOS systems provide. This is an important piece of most networks today.

The following is a short list of many of the services NOS systems may provide that most single-user systems do not:

- Directory services
- Internetworking, routing, and WAN support
- Support for remote dial-up users
- Clustering functionality
- Strong authentication, authorization, access control, and auditing
- File and printing services including backup and replication services
- Management and administration tools for remote clients
- Software distribution, and software and hardware inventory functionality
- Fault tolerance capabilities

When a user of a computer running a NOS needs to access a resource on the network, the NOS software uses a *redirector*, which points the computer to the actual requested resource. Often, this redirector functionality works at a lower layer of processing than the higher level requesting application. The application usually does not realize that the resource is not stored on the local computer. This reduces a lot of confusion and extra work for the programmers of the applications, because they do not need to figure out how to track down network resources themselves.

References

Network Operating Systems: **compnetworking.about.com/compute/ compnetworking/cs/networknos**

NOS Research Center: **www.nwfusion.com/netresources/nos.html**

Google listings for operating systems: **directory.google.com/Top/Computers/ Software/Operating_Systems**

DNS

Imagine how hard it would be to use the Internet if we had to remember actual specific IP addresses. The *Domain Name Service (DNS)* is a method of resolving hostnames to IP addresses so that names can be used instead of IP addresses when referencing unique hosts on the Internet. Not too many years ago, when the Internet was made up of about 100 computers, instead of more than 1 million now, a list used to be kept that mapped every user's hostname to their IP address. This list was kept on an FTP server so everyone could access it. It did not take long for the task of maintaining this list to become overwhelming, and the computing community looked to automate it.

A hierarchical system for domain names was developed, and in 1992 the National Science Foundation (NSF) awarded Network Solutions, Inc. (NSI) the contract to manage and maintain domain names and the registration process of those names. NSI handled the name registration and a hostname resolution directory of DNS servers. It also maintained the authoritative databases of the Internet, which are the root DNS servers. An authoritative root DNS server contained 13 files, one for each of the top-level domain servers.

Until 1999, the Internet Assigned Numbers Authority (IANA) maintained and coordinated the allocation of IP addresses. Large Internet service providers (ISPs) would apply to the registries for blocks of these IP addresses and allocate the blocks to smaller ISPs or individual users. However, after 1999 the Internet Corporation for Assigned Names and Numbers (ICANN) took over the responsibilities of IP address block allocation, DNS management, and root server system management. NSI still maintains the authoritative root databases.

Wonderful. We have had a history lesson, but how does DNS work and what is its place in a network?

When a user types in a uniform resource locator (URL) in his Web browser, it is made up of words or letters that are in a sequence that makes sense to that user, such as **www.isc2.org**. However, these words are only for humans—computers work with IP addresses. So after the user enters this URL and presses ENTER, behind the scenes his computer is actually being directed to a DNS server that will resolve this URL, or hostname, into an IP address the computer understands. Once the hostname has been resolved to an IP address, the computer knows how to get to the Web server holding the requested Web page.

Many companies have their own DNS servers to resolve their internal hostnames. These companies usually also use the DNS servers at their ISPs to resolve hostnames on the Internet. An internal DNS server can be used to resolve hostnames on the entire network, but usually more than one DNS server is used so that the load can be split up and redundancy and fault tolerance are in place.

Within DNS servers, networks are split up into *zones*. One zone may contain all hostnames for the marketing and accounting departments, and another zone may contain administration, research, and the legal departments. The DNS server that holds the files for one of these zones is said to be the *authoritative* name server for that particular zone. A zone may contain one or more domains, and the DNS server holding those host records is the authoritative name server for those domains.

The zone files contain records that map hostnames to IP addresses, which are referred to as *resource records*. When a user's computer needs to resolve a hostname to an IP address, it looks to its TCP/IP settings to find its DNS server. The computer then sends a request, containing the hostname, to the DNS server for resolution. The DNS server looks at its resource records and finds the record with this particular hostname, retrieves the address, and replies to the computer with the corresponding IP address.

It is recommended that a *primary* and *secondary* DNS server be placed in each zone. The primary contains the actual resource records for a zone, and the secondary contains copies of those records. Users can use the secondary DNS server to resolve names, which takes a load off of the primary server. If the primary server goes down for any reason or is taken offline, users can still use the secondary server for name resolution. Having a primary and secondary DNS provides fault tolerance and redundancy to ensure that users can continue to work if something happens to one of these servers.

Internet DNS and Domains

Networks on the Internet are connected in a hierarchical structure, as are the different DNS servers, as shown in Figure 7-40. While performing routing tasks, if a router does not know the necessary path to the requested destination, that router passes the packet up to a router above it. The router above it knows about all the routers below it. This router has a broader view of the routing that takes place on the Internet and has a better chance of getting the packet to the correct destination. This holds true with DNS servers also. If one DNS server does not know which DNS server holds the necessary resource record to resolve a hostname, it can pass the request up to a DNS server above it.

Figure 7-40   The DNS naming hierarchy is similar to the network and routing hierarchy on the Internet.

The naming scheme of the Internet resembles an inverted tree with the root servers at the top. Lower branches of this tree are divided into top-level domains with second-level domains under it. The most common top-level domains are listed here:

- **COM**   Commercial
- **EDU**   Education
- **MIL**   U.S. military organization
- **INT**   International treaty organization
- **GOV**   Government
- **ORG**   Organizational
- **NET**   Networks

The International Ad Hoc Committee created seven new generic top-level domains under which companies can register:

- **Firm** Business or firm
- **Arts** Cultural and entertainment
- **Nom** Individual nomenclature
- **Rec** Recreational entertainment
- **Info** Information services
- **Web** Web-related entities
- **Store** Merchants

So how do all of these DNS servers play together in the Internet playground? When a user types in a URL with the hopes of accessing a Web site that sells computer books, for example, his computer will ask its corporate authoritative DNS server if it can resolve this hostname to an IP address. Because this Web site is most likely not on the corporate network, this particular DNS server will not usually know the necessary IP address of that Web site. The DNS server does not just reject the user's request, but it passes it on to another DNS on the Internet. The request for this hostname resolution continues through different DNS servers until it reaches one that knows the IP address. This information is reported back to the user's computer. The user's computer then attempts to access the Web site using the IP address, and soon the user is buying computer books, happy as a clam.

DNS server and hostname resolution is extremely important in corporate networking and Internet use. Without it, users would have to remember and type in the IP address for each Web site and individual system, instead of the name. That would be a mess.

Directory Services

A *directory service* has a hierarchical database of users, computers, printers, resources, and attributes of each. The directory is mainly used for lookup operations, which enable users to track down resources and other users easily to facilitate access. Most directory service databases are built on the X.500 model and use the Lightweight Directory Access Protocol (LDAP) to access the directory database.

Directory services are often compared to telephone white and yellow pages, where, if you want to know how to contact someone, you can easily look though the white pages and find the necessary contact information. The same is true about directory services, although usually they contain much more than just phone numbers. (Actually, DNS is a type of directory service.)

The directory itself uses classes of objects and subclasses of those objects to provide organization to the directory repository, which is usually a database. Then policies can be applied to these objects in a central administration method. The entities within objects can be users, their location, and peripheral information, resources, profiles, electronic commerce information, network services, and much more. The administrator can then develop access control, security, and auditing policies that dictate who can access these objects and how the objects can be accessed, and then each of these actions are audited. Policies can also be developed and applied to control bandwidth management, firewall filtering, VPN access, and QoS.

Many different directories are developed and maintained. These directories can be based on business or security needs, and they can have different security policies, access control, and profiles applied to them. When more than one directory is in use, they need a way to communicate to each other; this takes place through *metadirectories. Metadata* is data about data. Metadirectories hold top-level information about the directory itself, which enables a user in one directory to locate the object he is looking for quickly in a totally different directory.

Each directory follows a specific *schema*, like regular databases. The schema provides structure to the directory repository and defines how objects and their relationships are to be represented. Each directory service vendor has a baseline schema that enables administrators to define their own objects and corresponding attributes. However, like many other types of products, interoperability issues can occur between vendors' schemas so that they cannot easily communicate with each other. If one company buys another company and their networks need to be merged and directory services combined, for example, this can turn into a tricky and hairy project.

Directory services offer rich services to users, administrators, and networks as a whole. They enable administrators to maintain and control all resources and users within an environment. The directory database acts as a holding place for almost all of the network's important information and enables users to track down needed services or resources easily and quickly. Two examples of directory services are Microsoft's Active Directory and Novell Directory Services (NDS). Although both are based on the X.500 model, they do not easily communicate with each other.

Many services are made available to users within a network, which is a big reason for constructing a network in the first place. This section described NOS, DNS, and directory services, but a network offers much more—for example, many offer print services that enable many users to share local and remote printers. The administrators have centralized network management services that let them view the network as a whole from one graphical application, add and delete users, troubleshoot network issues, audit activities, add and remove services, control remote user access, and more. Some networks have terminal emulation services, which enable users to have a lower-powered workstation that sees only the desktop. The operating system actually sits on a server somewhere else and does all the processor-intense activities.

Networks and networking are interesting, confusing, and rewarding constructs of today's computing world. However, networking complexity causes many errors, security holes, and vulnerabilities to occur, and this is what potential attackers are counting on. The more one knows and understands about networking and how each component works with other components, the more efficiently security mechanisms can be applied and a higher level of protection can be provided.

References

IETF LDAP Revision Charter: **www.ietf.org/html.charters/ldapbis-charter.html**

IETF Policy Framework Charter: **policywww.ietf.org/html.charters/policy-charter.html**

Intranets and Extranets

We kind of trust you, but not really. We're going to put you on the extranet.

Web technologies and their uses have exploded with functionality, capability, and popularity. Companies set up internal Web sites for centralized business information such as employee phone numbers, policies, events, news, and operations instructions. Many companies have also implemented Web-based terminals that enable employees to perform their daily tasks, access centralized databases, make transactions, collaborate on projects, access global calendars, use videoconferencing tools and whiteboard applications, and obtain often-used technical or marketing data.

Web-based clients are different from workstations that log into a network and have their own desktop. Web-based clients limit a user's abilities to access the computer's system files, resources, hard drive space, access back-end systems, and perform other tasks. The Web-based client can be configured to provide a graphical user interface (GUI) with only the buttons, fields, and pages necessary for the users to perform tasks. This gives all users a standard universal interface with similar capabilities.

When a company uses the Internet and Web-based technologies inside their networks, they are using an *intranet*. An intranet is a "private" network that uses Internet technologies, such as TCP/IP. The company has Web servers and client machines using Web browsers, and it uses the TCP/IP protocol suite. The Web pages are written in Hypertext Markup Language (HTML) or EXtensible Markup Language (XML) and are accessed via HTTP.

Another common element of intranets is that they usually use private IP addresses instead of publicly registered addresses. These addresses are free for any company to use and provide a degree of security because they cannot be routed on the Internet. The following lists current private IP address ranges:

- **10.0.0.0**   Class A network
- **172.16.0.0—172.31.255.255**   16 contiguous class B networks
- **192.168.0.0—192.168.255.255**   256 contiguous class C networks

Using Web-based technology has many pluses. It has been around for quite some time, it is easy to implement, no major interoperability issues occur, and with just a click on a link, a user can be taken to the location of the requested resource. Web technologies are not platform-dependent, meaning that all Web sites and pages may be maintained on a Unix server, while all different flavors of client workstations can access them. They only need a Web browser.

An *extranet* extends outside the bounds of the company's network to enable two or more companies to share common information and resources. Business partners commonly set up extranets to accommodate business-to-business communication. One business may post orders to the other business via the extranet, work on projects together, share marketing information, allow employees to communicate and work collaboratively on issues, and share catalogs, pricing structures, or upcoming event information. Trading partners often use electronic data interchange (EDI), which provides structure and organization to electronic documents, orders, invoices, purchase orders, and a data flow. EDI has evolved into Web-based technologies to provide easy access and easier methods of communication.

For many businesses, an extranet can provide a weakness or hole in their security if it is not implemented and maintained properly. Properly configured firewalls need to be in place to control who can use the extranet communication channels. Extranets used to be based mainly on dedicated links, which are more difficult for attackers to infiltrate, but today many extranets are set up over the Internet, which requires properly configured VPNs and security policies.

References

Intranet Road Map: **www.intranetroadmap.com**

Intranet/Extranet Research Center: **www.cio.com/forums/intranet**

Intranet Journal: **www.intranetjournal.com**

Network Address Translation

I have one address I would like to share with everyone!

When computers need to communicate with each other, they need to use the same type of addressing scheme so everyone understands how to find and talk to one another. The Internet uses the IP address scheme, and any computer or network that wants to communicate with other users on the network must conform to this scheme; otherwise, that computer will sit in a virtual room with only itself to talk to.

However, IP addresses have become scarce (until the full adoption of IPv6) and expensive. So some smart people came up with *network address translation (NAT)*, which enables a network that does not follow the Internet's addressing scheme to communicate over the Internet.

Private IP addresses were discussed in an earlier section of this chapter. These addresses can be used within the boundaries of a company, but they cannot be used on the Internet because they will not be properly routed. NAT enables a company to use these private addresses and still be able to communicate transparently with computers on the Internet.

NAT is a gateway that lies between a network and the Internet (or another network) that performs transparent routing and address translation. Because IP addresses were depleting fast, IPv6 was developed, which was intended to be the long-term fix to the address shortage problem. NAT was developed as the short-term fix to enable more companies to participate on the Internet. However, to date, IPv6 is extremely slow in acceptance and implementation, while NAT has caught on like wildfire. Many firewall vendors have implemented NAT into their products, and it has been found that NAT actually provides a great security benefit. When attackers want to hack a network, they first do what they can to learn all about the network, its topology, services, and addresses. Attackers cannot easily find out a company's addresses scheme and its topology when NAT is in place, because NAT acts like a large nightclub bouncer by standing in front of the network and hiding the true IP scheme. Because private IP addresses are not used on the Internet, attackers cannot find out the actual address a particular computer is using.

NAT hides internal addresses by centralizing them on one router, and any frames that leave that network have only the source address of that router, not the actual computer that sends the message. So when a message comes from an internal computer with the address of 10.10.10.2, for example, the message is stopped at the device running NAT software, which happens to have the IP address of 1.2.3.4. NAT changes the header of the frame from the internal address, 10.10.10.2, to the valid IP address of the NAT device, 1.2.3.4. (Yes, I know 1.2.3.4 isn't valid, but I think you get the concept.) When a computer on the Internet replies to this message, it replies to the address 1.2.3.4. The NAT device changes the header on this reply message to 10.10.10.2 and puts it on the wire for the internal user to receive.

In some cases, the NAT system has a pool of IP addresses to work with, which are used to translate between internal and external addresses. A company needs to have enough addresses to ensure that communication is not negatively affected. This means that, for example, if a company has only four public IP addresses and they are all used when another computer wants to communicate to the outside world, the last user has to wait until one of the addresses in the pool is freed up.

Most NAT implementations are *stateful*, meaning they keep track of a communication between the internal host and an external host until that session is ended. The NAT device needs to remember the internal IP address and port to send the reply messages back. This stateful characteristic is similar to stateful firewalls, but NAT does not perform scans on the incoming packets to look for malicious characteristics. Instead, NAT is a service usually performed on routers or firewalls within a company's screened subnet.

Although NAT was developed to provide a quick fix for the depleting IP address problem, it has actually put the problem off for quite some time. The more companies that implement private address schemes, the less the addresses become scarce. This has been helpful to NAT and the vendors that implement this technology, but it has put the acceptance and implementation of IPv6 much farther down the road.

References

Network Safety: **www.networksafety.com**

Network Address Translation: **www.tcpipprimer.com/nat.cfm**

NAT Basics: **www.homenethelp.com/web/explain/about-NAT.asp**

Metropolitan Area Network

Behind every good man… Response: Wrong MAN.

A *metropolitan area network (MAN)* is usually a backbone that connects LANs to each other and LANs to WANs, the Internet, and telecommunication and cable networks.

A majority of today's MANs are *Synchronous Optical Network (SONET)* or FDDI rings provided by the telecommunication service providers. These rings cover a large area and businesses can connect to the rings via T1, fractional T1s, and T3 lines. Figure 7-41 illustrates two companies connected via SONET ring and the devices usually necessary to make this type of communication possible. This is one example of a MAN, although in reality several businesses are usually connected to one ring.

FDDI technology was discussed earlier in the chapter; now we will quickly go over SONET. SONET is actually a standard for telecommunication transmissions over fiber-optic cables. Carriers and telephone companies have deployed SONET networks for North America, and if they follow the SONET standards properly, these various networks can communicate with little difficulty.

SONET is *self-healing*, meaning that if a break in occurs on one of its lines due to an earthquake or some other type of disaster, it can use a backup redundant ring to ensure that transmission continues. All SONET lines and rings are fully redundant. The redundant line is waiting in the wings in case anything happens to the primary ring or line.

SONET networks can transmit voice and data over optical networks. Slower-speed SONET networks often feed into larger, faster SONET networks, as shown in Figure 7-42. This enables businesses in different cities and regions to communicate.

References

IEC Online Tutorials: **www.iec.org/online/tutorials**

Wide Area Networks: **www.techfest.com/networking/wan.htm**

Wide Area Network

LAN technologies provide communication capabilities over a small geographic area, whereas *wide area network (WAN)* technologies are used when communication needs to travel over a larger geographical area. LAN technologies encompass how a computer puts its data onto a network cable, the rules and protocols of how that data is formatted

Figure 7-41   A MAN covers a large area and enables businesses to connect to each other, to the Internet, or to other WAN connections.

Figure 7-42   Smaller SONET rings connect to larger SONET rings to construct a MAN.

and transmitted, how errors are handled, and how the destination computer picks up this data from the cable. When a computer on one network needs to communicate with a network on the other side of the country or in a different country altogether, WAN technologies kick in.

The network must have some avenue to other networks, which is most likely a router that communicates with the company's service provider's routers or telephone company facilities. Just as several types of technologies lie within the LAN arena, several technologies lie within the WAN arena. This section touches on many of these.

Telecommunications Evolution

On the eighth day, God created the telephone.

Telephone systems have been around for about 100 years, and they started as copper-based analog systems. Central switching offices connected individual telephones by hand (a human operator) and then by electronic switching equipment. After two telephones were connected, they had an end-to-end connection, or an end-to-end circuit. Multiple phone calls were divided up and placed on the same wire, which is called multiplexing. *Multiplexing* is a method of combining multiple channels of data over a single transmission path. The transmission is so fast and efficient that the ends do not realize that they are sharing a line with many other entities. They think they have the line all to themselves.

In the mid-1960s, digital phone systems emerged with T1 trunks, which carried 24 voice communication calls over two pairs of copper wires. This provided a 1.544-Mbps transmission rate, which brought quicker service but also the capability to put more multiplexed calls on one wire. When calls take place between switching offices, say local phone calls, they are multiplexed on T1 lines. When a longer-distance call needs to take place, the calls coming in on the T1 lines are multiplexed on T3 lines, which can carry up to 28 T1 lines. This is shown in Figure 7-43.

The next entity to join the telecommunication party was fiber-optics, which enabled even more calls to be multiplexed on one trunk line over longer distances. Then came optical carrier technologies, SONET, which transmitted digitized voice signals in packets. SONET is a standard for telecommunication transmission over fiber-optic cables. This standard sets up the necessary parameters for transporting digital information over optical systems. Telecommunication carriers used this technology for lower-speed optical links to be multiplexed into higher-speed links, similar to how lower-speed LANs connect to higher-speed WAN links today. Figure 7-44 shows an example of SONET rings connected together.

Figure 7-44 shows how telecommunication carriers can provide telephone and Internet access to companies and individuals in large areas. The SONET standard allows all carriers the ability to interconnect.

The next evolutionary step in telecommunication's history is ATM. ATM encapsulates data in fixed cells and can be used to deliver data over the SONET network. The analogy of a highway and cars is used to describe the SONET and ATM relationship. SONET is the highway that provides the foundation, or network, for the cars, ATM packets, to travel on.

ATM is a high-speed network technology that is used in LAN and WAN implementations by carriers, ISPs, and telephone companies. ATM uses a fixed cell size instead of

Figure 7-43   Local calls are multiplexed on T1 lines and longer distance calls are moved from T1 lines to T3 multiplexed lines.

Figure 7-44 SONET technology enables several optical communication loops to communicate.

the variable frame size used by earlier technologies. This fixed size provides better performance and a reduced overhead for error handling. (More information on ATM technology is provided in the "WAN Technologies" section a little later.)

Here is a quick snapshot of telecommunication history:

- Copper lines carry purely analog signals
- T1 lines carry up to 24 conversations
- T3 lines carry up to 28 T1 lines
- Fiber-optics and the SONET network used
- ATM over SONET used

SONET was developed in the United States to achieve a data rate around 50Mbps to support the data flow from T1 lines (1.544 Mbps) and T3 lines (44.736 Mbps). Data travels over these T-carriers as electronic voltage to the edge of the SONET network. Then the voltage must be converted into light to run over the fiber-optical carrier lines, known as optical carrier (OC) lines. Each OC-1 frame runs at a signaling rate of 51.84 Mbps, with a throughput of 44.738 Mbps.

The Europeans had a different infrastructure and chose to use Synchronous Digital Hierarchy (SDH), which supports E1 lines (2.048 Mbps) and E3 lines (34.368 Mbps). SONET is a standard for North America and SDH is a standard for the rest of the world. SDH and SONET are similar but just different enough to be incompatible. For communication to take place between SDH and SONET lines, a gateway needs to do the proper signaling translation.

You've had only a quick glimpse at an amazing, complex giant referred to as *telecommunications*. Many more technologies are being developed and implemented to increase the amount of data that can be efficiently delivered in a short period of time.

Dedicated Links

A *dedicated link* is also called a *leased line* or *point-to-point* link. It is one single link that is pre-established for the purposes of WAN communications between two destinations. It is *dedicated*, meaning that only the destination points can communicate with each other. This link is not shared by any other entities at any time. This was the main way companies communicated in the past because not as many choices were available as there are today. A dedicated link is good for two locations that will communicate often and require fast transmission and a specific bandwidth, but it is expensive compared to other possible technologies that enable several companies to share the same bandwidth and also share the cost. This does not mean that dedicated lines are not in use; they definitely are used, but many other options are now available, as in SMDS, frame relay, and ATM technologies.

T-Carriers

T-carriers are dedicated lines that can carry voice and data information over trunk lines. The most commonly used T-carriers are T1 lines that provide up to 1.544 Mbps and T3 lines that provide up to 45 Mbps, as mentioned earlier. Both are digital circuits that multiplex several individual channels into a higher-speed channel.

These lines perform multiplex functionality through time-division multiplexing (TDM). What does this multiplexing stuff really mean? Consider a T1 line, which can multiplex up to 24 channels. If a company has a PBX connected to a T1 line, which in turn connects to the telephone company switching office, 24 calls can be chopped up and placed on the T1 line and transferred to the switching office. If this company did not use a T1 line, it would have to have 24 individual twisted pairs of wire to handle this many calls.

As shown in Figure 7-45, data is inputted into these 24 channels and transmitted. Each channel gets to insert up to 8 bits into its established time slot. Twenty-four of these 8-bit time slots make up a T1 frame. That does not sound like much information, but 8000 frames are built per second. Because this happens so quickly, the receiving end does not notice a delay and does not know that it is sharing its connection and bandwidth with up to 23 other devices.

Figure 7-45 Multiplexing puts several phone calls, or data transmissions, on the same wire.

Originally, T1 and T3 lines were used by the carrier companies, but they have been re-placed mainly with optical lines. Now T1 and T3 lines feed data into these powerful and super fast optical lines. The T1 and T3 lines are leased to companies and ISPs that need high-capacity transmission capability. Sometimes, T1 channels are split up between companies who do not really need the full bandwidth of 1.544 Mbps. These are called *fractional* T lines.

As mentioned earlier, dedicated lines have their drawbacks. They are expensive and inflexible. If a company moves to another location, a T1 line cannot easily follow them. It is expensive because companies have to pay for a dedicated connection with a lot of bandwidth even when they do not use the bandwidth. Not many companies require this level of bandwidth 24 hours a day. Instead, they may have data to send out here and there, but not continuously.

The cost of a dedicated line is determined by the distance to the destination. If a T1 line is run from one building to another building 2 miles away, it will be much cheaper than a T1 that covers 50 miles or a full state.

References

All You Wanted to Know About T1: **www.dcbnet.com/notes/9611t1.html**

Everything T1: **www.everythingt1.com**

S/WAN

Secure WAN (S/WAN) was originally an initiative of RSA Security, which worked with many firewall and protocol vendors in the efforts to build secure firewall-to-firewall connections through the Internet. S/WAN is based on VPNs that are created with *IPSec*, the newest and most secure tunneling protocol that provides hard-to-break encryption, the option of encrypting the header information and not just the payload data, and incor-porates authentication based off of the public-key technology.

One other advantage of using IPSec in S/WAN devices is that it will ensure that all firewalls are using the same protocol. This will help battle the ongoing interoperability issues when firewall, or VPN, vendors use their own proprietary protocols that other vendors cannot understand. IPSec is an integrated part of IPv6 and an add-on option for

IPv4. It performs authentication via the IP address and the use of certificates or symmetric keys instead of user authentication that usually requires a username and password.

An open-source version of S/WAN provides VPN services in Linux environments. It provides secure gateways and VPN connections and is called FreeS/WAN.

References

Linux FreeS/WAN Project: **www.freeswan.org**

RSA Security: **www.rsasecurity.com**

WAN Technologies

I can't throw my packets that far! Response: We have technology for that.

WAN technologies, as I am sure you have guessed, are used to enable networks to communicate over long distances. Several varieties of WAN technologies are available to companies today, and the information that is used to make the decision pertaining to which is the most appropriate usually includes functionality, bandwidth demands, service level agreements, required equipment, cost, and what is available from service providers. The following sections go over some of the WAN technologies available today.

CSU/DSU

A *Channel Service Unit/Data Service Unit (CSU/DSU)* is required when digital equipment will be used to connect a LAN network to a WAN network. This connection can take place with T1 and T3 lines, as shown in Figure 7-46. It is necessary because the signals and frames can vary between the LAN equipment and the WAN equipment used by service providers.

The DSU device converts digital signals from routers, bridges, and multiplexers into signals that can be transmitted over the telephone company's digital lines. The DSU device ensures that the voltage levels are correct and that information is not lost during the conversion. The CSU unit connects the network directly to the telephone company's line. The CSU/DSU is not always a separate device and can be part of a networking device.

Figure 7-46 A CSU/DSU is required for digital equipment to be able to communicate with telephone lines.

The CSU/DSU provides a digital interface for Data Terminal Equipment (DTE), such as terminals, multiplexers, or routers, and an interface to the Data Circuit-Terminating Equipment (DCE) device, such as a carrier's switch. The CSU/DSU basically works as a translator and at times as a line conditioner.

Switching

Dedicated links have one single path to transverse; thus, there is no complexity when it comes to determining how to get packets to different destinations. Only two points of reference are needed when a packet leaves one and heads toward the other. It gets much more complicated when thousands of networks are connected to each other, and this is often when switching comes in to play.

Two main types of switching can be used: circuit switching and packet switching. *Circuit switching* sets up a virtual connection that acts like a dedicated link between two systems. ISDN and telephone calls are examples of circuit switching, which is shown in Figure 7-47.

When the source system makes a connection with the destination system, they set up a communication channel. If the two systems are local to each other, fewer devices need to be involved with setting up this channel. The farther the two systems are from each

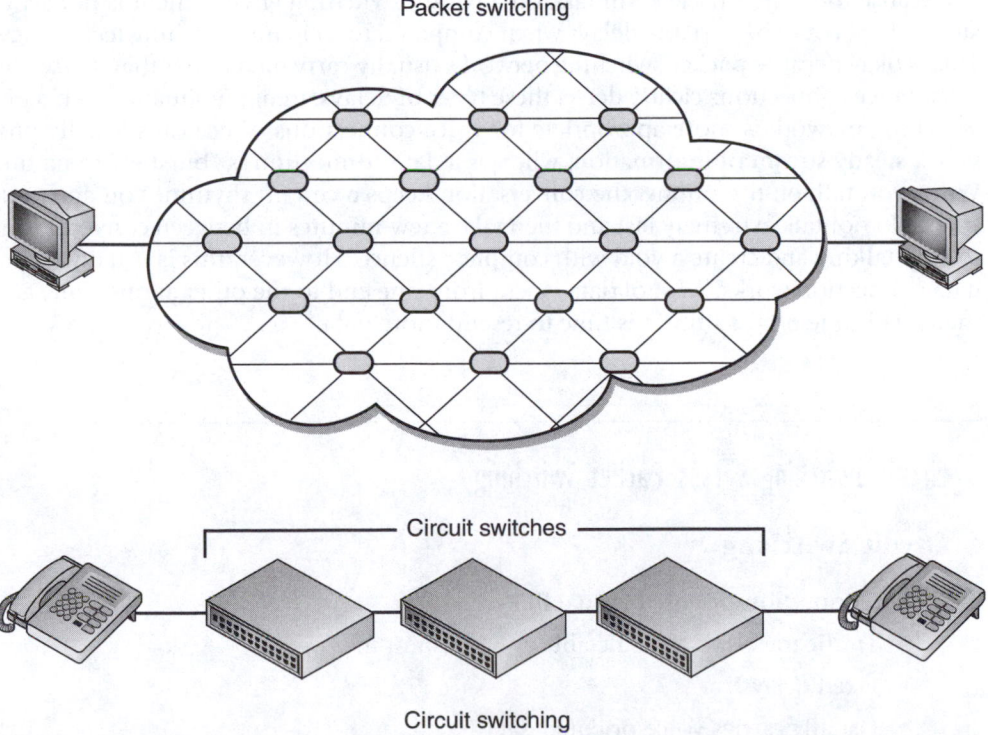

Packet switching

Circuit switches

Circuit switching

Figure 7-47   Circuit switching provides one road for a communication path, whereas packet switching provides many different possible roads.

other, the more the devices are required to be involved with setting up the channel and connecting the two systems.

An example of a circuit-switching system is daily telephone use. When one person calls another, the same type of dedicated virtual communication link is set up. Once the connection is made, the devices supporting that communication channel do not dynamically move the call through different devices, which is what takes place in a packet-switching environment. The channel remains configured at the original devices until the call, or connection, is done and torn down.

Packet switching, on the other hand, will not set up a dedicated virtual link, and packets from one connection can pass through a number of different individual devices, instead of all of them following one another through the same devices. Some examples of packet-switching technologies are the Internet, X.25, and frame relay. The infrastructure that supports these methods is made up of routers and switches of different types. They provide multiple paths to the same destinations, which provide a high degree of redundancy.

In a packet-switched network, the data is broken up into packets containing sequence numbers. These packets will go through different devices, and their path can be dynamically altered by a router or switch that determines a better route for a specific packet to take. Once the packets are received at the destination computer, all the packets are reassembled sequentially and interpreted.

Because the path a packet will take on a packet-switching environment is not set in stone, there could be variable delays when compared to a circuit-switching technology. This is okay because packet-switching networks usually carry data rather than voice. Because voice connections clearly detect these types of delays, in many situations a circuit-switching network is more appropriate for voice connections. Voice calls usually provide a steady stream of information, whereas a data connection is "burstier" in nature. When you talk on the phone, the conversation keeps a certain rhythm. You and your friend do not talk extremely fast and then take a few minutes in between conversations to stop talking and create a void with complete silence. However, this is usually how a data connection works. A lot of data is sent from one end to the other at one time, and then dead time occurs until it is time to resend more data.

Circuit Switching versus Packet Switching

Circuit Switching

- Connection-oriented virtual links
- Traffic travels in a predictable and constant manner
- Fixed delays
- Usually carries voice-oriented data

Packet Switching

- Packets can use many different dynamic paths to get to the same destination
- Traffic is usually bursty in nature
- Variable delays
- Usually carries data-oriented data

Reference

Packet Switching Simulation: **www.rad.com/networks/1998/packet/ps.htm**

Frame Relay

Why are there so many paths to choose from?

For a long time, many companies used dedicated links to communicate with other companies. Company A had a pipeline to company B that provided a certain bandwidth 24 hours a day and was not used by any other entities. This was great because only the two companies could use the line and a certain level of bandwidth was always available, but it was expensive and most companies did not use the full bandwidth each and every hour that this link was available. Thus, the companies spent a lot of money for a service that they did not use all the time. Today, instead of using dedicated lines, companies are turning to frame relay.

Frame relay is a WAN protocol that operates at the data link layer. It is a WAN solution that uses packet-switching technology that enables multiple companies and networks to share the same WAN media. Whereas direct point-to-point links have a cost based on the distance between the end points, the frame relay cost is based on the amount of bandwidth used. Because several companies and networks use the same media and devices (routers and switches), the cost can be greatly reduced per company compared to dedicated links.

If a company knows that it will usually require x amount of bandwidth each day, it can pay a certain fee to make sure that this amount of bandwidth will always be available to it. If another company knows that it will not have a high bandwidth requirement, it can pay a lower fee that does not guarantee the higher bandwidth allocation. This second company will have the higher bandwidth available to it anyway—at least until that link gets busy, and then the bandwidth level will reduce. (Companies that pay more to ensure that a higher level of bandwidth will always be available pay a *committed information rate,* or *CIR*.)

Two main types of equipment are used in frame relay connections: Data Terminal Equipment (DTE) and Data Circuit-Terminating Equipment (DCE). The DTE is usually a customer-owned device, such as a router or switch that provides connectivity between the company's own network and the frame relay network. DCE is the service provider's, or telecommunication company's, device that does the actual data transmission and switching in the frame relay cloud. So the DTE is a company's ramp way onto the frame relay network and the DCE devices actually do the work within the frame relay cloud.

The frame relay cloud is the collection of DCEs that provide switching and data communication functionality. Several service providers provide this type of service, and some providers use other provider's equipment—it can all get confusing because a packet can take so many different routes. This collection is called a *cloud* to differentiate it from other types of networks, and because when a packet hits this cloud, users do not usually know the route that their frames will take. The frames will either be sent through permanent or switched virtual circuits that are defined within the DCE, or they'll be sent through carrier switches.

Frame relay is an any-to-any service that is shared by many users. As stated earlier, this is good because the costs are much lower than those of dedicated leased lines. Because it is shared, if one subscriber is not using his bandwidth, it is available to others to use. On the other hand, when traffic levels increase, the available bandwidth decreases. This is why subscribers who want to ensure that a certain bandwidth is always available to them pay a higher committed rate.

Figure 7-48 shows five sites being connected via dedicated lines versus five sites connected through the frame relay cloud. The first solution requires many dedicated lines that are expensive and not flexible. The second solution is cheaper and provides companies much more flexibility.

Virtual Circuits
Frame relay forwards frames across virtual circuits. These circuits can be permanent, meaning that they are programmed in advance, or the circuits can be switched, meaning that the circuit is quickly built when it is needed and torn down when it is no longer needed. The *permanent virtual circuit (PVC)* works like a private line for a customer with an agreed-upon bandwidth availability. When a customer decides to pay for the committed rate, a PVC is programmed for that customer to ensure that he will always receive a certain amount of bandwidth.

Unlike PVCs, *switched virtual circuits (SVCs)* require steps similar to a dial-up and connection procedure. This is because a permanent path is set up for PVC frames, and when SVCs are used, a circuit needs to be built. It is similar to setting up a phone call over the public network. During the setup procedure, the required bandwidth is requested, the destination computer is contacted and must accept the call, a path is determined, and forwarding information is programmed into each switch along the SVC's path. SVCs are used for teleconferencing, establishing temporary connections to remote sites, data replication, and voice calls. Once the connection is no longer needed, the circuit is torn down and the switches forget that it ever existed.

Although a PVC provides a guaranteed level of bandwidth, it does not have the flexibility of a SVC. If a customer wants to use her PVC for a temporary connection, as mentioned earlier, the customer must call the carrier and have it set up, which can take hours.

Figure 7-48   A private network connection requires several expensive dedicated links. Frame relay enables users to share a public network.

References

Frame Relay Forum: **www.frforum.com**

RAD University Networking Tutorials: **www2.rad.com/networks/netterms.htm**

Frame Relay Resource Center: **www.alliancedatacom.com/framerelay.asp**

X.25

X.25 is an older WAN protocol that defines how devices and networks establish and maintain connections. Like frame relay, X.25 is a switching technology that uses carrier switches to provide connectivity for many different networks. It also provides an any-to-any connection, meaning that many users use the same service simultaneously. Subscribers are charged by the amount of bandwidth they use instead of a flat fee as in dedicated links.

Data is divided into 128 bytes and encapsulated in High-level Data Link Control (HDLC) frames. The frames are then addressed and forwarded across the carrier switches. Much of this sounds the same as frame relay—and it is, but frame relay is much more advanced and efficient when compared to X.25, because the X.25 protocol was developed and released in the 1970s. During this time, many of the devices that were connected to networks were dumb terminals, the networks did not have built-in functionality and fault tolerance, and the Internet overall was not as foundationally stable and resistant to errors as it is today. When these characteristics were not part of the Internet, X.25 was required to compensate for these deficiencies and to provide many layers of error checking, error correcting, and fault tolerance. This made the protocol fat, which was required back then; but today it clogs down the system and provides a lower performance rate than frame relay or ATM.

ATM

Asynchronous Transfer Mode (ATM) is another switching technology, but instead of being a packet-switching method, it uses a cell-switching method. ATM is a high-speed networking technology used for LAN, WAN, and service provider connections. Like frame relay, it is a connection-oriented switching technology. IP is an example of a connectionless-oriented switching technology. Within the TCP/IP protocol suite, IP is connectionless and TCP is connection-oriented. This means that IP segments can be quickly and easily routed and switched without each router or switch in between having to worry about whether the data actually made it to its destination; that is TCP's job. TCP works at the source and destination ends to ensure that data was properly transmitted, and it resends data that ran into some types of problems. When using ATM or frame relay, the devices in between the source and destination have to be more conscious of data and whether it gets to where it needs to go, unlike when purely IP is being used.

ATM is a cell-switching technology versus a packet-switching technology. Data is segmented into fixed-size cells of 53 bytes, instead of variable-size packets. This provides for more efficient and faster use of the communication paths. ATM sets up virtual circuits, which act like dedicated paths between the source and destination. These virtual circuits can guarantee bandwidth and QoS, unlike IP. For these reasons, ATM is a good carrier for voice and video transmission, because it promises a bandwidth level and a virtual dedicated path.

ATM technology is used by carriers and service providers and makes up part of the core technology of the Internet, but this technology can also be used for a company's private use in backbones and connections to the service provider's networks.

Traditionally, companies used dedicated lines, usually T-carrier lines, to connect to the public networks. However, companies have also moved to implementing an ATM switch on their network, which connects them to the carrier infrastructure. Because the fee is based on bandwidth used instead of a continual connection, it can be much cheaper. Some companies have replaced their Fast Ethernet and FDDI backbones with ATM. When ATMs are used as private backbones, the companies have ATM switches that take the Ethernet, or whatever data link technology is being used, and frame and convert them into the 53-byte ATM cells.

ATM supports various interfaces to provide this type of flexibility and use. A DSU device is used to connect a LAN to the public ATM network. This architecture is used when a company's network is connected to the ATM network via a router or bridge. The DSU device is necessary to make sure that the digital signals are converted to a signal type the ATM network can understand.

Like frame relay, ATM can set up PVCs, which are preprogrammed into the switches along that particular communication path, and SVCs, which are set up at the time they are required and torn down when they are done being used.

Reference

The ATM Forum: **www.atmforum.com**

SMDS

Switched Multimegabit Data Service (SMDS) is a high-speed packet-switched technology used to enable customers to extend their LANs across MANs and WANs. When a company has an office in one state that needs to communicate with an office in a different state, for example, the two LANs can use this packet-switching protocol to communicate across the already established public network. This protocol is connectionless and can provide bandwidth on demand.

Although some companies still use this technology, it has been greatly replaced with frame relay. Service providers usually maintain only the networks that currently use this technology instead of offering it to new customers.

SDLC

Synchronous Data Link Control (SDLC) protocol is based on networks that use dedicated, leased lines with permanent physical connections. It is used mainly for communication to IBM hosts within a Systems Network Architecture (SNA). Developed by IBM in the 1970s, it is a bit-oriented, synchronous protocol that has evolved into other communication protocols such as HDLC, Link Access Procedure (LAP), and Link Access Procedure-Balanced (LAPB).

SDLC was developed to enable mainframes to communicate with remote locations. The environments that use SDLC usually have primary systems that control secondary stations' communication. SDLC provides the polling media access technology, which is the mechanism that enables secondary stations to communicate on the network. Figure 7-49 shows the primary and secondary stations on an SDLC network.

HDLC

High-level Data Link Control (HDLC) protocol is also a bit-oriented link layer protocol used for transmission over synchronous lines. HDLC is an extension of SDLC, which is mainly used in SNA environments. HDLC provides high throughput because it supports full-duplex transmissions and is used in point-to-point and multipoint connections.

Like SDLC, HDLC works with primary stations that contact secondary stations to establish data transmission. Vendors have developed their own parameters within their version of HDLC, which has ended up with interoperability issues between vendor HDLC implementations.

HSSI

High-Speed Serial Interface (HSSI) is an interface used to connect multiplexers and routers to high-speed communication services such as ATM and frame relay. It supports speeds up to 52 Mbps as in T3 WAN connections, which are usually integrated with router and multiplex devices to provide serial interfaces to the WAN.

These interfaces define the electrical and physical interfaces to be used by DTE/DCE devices; thus, it works at the physical layer. The interface was developed by Cisco and T3plus Networking.

Figure 7-49   SDLC is used mainly in mainframe environments within an SNA network.

References

High-Speed Serial Interface: **www.cisco.com/univercd/cc/td/doc/cisintwk/ ito_doc/hssi.htm**

HSSI Design Specification: **cio.cisco.com/warp/public/459/8.html**

Multiservice Access Technologies

Let's see how many services we can shove onto this one cable.

Multiservice access technologies combine several types of communication categories (data, voice, and video) over one transmission line. This provides for higher performance, reduced operational costs, and greater flexibility, integration, and control for the customers. This advancement in technology is clearing up the usually blurred division lines between the ISPs and the telephone carriers.

The regular phone system is based on a circuit-switched, voice-centric network, referred to as public-switched telephone network (PSTN). PSTN uses circuit switching instead of packet switching. When a phone call is made, the call is placed at the PSTN interface, which is the user's telephone. This PSTN is connected to the telephone company's local loop via copper wiring. Once the signals for this phone call reaches the telephone company's central office (the end of the local loop), they are part of the telephone company's circuit-switching world. A connection is made between the source and the destination, and as long as the call is in session, the data flows through the same switches.

When a phone call is made, the connection has to be set up, signaling has to be controlled, and the session must be torn down. This takes place through the Signaling System 7 protocol. When Voice over IP (VoIP) is used, its protocols must be properly transmitted so the devices involved can understand this different signaling scheme.

This PSTN network is being replaced by data-centric, packet-oriented networks that can support voice, data, and video. The new VoIP networks use different switches, protocols, and communication links. This means that the VoIP has to go through a tricky transition stage that enables the old systems and infrastructures to communicate with the new systems until the old is dead and gone.

High-quality compression is used with VoIP technology and the identification numbers (phone numbers) are IP addresses. This technology gets around some of the barriers that are present in the PSTN today. The interface devices (telephones) have embedded functions and logic that make it more difficult to implement different types of services that the network as a whole can support. In VoIP, the interface to the network can be a computer, server, PBX, and anything else that runs a telephone application. This provides for more flexibility when it comes to adding new services and a lot more control and intelligence to the interfacing devices.

Because this is a packet-oriented switching technology, possible latency delays can occur. This manifests as longer delays within a conversation and lets the conversation seem to get out of synch a bit. When someone using VoIP for a phone call experiences these types of lags in the conversation, it is because the packets holding the other person's voice message got queued somewhere within the network and is on its way. This is referred to as *jittering*, but protocols are being developed to help smooth out these issues and provide a more continuous telephone call experience.

H.323 Gateways

The ITU-T recommendations cover a wide variety of multimedia communication services. H.323 is part of this family of recommendations, but it is also a standard that deals with video, real-time audio, and data packet-based transmissions where multiple users can be involved with the data exchange. An H.323 environment features terminals, which can be telephones or computers with telephony software, gateways that connect this environment to the public telephone network, multipoint control units, and gatekeepers that manage calls and functionality.

Like any type of gateway, H.323 gateways connect different types of systems and devices and provide the necessary translation functionality. The H.323 terminals are connected to these gateways and the gateways are connected to the PSTN. These gateways translate protocols used on the circuit-based telephone network and the packet-based VoIP network. The gateways also translate the circuits into packets and packets into circuits as required.

The technology is only a few years old, but it is catching on fast and the new devices and protocols are being implemented and used. Today it is necessary also to implement the gateways that enable the new technology to communicate with the old, but soon the old telephone network may be a thing of the past and all communication may take place over packets instead of circuits.

The newer technology looks to provide transmission mechanisms that will involve much more than just voice. Although we have focused mainly on VoIP, other technologies support the combination of voice and data over the same network, such as voice over ATM and voice over frame relay. ATM and frame relay are connection-oriented protocols and IP is connectionless. This means that frame relay and ATM provide better QoS and less jittering and latency.

The best of both worlds is to combine IP over ATM or frame relay. This allows for packet-oriented communication over a connection-oriented network that will provide an end-to-end connection. IP is at the network layer and is media independent—it can run over a variety of data link layer protocols and technologies.

Traditionally, a company has a PBX, which is a switch between the company and the PSTN, on its premises, and T1 or T3 lines connect the PBX to the telephone company's central office, which houses switches that act as ramps onto the PSTN. When WAN technologies are used instead of accessing the PSTN through the central office switches, the data is transmitted over the frame relay, or ATM, cloud. An example of this configuration is shown in Figure 7-50.

Because frame relay and ATM utilize PVCs and SVCs, they both have the ability to use SVCs for telephone calls. Remember that a CIR is used when a company wants to ensure that it will always have a certain bandwidth available. When a company pays for this guaranteed bandwidth, it is paying for a PVC where the switches and routers are programmed to control its connection and for that connection to be maintained. SVCs, on the other hand, are set up on demand and are temporary in nature. They are perfect for making telephone calls or transmitting video during videoconferencing.

We have covered several WAN technologies in these last sections. Table 7-10 provides a snapshot of the important characteristics for each.

Figure 7-50 Regular telephone calls connect phones to the PSTN. Voice over WAN technologies connect calls to the Internet cloud.

WAN Technology	Characteristics
Dedicated lines	–Dedicated, leased line that connects two locations –Expensive compared to other WAN options –Secure because only two locations are using the same media
Frame relay	–High-performance WAN protocol that uses packet-switching technology, which works over public networks –Shared media among companies –Uses SVCs and PVCs –Fee based on used bandwidth
X.25	–First packet-switching technology developed to work over public networks –Shared media among companies –Lower speed than frame relay because of its extra overhead –International standard and used more in countries other than the U.S.
SMDS	–High-speed switching technology used over public network
ATM	–High-bandwidth switching and multiplexing technology that has a low delay –Uses 53-byte fixed-size cells –Uses PVCs and SVCs –Very fast because of the low overhead
SDLC	–Enables mainframes to communicate with remote offices –Provides polling mechanism to allow primary and secondary stations to communicate
HDLC	–A data encapsulation method for synchronous serial links –Point-to-point and multipoint communication
HSSI	–DTE/DCE interface to enable high-speed communication over WAN links
VoIP	–Combines voice and data over the same IP network media and protocol –Reduces costs of implementing and maintaining two different networks

Table 7-10   The Characteristics of Discussed WAN Technologies

References

VoIP Quick Start Guide: www.cisco.com/univercd/cc/td/doc/product/access/acs_mod/cis3600/voice/4936vqsg.htm

IETF IP Telephony Charter: www.ietf.org/html.charters/iptel-charter.html

Frame Relay Forum: www.frforum.com

ATM Forum: www.atmforum.com/aboutatm/2.html

Voice Telephony Over ATM: www.iec.org/online/tutorials/vtoa/

Remote Access

I need to talk to you, but I am way over here!

Remote access covers several technologies that enable remote and home users to connect to networks, which will grant them access to network resources that help them to perform their tasks. Most of the time, these users must first gain access to the Internet through an ISP, which will set up a connection to the destination network.

For many corporations, remote access is a necessity because it enables users to obtain up-to-date information, it can reduce networking costs by using the Internet as the access media instead of expensive dedicated lines, and it extends the workplace for employees to their homes or on the road. Remote access can streamline access to resources and information through Internet connections and provides a competitive advantage by letting partners, suppliers, and customers have closely controlled links. The most common types of remote connectivity methods used are VPNs, dial-up connections, ISDN, cable modems, DSL connections, and wireless technologies.

Dial-Up and RAS

Remote access is usually gained by connecting to a network access server (NAS). The NAS acts as a gateway and an end point to a PPP session. Then NAS provides authentication and authorization and usually controls a bank of modems.

Users dial into a Remote Access Service (RAS) server, which performs authentication by comparing the provided credentials with the database of credentials it maintains. Another type of access authentication technology used in remote connection situations is RADIUS, which is covered in Chapter 4. An administrator can set several configurations to dictate what actions will take place when a remote user attempts to connect to the NAS. Usually a request for a username and password takes place, and the NAS may hang up the call to call the user back at a predefined phone number. This security activity is used to try and ensure that only authenticated users are given access to the network, and it reverses the long-distance charges back to the company. Even if an attacker finds out the logon credentials necessary to gain remote access, it is unlikely that the attacker will also be at the predefined phone number. However, this security measure can be compromised if someone implements call forwarding.

Remote access methods are highly targeted items when it comes to trying to find an entry point into a network. This is because many companies have a stack of modems to provide remote access to their network and somehow think that their firewall magically protects all access to their network. So when a company has a false sense of security because it has implemented a firewall but has not implemented any (or strong) access control over the modem pool, the attackers can easily walk into a network without ever having to bother with the firewall.

Wardialing is used by many attackers to identify remote access modems. Specially written program tools can be used to dial a large bank of phone numbers that is fed to them. The tools log valid data connections (modems used for data transmission) and attempt to identify the system on the other end of the phone line. Some of these tools have the option of performing a dictionary attack, which attempts many possible username and password combinations in the hopes of being authorized and allowed access to the network. Wardialing enables an attacker to find all the modems that provide remote access into a network. Once she finds a modem, she will attempt to access the network through this entry point. If modems are used within an infrastructure, they are usually much easier to compromise than a firewall.

Companies often have hanging modems off of workstations here or there without much ado. Employees may install them or the IT staff may install them and then forget about them. This is why it is important for companies to perform wardialing on their own network to make sure that no unaccounted for modems are attached.

ISDN

Integrated Services Digital Network (ISDN) is a communication protocol provided by telephone companies and ISPs. This protocol and the necessary equipment enable data, voice, and other types of traffic to travel over a medium in a digital manner that was previously used only for analog voice calls. Telephone companies went all digital many years ago, except for the local loops. The local loop consists of the copper wires that connect houses and businesses to their carrier provider's central offices. These central offices contain the telephone company's switching equipment, and it is here that the analog to digital transformation takes place. However, the local loop is always analog, and is therefore slower. ISDN was developed to replace the aging telephone analog systems, but it has yet to catch on to the level that was expected.

ISDN Examined

ISDN breaks the telephone line into different channels and transmits data in a digital form versus the old analog method. Three ISDN implementations are in use:

- **Basic Rate Interface (BRI) ISDN** This implementation operates over existing copper lines at the local loop and provides digital voice and data channels. It uses two B channels and one D channel with a combined bandwidth of 144 Kbps and is used usually for home subscribers.

- **Primary Rate Interface (PRI) ISDN** This implementation has up to 23 B channels and 1 D channel, at 64 Kbps per channel. The total bandwidth is equivalent to a T1, which is 1.544 Mbps. This would be more suitable for a company that requires a higher amount of bandwidth.

- **Broadband-ISDN (BISDN)** This implementation can handle many different types of services at the same time and is mainly used within telecommunication carrier backbones. When BISND is used within a backbone, ATM is used to encapsulate data at the data link layer into cells, which travel over a SONET network.

ISDN uses the same wires and transmission media used by analog dial-up technologies, but it works in a digital fashion. If a computer uses a modem to communicate with an ISP, it converts its data from digital to analog to be transmitted over the phone line. If that same computer were configured and had the necessary equipment to utilize ISDN, it would not need to convert the data from digital to analog, but would keep it in a digital form. This, of course, means that the receiving end would also require the necessary equipment to receive and interpret this type of communication properly. Communicating in a purely digital form provides higher bit rates that can be sent more economically.

ISDN is a set of telecommunication services that can be used over public and private telecommunication networks. It provides a digital point-to-point circuit-switched medium and establishes a circuit between the two communicating devices. An ISDN connection can be used for anything a modem can be used for, but it provides more functionality and higher bandwidth. This switched digital service can provide bandwidth on an as-needed basis and can be used for LAN-to-LAN on-demand connectivity instead of using an expensive dedicated link.

As stated earlier, analog uses a full channel for communication, but ISDN can break up this channel into multiple channels to provide full-duplex communication and a higher level of control and error handling. ISDN provides two basic home and business services: Basic Rate Interface (BRI) and Primary Rate Interface (PRI). BRI has two B channels that enable data to be transferred and one D channel that provides for call setup, connection management, error control, caller ID, and more. The bandwidth available with BRI is 144 Kbps, whereas the top modems can provide only 56 Kbps.

The D channel provides for a quicker call setup and process of making a connection. An ISDN connection may require only a 2 to 5–second setup connection time, whereas a modem may require a 45 to 90–second time frame. This D channel is an out-of-band communication link between the local loop equipment and the user's terminal. It is out of band because the control data is not mixed in with the user communication data. This makes it more difficult for a would-be defrauder to send bogus instructions back to the service provider's equipment in the hopes of causing a DoS, obtaining services not paid for, or conducting some other type of destructive behavior.

DSL

Digital Subscriber Line (DSL) is another type of high-speed connection technology used to access the Internet. It can provide 6 to 30 times higher bandwidth speeds than ISDN and analog technologies. It uses existing phone lines and provides a 24-hour connection to the Internet. This does indeed sound better than sliced bread, but only certain people can get this service because they need a service provider that provides this service, and they have to be within a 2.5-mile radius of the service provider's equipment. As the distance between a residence and the central office increases, the transmission rates for DSL decreases.

DSL is a broadband technology that can provide up to 52 Mbps transmission speed without replacing the carrier's copper wire. The end user and the carrier's equipment do need to be upgraded for DSL, though, and this is why many companies and residents cannot use this service at this time. The user and carrier must have DSL modems that use the same modulation techniques.

DSL offers several types of services. The services can be *symmetric*, which means that traffic flows at the same speed upstream and downstream, or they can be *asymmetric*, where the downstream speed is much higher than upstream. In most situations, an asymmetric connection is fine for residence users because they usually download items from the Web much more often than they upload data.

References

DSL Sourcebook: **www.paradyne.com/sourcebook_offer**

DSL Life: **www.dsllife.com**

Cable Modems

We already have a cable running to your house, so just buy this extra service.

The television cable companies have been delivering television services to homes for years, and they recently started delivering data transmission services for users who have cable modems and want to connect to the Internet at high speeds.

Cable modems provide high-speed access, up to 50 Mbps, to the Internet through existing cable coaxial and fiber lines. The cable modem provides upstream and downstream conversions.

Coaxial and fiber cables are used to bring hundreds of television stations to users, and one or more of the channels on these lines are dedicated to carrying data. The bandwidth is shared between users in a local area; therefore, it will not always stay at a static rate. So if Mike attempts to download a program from the Internet at 5:30 P.M., he most likely will have a much slower connection than if he attempted it at 10:00 A.M., because many people come home from work and hit the Internet at the same time. As more people access the Internet within his local area, Mike's Internet access performance drops.

Always Connected

Unlike modem connections, DSL lines and cable modems are connected to the Internet all the time. No dial-up steps are required as in modem connections. This can cause a huge security issue because many hackers look for just these types of connections. Systems using these types of connections are always online and available for scanning, probing, hacking, and attacking. However, these systems are often used in distributed DoS (DDoS) attacks. Because the systems are on all the time, attackers plant Trojan horses that lay dormant until they get the command from the attacker to launch an attack against a victim. Many of the DDoS attacks use systems with DSL and cable modems as their accomplices, and usually the owner of the computer has no idea of the vulnerabilities involved.

Sharing the same media brings up a slew of security concerns, because users with network sniffers can easily view their neighbors traffic and data as it travels to and from the Internet. Many cable companies are looking into encryption and other security mechanisms. The growth of cable modems has also increased the use of personal firewalls.

Reference

Cable Modem Info: **www.cablemodeminfo.com**

VPN

Here's the secret handshake. Now you can use the secret tunnel.

A *virtual private network (VPN)* is a secure, private connection through a public network or an otherwise unsecure environment, as shown in Figure 7-51. It is a *private* connection because the encryption and tunneling protocols are used to ensure the confidentiality and integrity of the data in transit. It is important to remember that VPN technology requires a tunnel to work and it assumes encryption. The protocols that can be used for VPNs are Point-to-Point Tunneling Protocol (PPTP), IPSec, and L2TP.

The sending and receiving ends must have the necessary hardware and software to set up an encrypted tunnel, which provides the private link. The tunneling encryption protocol that is used encrypts the data and protects it as it travels through the untrusted public network, usually the Internet.

Remote users, or road warriors, can use VPNs to connect to their company network to access their e-mail, network resources, and personal files. A remote user must have the necessary software loaded on his computer to use a VPN. The user first makes a PPP connection to an ISP, and the ISP makes a full connection for the user to the destination network. PPP encapsulates datagrams to be properly transmitted over an IP network. Once this connection has been made, the user's software initiates a VPN connection with the destination network. Because data exchanged between the two entities will be encrypted, the two entities go through a handshaking phase to agree upon the type of encryption that will be used and the key that will be employed to encrypt their data. The ISP is involved with the creation of the PPP connection, which is a type of foundation for the VPN connection. Once the PPP connection is set up, the ISP is out of the picture

Remote user   Private link provided by VPN   Server

Figure 7-51   A VPN provides a virtual dedicated link between two entities across a public network.

and the VPN parameters are negotiated and decided upon by the user and the destination network. After this is complete, the user and network can then communicate securely through their newly created virtual connection.

VPN connections can be used by remote users to access a network and they can also be used to provide a connection between two routers (many times called gateway-to-gateway connection) or two users. It is a flexible connection, and the only requirements are that each entity has a connection, VPN software, the necessary protocols, and the same encryption mechanisms. Once the VPN connection is made, the user can access network resources in the same manner that he can access them via dial-up connections.

Up to this point, we have been discussing VPN that takes place over dial-up connections; but a VPN can also take place between firewalls that have VPN functionality. Within a network, the VPN device sits on the outer edge of the security domain. When a company implements a firewall that has VPN functionality embedded, this allows for centralization of administration for the VPN and firewall. In this type of configuration, packets that enter the network can come in encrypted through the VPN connection and must be decrypted to allow the firewall to inspect the packets and either allow or deny them. Because extra work is being done on the packets as they enter and leave a network, much more overhead is generated, which causes degradation in performance. However, today most of the processing that takes place is being moved to hardware and integrated circuits, which can work at much faster speeds than pure software.

Tunneling Protocols

How do we get our message through this sea of packets? Answer: Create a tunnel.

It was mentioned that VPNs use tunneling protocols, but what the heck are they anyway? A *tunnel* is a virtual path across a network that delivers packets that are encapsulated and possibly encrypted. Encapsulation and encryption sound alike, but they describe two different reasons a tunnel would be used in the first place.

If one network uses NetBIOS Enhanced User Interface (NetBEUI) and needs to be connected to another network that also uses NetBEUI, but they are two states apart, what is the problem? NetBEUI is nonroutable. So for these two networks to communicate, the NetBEUI packets must be encapsulated within a routable protocol, such as IP. This type of encapsulation happens all the time on the Internet and between networks. When an Ethernet network is connected to an FDDI backbone, that FDDI network will not understand the Ethernet frame format; thus, the packets must be encapsulated within the FDDI protocol when they are to be sent over the FDDI network. If two networks use IPX and need to communicate across the Internet, these messages must also be encapsulated in a protocol that the Internet can understand, such as IP.

The second variation to a tunnel is encapsulation *and* encryption. The encapsulation reasons stay the same and the encryption is used to protect the data's confidentiality and integrity as it travels through untrusted environments. These are both ways of tunneling through another network.

Tunneling is the main ingredient to a VPN because that is how it creates its private connection. Three main tunneling protocols are used in VPN connections: PPTP, L2TP, and IPSec. (IPSec is described in depth in Chapter 8.)

PPP

Point-to-Point Protocol (PPP) is used to encapsulate messages and transmit them over a serial line. Therefore, PPP is used to allow TCP/IP and other protocols to be carried across dial-up lines. PPP is used to establish dial-up connections between routers, user-to-router, and user-to-user. PPP establishes a dial-up Internet connection between a computer and an Internet *point of presence* (PoP)—usually a bank of modems and access servers at an ISP location. The user dials into this PoP over a telecommunication line and communicates using the PPP.

When we connect to the Internet, we may be using a serial asynchronous dial-up connection or a point-to-point connection, such as a T1 line. It is a *serial* connection, meaning one bit follows the one in front of it, compared to a *parallel* connection, where channels of bits travel at one time. This serial connection is the telephone company's line, and it knows nothing about networking protocols such as IP, IPX, AppleTalk, and so on, which is what our computers use to communicate. Therefore, this traffic needs to be encapsulated before it is put onto this serial link, which is what the PPP does. PPP *encapsulates* the data coming from our computer or network, which means that it puts the data into the correct format to travel over the telecommunication link. PPP frames our data with start and stop bits so that the other end knows how to process the data. PPP allows us to set up and establish a dial-up Internet connection. Once a link is established, the user must authenticate to a network authentication server at the ISP site. PPP can use Password Authentication Protocol (PAP), Challenge Handshake Authentication Protocol (CHAP), or Extensible Authentication Protocol (EAP) to accomplish this task. If the user is attempting to dial into her company's network, another step must take place: a protocol must deliver this PPP session to the actual corporate network. So what does this mean? The data that is encapsulated within PPP must now travel over the Internet, which does not understand PPP, but instead uses IP. So another protocol must encapsulate the PPP data in IP packets and tunnel it through the Internet to the corporate network, as shown in Figure 7-52. PPP encapsulates data to travel over a private network (between you and your ISP), and a tunneling protocol encapsulates the data to travel over a public network, as in the Internet.

Two of the main tunnel protocols used today for setting up a VPN are PPTP and L2TP. Both reduce the cost of remote dial-up networking because the user can dial into a local ISP instead of dialing directly to the corporate network, which may accrue long-distance charges.

PPP has, for the most part, replaced *Serial Line Internet Protocol (SLIP)*, an older protocol that was used for encapsulating data to be sent over serial connection links. PPP has several capabilities that SLIP does not have:

- PPP implements header and data compression for efficiency and better use of bandwidth.
- PPP has error correction.
- PPP supports different authentication methods.
- PPP can encapsulate protocols other than just IP.
- PPP does not require both ends to have an IP address assigned before data transfer can occur.

Figure 7-52
A VPN
connection
can be used to
extend a PPP
connection
securely.

PPTP

The Internet does not understand my dial-up packets. Response: Wrap them up in PPTP.

Why do we need tunneling protocols? Because some protocols cannot be properly routed through specific networks. Here we are talking about PPP frames, which are not routable over the Internet, but the Internet does not understand some other protocols that we use today, such as IPX, NetBEUI, and AppleTalk. Alone, these frames could not find their way to the ultimate destination they are seeking when crossing the Internet, so they need a hand; that is what the tunneling protocol does—similar to a ferry taking cars across a body of water. The car could not get to the other side by itself because it was not built to deal with water, but the ferry can move and navigate in the water, as the tunneling protocol can move in the IP-based Internet.

PPTP, a Microsoft protocol, has been the de facto industry standard tunneling protocol for years that has allowed remote users to set up a PPP connection to a local ISP and then create a secure VPN to their destination.

Although tunneling does not by default mean that the user's data is encrypted, this is usually the case. When using PPTP, the PPP payload is encrypted with Microsoft Point-to-Point Encryption (MPPE) protocol using MS-CHAP or EAP-TLS. The keys used in encrypting this data are generated during the authentication process between the user and the authentication server.

Along with encryption, the frame has to be encapsulated as well. A series of encapsulation takes place in this technology. The user's data is encapsulated within PPP, and then this frame is encapsulated by PPTP with a Generic Routing Encapsulation (GRE) header and IP header, as shown in Figure 7-53. This encapsulation allows the resulting frame to be routable over public networks, such as in the Internet.

Figure 7-53
PPTP
encapsulates
a PPP frame.

One limitation of PPTP is that it can work only over IP networks, so other protocols must be used to move data, such as frame relay, X.25, and ATM links. Cisco started to develop a protocol, Layer 2 Forwarding (L2F), that would tunnel PPP traffic through these other types of networks, but it was asked by the IETF to combine its work with PPTP for interoperability sake. As a result, Cisco developed L2TP, which combines the best of PPTP and L2F.

L2TP

L2TP provides the functionality of PPTP, but it can work over networks other than just IP, and it provides a higher level of security when combined with IPSec. L2TP does not provide any encryption or authentication services, so it needs to be combined with IPSec if those services are required.

Similar encapsulation processes take place when compared to PPTP. The PPP frame is encapsulated with a L2TP and UDP header.

When the destination system receives the L2TP frame, it processes the headers. Once it gets to the IPSec trailer, it ensures the integrity and authentication of the frame. Then it uses the information in the ESP header to decrypt the rest of the headers and data payload properly.

- PPTP can run only on top of IP networks. It is dependent on IP. L2TP, on the other hand, can run on top and tunnel through networks that use other protocols, such as frame relay, X.25, and ATM.

- PPTP is an encryption protocol and L2TP is not; thus, L2TP lacks the security to be called a *true* VPN solution. L2TP is often used in conjunction with IPSec to provide the necessary encryption.

- L2TP supports TACACS+ and RADIUS, and PPTP does not.

PAP, CHAP, and EAP

Hey, how do I know you are who you say you are?

Password Authentication Protocol (PAP) is an authentication protocol used by remote users to authenticate over PPP lines. It provides identification and authentication of the user attempting to access a network from a remote system. This protocol requires a user to enter a password before being authenticated. The password and the username credentials are sent over the network to the authentication server after a connection has been established via PPP. The authentication server has a database of user credentials that are compared to the supplied credentials to authenticate users.

VPN Tunneling Protocols

The following provides an outline of VPN tunneling protocols:

Point-to-Point Tunneling Protocol (PPTP)

- Designed for client/server connectivity
- Sets up a single point-to-point connection between two computers
- Works at the data link layer
- Transmits over only IP networks

Layer 2 Forwarding (L2F)

- Created before L2TP by Cisco
- Merged with PPTP, which resulted in L2TP
- Provides mutual authentication
- No encryption

Layer 2 Tunneling Protocol (L2TP)

- Hybrid of L2F and PPTP
- Sets up a single point-to-point connection between two computers
- Works at the data link layer
- Transmits over multiple types of networks, not just IP
- Combined with IPSec for security

IPSec

- Handles multiple connections at the same time
- Provides secure authentication and encryption
- Supports only IP networks
- Focuses on LAN-to-LAN communication rather than a dial-up protocol
- Works at the network layer, and provides security on top of IP
- Can work in *tunnel mode*, meaning the payload and header are protected, or *transport mode*, meaning that only the payload is protected

PAP is one of the least secure ways of authentication, because the credentials are sent in clear text, which renders them easy to capture by network sniffers. Although it is not recommended, some systems revert to PAP if they cannot agree on any other authentication protocol. During the handshake process of a connection, the two entities negotiate how authentication is going to take place, what connection parameters to use, the speed of data flow, and other factors. Both entities will try to negotiate and agree upon the most secure method of authentication; they may start with EAP, and if one computer does not have EAP capability, they will try to agree upon CHAP. If one of the computers does not have CHAP capabilities, they may be forced to use PAP. If this type of authentication is unacceptable, the administrator will configure the RAS to accept only CHAP authentication and higher, and PAP cannot be used at all.

Challenge Handshake Authentication Protocol (CHAP) authentication protocol addresses some of the vulnerabilities found in PAP. It uses a challenge/response mechanism to authenticate the user instead of sending a password. When a user wants to establish a PPP connection and both ends have agreed that CHAP will be used for authentication purposes, the user's computer sends the authentication server a logon request. The server sends the user a challenge, which is a random value. This challenge is encrypted with the use of a predefined password as an encryption key, and the encrypted challenge value is returned to the server. The authentication server also uses the predefined password as an encryption key and encrypts the original challenge value, comparing the results to what was received from the user. If the two results are the same, the authentication server deduces that the user must have entered the correct password, and authentication is granted. The steps that take place in CHAP are depicted in Figure 7-54.

PAP versus CHAP

PAP Characteristics

- Sends credentials in cleartext during transmission
- Decreases in use because it does not provide a high level of security
- Supported by most networks and network access servers

CHAP Characteristics

- Used the same way PAP is used but provides a higher degree of security
- Authenticates using a challenge/response method
- Used by remote users, routers, and NASs to provide authentication before providing connectivity

Figure 7-54
CHAP uses
a challenge/
response
mechanism
instead of having
the user send the
password over
the wire.

PAP is vulnerable to sniffing because it sends the password and data in plaintext, but it is also vulnerable to man-in-the-middle attacks. CHAP is not vulnerable to man-in-the-middle attacks because it continues this challenge/response activity throughout the connection to ensure that the authentication server is still communicating with a user who holds the necessary credentials.

Extensible Authentication Protocol (EAP) is also supported by PPP. Actually, EAP is not a specific authentication mechanism as are PAP and CHAP; instead, it provides a framework to enable many types of authentication techniques to be used during PPP connections. As the name states, it extends the authentication possibilities from the norm (PAP and CHAP) to other methods such as one-time passwords, token cards, biometrics, Kerberos, and future mechanisms. So when a user dials into an authentication server and both have EAP capabilities, they can negotiate between a longer list of possible authentication methods.

References

"If Your PPP Server Uses PAP": **en.tldp.org/HOWTO/PPP-HOWTO/pap.html**

PPP Extensible Authentication Protocol: **www.msg.net/kadow/answers/extras/rfc/rfc2284.html**

Remote Access Guidelines

Many companies do not exactly know who is accessing their network remotely or why. Remote users should be identified and authenticated and their activities audited to ensure that no malicious activity is taking place and that no one is abusing access rights. All remote users should be justified in their right to access the network, and this should be reviewed on an annual basis. For example, if Brian worked in the software development group and required remote access to work from home, and then six months later he was moved into the logistics group, he might not require remote access any longer; thus, remote access should no longer be available to him.

Expected activity and behavior pertaining to remote access should be within the company's security policy or in an issue-specific policy that outlines who should do what and when. This policy should be presented and available to all users to help clear up confusion and enable the company to take steps if someone is abusing her use of remote access.

The access modems should be set to answer after the fourth ring. Wardialers are often configured to move to another phone number if the number they are dialing rings longer than two or three times. This is because connections that ring more than three times are usually telephone lines and not data lines. Configuring the modem to answer on the fourth ring or higher is done in the hopes that attackers will not be able to tell that the telephone line is actually being used for remote data access.

The remote access facilities should be consolidated when possible. This means that all access servers and modem pools are housed in the same server room and administered by the same person or group. This helps ensure consistency in how remote entry points are maintained and monitored, and when changes take place they happen to all entry points. This would also allow for centralized auditing and logging, and it makes it more difficult for administrators to forget all the ways the company is allowing users to access the environment.

Strong two-factor user authentication should be used via RADIUS or TACACS+ servers, which are explained in Chapter 4. If the data that users and the company will be transmitting is confidential or sensitive, users should connect via VPN. Various levels of security should be provided to various types of users entering the network to help ensure that each user has only the necessary access rights and permissions he needs.

Companies often restrict access based on the address of the source computer trying to gain access. If the address is unknown or not on the ACL, the connection should be denied. A firewall can also be implemented to ensure that remote users access only the services and ports the network administrator wants them to access.

Caller ID and/or callback settings should be configured on the RAS server, as well as two-factor authentication. The *caller ID* functionality can see the source telephone number and make a decision as to whether access is to be allowed or not based on a predefined list of approved phone numbers. For an attacker to get around this, she must call from a preauthorized telephone number or compromise the telephone company's central office equipment. The *callback* option requires the RAS to call the user requesting access in return. This is when a user authenticates to the RAS and it drops the connection and calls the user back at a preconfigured telephone number. This does not protect unauthorized access from an authorized location and can be bypassed by call forwarding.

Caller ID and callback options are great, but they are usually not practical because they require users to call in from a static phone number each time they access the network. Most users are accessing the network remotely because they are on the road and moving from place to place.

References

Remote Access: **www.microsoft.com/windows2000/techinfo/howitworks/communications/remoteaccess**

Remote Access Market and Product Evolution: **www.firstvpn.com/papers/ nortel/remote.pdf**

IETF Network Access Server Requirements: **www.ietf.org/html.charters/ nasreq-charter.html**

Network and Resource Availability

In the triangle of security services, *availability* is one of the foundation components, the other two being *confidentiality* and *integrity*. Network and resource availability often is not fully appreciated until it is gone. That is why administrators and engineers need to implement effective backup and redundant systems to make sure that when something happens (and something will happen), users' productivity will not be drastically affected.

The network needs to be properly maintained to make sure that the network and its resources will always be available when they're needed. The cables need to be the correct type for the environment and technology used, and cable runs should not exceed the recommended lengths. Older cables should be replaced for newer ones, and possible cable cuts and malfunctions should be periodically checked.

A majority of networks use Ethernet technology, which is very resistant to failure. Token Ring was designed to be fault tolerant and does a good job when all the computers within this topology are configured and act correctly. If one NIC is working at a different speed than the others, the whole ring can be affected and traffic may be disrupted. Also, if two systems have the same MAC address, the whole network can be brought down. These issues need to be considered when maintaining an existing network. If an engineer is installing an NIC on a Token Ring network, he should ensure that it is set to work at the same speed as the others and that there is no possibility for duplicate MAC addresses.

Single Points of Failure

Don't put all your eggs in one basket or all your electrons in one device.

A *single point of failure* can bring a lot of potential risk to a network, because if the device fails, a segment or the entire network is negatively affected. Devices that could provide single points of failure are firewalls, routers, network access servers, T1 lines, switches, bridges, hubs, and authentication servers—to name a few. The best defense against being vulnerable to these are proper maintenance, regular backups, and redundancy.

Multiple paths should exist between routers in case one router goes down, and dynamic routing protocols should be used so that each router will be informed when a change to the network takes place. For WAN connections, a failover option should be configured to enable an ISDN or modem connection to be available if the WAN router fails.

Uninterruptible power supply (UPS) and redundant array of inexpensive disks (RAID) should be in place and properly configured. UPS is addressed in Chapter 6, so we will just touch on it here and show how it relates to network availability.

The UPS should be able to provide a clean and steady power source to the crucial systems and resources on the network. RAID provides fault tolerance for hard drives and can improve system performance. Redundancy and speed are provided by breaking up the data and writing it across several disks so that different disk heads can work simultaneously to retrieve the requested information. Control data is also spread across each disk—this is called *parity*—so that if one disk fails, the other disks can work together and restore its data.

RAID

Everyone be calm—this is a raid. Response: Wrong raid.

Redundant array of inexpensive disks (RAID) is a technology used for redundancy and performance improvement. It combines several physical disks and aggregates them into logical arrays. When data is saved, it is written across all drives. A RAID appears as a single drive to applications and other devices.

When data is written across all drives, the technique of *striping* is used. This activity divides and writes the data over several drives. The write performance is not affected, but the read performance is increased dramatically because more than one head is retrieving data at the same time. It might take the RAID system 6 seconds to write a block of data to the drives and only 2 seconds or less to read the same data from the disks.

Various levels of RAID dictate the type of activity that will take place within the RAID system. Some levels deal only with performance issues, while other levels deal with performance and fault tolerance. If fault tolerance is one of the services that a RAID level is providing, parity is involved. **Parity** data can be written to each disk, which works as a backup. If a drive fails, the parity data is used to rebuild a new drive and all the information is restored. Most RAID systems have *hot-swapping* disks (they can replace drives while the system is running). When a drive is swapped out, or added, the parity data that is written to each disk rebuilds the data on the new disk that was just added.

The most common RAID levels used today are levels 1, 3, and 5. Table 7-11 describes each of the possible RAID levels.

 NOTE RAID level 15 is actually a combination of levels 1 and 5, and RAID 10 is a combination of levels 1 and 0.

The RAID Advisory Board (RAB) has developed the following new classifications:

- **Failure Resistant Disk Systems** Protects against loss of data or access due to a disk failure.

- **Failure Tolerant Disk Systems** Protects against loss of data access due to failure of any single component and offers continuous data availability.

- **Disaster Tolerant Disk Systems** Two or more zones are used to provide access to stored data. These systems describe server systems that are divisible into two or more zones. The mechanisms within the zones cooperate to protect against the loss of access, possibly caused by a power outage, cooling system, or component failure.

RAID Level	Activity	Name
0	Data striped over several drives. No redundancy or parity is involved. If one volume fails, the entire volume is unusable. It is used for performance only.	Striping
1	Mirroring of drives. Data is written to two drives at once. If one drive fails, the other drive has the exact same data available.	Mirroring
2	Data striping over all drives at the bit level. Parity data is created with a hamming code, which identifies any errors. This level specifies the use of up to 39 disks: 32 for storage and 7 for error recovery data. This is not used in production today.	Hamming code parity
3	Data striping over all drives and parity data held on one drive. If a drive fails, it can be reconstructed from parity drive.	Byte-level parity
4	Same as level 3, except data is striped at the block level instead of the byte level.	Block-level parity
5	Data is written in disk sector units to all drives. Parity is written to all drives also, which ensures that there is no single point of failure.	Interleave parity
6	Similar to level 5 but with added fault tolerance, which is a second set of parity data written to all drives.	Second parity data (or double parity)
10	Data is simultaneously mirrored and striped across several drives and can support multiple drive failures.	Striping and mirroring

Table 7-11 Explanations of the Different RAID Levels

Two other backup technologies, Hierarchical Storage Management (HSM) and storage area network (SAN), can also be used. HSM provides continuous online backup functionality. It combines hard disk technology with the cheaper and slower optical or tape juke boxes. In SAN, storage systems are connected together to form a single backup network. Private channels or storage controllers are implemented so hosts can access the different backup devices transparently.

Reference

RAID Basics: **www.raidweb.com/whatis.html**

Clustering

Okay, everyone gather over here and perform the same tasks.

Clustering is a fault-tolerant server technology that is similar to redundant servers, except each server takes part in processing services that are requested. A *server cluster* is a group of servers that are viewed logically as one server to users and can be managed as a single logical system. Clustering provides for availability and scalability. It groups physically different systems and combines them logically, which provides immunity to faults and improves performance. Clusters work as an intelligent unit to balance traffic, and users who access the cluster do not know that they may be accessing different systems at different times. To the users, all servers within the cluster are seen as one unit.

If one of the systems within the cluster fails, processing continues because the rest pick up the load, although degradation in performance could occur. This is more attractive, however, than having a secondary server that waits in the wings in case a primary server fails, because this secondary server may just sit idle for a long period of time, which is wasteful. When clustering is used, all systems are used to process requests and none sit in the background waiting for something to fail.

Clustering brings a lot to the table instead of just availability. It provides load balancing (each system takes a part of the processing load), redundancy, and failover (other systems will continue to work if one fails).

Backups

Backing up software and having backup hardware devices is a large part of network availability. (These issues are covered extensively in Chapters 6 and 9 so they are discussed only briefly here.)

It is important that you be able to restore data if a hard drive fails, a disaster takes place, or some type of software corruption occurs.

A policy should be developed that indicates what gets backed up, how often, and how these processes should occur. If users have important information on their workstations, a method needs to be detailed that indicates that backups include certain directories on users' workstations or that users move their critical data to a server share at the end of each day to ensure that it gets backed up. Backups may occur once or twice a week, every day, or every three hours. It is up to the company to determine this routine. The more frequent the backups, the more staff time will be dedicated to it, so there needs to be a balance between backup costs and the actual risk of potentially losing data.

A company may find that it is more economical and effective to conduct automatic backups through specialized software instead of spending IT work hours toward the task. It is important that the integrity of these backups is checked to ensure that backups are happening as expected—rather than finding out right after two major servers blow up that the automatic backups were saving only temporary files. Please review Chapters 6 and 9 for more information on backup issues.

Wireless Technologies

Look, Mom, no wires!

Wireless communication takes place much more often than we think, and a wide range of broadband wireless data transmission technologies occur in various frequency ranges. Broadband wireless signals occupy frequency bands that may be shared with microwave, millimeter-wave, satellite, radar, and ham radio use, for example. We use these technologies for television transmissions, cellular phones, satellite transmissions, spying, surveillance, and garage door openers.

Wireless Communications

When two people are talking, they are using wireless communication because their vocal cords are altering airwaves, which are signals that travel to another person with no cables attached. Wireless communication involves transmitting signals via radio waves through air and space, which also alters airwaves.

Signals are measured in *frequency* and *amplitudes*. The frequency of a signal dictates how much data can be carried and how far. The higher the frequency, the more data the signal can carry, but the higher the frequency, the more susceptible the signal is to atmospheric interference. A higher frequency can carry more data but over a shorter distance.

In a wired network, each computer and device has its own cable connecting it to the network in some fashion. In wireless technologies, each device must instead share the allotted radio frequency spectrum with all other wireless devices that need to communicate. This spectrum of frequencies is finite in nature—it cannot grow if more and more devices need to use it. The same thing happens with Ethernet—all the computers on a segment share the same medium and only one computer can send data at any given time, otherwise a collision can take place. Wired networks using Ethernet employ the CSMA/CD technology. Wireless technology, on the other hand, uses CSMA/CA, which means that the wireless device sends out a broadcast indicating that it is going to transmit data. This is received by other devices on the shared medium, which causes them to hold off on transmitting information. It is all about trying to eliminate or reduce collisions. (The two versions of CSMA are explained earlier in this chapter in the section "CSMA.")

A number of technologies have been developed to allow wireless devices to access and share this limited amount of medium for communication purposes. We will look at two different types of spread spectrum techniques: frequency hopping and direct sequence. The goal of each of these wireless technologies is to split the available frequency into usable portions, since it is a limited resource, and to allow the devices to share them efficiently.

Spread Spectrum

Can I spread these signals with a butter knife? Answer: Whatever.

In wireless technologies, certain technologies and industries are allocated specific *spectrums*, or frequency ranges, to be used for transmissions. In the United States, the Federal Communications Commission (FCC) decides upon this allotment of frequencies and enforces its own decisions. *Spread spectrum* means that something is distributing individual signals across the allocated frequencies in some fashion. So when a spread spectrum technology is used, the sender will spread its data across the frequencies over which it has permission to communicate. This allows for more effective use of the available bandwidth, because the sending system can use more than one frequency at a time. Think of it in the terms of serial versus parallel communication. In serial transmissions, all the bits have to be fed into one channel, one after the other. In parallel transmissions, the bits can take several channels to arrive at their destination. Parallel is a faster approach because more channels can be used at one time. This is similar to moving water through a water hose—more water can come out of a fire hose than a garden hose because the former has more bandwidth, or a larger diameter to move its substance.

So spreading the signal allows the data to travel in a parallel fashion by allowing the sender and receiver to send data over more than one frequency.

We will look at two types of spread spectrum: frequency hopping spread spectrum (FHSS) and direct sequence spread spectrum (DSSS).

References

802.11 and Spread Spectrum: **www.networkmagazine.com/article/ NMG20000726S0001**

Spread Spectrum Primer: **www.sss-mag.com/primer.html**

Guide to Wireless LAN Technologies: **www.utdallas.edu/ir/wlans/ whitepapers/wlan_wp.pdf**

Frequency Hopping Spread Spectrum   FHSS takes the total amount of bandwidth (spectrum) and splits it into smaller subchannels. The sender and receiver work at one of these channels for a specific amount of time and then move to another channel. The signal will be traveling over one frequency and then change, or hop, to another frequency. The FHSS algorithm determines the frequency to which the signal will hop and the sender and receiver's hop sequence.

Interference is a large issue in wireless transmissions because it can corrupt signals as they travel. Interference can be caused by other devices working in the same frequency space. The devices' signals step on each other's toes and distort the data that is being sent. The FHSS approach to this is to hop between different frequencies so that if another device is operating at the same frequency, it will not be drastically affected. Consider another analogy: Suppose George and Marge have to work in the same room. They could get into each other's way and affect each other's work. But if they periodically change rooms, the probability of them bumping into each other is reduced.

This hopping approach also makes it much more difficult for eavesdroppers to listen in and reconstruct the data being transmitted. FHSS has been used extensively in military wireless communication devices because the only way that the enemy could intercept and capture the transmission is by knowing the hopping sequence.

So how does this FHSS stuff work? The sender and receiver hop from one frequency to another based on a predefined hop sequence. Several pairs of senders and receivers can move their data over the same set of frequencies because they are all using different hop sequences. Let's say you and I share a hop sequence of 1,5,3,2,4, and Nicole and Ed have a sequence of 4,2,5,1,3. I can send a message on frequency 1, and Nicole sends her first message on frequency 4 at the same time. My message will hop from frequency 1 to frequency 5 and then to 3, and so on until it reaches its destination, which is your wireless device. So your device will listen on frequency 1 for a half of a second, then listen on frequency 5, and so on, until it receives the messages that are on the line on those frequencies at that time. Ed's device is listening to the same frequencies but at different times and in a different order, so he will ignore my message because it is out of synch with his predefined sequence. Without knowing the right code, Ed treats my messages as background noise and does not process it.

Direct Sequence Spread Spectrum DSSS takes a different approach by applying sub-bits to a message. The sub-bits are used by the sending system to generate a different format of the data before it is transmitted. The receiving end uses these bits to reassemble the signal into the original data format. The sub-bits are collectively called a *chip* and the sequence of how the sub-bits are applied is referred to as the *chipping code*.

When the sender's data is combined with the chip, to anyone who does not know the chipping sequence, these signals appear as random noise; this is why the sequence is sometimes called a *pseudo-noise* sequence. Once the sender combines the data with the chipping sequence, the new form of the information is modulated with a radio carrier signal, and it is shifted to the necessary frequency and transmitted. What the heck does that mean? When using wireless transmissions, the data is actually moving over radio signals that work in specific frequencies. Any data that is to be moved in this fashion must have a carrier signal, and this carrier signal works in its own specific range, which is a *frequency*. So you can think of it this way: once the data is combined with the chipping code, it is put into a car (carrier signal), and the car travels down its specific road (frequency) to get to its destination.

The receiver will basically reverse the process, first by demodulating the data from the carrier signal (removing it from the car). The receiver has to know the correct chipping sequence to change the received data into its original format. This means that the sender and receiver must be properly synchronized.

The sub-bits provide error recovery instructions, just as parity does in RAID technologies. If a signal is corrupted using FHSS, it will have to be resent, but by using DSSS, even if the message is a somewhat distorted, the signal can still be regenerated because it can be rebuilt from the chipping code bits. The use of this code allows for prevention of interference, allows for tracking of multiple transmissions, and provides a level of security.

FHSS versus DSSS FHSS uses only a portion of the total bandwidth available at any one time, while the DSSS technology uses all of the available bandwidth continuously. DSSS provides more security because the signals are more difficult to detect from background noise without knowing the specific code. And DSSS is less affected than FHSS by fading and the negative affects of jumping from one path to another. DSSS spreads the signals over a wider frequency band, where FHSS uses a narrow band carrier.

Since DSSS sends data across all frequencies at once, it has a higher data throughput than FHSS. The first WAN standard, 802.11, used FHSS, but as bandwidth requirements increased DSSS was implemented. By using FHSS, the 802.11 standard can only provide a throughput of 1–2 Mbps. By using DSSS instead, 802.11b provides a data throughput of up to 11 Mbps.

Wireless Standards

We don't need no stinking standards! Response: Uh, yeah we do.

Standards are developed so that the many vendors can create various products that will work together seamlessly. Standards are usually developed on a consensus basis among the different vendors in a specific industry. The Institute of Electrical and Electronics Engineers (IEEE) develops standards for a wide range of technologies—wireless being one of them.

The first wireless LAN (WLAN) standard, 802.11, was developed in 1997 and provided a 1–2 Mbps transfer rate. It worked in the 2.4 GHz frequency range. This fell into the available range that is unlicensed by the FCC, which means that companies and users do not need to pay to use this range. Free is better and less complicated.

The 802.11 standard outlines how wireless clients and access points communicate, lays out the specifications of their interfaces, dictates how signal transmission should take place, and describes how authentication, association, and security should be implemented.

Now just because life is unfair, a long list of standards actually fall under the 802.11 main standard. You may have seen this alphabet soup (802.11a, 802.11b, 802.11i, 802.11g, 802.11h, and so on) and not clearly understood the difference among them. IEEE created several task groups to work on specific areas within wireless communication. Each group had its own focus and was required to investigate and develop standards for its specific section. The letter suffixes indicate the order in which they were proposed and accepted.

802.11b This standard was the first extension to the 802.11 wireless LAN (WLAN) standard and is the most common standard used today. (Although 802.11a was conceived and approved first, it was not released first because of the technical complexity that was involved with this proposal, and it required special approval from the FCC to be able to use the OFMD signaling technique.) 802.11b provides up to 11 Mbps in transfer rates and works in the 2.4 GHz frequency range. It uses DSSS and is backward compatible with 802.11 implementations.

802.11a This standard uses a different method of modulating data onto the necessary radio carrier signals. Where 802.11b uses DSSS, 802.11a uses OFDM and works in the 5 GHz frequency band. Because of these differences, 802.11a is not backward compatible with 802.11b or 802.11. Several vendors have developed products that can work with both 802.11a and 802.11b implementations; the devices must be properly configured or may be able to sense the technology already being used and configure themselves appropriately.

This technology offers a couple of advantages: speed and frequency issues. 802.11a provides up to 54 Mbps, and it does not work in the already very crowded 2.4 GHz spectrum. The 2.4 GHz frequency band is referred to as a "dirty" frequency because several devices already work there—microwaves, cordless phones, baby monitors, and so on. In many situations, this means that contention for access and use of this frequency can cause loss of data or inadequate service.

One downfall of using this frequency range is that other countries have not necessarily allocated this band for use of WLAN transmissions. So 802.11a products may work in the United States, but they may not necessarily work in other countries around the world.

802 11.e   This working group has provided QoS and proper support of multimedia traffic. Multimedia and other types of time-sensitive applications have a lower tolerance of delays in data transmission. QoS provides the ability to prioritize traffic, and it affords guaranteed delivery. This specification and its capabilities can open the door to allow many different types of data to be transmitted over wireless connections.

802 11.f   When a user moves around in a WLAN, many times her wireless device will need to communicate with different access points. This is because an access point can cover only a certain distance, and as she moves out of the range of the first access point, another access point will need to pick up and maintain her signal to ensure that she does not lose network connectivity. This is referred to as *roaming*, and for this to happen seamlessly, the access points may need to communicate with each other. If the second point needs to take on this user's communication, it may need to be assured that this user has been properly authenticated and must know the necessary settings for this user's connection. This means the first access point would need to be able to convey this information to the second access point. The conveying of this information between the different access points during roaming is what 802.11f deals with. It outlines how this data can be properly shared.

802 11.g   We are never happy with what we have; we always need more functions, more room, and more speed. The 802.11g standard provides for higher data transmission—up to 54 Mbps. This is basically a speed extension for current 802.11b products. If a product meets the specifications of 802.11b, its data transfer rates are up to 11 Mbps; and if a product is based on 802.11g, that new product can be backward compatible with older equipment but work at a much higher transfer rate.

So do we go with 802.11g or with 802.11a? They both provide higher bandwidth. 802.11g is backward compatible with 802.11b, so that is a good thing if you already have a current infrastructure. But 802.11g still works in the 2.4 GHz range, which is continually getting crowded. 802.11a works in the 5 GHz band and may be a better bet if you use other devices in that frequency range. But your decision will also come down to what standard wins out in the standards war. Most likely, one or the other standard will eventually be dropped, so you will not have to worry about making this decision. Only time will tell which one will be the keeper.

802 11.h   As stated earlier, 802.11a works in the 5 GHz range, which is not necessarily available in countries other than the United States for this type of data transmission.

The 802.11h standard builds upon the 802.11a specification to meet the requirements of European wireless rules so that products working in this range can be properly implemented in European countries.

80211.i A wide range of security flaws have been documented in 802.11, which has reduced the possible implementations of WLANs and has caused serious security breaches for those who choose to implement them anyway. Each of the mentioned WLAN standards is based on the same security model, so they have all inherited the same deficiencies. The 802.11i working group has been trying to improve this security model and addressing all the current issues by using the Temporal Key Integrity Protocol, Extensible Authentication Protocol, 802.1x, and more. These technologies and approaches are covered in detail in Appendix F of this book.

80211.j *Can't we all get along and fall into step?* Many countries have been developing their own wireless standards, which inevitably causes massive interoperability issues. This can be frustrating for the customer because he cannot use certain products, and it can be frustrating and expensive for vendors because they have a laundry list of specifications to meet if they want to sell their products in various countries. If vendors are unable to meet these specifications, whole customer bases are unavailable to them. This task group has been working on bringing together many of the different standards and streamlining their development to allow for better interoperability across borders.

Not enough different wireless standards for you? You say you want some more? Okay. here you go!

802.16 All the wireless standards covered so far are WLAN-oriented standards. 802.16 is a metropolitan area network (MAN) wireless standard, which allows for wireless traffic to cover a much wider geographical area. This technology is also referred to as *broadband* wireless access.

802.15 This standard deals with a much smaller geographical network, which is referred to as a wireless personal area network (WPAN). This technology allows for connectivity to take place among local devices, as in a computer communicating to PDA, a cellular phone communicating to a computer, or a headset communicating to another device. The goal here is to allow for data transfer without all of those pesky cables—as it is with all wireless technologies. Although incredible growth in this field is continuing to occur, consumers have not yet jumped on this bandwagon as much as vendors have hoped.

The Bluetooth wireless technology provides access similar to that of the 802.15 standard, with a 1–20 Mbps transfer rate. It works in a range of approximately 10 meters. If a cell phone and a PDA are Bluetooth enabled, and they both have calendar functionality, they could update each other without your needing to connect them physically. If you added some information to your cell phone contacts list and task list, for example, you could just place the phone close to your PDA. The PDA would sense that the other device was nearby, and it would then attempt to set up a network connection with it. Once the connection is made, synchronization between the two devices would take place and the PDA would add the new contact and task list data. This sounds very much like a "Jetson's" scenario, but several types of devices already work this way.

Bluetooth works in the frequency range of 802.11 (2.4 GHz), and plans are currently underway to make various technologies interoperable.

 NOTE Some of these standards are still being developed. Not all of these standards and technologies will survive; it will take time to see which catch on and are accepted by vendors and customers alike. Wireless is still an immature technology that is currently undergoing painful growth spurts, and it is difficult to determine at this stage of the game the true future of each standard. But wireless has caught on like wildfire, and it will be interesting to watch it grow and consume the market.

References

IEEE Wireless Standards Zone: **standards.ieee.org/wireless**

"802.11 Alphabet Soup": **www.smallbusinesscomputing.com/buyersguide/article.php/1440011**

WAP

There is a hole in this security. Response: Yep, we call it the gap in the WAP.

Wireless Application Protocol (WAP) is not a standard per se. Instead, WAP is a market and industry-driven protocol stack. What's the difference? When a governing body, as in IEEE, determines that there is a need for a new technology, it creates a working group to develop the corresponding standard. This standard works as a blueprint for all of the vendors that want to develop this type of technology. If no recognized standard is in place, organizations can come together and outline specifications for the new technology for all to follow.

WAP provides a common architecture for wireless devices to be able to communicate over the Internet. It allows traditionally used voice wireless devices to be able to move data, meaning cell phones can now connect to content providers on the Internet and find out stock quotes, weather updates, access e-mail, and more. It also opened the door for new types of wireless devices to be created and sold.

Some of these wireless devices do not have the full resources that PCs and laptops have—they do not have the same amount of processing power, memory, storage space, and supporting circuitry. This means that these devices cannot use the same protocol stack used by these more powerful systems, and they cannot run the same type of applications. The WAP protocol stack was developed to be used with the limited resources and applications that have been created to work in this new environment.

WAP is a set of communications protocols used to standardize the way that wireless devices interface with each other and the Internet. The WAP model contains protocols that perform similar functionalities when compared to the TCP/IP stack. Because wireless is a Web-based technology, there must be a way to present Web pages. Personal computers and servers use HTML or XML to present Web-based material and JavaScripts to perform the processing in the background. WAP uses Wireless Markup Language (WML) and WMLScript to perform these similar tasks. WAP has its own session and transaction protocols and transport layer security protocol called *Wireless Transport Layer Security (WTLS)*, which is similar to TLS and SSL. The wireless device has a WAP microbrowser that displays the Web pages to the user.

The vision for developing this type of technology and these devices is to provide users with the functionality to check e-mail, voice messages, a calendar, and more from anywhere without needing physically to plug into any network. A user can watch the stock market on her PDA while riding a bus and hit a few buttons when she wants to sell her stocks because of a dip in the market. Users can also transfer funds from one bank account to another on their mobile phones, receive the daily news, and much more. The devices could be used to communicate with financial institutions or other organizations that provide information and wireless capabilities through the Internet.

Because these devices use a different set of protocols, a gateway is required to translate between WAP and the Internet's protocols and application types, as shown in Figure 7-55. Service providers can provide this gateway much as they can provide the service for users and companies to access the Internet today.

When data comes from the wireless mobile device, it can be encrypted with WTLS, which must be translated into TLS or SSL by the gateway. Because the wireless devices use the Internet for transmission, and the Internet does not understand WTLS, it must be translated into a protocol it does understand. This translation takes place at the server provider's gateway.

A security concern is that this data will be decrypted at the service provider's site and then encrypted with SSL or TLS. That means for a second or two, the data is not protected. This is referred to as the *gap in the WAP*, and it has caused a lot of concern for businesses and security professionals and is still one of the issues that needs to be dealt with.

WTLS works similarly to SSL/TLS, by encrypting data and allowing for authentication to take place between the communicating devices. WTLS has three classes that define how authentication will take place between a wireless devices and a gateway server:

- **Class 1 = Anonymous authentication**   The wireless device and server do not authenticate to each other.

- **Class 2 = Server authentication**   The server authenticates to the wireless device.

- **Class 3 = Two-way client and server authentication**   The server and the wireless device authenticate to each other.

In most cases, the gateway server will dictate which type of authentication will be used, but the wireless device needs to be properly configured so that it can actually work in this type of implementation.

Figure 7-55   A WAP gateway is required to translate WAP protocols to Internet protocols.

References

"Wireless Goal: Don't Get Whacked": **www.informationweek.com/story/ IWK20010705S0013**

WAP Forum Releases: **www.wapforum.org/what/technical.htm**

WAP Gateway Security Risks: **aphy.ku.edu.pk/resources/res2001/ Faraz-Haider/gateway.htm**

WLAN Components

A WLAN uses a transceiver, called an *access point (AP)*, that connects to an Ethernet cable, which is the link that wireless devices use to access resources on the wired network, as shown in Figure 7-56. The APs are in fixed locations throughout a network and work as communication *beacons*. A wireless user has a device with a wireless interface card, which modulates her data onto radio frequency signals that are accepted and processed by the AP. The signals that are transmitted from the AP are received by the wireless NIC and converted into a digital format, which the device can understand.

When APs are used to bridge wireless and wired networks, this is referred to as an *infrastructure WLAN*. An infrastructure WLAN is used to extend an existing wired network. In an *ad hoc WLAN*, there are no APs. The wireless devices communicate to each other through their wireless NICs instead of going through a centralized device.

To construct an ad hoc network, wireless client software is installed on contributing hosts and configured for peer-to-peer operation mode. Then the user clicks Network

Station

Access
Point

Figure 7-56   A wireless device must authenticate with an access point.

Neighborhood in a Windows platform, and the software searches for other hosts operating in this similar mode and shows them to the user.

For a wireless device and AP to communicate, they must be configured to communicate over the same channel. A *channel* is a certain frequency within a given frequency band. The AP is configured to transmit over a specific channel, and the wireless device will "tune" itself to be able to communicate over this same frequency.

Any hosts that wish to participate within a particular WLAN must be configured with the proper *Service Set ID (SSID)*. Various hosts can be segmented into different WLANs by using different SSIDs. The reasons to segment a wireless LAN into portions are the same reasons wired systems are segmented on a network: the users require access to different resources, the users have different business functions, or they have different levels of trust.

The SSID is usually required when a wireless devices wants to authenticate to an AP. For the device to prove that it should be allowed to communicate with the wired network, it must first provide a valid SSID value. The SSID should not be seen as a reliable security mechanism because many APs broadcast their SSIDs, which can be easily sniffed and used by attackers.

The wireless device can authenticate to the AP in two main ways: open system authentication (OSA) and shared key authentication (SKA). OSA does not require the wireless device to prove to the AP that it has a specific cryptographic key to allow for authentication purposes. In many cases, the wireless device needs to provide only the correct SSID value. In OSA implementations all transactions are in cleartext because no encryption is involved. So an intruder can sniff the traffic, capture the necessary steps of authentication, and walk through the same steps to be authenticated and associated to an AP.

When an AP is configured to use SKA authentication, the AP will send a random value to the wireless device. The device will encrypt this value with its cryptographic key and return it. The AP will decrypt and extract the response, and if it is the same as the original value, the device is authenticated. In this approach, the wireless device is authenticated to the network by proving that it has the necessary encryption key. This method is based on the wired equivalent privacy (WEP) protocol, which also allows for data transfers to be encrypted. A long list of deficiencies in this protocol have been uncovered, and the new solutions that are being developed are explained in Appendix F.

War Driving   *Here, hold my Pringles can. I am looking for wireless networks. Response: Hold it yourself.* A common attack on wireless networks is *war driving*, when one or more people either drive around with a wireless device equipped with the necessary equipment and software with the intent of identifying APs and breaking into them. Traditionally, this activity has taken place by using a laptop and driving in the proximity of buildings that have WLANs implemented, but today even PDAs can be used for this type of attack.

NetStumbler is a shareware program that sniffs for APs. When it identifies an AP's signal, it logs the network name, SSID, MAC address of the AP, manufacturer of the AP, channel it was heard on, signal strength, signal noise ratio, and whether WEP is enabled. Attackers will drive around in their cars with a laptop running NetStumbler, actively looking for APs. They can usually find APs within a range of up to 350 feet, but with a more powerful antenna, the attacker can locate APs much farther away. The NetStumbler will broadcast probes once each second, waiting for APs to respond. AirSnort and WEPCrack are utilities that can use to break WEP encryption if it is enabled.

 NOTE Inventive individuals have used Pringles cans and beverage cans as inexpensive antennas for war driving endeavors.

IEEE has developed a working group, 802.11i, that has created solutions for the security weaknesses in the 802.11 standards. (This is explained fully in Appendix F.) The 802.11i has not been released as of this writing, so in the meantime, an individual or company can follow some best practices to implement a wireless network and reduce the amount of vulnerabilities that it brings along with it:

- *Enable WEP.* Even though it can be broken into, it might deter attackers.

- *Change default SSID.* Each AP comes with a preconfigured default SSID value.

- *Disable "broadcast SSID" on the AP.* Most APs allow for this to be turned off.

- *Implement another layer of authentication (RADIUS, Kerberos).* Before the user can access the network, require him to authenticate again.

- *Physically put AP at the center of the building.* The AP has a specific zone of coverage it can provide.

- *Logically put the AP in a DMZ with a firewall between the DMZ and internal network.* Allow the firewall to investigate the traffic before it gets to the wired network.

- *Use 104-bit WEP, not 40-bit.* This may, or may not, provide more protection.

- *Implement VPN for wireless devices to use.* This adds another layer of protection for data being transmitted.

- *Configure the AP to allow only known MAC addresses into the network.* Allow Only known devices to authenticate.

- *Assign static IPs to wireless devices and disable DHCP.* If an attacker gains access and DHCP is enabled, you have just given the attacker a valid working IP address to use.

References

WarDriving.com: **www.wardriving.com**

"War Driving by the Bay": **online.securityfocus.com/news/192**

War Driving: **www.infosecuritymag.com/articles/november01/ technology_wardriving.shtml**

Summary

This chapter touched on many of the different players within different types of networks, including how they work together to provide an environment for users to communicate, share resources, and be productive. Each piece of networking is important to security, because almost any piece can introduce unwanted vulnerabilities and weaknesses in the infrastructure. It is important that the security professional understands how the various devices, protocols, authentication mechanisms, and services work individually and how they interface and interact with other entities. This can be an overwhelming task because of all the possible technologies involved. However, knowledge and hard work will keep security professionals up to speed and hopefully in front of the hackers and attackers.

Quick Tips

- Dual-homed firewalls can be compromised if the operating system does not have packet forwarding or routing disabled.

- A protocol is a set of rules that dictate how computers will communicate over networks.

- The application layer, layer 7, has services and protocols required by the user's applications.

- The presentation layer, layer 6, formats data into a standardized format and deals with the syntax of the data, not the meaning.

- Routers work at the network layer, layer 3.

- The session layer, layer 5, sets up, maintains, and breaks down the dialog (session) between two applications. It controls the dialog organization and synchronization.

- The transport layer, layer 4, deals with error detection and correction, regulates the flow of traffic, and multiplexes data. It provides end-to-end connectivity, sequencing, and virtual circuits.

- The network layer, layer 3, provides routing, segmenting, and relaying of data. This layer can determine alternative routes to avoid network congestion.

- The data link layer, layer 2, prepares data for the network wire by framing it. This is where the different LAN and WAN technologies live.

- The physical layer, layer 1, provides physical connections for transmission and performs electrical encoding of data. This layer transforms bits to electrical signals.

- TCP/IP is a suite of protocols that is a de facto standard for transmitting data across the Internet. TCP is a reliable connection-oriented protocol, and IP is an unreliable connectionless-oriented protocol.

- Data is encapsulated as it travels down the OSI model on the source computer, and the process is reversed on the destination computer. During encapsulation, each layer adds its own information so that the corresponding layer on the destination computer knows how to process the data.

- The data link layer defines how the physical layer transmits the network layer packets. ARP and RARP are two protocols at this layer.

- Two main protocols at the transport layer are TCP and UDP.

- UDP is connectionless-oriented protocol that does not send or receive acknowledgments when a datagram is received. It does not ensure that data arrives at its destination. It provides "best-effort" delivery.

- TCP is a connection-oriented protocol that sends and receives acknowledgments. It ensures that data arrives at its destination.

- ARP translates the IP address into a MAC address (physical Ethernet address), and RARP translates a MAC address into an IP address.

- ICMP works at the network layer and informs hosts, routers, and devices of network or computer problems. It is the major component of the ping utility.

- DNS resolves hostnames into IP addresses and has distributed databases all over the Internet to provide name resolution.

- Altering an ARP table so that an IP address is mapped to a different MAC address is ARP poisoning and can redirect traffic to an attacker's computer or unattended system.

- Packet filtering (screening routers) is accomplished by ACLs and is a first-generation firewall. Traffic can be filtered by addresses, ports, and protocol types.

- Tunneling protocols move frames from one network to another by placing them inside of routable encapsulated frames.

- Packet filtering provides application independence, high performance, and scalability, but it provides low security and no protection above the network layer.

- Firewalls that use proxies transfer an isolated copy of each approved packet from one network to another network.

- An application proxy requires a proxy for each approved service and can understand and make access decisions on the protocols used and the commands within those protocols. Circuit-level firewalls also use proxies but at a lower layer. Circuit-level firewalls do not look as deep within the packet as application proxies.

- A proxy server is the middleman in communication. It does not allow anyone to connect directly to a protected host within the internal network. Proxy firewalls are second-generation firewalls.

- Application proxy firewalls provide good security and have full application layer awareness, but they have poor performance, limited application support, and poor scalability.

- Stateful inspection keeps track of each communication session and lets in only those packets that are responding to an internal host's request. It must maintain a state table that contains data about each connection. It is a third-generation firewall.

- VPN uses tunneling protocols and encryption to provide a secure network link between two networks or hosts. A private and secure connection can be made across an unsecure network.

- VPN can use PPTP, L2F, L2TP, or IPSec as a tunneling protocol.

- PPTP works at the data link layer. IPSec works at the network layer and can handle multiple tunnels at the same time.

- Dedicated links are usually the most expensive type of WAN connectivity method because the fee is based on distance between the two destinations versus amount of bandwidth used. T1 and T3 are examples of dedicated links.

- Frame relay and X.25 are packet-switched WAN technologies, which use virtual circuits instead of dedicated ones.

- An intranet is an internal network using Web-based technology, and an extranet is a private network that connects to an external network using Internet protocols. An extranet is usually set up between partners, suppliers and vendors, and with customers.

- A hub (concentrator) in star topologies serves as the central meeting place for all cables from computers and devices.

- A bridge divides networks into more controllable segments to ensure more efficient use of bandwidth. Bridges work at the data link layer and understand MAC addresses, not IP addresses.

- A switch is a device with combined repeater and bridge technology. It works at the data link layer and understands MAC addresses.

- Routers link two or more network segments, where each segment can function as an independent network. A router works at the network layer, works with IP addresses, and has more network knowledge than bridges, switches, or repeaters.

- A bridge filters by MAC addresses, and a router filters by IP addresses. Bridges forward broadcast traffic and routers do not.

- Layer 3 switching combines switching and routing technology.

- Attenuation is the loss of signal strength when a cable exceeds its maximum length.

- STP and UTP are twisted-pair cabling types that are the most popular, cheapest, and easiest to work with. However, they are the easiest to tap into, have crosstalk issues, and are vulnerable to electromagnetic interference (EMI).

- Coaxial cable is more expensive than UTP and STP, is more resistant to EMI, and can carry baseband and broadband technologies.

- Fiber-optic cabling carries data as light waves, is expensive, can transmit data at high speeds, is difficult to tap into, and is resistant to EMI. If security is extremely important, fiber cabling should be used.

- ATM transfers data in fixed cells, is a WAN technology, and transmits data at very high rates. It supports voice, data, and video applications.

- FDDI is a LAN and MAN technology, usually used for backbones, uses token-passing technology, and has redundant rings in case the primary ring goes down.

- Ethernet, 802.3, is the most used LAN implementation today and can operate at 10 to 1000 Mbps.

- Token Ring, 802.5, is an older LAN implementation that uses a token-passing technology.

- Ethernet uses CSMA/CD, which means all computers compete for the shared network cable, listen to see when they can transmit data, and are susceptible to data collisions.

- WAN circuit-switching technologies set up a circuit that will be used during a data transmission session, just like making a phone call. Packet-switching technologies do not set up circuits—instead, packets can travel along many different routes to arrive to the same destination.

- A PVC is a permanent virtual circuit that is programmed into WAN devices, and SVCs are temporary. SVCs are set up and then torn down quickly when they are no longer needed.

- CSU/DSU is used when a LAN device needs to communicate with WAN devices. It ensures that the necessary electrical signaling and format are used. It interfaces between a DTE and a DCE.

- ISDN has a BRI rate that uses two B channels and one D channel, and a PRI that uses up to 23 B channels. They support voice, data, and video.

- Frame relay is a WAN protocol that works at the data link layer and performs packet switching. It is an economical choice because the fee is based on bandwidth usage.

- PPP is an encapsulation protocol for dial-up connections. It replaced SLIP and is ideal for connecting different types of devices over serial lines.

- DSL transmits high-speed bandwidth over existing phone lines.

- Remote access servers can be configured to call back remote users, but this can be compromised by enabling call forwarding.

- PAP sends credentials in cleartext, and CHAP authenticates using a challenge/response mechanism and therefore does not send passwords over the network.

- SOCKS is a proxy-based firewall solution. It is a circuit-based proxy and does not use application-based proxies.

- IPSec tunnel mode protects payload and header information of a packet, and transport mode protects only the payload.

- RAID can provide increased performance and fault tolerance depending on the level used.

- A screened-host firewall lies between the perimeter router and the LAN.

- A screened-subnet is a subnet that is sandwiched between two screening devices.

- NAT is used when companies do not want systems to know internal hosts' addresses and enables companies to use private, nonroutable IP addresses.

- The 802.11 standard is a WLAN technology and has several variations—802.11a, 802.11b, 802.11f, 802.11g, and 802.11i.

- The 802.15 standard outlines wireless personal area network (WPAN) technologies, and 802.16 addresses wireless MAN technologies.

- WAP is a protocol stack used instead of TCP/IP on wireless devices.

- Environments can be segmented into different WLANs by using different SSIDs

- The 802.11b standard works in the 2.4Ghz range at 11 Mbps, and 802.11a works in the 5 Ghz range at 54 Mbps.

Questions

Please remember that these questions are formatted and asked in a certain way for a reason. You must remember that the CISSP exam is asking questions at a conceptual level. Questions may not always have the perfect answer, and the candidate is advised against always looking for the perfect answer. The candidate should look for the best answer in the list.

1. Which of the following is not considered a passive attack?

   A. Spoofing

   B. Network sniffing

   C. Wiretapping

   D. Traffic analysis

2. What does the term *phreaking* pertain to?

   A. Spamming mail servers in the hopes of bringing them down

   B. Footprinting and port scanning networks

   C. Fraudulent use of telephone services

   D. Compromising tunneling protocols

3. What does a packet sniffer do?

   A. It performs port scans and footprinting.

   B. It identifies cabling faults.

   C. It detects hanging modems not protected by the firewall.

   D. It captures traffic for data analysis.

4. What can be used to compromise and defeat callback security?

   A. Passive wiretapping

   B. Call forwarding

   C. Packet spoofing

   D. Brute force attack

5. Which is not considered a firewall architecture used to protect networks?

   A. Screened host

   B. Screened subnet

   C. NAT gateway

   D. Dual-homed host

6. Why are switched infrastructures safer environments compared to routed networks?

   A. It is more difficult to sniff traffic since the computers have virtual private connections.

   B. They are just as unsafe as non-switched environments.

   C. The data link encryption does not permit wiretapping.

   D. Switches are more intelligent than bridges and implement security mechanisms.

7. What functionality hangs up on a remote caller and looks at a table of predefined valid phone numbers?

   A. Caller ID

   B. RAS

   C. Callback

   D. NOS

8. Which of the following protocols is considered connection oriented?

   A. IP

   B. ICMP

   C. UDP

   D. TCP

9. Which of the following best describes Ethernet transmissions over a LAN?

    A. Traffic is sent to a gateway that sends it to the destination system.

    B. Traffic is bursty in nature and broadcasts data to all hosts on the subnet.

    C. Traffic streams and does not broadcast data.

    D. Traffic is contained within collision domains but not broadcast domains.

10. Which of the following proxies cannot make access decisions on protocol commands?

    A. Application

    B. Packet filtering

    C. Circuit

    D. Stateful

11. A security concern that is prevalent in distributed environments and systems is
_____.

    A. Knowing the proper proxy and default gateway

    B. Knowing whom to trust

    C. Knowing what authentication method is most appropriate

    D. Knowing how to resolve hostnames

12. Which protocol is commonly used to authenticate users on dial-up connections?

    A. PPTP

    B. IPSec

    C. CHAP

    D. L2F

13. Which of the following shows the sequence of layers as layer 2, 5, 7, 4, and 3?

    A. Data link, session, application, transport, and network

    B. Data link, transport, application, session, and network

    C. Network, session, application, network, and transport

    D. Network, transport, application, session, and presentation

14. What is another name for a VPN?

    A. Transport session

    B. Tunnel

    C. End-to-end connection

    D. Bandwidth

15. When security is a high priority, why is fiber cabling used?

    A. It has high data transfer rates and is less vulnerable to EMI.

    B. It multiplexes data, which can confuse attackers.

    C. It has a high degree of data detection and correction.

    D. Data interception is next to impossible.

16. Why are mainframe environments considered more secure than LAN environments?

    A. They have fewer entry points.

    B. They have stronger authentication mechanisms.

    C. They have more auditing and encryption implemented.

    D. They are actually weaker than LANs.

17. What does it mean when computers communicate logically and physically to each other?

    A. They speak physically through headers and trailers and logically through physical connections.

    B. They speak physically through PVCs and logically through SVCs.

    C. They speak physically when connected to a backbone network and logically when they speak to each other within the same LAN.

    D. They speak physically through electrons and network cables and logically through layers in the OSI model.

18. How does data encapsulation and the protocol stack work?

    A. Each protocol or service at each layer in the OSI model multiplexes other packets to the data as it is passed down the protocol stack.

    B. Each protocol or service at each layer in the OSI model adds its own information to the data as it is passed down the protocol stack.

    C. The packet is encapsulated and grows as it hops from router to router.

    D. The packet is encapsulated and grows when it is passed up the protocol stack.

19. Systems that are built on the OSI framework are considered open systems. What does this mean?

    A. They do not have authentication mechanisms configured by default.

    B. They have interoperability issues.

    C. They are built with internationally accepted protocols and standards so that they can easily communicate with other systems.

    D. They are built with international protocols and standards so that they can choose what types of systems they will communicate with.

20. Which of the following protocols works in the following layers: application, data link, network, and transport?

    A. FTP, ARP, TCP, and UDP

    B. FTP, ICMP, IP, and UDP

    C. TFTP, ARP, IP, and UDP

    D. TFTP, RARP, IP, and ICMP

21. What is the purpose of the presentation layer?

    A. Addressing and routing

    B. Data syntax and formatting

    C. End-to-end connection

    D. Framing

22. What is the purpose of the data link layer?

    A. End-to-end connection

    B. Dialog control

    C. Framing

    D. Data syntax

23. What takes place at the session layer?

    A. Dialog control

    B. Routing

    C. Packet sequencing

    D. Addressing

24. At what layer does a bridge work?

    A. Session

    B. Network

    C. Transport

    D. Data link

25. Which best describes the IP protocol?

    A. Connectionless protocol that deals with dialog establishment, maintenance, and destruction

    B. Connectionless protocol that deals with addressing and routing of packets

    C. Connection-oriented protocol that deals with addressing and routing of packets

    D. Connection-oriented protocol that deals with sequencing, error detection, and flow control

Answers

1. **A.** A passive attack means that an attacker is monitoring a connection but not doing anything to it. Passive attacks can be carried out through sniffing, traffic analysis, or wiretapping. An active attack means the attacker is carrying out some type of activity. Active attacks can be DoS, brute force, or dictionary attacks.

2. **C.** A phreaker is a type of hacker who specializes in telephone fraud. This can be carried out by reconfiguring a telecommunication device, social engineering, or attacking a company's PBX system.

3. **D.** A sniffer is some type of tool that has been developed to capture frames from a network for viewing purposes. Most sniffers put the system's NIC into promiscuous mode so that all traffic can be monitored.

4. **B.** A remote access server can be configured to drop a remote user's connection and call him back at a predefined number. If call forwarding is enabled, this security measure can be compromised.

5. **C.** The other answers describe basic firewall architectures, meaning where they can be placed within an environment. Network address translation (NAT) maps public to private addresses and does not provide traffic monitoring capabilities. Some firewalls provide NAT services, but the goals of the services are different.

6. **A.** Switched environments use switches to allow different network segments and/or systems to communicate. When this communication takes place, a virtual connection is set up between the communicating devices. Since it is a dedicated connection, broadcast and collision data are not available to other systems, as in an environment that uses purely bridges and routers.

7. **C.** The goal of a callback system is to provide another layer of authentication. For an attacker to compromise this set up successfully and obtain unauthorized access, she would need to be at the preconfigured phone number or reconfigure the telephone company's equipment to forward the call on to her.

8. **D.** TCP is the only connection-oriented protocol listed. A connection-oriented protocol provides reliable connectivity and data transmission, while connectionless provides unreliable connections and does not promise or ensure data transmission.

9. **B.** Ethernet is a very "chatty" protocol because it allows all systems to hear each other's broadcasts, and the technology has many collisions because all systems have to share the same medium.

10. **C.** Application and circuit are the only types of proxy-based firewall solutions listed here; the others do not use proxies. Circuit-based proxy firewalls make decisions based on header information and not the protocol's command structure. Application-based proxies are the only ones that understand this level of granularity about the individual protocols.

11. **B.** Distributed environments brings about a lot more complexity and drastically increases the difficulty of access control. Since you now have many different

applications, devices, services, and users, it is much more difficult to know which entities to trust and to what degree.

12. **C.** The other protocols listed are used for tunneling and/or VPN connectivity, not user authentication. CHAP uses the challenge-response method of authenticating a user.

13. **A.** The OSI model is made up of seven layers: application (layer 7), presentation (layer 6), session (layer 5), transport (layer 4), network (layer 3), data link (layer 2), and physical (layer 1).

14. **B.** A VPN sets up a private and secure tunnel by encapsulating and encrypting data. This allows data to be safely transmitted over untrusted networks.

15. **D.** It is difficult to tap into a fiber line, and fiber does not radiate signals as the other cable types do.

16. **A.** This is a relative and general statement. Mainframes are more closed systems and work in more closed environments when compared to the distributed environments we work in today. Mainframes usually have a smaller amount of entry points, which are generally very controlled.

17. **D.** Systems, of course, communicate physically using network cables or airwaves. But they also communicate logically. An FTP service on one system "speaks" to the FTP service on another system and is not aware that many other protocols, devices, and cables are involved. Protocols, services, and applications communicate logically, and this communication is transmitted over physical means.

18. **B.** Data encapsulation means that a piece of data is put inside another type of data. This usually means that individual protocols apply their own instruction set in the form of headers and trailers. As a data package goes down the OSI, or protocol stack, of a system, each protocol that is involved adds its own instructions. This process is reversed at the destination.

19. **C.** An open system is a system that has been developed based on standardized protocols and interfaces. Following these standards allows the systems to interoperate more effectively with other systems that follow the same standards.

20. **C.** Different protocols have different functionalities. The OSI model is an attempt to describe conceptually where these different functionalities take place in a networking stack. The model attempts to draw boxes around reality to help people better understand the stack. Each layer has specific functionality, and the layer has several different protocols that can live at that layer that can carry out that specific functionality.

21. **B.** No protocols work at the presentation layer, but services that carry out data formatting, compression/decompression, and encryption/decryption processes do occur at that layer. Putting data into a standardized format allows for a large subset of applications to be able to understand and interpret it.

22. **C.** The data link layer, in most cases, is the only layer that understands the environment in which the system is working, whether it be Ethernet, Token Ring, wireless, or connection to a WAN link. This layer adds the necessary headers and trailers to the data, which frames it. Other systems on the same network using the same technology understand only the specific header and trailer format used in its technology.

23. **A.** The session layer is responsible for controlling how applications communicate, not how computers communicate. Not all applications use protocols that work at the session layer, so this layer is not always used in networking functions. A session layer protocol will set up the connection to the other application logically and control the dialog going back and forth. Session layer protocols allow applications to keep state of the dialog.

24. **D.** A bridge will read header information only in the data link layer and no higher because it makes forwarding and filtering decisions based on what is held within this header, which is the MAC address.

25. **B.** The IP protocol is connectionless and works at the network layer. It will add source and destination addresses to a packet as it goes through its data encapsulation process. IP can also make routing decisions based on the destination address.

Cryptography

In this chapter, you will learn about the following items:

- History of cryptography
- Cryptography components and their relationships
- Government involvement in cryptography
- Symmetric and asymmetric key algorithms
- Public key infrastructure (PKI) concepts and mechanisms
- Hashing algorithms and uses
- Types of attacks on cryptosystems

Cryptography is a method of storing and transmitting data in a form that only those it is intended for can read and process. It is considered a science of protecting information by encoding it into an unreadable format. Cryptography is an effective way of protecting sensitive information as it is stored on media or transmitted through untrusted network communication paths.

The ultimate goal of cryptography, and the mechanisms that make it up, is to hide information from unauthorized individuals. However, most algorithms can be broken, and the information can be revealed if the attacker has enough time, desire, and resources. So a more realistic goal of cryptography is to make obtaining the information too work-intensive or time-consuming to be worth it to the attacker.

The first encryption methods date back to 4,000 years ago and were considered more of an ancient art. As encryption evolved, it was mainly used to pass messages through hostile environments of war, crisis, the Internet, and for negotiation processes between conflicting groups of people. Throughout history, individuals and governments have worked to protect communication by encrypting it. The encryption algorithms and the devices that used them increased in complexity, new methods and algorithms were continually introduced, and encryption became an integrated part of the computing world.

Cryptography

Cryptography has had an interesting history and has undergone many changes through the centuries. It seems that keeping secrets has been important throughout the ages of civilization. Keeping secrets gives individuals or groups the ability to hide true intentions, gain a competitive edge, and reduce vulnerability.

The changes that cryptography has undergone closely follow advances in technology. Cryptography methods began with a person carving messages into wood or stone, which were then passed to the intended individual who had the necessary means to decipher the messages. This is a long way from how cryptography is being used today. Cryptography that used to be carved into materials is now being inserted into streams of binary code that passes over network wires, Internet communication paths, and airwaves, as shown in Figure 8-1.

In the past, messengers were used as the transmission mechanism, and encryption helped protect the message in case the messenger was captured. Today, the transmission mechanism has changed from human beings to packets carrying 0s and 1s passing through network cables or open airwaves. The messages are still encrypted in case an intruder captures the transmission mechanism (the packets) as they travel along their paths.

History of Cryptography

Look, I scrambled up the message so no one can read it. Response: Yes, but now neither can we.

Cryptography has roots that began around 2000 B.C. in Egypt, when hieroglyphics were used to decorate tombs to tell the story of the life of the deceased. The practice was not as much to hide the messages themselves, but to make them seem more noble, ceremonial, and majestic. An illustration of hieroglyphics is shown in Figure 8-2.

Encryption methods evolved from being mainly for show into practical applications used to hide information from others.

A Hebrew cryptographic method required the alphabet to be flipped so that each letter in the original alphabet is mapped to a different letter in the flipped, or shifted, alphabet. The encryption method was called *atbash*. An example of an encryption key used in the atbash encryption scheme is shown here:

```
ABCDEFGHI JK LMNOPQ R STU VW XYZ
ZYXWVUTSR QP ONMLKJ I HGF ED CBA
```

For example, the word "security" is encrypted into "hvxfirgb." What does "xrhhk" come out to be? This is a *substitution cipher*, because one character is replaced with another character. This type of substitution cipher is referred to as a *monoalphabetic substitution* cipher because it uses only one alphabet, compared with other ciphers that use multiple alphabets at a time, referred to as *polyalphabetic substitution*.

Figure 8-1

Today, encrypted binary data passes through network cables and airwaves.

11001010101100001101010101011000100011111001010101010011011001010 ⟶

Figure 8-2
Hieroglyphics
are the first
recorded use
of cryptography.

This simplistic encryption method worked for its time and for particular cultures, but eventually more complex mechanisms were required.

Around 400 B.C., the Spartans used a system of encrypting information by writing a message on a sheet of papyrus (a type of paper), which was wrapped around a staff. (This would look like a piece of paper wrapped around a stick or wooden rod.) The message was only readable if it was wrapped around the correct size staff, which allowed the letters to properly match up. This is referred to as the *scytale* cipher, as shown in Figure 8-3. When the papyrus was removed from the staff, the writing appeared as just a bunch of random characters. The Greek government had carriers run these pieces of papyrus to different groups of soldiers. The soldiers would then wrap the papyrus around a staff of the right diameter and length, and all the seemingly random letters would match up and form an understandable message. These could be used to instruct the soldiers on strategic moves and provide them with military directives.

In another time and place, Julius Caesar developed a simple method of shifting letters of the alphabet, similar to the atbash scheme. He simply shifted the alphabet by three positions. Today this technique seems too simplistic to be effective, but in that day not many people could read in the first place, so it provided a high level of protection. The evolution of cryptography continued as countries refined their practices using new methods, tools, and practices throughout the Middle Ages. By the late 1800s, cryptography was commonly used in the methods of communication between military factions.

Figure 8-3
The scytale was
used by the
Spartans to
decipher
encrypted
messages.

During World War II, simplistic encryption devices were used for tactical communication, which drastically improved with the mechanical and electromechanical technology that provided the world with telegraphic and radio communication. The rotor cipher machine, which is a device that substitutes letters using different rotors within the machine, was a huge breakthrough in military cryptography that provided complexity that proved difficult to break. This work gave way to the most famous cipher machine in history to date: Germany's *Enigma* machine. The Enigma machine had three rotors, a plugboard, and a reflecting rotor.

The originator of the message configured the Enigma machine to its initial settings before starting the encryption process. The operator would type in the first letter of the message, and the machine would substitute the letter with a different letter and present it to the operator. This encryption was done by moving the rotors a predefined number of times, which would substitute the original letter with a different letter. So if the operator typed in a *T* as the first character, the Enigma machine might present an *M* as the substitution value. The operator would write down the letter *M* on his sheet. The operator would then advance the rotors and enter the next letter. Each time a new letter was to be encrypted, the operator advanced the rotors to a new setting. This process was done until the whole message was encrypted. Then the encrypted text was transmitted over the airwaves, most likely to a U-boat. The chosen substitution for each letter was dependent upon the rotor setting, so the crucial and secret part of this process (the key) was the initial settings and how the operators advanced the rotors when encrypting and decrypting a message. The operators at each end needed to know this sequence of increments to advance each rotor in order to enable the German military units to properly communicate.

Although the mechanisms of the Enigma were complicated for the time, a team of Polish cryptographers broke its code and gave Britain insight into Germany's attack plans and military movement. It is said that breaking this encryption mechanism shortened World War II by two years. After the war, details about the Enigma machine were published—one of the machines is exhibited at the Smithsonian Institute.

Cryptography has a deep, rich history. Mary, Queen of Scots, lost her life in the 16th century when an encrypted message she sent was intercepted. During the Revolutionary War, Benedict Arnold used a codebook cipher to exchange information on troop movement and strategic military advancements. The military has always played a big part in using cryptography by encoding information and attempting to decrypt their enemy's encrypted information. William Frederick Friedman published *The Index of Coincidence and Its Applications in Cryptography*. He is called the "Father of Modern Cryptography" and broke many messages that were intercepted during WWII. Encryption has been used by many governments and militaries and has contributed great victory for some because of the covert maneuvers that could be accomplished in secrecy. It has also brought great defeat to others when their cryptosystems were discovered and deciphered.

As computers were invented, the possibilities for encryption methods and devices advanced, and cryptography efforts expanded exponentially. This era brought unprecedented opportunity for cryptographic designers and encryption techniques. The most well-known and successful project was *Lucifer*, which was developed at IBM. Lucifer introduced complex mathematical equations and functions that were later adopted and modified by the U.S. National Security Agency (NSA) to come up with the U.S. Data Encryption Standard (DES). DES has been adopted as a federal government standard, is used worldwide for financial and other transactions, and is imbedded into numerous commercial applications. DES has had a rich history in computer-oriented encryption and has been in use for over 25 years.

Governments have enforced trans-border restrictions and hindered the use of cryptography in certain sectors by imposing export regulations. The U.S. government developed their own encryption chip, the *Clipper Chip,* to decipher communication that had to do with suspected criminal activity and drug movements, which has raised many questions about the public's privacy versus the government's right to eavesdrop. (These issues are addressed further in "The Government's Involvement with Cryptography" section.)

A majority of the protocols developed at the dawn of the computing age have been upgraded to include cryptography to add necessary layers of protection. Encryption is used in hardware devices and in software to protect data, banking transactions, corporate extranet transmissions, e-mail, Web transactions, wireless communication, storing of confidential information, faxes, and phone calls.

The code breakers and cryptanalysis efforts and the amazing number-crunching capabilities of the microprocessors hitting the market each year have quickened the evolution of cryptography. As the bad guys get smarter and more resourceful, the good guys must increase efforts and strategy. *Cryptanalysis* is the science of studying and breaking the secrecy of encryption algorithms and their necessary pieces. It is performed in academic settings and by curious and motivated hackers, either to satisfy their inquisitiveness or to use their findings to commit fraud and destruction. Different types of cryptography have been used throughout civilization, but today cryptography is deeply rooted in every part of our communication and computing world. Automated information systems and cryptography play a huge role in the effectiveness of militaries, functionality of governments, and economics of private businesses. As our dependency upon technology increases, so does our dependency upon cryptography, because secrets will always need to be kept.

References

Security Strategies for E-Companies: **www.infosecuritymag.com/articles/ july01/columns_logoff.shtml**

A Short History of Cryptography: **all.net/books/ip/Chap2-1.html**

An Introduction to Cryptography: **home.earthlink.net/~mylnir/ crypt.intro.html**

Historical Cryptography: **starbase.trincoll.edu/~crypto/**

Historical Cryptography: **dmoz.org/Science/Math/Applications/ Communication_Theory/Cryptography/Historical**

Cryptography Definitions

Why can't I read this? Answer: It is in ciphertext.

Encryption is a method of transforming original data, called *plaintext* or *cleartext*, into a form that appears to be random and unreadable, which is called *ciphertext*. Plaintext is either in a form that can be understood by a person (a document) or by a computer (executable code). Once it is transformed into ciphertext, neither human nor machine can properly process it until it is decrypted. This enables the transmission of confidential information over insecure channels without unauthorized disclosure. When data is stored on a computer, it is usually protected by logical and physical access controls. When this same sensitive information is sent over a network, it can no longer take these controls for granted, and the information is in a much more vulnerable state.

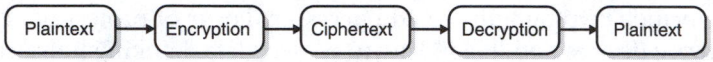

A system that provides encryption and decryption is referred to as a *cryptosystem* and can be created through hardware components or program code in an application. The cryptosystem uses an encryption algorithm, which determines how simple or complex the encryption process will be. Most algorithms are complex mathematical formulas that are applied in a specific sequence to the plaintext. Most encryption methods use a secret value called a key (usually a long string of bits representing a number), which works with the algorithm to encrypt and decrypt the text, as depicted in Figure 8-4.

The *algorithm*, the set of mathematical rules, dictates how enciphering and deciphering take place. Many algorithms are publicly known and are not the secret part of the encryption process. In fact, it is often said that secrecy of the algorithm is not something that you should base your security on. The way that encryption algorithms work can be kept secret from the public, but many of them are publicly known and well understood. If the internal mechanisms of the algorithm are not a secret, then something must be. The secret piece of using a well-known encryption algorithm is the key. The *key* is a value that is made up of a large sequence of random bits. Is it just any random number of bits crammed together? Not really. An algorithm contains a *keyspace*, which is a range of values that can be used to construct a key. The key is made up of random values within the keyspace range. The larger the keyspace, the more available values can be used to

Figure 8-4
The key is inserted into the mathematical algorithm, and the result is applied to the message, which ends up in ciphertext.

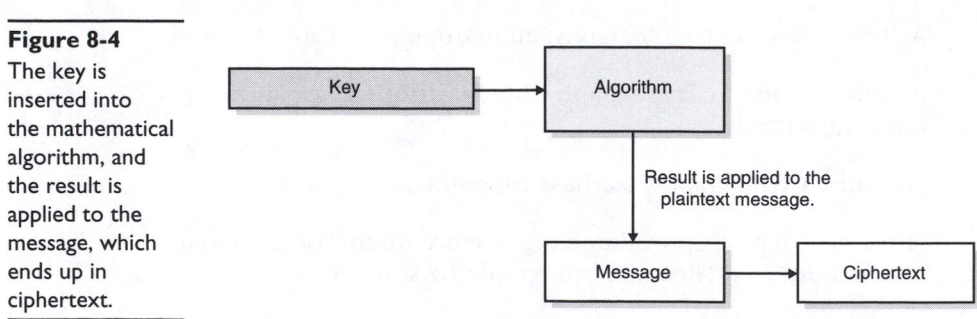

represent different keys—and the more random the keys are, the harder it is for intruders to figure them out. For example, if an algorithm allows a key length of 2 bits, the keyspace for that algorithm would be 4, which indicates the total number of different keys that would be possible. That would not be a very large keyspace, and certainly it would not take an attacker very long to find the correct key that was used.

A large keyspace allows for more possible keys. The encryption algorithm should use the entire keyspace and choose the values to make up the keys as randomly as possible. If a smaller keyspace were used, there would be fewer values to choose from when generating a key, as shown in Figure 8-5. This would increase an attacker's chance of figuring out the key value and deciphering the protected information.

If an eavesdropper captures a message as it passes between two people, she can view the message, but it appears in its encrypted form and is therefore unusable. Even if this attacker knows the algorithm that the two people are using to encrypt and decrypt their information, without the key, this information remains useless to the eavesdropper, as shown in Figure 8-6.

NOTE Cryptography is the science of encrypting and decrypting information. It comes from the Greek words "kryptos," meaning hidden, and "graphia," meaning writing. Cryptography involves developing, testing, and studying the science of encryption methods. Cryptanalysis is the process of trying to decrypt encrypted data without the key. When new algorithms are tested, they go through stringent processes of cryptanalysis to ensure that the new encryption process is unbreakable or that it takes too much time and resources to break.

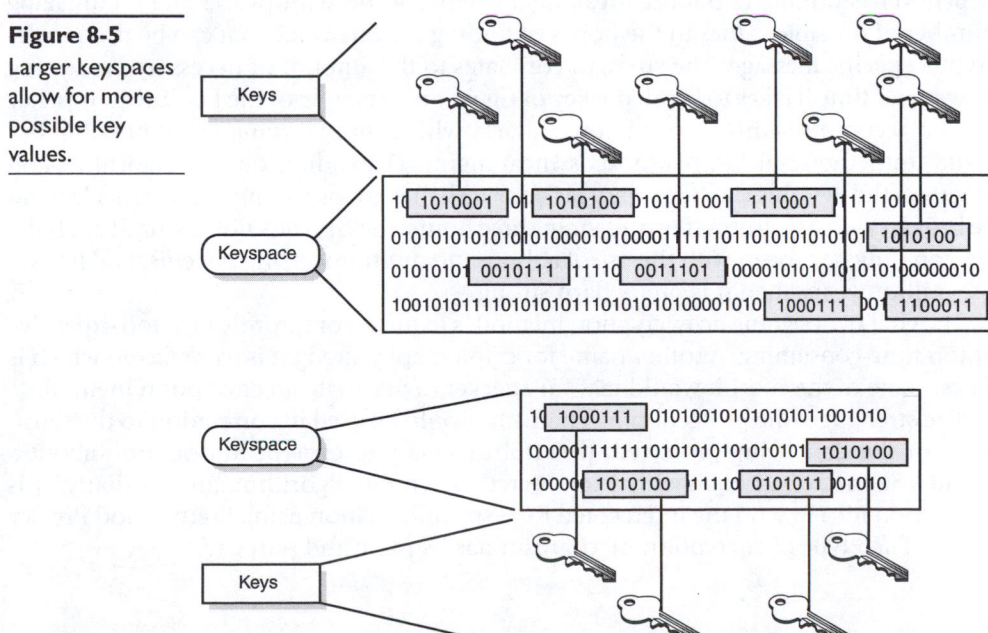

Figure 8-5
Larger keyspaces allow for more possible key values.

Figure 8-6
Without the right key, the captured message is useless to an attacker.

Encrypted Message

askfjaoiwenh220va8fjsdnv jaksfue92v8ssk

Intruder obtains the message but its encryption makes it useless to her.

Intruder

askfjaoiwenh220va8fjsdnv jaksfue92v8ssk

Strength of the Cryptosystem

You are the weakest link. Goodbye!

The *strength* of the encryption method comes from the algorithm, secrecy of the key, length of the key, initialization vectors, and how they all work together. When strength is discussed in encryption, it refers to how hard it is to figure out the algorithm or key, whichever is not made public. Breaking a key has to do with processing an amazing number of possible values in the hopes of finding the one value that can be used to decrypt a specific message. The strength correlates to the amount of necessary processing power and time it takes to break the key or figure out the value of the key. Breaking a key can be accomplished by a brute force attack, which means trying every possible key value until the resulting plaintext is meaningful. Depending on the algorithm and length of the key, this can be an easy task or a task that is close to impossible. If a key can be broken with a Pentium II processor in three hours, the cipher is not strong at all. If the key can only be broken with the use of a thousand multiprocessing systems, and it takes 1.2 million years, then it is pretty darn strong.

The goal of designing an encryption method is to make compromising it too expensive or too time-consuming. Another name for cryptography strength is *work factor*, which is an estimate of the effort it would take an attacker to penetrate an encryption method.

The strength of the protection mechanism should be used in correlation to the sensitivity of the data being protected. It is not necessary to encrypt information about a friend's Saturday barbeque with a top-secret encryption algorithm, and similarly, it is not a good idea to send the intercepted KGB spy information using Pretty Good Privacy (PGP). Each type of encryption mechanism has its place and purpose.

Even if the algorithm is very complex and thorough, other issues within encryption can weaken encryption methods. Because the key is usually the secret value needed to actually encrypt and decrypt messages, improper protection of the key can weaken the encryption. An extremely strong algorithm can be used, using a large keyspace, and a large and random key value, which are all the requirements for strong encryption, but if a user shares her key with others, these other pieces of the equation really don't matter.

Important elements of encryption are using an algorithm without flaws, using a large key, using all possible values within a keyspace, and protecting the actual key. If one element were weak, it could be the link that dooms the whole process.

Goals of Cryptosystems

Cryptosystems can provide confidentiality, authenticity, integrity, and nonrepudiation services. They do not provide availability of data or systems. *Confidentiality* means that unauthorized parties cannot access information. *Authenticity* refers to validating the source of the message to ensure the sender is properly identified. *Integrity* provides assurance that the message was not modified during transmission, accidentally or intentionally. *Nonrepudiation* means that a sender cannot deny sending the message at a later date. If your boss sends you a message telling you that you will be receiving a raise that doubles your salary and it is encrypted, encryption methods can ensure that it really came from your boss, that someone did not alter it before it arrived at your computer, that no one else was able to read this message as it traveled over the network, and that your boss cannot deny sending the message later when he comes to his senses.

Different types of messages and transactions require a higher degree of one or all of the services that encryption methods can supply. Military and intelligence agencies are very concerned about keeping information confidential, so they would choose encryption mechanisms that provide a high degree of secrecy. Financial institutions care about confidentiality, but care also about the integrity of the data being transmitted, so the encryption mechanism they would choose may differ from the military's encryption methods. If messages were accepted that had a misplaced decimal point or zero, the ramifications could be far reaching in the financial world. Legal agencies may care more about the authenticity of messages that they receive. If information that was received ever needed to be presented in a court of law, its authenticity would certainly be questioned; therefore, the encryption method used should ensure authenticity, which confirms who sent the information.

 NOTE If David sends a message and then later claims that he did not send the message, this is an act of repudiation. When an encryption mechanism provides nonrepudiation, it means that the sender cannot deny sending the message. It's a way of keeping the sender honest.

Cryptography Definitions

- **Algorithm**   Set of mathematical rules used in encryption and decryption
- **Cryptography**   Science of secret writing that enables you to store and transmit data in a form that is available only to the intended individuals
- **Cryptosystem**   Hardware or software implementation of cryptography that transforms a message to ciphertext and back to plaintext
- **Cryptanalysis**   Practice of obtaining plaintext from ciphertext without a key or of breaking the encryption
- **Cryptology**   The study of both cryptography and cryptanalysis
- **Ciphertext**   Data in encrypted or in unreadable format
- **Encipher**   Act of transforming data into an unreadable format
- **Decipher**   Act of transforming data into a readable format
- **Key**   Secret sequence of bits and instructions that governs the act of encryption and decryption
- **Key clustering**   Instance when two different keys generate the same ciphertext from the same plaintext
- **Keyspace**   Possible values used to construct keys
- **Plaintext**   Data in readable format, also referred to as cleartext
- **Work factor**   Estimated time, effort, and resources necessary to break a cryptosystem

Types of Ciphers

There are two basic types of encryption ciphers: substitution and transposition (permutation). The *substitution cipher* replaces bits, characters, or blocks of characters with different bits, characters, or blocks. The *transposition cipher* does not replace the original text with different text, but moves the original text around. It rearranges the bits, characters, or blocks of characters to hide the original meaning.

Substitution Cipher

Give me your A and I will change it out for an M. Now, no one can read your message. Response: That will fool them.

A substitution cipher uses a key to know how the substitution should be carried out. In the *Caesar Cipher*, each letter is replaced with the letter three places beyond it in the alphabet. This is referred to as a shift alphabet.

If the Caesar Cipher were used with the English alphabet, when George wants to encrypt the important message of "meow," the encrypted message would be "phrz." Substitution is used in today's algorithms, but it is extremely complex compared with this example. Many different types of substitutions take place, usually with more than one alphabet. This example is only meant to show you the concept of how a substitution cipher works in its most simplistic form.

Transposition Cipher

In a *transposition cipher*, permutation is used, meaning that letters are scrambled. The key determines the positions that the characters are moved to, as illustrated in Figure 8-7.

This is a simplistic example of a transposition cipher and only shows one way of performing transposition. When implemented with complex mathematical functions, transpositions can become quite sophisticated and difficult to break. Most ciphers used today use both long sequences of complicated substitutions and permutations on messages. The key value is inputted into the algorithm, and the resulting ciphertext is produced by the sequence of operations (substitutions and permutations) that is performed on the plaintext.

Simple substitution and transposition ciphers are vulnerable to attacks that perform *frequency analysis*. In every language, some words and patterns are used more often than others. For instance, in the English language, the words "the," "and," "that," and "is" are frequent patterns of letters used in messages and conversation. Messages usually start with "Hello" or "Dear" and end with "Sincerely." These patterns help attackers figure out the transformation from plaintext to ciphertext, which enables them to figure out the key that was used to perform the transformation. It is important for cryptosystems to not reveal these patterns.

More complex algorithms usually use more than one alphabet for substitution and permutation, which reduces the vulnerability to frequency analysis. The more complicated the algorithm, the more the resulting text (ciphertext) differs from the plaintext. Thus, the matching of these types of patterns becomes more difficult.

Figure 8-7
Transposition
cipher

Running and Concealment Ciphers

I have my decoder ring, spyglasses, and secret handshake. Now let me figure out how I will encrypt my messages.

Two more of the spy-novel-type ciphers are the running key cipher and the concealment cipher. The *running key cipher* could use a key that does not require an electronic algorithm and bit alterations, but clever steps in the physical world around you. For instance, a key in this type of cipher could be a book page, line number, and column count. If I get a message from my super-secret spy buddy and the message reads "149l6c7.299l3c7.911l5c8," this could mean for me to look at the first book in our predetermined series of books, the 49th page, 6th line down the page, and the 7th column. So I write down the letter in that column, which is *m*. The second set of numbers starts with 2, so I go to the 2nd book, 99th page, 3rd line down, and then to the 7th column, which is *p*. The last letter I get from the 9th book in our series, the 11th page, 5th row, and 8th column in that row, which is *t*. So now I have come up with my important secret message, which is *mpt*. This means nothing to me, and I need to look for a new spy buddy. Running key ciphers can be used in different and more complex ways, but I think you get the point.

Another type of spy-novel cipher is the *concealment cipher*. If my other super-secret spy buddy and I decide our key value is every third word, then when I get a message from him, I will pick out every third word and write it down. Suppose he sends me a message that reads, "The saying, 'The time is right' is not cow language, so is now a dead subject." Because my key is every third word, I come up with "The right cow is dead." This again means nothing to me, and I am now turning in my decoder ring.

No matter which type of cipher is used, the roles of the algorithm and key are the same, even if they are not mathematical equations. In the running key cipher, the algorithm states that encryption and decryption will take place by choosing characters out of a predefined set of books. The key indicates the book, page, line, and word within that line. In substitution ciphers, the algorithm dictates that substitution will take place using a predefined alphabet or sequence of characters, and the key indicates that each character will be replaced with the third character that follows it in that sequence of characters. In actual mathematical structures, the algorithm is a set of mathematical functions that will be performed on the message, and the key can indicate in which order these functions take place. So even if an attacker knows the algorithm, and we have to assume that he does, if he does not know the key, the message is still useless to him.

References

Classical Cryptography: **www-math.cudenver.edu/~wcherowi/courses/m5410/ m5410cc.html**

Methods of Transposition: home.ecn.ab.ca/~jsavard/crypto/pp0102.htm

Steganography

Where's the top-secret message? Answer: In this picture of my dogs.

   Steganography is a method of hiding data in another media so that the very existence of the data is concealed. Steganography is mainly used by hiding messages in graphic images. The least significant bit of each byte of the image can be replaced with bits of the secret message. This practice does not affect the graphic enough to be detected.

   Steganography does not use algorithms or keys to encrypt information. This is a process to hide data within another object so no one will detect its presence. A message can be hidden in a wave file, in a graphic, or in unused spaces on a hard drive or sectors that are marked as unusable. Steganography can also be used to insert a digital watermark on digital images in the hopes of detecting illegal copies of the images.

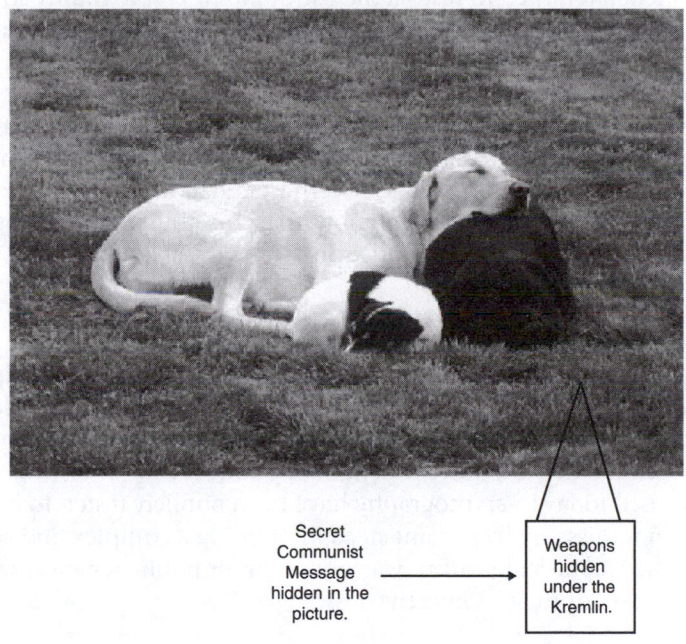

Secret Communist Message hidden in the picture. → Weapons hidden under the Kremlin.

References

Steganography and Digital Watermarking: **www.jjtc.com/Steganography**

Steganography: A Cryptography Layer: **www.rit.edu/~vxr8205/crypto2/ cryptopaper.html**

The Government's Involvement with Cryptography

Big Brother is watching you! Um, I mean we are only watching the bad guys.

In the United States, the government's cryptographic agency, the NSA (National Security Agency), was granted the power to regulate the export of cryptographic mechanisms and equipment. This was done with the hopes of making encryption technology harder to be obtained and used by terrorists and criminals. Harry Truman created the NSA in 1952, and its main mission is to listen in on communications in the interest of national security for the United States. The NSA keeps an extremely low profile, and its activities are highly secret. The NSA also conducts research in cryptology to create secure algorithms and to break other cryptosystems to enable eavesdropping and spying.

The government attempted to restrict the use of public cryptography so that enemies of the United States could not employ encryption methods that were too strong for it to break. These issues have caused tension and controversy between cryptography researchers, vendors, and the NSA pertaining to new cryptographic methods and the public use of them. The fear is that if the government controls all types of encryption and is allowed to listen in on private citizens' conversations, the obtained information may be misused in Big Brother ways. Also, if the government had the ability to listen in on everyone's conversations, there is little certainty that this ability would not fall into the wrong hands, to be used for the wrong reasons.

Clipper Chip

In 1993, the U.S. government proposed placing their own encryption chip, the *Clipper Chip*, in every American-made communication device. This included telephones, cell phones, personal computers, and more. The Clipper Chip was based on the SkipJack algorithm that was classified and never opened for public review or testing. A majority of the algorithms used today in cryptography have been publicly tested to ensure that the developers did not miss any important steps in building a complex and secure mechanism. Because the SkipJack algorithm was not open for public review, many people in the public sector do not trust its effectiveness.

Kerckhoff's Principle

Auguste Kerckhoff published a paper in 1883 stating that the only secrecy involved with a cryptography system should be the key. He claimed the algorithm should be publicly known. He asserted that if security were based on too many secrets, there would be more vulnerabilities.

This is a common mentality of cryptographers in the private sector, but not so in military and government agencies. Governments around the world create their own algorithms that are not released to the public.

The Clipper Chip is an NSA-designed tamperproof chip for encrypting data. It is one of the two chips implemented in the U.S. government's Escrowed Encryption Standard (EES). Each chip has a unit key, which is used to encrypt a copy of each user's session key, not the message itself. Each Clipper Chip has a unique serial number, and a copy of the unit key is stored in the database under this serial number. The sending Clipper Chip generates and sends a Law Enforcement Access Field (LEAF) value included in the transmitted message. This field value contains the serial number of the Clipper Chip used to encrypt the message in the first place. This is how the government, or law enforcement, knows which unit key to retrieve from the database. This unit key enables them to decrypt and find out the session key, which enables them to actually decrypt the message and eavesdrop on the conversation, as shown in Figure 8-8. The unit key is split into two pieces and kept in different databases maintained by two different escrow agencies.

Figure 8-8
The unit key decrypts the session key.

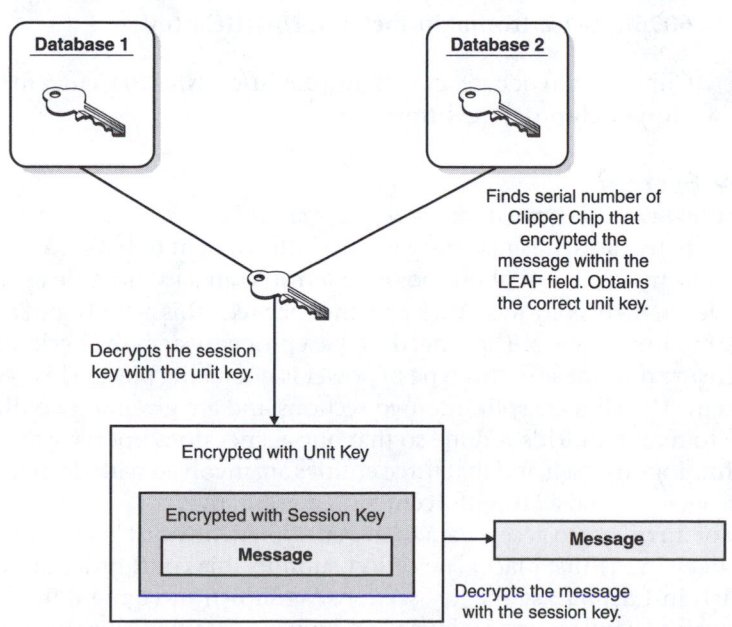

Some Weaknesses Found in the Clipper Chip

- The SkipJack algorithm was never publicly scrutinized and tested.
- An 80-bit key is very weak.
- A 16-bit checksum can be defeated.
- The Clipper Chip ID tagged and identified every communication session.

There was quite a public outcry pertaining to the Clipper Chip and its threat to personal privacy. Eventually, the government stopped supporting the Clipper Chip, and most companies turned to software-based encryption programs (fair crypto systems) instead of an actual hardware chip. Several deficiencies were found in the Clipper Chip, and because it was considered invasive to the public's privacy, it quickly lost support and was dropped. The Clipper Chip initiative was abandoned and replaced with policies aimed at controlling the proliferation and use of cryptography in the public. It was just too Big Brother for society.

References

Cryptography, the Clipper Chip, and the Constitution: **www.swiss.ai.mit.edu/ 6095/articles/froomkin-metaphor/partIC.html**

Clipper Chip debate: **cse.stanford.edu/class/cs201/current/Projects/ clipper-chip/debate.html**

Key Escrow

Hi, could you hold on to a copy of this key, please?

In many cases, it is necessary for law enforcement to have access to certain conversations to try and learn about possible terrorist attacks, drug deals, or murder attempts. However, there is always a tricky balance between this activity and a citizen's right to private communication. There needs to be a proper system of checks and balances in place to ensure that abuse of this type of power is not taking place. This is where *key escrow* comes in. The keys are split into two sections and are given to two different escrow agencies to maintain. This is done so that one agency does not have the ability to abuse this technology by itself and that three entities are involved with decrypting this type of data: two agencies and a law enforcement representative.

For an officer to access data that is encrypted, he must get a court order to request the unit key in the first place. The officer submits this court order to both escrow agencies, which in turn release the key sections, as shown in Figure 8-9. The sections are combined into a full key, and it is used on only the specified data that is outlined in the court order. This is all outlined in the U.S. Escrow Encryption Standard.

Figure 8-9

In a key escrow arrangement, the key necessary to decrypt traffic is split and kept by at least two different parties.

The Clipper Chip uses the concept of key escrow and key recovery. A key escrow implementation can also be used in software using public key cryptography. In these cases, the public key is available to encrypt and decrypt messages, but the private key is split up into two or more pieces and stored by different entities. When it is necessary to decrypt information, say during a wiretap, then each entity must supply its piece of the private key, which will be combined to create one useful key. This provides another layer of protection because two or more people would have to supply part of the private key to decrypt information. This is referred to as a *fair cryptosystem*, which uses software instead of hardware chips. The algorithm in fair cryptosystems does not need to be secret; thus, well-tested and well-known algorithms and protocols can be used.

Although these examples are U.S. centric, many governments have similar systems in use today. Key escrow is an important concept for you to understand. It means that the keys (or key parts) are kept by third parties to implement the separations of duties concept. It is not specifically tied just to the Clipper Chip or to fair cryptosystems and can be used in other situations.

References

Escrowed Encryption Standard (EES): **www.itl.nist.gov/fipspubs/fip185.htm**

Key Escrow Encryption Available: **www.cs.georgetown.edu/~denning/crypto/ Lathe-Gambit.txt**

Security Technology Issues: **www.sims.berkeley.edu/courses/is224/s99/ GroupC/pr2/s4.html**

Methods of Encryption

Although there can be several pieces to an encryption method, the two main pieces are the algorithms and the keys. As stated earlier, algorithms are usually complex mathematical formulas that dictate the rules of how the plaintext will be turned into ciphertext. A key is a string of random bits that will be inserted into the algorithm. For two entities to be able to communicate via encryption, they must use the same algorithm and, many times, the same key. In some encryption methods, the receiver and the sender use the same key, and in other encryption methods, they must use different, but related keys for encryption and decryption purposes. The following sections explain the difference between these two types of encryption methods.

Symmetric versus Asymmetric Algorithms

Cryptography algorithms use either *symmetric keys*, also called secret keys, or *asymmetric keys*, also called public and private keys. As if encryption were not complicated enough, the terms that are used to describe the key types only make it worse. Just pay close attention and we will get through this just fine.

Symmetric Cryptography

In a cryptosystem that uses symmetric cryptography, both parties will be using the same key for encryption and decryption, as shown in Figure 8-10. This provides dual functionality.

Figure 8-10
When using symmetric algorithms, the sender and receiver use the same key for encryption and decryption functions.

Symmetric encryption uses the same keys.

Encrypt Message

Decrypt Message

Message

Message

Symmetric keys are also called secret keys because this type of encryption relies on each user to keep the key a secret and properly protected. If an intruder were to get this key, the intruder could decrypt any intercepted message encrypted with this key.

Each pair of users who want to exchange data using symmetric key encryption must have their own set of keys. This means if Dan and Iqqi want to communicate, both need to obtain a copy of the same key. If Dan also wants to communicate using symmetric encryption with Norm and Dave, he now needs to have three separate keys, one for each friend. This might not sound like a big deal until Dan realizes that he may communicate with hundreds of people over a period of several months, and keeping track and using the correct key that corresponds to each specific receiver can become a daunting task. If ten people needed to communicate securely with each other using symmetric keys, then 45 keys would need to be kept track of. If 100 people were going to communicate, then 4,950 keys would be involved. The equation that is used to calculate the number of symmetric keys needed is

$$N(N - 1)/2 = \text{number of keys}$$

The security of the symmetric encryption method is completely dependent on how well users protect the key. This should raise red flags for you if you have ever had to depend on a whole staff of people to keep a secret. If a key is compromised, then all messages encrypted with that key can be decrypted and read by an intruder. This is complicated further by how symmetric keys are actually shared and updated when necessary. If Dan wants to communicate to Norm for the first time, Dan has to figure out how to get Norm the right key. It is not safe to just send it in an e-mail message, because the key is not protected and can be easily intercepted and used by attackers. Dan has to get the key to Norm through an *out-of-band method*. Dan can save the key on a floppy disk and walk over to Norm's desk, or have a secure carrier deliver it to Norm. This is a huge hassle, and each method is very clumsy and insecure.

Because both users employ the same key to encrypt and decrypt messages, symmetric cryptosystems can provide confidentiality, but they cannot provide authentication or nonrepudiation. There is no way to prove who actually sent a message if two people are using the same key.

If symmetric cryptosystems have so many problems and flaws, why use them at all? They are very fast and can be hard to break. Compared with asymmetric systems, symmetric algorithms scream in speed. They can encrypt and decrypt large amounts of data that would take an unacceptable amount of time if an asymmetric algorithm were used instead. It is also difficult to uncover data that is encrypted with a symmetric algorithm if a large key size was used. For many of our network applications that require quick encryption, symmetric key cryptography is the only option.

The following list outlines the strengths and weakness of symmetric key systems:

- Strengths:
  - Much faster than asymmetric systems
  - Hard to break if using a large key size

- Weaknesses:
  - Requires a secure mechanism to deliver keys properly.
  - Each pair of users needs a unique pair of keys, so the number of keys grows, and key management can become overwhelming.
  - Provide confidentiality, but not authenticity or nonrepudiation.

The following are examples of symmetric algorithms and will be explained in the "Stream and Block Ciphers" section:

- Data Encryption Standard (DES)
- Triple-DES (3DES)
- Blowfish
- IDEA
- RC4, RC5, and RC6
- Advanced Encryption Standard (AES)

References

Symmetric Key Cryptography: **csrc.nist.gov/publications/nistpubs/800-7/ node208.html**

Public Key Cryptography: **developer.netscape.com/docs/manuals/security/ pkin/contents.htm**

Asymmetric Cryptography

Some things you can tell the public, but some things you just want to keep private.

In symmetric key cryptography, a single secret key is used between entities, whereas in public key systems, each entity has different keys, or *asymmetric keys*. The two different asymmetric keys are mathematically related. If a message is encrypted by one key, the other key is required in order to decrypt the message.

In a public key system, the pair of keys is made up of one public key and one private key. The *public key* can be known to everyone, and the *private key* must only be known and used by the owner. Many times, public keys are listed in directories and databases of e-mail addresses so they are available to anyone who wants to use these keys to encrypt or decrypt data when communicating with a particular person. Figure 8-11 illustrates the use of the different keys.

The public and private keys of an asymmetric cryptosystem are mathematically related. If someone gets another person's public key, she should not be able to figure out the corresponding private key. This means that if an evildoer gets a copy of Bob's public key, it does not mean he can now use some mathematical magic and find out Bob's private key. But if someone got Bob's private key, the corresponding public key can be derived more easily.

Figure 8-11
Asymmetric
cryptosystem

Asymmetric systems use two different keys
for encryption and decryption purposes.

Encrypt
Message

Decrypt Message
with different key

Message

Message

If Bob encrypts a message with his private key, the receiver must have a copy of Bob's public key to decrypt it. The receiver can decrypt Bob's message and decide to reply back to Bob in an encrypted form. All she needs to do is encrypt her reply with Bob's public key, and then Bob can decrypt the message with his private key. It is not possible to encrypt and decrypt using the same key when using an asymmetric key encryption technology, and that is because, once again, the two keys are related to each other mathematically.

Bob can encrypt a message with his private key, and the receiver can then decrypt it with Bob's public key. By decrypting the message with Bob's public key, the receiver can be sure that the message really came from Bob. A message can only be decrypted with a public key if the message was encrypted with the corresponding private key. This provides authentication, because Bob is the only one who is supposed to have his private key. When the receiver wants to make sure Bob is the only one that can read her reply, she will encrypt the response with his public key. Only Bob will be able to decrypt the message because he is the only one who has the necessary private key.

Now the receiver can also encrypt her response with her private key instead of using Bob's public key. Why would she do that? She wants Bob to know that the message came from her and no one else. If she encrypted the response with Bob's public key, it does not provide authenticity because anyone can get Bob's public key. If she uses her private key to encrypt the message, then Bob can be sure that the message came from her and no one else. Symmetric keys do not provide authenticity because the same key is used on both ends. Using one of the secret keys does not ensure that the message originated from a specific entity.

If confidentiality is the most important security service to a sender, she would encrypt the file with the receiver's public key. This is called a *secure message format* because it can only be decrypted by the person who has the corresponding private key.

If authentication is the most important security service to the sender, then she would encrypt the data with her private key. This provides assurance to the receiver that the only person who could have encrypted the message is the individual who has possession of that private key. If the sender encrypted the message with the receiver's public key, authentication is not provided because this public key is available to anyone.

Encrypting a message with the sender's private key is called an *open message format* because anyone with a copy of the corresponding public key can decrypt the message. Confidentiality is not ensured.

For a message to be in a *secure and signed format*, the sender would encrypt the message with her private key and then encrypt it again with the receiver's public key. The receiver would need to decrypt the message with his own private key and then decrypt it again with the sender's public key. This provides confidentiality and authentication for that delivered message. The different encryption methods are shown in Figure 8-12.

Each key type can be used to encrypt and decrypt, so do not get confused and think the public key is only for encryption and the private key is only for decryption. They both have the capability to encrypt and decrypt data. However, if data is encrypted with a private key, it cannot be decrypted with a private key. If data is encrypted with a private key, it must be decrypted with the corresponding public key. If data is encrypted with a public key, it must be decrypted with the corresponding private key. Figure 8-13 further explains the steps of a signed and secure message.

An asymmetric cryptosystem works much more slowly than symmetric systems, but can provide authentication and nonrepudiation, depending on its configuration and use. Asymmetric systems also provide for easier and more manageable key distribution than symmetric systems and do not have the scalability issues of symmetric systems. The "Hybrid Encryption Methods" section will show how these two systems can be used together to get the best of both worlds.

Figure 8-12
The way that the sender encrypts the message dictates the type of security service that will be provided.

Figure 8-13 A secured and signed message is encrypted twice with two different keys.

 NOTE "Public key cryptography" is "asymmetric cryptography." The terms can be used interchangeably.

The following outlines the strengths and weaknesses of asymmetric key systems:

- Strengths:
  - Better key distribution than symmetric systems
  - Better scalability than symmetric systems
  - Can provide authentication and nonrepudiation
- Weaknesses:
  - Works much more slowly than symmetric systems
  - Mathematically intensive tasks

The following are examples of asymmetric key algorithms:

- RSA
- Elliptic Curve Cryptosystem (ECC)
- Diffie-Hellman
- El Gamal
- Digital Signature Algorithm (DSA)
- Knapsack

These will be explained further in the sections following "Asymmetric Encryption Algorithms" later in the chapter.

References

Asymmetric Key Cryptography: **csrc.nist.gov/publications/nistpubs/800-7/ node210.html**

Cryptography Define/Brief History: **www.eco.utexas.edu/~norman/BUS.FOR/ course.mat/SSim/history.html**

Asymmetric Cryptography: **www.maths.mq.edu.au/~steffen/old/PCry/report/ node8.html**

Stream and Block Ciphers

Which should I use, the stream or block cipher? Answer: The stream cipher because it makes you look skinnier.

There are two main types of symmetric algorithms: stream and block ciphers. Like their names sound, block ciphers work on blocks of plaintext and ciphertext, whereas stream ciphers work on streams of plaintext and ciphertext, one bit at a time.

Block Cipher

When a *block cipher* algorithm is used for encryption and decryption purposes, the message is divided into blocks of bits. These blocks are then put through substitution, transposition, and other mathematical functions, one block at a time. The algorithm dictates all the possible functions available to be used on the message, and it is the key that will determine in what order these functions will take place. Strong algorithms make reengineering, or trying to figure out all the functions that took place on the message, basically impossible.

The properties of a cipher should contain confusion and diffusion. The complexity of the algorithm and not knowing the key value cause confusion, and diffusion is accomplished by putting the bits within the plaintext through many different functions so that they are dispersed throughout the algorithm. An analogy is an example where Dusty is given the task of finding 25 people. The 25 people start off as one group in his living room and have their own maps that lay out paths to their destinations. Each person has a destination of a particular city in a different state. The 25 people disperse and reach their destinations, and it is up to Dusty to find them. Because he does not have a copy of each person's map (or their keys), it brings confusion to the game. Because each person is in a different state throughout the United States, it adds diffusion.

Block ciphers use diffusion and confusion in their methods. Figure 8-14 shows a conceptual example of a simplistic block cipher. It has 16 inputs and each input represents a bit. This block cipher has two layers of 4-bit substitution boxes called *S-boxes*, or substitution boxes. Each S-box contains a lookup table that instructs how the bits should be encrypted. The key that is used in the encryption process dictates what S-boxes are used and in what order.

Figure 8-14 In block cipher algorithms, a message is divided into blocks of bits, and mathematical functions are performed on those blocks.

Figure 8-14 shows that the key dictates what S-boxes are to be used when scrambling the original message from readable plaintext to encrypted nonreadable ciphertext. Each S-box can have different types of functions, mathematical formulas, and methods to be performed on each bit. The key provides the confusion because the attacker does not know which S-boxes would be used during the encryption process. All the permutations that happen on the bits are the diffusion, because they are moved between different S-boxes and put through different steps of scrambling. In this example, only two rounds are performed on the message.

This example is simplistic—most block ciphers work with blocks of 64 bits, and many more S-boxes are usually involved. Strong and efficient block cryptosystems use random key values so an attacker cannot find a pattern as to which S-boxes are chosen and used.

Stream Cipher

As stated earlier, a block cipher performs mathematical functions on blocks of data. A stream cipher does not divide a message into blocks; instead, a *stream cipher* treats the message as a stream of bits and performs mathematical functions on them individually.

When using a stream cipher, the same plaintext bit will be transformed into a different ciphertext bit each time it is encrypted. Some stream ciphers use a *keystream generator*, which produces a stream of bits that is XORed with the plaintext bits to produce ciphertext, as shown in Figure 8-15. ("XOR" stands for "exclusive OR.")

 NOTE XOR is an operation that is applied to two bits. It is a function in binary mathematics. When combining them, if both bits are the same, the result is zero (1 + 1 = 0). If the bits are different from each other, the result is one (1 + 0 = 1).

Example:
Message stream   1001010111
Keystream   0011101010
Ciphertext stream   1010111101

If the cryptosystem were only dependent upon the symmetric stream algorithm, an attacker could get a copy of the plaintext and the resulting ciphertext, XOR them together, and find the keystream to use in decrypting other messages. So the smart people decided to stick a key into the mix.

In block ciphers, it is the key that determines what functions are applied to the plaintext and in what order. The key provides the randomness of the encryption process. As stated earlier, most encryption algorithms are public, so people know how they work. The secret to the secret sauce is the key. In stream ciphers, the key also provides randomness, but to the keystream that is actually applied to the plaintext. The key is a random value input into the stream algorithm, which it uses to ensure the randomness of the keystream data. This concept is shown in Figure 8-16. As you can see in this graphic, both the sending and receiving end must have the same key to generate the same keystream for proper encryption and decryption purposes.

Figure 8-15
The value that is generated by the keystream generator is XORed with the bits of the plaintext message.

Figure 8-16
A keystream and key are needed for the encryption and the decryption process.

A strong and effective stream cipher algorithm contains the following characteristics:

- Long periods of no repeating patterns within keystream values
- Statistically unpredictable keystream
- A keystream not linearly related to the key
- Statistically unbiased keystream (as many 0s as 1s)

Because stream ciphers encrypt and decrypt one bit at a time, they are more suitable for hardware implementations. Block ciphers are easier to implement in software because they work with blocks of data that the software is used to working with. Stream ciphers are intensive because each bit must be manipulated, which works better at the silicon level. To make things just a little more confusing, block ciphers sometimes work in a mode that emulates a stream cipher. No one said cryptography was easy, and we have not even touched any of the mathematics involved!

Types of Symmetric Systems

There are several types of symmetric algorithms used today. They have different methods of providing encryption and decryption functionality. The one thing they all have in common is that they are symmetric algorithms, meaning two identical keys are used to encrypt and decrypt the data.

Data Encryption Standard (DES)

Data Encryption Standard (DES) has had a long and rich history within the computer community. The National Institute of Standards and Technology (NIST) researched the need for the protection of sensitive but unclassified data during the 1960s and initiated a cryptography program in the early 1970s. NIST invited vendors to submit data encryption algorithms to be used as a cryptographic standard. IBM had already been developing encryption algorithms to protect financial transactions. In 1974, IBM's 128-bit algorithm, named *Lucifer*, was submitted and accepted. The NSA modified this algorithm to use a key size of 64 bits (8 bits used for parity, resulting in an effective key length of 56 bits) instead of the original 128 bits, and named it the Data Encryption Algorithm (DEA). There was controversy about whether the NSA weakened Lucifer on purpose to give the agency the ability to decrypt messages not intended for them, but in the end, the modified Lucifer became a national cryptographic standard in 1977 and an American National Standards Institute (ANSI) standard in 1978.

DES has been implemented in a majority of commercial products using cryptography functionality and in almost all government agencies. It was tested and approved as one of the strongest and most efficient cryptographic algorithms available. The continued overwhelming support of the algorithm is what caused the most confusion when NSA announced in 1986 that as of January 1988, the agency would no longer endorse DES and that DES-based products would no longer fall under compliance with the Federal Standard 1027. The NSA felt that because DES had been so popular for so long, it would surely be targeted for penetration and become useless as an official standard. Many researches disagreed, but NSA wanted to move on to a newer, more secure, and less popular algorithm as the new standard.

NSA's decision to drop its support for DES caused major concern and negative feedback. At that time, it was shown that DES still provided the necessary level of protection, it was projected that it would take a computer thousands of years to crack it, it was already embedded in thousands of products, and that there was no equivalent substitute. NSA reconsidered its decision and NIST ended up recertifying DES for another five years.

In 1998, the Electronic Frontier Foundation built a computer system for $250,000 that broke DES in three days using a brute force attack against the keyspace. It contained 1,536 microprocessors running at 40 MHz, which performed 60 million test decryptions per second per chip. Although most people do not have these types of systems to conduct such attacks, as Moore's Law holds true and microprocessors increase in processing power, this type of attack will become more feasible for the average attacker. This brought about 3DES, which provides stronger protection. 3DES performs encryption, decryption, and then encryption on a message with independent keys.

NOTE In 1965, Gordon Moore, co-founder of Intel, made an observation that the number of transistors per square inch on integrated circuits had doubled every year since the integrated circuit was invented. Moore predicted that this trend would continue. In subsequent years, the pace slowed a bit, but data density has doubled approximately every 18 months, and this is the current definition of Moore's Law. Most experts, including Moore himself, expect Moore's Law to hold for at least another 20 years or so.

DES was later replaced by the Rijndael algorithm as the *Advanced Encryption Standard (AES)* by NIST. This means that Rijndael is the new approved method of encrypting sensitive but unclassified information for the U.S. government and will most likely be accepted and widely used in the public arena in the future.

How Does DES Work?

How does DES work again? Answer: Voodoo magic and a dead chicken.

DES is a block symmetric encryption algorithm. When 64-bit blocks of plaintext go in, 64-bit blocks of ciphertext come out. It is also a symmetric algorithm, meaning the same key is used for encryption and decryption. It uses a 64-bit key: 56 bits make up the true key, and 8 bits are used for parity.

When the DES algorithm is applied to data, it divides the message into blocks and operates on them one at a time. A block is made up of 64 bits and is divided in half, and each character is encrypted one at a time. The characters are put through 16 rounds of transposition and substitution functions. The order and type of transposition and substitution functions depend on the value of the key that is inputted into the algorithm. The result is a 64-bit block of ciphertext.

There are several modes of operation when using block ciphers. Each mode specifies how a block cipher will operate. One mode may work better in one type of environment for specific functionality, whereas another mode may work in another environment with totally different requirements. It is important that vendors who employ DES understand the different modes and which one to use for which purpose.

DES has several distinct modes of operation that are used in different situations for different results; we just need to understand four of them.

Electronic Code Book (ECB) Mode This operates like a code book. A 64-bit data block is entered into the algorithm with a key, and a block of ciphertext is produced. For a given block of plaintext and a given key, the same block of ciphertext is always produced. Not all messages end up in neat and tidy 64-bit blocks, so ECB incorporates padding to address this problem. This mode is usually used for small amounts of data like encrypting and protecting encryption keys.

Every key has a different code book. The code book provides the recipe of substitutions and permutations that will be performed on the block of plaintext. Because this mode works with blocks of data independently, data within a file does not have to be encrypted in a certain order. This is very helpful when using encryption in databases. A database has different pieces of data accessed in a random fashion. If it is encrypted in ECB mode, then any record or table can be added, encrypted, deleted, or decrypted independent of any other table or record. Other DES modes are dependent upon the text that was encrypted before them; this dependency makes it harder to encrypt and decrypt smaller amounts of text because the previous encrypted text would need to be decrypted first.

This mode is used for challenge-response encryption operations and some key management tasks. It is also used to encrypt personal identification numbers (PINs) in ATM machines for financial institutions. It is not used to encrypt large amounts of data because patterns would eventually show themselves since this mode uses no chaining, which is explained in the next section.

Cipher Block Chaining (CBC) Mode *Take a little bit from what you just created and throw it in the mix.* In ECB mode, a block of plaintext and a key will always give the same ciphertext. This means that if the word "balloon" were encrypted and the resulting ciphertext were "hwicssn," each time it was encrypted using the same key, the same ciphertext would always be given. This can show evidence of a pattern, which if an evil-doer put some effort into revealing, could get him a step closer to compromising the encryption process. *Cipher Block Chaining (CBC)* does not reveal a pattern because each block of text, the key, and the value based on the previous block is processed in the algorithm and applied to the next block of text, as shown in Figure 8-17. This gives a more random resulting ciphertext. Ciphertext is extracted and used from the previous block of text.

Figure 8-17 In CBC mode, ciphertext from the pervious block of data is used in encrypting the next block of data.

This provides dependence between the blocks, and in a sense they are chained together. This is where the name of Cipher Block Chaining (CBC) comes from, and it is this chaining effect that hides any patterns.

The results of one block are fed into the next block, meaning that each block is used to modify the following block. This chaining effect means that a particular ciphertext block is dependent upon all blocks before it, not just the previous block.

Cipher Feedback (CFB) Mode   In this mode, the previously generated ciphertext from the last encrypted block of data is inputted into the algorithm to generate random values. These random values are processed with the current block of plaintext to create ciphertext. This is basically the same as the CBC mode, except the CFB mode emulates a stream cipher by using a keystream generator, and CBC works purely as a block cipher. This mode is used when encrypting individual characters is required.

Output Feedback (OFB) Mode   This mode is very similar to *Cipher Feedback (CFB)* mode, but if DES is working in *Output Feedback (OFB)* mode, it is functioning like a stream cipher by generating a stream of random binary bits to be combined with the plaintext to create ciphertext. The ciphertext is fed back to the algorithm to form a portion of the next input to encrypt the next stream of bits.

As previously stated, block ciphers work on blocks of data, and stream ciphers work on a stream of bits. Stream ciphers use a keystream method of applying randomization and encryption to the text, whereas block ciphers use an S-box method. In OFB and CFB modes, the DES block cipher crosses the line between block cipher and stream cipher and uses a keystream for encryption and decryption purposes. The differences between how CFB and OFB work are illustrated in Figure 8-18.

References

Cryptography: **axion.physics.ubc.ca/crypt.html**

Cryptography Research Inc.: **www.cryptography.com/**

Figure 8-18
CFB and OFB
modes allow a
block cipher to
emulate a stream
cipher.

Triple-DES (3DES)

We went from DES to Triple-DES (3DES), so it might seem that we skipped Double-DES. We did. Double-DES has a key length of 112 bits, but there is a specific attack against Double-DES that reduces its work factor to about the same as DES. Thus, it is no more secure than DES. So we will move on to 3DES.

Many successful attacks against DES and the realization that the useful lifetime of DES was about up brought much support for 3DES. NIST knew that a new standard had to be created, which ended up being AES, but a quick fix was needed in the meantime to provide more protection for sensitive data. The result: 3DES.

3DES uses 48 rounds in its computation, which makes it highly resistant to differential cryptanalysis and approximately 2^{56} times stronger than DES. However, because of the extra work that 3DES performs, there is a heavy performance hit. It can take up to three times longer than DES to perform encryption and decryption.

Although NIST has selected the Rijndael algorithm to replace DES as the AES, NIST and others expect 3DES to be around and used for quite some time.

3DES can work in different modes:

- DES-EEE3 uses three different keys for encryption.

- DES-EDE3 uses three different keys, and it encrypts, decrypts, and encrypts data.

- DES-EEE2 and DES-EDE2 are the same as the previous mode, but the first and third operations use the same key.

The mode that is chosen will dictate the number of keys that are used and what functions are carried out. If 3DES is working in EEE3, three keys are used and the data is

Advanced Encryption Standard (AES)

After DES was used as an encryption standard for over 20 years and it was cracked in a relatively short time, NIST decided a new standard, the Advanced Encryption Standard (AES), needed to be put into place. This decision was announced in January 1997, and a request for AES candidates was made. The AES was to be a symmetric block cipher algorithm supporting keys sizes of 128-, 192-, and 256-bit keys. The following five algorithms were the finalists:

- **MARS**   Developed by the IBM team that developed Lucifer
- **RC6**   Developed by the RSA Laboratories
- **Serpent**   Developed by Ross Anderson, Eli Biham, and Lars Knudsen
- **Twofish**   Developed by Counterpane Systems
- **Rijndael**   Developed by Joan Daemon and Vincent Rijmen

Rijndael was NIST's choice in replacing DES. It is now the algorithm that is required to protect sensitive but unclassified U.S. government information. Rijndael is a block cipher with a variable block length and key length.

encrypted, encrypted, encrypted. If EDE3 is used, then three keys are used and the data is encrypted, decrypted, and encrypted. And if the EEE2 or EDE2 is used, then only two keys are used. The first and last encryption processes use the same key.

EDE may seem a little odd at first. How much protection could be provided by encrypting something, decrypting it, and encrypting it again? The decrypting portion here is decrypted with a different key. When data is encrypted with one symmetric key and decrypted with a different symmetric key, it is jumbled even more. So the data is not actually decrypted in the middle function, it is just run through a decryption process with a different key. Pretty tricky.

IDEA

International Data Encryption Algorithm (IDEA) is a block cipher and operates on 64-bit blocks of data. The 64-bit data block is divided into 16 smaller blocks, and each has eight rounds of mathematical functions performed on it. The key is 128 bits long.

The IDEA algorithm offers different modes similar to the modes described in the DES section, but it is much harder to break than DES. IDEA is used in the PGP encryption software. It was thought to replace DES, but it is patented, meaning that licensing fees would have to be paid to use it.

Blowfish

One fish, two fish, red fish, blowfish. Response: Hmm, I thought it was blue fish.

Blowfish is a block cipher that works on 64-bit blocks of data. The key length can be up to 448 bits, and the data blocks go through 16 rounds of cryptographic functions. Bruce Schneier designed it.

RC5

RC5 is a block cipher that has a variety of parameters it can use for block size, key size, and the number of rounds used. It was created by Ron Rivest and analyzed by RSA Data Security, Inc. The block sizes used in this algorithm are usually 32, 64, or 128 bits, and the key size goes up to 2,048 bits. RC5 was patented by RSA Data Security in 1997.

Asymmetric Encryption Algorithms

Several types of asymmetric algorithms are used in the computing world today. They may have different internal mechanisms and methods, but what they have in common is that they are all asymmetric. As discussed earlier, this means that a different key is used to encrypt a message than the key that is used to decrypt the message.

RSA

Give me an R, give me an S, give me a…How do you spell "RSA" again? Answer: Sigh.

RSA, named after its inventors Ron Rivest, Adi Shamir, and Leonard Adleman, is a public key algorithm that is the most popular when it comes to asymmetric algorithms. RSA is a worldwide de facto standard and can be used for digital signatures, key exchange, and encryption. It was developed in 1978 at MIT and provides authentication as well as encryption.

The security of this algorithm comes from the difficulty of factoring large numbers. The public and private keys are functions of a pair of large prime numbers, and the necessary activities required to decrypt a message from ciphertext to plaintext using a private key is comparable to factoring a product into two prime numbers. (A prime number is a positive whole number with no proper divisors, meaning the only numbers that can divide a prime number are one and the number itself.)

One advantage of using RSA is that it can be used for encryption and digital signatures. Using its one-way function, RSA provides encryption and signature verification, and the inverse direction performs decryption and signature generation.

RSA is used in many Web browsers with the Secure Sockets Layer (SSL) protocol. PGP and government systems that use public key cryptosystems also use RSA, and indeed, RSA is used in many products that incorporate the need to have asymmetric cryptography integrated into the product.

One-Way Function   A *one-way function* is a mathematical function that is easier to compute in one direction than in the opposite direction. An analogy of this is when you drop a glass on the floor. Although dropping a glass on the floor is easy, putting all the pieces back together again to have the original glass is next to impossible. This concept is similar to how a one-way function is used in cryptography, which is what the RSA and all other asymmetric algorithms are based upon.

The easy direction of computation in the one-way function that is used in the RSA algorithm is the process of multiplying two large prime numbers. It is easy to multiply the two numbers and get the resulting product, but it is much harder to factor the product and recover the two initial large prime numbers. RSA is based on the difficulty of factoring large numbers that are the product of two large prime numbers. When there are attacks on these types of cryptosystems, the attack is not necessarily trying every possible key value, but trying to factor the large number, which will give the attacker the private key. The easy process in a one-way function is multiplying two large prime numbers, and the hard function is working backwards by figuring out the large prime numbers that were used to calculate the obtained product number.

When a user encrypts a message with a public key, this message is encoded with a one-way function (breaking a glass). This function supplies a trapdoor (knowledge of how to put the glass back together), but the only way the trapdoor can be taken advantage of is if it is known about and the correct code is applied. The private key provides this service. The private key knows about the trapdoor, it knows how to derive the original prime numbers, and has the necessary programming code to take advantage of this secret trapdoor to unlock the encoded message (reassembling the broken glass). Knowing about the trapdoor and having the correct functionality to take advantage of it make a private key a private key.

Only the corresponding Private Key will know how to open the one-way function trap door.

One-way
Function Trap Door

The crux of this section is that RSA provides security by using mathematical equations that are easy to perform one way and next to impossible to perform the other way. An attacker would have to go through a lot of work to perform the mathematical equations in reverse (which is the process of figuring out the private key).

El Gamal

El Gamal is a public key algorithm that can be used for digital signatures, encryption, and key exchange. It is not based on the difficulty of factoring large numbers, but is based on calculating discrete logarithms in a finite field.

Elliptic Curve Cryptosystems (ECCs)

Elliptic curves. That just sounds like fun.

Elliptic curves are rich mathematical structures that have shown usefulness in many different types of applications. An *Elliptic Curve Cryptosystem (ECC)* provides much of the same functionality that RSA provides: digital signatures, secure key distribution, and encryption. One differing factor is ECC's efficiency. Some devices have limited processing capacity, storage, power supply, and bandwidth like wireless devices and cellular telephones. With these types of devices, efficiency of resource use is very important. ECC provides encryption functionality requiring a smaller percentage of the resources required by RSA and other algorithms, so it is used in these types of devices.

In most cases, the longer the key length, the more protection provided, but ECC can provide the same level of protection with a key size that is smaller than what RSA requires. Because longer keys require more resources to perform mathematical tasks, the smaller keys used in ECC require fewer resources of the device.

ECC algorithm use the properties of elliptic curves. The elliptic curves provide ways of constructing groups of elements and specific rules of how the elements within these groups combine. The properties between the groups are used to build cryptographic algorithms.

References

Cryptography information: **www.cs.berkeley.edu/~daw/crypto.html**

Advanced Encryption Standard: **csrc.nist.gov/encryption/aes**

History of Cryptography: **www.sans.org/infosecFAQ/encryption/blowfish.htm**

Elliptic Curve Cryptography: **www.cryptoman.com/elliptic.htm**

Hybrid Encryption Methods

Comparisons were made between symmetric and asymmetric algorithms earlier. Because symmetric has some downfalls, surely asymmetric will be our saving grace, right? Not so fast.

Asymmetric algorithms do provide more security services than the symmetric methods. It provides authenticity and nonrepudiation when a sender encrypts some data using his private key and provides access control because only the people with the private key and corresponding public key can access the encoded data. However, asymmetric algorithms are very slow. Their algorithms are so complex and intensive that they require more system resources and take too long to encrypt and decrypt full messages.

We just can't seem to win. So we turn to a hybrid system that uses symmetric and asymmetric encryption methods together.

Asymmetric and Symmetric Used Together

Public key cryptography uses two keys (public and private) generated by an asymmetric algorithm for protecting encryption keys and key distribution, and a secret key is generated by a symmetric algorithm and used for bulk encryption. It is a hybrid use of the two different algorithms: asymmetric and symmetric. Each algorithm has its pros and cons, so using them together can bring together the best of both worlds.

How Do These Algorithms Work Together? We have established that symmetric cryptography provides limited security because two users use the same key, and although asymmetric cryptography enables the two users to use different keys, it is too slow when compared with symmetric methods. So some really smart people decided to use them together to accomplish a high level of security in an acceptable amount of time.

In the hybrid approach, the two technologies are used in a complementary manner, with each performing a different function. A symmetric algorithm creates keys that are used for encrypting bulk data, and an asymmetric algorithm creates keys that are used for automated key distribution.

When a symmetric key is used for bulk data encryption, this key is used to encrypt the message you want to send. When your friend gets the message you encrypted, you want him to be able to decrypt it. So you need to send him the necessary key to use to decrypt the message. You do not want this key to travel unprotected, because if the message were intercepted and the key were not protected, an evildoer could intercept the message that contains the necessary key to decrypt your message and read your information. If the symmetric key that is needed to decrypt your message is not protected, there is no use encrypting the message in the first place. So we use an asymmetric algorithm to encrypt the symmetric key, as depicted in Figure 8-19. Why do we use the symmetric key on the message and the asymmetric key on the symmetric key? We said earlier that the asymmetric algorithm takes longer because the math is more complex. Because your message is

Figure 8-19
In a hybrid system, the asymmetric key is used to encrypt the symmetric key, and the symmetric key is used to encrypt the message.

Message and key will be sent to receiver.

Symmetric key encrypted with an asymmetric key

Message encrypted with symmetric key

Receiver decrypts and retrieves the symmetric key, then uses this symmetric key to decrypt the message.

most likely going to be longer than the length of the key, we use the faster algorithm on the message (symmetric) and the slower algorithm on the key (asymmetric).

How does this actually work? Let's say Bill is sending Paul a message that Bill wants only Paul to be able to read. Bill encrypts his message with a secret key, so now Bill has ciphertext and a secret key. The key needs to be protected, so Bill encrypts the secret key with an asymmetric key. Remember that asymmetric algorithms use private and public keys, so Bill will encrypt the secret key with Paul's public key. Now Bill has ciphertext from the message and ciphertext from the secret key. Why did Bill encrypt the secret key with Paul's public key instead of his own private key? Because if Bill encrypted it with his own private key, then anyone with Bill's public key could decrypt it and retrieve the secret key. However, Bill does not want anyone who has his public key to read his message to Paul. Bill only wants Paul to be able to read it. So Bill encrypts the secret key with Paul's public key. If Paul has done a good job protecting his private key, he will be the only one who can read Bill's message.

Paul receives Bill's message and Paul uses his private key to decrypt the secret key. Paul then uses the secret key to decrypt the message. Paul then reads Bill's very important and confidential message that asks Paul how his day is.

Now when I say that Bill is using this key to encrypt and that Paul is using that key to decrypt, those two individuals do not necessarily need to find the key on their hard drive and know how to properly apply it. We have software to do this for us—thank goodness.

If this is your first time with these issues, don't worry. I remember when I first started with these concepts, and they turned my brain into a pretzel.

Just remember the following points:

- An asymmetric algorithm performs encryption and decryption by using public and private keys that are related to each other mathematically.

- A symmetric algorithm performs encryption and decryption by using a secret key.

- A secret key is used to encrypt the actual message.

- Public keys are used to encrypt the secret key for key distribution.

- A secret key is synonymous to a symmetric key.

- An asymmetric key refers to a public or private key.

That is how a hybrid system works. The symmetric algorithm creates a secret key that will be used to encrypt the bulk, or the message, and the asymmetric key encrypts the secret key. Table 8-1 outlines the differences between symmetric and asymmetric algorithms.

Session Keys

Hey, I have a disposable key! Response: Amazing. Now go away.

A *session key* is a secret key that is used to encrypt messages between two users. A session key is no different than the secret key that was described in the previous section, but it is only good for one communication session between users.

If Tanya had a secret key she used to encrypt messages between Lance and herself all the time, then this secret key would not be regenerated or changed. They would use the same key every time they communicated using encryption. However, using the same key repeatedly increases the chances of the key being captured and the secure communication being compromised. If, on the other hand, a new secret key were generated each time Lance and Tanya wanted to communicate, as shown in Figure 8-20, it would only be used during their one dialogue and then destroyed. If they wanted to communicate an hour later, a new session key would be created and shared.

A session key provides security because it is only valid for one session between two computers. If an attacker captured the session key, she would have a very small window of time to use it to try and decrypt messages being passed back and forth.

When two computers want to communicate using encryption, they must first go through a handshaking process. The two computers agree on the encryption algorithms

Diffie-Hellman Key Exchange

In 1976, Dr. W. Diffie and Dr. M.E. Hellman performed open research in cryptography and were the first to introduce the notion of public key cryptography. This notion allowed users to handle key distribution electronically in a secure fashion. This evolved into the Diffie-Hellman key exchange.

This method of key exchange enables users to exchange secret keys over a nonsecure medium. The Diffie-Hellman algorithm is used for key distribution, and it cannot be used to encrypt and decrypt messages or for digital signatures.

Dr. Diffie and Dr. Hellman originated the whole public key/private key concept.

Table 8-1	Attribute	Symmetric	Asymmetric
Various Characteristics Between Symmetric and Asymmetric Systems	Keys	One key is shared between two or more entities.	One entity has a public key and the other entity has a private key.
	Key exchange	Out-of-band.	Symmetric key is encrypted and sent with message; thus, the key is distributed by inbound means.
	Speed	Algorithm is less complex and faster.	Algorithm is more complex and slower.
	Use	Bulk encryption, which means encrypting files and communication paths.	Key encryption and distributing keys.
	Security service provided	Confidentiality.	Authentication and nonrepudiation.

that will be used and exchange the session key that will be used for data encryption. In a sense, the two computers set up a virtual connection between each other and are said to be in session. When this session is done, each computer tears down any data structures it built to enable this communication to take place, the resources are released, and the session key is destroyed.

Figure 8-20

A session key is generated so that all messages can be encrypted during one particular session between users.

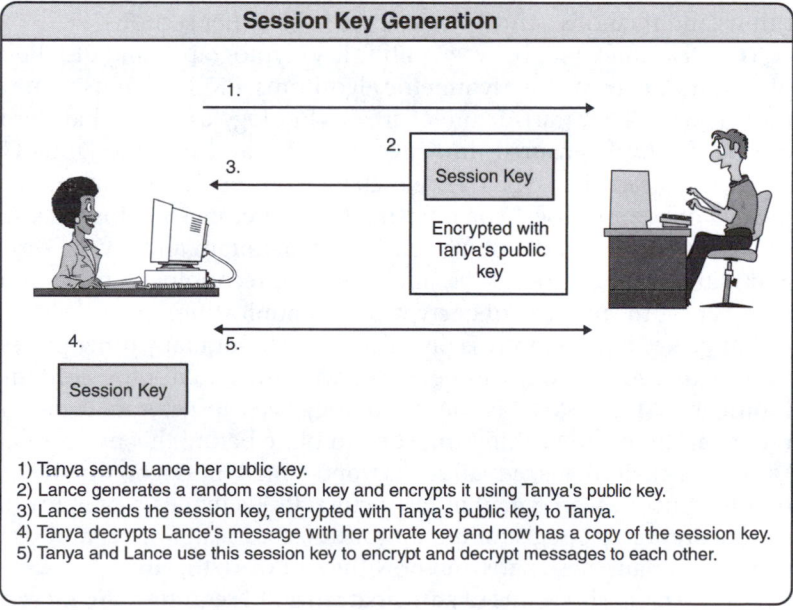

1) Tanya sends Lance her public key.
2) Lance generates a random session key and encrypts it using Tanya's public key.
3) Lance sends the session key, encrypted with Tanya's public key, to Tanya.
4) Tanya decrypts Lance's message with her private key and now has a copy of the session key.
5) Tanya and Lance use this session key to encrypt and decrypt messages to each other.

Some keys are used to encrypt data, and other types of keys are used to encrypt keys. These keys must be kept separate from each other, and neither should try to perform the other key's job. A key meant to encrypt keys should not be used to encrypt data, and no keys should appear in cleartext. This will reduce the vulnerability to certain brute force attacks.

These things are taken care of by operating systems and applications in the background, so a user would not necessarily need to be worried about using the wrong type of key for the wrong reason. The software will handle this, but it is important for security professionals to understand the difference between the key types and the issues that surround them.

Public Key Infrastructure (PKI)

Public key infrastructure (PKI) consists of programs, data formats, procedures, communication protocols, security policies, and public key cryptographic mechanisms working in a comprehensive manner to enable a wide range of dispersed people to communicate in a secure and predictable fashion. In other words, a PKI establishes a level of trust within an environment. PKI is an ISO authentication framework that uses public key cryptography and the X.509 standard protocols. The framework was set up to enable authentication to happen across different networks and the Internet. Particular protocols and algorithms are not specified, which is why PKI is called a framework and not a specific technology.

PKI provides authentication, confidentiality, nonrepudiation, and integrity of the messages exchanged. PKI is a *hybrid* system of symmetric and asymmetric key algorithms and methods, which was discussed in earlier sections.

There is a difference between public key cryptography and PKI. Public key cryptography is another name for asymmetric algorithms. PKI is what its name states—it is an infrastructure. The infrastructure of this technology assumes that the receiver's identity can be positively ensured through certificates and that the Diffie-Hellman exchange protocol (or another type of key exchange protocol) will automatically negotiate the process of key exchange. The infrastructure therefore contains the pieces that will identify users, create and distribute certificates, maintain and revoke certificates, distribute and maintain encryption keys, and enable all technologies to communicate and work together for the purpose of encrypted communication.

Public key cryptography is one piece in PKI, but many other pieces make up this infrastructure. An analogy can be drawn with the e-mail protocol Simple Mail Transfer Protocol (SMTP). SMTP is the technology used to get e-mail messages from here to there, but many other things must be in place before this protocol can be productive. We need e-mail clients, e-mail servers, and e-mail messages, which together build a type of infrastructure—an e-mail infrastructure. PKI is made up of many different parts: certificate authorities, registration authorities, certificates, keys, and users. The following sections explain these parts and how they all work together.

Each person who wants to participate in a PKI requires a *digital certificate*, which is a credential that contains the public key for that individual along with other identifying information. The certificate is created and signed (digital signature) by a trusted third party or a *certificate authority (CA)*. When the CA signs the certificate, it binds the individual's identity to the public key, and the CA takes liability for the authenticity of that public key. It is this trusted third party (the CA) that allows people who have never met to authenticate to each other and communicate in a secure method. If Kevin has never met David, but would like to communicate securely with him and they both trusted the same CA, then Kevin could retrieve David's public key from that CA and start the process.

Certificate Authorities

How do I know I can trust you? Answer: The CA trusts me.

A CA is a trusted organization that maintains and issues digital certificates. When a person requests a certificate, the registration authority (RA) verifies that individual's identity and passes the certificate request off to the CA. The CA constructs the certificate, signs it, delivers it to the requester, and maintains the certificate over its lifetime. When another person wants to communicate with this person, the CA will basically vouch for that person's identity. When David receives a message from Kevin, which contains Kevin's public key, David will go back to the CA and basically say, "Hey, is this guy really Kevin Chiasson?" The CA will look in its database and reply, "Yep, that's him, and his certificate is valid." Then David feels more comfortable and allows Kevin to communicate with him.

Certificate Authority

Dave and Kevin trust each other indirectly.

Kevin trusts the
CA

Dave trusts the
CA

The CA can be internal to an organization. Such a setup would enable the company to control the CA server, configure how authentication will take place, maintain the certificates, and recall certificates when necessary. Other CAs are organizations dedicated to this type of service, and other individuals and companies pay them to supply it.

Some well-known CAs are Entrust and VeriSign. Many browsers have several well-known CAs configured by default, so the user does not need to figure out how to contact the CA and go through the processes of verifying other users' certificates. It is all handled in the background processing of the Web browser.

The CA is responsible for creating and handing out certificates, maintaining them, and revoking them if necessary. Revocation is handled by the CA and stored on a *certificate revocation list (CRL)*. This is a list of every certificate that has been revoked. This list is maintained and updated periodically. A certificate may be revoked because the key holder's private key was compromised or because the CA discovered that the certificate was issued to the wrong person. An analogy to the use of a CRL is how a driver's license is used by a police officer. If an officer pulls over Sean for speeding, the officer will ask to see Sean's license. The officer will then run a check on the license to find out if Sean is wanted for any other infractions of the law and to verify that the license has not expired. The same thing happens when a person checks with a CA pertaining to another's certificate. If the certificate became invalid for some reason, the CRL is the mechanism for the CA to let others know this information.

Certificates

One of the most important pieces of a PKI is its public key certificate. A *certificate* is the mechanism used to associate a public key with a collection of components sufficient to uniquely authenticate the claimed owner. Each certificate has a unique serial number within the CA, which binds that certificate to its particular owner. The standard for how the CA creates the certificate is X.509, which dictates the different fields used in the certificate and the valid values that can populate those fields. We are currently at version 3 of this standard, which is often denoted as X.509v3. Many cryptographic protocols use this type of certificate, including SSL.

The certificate includes the serial number, version number, identity information, algorithm information, lifetime dates, and the signature of the issuing authority, as shown in Figure 8-21.

Registration Authority

The *registration authority (RA)* performs the certification registration duties. The RA establishes and confirms the identity of an individual, initiates the certification process with a CA on behalf of an end user, and performs certificate life cycle management functions. The RA cannot issue certificates, but can act as a middleman between the user and the CA. When new certificates are needed, users will make requests to the RA, and the RA verifies all necessary identification information before a request to the CA can be made.

PKI Steps

Now that we know some of the main pieces of a PKI and how they actually work together, let's walk through an example.

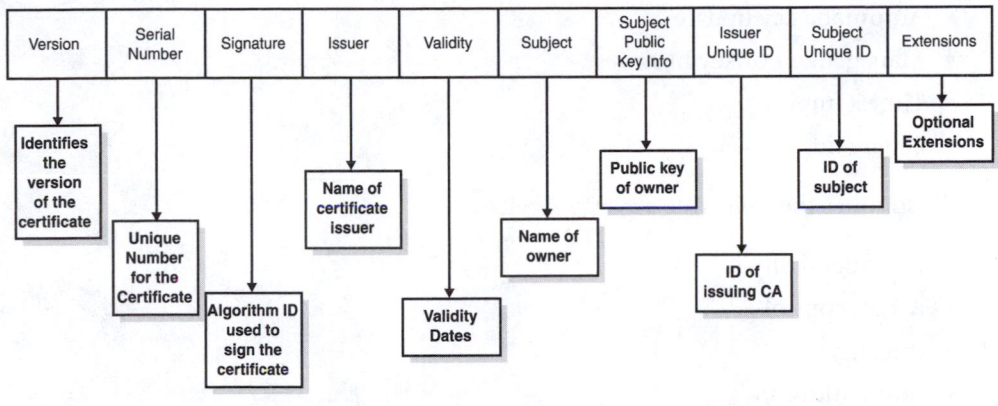

Figure 8-21 Each certificate has a structure with all the necessary identifying information in it.

John needs to obtain a digital certificate for himself so that he can participate in a PKI, so he makes a request to the RA. The RA requests certain identification from John, like a copy of his driver's license, his phone number, address, and other identification information. Once the RA receives the required information from John and verifies it, the RA sends his certificate request to the CA. The CA creates a certificate with John's public key and identity information embedded. (The private/public key pair is either generated by the CA or on John's machine, which depends on the systems' configurations. If it is created at the CA, his private key needs to be sent to him by secure means. In most cases the user generates this pair and sends in his public key during the registration process.) Now John is registered and can participate in a PKI. John decides he wants to communicate with Diane, so he requests Diane's public key from a public directory. The directory, sometimes called a repository, sends Diane's public key, and John uses this to encrypt a session key that will be used to encrypt their messages. John sends the encrypted session key to Diane. John then sends his certificate, containing his public key, to Diane. When Diane receives John's certificate, her browser looks to see if it trusts the CA that digitally signed this certificate. Diane's browser trusts this CA, and she makes a request to the CA to see if this certificate is still valid. The CA responds that the certificate is valid, so Diane decrypts the session key with her private key. Now they can both communicate using encryption. These concepts are shown in Figure 8-22.

PKI may be made up of the following entities and functions:

- CA
- RA
- Certificate repository
- Certificate revocation system
- Key backup and recovery system

- Automatic key update
- Management of key histories
- Timestamping
- Client-side software

PKI supplies the following security services:

- Confidentiality
- Access control
- Integrity
- Authentication
- Nonrepudiation

References

Public Key Infrastructure (PKI): **www.pki-page.org**

Cryptography info: **www.nwfusion.com/research/crypto.html**

Figure 8-22
CA and user
relationships

Message Integrity

My message was altered, thus it has character flaws. Response: So do you.

Cryptography can detect if a message has been modified in an unauthorized manner in a couple of ways. The first way is that the message will usually not decrypt properly if parts of it have been changed. The same type of issue happens in compression. If a file is compressed and then some of the bits are modified, either intentionally or accidentally, many times the file cannot be uncompressed because it cannot be successfully transformed from one form to another. But encryption algorithms have been built to encrypt and decrypt data, not necessarily to look out for integrity issues, so other types of algorithms have been created that deal specifically with integrity.

Parity bits have been used in protocols to detect modifications in streams of bits as they are passed from one computer to another, but parity bits can usually only detect unintentional modifications. Unintentional modifications can happen if there is a spike in the power supply, if there is interference or attenuation on a wire, or if some other type of physical condition occurs that causes the corruption of bits as they travel from one destination to another. Parity bits cannot identify if a message was captured by an intruder, altered, and then sent on to the intended destination. The intruder can just recalculate a new parity value that includes his changes, and the receiver would never know the difference. For this type of protection, hash algorithms are required to successfully detect intentional and unintentional unauthorized modifications to data.

One-Way Hash

Now, how many times does the one-way hash run again? Answer: One, brainiac.

A **one-way hash** is a function that takes a variable-length string, a message, and produces a fixed-length value called a hash value that represents that original data. A hash value is also called a **message digest**. I know, more confusing names!

The reason to go through these steps is to create a fingerprint of this message. Just as fingerprints can be used to identify individuals, hash values can be used to identify a specific message or piece of data. If Kevin wants to send a message to Maureen, and he wants to ensure that the message does not get altered in an unauthorized fashion while it is being transmitted, he would calculate a hash value for the message and append it to the message itself. When Maureen receives the message, she performs the same hashing function Kevin used and compares her result with the hash value that was sent with the message. If the two values are the same, Maureen can be sure that the message was not altered during transmission. If the two values are different, Maureen knows that the message was altered, either intentionally or unintentionally, and she discards the message.

The hashing function is not a secret—it is publicly known. The secrecy of the one-way hashing function is its "one-wayness." The function is only run in one direction, not the other direction. This is different than the one-way function used in public key cryptography. In public key cryptography, the security is provided because it is very hard, without knowing a trapdoor, to perform the one-way function backwards on a message and come up with readable plaintext. However, one-way hash functions are never used in reverse; they create a hash value and call it a day. The receiver does not attempt to reverse the process at the other end, but instead runs the same hashing function one way and compares the two results. (Several hashing algorithms are described in the section "Various Hashing Algorithms.")

The hashing one-way function takes place without the use of any keys. This means that if Cheryl writes a message, calculates a message digest, appends the digest to the message, and sends it on to Scott, Bruce can intercept this message. Bruce can alter Cheryl's message and recalculate another message digest, append it to the message, and send it on to Scott. When Scott receives it, he verifies the message digest, but never knows that the message was actually altered by Bruce. Scott thinks the message came straight from Cheryl and that it was never modified. Now if Cheryl wanted more protection than this, she would need to use something different than just a hashing algorithm—she would need to use *message authentication code (MAC)*.

If Cheryl used MAC instead, a symmetric key would be concatenated with her message. Now the result of this process would be put through a hashing algorithm, and the result would be a MAC value. This MAC value is then appended to her message and sent to Scott. If Bruce did intercept this message and modify it, he does not have the necessary symmetric key to create the MAC value that Scott will attempt to generate.

In Figure 8-23 we will walk through these steps.

In the top portion of this figure we see the steps of a hashing process. Here is what is going on:

1. The sender puts the message through a hashing function.

2. A message digest value is generated.

3. The message digest is appended to the message.

4. The sender sends the message to the receiver.

5. The receiver puts the message through a hashing function.

6. The receiver generates her own message digest value.

7. The receiver compares the two message digest values. If they are the same, the message has not been altered.

In the second portion of the graphic we are looking at the steps of a MAC.

1. The sender concatenates a symmetric key with the message.

2. The result is put through a hashing algorithm.

3. A MAC value is generated.

4. The MAC value is appended to the message.

5. The sender sends the message to the receiver.

6. The receiver concatenates a symmetric key with the message.

7. The receiver puts the results through a hashing algorithm and generates her own MAC value.

8. The receiver compares the two MAC values. If they are the same, the message has not been modified.

The use of the symmetric key ensures that the only person who can verify the integrity of the message is the person who has a copy of this key. No one else can verify the data's integrity, and if someone were to make a change to the data, he could not generate the MAC value the receiver would be looking for. Any modifications would be detected by the receiver.

Figure 8-23

Steps of using a hashing algorithm and MAC function

One-Way Function Used in Encryption versus One-Way Hashing

One-Way Hashing Function

- It provides integrity of a message, not confidentiality or authentication.
- The result of a one-way hash is a hashing value also referred to as a message digest.
- The hashing value is used in hashing to create a fingerprint for a message.

Message Authentication Code

- A symmetric key is combined with the message before being put through a hashing algorithm.
- It provides integrity and data origin authentication.

Now the receiver knows that the message came from whoever has the other copy of the same symmetric key, so MAC provides a form of authentication. It provides *data origin authentication*, sometimes referred to as *system authentication*. This is different than user authentication, which would require the use of a private key. A private key is bound to an individual; a symmetric key is not. DES uses MAC for data origin authentication.

Digital Signatures

To do a digital signature, do I sign my name on my monitor screen? Answer: Sure.

A digital signature is a hash value that has been encrypted with the sender's private key. The act of signing means encrypting the message's hash value with a private key, as shown in Figure 8-24.

From our previous example, if Kevin wanted to ensure that the message he sent to Maureen was not modified *and* he wants her to be sure that it came only from him, he can digitally sign the message. This means that a one-way hashing function would be run on the message, and then Kevin would encrypt that hash value with his private key.

When Maureen receives the message, she will perform the hashing function on the message and come up with her own hash value. Then she will decrypt the sent hash value with Kevin's public key. She then compares the two values, and if they are the same, she can be sure that the message was not altered during transmission. She is also sure that the message came from Kevin because the value was encrypted with his private key.

Figure 8-24
Creating a digital signature for a message

The hashing function ensures the integrity of the message, and the signing of the hash value provides authentication and nonrepudiation. The act of signing just means that the value was encrypted with a private key. The steps of a digital signature are outlined in Figure 8-25.

Figure 8-25
Steps of digital signature

We need to be clear on all the available choices within cryptography, because different steps and algorithms provide different types of security services:

- A message can be encrypted, which provides confidentiality.
- A message can be hashed, which provides integrity.
- A message can be digitally signed, which provides authentication, nonrepudiation, and integrity.
- A message can be encrypted and digitally signed, which provides confidentiality, authentication, nonrepudiation, and integrity.

Some algorithms can only perform encryption, whereas others can perform digital signatures and encryption. When hashing is involved, a hashing algorithm is used, not an encryption algorithm.

It is important to understand that all encryption algorithms cannot necessarily provide all security services. Most of these algorithms are used in some type of combination to provide all the necessary security services required of an environment.

Table 8-2 shows the services provided by the algorithms.

Digital Signature Standard (DSS)

Because digital signatures are so important in proving who sent what messages, the U.S. government decided to establish standards pertaining to their functions and acceptable use. In 1991, NIST proposed a federal standard called the Digital Signature Standard (DSS). It was developed for federal departments and agencies, but most vendors designed their products to meet these specifications also. The federal government requires its departments to use the Digital Signature Algorithm (DSA), RSA, or the elliptic curve digital signature algorithm (ECDSA) and the Secure Hash Algorithm (SHA). The SHA creates a 160-bit message digest output, which is then inputted into one of the three mentioned digital signature algorithms. The SHA is used to ensure the integrity of the message, and the other algorithms are used to digitally sign the message. This is an example of how two different algorithms are combined to provide the right combination of security services.

RSA and DSA are the best known and most widely used digital signature algorithms. Unlike RSA, DSA can only be used for digital signatures. RSA can be used for digital signatures, message encryption, *and* secure distribution of symmetric keys.

Various Hashing Algorithms

As stated in an earlier section, the goal of using a one-way hash function is to provide a fingerprint of the message. If two different messages produced the same hash value, then it would be easier for an attacker to break that security mechanism, because patterns would be revealed.

A strong one-hash function does not provide the same hash value for two or more different messages. If a hashing algorithm takes steps to ensure that it does not create the same hash value for two or more messages, it is said to be *collision free*.

Table 8-2
Various Functions
of Different
Algorithms

Algorithm Type	Encryption	Digital Signature	Hashing Function	Key Distribution
Asymmetric Key Algorithms				
RSA	x	x		x
ECC	x	x		x
Diffie-Hellman				x
El Gamal	x	x		x
Digital Signature Algorithm		x		
Symmetric Key Algorithms				
DES	x			
3DES	x			
Blowfish	x			
IDEA	x			
RC4	x			
SAFER	x			
Hashing Algorithms				
Ronald Rivest family of hashing functions: MD2, MD4, and MD5			x	
Secure Hash Algorithm (SHA)			x	
HAVAL (variable-length hash values using a one-way function design)			x	

Good cryptographic hash functions should have the following characteristics:

- The hash should be computed over the entire message.
- The hash should be a one-way function so that messages are not disclosed by their values.
- It should be impossible, given a message and its hash value, to compute another message with the same hash value.
- It should be resistant to birthday attacks, meaning an attacker should not be able to find two messages with the same hash value.

Table 8-3 and the following sections quickly describe some of the available hashing algorithms used in cryptography today.

Algorithm	Description
Message Digest 2 (MD2) algorithm	One-way function. Produces a 128-bit hash value. Much slower than MD4 and MD5.
Message Digest 4 (MD4) algorithm	One-way function. Produces a 128-bit hash value.
Message Digest 5 (MD5) algorithm	One-way function. Produces a 128-bit hash value. More complex than MD4.
HAVAL	One-way function. Variable-length hash value. Modification of MD5 algorithm and provides more protection against attacks that affect MD5.
SHA	One-way function. Produces a 160-bit hash value. Used with DSA.

Table 8-3   The Different Hashing Algorithms Available

MD4

MD4 is a one-way hash function designed by Ron Rivest. It produces 128-bit hash, or message digest, values. It is used for high-speed computation in software implementations and is optimized for microprocessors.

MD5

MD5 is the newer version of MD4. It still produces a 128-bit hash, but the algorithm is more complex, which makes it harder to break. MD5 added a fourth round of operations to be performed during the hashing functions and makes several of its mathematical operations carry out more steps or more complexity to provide a higher level of security.

MD2

MD2 is also a 128-bit one-way hash function designed by Ron Rivest. It is not necessarily any weaker than the previously mentioned hash functions, but it is much slower.

SHA

SHA was designed by NIST and NSA to be used with the DSS. The SHA was designed to be used in digital signatures and was developed when a more secure hashing algorithm was required for federal applications.

SHA produces a 160-bit hash value, or message digest. This is then inputted into the DSA, which computes the signature for a message. The message digest is signed instead of the whole message because it is a much quicker process. The sender computes a 160-bit hash value, encrypts it with his private key (signs it), appends it to the message, and sends it. The receiver decrypts the value with the sender's public key, runs the same hashing function, and compares the two values. If the values are the same, the receiver can be sure that the message has not been tampered with in transit.

SHA is similar to MD4. It has some extra mathematical functions and produces a 160-bit hash instead of 128-bit, which makes it more resistant to brute force attacks, including birthday attacks. (Birthday attacks are described in the "Attacks Against One-Way Hash Functions" section.)

HAVAL

HAVAL is a variable-length one-way hash function and is the modification of MD5. It processes message blocks twice the size of those used in MD5; thus, it processes blocks of 1,024 bits.

References

Advanced Encryption Standard: **csrc.nist.gov/encryption/aes**

Counterpane Internet Security Inc.: **www.counterpane.com**

Cryptography Search Directory: **www.the-search-directory.com/cryptography**

MD5 Message-Digest Algorithm: **theory.lcs.mit.edu/~rivest/rfc1321.txt**

Attacks Against One-Way Hash Functions

A good hashing algorithm should not produce the same hash value for two different messages. If the algorithm does produce the same value for two distinctly different messages, this is called a *collision*. If an attacker finds an instance of a collision, he has more information to use when trying to break the cryptographic methods.

A complex way of attacking a one-way hash function is called the *birthday attack*. Now hold on to your hat while we go through this—it is a bit tricky.

In standard statistics, a birthday paradox exists. It goes something like this:

> How many people must be in the same room for the chance to be greater than even that another person has the same birthday as you?
>
> **Answer:** 253
>
> How many people must be in the same room for the chance to be greater than even that at least two people share the same birthday?
>
> **Answer:** 23

This seems a bit backwards, but the difference is that in the first instance, you are looking for someone with a specific birthday date that matches yours. In the second instance, you are looking for any two people who share the same birthday. There is a higher probability of finding two people who share a birthday than you finding another person sharing your birthday—thus, the birthday paradox.

Why do we care? It can apply to cryptography also. The main way that an attacker can find the corresponding hashing value that matches a specific message is through a brute force attack. If he finds a message with a specific hash value, it is equivalent to finding someone with a specific birthday. If he finds two messages with the same hash values, it is equivalent to finding two people with the same birthday.

The output of a hashing algorithm is n, and to find a message through a brute force attack that results in a specific hash value would require hashing 2^n random messages. Then to take this one step further, finding two messages that hash to the same value would only require $2^{n/2}$ messages to be reviewed.

This means that if an attacker has one hash value and wants to find a message that hashes to that same hash value, this process could take him years. However, if he just wants to find any two messages with the same hashing value, it could take him only a couple of hours.

The hash function used in digital signatures usually uses the value of n that is large enough to make it collision free. So the MD5 algorithm that has a 128-bit output will require 2^{64} computations to break. An algorithm that has 160-bit output, like SHA1, will require 2^{80} computations to break. This means that there is a less than 1 in 2^{80} chance that someone will break an encryption system.

The main point of this paradox and this section is to show how important longer hashing values truly are. A hashing algorithm that has a larger bit output is less vulnerable to brute force attacks such as a birthday attack.

Reference

One-Way Hash FAQ: **www.stack.nl/~galactus/remailers/attack-3.html**

One-Time Pad

I want to use my one-time pad three times. Response: Not a good idea.

A **one-time pad** is a perfect encryption scheme because it is unbreakable by brute force, and each pad is used exactly once. A one-time pad uses a truly nonrepeating set of random bits that are combined bitwise using the binary XOR function. The bits of the message are XORed to the bits in the pad to generate ciphertext. The random pad is the same size as the message and is only used once. Because the entire pad is random and as long as the message, it is said to be unbreakable even with infinite resources. Each bit in the pad is XORed with each bit of the message, and this ensures that each bit is encrypted by a nonrepeating pattern of bits. The sender encrypts the message and then destroys the one-time pad. After the receiver decrypts the message, he destroys his copy of the one- time pad.

One-time pads are integrated into some applications. A pseudorandom sequence generator feeds values to the algorithm, which in turn creates the one-time pad and then XORs it to the message. A pad is unbreakable if the same pad is never used more than once and the bits used in the pad are truly random. This ensures that even if an attacker were to intercept a message, he would not be able to decrypt it without the one-time pad value. If an attacker were actually successful in intercepting a copy of the one-time pad key, it would not be useful because the pad is only good for a one-time use.

Let's walk through this. Two copies of a pad containing a set of completely random bits are created. This set contains at least as many bits as the bits in the message that is to be encrypted. The bits within the pad are produced by a secure random number generator, which can be seeded by the date, time, or other sources. The seed is the starting value, which determines all subsequent values in the sequence used to generate the one-time pad.

Figure 8-26

A one-time pad

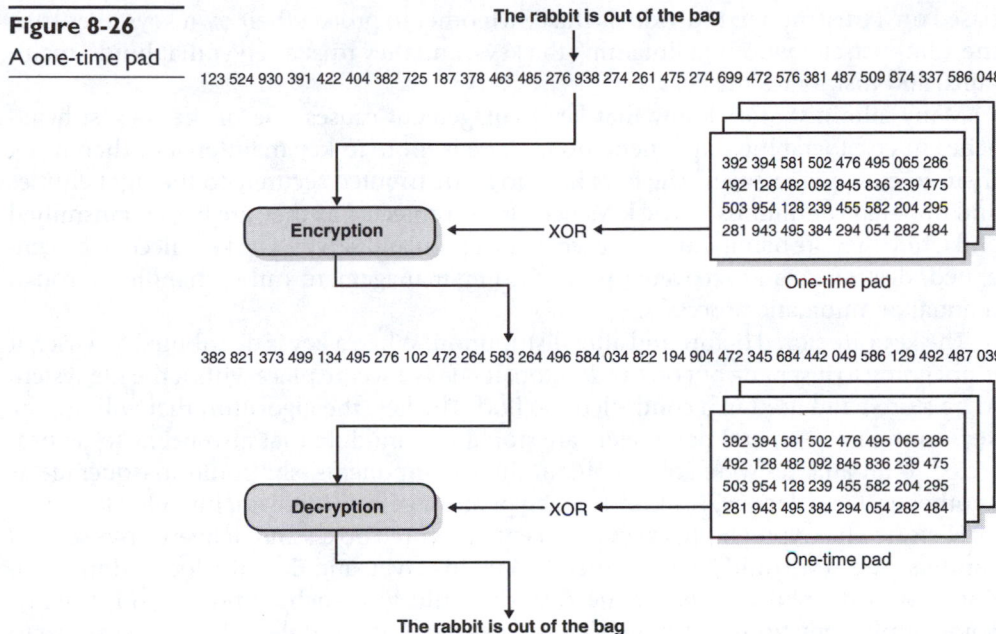

The rabbit is out of the bag

123 524 930 391 422 404 382 725 187 378 463 485 276 938 274 261 475 274 699 472 576 381 487 509 874 337 586 048

392 394 581 502 476 495 065 286
492 128 482 092 845 836 239 475
503 954 128 239 455 582 204 295
281 943 495 384 294 054 282 484

Encryption ← XOR ←

One-time pad

382 821 373 499 134 495 276 102 472 264 583 264 496 584 034 822 194 904 472 345 684 442 049 586 129 492 487 039

392 394 581 502 476 495 065 286
492 128 482 092 845 836 239 475
503 954 128 239 455 582 204 295
281 943 495 384 294 054 282 484

Decryption ← XOR ←

One-time pad

The rabbit is out of the bag

Although this approach to encryption can provide a very high degree of security, it is impractical in most situations because it is difficult to distribute the pads to all the necessary parties. Each possible pair of entities that might want to communicate in this fashion must receive the pad that is as long, or longer, than the actual message in a secure fashion. This type of key management can be overwhelming and require more overhead than it is worth. The distribution of the pad can be challenging, and the sender and receiver must be perfectly synchronized so that each is using the same pad. The steps of encryption using a one-time pad are shown in Figure 8-26.

Key Management

I am the manager of all keys! Response: I am sorry.

Cryptography can be used as a security mechanism to provide confidentiality, integrity, and authentication, but not if the keys are compromised in any way. The keys can be captured, modified, corrupted, or disclosed to unauthorized individuals. Cryptography is based on a trust model. Individuals trust each other to protect their own keys, they trust the administrator who is maintaining the keys, and they trust a server that holds, maintains, and distributes the keys.

Many administrators know that key management causes one of the biggest headaches in cryptographic implementation. There is more to key maintenance than using them to encrypt messages. The keys have to be distributed securely to the right entities and updated continuously. The keys need to be protected as they are being transmitted and while they are being stored on each workstation and server. The keys need to be generated, destroyed, and recovered properly. Key management can be handled through manual or automatic processes.

The keys are stored before and after distribution. When a key is distributed to a user, it is not going to just hang out on the desktop; it needs a secure place within the file system to be stored and used in a controlled method. The key, the algorithm that will use the key, configurations, and parameters are stored in a module that also needs to be protected. If an attacker were able to obtain these components, she could masquerade as another user and decrypt, read, and reencrypt messages that were not intended for her.

Historically, cryptographic keys were kept in secured boxes and delivered by escorted couriers. The keys could be distributed to a main server, and then the local administration would distribute them, or the courier would visit each computer individually. Some implementations distributed a master key to a site, and then that key was used to generate unique secret keys to be used by individuals at that location. Today most key distributions are handled by a protocol through automated means and not manually by an individual. The overhead of key management, required security level, and cost-benefit issues needs to be evaluated for a company to decide on how it will conduct key management, but overall, automation provides a more accurate and secure approach.

When using the Kerberos protocol (described in Chapter 4), a Key Distribution Center (KDC) is used to store, distribute, and maintain cryptographic session and secret keys. This method provides an automated method of key distribution. The computer that wants to access a service on another computer will request access via the KDC. The KDC then generates a session key to be used between the requesting computer and the computer providing the requested resource or service. The automation of this process reduces the possible errors that can happen through a manual process, but if the KDC gets compromised in any way, then all the computers and their services are affected and possibly compromised.

Other key exchange protocols are RSA and Diffie-Hellman, discussed earlier, and a variation of the Diffie-Hellman algorithm called the key exchange algorithm (KEA).

Unfortunately, many companies use cryptographic keys, but rarely if ever change them. This is because of the hassle of key management and because the network administrator is already overtaxed with other tasks or does not realize the task actually needs to take place. The frequency of use of a cryptographic key can have a direct correlation to how often the key should be changed. The more a key is used, the more likely it is to be captured and compromised. If a key is used infrequently, then this risk drops dramatically. The necessary level of security and the frequency of use can dictate the frequency of key updates. A mom-and-pop diner might only change their cryptography keys every six months, whereas an information warfare military unit might change them every day or every week. The important thing is that the keys are being changed in a secure method.

Key management is the most challenging part of cryptography and also the most crucial. It is one thing to develop a very complicated and complex algorithm and key method, but if the keys are not securely stored and transmitted, it does not really matter how strong the algorithm is. Keeping keys secret is a challenging task.

Key Management Principles

Keys should not be in cleartext outside the cryptography device. As stated previously, many cryptography algorithms are known publicly, which puts more stress on protecting the secrecy of the key. If attackers know how the actual algorithm works, then in many cases, all they need to figure out is the key to compromise a system. This is why keys should not be available in cleartext; the key is what brings secrecy to encryption.

These steps, and all of key distribution and maintenance, should be automated and hidden from the user. These processes should be integrated into software or the operating system. It only adds complexity and opens the doors for more errors when processes are done manually and if the process depends upon end users to perform certain functions.

Keys are at risk of being lost, destroyed, or corrupted. Backup copies should be available and easily accessible when required. If data is encrypted and then the user accidentally loses the necessary key to decrypt it, this information would be lost forever if there were not a backup key to save the day. The application being used for cryptography may have key recovery options, or it may require copies of the keys to be kept in a secure place. There are different scenarios that can show the need for key recovery or backup copies of keys. If Bob has possession of all the critical bid calculation, stock value information, and the corporate trend analysis needed for tomorrow's senior executive presentation, and Bob has an unfortunate confrontation with a bus, someone is going to need to access this data after the funeral. If an employee left the company and encrypted important documents on her computer before departing, the company would probably want to have a way to still have access to that data. Similarly, if the vice president did not know that running a large magnet over the floppy disk that holds his private key was not a good idea, he would want his key replaced immediately instead of listening to a lecture about electromagnetic fields and how they rewrite sectors on media.

Of course, having more than one key can increase the chance of disclosure, so a company needs to decide if it will have key backups and what precautions will be put into place to protect them properly. A company can choose to have multiparty control for emergency key recovery. This means that if a key needs to be recovered, more than one person is required to be involved with this process. The key recovery process could require two other individuals to present their private keys or three individuals to supply their individual PINs. These individuals should not all be members of the IT department. There should be a member from management, maybe an individual from auditing, and one individual from the IT department. All of these requirements reduce the potential for abuse and would require collusion for fraudulent activities to take place.

Rules for Keys and Key Management

- The key length should be long enough to provide the necessary level of protection.

- Keys should be stored and transmitted by secure means.

- Keys should be extremely random and use the full spectrum of the keyspace.

- The key's lifetime should correspond with the sensitivity of the data it is protecting. (Less secure data may allow for a longer key lifetime, whereas more sensitive data might require a shorter key lifetime.)

- The more the key is used, the shorter its lifetime should be.

- Keys should be backed up or escrowed in case of emergencies.

- Keys should be properly destroyed when their lifetime comes to an end.

References

Cryptography Compendium: **home.ecn.ab.ca/~jsavard**

Product Ciphers FAQ: **www.faqs.org/faqs/cryptography-faq/part05**

The Cryptography Project: **www.cs.georgetown.edu/~denning/crypto**

Cryptography A–Z: **www.ssh.fi/tech/crypto/intro.html**

Link versus End-to-End Encryption

Encryption can be performed at two communication levels, each with different types of protection and implications. These two general modes of encryption implementation are link and end-to-end. *Link encryption* encrypts all the data along a specific communication path as in a satellite link, T3 line, or telephone circuit. Not only is the user information encrypted, but the header, trailers, addresses, and routing data that are part of the packets are also encrypted. The only traffic that is not encrypted in this technology is the data link control messaging information, which includes instructions and parameters that the different link devices use to synchronize communication methods. Link encryption provides extra protection against packet sniffers and eavesdroppers. In *end-to-end encryption*, the headers, addresses, routing, and trailer information are not encrypted, enabling attackers to learn more about a captured packet and where it is headed.

Link encryption, which is sometimes called online encryption, is usually provided by service providers and is incorporated into network protocols. All of the information is encrypted, and the packets have to be decrypted at each hop so the router, or other intermediate device, knows where to send the packet next. The router must decrypt the header portion of the packet, read the routing and address information within the header, and then reencrypt it and send it on its way.

With end-to-end encryption, the packets do not need to be decrypted and then encrypted again at each hop because the headers and trailers are not encrypted. The devices in between the origin and destination just read the necessary routing information and pass the packets on their way. Although link encryption provides extra protection as it travels though the communication path, it does expose the packets' headers at each hop that has to decrypt it. There is always a little bad with the good, isn't there?

End-to-end encryption is usually initiated by the user of the originating computer. It provides more flexibility for the user to be able to determine if certain messages will get encrypted or not. It is called "end-to-end" because the message stays encrypted from one end of its journey to the other. Link encryption has to decrypt the packets at every computer between the two ends.

Encryption can happen at the highest or the lowest levels of the OSI model. If the encryption happens at the lower layers, then it is link encryption; at the higher levels, it is considered end-to-end encryption.

Link encryption is at the data link and the physical layers, as depicted in Figure 8-27. Hardware encryption devices interface with the physical layer and encrypt all data that passes through them. All data, routing, and protocol information is encrypted through these devices if link encryption is in place. Because no part of the data is available to an attacker, she cannot learn basic information about how data flows through the environment. This is referred to as *traffic-flow security*.

NOTE A hop is a computer that helps a packet reach its destination. It is usually a router that looks at the packet address to determine where the packet needs to go next. Packets usually go through many hops between the sending and receiving computers.

Figure 8-27
Link and end-to-end encryption happen at different OSI layers.

Encryption can take place within software or through specialized devices. If a device is going to encrypt the data, then the computer sends its data to the specialized hardware device for encryption before sending it to the lower layers of communication to prepare for transmission.

The following section outlines the advantages and disadvantages of end-to-end and link encryption methods.

Advantages of end-to-end encryption include the following:

- It protects information from start to finish throughout the network.
- It provides more flexibility to the user in choosing what gets encrypted and how.
- Higher granularity of encryption is available because each application or user can use a different key.
- Each hop computer on the network does not need to have a key to decrypt each packet.

Disadvantages of end-to-end encryption include the following:

- Headers, addresses, and routing information are not encrypted, and therefore not protected.
- The destination system needs to have the same encryption mechanisms to properly decrypt the message.

Advantages of link encryption include the following:

- All data is encrypted, including headers, addresses, and routing information.
- Users do not need to do anything to initiate it; it works at a lower layer in the OSI model.

Disadvantages of link encryption include the following:

- Key distribution and management is more complex because each hop device must receive a key, and when the keys change, each must be updated.
- Messages are decrypted at each hop; thus, there are more points of vulnerability.

Reference

Some Fundamentals of Cryptography: **www.rand.org/publications/RM/ RM3765/RM3765.chapter3.html**

Hardware versus Software Cryptography Systems

Encryption can be done through software or hardware, and there are trade-offs with each. Generally, software is less expensive and provides a slower throughput than hardware mechanisms. Software cryptography methods can be more easily modified and disabled compared with hardware systems, but it depends on the application and the hardware product.

If a company needs to perform high-end encryption functions at a higher speed, the company will most likely implement a hardware solution.

E-mail Standards

Just like in other types of technologies, cryptography has industry standards and de facto standards. Standards are necessary because they help ensure interoperability among vendor products. Standards usually mean that a certain technology has been under heavy scrutiny and properly tested and accepted by many similar technology communities. A company will still need to decide on what type of standard to follow and what type of technology to implement.

The goals of the technology need to be evaluated and a cost-benefit analysis needs to be performed on the competing standards and products within the chosen standards. For cryptography implementation, the company would need to decide on what needs to be protected by encryption, if digital signatures are necessary, how key management should take place, what type of resources are available to implement and maintain the technology, and what the overall cost will amount to.

If a company only needs to encrypt some e-mail messages here and there, then PGP may be the best choice. If the company wants all data encrypted as it goes throughout the network and to sister companies, then a link encryption implementation may be the best choice. If a company wants to implement a single sign-on environment where users need to authenticate to use different services and functionality throughout the network, then implementing a PKI or Kerberos might serve them best. Each type of technology and standard should be understood to help make the most informative decision, and each competing product within the chosen technology should be researched and tested before making the final purchase. Cryptography can be a complicated subject, and so is implementing and maintaining it. Doing homework versus buying into buzzwords and flashy products might help a company reduce its headaches down the road.

The following sections briefly describe some of the most popular e-mail standards in use.

MIME

Multipurpose Internet Mail Extension (MIME) is a technical specification indicating how multimedia data and e-mail attachments are to be transferred. The Internet has mail standards that dictate how mail is to be formatted, encapsulated, transmitted, and opened. If a message or document contains a multimedia attachment, MIME dictates how that portion of the message should be handled.

When a user requests a file from a Web server that contains an audio clip, graphic, or some other type of multimedia component, the server will send the file with a header that describes the file type. For example, the header might indicate that the MIME type is Image and the subtype is jpeg. Although this will be in the header, many times systems also use the file's extension to identify the MIME type. So in our example, the file's name might be stuff.jpeg. The user's system will see the extension jpeg, or see the data in the header field, and look in its association list to see what program it needs to initialize to open this particular file. If the system has JPEG files associated with the Explorer application, then Explorer will open and present the picture to the user.

Sometimes systems either do not have an association for a specific file type or do not have the helper program necessary to review and use the contents of the file. When a file has an unassociated icon assigned to it, it might require the user to choose the Open With command and choose an application in the list to associate this file with that program. So when the user double-clicks on that file, the associated program will initialize and present the file. If the system does not have the necessary program, the Web site might offer the necessary helper program, like Acrobat or an audio program that plays wave files.

MIME is a specification that dictates how certain file types should be transmitted and handled. This specification has several types and subtypes, enables different computers to exchange data in varying formats, and provides a standardized way of presenting the data. So if Sean views a funny picture that is in GIF format, he can be sure that when he sends it to Debbie, it will look exactly the same.

S/MIME

Secure MIME (S/MIME) is a standard for encrypting and digitally signing electronic mail that contains attachments and for providing secure data transmissions. S/MIME extends the MIME standard by allowing for the encryption of e-mail and attachments. The encryption and hashing algorithms can be specified by the user of the mail package instead of having it dictated to them.

S/MIME provides confidentiality through the user's encryption algorithm, integrity through the user's hashing algorithm, authentication through the use of X.509 public key certificates, and nonrepudiation through cryptographically signed messages.

Privacy-Enhanced Mail

Privacy-Enhanced Mail (PEM) is an Internet standard to provide secure e-mail over the Internet and for in-house communication infrastructures. The protocols within PEM provide authentication, message integrity, encryption, and key management. This standard was developed to provide compatibility with many types of key-management processes and symmetric and public key methods of encryption.

PEM is a series of message authentication and encryption procedures developed by several governing groups. PEM can use DES for encryption and RSA for sender authentication and key management. It also provides support for nonrepudiation. The following are specific components that can be used in PEM:

- Messages encrypted with DES in CBC mode
- Public key management provided using RSA
- X.509 standard used for certification structure and format

PEM has not caught on to the extent that the developers planned. The main issue is that PEM provides too much structure for different environments that require more flexibility in their secure communication infrastructure.

Message Security Protocol

The military has their own way to secure messages. Response: They have their own way of doing most things.

The *Message Security Protocol (MSP)* is the military's PEM. It was developed by the NSA and is an X.400-compatible application-level protocol used to secure e-mail messages. MSP can sign and encrypt messages and perform hashing functions. Like PEM, applications that incorporate MSP enable different algorithms and parameters to be used to provide greater flexibility.

References

Encryption and Security Tutorial: **www.cs.auckland.ac.nz/~pgut001/tutorial**

Secure Electronic Commerce System: **www.informweb.com/webportal/ articles/tosecs.htm**

Pretty Good Privacy (PGP)

Pretty Good Privacy (PGP) was designed by Phil Zimmerman as a freeware e-mail security program and released in 1991. It was the first widespread public key encryption program. PGP is a complete working system that uses cryptographic protection to protect e-mail and files. It can use RSA public key encryption for key management and IDEA symmetric cipher for bulk encryption of data, although the user has the option of picking different types of algorithms for these functions. PGP can provide confidentiality through the IDEA encryption algorithm, integrity by using the MD5 hashing algorithm, authentication by using the public key certificates, and nonrepudiation through the use of cryptographically signed messages. PGP uses its own type of digital certificates rather than what is used in PKI, but they both have similar purposes.

The user's private key is generated and encrypted when the application asks the user to randomly type on her keyboard for a specific amount of time. Instead of using passwords, PGP uses passphrases. The passphrase is used to encrypt the user's private key that is stored on her hard drive.

PGP does not use a hierarchy of CAs, or any type of formal trust certificates, but relies on a "web of trust" in its key management approach. Each user generates and distributes his or her public key, and users sign each other's public keys, which creates a community of users who trust each other. This is different than the CA approach where no one trusts each other; they only trust the CA.

For example, if Mark and Mike want to communicate using PGP, Mark can give his public key to Mike. Mike signs Mark's key and keeps a copy for himself. Then Mike gives a copy of his public key to Mark so they can start communicating securely. Later, Mark would like to communicate with Joe, but Joe does not know Mark, and does not know if he can trust him. Mark sends Joe his public key, which has been signed by Mike. Joe has Mike's public key, because they have communicated before, and trusts Mike. Because Mike signed Mark's public key, Joe now also trusts Mark and sends his public key and begins communicating with him.

So basically it is a system of "I don't know you, but my buddy Mike says you are an alright guy, so I will trust you on behalf of Mike's word."

Each user keeps a collection of signed public keys he has received from other users in a file referred to as a *key ring*. Each key in that ring has a parameter that indicates the level of trust assigned to that user and the validity of that particular key. If Steve has known Liz for many years and trusts her, he might have a higher level of trust indicated on her stored public key than Tom, whom he does not trust much at all. There is also a field indicating who can sign other keys within Steve's realm of trust. If Steve receives a key from someone he doesn't know, like Kevin, and the key is signed by Liz, he can look at the field that pertains to whom he trusts to sign other people's keys. If the field indicates that Steve trusts Liz enough to sign another person's key, then Steve will accept Kevin's key and communicate with him because Liz is vouching for him.

However, if Steve receives a key from Kevin and it is signed by untrustworthy Tom, then Steve might choose to not trust Kevin and not communicate with him.

These fields are available for updating and alteration. If one day Steve really gets to know Tom and finds out he is okay after all, he can modify these parameters within PGP and give Tom more trust when it comes to cryptography and secure communication.

Because the web of trust does not have a central leader, like a CA, certain standardized functionality is harder to accomplish. If Steve were to lose his private key, anyone else trusting his public key would have to be notified that it should no longer be trusted. In a PKI, Steve would only need to notify the CA, and anyone attempting to verify the validity of Steve's public key would be told not to trust it when the other users contacted the CA. This is carried out by PKI's CRL functionality. In the PGP world, this is not as centralized and organized. Steve can send out a key revocation certificate, but there is no guarantee that it will reach each user's key ring file.

PGP is a public domain software that uses public key cryptography. It has not been endorsed by the NSA, but because it is a great product and free for individuals to use, it has become somewhat of an encryption standard on the Internet.

 NOTE PGP is considered a cryptosystem because it has all the necessary components: symmetric key algorithms, asymmetric key algorithms, message digest algorithms, keys, protocols, and the necessary software components.

References

Distribution Center for PGP: **web.mit.edu/network/pgp.html**

How PGP Works: **www.pgpi.org/doc/pgpintro**

Cryptography Systems: **axion.physics.ubc.ca/crypt.html**

International PGP Home Page: **www.pgpi.org**

Internet Security

Is the Internet tied up into a Web? Answer: Well, kind of.

The Web is not the Internet. The Web runs on top of the Internet, in a sense. The Web is the collection of Hypertext Transfer Protocol (HTTP) servers that hold and process Web sites that we see. The Internet is the collection of physical devices and communication protocols used to transverse these Web sites and interact with them. (These issues were touched upon in Chapter 2.) The Web sites look the way they look because the creator used a language that dictates the look, feel, and functionality of the page. The Web browser lets users read Web pages by enabling them to request and accept Web pages via HTTP, and the user's browser converts the language (HTML, DHTML, and XML) into a format that can be viewed on the monitor. The browser is the user's window to the World Wide Web.

Browsers can understand a variety of protocols and have the capability to process many types of commands, but they do not understand them all. For the protocols or commands they do not know how to process, the user must download a viewer or plug-in. This is a quick and easy way to expand the functionality of the browser by installing a modular component of code that integrates itself into the system or browser. This has caused serious security compromises because the payload of the module can easily carry viruses and malicious software that the users do not know about until it is already installed and has started to do damage.

Start with the Basics

Why do we connect to the Internet? This is a basic question at first, but as we dive deeper into the question, the complexity creeps in. We connect to download MP3s, check e-mail, order security books, look at Web sites, communicate with friends, and much more. But what are we really doing? We are using services provided by a computer's protocols and software. The services can be file transferring provided by FTP, remote connectivity provided by Telnet, Internet connectivity provided by HTTP, secure connections provided by SSL, and much, much more. Without these protocols, there would be no way to even connect to the Internet.

Management needs to decide what functionality employees should have pertaining to Internet use, and the administrator needs to implement these decisions by controlling services that can be used inside and outside the network. There are different ways of restricting services: allow certain services to only run on a particular system and restrict access to that system, employ a secure version of a service, filter the use of services, or block them altogether. These choices will determine how secure the site will be and indicate what type of technology is needed to provide this type of protection.

HTTP

TCP/IP is the protocol suite of the Internet, and HTTP is the protocol of the Web. HTTP sits on top of TCP/IP. When a user clicks her mouse on a link within a Web page, her browser uses HTTP to send a request to the Web server hosting that Web site. The Web server finds the corresponding file to that link and sends it to the user via HTTP. So where is TCP/IP in all of this? The TCP protocol controls the handshaking and maintaining the connection between the user and the server, and the IP protocol makes sure that it is routed properly throughout the Internet to get from the Web server to the user. So the IP protocol finds the way to get from A to Z, TCP makes sure that the origin and destination are correct and that no packets are lost along the way, and upon arrival at the destination, HTTP presents the payload, which is a Web page.

HTTP is a stateless protocol, which means the client and Web server make and break a connection for each operation. When a user requests to view a Web site, that Web server finds the requested Web site, presents it to the user, and then terminates the connection. If the user requests a link within the newly received Web page, a new connection has to be set up, the request goes to the Web server, and the Web server sends the requested item and breaks the connection. The Web server never "remembers" the users that ask for different Web pages. This is done because for the Web server to have to remember and keep track of these connections would require it to use and commit a lot of resources.

S-HTTP

Secure Hypertext Transport Protocol (S-HTTP) is HTTP with added-on security features. It was developed to provide secure communication between a client and a server over the Internet. The client and server both have a list of cryptographic preferences and keying material. When a client makes a request to a server and the server deems that this type of communication should be protected, the server will query the client about the type of encryption methods it is configured to use. Once the client and server agree upon a specific encryption method, the client sends the server its public key. The server generates a session key, encrypts the session key with the client's public key, and sends it back. From here on out, the client and server encrypt their messages with the newly calculated session key.

S-HTTP can also provide data integrity and sender authentication capabilities. S-HTTP computes a hash value of the message, and the value can then be digitally signed. It was stated earlier that HTTP is a stateless protocol, meaning that after an operation is complete, the connection is terminated. This is not the case with S-HTTP because it would require too much overhead if the client and server had to handshake and agree upon security parameters for each and every operation.

S-HTTP can support multiple encryption modes and types. It can use public key technology, PEM, and symmetric key encryption. S-HTTP does not require the client to obtain a public key certificate if symmetric session key operations are allowed. This is a much less secure way of communicating, but it shows the flexibility of S-HTTP.

HTTPS

There is a difference between S-HTTP and HTTPS. S-HTTP is a technology that protects each message that is sent between two computers. *HTTPS* protects the communication channel between two computers, messages and all. HTTPS uses SSL and HTTP to provide a protected circuit between a client and server. So S-HTTP is used if an individual message needs to be encrypted, but if all information that passes between two computers needs to be encrypted, then HTTPS is used, which is SSL over HTTP.

SSL

Secure Sockets Layer (SSL) is similar to S-HTTP, but it protects a communication channel instead of individual messages. It uses public key encryption and provides data encryption, server authentication, message integrity, and optional client authentication. When a client accesses a Web site, it is possible for that Web site to have secured and public portions. The secured portion would require the user to be authenticated in some fashion. When the client goes from a public page on the Web site to a secured page, the Web server will start the necessary tasks to invoke SSL and protect this type of communication.

The server sends a message back to the client indicating that a secure session needs to be established, and the client sends its security parameters. The server compares those security parameters to its own until it finds a match. This is the handshaking phase. The server authenticates to the client by sending it a digital certificate, and if the client decides to trust the server, the process continues. The server can require the client to send over a digital certificate for mutual authentication, but that is rare.

The client generates a session key and encrypts it with the server's public key. This encrypted key is sent to the Web server, and they both use this symmetric key to encrypt the data they send back and forth. This is how the secure channel is established.

Just like S-HTTP, SSL keeps the communication path open until one of the parties requests to end the session. The session is usually ended when the client sends the server a FIN packet, which is an indication to close out the channel.

SSL protocol requires an SSL-enabled server and browser. SSL will provide security for the connection, but does not provide security for the data once it is received. This means the data is encrypted while it is being transmitted, but once it is received by a computer, it is no longer encrypted. So if a user sends bank account information to a financial institution via a connection protected by SSL, that communication path is protected, but the user must trust the financial institution that receives this information because at this point, SSL's job is done.

The user can verify a secure connection by looking at the URL to see that it includes "https://." The same is true for a padlock or key icon, depending on the browser type, at the bottom corner of the browser window.

In the protocol stack, SSL lies beneath the application layer and above the network layer. This ensures that SSL is not limited to specific application protocols and can still use the communication transport standards of the Internet. Different books and technical resources place SSL at different layers of the OSI model, which may seem confusing at first. But the OSI model is a conceptual construct that is trying to describe the reality of networking. This is like trying to draw nice neat boxes around life; some things don't fit perfectly and hang over the sides. SSL is actually made up of two protocols: one works at the lower end of the session layer, and the other works at the top of the transport layer. This is why one resource will state that SSL works at the session layer and another resource puts it in the transport layer. For our purpose, which is to pass the CISSP exam, the SSL protocol works at the transport layer.

Although SSL is almost always used with HTTP, it can be used with other types of protocols. So if you see a common protocol that is followed by an *s*, that protocol is using SSL to encrypt its data.

References

S/MIME and OpenPGP: **www.imc.org/smime-pgpmime.html**

Security Issues in WWW: **nsi.org/Library/Internet/security.htm**

Security Links: **www.ece.umn.edu/users/kjhan/security**

SET

Secure Electronic Transaction (SET) is a security technology proposed by Visa and MasterCard to allow for more secure credit card transaction possibilities than what is currently available. SET has been waiting in the wings for full implementation and acceptance as a standard for quite some time. Although SET provides an effective way of transmitting credit card information, businesses and users do not see it as efficient because it requires more parties to coordinate their efforts, more software installation and configuration for each entity involved, and more effort and cost than the widely used SSL method.

SET is a cryptographic protocol and infrastructure developed to send encrypted credit card numbers over the Internet. The following entities would be involved with a SET transaction, which would cause each of them to upgrade their software and possibly hardware:

- **Issuer—cardholder's bank**   Financial institution that provides a credit card to individual
- **Cardholder**   Individual authorized to use credit card
- **Merchant**   Entity providing goods
- **Acquirer—merchant's bank**   Financial institution that processes payment cards
- **Payment gateway**   Processes merchant payment. Can be acquirer

To use SET, a user must enter her credit card number into her electronic wallet software. This information will be stored on the user's hard drive or on a smart card. The software will then create a public and private key used specifically for encrypting financial information before it is sent.

Let's say Tanya wants to buy her mother a gift from a Web site using her electronic wallet. When she finds the perfect gift and decides to purchase it, her encrypted credit card information is sent to the merchant's Web server. The merchant does not decrypt the credit card information, but instead digitally signs it and sends it on to its processing bank. At the bank, the payment server decrypts the information, verifies that Tanya has the necessary funds, and transfers the funds from Tanya's account to the merchant's account. Then the payment server sends a message to the merchant telling it to finish the transaction, and a receipt is sent to Tanya and the merchant.

This is basically a very secure way of doing business over the Internet, but today everyone seems to be happy enough with the security SSL provides. They do not feel motivated enough to move to a different and more encompassing technology.

Cookies

Hey, I found a Web site that is giving out free cookies! Response: Great, I will bring the milk!

HTTP is a stateless protocol, meaning that each HTTP connection has no memory of any prior connections. This is one main reason to use cookies. They retain the memory between HTTP connections by saving prior connection data to the client's computer.

Cookies are text files that a browser maintains on a user's hard drive. There are different uses for cookies, but they can be used for demographic and advertising information. As a user travels from site to site on the Internet, the sites could be writing data to the cookies stored on the user's system. The sites can keep track of the user's browsing and spending habits and user's specific customization for certain sites. For example, if Emily goes to mainly Christian sites on the Internet, those sites will most likely be recording this information and the types of items in which she shows most interest. Then when Emily comes back to one of the same or similar sites, it will retrieve her cookies, find that she has shown interest in Christian books in the past, and present her with their line of Christian books. This increases the likelihood of Emily purchasing a book of her liking. This is a way of zeroing in on the right marketing tactics for the right person.

The servers at the Web site determine how cookies are actually used. When a user adds items to his shopping cart on a site, this data is usually added to a cookie. Then when the user is ready to check out and pay for his items, all the data in this specific cookie is extracted and the totals are added.

Cookies can also be used as timestamps to ensure that a session between a user and a server is restricted to a specific length of time. For example, if a user enters her credentials to access her banking information through her online bank account, she will need to be authenticated. Once she is authenticated, the server puts a cookie on her hard drive with a timestamp of four minutes. When she requests to go to another secure page within the site, the server will query the cookie to see if the session has timed out yet. If the session did time out, the user is asked to reenter her credentials to initiate another session.

A majority of the data within a cookie is meaningless to any entities other than the servers at specific sites, but some cookies can contain usernames and passwords for different accounts on the Internet. The cookies that contain sensitive information should be encrypted by the server at the site that distributes them, but this does not always happen, and a nosey attacker can find this data on the user's hard drive and attempt to use it for mischievous activity. Some people who live on the paranoid side of life do not allow cookies to be downloaded to their systems (controlled through browser security controls). Although this provides a high level of protection against different types of cookie abuse, it also reduces their functionality on the Internet. Some sites require cookies because there is specific data within the cookies that the site needs to perform correctly and to be able to provide the user with the services she requested.

There are third-party products that can limit the type of cookies downloaded, hide the user's identities as he travels from one site to the next, or mask the user's e-mail addresses and the mail servers he uses if he is concerned about concealing his identity and his tracks.

SSH

Secure Shell (SSH) functions as a type of tunneling mechanism that provides terminal-like access to remote computers. SSH is a program that can be used to log into another computer over a network. The program can let Paul, who is on computer A, access computer B's files, run applications on computer B, and retrieve files from computer B without ever physically touching that computer. SSH provides authentication and secure transmission over vulnerable channels like the Internet.

SSH should be used instead of Telnet, FTP, rlogin, rexec, or rsh, which provides the same type of functionality that SSH provides but in a much less secure manner. SSH is a program and a set of protocols that work together to provide a secure tunnel between two computers. The two computers go through a handshaking process and exchange a session key via Diffie-Hellman algorithm that will be used during the session to encrypt and protect the data that is exchanged. The steps of an SSH connection are outlined in Figure 8-28.

Figure 8-28
SSH is used for remote terminal-like functionality.

Once the handshake takes place and a secure channel is established, the two computers now have a pathway to exchange data with the assurance that the information will be encrypted and its integrity will be protected.

Secure Channel

References

SSH FAQ: **www.uni-karlsruhe.de/~ig25/ssh-faq**

Secure Shell FAQ: **www.onsight.com/faq/ssh/ssh-faq.html**

Secure Shell (SSH): **wks.uts.ohio-state.edu/sysadm_course/html/ sysadm-558.html**

IPSec

Hey, is there a real complex protocol to provide me network layer protection? Answer: Yep, IPSec.

The **Internet Protocol Security (IPSec)** protocol suite is a method of setting up a secure channel for protected data exchange between two devices. The devices that share this secure channel can be two servers, two routers, a workstation and a server, or two gateways between different networks. IPSec is a widely accepted standard for providing network layer protection. It can be more flexible and less expensive than application- and link-layer encryption methods.

IPSec has strong encryption and authentication methods, and although it can be used to enable communication between two computers, it is usually used to establish virtual private networks (VPNs) among networks across the Internet.

IPSec is not a strict protocol that dictates the type of algorithm, keys, and authentication method to be used, but it is an open, modular framework that provides a lot of flexibility for companies when they choose to use this type of technology. IPSec uses two basic security protocols: **Authentication Header (AH)** and the **Encapsulating Security Payload (ESP)**. AH is the authenticating protocol, and ESP is an authenticating and encrypting protocol that uses cryptographic mechanisms to provide source authentication, confidentiality, and message integrity.

IPSec can work in one of two modes: *transport mode*, where the payload of the message is protected, and *tunnel mode*, where the payload and the routing and header information is also protected. ESP in transport mode encrypts the actual message information so that it cannot be sniffed and uncovered by an unauthorized entity. The tunnel mode provides a higher level of protection by also protecting the header and trailer data that an attacker may find useful. Figure 8-29 shows the high-level view of the steps of setting up an IPSec connection.

Figure 8-29
Steps that two computers follow when using IPSec

Each device will have at least one *security association (SA)* for each session that it uses. The SA is critical to the IPSec architecture and is a record of the configurations the device needs to support an IPSec connection. When two devices complete their handshaking process, which means that they agree upon a long list of parameters they will use to communicate, this data must be recorded and stored somewhere, which is in the SA. The SA can contain the authentication and encryption keys, the agreed-upon algorithms, key lifetime, and the source IP address. When a device receives a packet via the IPSec protocol, it is the SA that tells the device what to do with the packet. So if device B received a packet from device C via IPSec, device B will look to the corresponding SA to tell it how to decrypt the packet, how to properly authenticate the source of the packet, which key to use, and how to reply to the message if necessary.

SAs are directional, so a device will have one SA for outbound traffic and a different SA for inbound traffic for each individual communication channel. If it is connecting to three devices, it will have at least six SAs, one for each inbound and outbound connection per remote device. So how can a device keep all of these SAs organized and ensure that the right SA is invoked for the right connection? With the mighty *security parameter index (SPI)*, that's how. Each device has an SPI index that keeps track of the different SAs and tells the device which one is appropriate to invoke for the different packets it receives. The SPI value is in the header of an IPSec packet, and the device reads this value to tell it which SA to consult as depicted in Figure 8-30.

The AH protocol can authenticate the sending devices of the packet by using message authentication code (MAC), which also provides data integrity. (MAC was covered in the earlier section "One-Way Hash.") The ESP protocol can provide authentication,

Figure 8-30
The SPI and SA help the system process IPSec packets.

integrity, and confidentiality if the devices are configured for this type of functionality. So if a company just needed to make sure it knows the source of the sender and needs to be assured of the integrity of the packets, it would choose to use AH. If the company would like to use these services and also confidentiality, then it would use the ESP protocol because it provides encryption functionality. In most cases ESP will be employed because the company needs to set up a VPN connection.

It may seem odd to have two different protocols that provide overlapping functionality. AH provides authentication and integrity, and ESP can provide those two functions and confidentiality. Why even bother with AH then? In most cases it has to do with whether the environment is using network address translation (NAT). IPSec will generate an ICV value, which is really the same thing as a MAC value, over a portion of the packet. Remember that the sender and receiver generate their own values. In IPSec it is called an ICV value, and the receiver will compare her ICV value with the one that was sent by the sender. If the values match, the receiver can be assured that the packet has not been modified during transmission. If the values are different, the packet has been altered and the receiver discards the packet.

The AH protocol calculates this ICV over the data payload, transport, and network headers. If the packet then goes through a NAT device, the NAT device will change the IP address of the packet; that is its job. This means that a portion of the data (network header) that was included to calculate the ICV value has now changed, and the receiver will generate an ICV value that is different from the one that was sent with the packet, which means the packet will be discarded automatically.

The ESP protocol follows similar steps, except it does not include the network header portion when calculating its ICV value. When the NAT device changes the IP address, it will not affect the receiver's ICV value because it does not include the network header when calculating the ICV. The differences are shown in Figure 8-31.

Figure 8-31
AH and ESP use
different portions
of the packet
to calculate
the ICVs.

Because IPSec is a framework, it does not dictate which hashing and encryption algorithms are to be used or how keys are to be exchanged between devices. Key management can be handled manually or automated by a key management protocol. The de facto standard for IPSec is to use Internet Key Exchange (IKE), which is a combination of the ISAKMP and OAKLEY protocols. The *Internet Security Association and Key Management Protocol (ISAKMP)* is an authentication and key exchange architecture that is independent of the type of keying mechanisms used. Basically, the ISAKMP provides the framework of what can be negotiated to set up an IPSec connection (algorithms, protocols, modes, keys). The OAKLEY protocol is the one that carries out the negotiation process. You can think of ISAKMP as providing the playing field (the infrastructure) and OAKLEY is the guy running up and down the playing field (carrying out the steps of the negotiation).

 NOTE Simple Key management Protocol for IP (SKIP) is another key exchange protocol that provides basically the same functionality as IKE. It is important to know that all of these protocols work at the network layer.

IPSec is very complex with all of its components and possible configurations. This complexity is what provides for a great degree of flexibility, because a company has many different configuration choices to achieve just the right level of protection. If this is all new to you and still confusing, please review one or more of the following references to help fill in the gray areas.

References

IPSec Charter: **www.ietf.org/html.charters/ipsec-charter.html**

IETF IPSec Working Group News: **www.cs.arizona.edu/xkernel/www/ipsec/ipsec.html**

Cisco IPSec White Paper: **www.cisco.com/warp/public/cc/so/neso/sqso/eqso/ipsec_wp.htm**

A Cryptographic Evaluation of IPSec: **www.counterpane.com/ipsec.html**

Attacks

Eavesdropping, network sniffing, and capturing data as it passes over a network are considered passive because the attacker is not affecting the protocol, algorithm, key, message, or any parts of the encryption system. *Passive attacks* are hard to detect, so methods are put in place to try and prevent them rather than detect and stop them.

Altering messages, modifying system files, and masquerading as another individual are acts that are considered *active attacks* because the attacker is actually doing something instead of sitting back gathering data. Passive attacks are usually used to gain information prior to carrying out an active attack. The following sections address some active attacks that relate to cryptography.

Ciphertext-Only Attack

In this type of attack, the attacker has the ciphertext of several messages. Each of the messages has been encrypted using the same encryption algorithm. The attacker's goal is to discover the key that was used in the encryption process. Once the attacker figures out the key, she can decrypt all other messages encrypted with the same key.

A ciphertext-only attack is the most common because it is very easy to get ciphertext by sniffing someone's traffic, but it is the hardest attack to actually be successful at because the attacker has so little information about the encryption process.

Known-Plaintext Attack

In this type of attack, the attacker has the plaintext and ciphertext of one or more messages. Again, the goal is to discover the key used to encrypt the messages so that other messages can be deciphered and read.

Messages usually start with the same type of beginnings and ends. An attacker might know that each message a general sends out to his commanders always starts with certain greetings and ends with specific salutations and the general's name and contact information. In this instance, the attacker has some of the plaintext (the data that is the same on each message) and can capture an encrypted message, and therefore capture the ciphertext. Once a few pieces of the puzzle are discovered, the rest is accomplished by reverse-engineering and trial-and-error attempts. Known-plaintext attacks were used by the United States against the Germans and the Japanese during World War II.

Chosen-Plaintext Attack

In this attack, the attacker has the plaintext and ciphertext, but the attacker can choose the plaintext that gets encrypted to see the corresponding ciphertext. This gives her more power and possibly a deeper understanding of the way that the encryption process works so that she can gather more information about the key that is being used. Once the key is discovered, other messages encrypted with that key can be decrypted.

How would this be carried out? I can e-mail you a message that I think you not only will believe, but also will panic about, encrypt, and send to someone else. Suppose I send you an e-mail that states, "The meaning of life is 42." You may think you have received an important piece of information that should be concealed from others, everyone except your friend Bob, of course. So you encrypt my message and send it to Bob. Meanwhile I am sniffing your traffic and now have a copy of the plaintext of the message, because I wrote it, and a copy of the ciphertext.

Chosen-Ciphertext Attack

In this attack, the attacker can choose the ciphertext to be decrypted and has access to the resulting decrypted plaintext. Again, the goal is to figure out the key. This would be a harder attack to carry out, and the attacker may need to have control of the system that contains the cryptosystem.

All of these attacks could have a derivative with the word "adaptive" in front of it: adaptive ciphertext-only, adaptive chosen-plaintext, adaptive known-plaintext, adaptive chosen-ciphertext. What this means is that the attacker can carry out one of these attacks, and depending upon what she gleaned from that first attack, can modify her next attack. This is the process of reverse-engineering or cryptanalysis attacks, using what you learned to improve your next attack.

The public mainly uses algorithms that are known and understood versus the secret algorithms where the internal processes and functions are not released to the public. In general, the strongest and best-engineered algorithms are the ones that are released for peer review and public scrutiny, because a thousand brains are better than five, and many times some smarty-pants within the public population can find problems within an algorithm that the developers did not think of. This is why vendors and companies have competitions to see if anyone can break their code and encryption processes. If someone does break it, that means the developers must go back to the drawing board and strengthen this or that piece.

Not all algorithms are released to the public, such as the ones developed by the NSA. Because the sensitivity level of what they are encrypting is so important, they want as much of the process as secret as possible. It does not mean that their algorithms are weak because they are not released for public examination and analysis. Their algorithms are developed, reviewed, and tested by many of the top cryptographic smarty-pants and are of very high quality.

Man-in-the-Middle Attack

If David is eavesdropping on different conversations that happen over a network and would like to know the juicy secrets that Lance and Tanya pass between each other, he can perform a *man-in-the-middle* attack. The following are the steps for this type of attack:

1. Tanya sends her public key to Lance, and David intercepts this key and sends Lance his own public key. Lance thinks he has received Tanya's key, but in fact received David's.

2. Lance sends Tanya his public key. David intercepts this key and sends Tanya his own public key.

3. Tanya sends a message to Lance, encrypted in what she thinks is Lance's public key. David intercepts the message and can decrypt it because it is encrypted with his own public key, not Lance's. David decrypts it with his private key, reads the message, and reencrypts it with Lance's real public key and sends it to Lance.

4. Lance answers Tanya by encrypting his message with "Tanya's" public key. David intercepts it, decrypts it with his private key, reads the message, and encrypts it with Tanya's real public key and sends it on to Tanya.

Public keys are often kept on a public server for anyone to access. David can intercept queries to the database for individual public keys, or David can substitute his public key in the database itself in place of Lance and Tanya's public keys.

The SSL protocol has been known to be vulnerable to some man-in-the-middle attacks. The attacker injects herself right at the beginning of the authentication phase so that she obtains both parties' public keys. This enables her to decrypt and view messages that were not intended for her.

Using digital signatures during the session-key exchange can circumvent the man-in-the-middle attack. If using PKI, when Lance and Tanya obtain each other's public keys from the certificate repository, the certificates containing their public keys are signed by the CA. Because Tanya and Lance have the public key of the CA, they both can verify the signature on each other's digital certificate and be sure that it came from the CA itself. Because David does not have the private key of the CA, he cannot substitute his public key during this type of transmission. So PKI has protections built in to protect against these types of man-in-the-middle attacks.

When Lance and Tanya communicate, they can use digital signatures, which means they sign the message with their private keys. Because David does not have Tanya or Lance's private key, he cannot intercept the messages, read them, and encrypt them again as he would in a successful man-in-the-middle attack.

Dictionary Attacks

If Daniel steals a password file that is filled with one-way function values, how can this be helpful to him? He can take 100,000, or 1,000,000 if he is more motivated, of the most commonly used passwords and run them through the same one-way function and store them in a file. Now Daniel can compare his file results of the hashed values of the common passwords to the password file he stole from an authentication server. The ones that match will correlate to the passwords he entered as commonly used passwords.

For example, Table 8-4 represents Daniel's homemade password file that he ran through a one-way function. Table 8-5 represents the stolen password file.

Comparing the two results, Daniel now knows that STomaino is using the password "Computer02," StSheperson is using "Server1," and that SFoster is using the password "Debbie04." Now Daniel can log on as these individuals and access the network resources using their security credentials.

This process is an example of how dictionary attacks take place. Most of the time the attacker does not need to come up with thousands or millions of passwords. This work is already done and is readily available at many different hacker sites on the Internet. The attacker only needs a dictionary program, and he can then insert the file of common passwords, or a dictionary file, into the program and run it against a captured password file.

Replay Attack

A big concern in distributed environments is replay attacks. A *replay attack* is when an attacker captures some type of data and resubmits it with the hopes of fooling the

Table 8-4	Commonly Used Password	One-Way Function Value
Daniel's Homemade Password File	Password	abc
	Kristy01	124
	Cowboys	8yt
	Computer02	83d
	Administrator	dks
	Server1	qwk
	Lab003	39c
	Elvis03	Dk7
	Debbie04	3k5

Table 8-5	User	One-Way Function Value
The Password File that Daniel Stole	EmGorenz	329
	MitHockabout	aks
	MarFairbairn	12p
	STomaino	83d
	SKowtko	00d
	StSheperson	qwk
	DKress	8sn
	DFerguson	0d0
	SFoster	3k5

receiving device into thinking it is legitimate information. Many times the data that is captured and resubmitted is authentication information, and the attacker is trying to authenticate herself as someone else to gain unauthorized access.

Timestamps and sequence numbers are two countermeasures to the replay vulnerability. Packets can contain sequence numbers so each machine will be expecting a specific number on each receiving packet. If a packet has a sequence number that had been previously used, this is an indication of a replay attack. Packets can also be timestamped. A threshold can be set on each computer to only accept packets within a certain time frame. If a packet is received that is past this threshold, it can help identify a replay attack.

Side Channel Attacks

All of the attacks we have covered till now have been based mainly on the mathematics of cryptography. Using plaintext and ciphertext involves high-powered mathematical tools that are needed to uncover the key used in the encryption process.

But what if we took a different approach? Let's say we see something that looks like a duck, walks like a duck, sounds like a duck, swims in water, and eats bugs and small fish. We could be able to conclude that this is a duck.

In cryptography, what if we detect how much power consumption is used for encryption and decryption (the fluctuation of electronic voltage)? We could also intercept the radiation emissions that are released and calculate how long the processes take. Looking around the cryptosystem, or its physical implementation, is different than looking into the cryptosystem and trying to defeat it through mathematical computations. Looking around something is referred to as looking at that item's side channels.

If I wanted to figure out what you do for a living, but I don't want you to know I am doing this type of reconnaissance work, I won't ask you directly. What I will do is find out when you go to work and come home, the types of clothing that you wear, the items that you carry, whom you talk to, and I can just follow you to work. These are examples of side channels.

So in cryptography this is just another way of attacking a cryptosystem by gathering "outside" information with the goal of uncovering the encryption key instead of trying to work on the "inside."

Summary

Cryptography has been used in one form or another for over 4,000 years, and the attacks on cryptography have probably been in place for 3,999 years and 364 days. As one group of people works to find new ways to hide and transmit secrets, another group of people is right on their heels finding holes in the newly developed ideas and products. This can be viewed as evil and destructive behavior, or hackers can be viewed as the thorn in the side of the computing world that requires the building of better and more secure products and environments.

Cryptographic algorithms provide the underlying tools to most security protocols used in today's infrastructures. The algorithms work off of mathematical functions and provide various types of functionality and levels of security. A big leap was made when encryption went from purely symmetric key use to public key cryptography. This evolution provided users and maintainers much more freedom and flexibility when it came to communicating with a variety of users all over the world.

Encryption can be supplied at different layers of the OSI model by a range of applications, protocols, and mechanisms. Today not much thought has to be given to cryptography and encryption because it is taken care of in the background by many operating systems, applications, and protocols. However, for administrators who maintain these environments, security professionals who propose and implement security solutions, and for those interested in obtaining a CISSP certification, knowing the ins and outs of cryptography is essential.

Quick Tips

- Cryptography is the science of protecting information by encoding it into an unreadable format.
- The most famous rotor encryption machine is the Enigma used by the Germans in WWII.
- A readable message is in a form called plaintext, and once it is encrypted, it is in a form called ciphertext.
- The process of encryption turns plaintext into ciphertext, and decryption transforms ciphertext back into the original plaintext.
- Cryptographic algorithms are the mathematical rules that dictate the functions of enciphering and deciphering.
- Cryptanalysis is the study of breaking cryptosystems.

- Nonrepudiation is a service that ensures that the sender cannot later falsely deny sending a message.

- Key clustering is an instance when two different keys generate the same ciphertext from the same plaintext.

- The range of possible keys is referred to as the keyspace. A larger keyspace and the full use of the keyspace allows for more random keys to be created. This provides more protection.

- The two basic types of encryption ciphers are substitution and transposition. Substitution ciphers change a character (or bit) out for another, and transposition ciphers scramble the characters (or bits).

- A polyalphabetic cipher uses more than one alphabet to defeat frequency analysis.

- Steganography is a method of hiding data within another media type, like a graphic, wave file, or document. This method is used to hide the existence of the data.

- The Clipper Chip was an encryption chip the U.S. government wanted to implement into many American-made devices so that they could listen to communication that contained suspected information about illegal activities.

- The Clipper Chip used the SkipJack algorithm, which was developed by the NSA to enable the government to decrypt any traffic encrypted using the Clipper Chip.

- Key escrow is a practice that splits up the necessary key required to decrypt information. Different agencies, or entities, hold on to the different pieces and come together when decryption is necessary.

- Fair cryptosystems also separate the necessary key required for decryption, but this method takes place in software encryption processes using public key cryptography.

- A key is a random string of bits that is inserted into an encryption algorithm. The result determines what encryption functions will be carried out on a message and in what order.

- In symmetric key algorithms, the sender and receiver use the same key for encryption and decryption purposes.

- In asymmetric key algorithms, the sender and receiver use different keys for encryption and decryption purposes.

- Symmetric key processes provide barriers of key distribution and scalability. However, symmetric key algorithms perform much faster than asymmetric key algorithms.

- Symmetric key algorithms can provide confidentiality, but not authentication or nonrepudiation.

- Examples of symmetric key algorithms include DES, 3DES, Blowfish, IDEA, RC4, RC5, RC6, and Rijndael.

- Asymmetric algorithms are used to encrypt keys, and symmetric algorithms are used to encrypt bulk data.

- If a user encrypts data with his private key, it can only be decrypted by his public key.

- Public and private keys can be used for encryption and decryption processes. If a message is encrypted with a public key, it is decrypted with a private key and vice versa.

- Asymmetric key algorithms are much slower than symmetric key algorithms, but can provide authentication and nonrepudiation services.

- Examples of asymmetric key algorithms include RSA, ECC, Diffie-Hellman, El Gamal, Knapsack, and DSA.

- Two main types of symmetric algorithms are stream and block ciphers. Stream ciphers use a keystream generator and encrypt a message one bit at a time. A block cipher divides the message into groups of bits and encrypts them.

- Block ciphers are usually implemented in software, and stream ciphers are usually implemented in hardware.

- Many algorithms are publicly known, so the secret part of the process is the key. The key provides the necessary randomization to encryption.

- Data Encryption Standard (DES) is a block cipher that divides a message into 64-bit blocks and employs S-box-type functions on them.

- As technology has allowed the DES keyspace to be successfully broken, Triple-DES (3DES) was developed to be used instead. 3DES uses 48 rounds of computation and up to three different keys.

- International Data Encryption Algorithm (IDEA) is a block symmetric cipher with a key of 128 bits.

- RSA is an asymmetric algorithm developed by Rivest, Shamir, and Adleman and is the de facto standard for digital signatures.

- Elliptic Curve Cryptosystems (ECCs) are used as asymmetric algorithms and can provide digital signature, secure key distribution, and encryption functionality. They use much less resources, which makes them better for wireless device and cell phone encryption use.

- When symmetric and asymmetric key algorithms are used together, this is called a hybrid system. The asymmetric algorithm encrypts the symmetric key, and the symmetric key encrypts the data.

- A session key is a symmetric key used by the sender and receiver of messages for encryption and decryption purposes. The session is only good while that communication session is active and then it is destroyed.

- A public key infrastructure (PKI) is a framework of programs, procedures, communication protocols, and public key cryptography that enables a diverse group of individuals to communicate securely.

- A certificate authority (CA) is a trusted third party that generates and maintains user certificates, which hold their public keys.

- The CA uses a certification revocation list (CRL) to revoke certificates when they have been compromised in some fashion.

- A certificate is the mechanism the CA uses to associate a public key to a person's identity.

- A registration authority (RA) validates the user's identity and then sends the request for a certificate to the CA. The RA cannot generate certificates.

- A one-way function is a mathematical function that is easier to compute in one direction than in the opposite direction.

- RSA is based on a one-way function that factors large numbers into prime numbers. Only the private key knows how to use the trapdoor and decrypt messages that were encrypted with the corresponding public key.

- Hashing algorithms provide data integrity only.

- When a hash algorithm is applied to a message, it produces a message digest, and this value is signed with a private key to produce a digital signature.

- Some examples of hashing algorithms include SHA-1, MD2, MD4, MD5, and HAVAL.

- HAVAL produces a variable-length hash value, whereas the others produce a fixed-length value.

- SHA-1 produces a 160-bit hash value and is used in DSS.

- A birthday attack is an attack on hashing functions through brute force. The attacker tries to find two messages with the same hashing value.

- A one-time pad uses a pad with random values that are XORed against the message to produce ciphertext. The pad is at least as long as the message itself and is used once and then discarded.

- A digital signature is the result of a user signing a hash value with a private key. It provides authentication, data integrity, and nonrepudiation. The act of signing is the actual encryption of the value with the private key.

- Examples of algorithms used for digital signatures include RSA, El Gamal, ECDSA, and DSA.

- Key management is one of the most challenging pieces of cryptography. It pertains to creating, maintaining, distributing, and destroying cryptographic keys.

- The Diffie-Hellman protocol is a key exchange protocol and does not provide encryption for data and cannot be used in digital signatures.

- Link encryption encrypts the entire packet, including headers and trailers, and has to be decrypted at each hop. End-to-end encryption does not encrypt the headers and trailers, and therefore does not need to be decrypted at each hop.

- Privacy-Enhanced Mail (PEM) is an Internet standard that provides secure e-mail over the Internet by using encryption, digital signatures, and key management.

- Message Security Protocol (MSP) is the military's PEM.

- Pretty Good Privacy (PGP) is a freeware e-mail security program that uses public key encryption. It uses a web of trust instead of the hierarchical structure used in PKI.

- S-HTTP provides protection for each message that is sent between two computers, but not the actual link. HTTPS protects the communication channel. HTTPS is HTTP that uses SSL for security purposes.

- Secure Electronic Transaction (SET) is a proposed electronic commerce technology that provides a safer method for customers and merchants to perform transactions over the Internet.

- In IPSec, AH provides integrity and authentication, and ESP provides those plus confidentiality.

- IPSec protocols can work in transport mode (data payload is protected) or tunnel mode (payload and headers are protected).

- IPSec uses IKE as its key exchange protocol. IKE is the de facto standard and is a combination of ISAKMP and OAKLEY.

- DES uses MAC for authentication and integrity.

- DEA is the algorithm that was used for the DES standard.

Questions

Please remember that these questions are formatted and asked in a certain way for a reason. You must remember that the CISSP exam is asking questions at a conceptual level. Questions may not always have the perfect answer, and the candidate is advised against always looking for the perfect answer. The candidate should look for the best answer in the list.

1. What is the goal of cryptanalysis?

    A. To determine the strength of an algorithm

    B. To increase the substitution functions in a cryptographic algorithm

    C. To decrease the transposition functions in a cryptographic algorithm

    D. To determine the permutations used

2. The brute force attacks have increased because:

    A. The use of permutations and transpositions in algorithms has increased.

    B. As algorithms get stronger, they get less complex, and thus more susceptible to attacks.

   C. The increase in processor speed and power has increased.

   D. Key length reduces over time.

3. Which of the following is not a property or characteristic of a one-way hash function?

   A. It converts a message of arbitrary length into a value of fixed length.

   B. Given the digest value, it should be computationally infeasible to find the corresponding message.

   C. It should be impossible or rare to derive the same digest from two different messages.

   D. It converts a message of fixed length to an arbitrary length value.

4. What would indicate that a message had been modified?

   A. The public key has been altered.

   B. The private key has been altered.

   C. The message digest has been altered.

   D. The message has been encrypted properly.

5. Which of the following is a U.S. algorithm developed for creating secure message digests?

   A. Data Encryption Algorithm

   B. Digital Signature Standard

   C. Secure Hash Algorithm

   D. Data Signature Algorithm

6. If an attacker were to steal a password file that contained one-way encrypted passwords, what type of attack would she perform to find the encrypted passwords?

   A. Man-in-the-middle attack

   B. Birthday attack

   C. Denial of service attack

   D. Dictionary attack

7. What is an advantage of RSA over the DSA?

   A. It can provide digital signature and encryption functionality.

   B. It uses fewer resources and encrypts faster because it uses symmetric keys.

   C. It is a block cipher versus a stream cipher.

   D. It employs a one-time encryption pad.

8. Many countries restrict the use or exportation of cryptographic systems. What is the reason given when these types of restrictions are put into place?

   A. Without standards, there would be many interoperability issues when trying to employ different algorithms in different programs.

   B. The systems can be used by some countries against their local people.

   C. Criminals could use encryption to avoid detection and prosecution.

   D. Laws are way behind, so adding different types of encryption would confuse the laws more.

9. What is used to create a digital signature?

   A. The receiver's private key

   B. The sender's public key

   C. The sender's private key

   D. The receiver's public key

10. Which of the following best describes a digital signature?

    A. A method of transferring a handwritten signature to an electronic document

    B. A method to encrypt confidential information

    C. A method to provide an electronic signature and encryption

    D. A method to let the receiver of the message prove the source and integrity of a message

11. How many bits make up the effective length of the DES key?

    A. 56

    B. 64

    C. 32

    D. 16

12. When would a certificate authority revoke a certificate?

    A. If the user's public key has become compromised

    B. If the user changed over to using the PEM model that uses a web of trust

    C. If the user's private key has become compromised

    D. If the user moved to a new location

13. What does DES stand for?

    A. Data Encryption System

    B. Data Encryption Standard

    C. Data Encoding Standard

    D. Data Encryption Signature

14. Which of the following best describes a certificate authority?

    A. An organization that issues private keys and the corresponding algorithms

    B. An organization that validates encryption processes

    C. An organization that verifies encryption keys

    D. An organization that issues certificates

15. What does the acronym "DEA" stand for?

    A. Data Encoding Algorithm

    B. Data Encoding Application

    C. Data Encryption Algorithm

    D. Digital Encryption Algorithm

16. Who was involved in developing the first public key encryption system?

    A. Adi Shamir

    B. Ross Anderson

    C. Bruce Schneier

    D. Martin Hellman

17. What process takes place after creating a DES session key?

    A. Key signing

    B. Key escrow

    C. Key clustering

    D. Key exchange

18. DES performs how many rounds of permutation and substitution?

    A. 16

    B. 32

    C. 64

    D. 56

19. Which of the following is a true statement pertaining to data encryption when it is used to protect data?

    A. It verifies the integrity and accuracy of the data.

    B. It requires careful key management.

    C. It does not require much system overhead in resources.

    D. It requires keys to be escrowed.

20. If different keys generate the same ciphertext for the same message, what is this called?

    A. Collision

    B. Secure hashing

    C. MAC

    D. Key clustering

21. What is the definition of an algorithm's work factor?

    A. Time it takes to encrypt and decrypt the same plaintext

    B. Time it takes to break the encryption

    C. Time it takes to implement 16 rounds of computation

    D. Time it takes to apply substitution functions

22. What is the primary purpose of using one-way hashing on user passwords?

    A. Minimizes the amount of primary and secondary storage needed to store passwords

    B. Prevents anyone from reading passwords in plaintext

    C. Avoids excessive processing required by an asymmetric algorithm

    D. Prevents replay attacks

23. Which of the following is based on the fact that it is hard to factor large numbers into two original prime numbers?

    A. ECC

    B. RSA

    C. DES

    D. Diffie-Hellman

24. Which of the following describes the difference between the Data Encryption Standard and the Rivest-Shamir-Adleman algorithm?

    A. DES is symmetric, while RSA is asymmetric.

    B. DES is asymmetric, while RSA is symmetric.

    C. They are hashing algorithms, but RSA produces a 160-bit hashing value.

    D. DES creates public and private keys, while RSA encrypts messages.

25. Which of the following uses a symmetric key and a hashing algorithm?

    A. MAC

    B. Triple-DES

    C. ISAKMP-OAKLEY

    D. RSA

Answers

1. **A.** Cryptanalysis is the process of trying to reverse-engineer a cryptosystem with the goal of uncovering the key that was used. Once this key is uncovered, all other messages encrypted with this key can be accessed. Cryptanalysis is carried out by the white hats to test the strength of the algorithm.

2. **C.** A brute force attack is resource intensive. It guesses values until the correct one is obtained. As computers have more powerful processors added to them, attackers can carry out more powerful brute force attacks.

3. **D.** A hashing algorithm will take a string of variable length, the message can be of any size, and compute a fixed-length value. The fixed-length value is the message digest. The MD family creates the fixed-length value of 128 bits, and SHA creates one of 160 bits.

4. **C.** Hashing algorithms generate message digests to detect if modification has taken place. The sender and receiver independently generate their own digests, and the receiver compares these values. If they differ, the receiver knows the message had been altered.

5. **C.** SHA was created to generate secure message digests. Digital Signature Standard (DSS) is the standard to create digital signatures, which dictates that SHA must be used. DSS also outlines the digital signature algorithms that can be used with SHA: RSA, DSA, ECDSA.

6. **D.** A dictionary attack is carried out by comparing a captured password against a list of commonly used words. The list is usually fed into a dictionary attacking tool.

7. **A.** RSA can be used for data encryption, key exchange, and digital signatures. DSA can only be used for digital signatures.

8. **C.** The U.S. government has greatly reduced their restrictions on cryptography exportation, but there are still some restrictions in place. Products that use encryption cannot be sold to any country the United States has declared as terrorist in nature. The fear is that the enemies of the country would use encryption to hide their communication, and the government would be unable to break this encryption and spy on their data transfers.

9. **C.** A digital signature is a message digest that has been encrypted with the sender's private key. A sender, or anyone else, should never have access to the receiver's private key.

10. **D.** A digital signature provides authentication (knowing who really sent the message), integrity (because a hashing algorithm is involved), and nonrepudiation (sender cannot deny sending the message).

11. **A.** DES has a key size of 64 bits, but 8 bits are used for parity, so the true key size is 56 bits. Remember that DEA is the algorithm used for the DES standard,

so DEA has a true key size of 56 bits also because we are actually talking about the same algorithm here. DES is really the standard and DEA is the algorithm, we just call it DES in the industry because it is easier.

12. **C.** The reason that a certificate is revoked is to warn others who use that person's public key that they should no longer trust the public key. For some reason that public key is no longer bound to that particular individual's identity. This could be because an employee left the company, or changed his name and needed a new certificate, but most likely it is because the person's private key was compromised.

13. **B.** Data Encryption Standard was developed by NIST and NSA to be used to encrypt sensitive but unclassified government data.

14. **D.** A registration authority (RA) will accept a person's request for a certificate and verify that person's identity. Then the RA sends this request to a certificate authority (CA), which generates and maintains the certificate. Some companies are in business solely for this purpose; Entrust and VeriSign are just two examples.

15. **C.** DEA is the algorithm that fulfilled the DES standard. So DEA has all of the attributes of DES: block symmetric cipher that uses 64-bit blocks, 16 rounds, and a 56-bit key.

16. **D.** The first released public key cryptography algorithm was developed by Whitfield Diffie and Martin Hellman.

17. **D.** After a session key has been created, it has to be exchanged securely. In most cryptosystems an asymmetric key (the receiver's public key) is used to encrypt this session key, and it is sent to the receiver.

18. **A.** DES carries out 16 rounds of mathematical computation on each 64-bit block of data it is responsible for encrypting. A round is a set of mathematical formulas that is used for encryption and decryption processes.

19. **B.** Data encryption always requires careful key management. Most algorithms are so strong today that it is much easier to go after key management rather than launch a brute force attack. Hashing algorithms are used for data integrity, encryption does require a good amount of resources, and keys do not have to be escrowed for encryption.

20. **D.** Message A was encrypted with key A and the result is ciphertext Y. If that same message A were encrypted with key B, the result should not be ciphertext Y. The ciphertext should be different since a different key was used. But if the ciphertext is the same, it is referred to as key clustering.

21. **B.** The work factor of a cryptosystem is the amount of time and resources necessary to break the cryptosystem or its encryption process. The goal is to make the work factor so high that an attacker could not be successful at this type of attack.

22. **B.** Passwords are usually run through a one-way hashing algorithm so that the actual password is not transmitted across the network or stored on the authentication server in plaintext. This greatly reduces the risk of an attacker being able to obtain the actual password.

23. **B.** The RSA algorithm's security is based on the difficulty of factoring large numbers into their original prime numbers. This is a one-way function. It is easier to calculate the product than it is to identify the prime numbers that were used to generate that product.

24. **A.** DES is a symmetric algorithm. RSA is a public key algorithm. DES is used to encrypt data, and RSA is used to create public/private key pairs.

25. **A.** When a MAC function is used, a symmetric key is combined with the message, and then that result is put though a hashing algorithm. The result is a MAC value. MAC provides data origin authentication and data integrity.

Business Continuity Planning

In this chapter, you will learn about the following items:

- Business impact analysis
- Types of drills and tests
- Recovery and continuity planning requirements
- Selecting, developing, and implementing disaster and continuity plans
- Backup and offsite facilities

We can't prepare for every possibility, as recent events have proved. An earthquake that hit Seattle in 2001 did not do as much damage as it could have, but many businesses were hit with a disaster they did not expect. Hurricane Andrew, in Miami, Florida, could hardly have caused any more damage than it did to that area. Businesses were not merely affected—their buildings were destroyed and lives were lost. Kobe, Japan, was hit by an earthquake whose aftermath was full of damage and destruction. California had power fluctuations because of the lack of power supplies in the summer of 2001, which several businesses were clearly not ready to deal with. The World Trade Center towers coming down after terrorists crashed planes into them affected many surrounding businesses, U.S. citizens, the government, and the world in a way that most people would have never dreamed. Every year, thousands of businesses are affected by floods, fires, tornadoes, terrorist attacks, and vandalism in one area or another. The companies that survive these traumas are the ones that thought ahead, planned for the worst, estimated the possible damages that could occur, and put the necessary controls in place to protect themselves. This is a very small percentage of businesses today. Most businesses affected by these events have to close their doors forever. The companies that have survived these negative eventualities had a measured, approved set of advance arrangements and procedures.

An organization is dependent upon resources, personnel, and tasks that are performed on a daily basis in order to stay healthy, happy, and profitable. Most organizations have tangible resources, intellectual property, employees, computers, communication links, facilities, and facility services. If any one of these is damaged or inaccessible for one reason or another, the company can be crippled. If more than one is damaged, the company may be in a darker situation. The longer these items are unusable, the longer it will probably take for an organization to get back on its feet. Some companies are never able to recover after certain disasters. However, the companies that thought ahead, planned for the possible disasters, and did not put all of their eggs in one basket have had a better chance of coming back to business and in time thrive in the market again.

Business Continuity and Disaster Recovery

What do we do if everything blows up? And how can we still make our widgets?

Disaster recovery has the goal of minimizing the effects of a disaster and taking the necessary steps to ensure that the resources, personnel, and business processes are able to resume operation in a timely matter. This is different from continuity planning, which deals with providing methods and procedures for dealing with longer-term outages and disasters. A disaster recovery plan has the goal of dealing with the disaster and its ramifications right after the disaster hits. A disaster recovery plan will be carried out when everything is still in emergency mode and scrambling to get critical systems back online. A continuity plan takes a longer look at the problem. This includes getting critical systems to another environment while repair of the original facilities is taking place, getting the right people to the right places, and performing business in a different mode until regular conditions are back in place. It also involves dealing with customers, partners, and shareholders through different channels until everything returns to normal. So disaster recovery deals with, "Oh my goodness, the sky is falling," and continuity planning deals with, "Okay, the sky fell. Now, how do we stay in business until someone can put the sky back where it belongs?" Figure 9-1 is an example of the proverbial sky in the process of falling.

NOTE $(ISC)^2$ used to distinguish between disaster recovery plans and business continuity plans. In their current materials they have combined them as one plan. All of the items that are discussed in this chapter will be addressed on the exam as business continuity.

There is a continual theme throughout many of the chapters in this book: availability, integrity, and confidentiality. Because each chapter is dealing with a different topic, it looks at these three security characteristics in slightly different ways. In Chapter 4, which discussed access control, availability meant that resources should always be available to users and subjects and not be hindered by any access control methods. The access control method should protect the integrity and/or confidentiality of a resource. In fact, it must take many steps to ensure that the resource is kept confidential and that there is no possibility of altering its contents while they are being accessed. In this chapter, integrity and confidentiality need to be considered not in everyday procedures, but in the procedures that will be taking place right after a disaster or disruption. It may not be appropriate to leave a server that holds confidential information in one building while everyone else moves to another building. A company is much more vulnerable after a disaster hits, so it is important that the secret stuff still stays secret and the integrity of data and systems is ensured even when people and the company are in dire

Figure 9-1   Disasters are unpredictable, and sometimes the best protection is good planning.

straits. Availability is extremely important in business continuity. The resources that keep the business going must be available to the people and systems that rely upon them. This may mean that backups need to be done religiously and redundancy factored into the architecture. If communication lines are disabled, there must be a quick and sure way of establishing other methods of communication.

When looking at business continuity planning, some companies focus mainly on backing up data and providing redundant hardware. Although these items are extremely important, they are just small pieces of the company's pie. Hardware and computers need people to configure and operate them, and data is usually not useful unless it is accessible by other systems and possibly outside entities. Thus, a large picture of how

Recovery Planning Definition

Recovery planning involves developing a plan and preparing for a disaster before it takes place in the hope of minimizing loss and ensuring the availability of critical systems and personnel.

the business works needs to be understood. Planning needs to include getting the right people to the right places, documenting the necessary configurations, and making sure a redundant power supply is available. It is also important to understand how automated tasks can be carried out manually, if necessary, and how business processes can be safely altered to keep the operation of the company going. Without this type of vision and planning, after a disaster hits a company could have its backup data and redundant servers, but people would be standing around in a daze not knowing where to start or how to perform in such a different environment.

Make It Part of the Security Policy and Program

Why would we need to combine business and security plans anyway? Answer: They both protect the business, unenlightened one.

As stated in Chapter 5, each and every company should have security policies, procedures, standards, and guidelines. When all of these come together, they are considered a security program that should be a living entity. This means that because a company will always go through changes, the program should also go through changes to stay current, usable, and effective.

Business continuity should be a part of the security policy and program and not an entity that stands off in a corner by itself. If it is properly integrated with other security issues, it has a better chance of being continually updated and improved upon. This can help ensure that security is thought of in each step of the business and disaster plans. Business continuity is a foundational piece of an effective security program.

A very important question to be asked when first developing a business continuity plan is why. This may seem silly and the answer obvious, but not always. One would think that the reason to have these plans is to deal with an unexpected disaster and to get people back to their tasks at hand. Why are most companies in business? To make money and be profitable. If these are usually the main goals of businesses, then the plans need to be developed to help achieve these goals also. The main reason to develop these plans in the first place is to reduce the risk of financial loss by improving the company's ability to recover and restore operations. This encompasses the goals of mitigating the effects of the disaster.

 NOTE Small companies may have their continuity plan as part of their overall security plan. Larger, more complex companies should contain a synopsis of the continuity plan within the security plan, but each should be separate documents.

The most critical part of continuity planning is management support. Management must be convinced of the necessity for such a plan. Therefore, a business case must be made to obtain this support. The business case can include current vulnerabilities, regulatory and legal obligations, current status of recovery plans, and recommendations. Management will be mostly concerned with cost/benefit issues, so preliminary numbers will need to be gathered and potential losses estimated. The decision of how a company should plan to recover is purely a business decision and should be treated as such.

Business Impact Analysis

How bad is it going to hurt and how long can we deal with this level of pain?

Business continuity planning deals with uncertainty and chance. The point of making these plans is to try and think of all the possible disasters that could take place, estimate the potential damage and loss, and develop viable alternatives in case those events do actually happen.

Risk assessment and analysis need to be performed to evaluate all potential threats. (For a full examination of risk analysis, refer to Chapter 3.) Threats can be manmade, natural, or technical. A manmade threat may be an arsonist, a terrorist, or simple mistakes that can have serious outcomes. Natural threats can be tornadoes, floods, hurricanes, and earthquakes. Technical threats can be data corruption, loss of power, device failure, or loss of a T1 line. It is important to identify all possible threats and estimate the probability of them happening. Some issues may not come to mind when developing these plans, such as an employee strike, vandals, disgruntled employees, or hackers. These issues are best addressed in a group with scenario-based exercises. This ensures that if a threat became reality, the plan includes the ramifications on *all* business tasks, departments, and critical operations. The more issues that are thought of, the better prepared a company will be when these events take place.

The next step in the risk analysis is assigning a value to the assets that could be affected by each threat. This helps in establishing economic feasibility of the overall plan. Once the team knows about the possible threats and the amount of potential loss, they can look at the top five or ten issues and document this information so that management can clearly understand the threats the company faces.

These issues are part of a *business impact analysis (BIA)*, which is a crucial first step in business continuity planning. Qualitative and quantitative impact information should be gathered and then properly analyzed and interpreted. The goal is to see exactly how a business will be affected by different threats. The effects can be economical, operational, or both. This information can be gathered through standard survey tools or questionnaires given to the most knowledgeable people within the company. This will give a fuller understanding of all the possible business impacts.

This information should be gathered and documented in a clear and understandable format, which is presented to management, as shown in Figure 9-2. It is one thing to know that if a tornado hit, it would be *really bad*, and it is another thing to know that if a tornado hit that affected 65 percent of the facility, the company could be at risk of losing computing capabilities for up to 72 hours, power supply up to 24 hours, and a full stop of operations for 76 hours, which equates to a loss of $125,000 each day. Management has a hard time dealing with *really bad* compared to real numbers.

Business continuity planning should be brought into normal business decision making. This ensures that it is considered and dealt with when other business changes are introduced.

 NOTE A BIA is performed at the beginning of business continuity planning to identify the areas that would suffer the greatest financial or operational loss in the event of a disaster or disruption. It identifies the company's critical systems needed for survival and estimates the outage time that can be tolerated by the company as a result of a disaster or disruption.

Figure 9-2   Continuity plans are business decisions that should be based on real numbers and facts.

Essential business functions need to be identified, and a loss criteria needs to be developed. The business functions can include and may not be limited to:

- IT network support
- Data processing
- Accounting
- Software development
- Payroll
- Customer support
- Order entry
- Production scheduling
- Purchasing
- Communications

There may be interdependencies between these departments and functions that need to be identified so they are also properly protected and put back into place during a recovery procedure.

Once threats are identified and critical business functions acknowledged, a specific loss criteria must be applied. The criteria can contain

- Loss in reputation and public confidence
- Loss in profits
- Loss of competitive advantages
- Increase in operational expenses
- Violations of contract agreements
- Violations of legal and regulatory requirements
- Delayed income costs
- Loss in revenue
- Loss in productivity

These costs can be direct or indirect and must be properly accounted for.

So if the business continuity planning team is looking at the threat of a terrorist bombing, it is important to identify which business function would be most likely targeted, how all business functions could be affected, and how each bulleted item in the loss criteria would be directly or indirectly affected. Many times the timeliness of the disruption can cause permanent effects. It may be acceptable to have the customer support functionality out of commission for two days, but if it is out five days, the company could be in financial ruin. So time-loss curves that show the total impact over specific time periods should be developed and analyzed, as shown in Figure 9-3.

The BIA identifies the company's critical systems needed for survival and estimates the outage time that can be tolerated by the company as a result of various unfortunate events. The outage time that can be endured by a company is referred to as the *maximum tolerable downtime (MTD)*.

Here are some MTD estimates that may be used within an organization:

- Non-essential = 30 days
- Normal = 7 days
- Important = 72 hours
- Urgent = 24 hours
- Critical = Minutes to hours

Each critical business function and asset should be placed in one of these categories, depending upon how long the company can survive without it. These estimates will

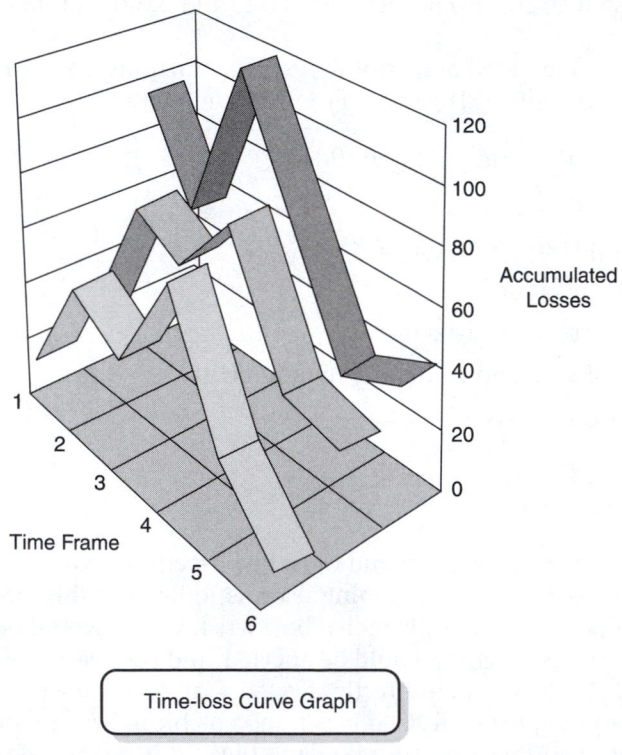

Time-loss Curve Graph

Figure 9-3   Time-loss curves should be constructed to portray the real effects a company would experience if it were out of commission for certain periods of time.

help the company determine what backup procedures are necessary to ensure the availability of these resources. For example, if being without a T1 communication line for three hours would cost the company $130,000, they should put in a backup T1 line from a different carrier. If a server going down and being unavailable for ten hours will only cost the company $250 in revenue, they may not need to have a fully redundant server waiting to be swapped out. Instead, they may choose to count on their vendor service level agreement (SLA), which promises to have it back online in eight hours.

It is necessary to try and think of all the possible events that could take place which could turn out to be detrimental to a company. It is also necessary to understand that not all events will be thought of, and protection may not be available for each and every scenario introduced. This goes back to a main reason that companies are in business: to be profitable. Business continuity plans should provide the necessary level of security within the economical constraints. This requires comprehensive risk analysis to understand the possible events and estimate the potential damage, which will provide economical justification. In other words, if the company has a facility in a flood zone and they could lose up to $1.2 million if a large flood hit, it would not make sense for the company to spend $2 million in protection against a flood. If the company has a facility in a flood zone, there is a high probability that a flood would take place; therefore, this disaster should be dealt with and planned for first. It is also possible that the company could experience a massive alien abduction, but that disaster should be way down on the list because it is not as common as a flood.

Interdependencies

Operations depend on manufacturing, manufacturing depends on R & D, payroll depends on accounting, and they all depend on IT. Response: Hold on. I need to write this down.

It is important to look at a company as a complex animal instead of a static two-dimensional entity. It is comprised of many types of equipment, people, tasks, departments, communication, and interfaces to the outer world. The complexity of true continuity planning is understanding all of these intricacies and their interrelationships. A team may develop plans to back up and restore data, implement redundant data processing equipment, educate employees on how to carry out automated tasks manually, and obtain redundant power supplies. But if all of these components have no idea how to work together in a different environment to get the products out the door, it might all be a waste of time.

The following interrelation and interdependency issues should be researched and addressed in the resulting plan:

- Define essential business functions and supporting departments.
- Identify interdependencies between these functions and departments.
- Discover all possible disruptions that could affect the mechanisms necessary to allow these departments to function together.
- Identify and document potential threats that could disrupt interdepartmental communication.
- Gather quantitative and qualitative information pertaining to those threats.
- Provide alternative methods of restoring functionality and communication.
- Provide a brief statement of rationale for each threat and corresponding information.

This information, along with other data explained in previous sections, should be presented to the senior management staff. After their approval of the information, the actual development of the plan should begin.

Reference

Business Impact Analysis: **www.disasterrecoveryworld.com/bia.htm**

Business Continuity Planning Requirements

A major requirement for anything that has such far-reaching ramifications as business continuity planning is management support. It is very important that management understands what the real risks are to the company, the consequences of those risks, and the potential loss values for each and every risk. Without this understanding, management may only give lip service to continuity planning, and in some cases, this is worse than not having any plans at all, because of the false sense of security. Without management support, the necessary resources, funds, and time will not be devoted, which could result in bad plans that again can provide a false sense of security. Failure of these plans usually means a failure in management understanding, vision, and due care responsibilities.

Executives may be held responsible and liable under various laws and regulations. They could be sued by stockholders and customers if they do not practice due diligence and due care and fulfill all of their responsibilities when it comes to disaster recovery and business continuity items. Some business types have strict regulatory rules and laws that they have to abide by, and these should be researched and integrated into the plan from the beginning. For example, banking and investment organizations must ensure that even if a disaster occurs, their customers' confidential information would not be disclosed to unauthorized individuals or be vulnerable in any way. Disaster recovery, continuity development, and planning work best in a top-down approach, not a bottom-up approach.

Many companies do not see the benefit in spending time and resources on disaster recovery issues because they are running so fast to try and keep up with a dynamic and changing business world. Those who *do* see the value in these efforts often have a hard time convincing top management because management does not see a profit margin or increase in market shares as a result. But if a disaster does hit and they did put in the effort to properly prepare, the result is priceless. Today's business world requires two important characteristics: the drive to produce a great product or service and get it to the market, and the insight and wisdom to know that unexpected trouble can easily find its way to one's doorstep.

The policies and goals of the planning effort need to be established by management. The management sees the company in a much larger view than individual employees. They should have an understanding of the complexity of keeping a business going and thriving and how a disruption to any of these processes can have far-reaching effects. It is important that management set the overall goals of continuity planning, and they must make the priorities of what should be dealt with first. Once management sets the goals, policies, and priorities, other staff members who are responsible for these plans can fill in the rest. However, management's support does not just stop there. They need to make sure that the plans and procedures developed are actually implemented. Management needs to make sure that the plans stay updated and represent the priorities of a company, which can change over time.

The main goals of a business continuity plan are to improve responsiveness by the employees in different situations, ease confusion by providing written procedures and participation in drills, and help make logical decisions during a crisis. If the employees know where to go when the all-hands-on-deck alarm is called, and are familiar with what tasks are expected of them and how to perform these tasks, then the people in position to make decisions on how to properly deal with the event can do so in a calmer and more controlled manner. This can prove to be a crucial element in business continuity.

 NOTE Another requirement is performing continual data backups. This task can seem like an irritating day-in-day-out task, but if everything else failed and the company's information was still saved, this irritating task could be the actual event that helped the company stay afloat. These data files can be restored to enable the company to start reconstruction. Not only should crucial files be backed up, but the programs used to access these files should also be backed up. Even if no other steps are taken for disaster recovery and business continuity, backing up critical information and vital records should always be performed.

The parameters of the plan need to be established. This would happen by interviewing senior management and personnel in each department and function, as shown in Figure 9-4. First, the concerns and priorities of management need to be determined, which will basically dictate a majority of the scope of the project and plan. The scope may be broken down geographically, organizationally, or functionally. Representatives from each department and management personnel should be interviewed to ensure that all of the company's concerns and priorities pertaining to business continuity are covered.

Developing Goals for the Plans

My goals are to own a boat, retire at 55, and grow more hair. Response: Wrong goals.

If you do not have established goals, then how do you know that you are done and if your efforts were actually successful? Goals are established so that everyone knows the ultimate objectives. Establishing goals is important for any task, but especially for business continuity and recovery plans. The definition of the goals helps direct the proper allocation of resources and tasks, develops necessary strategies, and assists in economical justification of the plans and program overall. Once the goals are set, they provide a guide to the development of the actual plans themselves. Anyone who has been involved in large projects that must also deal with many small, complex details knows that at times it is easy to get off track and not actually accomplish the major goals of the project. Goals are established to keep everyone on track and ensure that the efforts pay off in the end. A simple outline of how goals are accomplished is depicted in Figure 9-5.

Great, we have established that goals are important. But the goal could be, "Keep the company in business if an earthquake hits." Good goal, but not overly useful without

Figure 9-4   Representatives from each department and management personnel should be interviewed.

Figure 9-5 Goals, strategies, and actions have an integrated relationship.

more clarity and direction. To be useful, a goal must contain certain key information such as the following:

- **Responsibility** Each individual involved with recovery and continuity should have his responsibilities spelled out in writing to ensure a clear understanding in a chaotic situation. Each task should be assigned to the most logical individual. These individuals must know what is expected of them, which is done through training, drills, communication, and documentation. So instead of just running out of the building screaming, an individual knows she is responsible for shutting down the servers before she can run out of the building screaming.

- **Authority** In times of crisis, it is important to know who is in charge. Teamwork is important in these situations and almost every team does much better with an established and trusted leader. These people must know that they will be expected to step up to the plate and understand what type of direction they should be providing to the rest of the employees. Clear-cut authority will aid in reducing confusion and increasing cooperation.

- **Priorities** It is extremely important to know what is critical versus nice to have. Different departments provide different functionality for an organization. The critical departments must be singled out versus the departments that provide functionality that the company can live without for a week or two. It is necessary to know which department must come online first, which second, and so on. This way, the efforts are used in the most useful, effective, and focused manner. Along with the priorities of departments, the priorities of systems, information, and programs must be established. It may be necessary to ensure that the database is up and running before working to bring the file server online. The general priorities must be set by the management with the help of the different departments and IT staff.

- **Implementation and testing** It is great to write down very profound ideas and develop plans, but unless they are actually implemented, carried out, and tested, they may not add up to a hill of beans. Once a continuity plan is developed, it actually has to be put into action. It needs to be documented and put in places that are easily accessible in times of crisis. The people who are assigned specific tasks need to be taught and informed, and dry runs need to be done to walk people through different situations. The drills should take place at least once a year, and the entire program should be continually updated and improved.

Studies have shown that 65 percent of businesses that lose computing capabilities for over one week are never able to recover and go out of business. Not being able to bounce back quickly or effectively by setting up shop somewhere else can make a company lose business, and more importantly, its reputation. In such a competitive world, customers have a lot of options. If one company is not prepared to bounce back after a disruption or disaster, customers may go to another vendor and stay there.

Developing the Team

I don't want him on the team. He smells.

Once it is decided that these plans are needed, senior management must appoint specific people to perform the necessary tasks. Knowing the actual tasks of the job will help management ensure that they appoint the right people to the team.

The team must then work with the management staff to develop the ultimate goals of the plan, identify the critical parts of the business that must be dealt with first during a disaster, and the priorities of departments and tasks. Once these directives are handed down from management, the team now has goals, objectives, and priorities with which to shape the program. The team must focus on each threat and how that threat can affect the issues deemed most important by management. They develop procedures and tasks that must be performed in each situation and assign responsibility to employees in charge of the tasks. The more time given to this step in the process will result in a more useful, effective, and complete plan.

The team may need to contact outside vendors to establish offsite solutions, redundant communication methods, data backup services, and redundant hardware. All agreements must be documented and outlined so there is less confusion in time of crisis.

It is important that the team is made up of people who are familiar with every department within the company or of representatives from each department. This is because each department is unique in its functionality and has unique risks and threats. The best plan is when all issues and threats are brought to the table and discussed. This cannot be done effectively with a few people who are only familiar with a couple of departments. It is important that representatives from each department are involved with not only the planning stages, but also the testing and implementation stages.

Business continuity planning has various phases of development, shown in Figure 9-6. We have only addressed a few of these phases so far (the rest will be addressed throughout this chapter), however, it is important to see the phases together as one complete program.

Advance planning for emergencies covers issues that were thought of and foreseen. Many other problems may arise that are not covered in the plan; thus flexibility in the plan is crucial. The plan is a systematic way of providing a checklist of actions that should take place right after a disaster. These actions have been thought through in advance to help the people involved be more efficient and effective in dealing with traumatic situations.

Figure 9-6   The phases of a continuity plan

Enterprise-Wide

The main goal of business continuity is to resume business as quickly as possible spending the least amount of money. The main plan must be enterprise-wide. In large corporations, individual departments should have their own disaster recovery and continuity plans because it would be hard to create one large plan that would provide enough granularity to be useful to each and every department. Each department's plan is then integrated with other departments' plans into the overall recovery plan for the company, as shown in Figure 9-7.

The overall business interruption and resumption plan should cover all organizational elements, identify critical services and functions, provide alternatives for emergency operations, and integrate each departmental plan. This can be accomplished by in-house appointed employees, outside consultants, or a combination of both. A combination can bring many benefits to the company because the consultants are experts in this field and know the necessary steps, questions to ask, issues to look out for, and general reasonable advice. In-house employees know their company intimately and have a full understanding of how certain threats can affect operations. It is good to cover all the necessary ground, and many times a combination of consultants and employees provides just the right recipe.

Figure 9-7 Each department should have its own disaster recovery plan, which is integrated into the overall enterprise business continuity plan.

Up until now, we have established management's responsibilities as the following:

- Full commitment
- Policy and goal setting
- Making available the necessary funds and resources
- Taking responsibility for the outcome of the development of the business continuity plan
- Appointing a team for the process

The team's responsibilities are as follows:

- Identifying regulatory and legal requirements that must be met
- Identifying all possible threats and risks
- Estimating the possibilities of these threats and the loss potential
- Performing a BIA
- Outlining which departments, systems, and processes must be up and running before any others
- Developing procedures and steps in resuming business after a disaster

There are several software tools available for developing a business continuity plan that simplify the process. Automation of these procedures can quicken the pace of the project and allow easier gathering of the massive amount of information. Many of the necessary items are provided in the boilerplate templates.

Plan Development

The plan should address all sections described in the previous sections in detail. The actual format of the plan will depend on the environment, goals of the plan, priorities, and identified risks. After each of those items are examined and documented, the following parts of the plan can be divided into four categories: end-user environment, backup alternatives, recovery, and restoration. There may be more sections depending on the company and its needs. It also will depend upon the identified disaster effects. One type of disaster could require that only the data center be relocated to a different site, another disaster could require a majority of the users to be relocated, or a disruption of communication could require an alternate communication method be implemented.

The reasons plans become outdated include the following:

- Infrastructure and environment changes.
- Reorganization of company, layoffs, and merges.
- Changes in hardware, software, and applications.
- After plan is constructed, people feel their job is done.
- Personnel turnover.
- Large plans can take a lot of work to maintain.
- Does not have a direct line to profitability.

Keep the plan updated by take the following actions:

- Make business continuity a part of every business decision.
- Insert the maintenance responsibilities into job descriptions.
- Include maintenance in personnel evaluations.
- Perform internal audits that include disaster recovery and continuity documentation and procedures.
- Perform regular drills that use the plan.

A general six-step approach to contingency planning is described in the following sections. The goal of each is to avert potential contingencies and disasters or minimize the damage an organization may endure.

References

Disaster Recovery World: **www.disasterrecoveryworld.com**

Business Continuity Planning Directory: **www.business-continuity-and-disaster-recovery-world.co.uk**

Business Impact Analysis: **www.dri.ca/dric_pp3.html**

Identifying Business Critical Functions

It is difficult to protect what is most important to a company if it is not first identified. Senior management is usually involved with this step because they have a point of view that extends beyond each function manager's focus area of responsibility. The company's business plan usually defines the company's critical mission and business function. The functions must have priorities set upon them to indicate which is most crucial to a company's survival.

Identifying the Resources and Systems that Support the Critical Functions

After identifying the critical functions, it is necessary to find out exactly what is required for these functions to take place. These are not necessarily just computer systems, but can include personnel, procedures, tasks, supplies, and vendor support. It needs to be understood that if one or more of these support mechanisms is not available, the critical function may be doomed. The team must determine what type of effect unavailable resources and systems will have on these critical functions.

An analysis of these resources should be done by people who understand them and how they provide functionality to the company. These are the people that would mostly understand the interdependencies between the different resources and the true effects of their absence.

Estimating Potential Disasters

This step can be challenging in identifying all possible disruptions and disasters. This is one reason why outside consultants can be beneficial: they may be able to think of issues the team cannot. Scenarios are usually used to step through specific threats to estimate all possible risks in each threat type.

Selecting Planning Strategies

This step includes developing plans on how to recover the critical resources and evaluate alternatives. A disaster recovery plan usually consists of emergency response, recovery, and resumption activities. Emergency response deals with protecting lives and limiting further damages. Recovery encompasses the steps necessary to get the critical functions back online, and resumption is the acts taken to return the company back to original operations.

The strategy is based on logical, feasible, and cost-effective measures. Decisions need to be made pertaining to certain sacrifices that might have to be made in order to recover the critical functions.

Implementing Strategies

Once the strategies have been decided upon, they need to be documented and put into place. This moves the efforts from a purely planning stage to an actual implementation and action phase.

It is important that copies of the plans are kept in one or more locations other than the primary site. If the primary site is destroyed or negatively affected, the continuity plan is still available to the teams.

Testing and Revising the Plan

The business continuity plan should be tested regularly because an environment continually changes. Each time it is tested, more improvements may be uncovered. The responsibility of periodic tests and maintaining the plan should be assigned to a specific person or persons.

The plan's maintenance can be incorporated into change management procedures so that any changes in the environment will be sure to be reflected in the plan itself.

References

Business Continuity Planning Model: **www.drj.com/new2dr/model/ bcmodel.htm**

Disaster Prevention and Recovery Program: **www.so.cc.va.us/its/models/ secpl.htm**

End-User Environment

I have no idea how my network works. Response: Then how can you rebuild it after a disaster?

Because the end-users are usually the worker bees of a company, it is important that they are provided a functioning environment as soon as possible after a disaster hits. This means the current functioning environment needs to be understood and critical pieces examined so they can be replicated.

The first issue pertaining to users is how they will be notified of the disaster and who will tell them where to go and when. A tree structure of managers can be developed so that once a disaster hits, the person at the top of the tree calls two managers, and they in turn call three managers, and so on until all managers are notified. Each manager would be responsible for notifying the people he is responsible for until everyone is on the same page. Then, one or two people must be in charge of coordinating the issues pertaining to users. This could mean directing them to a new facility, making sure they have the necessary resources to complete their tasks, restoring data, and being a liaison between the different groups.

The user environment must be understood, which means the planners have to know issues such as whether the users can work on stand-alone PCs or if they have to be connected in a network to fulfill specific tasks. For example, in a financial institution, users who work on stand-alone PCs might be able to accomplish some small tasks like filling out account forms, word processing, and accounting tasks, but would need to be connected to a host system to update customer profiles and to interact with the database.

Also, some or all data from user machines may be backed up and kept offsite. The planners must be aware of this fact and provide procedures for retrieving the data and installing it after a disruption or disaster. If the users' systems were destroyed, do they need to be replaced with the exact same hardware or similar hardware? If backups are done on images, the exact same hardware may be required, but if the backup only contains files, other hardware may suffice.

Backup Alternatives

Backup alternatives can come in the form of hardware, data, personnel, and offsite facilities. It is up to each company and its continuity team to decide if all of these components are necessary for its survival. The following sections explain how these backup alternatives can be initiated.

Hardware Backup

I don't like to be hot or cold, so I want a warm site. Response: So be it.

Backups for physical equipment are important elements in contingency plans because companies are so dependent upon them. The hardware backup procedures should address onsite and offsite strategies. Because most disruptions or disasters are small in nature, localized single pieces of hardware should be able to be quickly and easily replaced. A company can choose to have redundant devices so that an extra device can be quickly exchanged, but this approach is usually too expensive for most companies. The next step is to have a service agreement with a vendor so that the device would be repaired within a number or hours or days, or a replacement would be shipped in a reasonable amount of time.

There are three main categories of disruptions; they are usually classified as nondisasters, disasters, and catastrophes. A *nondisaster* is a disruption in service as a result from a device malfunction or failure. The solution could include hardware, software, or file restoration. A *disaster* is an event that causes the entire facility to be unusable for a day or longer. This usually requires the use of an alternate processing facility and restoration of software and data from offsite copies. The alternate site must be available to the company until their main facility is repaired and usable. A *catastrophe* is a major disruption that destroys the facility altogether. This requires a short-term solution, which would be an offsite facility, and a long-term solution, which may require rebuilding the original facility.

Disasters and catastrophes are rare compared to nondisasters, thank goodness. Nondisasters can usually be taken care of by replacing a device or restoring files from onsite backups. Onsite backup requirements need to be thought out, and decisions should be made with good judgment. It might make sense for a company to have an onsite backup of the server that processes all of their important transactions and customer purchases, but not so smart to have a backup of the file server that is hardly used. The critical equipment needs to be identified and their mean time between failure (MTBF) and mean time to repair (MTTR) should be estimated to provide the necessary statistics of when a device may be meeting its maker and a new device may be required.

For larger disasters that affect the primary facility, an offsite backup facility must be accessible. Companies can choose from three main types:

- **Hot site** This is a facility that is fully configured and would be ready to operate within a few hours. The only missing resources from a hot site are usually the data, which will be retrieved from a backup site, and the people who will be processing the data. The equipment and system software must be compatible with the data being backed up from the main site and cause no negative interoperability issues. These sites are a good choice for a company that needs to ensure that a site will be available for them as soon as possible. A hot site can support a short- or long-term outage. Most hot site facilities support annual tests that can be done by the company to ensure the site is functioning in the necessary state. This is the most expensive of the three types of offsite facilities and can have problems if a company requires proprietary or unusual hardware or software.

- **Warm site** These facilities are usually partially configured with some equipment, but not the actual computers. In other words, a warm site is usually a hot site without the expensive equipment. Filling a facility with duplicate hardware and computers configured for immediate operation is extremely expensive, so a warm site provides the facility and some peripheral devices. This is the most widely used model. It is less expensive than a hot site and can be up and running within an acceptable time period. It may be a better choice for companies that depend upon proprietary and unusual hardware and software, because they will be bringing their own hardware and software with them to the site after the disaster hits. However, the annual testing available with hot site contracts is not usually available with warm site facilities, and a company cannot be sure that they will be back to operations within hours.

- **Cold site** These facilities do supply the basic environment, electrical wiring, air conditioning, plumbing, and flooring, but it may take weeks to get the site activated and ready for work. The cold site can receive equipment, but does not provide any. The cold site is the least expensive option, but will take the most time and effort to actually get up and functioning right after a disaster.

NOTE It is important to understand the different site types listed here are service bureaus, meaning a company pays a monthly subscription fee to another company for this space and service. A hot site is a subscription service. A *redundant site* is a site owned and maintained by the company, thus they do not pay anyone else for this site. A redundant site might be "hot" in nature, meaning it is ready for production quickly, but the exam differentiates between a hot site (subscription service) and redundant site (owned by the company).

A company would choose a hot site only if downtime cost them a major amount of money and they needed to have operations back in place within hours. The company must also be able to afford to keep a hot site fully loaded with redundant systems and devices. Commercial companies that specialize in subscription service provide these facilities. The cost for the use of a commercial hot site usually includes a basic subscription cost, an activation cost when the site is actually used, and an hourly or daily use charge. Hot sites are usually used for short-term solutions because of the added expenses to regular operational cost.

Most companies use warm sites, which have some devices such as disk drives, tape drives, and controllers, but nothing else. These companies usually cannot afford a hot site, and the extra downtime would not be detrimental. A warm site can provide a longer-term solution than a hot site. Companies that decide to go with a cold site must be able to be out of operation for a week or two. The cold site usually includes power, raised flooring, climate control, and wiring.

The following provides a quick overview of the differences between offsite facilities:

- Hot Site Advantages:
  - Ready within hours for operations
  - Highly available
  - Usually used for short-term solutions, but available for longer stays
  - Annual testing available
- Hot Site Disadvantages:
  - Very expensive
  - Limited on hardware and software choices
- Warm and Cold Site Advantages:
  - Less expensive
  - Availability for longer timeframes because of the reduced costs
  - Practical for proprietary hardware or software use
- Warm and Cold Site Disadvantages:
  - Not immediately available
  - Operational testing not usually available
  - Resources for operations not immediately available

Backup tapes or other media should be tested periodically on the equipment kept at the hot site to make sure the media is readable by those systems. If a warm site is used, the tapes should be brought to the original site and tested on those systems. The reason for the difference is that when a company uses a hot site, it will be depending on the systems kept there all the time; therefore, the media needs to be readable by those systems. If a company is depending on a warm site, they will most likely be bringing their original equipment with them, so the media needs to be able to be read by the original systems.

NOTE   When choosing a facility, it should be far enough away from the original site so that it will not be affected by a disaster that the original site was affected by. In other words, it is not logical to have the backup site only a few miles away if the company is concerned about tornado damage because the backup site could also be affected or destroyed. The backup site should be at least 25 miles away from the primary site to give maximum protection in cases of regional disasters.

Another approach to alternate offsite facilities is establishing a *reciprocal agreement*, also referred to as mutual aid, with another company. This means that Company A agrees to allow Company B to use its facilities if Company B is hit by a disaster. This is a cheaper way to go than the other offsite choices, but it is not necessarily a good choice. Most environments are maxed out pertaining to the use of facility space, resources, and computing capability. To allow another company to come in and work out of the same shop could prove to be detrimental to both companies. The stress of two companies working in the same environment could cause tremendous levels of tension, comically shown in Figure 9-8. If it did work out, it would only provide a short-term solution. Configuration management could be a nightmare, and the mixing of operations could introduce many security issues.

There is also another large concern pertaining to security with reciprocal agreements. If you allow another company to move into your facility and work from there, you may have a solid feeling about your friend, the CEO, but what about all of her employees whom you do not know? Now you have a new subset of people who have privileged and direct access to your resources. This other company could be your competitor in the business world, so many of the employees may see you and your company more as a threat instead of one that is offering a helping hand in need. Close attention needs to be paid when assigning these other people access rights and permissions to your critical assets and resources, if they need access at all.

Reciprocal agreements are at best a secondary option for disaster protection. The agreements are not enforceable, so there is no guarantee that this facility will really be available to the company in a time of need. However, many companies do opt for this solution because of the low cost, and in some cases, it may be the only viable solution.

There are important issues that need to be addressed before a disaster hits if a company decides to participate in a reciprocal agreement with another company:

- How long will the facility be available to the company in need?
- How much assistance will the staff supply in integrating the two environments and ongoing support?

Figure 9-8 A reciprocal agreement can result in stress and conflicts not previously imagined.

- How quickly can the company in need move into the facility?
- What are the issues pertaining to interoperability?
- How many of the resources will be available to the company in need?
- How will differences and conflicts be addressed?
- How does change control and configuration management take place?
- How often can drills and testing take place?

Some companies choose to have *redundant sites*, meaning one site is equipped and configured exactly like the primary site, which serves as a redundant environment. These sites are owned by the company and are mirrors of the original production environment. This is one of the most expensive backup facility options because a full environment must be maintained and usually not used for any production activities until after a disaster takes place. But expensive is relative here. If the company would lose a million dollars if they were out of business for 5 to 12 hours, the loss potential would override the cost of this option. Many organizations are subjected to regulations that dictate that they must have redundant sites in place, so expense is not an issue in these situations.

The other types of facility backups include *rolling hot sites*, or mobile hot sites, where the back of a large truck or a trailer is turned into a data processing or working area. The trailer can be brought to the company's parking lot or another location. Another solution is prefabricated buildings that can be easily and quickly put together.

It is best if a company is aware of all available options for hardware and facility backups so they can have many options to make the best decision for themselves.

Software Backup

I have a backup server and my backed-up data, but no operating system or applications. Response: Good luck.

Hardware is usually not worth much to a company without the software required to run on it. The software that needs to be backed up can be in the form of applications, files, utilities, databases, and operating systems. The continuity plan must have provisions to back up and protect these items along with hardware and facilities.

Software usually changes more often than hardware, so backup procedures must happen on a continual basis. It is important that the software backup process makes sense. If data in the files changes several times a day, backup procedures should happen a couple times a day or nightly to ensure that all the changes are captured and kept. If data is changed once a month, backing up software every night is a waste of time and resources. It is usually desirable to back up a file and its corresponding changes instead of having multiple copies of that one file. Online files usually have the changes to a file made to a transaction log, which is separate from the original file.

Important data should be backed up to an onsite area and an offsite area. The onsite backup copies should be easily accessible in the case of nondisasters and provide a quick restore process so operations can return to normal. However, onsite backup copies are not enough to provide real security. The software should also be held in an offsite facility in case of actual disasters. One choice that needs to be made is where the offsite location should be located in reference to the main facility. The closer the offsite backup storage site is, the easier it is to access, but this can put the backup copies in danger if a disaster took out the company's main facility and backup facility. It may be wiser to choose a backup facility farther away, which makes accessibility harder. Some companies choose to have more than one backup facility: one that is close and one that is farther away.

The onsite backup information should be stored in a fire-resistant safe. The procedures for backing up and restoring data should be easily accessible and comprehensible. In an emergency situation, the same guy who always does the backing up and restoring may not be around, so this information should be readily available to others.

Master files should be updated at sensible intervals and transaction files should be preserved to coincide with those master files. This enables a prior generation master file to be easily brought up to date to recreate the current master file that represents all of the new data. Backup strategy must take into account that failure can take place at any step of the process, so if there is a problem during the backing up or restoring process that could corrupt the data, there should be a graceful way of backing out or reconstructing the data from the beginning.

Databases require specialized backup operations, which is why backup operations are usually integrated into the database management software as a feature. Databases can be configured to use *disk-shadowing*, or data-mirroring, technologies. A disk-shadowing subsystem uses two physical disks and the data is written to both at the same time for redundancy purposes. This subsystem performs data-mirroring functionality. If one disk fails, the other is readily available. This is different from *disk duplexing*, which has more than one disk controller. If one disk controller fails, the other is ready and available.

File descriptions need to be maintained along with separate data dictionaries. Each of these needs to coincide with the file version, so the backup procedures should happen in a predictable way each time and in concert. Databases have functionality that enables them to be restored and have roll-forward processes. (Database concepts and issues are addressed in Chapter 11.)

Manually backing up systems and data can be time consuming, error prone, and costly. There are several technologies that serve as automated backup alternatives. These are usually more expensive, but are quicker and more accurate, which may be necessary for online information that changes often. *Electronic vaulting* makes an immediate copy of a changed file or transaction and sends it to a remote location where the original backup is stored. The information can be stored in an offsite facility and retrieved from that facility in a short period of time. This takes place in many financial institutions, so when a bank teller accepts a deposit or withdrawal, the change to the customer's account is made locally to that branch and to the remote site that maintains the backup copies of all customer records.

Various Backup Types

- **Incremental backup** A procedure that backs up only those files that have been modified since the pervious backup of any sort. It does remove the archive attribute.

- **Differential backup** A procedure that backs up all files that have been modified since the last full backup. It does not remove the archive attribute.

- **Full backup** A procedure that backs up all files, modified or not, and removes the archive attribute.

Incremental backups finish more quickly than differential backups, but they take longer to restore because each incremental backup has to be restored since the last full backup.

Transaction Redundancy

Electronic Vaulting

- Copy of modified file is sent to a remote location where an original backup of the file is stored
- Transfers bulk backup information
- Batch process of moving data

Remote Journaling

- Moves the journal or transaction log to a remote location, not the actual files
- Parallel processing of transactions to an alternate site
- Communication line used to transmit data as it is generated

Electronic vaulting is a method of transferring bulk information to offsite facilities for backup purposes. *Remote journaling* is another method of transmitting data offsite, but this usually only includes moving the journal or transaction logs to the offsite facility, not the actual files.

It may be necessary to keep different versions of software and files, especially in a software development environment. The object and source code should be backed up along with libraries, patches, and fixes. The offsite facility should mirror the onsite facility, meaning it does not make sense to keep all of this data at the onsite facility and only the source code at the offsite facility. Each site should have a full set of the most current and updated information and files.

Two other backup technologies are hierarchical storage management (HSM) and storage area network (SAN). HSM provides continuous online backup functionality. It combines hard disk technology with the cheaper and slower optical or tape jukeboxes. In this situation, the HSM system dynamically manages the storage and recovery of files, which are copied to storage media devices that vary in speed and cost. The faster media holds the data that is accessed more often, and the seldom-used files are stored on the slower devices, or *near-line* devices. The storage media could include optical disks, magnetic disks, and tapes. This functionality happens in the background without the knowledge of the user or need for user intervention. SAN is made up of several storage systems that are connected together to form a single backup network. A SAN is a networked infrastructure that allows several systems to be connected to any storage device. This is usually provided by using switches to create a switching fabric, as shown in Figure 9-9. The switching fabric allows for several devices to be able to communicate with back-end storage devices and provides redundancy and fault tolerance by not depending upon one specific line or connection. Private channels or storage controllers are implemented so hosts can access the storage devices transparently.

Figure 9-9   SAN can provide a switched fabric that allows all systems to communicate with the storage device.

The last software backup technology we will discuss is referred to as tape vaulting. Many businesses back up their data to tapes that are then manually transferred to an offsite facility by a courier or an employee. The data can be at risk while it is in transit. There have been many interesting stories of couriers setting the tapes down on the floor in a subway station while waiting for a subway car. The subway station is full of large engines that continually run. Engines produce electromagnetic fields that can corrupt or erase the data on the tapes. Also there can be problems retrieving the data in a manual way. If a company needs to restore its data, it probably needs to restore it now, not in three days.

With automatic *tape vaulting* the data is sent over a serial line to a backup tape system at the offsite facility. The company that is maintaining the offsite facility will maintain the systems and change out tapes when necessary. Data can be quickly backed up and retrieved when necessary. This technology reduces the manual steps in the traditional tape backup procedures.

Choosing a Software Backup Facility

I like this facility because it is pink.

There are several issues that need to be addressed and questions that need to be asked when a company is deciding upon a storage facility for its backup materials. The following provides a list of just some of the issues that need to be thought through before committing to a specific facility:

- Can the records or redundant hardware be accessed in the necessary timeframe?
- Is the facility closed on weekends, holidays, and does it only operate during specific hours of the day?
- Are the access control mechanisms tied to an alarm and/or the police station?
- Is the facility fire resistant in its construction?
- What is the physical layout of the facility?
- Will the physical layout provide any obstacles to its use?
- Does the facility have the capability to properly store the media that the company's backups are stored on?
- What is the availability of a bonded transport service?
- Are there any geographical environmental hazards such as floods, earthquakes, tornadoes, and so on?
- Is there a fire detection and suppression system?
- Does the facility provide temperature and humidity monitoring and control?

The questions and issues that need to be addressed will vary depending on the type of company, its needs, and the requirements of a backup facility.

Documentation

We came up with a great plan six months ago. Did anyone write it down?

Documentation seems to be a dreaded task to most people, who will find many other tasks to take on to ensure that they are not the ones stuck with documenting processes and procedures. However, a company can do a great and responsible job of backing up hardware and software to an offsite facility, maintaining it, keeping everything up to date and current, and yet, when a disaster hits, no one knows how to put Humpty-Dumpty back together again.

Restoration of files can be challenging, but restoring a whole environment that was swept away in a tornado can be overwhelming if not impossible. Procedures need to be documented because when they are actually needed, it will most likely be a chaotic and frantic time with a demanding time schedule. The documentation may need to include how to install images, configure operating systems and servers, and properly install utilities and proprietary software.

Most environments have evolved over time. Software has been installed on top of other software, configurations have been altered over the years to properly work in a unique environment, and service packs and patches have been installed to fix this problem or that issue. To expect one person or a group of people to go through all of these steps and end up with an environment exactly like the original environment that works together seamlessly may be a lofty dream.

So the dreaded task of documentation may be the saving grace one day. It is an essential piece of business, and therefore an essential piece in disaster recovery and business continuity.

Human Resources

We have everything up and running now—where are all the people to run these systems?

One of the resources that is commonly left out of the equation is people. A company can restore their networks and critical systems, get business functions up and running, and then it finally dawns on them, "Who will take it from here?" Human resources is a critical component to any recovery and continuity process, and it needs to be fully thought out and integrated into the plan.

What happens if we have to move an offsite facility that is 250 miles away? We cannot expect people to drive back and forth from home to work. Should we pay for temporary housing for the necessary employees? Do we have to pay their moving costs? Do we need to hire new employees in the area of the offsite facility? If so, what skill set do we need?

If a large disaster took place that affected not only the company's facility but surrounding areas and housing areas, do you think your employees will be more worried about your company or their families? Some companies assume that employees will be ready and available to help them get back into production, when in fact they may need to be at home because they have responsibilities to their family.

Regrettably, some employees may be killed in the disaster and the team may need to look at how they will be able to replace employees quickly through a temporary agency or a headhunter. This is extremely unfortunate, but it is part of reality. The team that identifies all threats and is responsible for identifying solutions needs to think about all of these issues and more.

Recovery and Restoration

A restoration team should be identified and trained in their tasks as part of the business continuity plan. There should be one team that has the responsibility of getting the alternate site into a working and functioning environment and another team, referred to as the salvage team, to start the recovery of the original site. The teams must know how to do many tasks, such as how to install operating systems, configure workstations and servers, string wire and cabling, set up the network and configure networking services, and install equipment and applications. The team must also know the proper steps of restoring data from backup facilities, which can be harder than it sounds.

A company is not out of an emergency state until it is back in operation at the original primary site or a new site that was constructed to replace the primary site. This is because the company is in a vulnerable state while operating in a backup facility, which continues until things are returned to the way they were before the disaster. There are many logistic issues to consider when a company must return from the alternate site to the original site. The least critical functions should be moved back first, so if there are issues in network configurations or connectivity, or important steps were not carried out, the critical operations of the company are not negatively affected.

Testing and Drills

We made a plan and tested it and it doesn't work. Response: That is why you test it.

Tests and disaster recovery drills should be performed at least once a year. A company should have no real confidence in a developed plan until it has actually been tested. The tests and drills prepare personnel for what they may be faced with and enable them to learn the tasks expected of them. These tests and drills also point out issues to the planning team and management that were not previously thought about and addressed. The tests and drills will demonstrate if a company can actually recover after a disaster.

The test should have a predetermined scenario that the company may indeed be faced with one day. Specific parameters and a scope of the test must be worked out before sounding the alarms. The team of testers must agree upon what exactly is getting tested and how to properly determine success or failure. The timing and duration of the test, who will participate in the test, who will receive which assignments, and what steps should be taken, must be agreed upon. Also, it needs to be determined if hardware, software, personnel, procedures, and communication lines are going to be tested, and whether it is some, all, or a subset combination. If the test will include moving some equipment to an alternate site, then transportation, extra equipment, and alternate site readiness must be addressed.

Most companies cannot afford for these tests to interrupt production or productivity, so the tests may need to take place in sections, which will require logistics planning. Written test plans should be developed that will test for specific weaknesses in the overall disaster recovery plan. The first test should not include all 3,500 employees, but a small group of people here and there until each learns his or her responsibilities. Then larger drills can take place so that overall operations will not be negatively affected. The people carrying out these drills should expect problems and mistakes; this is why they are having the drills in the first place. A company would want employees to make mistakes during a drill so that they can learn from them and perform more effectively during a real disaster.

NOTE After a disaster, telephone service may not be available. For communication purposes there should be alternatives in place, such as cell phones or ham radios.

There are a few different types of drills and tests that can take place, each with its own pros and cons. The following sections explain the different types of drills.

Checklist Test

In this type of test, copies of the business continuity plan are distributed to the different departments and functional areas for review. This is done so that each functional manager or team can review the plan and indicate if anything has been left out or if some approaches should be modified or deleted. This is a method that ensures that some things have not been taken for granted or omitted. Once the departments have reviewed their copies and made suggestions, the planning team then integrates those changes into the master plan.

Structured Walk-Through Test

Let's get in a room and talk about this.

In this test, representatives from each department or functional area come together to go over the plan to ensure its accuracy. The group will go over the objectives of the plan, discuss the scope and assumptions of the plan, review the organization and reporting structure, and evaluate the testing, maintenance, and training requirements described. This gives the people who will be responsible for making sure that a disaster recovery happens effectively and efficiently a chance to review what has been decided upon and what is expected of them.

The group will walk through different scenarios of the plan from beginning to end to make sure nothing was left out. This also raises the awareness of the recovery procedures to team members.

Simulation Test

Everyone take your places. Okay, action!

This type of test takes a lot more planning and people. In this situation, all employees who participate in operational and support functions, or their representatives, come together to practice executing the disaster recovery plan based on a specific scenario. The scenario is used to test the reaction of each operational and support representative. Again, this is done to ensure that specific steps were not left out and certain threats were not overlooked. It will act as a catalyst to raise the awareness of the people involved.

The drill will have only those materials that will be available in an actual disaster to portray a more realistic environment. The simulation test continues up to the point of actual relocation to an offsite facility and actual shipment of replacement equipment.

Parallel Test

A parallel test is done to ensure that the specific systems can actually perform adequately at the alternate offsite facility. The systems are moved to the alternate site and processing takes place. The results are compared with the regular processing that is done at the original site. This points out any necessary tweaking, reconfiguring, or steps that need to take place.

Full-Interruption Test

This type of test is the most intrusive to regular operations and business productivity. The original site is actually shut down and processing takes place at the alternate site. The recovery team fulfills their obligations in preparing the systems and environment for the alternate site. All processing will be done only on devices at the alternate offsite facility.

This is a full-blown drill that takes a lot of planning and coordination, but it can reveal many holes in the plan that need to be fixed before an actual disaster hits.

The type of organization will dictate what type of training approach is most effective. Each organization can have a different approach and unique aspects. If detailed planning methods and processes are going to be taught, then specific training may be required, rather than general training that provides an overview. Higher quality training will result in an increase of interest and commitment.

During and after each type of test, a record of the significant events should be recorded and reported to management so that they are aware of the outcome of the test.

Other Types of Training

I think I stopped breathing. Quick, blow into my mouth! Response: Leave me alone.

There are other issues employees need to be trained on besides disaster recovery drills. These include first aid and CPR, how to properly use a fire extinguisher, evacuation routes and methods, emergency communication procedures, and how to properly shut down equipment in different types of disasters.

The more technical employees may need to know how to redistribute network resources and use different telecommunication lines if the main one goes down. A redundant power supply needs to be investigated, and the procedures of how to move critical systems from one power supply to the next should be understood and tested.

Emergency Response

You must save your fellow man before equipment. Response: But I like my computer more than anyone I know.

Many times how an emergency is initially responded to can affect the ultimate outcome. Emergency response procedures are the prepared actions that are developed to help people in a crisis situation better cope with the disruption. They are the first line of defense when dealing with a crisis situation.

People who are up to date on their knowledge pertaining to disaster recovery will perform the best, which is why training and drills are very important. Emergencies are unpredictable, and no one knows when they will be called to perform.

Protection of life is of the utmost importance and should be dealt with first before looking to save material objects. Training and drills should show the people with the responsibility of authority how to evacuate personnel. All personnel should know their designated emergency exits and destinations. One person in each designated group is often responsible for making sure that all people are accounted for. One person in particular should be responsible for notifying the appropriate authorities: the police department, security guards, fire department, emergency rescue, and management. With proper training, employees will be better equipped to handle emergencies rather than just running to the exit as shown in Figure 9-10.

Figure 9-10   Untrained employees may forget all responsibilities and head for the door during an emergency.

If the situation is not life threatening, systems should be shut down in an orderly fashion, and critical data files or resources should be removed during evacuation. The documented continuity plan should be found and the necessary activities carried out.

Once things have approached a reasonable plateau of activity, one or more people will most likely be required to interface with external entities. These entities can be the press, customers, shareholders, and civic officials. One or more people should be prepped in their reaction and response to the recent disaster so that a uniform and reasonable reaction is given to explain the circumstances, how the company is dealing with the disaster, and what customers and others should now expect from the company. The company should quickly present this information instead of having others come to their own conclusions and start false rumors. At least one person should be available to the press to ensure that proper messages are being reported and sent out.

Another unfortunate issue needs to be addressed prior to an emergency and that is looting, vandalism, and fraud opportunities. After a company is hit with a large disturbance or disaster is usually when it is most vulnerable and others may take advantage of this, as shown in Figure 9-11. It needs to be thought through how these issues will be dealt with so the necessary and expected level of protection is provided at all times.

Reference

Disaster Recovery Planning: **www.utoronto.ca/security/drp.htm**

Figure 9-11   In emergency situations, security needs to be strictly enforced so that others do not take advantage of the situation.

Summary

Although business continuity is usually pushed to the back of the bus in most organizations today, this in no way means that it is not important and crucial. Unfortunately, many companies have to experience the pain of a disaster to understand how they could have circumvented or mitigated the events that caused the pain to occur.

To develop and carry out business continuity efforts successfully, plenty of thought, planning, time, and effort must go into the different phases of this activity. The real threats must be identified and understood, reasonable countermeasures put into place, and detailed plans outlined for the unfortunate day when they are needed.

Quick Tips

- A business continuity plan is created in advance to minimize loss and ensure availability of critical systems.

- A business continuity plan ensures continuity of critical business functions and provides rapid recovery to reduce the overall impact of a disaster or disruption.

- A business continuity plan provides procedures for emergency responses, extended backup operations, and post-disaster recovery.

- There should be an enterprise-wide plan, and each individual organizational unit should also have its own disaster recovery plan.

- The executive management should support and perform the final approval of the plan. Senior management should identify and prioritize the critical missions of the company.

- Executives may be held liable if proper business continuity plans are not developed and used.

- Threats can be natural, manmade, or technical.

- Continuity planning involves identifying critical resources, identifying potential threats and possible damages, and developing plans to respond to those threats.

- The steps of recovery planning include initiating the project, performing business impact analysis, developing a recovery strategy, developing a recovery plan, implementing, testing, and maintaining.

- The project initiation phase involves getting management support, developing the scope of the plan, and securing funding and resources.

- The business impact analysis is one of the most important first steps in the planning development. Qualitative and quantitative data needs to be gathered, analyzed, interpreted, and presented to management.

- Executive commitment and support are the most critical elements in developing the business continuity plan.

- A business case must be presented to gain executive support. This is done by explaining regulatory and legal requirements, exposing vulnerabilities, and accompanying these with recommendations.

- Plans should be prepared by the people who will actually carry them out.

- The planning group should be made up of representatives from all departments or organizational units.

- The plan should include individuals who will interact with external entities such as the press, shareholders, customers, and civic officials. Response to the disaster should be given quickly and honestly, and should be uniform with any other employee response.

- Disaster recovery and continuity planning should be brought into normal business decision-making procedures.

- The loss criteria for disasters are much more than direct dollar loss. It can be added operational costs, loss in reputation and public confidence, loss of competitive advantage, violation of regulatory or legal requirements, loss in productivity, delayed income, interest costs, and loss in revenue.

- A survey should be developed and given to the most knowledgeable people within the company to obtain the most realistic information pertaining to a company's risk and recovery procedures.

- The plan's scope can be determined by geographical, organizational, or functional means.

- Many things need to be understood pertaining to the working environment so that it can be replicated at an alternate site after a disaster.

- Subscription services can supply hot, warm, or cold sites.

- A reciprocal agreement is when one company promises another company that they can move in if they experience a disaster. These agreements are hard to enforce and rarely work out. However, they are cheap and sometimes the only choice.

- A hot site is fully configured with hardware, software, and environmental needs. It can usually be up and running in a matter of hours. It is the most expensive option, but some companies cannot be out of business longer than a day without detrimental results.

- A warm site does not have computers, but it does have some peripheral devices such as disk drives, controllers, and tape drives. This is less expensive than hot sites, but takes more effort and time to get operational.

- A cold site is just the shell of a building with power, raised floors, and utilities. There are no devices available. This is the cheapest of the three options, but can take weeks to get up and operational.

- Electronic vaulting is the process of backing up bulk data to an offsite facility.

- When returning to the original site, the least critical organizational units should go back first.

- An important part of the disaster recovery and continuity plan is to communicate its requirements and procedures to all employees.

- Testing and drills demonstrate the actual ability to recover and can verify compatibility of backup facilities.

- Before tests are performed, there should be a clear indication of what is being tested, how success will be determined, and how mistakes should be expected and dealt with.

- Checklist testing is when copies of the plan are handed out to each functional area to ensure that the plan properly deals with their needs and vulnerabilities.

- A structured walk-through test is when representatives from each functional area or department get together and walk through the plan from beginning to end.

- A simulation test is when a practice execution of the plan takes place. A specific scenario is established and the simulation continues up to the point of actual relocation to the alternate site.

- A parallel test is when some systems are actually run at the alternate site. The results from this processing are compared to the processing done at the original site.

- A full-interruption test is when regular operations are stopped and processing is moved to the alternate site.

- Remote journaling is transmitting the journal or transaction log offsite to a backup facility.

Questions

Please remember that these questions are formatted and asked in a certain way for a reason. You must remember that the CISSP exam is asking questions at a conceptual level. Questions may not always have the perfect answer, and the candidate is advised against always looking for the perfect answer. The candidate should look for the best answer in the list.

1. What procedures should take place to restore a system and its data files after a system failure?

   A. Restore from storage media backup

   B. Perform a parallel test

   C. Implement recovery procedures

   D. Perform a walk-through test

2. What is the first step in developing a business continuity plan?

   A. Identify all critical systems and functions of the company

   B. Decide if the company needs to perform a walk-through, parallel, or simulation test

C. Perform a business impact analysis

D. Interview a representative from each department

3. How often should a business continuity plan be tested?

A. At least every six months

B. Only when the infrastructure or environment changes

C. At least every two years

D. Whenever there are significant changes in the organization

4. During a test recovery procedure, one important step is to maintain records of important events that happen during the procedure. What other step is just as important?

A. Schedule another test to address issues that took place during that procedure

B. Make sure someone is prepared to talk to the media with the appropriate responses

C. Report the events to management and the appropriate agencies

D. Identify essential business functions

5. Which of the following issues is least important when quantifying risks associated with a potential disaster?

A. Information gathered from agencies that report the probability of certain natural disasters taking place in that area

B. Identifying the company's key functions and business requirements

C. Identifying critical systems that support the company's operations

D. Estimation of the potential loss and impact the company would face based on how long the outage lasted

6. The purpose of initiating emergency actions right after a disaster takes place is to prevent loss of life, injuries, and _____.

A. Secure the area to ensure that no looting or fraud takes place

B. Mitigate further damage

C. Protect evidence and clues

D. Investigate the extent of the damages

7. Which of the following is the best way to ensure that the company's backup tapes are being properly maintained at a warm site?

A. Retrieve the tapes from the offsite facility and verify that the equipment at the original site can read them

B. Ask the offsite vendor to test them and label the ones that were properly read

C. Test them on the vendor's machine, which won't be used during an emergency

D. Inventory each tape kept at the vendor's site twice a month

8. Which best describes a hot-site facility versus a warm- or cold-site facility?

   A. A site that has disk drives, controllers, and tape drives

   B. A site that has all necessary PCs, servers, and telecommunications

   C. A site that has wiring, central air, and raised flooring

   D. A site that is mobile that can be brought to the company's parking lot

9. Which is the best description of remote journaling?

   A. Backing up bulk data to an offsite facility

   B. Backing up transaction logs to an offsite facility

   C. Capturing and saving transactions to two mirrored servers in-house

   D. Capturing and saving transactions to different media types

10. Which of the following is something that should be required of an offsite backup facility that stores backed-up media for companies?

   A. The facility should be within 10 to 15 minutes of the original facility to ensure easy access.

   B. The facility should contain all necessary PCs, servers, and raised flooring.

   C. The facility should be protected by an armed guard.

   D. The facility should protect against unauthorized access and entry.

11. Which item will a business impact analysis not identify?

   A. If the company is best suited for a parallel or full-interrupt test

   B. What areas would suffer the greatest operational and financial loss in the event of a particular disaster or disruption

   C. What systems are critical for the company and must be highly protected

   D. What amount of outage time a company can endure before it is permanently crippled

12. Which areas of a company are recovery plans recommended for?

   A. The most important operational and financial areas

   B. The areas that house the critical systems

   C. All areas

   D. The areas that the company cannot survive without

13. Who has the final approval of the business continuity plan?

   A. The planning committee

   B. Each representative of each department

   C. Management

   D. External authority

14. Which are the proper steps for developing a continuity plan?

    A. Project initiation, strategy development, business impact analysis, plan development, implementation, testing, and maintenance

    B. Strategy development, project initiation, business impact analysis, plan development, implementation, testing, and maintenance

    C. Implementation and testing, project initiation, strategy development, business impact analysis, and plan development

    D. Plan development, project initiation, strategy development, business impact analysis, implementation, testing, and maintenance

15. What is the most crucial piece of developing a business continuity plan?

    A. Business impact analysis

    B. Implementation, testing, and following through

    C. Participation from each and every department

    D. Management support

16. During development, testing, and maintenance of the continuity plan, a high degree of interaction and communication is crucial to the process. Why?

    A. This is a regulatory requirement of the process.

    B. The more people that talk about it and are involved, the more awareness will increase.

    C. This is not crucial to the plan and should not be interactive because it will most likely affect operations.

    D. Management will more likely support it.

17. To get proper management support and approval of the plan, a business case must be made. Which of the following is least important to this business case?

    A. Regulatory and legal requirements

    B. Company vulnerabilities to disasters and disruptions

    C. How other companies are dealing with these issues

    D. The impact the company can endure if a disaster hit

18. Which of the following describes a parallel test?

    A. It is performed to ensure that some systems will run at the alternate site.

    B. All departments receive a copy of the disaster recovery plan and walk through it.

    C. Representatives from each department come together and go through the test collectively.

    D. Normal operations are shut down.

19. Which of the following describes a structured walk-through test?

    A. It is performed to ensure that critical systems will run at the alternate site.

    B. All departments receive a copy of the disaster recovery plan and walk through it.

    C. Representatives from each department come together and go through the test collectively.

    D. Normal operations are shut down.

20. When is the emergency actually over for a company?

    A. When all people are safe and accounted for

    B. When all operations and people are moved back into the primary site

    C. When operations are safely moved to the off-site facility

    D. When a civil official declares that all is safe

21. Which of the following does not describe a reciprocal agreement?

    A. Agreement is enforceable.

    B. It is a cheap solution.

    C. It may be able to be implemented right after a disaster.

    D. It could overwhelm a current data processing site.

22. Which of the following describes a cold site?

    A. Fully equipped and operational in a few hours

    B. Partially equipped with data processing equipment

    C. Expensive and fully configured

    D. Providing environmental measures and no equipment

23. Which of the following best describes what a disaster recovery plan should contain?

    A. Hardware, software, people, emergency procedures, recovery procedures

    B. People, hardware, off-site facility

    C. Software, media interaction, people, hardware, management issues

    D. Hardware, emergency procedures, software, identified risk

24. Which of the following is not an advantage of a hot site?

    A. Offers many hardware and software choices

    B. Is readily available

    C. Can be up and running in hours

    D. Annual testing is available

25. Disaster recovery plans can stay updated by doing any of the following except:

    A. Make disaster recovery a part of every business decision

B. Make sure it is part of employees' job descriptions

C. Perform regular drills that use the plan

D. Make copies of the plan and store them in an offsite facility

Answers

1. **C.** In this and similar situations, recovery procedures should be followed, which most likely includes recovery data from the backup media. Recovery procedures could include proper steps of rebuilding a system from the beginning, applying the necessary patches and configurations, and ensuring that what needs to take place to ensure productivity is not affected. Some type of redundant system may need to be put into place.

2. **C.** A business impact analysis includes identifying critical systems and functions of a company and interviewing representatives from each department. Once management's support is solidified, a business impact analysis needs to be performed to identify the threats the company faces and the potential costs of these threats.

3. **D.** The plans should be tested if there have been substantial changes to the company or the environment. They should also be tested at least once a year.

4. **C.** When recovery procedures are carried out, the outcome of those procedures should be reported to the individuals who are responsible for this type of activity. This is usually some level of management. If the procedures worked properly, they should know it, and if problems were encountered, they should definitely be made aware of this. They are the ones responsible for fixing the recovery system and will be the ones to delegate this work and provide the necessary funding and resources.

5. **A.** The question is asking you about quantifying the risks, which means to calculate the potential business impact of specific natural disasters. The core components of a business impact analysis are

   - Identifying the company's key functions and business requirements
   - Identifying critical systems that support the company's operations
   - Estimation of the potential loss and impact the company would face based on how long the outage lasted

   Information gathered from agencies that report the probability of certain natural disasters taking place in that area is an important piece in determining the probability of these threats. But it is considered least necessary when quantifying the potential damage that could be experienced.

6. **B.** The main goal of disaster recovery and business continuity plans is to mitigate all risks that could be experienced by a company. Emergency procedures first need to be carried out to protect human life and then other procedures need to be executed to reduce the damage from further threats.

7. **A.** A warm site is a facility that will not be fully equipped with the company's main systems. The goal of using a warm site is that if a disaster takes place, the company would bring their systems with them. If they cannot bring the systems with them because they are damaged, the company must purchase new systems that are exactly like their original systems. So to properly test backups, the company needs to test them by recovering the data on their original systems at their main site.

8. **B.** A hot site is a facility that is fully equipped and properly configured so that it can be up and running within hours to get a company back into production. Answer B gives the best definition of a fully functionally environment.

9. **B.** Remote journaling is a technology used to transmit data to an offsite facility, but this usually only includes moving the journal or transaction logs to the offsite facility, not the actual files.

10. **D.** This question is addressing a facility that is used to store backed-up data, it is not talking about an offsite facility used for disaster recovery purposes. The facility should not be 10–15 minutes away because if there was some type of disaster, the company's main facility and this facility could be destroyed and the company would lose all of its information. The facility should have the same security standards as the company's security, including protecting against unauthorized access.

11. **A.** All of the other answers address the main components of a business impact analysis. Determining the best type of exercise or drill to carry out is not covered under this type of analysis.

12. **C.** It is best if every department within the company has its own continuity plan and procedures in place. These individual plans would "roll up" into the overall enterprise plan.

13. **C.** Management really has the final approval over everything within a company, including these plans.

14. **A.** These steps outline the processes that should take place from beginning to end pertaining to these types of plans.

15. **D.** Management's support is the first thing to be obtained before putting any real effort into developing these plans. Without management's support the effort will not receive the necessary attention, resource, funds, or enforcement.

16. **B.** Communication not only provides awareness of these plans and their contents, but allows more people to discuss the possible threats and solutions that the original team may not uncover.

17. **C.** The other three answers are key components when building a business case. Although it is a good idea to investigate and learn about how other companies are dealing with similar issues, it is the least important of the four items listed.

18. **A.** In a parallel test, some systems are run at the alternate site and results are compared with how processing takes place at the primary site. This is to ensure the systems work in that area and productivity is not affected. This also extends the previous test and allows the team to walk through the steps of setting up and configuring systems at the offsite facility.

19. **C.** During a structured walk-through test, functional representatives review the plan to ensure its accuracy and that it correctly and accurately reflects the company's recovery strategy.

20. **B.** The emergency is not actually over until the company moves back into its primary site. The company is still vulnerable and at risk while it is operating in an altered or crippled state. This state of vulnerability is not over until the company is operating in the way it was prior to the disaster. Of course, this may mean that the primary site has to be totally rebuilt if it was destroyed.

21. **A.** A reciprocal agreement is not enforceable, meaning that the company that agreed to let the damaged company work out of its facility can decide not to allow this to take place. A reciprocal agreement is a better secondary backup option if the original plan falls through.

22. **D.** A cold site only provides environmental measures, wiring, air conditioning, raised floors, basically a shell of a building and no more.

23. **A.** The recovery plan should contain information about how to deal with people, hardware, software, emergency procedures, recovery procedures, facility issues, and supplies.

24. **A.** Because hot sites are fully equipped, they do not allow for different hardware and software choices. The subscription service offers basic software and hardware products and does not usually offer a wide range of proprietary items.

25. **D.** Storing the plan in an offsite facility is one sure way of ensuring the plan will become outdated. The plan should be part of normal business activities. A lot of time and resources go into creating disaster recovery plans and then they are usually pushed to the back of the bus and forgotten about. They need to be updated continuously as the environment changes to ensure that the company can properly react to any type of disaster or disruption.

Law, Investigation, and Ethics

In this chapter, you will learn about the following items:

- Ethics, pertaining to information security professionals and best practices
- Computer crimes and computer laws
- Motives and profiles of attackers
- Computer crime investigation process and evidence collection
- Incident-handling procedures
- Various types of evidence
- Laws and acts put into effect to fight computer crime

Computer and information crimes can be looked at as the result of the growing trend of society depending upon and improving its use of technology. However, crime has always taken place, with or without a computer. A computer is just another tool and like other tools in the past, it can be used for good or evil.

Fraud, theft, and embezzlement have always been part of life, but the computer age has brought on new opportunities for thieves and crooks. A new degree of complexity has been added to accounting, record keeping, communication, and funds transfer. This degree of complexity brings along its own set of vulnerabilities, which many crooks are all too eager to take advantage of.

Companies are being blackmailed by cybercriminals who discover vulnerabilities in their networks. Company trade secrets and confidential information are being stolen when security breaches take place. Online banks are seeing a rise in fraud, and retailers' databases are being attacked and credit card information is being stolen. More and more companies are losing money in profits and productivity because of the rise in denial-of-service (DoS) attacks.

As e-commerce and online business become a part of today's business world, these types of issues become more important and more dangerous. Hacking and attacks are continually on the rise, and companies are well aware of it. The legal system and law enforcement seem to be behind in their efforts to track down cybercriminals and successfully prosecute them. New technologies to fight many types of attacks are on their way, but there need to be proper laws, policies, and methods of actually catching the perpetrators and making them pay for the damage they cause. This chapter looks at some of these issues.

The Many Facets of Cyberlaw

Legal issues are very important to companies because a violation in legal commitments can be damaging. A company has many liable, ethical, and legal responsibilities to live up to pertaining to computer fraud. The more knowledge one has about these responsibilities, the easier it is to stay within the proper boundaries.

These issues can fall under laws and regulations, incident handling, privacy protection, computer abuse, control of evidence, and the ethical conduct expected of companies, their management, and employees. This is an interesting time for law and technology because technology is changing at an exponential rate. Laws, the courts, judges, law enforcement, and lawyers are behind the eight ball because of their lack of skill in the computing world and the complexity of the issues involved. Law enforcement needs to know how to capture a cybercriminal, properly seize and control evidence, and hand it over to the prosecutor and defense teams. Both of these teams must understand what actually took place in a computer crime, how it was carried out, and what legal precedents to use to prove their points. Many times judges and juries are confused by the technology, terms, and concepts used in these types of trials, and laws are not written fast enough to properly punish the guilty cybercriminals. Law enforcement, the court system, and the legal community are definitely experiencing growth pains as they are being pulled into the technology of the twenty-first century.

Many companies are doing business across state lines and in different countries. This brings even more challenges when it comes to who has to follow what laws. Different states can interpret the same law differently. One country may not consider some issues against the law at all, whereas another country may determine that the same issue demands five years in prison. One of the complexities in these issues is jurisdiction. If a cracker from another country steals a bunch of credit card numbers from an American financial institution and he is caught, a court in America would want to prosecute him. His homeland may not see this issue as illegal at all. Although the attackers are not restricted or hampered by country borders, the laws are in many cases.

Despite all this confusion, there are some clear-cut responsibilities that companies have pertaining to computer security issues and specifics on how companies are expected to prevent, detect, and report crimes.

Ethics

Just because something is not illegal does not make it right.

Ethics are based on many different issues and foundations. They can be relative to different situations and interpreted differently from individual to individual. Therefore, they are often a topic of debate. However, some ethics are less controversial than others, and these types of ethics are easier to expect of all people.

(ISC)^2 requires all certified system security professionals to commit to fully supporting its Code of Ethics. If a CISSP intentionally or knowingly violates this Code of Ethics, he or she can be subject to a peer review panel who will decide if the certification should be relinquished.

The full set of (ISC)^2 Code of Ethics for the CISSP is listed on the (ISC)^2 site at **www .isc2.org**. The following list is an overview, but each CISSP candidate should read the full version and understand the Code of Ethics before attempting this exam.

A summary of the Code of Ethics is as follows:

- Act honestly, justly, responsibly, and legally, and protect society.

- Work diligently and provide competent services and advance the security profession.

- Encourage the growth of research—teach, mentor, and value the certification.

- Discourage unnecessary fear or doubt, and do not consent to bad practices.

- Discourage unsafe practices, and preserve and strengthen the integrity of public infrastructures.

- Observe and abide by all contracts, expressed or implied, and give prudent advice.

- Avoid any conflict of interest, respect the trust that others put in you, and take on only those jobs you are fully qualified to perform.

- Stay current on skills, and do not become involved with activities that could injure the reputation of other security professionals.

There is an interesting relationship between law and ethics. Most often, laws are based on ethics and are put in place to ensure that others act in an ethical way. However, laws do not apply to everything—that is when ethics should kick in. Some things may not be illegal, but it does not mean they are ethical.

Corporations should have a guide developed on computer and business ethics. This can be part of an employee handbook, used in orientation, posted, and made a part of training sessions.

There are common ethical fallacies that are used by many in the computing world in order to justify their unethical acts. They exist because people look at issues differently and interpret (or misinterpret) rules and laws that have been put into place. The following are examples of these ethical fallacies:

- Hackers only want to learn and improve their skills. Many of them are not making a profit off of their deeds, thus it should not be illegal or unethical.

- The First Amendment protects and provides the right of U.S. citizens to write viruses.

- Information should be shared freely and openly, thus sharing confidential information and trade secrets should be legal and ethical.

- Hacking does not actually hurt anyone.

Computer Ethics Institute

The Computer Ethics Institute is a nonprofit organization that works to help advance technology by ethical means. This is "a public-interest alliance of computer scientists and others who are concerned about the impact of computer technology on society," as stated on their Web site at **www.brook.edu/its/cei**.

The Computer Ethics Institute has developed its own Computer Ethics.

This institute has developed its own Ten Commandments of Computer Ethics:

1. Thou shalt not use a computer to harm other people.
2. Thou shalt not interfere with other people's computer work.
3. Thou shalt not snoop around in other people's computer files.
4. Thou shalt not use a computer to steal.
5. Thou shalt not use a computer to bear false witness.
6. Thou shalt not copy or use proprietary software for which you have not paid.
7. Thou shalt not use other people's computer resources without authorization or proper compensation.
8. Thou shalt not appropriate other people's intellectual output.
9. Thou shalt think about the social consequences of the program you are writing or the system you are designing.
10. Thou shalt always use a computer in ways that ensure consideration and respect for your fellow humans.

Internet Architecture Board

The *Internet Architecture Board (IAB)* is the coordinating committee for Internet design, engineering, and management. It is an independent committee of researchers and professionals with a technical interest in the health and evolution of the Internet. The IAB has two principal subsidiary task forces: the Internet Engineering Task Force (IETF) and the Internet Research Task Force (IRFT). As such they issue ethics-related statements concerning the use of the Internet.

The IAB considers the Internet to be a resource that depends upon availability and accessibility to be useful to a wide range of people. It is mainly concerned with irresponsible acts on the Internet that could threaten its existence or negatively affect others. It sees the Internet as a great gift and works hard to protect it for all who depend upon it. IAB sees the use of the Internet as a privilege, which should be treated as such and used with respect.

The IAB considers the following acts as unethical and unacceptable behavior:

- Purposely seeking to gain unauthorized access to Internet resources
- Disrupting the intended use of the Internet
- Wasting resources (people, capacity, and computers) through purposeful actions
- Destroying the integrity of computer-based information
- Compromising the privacy of others
- Involving negligence in the conduct of Internet-wide experiments

The IAB vows to work with federal agencies to take whatever actions are necessary to protect the Internet. This could be through new technologies, methods, or procedures that are intended to make the Internet more resistant to disruption. There is a balance between protection and reducing functionality. One of the Internet's main purposes is to enable information to flow freely and not be prohibited, thus the IAB must be logical and flexible in its approaches and the restrictions it attempts to implement. The Internet is everyone's tool, therefore everyone should work together to protect it.

Generally Accepted System Security Principles (GASSP)

The *Generally Accepted System Security Principles (GASSP)* Committee seeks to develop and maintain GASSP with guidance from security professionals, IT product developers, information owners, and other organizations having extensive experience in defining and stating the principles of information security.

The committee creates, maintains, and monitors the adherence to GASSP for information security on an international level. The following lists the committee's objectives:

- Identify and develop pervasive, broadly functional, and detailed GASSP and protection profiles in a comprehensive framework of emergent principles, standards, conventions, and mechanisms that will preserve the availability, confidentiality, and integrity of information.
- Be an authoritative source for opinions, practices, and principles for information owners, information security practitioners, information technology products, and information systems.
- Define, implement, and subsequently operate under the governing GASSP infrastructure.
- Define and establish linkage to the Common Criteria Project.
- Maintain close liaison and coordination with other international authoritative bodies that have developed related works to establish and maintain GASSP based on these efforts.

- Define and establish liaison with bodies responsible for certifying professionals to encourage convergence.

- Promote broad awareness of information security and GASSP.

- Address management, user, and other interested parties' concerns at all levels to gain the broadest acceptance.

It would be great if everyone played by all of the rules that different organizations have laid out. However, we know they do not, and in fact, security would not be such an important subject in the computing world if everyone did play by the rules.

Many times when figuring out a computer crime, or any type of crime, one has to understand why crimes are committed and how. To be a good detective, one would need to know how a criminal thinks, what motivates him to do the things he does, what his goals and demons are, and how these are reflected in the crimes he commits. This is how the detective gets inside the criminal's mind so he can predict his next move as well as understand what circumstances and environments are more prone to fraud and illegal acts. This is true with cybercrime. To properly stop, reduce, or prohibit cybercrime, it is best to know why people do what they do in the first place.

References

(ISC)^2: **www.isc2.org**

Internet Architecture Board: **www.iab.org/iab**

Generally Accepted System Security Principles: **web.mit.edu/security/www/ GASSP/gassp021.html**

Motive, Opportunity, and Means

MOM did it.

To understand the "whys" in crime, it is necessary to understand the motive, opportunity, and means—or MOM.

Motive is the "who" and "why" of a crime. These motives can be induced by either internal or external conditions. A person may be driven by the excitement, challenge, and adrenaline of committing a crime, which would be an internal condition. Examples of external conditions might include financial trouble, a sick family member, or other dire straits. Understanding the motive for a crime is an important piece of figuring out who would engage in such an activity. For example, many hackers attack big name sites because when the sites go down, it is splashed all over the news. However, once technology advances to where attacks cannot bring down these sites and/or once these activities are not so highly publicized, the individuals will eventually stop initiating these types of attacks because their motive will have been diminished.

Opportunity is the "where" and "when" of a crime. Opportunities usually arise when certain vulnerabilities or weaknesses are present. If a company does not have a firewall, hackers and attackers have all types of opportunities within that network. If a company does not perform access control, auditing, and supervision, employees can have many opportunities to embezzle funds and defraud the company. Once a crime fighter finds out why a person would want to commit a crime (motive), he will look at what could allow the criminal to be successful (opportunity).

Means pertains to the capabilities a criminal would need to be successful. Say a crime fighter was asked to investigate a complex embezzlement that took place within a financial institution. If the suspects were three people who knew how to use the mouse, keyboard, and a word processing application, and the other person was a programmer and a system analyst, the crime fighter would see that the last person may have the means to commit this crime much more successfully than the other three individuals.

Hackers and Crackers

A majority of the hackers, sometimes called crackers, are usually curious and interested to see how far their skill will take them, or they are interested in seeing what type of destruction a new tool can cause. They see hacking as a type of intellectual game where only the smartest people actually win. However, it is the definition of winning that can get disturbing. People who write viruses usually do so to see how far the virus can spread and how much damage one small program they wrote can cause. It usually is not an act of vengeance against a particular target, although that does happen.

Some hackers may get a thrill about being able to break into a corporation's network and snoop around. This was Kevin Mitnick's drive. He did not intend to hurt anyone or any company per se—he just wanted to see what he could get away with. It is the thrill of the challenge. Other hackers like to see their acts in headlines and will work to bring down large Web sites like Microsoft, Yahoo!, eBay, and Excite. This gives them self-satisfaction and bragging rights to other hackers.

There is another breed of hackers who are usually more serious in nature, as depicted in Figure 10-1. These hackers usually work in small groups and have goals of stealing funds, credit card information, confidential information, and military secrets. These groups are usually much more organized and driven than the other types of hackers who are just curious, and they are therefore more dangerous. An example of this type of hacker is the group of Ukrainian hackers who stole credit card information from financial institutions in the United States, which affected several thousands of people. This group then threatened the institutions with publishing the credit cards on a public Web site if they were not paid hundreds of thousands of dollars, which was extortion. (This case is discussed further in Chapter 2.) It is similar to the evolution of the bank robber, who enters a bank through the front door with a gun. Hackers enter the bank through telephone lines with a set of potentially dangerous tools. Why do people rob banks? Because that's where the money is.

Therefore, the people who want to be successful in fighting crime over computer wires and airwaves must understand the mentality of the enemy, just like the cops on the street who must understand their type of criminal.

Figure 10-1   Another type of hacker knows the extent of the damage he can cause and hacks with malicious intent.

Operations Security

There are several categories of computer crimes that can be committed and different methods of committing those crimes. The following sections go over the more popular types of computer fraud and abuses.

Salami

I will take a little bit of your salami, and your salami, and your salami and no one will ever notice.

A *salami* attack is committing several small crimes with the hope that the overall larger crime will go unnoticed. The most common example of a salami attack involves subtracting a small amount of funds from several accounts with the hope that such an insignificant amount would be overlooked. An example would be if an employee altered a banking software program to subtract 5 cents from each of the bank's customers' accounts once a month and moved this amount to the employee's bank account. If this happened to all of the bank's 50,000 customer accounts, the intruder could make up to $30,000 a year.

Salami attacks usually take place in the accounting departments of companies.

Script Kiddies

Script kiddies are hackers who do not necessarily have the skill to carry out specific attacks without the tools that are provided for them on the Internet and through friends. Since these people do not necessarily understand how the attacks are actually carried out, they most likely do not understand the extent of damage they can cause.

Data Diddling

Can I just diddle the data a little? Answer: Nope, it's illegal.

Data diddling refers to the alteration of existing data. Many times this modification happens before it is entered into an application or as soon as it completes processing and is outputted from an application. For instance, if a loan processor was entering information for a customer's loan of $100,000, but instead entered $150,000 and then moved the extra approved money somewhere else, this would be a case of data diddling. Another example is if a cashier entered an amount of $40 into the cash register, but really charged the customer $60 and kept the extra $20.

There was an incident in 1997, in Maryland, where a Taco Bell employee was sentenced to ten years in jail because he reprogrammed the drive-up window cash register to ring up every $2.99 order as one penny. He collected the full amount from the customer, put the penny in the till, and pocketed the other $2.98. He made $3,600 before his arrest.

There are many reasons to enter false information into a system or application, but the usual reason is to overstate revenue and assets and understate expenses and liabilities. Sometimes managers do this to deceive shareholders, creditors, superiors, and partners.

This type of crime is extremely common and one of the crimes easiest to prevent by using access and accounting controls, supervision, auditing, separation of duties, and authorization limits. This is just one example of how insiders can be more dangerous than outsiders.

Excessive Privileges

This is a common security issue that is extremely hard to control in vast, complex environments. It occurs when a user has more computer rights, permissions, and privileges than what is required for the tasks she needs to fulfill. If a user only needs to be able to read and print materials on the file server, she should not be granted full control. A common example of this is when a manager in accounting is granted full control of all files on a specific server, including payroll information. When this person is moved from accounting to the research department, his rights should be revoked or at least reduced, but most companies do not have procedures in place to make sure this happens. (This is referred to as *authorization creep*.) Now he has full control over the account records and the research records, thus he has *excessive privileges*. If he ever became disgruntled for one reason or another, the company could have much more damage to deal with than if they had properly restricted his access.

Password Sniffing

I think I smell a password!

Password sniffing is just what it sounds like—sniffing network traffic with the hope of capturing passwords being sent between computers. There are several tools available on the Internet that provide this functionality. It is tricky to capture a password because it is a piece of data that is usually only used when a user wants to authenticate into a domain or access a resource. Once the password is caught, it can also be tricky to decipher because it is usually encrypted or only the hash value of the password is sent. Some systems and applications do send passwords over the network in cleartext, but a majority of them do not anymore. Instead, the user's workstation performs a one-way hashing function on the password and sends only the resulting value to the authenticating system or service. The authenticating system has a file containing all users' password hash values, not the passwords themselves, and when the authenticating system is asked to verify a user's password, it compares the hashing value sent to what it has in its file.

Many of the tools that are used to capture passwords also have the functionality of breaking the encryption of the password. They have several dictionaries of words that are commonly used as passwords, and these tools run all of these possibilities against the captured password until a match is found. This is called a *dictionary attack*.

IP Spoofing

I couldn't have carried out that attack. I have a different address! Response: I'm not convinced.

Networks and the Internet use IP addresses like we use building numbers and street names to find our way from one place to another. Each computer is assigned an IP address so that packets know where they came from and where they are going. However, many attackers do not want anyone to know their real location, so they either manually change the IP address within a packet to show a different address, or more likely, they use a tool that is programmed to provide this functionality for them. This type of activity is referred to as *IP spoofing*. Almost all attacks that take place use spoofed IP addresses, which gives the victim little hope of finding the real system and individual who initiated the attack.

One reason that IP spoofing is so easily accomplished is because the protocol of the Internet, IP, was developed in a time when security was rarely considered. At that point in time, the developers were much more focused on functionality and probably could not imagine all the types of attacks that would be carried out using the protocols they developed.

IPv6 and IPv4 using IPSec, described in Chapter 8, can be used to help fight IP spoofing, but for this to be successful, everyone would need to use this technology. Change is hard when it means that millions of people would need to modify the way they do things.

 NOTE Spoofing can be considered a masquerading attack. Masquerading is the act of trying to pretend to be someone else.

Denial of Service

I'm going to keep bothering you until you do not have the time or energy to carry out your job.

Denial of service (DoS) is a general term for many different types of attacks. However, each attack has one thing in common, which is denying others the service that the victim system usually provides.

Most DoS attacks occur over the Internet and are pointed at a company's Web servers, routers, or firewalls. Each of these devices has a finite set of resources, and the attacks that are waged on them have the goal of using up these resources so that no resources are left. Once a system has no resources available, they cannot fulfill requests from legitimate systems. An analogy is a bank. If a bank's main purpose is to lend others money and a bank robber takes all the money, then when people request a loan from the bank, the bank no longer has the necessary resources to fulfill its main purpose. (Simplistic example, I know, but I think you get the point.)

Some attackers like to target well-known Web sites like Yahoo!, Microsoft, eBay, and others with DoS attacks because when these sites are brought down, the event will be on the news and in the headlines. This type of attention strokes certain attackers' egos. At the time of this writing, it is estimated that 4,000 DoS attacks happen each and every week.

There are several types of tools available to perform DoS attacks, which makes DoS attacks extremely easy to carry out. Most systems are vulnerable to SYN attacks, Ping of Death, fragment attacks, and distributed denial-of-service (DDoS) attacks. This is because these attacks are mainly aimed at the use of the protocols within the TCP/IP stack, which almost all computers have to use. (These attacks are examined in Chapter 12.)

There are not many successful methods of fighting DoS attacks because they come in so many different forms, originate from all over the Internet, and use fake or spoofed addresses. Only recently have service providers and ISPs started looking at new technology and products that will help them stop DoS attack traffic so that it does not pass through their networks and onto their customers' networks.

Dumpster Diving

I went through your garbage and found your Social Security number, credit card number, network schematics, mother's maiden name, and that you wear funny underwear.

Dumpster diving refers to the concept of rummaging through a company's or individual's garbage for discarded documents, information, and other precious items that could then be used in an attack against that person or company. The intruder would have to gain physical access to the premises, but the area where the garbage is kept is usually not highly guarded. Dumpster diving is unethical, but it's legal unless it's done by trespassing on someone else's property.

Industrial spies can raid corporate dumpsters to find proprietary and confidential information. Credit card thieves can go through dumpsters to retrieve credit card information from discarded receipts. Phreakers have been known to dumpster dive at telephone companies hoping to find manuals on how the internals of the telephone systems worked. (Phreakers are described in the "Well-Known Computer Crimes" section.)

Most companies do not think about the confidential information that others could be extracting from their garbage.

Emanations Capturing

Do you think we should be worried about that white van in the parking lot with the huge antenna, large amount of power cords, and pizzas continually delivered to it? Answer: Nope.

Emanations, and the way that attackers eavesdrop on them, are addressed in Chapter 4 in the "Tempest" section. Basically, every electrical device emits electrical waves into the surrounding environment. These waves contain information comparable to how wireless technologies work. These waves can be carried over a distance, depending on the strength of the signals and the material and objects in the surrounding area. Attackers have used devices to capture these waves and port them to their own computer systems so that they can have access to information not intended for them.

Attackers need to have specialized tools that tune into the frequency that these waves are carried over. They also have to be within close proximity to the building that is emitting the waves. Companies having such sensitive information that would cause attackers to go through this much trouble usually have special computer systems with coverings that permit only a small amount of electrical signals to be emitted—one example is Tempest. The companies can also use material within the walls of the building to stop these types of electrical waves from bypassing them.

These types of attacks are usually the stuff of spy novels, with three guys in a service van full of high-grade technological devices in the parking lot of a company. However, a recent development has caused this type of eavesdropping to happen without such spy-like activities: wireless networks. When a company installs a wireless network, there are certain configurations that can be set to prevent outsiders from being able to eavesdrop on their employees' network traffic. Unfortunately, most companies do not employ these configurations for one reason or another. This enables anyone with a laptop and a wireless network interface card to drive into a company's parking lot and be able to eavesdrop on network traffic. (Wireless technology and its security ramifications are covered in Chapter 7.)

Wiretapping

Most communication signals are vulnerable to some type of *wiretapping* or eavesdropping. It can usually be done undetected and is referred to as a passive attack versus an active attack. Tools used to intercept communication can be cellular scanners, radio receivers, microphone receivers, tape recorders, network sniffers, and telephone-tapping devices.

It is illegal to intentionally eavesdrop on another person's conversation under many countries' existing wiretap laws. In many cases, this action is only acceptable if the person consents or there is a court order allowing law enforcement to perform these types of activities. Under these circumstances, the law enforcement officers must have probable cause of criminal activity and can only listen to relevant conversations. These regulations are in place to protect an individual's privacy expectations.

Social Engineering

Hi, I am someone else. Now, tell me all your secrets!

Social engineering plays a very important role in many types of attacks. It is the art of tricking people and maliciously using the information they unknowingly supply. For example, if a technical help-desk employee gets a frantic call from someone who claims to be the vice president of the company, saying he forgot his password and needs it right now or heads are going to roll, the help-desk employee may quickly hand over this information. If this person was not the vice president, the employee was just a victim of social engineering. If the person was the vice president, he should understand that he is not above the rules of security and should not put the employee in such a tough position.

Social engineering can come in many forms. Sometimes employees are called by someone claiming to be the network administrator who explains to the employee that there have been some technical difficulties pertaining to some accounts and to please change her current password to "password". If the employee believes this person and does what was asked of her, an attacker would now know that employee's password and could use it for malicious purposes.

Social engineering can be in the form of an e-mail message with a source address of someone the victim knows, or someone spinning a tale in person for others to believe in the hope of accessing information not intended for him. One example is a person who goes to an office in a uniform and says he is there to work on a broken device or network problem. If he convinces the person at the greeting desk, he can then go into the facility and attempt to sniff the network, break into computers and servers, or plant Trojan horses, viruses, or backdoors. The possibilities are overwhelming.

References

Law, Investigation, and Ethics: **www.cccure.org/Documents/HISM/ 522-525.html**

Introduction to Computing Security: **cui.unige.ch/OSG/courses/infrcom/ lectures/security/security.html**

Introduction to Security: **www.uwsg.iu.edu/usail/tasks/security/security.html**

Computer Crime and Security: **courses.cs.vt.edu/~cs3604/lib/Crime/ notes.html**

Social Engineering and Malware: **www.sans.org/infosecFAQ/securitybasics/ awareness.htm**

Social Engineering: **www.sans.org/rr/social/**

Well-Known Computer Crimes

Most computer crimes do not hit the news and headlines because companies choose to keep them quiet. This is done mainly for two reasons: to avoid the embarrassment of everyone finding out their dirty laundry and the fact that they have vulnerabilities, and also to avoid pointing out the vulnerabilities to other opportunistic hackers.

However, there are some computer crimes that have gone down in the history book of hacking and this section takes a quick look at some of them.

The 2600 group publishes the *2600: The Hacker Quarterly* magazine, which is full of ways to hack into computers and telephone systems. The name 2600 stands for the tone that phreakers used to send down a telephone line and get free long distance service in return. This 2600 tone tricked the system at the other end into thinking that the person making the call was authorized to receive long distance access, so it opened up a line and let the person make that type of a call. The 2600 group is basically made up of *phreakers,* who are hackers specializing in telephone and Private Branch Exchange (PBX) fraud.

One of the earliest actual phreaking clubs called itself the *414 Club* because they all lived in that area code. This group of hackers was suspected of breaking into more than 60 businesses and government systems in the United States and Canada in the early 1980s. Today a group of hackers breaking into 60 businesses would not cause the stir that it did in 1983. *Newsweek* magazine even ran a story on this group in the mid-1980s with a picture of one of the group members and his TRS-80 computer.

The Cuckoo's Egg

The Cuckoo's Egg is a book describing how Cliff Stoll, an astronomy student at the University of California at Berkeley, was assigned to track down a 75-cent accounting error in the late 1980s. This small error started him on an investigation only to find that someone was on the school's network who was not supposed to be. He tracked this intruder, back in the days when no sophisticated software tools were available to do this, and found out that the intruder had been breaking into U.S. military systems and stealing sensitive information. He set up one of the first known honeypots and lured the hacker into one of the university's servers claiming to be holding confidential information. Cliff then worked with people and companies all over the United States and other countries to track this intruder while the connection was still active. This mainly had to be done by workers at the phone company. At the time, the ability to perform these types of tasks was far from as automated as it is today. After many attempts, he finally got the U.S. counterintelligence agents involved. It ended up being a small group of hackers in the former Soviet Union working for the KGB.

This is an amazing and true story of someone who stumbled onto an intruder, did not have any sophisticated tracking tools (because they did not exist yet), and was incredibly creative, intelligent, and motivated enough to make many people all over the world help him.

Kevin Mitnick

Kevin Mitnick is one of the most well-known hackers and at one time was one of the FBI's most wanted criminals. He was in jail for almost five years for wire fraud and illegally stealing files from Sun Microsystems, Nokia, Motorola, and others.

Mitnick violated his previous probation terms in 1992, three years before his arrest and five-year jail term, and went into hiding for two years. During that time, he stole corporate secrets, hacked into computers, broke into the national defense warning system, and scrambled telephone networks. He was finally caught, charged, and pled guilty to five felony charges.

The main reason that he is so popular is because he is a martyr to many hackers. He claims he did not do any damage and that he could have done massive damage if his intentions were malicious. Mitnick, like many others, views hacking as an intellectual challenge and said he did it mainly to learn how different systems worked and were integrated.

Chaos Computer Club

This club is a group of German hackers committed to freedom of information across borders. It was formed in 1981 and has tested many corporations' technologies in their security strength and made demonstrations of the ones they found lacking. They demonstrated how easy it was to clone information from European ATM cards and defraud financial institutions. They also demonstrated how a Web-based Trojan horse could siphon money from a bank account. This ActiveX application scanned users' computers to see which had Quicken installed and extracted bank account information from that program. The Trojan horse then made a bogus transaction to one of the hackers' own bank accounts.

The hackers who make up these different groups are quite talented and computer-saavy individuals.

Cult of the Dead Cow

This is a group of hackers who have come up with many different hacking tools. The bestknown tool that they developed was Back Orifice, which was designed to remotely take over Windows 95 and Windows 98 systems. It can record keystrokes, record logins and passwords, take screen shots, delete files, and run programs.

Phone Phreakers

You're a phreak. Response: I know, now give me the phone.

This is not a specific group, but a classification of hackers who specialize in telephone fraud. The first known case of toll fraud was committed in 1961 when the Bell Telephone Company uncovered a method, called *Blue Boxing*, that enabled people to make free long-distance phone calls. At that time, all long-distance trunks were sensitive to signals at the 2,600-Hz frequency. The Blue Box device simulated this tone and other tones to trick telephone systems and gain free, unauthorized long-distance access.

Later came *Red Boxes*, which simulated the tones of coins being deposited into a pay phone. This enabled phreakers to also get free local and long-distance calls. Then came *Black Boxes*, which is a method to manipulate line voltage to enable people to call toll-free.

As the telephone companies advanced their systems and went digital, most of the phreaker phone tricks were no longer effective.

> **NOTE** Much of the "boxing" technology described above has been rendered useless because of the advances of switching technologies in the telecommunications industry. At one time the telecommunications networks were purely analog and the control information used to set up calls were in-band. Today those networks are digital and the control information is sent out-of-band, so phreakers cannot have as much fun and cause as much damage as they used to.

Phreakers specialize in getting long-distance phone calls for free.

In 1972, a phreaker called Cap'n Crunch made it known that a toy whistle in Cap'n Crunch cereal could generate the 2,600-Hz tone used to fool the telephone company systems and give anyone free long-distance phone calls.

Although these types of crimes are no longer effective, there is still a lot of fraud that takes place at PBXs. Today, phreakers still steal phone services from PBXs and other systems, and pass the long-distance charges to the owners of those systems. This crime is very hard to trace and is mainly successful because many large companies do not audit their phone bills.

As stated earlier, many attacks are carried out by curious semitalented, or very talented, individuals who want to see how far they can go. Although the individuals may not be out to cause massive damage or actually harm others directly, their efforts can cost companies thousands or millions of dollars. Therefore, companies and authorities take these acts very seriously.

Some attackers have specific goals in sight, instead of trying to bring down a system they come across here or there. One company can perform espionage on their competitors by breaking into networks and servers and stealing trade secrets and copyright information. Countries can also do this to other countries, which is referred to as *international economic espionage* or *information warfare*. (In Chapter 2, information warfare is described at some length.) Information warfare and international espionage will most likely only increase because society is becoming more and more dependent upon technology.

Governments are looking at these issues much more seriously and are putting the funds and resources toward training their own soldiers to be able to participate in this type of warfare. You can be sure that many of these activities will not be in the news or headlines like we see when a Microsoft site is brought down. These activities are much more covert in nature.

References

Hacking groups: **dmoz.org/Computers/Hacking/Groups**

AntiOnline Computer Security: **anticode.antionline.com/text-archive.php**

Security information links: **www.qub.ac.uk/mgt/itsoc/security.html**

CNN, "The Trials of Kevin Mitnick": **www3.cnn.com/specials/1999/mitnick.background**

Computer Underground Digest: **www.soci.niu.edu/~cudigest**

Identification, Protection, and Prosecution

Hacking, cracking, and attacking have only increased over the years and will not stop anytime soon. There are several issues that deal with why these activities have not been properly stopped or even curbed. These include proper identification of the attackers, the necessary level of protection for networks, and successful prosecution once an attacker is captured.

Most attackers are never caught because they spoof their addresses and use methods to cover their footsteps. Many attackers break into networks, take whatever resources they were after, and clean the logs that tracked their movements and activities. Because of this, many companies do not even know that they have been violated. Even if an attacker's activities trigger an intrusion detection system (IDS) alert, it does not usually find the true identity of the individual, though it does alert the company that a specific vulnerability was exploited.

The FBI and Secret Service are responsible for investigating computer crimes.

Law enforcement, the FBI, and the Secret Service are called in for a range of computer crimes. Although each of these entities works to train their people to identify and track computer criminals, they are very far behind the times in their skill and tools, and they are outnumbered by the number of hackers actively attacking networks. Because the attackers use tools that are automated, they can perform several serious attacks in a short time frame. When law enforcement is called in, their efforts are usually purely manual in checking logs, interviewing people, scanning for vulnerabilities, and setting up traps in case the attacker comes back. Each agency can only spare a small number of people for computer crimes, their steps are manual, and they are behind in their expertise compared to many hackers. Because of this, most attackers are never found, much less prosecuted.

As mentioned earlier, there are only a handful of laws that deal specifically with computer crimes so it is more challenging to successfully prosecute the attackers who are caught. Many companies that are victims of an attack usually just want to ensure that the vulnerability the attacker exploited is patched and removed instead of spending the time and money toward going after and prosecuting the attacker.

NOTE The author of the ILOVEYOU virus was caught, but could not be prosecuted because there was no specific law indicating that his actions were wrong. This virus cost companies millions of dollars, and the responsible person did not get fined a dollar or spend any time in jail.

These trends will most likely change, but changes will probably happen a lot slower than most would like. As companies lose more and more money to attacks, there will be more and more pressure on law enforcement agencies to stop this type of crime. Each agency will put more money and resources into this problem, and the courts will devise useful laws to hold individuals who are doing these acts accountable. Down the road, people will most likely think twice about letting loose a crippling e-mail virus after 20 other people have been jailed for the same actions.

NOTE Portions of the U.S. Homeland Security Act are dedicated to computer crimes. This trend is happening more and more across the entire globe in most countries. This means that a lot more attention and funds are being put into place to improve the current ways of protecting against, investigating, and prosecuting computer criminals.

Another thing that is changing every day is how companies are protecting themselves from these attacks. Five to ten years ago, most companies had never heard of a firewall, but today it is a known essential. Five to ten years ago, someone would only have a full-time position in computer security if he worked for a government, but today most organizations are screaming for help when it comes to their network and information security. Security is not only part of the IT staff's vocabulary, it is also an issue that has forced itself into board meetings and shareholders' concerns. It has cost executives their jobs if they did not make sure computer security took place correctly within their organization. As the attackers and hackers evolve in their skills and numbers, many business-oriented individuals who would rather deal with other issues have been forced to make security a priority.

Because an attacker must have access to the systems holding the wanted resources, it is usually easier for insiders than outsiders to access resources that companies fight to protect. In this sense, employees can present a greater potential for computer crimes than outsiders trying to get in. Many statistics and security professionals have indeed indicated that employees cause more security breaches and computer fraud than outside attackers, but the media usually only touts the stories about external hackers and crackers. Therefore, more attention and effort are put toward fighting off that group of people rather than the threat of employees taking advantage of their position and access.

Liability and Its Ramifications

As the courts, law enforcement, laws, and legal methods evolve in their approaches to computer crimes, so must corporations. They should evolve not only their preventive, detective, and corrective approaches, but also their liability and responsibility approaches. As these crimes increase in frequency and sophistication, so will their destruction and lasting effects. In most cases, the attackers are not caught, but there is enough blame to be passed around, so corporations will need to take many steps to ensure that the blame and liability do not land clearly at their doorstep.

The same is true for other types of threats that corporations have to deal with today. If a company has a facility that burns to the ground, the arsonist is only one small piece of this tragedy. The company is responsible for providing fire detection and suppression systems, fire-resistant construction material in certain areas, alarms, exits, fire extinguishers, and backups of all the important information that could be affected by a fire. If a building burns to the ground and takes all the records (information, customer data, inventory records, and the like that is necessary to rebuild), then this company did not perform due care in ensuring that it is protected from such disasters. In this case, the employees, shareholders, customers, and everyone affected could successfully sue the company. However, if the company did everything expected of it in the previously listed respects, it could not be successfully sued for negligence and not practicing due care.

Due care means that a company did all that it could have reasonably done to try and prevent security breaches, and also took the necessary steps to ensure that if a security breach did take place, the damages were reduced because of the controls or countermeasures that existed. Due care means that a company practiced common sense and prudent management practices with responsible actions. *Due diligence* means that the company properly investigated all of their possible weaknesses and vulnerabilities before carrying out any due care practices.

Before you know how to properly protect yourself, you need to find out what you are supposed to be afraid of. This is what due diligence is all about, researching and assessing the current level of vulnerabilities so that the true risk level is understood. Only after these steps and assessments can effective controls and safeguards be identified and implemented.

The same type of responsibility is starting to be expected of corporations pertaining to computer crime and resource protection. Information security is developed and implemented to protect an organization's valuable resources, thus appropriate safeguards need to be in place to protect the company's mission by protecting its tangible and intangible resources, reputation, employees, customers, shareholders, and legal position. Security is one piece of this that works as a means to an end and not an end within itself. Security is not practiced just for the sake of doing it. Security should be practiced in a way to accomplish fully understood, planned, and attainable goals.

 NOTE In the United States, in 1997, the Federal Sentencing Guidelines were extended to cover computer crimes and specified that senior corporate officers could be personally responsible to pay up to $290 million in fines if their company did not comply with the laws set out for them.

Senior management has an obligation to protect the company from a long list of activities that can negatively affect the company, including protection from malicious code, natural disasters, privacy violation, infraction of the law, and more.

It is dictated that management must follow the *prudent person rule*, which requires them to perform duties that prudent and responsible people would exercise in similar circumstances. They are to perform these duties with diligence and care when carrying out their responsibilities.

The costs and benefits of security should be evaluated in monetary and nonmonetary terms to ensure that the cost of security does not outweigh the expected benefits. Security should be proportional to the value of and degree of reliance required by the company pertaining to the severity, likelihood, and extent of potential damage.

Security mechanisms should be employed to reduce the frequency and severity of security-related losses. A sound security program is a smart business practice.

The senior management needs to decide upon the amount of risk they are willing to take on, pertaining to computer and information security, and implement security in a cost/benefit manner. (These issues are discussed in great detail in Chapter 3.) These risks do not always stop at the boundaries of the organization. Many companies have extranets set up with other companies, value-added networks (VAN), telecommunication lines, and more to enable them to work quickly and efficiently with other organizations. However, these relationships can get more complicated when it comes to liability and responsibilities.

When companies come together to work in an integrated manner, such as extranets and VANs, special care must be taken to ensure that each party promises to provide the necessary level of protection, liability, and responsibility needed, which should be clearly defined in the contracts that each party signs. Auditing and testing should be performed to ensure that each party is indeed holding up its side of the bargain and that its technology integrates properly with all the other parties. Interoperability can become a large, frustrating, and expensive issue in these types of arrangements.

If one of the companies does not provide the necessary level of protection and their negligence affects a partner they are working with, the affected company can sue the upstream company. For example, let's say company A and company B have constructed an extranet. Company A does not put in controls to detect and deal with viruses. Company

A gets infected with a destructive virus and it is spread to company B through the extranet. The virus corrupts critical data and causes massive disruption to company B's production. Company B can sue company A for being negligent. Both companies need to make sure that they are doing their part to ensure that their activities, or lack of them, will not negatively affect another company, which is referred to as *downstream liability*.

 NOTE Responsibility generally refers to the obligations and expected actions and behaviors of a particular party. An obligation can have a defined set of specific actions required or a more general and open approach, which enables the party to decide how it will fulfill the particular obligation. Accountability refers to the ability to hold a party responsible for certain actions or inaction.

Computer security usually has some interesting interdependencies with other factions of the company such as management functions, legal issues, employee privacy, disaster recovery and business continuity plans, and daily operations. The company that can clearly understand these types of issues and the interrelations between them can better plan, implement, and maintain their security program.

The following list describes some of the actions required to show that due care is being properly practiced in a corporation:

- Adequate physical and logical access controls
- Adequate telecommunication security, which could require encryption
- Proper information, application, and hardware backups
- Disaster recovery and business continuity plans
- Periodic review, drills, tests, and improvement in disaster recovery and business continuity plans
- Properly informing employees of expected behavior and ramifications of not following these expectations
- Developing a security policy, standards, procedures, and guidelines
- Performing security awareness training
- Running updated antivirus software
- Periodically performing penetration tests from outside and inside the network
- Implementing dial-back or preset dialing features on remote access applications
- Abiding by and updating external service level agreements (SLAs)
- Ensuring that downstream security responsibilities are being met
- Implementing measures that ensure that software piracy is not taking place
- Ensuring that proper auditing and reviewing of those audit logs are taking place
- Conducting background checks on potential employees

Each company will have different requirements when it comes to this list of due care responsibilities. If these steps are not taken, the company can be charged with negligence. For negligence to be proven in court, there usually needs to be a *legally recognized obligation*, which means there is a standard of conduct expected of the company to protect others from unreasonable risks. The company must fail to conform to this standard, which results in injury or damage to another. There must also be *proximate causation*, meaning someone can prove that the damage that was caused was the company's fault.

The following are some scenarios that show how a company can be proved negligent in its action and responsibilities.

Personal Information

A company that holds medical information, Medical Information Inc., does not have strict procedures on how patient information is disseminated or shared.

A person pretends to be a physician and calls into Medical Information Inc. and requests medical information on the patient Don Hammy. The receptionist does not question the caller and explains that Don Hammy has a brain tumor. A week later, Don Hammy does not receive the job he interviewed for and finds out that the employer called Medical Information Inc. for his medical information.

So what was improper about this activity and how would liability be determined? If and when this case went to court, the following items would be introduced and addressed:

- Legally recognized obligation:
  - The Medical Information Inc. company does not have policies and procedures in place to protect patient information.
  - The employer does not have the right to make this kind of call and is not able to use medical information against potential employees.

- Failure to conform to the required standard:
  - Sensitive information was released to an unauthorized person by a Medical Information Inc. employee.
  - The employer requested information it did not have a right to.

- Proximate causation and resulting in injury or damage:
  - The information leaked by Medical Information Inc. caused Don Hammy great embarrassment and prevented him from obtaining a specific job.
  - The employer made his decision based on information he did not have a right to inquire about in the first place. The illegally obtained information was used in a decision-making process.

The outcome was a long legal battle, but Don Hammy ended up successfully suing both companies, recovered from his brain tumor, bought an island, and has never had to work again.

Hacker Intrusion

A financial institution, Cheapo Inc., buys the necessary middleware to enable it to offer online bank account transactions for its customers. It does not add any of necessary security safeguards required for this type of communication and transactions to take place over the Internet.

Within the first two weeks, 22 customers had their checking and savings accounts hacked into, with a combined loss of $439,344.09.

What was improper about this activity and how would liability be determined? If and when this case went to court, the following items would be introduced and addressed:

- Legally recognized obligation:
  - Cheapo Inc. did not implement a firewall or IDS, harden the database holding the customer account information, or use encryption for customer transactions.
  - Cheapo Inc. did not effectively protect its customers' assets.
- Failure to conform to the required standard:
  - By not erecting the proper security policy and program and implementing the necessary security controls, Cheapo Inc. broke 12 federal regulations used to govern financial institutions.
- Proximate causation and resulting injury or damage:
  - The fact that 22 individuals lost $439,344.09 was directly related to the financial institution's lack of implementing the basic requirements of online banking and not practicing due care.

Eventually, a majority of the accounts were attacked and drained, a class action suit was brought against Cheapo Inc., a majority of the people got most of their money back, and the facility Cheapo Inc. was using as a financial institution is now used to sell tacos.

These scenarios are simplistic and described in jest, but failure to implement computer and information security properly can expose a company and its board of directors to litigation and legal punishment. Many times people cannot hide behind the corporation, but will be held accountable individually and personally. The board of directors can compromise its responsibilities to the stockholders, customers, and employees by not ensuring that due care is practiced and that the company was not being negligent in any way.

Types of Laws

There have always been various types of laws and computer crime laws are no different. The three main categories of laws are civil, criminal, and administrative (regulatory).

Civil law, also called *tort*, deals with wrongs against individuals or companies that result in damages or loss. A civil lawsuit would result in financial restitution and/or community service instead of jail sentences. If someone took another person to a civil court, the jury would decide upon liability instead of innocence or guilt, and if the person was determined to be liable for the act, then the jury would decide upon the punitive damages of the case.

Criminal law is used when an individual's conduct violates the government laws, which have been developed to protect the public. Jail sentences are commonly the punishment for criminal law cases, whereas in civil law cases the punishment is usually an amount of money that the guilty individual has to pay to the victim. In the O.J. Simpson case, he was first tried and found not guilty in the criminal law case and then found guilty in the civil law case. This can happen because the burden of proof is less in civil cases compared to criminal cases.

Administrative/regulatory law deals with regulatory standards that regulate performance and conduct. Government agencies create these standards, which are usually applied to companies and individuals within those companies. Some examples of administrative law standards could be that every building used for business must have a fire detection and suppression system, they must have easily seen exit signs, and the doors cannot be blocked in case of a fire. Companies that produce and package food and drug products are regulated by many standards they must live up to so the public is protected and aware of their actions. If a case was made that specific standards were not abided by, high officials in the companies usually would be held accountable, as in a company that makes tires that shred after a couple of years of use. The people who were in high positions of this company were most likely aware of these conditions but chose to ignore them to keep profits up. Under administrative, criminal, and civil law, they will most likely pay dearly for these decisions.

Not every country uses each category of these laws, and many countries interpret or use them differently for different reasons. This is one challenge of fighting cybercrime. If someone from Germany broke into a financial institution in Russia, but each country had different laws with different meanings applied to this type of action, which law is used to punish the criminal? Is it the German version because the criminal committed the crime from Germany or is the Russian version used because the actual crime took place there? These issues and more are being debated, but clear-cut resolutions are much farther down the road.

Intellectual Property Laws

Intellectual property laws are different from the three previously mentioned categories of law. These laws are not necessarily looking at who is right or wrong, but how a company can protect what is rightfully theirs and what can be done if these laws are violated.

A major issue in many intellectual property cases is what the company did to protect the resources it claims had been violated in one fashion or another. A company must go through many steps to protect resources that it claims to be intellectual property and must show due care in its efforts to protect those resources. If an employee sent a file to a friend and the company charged that employee with illegally sharing intellectual property, it must show the court and jury why this file is so important to the company, what type of damage it could cause if it was indeed shared, and most importantly, what the company had done to protect that file. If the company did not secure the file and tell the employees that they were not allowed to copy and share that file, then the company will most likely lose the case. However, if the company went through many steps to protect that file, explained to the employees that it was wrong to copy and share the information within the file, and that the punishment could be termination, then the company could not be charged with falsely terminating an employee.

Intellectual property can be protected by several different laws, depending upon the type of resource it is.

Trade Secret

Trade secret law protects certain types of information or resources from unauthorized use or disclosure. For a company to have their resource qualify as a trade secret, the resource must provide the company with some type of competitive value or advantage. A resource can be protected by law if it is not generally known and if it requires special skill, ingenuity, and/or expenditure of money and effort to develop it. This means that a company cannot say that the sky is blue and call it a trade secret.

A trade secret is something that is proprietary to that company and important for its survival and profitability. An example of a trade secret is the formula used for a soft drink, such as Coke or Pepsi. The resource that is claimed to be a trade secret must be confidential and protected with certain security precautions and actions. A trade secret could also be a new form of mathematics, source code of a program, method of making the perfect jellybean, or ingredients for a special, secret sauce.

Many companies require their employees to sign a nondisclosure agreement contract indicating that they understand and promise not to share the company's trade secrets with competitors. Companies do this to inform the employees of the importance of keeping certain information secret and to deter the act of sharing this information. Doing so gives them the ability to fire the employee or bring charges if the employee does not uphold his part of the contract.

Copyright

In the United States, copyright law protects the right of an author to control the public distribution, reproduction, display, and adaptation of his original work. The law covers many categories of work: pictorial, graphic, musical, dramatic, literary, pantomimes, motion picture, sculptural, sound recording, and architectural. A copyright law does not cover the specific resource like trade secret law does. It protects the expression of the idea of the resource instead of the resource itself. A copyright law is usually used to protect an author's writings, an artist's drawings, a programmer's source code, or specific rhythms and structures of a musician's creation. Computer programs and manuals are just two examples of items protected under the Federal Copyright Act. The item is covered under copyright law once the program or manual has been written. Although it is not required to include a warning and the copyright symbol (©), it is encouraged so that others cannot claim innocence after copying another's work.

The protection does not extend to any method of operations, process, concept, or procedure, but it does protect from unauthorized copying and distribution of a work. It protects the form of expression rather than the subject matter. A patent deals more with the subject matter of an invention; copyright deals with how that invention is represented.

NOTE A copyright protects the expression of ideas rather than the ideas themselves. A trade secret or patent protects the idea itself.

Computer programs can be protected under the copyright law as literary works. The law protects both the source and object code, which can be an operating system, application, or database. In some instances, the law can protect not only the code, but also the structure, sequence, and organization. The user interface is part of the definition of a software application structure, therefore one vendor could not copy the exact composition of another vendor's user interface.

Trademark
My trademark is my stupidity. Response: Good for you!

A trademark is slightly different from a copyright in that it is used to protect a word, name, symbol, sound, shape, color, or combination of these. The reason a company would trademark one of these, or a combination, is because it represents their company to a group of people or to the world. Companies have marketing departments that work very hard in coming up with something new that will make them be noticed and stand out in a crowd of competitors, and trademarking the result of this work is a way of properly protecting it and ensuring that others cannot copy and use it.

Patent
Patents are given to individuals or companies to grant the owner legal ownership and enable the owner to exclude others from using or copying the invention covered by the patent. The invention must be novel, useful, and not obvious—which means, for example, that a company could not patent air. Thank goodness. If a company figured out how to patent air, we would have to pay for each and every breath we took!

After the inventor completes an application for a patent and it is approved, the patent grants a limited property right to exclude others from making, using, or selling the invention for a specific period of time. This has been used by pharmaceutical companies where one company develops a specific drug and acquires a patent for it. This company is the only one that can manufacture and sell this drug until the stated year in the patent is up. After that, all companies are allowed to manufacture and sell this product. This is why a new little white pill is $17 each for ten years. After ten years (or however long the patent is), all pharmaceutical companies can make the same drug, which then costs 2 cents per pill.

This also takes place with algorithms. If an inventor of an algorithm acquires a patent, she has full control over who can use it in their products. If the inventor lets a vendor incorporate the algorithm, then she will most likely get a fee and possibly a royalty fee on each instance of the product sold.

Internal Protection of Intellectual Property

Ensuring that specific resources are protected by the previously mentioned laws is very important, but there are other measures that must be taken internally to make sure the resources that are confidential in nature are properly identified and protected.

The resources protected by one of the previously mentioned laws need to be identified and integrated into the company's data classification scheme. This should be directed by management and carried out by the IT staff. The identified resources should have the necessary level of access control protection, auditing enabled, and proper storage environment. If it is deemed secret, then not everyone in the company should be able to access it. Once the individuals who are allowed to have access are identified, their level of access and interaction with the resource should be defined in a granular method. The attempts of access and manipulation should be properly audited, and the resource should be stored on a protected server with the necessary security mechanisms.

Employees must be informed of the level of secrecy or confidentiality of the resource, and their expected behavior, pertaining to that resource, must be explained.

If a company fails in one or all of these steps, they may not be covered by the laws described previously because they are not practicing due care and properly protecting the resource they have vowed to be so important to the survival and competitiveness of their company.

References

United States Copyright Office: **www.loc.gov/copyright**

Patent/Trademark/Copyright Archive: **www.eff.org/Intellectual_property**

Office of the Intellectual Property Counsel: **www.caltech.edu/ott/security/ OIPC_Home.htm**

Copyright Tutorials: **www.ksu.edu/uauc/intprop/tutorial.htm**

Software Piracy

Software piracy indicates that the intellectual or creative work of an author has been used or duplicated without permission or compensation to the author. It is an act of infringement on ownership rights and if someone is caught, the person could be sued civilly for damages, be criminally prosecuted, or both. Duplicate software is everywhere and software piracy is everywhere. Up until now, there have not been efficient mechanisms put into place to ensure that software could not be copied and illegally used. Companies are testing out new features, and within time, it will most likely not be as easy to illegally copy and use software as it is now.

When a vendor develops an application, the program is usually licensed rather than sold outright. The license agreement contains provisions relating the use and security of the software and the corresponding manuals. If an individual or company fails to observe and abide by those requirements, the license may be terminated, and depending on the actions, criminal charges may be implemented. The risk to the vendor developing and selling the software is the loss of profits that it would have earned. Many companies and their employees do not abide by their software licenses and the employees use the company's software for their home use.

Some software vendors sell bulk licenses, which enable several users to use the product simultaneously. The vendor could have incorporated a monitoring system that keeps track of the usability to ensure that the customer does not go over this limit. The network administrator or security officer should be aware of all of these types of contractual commitments required by software companies. This person needs to be educated on the restrictions the company is under and make sure proper enforcement mechanisms are in place. If a company is found guilty of illegally copying software or using more copies than their license permits, the network administrator or security officer who was put in charge of this task will be the first called on the carpet.

The Software Protection Association (SPA) has been formed by major companies to enforce proprietary rights of software. The association was formed to protect the founding companies' software developments, but it also helps others to ensure that their software is properly licensed. These are huge issues for companies that develop and produce software because a majority of their revenue comes from licensing fees.

Other international groups have been formed to protect against software pirates and stealing. These include the Federation Against Software Theft (FAST), headquartered in London, and the Business Software Alliance (BSA), based in Washington, D.C. They provide similar functionality as the SPA and make efforts to protect software around the world.

One of the offenses an individual or company can commit is decompiling vendor object code. This is usually done to figure out how the application works by obtaining the original source code, which is confidential, and perhaps to reverse-engineer it in the hope of understanding the intricate details of its functionality. Another purpose of reverse-engineering products is to be able to detect security flaws within the code that can later be exploited. This is how some buffer overflows are discovered.

Many times the object code is decompiled into source code and the individual either finds security holes to take advantage of or alters the source code to produce some type of functionality that the original vendor did not want to exist. One example is an individual who decompiled a program that displays e-books and publications. The vendor did not want anyone to be able to copy the e-publications its product displayed and inserted an encoder that enforced this limitation within the object code of their product. The individual decompiled the object code and figured out how to create a decoder that would overcome this restriction and enable users to make copies of the e-publications, which infringed upon those authors' and publishers' copyrights.

The individual was arrested and prosecuted under the new Digital Millennium Copyright Act (DMCA), which makes it illegal to create products that circumvent copyright protection mechanisms. As of this writing, this new act and how it will be enforced have caused many debates and controversy because of its possible negative effects on free speech and legitimate research.

Interestingly enough, many computer-oriented individuals protested this individual's arrest, several marches took place, and the company that was pressing charges (Adobe) quickly decided to drop all charges.

Discarding Equipment and Software Issues

When equipment is being discarded, sold, or moved to a different department or company, all previous information and files should be completely erased. This is logical, however, there could be some not so obvious requirements pertaining to the hardware and the software that is loaded on it. Depending on the vendor of the system, it may be illegal to sell a computer with an operating system without proper licensing, or it may be illegal to sell the system without an operating system at all.

In one example, a company wanted to sell 2,000 of its older 486 and lower-end Pentium systems. The network administrator instructed the network engineers to format and fdisk each and every system. After this task was complete, the network administrator found out that through its agreement with the vendor of the computers, it would be illegal to sell even one of those computers without a functioning operating system. The network administrator or security officer should investigate the proper procedures to protect the company pertaining to license and vendor agreements at each stage of a system's life-cycle. In this instance, the network engineers had to go back and reinstall the necessary operating system on each of the 2,000 computers.

 NOTE Most reporting of illegal use of software comes from disgruntled employees.

Trade secret, copyright, patent, and trademark laws can differ from country to country. Any vendor that is interested in selling its product should be aware of these differences and should take the necessary steps to properly protect its product.

Computer Crime Investigations

As mentioned earlier in the chapter, law enforcement has many challenges and barriers when it comes to fighting cybercrime. In most instances, they only have a small force that is properly trained, the rules of jurisdiction can get fuzzy, and determining exactly what laws have been broken in this quickly evolving computing age can be overwhelming at best. Another issue that law enforcement has to deal with is properly gathering evidence from a computer or media, which is very different from collecting evidence from a regular crime scene. This section will go over some of these barriers and many of the issues that have been addressed, as well as guidelines that have been developed to help with future investigations.

A Different Approach

Many computer crimes go unreported because the victim, in many cases, is not aware of the incident or wants to just patch the hole the hacker came in through and keep the details quiet to escape embarrassment or the risk of hurting its reputation. This makes it harder to know the real statistics of how many attacks happen each day, what degree of damage that is caused, and what types of attack and methods are being used.

This lack of reporting crimes does not make fighting this type of crime any easier. A law enforcement agent who investigates a computer crime has to deal with a shift from physical damage and thefts to an intangible electronic environment that requires a different type of skill to get around in, identify clues, and be able to obtain usable evidence. The ease of committing a cybercrime, the relative anonymity available to the attacker, and the difficulty in tracking down the attacker usually gives the criminal more advantages than the cybercop. The Internet and interconnection of computers are making targets much more accessible than ever before, and the criminals have much lower risk of getting caught.

Law enforcement agents who fight cybercrime must be very talented.

Many of the existing theft, damage, and extortion laws are written to protect physical property, not necessarily the type of damage that can be done by bytes over a phone line or network wire.

When a company endures a computer crime, they should leave the environment and evidence unaltered and contact the authorities. Someone who is unfamiliar with the proper process of collecting data and evidence from a crime scene could destroy evidence. All hope of prosecuting and achieving a conviction would be lost. Companies should have procedures for many issues in computer security such as enforcement procedures, disaster recovery and continuity procedures, and backup procedures. It would be best if they also had a procedure for dealing with a cybercrime or incident. Most companies do not have a clue who to call or what to do right after they have been the victim of a cybercrime. This means the company should have an incident response policy and procedures set up just for this type of event before it actually takes place.

The incident response policy should indicate if systems can be taken offline to try and save evidence or if systems have to continue functioning with the risk of destroying evidence. Each system and functionality should have a priority assigned to it. For instance, if the file server is hit, it should be removed from the network, but not shut down. However, if the mail server is hit, it should not be removed from the network or shut down because of the priority the company attributes to the mail server over the file server. Trade-offs and decisions will have to be made, but it is better to think through these issues before the situation occurs because better logic is usually possible before a crisis, with less emotion and chaos.

If the company would like to handle these types of issues in-house, an *incident response team* should be developed who is responsible for responding to major security incidents. The team should have someone from senior management, the network administrator, security officer, possibly a network engineer and/or programmer, and a liaison for public affairs. The purpose of having an incident response team is to ensure that there is a group of people who are properly skilled, who follow a standard set of procedures, and who are singled out and called upon when this type of event takes place.

 NOTE In reality, usually the technical team members are called to the scene to carry out their functions and the other team members may be called to update them on the situation and possibly ask them for direction pertaining to specific issues of the situation.

The team should have proper reporting procedures established, have the ability to provide prompt reaction, have coordination with law enforcement, and be an important element of the overall security program.

The incident response team should have the following basic items:

- List of outside agencies and resources to contact or report to
- List of computer or forensics experts to contact
- Steps on how to search for evidence
- Steps on how to secure and preserve evidence
- List of items that should be included on the report

- A list that indicates how the different systems should be treated in this type of situation (removed from the Internet and the network and powered down)

When a suspected crime is reported, there are some steps that should be followed that ensure uniformity in approach and help to make sure steps have not been skipped. First, the report should be investigated and it should be determined that an actual crime has been committed. Senior management should be informed immediately. If the suspect is an employee, a human resources representative must be called right away. The sooner the documenting of events begins, the better, so if the starting time of the crime could be documented along with the company employees and resources involved, it would provide a good start. At this point, the company must decide if it wants to conduct its own forensics investigation or call in the big guns. If experts are going to be called in, the system that was attacked should be left alone to try to preserve as much evidence of the attack as possible. If the company decides to conduct its own forensics, there are many issues to deal with and tricky elements to address.

Computer Forensics and Proper Collection of Evidence

I just spilled coffee on our only evidence. Response: Case closed. Let's all go home.

It is very important that the people conducting the forensics investigation are properly skilled in this trade and know what to look out for. If someone reboots the attacked system or goes around looking at different files, it could corrupt viable evidence, change timestamps on key files, and erase footprints the criminal may have left. In most situations, it is best to remove the system from the network, dump the contents of the memory, power down the system, and make a sound image of the attacked system and perform forensic analysis on this copy. Working on the copy instead of the original drive will ensure that the evidence stays unharmed on the original system in case some steps in the investigation actually corrupt or destroy data. Dumping the memory contents to a file before doing any work on the system or powering it down is a crucial step because of the information that could be stored there. This is another method of capturing fragile information.

The response team will need specialized forensics tools, an evidence collection notebook, containers, a camera, and evidence identification tags. It is important that the notebook is not a spiral notebook, but a notebook that is bound in a way that one can tell if pages have been removed.

 NOTE In most cases, an investigator's notebook cannot be used as evidence in court. It can only be used by the investigator to refresh his memory during a proceeding, but it cannot be submitted as evidence in any form.

The next crucial piece is to keep a proper *chain of custody* of the evidence. Because evidence from these types of crimes can be very volatile and easily dismissed from court because of improper handling, it is important to follow very strict and organized procedures when collecting and tagging evidence.

When copies of data need to be made, this process must meet certain standards to ensure quality and reliability. Specialized software for this purpose can be used. The copies must be able to be independently verified and tamperproof.

Each piece of evidence should be marked in some way with the date, time, initials of the collector, and a case number if one has been assigned. Magnetic disk surfaces should not be marked on, and floppy disks should only be marked with a felt tip pen. Reel-to-reel magnetic tape can be marked on the non-shiny side of the tape within the first 10 to 15 feet, also known as the *leader* part. The piece of evidence should then be sealed in a container and the container should be marked with the same information. The container should be sealed with evidence tape and if possible, the writing should be on the tape so a broken seal can be detected.

NOTE The chain of custody of evidence dictates that all evidence be labeled with information indicating who secured and validated it.

Wires and cables should be labeled, and a photograph of the labeled system should be taken before it is actually disassembled. Media should be write-protected. Storage should be dust free, kept at room temperature without much humidity, and, of course, not close to any strong magnets.

If possible, the crime scene should be photographed, including behind the computer if the crime involved some type of physical break in. Documents, papers, and devices should be handled with cloth gloves and placed into containers and sealed. All storage media should be contained, even if it has been erased, because data still may be obtainable.

Because this type of evidence can be easily erased or destroyed and is complex in nature, identification, recording, collection, preservation, transportation, and interpretation are all important. After everything is properly labeled, a chain of custody log should be made of each container and an overall log should be made capturing all events.

For a crime to be successfully prosecuted, solid evidence is required. Computer forensics is the art of retrieving this evidence and preserving it in the proper ways to make it admissible in court. Without proper computer forensics, hardly any computer crimes could ever be properly and successfully presented in court.

The most common reasons for improper evidence collection are no established incident response team, no established incident response procedures, poorly written policy, and a broken chain of custody.

NOTE A chain of custody is a history that shows how evidence was collected, analyzed, transported, and preserved in order to be presented as evidence in court. Because electronic evidence can be easily modified, a clearly defined chain of custody demonstrates that the evidence is trustworthy.

There are other issues to think through when a company is developing incident response procedures, such as how the issue will be explained to the press, customers, and shareholders. This could require the collaboration of the public relations department, management, human resources (if employees are involved), IT department, and the legal department. There can be legal ramifications in a cybercrime that do not seem apparent right from the beginning and must be handled delicately. The company should decide how it will report the matter to outsiders, because if they do not present it the way they want it to be viewed, it could be presented in a totally different light.

Incident Handling

In the previous sections, incident handling was addressed in an indirect manner, but a clear definition of incident handling and its place within a company is important.

There are many types of threats a computer and network can face, each requiring a specialized way to properly recover. However, a basic outline of how all incidents are to be handled should be drafted and enforced. This is a much better approach than the way that most companies deal with these threats, which is usually in an ad hoc, reactive and confusing manner. A clearly defined incident-handling process can be more cost effective, enable recovery to happen more quickly, and provide a uniform approach with certain expectation of its results.

Incident handling should be closely related to disaster recovery planning and should be part of the company's disaster recovery plan. Both are reacting to some type of incident that can require a quick reaction so that the company can return to normal operations. Incident handling can be the portion of a recovery plan that responds to malicious technical threats.

The primary goal of incident handling is to contain and repair any damage caused by an event and to prevent any further damage. It can also improve internal communications and a company's ability to be prepared for threats and disasters.

Without an effective incident-handling program, individuals who have the best intentions can sometimes make the situation worse by damaging evidence, systems, or spreading malicious code. Many times the attacker booby-traps the compromised system to erase specific critical files if a user does something as simple as list the files in a directory. A compromised system can no longer be trusted because the internal commands listed in the path could be altered to perform unexpected activities. The system could now have a backdoor for the attacker to enter when he wants, or there could be Trojan horses silently waiting for a user to start snooping around only to destroy any and all evidence.

Incident handling should be closely linked to the company's security training and awareness program to ensure that these types of mishaps do not take place. The past issues that the incident recovery team encountered can be used in future training sessions to help others learn what the company is faced with.

It is important that employees know how to report an incident to the incident-handling team. The process must be centralized, easy to accomplish (or they won't bother), convenient, and welcomed. Some employees feel reluctant to report incidents because they are afraid they will get pulled into something they do not want to be involved with or accused of something they did not do. There is nothing like trying to do the right thing and getting hit with a big stick. Employees should feel comfortable about the process, which means suggestions on improving the process should be looked at seriously.

A sound incident-handling program works with outside agencies and counterparts. The members of the team should be on the mailing list of the Computer Emergency Response Team (CERT) so they can be aware of new issues and can spot malicious events, hopefully, before they get out of hand. CERT is responsible for monitoring and advising users and companies about security preparation and security breaches on the Internet. The team tracks and reports security issues and develops recommendations with clearly written steps to be taken if faced with specific threats.

References

CERT Coordination Center: **www.cert.org**

Computer Security and Ethics: **www.uga.edu/compsec**

Bibliography of Incident Handling Documents: **www.cert.dfn.de/eng/ pre99papers/certbib.html**

Incident Handling Information: **csrc.nist.gov/topics/inchand.html**

What Is Admissible in Court?

He is guilty because I don't like him. Response: Um, I need more than that.

Computer logs are important in many aspects of the IT world. They are usually used to troubleshoot an issue or to try to understand the events that took place at a specific moment in time. When computer logs are to be used as evidence in court, they must be collected in the regular course of business. Most of the time, computer-related documents are considered *hearsay*, meaning the evidence is secondhand evidence. Hearsay evidence is not normally admissible in court unless it has firsthand evidence that can be used to prove the evidence's accuracy, trustworthiness, and reliability, such as a businessperson who generated the computer logs and collected them. It is important that this person generates and collects logs as a normal part of his business and not just this one time for court. The value of evidence depends upon the genuineness and competence of the source.

It is important to show that the logs, and all evidence, have not been tampered with in any way, which is the reason for the chain of custody of evidence. There are several tools that run some type of checksum or hashing function on the logs, which will allow the team to be alerted if something has been modified.

When evidence is being collected, one issue that can come up is the user's expectation of privacy. If an employee is suspected of and being charged for a computer crime, he might claim that his files on the computer he uses are personal and not available to law enforcement and the courts. This is why it is important for companies to conduct security awareness training, have employees sign contracts pertaining to the acceptable use of the company's computers and equipment, and to have legal banners pop up on each and every employees' computer when they log on. These are key elements to establish that a user has no right to privacy when he is using company equipment. The following banner is suggested by CERT Advisory:

"This system is for the use of authorized users only. Individuals using this computer system without authority, or in excess of their authority, are subject to having all of their activities on this system monitored and recorded by system personnel.

In the course of monitoring an individual improperly using this system, or in the course of system maintenance, the activities of authorized users may also be monitored.

Anyone using this system expressly consents to such monitoring and is advised that if such monitoring reveals possible evidence of criminal activity, system personnel may provide the evidence of such monitoring to law enforcement officials."

This explicit warning strengthens a legal case that can be brought against an employee or intruder because the continued use of the system after viewing this type of warning implies that the person acknowledges the security policy and gives permission to be monitored.

Evidence has its own life cycle and it is important that the individuals involved with the investigation understand the phases of the life cycle and properly follow them.

The life cycle of evidence includes:

- Collection and identification
- Storage, preservation, and transportation
- Presentation in court
- Being returned to victim or owner

There are several types of evidence that can be used in a trial: written, oral, computer generated, and visual or audio. Oral evidence is a testimony of a witness. Visual or audio is usually a captured event during the crime or right after it.

Not all evidence is equal in the eyes of the law and some types of evidence have more clout, or weight, than other types. The following sections quickly describe the different ways evidence can be categorized and valued.

Best Evidence

Best evidence is the primary evidence used in a trial because it provides the most reliability. An example of something that would be categorized as best evidence is an original signed contract. Oral evidence is not considered best evidence because there is no first-hand reliable proof that supports its validity, and it therefore does not have as good of a standing as legal documents. Oral evidence cannot be used to dispute a legal document, but it can be used to interpret the document.

Secondary Evidence

Secondary evidence is not viewed as reliable and strong in proving innocence or guilt when compared to best evidence. Oral evidence, such as a witness testimony, and copies of original documents are placed in the secondary evidence category.

Direct Evidence

Direct evidence can prove a fact all by itself instead of needing backup information to refer to. When using direct evidence, presumptions are not required. One example of direct evidence is the testimony of a witness who saw a crime take place. Although this oral evidence would be secondary in nature, meaning a case could not rest on just it alone, it is also direct evidence, meaning the lawyer does not necessarily need to provide other evidence to back it up. Many times direct evidence is based on information gathered from a witness's five senses.

Conclusive Evidence

Conclusive evidence is irrefutable and cannot be contradicted. Conclusive evidence is very strong all by itself and does not require corroboration.

Circumstantial Evidence

Circumstantial evidence can prove an intermediate fact that can then be used to deduce or assume the existence of another fact. This type of fact is used so that the judge or jury will logically assume the existence of a primary fact. For example, if a suspect told a friend he was going to bring down eBay's Web site, a case could not rest on that piece of evidence alone because it is circumstantial. However, this evidence can cause the jury to assume that because the suspect said he was going to do it and hours later it happened, maybe he was the one who did the crime.

Corroborative Evidence

Corroborative evidence is supporting evidence used to help prove an idea or point. It cannot stand on its own, but is used as a supplementary tool to help prove a primary piece of evidence.

Opinion Evidence

When a witness testifies, the *opinion rule* dictates that she must testify to only the facts of the issue and not her opinion of the facts. This is slightly different from when an expert witness is used because he is used primarily for his educated opinion. Most lawyers will call in expert witnesses to testify and help the defending or prosecuting sides to better understand the subject matter so that they can help the judge and jury to better understand the matters of the case.

Hearsay Evidence

Hearsay evidence pertains to oral or written evidence presented in court that is secondhand and that has no firsthand proof of accuracy or reliability. If a witness testifies about something he heard someone else say, it is too far removed from fact and has too many variables that can cloud the truth. If business documents were made during regular business routines, they can be admissible. However, if these records were made just to be presented in court, they could be categorized as hearsay evidence.

It is important that evidence be sufficient, reliable, and relevant to the case at hand. These characteristics of evidence provide a foundation for a case and help ensure that the evidence is legally permissible.

For the evidence to be *sufficient*, it must be persuasive enough to convince a reasonable person of the validity of the findings. This means that the evidence cannot be wishy-washy in that one person interprets it to mean one thing and another person in terprets it to mean something else. Sufficient evidence also means that it cannot be easily doubted.

For evidence to be *reliable*, or competent, it must be consistent with fact. Evidence cannot be reliable if it is based on someone's opinion or copies of an original document, because there is too much room for error. Reliable evidence means that it is factual and not circumstantial.

For evidence to be *relevant*, it must have a reasonable and sensible relationship to the findings. If a judge rules that a person's past traffic tickets cannot be brought up in a murder trial, this means that the judge has ruled that the traffic tickets are not relevant to the case at hand. Thus, the prosecuting lawyer cannot even mention them in court.

If a piece of evidence is found to be sufficient, reliable, and relevant to the case, it must also be legally permissible, meaning that it was obtained in a legal way. The evidence must not have been obtained through an unlawful search and seizure, recorded illegally, or through a coerced confession. All of these steps must be taken to ensure that the evidence will not be thrown out once it gets to court. (This section will not only help you on the CISSP exam, but will also come in handy the next time you watch *Law & Order*.)

Surveillance, Search, and Seizure

There are two main types of surveillance when it comes to identifying computer crimes: physical and via the computer. Physical surveillance pertains to security cameras, security guards, and closed-circuit TV (CCTV), illustrated in Figure 10-2, which may capture evidence. Physical surveillance can also be used by an undercover agent who learns about the suspect's spending activities, family and friends, and personal habits in the hope of gathering more clues for the case.

Computer surveillance pertains to auditing events, which passively monitors events by using network sniffers, keyboard monitors, wiretaps, and line monitoring. In most jurisdictions, active monitoring may require a search warrant. In most workplace environments, to legally monitor an individual, the person had to have been warned ahead of time that her activities may be subject to this type of monitoring.

Figure 10-2 Surveillance can happen through CCTVs, cameras, keyboard monitoring, network sniffers, or line monitors.

Search and seizure activities can get tricky depending on what is being searched for and where. For example, American citizens are protected by the Fourth Amendment against unlawful search and seizure. So law enforcement agencies must have probable cause and request a search warrant from a judge or court. The actual search can only take place in the areas outlined by the warrant. Private citizens are not subjected to protecting these Fourth Amendment rights of others unless they are acting as police agents. So if Kristy's boss warned all employees that the management could remove files from their computers at any time, and her boss was not a cop or acting as a police agent, she could not successfully claim that her Fourth Amendment rights were violated. Kristy's boss may have violated some specific privacy laws, but he did not violate Kristy's Fourth Amendment rights.

There are circumstances that could allow a law enforcement agent to seize evidence that is not included in the warrant, such as if the suspect tries to destroy the evidence. In other words, there is an impeding possibility that evidence might be destroyed, therefore there is a requirement for law enforcement to quickly seize the evidence. This is referred to as *exigent circumstances*, and a judge will later decide if this was carried out properly and legally so that the evidence can be admitted. For example, if a police officer had a search warrant that allowed him to search a suspect's living room but no other rooms, and then he saw the suspect dumping cocaine down the toilet, the police officer could obtain the cocaine even though it was in a room not covered under his search warrant.

After evidence is gathered, the chain of custody needs to be enacted and enforced to make sure the evidence's integrity is not compromised.

Enticement and Entrapment

There can be a thin line between enticement and entrapment when it comes to capturing a suspect's actions. *Enticement* is legal and ethical, and *entrapment* is neither legal nor ethical. In the world of computer crimes, a honeypot is always a good example to show the difference between enticement and entrapment. Companies put systems in their screened subnets that either emulate services attackers usually like to take advantage of or actually have the services enabled on those systems. The hope is that if an attacker breaks into the company's network, she will go right to the honeypot instead of the systems that are actual production machines. The attacker will be enticed to go to the honeypot system because it has many open ports and services running and exhibits vulnerabilities that the attacker would want to exploit. The company can log the attacker's actions and later attempt to prosecute. This example is legal unless the company crosses the line to entrapment. For example, say there is a link on a Web page that indicates that if the attacker clicks on it, she could then download thousands of MP3 files for free. However, when the attacker clicks on that link, she is taken to the honeypot system instead and the company records all of her actions and attempts to prosecute. Entrapment does not prove that the suspect had the intent of committing a crime; it only proves that she was successfully tricked.

Interviewing and Interrogating

Once surveillance and search and seizure activities have been performed, it is very likely that suspects must be interviewed and interrogated. When this is needed, there should be one person in charge of the interview or interrogation, with one or two others present. The topics of discussion and questions should be prepared beforehand and asked in a calm fashion. The purpose of an interrogation is to obtain evidence for a trial, therefore it should be properly planned and carried out.

Interrogating employees requires specific guidelines and procedures to make it successful.

The employee interrogator should be in a position that is senior to the employee suspect. A vice president is not going to be very intimidated or willing to spill his guts to the mailroom clerk. The interrogation should be held in a private place, and the suspect should be relatively comfortable and at ease. If exhibits are going to be shown to the suspect, they should be shown one at a time, and otherwise kept in a folder. It is not necessary to read a person their rights before questioning unless law enforcement officers do the interview.

What the interrogators do not want to happen during an interrogation is to be deceived by the suspect, to relinquish important information pertaining to the investigation, or to have the suspect flee before a trial date is set.

Import and Export Laws

As stated earlier, various countries have different laws pertaining to copyright, trade secrets, trademarks, and such. Countries also have different import and export restrictions.

The main technology that countries restrict in transborder issues is encryption. Some countries restrict the type or strength of encryption that can be used between countries or that can be bought and sold between different countries. This is because governments want to be able to break the encryption and listen in on communications if they are suspected of being about illegal activities.

 NOTE There are no restrictions on domestic use in the United States pertaining to encryption products.

If a vendor wants to sell encryption technologies to another country or include encryption within its product, it must thoroughly research the restrictions of the source and destination countries and seek legal advice to ensure that no laws or regulations are being broken accidentally.

In the United States, the Bureau of Export Administration (BXA), in the U.S. Department of Commerce, governs exportation of encryption mechanisms. In the past, exportation of these technologies has been extremely strict. In October 2000, the BXA published a rule creating a "free-trade zone" approved by the President and Vice President, which enables U.S. exporters to export most encryption products to 15 European Union member states and 8 additional trading partners. This included PCs, laptops, handheld devices, wireless technologies, software, and network devices that use encryption technologies. This greatly reduced the process vendors had to go through to get their products approved to be sold in other countries.

There are still strict exportation regulations on the countries considered terrorist-supporting states. For further information on these issues, please refer to the references provided.

Transborder Information Flow

Many companies communicate internationally every day through e-mail, telephone lines, satellites, fiber cables, and long distance wireless transmission. It is important for a company to research the laws of different countries pertaining to information flow and privacy.

Data can route through many different countries before arriving at its destination. Network routing should be analyzed regularly to understand how data moves from one place to another. Some countries restrict the flow of personal information and financial data, or deem it illegal. Wiretapping may be able to occur without any legal consequence. It all depends on the laws of the countries you are passing data through, thus you should be aware of them.

Other issues to consider pertaining to the privacy of confidential information:

2

- **Data retrieval advances**   Ways of collecting a vast amount of personal data and storing it in central repositories

- **Convergent technologies**   Technical methods of gathering, analyzing, and distributing information

- **Globalization**   Distributing information beyond national borders

If these technologies and methods are used to collect and store private data, the data must be properly secured and access drastically restricted.

References

U.S. Bureau of Industry and Security: **www.bxa.doc.gov**

Export Administration Regulations FAQ: **chaos.fedworld.gov/bxa/faq.html**

Privacy

There is a sense that privacy is becoming more threatened as the world relies more and more on technology.

For example, in the United States, there have been privacy laws enacted and enforced, such as the Federal Privacy Act of 1974, and new laws, such as the Gramm-Leach-Bliley Act of 1999 and the Health Insurance Portability and Accountability Act (HIPAA), which show an increase in the need to protect personal privacy information.

The Federal Privacy Act was put into place to protect the U.S. citizens' sensitive information that was collected by government agencies. It states that any data collected must be done in a fair and lawful manner. The data is only to be used for the purposes it was collected for and held only for a reasonable amount of time. If an agency collects data on a person, that person has the right to receive a report outlining data collected about him if it is requested. Similar laws exist in many countries around the world.

Many of the privacy principles addressed in most countries' privacy laws state that the information must be accurate, kept up-to-date, and cannot be disclosed to a third party unless authorized by statute or consent of that individual. People also have the right to make a correction to their personal information. If data is to be transmitted to a location where the equivalent security protection cannot be ensured, then transmission is prohibited.

Within a corporation, there are several employee privacy issues that must be thought through and addressed if the company wants to be properly protected. An understanding that each state can have different privacy regulations should prompt the company to investigate exactly what they can and cannot monitor before doing so.

If a company has learned that the state the facility is located in permits keyboard, e-mail, and surveillance monitoring, they must take the proper steps in ensuring that the employees know that these types of monitoring may be put into place. This is the best way for a company to protect itself, make sure it has a legal leg to stand on if necessary, and not present the employees with any surprises.

The monitoring has to be work related, meaning that a manager may have the right to listen in on his employees' conversations with customers, but he does not have the right to listen in on personal conversations that are not work related. Monitoring also must happen in a consistent way where all employees are subjected to monitoring instead of picking out one or two people.

If a company feels that it may be necessary to monitor e-mail messages and usage, this needs to be explained to the employees first of all through policy, and then through a constant reminder such as a banner or regular training. It is best to have an employee read a document describing what type of monitoring they could be encountered with, what is considered acceptable behavior, and what the consequences of not meeting those expectations are. The employees should sign this document, which can later be treated as a legal document if necessary.

A company that wants to be able to monitor e-mail should have this addressed in their security policy. It should outline who can and cannot read employee messages, describe the circumstances where e-mail monitoring may be acceptable, and where the e-mail can be accessed. Some companies indicate that they will only monitor e-mail that lives on the mail server, whereas other companies declare the right to read employee messages if they reside on the mail server or the employee's computer. It is important that the company does not promise privacy to employees that may not be provided, because that could initiate a lawsuit.

Although IT and security professionals have access to many parts of computer systems and the network, this does not mean it is ethical and right to overstep the bounds that could threaten a user's privacy. Only the tasks necessary to enforce the security policy should take place and nothing further that could compromise another's privacy.

Prescreening Personnel

Chapter 3 described why it is important to properly screen individuals before hiring them into a corporation. These steps are necessary to help the company protect itself and to ensure that it is getting the type of employee that is required for the job. This chapter will look at some of the issues from the other side of the table, which deals with that individual's privacy rights.

There are limitations on the type and amount of information an organization can obtain on a potential employee. The limitations and regulations for background checks vary from jurisdiction to jurisdiction, so the hiring manager will want to consult the legal department. Usually human resources will develop an outline for hiring managers to follow when it comes to interviews and background checks.

There are also potential problems when an employee leaves the company. If the employee is terminated, laid off, moves on to a competitor company, or has any unresolved issues with the company, there may be instances of fraud, destruction, or sharing of confidential information. An exit interview should be performed that requires the employee to sign a document indicating he does not have any confidential papers and promises not to violate the trade secret and confidential information rules that he agreed to when he was hired.

Laws, Directives, and Regulations

Regulation in computer and information security can cover many areas for many different reasons. Some issues that require regulation are data privacy, computer misuse, software copyright, data protection, and controls on cryptography. These regulations can be implemented in various arenas such as government and private sectors for reasons dealing with environmental protection, intellectual property, national security, personal privacy, public order, health and safety, and prevention of cruelty and corruption. Regulations have had to provide an interesting, and many times debated, balance between the individual and the corporation.

Security professionals need to keep up-to-date on computer laws and regulations.

Security professionals have so much to keep up with these days, from understanding how the latest worm attacks work and how to properly protect against them. They need to grasp how new versions of DoS attacks take place and what tools are used to accomplish them. Professionals also need to follow what new security products are released and how they compare to the existing products. This is followed up by keeping track of new technologies, service patches, hotfixes, encryption methods, access control mechanisms, telecommunication security issues, social engineering, and physical security. Laws and regulations are not usually at the top of security professionals' list of interests or things to know. However, they are important, especially if you are asked to be involved with identifying and investigating a computer crime or asked to provide your professional opinion or work as an expert witness. Laws and regulations can be another item on the large heap of information a security professional is expected to keep current on, but in many situations it is just as important as any other security issues.

NOTE In many countries, to deal more effectively with computer crime, legislative bodies have broadened the definition of property to include data.

Laws, regulations, and directives developed by governments or appointed agencies do not usually provide detailed instructions to follow to properly protect computers and company assets. Each environment is too diverse in topology, technology, infrastructure, requirements, functionality, and personnel. Because technology changes at such a fast pace, these laws and regulations could never successfully represent reality. Instead, they specify requirements expected from different business types. They work as a framework of rules, and it is up to each company to fill in that framework, but properly stay within the bounds.

 NOTE Over time, the CISSP exam has become more global in nature instead of U.S.-centric. Specific laws have been taken out of the test recently so you do not need to spend a lot of time learning them. Be familiar with why laws are developed and put in place and their overall goals, instead of memorizing specific laws and dates.

Health Insurance Portability and Accountability Act (HIPAA)

The *Health Insurance Portability and Accountability Act (HIPAA) of the United States*, a new federal regulation, has been mandated to provide national standards and procedures for the storage, use, and transmission of personal medical information and health care data. This regulation provides a framework and guidelines to ensure security, integrity, and privacy when handling confidential medical information. HIPAA outlines how security should be managed for any facility that creates, accesses, shares, or destroys medical information.

People's health records can be used and misused in different scenarios for many reasons. As health records migrate from a paper-based system to an electronic system, they become easier to maintain, access, and transfer, but they also become easier to manipulate and access in an unauthorized manner. Traditionally, health care facilities have lagged behind other businesses in their information and network security mechanisms, architecture, and security enforcement because there was no real business need to expend the energy and money to put these items in place. Now there is.

HIPAA brings steep federal penalties for noncompliance. If medical information is used in a way that violates the privacy standards dictated by HIPAA, even by mistake, there are monetary penalties of $100 per violation up to $25,000 per year, per standard. If protected health information is obtained or disclosed knowingly, the fines can be as much as $50,000 and one year in prison. If the information is obtained or disclosed under false pretenses, the cost can go up to $250,000 and ten years in prison if there is intent to sell or use the information for commercial advantage, personal gain, or malicious harm. This is serious business. (Please review Appendix C for more indepth information on HIPAA, including a compliancy matrix.)

Gramm-Leach-Bliley Act of 1999

This act requires financial institutions to develop privacy notices and give their customers the option to prohibit the banks from sharing their information with nonaffiliated third parties. The act dictates that the board of directors is responsible for many of the security issues within a financial institution, indicates that risk management must be implemented, all employees need to be trained on information security issues, and implemented security measures must be fully tested. It also required these facilities to have a written security policy in place. (Please review Appendix F for further information pertaining to this act.)

Computer Fraud and Abuse Act

This act was written in 1986 and amended in 1996 and is the primary federal antihacking statute. It categorizes seven forms of activity as federal crimes:

- Prohibits the knowing access of computers of the federal government to obtain classified information without authorization or access through the use of excess of authorization

- Prohibits the intentional access of a computer to obtain information from a financial institution, the federal government, or any protected computer involved in interstate or foreign communications without authorization or through the use of excess of authorization

- Prohibits the intentional and unauthorized access of computers of the federal government, or computers used by or for the government when the access affects the government's use of that computer

- Prohibits the knowing access of a protected computer without authorization or in excess of authorization with the intent to defraud

- Prohibits anyone from knowingly causing the transmission of a program, information, code, or command, and as a result of such conduct, intentionally causing damage without authorization to a protected computer

- Prohibits the knowing trafficking of computer passwords with the intent to defraud

- Prohibits the transmission of communications containing threats to cause damage to a protected computer

These acts range from felonies to misdemeanors with small to large fines and jail sentences if any of these listed activities are committed.

Federal Privacy Act of 1974

In the mid-1960s, there was a proposal that the U.S. government would collectively hold each individual's information, pertaining to Social Security, Census, Internal Revenue Service, Bureau of Labor Statistics, and other limbs of the government, which would be compiled and held in a main federal data bank. The committee that proposed it saw this as an efficient way of gathering and centralizing data. Others saw it as a dangerous move against individual privacy. The federal data bank never came to pass because of strong opposition.

The Privacy Act of 1974

This act requires the following stipulations:

- Disclosure of personal information is limited to only authorized persons.
- The records must be accurate, relevant, timely, and complete.
- Safeguards are required to ensure security and confidentiality of records.

To keep the government in check on gathering information on U.S. citizens and other matters, a majority of its files are considered open to the public. Government files are open to the public unless there are specific issues enacted by legislature deeming specific files unavailable. This is what is explained in the Freedom of Information Act. This is different from what the Privacy Act outlines and protects. The Privacy Act applies to records and documents developed and maintained by specific branches of the federal government such as executive departments, government corporations, independent regulatory agencies, and government-controlled corporations. It does not apply to congressional, judiciary, or territorial subdivisions.

An actual *record* is information about an individual's education, medial history, financial history, criminal, employment, and other similar types of information. Agencies can only maintain this type of information if it is necessary and relevant to accomplishing the agency's purpose. The Privacy Act dictates that an agency cannot disclose this information without written permission from the individual. However, like most government acts, legislation, and creeds, there is a list of exceptions.

So what does all of this dry legal mumbo-jumbo mean? Basically, agencies can gather information about individuals, but it must be relevant and necessary for its approved cause. In addition, that agency cannot go around town sharing other people's private information. If they do, private citizens have the right to sue in order to protect their privacy.

This leaks into the computer world because this information is usually held by one type of computer or another. If an agency's computer is holding an individual's confidential information, it must provide the necessary security mechanisms to ensure it cannot be compromised or copied in an unauthorized way.

European Union Principles on Privacy

European countries have strict laws pertaining to data that is considered private in nature compared to many other countries. The *European Union Principles on Privacy* has six areas that addresses using and transmitting data considered sensitive in nature. All states in Europe must abide by these six principles to be in compliance. The following gives a quick overview of the different areas of privacy that are addressed under this law:

- *The reason for gathering of data must be specified at the time of collection.* This helps reduce the possible misuse of data and forces the individual to justify the reason for gathering the information.

- *Data cannot be used for other purposes.* The data can only be used for the original reason it was gathered.

- *Unnecessary data should not be collected.* Only information that is required to meet the stated purpose should be gathered and no more.

- *Data should only be kept for as long as it is needed to accomplish the stated task.* This helps ensure that the data is current and prevents indefinite archiving of data.

- *Only the necessary individuals who are required to accomplish the stated task should be allowed access to the data.* This helps prevent the selling of private data to others.

- *Whoever is responsible for securely storing the data should not allow unintentional "leaking" of data.* This helps enforce strong security for those who are responsible for storing private information.

Computer Security Act of 1987

This act requires federal agencies to identify computer systems that will contain sensitive information. The agency must develop a security policy and plan for each of these systems and conduct periodic training for individuals who operate, manage, or use these systems. Federal agency employees must be provided with security awareness training and be informed of how the agency defines acceptable computer use and practices.

Because the federal government deals with a lot of important, confidential, and secret information, it wants to make sure that all individuals and systems within all federal government agencies meet a certain level of awareness and protection.

Security and Freedom Through Encryption Act

This was approved in 1997 and guarantees the right of all U.S. citizens and residents to be able to use and sell encryption products and technology. This act was developed to relax encryption export controls and to make it legal for people to own and use encryption software no matter what algorithm it employs or key length it uses. It also prohibits state and federal governments from requiring anyone to relinquish his encryption key so these agencies can snoop on conversations or decrypt information. This means the government cannot require key escrow.

Federal Sentencing Guidelines

In 1991, U.S. Federal Sentencing Guidelines were developed and passed down to provide judges with courses of action to take when overseeing white collar crimes that take place within organizations. These guidelines deal with antitrust, federal securities, mail and wire fraud, bribery, contracts, and money laundering.

These guidelines provided ways in which companies and law enforcement should prevent, detect, and report computer crimes. They outlined how senior executives are responsible for the computer and information security decisions they make and what actually takes place within their organizations, and set a maximum fine of $290 million dollars.

The actual punishments and fines could be reduced if the company in question exercised due diligence and showed steps of responsible behavior. The guidelines required companies to develop security policies, standards, and procedures, and to properly inform employees of these issues.

Economic Espionage Act of 1996

Industry and corporate espionage was taking place with no real guidelines for who could properly investigate the events. This act provided the necessary structure when dealing with these types of cases and further defined trade secrets to be technical, business, engineering, scientific, or financial. This meant that an asset did not necessarily need to be tangible to be protected or to be stolen. This act enables the FBI to investigate industrial and corporate espionage cases.

International Cooperation Efforts

Governments all over the world have realized that they must cooperate with each other if they hope to properly deal with computer crimes. This means different channels of communication had to be opened, agreements on the meaning and definitions of specific crimes had to be made, and barriers that usually stood in the way of effective investigative work that crossed geographical boundaries had to be lessened or erased. The following sections quickly describe some of the organizations that are involved with this type of work.

G8

The G8 group represents the world's leading industrialized countries and Russia. During a Paris meeting in May 2000, they agreed to cooperate to fight cybercrime. This was prompted by the global concern over the growing threat of cybercrime, and the success of viruses like ILOVEYOU, which cost companies all over the world thousands to millions of dollars. G8 vowed to extend the powers of the European law enforcement agency, Europol, to fight illegal acts committed with technology.

This was done so that countries would work together to develop similar laws and open doors to help each other enforce laws and regulations pertaining to computer and information crimes.

Interpol

The international police organization, Interpol, collects and distributes information about cross-border crimes. It works to keep companies, law enforcement agencies, and governments informed about cybercrimes and who is becoming a target of malicious hackers.

European Commission

In January 2000, the European Commission revealed its proposals on fighting cybercrime. The Commission presented its paper to the Council of Ministers of the European Union and Parliament, which outlined a policy that describes the methods necessary to fight computer crimes without hindering e-commerce. The proposal suggests harmonizing the member states' laws to deal with criminal law on high-tech crimes, including hacking and DoS attacks.

References

IT Security and Crime Prevention Methods: **www.interpol.int/Public/ TechnologyCrime/CrimePrev/ITSecurity.asp**

Interpol and Information Technology Crime: **www.interpol.com/Public/ TechnologyCrime**

Internet Security Recommendations: **www.cnn.com/2000/TECH/computing/ 05/18/global.security.idg**

Summary

Law, ethics, and investigations are very important parts of computer and information security. They are elements not usually brought to mind when one speaks of information security, but they are a must if a society is serious about controlling this type of crime and punishing the guilty.

In many ways, the laws and courts are in their infancy stages when attempting to deal with computer crimes. They are faced with not having many precedents to fall back on when interpreting what is legal and illegal and what the proper punishments are for each type of computer crime. However, the legal system is quickly developing laws and providing ways for proper interpretation of these laws to help all arms of the law enforcement agencies and the victims. Over the last few years, hacking and attacking have been performed for fun, mainly by curious computer individuals, but as the punishments increase, the fun may quickly come to an end.

Security professionals should be aware of and well versed in computer security laws and regulations that apply in their environments. They should be able to properly inform their management and customers of expected responsibilities, as well as know what boundaries they are expected to work within themselves.

Quick Tips

- Dumpster diving is going through someone's trash to find confidential or useful information. It is legal, unless trespassing, but in all cases considered unethical.

- Wiretapping is a passive attack that eavesdrops on communication. It is only legal with prior consent or a warrant.

- Social engineering is the act of tricking or deceiving a person into giving confidential or sensitive information that could then be used against him or his company.

- Data diddling is the act of willfully modifying information, programs, or documentation in an effort to commit fraud.

- Excessive privileges means that an employee has more rights than necessary to complete her tasks.

- Criminal law deals with an individual's conduct that violates the government laws, which were developed to protect the public.

- Civil law deals with wrongs committed against individuals or companies that result in injury or damages. Civil law does not use prison time as a punishment, but usually financial restitution.

- Administrative, or regulatory, law covers standards of performance or conduct expected by government agencies from companies, industries, and certain officials.

- A patent grants ownership and enables that owner to legally enforce his rights to exclude others from practicing the invention covered by the patent.

- Copyright covers the expression of ideas rather than the ideas themselves.

- Trademarks cover words, names, product shape, symbol, color, or a combination of these used to identify products. These items are used to distinguish products from the competitors' products.

- Trade secrets are deemed proprietary to a company and can be information that provides a competitive edge. The information is protected as long as the owner takes the necessary protective actions.

- Crime over the Internet has brought about jurisdiction problems for law enforcement and the courts.

- Privacy laws dictate that data collected by agencies must be collected fairly and lawfully, must be used only for the purpose it was collected, must only be held for a reasonable amount of time, and must be accurate and timely.

- If companies are going to use any type of monitoring, they need to make sure it is legal in their area and inform all employees that they may be subjected to monitoring.

- Employees need to be informed regarding what is expected behavior pertaining to computer systems, network use, e-mail, and phone use. They need to also know what the ramifications are for not meeting those expectations. These requirements are usually communicated through policies.

- Logon banners should be used to inform users of what could happen if they do not follow the rules pertaining to using company resources. This provides legal protection for the company.

- Countries differ in their view of the seriousness of computer crime or have different penalties for certain crimes. This makes enforcing laws much harder across country borders.

- The three main types of harm addressed in computer crime laws pertain to unauthorized intrusion, unauthorized alteration or destruction, and using malicious code.

- The Federal Sentencing Guidelines of the United States gave judges and courts procedures for how prevention, detection, and reporting of computer crimes should take place along with penalty ranges. This also made senior executives responsible for their company's actions.

- Law enforcement and the courts have a hard time with computer crimes because of the newness of the types of crimes, the complexity involved, jurisdiction issues, and evidence collection. New laws are being written to properly deal with cybercrime.

- If a company does not practice due care in its efforts to protect itself from computer crime, it can be found to be negligent and legally liable for damages.

- Elements of negligence include not fulfilling a legally recognized obligation, failure to conform to a standard, and proximate causation, which result in injury or damage.

- Most computer crimes are not reported because the victims are not aware of the crime or are too embarrassed to let anyone else know.

- Theft is no longer restricted to physical constraints. Assets are now viewed as intangible objects that can also be stolen or disclosed via technology means.

- The primary reason for the chain of custody for evidence is to ensure that it will be admissible in court by showing that it was properly controlled before being presented in court.

- Companies should develop their own incident response team, which is made up of people from management, IT, legal, human resources, public relations, and security and other key areas of the organization.

- Hearsay evidence is secondhand and usually not admissible in court.

- To be admissible in court, business records have to be made and collected in the normal methods of business, not specially generated for a case in court. Business records can easily be hearsay if there is no firsthand proof of their accuracy and reliability.

- The life cycle of evidence includes identification and collection of the evidence, storage, preservation, transportation, presentation in court, and return back to the owner.

- Collection of computer evidence is a very complex and detail-oriented task. Only skilled people should attempt it, otherwise evidence can be ruined forever.

- When looking for suspects, it is important to consider the motive, opportunity, and means (MOM).

- For evidence to be admissible in court, it needs to be relevant, sufficient, and reliable.

- Evidence must be legally permissible, meaning that it was seized legally and the chain of custody was not broken.

- All evidence should be marked and stored in a container, which is also marked.

- In many jurisdictions, law enforcement agencies must obtain a warrant to search and seize an individual's property, as stated in the Fourth Amendment. Private citizens are not subject to protecting the Fourth Amendment of others unless acting as a police agent.

- Enticement is luring an intruder and is legal. Entrapment induces a crime, tricks a person, and is illegal.

- Know what issues the Internet Architecture Board (IAB) considers unethical.

- The salami attack is carrying out smaller crimes with the hope that the larger crime will not be noticed. The common salami attack is the act of skimming off a small amount of money.

- Phreakers are hackers who specialize in committing telephone fraud.

- Blue Boxing simulates a tone that tricks the telephone company's system into thinking the user is authorized for long distance service, which enables him to make the call for free.

- Red Boxing simulates the sound of coins being dropped into a pay phone.

- Black Boxing manipulates the line voltage to receive a toll-free call.

- After a computer system is seized, the investigators should make a bit mirror image copy of the storage media before doing anything else.

Questions

Please remember that these questions are formatted and asked in a certain way for a reason. You must remember that the CISSP exam is asking questions at a conceptual level. Questions may not always have the perfect answer, and the candidate is advised against always looking for the perfect answer. The candidate should look for the best answer in the list.

1. Which of the following does the IAB consider unethical?

   A. Creating a computer virus

   B. Entering information into a Web page

   C. Performing a penetration test on a host on the Internet

   D. Disrupting Internet communications

2. What is the study of computers and surrounding technologies and how they relate to crime?

   A. Computer forensics

   B. Computer vulnerability analysis

   C. Incident handling

   D. Computer information criteria

3. Which of the following does IAB consider unethical behavior?

   A. Internet users who conceal unauthorized accesses

   B. Internet users who waste computer resources

   C. Internet users who write viruses

   D. Internet users who monitor traffic

4. After a forensics investigator seizes a computer during a crime investigation, what is the next step?

   A. Label and put it into a container, and label the container

   B. Dust the evidence for fingerprints

   C. Make an image copy of the disks

   D. Lock the evidence in the safe

5. A CISSP candidate signs an ethics statement prior to taking the CISSP examination. Which of the following would be a violation of the $(ISC)^2$ Code of Ethics that could cause the candidate to lose his/her certification?

   A. E-mailing information or comments about the exam or information taught in the class to other CISSP candidates

   B. Submitting comments on the questions of the exam to $(ISC)^2$

   C. Submitting comments to the board of directors regarding the test and content of the class

   D. Conducting a presentation about the CISSP certification and what the certification means

6. If your company gives you a new PC and you find residual information about confidential company issues, what should you do based on the $(ISC)^2$ Code of Ethics?

   A. Contact the owner of the file and inform him about it. Copy it to a disk, give it to him, and delete your copy.

    B. Delete the document because it was not meant for you.

    C. Inform management of your findings so they can make sure this type of thing does not happen again.

    D. E-mail it to the author and to management so that everyone is aware of what is going on.

7. Why is it difficult to investigate computer crime and track down the criminal?

    A. Privacy laws are written to protect people from being investigated for these types of crimes.

    B. Special equipment and tools are necessary to detect these types of criminals.

    C. Criminals can spoof their address and hop from one network to the next.

    D. The police have no jurisdiction over the Internet.

8. Protecting evidence and providing accountability for who handled it at different steps during the investigation is referred to as what?

    A. Rule of best evidence

    B. Hearsay

    C. Evidence safety

    D. Chain of custody

9. If an investigator needs to communicate to another investigator, but does not want the criminal to be able to eavesdrop on this conversation, what type of communication should be used?

    A. Digitally signed messages

    B. Out-of-band messages

    C. Forensics frequency

    D. Authentication and access control

10. Why is it challenging to collect and identify computer evidence to be used in a court of law?

    A. The evidence is mostly intangible.

    B. The evidence is mostly corrupted.

    C. The evidence is mostly encrypted.

    D. The evidence is mostly tangible.

11. The chain of custody of evidence describes who obtained the evidence and _____.

    A. Who secured it and stole it

    B. Who controlled it and broke it

    C. Who secured it and validated it

    D. Who controlled it and duplicated it

12. Before shutting down a system suspected of an attack, the investigator should do what?

    A. Remove and back up the hard drive

    B. Dump memory contents to disk

    C. Remove it from the network

    D. Save data in spooler queue and temporary files

13. Why is computer-generated documentation usually considered unreliable evidence?

    A. It is primary evidence.

    B. It is too difficult to detect prior modifications.

    C. It is corroborative evidence.

    D. It is not covered under criminal law, but it is covered under civil law.

14. Which of the following is a necessary characteristic of evidence for it to be admissible?

    A. It must be real.

    B. It must be noteworthy.

    C. It must be reliable.

    D. It must be important.

15. In the United States, what agency usually works with the FBI when investigating computer crimes?

    A. (ISC)^2

    B. Secret Service

    C. CIA

    D. State police

16. If a company deliberately planted a flaw in one of their systems in the hope of detecting an attempted penetration and exploitation of this flaw, what would this be called?

    A. Incident recovery response

    B. Entrapment

    C. Illegal

    D. Enticement

17. If an employee is suspected of wrongdoing in a computer crime, what department must be involved?

    A. Human resources

    B. Legal

C. Auditors

D. Payroll

18. When would an investigator's notebook be admissible in court?

   A. When he uses it to refresh memory

   B. When he cannot be present for testimony

   C. When requested by the judge to learn the original issues of the investigations

   D. When no other physical evidence is available

19. Disks and other media that are copies of the original evidence are considered what?

   A. Primary evidence

   B. Reliable and sufficient evidence

   C. Hearsay evidence

   D. Conclusive evidence

20. If a company does not inform employees that they may be monitored and does not have a policy stating how monitoring should take place, what should a company do?

   A. Don't monitor employees in any fashion.

   B. Monitor during off-hours and slow times.

   C. Obtain a search warrant before monitoring an employee.

   D. Monitor anyway—they are covered by two laws allowing them to do this.

21. What is one reason why successfully prosecuting computer crimes is so challenging?

   A. There is no way to capture electrical data reliably.

   B. The evidence in computer cases does not follow best evidence directives.

   C. These crimes do not always fall into the traditional criminal activity.

   D. Wiretapping is hard to do legally.

22. When can executives be charged with negligence?

   A. If they do not follow the transborder laws

   B. If they do not properly report and prosecute attackers

   C. If they do not properly inform users that they may be monitored

   D. If they do not practice due care when protecting resources

23. To better deal with computer crime, several legislative bodies have taken what steps in their strategy?

   A. Expanded several privacy laws

   B. Broadened the definition of property to include data

C. Required corporations to have computer crime insurance

D. Redefined transborder issues

24. Many privacy laws dictate which of the following rules?

A. Individuals have a right to remove any data they do not want others to know.

B. Agencies do not need to ensure that the data is accurate.

C. Agencies need to allow all government agencies access to the data.

D. Agencies cannot use collected data for a purpose different from what it was collected for.

25. Which of the following is not true about dumpster diving?

A. It is legal.

B. It is illegal.

C. It is a breach of physical security.

D. It is gathering data from places people would not expect to be raided.

Answers

1. **D.** The Internet Architecture Board (IAB) is a committee for Internet design, engineering, and management. It considers the use of the Internet to be a privilege that should be treated as such.

The IAB considers the following acts unethical and unacceptable behavior:

- Purposely seeking to gain unauthorized access to Internet resources
- Disrupting the intended use of the Internet
- Wasting resources (people, capacity, and computers) through purposeful actions
- Destroying the integrity of computer-based information
- Compromising the privacy of others
- Involving negligence in the conduct of Internet-wide experiments

2. **A.** Computer forensics is a field that specializes in understanding and properly extracting evidence from computers and peripheral devices for the purpose of prosecution. Collecting this type of evidence requires a skill set and understanding of several relative laws.

3. **B.** This question is similar to question 1. The IAB has declared wasting computer resources through purposeful activities unethical because it sees these resources as assets that are to be available for the computing society.

4. **C.** There are several steps that need to be followed when gathering and extracting evidence from a scene. Once a computer has been confiscated, the first thing the forensics team should do is to make an image of the hard drive. The team

will work from this image instead of the original hard drive so that it stays in a pristine state and the evidence on the drive is not accidentally corrupted or modified.

5. **A.** A CISSP candidate and a CISSP holder should never discuss with others what was on the exam. This degrades the usefulness of the exam to be used as a tool to test someone's true security knowledge. If this type of activity is uncovered, the person could be stripped of their CISSP certification.

6. **C.** When dealing with the possible compromise of confidential company information or intellectual property, management should be informed and be involved as soon as possible. They are the ones who are ultimately responsible for this data and who understand the damage its leakage can cause. An employee should not attempt to address and deal with these issues on his own.

7. **C.** Spoofing one's identity and being able to transverse anonymously through different networks and the Internet increase the complexity and difficulty of tracking down criminals who carry out computer crimes. It is very easy to commit many damaging crimes from across the country or world, and this type of activity can be difficult for law enforcement to track down.

8. **D.** Properly following the chain of custody for evidence is crucial for it to be admissible to court. A chain of custody is a history that shows how evidence was collected, analyzed, transported, and preserved in order to be presented as evidence in court. Because electronic evidence can be easily modified, a clearly defined chain of custody demonstrates that the evidence is trustworthy.

9. **B.** Out-of-band communication means to communicate through some other type of communication channel. For example, if law enforcement agents were investigating a crime on a network, they should not share information through e-mail that passes along this network. The criminal could have sniffers still installed, thus this data may be available to her.

10. **A.** The evidence in computer crimes usually comes straight from computers themselves. This means that the data is held as electronic voltages, which are represented as binary bits. Some data can be held on hard drives and peripheral devices, and some data may be held in the memory of the system itself. This type of evidence is intangible in that it is not made up of objects one can hold, see, and easily understand. Other types of crimes usually have evidence that is more tangible in nature, which is easier to handle and control.

11. **C.** The chain of custody outlines a process to ensure that who obtained, validated, secured, and controlled the evidence is documented to ensure that under no circumstance was there a possibility for the evidence to be tampered with. If the chain of custody is broken, there is a high probability that the evidence will not be admissible into court. If it is admitted, it will not carry as much weight.

12. **B.** If the computer was actually attacked or involved in a computer crime, there is a good possibility that useful information could still reside in memory. Specific tools can be used to actually dump this information and save it for analysis before the power is removed.

13. **B.** It can be very difficult to determine if computer-generated material has been modified before it is presented in court. Since this type of evidence can be altered without being detected, the court cannot put a lot of weight on this evidence. Many times computer-generated evidence is considered hearsay, in that there is no firsthand proof backing it up.

14. **C.** For evidence to be admissible, it must be sufficient, reliable, and relevant to the case. For evidence to be reliable, it must be consistent with fact and not based on opinion or circumstantial.

15. **B.** The FBI and Secret Service are both responsible for investigating computer crimes. They have their own jurisdictions and rules outlining who investigates which types of crimes.

16. **D.** Companies need to be very careful about the items they use to entice intruders and attackers, because this may be seen as entrapment by the court. It is best to get the legal department involved before implementing these items. Putting a pseudo-flaw or honeypot in place is usually seen as the use of enticement tools.

17. **A.** It is imperative that the company gets human resources involved if an employee is considered a suspect in a computer crime. This department knows the laws and regulations pertaining to employee treatment and can work to protect the employee and the company at the same time.

18. **A.** Notes that are taken by an investigator will, in most cases, not be admissible in court as evidence. This is not seen as reliable information and can only be used by the investigator to help him remember activities during the investigation.

19. **C.** In most cases, computer-related evidence will fall under the hearsay category because it is seen as copies of the original data that is held in the computer itself and can be modified without any indication. Evidence is considered hearsay when there is no firsthand proof in place to validate it.

20. **A.** Before a company can monitor its employees, it is supposed to inform them that this type of activity can take place. If a company monitors an employee without telling him, this could be seen as an invasion of privacy. The employee had an expected level of privacy that was invaded. The company should implement monitoring capabilities into its security policy and employee awareness programs.

21. **C.** We have an infrastructure set up to investigate and prosecute crimes: law enforcement, laws, lawyers, courts, juries, judges, and so on. This infrastructure has a long history of prosecuting "traditional" crimes. Only in the last five years have computer crimes been prosecuted more regularly, thus these types of crimes are not fully rooted in the legal system with all of the necessary and useful precedents.

22. **D.** Executives are held to a certain standard and are expected to act responsibly when running and protecting a company. These standards and expectations equate to the due care concept under the law. Due care means to carry out activities that a reasonable person would be expected to do in the same situation. If an executive

acts irresponsibly in any way, she can be seen as not practicing due care and be held negligent.

23. **B.** Many times what is corrupted, compromised, or taken from a computer is data, so for standing laws (which outlined ramifications of taking or damaging another's property) to be applied to computer crimes, property had to also include data. Over the years, data and information have become many companies' most valuable asset, which must be protected by the laws.

24. **D.** The Federal Privacy Act of 1974 and European Union Principles on Privacy were created to protect citizens from government agencies using information that they collected improperly. These acts have many stipulations, including that the information can only be used for the reason it was collected.

25. **B.** Dumpster diving is the act of going through someone's trash with the hope of uncovering useful information. Dumpster diving is legal, but unethical.

Application and System Development

In this chapter, you will learn about the following items:
- Various types of software controls and implementation
- Database concepts and security issues
- Data warehousing and data mining
- Software life cycle development processes
- Change control concepts
- Object-oriented programming components
- Expert systems and artificial intelligence

Applications and computer systems are usually developed for functionality first, not security first. To get the best of both worlds, security and functionality would have to be designed and developed at the same time. Security should be interwoven into the core of a product and provide protection at different layers; this is a better approach than trying to develop a front end or wrapper that may reduce the overall functionality and leave security holes when this product has to be integrated with other applications.

Software's Importance

Application system controls come in various flavors with many different goals. They can control input, processing, number-crunching methods, interprocess communication, interfacing to the system and other programs, access, and output. They should be developed with the potential risks in mind, and many types of threat models and risk analyses should be invoked at different stages of development. The goal is to prevent security compromises and to reduce the vulnerabilities and the possibility of data corruption. The controls can be preventive, detective, or corrective. They can come in the form of administrative and physical controls, but are usually more technical in this context (see Figure 11-1).

The specific application controls depend upon the application itself, its objectives, the security goals of the developers, and the environment the application will be placed in. If an application is purely proprietary and will only run in closed trusted environments,

Figure 11-1

Applications and operating systems have various types of controls, but most of them are technical in nature.

Administrative Physical Technical

System Control Type

fewer security controls may be needed than those required for applications that will connect businesses over the Internet and provide financial transactions. The trick is in understanding the security needs of an application, implementing the right controls and mechanisms, thoroughly testing the mechanisms and how they integrate into the application, following structured development methodologies, and providing secure and reliable distribution methods. This can be harder than it sounds.

Device versus Software Security

Today, many security efforts look to devices to solve security problems. These devices are firewalls, intrusion detection systems (IDSs), sensors, and vulnerability scanners. This occurs because networks, and how they are thought of, work on a basic outside and inside notion. The bad people and potential threats are on the outside, and what needs to be protected is on the inside. This notion has worked, to an extent, because networks were closed environments, which usually meant controlled environments. However, our environments then incorporated electronic data interchange (EDI), remote dial-in capabilities, Internet sites, and virtual private networks (VPNs). Now environments are incorporating wireless communication, value-added networks (VANs), and business-to-business (B2B) capabilities, which add complexity to the concept of us and them and inside and outside.

The division between software security and device security deals with providing security at the beginning stages of software development versus providing devices that protect the perimeters of networks. The perimeter devices try to prevent attackers from exploiting the security holes that reside in the software. Firewalls and IDSs are studied and talked about within circles of security much more than inadvertent flaws in design and poorly written software. In reality, the flaws within the software cause a majority of the vulnerabilities in the first place. Figure 11-2 illustrates two distinct approaches to security.

Figure 11-2
The two main ways to approach security

Approaches to Security

Option 1 = firewalls, routers, ACLs, IDS, bastion hosts

Option 2 = design and develop software with security in mind

Software with security flaws

Firewall

Firewall

Firewall

Perimeter devices are more often considered than software development for security for several reasons:

- In the past, it was not crucial to implement security during the software development stages; thus, many programmers do not practice these procedures.
- Many security professionals are not software developers.
- Many software developers do not have security as a main focus.
- Software vendors are trying to rush their products to market with their eyes set on functionality, not security.
- The computing community is used to receiving software with bugs and applying patches.
- A combination of all the preceding.

Finger-pointing and quick judgments are neither useful nor necessarily fair at this stage of our computing evolution. Twenty years ago, mainframes had tight security because a handful of people knew how to run them, users worked on computers (dumb terminals) that could not introduce malicious code to the mainframe, and environments were closed. The core protocols and framework were developed at a time when threats and attacks were not prevalent. There was no need for such stringent security. Then computer and software evolution took off, and the possibilities splintered into a thousand different directions. The high demand for computer technology and different types of software increased the demand for programmers, system designers, administrators, and engineers. This demand brought in a wave of people who had little experience. The lack of experience, the high change rate of technology, and the race to market add problems to security that are not always clearly understood. Although it is easy to blame the big software vendors in the sky for producing flawed or buggy software, this is driven by the customer demand. Understanding how security works within programs, how programs integrate into environments, and how compromises take place will cause consumers to demand more security-oriented software and better programming and development practices.

This chapter is an attempt to show how to address security at its source, which is at the software and development level. This requires a shift from *reactive* to *proactive* actions toward security problems to ensure they do not happen in the first place, or at least happen to a smaller extent. Figure 11-3 illustrates our current way of dealing with security issues.

Different Environments Demand Different Security

Today, a network administrator is in an overwhelming position of integrating different applications and computer systems to keep up with his company's demand on expandable functionality and the new gee-whiz components that executives buy into and demand quick implementation of. This integration is further frustrated by the company's race to provide a well-known presence on the Internet by implementing Web sites with the capabilities of taking online orders, storing credit card information, and setting up

Figure 11-3   The usual trend of software being released to the market and how security is dealt with

extranets with partners. This can quickly turn into a confusing ball of protocols, devices, interfaces, incompatibility issues, routing and switching techniques, telecommunication routines, and management procedures. It could make an administrator choose to buy some land in Montana and raise goats instead.

On top of this, security is expected, required, and depended upon. When security compromises creep in, the finger-pointing starts, liability issues are tossed like hot potatoes, and heads might even roll. An understanding of the environment, what is currently in it, and how it works is required, so the new technologies can be implemented in a more controlled and comprehendible fashion.

E-Commerce

The days of developing a simple Web page and posting it on the Internet to sell candles are long gone. Today, customer front-end, complex middleware, and third-tier data warehousing must be developed and work seamlessly. As the complexity of this type of environment grows, tracking down errors and security compromises becomes an awesome task. (This type of environment will be described throughout this chapter.)

Client/Server Model

Basically, the client/server architecture enables an application system to be divided across multiple platforms that can vary in operating systems and hardware. The client requests services and the server fulfills these requests. The server handles the data-processing services and provides the processed result to the client. The client performs the front-end portion of an application, and the server performs the back-end portion, which is usually more labor intensive.

The front end usually includes the user interface and local data manipulation capabilities, and provides the communication mechanisms that can request services from the server portion of the application.

Environment versus Application Controls

Software controls can be implemented by the operating system, application, or through database management controls, and usually a combination of all three. Each has its strengths and weaknesses, but if they are all understood and programmed to work in a concerted effort, then many different scenarios and types of compromises can be thwarted. One downside to relying mainly on operating system controls is that they can control a subject's access to different objects and restrict the actions of that subject within the system, but not necessarily within an application. If an application has a security compromise that is created by the programming code, it is hard for the operating system to predict that this type of compromise could take place or to audit it once it does happen. A file system is a broad environment for many applications to work within. It is unfair to expect the operating system to understand all the nuances of different programs and their internal mechanisms.

On the other hand, application controls and database management controls are very specific to their needs and in the security compromises they understand. Although an application might be able to protect data by allowing only certain types of input and not allowing certain users to view data kept in sensitive database fields, it cannot prevent the user from deleting system files or inserting bogus data into the Address Resolution Protocol (ARP) table. Operating system and application controls have their place and limitations. The trick is to find out where one type of control stops so the next type of control can kick into action.

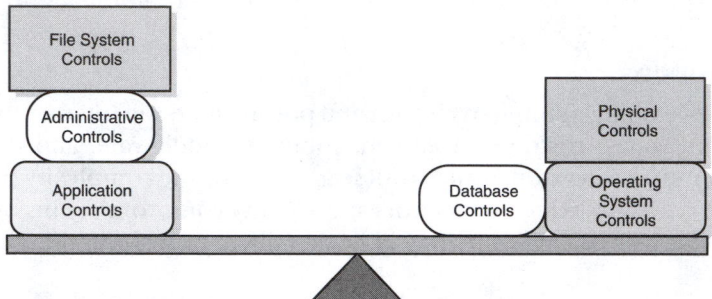

The different types of controls need to be understood
and utilized to provide a balanced and useful security level.

Security has been mainly provided by environmental and perimeter devices rather than controls built into applications. The devices can cover a wide range of applications, they can be controlled by a centralized management console, and they are further away from application control. However, this approach does not always provide the necessary level of granularity, and it does not approach compromises that can take place because of problematic coding and programming routines. Firewalls and access control mechanisms can provide a level of protection by preventing attackers from exploiting buffer overflows, but the real protection happens at the core of the problem—proper software development and coding practices must be in place.

Complexity of Functionality

Programming is a complex trade—the code itself, routine interaction, global and local variables, input received from other programs, output fed to different applications, attempts to envision future user inputs, calculations, and restrictions form a laundry list of possible consequences. Many times trying to account for all the what-ifs and programming on the side of caution can reduce the overall functionality of the application. As you limit the functionality and scope of an application, the market share and potential profitability of that program could be reduced. A balance always exists between functionality and security, and in the development world, functionality is usually deemed the most important.

So this means programmers and application architects need to find a happy medium between the necessary functionality of the program, the security requirements, and the mechanisms that should be implemented to provide this security. This can add more complexity to an already complex task.

More than one road may lead to enlightenment, but as these roads increase in number, it is hard to know if a path will eventually bring you to bliss or to a fiery doom of unpleasantness. Many programs accept data from different parts of the program, other programs, the system itself, and user input. Each of these paths needs to be followed in a methodical way, and each possible scenario and input needs to be thought through and tested to provide a deep level of assurance. It is important that each module be capable of being tested individually and in concert with other modules. This level of understanding and testing will make the product more secure by catching flaws that could be exploited.

Data Types, Format, and Length

We have all heard about the recent uproar pertaining to buffer overflows, as if they were new to the programming world. They are not new, but are now being exploited on a reoccurring basis.

Buffer overflows were discussed in Chapter 5, and it was explained that attacks are carried out when the application does not check the length of input that is actually being accepted. Extra data could be executed in a privileged mode that would enable an attacker to take control of the system. If a programmer wrote a program that expected the input length to be 5KB, then this needs to be part of the code so that the right amount of buffer space is available to hold this data when it actually comes in. However, if that program does not make sure the 5KB is accepted, and only 5KB is accepted, an evildoer can input the first 5KB for the expected data to process, and then another 50KB that contains malicious instructions can also be processed by the CPU.

Length is not the only thing programmers need to be worried about when it comes to accepting input data. Data also needs to be in the right format and data type. If the program is expecting alpha ASCII characters, it should not accept hexadecimal or binary values.

The accepted value also needs to be reasonable. This means that if an application asks Stacy to enter the amount she would like to transfer from her checking account to her savings account, she should not be able to enter "Bob." This can fall under data format and data type (numbers versus alphabet characters), but parameters also need to be in place to watch for bogus entries so errors can be stopped at their origin instead of being passed to calculations and logic procedures.

These examples are extremely simplistic compared with what programmers have to face in the real programming world. However, they are presented to show that software needs to be developed to accept the correct data types, format, and length of inputted data for security and functionality purposes.

Implementation and Default Issues

If I have not said "yes," then the answer is "no."

As many people in the computer field know, out-of-the-box implementations are usually far from secure. Most security has to be configured and turned on after installation;

not being aware of this can be dangerous for the inexperienced IT person. Windows NT has received its share of criticism for lack of security, but in many ways the platform can be secured. It just comes out of the box in an insecure state. This is done because settings will have to be configured to properly integrate into different environments, and this is a friendlier way of installing the product for users. If Mike installed a new software package that continually threw messages of "Access Denied" when he was attempting to configure it to interoperate with other applications and systems, his patience might wear thin, and he might decide to hate that vendor for years to come because of the stress and confusion inflicted upon him.

Yet again we are at a hard place for developers and architects. When a security application or device is installed, it should default to "No Access." This means that when Lance installs a packet-filter firewall, it should not allow any packets to pass into the network that were not specifically granted access. However, this requires Lance to know how to configure the firewall for it to ever be useful. There is a fine line between security, functionality, and user-friendliness. If an application is extremely user-friendly, it is probably not as secure. For an application to be user-friendly, it usually requires a lot of extra coding for errors, dialog boxes, wizards, and step-by-step instructions. This extra coding can result in bloated code that can create unforeseeable compromises. So vendors have a hard time winning, but they usually keep making money as they keep trying.

Implementation

Implementation errors and misconfigurations are common issues that cause a majority of the security issues in networked environments. Many people do not realize that various services are enabled when a system is installed. These services can provide evildoers with information that can be used during an attack. Many services provide an actual way into the environment itself. NetBIOS services can be enabled to permit sharing resources in Windows environments and remote procedure call (RPC) services, which let remote users run command shells, and other programs can be enabled with no restrictions. Many systems have File Transfer Protocol (FTP), Telnet, and Internet Relay Chat (IRC) services enabled that are not being used and have no real safety measures in place. Some of these services are enabled by default, so when an administrator installs an operating system and does not check these services to properly restrict or disable them, they are available for attackers to uncover and use.

Because vendors have user-friendliness and user functionality in mind, the product will usually be installed with defaults that provide no or very low security protection. It would be very hard for vendors to know the security levels required in all the environments that the product will be installed in, so they usually do not attempt it. It is up to the person installing the product to learn how to properly configure the settings to achieve the necessary level of protection.

Another problem in implementation and security is the number of unpatched systems. Once security issues are identified, vendors develop patches to address and fix these security holes. However, many times they do not get installed on the systems that are vulnerable. The reasons for this vary: an administrator may not keep up-to-date on the recent security vulnerabilities and patches, he does not fully understand the importance of these patches, or he is afraid that the patches will cause other problems. All of these reasons are quite common, but they all have the same result—insecure systems. Many vulnerabilities that are being exploited have had patches developed and released months or years ago.

It is unfortunate that adding security (or service) patches can adversely affect other mechanisms within the system. The patches should be tested for these types of activities before they are applied to production servers and workstations, to help prevent service disruptions that can affect network and employee productivity.

Failure States

Many circumstances are unpredictable and are therefore hard to plan for. However, unpredictable situations can be planned for in a general sense rather than trying to plan and code for every situation. If an application fails for any reason, it should return to a safe and more secure state. This could require the application to shut down or present the user with a logon screen to start the application from its initialization state. This is why some systems "blue-screen" and/or restart. When this occurs, something is going on within the system that is unrecognized or unsafe, so the system dumps its memory contents and starts all over.

Different system states were discussed in Chapter 5, which described how processes can be executed in a privileged or user state. If an application fails and is executing in a privileged state, these processes should be shut down properly and released to ensure that disrupting a system could not provide compromises that could be exploited. If a privileged process does not shut down properly and it stays active, an attacker can figure out how to access the system, using this process, in a privileged state. This means that the attacker could have administrative or root access to a system, which opens the door for more severe destruction.

Database Management

Databases have a long history of storing important intellectual property and items that are considered valuable and proprietary to companies. Because of this, they usually live in an environment of mystery to all but the database and network administrators. The less anyone knows about the databases, the better. Users usually access databases indirectly through a client interface, and their actions are restricted to ensure the confidentiality and integrity of the data held within the database and the structure of the database itself.

NOTE A database management system (DBMS) is usually a suite of programs used to manage large sets of structured data with ad hoc query capabilities for many types of users. These can also control the security parameters of the database.

This norm is changing as companies run to connect their networks to the Internet, which usually includes indirect access to a back-end database. In the past, employees accessed customer information held in databases instead of customers accessing it themselves. Today, many companies allow their customers to access data in their databases through a browser. The browser makes a connection to the company's middleware, which then connects them to the back-end database. This adds levels of complexity, and the database will be accessed in new and unprecedented ways.

One example is in the banking world, where online banking is all the rage. Many financial institutions want to keep up with the times and add the services they think their customers will want. But online banking is not just another service like being able to order checks. Most banks work in closed (or semiclosed) environments, and opening their environments to the Internet is a huge undertaking. The perimeter network needs to be secured, middleware software has to be developed or purchased, and the database should be behind one, preferably two, firewalls. Many times components in the business application tier are used to extract data from the databases and process the customer requests.

Access control can be restricted by only allowing roles to interact with the database. The database administrator can define specific roles that are allowed to access the database. Each role will have assigned rights and permissions, and customers and employees are then ported into these roles. Any user who is not within one of these roles is denied access. This means that if an attacker were able to compromise the firewall and other perimeter network protection mechanisms and were then able to make requests to the database, if he were not in one of the predefined roles, the database would still be safe. This process streamlines access control and ensures that no users or evildoers can access the database directly, but must access it indirectly through a role account. Figure 11-4 illustrates these concepts.

Figure 11-4   One type of database security is employing roles.

Database Management Software

A *database* is a collection of data stored in a meaningful way that enables multiple users and applications to access, view, and modify data as needed. Databases are managed with software that provides these types of activities. It also enforces access control restrictions, provides data integrity and redundancy, and sets up different procedures for data manipulation. This software is referred to as the *database management system (DBMS)* and is usually controlled by a database administrator. Databases not only store data, but they also process data and represent it in a more usable and logical form. Database management systems interface with programs, users, and data within the database. They help us store, organize, and retrieve information effectively and efficiently.

A database is the mechanism that provides structure for data that is collected. The actual specifications of the structure can be different per database implementation because different organizations or departments work with different types of data and need to perform diverse functions upon that information. There may be different workloads, relationships between the data, platforms, performance requirements, and varying security goals.

Because the needs and requirements for databases vary, different data models can be implemented that align with different business and organizational needs.

Database Jargon

- **Record**   Collection of related data items
- **File**   Collection of records of the same type
- **Database**   Cross-referenced collection of files
- **DBMS**   Manages and controls the database
- **Base relation**   A table stored in a database
- **Tuple**   A row in a two-dimensional database
- **Attribute**   A column in a two-dimensional database
- **Primary key**   Columns that make each row unique (A table must include a primary key for every row.)
- **View**   Virtual relation defined by the database to keep subjects from viewing certain data
- **Foreign key**   Attribute of one table that is the primary key of another table
- **Cell**   Intersection of a row and column
- **Schema**   Holds data that describes a database
- **Data dictionary**   Central repository of data elements and their relationships

Database Models

Ohhh, that database model is very pretty, indeed. Response: You have problems.

The database model defines the relationships between different data elements, dictates how data can be accessed, and defines acceptable operations, the type of integrity offered, and how the data is organized. This model provides a formal method of representing data in a conceptual form and provides the necessary means of manipulating the data held within the database. There are several types of data models for databases; we will only touch on a few of them.

A *relational data model* uses attributes (columns) and tuples (rows) to contain and organize information (see Figure 11-5). The relational model is the most widely used method of organizing databases today. It presents information in the form of tables. A relational database is composed of two-dimensional tables, and each table contains unique rows, columns, and cells (the intersection of a row and a column). A primary key is a field that links all the data within a record to a corresponding value. For example, in the following table, the primary keys are Product G345 and G978. When an application or another record refers to this primary key, it is actually referring to all the data within this one row.

A *hierarchical data model* is another database model (see Figure 11-6). The structure and relationship between the data elements are different than those in a relational database. A hierarchical model combines records and fields that are related in a logical tree structure.

The parents can have one child, many children, or no children. The tree structure contains branches, and each branch has a number of leaves, or data fields. These databases have well-defined, prespecified access paths, but they are not as flexible in relating information as a relational database. Hierarchical databases are useful for mapping one-to-many relationships.

A *distributed data model* has data stored in more than one database, but it is logically connected (see Figure 11-7). Different databases may live at different places on a network or reside in totally different networks. Because they are logically connected, the users see the database as one full entity, instead of several entities. When users access data, they do not need to know which database they are accessing; one database may transfer a user to another database, which is transparent to the user.

Figure 11-5   Relational databases hold data in table structures.

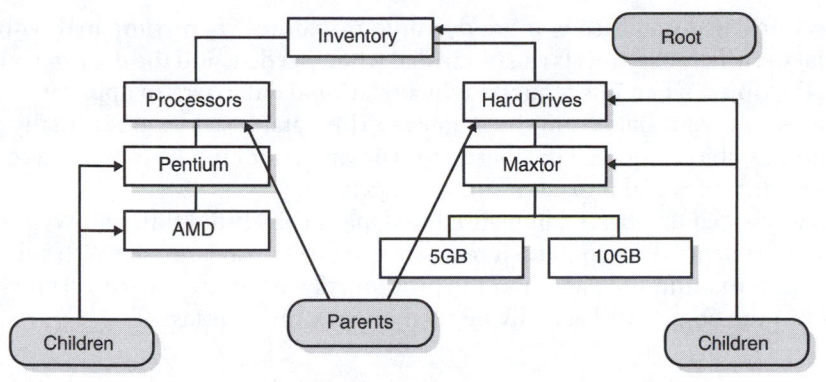

Figure 11-6   Hierarchical databases use a tree structure and a parent/child relationship.

This model enables different databases to be managed by different administrators, although one person or group must manage the entire logical database. This may be useful if each database contains information that is specialized, but the complexity of load balancing, fault tolerance, and shifting of users is quite high.

An *object-oriented database* is designed to handle a variety of data (images, audio, documents, video). The objects within the database contain information that is used to access the objects actually containing these different data types and defines their properties.

Figure 11-7
A distributed database may contain databases in different areas, which are logically connected and viewed as one database.

An object-oriented database is more dynamic in nature when compared with a relational database because objects can be created when needed, and the data *and* procedure go with the object when it is requested. In a relational database, an application uses its procedures to obtain data from the database. The database does not actually provide procedures as object-oriented databases do. The object-oriented database has classes to define the attributes and procedures of its objects.

Object-oriented databases can be used to dynamically build different Web pages for different users depending upon their requests and input to a particular Web site. The objects are used to build the page, and the procedures within the objects dictate how the data within the objects will actually be used to perform their tasks.

Database Interface Languages

Data is of no use if you can't get to it and do something with it. Applications need to be able to obtain and interact with the information stored in databases. They need some type of interface and communication mechanism. The following sections address several interface languages:

- **Open Database Connectivity (ODBC)** An application programming interface (API) that allows an application to communicate with a database either locally or remotely. The application sends requests to the ODBC, which in turn translates them into database commands. ODBC tracks down the necessary database driver for the application.

- **Object Linking and Embedding Database (OLE DB)** Separates data into components that run as middleware on a client or server. It provides a low-level interface to link information across different databases and provides access to data no matter where it is located or how it is formatted.

- **ActiveX Data Objects (ADO)** An API that allows applications to access back-end database systems. It is a set of ODBC interfaces that expose the functionality of a database through accessible objects. The ADO uses the OLE DB interface to connect with the database and can be developed with many different scripting languages.

- **Java Database Connectivity (JDBC)** An API that allows a Java application to communicate with a database. The application can connect through ODBC or directly to the database.

- **EXtensible Markup Language (XML)** A standard for structuring data so that it can be easily shared by applications using Web technologies. It is a markup language that is self-defining and provides a lot of flexibility in how information within the database is presented. The Web browser interprets the XML tags.

Relational Database Components

Like all software, databases are built with programming languages. Some database languages include a *data definition language (DDL)*, which defines the schema; a *data manipulation language (DML)*, which examines and manipulates the data within the database; a *data control language (DCL)*, which defines the internal organization of the database; and an ad hoc *query language (QL)* for users to make queries and access the data within the database.

Each type of database model can have many other differences, which vary from vendor to vendor. Most, however, contain the following basic core functionalities:

- Data definition language (DDL)
- Data manipulation language (DML)
- Query language (QL)
- Report generator

DDL defines the structure and schema of the database. The structure could mean the table size, key placement, views, and data element relationship. The **schema** describes the type of data that will be held and manipulated, and its properties. It defines the structure of the database, access operations, and integrity procedures.

DML contains all the commands that enable a user to view, manipulate, and use the database (view, add, modify, sort, and delete commands). QL enables users to make requests of the database, and the report generator produces printouts of data in a user-defined manner.

Data Dictionary

Will the data dictionary explain all the definitions of database jargon to me? Answer: Wrong dictionary.

A **data dictionary** is a central repository of data elements and their relationships. It stores critical information about data usage, data relationships, data sources, and data formats. It is a tool used to centrally manage parts of a database by controlling data about the data (referred to as metadata) within the database. It provides a cross-reference between groups of data elements and the databases.

A data dictionary is a central collection of data element definitions, schema objects, and reference keys. The schema objects can contain tables, views, indexes, procedures, functions, and triggers. A data dictionary can contain the default values for columns, integrity information, the names of users, the privileges and roles for users, and auditing information.

The database management software reads the data dictionary to ascertain that schema objects exist and checks to see if specific users have the process access rights to view them (see Figure 11-8). When users look at the database, they can be restricted by specific views. The different view settings for each user are held within the data dictionary. When new tables, new rows, or new schema are added, the data dictionary is updated to reflect this.

Primary versus Foreign Key

The primary key is an identifier of a row and it must be unique. Each row must have a primary key. When a user requests to view a record, the database tracks this record by its

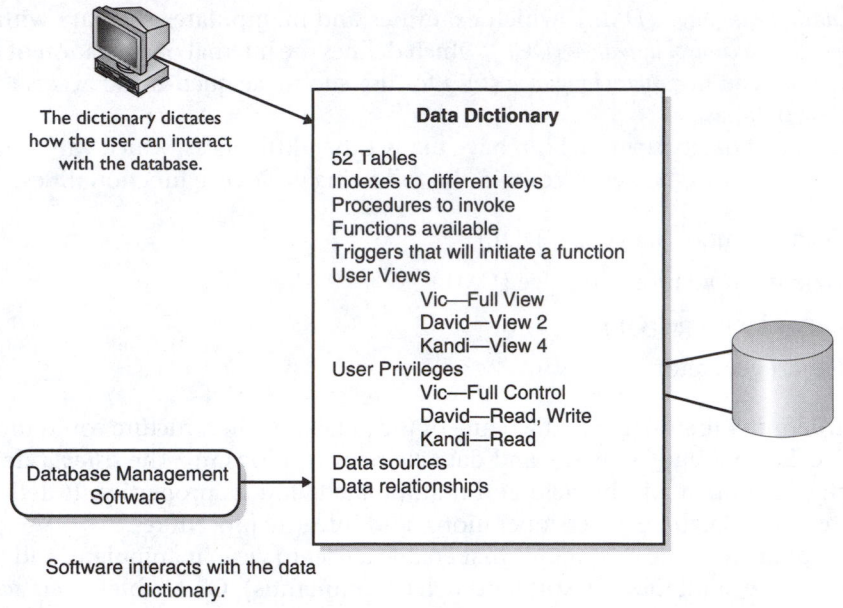

Figure 11-8   The data dictionary is a centralized program that contains information about a database.

unique primary key. If the primary key were not unique, the database would not know which record to present to the user. In the following illustration, the primary keys for Table A are the dogs' names.

A primary key is different from a foreign key, although they are closely related. If an attribute in one table has a value matching the primary key in another table, this attribute is considered a foreign key. This foreign key is not necessarily the primary key in its current table; it only has to contain the same information that is held in another table's primary key. In the following illustration, a primary key for Table A is Dallas. Because Table B has an attribute that contains the same data as this primary key and there is a relationship set up between these two keys, it is referred to as a foreign key. This is another way for the database to track relationships between data that it houses.

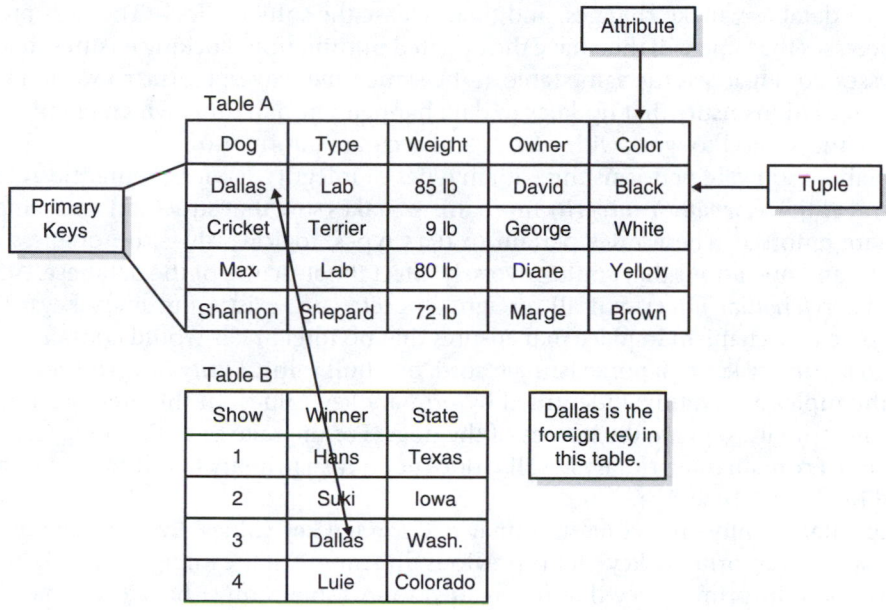

Integrity

You just wrote over my table! Response: Well my information is more important than yours.

Like other resources within a network, a database can run into **concurrency** problems. Concurrency has to do with making sure that different subjects receive the most up-to-date information and ensures that the database can properly handle various requests at the same time. If a group uses one price sheet to know how many supplies to order for the next week and also to calculate the expected profit, this is an important file. If Dan and Elizabeth copy this price sheet from the file server to their workstations, they each have a copy of the original file. Dan changes the stock level of computer books from 120 to 5, because they sold 115 in the last three days. He also uses the current prices listed in the price sheet to estimate his expected profits for the next week. Elizabeth reduces the price on several software packages and sees that the stock level of computer books is still over 100, so she chooses not to order any more for next week. Dan and Elizabeth do not communicate this different information to each other, but place it on this price sheet for everyone to view and use.

Dan copies his changes back to the file server, and then 30 seconds later Elizabeth copies her changes over Dan's changes. So the file only reflects Elizabeth's changes. Because they did not synchronize their changes, they are both now using incorrect data. Dan's profits are off because he does not know that Elizabeth reduced the prices, and next week Elizabeth will have no computer books because she did not know that the stock level had dropped to five.

The same thing happens in databases. If controls are not in place, two users can access and modify the same data at the same time, which can be detrimental to a dynamic environment. To ensure that concurrency problems do not exist, processes can *lock* tables within a database, make changes, and then release the software lock. The next process that accesses the table will then have the updated information. Locking ensures that two processes do not access the same table at the same time. Pages, tables, rows, and fields can be locked to ensure that updates to data happen one at a time, which enables each process and subject to work with correct and accurate information.

Database software performs three main types of integrity services: semantic, referential, and entity. A *semantic integrity* mechanism makes sure that structural and semantic rules are enforced. These rules pertain to data types, logical values, uniqueness constraints, and operations that could adversely affect the structure of the database. A database has *referential integrity* if all foreign keys reference existing primary keys. There should be a mechanism in place that ensures that no foreign key would contain a reference to a primary key of a nonexisting record, or a null value. *Entity integrity* guarantees that the tuples are uniquely identified by primary key values. In the previous illustration, the primary keys are the names of the dogs. For the sake of entity integrity, every tuple must contain one primary key. If it does not have a primary key, it cannot be referenced by the database.

The database must not contain unmatched foreign key values. Every foreign key refers to an existing primary key. In the previous illustration, if the foreign key in Table B is Dallas, then the primary key that it is related to in Table A must have the same value, which is Dallas. If these values do not match, then their relationships can be broken, and again the database cannot reference the information properly.

Other configurable operations are available to help protect the integrity of the data within a database. These operations are rollbacks, commits, and savepoints and checkpoints.

The *rollback* is a statement that ends a current transaction and cancels all other changes to the database. These changes could have taken place with the data itself or with schema changes that were typed in. When a rollback statement is executed, the changes are cancelled, and the database returns to its previous state. A rollback can take place if the database has some type of unexpected glitch or if outside entities disrupt its processing sequence. Instead of transmitting and posting partial or corrupt information, the database will roll back to its original state, and log these errors and actions so that they can be reviewed later.

The *commit* statement terminates a transaction and executes all changes that were just made by the user. Just like its name indicates, once the commit command is executed, the changes are committed and reflected in the database. These changes can be made to data or schema information. By committing these changes, they are then available to all other applications and users. If a user attempts to commit a change and it cannot complete correctly, a rollback is performed. This ensures that partial changes do not take place and that data is not corrupted.

Savepoints are used to make sure that if a system failure occurs, or if an error is detected, the database can attempt to return to a point before the system crashed or hiccupped. For a conceptual example, say Dave typed, "Jeremiah was a bullfrog. He was

<savepoint> a good friend of mine." (The system inserted a savepoint.) Then a freak storm came through and rebooted the system. When Dave got back into the database application, he might see "Jeremiah was a bullfrog. He was," but the rest was lost. Therefore, the savepoint saved some of his work. The database will use this tool to attempt to restore the user's work and the state of the database after a glitch, but some glitches are just too large and invasive to overcome.

Savepoints are easy to implement within databases, but a balance has to be struck between too many and not enough. Having too many savepoints can degrade the performance of the database, whereas having not enough savepoints runs the risk of losing data and decreasing user productivity because the lost data would have to be reentered. Savepoints can be initiated by a time interval, a specific action by the user, or the number of transactions or changes made to the database. For example, a database can set a savepoint every 15 minutes, every 20 transactions completed, each time a user gets to the end of a record, or every 12 changes made to the databases.

So a savepoint restores data by enabling the user to go back in time before the system crashed or hiccupped. This can reduce frustration and help us all live in harmony.

 NOTE "Checkpoints" are very similar to savepoints. When the database software fills up a certain amount of memory, a checkpoint is initiated, which saves the data from the memory segment to a temporary file. If a glitch is experienced, the software will try and use this information to restore the user's working environment to its previous state.

Reference

Security Issues in SQL: **csrc.nist.gov/publications/nistpubs/800-8/800-8.txt**

Database Security Issues

Oh, I know this and now that. Now I know the big secret! Response: Then I am changing the big secret—hold on.

The two main security issues we are going to address are aggregation and inference. *Aggregation* happens when a user does not have the clearance or permission to access specific information, but she does have the permission to access components of this information. She can then figure out the rest and obtain restricted information. She can learn of information from different sources and combine it to learn something that she does not have the clearance to know.

 NOTE Aggregation is the act of combining information from separate sources. The combination of the information forms new information, which the subject does not have the necessary rights to access. The combined information has a sensitivity that is greater than the individual parts.

The following is a silly conceptual example. Let's say a database administrator does not want anyone in the Users group to be able to figure out a specific sentence, so he segregates the sentence into components and restricts the Users group from accessing it, as represented in Figure 11-9. However, Emily can access components A, C, and F. Because she is particularly bright, she figures out the sentence and now knows the restricted secret.

To prevent aggregation, the subject, and any application or process acting on the subject's behalf, needs to be prevented from gaining access to the whole collection, including the independent components. The objects can be placed into containers, which are classified at a higher level to prevent access from subjects with lower-level permissions or clearances. A subject's queries can also be tracked and context-dependent access control can be enforced. This would keep a history of the objects a subject has accessed and restrict an access attempt if there was an indication that an aggregation attack is under way.

The other security issue is *inference*, which is similar to aggregation. The inference problem happens when a subject deduces, or figures out, the full story from the pieces he learned of through aggregation. This is seen when data at a lower security level indirectly portrays data at a higher level.

 NOTE Inference is the ability to derive information that is not explicitly available.

For example, if a clerk were restricted from knowing the planned movements of troops based in a specific country, but did have access to food shipment requirements forms and tent allocation documents, he could figure out that the troops were moving to a specific place because that is where the food and tents are being shipped. The food shipment and tent allocation documents were classified as confidential, and the troop movement was classified as top secret. Because of the varying classifications, the clerk could access and ascertain information he was not supposed to know.

The trick is to prevent the subject, or any application or process acting on behalf of that subject, from indirectly gaining access to the inferable information. This problem is

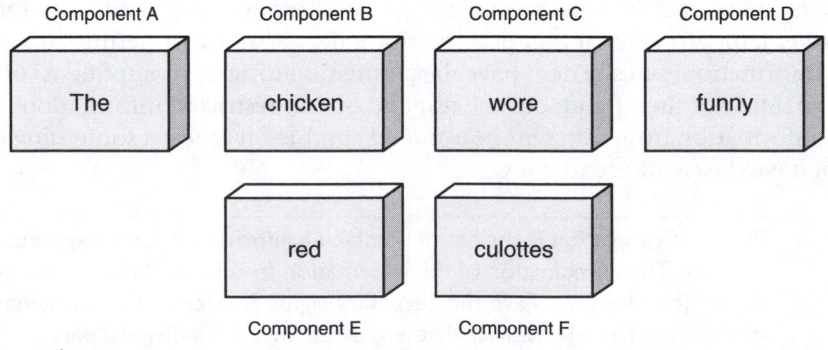

Figure 11-9   Because Emily has access to components A, C, and F, she can figure out the secret sentence through aggregation.

usually dealt with in the development of the database by implementing content- and context-dependent access control rules. Such rules track the subject's query requests and restrict patterns that represent inference.

Database security takes a different approach than operating system security. In an operating system, the identity and authentication of the subject controls access. This is done through access control lists (ACLs), capability tables, roles, and security labels. The operating system only makes decisions about whether a subject can access a file; it does not make this decision based on the contents of the file itself. If Mitch can access file A, it does not matter if that file contains information about a cookie recipe or secret information from the Cold War. On the other hand, database security does look at the contents of a file when it makes an access control decision, which is referred to as *content-dependent access control*. This type of access control increases processing overhead, but it provides higher granular control.

Common attempts to prevent inference attacks are cell suppression, partitioning the database, and noise and perturbation. *Cell suppression* is a technique used to hide or not show specific cells that contain information that could be used in inference attacks. *Partitioning* a database involves dividing the database into different parts, which makes it much harder for an unauthorized individual to find connecting pieces of data that can be brought together and other information that can be deduced or uncovered. *Noise and perturbation* is a technique of inserting bogus information in the hopes of misdirecting an attacker or confusing the matter enough that the actual attack will not be fruitful.

Often security is not integrated into the planning and development of a database. Security is an afterthought and a trusted front end is developed to be used with the database instead. This approach is limited in the granularity of security and in the types of security functions that can take place.

A common theme in security is a balance between effective security and functionality. In many cases, the more you secure something, the less functionality you have. Although this could be the desired result, it is important to not impede user productivity when security is being introduced.

Database Views

Don't show your information to everybody, only a select few.

Databases can permit one group, or a specific user, to see certain information, while restricting another group from viewing it altogether. This functionality happens through the use of *database views*. If a database administrator wants to allow middle management to see their departments' profits and expenses, but not show them the whole company's profits, she can implement views. Senior management would be given all views, which contain all the departments' and the company's profit and expense values, whereas each individual manager would only be able to view his or her department values.

Like operating systems, databases can employ discretionary access control (DAC) and mandatory access control (MAC) (explained in Chapter 4). Views can be displayed according to group membership, user rights, or security labels. If a DAC were being employed, then groups and users could be granted access through views based on their identity, authentication, and authorization. If a MAC were in place, then groups and users would be granted access based on their security clearance and the data's classification level.

Polyinstantiation

Polyinstantiation. Response: Gesundheit.

Sometimes a company does not want users at one level to access and modify data at a higher level. There are different ways of handling this type of situation. One approach is when a lower-level user attempts to access a higher-level object, access is denied. However, this gives away information indirectly by telling the lower-level entity that something sensitive lives inside that object at that level.

Another way of dealing with this issue is *polyinstantiation*. This enables a relation to contain multiple tuples with the same primary keys, with each instance distinguished by a security level. When this information is inserted into a database, lower-level subjects need to be restricted from it. Instead of just restricting access, another set of data is created to fool the lower-level subjects into thinking that the information actually means something else. For example, if a naval base has a cargo shipment going from Delaware to the Ukraine that contains weapons via the *Oklahoma* ship, this type of information could be classified as top secret. Only the subjects with the security clearance of top secret and above should know this information, so a dummy file is created that states that the *Oklahoma* is carrying a shipment from Delaware to Africa containing food, and it is given a security clearance of unclassified, as shown in Table 11-1. It will be obvious that the *Oklahoma* is gone, but individuals at lower security levels will think that the ship is on its way to Africa, instead of to the Ukraine. This will also make sure that no one at a lower level will try to commit the *Oklahoma* for any other missions. The lower-level subjects know that the *Oklahoma* is not available, and they will use other ships for cargo shipments.

 NOTE Polyinstantiation is a process of interactively producing more detailed versions of objects by populating variables with different values or other variables. It is often used to prevent inference attacks.

In this example polyinstantiation was used to create two versions of the same object so the lower-level subjects will not know the true information, and it stops them from attempting to use or change that data in any way. It is a way of providing a cover story for the entities that do not have the necessary security level to know the truth. This is just one example of how polyinstantiation can be used. Polyinstantiation is not strictly related to security, although that is the most common use for it. Whenever a copy of an object is created and populated with different data, meaning two instances of the same object have different attributes, polyinstantiation is in place.

Online Transaction Processing (OLTP)

What if our databases get overwhelmed? Answer: OLTP to the rescue!

Online transaction processing (OLTP) is usually used when databases are clustered to provide fault tolerance and higher performance. OLTP provides mechanisms that watch for problems and that deal with them appropriately when they do occur. For example, if a process stops functioning, the monitor mechanisms within OLTP can detect this and attempt to restart the process. If the process cannot be restarted, then the transaction that was taking place will be rolled back to ensure that no data is corrupted or that only

Level	Ship	Cargo	Origin	Destination
Top Secret	Oklahoma	Weapons	Delaware	Ukraine
Unclassified	Oklahoma	Food	Delaware	Africa

Table 11-1 An Example of Polyinstantiation by Providing a Cover Story to Subjects at a Lower Level

part of a transaction happens. Any erroneous or invalid transactions that are detected should be written to a transaction log and to a report log to be reviewed at a later time.

OLTP will load balance incoming requests if it is necessary. This means that if requests to update databases increase, and one system reduces in performance because of the large volume, OLTP can move some of these requests to other systems. This makes sure that all requests are handled and that the user, or whoever is making the requests, does not have to wait a long time for the transaction to complete.

When there is more than one database, it is important that they all contain the same information. If database A has a value for Katie's checking account of $3,500, and database B has the value of $10,000, this could cause some problems, as illustrated in Figure 11-10. The reason the difference would occur is that Katie withdrew a lot of money, and only one database received that request and did not update any of the other databases. If the real value is $3,500 and Katie makes a request to check her checking account balance a few minutes later, this request may go to the database that still has the old value of $10,000. Although this information might make Katie surprised and happy, it is incorrect information. OLTP will make sure that a transaction is not complete until all databases receive and reflect this change. This is a *two-phase commit* service.

OLTP records transactions as they occur (in real time), which usually updates more than one database in a distributed environment. This type of complexity can introduce many integrity threats, so the database software should implement the characteristics of what's known as the ACID test:

- **Atomicity** Divides transactions into units of work and ensures that all modifications take effect or none takes effect. The changes are either committed, or the database is rolled back.

- **Consistency** A transaction must follow the integrity policy developed for that particular database and ensure that all data is consistent in the different databases.

Checking account debited $6,500. New balance is $3,500.

Transaction not carried over to this database. Balance is still set at $10,000.

User withdraws $6,500 from checking account.

Figure 11-10 If each database is not updated with the correct information, many types of problems can take place.

- **Isolation** Transactions execute in isolation until completed, without interacting with other transactions. The results of the modification are not available until the transaction is completed.

- **Durability** Once the transaction is verified as accurate on all systems, it is committed, and the databases cannot be rolled back.

 Atomicity is used so that if one step in the transaction fails, subsequent steps are not processed.

Data Warehousing and Data Mining

Oh, so that is what is in our data warehouse. I had no idea.

Data warehousing combines data from multiple databases or data sources into a large database with the purpose of a fuller extent of information retrieval and data analysis. Data from different databases is extracted and transferred to a central data storage device called a warehouse. This enables users to query one entity rather than accessing and querying different databases.

This is not a process of just mirroring data from different databases and presenting the data in one place. It is a method of selecting useful information that is then processed and presented in a more useful and understandable way. Related data is summarized and correlated before it is presented to the user. Instead of having every piece of data presented, the user is given data in a more abridged form that best fits her needs.

Although this provides easier access and control, because the data warehouse is in one place, it also requires more stringent security. If an intruder were to get into the data warehouse, he could access all of the company's information at once.

Data mining is the process of massaging the data held in the data warehouse into more useful information. Data mining tools are used to find an association and correlation in data to produce *metadata*. Metadata can show previously unseen relationships between individual subsets of information. It can find abnormal patterns that were not previously apparent. A simplistic example could be detecting insurance fraud. Suppose millions of customers, their information, claims, and specific habits were kept in a database, or warehouse, and a mining tool were to look for certain patterns in claims. It might find that each time John Smith moved, he had an insurance claim two to three months following the move. If he moved in 1967 and two months later had a suspicious fire, then moved in 1973 and had a motorcycle stolen three months after that, and then moved again in 1984 and had a burglary break-in two months afterwards, a pattern arises. This might be hard for people to manually catch because he had different insurance agents over the years, the files were just updated and not reviewed, or the files were not kept in a centralized place for agents to review.

Data mining can look at complex data and simplify it by using Fuzzy logic, a set theory, and expert systems to perform the mathematical functions and look for patterns in data that are not so apparent. In many ways, the metadata is more valuable than the data it was derived from; thus, it must be highly protected. (Fuzzy logic and expert systems are discussed later in the "Artificial Neural Networks" section.)

NOTE *Data mining* is the process of analyzing a database using tools that look for trends, correlations, relationships, and anomalies without having the knowledge of the meaning of the data. *Metadata* is the result of storing data within a database and mining the data with tools (see Figure 11-11). Data goes into a database and metadata comes out of the database.

Data mining is also known as ***Knowledge Discovery in Database (KDD),*** and is a combination of techniques to identify valid and useful patterns. Different types of data can have various interrelationships, and the method used depends on the type of data and patterns that are sought. The following are three approaches used in KDD systems to uncover these patterns:

- **Classification**   Data is grouped together according to shared similarities.

- **Probabilistic**   Data interdependencies are identified and probabilities are applied to their relationships.

- **Statistical**   Identifies relationships between data elements and uses rule discovery.

Figure 11-11   Mining tools are used to extract data from a data warehouse, identify patterns, and present it in useful formats for users.

System Development

Security is most effective if it is planned and managed throughout the life cycle of a system or application rather than applying a third-party package as a front end at the end of development. Many security risks, analyses, and events occur during its lifetime, and these issues should be dealt with from the initial planning stage and continue through the design, coding, implementation, and operational stages. If security is added at the end of a project development versus being involved with each and every step of the life cycle, the cost and time of adding security increases dramatically. Security should not be looked at as a short sprint, but should be seen as a long run with many hills and obstacles.

Security should be implemented at each developmental phase.
Adding security at the end costs a lot more money.

Many developers, programmers, and architects know that security is much more expensive and complicated when it is added at a later phase of the system's life cycle instead of integrating it into the planning and designing phase. Different security components can affect many different aspects of a system, and if they are thrown in at the last moment, they will surely affect other mechanisms negatively, restrict some already developed functionality, and cause the system to perform in unusual and unexpected ways. This approach costs more money because of the number of times the developers have to go back to the drawing board, recode completed work, and rethink different aspects of the system's architecture.

Management of Development

Many developers know that good project management keeps the project moving in the right direction, allocates the necessary resources, provides the necessary information, and plans for the worst and hopes for the best. Project management is an important part of product development, and security management is an important part of project management.

A security plan should be drawn up at the beginning of a development project and integrated into the functional plan to ensure that security is not overlooked. The first plan is broad, covers a wide base, and refers to documented references for more detailed information. The references could include computer standards (RFCs, IEEE standards, and best practices), documents developed in previous projects, security policies, accreditation statements, incident-handling plans, and national or international guidelines (Orange Book, Red Book, and Common Criteria). This makes the plan easier to read and more usable.

The security plan should have a lifetime of its own. It will need to be added to, subtracted from, and explained in more detail as the project continues. It is important to keep it up-to-date for future reference. It is always easy to lose track of actions, activities, and decisions once a large and complex project gets underway.

The security plan and project management activities will most likely be audited so that security-related decisions can be understood. When assurance in the system needs to be guaranteed, indicating that security was fully considered in each phase of the life cycle, the procedures, development, decisions, and activities that took place during the project will be reviewed. It is important that the documentation accurately reflects how the system or product was built and how it operates once implemented into an environment.

Life Cycle Phases

There is a time to live, a time to die, a time to love... Response: And a time to shut up.

Several types of models are used for system or application development, which include varying life cycles. This section outlines the core components that are common to all of them. Each model basically accomplishes the same thing; the main difference is how the development and lifetime of a system is broken into sections.

A project can start with a good idea, and then the programmers and engineers just wing it, or the project can be carefully thought out and structured to follow the necessary life cycles. The first option may seem more fun in the beginning because stuffy requirements and steps can be skipped, documentation can be blown off, and the product can get out the door in a shorter time and under budget. However, more fun would actually be had by the team that took its time to think through all of the scenarios of each phase of the life cycle because its product would be more sound, become more trustworthy by the market, the team would make more money in the long run, and it would not need to chaotically develop several service and security patches to fix problems missed the first time around.

The different models integrate the following phases in one fashion or another:

- Project initiation
- Functional design analysis and planning
- System design specifications
- Software development
- Installation/implementation
- Operational/maintenance
- Disposal

You may notice that security is not listed as a bullet point that would indicate it is dealt with in one phase or another. This is because security should be embedded throughout all phases. It costs a lot more money to address security issues after the product is released compared with addressing it during the development of the product. Functionality is the main driving force of developing products, and several considerations need to take place within that realm, but we will be addressing the *security* issues that also need to be examined at each phase of the product's life cycle.

Project Initiation
So what are we building and why?

This is the phase when everyone involved attempts to understand why the project is needed and what the scope of the project entails. Either a specific customer needs a new system or application, or there is a demand for the product in the market. At this point, the characteristics of the system and proposed functionality are discussed, brainstorming sessions take place, and obvious restrictions are reviewed.

A conceptual definition of the project needs to be initiated and developed to ensure that everyone is on the right page and that this is a proper product to develop that will be, hopefully, profitable. This phase could include evaluating products that are currently on the market and could identify any demands that are not being met by current vendors. It could also be a direct request for a specific product from a current or future customer.

In either case, because this is for a specific client or market, an initial study of the product needs to be started, and a high-level proposal should be drafted that outlines the necessary resources for the project and the predicted timeline of development. The estimated profit expected from the product also needs to be conducted. This information is submitted to senior management who will determine if the next phase should begin or if further information is required.

In this phase, the user needs are identified and basic security objectives of the product are acknowledged. It must be determined if the product will be processing sensitive data, and if so, the levels of sensitivity involved should also be defined. An initial risk analysis should be initiated that evaluates threats and vulnerabilities to estimate the cost/benefit ratios of the different security countermeasures. Issues pertaining to security integrity, confidentiality, and availability need to be addressed. The level of each security attribute should be focused upon so that a clear direction of security controls can begin to take shape.

A basic security framework is designed for the project to follow, and risk management processes are established. Risk management will continue throughout the lifetime of the project. Some of the following risk information may start to be gathered and evaluated in the project initiation phase, but it will become more granular in nature as the phases graduate into the functional design and design specification phase.

Risk Management

Okay, question one. How badly can we screw up?

One of the most important pieces of risk management is to know the right questions to ask. Risk management was discussed in Chapter 3, but it dealt with identifying and mitigating risks that directly affect the business as a whole. Risk management must also be performed when developing and implementing software. Although the two functions are close in concepts, goals, and objectives, they have different specific tasks and focus.

Software development usually has a focus on rich functionality and getting it out the door and on the shelves for customers to buy as soon as possible. Most of the time security is not part of the process or quickly falls by the wayside when a deadline seems imminent. It is not just the programmer who should be thinking about coding in a secure manner, but the design of the product should have security integrated and layered throughout the project. Software engineering should address security threat scenarios and solutions during their tasks. It is not just one faction of a development team that might fall down when it comes to security. Security has never really been treated as an important function of the process—that is, until the product is bought by several customers who undergo attacks and compromises that tie directly to how the product was developed and programmed. Then security is quite a big deal, but it is too late to integrate security into the project; instead, a patch is developed and released.

The first step in risk management is to identify the threats and vulnerabilities and to calculate the level of risk involved. When all the risks are evaluated, management will decide upon the acceptable level of risk. Of course, it would be nice for management to not accept any risks and for the product to be designed and tested until it is foolproof; however, this would cause the product to be in development for a long time and to be too expensive to purchase. Compromises and intelligent business decisions need to be made to provide a balance between risks and economic feasibility.

Risk Analysis

A risk analysis is performed to identify the relative risks and the potential consequences. This process usually involves asking many, many questions to find out the laundry list of vulnerabilities and threats, the probability of these vulnerabilities being exploited, and the outcome if one of these threats actually becomes real and a compromise takes place. The questions vary from product to product—its intended purpose, the expected environment it will be implemented into, the personnel involved, and the types of businesses that would purchase and use this type of product. The following is a small list of the types of questions that should be asked during a software risk analysis:

- What is the possibility of buffer overflows, and what type of outcome would result?
- Are threat agents outside and inside the environment? What are those threat agents?

- What type of businesses would depend on this product, and what type of business loss would it cause if the product were to go offline for a specific period?

- Are there covert channel issues that need to be dealt with?

- What type of fault tolerance is integrated into the product, and when would it be initiated?

- Is encryption needed? Which type? What strength?

- Are contingency plans needed for emergency issues?

- Would another party (ISP or hosting agency) be maintaining this product for the customer?

- Is mobile code necessary? How and why?

- Will this product be in an environment that is connected to the Internet? What effects could this have on the product?

- Does this product need to interface to vulnerable systems?

- How could this product be vulnerable to denial of service (DoS) attacks?

- How could this product be vulnerable to viruses?

- Are intrusion alert mechanisms necessary?

- Would there be motivation for insiders or outsiders to sabotage this product? How and why?

- Would competitor companies of the purchaser want to commit fraud via this product? How and why?

- What other systems would be affected if this product failed?

This is a short list, and each question can branch off into other questions to ensure that all possible threats and risks are identified and thought through.

Once all the risks are identified, the probability of them actually taking place needs to be quantified, and the consequences of these risks need to be properly evaluated to ensure that the right countermeasures are implemented within the development phase and the product itself. If a product will only be used to produce word documents, a lower level of security countermeasures and tests would be needed compared with a product that maintains credit card data.

Many of the same risk analysis steps outlined in Chapter 3 can be applied in the risk analysis that needs to be performed when developing a product. Once the threats are identified, the probability of occurring is estimated, and their consequences are calculated, the risks can be listed in order of importance. If the possibility of a DoS taking place is high and could devastate a customer, then this is at the high end of importance. If the possibility of fraud is low, then this is pushed to the back of the bus. The most probable and potentially devastating risks are approached first, and the less likely and less damaging are dealt with after the more important risks.

These risks need to be addressed in the design and architecture of the product as well as in the functionality the product provides, the implementation procedures, and the required maintenance. A banking software product may need to be designed to have Web server farms within a demilitarized zone (DMZ) of the branch, but have the components and databases behind another set of firewalls to provide another layer of protection. This would mean that the architecture of the product would include splitting it among different systems and developing communication methods between the different parts. If the product is going to provide secure e-mail functionality, then all the risks involved with just this service need to be analyzed and properly accounted for. Implementation procedures need to be thought through and addressed. How will the customer set up this product? What are the system and environment requirements? Does this product need to be supplied with a public key infrastructure (PKI)? The level of maintenance required after installation is important to many products. Will the vendor need to keep the customer abreast of certain security issues? Should any logging and auditing take place? The more these things are thought through in the beginning, the less scrambling will be involved at the end of the process.

It is important to understand the difference between project risk analysis and security risk analysis. Many times they are confused or combined. The project team may do a risk analysis pertaining to the risk of the project failing. This is much different than the security risk analysis, which has different threats and issues. The two should be understood and used, but in a distinctively different manner.

Functional Design Analysis and Planning

I would like to design a boat to carry my yellow ducky. Response: You are in the wrong meeting.

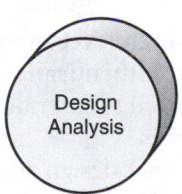

In this phase, a project plan is developed to define the security activities and to create security checkpoints to ensure that quality assurance for security controls takes place and that the configuration and change control process is identified. At this point in the project, resources are identified, test schedules start to form, and evaluation criteria are developed to be able to properly test the security controls. A formal functional baseline is formed, meaning the expectations of the product are outlined in a formal manner, usually through documentation. A test plan is developed, which will be updated through each phase to ensure that all issues are properly tested.

Determining security requirements can be derived from several different sources:

- Functional needs of the system or application
- National, international, or organizational standards and guidelines
- Export restrictions

- Sensitivity level of data being processed (military strategic data versus private sector data)
- Relevant security policies
- Cost/benefit analysis results
- Required level of assurance to achieve the targeted security level rating

The initial risk assessment will most likely be updated throughout the project as more information is uncovered and learned. In some projects, more than one risk analysis needs to be performed at different stages of the life cycle. For example, if the project team knows that the product will need to identify and authenticate users in a domain setting requiring a medium level of security, an initial risk analysis is performed. Later in the life cycle, if it is determined that this product should work with biometric devices and have the capability to integrate with systems that require high security levels, a whole new risk analysis will need to be performed because new morsels have been added to the mix.

This phase addresses the functionality required out of the product and is captured in a design document. If the product is being developed for a customer, the design document is used as a tool to explain to the customer what the developing team understands of the requirements of the product. A design document is usually drawn up by analysts, with the guidance of engineers and architects, and presented to the customer. The customer can then decide if more functionality needs to be added or subtracted, and dialogues between the customer and development team begin hammering out exactly what is expected from the product.

In security issues, this is where high-level questions are asked. Examples of these questions include the following: Are authentication and authorization necessary? Is encryption needed? Will the product need to interface with other systems? Will the product be directly accessed via the Internet?

Many companies skip the functional design phase and jump right into developing specifications for the product. Or a design document is not shared with the customer. This can cause major delays and rework efforts, because a broad vision of the product needs to be developed before looking strictly at the details. If the customer is not involved at this stage, the customer most likely thinks the developers will be developing a product that accomplishes X, while the development team thinks that the customer wants Y. A lot of wasted time can go into developing a product that is not what is actually wanted by the customer, so clear direction and goals need to be drawn up before the beginning of coding. This is usually an important function of the project management team.

System Design Specifications

Software requirements come from informational, functional, and behavioral models. The informational model dictates the type of information to be processed and how it will be processed. The functional model outlines the tasks and functions that the application needs to carry out. The behavioral model explains the states that the application will be in during and after specific transitions take place. For example, an antivirus software application may have an informational model that dictates what information is to be processed by the program, such as virus signatures, modified system files, checksums on critical files, and virus activity. It would also have a functional model that dictates that the application should be able to scan a hard drive, check e-mail for known virus signatures, monitor critical system files, and update itself. The behavioral model would indicate that when the system starts up, the antivirus software application will scan the hard drive. The computer coming online would be the event that changes the state of the application. If a virus were found, the application would change state and deal with the virus appropriately. The occurrence of the virus is the event that would change the state. Each state has to be accounted for to ensure that the product does not go into an insecure state and act in an unpredictable way.

The informational, functional, and behavioral model data go into the software design as requirements. What comes out of the design is the data, architectural, and procedural design, as shown in Figure 11-12.

The data design takes the informational model information and transforms it into data structures that will be required to implement the software. The architectural design defines the relationships between the major structures and components of the application. The procedural design transforms structural components into descriptive procedures.

This is the point where access control mechanisms are chosen, subject rights and permissions are defined, the encryption method and algorithm are chosen, the handling of sensitive data is ironed out, the necessary objects and components are identified, the interprocessing communication is evaluated, the integrity mechanism is identified, and any other security specifications are appraised and solutions are determined.

Figure 11-12
Information from three models can go into the design.

The work breakdown structure (WBS) for future phases needs to be confirmed, which includes the development and implementation stages. This includes a timeline and detailed activities for testing, development, staging, integration testing, and product delivery.

The system design is a tool used to describe the user requirements and the internal behavior of a system. It then maps the two elements to show how the internal behavior actually accomplishes the user requirements.

This phase starts to look at more details of the product and the environment that it will be implemented within. The required functionality was determined in the last phase. This phase addresses what mechanisms are needed to provide this functionality and determines how it will be coded, tested, and implemented.

The modularity and reusability of the product, or the components of the product, need to be addressed. Code that provides security-critical functions should be simple in design in order to catch errors in a less confusing fashion, and be small enough to be fully tested in different situations. Components can be called and used by different parts of the product or by other applications. This attribute, reusability, can help streamline the product and provide for a more efficient and more structured coding environment.

The product could have portability issues that need to be dealt with and handled at the early stages of the product development. If the product needs to work on Unix and Windows systems, then different coding requirements are needed compared with a product that will only be installed on mainframes. Also, the environment that will implement this product needs to be considered. Will this product be used by individual users, or will all the users within the network access this product in one fashion or another? Being a single-user product rather than a multiuser product has large ramifications on the development of the necessary specifications.

The testability of the product and components need to be thought about at this early phase instead of at later phases. Programmers can code in *hooks* that show the testers the state of the product at different stages of data processing. Just because the product appears to act correctly and produces the right results at the end of the processing phases, does not mean that internal errors are not taking place. This is why testing should happen in modular ways, the flow of data through the product needs to be followed, and each step should be analyzed.

This phase should look closely at all the questions asked at the project initiation and ensure that specifications are developed for each issue addressed. For example, if authentication is required, this phase will lay out all the details necessary for this process to take place. If fraud is a large risk, then all the necessary countermeasures should be identified and how they integrate into the product should be shown. If covert channels are a risk, then these issues should be addressed, and pseudocode should be developed to show how they will be reduced or eliminated.

If the product is being developed for a customer, the specifications of the product should be shared with them to again ensure that everyone is still on the same page and headed in the right direction. This is the stage to work out any confusion or misunderstanding before the actual coding begins.

The decisions made during the design phase are pivotal steps to the development phase. The design is the only way that the customer requirements are translated into software components; thus, software design serves as the foundation. Software quality and maintenance are greatly affected by the design of the product, as indicated in Figure 11-13.

Figure 11-13 If good product design is not put into place in the beginning, the following phases will be much more challenging.

Software Development
Code jockeys to your cubes and start punching those keys!

This is the phase where the programmers and developers become deeply involved. They are usually involved up to this point for their direction and advice, but at this phase, it is basically put into their laps. Let the programming and testing begin!

This is the stage where the programmers should code in a way that does not permit software compromises. Checking input lengths so buffer overflows cannot take place, coding to prevent the presence of covert channels, checking for proper data types, making sure checkpoints cannot be bypassed by users, syntax verification, and performing checksums are just some of the issues to be addressed. Different attack scenarios should be played out to see how the code could be attacked or modified in an unauthorized

Verification versus Validation

Verification determines if the product accurately represents and meets the specifications. A product can be developed that does not match the original specifications. This step ensures that the specs are properly met.

Validation determines if the product provides the necessary solution for the intended real-world problem. In large projects it is easy to lose sight of the overall goal. This exercise ensures that the main goal of the project is met.

fashion. Debugging and code reviews should be carried out by peer developers, and everything should be clearly documented.

Most programmers do not like to document and will find a way to get out of the task. Six to 12 months later, no one will remember specific issues that were addressed, how they were handled, or the solutions to problems that have already been encountered—or the programmer who knew all the details went to work for a competitor or won the lottery and moved to an island. This is another cause of rework and wasting of man-hours. Documentation is extremely important for many different reasons and can save a company a lot of money in the long run.

Formal and informal testing should begin as soon as possible. Unit testing can start very early in development. After a programmer develops a component, or unit of code, it is tested with several different input values and in many different situations. Unit testing usually continues throughout the development phase. A totally different group of people should carry out the formal testing. This is an example of *separation of duties*. A programmer should not develop, test, and release software. The more eyes upon the code and the more fingers punching keys, the greater the chance that bugs will be found before the product is released.

Of course, any software hooks inserted for testing or modification purposes need to be removed prior to being released to production because these can easily provide attackers back doors into the product.

There is no cookie-cutter recipe for security testing, because the applications and products can be so diverse in functionality and security objectives. It is important to map security risks to test cases and code. Linear thinking can be followed by identifying a risk, providing the necessary test scenario, performing the test, and reviewing the code for how it deals with such a risk, as illustrated in Figure 11-14. At this phase, tests are conducted in an actual network, which should mirror the production environment to ensure the code does not only work in the labs.

Security attacks and penetrations usually take place during this phase to identify any missed vulnerabilities. Functionality, performance, and penetration resistance are evaluated. All the necessary functionality required of the product should be in a checklist to ensure that each one is accounted for.

Security tests should be run to test against the risks identified earlier within the project. Buffer overflows should be attempted, the product should be hacked and attacked, interfaces should be hit with unexpected inputs, DoS situations should be tested, unusual user activity should take place, and if a system crashes, the product should react by

Separation of Duties

Different environmental types (development, testing, and production) should be properly separated, and functionality and operations should not overlap. Developers should not have access to code used in production. The code should be tested, submitted to the library, and then sent to the production environment.

Figure 11-14
After risks are identified, test scenarios need to be developed and used to verify that those risks are addressed.

reverting back to a more secure state. The product should be tested in various environments with different applications, configurations, and hardware platforms. A product may respond fine when installed on a clean Windows 2000 installation on a stand-alone PC, but it may throw unexpected errors when installed on a laptop that is remotely connected to a network and that has an SMS client installed.

At this stage, issues found in unit and formal testing are relayed to the development team in problem reports. The problems are fixed and retesting occurs. This is a continual process until everyone is satisfied that the product is ready for production. If there is a specific customer, the company would run through a range of tests before formally accepting the product. Then the product is formally released to the market or customer.

 NOTE Sometimes developers enter lines of code in a product that will allow them to do a few keystrokes and get right into the application. This allows them to bypass any security and access controls so that they can quickly access the application's code. This is referred to as a "trapdoor" or "maintenance hook" and should be removed before the code goes into production.

Installation/Implementation

The implementation stage focuses on how to use and operate the developed system or application.

At this phase, the customer has purchased the developed product and installed it into their environment. The product would then be configured for the right level of protection. Functionality and performance tests can be performed, and the results can be analyzed and compared with the company's security requirements.

The configurations should be documented. User guides and operation and maintenance manuals are developed so users know how to properly use the systems, and so the technical staff know how to properly configure the product if needed. Monitoring security activities needs to be performed to ensure that the system or application performs in the manner promised by the service level agreement.

Accreditation should occur between the implementation and the beginning of operational use of the system or application. This process follows the certification process, which formally or informally tests all the security features to determine if they accomplish the required security needs. Certification is the process of reviewing and evaluating security controls and functionality. It is usually a task assigned to an outside, independent reviewer. (Certification and accreditation were covered in detail in Chapter 5.)

The accreditation is the formal acceptance of the system by management and an explicit acceptance of risk. The accreditation looks at the whole system, not just at an application or a newly upgraded feature. This is because security is not a compartmentalized attribute, but is a service that takes place at different layers of the system and can be manifested in many ways. The accreditation process forces the management and technical staff to work together to ensure quality and a level of protection provided by purchased and implemented technologies. The technical staff understand operational and mechanical issues, and the management staff understand mission, financial, and liability issues. Together, they can cover a lot of ground during the certification accreditation processes.

Once they are sure of the security provided by the new system and understand and accept the risk, management should issue a formal accreditation statement.

Auditing needs to be enabled and monitored, and contingency recovery plans and procedures should be developed and tested to make sure the system and product react as planned in the event of a system failure or emergency situation.

Operational and Maintenance
Okay, the thing is out there. Now someone has to take care of that thing.

Operational

This is not a phase where you can think that security is done and in control, and that all you have to do now is sit back and eat donuts. On the contrary, security is just as, or more, important during the operational phase than during earlier phases.

The initial part of this phase includes the configuration of the new system and inserting it properly into the network and environment. Many times security controls are not enabled or properly configured for the environment, so even if they were correctly coded from the beginning, it does not really matter if they are not actually used or are used in an unintended way.

Operational assurance is carried out by continually conducting vulnerabilities tests, monitoring activities, and auditing events. It is through operational assurance activities that an administrator learns of new vulnerabilities or security compromises, so the proper actions can take place.

If major changes happen to the system, product, or environment, a new risk analysis may need to be performed along with a new certification and accreditation process. These major changes could include adding new systems and/or new applications, relocating the facility, or changing data sensitivity or criticality.

Disposal
All good things must come to an end.

When it is time for "out with the old and in with the new," certain steps may need to take place to make sure this transition happens in a secure manner. Depending on the sensitivity level of the data held on a system, various disposal activities may be necessary. Information may need to be archived, backed up to another system, discarded, or destroyed. If the data is sensitive and needs to be destroyed, it may need to be purged by overwriting, degaussing, or physically destroying the media. It depends on the data and the company's policy in destroying sensitive information.

If the product that is being replaced is just a word processor or an antivirus software package, this phase can be easily taken care of. But if the software is integrated into every part of the company's processing infrastructure, properly extracting it without affecting productivity and security can be an overwhelming task.

Postmortem Review
It is important that the team gather after the completion of a project to exhale, talk about the overall project, and discuss things that should be improved for the next time. If this phase is taken seriously and handled properly, the company can save money and time on future projects because lessons will have been learned, mistakes will not be repeated, and the process will be streamlined. All of these activities will help the next project run more smoothly with fewer mistakes and in less time.

This should be a structured event where someone is leading the meeting(s) and notes are being taken, but it should be a relaxed atmosphere for each team member to feel comfortable in expressing opinions and ideas. It is important that the review does not come down to a finger-pointing session or become a cesspool of complaining. It is a method of looking at the project from an objective view and identifying issues that could be improved upon the next time around.

Some companies do not see the value in this exercise and just race off to start the next project, which will most likely be cursed with the problems of the prior project. Projects are learning processes, and business is about making the best product in the least amount of time for the least amount of money. It is beneficial for management to understand how the two go together and to make sure that a postmortem review is part of every project. The most successful businesses streamline the processes of projects and project management and hone them to become a repeatable procedure that produces the expected level of quality. These businesses continually take the time to look at how processes can be improved and built upon.

This chapter explains a life cycle containing seven phases. Other models can use different cycles and a different number of phases, but they accomplish the basic components shown in Figure 11-15.

System Life Cycle Phases

- Project initiation:
  - Conception of project definition
  - Proposal and initial study
  - Initial risk analysis
- Functional design analysis and planning:
  - Requirements uncovered and defined
  - System environment specifications determined
  - Formal design created
- System design specifications:
  - Functional design review
  - Functionality broken down
  - Detailed planning put into place
  - Code design
- Software development:
  - Developing and programming software
- Installation:
  - Product installation and implementation
  - Testing and auditing
- Maintenance support:
  - Product changes, fixes, and minor modifications
- Disposal:
  - Replace product with new product

Figure 11-15
Phases to
a software
development
project

Software Development Methods

There are several different life cycle models that outline the significant phases of software development. The following list provides a quick glimpse at some of these different models:

- **Waterfall**   A classical method that uses discrete phases of development that require formal reviews and documentation before moving into the next phase of the project.

- **Spiral Model**   A method that builds upon the waterfall method with an emphasis on risk analysis, prototypes, and simulations at different phases of the development cycle.

- **Joint Analysis Development (JAD)**   Uses a team approach in application development in a workshop-oriented environment.

- **Rapid Application Development (RAD)**   A method of determining user requirements and developing systems quickly to satisfy immediate needs.

- **Cleanroom**   An approach that attempts to prevent errors or mistakes by following structured and formal methods of developing and testing. This approach is used for high-quality and critical applications that will be put through a strict certification process.

References

Software Lifecycles: **www.cs.toronto.edu/~sme/CSC444F/slides/ L04-Lifecycles.pdf**

The Software Life Cycle: **bmrc.berkeley.edu/courseware/cs169/spring01/ lectures/lifecycle**

Change Control

I am changing stuff left and right. Response: Was it approved and tested first?

Changes during development or production can cause a lot of havoc if not done properly. There are several reasons for changes to take place. During the development phases, a customer may alter requirements and ask that certain functionality be added, removed, or modified. In production, changes may need to happen because of other changes in the environment, new requirements of a product or system, or newly released patches or upgrades. These changes should be controlled to make sure they are approved, incorporated properly, and that no original functionality was affected in an adverse way. Configuration management is the process of controlling the life cycle of an application and documenting the necessary change control activities.

 NOTE I have found that "change control" and "configuration management" mean different things to different people and companies, usually to best fit their internal environment. Change control is a *process* to manage and approve of any type of change within the environment. Configuration management is the *procedures* that are used to carry out changes that affect the network, individual systems, or software.

A process for dealing with changes needs to be in place at the beginning of a project, so everyone knows how changes are dealt with and what is expected of each entity when a change request is made. Some projects have been doomed from the start because proper change control was not put into place and enforced. Many times in development,

Official Definition of Configuration Management

- Identifying, controlling, accounting for and auditing changes made to the baseline TCB, which includes changes to hardware, software, and firmware.
- A system that will control changes and test documentation through the operational life cycle of a system.

Change Control

Changes must be authorized, tested, and recorded. Changed systems may require re-certification and re-accreditation.

the customer and vendor agree on the design of the product, requirements, and specifications. The customer is then required to sign a contract saying that this is the agreement, and if they want any further modifications, they will need to pay the vendor for that extra work. If this is not put into place, then the customer can continually request changes, the development team puts in the extra hours to provide these changes, the vendor loses money, and the product does not meet its completion deadline.

There are other reasons to have change control in place. These reasons deal with organization, standard procedures, and expected results. If a product is in the last phase of development and a change request comes in, the team should know how to deal with this. Usually the team leader must tell the project manager how much extra time will be required to complete the project if this change is incorporated and what steps need to be taken to ensure that this change does not affect other components within the product. In addition, security cannot be compromised, and management must approve the change. If these processes are not controlled, one part of a development team could implement the change, while another part of the team is unaware of the change. This could break some of their pieces. When the pieces of the product are integrated and it is found that some pieces are incompatible, heads might roll because management never approved the change in the first place.

The change must be approved, documented, and tested. Some tests may need to be rerun to ensure that the change does not affect the product's capabilities. When a programmer makes a change to source code, it should be done on the test version of the code. Under no conditions should a programmer change the code that is already in production. The changes to the code should be made, and then the new code should go to the librarian. Production code should come only from the librarian and not from a programmer or directly from a test environment.

Change control should be evaluated during system audits. It is possible to overlook a problem that a change has caused in testing, so the procedures of how change control is implemented and enforced should be examined during a system audit.

The following are some necessary steps for a change control process:

1. Make a formal request for a change.

2. Analyze the request.

   a. Develop the implementation strategy.

    b. Calculate the costs of this implementation.

    c. Review any security implications.

3. Record the change request.

4. Submit the change request for approval.

5. Develop the change.

    a. Recode segments of the product, and add or subtract functionality.

    b. Link these changes in the code to the formal change control request.

    c. Submit software for testing and quality approval.

    d. Repeat until quality is adequate.

    e. Make version changes.

6. Report results to management.

The changes to systems may require another round of certification and accreditation. If the changes to a system are significant, then the functionality and level of protection may need to be reevaluated (certified), and management would have to approve the overall system, including the new changes (accreditation).

Capability Maturity Model

The *Capability Maturity Model (CMM)* describes procedures, principles, and practices that underlie software development process maturity. This model was developed to help software vendors improve their development processes by providing an evolutionary path from an ad hoc, "fly by the seat of your pants" approach, to a more disciplined and repeatable approach that improves software quality, reduces the life cycle of development, provides better project management capabilities, allows for milestones to be created and met in a timely manner, and takes a more proactive approach versus the less effective reactive approach.

This model provides policies, procedures, guidelines, and best practices to allow an organization to develop a standardized approach to software development that can be used across many different groups. The goal is to continue to review and improve upon the processes to optimize output, increase capabilities, and provide higher quality software at a lower cost.

The model provides a layered framework that allows different organizations the ability to implement continuous improvement. It is a tool for the software development company and a tool for those wanting to assess a vendor's development consistency and quality. If the company StuffRUs wants a software developing company, SoftwareRUs, to develop an application for them, they can choose to buy into the sales hype about how wonderful SoftwareRUs is, or they can ask for the company to be evaluated against the CMM model. Third-party companies evaluate software development companies to certify the organizations' product development processes. Many software companies have this evaluation done so they can use this as a selling point to attract new customers.

There are five maturity levels used:

- **Initial**   Development process is ad hoc or even chaotic. The company does not use effective management procedures and plans. There is no assurance of consistency, and quality is unpredictable.

- **Repeatable**   A formal management structure, change control, and quality assurance is in place. The company can properly repeat processes throughout each project. The company does not have formal process models defined.

- **Defined**   Formal procedures are in place that outline and define processes that are carried out in each project. The organization has a way to allow for quantitative process improvement.

- **Managed**   The company has formal processes in place to collect and analyze qualitative data, and metrics are defined and fed into the process improvement program.

- **Optimizing**   The company has budgeted and integrated plans for continuous process improvement.

Software Escrow

Will someone keep a copy of my source code?

If a company pays another company to develop software for them, they should have some type of *software escrow* in place for protection. Software escrow means that there is a third party involved. This third party will keep a copy of the source code, and possibly other materials, which will only be released to the customer if specific circumstances arise, mainly if the vendor who developed the code goes out of business or for some reason is not meeting its obligations and responsibilities. This procedure protects the customer because they are paying the vendor to develop software code for them, and if the software company goes out of business, then the customer no longer has access to the actual code. This means that the code could never be updated or maintained properly.

A logical question would be, "Why doesn't the vendor just hand over the source code to the customer, since they paid for it to be developed in the first place?" Nope. It does not work that way. The code is the vendor's intellectual property. They employ and pay people with the necessary skills to develop that code, and if they just hand it over to the customer, they are giving away their intellectual property, their secrets. The customer gets compiled code instead of source code. This is code that has been put through a compiler and is unreadable to humans. Most software profits are based on licensing, which outlines what customers can do with the compiled code.

Application Development Methodology

Applications are written in programming code, and it is this code that tells the operating system and processor what needs to happen to accomplish the user's requirements when operating a specific application. Programming languages have gone through several generations, each generation building on the next, providing richer functionality and giving the programmers more powerful tools as the languages evolve.

There are different types of languages: machine language, assembly language, and high-level languages. *Machine language* is in a form that the processor can understand and work with directly. *Assembly* and *high-level languages* cannot be understood directly by the processor and must be translated, which results in machine language. The process is typically done by a compiler, whose function is to turn human-understandable programming language into machine-understandable language, or object code.

When a customer purchases a program, it is in object code form. The program has already been compiled, and it is ready to be executed and set up on the system. The compiler will put it into a form that specific processors can understand. This is why a program that works on a computer with an Alpha processor may not work on a computer with a Pentium processor. They use different processors and require a different form of machine language.

If the program was actually sold in the form of original source code, it would have to be complied on the customer's computer; thus, the customer must have the correct complier. Also, original source code would enable competing vendors to view each other's original ideas and techniques. Source code is considered intellectual property by vendors who develop software and should be highly protected.

Various programs are used to turn high-level programming code (or source code) into object code. They are compilers, assemblers, and interpreters. They work as translators. *Interpreters* translate one command at a time during execution, and *compilers* translate large sections of code at a time. *Assemblers* translate assembly language into machine language. Most applications are compiled, whereas many scripting languages are interpreted. The relationship between these entities is shown in Figure 11-16.

Object-Oriented Concepts

Objects are so cute, and small, and modular. I will take one in each color!

Software development used to be done by classic input-processing-output methods. This used an information flow model from hierarchical information structures. Data was inputted into a program, and the program passed the data from the beginning to end, performed logical procedures, and returned a result, as illustrated in Figure 11-17.

Object-oriented programming (OOP) methods perform the same functionality with different techniques that work in a more efficient manner. First, the basic concepts of OOP need to be understood.

Figure 11-16
Different types of programs are used to translate source code to object or machine code.

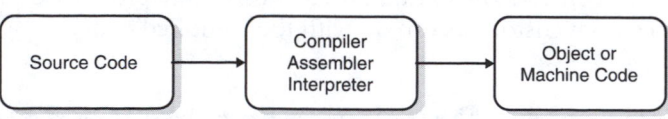

Compiled or Interpreted

Interpreted programs have instructions that are read and interpreted by a program one instruction at a time. This program, the interpreter, converts high-level instructions into machine-readable format in real time.

Compiled programs are written in a high-level language and turned into machine-readable format by a program called a compiler.

OOP works with classes and objects. A real-world object, such as a table, is a member (or instance) of a larger class of objects called "furniture." The class can have a set of attributes associated with it, and when an object is generated, it inherits these attributes. The attributes can be color, dimensions, weight, style, and cost. These attributes apply if a chair, table, or loveseat object is generated or instantiated. Because the table is a member of the class furniture, the table inherits all attributes defined for the class (see Figure 11-18).

Once the class is defined, the attributes can be reused for each new member, or instance, of the class that is created.

A *method* is the functionality or procedure that an object can carry out. An object may be constructed to accept data from a user and to reformat the request so that a back-end server can understand and process it. Another object may perform a method that extracts data from a database and populates a Web page with this information. Or an object may carry out a withdrawal procedure to allow a user of an ATM to be able to extract money from her account.

NOTE   In object-oriented programming (OOP), objects are unique instances of a data structure defined by the template provided by their corresponding classes.

Figure 11-17
The non-object-oriented approach to programming usually inputs data into the beginning of the program, which results in the output.

Figure 11-18
Each object belongs to a class and takes on the attributes of that class.

The objects encapsulate the attribute values, which means that this information is packaged under one name and can be reused as one entity by other objects. Objects need to be able to communicate to each other, and this happens by using *messages.* If Object A needs to tell Object B that a user's checking account needs to be reduced by $40, it will send the object a message. The message is made up of the destination, the method that needs to be performed, and the corresponding arguments. Figure 11-19 shows this example.

An object can have a shared portion and a private portion. The shared portion is the interface that enables it to interact with other components. Messages enter through the interface to specify the requested operation, or method, to be performed. The private part of an object can be how it actually works and performs the requested operations. Other components need not know how each object works internally—only that it does the job requested of it. This is how *information hiding* is possible. The details of the processing are hidden from all other program elements outside the object. Objects communicate through well-defined interfaces; therefore, they do not need to know how each other works.

 NOTE Data hiding is provided by encapsulation, which protects an object's private data from outside access. No object should be allowed to or have the need to access another object's internal data or processes.

Figure 11-19
Objects communicate via messages.

Figure 11-20
A classification structure can be developed to provide better organization of the relationships between the objects.

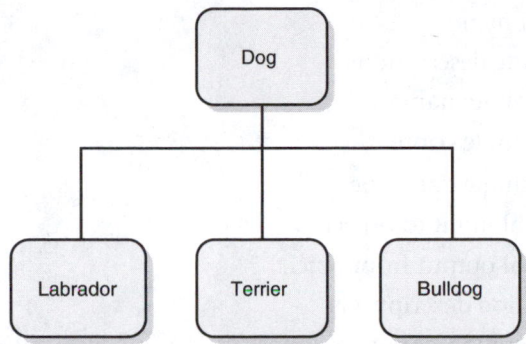

Once the objects are defined, it might be necessary to develop a classification structure. This means that instances of an object are defined and named. If the main object is named Dog, then the three objects under and related to this object could be Labrador, Terrier, and Bulldog. Figure 11-20 shows the relationship between these objects. This gives structure to the classification and defines the necessary relationships between the objects. Structure representation is a way of partitioning the requirements of the model.

These objects can grow to great numbers, so the complexity of understanding, tracking, and analyzing can get a bit overwhelming. Many times the objects are shown in connection to a reference or pointer in documentation. Figure 11-21 shows how related objects are represented as a specific piece, or reference, in an ATM system. This enables analysts and developers to look at a higher level of operation and procedures without having to look at each individual object. This modularity provides for a more easily understood model.

Abstraction is the capability to suppress unnecessary details so that the important, inherent properties can be examined and reviewed. It enables the separation of conceptual aspects of a system. For example, if a software architect needed to understand how data flows through the program, she would want to understand the big pieces of the program and trace the steps that the data takes from first being inputted into the program all the way until it exits the program as output. It would be difficult to understand this concept if the small details of every piece of the program were presented. Instead, through abstraction, all the details are suppressed so that she can understand a crucial part of the product.

Messaging can happen in several ways. Two objects can have a single connection (one to one), a multiple connection (one to many), and a mandatory connection or an optional connection. It is important to map these communication paths to identify if information can flow in a way that is not intended. This will help ensure that sensitive data cannot be passed to objects of a lower security level.

Each object should have specifications that it should adhere to. This discipline will provide cleaner programming and reduce programming errors and omissions. The following list is an example of what should be developed for each object.

- Object name
- Attribute descriptions
  - Attribute name
  - Attribute content
  - Attribute data type
- External input to object
- External output from object
- Operation descriptions
  - Operation name
  - Operation interface description
  - Operation processing description
  - Performance issues
  - Restrictions and limitations
- Instance connections
- Message connections

The developer creates a class that outlines these specifications. When objects are instantiated, they inherit these attributes. This is referred to as *abstraction*.

Figure 11-21 Programs can get very complicated with many different objects. They are usually represented by references, which point to several objects, to show the main functionality of the application itself.

Each object can be reused, which is the beauty of OOP. This enables more efficient use of resources and the programmer's time. Different applications can use the same objects so that there is a reduction in redundant work, and as an application grows in functionality, objects can be easily added and integrated into the original structure.

The objects can be catalogued in a library, which provides an economical way for more than one application to call upon the objects (see Figure 11-22). The library provides an index and pointers to where the objects actually live within the system or on another system.

When applications are developed in a modular approach, like object-oriented methods, components can be reused, complexity is reduced, and parallel development can be done. These characteristics allow for fewer mistakes, easier modification, resource efficiency, and more timely coding than the classic information flow models. OOP also provides functional independence, which means that each module addresses a specific subfunction of requirements and has an interface that is easily understood by other parts of the application.

An object is encapsulated, meaning that the data structure (the operation's functionality) and the acceptable ways of accessing are grouped into one entity. Other objects, subjects, and applications can use this object and its functionality by accessing it through controlled and standardized interfaces and sending it messages (see Figure 11-23).

Object-oriented design (OOD) creates a representation of a real-world problem and maps it to a software solution. The result of an OOD is a design that modularizes data and procedures. The design interconnects data objects and processing operations. This programming approach is different from others because it allows for abstraction, modularity, and information hiding. Modularity is accomplished by using objects, applets, and agents.

 NOTE Object-oriented design (OOD) is a design method where a system is modeled as a collection of cooperating objects. Each individual object is treated as an instance of a class within a class hierarchy.

Figure 11-22
Applications can access and reuse components by using indexes within the component library.

Figure 11-23
The different components of an object and the way that it works are hidden from other objects.

Data Encapsulation

Polymorphism

Polymorphism is a funny name. Response: You are funny looking.

Polymorphism adds another dimension to an object's behavior and aids in providing a better description for the object. *Polymorphism* means that an object's response to a message is determined by the class to which the object belongs. Different objects that belong to different classes can be addressed in a uniform manner, but they exhibit different behaviors.

A simplistic example of polymorphism would be three different objects that receive the input "Bob." Object A would process this input and produce the output "43-year-old white male." Object B would receive the input "Bob" and produce the output "Husband of Sally." Object C would produce the output of "Member of User group." Each object received the same input, but responded with a different output.

 NOTE Polymorphism is when different objects respond to the same command, input, or message in different ways.

Object-oriented analysis (OOA) is the process of classifying objects that will be appropriate for a solution. A problem is analyzed to determine the classes of objects to be used in the application.

OOD enables an engineer or developer to indicate the objects that will derive from each class and how these objects will work together. So the problem needs to be analyzed, and a solution should be decided upon. Then the details of that solution are attacked and hammered out.

OOP is a class of programming languages and techniques that are based on the concepts of objects and a set of routines and methods, which operate on the data.

Data Modeling

Let's see. The data went thataway. Oh no, it went thataway. I lost the data.

The previous paragraphs have provided a simple look at a ***structured analysis approach***. A full structured analysis approach looks at all objects and subjects of an application, and maps the interrelationships, communication paths, and inheritance properties. This is different than ***data modeling***. Data modeling considers data independently of the way that the data is processed and of the components that process the data. A data model will follow an input value from beginning to end and verify that the output is correct. OOA is an example of a structure analysis model approach. If an analyst is reviewing the OOA of an application, she will make sure that all relationships are set up correctly, that the inheritance flows in a predictable and usable manner, that the instances of objects are practical and provide the necessary functionality, and that the attributes of each class cover all the necessary values used by the application. When another analyst does a data model review of the same application, he will follow the data and the returned values after processing takes place. An application can have a perfect OOA structure, but when 1 + 1 is entered and it returns –3, something is wrong. This is what the data modeling looks at.

Another example of data modeling deals with databases. Data modeling can be used to provide insight into the data and the relationships that govern it. A data item in one file structure, or data store, might be a pointer to another file structure or to a different data store. It is important that these pointers are actually pointing to the right place. Data modeling would verify this, not OOA structure analysis.

Software Architecture

Software architecture relates the components that make up a software solution to the parts of a real-world problem. It is a higher point of view than the programmers who are focused on data structures, coding rules, variables, and communication paths between objects. An architectural view looks at how the application actually meets and fulfills the requirements recognized and agreed upon in the design phase.

Software architecture involves the process of partitioning requirements into individual problems that can be solved by individual software solutions. This process is the transition phase between the software requirement analysis and the design of the actual components that make up the resulting application, as shown in Figure 11-24.

Figure 11-24
Software architects look at real-world problems and break them down into pieces that can be solved by software components.

If the requirements are that the application will scan hard drives and e-mail messages for viruses, the software architecture will break these requirements into individual units that need to be achieved by functionality within that application. These units can include

- Virus signature storage
- An agent that compares software strings on hard drives to virus signatures
- A process of parsing an e-mail message before the user can view it
- Procedures necessary if data on a hard drive is compressed
- Actions taken if a virus is found
- Actions taken if an e-mail attachment is encrypted

This way of developing a product provides more control and modularity of issues and solutions. If a group of programmers is told to develop an antivirus software package, the group may sit there like deer caught in headlights. However, if one developer is told to write a piece of the program that holds and updates signature files, another developer is told to determine how data on the hard drive will be compared with the signatures within the signature files, and another developer is instructed to program a way to read compressed files, then the programmers will have set goals and start pounding at the keyboards.

Software architects need to provide this type of direction: a high-level view of the application's objectives and a vision of the overall goals of the project.

Data Structures

A *data structure* is a representation of the logical relationship between elements of data. It dictates the degree of association between elements, methods of access, processing alternatives, and the organization of data elements.

The structure can be simple in nature, like the scalar item, which represents a single element that can be addressed by an identifier and accessed by a single address in storage. The scalar items can be grouped in arrays, which provide access by indexes. Other data structures include hierarchical structures by using multilinked lists that contain scalar items, vectors, and possibly arrays. The hierarchical structure provides categorization and association. If a user can make a request of an application to find all computer books written on security and that application returns a list, then this application is using a hierarchical data structure of some kind. Figure 11-25 shows simple and complex data structures.

Cohesion and Coupling

I am very needy and like to talk to others a lot. Response: Low cohesion and high coupling describes you best, then.

A *cohesive* module can perform a single task with little or no help from other modules. A cohesive module does just one function, and it does it with little interaction from other modules. The more a module can do on its own, the better, because requiring a lot of interaction between modules makes it harder to modify one module down the road without affecting other modules. Similarly, the more interactions there are, the more complexity, which makes it harder to track down problems. The best programming uses the most cohesive modules possible, but because different modules need to pass data and communicate, they usually cannot be totally cohesive. Figure 11-26 shows a linear approach of looking at cohesion.

Figure 11-25
Data structures
can be very
simple to
very complex
in nature.

Figure 11-26
A cohesion spectrum shows the different levels of cohesion that a module can obtain.

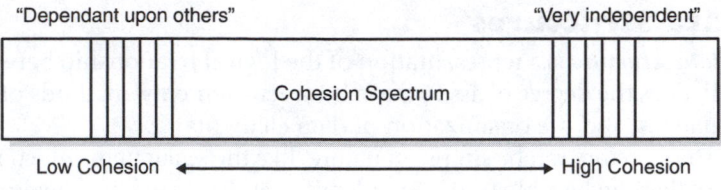

"Dependant upon others"   "Very independent"

Cohesion Spectrum

Low Cohesion ← → High Cohesion

Coupling is a measure of interconnection among modules in an application. The level of coupling involved between modules depends on the interface's complexity, the data being passed between modules, and the point of entry or reference made to the module itself. The lower the coupling, the better the software design, because it promotes module independence. The more independent a component is, the less complex the application is, and the easier it is to modify and troubleshoot.

An example of low coupling would be one module passing a variable value to another module. An example of a high coupling situation is when Module A passes a value to Module B, which performs calculations on the data and passes it to Module C. Module C then performs a lookup in a database to make sure this value is within a range and then passes the resulting value back to Module A. This high level of interconnection and interdependence is referred to as high coupling.

NOTE Modules should be self-contained and perform a single logical function, which is high cohesion. Modules should not drastically affect each other, which is low coupling.

ORBs and CORBAs

Has anyone seen my ORB? I need to track down an object.

The Object Management Architecture (OMA) provides standards to accomplish a complete distributed environment. It contains two main parts: system-oriented components (*object request brokers [ORBs]* and object services) and application-oriented components (application objects and common facilities). ORB manages all communication between components and enables them to interact in a heterogeneous and distributed environment, as shown in Figure 11-27. ORB works independently of the platforms where the objects reside, which provides greater interoperability.

ORB relies on object services to provide access control, track relocated objects, and create objects. The application objects and common facilities are farther from the system and closer to the end user. When they need services from the system, they invoke services from ORB and object services.

Common Object Request Broker Architecture (CORBA) provides interoperability among the vast array of software, platforms, and hardware in environments today. CORBA enables applications to communicate with one another no matter where the application is located or who developed it.

Figure 11-27
The ORB enables different components throughout a network to communicate and work with each other.

The Object Management Group (OMG) developed a model for the use of these different services in an environment. The model defines object semantics so that the external visible characteristics are standard and viewed the same by all other objects in the environment. This standardization enables many different developers to write hundreds or thousands of components that can interact with other components in an environment without having to know how the component actually works. The developers know how to communicate with the components because the interfaces are uniform and follow the rules of the model.

In the model, clients request services from objects. The client passes the object a message that contains the name of the object, the requested operation, and any necessary parameters.

ORB is the middleware that establishes the client/server relationship between objects. When a client needs to access an object on a server for that object to perform an operation or method, the ORB intercepts the request and is responsible for finding the object. Once the object is found, ORB invokes a method (or operation), passes the parameters, and returns the result to the client. The client software does not need to know where the object resides and go through the trouble of finding it. That is the ORB's job. The objects can be written in different languages and reside on different operating systems and platforms, but the client does not need to worry about any of this (see Figure 11-28).

When objects communicate to each other, they use pipes, which are intercomponent communication services. There are different types of pipes like remote procedure calls (RPCs) and ORBs. ORBs provide communication between distributed objects. If an object on a workstation needs to have an object that is on a server process data, it can make a request through ORB, which will track down the needed object and facilitate the communication path between these two objects until the process is complete. This is the client/server communication pipe used in many networking environments.

ORBs are mechanisms that enable objects to communicate locally or remotely. They enable objects to make requests to objects and receive responses. This happens transparently to the client and provides a type of pipeline between all corresponding objects. CORBA specifies interface definitions and APIs that interface to the ORB. Using CORBA enables an application to be usable with many different types of ORBs. It provides

Figure 11-28
CORBA provides standard interface definitions between OMG-compliant objects, which provides greater interoperability in heterogeneous environments.

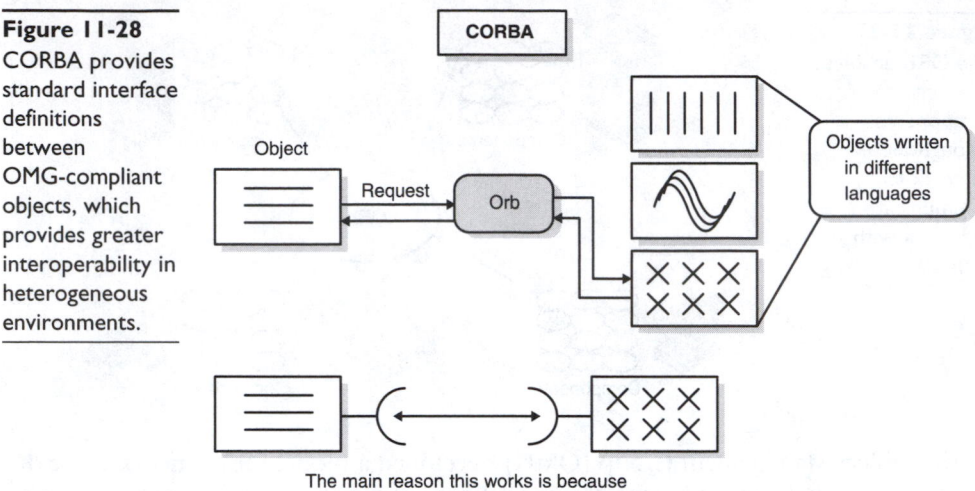

The main reason this works is because standardized interfaces are used.

portability for applications and tackles many of the interoperability issues that many vendors and developers run into when their product is implemented into different environments.

Computer-Aided Software Engineering (CASE)

Computer-aided software engineering (CASE) tools are broad and far reaching in functionality and uses. "CASE tools" is a general term for many types of tools used by programmers, developers, project managers, and analysts that help them make program applications more quickly and with fewer errors in an automated fashion and run the project in a controlled and organized manner. Different tools provide managerial, administrative, and technical help in software projects. They provide several layers of organization that are not available when a developer is just programming by hand, notes are written in word processors, and timetables are inputted into static spreadsheets.

The first CASE tools were translators, compilers, assemblers, linkers, and loaders. However, as programming and projects became more complex, the need for more complex tools grew. The tools graduated into program editors, debuggers, code analyzers, and version control mechanisms. The tools aid in keeping more detailed records of requirements, design, implementation, and in testing the program and project overall. A CASE tool is aimed at supporting one or more software engineering tasks and activities in the process of developing software. It applies engineering principles to the development and analysis of specifications using specific tools.

Many vendors can get their products to the market faster because they are "computer aided." The CASE tools enable software engineering to be done correctly and fast, relatively speaking.

When the automation covers the complete life cycle of a product, the tools are referred to as *integrated computer-aided software engineering (I-CASE)*, and if tools are used for one specific part of the life cycle, then the tools are referred to as *CASE tools*.

Many CASE tools utilize **rapid prototyping** technologies that enable applications to be developed faster with higher quality and lower cost. A prototype can be made so that testing can begin earlier in the development process. The more testing, the more errors can be caught. Because it costs more to find and fix problems at the end of a project compared with the beginning of a project, prototyping can save a lot of time and money.

As previously stated, a wide range of tools falls into the category of CASE tools. The tools can provide and support the data flow, aid structured development, produce documentation, provide design method support, and generate application code for a specific goal within the project. They also help when a project is large with many developers working on specific pieces of the product. It is easy to get disjointed when everyone has his own little piece he is responsible for, and when the different pieces come together, they may not integrate properly. The different tools can work together with a shared database and a conceptual notion, like a shared philosophy on architecture and common semantics about the objects and the tools that manipulate them.

Prototyping

I would like a prototype of a mini-me. Response: One of you is enough.

Many times it is necessary to build a model of the gathered requirements of a software product to be used for a customer and the developers. This model, called a **prototype**, can show the customer where the development team is headed and its interpretation of the customer's stated requirements. This enables the customer to agree on the direction the team is headed and get an idea of what the product will look like, or enables the customer to make changes and further explain any requirements that were gray or confusing. The prototype also enables testing to begin earlier in the development process so that errors or problems can be uncovered and addressed.

Some projects are very large and may require that partitioning the product is necessary so that each part has its own prototype to be reviewed and built upon. In either case, partitioning or prototyping the full product, an analyst will develop an abbreviated representation of the requirements for the prototype. The software can be created using prototyping tools, which speed up the process. This enables the design to be translated into executable form.

Security testing can begin at an earlier stage if a prototype is developed. Penetration, vulnerability, and data format tests can be performed at each stage of development and with each prototype developed.

If a software prototype is impractical, paper prototypes can be developed where interaction, queries, displays, and logic are shown on paper for the customer to see and the developers to walk through. A series of storyboard sheets can be used to represent each screen shot and the actions that take place behind the screen.

COM and DCOM

Component Object Model (COM) defines how components interact and provides an architecture for simple interprocess communication (IPC). *Distributed Component Object Model (DCOM)* supports the same model for component interaction, but supports distributed IPC. COM enables applications to use components on the same systems, and DCOM enables applications to access objects that reside in different parts of a network.

Without DCOM, programmers would have to write much more complicated code to find necessary objects, set up network sockets, and incorporate the services necessary to allow communication. DCOM takes care of these issues and more, and enables the programmer to focus on his tasks at hand. DCOM has a library that takes care of session handling, synchronization, buffering, fault identification and handling, and data format translation.

DCOM works as the middleware that enables distributed processing and provides developers with services that support process-to-process communication across networks (see Figure 11-29).

Other types of middleware provide similar functionality: ORB, message-oriented middleware (MOM), RPC, open database connectivity (ODBC), and so on. DCOM provides ORB services, data connectivity services, distributed messaging services, and distributed transaction services layered over its RPC mechanism. DCOM integrates all these functionalities into one technology that uses the same interface as COM (see Figure 11-30).

Open Database Connectivity (ODBC)

Open database connectivity (ODBC) is a de facto standard that provides a standard SQL dialect that can be used to access many types of rational databases. ODBC is the middleman between applications and databases. An application makes a request to the ODBC driver manager. The ODBC driver manager decides which driver needs to be used for communication purposes. (The driver is a piece of software that will provide communication between a system and a database. Different databases require different drivers.) The request is passed through the ODBC manager, through the driver, and to the database, as shown in Figure 11-31. The database answers the request, which goes back through the driver, through ODBC, and to the application.

Figure 11-29
Although DCOM provides communication mechanisms in a distributed environment, it still works off of the COM architecture.

It is the middleware portion of DCOM that allows different processes to communicate across a network.

Figure 11-30
DCOM provides
several services
over its RPC
mechanism and
a COM interface.

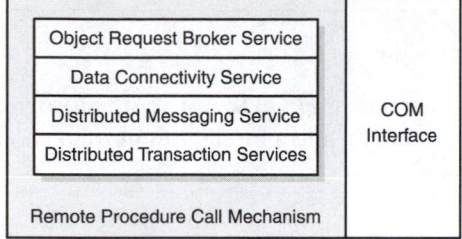

Object Linking and Embedding (OLE)

Object linking and embedding (OLE) provides a way for objects to be shared on a local personal computer and to use COM as their foundation. OLE enables objects to be embedded into documents, like graphics, pictures, and spreadsheets. In this book, there are many graphics placed throughout the text. The OLE technology puts the graphics into the text documents that make up this book.

OLE also allows for linking different objects and documents. When Chrissy creates a document that contains a uniform resource locator (URL), that URL turns blue and is underlined, indicating that a user can just double-click on it, and he will be taken to the appropriate Web site. This is an example of linking capabilities. If Chrissy adds a spreadsheet to her document, this is an example of embedding. If she needs to edit the spreadsheet, she can double-click on the spreadsheet, and the operating system will open the correct environment (which might be Excel) to let her make her changes.

This technology was evolved to work on the World Wide Web (WWW) and is called ActiveX. The components are like other components, but are meant to be portable. ActiveX components can run on any platform supporting DCOM, using the COM model, or communicating using DCOM services.

Figure 11-31
ODBC provides
a standardized
interface for
many different
applications
to be able to
communicate
with many
different types
of databases.

OLE

The capability for one program to call another program is *linking*. The capability to place a piece of data inside a foreign program or document is *embedding*.

Dynamic Data Exchange

Dynamic Data Exchange (DDE) enables applications to share data by providing IPC. It is based on the client/server model and enables two programs to send commands to each other directly. DDE is a communication mechanism that enables direct conversation between two applications. The source of the data is called the *server*, and the receiver of the data is the *client*.

A spreadsheet can use a DDE link to another program that keeps track of stock prices. The spreadsheet can display the current trading information because updates are being received from the server via a DDE communication link.

Distributed Computing Environment

Distributed Computing Environment (DCE) is a standard that was developed by the Open Software Foundation (OSF), also called Open Group. It is basically middleware that is available to many vendors to use within their products. This middleware has the capability to support many types of applications across an enterprise. DCE provides an RPC service, security service, directory service, time service, and distributed file support.

DCE is a set of management services with a communication layer based on RPC. It is a layer of software that sits on the top of the network layer and provides services to the applications above it. DCE and DCOM provide a lot of the same functionality. DCOM was developed by Microsoft and is more proprietary in nature.

DCE's time service provides host clock synchronization and enables applications to determine sequencing and schedule events based on this clock synchronization. This time synchronization is for applications. Users cannot access this functionality directly. The directory service enables users, servers, and resources to be contacted anywhere on the network. When the directory service is given the name, it returns the network address of the resource along with other necessary information. DCOM uses a *globally unique identifier (GUID)*, and DCE uses a *universal unique identifier (UUID)*. They are both used to uniquely identify users, resources, and components within an environment. DCE is illustrated in Figure 11-32.

The RCP function collects the arguments and commands from the sending program and prepares them for transmission over the network. RCP determines the network transport protocol that is to be used and finds the receiving host's address in the directory service. The threads service provides real-time priority scheduling in a multithreading environment. The security services support authentication and authorization services. The distributed file service (DFS) provides a single integrated file system that all DCE users

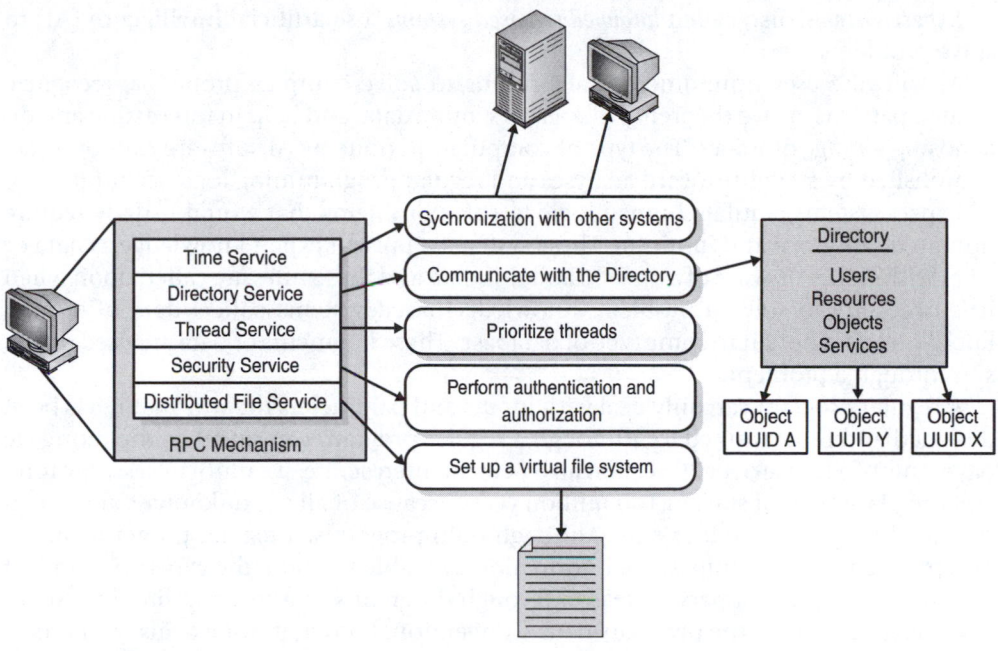

Figure 11-32 DCE provides many services wrapped into one technology.

can use to share files. This is important because many environments have different operating systems that cannot understand other file systems. However, if DCE is being used, a DCE local file system exists alongside the native file system.

Enterprise Java Bean

Enterprise Java Bean (EJB) is a structural design for the development and implementation of distributed applications written in Java. The EJB provides interfaces and methods to allow different applications to be able to communicate across a networked environment. By using the Internet Inter-ORB Protocol (IIOP), the client portion does not have to be a program written in Java, but can be any valid CORBA client.

NOTE A Java component is called a Java Bean.

Expert Systems and Knowledge-Based Systems

Hey, this computer is smarter than me! Response: No surprise there.

Expert systems, also called *knowledge-based systems*, use artificial intelligence (AI) to solve problems.

AI software uses nonnumerical algorithms to solve complex problems, recognize hidden patterns, prove theorems, play games, mine data, and help in forecasting and diagnosing a range of issues. The type of computation done by AI software cannot be accomplished by straightforward analyses and regular programming logic techniques.

Expert systems emulate human logic to solve problems that would usually require human intelligence and intuition. These systems represent expert knowledge as data or rules within the software of a system, and this data and these rules are called upon when it is necessary to solve a problem. Knowledge-based systems collect data of human know-how and hold it in some type of database. These fragments of data are used to reason through a problem.

A regular program can only deal with inputs and parameters the way that it has been designed and programmed to. Although a regular program can calculate the mortgage payments of a house over 20 years at an 8 percent interest rate, it cannot necessarily forecast the placement of stars in 100 million years because of all the unknowns and possible variables that come into play. Although both programs, a regular program and an expert system, have a finite set of information available to them, the expert system will attempt to think like a person, reason through different scenarios, and provide an answer even without all the necessary data. Conventional programming deals with procedural manipulation of data, whereas humans attempt to solve complex problems using abstract and symbolic approaches.

A book may contain a lot of useful information, but a person has to read that book, interpret its meaning, and then attempt to use those interpretations within the real world. This is what an expert system attempts to do.

AI is the development of techniques that provide the modeling of information at higher levels of abstraction. The techniques are part of the languages and tools used, which enable programs to be developed that closely resemble human logic. The programs that can emulate human expertise in specific domains are called expert systems.

Rule-based programming is a common way of developing expert systems. The rules are based on if-then logic units. This specifies a set of actions to be performed for a given situation. This is one way that expert systems are used to find patterns, which is called *pattern matching*. A mechanism, called the *inference engine*, automatically matches facts against patterns and determines which rules are applicable. The actions of the corresponding rules are executed when the inference engine is instructed to begin execution.

Expert System

An expert system is a computer program containing a knowledge base and a set of algorithms and rules used to infer new facts from knowledge and incoming data.

Huh? Okay, let's say Dr. Gorenz is puzzled by a patient's symptoms and is unable to match the problems the patient is having to a specific ailment and find the right cure. So he uses an expert system to help him in his diagnosis. Dr. Gorenz can initiate the expert system, which will then take him through question-and-answer scenarios. The expert system will use the information gathered through this interaction, and it will go step by step through the facts looking for patterns that can be tied to known diseases, ailments, and medical issues. Although Dr. Gorenz is very smart and one of the top doctors in his field, he cannot necessarily recall all possible diseases and ailments. The expert system can know this information because it is working off of a database that has been stuffed full of medical information that can fill up several libraries.

As the expert system goes through the medical information, it may see that the patient had a case of severe hives six months ago, a case of ringing in the ears and blurred vision three months ago, and a history of diabetes. The system will look at the patient's recent complaints of joint aches and tiredness. With each finding, the expert system will dig deeper looking for further information, and then use all information obtained and compare it with the knowledge base that is available to it. In the end, the expert system returns a diagnosis to Dr. Gorenz that says that the patient is suffering from a rare disease found only in Brazil that is caused by a specific mold that grows on bananas. Because the patient has diabetes, his sensitivity is much higher to this contaminant. The system spits out the necessary treatment. Then Dr. Gorenz marches back into the room where the patient is waiting and explains the problem and protects his reputation of being a really smart doctor.

The system not only uses a database of facts, but it also collects a wealth of knowledge from experts in a specific field. This knowledge is captured by using interactive tools that have been engineered specifically to capture human knowledge. This knowledge base is then transferred to automated systems that help in human decisions by offering advice, free up experts from repetitive routine decisions, ensure that decisions are made in a consistent manner in a quicker fashion, and that help a company retain its organization's expertise even as employees come and go.

An expert system usually consists of two parts: an inference engine and a knowledge base. The inference engine handles the user interface, external files, scheduling, and program-accessing capabilities. The knowledge base contains data pertaining to a specific problem or domain. Expert systems use the inference engine to decide how to execute a program or how the rules should be initiated and followed. The inference piece of a knowledge-based system provides the necessary rules for the system to take the original facts and combine them to form new facts.

The systems employ AI programming languages to allow for real-world decision making. The system is built by a knowledge system builder (programmer), a knowledge engineer (analyst), and subject matter expert(s), as shown in Figure 11-33. The system is built on facts, rules of thumb, and the expert's advice. The information gathered from the expert(s) during the development of the system is kept in a knowledge base and is used during the question-and-answer session with the end user. The system works as a consultant to the end user and can recommend several alternative solutions by considering competing hypotheses at the same time.

Figure 11-33 This graphic shows what goes into developing an expert system and how it is used once developed.

Expert systems are commonly used to automate a security log review for an IDS.

NOTE Expert systems use automatic logical processing, inference engine processing, and general methods of searching for problem solutions.

Artificial Neural Networks

An *artificial neural network (ANN)* is an electronic model based on the neural structure of the brain. Computers perform activities like computing large numbers, keeping large ledgers, and performing complex mathematical functions, but they cannot recognize patterns or learn from experience as the brain can. ANNs contain many units that stimulate neurons, each with a small amount of memory. The units work on data that is inputted through their many connections. Through training rules, the systems are able to learn from examples and have the capability to generalize.

The brain stores information in forms of patterns. People have the ability to recognize another person's face from several different angles. Each angle of that person's face is made up of a complex set of patterns. Even if only half the face is seen or the face is viewed in a shadow or dark lighting, the human brain can insert the missing pieces, and people can recognize their friends and acquaintances. A computer that uses conventional programming and logic would have to have each piece of the pattern and the full face in one particular angle to be able to match or recognize it.

The brain uses neurons to remember, think, apply previous experiences, perform logic, and recognize patterns. The capacity of the brain comes from the large number of neurons and the multiple connections between them. The power of the brain comes from genetic programming and learning.

ANNs try to replicate the basic functions of neurons and their circuitry to solve problems in a new way. They consist of many simple computational neural units connected to each other. An input value is presented to one, some, or all the units, which will in turn perform functions on the data.

The brain has clusters of neurons that process in an interactive and dynamic way. Biologically, neurons have no restrictions of interconnections between themselves; therefore a neuron can have thousands of connections. In addition, the neurons in the brain work in a three-dimensional world, whereas the electronic units in ANN have a physical limitation on the possible number of connections and operate in a two-dimensional world.

Like the brain, the ANN's real power comes from its capability to learn. Within the brain, when something is learned and used often, the connection path to where that information is stored is strengthened to provide quicker access. This is why sometimes you know something but "can't put your finger on it." This means that there is not a pronounced pathway to the information that is stored somewhere in the brain. If a person is asked her phone number, she can rattle it off without any real energy. But if you ask her who her third-grade teacher was, it might take more time and energy. Both facts are held within her brain, but the phone number has a more pronounced connection path and comes to mind more quickly and easily. In ANN, a connection between two units that is often activated might be strengthened, which is a form of learning.

It is known that when something happens to someone in a highly emotional state, that person is more likely to remember specifics about a situation or incident. If Joyce had a surprise party on her 35th birthday, which was filled with fun and emotion, she will most likely remember that birthday more than her 36th birthday, when her husband only bought her a card. But she and her husband will probably remember her 45th birthday, when her husband forgot her birthday, because the fight that occurred was full of emotion and activity. The reason that some memories are more vivid than others is because more emotion is tied to them, or more weight is assigned to them. In ANN, some inputs have higher weights assigned to them than other inputs, which amplifies the meaning or importance of the inputs just like emotion does with human beings.

 NOTE Decisions by neural networks are only as good as the experiences they are given.

Intuition is a hard issue to replicate in electrical circuits and logic gates. Fuzzy logic and other mathematical disciplines are used for intuition, forecasting, and intelligent guessing. These approaches work with types of probability within mathematics and memberships of different sets. One simple example of the use of Fuzzy logic is a washing machine that has built-in intelligence. When a person puts a load of clothes in the washing machine and the tank fills with water, the machine that is using Fuzzy logic sends a beam from one part of the tank to the other. Depending on how much light actually was received at the other end, it can determine how dirty the clothes are because of the density of the dirt in the water. Then there are other tests to see if the dirt is oily or dry and other relevant attributes. The washing machine will take in all this information and guess at the right temperature and the right amount of laundry soap to use. This will provide a more efficient way of washing by saving on water and soap and washing the clothes in the right temperature for the right amount of time. The washing machine does not necessarily know all the facts or know that the information that it gathered is 100 percent correct, but it can make guesses that will be pretty close to reality.

Neural networks are programmed with the capability to decide and learn to improve their functionality through massive trial-and-error decision making.

Fuzzy logic is necessary because a regular computer system does not see the world in shades of gray. It cannot differentiate between good, bad, few, and many. Fuzzy logic is an approach to enable the computer to use these vague values that mean something to humans but nothing to computers.

Stock market forecasting and insurance and financial risk assessments are examples of where Fuzzy logic can be used and is most beneficial. They require a large number of variables and decision-making information from experts in those particular domains. The system can indicate which insurance or financial risks are good or bad without the user having to input a stack of conditions, if-then statements, and variable values.

Conventional systems see the world in black and white, and work in a sea of precision and decimal points. Fuzzy logic enables the computer to incorporate imprecision into the programming language, which opens up a whole new world for computing and attacking complex issues. Neural network researchers attempt to understand more of how the brain works and of nature's capabilities so that more complex problems can be solved by newly engineered ANN solutions versus the traditional computing means.

Java

Java is an object-oriented, platform-independent programming language. It is used as a full-fledged programming language and used to write full-fledged programs and short programs, *applets*, which run on a user's browser.

Other languages are compiled to object code, but each processor type understands a different object code. This is why an application may run on Windows, but not run on Macintosh. An Intel processor does not necessarily understand machine code compiled for an Alpha processor and vice versa. Java is platform independent because it creates intermediate code, bytecode, which is not processor specific. The Java Virtual Machine then converts the bytecode to the machine code that the processor on that particular system can understand (see Figure 11-34). Let's quickly walk through these steps:

1. A programmer creates a Java applet and runs it through a compiler.

2. The Java compiler converts the source code into bytecode (non–processor specific).

Object versus Machine Code

When source code is processed by a compiler, the result is object code, which is written for a specific platform and processor. This object code is the executable form of an application that a user purchases from a vendor. When the object code runs, it must be converted into binary machine code, which is what the processor actually understands.

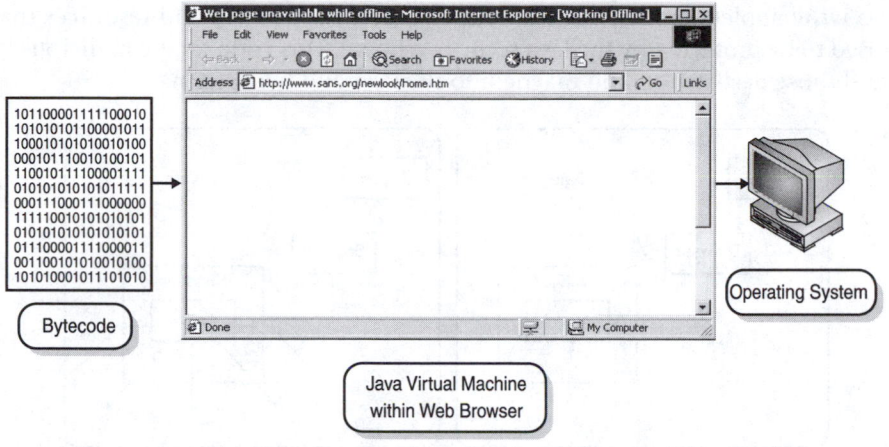

Figure 11-34 Java is platform independent because it is not compiled to processor-specific machine code. The Java Virtual Machine interprets bytecode to machine code for that specific computer system.

3. The user downloads the Java applet.

4. If the user's browser is Java-enabled and has a Java Virtual Machine installed, the browser knows what to do.

5. The Java Virtual Machine converts the bytecode into machine-level code (processor specific).

6. The applet runs.

Java Security

Java applets use a security scheme that employs a *sandbox* to limit the applet's access to certain specific areas within the user's system and protects the system from malicious or poorly written applets. The applet is supposed to run only within the sandbox. The sandbox restricts the applet's environment by restricting access to a user's hard drives and system resources. If the applet does not go outside the sandbox, it is considered safe.

However, as with many other things in the computing world, the bad guys have figured out how to escape their confines and restrictions. Programmers have figured out

Browser Settings

Java applets and the actions that they perform can be prevented and controlled by specific browser settings. These settings do not affect full-fledged Java applications running outside of the browser.

how to write applets that enable the code to access hard drives and resources that are supposed to be protected by the Java security scheme. This code can be malicious in nature and cause destruction and mayhem to the user and her system.

Java employs a sandbox in its security scheme, but if an applet can escape the confines of the sandbox, the system can be easily compromised.

There is a different type of Java applet, which is deemed *trusted* because it provides a digital signature. This type of applet has access to all system resources and is not confined to a sandbox. This type of applet is usually not a component on the Internet for users to download and install, but is developed by in-house programmers and distributed within an intranet to provide some type of business-oriented functionality. The browser will check the digital signature presented by the Java applet and make a decision on whether it comes from a known, trusted source before allowing it to execute.

ActiveX

ActiveX is a Microsoft technology that is used to write controls that Internet users can download to increase their functionality and Internet experience. Instead of trying to keep ActiveX components in a safe area for its computations and activities, this language practices security by informing the user where the program came from. The user can decide whether to trust this origin or not.

ActiveX technology provides security levels and authentication for users to be able to control the security of the ActiveX components they download. Unlike Java applets, ActiveX components are downloaded to a user's hard drive when he chooses to add the functionality that the component provides. This means the ActiveX has far greater access to the user's system.

The security level setting of the user's browser dictates if an ActiveX component is downloaded automatically or if the user is first prompted with a warning. The security level is configurable by the user via his browser controls. As the security level increases, it increases the browser's sensitivity level to signed and unsigned components and controls, and to the initialization of ActiveX scripts.

The main difference between Java and ActiveX security is that Java sets up a sandbox for the code to execute in, and this restricts the code's access to resources within the user's computer. ActiveX uses Authenticode technology that relies on digital certificates and trusting certificate authorities. (Signing, digital certificates, and certificate authorities are explained in detail in Chapter 8.) Although both are good and interesting technologies, there are inherent flaws. Java has not been able to ensure that all code stays within the sandbox, which has caused several types of security compromises; these instances are examples of malware. (*Malware* is a general term for malicious code.) ActiveX doesn't necessarily provide security, but it presents annoying dialog boxes to users. The users do not necessarily know what they are viewing and can become confused and scared or continually click OK because they don't understand the risks involved.

Malicious Software (Malware)

There are several types of malicious code: viruses, worms, Trojan horses, and logic bombs. They usually are dormant until activated by an event the user or system initiates. They can be spread through using e-mail, sharing media (floppy disks), sharing documents and programs, downloading things from the Internet, or they can be purposely inserted by an attacker.

The usual rule of not opening an e-mail attachment that comes from an unknown source is one of the best ways of combating malicious code. However, recent viruses and worms have infected personal e-mail address books, so this precaution is not a sure thing to protect systems from malicious code. If an address book is infected and used during an attack, the victim gets an e-mail message that seems to have come from a person he knows. Because he knows this person, he will proceed to open the e-mail message, and double-click on the attachment. Bam! His address book is now infected, and his system just spread the virus to all his friends and acquaintances.

Antivirus software should be installed to watch for known virus signatures, and host intrusion detection software can watch for suspicious activity, file access, and changes to help detect evildoers and their malicious activity.

Malicious code can be detected by the following ways:

- File size increase
- Many unexpected disk accesses
- Change in update or modified timestamp

- Sudden decrease of hard drive space
- Unexpected and strange activity by applications

The following section gives a quick look at a few types of malicious code.

 NOTE A "pseudo-flaw" is code inserted into an application on purpose to trap potential intruders.

Virus

A *virus* is a small application, or string of code, that infects applications. The main function of a virus is to reproduce, and it requires a host application to be able to do this. In other words, viruses cannot replicate on their own. A virus infects files by inserting or attaching a copy of itself to the file. The virus may also cause destruction by deleting system files, displaying graphics, reconfiguring systems, or overwhelming mail servers.

Several viruses have been released that achieved self-perpetuation by mailing themselves to every entry in a victim's personal address book. The virus masqueraded as coming from a trusted source. The ILOVEYOU, Melissa, and Naked Wife viruses used the programs Outlook and Outlook Express as their host applications and were replicated when the victim chose to open the message.

Macros are programs written in Word Basic, Visual Basic, or VBScript and are usually used with Microsoft Office products. Macros automate tasks that users would otherwise have to carry out themselves. Users can define a series of activities and common tasks for the application to perform when a button is pushed, instead of doing each of those tasks individually. A *macro virus* is a virus written in one of these macro languages and is platform independent. They infect and replicate in templates and within documents. Macro viruses are common because they are extremely easy to write, and Office products are in wide use.

Some viruses infect the boot sector (*boot sector viruses*) of a computer and either move data within the boot sector or overwrite the sector with new information. Some boot sector viruses have part of their code in the boot sector, which can initiate the virus, and have the rest of the virus code in sectors on the hard drive it has marked off as bad. Because the sectors are marked as bad, the operating system and applications will not attempt to use those sectors; thus, they will not get overwritten.

Virus

A virus is a program that searches out other programs and infects them by embedding a copy of itself. When the infected program executes, the embedded virus is executed, which propagates the infection.

Macro Languages
Macro languages enable users to edit, delete, and copy files. Because these languages are so easy to use, many more types of macro viruses are possible.

Other types of viruses append themselves to executables on the system and compress them using the user's permissions (*compression viruses*). When the user chooses to use that executable, the system automatically decompresses it and the malicious code, which usually causes the malicious code to initialize and perform its dirty deeds.

A *stealth virus* hides the modifications that it has made to files or boot records. This can be accomplished by monitoring system functions used to read files or sectors and forging the results. This means that when applications or users attempt to read an infected file, or sector, the original, uninfected form will be presented instead of the actual infected form.

So a stealth virus is a virus that hides its tracks after infecting a system. Once infected, the virus can make modifications to make the computer appear the same as before. The virus can show the original file size of a file it infected instead of the new larger size to try and trick the antivirus software into thinking that no changes have been made.

A *polymorphic virus* produces varied but operational copies of itself. This is done in the hopes of outwitting a virus scanner. Even if one or two copies are found and disabled, other copies may still remain active within the system.

The polymorphic virus can use different encryption schemes requiring different decryption routines. This would require an antivirus scan to have to exploit several scan strings, one for each possible decryption method, in order to identify all copies of this type of virus.

These viruses can also vary the sequence of their instructions by including *noise*, or bogus instructions, with other useful instructions. They can also use a mutation engine and a random-number generator to change the sequence of their instructions in the hopes of not being detected. A polymorphic virus has the capability of changing its own code, enabling the virus to have hundreds or thousands of variants. These activities can cause the virus scanner to not properly recognize the virus and to leave it alone.

A *multipart virus* infects both the boot sector of a hard drive and executable files. The virus first becomes resident in memory and then infects the boot sector. Once it is in memory, it can infect the entire system.

A *self-garbling virus* attempts to hide from antivirus software by garbling its own code. As the virus spreads, it changes the way its code is formatted. A small portion of the virus code decodes the garbled code when activated.

Meme viruses are not actual computer viruses but types of e-mails that continually get forwarded around the Internet. They can be chain letters, e-mail hoax virus alerts, religious messages, or pyramid selling schemes. They are replicated by humans, not software, and can waste bandwidth and spread fear. There are several e-mails that are passed around describing dangerous viruses, even though the viruses are not real. People believe the e-mails and feel as though they are doing the right thing by passing them on and telling their friends about this supposedly dangerous malware, but really the people have been duped and are themselves spreading a meme virus.

 NOTE An EICAR test is done with antivirus software by introducing a benign virus to test the detection and reaction activities of the software.

Worm

Worms are different than viruses in that they can reproduce on their own without a host application and in that they are self-contained programs. A worm can propagate itself by using e-mail, TCP/IP, and disk drives. The definitions of a worm and virus are continually merging, and the distinction is becoming more blurred. The ILOVEYOU program was a worm. When the user executed an e-mail attachment, several processes were spawned automatically. The worm was copied and sent to all addresses within the victim's address book. Some files on the hard drive were deleted and replaced. If these were opened, the worm self-propagation started again. ILOVEYOU acts as a virus by requiring the use of an e-mail client, like Outlook, and works as a worm by reproducing itself when the user opens infected files that reside on his hard drive.

Logic Bomb

A *logic bomb* will execute a program, or string of code, when a certain event happens or a date and time arrives. For example, if a user accesses her bank account software, a logic bomb may be initiated, and a program may be triggered to copy the user's account number and transaction codes. Another example is when a user accesses the Internet through his modem, as shown in Figure 11-35. This action can initiate a planted bomb that will send a message to an attacker over the Internet to let him know that the user is online and in position for an attack.

Trojan Horse

A *Trojan horse* is a program that is disguised as another program. For example, a Trojan horse can be named Notepad.exe and have the same icon as the regular Notepad program. However, when a user executes Notepad.exe, the program can delete system files. Trojan horses will perform the useful functionality in addition to the malicious functionality in the

Trojan Horse

A Trojan horse is a useful program that contains hidden code exploiting the authorization process to violate security.

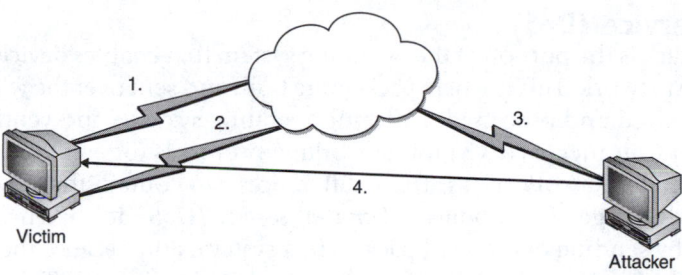

1. Victim connects to the Internet, which is the event that kicks off a logic bomb.
2. The logic bomb "calls" the attacker to indicate that the victim is on the Internet.
3. The attacker receives the message.
4. The attacker attacks the victim.

Figure 11-35 A logic bomb is initiated by specific events.

background. So the Trojan horse named Notepad.exe may still run the Notepad program for the user and in the background manipulate files or cause some other malicious acts. A host IDS can be configured to watch certain files and detect when they grow in size, which is often a sign of a Trojan horse. If the original Notepad.exe was 50KB in size and then grew to 2MB, it may indicate that a Trojan horse has infected that program.

Remote access Trojans are malicious programs that run on systems and allow intruders to access the system remotely. They mimic the functionality of legitimate remote control programs used for remote administration, but they are used for sinister purposes instead of helpful activities. They are developed to allow for stealth installation and operation. They are usually hidden in some type of mobile code, such as in Java Applets or ActiveX controls that are downloaded from Web sites.

The Trojan can send an e-mail to the attacker to indicate that the system has been infected. The Trojan and attacker work in a client/server model. The remote access Trojan installed on the victim's system is the server portion, and the attacker has a client piece. The server portion of the Trojan listens on a specific port, which allows a remote backdoor into the victim's system. The fun never ends.

So a Trojan horse appears to serve one purpose, but in reality, it performs different and often malicious tasks. This malware was named after the Trojan horse of Greek mythology that Greek soldiers used to sneak into the city of Troy. The horse looked like a gift, but it was filled with Greek soldiers ready for battle.

Attacks

This section will attempt to show how software weaknesses and bugs are used to provide methods of bringing down systems and/or networks. The weaknesses can reside in the applications, the operating system, protocols, and the network stack.

Denial of Service (DoS)

The network stack is the portion of the operating system that enables devices to communicate over the network. This is where packets are built and sent over the wire and where packets are received and processed. Different operating systems and vendors interpret the Request for Comments (RFCs) for networking protocols differently, which end up in slightly different network stacks. These differences can contain their own flaws that can be taken advantage of to produce a *denial-of-service (DoS)* attack. These attacks can be performed by sending malformed packets to a system, and because the system does not recognize the format, it does not know how to properly process it. This can cause the system to crash or stop processing other packets (denial of service).

DoS attacks cost businesses millions of dollars each year because of system downtime, lost revenue and productivity, reputation, and the man-hours involved in tracking down the problem and fixing it. DoS can interrupt service or completely deny legitimate users of needed system resources.

DoS attacks can consume a victim's bandwidth by flooding the network connection either from an attacker with more bandwidth than the victim, or from several attackers working together to saturate the victim's network and bring it to its knees. If more than one attack is involved, each attacker amplifies the effects of the other attackers by combining their bandwidth capabilities and overwhelming the victim's network segment, as Figure 11-36 illustrates.

Another type of DoS attack can use up all of the victim's resources instead of consuming the network's bandwidth. The resources can be processes, file system quotas, memory allocation, and CPU utilization. The following sections discuss some of the possible DoS attacks available.

Smurf

Oh, a cute little blue attack.

The Internet Control Message Protocol (ICMP) is the mini-messenger of Internet Protocol (IP) and is used to find out what systems are up and running (or alive). It reports status reports and error messages. When a user pings another computer, the ping utility actually sends an ICMP ECHO REQUEST message, and if the system is up and running, it will answer back with an ECHO REPLY message. It basically says, "Hello, computer 10.10.10.1, are you up and running?" and that computer answers back, "Yep."

The *smurf* attack requires three players: the attacker, the victim, and the amplifying network, as shown in Figure 11-37. The attacker spoofs, or changes the source IP address in a packet header, to make an ICMP ECHO REQUEST packet seem as though it originated at the victim's system. This ICMP ECHO REQUEST message is broadcast to the amplifying network, which will reply to the message in full force. The victim system and victim's network are overwhelmed. The ECHO functions of ICMP are there to determine if a computer is up and running and accepting requests. However, this attack takes advantage of the protocol not having certain safety measures built in to protect computers from being overwhelmed with ECHO messages.

Figure 11-36
DoS attacks can
be amplified by
several attackers
combining their
bandwidth and
attacking at once.

Figure 11-37 A smurf attack requires the attacker, the victim, and the amplifying network.

Countermeasures

- To make sure a certain network is not used as an amplifying site, direct broadcast functionality can be disabled at border routers.

- Packets that contain internal source IP addresses should not be accepted by perimeter routers as incoming messages. These packets are spoofed.

- Only the necessary ICMP traffic should be allowed into and out of an environment.

- A network IDS should be employed to watch for suspicious activity.

- Some systems are more sensitive to certain types of DoS, and patches have already been released. The appropriate patches should be applied.

Fraggle

Fraggle is an attack similar to smurf, but instead of using ICMP, it uses User Datagram Protocol (UDP) as its weapon of choice. The attacker broadcasts a spoofed UDP packet to the amplifying network, which in turn replies to the victim's system. The larger the amplifying network, the larger the amount of traffic that is pointed at the victim's system.

Different ICMP and UDP packets should be restricted from entering a network for many reasons. Many times an attacker uses these protocols to learn the topology of a network, locate routers, and learn about the type of systems within the network. Because we want to limit the amount of information available to attackers, these restrictions should take place at the network's perimeter routers:

- To make sure a certain network is not used as an amplifying site, direct broadcast functionality can be disabled at perimeter routers.

- Packets that contain internal source IP addresses should not be accepted by perimeter routers as incoming messages. These packets are spoofed.

- Only the necessary UDP should be allowed into and out of an environment.

- Network IDS should be employed to watch for suspicious activity.

- Some systems are more sensitive to certain types of DoS, and patches have already been released. The appropriate patches should be applied.

SYN Flood

Wanna talk? Wanna talk? Wanna talk? Wanna talk? Wanna talk? Wanna talk? Answer: This is looking like a SYN attack.

Because TCP is a connection-oriented protocol, it must set up a virtual connection between two computers. This virtual connection requires handshaking, and when using the TCP protocol, this requires a three-way process (see Figure 11-38). If computer Blah would like to communicate with computer Yuck, Blah will send a synchronous (SYN) packet to a specific port on Yuck that is in a LISTEN state. If Yuck is up, running, and accepting calls, it will reply to Blah with an SYN/ACK acknowledgment message. After receiving that message, Blah will send an ACK message to Yuck, and the connection will be established.

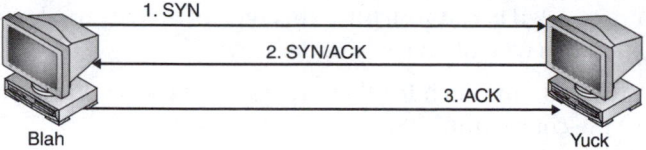

Figure 11-38
When using TCP, a three-way handshake must take place to establish a connection.

Systems, and their network stack, are expected to only have to deal with a certain number of these types of connections, so they have allocated only a certain amount of resources necessary for these types of functions. A quick analogy is in order. If Katie is only expecting three to five friends to show up at her house for a get together on Friday night, she will most likely only buy a couple of six packs of beer and munchies. When Friday night comes around and over 100 people show up, the party comes to a standstill when there is no more beer and only a bag of pretzels to go around. The same sort of thing is true within the network stack. Once 10 to 12 SYN requests are received, the system runs out of resources to process any more requests to set up communication paths.

Attackers can take advantage of this design flaw by continually sending the victim SYN messages with spoofed packets. The victim will commit the necessary resources to set up this communication socket, and it will send its SYN/ACK message waiting for the ACK message in return. However, the victim will never receive the ACK message, because the packet is spoofed, and the victim system sent the SYN/ACK message to a computer that does not exist. So the victim system receives a SYN message, and it dutifully commits the necessary resources to set up a connection with another computer. This connection is queued waiting for the ACK message, and the attacker sends another SYN message. The victim system does what it is supposed to and commits more resources, sends the SYN/ACK message, and queues this connection. This may only need to happen a dozen times before the victim system no longer has the necessary resources to open up another connection. This makes the victim computer unreachable from legitimate computers, denying other systems service from the victim computer.

The SYN message does not take a lot of bandwidth, and this type of attack can leave the victim computer in this state from about a minute and a half up to 23 minutes, depending on the TCP/IP stack. Because the SYN packet is spoofed, it makes it more difficult to track down the evildoer. Vendors have released patches that will increase the connection queue and/or decrease the connection establishment timeout period, which will enable the system to flush its connection queue.

Countermeasures

- Decrease the connection-established timeout period. (This will only lessen the effects of a SYN attack.)
- Increase the size of the connection queue in the IP stack.
- Different vendors have different ways of dealing with SYN attacks, and many patches have been developed to address them. The proper patches should be installed.

- A network IDS can watch for this type of activity to alert the responsible parties when this type of attack is under way.

- A firewall can watch for these types of attacks and alert the administrator or cut off the connection.

Teardrop

When packets travel through different networks, they may need to be fragmented and recombined depending on the network technology of each specific network. Each network technology has a maximum transmission unit (MTU), which indicates the largest packet size it can process. Some systems make sure that packets are not too large, but do not check to see if a packet is too small. The receiving system, the victim, would receive the fragments and attempt to recombine them, but these fragments have been made in such a way by an attacker that they cannot be properly reassembled. Many systems do not know how to deal with this situation. Attackers can take advantage of this design flaw and send very small packets that would cause a system to freeze or reboot.

Countermeasures

- Install necessary patch or upgrade operating system.

- Disallow malformed fragments of packets to enter environment.

- Use a router that will combine all fragments into a full packet prior to routing it to the destination system.

Distributed Deial of Service (DDoS)

A *distributed denial-of-service (DDoS)* attack is a logical extension of the DoS that gets more computers involved in the act. DoS attacks overwhelm computers by one computer sending bad packets or continually requesting services until the system's resources are all tied up and cannot honor any further requests. The DDoS uses hundreds or thousands of computers to request services from a server or server farm until the system or Web site is no longer functional.

The more recent victims of this type of attack have been Yahoo!, CNN.com, ZDNet, and E*Trade. These sites are developed to handle many hits to their sites and have the capability to process a large number of service requests each hour. However, a DDoS implements a volume of service requests that could overload any site. The attack can use other computers that knowingly participate, but most likely are unknowingly used as slaves in the process. The attacker creates master controllers that can in turn control slaves, or *zombie* machines. The master controllers are systems that an attacker is able to achieve administrative rights to so that programs can be loaded that will wait and listen for further instructions. The components of the third tier of computers are referred to as zombies because they do not necessarily know that they are involved in an attack. Scripts that have been put on their hard drives execute, and together all the zombie slaves work in concert to overwhelm a victim. An example of a DDoS attack is shown in Figure 11-39.

Figure 11-39
In a DDoS attack, the attacker uses masters to control zombies to overwhelm the victim with requests.

Countermeasures

- Perimeter routers restrict unnecessary ICMP and UDP traffic.
- A network IDS can be employed to watch for this type of suspicious activity.
- Disable unused subsystems and services on computers.
- Rename administrator account and implement strict password management so systems cannot be used unknowingly.
- Packets that contain internal source IP addresses should not be accepted by perimeter routers as incoming messages. These packets are spoofed.

DNS DoS Attacks

Domain Name Service (DNS) servers are used to map hostnames to IP addresses. It is a service used on almost every network and all over the Internet. People understand hostnames (**www.isc2.org**), and the network layer of the network stack understands IP addresses. So when a user types in a URL, it is a DNS server that transforms this address into something understandable by computers and network devices. Once the system and network devices know the right IP address, they know how to route the packets properly and communicate with the destination computer. It is like stopping at a gas station for directions. If you tell the guy behind the counter that you are looking for the post office, he will tell you that the post office is on Main Street and proceed to tell you the streets and turns to get to this destination. Thank goodness for gas stations and DNS servers!

Each DNS server is responsible for certain hosts, which are collectively referred to as a *zone*. Each host has its own record within the DNS server that contains its IP addresses, and this is how the DNS translates the hostname to the IP address. If a record that indicates that **www.isc2.org** is mapped to 10.10.10.1 is replaced with a record that says that **www.isc2.org** is mapped to 10.10.10.2 instead, the real Web site would not be able to receive hits. Users would not be able to get to this site, resulting in a DoS.

This is how DNS DoS attacks can occur. If the actual DNS records are unattainable to the attacker for him to alter in this fashion, which they should be, the attacker can insert this data into the cache of the server instead of replacing the actual records, which is referred to as *cache poisoning*. Many times DNS servers will cache previously resolved requests to make the next request for that hostname quicker. If the attacker replaces real data with bogus information in the server's cache, the DNS server and user would not necessarily know about this violation.

Because DNS servers are responsible only for a finite number of clients, many times one DNS server will have to ask another DNS server for help in finding out the requested information for the user. The DNS server can ask a root server for the address of the DNS server that is authoritative for the destination domain. This recursively resolves DNS names, and the original DNS server acts as a middleman by sending the user the address of the DNS responsible for the host the user is asking about. An attacker can send a bogus response to the requesting DNS server, and the DNS server will in turn send this bogus information to the requesting user. This will point the user to a different site than what was planned, and DoS has been committed because the user cannot get the service he requested.

Countermeasures

- DNS servers should have public and internal records. The public records serve Internet requests and contain no sensitive information pertaining to the internal network. The internal records should be unreachable from the Internet and are used to resolve queries from internal users.

- DNS servers should also be redundant by using a primary and secondary DNS server per zone.

- Different DNS BIND versions have different vulnerabilities. The BIND version should be updated.

- Employ secure DNS, which is explained in the next section.

Secure DNS

DNS servers contain records that enable the mapping between hostnames and IP addresses, as stated earlier. Primary DNS servers make all the necessary changes to the records when host and/or IP addresses change, and these records are then distributed to the secondary DNS servers. If a secondary server received bogus records from an attacker instead of the primary DNS server, it would not know the difference and update its records accordingly. Then when a user's computer contacted this secondary DNS server to translate hostnames to IP addresses, the records could contain incorrect information. Attacks like this have taken place mainly to embarrass businesses because users were redirected to indecent sites or to competitors' sites. However, this also causes DoS because the users cannot get where they need to go.

When Security DNS (DNSSEL) is implemented, the secondary DNS servers must authenticate the systems that are updating their records. Integrity checks are also performed to ensure that records were not modified or corrupted during transmission. Secure DNS protects DNS servers from having their records updated by unauthorized sources.

Timing Attacks

Attacks work because computers act in a predictable manner. They have to follow a sequence of steps, and when an attacker understands these steps and figures out how to take advantage of them, she can perform a type of timing attack. The following are three types of timing attacks you should be familiar with:

- **Between the lines entry attack** The attacker taps into and uses an active communication line. The user may not be using the connection at that time, but it is still active, so the attacker jumps in and uses it.

- **NAK/ACK attack** A NAK is a negative acknowledgement to tell a system that a certain piece of information was not received or that a certain message or parameter is unacceptable. Some systems do not deal with negative acknowledgements properly, and attackers use this weakness to their advantage.

- **Line disconnect attack** An attacker may access and keep a communication session open after the user attempts to terminate it. In this case the user drops off, thinking the connection is closed, but actually the attacker kept the connection active and is now using it.

Summary

Although functionality is the first concern when developing software, it would be beneficial if security were brought into the mix before the project started and were integrated into every step of the development process. Although many companies do not view this as the most beneficial approach to software development, they are becoming convinced of it over time as more security patches and fixes have to be developed and released, and as their customers continually demand more secure products.

Software development is a complex task, especially as technology changes at the speed of light, environments evolve, and more expectations are brought to vendors wishing to be the "king of the mountain" within the software market. This complexity also makes implementing effective security more challenging. For years programmers and developers did not need to consider security issues within their code, but this trend is changing. Education, experience, awareness, enforcement, and the demands of the consumers are all necessary pieces to bring more secure practices and technologies to the program code we all use.

Quick Tips

- Buffer overflows happen when an application does not check the length of data that is inputted and can cause the elevation of privilege for malicious code.

- If an application fails for any reason, it should go directly to a secure state.

- A database management system (DBMS) is the software that controls the access restrictions, data integrity, redundancy, and the different types of manipulation available for a database.

- In relational database terminology, a database row is called a tuple.

- A database primary key is how a specific row is located from other parts of the database.

- A view is an access control mechanism used in databases to ensure that only authorized subjects can access sensitive information.

- A relational database uses two-dimensional tables with rows (tuples) and columns (attributes).

- A hierarchical database uses a tree-like structure to define relationships between data elements, using a parent/child relationship.

- A distributed database, or network database, has databases that are physically in different areas but logically connected to represent one main database.

- Most databases have data definition language (DDL), data manipulation language (DML), query language (QL), and a report generator.

- A pseudo-flaw is code inserted into an application or system on purpose with the intention of trapping future intruders.

- A data dictionary is a central repository that describes the data elements within a database and their relationships. A data dictionary contains data about a database, which is called metadata.

- Database integrity is provided by concurrency mechanisms. One concurrency control is locking, which prevents users from accessing and modifying data that is being used by someone else.

- Entity integrity makes sure that a row, or tuple, is uniquely identified by a primary key, and referential integrity ensures that every foreign key refers to an existing primary key.

- A rollback cancels changes and returns the database to its previous state. This takes place if there was a problem during a transaction.

- A commit statement terminates a transaction and saves all changes to the database.

- A checkpoint is used if there is a system failure or problem during a transaction. The user is returned to the state of the last checkpoint.

- Aggregation can happen if a user does not have access to a group of elements, but has access to some of the individual elements within the group. Aggregation happens if the user combines the information of these individual elements and figures out the information of the group of data elements, which is at a higher sensitivity level.

- Inference is the capability to derive information that is not explicitly available.

- Common attempts to prevent inference attacks are partitioning the database, cell suppression, and adding noise to the database.

- Polyinstantiation is the process of allowing a table to have multiple rows with the same primary key. The different instances are distinguished by their security levels or classifications.

- Polymorphism is when different objects are given the same input and react differently.

- The two largest security problems associated with database security are inference and aggregation.

- Data warehousing combines data from multiple databases and data sources.

- Data mining is the process of massaging data held within a data warehouse to provide more useful information to users.

- Data mining tools produce metadata, which can contain previously unseen relationships and patterns.

- Security should be addressed in each phase of system development. Security should not be addressed at the end of development because of the added cost, time, effort, and lack of functionality.

- Systems and applications can use different models that use different life cycles, but they all contain project initiation, functional design analysis and planning, system design specifications, software development, installation, operations and maintenance, and disposal in some form or fashion.

- Risk management and assessments should start at the beginning of a project and continue throughout the lifetime of the product.

- If proper design for a product is not put into place in the beginning, more effort will have to take place in the implementation, testing, and maintenance phases.

- Separation of duties should be practiced in roles, environments, and functionality pertaining to development of a product.

- A programmer should not have direct access to code in production. This is an example of separation of duties.

- Certification deals with testing and assessing the security mechanism in a system, and accreditation pertains to the management formally accepting the system and its security level.

- Media that contain sensitive information must be disposed of in a controlled and secure way. This may mean physical destruction of the media.

- Change control needs to be put in place at the beginning of a project and must be enforced through each phase.

- Changes must be authorized, tested, and recorded. The changes must not affect the security level of the system or its capability to enforce the security policy.

- High-level programming languages are translated into machine languages for the system and its processor to understand.

- Source code is translated into machine code, or object code, by compilers, assemblers, and interpreters.

- Object-oriented programming provides modularity, reusability, and more granular control within the programs themselves.

- Objects are members, or instances, of classes. The classes dictate the objects' data types, structure, and acceptable actions.

- Objects communicate with each other through messages.

- A method is the functionality an object can carry out.

- Data and operations internal to objects are hidden from other objects, which is referred to as data hiding. Each object encapsulates its data and processes.

- Objects can communicate properly because they are using standard interfaces.

- Object-oriented design represents a real-world problem and modularizes the problem into cooperating objects that work together to solve the problem.

- If an object can perform a function without the help of others, it has high cohesion.

- If an object does not require much interaction with other modules, it has low coupling.

- The best programming design enables objects to be as independent and modular as possible; therefore, the higher the cohesion and the lower the coupling, the better.

- An object request broker (ORB) manages communication between objects and enables them to interact in a heterogeneous and distributed environment.

- Common Object Request Broker Architecture (CORBA) provides a standardized way for objects within different applications, platforms, and environments to communicate. It accomplishes this by providing standards for interfaces between objects.

- Component Object Model (COM) provides an architecture for components to interact on a local system. Distributed COM (DCOM) uses the same interfaces as COM, but enables components to interact over a distributed, or networked, environment.

- Open database connectivity (ODBC) enables several different applications to communicate with several different types of databases by calling the required driver and passing data through that driver.

- Object linking and embedding (OLE) enables a program to call another program (linking) and enables a piece of data to be inserted inside another program or document (embedding).

- Dynamic Data Exchange (DDE) enables applications to work in a client/server model by providing the interprocess communication (ICP) mechanism.

- Distributed Computing Environment (DCE) provides much of the same functionality as DCOM, which enables different objects to communicate in a networked environment.

- DCE uses universal unique identifiers (UUIDs) to keep track of different subjects, objects, and resources.

- An expert system uses a knowledge base full of facts, rules of thumb, and expert advice. It also has an inference machine that matches facts against patterns and determines which rules are to be applied.

- Expert systems are used to mimic human reasoning and replace human experts.

- Artificial neural networks (ANNs) attempt to mimic a brain by using units that react like neurons.

- ANNs can learn from experiences and can match patterns that regular programs and systems cannot.

- Java security employs a sandbox so that the applet is restricted from accessing the user's hard drive or system resources. Programmers have figured out how to write applets that escape the sandbox.

- ActiveX uses a security scheme that includes digital signatures. The browser security settings determine how ActiveX controls are dealt with.

- A virus is an application that requires a host application for replication.

- Macro viruses are common because the languages used to develop macros are easy to use and they infect Office products, which are everywhere.

- A boot sector virus overwrites data in the boot sector and can contain the rest of the virus in a sector it marked as "bad."

- A stealth virus hides its tracks and its actions.

- A polymorphic virus tries to escape detection by making copies of itself and modifying the code and attributes of those copies.

- Multipart viruses can have one part in the boot sector and another part of the virus on the hard drive.

- A self-garbling virus tries to escape detection by changing, or garbling, its own code.

- A worm does not require a host application to replicate.

- A logic bomb executes a program when a predefined event takes place, or a date and time are met.

- A Trojan horse is a program that performs useful functionality and malicious functionally without the user knowing it.

- Smurf and Fraggle are two examples of DoS attacks that take advantage of protocol flaws and use amplifying networks.

- Expert systems use inference engine processing, automatic logical processing, and general methods of searching for problem solutions.

Questions

Please remember that these questions are formatted and asked in a certain way for a reason. You must remember that the CISSP exam is asking questions at a conceptual level. Questions may not always have the perfect answer, and the candidate is advised against always looking for the perfect answer. The candidate should look for the best answer in the list.

1. What is the final stage in the change control management process?

    A. Configure the hardware properly.

    B. Update documentation and manuals.

    C. Inform users of the change.

    D. Report the change to management.

2. Which best describes a logic bomb?

    A. Used to move assets from one computer to another

    B. Action triggered by a specified condition

    C. Self-replicating

    D. Performs a useful action and a malicious action

3. An application is downloaded from the Internet to perform disk cleanup and to delete unnecessary temporary files. The application is also recording network login data and sending it to another party. This application is best described as which of the following?

    A. Virus

    B. Trojan horse

    C. Worm

    D. Logic bomb

4. Why are macro viruses so prevalent?

    A. They replicate quickly.

    B. They infect every platform in production.

    C. The languages used to write macros are very easy to use.

    D. They are activated by events that happen commonly on each system.

5. Which action is not part of configuration management?

    A. Submitting a formal request

    B. Operating system configuration and settings

    C. Hardware configuration

    D. Application settings and configuration

6. Expert systems are used to automate security log review for what purpose?

    A. To develop user behavioral models

    B. To ensure best access methods

    C. To detect intrusion

    D. To provide statistics that will not be used for baselines

7. Which form of malware has a purpose of reproducing itself utilizing system resources?

    A. Worm

    B. Virus

    C. Trojan horse

    D. Multipart virus

8. Expert systems use each of the following items except for _____.

    A. Automatic logical processing

    B. General methods of searching for problem solutions

    C. Inference engine

    D. Cycle-based reasoning

9. Which of the following replicates itself by attaching to other programs?

    A. Worm

    B. Virus

    C. Trojan horse

    D. Malware

10. What is the importance of inference in an expert system?

    A. The knowledge base contains facts, but must also be able to combine facts to derive new information and solutions.

    B. The inference machine is important to fight against multipart viruses.

    C. The knowledge base must work in units to mimic neurons in the brain.

    D. The access must be controlled to prevent unauthorized access.

11. A system has been patched many times and has recently become infected with a dangerous virus. If antivirus software indicates that disinfecting a file may damage it, what is the correct action?

   A. Disinfect the file and contact the vendor.

   B. Back up the data and disinfect the file.

   C. Replace the file with the file saved the day before.

   D. Restore an uninfected version of the patched file from backup media.

12. Which of the following centrally controls the database and manages different aspects of the data?

   A. Data storage

   B. Database

   C. Data dictionary

   D. Access control

13. What is the purpose of polyinstantiation?

   A. To restrict lower-level subjects from accessing low-level information

   B. To make a copy of an object and modify the attributes of the second copy

   C. To create different objects that will react in different ways to the same input

   D. To create different objects that will take on inheritance attributes from their class

14. When a database detects an error, what enables it to start processing at a designated place?

   A. Checkpoint

   B. Data dictionary

   C. Metadata

   D. Data mining tool

15. Database views provide what type of security control?

   A. Detective

   B. Corrective

   C. Preventive

   D. Administrative

16. If one department can view employees' work history and another group cannot view their work history, what is this an example of?

   A. Context-dependent access control

   B. Content-dependent access control

   C. Separation of duties

   D. Mandatory access control

17. Which of the following is used to deter database inference attacks?

    A. Partitioning, cell suppression, and noise and perturbation

    B. Controlling access to the data dictionary

    C. Partitioning, cell suppression, and small query sets

    D. Partitioning, noise and perturbation, and small query sets

18. What is a disadvantage of content-dependent access control when it comes to databases?

    A. It can access other memory addresses.

    B. It can cause concurrency problems.

    C. It increases processing and resource overhead.

    D. It can cause deadlock situations.

19. If security was not part of the development of a database, how is it usually handled?

    A. Cell suppression

    B. Trusted back end

    C. Trusted front end

    D. Views

20. What is an advantage of content-dependent access control in databases?

    A. Processing overhead

    B. Ensures concurrency

    C. Disallows data locking

    D. Granular control

21. Which of the following is used in the Distributed Computing Environment technology?

    A. Global unique identifier (GUID)

    B. Universal unique identifier (UUID)

    C. Universal global identifier (UGID)

    D. Global universal identifier (GUID)

22. When should security first be addressed in a project?

    A. During requirements development

    B. During integration testing

    C. During design specifications

    D. During implementation

23. Online application systems that detect an invalid transaction should do which of the following?

    A. Roll back and rewrite over original data.

    B. Terminate all transactions until properly addressed.

    C. Write a report to be reviewed.

    D. Checkpoint each data entry.

24. What is the final phase of the system development life cycle?

    A. Certification

    B. Unit testing

    C. Development

    D. Accreditation

25. Which of the following are rows and columns within relational databases?

    A. Rows and tuples

    B. Attributes and rows

    C. Keys and views

    D. Tuples and attributes

Answers

1. **D.** A common CISSP theme is to report to management, get management's buy in, get management's approval, and so on. The change must first be approved by the project or program manager. Once the change is completed, it is reported to senior management, usually as a status report in a meeting or a report that addresses several things at one time, not necessarily just this one item.

2. **B.** A logic bomb is a program that has been coded to carry out some type of activity when a certain event takes place, or a time and date are met. An attacker may have a computer attack another computer on Michelangelo's birthday, it may be set to execute in two weeks and three minutes, or it may initiate after a user strikes specific keys in a certain sequence.

3. **B.** A Trojan horse looks like an innocent and helpful program, but in the background it is carrying out some type of malicious activity unknown to the user. The Trojan horse could be corrupting files, sending the user's password to an attacker, or attacking another computer.

4. **C.** A macro language is written specifically to allow non-programmers to program macros. Macros are sequences of steps that can be executed with one keystroke, and they were developed to reduce the repetitive activities of users. The language is very simplistic, which is why macro viruses are so easy to write.

5. **A.** Submitting a formal request would fall under the change control umbrella. Most environments have a change control process that dictates how all changes will be handled, approved, and tested. Once the change is approved, there needs to be something in place to make sure the actual configurations that are implemented to carry out this change take place properly. This is the job of configuration management.

6. **C.** An IDS can be based on an expert system or have an expert system component. The job of the expert system is to identify patterns that would represent an intrusion or an attack that an IDS without this component may not pick up on. The expert system will look at a history of events and identify a pattern that would be otherwise very hard to uncover.

7. **A.** A worm does not need a host to replicate itself, but it does need an environment, which would be an operating system and its resources. A virus requires a host, which is usually a specific application.

8. **D.** An expert system attempts to reason like a person by using logic that works with the gray areas in life. It does this by using a knowledge base, automatic logical processing components, general methods of search for solutions, and an inference engine. It carries out its logical processing with rule-based programming.

9. **B.** As stated in an earlier answer, a virus requires a host to replicate, which is usually a specific application.

10. **A.** The whole purpose of an expert system is for it to look at the data it has to work with and what the user presents to it and to come up with new or different solutions. It will basically perform data mining activities, identify patterns and relationships the user could not see, and provide solutions. This is the same reason you would go to a human expert. You would give her your information, and she would combine it with the information she knows and give you a solution or advice, which is not necessarily the same data you gave her.

11. **D.** Some files cannot be properly sanitized by the antivirus software without destroying it or affecting its functionality. So the administrator must replace the file with a known uninfected file. And the administrator needs to make sure he has the patched version of the file, or else he could be introducing other problems. Answer C is not the *best* answer because the administrator may not know that the file was clean yesterday, so just restoring yesterday's file may get him into the same boat.

12. **C.** A data dictionary holds the schema information about the database. This schema information is represented as metadata. When the database administrator modifies the database attributes, he is modifying the data dictionary because it is the central component that holds this type of information. When a user attempts to access the database, the data dictionary will be consulted to see if this activity is deemed appropriate.

13. **B.** Instantiation is what happens when an object is created from a class. Polyinstantiation is when more than one object is made, and the other copy is modified to have different attributes. This can be done for several reasons. The example that was given in the chapter was a way to use polyinstantiation for security purposes, to ensure that a lower-level subject could not access an object at a higher level.

14. **A.** Savepoints and checkpoints are similar in nature. A savepoint is used to periodically save the state of the application and the user's information. A checkpoint will save data held in memory off to a temporary file. Both are used so that if the application endures a glitch, it has the necessary tools to bring the user back to his working environment without losing any data. You experience this with word processors when it asks you if you want to review the recovered version of a file you were working on.

15. **C.** A database view is put into place to prevent certain users from viewing specific data. This is a preventive measure because the administrator is preventing the users from seeing data that is not meant for them. This is one control to use to prevent inference attacks.

16. **B.** Content-dependent access control carries out its restrictions based upon the sensitivity of the data. Context-dependent control will review the previous access requests and make an access decision based on the previous activities.

17. **A.** Partitioning means to logically split the database into parts, and then views will dictate what users can view specific parts. Cell suppression means that specific cells are not viewable by certain users. And noise and perturbation is when bogus information is inserted into the database to try and give potential attackers incorrect information.

18. **C.** Relative to other types of access control, content-dependent control requires a lot of overhead and processing because it makes decisions based on the sensitivity of the data instead of purely on the identity of the requesting subject.

19. **C.** A trusted front end can be developed to implement more security that the database itself is lacking. It can require a more granular and stringent access control policy by requiring tighter identification and authorization pieces than what is inherent in the database. Front ends can also be developed to provide more user friendliness and interoperability with other applications.

20. **D.** As stated in an earlier question, content-dependent access control bases its access decision on the sensitivity of the data. This provides more granular control, which almost always means more processing is required.

21. **B.** Universal unique identifier (UUID) is used by DCE, and global unique identifier (GUID) is used by DCOM. DCE and DCOM both need a naming structure to keep track of their individual components, which is what these different naming schemes provide.

22. **A.** The trick to this question, and any one like it, is that security should be implemented at the first possible phase of a project. Requirements are gathered and developed at the beginning of a project, which is project initiation. The other answers are steps that follow this phase, and security should be integrated right off the bat instead of in the middle or at the end.

23. **C.** This can seem like a tricky question. It is asking you if the system detected an invalid transaction, which is most likely a user error. This error should be logged so it can be reviewed. After the review, the supervisor, or whoever makes this type of decision, will decide if it was a mistake or not and investigate it as needed. If the system had a glitch, power fluctuation, hangup, or any other software- or hardware-related error, that would not be an invalid transaction, and in that case the system would carry out a rollback function.

24. **D.** Out of this list the last phase is accreditation, which is where management formally approves of the product. Now the question could have different answers. For example, if it listed disposal, that would be the right answer because that would be the last phase listed.

25. **D.** In a relational database a row is referred to as a tuple, and a column is referred to as an attribute.

Operations Security

In this chapter, you will learn about the following items:

- Administrative management responsibilities
- Product evaluation and operational assurance
- Configuration management
- Trusted recovery states
- E-mail security
- Threats to operational security

Operation security pertains to everything that takes place to keep a network, computer systems, applications, and environment up and running in a secure and protected manner. Operations take place after the network is developed and implemented. This includes the continual maintenance of an environment and the activities that should take place on a day-to-day or week-to-week basis. These activities are routine in nature and enable the network and individual computer systems to continue to run correctly and securely.

Networks and computing environments are evolving entities; just because they are secure one week does not mean that they are still secure three weeks later. Many companies have paid security consultants who come in and advise them on how to improve their infrastructure, policies, and procedures. A company can then spend thousands of dollars to implement the consultant's suggestions and install properly configured firewalls, intrusion detection systems (IDSs), antivirus software, and patch vulnerable systems. However, if the IDS and antivirus software do not continually have updated signatures, if the systems are not continually patched, and if firewalls and devices are not tested for vulnerabilities, then the company can easily slip back into an insecure and dangerous place. This would happen because it did not keep up on its operational security tasks.

Most of the necessary operational security issues have been addressed in earlier chapters. They were integrated with related topics and not necessarily pointed out as actual operational security issues. So instead of repeating what has already been previously stated, this chapter will review and point out the operational security topics that are important for organizations and CISSP candidates.

Operational Security

I am a very prudent man. Response: That is debatable.

The continual effort of making sure that the correct policies, procedures, standards, and guidelines are in place and being followed is an important piece of the *due care* and *due diligence* that companies need to perform. Due care and due diligence are comparable to the "prudent person" concept. A prudent person is seen as responsible, careful, cautious, and practical, and a company practicing due care and due diligence is seen in the same light. The right steps need to be taken to achieve the necessary level of security, but it takes continued effort and discipline to retain this level of security. This is what operational security is all about.

Although operational security is the practice of continual maintenance to keep an environment running at a necessary security level, there can also be liability and legal responsibilities when it comes to performing these tasks. Companies, and senior executives at those companies, often have legal obligations to ensure that resources are protected, safety measures are in place, and security mechanisms are tested to guarantee they are actually providing the necessary level of protection. If these operational security responsibilities are not fulfilled, the company may have more than antivirus signatures to be concerned about. (Please refer to Chapter 10 to learn more about the legal, regulatory, and ethical responsibilities of companies when it comes to security.)

Administrative Management

I think our tasks should be separated because I don't trust you. Response: Fine by me.

Administrative management is a very important piece of operational security. One aspect of administrative management is dealing with personnel issues. This includes separation of duties and job rotation. The objective of *separation of duties* is to ensure that one person acting alone cannot compromise the company's security in any way. High-risk activities should be broken up into different parts and distributed to different individuals. This way the company does not need to put a dangerously high level of trust on certain individuals. If fraud were to take place, collusion would need to be committed, meaning more than one person would have to be involved in the fraudulent activity. Separation of duties, therefore, is a preventive measure that forces collusion in order for someone to commit something against policy.

Separation of duties also helps prevent mistakes that can take place if one person is performing a task from beginning to end. For instance, a programmer should not be the only one to test her own code. Another person with a different job and agenda should perform functionality and integrity testing on the programmer's code because the programmer may have a focused view of what the program is supposed to accomplish and only test certain functions, input values, and in certain environments.

Another example of separation of duties is the difference between the functions of a computer user versus the functions of a system administrator. There must be clear-cut lines drawn between system administrator duties and computer user duties. These will vary from environment to environment and will depend on the level of security required within the environment. System administrators usually have the responsibility of performing backups and recovery procedures, setting permissions, adding and removing users, and developing user profiles. The computer user, on the other hand, may be allowed to install software, set an initial password, alter desktop configurations, and modify certain system parameters. The user should not be able to modify her own security profile, add and remove users globally, or make critical access decisions pertaining to network resources. This would breach the concept of separation of duties.

Job rotation means that more than one person fulfills the tasks of one position within the company. This enables the company to have more than one person who understands tasks and responsibilities of a specific job title, which provides backup and redundancy if a person leaves the company or is absent. Job rotation also helps identify fraudulent activities, and therefore can be considered a detective type of control. If Keith has performed David's position, he knows the regular tasks and routines that are to be completed to fulfill the responsibilities of that job. This would allow Keith to better identify if David does something out of the ordinary and suspicious. Job rotation can sometimes also be considered a preventive control, because if someone knows that a specific individual is going to be replacing him/her in that job function, it may prevent that person from committing a violation against policy. (Please refer to Chapters 4 and 6 for further examples pertaining to job rotation.)

Least privilege and need-to-know are also administrative-type controls that should be implemented in an operations environment. *Least privilege* means that an individual should have just enough permissions and rights to fulfill his role in the company and no more. If an individual has excessive permissions and rights, it could open the door to abuse of access and put the company at more risk than is necessary. If Dusty is a technical writer for a company, he does not necessarily need to have access to the company's source code. So the mechanisms that control Dusty's access to resources should not let him access source code. This would be properly fulfilling operational security controls that are in place to protect resources.

Least privilege and need-to-know have a symbiotic relationship. Each user should have a need-to-know of the resources that he is allowed to access. If Mike does not have a need-to-know of how much the company paid last year in taxes, then his system rights should not include access to these files, which would be an example of exercising least privilege.

A user's access rights can be a combination of the least privilege attribute, the user's security clearance, the need-to-know, the sensitivity level of the resource, and the mode

Rotation of Duties Definition

"Interrupt opportunity to create collusion to subvert operation for fraudulent purposes." This definition may be necessary to know for test purposes. It means that if employees rotated jobs, it would make it harder for one employee to commit fraudulent activities without other employees finding out.

at which the computer operates. A system can operate at different types of modes depending on the sensitivity of the data being processed, the clearance level of the users, and what those users are authorized to do. The mode of operation describes the conditions under which the system actually functions. These are clearly defined in Chapter 5.

Mandatory vacations is another type of administrative control that may sound a bit odd at first. Chapter 3 touches on reasons to make sure that employees take their vacations; this has to do with being able to identify fraudulent activities and enable job rotation to take place. If an accounting employee has been performing a salami attack by shaving off pennies from multiple accounts and putting the money into his own account, a company would have a better chance of figuring this out if that employee was required to take a vacation for a week or longer. When the employee is on vacation, another employee has to fill in. She might uncover questionable documents and clues of previous activities, or the company may see a change in certain patterns once the employee who is committing fraud is gone for a week or two. The idea behind mandatory vacations is that, traditionally, those employees who have committed fraud are usually the ones who have resisted going on vacation because of their fear of being found out while away.

Accountability

I am going to bring down the servers, change configuration files, and cause chaos without anyone knowing it. Response: Nope, we have auditing enabled.

User access to resources must be limited and properly controlled to ensure that excessive privileges do not provide the opportunity to cause damage to a company and its resources. Users' access attempts and activities while using a resource need to be properly monitored, audited, and logged. The individual user ID needs to be included in the audit logs to enforce individual responsibility. Each user should understand his responsibility when using company resources and be accountable for his actions.

Capturing and monitoring audit logs helps determine if a violation has actually occurred or if system and software reconfiguration is needed to better capture only the activities that fall outside of established boundaries. If user activities were not captured and reviewed, it would be very hard to determine if users have excessive privileges or if there has been unauthorized access.

Auditing needs to take place in a routine manner. Also, there is really no reason to audit and log events if no one looks at the output. Audit and function logs often contain too much cryptic or mundane information to be interpreted manually. This is why there are products that parse logs for companies and report important findings. Logs should be monitored and reviewed either through manual or automatic methods to uncover suspicious activity or if an environment is shifting away from its original baselines. This is how administrators can be warned of many problems before they become too big and out of control. (Please look at Chapters 3, 6, and 10 for auditing, logging, and monitoring issues.)

Certain questions need to be asked when monitoring, which pertain to the users, their actions, and the current level of security and access:

- *Are users accessing information and performing tasks that are not necessary for their job description?* This would indicate if users' rights and permissions need to be reevaluated and possibly modified.

- *Are repetitive mistakes being made?* This would indicate if users need to have further training.

- *Do too many users have rights and privileges to sensitive or restricted data or resources?* This would indicate if access rights to the data and resources need to be reevaluated, the number of individuals accessing them needs to be reduced, and/or the extent of their access rights should be modified.

Security Operations and Product Evaluation

When products are evaluated for the level of trust and assurance they provide, many times operational assurance and life cycle assurance are part of the evaluation process. *Operational assurance* concentrates on the architecture of the product, embedded features, and functionality that enable a customer to continually obtain the necessary level of protection when using the product. Examples of operational assurances examined in the evaluation process are access control mechanisms, the separation of privileged and user program code, auditing and monitoring capabilities, covert channel analysis, and trusted recovery when the product experiences unexpected circumstances.

Life cycle assurance pertains to how the product was developed and maintained. Each stage of the product's life cycle has standards and expectations it must fulfill before it can be deemed a highly trusted product. Examples of life cycle assurance standards are design specifications, clipping level configurations, unit and integration testing, configuration management, and trusted distribution. Products that are looking to achieve one of the higher security ratings will have each of these issues evaluated and tested.

The following sections address several of these types of operational assurance and life cycle assurance issues as they pertain to evaluation, but also as they pertain to a company's responsibilities once the product is implemented. A product is just a tool for a company to use for functionality and security; it is up to the company to ensure that this functionality and security are continually available through responsible and proactive steps.

Clipping Levels

I am going to keep track of how many mistakes you make.

Companies set certain thresholds for certain types of errors or mistakes allowed and the number of these mistakes that can take place before it is considered suspicious. The threshold is a baseline for violation activities that may be normal for a user to commit before alarms are raised. This baseline is referred to as a *clipping level*. Once this clipping level has been exceeded, further violations are recorded for review. Most of the time IDS software is used to track these activities and behavior patterns because it would be too overwhelming for an individual to continually monitor stacks of audit logs and properly identify certain activity patterns. Once the clipping level is exceeded, the IDS can e-mail a message to the network administrator, send a message to his pager, or just add this information to the logs, depending on how the IDS software is configured.

Clipping levels, auditing, and monitoring are done with the hope of discovering problems before major damage occurs and, at times, being alerted if a possible attack is underway within the network.

NOTE It is important that the security controls and mechanisms that are in place have a degree of transparency. This enables the user to perform tasks and duties without having to go through extra steps because of the presence of the security controls. Transparency also does not let the user know too much about the controls, which helps prevent him from figuring out how to circumvent them. If the controls are too obvious, an attacker can figure out how to compromise them more easily.

Change Management Control
The only thing that is constant is change.

Every company should have a policy indicating how changes take place within a facility, who can make the changes, how they are approved, and how these changes are documented and communicated to other employees. Without these policies in place, people can make changes that others do not know about and have not been approved, which can result in a confusing mess. This is usually when vulnerabilities are introduced into an environment, and tracking down and reversing the changes can be a complicated task.

The changes can happen to network configurations, system parameters, applications, and settings by adding new technologies, application configurations, devices, or modifying the facility's environmental devices. Change control is important for an environment, but also for a product during its development and life cycle. It is important that changes be effective and orderly because it is easy to waste time and money by continually making changes that do not meet an ultimate goal.

NOTE Change control is the management of security features and a level of assurance provided through the control of the changes made to the system's hardware, software, and firmware configurations throughout the development and operational life cycle.

Some changes can cause a serious disruption to a network and affect systems' availability. This means that changes must be thought through, approved, and carried out in a structured fashion. Backup plans may be necessary in case the change causes unforeseen negative effects. For example, if a facility is changing its power supply, there should be backup generators on hand in case the transition does not take place as smoothly as planned. Or if a server is going to be replaced with a different server type, there could be interoperability issues that could prevent users from accessing specific resources, so a backup or redundant server should be in place to ensure availability and continued productivity.

A well-structured change management process should be put into place to aid staff members through many different types of changes to the environment. This process would be laid out in the change control policy. Although the types of changes vary, a standard list of procedures can help keep the process under control and ensure that it is carried out in a predictable manner. The following steps are examples of the types of procedures that should be part of any change control policy:

1. **Request for a change to take place**   Requests should be presented to an individual or group that is responsible for approving changes and overseeing the activities of changes that take place within an environment.

2. **Approval of the change**   The individual requesting the change must justify the reasons and clearly show the benefits and possible pitfalls of the change. Sometimes the requester is asked to conduct more research and provide more information before the change is approved.

3. **Documentation of the change**   Once the change is approved, it should be entered into a change log. The log should be updated as the process continues toward completion.

4. **Tested and presented**   The change must be fully tested to uncover any unforeseen results. Depending on the severity of the change and the company's organization, the change and implementation may need to be presented to a change control committee. This helps show different sides to the purpose and outcome of the change and the possible ramifications.

5. **Implementation**   Once the change is fully tested and approved, a schedule should be developed that outlines the projected phases of the change being implemented and the necessary milestones. These steps should be fully documented and progress should be monitored.

6. **Report changes to management**   A full report should be submitted to management summarizing the change. This report can be submitted on a periodic basis to keep management up to date and ensure continual support.

These steps, of course, usually apply to large changes that take place within a facility. These types of changes are usually expensive and can have lasting effects on a company. However, smaller changes should also go through some type of change control process. If a server needs to have a patch applied, it is not good practice to have an engineer just apply it without properly testing it on a non-production server, without having the approval of the manager of the IT department or network administrator, and without having backup plans in place in case the patch causes some negative effect on the production server. Of course, these changes need to be documented. (Please refer to Chapter 7 for a further look at change control procedures.)

Change Control Documentation   *I wrote down my changes on this napkin with crayons. Response: Um, thanks.* Documentation should be done on a regular basis so that changes are identified and written down and available for future use. There are numerous changes that can take place in a company:

- New computers installed
- New applications installed
- Different configurations implemented
- Patches and updates installed
- New technologies integrated
- Updated policies, procedures, and standards
- New regulations and requirements
- Identified and implemented fixes for network or system problems
- Different network configuration
- New networking devices integrated into the network

The list can go on and on and can be general or detailed. Many companies have experienced some major problem that affects the network and employee productivity. The IT department may run around trying to figure out the issue and go through hours or days of trial-and-error exercises of finding and applying the necessary fix. If no one properly documents the incident and what was done to fix the issue, the company can be doomed to repeat the same dance six months to a year down the road.

Media Controls

Media and devices that can be found in an operations environment require a variety of controls to ensure that they are properly preserved and that the integrity, confidentiality, and availability of the data that is held on them are not compromised.

The operational controls that pertain to these issues come in many flavors. The first are controls that prevent unauthorized access, which can require physical, administrative, and technical controls to be put into place. If the company's backup tapes are to be properly protected, they need to be in a place where only the necessary people have access to them, which could be in a locked server room or off-site facility. If the tapes need to be protected from environmental issues such as humidity, heat, cold, fire, and natural disasters, they should be kept in a fireproof safe in a regulated environment or in an off-site facility that controls the environment to be hospitable to data processing components. These issues are covered in detail in Chapter 6.

Companies often have a media library with a librarian in charge of protecting its resources. Users may be required to check out specific types of media and resources instead of having the resources readily available for anyone and everyone to access them. If the library controls backed up data, each tape should be labeled with the following information:

- The date of creation
- The individual who created the backup
- The retention period (how long the data is good for)
- The classification
- The volume name and version

Media should be clearly marked and logged, its integrity should be verified, and it should be properly erased of data when necessary. When media is cleared of its contents, it is said to be *sanitized*. There are several methods for sanitation: overwriting (zeroization), degaussing, and destruction. As stated in earlier chapters, deleting files on a piece of media does not actually make the data disappear; it only deletes the pointers to where those files still live on the disk. This is how companies that specialize in restoration can recover the deleted files intact after they have been apparently destroyed.

NOTE A device that performs degaussing generates a coercive magnetic force that reduces the magnetic flux density of the storage media to zero. This magnetic force is what properly erases data from media.

Data remanence is the residual physical representation of information that was saved and then erased in some fashion. This remanence may be enough to enable the data to be reconstructed and restored back into a readable form. This can cause a security threat to a company that thought they properly erased confidential data from their media.

If the media does not hold confidential or sensitive information, overwriting or deleting the files may be the appropriate steps to take. If the data is sensitive, degaussing may be required. If the data is highly confidential or the media cannot be properly degaussed, the appropriate action would be to physically destroy it. (Please refer to Chapters 3 and 4 for further discussion on these issues.)

System Controls

System controls are also part of operational security. Within the operating system itself, certain controls must be in place to ensure that instructions are being executed in the correct security context. The system has mechanisms that restrict the execution of certain types of instructions, which can only take place when the operating system is in a privileged or supervisor state. This protects the overall security and state of the system and helps ensure that it runs in a stable and predictable manner.

An operating system does not provide direct access to hardware by processes of lower privilege, which are usually processes used by user applications. If a program needs to send instructions to hardware devices, the request is passed off to a process of higher privilege. To execute privileged hardware instructions, a process must be running in a restrictive and protective state. This is an integral part of the operating system's architecture, and the determination of what processes can submit what type of instructions is made based on the operating system's control tables.

Many input/output (I/O) instructions are defined as privileged and can only be executed by the operating system kernel processes. When a user program needs to send I/O information, it must notify the system's core, privileged processes that work at the inner rings of the system. These processes (called system services) either authorize the user program processes to perform these actions and temporarily increase their privileged state or the system's processes complete the request on behalf of the user program. (Please review Chapter 5 for a more in-depth understanding of these types of system controls.)

Trusted Recovery

What if my application or system blows up? Answer: It should do so securely.

When an operating system or application crashes or freezes, it should not put the system in any type of insecure state. The usual reason for a system crash in the first place is because it encountered something that it perceived as insecure or did not understand and decided that it was safer to freeze, shut down, or reboot than perform the current activity.

An operating system's response to a type of failure can be classified as one of the following:

- System reboot
- Emergency system restart
- System cold start

A *system reboot* takes place after shutting down the system in a controlled manner in response to a trusted computing base (TCB) failure. If the system finds inconsistent object data structures or if there is not enough space in some critical tables, a system reboot may take place. This releases resources and returns the system to a more stable and safe state.

An *emergency system restart* takes place after a system failure happens in an uncontrolled manner. This can be a TCB or media failure that could be caused by lower-privileged user processes attempting to access memory segments that are restricted. The system sees this as an insecure activity that it cannot properly recover from without rebooting. The system goes into a maintenance mode and recovers from the actions taken. The system is brought back up in a consistent and stable state.

A *system cold start* takes place when an unexpected TCB or media failure happens and the regular recovery procedure cannot recover the system to a more consistent state. The system, TCB, and user objects may remain in an inconsistent state while the system attempts to recover itself, and intervention may be required by the user or administrator to restore the system.

It is important that the system does not enter an insecure state when it is affected by any of these types of problems, and that it shuts down and recovers properly to a secure and stable state. (Please refer to Chapter 5 for more information on TCB components and activities.)

Input and Output Controls

Garbage in, garbage out.

What is inputted into an application has a direct correlation to what that application outputs; thus, it needs to be monitored for errors and suspicious activity. If a checker at a grocery store continually puts in the amount of $1.20 for each prime rib steak that customers buy, the store could eventually lose a good amount of money. This activity could be done by accident, which would require proper training, or done on purpose, which would require disciplinary actions.

Because so many companies are extremely dependent upon computers and applications to process their data, input and output controls are very important. Chapter 10 addresses illegal activities that take place when users alter the data going into a program or the output generated by a program, usually for financial gain.

The applications themselves also need to be programmed to only accept certain types of values inputted into them and to do some type of logic checking about the received input values. If an application requests the user to input a mortgage value of a property and the user enters 25 cents, the application should ask the user for the value again so that wasted time and processing is not done on an erroneous inputted value. Also, if an application has a field that is to be used for holding monetary values, a user should not be able to enter "bob" in the field without the application barking. These and many more input and output controls are discussed in Chapter 11.

It is important that all of the controls mentioned in the previous sections are in place and continue to function in a predictable and secure fashion so that the systems, applications, and the environment as a whole continue to be operational.

Electronic Mail Security

The Internet was first developed mainly for government agencies and universities to communicate and share information, but today businesses depend upon it for productivity and profitability. Millions of individuals depend upon it for their window to a larger world and as a quick and efficient communication tool.

E-mail has become an important and integrated part of people's lives. It is used to communicate with family and friends, business partners and customers, coworkers and management, and online merchants and government offices. Generally, the security, authenticity, and integrity of an e-mail message are not considered in day-to-day use. Users are more aware that attachments can carry viruses than of the fact that an e-mail can be easily spoofed and its contents can be changed while in transmission.

It is very easy to spoof e-mail messages, meaning altering the name in the From field. All a user needs to do is modify information within the preferences section of his mail client and restart the application. An attacker could send a message to the CEO's secretary telling her that the IT department is having problems with some servers, and if she could change her network logon to "password" it would really help them out. If she receives this e-mail and the From field has the network administrator's name in it, she will probably fulfill this request without thinking twice.

This type of activity is rare today, but will probably become more used as a social engineering tactic. The solution requires proper authentication to ensure that the message actually came from the source indicated. Companies that regard security as one of their top priorities would implement an e-mail protection application like Pretty Good Privacy (PGP) or use a public key infrastructure (PKI) and digital signatures. These companies may also consider using an encryption protocol to help fight against network sniffing and the unauthorized interception of messages.

An e-mail message that travels from Arizona to Maine has many hops in between the source and destination. There are several potential interception points that can allow an attacker to intercept, view, modify, or delete the message during its journey, as shown in Figure 12-1.

If a user is going to use a security scheme to protect his messages from eavesdropping, modification, and forgery, he and the recipient must use the same encryption scheme. If public key cryptography is going to be used, both users must have a way to exchange encryption keys. This is true for PGP, digital signatures, and S/MIME, which are discussed in detail in Chapter 8. This type of protection happens at the application and presentation layers of the Open System Interconnect (OSI) model. If an administrator, or security professional, wants to ensure that all messages are encrypted between two points and does not want to have to depend on the users to properly encrypt their messages, she can implement Secure Sockets Layer (SSL) (also discussed in Chapter 8).

How E-mail Works

I think e-mail is delivered by an e-mail fairy wearing a purple dress. Response: Exactly.

A user has a mail client that is used to create, modify, address, send, receive, and forward messages. This client can provide other functionality such as using a personal

Figure 12-1   There are several possible points where an e-mail message can be intercepted.

address book, adding attachments, setting flags, recalling messages, and storing messages within different folders.

Great, the user has created a lovely message through his e-mail client, but the message is of no use unless it is actually sent somewhere. This is where *Simple Mail Transfer Protocol (SMTP)* comes in. SMTP works as a message transfer agent, as shown in Figure 12-2, and moves the message from the user's computer to the mail server when the user clicks the Send button. SMTP is also a message-exchange standard and most people are used to seeing its familiar addressing scheme: *something@somewhere.com*.

Many times a message will need to travel throughout the Internet and through different mail servers before arriving at its destination mail server. SMTP is the protocol that will carry this message and it works on top of the Transmission Control Protocol (TCP). TCP is used as the transport protocol because it is a reliable protocol and will provide sequencing and acknowledgments to ensure that the e-mail message arrived successfully at its destination.

The user's e-mail client must be SMTP compliant to be properly configured to use this protocol. The client provides an interface to the user so that he can create and modify messages as needed, and then the client passes the message off to SMTP. So if the analogy of a post office was used, the e-mail client could be the typewriter a person uses to write the message, SMTP could be the mail courier who picks up the mail and delivers it to the post office, and the post office could be the mail server. The mail server has the responsibility of understanding where the message is heading and properly routing the message to that destination. The mail server is often referred to as an SMTP server.

The most common SMTP server software within the Unix world is Sendmail, which is actually an e-mail server application. This means that Unix uses Sendmail software to store, maintain, and route e-mail messages. Within the Microsoft world, Microsoft Exchange is mostly used, and in Novell, Groupwise is the common SMTP server. SMTP works

Figure 12-2 SMTP works as a transfer agent for e-mail messages.

closely with two mail server protocols, POP and IMAP, which are explained in the following sections.

POP   *Post Office Protocol (POP)* is an Internet mail server protocol that supports incoming and outgoing messages. The mail server using POP stores and forwards e-mail messages and works with SMTP to move messages between mail servers.

A company may have one POP server that holds employee mailboxes, and larger companies may have several POP servers, one for each department within the organization. There are also Internet POP servers that enable people all over the world to exchange messages.

This system is useful because the messages will be held on the mail server until users are ready to download their messages instead of trying to push messages right to a person's computer, which may be down or offline. The e-mail server can implement different authentication schemes to ensure that an individual is authorized to access a particular mailbox, but it is usually handled through usernames and passwords.

IMAP   *Internet Message Access Protocol (IMAP)* is also an Internet protocol that enables users to access mail on a mail server. IMAP provides the same types of functionality as POP, but has more capabilities and functionality. If a user is using POP, when he accesses his mail server to see if he has received any new messages, all messages are automatically downloaded to his computer. Once the messages are downloaded from the POP server, they are usually deleted from that server. POP can cause frustration for mobile users because the messages are automatically pushed down to their computer or device and they may not have the necessary space to hold all these messages. This is especially true for mobile devices that can be used to access e-mail servers. This is also inconvenient for people checking their mail on other people's computers. If Christina checks her e-mail on Jessica's computer, all of Christina's new mail could be downloaded to Jessica's computer.

If a user uses IMAP instead of POP, she can download all the messages or leave them on the mail server within her remote message folder, referred to as a mailbox. The user can also manipulate the messages within this mailbox on the mail server as if the messages resided on her local computer. She can create or delete messages, search for specific messages, and set and clear flags. This gives the user much more freedom and keeps the messages in a central repository until the user specifically chooses to download all messages from the mail server.

IMAP is a store-and-forward mail server protocol that is considered POP's successor. IMAP also gives administrators more capabilities when it comes to administering and maintaining the users' messages.

E-mail Relaying   *Could you please pass on this irritating message that no one wants? Answer: Sure.* E-mail has changed drastically from the purely mainframe days. In those days, mail used simple Systems Network Architecture (SNA) protocols and ASCII format. Today there are several types of mail systems that run on different operating systems offering a wide range of functionality. Sometimes companies need to implement different types of mail servers and services within the same network, which can become a bit overwhelming and a challenge to secure.

Most companies have their public mail servers in their demilitarized zone (DMZ) and may have one or more mail servers within their local area networks (LANs). The mail servers in the DMZ are in this protected space because they are directly connected to the Internet. These servers should be tightly locked down and their relaying mechanisms should be correctly configured. Mail servers use a *relay agent* to send a message from one mail server to another. This needs to be properly configured so that a company's mail server is not used by another for spamming activity. Spamming is often actually illegal, so the people doing the spamming do not want the traffic to seem as though it originated from their equipment. They will find mail servers on the Internet, or within company DMZs, that have loosely configured relaying mechanisms and use these computers to send their spam. If relays are configured "wide open" on a mail server, it can be used to receive *any* mail message and send it on to the intended recipient, as shown in Figure 12-3. This means that if a company does not properly configure their mail relaying, their server can be used to distribute advertisements for other companies, spam messages, and pornographic material. It is important that mail servers have proper antispam features enabled, which are actually antirelaying features. A company's mail server should only accept mail destined for its domain and not forward messages on to other mail servers and domains.

Many companies employ antivirus and content-filtering applications on their mail servers to try to stop the spread of malicious code and not allow unacceptable messages through the e-mail gateway. It is important to filter both incoming and outgoing messages. This helps ensure that inside employees are not spreading viruses or sending out messages that are against company policy.

References

S/MIME Mail Security: **www.ietf.org/html.charters/smime-charter.html**

Internet Mail Consortium: **www.imc.org**

eMailman: **www.emailman.com**

Internet Message Access Protocol (IMAP): **idm.internet.com/foundation/imap4.shtml**

Facsimile Security

Your covert strategic plans on how we are going to attack Canada are sitting in a fax bin in the front office.

Faxing data is a very popular way of delivering information today and like other types of communication channels, it must be incorporated into the security policy and program of companies.

Fax machines can present some security issues if they are being used to transmit sensitive or confidential information. The information is scanned into the device, transmitted over a phone line, and printed out on the destination fax machine. Many times the

Figure 12-3   Mail servers can be used for spamming if relay functionality is enabled.

received fax just sits in a bin until the recipient walks over to retrieve it. If it contains confidential information, it might not be a good idea to have it just lying around for anyone to see it.

Some companies use *fax servers*, which are systems that manage incoming and outgoing faxed documents. When a fax is received by the fax server, it properly routes it to the individual it is addressed to so that it is not actually printed, but held in an electronic form. Many times the received fax is routed to the recipient's electronic mailbox.

The fax server lets many users transmit documents from their computers to the fax server, as illustrated in Figure 12-4, without having to pass the document through a fax device. This

Figure 12-4   A fax server can be used instead of stand-alone fax devices.

reduces the amount of sensitive documentation that needs to be properly destroyed and can save money on printing and thermal paper required by stand-alone fax machines.

A fax server usually has the capability of enabling someone to print the received faxes, but this can present the same security breaches as a stand-alone fax device. In environments that demand high security levels, the print feature should be disabled so that sensitive documents can be stored and viewed by authorized individuals only and never printed.

Extensive logging and auditing is available for fax servers and should be implemented and monitored in companies that require this level of security. Because data will be traveling to and from the fax server in a cleartext form, some companies may want to implement encryption for faxed materials. A *fax encryptor*, a bulk data link encryption mechanism, may be put into place. The fax encryptor encrypts any and all fax data that hits the network cable or telephone wire. This would be put into place if a company did not want to depend on each individual user to encrypt documents that are faxed; instead, the company is sure that all data leaving that system is properly encrypted.

References

Faximim Fax FAQ: **www.faximum.com/faqs/fax**

Interstar Fax Server: **www.faxserver.com**

Hack and Attack Methods

Several types of attacks have been explained in the chapters throughout this book. This section brings these attack methods, and others that have not be presented, together to show how they are related, how they can be detected, and how they can be countered.

A majority of the tools used by hackers have dual capabilities in that they can be used for good or evil. An attacker could use tool "ABC" to find a vulnerability to exploit, and a security professional could use the same tool to identify a vulnerability so that she could fix it. When this tool is used by black hats (attackers), it is referred to as *hacking*. When a white hat (security professional) uses this tool, it is considered *ethical hacking* or *penetration testing*.

The evolution of the tools used to perform attacks on networks and systems has allowed a moderately skilled individual (sometimes called a *script kiddie*) to perform damaging attacks. This is because the tools are simple to use and often come with a graphical user interface (GUI) that walks the person through the steps of resource identification, network mapping, and the actual attack. The person no longer needs to understand protocol stacks, know what protocols fields are used by different systems, understand how operating systems process program and assembly code, or know how to write program code at all. The user just needs to insert an IP range within a GUI and click Go.

Hacking tools are easily and widely available to anyone who wants them. At one time, these types of tools were only available to a small group of highly skilled people, but today there are hundreds of Web sites devoted to telling people how to perform exploits and providing the tools for a small fee or for free. The ease of use of these tools, the increased interest in hacking, and the deep dependence that companies and people have upon technology have provided the ingredients to a recipe that can cause continuous damage.

Any network administrator who maintains a firewall, or any person who runs a personal firewall on a computer, knows how active the Internet is with probes and port scanners. These front-end protection devices are continually getting hit with packets requesting information. Some probes are looking for specific types of computers such as Unix systems, Web servers, or databases because the attacker has specific types of attacks she wants to carry out and these attacks target specific types of operating systems or applications. These probes could also be looking to plant Trojan horses or viruses in computers in the hope of causing destruction or compromising the systems so that they can be used in future distributed denial-of-service (DDoS) attacks. These probes scan thousands of networks and computers with no one target in mind. They just look for any and all vulnerabilities, and the attacker does not necessarily care where the vulnerable system happens to be located.

Sometimes the attacker has a specific target in mind and thus does not send out a wide sweeping probe. When an attacker identifies her target, she will do network mapping and port scanning. Network-mapping tools send out seemingly benign packets to many different systems on a network. These systems respond to the packets, and the mapping tool interrogates the returned packets to find out what systems are up and running, the types of systems that responded, and possibly their place within the network. This might seem like a lot of information from just some packets being sent out, but these tools are highly calibrated to dig as much data from the returned packet as possible. Different operating systems vary in their protocol stacks, meaning they use different fields within protocol frames or populate those fields differently than other operating systems. So if the tool sent a message to two computers running different operating systems, they may respond with two slightly different answers. They may both respond with the same basic answer using the same protocol, but because the two operating systems use varied protocol stacks, one computer may use a certain value within the response and the other system may use a different value within its response, as shown in Figure 12-5. When the tool receives these two slightly different responses, it can determine what type of operating system just replied. The tool and the attacker start to put together the topology of the victim's network.

The network-mapping tool has a database that maps operating systems, applications, and versions to the type of responses and message field they use. So if the networking tool received a reply from its ICMP ping sweep, which sends out ICMP packets to targets within a configured IP address range, and one reply has the ICMP "Don't fragment" bit enabled, the tool may determine that the target is a Unix host. Or if the tool sent out a TCP SYN packet and the response received was a FIN/ACK, the tool may determine that the target is a Windows NT system. This activity is referred to as *operating system fingerprinting*.

Figure 12-5   A tool can be used to determine the type of operating system with which an attacker is communicating.

It is important to the attacker to know what systems are alive on the network. When the tool first sends out packets, it is looking to see what computers respond, which indicates they are powered on and alive. Normally, when a computer sends a SYN packet, it is requesting to set up a conversation channel with the destination computer and is the first step in the TCP handshaking procedure. However, hacking tools that use the SYN packet have no intention of setting up a real conversation channel, but hope to trick the target system into replying. The normal response to a SYN packet is SYN/ACK, but the network administrator may have blocked this type of traffic at the firewall or router or disabled the port on the computer. The attacker may receive no response or receive a message saying "Port Unreachable." This response tells the network-mapping tool that the company's firewall allows this type of traffic to enter the network, but that specific port is closed on the target machine. These are all clues used by the attacker to learn more and more about an environment. This knowledge enables her to figure out the most successful ways of attacking.

So, the first step for the attacker is to find out what systems are alive, attempt to find out what type of operating systems the targets are running, and start to build the network's topology. The next step for an attacker is to do a port scanning on the target machines. *Port scanning* identifies open ports on a computer. Ports provide doors into the operating system for other computers, processes, protocols, and attackers. If an attacker can find out what ports are open, she can have a pretty good idea of what services are running on the systems. Knowing what services are available can further clarify the type of system the target is. For example, if a target computer responds to an SMTP packet sent to its port 25, the attacker could think that this computer may be an e-mail server. However, more work would need to be done to confirm this.

The attacker wants to know what operating systems, applications, and services are running so that she knows what type of attacks to run. If she finds a Unix server running Apache, she must run totally different types of attacks on it than if she found a Windows 2000 server running Exchange. Each operating system, application, and service has its own vulnerabilities, and properly identifying these enables the attacker to be more successful in her attack.

There are 65,535 TCP and 65,535 UDP ports on every computer system. The first 1,024 are said to be well-known ports. This means that a specific port number under 1,025 is usually mapped to a well-known and used protocol. For instance, port 80 is almost always mapped to the Hypertext Transfer Protocol (HTTP) protocol, port 21 is mapped to the File Transfer Protocol (FTP), and port 25 is mapped to SMTP. These ports can be reconfigured so that port 21 is mapped to HTTP, let's say, but that is very uncommon.

A port scanning utility is used to find out what ports are open on a system so the attacker knows what doors are available to her. This tool will send packets to each and every port on a system and listen for its response. If there is no response or a message indicating "Port Unreachable," this usually indicates that the port and its corresponding service is disabled. If a predictable response comes from the port, the attacker knows the port is open and available for attack.

A port needs to be open and available for functionality. For example, most networks require the use of SMTP, port 25, for e-mail activity. The administrator needs to put a

Countermeasures to Port Scanning and Network Mapping

- Disable unnecessary ports and services.
- Block access at the perimeter network using firewalls, routers, and proxy servers.
- Use an IDS to identify this type of activity.
- Use TCP Wrappers on vulnerable services that have to be available.
- Remove as many banners as possible within operating systems and applications.
- Upgrade or update to more secure operating systems, applications, and protocols.

barrier between the potential attackers and this vulnerable port and its service. Of course, the first step is to implement a perimeter network with firewalls, proxy servers, and routers that only permit acceptable connections to the internal hosts. However, if an administrator or security professional wanted to add another layer of protection, he could implement *TCP Wrappers*. These wrappers monitor incoming network traffic and control what can and cannot access the services mapped to specific ports. When a request comes to a computer at a specific port, the target operating system will check to see if this port is enabled. If it is enabled and the operating system sees that the corresponding service is wrapped, it knows to look at an access control list, which spells out who can access this service. If the person or computer attempting to access this service is allowed within the access control list, the operating system allows the connection to be made. If this person or computer is not allowed, the packet is dropped or a message is sent back to the initiator of the request indicating that the request is refused.

At this point, the attacker has an idea of what systems are alive, what ports are open, and what services are listening and available for attack. Although the search for exploitable vulnerabilities is becoming more focused, there is still an incredible amount of possible vulnerabilities one network can have. Sometimes attackers specialize in a few specific attacks that they know well enough to carry out manually or have scripts that carry out specific attacks for them. But many attackers want a large range of possible attacks available to them, so they use *vulnerability scanning tools*.

Vulnerability scanning tools have a large database of vulnerabilities and the capability to exploit many of the vulnerabilities they identify. New vulnerabilities are found each week in operating systems, Web servers, database software, and applications. It can be overwhelming to try to keep up to date on each of these and the proper steps to carry them out. The vulnerability scanners can do this for the security professional—and unfortunately, for the attacker. These tools have an engine that can connect to the target machine and run through its database of vulnerabilities to see which apply to the target machine. Some tools can even go a step further and attempt the exploit to determine the actual degree of vulnerability.

There are several types of vulnerability scanners available. Security Administrator Tool for Analyzing Networks (SATAN) and Nessus are two products.

As stated earlier, these tools are dual in nature. Network administrators and security professionals should be using these types of tools on their environments to see what vulnerabilities are present and available to potential attackers. This way when a vulnerability or weakness is uncovered, the security professional can fix it before an attacker finds it.

Superzapping

I am going to use my magic tool and you will never know about my activities.

Computer systems sometimes malfunction, freeze, or enter a state that cannot be fixed by normal recovery procedures. This is the reason that superzapper programs were written. A *superzapping* program is a utility used in IBM mainframe centers that has the capability to bypass access controls within the mainframe's operating system. An administrator would use this tool in the rare cases when nothing else seems to work and the operating system, or program, needs specific attention and possibly reconfiguration.

These programs can be very useful to administrators, but are dangerous if they are not properly protected and end up in an attacker's hands. The tool can enable changes to take place to operating systems and system files that cannot be easily detected, because this type of activity is not usually logged. In many cases, the only way to detect the improper use of a superzapping utility is by comparing the sizes of the files to the original or parent files. This is a functionality that intrusion detection systems carry out.

Today the label "superzapper" has been expanded upon to be any tool that can make modifications that are not auditable or logged.

Browsing

I am looking for something, but I have no idea what it looks like.

Browsing is a general term used by intruders to obtain information that they are not authorized to access. This type of attack takes place when an attacker is looking for sensitive data, but does not know the format the data is in (word processing document, spreadsheet, database, piece of paper). Browsing can be accomplished by looking through another person's files kept on a server or workstation, rummaging through garbage looking for information that was carelessly thrown away, or reviewing information that has been saved on floppy disks. A more advanced and sophisticated example of browsing is when an intruder accesses residual information on storage media. The original user may have deleted the files from a floppy disk, but as stated earlier, this only removes the pointers to the files within the file system on that disk. The talented intruder can access this data (residual information) and access information that he is unauthorized to obtain.

Another type of browsing attack is called *shoulder surfing*, where a user looks over another's shoulder to see items on that person's monitor or what is being typed in at the keyboard.

Sniffers

A *network sniffer* is a tool that monitors traffic as it passes by. Administrators and network engineers often use sniffers to diagnose network problems. Sniffers are also referred to as network analyzers or protocol analyzers. When used as a diagnostic tool, a sniffer enables the administrator to see what type of traffic is being generated in the hope of getting closer to the root of the network problem. When it is used as a tool by an attacker, usernames, passwords, and confidential information can be captured as they travel over the network.

The tool is usually a piece of software that runs on a computer with its network interface card (NIC) in promiscuous mode. NICs usually only pay attention to traffic addressed to them, but if they are in promiscuous mode, they see all traffic that is going past them on the network wire. Once a computer has been compromised by an attacker, the attacker will often install a sniffer on that system to look for interesting traffic. Some sniffers only look for passwords that are being transmitted and ignore the rest. Sniffers have been very successful because a majority of LANs use Ethernet, which is a broadcast technology. Because so much data is continually broadcast, it is easily available for an attacker who has planted a sniffer on a network segment. However, sniffers are becoming less successful because of the move to switched environments. Switched environments separate network segments by broadcast and collision domains. If the attacker is not within the broadcast and collision domain of the environment she is interested in sniffing, she will not receive the information she is looking for. This is because a switch is usually configured so that the required source and destination ports on the switch carry the traffic; thus, it is not blasted for everyone in the vicinity to hear. Switched traffic travels from point A to point B through the switch and does not spill over to every computer on the network like purely Ethernet networks do. (Broadcast and collision domains are discussed in detail in Chapter 7.)

To combat sniffers within an environment, secure versions of services and protocols should be used whenever possible. Many services and protocols were developed to provide functionality and not security, but once it was figured out that security is also required in many environments, the protocols and services were improved upon to provide the same functionality and security. Several protocols have a secure version. This means the regular protocol operates in a way that has vulnerabilities that can be exploited and a more secure version has been developed to counter those vulnerabilities. One example is *Secure RPC (S-RPC)*, which uses Diffie-Hellman public key cryptography to determine the shared secret key for encryption with the DES algorithm. If S-RPC is used in an environment, a sniffer can capture this data, but not necessarily decrypt it.

Most protocols are vulnerable because they do not require strong authentication, if it is required at all. For example, the *r-utilities* used in Unix (rexec, rsh, rlogin, and rcp) are known to have several weaknesses. Authentication is usually provided through a .rhosts file that looks at IP addresses instead of individual usernames and passwords. These utilities should be replaced with ones that require stronger authentication like S-RPC and Secure Shell (SSH).

Session Hijacking

Many attackers spoof their addresses, meaning that the address within the frame that is used to commit the attack has an IP address that is not theirs. This makes it much harder to track down the attacker, which is the attacker's purpose for spoofing in the first place. This also enables an attacker to hijack sessions between two users without being noticed.

If an attacker wanted to take over a session between two computers, she would need to put herself in the middle of their conversation without being detected. Two tools used for this are Juggernaut (**www.packetfactory.net**) and the HUNT project (**lin.fsid.cvut.cz/~kra**). These tools enable the attacker to spy on the TCP connection and then hijack it if the attacker decides that is what she wants to do.

If Kristy and David were communicating over a TCP session and the attacker wanted to bump David off and trick Kristy into thinking she is still communicating with David, the attacker would use a tool to spoof her address to be the same as David's and temporarily take David off the network with a type of DoS attack. Once this is in place, when Kristy sends a message to David, it actually goes to the attacker and the attacker can respond to Kristy. Kristy thinks she is getting a reply from David. The attacker may also choose to leave David on the network and intercept each of the users' messages, read them, and repackage them with headers that indicate that no session hijacking took place, as shown in Figure 12-6.

If session hijacking is a concern on a network, the administrator can implement a protocol that requires mutual authentication between users or systems like IPSec or

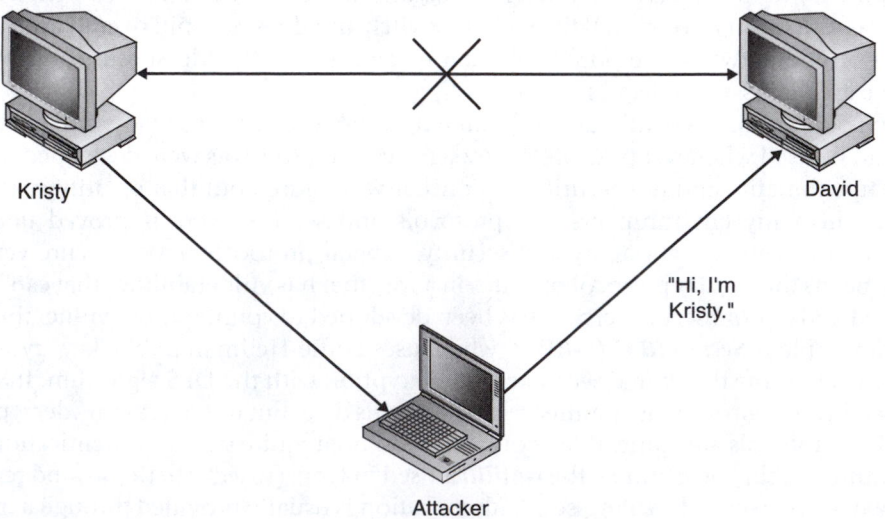

Figure 12-6   Session hijacking between Kristy and David

Kerberos. Because the attacker will not have the necessary credentials to authenticate to a user, she cannot act as an imposter and hijack sessions.

Password Cracking

Chapter 4 discussed access control and authentication methods in depth. Although there are various ways of authenticating a user, most of the time a static password is the method of choice for many companies. This is because the computing society is used to using static passwords; this is how many systems and applications have their authentication processes coded, and it is an easier technique to maintain and cheaper than other options such as smart cards or biometrics.

However, this static password method is easily cracked when a determined attacker has the right tools. John the Ripper is an example of a sniffer and password cracker that listens for authentication data being passed over network cables. Once the data is captured, the attacker can initiate a dictionary attack using the same tool to try and reveal the captured password. The powerful tools Crack and L0phtcrack are also used to perform dictionary and brute force attacks on the captured password or password file.

A strong password policy is a major countermeasure to password-cracking efforts. The policy should dictate that passwords should be at least eight characters with upper- and lowercase letters and two special characters (*.,$@). If the passwords are long, contain special characters, and are hard to guess, it will take cracking tools much longer to uncover them. The longer this process takes, the higher the chance of the attacker moving on to an easier victim. Software applications and add-ons are available to ensure that the password that each user chooses meets the company's security policy.

Backdoors

In Chapter 5, backdoors and some of the potential damage that can be caused by them are discussed. We also looked at how backdoors are inserted into the code so a developer

---

Dictionary and Brute Force Attacks

A *dictionary attack* is when a large list of words is fed into a password hacking tool. This tool runs a one-way hash on the captured password and on each word in the list. The tool compares the hashing results to see if they match. If they do match, the tool has discovered the password; if not, it moves to the next word in the list.

In a *brute force attack*, a tool will try many different variations of characters, run a hash value on each variation, and compare it to the hash value of the captured password. A dictionary attack and a brute force attack are often used together. If a tool first runs a dictionary attack and figures out that the first seven characters of the captured password are Jeffery, the brute force piece will kick in and try different variations of this password, like Jeffery1, Jeffery001, Jeffery01, Jeffery2, JefferyL, and so on until it finds a match.

can access the software at a later time, bypassing the usual security authentication and authorization steps. Now we will look at how and why attackers install backdoors on victims' computers.

A backdoor is a program that is installed by an attacker to enable her to come back into the computer at a later date without having to supply login credentials or go through any type of authorization process. Access control is thwarted by the attacker because she can later gain access to the compromised computer. The backdoor program actually listens on specific ports for the attacker, and once the attacker accesses those ports, the backdoor program lets her come right in.

An attacker can compromise a computer and install the backdoor program or hide the code within a virus or Trojan horse that will install the backdoor when a predefined event takes place. Many times these backdoors are installed so that the attacker can later control the computer remotely to perform the tasks she is interested in. The tools used for backdoor remote control actions are Back Orifice (**www.bo2k.com**), NetBus, and SubSeven (**www.subseven.ws**). A comprehensive list of backdoors and Trojans can be found at **www.tlsecurity.net/tlfaq.htm**.

Today many antivirus software applications and IDSs look for signatures of these tools and scan for the known behavior patterns that they commit. Host-based IDS can be one of the best attempts to detect a backdoor or to install one. Because the backdoor will be listening on specific ports, the host IDS can be configured to detect suspicious port activity. The administrator can also scan for known executables used by backdoor programs, view the startup files and registry entries for suspicious executables, and run checksums on system files to see if any have been altered. These activities are not usually done manually because of the time involved, but are done automatically through the use of antivirus and IDS software. But because attackers are smart and tricky, new tools are continually developed and old tools are morphed so that they will not be detected by these detection applications. The inevitable cat-and-mouse game continues between the hackers and the security community.

The following list contains a brief description of a sampling of attack types you should be familiar with:

- **Denial-of-service (DoS) attack** An attacker sends multiple service requests to the victim's computer until it eventually overwhelms the system, causing it to freeze, reboot, and ultimately not be able to carry out regular tasks.

- **Man-in-the middle attack** An intruder injects herself into an ongoing dialog between two computers so that she can intercept and read messages being passed back and forth. These attacks can be countered with digital signatures and mutual authentication techniques.

- **Spamming** This is an attack used to overwhelm mail servers and clients with unrequested e-mails. E-mail filtering and properly configuring mail relay functionality on mail servers can be used to protect against spamming.

- **Wardialing** This is a brute force attack in which an attacker has a program that systematically dials a large bank of phone numbers with the goal of finding ones that belong to modems instead of telephones. These modems can provide easy access into an environment. The countermeasures are not to publicize these telephone numbers and implement tight access control for modems and modem pools.

- **Ping of Death**   This is a type of DoS attack where oversized ICMP packets are sent to the victim. Systems that are vulnerable to this type of attack do not know how to handle ICMP packets over a specific size and may freeze or reboot. Countermeasures are patching the systems and implementing ingress filtering to detect these types of packets.

- **WinNuk**   This type of DoS attack sends out-of-band packets to port 139. Windows 9x and NT can be vulnerable to this kind of attack. The countermeasures to this attack are to patch the system or upgrade to a later operating system version.

- **Fake login screens**   A fake login screen is created and installed on to the victim's system. When the user attempts to log in to the system, this fake screen is presented to the user and he enters his credentials into it. The screen captures the credentials and exits showing the user the actual login screen for his system. Usually the user just thinks he mistyped his password and attempts to authenticate again without knowing anything malicious just took place. A host-based IDS can be used to detect this type of activity.

- **Teardrop**   This attack sends malformed fragmented packets to a victim. The victim's system usually cannot reassemble the packets correctly and freezes as a result. Countermeasures to this attack are patching the system and using ingress filtering to detect these packet types.

- **Traffic analysis**   This is a method of uncovering information by watching traffic patterns on a network. For example, heavy traffic between HR and headquarters could indicate an upcoming layoff. Traffic padding can be used to counter this kind of attack, in which decoy traffic is sent out over the network to disguise patterns and make it more difficult to uncover patterns.

- **Slamming and cramming**   Slamming is when a user's telephone service provider has been changed without that user's consent. Cramming is adding on charges that are bogus in nature that the user did not request.

This section only talked about some of the possible attacks, and many other types of attacks have been addressed in earlier chapters. One of the most beneficial things a company, network administrator, network engineer, or security professional can do is to develop some good habits that deal with the previously mentioned items. Although it is great that an administrator installs a security patch after he reads about a dangerous attack that has recently become popular, it is more important that he continues to stay on top of all potential risks and vulnerabilities, scans his network regularly, and is aware of some symptomatic effects of particular attacks, viruses, Trojan horses, and backdoors. It can be a tall order to follow, but these good habits, once developed, will keep a network healthy and the administrator's life less chaotic.

Penetration Testing

Penetration testing is a set of procedures designed to test and possibly bypass security controls of a system. Its goal is to measure an organization's resistance to an attack and to uncover any weaknesses within the environment. Organizations need to determine the effectiveness of their security measures and not just trust the promises of the security vendors. Good computer security is based on reality, not on some lofty goals of how things are supposed to work.

A penetration test will emulate the same methods that attackers would use. Attackers can be clever, creative, and resourceful in their techniques, so penetration attacks should align with the newest hacking techniques along with strong foundational testing methods. The test should look at each and every computer in the environment, as shown in Figure 12-7, because an attacker will not necessarily scan one or two computers only and call it a day.

The type of penetration test depends on the organization, its security objectives, and the management's goals. Some corporations perform periodic penetration tests on themselves using different types of tools or they may use scanning devices that continually

Figure 12-7 Penetration tests should be run against all systems periodically.

examine the environment for new vulnerabilities in an automated fashion. Other corporations ask a third party to perform the vulnerability and penetration tests to provide a more objective view.

Penetration tests can evaluate Web servers, DNS servers, router configurations, workstation vulnerabilities, access to sensitive information, remote dial-in access, open ports, and available services properties that a real attacker might use to compromise the company's overall security. Some tests can be quite intrusive and disruptive. The timeframe for the tests should be agreed upon so that productivity is not affected and personnel can bring systems back online if necessary.

The result of a penetration test is a report given to management describing the vulnerabilities that were identified and the severity of those vulnerabilities along with suggestions on how to deal with them properly. From here, it is up to management to determine how the vulnerabilities are actually dealt with and what countermeasures are implemented.

Operations Department

I think this computer is possessed by the devil. Response: Call the operations guy.

Operations security encompasses safeguards and countermeasures to protect resources, information, and the hardware that they reside on. The goal is to reduce the possibility of damage that could result from unauthorized access or disclosure by limiting the opportunities of misuse.

Some organizations may have an actual operations department that is responsible for activities and procedures that are required to keep the network running smoothly and to keep productivity at a certain level. Other organizations may have individuals who are responsible for these things, but there is no structured department dedicated just to operations. Either way there are certain things that people who hold these responsibilities are accountable for and specific issues that must be monitored and controlled.

Operations within a computing environment can pertain to software, personnel, and hardware, but an operations department often focuses on the hardware and software aspects. Management is responsible for employees' behavior and responsibilities. The people within the operations department are responsible for ensuring that systems are protected and that they continue to run in a predictable manner.

The operations department usually has the objectives of preventing reoccurring problems, reducing hardware failures to an acceptable level, and reducing the impact of hardware failure or disruption. This group should investigate any unusual or unexplained occurrences, unscheduled initial program loads, deviations from standards, or other odd or abnormal conditions that take place on the network.

Unusual or Unexplained Occurrences

Networks, and the hardware within them, can be complex and dynamic. At times, conditions occur that are at first confusing and possibly unexplainable. It is up to the operations department to investigate these issues, understand the problem, and come up with a logical solution.

One example could be a network that has hosts that are continually kicked off the network for no apparent reason. Controlled troubleshooting should take place to make sure no possibilities are overlooked and that different types of problems are investigated. The team may look at connectivity issues between the hosts and the wiring closet, the hubs and switches that control their connectivity, and any possible cabling defects. The team should work methodically until it finds that one of the NICs on this Token Ring network is malfunctioning and sending out bogus traffic that affects other hosts' connection to the network.

Deviations from Standards

In this instance, standards pertain to computing service levels and how they are measured. Each device can have certain standards applied to it: the hours of time to be online, the number of requests that can be processed within a defined period of time, bandwidth usage, performance counters, and more. These standards provide a baseline that is used to determine if there is a problem with the device or not. For example, if a device usually accepts approximately 300 requests per minute, but suddenly it was only able to accept 3 per minute, the operations team would need to investigate the deviation of this standard that is usually provided by this device. The device may be failing or under a DoS attack.

Sometimes the standard needs to be recalibrated so that it portrays a realistic view of the service level it can provide. If a server was upgraded from a Pentium II to a Pentium III, the memory was quadrupled, the swap file was increased, and three extra hard drives were added, the service level of this server should be reevaluated.

Unscheduled Initial Program Loads (IPLs)

Initial program load (IPL) is a mainframe term for loading the operating system's kernel into the computer's main memory. On a personal computer, booting into the operating system is the equivalent to IPLing. This activity takes place to prepare the computer for user operation.

The operations team needs to investigate computers that reboot for no reason, which could indicate that the operating system is experiencing major problems.

Summary

Operational security has to do with keeping up with implemented solutions, keeping track of changes, properly maintaining systems, continually enforcing necessary standards, and following through with security practices and tasks. It does not do much good for a company to develop a strong password policy if after a few months enforcement gets lax and users can use whatever passwords they want. It is similar to working out and staying physically fit. Just because someone lifts weights and jogs for a week does not mean he can spend the rest of the year eating jelly donuts and expect to stay physically fit. It requires discipline day in and day out, sticking to a regime, and practicing due care.

Quick Tips

- Facilities that house systems that process sensitive information should have physical access controls to limit access to authorized personnel.

- Data should be classified, and the necessary technical controls should be put into place to protect its integrity, confidentiality, and availability.

- System and audit logs should be monitored and protected from unauthorized modification.

- Sensitive data should not be printed and left at stand-alone printers or fax devices.

- Users should have the necessary security level to access data and resources, but must also have a need-to-know.

- Clipping levels should be implemented, which establishes a baseline of user activity and acceptable errors.

- Separation of responsibilities and duties should be in place so that if fraud takes place it requires collusion.

- Sensitive information should contain the correct markings and labels to indicate the corresponding sensitivity level.

- Contract and temporary staff members should have more restrictive controls put upon their accounts.

- Access should be restricted to printed output storage areas.

- Change control and configuration management should be put into place so that changes are approved, documented, tested, and properly implemented.

- Systems should not allow their bootup sequences to be altered in a way that could bypass operating system security mechanisms.

- Potential employees should have background investigations, references, experience, and education claims checked out.

- Proper fault tolerant mechanisms should be put into place to counter equipment failure.

- Antivirus and IDS signatures should be updated on a continual basis.

- System, network, policy, and procedure changes should be documented and communicated.

- When media is reused, it should contain no residual data.

- Media holding data must be properly purged, which could be zeroization, degaussing, or media destruction.

- Penetration testing should be done on a regular basis to identify new vulnerabilities.

- The operations department is responsible for any unusual or unexplained occurrences, unscheduled initial program loads, and deviations from standards.

- A teardrop attack involves malformed fragmented packets sent to a vulnerable system.

- A superzapper program is a utility used in IBM mainframe centers that has the capability to bypass access controls. Their activities are not logged.

- Improper mail relay configurations allow for mail servers to be used to forward spam messages.

- A browsing attack is when an attacker is looking for sensitive information without knowing what format it is in.

- A fax encryptor will encrypt all fax data leaving a fax server.

- A system can fail in one of the following manners: system reboot, emergency system restart, and system cold start.

- The main goal of operation security is to protect resources.

- Operational assurance looks at how a product was developed and tested. Life cycle assurance looks at each phase of the product, including maintenance procedures used in the production environment.

Questions

Please remember that these questions are formatted and asked in a certain way for a reason. You must remember that the CISSP exam is asking questions at a conceptual level. Questions may not always have the perfect answer, and the candidate is advised against always looking for the perfect answer. The candidate should look for the best answer in the list.

1. Which of the following best describes operation security?

   A. Continual vigilance about hacker activity and possible vulnerabilities

   B. Enforcing access control and physical security

   C. Taking steps to make sure an environment, and the things with in it, stay at a certain level of protection

   D. Doing strategy planning to develop a secure environment and then implementing it properly

2. Which of the following describes why operation security is important?

   A. An environment continually changes and has the potential of lowering its level of protection.

   B. It helps an environment be functionally sound and unproductive.

   C. It ensures that there will be no unauthorized access to the facility or its resources.

   D. It continually raises a company's level of protection.

3. What is the difference between due care and due diligence?

   A. Due care is the continual effort of ensuring that the right thing takes place, and due diligence is the continual effort to stay compliant to regulations.

   B. Due care and due diligence are in contrast to the "prudent person" concept.

   C. They mean the same thing.

   D. Due diligence is investigating the risks, and due care is carrying out the necessary steps to mitigate these risks.

4. Why should employers make sure employees take their vacations?

   A. They have a legal obligation.

   B. It is part of due diligence.

   C. It is a way that fraud can be uncovered.

   D. To ensure the employee does not get burnt out.

5. Which of the following best describes separation of duties and job rotation?

   A. Separation of duties ensures that more than one employee knows how to perform the tasks of a position, and job rotation ensures that one person cannot perform a high-risk task alone.

   B. Separation of duties ensures that one person cannot perform a high-risk task alone, and job rotation can uncover fraud and ensure that more than one person knows the tasks of a position.

   C. They are the same thing with different titles.

   D. They are administrative controls that enforce access control and protect the company's resources.

6. If a programmer is restricted from updating and modifying production code, what is this an example of?

   A. Rotation of duties

   B. Due diligence

   C. Separation of duties

   D. Controlling input values

7. Why is it important to control and audit input and output values?

   A. Incorrect values can cause mistakes in data processing and can be evidence of fraud.

   B. Incorrect values can be the fault of the programmer and not comply with the due care clause.

   C. Incorrect values can be caused by brute force attacks.

   D. Incorrect values are not security issues.

8. What is the difference between least privilege and need-to-know?

A. A user should have least privilege that restricts her need-to-know.

B. A user should have a security clearance to access resources, a need-to-know about those resources, and least privilege to give her full control of all resources.

C. A user should have a need-to-know to access particular resources, and least privilege should be implemented to ensure she only accesses the resources she has a need-to-know.

D. They are two terms for the same issue.

9. Which of the following would not require updated documentation?

A. Antivirus signature update

B. Reconfiguration of a server

C. Change in security policy

D. Installing a patch to a production server

10. If sensitive data is stored on a CD-ROM and it is no longer needed, which would be the proper way of disposing of the data?

A. Degaussing

B. Erasing

C. Purging

D. Physical destruction

11. If SSL is being used to encrypt messages that are transmitted over the network, what is a major concern of the security professional?

A. The network segments that have systems that use different versions of SSL.

B. If the user encrypted the message with an application layer product, it will be incompatible with SSL.

C. Network tapping and wiretapping.

D. The network segments that the message will travel on that the company does not control.

12. What is the purpose of SMTP?

A. To enable users to decrypt mail messages from a server

B. To enable users to view and modify mail messages from a server

C. To transmit mail messages from the client to the mail server

D. To encrypt mail messages before being transmitted

13. If a company has been contacted because its mail server has been used to spread spam, what is most likely the problem?

    A. The internal mail server has been compromised by an internal hacker.

    B. The mail server in the DMZ has private and public resource records.

    C. The mail server has e-mail relaying enabled.

    D. The mail server has SMTP enabled.

14. Which of the following is not a reason that fax servers are used in many companies?

    A. They save money by not needing individual fax devices and the constant use of fax paper.

    B. They provide a secure way of faxing instead of having faxed papers sitting in bins waiting to be picked up.

    C. Faxes can be routed to employees' electronic mailboxes.

    D. They reduce the need for any other communication security mechanisms.

15. If a company wants to protect fax data while it is in transmission, which of the following are valid mechanisms?

    A. PGP and MIME

    B. PEM and TSL

    C. Data link encryption or fax encryptor

    D. Data link encryption and MIME

16. What is the purpose of TCP Wrappers?

    A. Monitor requests for certain ports and control access to sensitive files

    B. Monitor requests for certain services and control access to password files

    C. Monitor requests for certain services and control access to those services

    D. Monitor requests to system files and ensure they are not modified

17. How do network sniffers work?

    A. They probe systems on a network segment.

    B. They listen for ARP requests and ICMP packets.

    C. They require an extra NIC to be installed and configured.

    D. They put the NIC into promiscuous mode.

18. Which of the following is not an attack against operations?

    A. Brute force

    B. Denial of service

    C. Buffer overflow

    D. Known plaintext attack

19. Why should user IDs be included in data captured by auditing procedures?

    A. Shows what files were attacked

    B. Establishes individual accountability

    C. Needed to detect a denial-of-service attack

    D. Activates corrective measures

20. Which of the following controls requires separate entities, operating together, to complete a task?

    A. Least privilege

    B. Data hiding

    C. Dual control

    D. Administrative

21. Which of the following would not be considered an operations media control task?

    A. Compressing and decompressing storage materials

    B. Erasing data when its retention period is over

    C. Storing backup information in a protected area

    D. Controlling access to media and logging activities

22. How are clipping levels a way to track violations?

    A. They set a baseline for normal user errors, and any violations that exceed that threshold should be recorded and reviewed to understand why they are happening.

    B. They enable the administrator to view all reduction levels that have been made to user codes, which have incurred violations.

    C. They disallow the administrator to customize the audit trail to record only those violations that are deemed security related.

    D. They enable the administrator to customize the audit trail to capture only access violations and denial-of-service attacks.

23. Tape library management is an example of operations security through which of the following?

    A. Archival retention

    B. Reviewing clipping levels

    C. Resource protection

    D. Change management

24. A device that generates coercive magnetic force for the purpose of reducing magnetic flux density to zero on media is called:

    A. Magnetic saturation

    B. Magnetic field

    C. Physical destruction

    D. Degausser

25. Which of the following controls might force a person in operations into collusion with personnel assigned organizationally within a different function for the sole purpose of gaining access to data he is not authorized to access?

    A. Limiting the local access of operations personnel

    B. Enforcing auditing

    C. Enforcing job rotation

    D. Limiting control of management personnel

Answers

1. C. All of these are necessary security activities and procedures; they just don't all fall under the operations umbrella. Operations is about keeping production up and running in a healthy and secure manner. Operations is not usually the entity that reviews hacker activities and researches vulnerabilities. They do not enforce access control and physical security, and they do not do the necessary strategic planning. They work at an operational day-to-day level, not the higher strategic level.

2. A. This is the best answer because operations has the goal of keeping everything running smoothly each and every day. They will implement new software and hardware and carry out the necessary security tasks passed down to them. As the environment changes and security is kept in the loop with these changes, there is a smaller likelihood of opening up vulnerabilities.

3. D. Due care and due diligence are legal terms that do not just pertain to security. Due diligence is going through the necessary steps to know what a company or individual's actual risks are, and due care is carrying out responsible actions to reduce those risks. These concepts correspond with the "prudent person" concept.

4. C. Many times employees who are carrying out fraudulent activities do not take the vacation they have earned because they do not want anyone to find out what they have been doing. Forcing employees to take vacations means that someone else has to do that person's job and possibly uncover any misdeeds.

5. **B.** Rotation of duties allows for a company to have more than one person trained in a position and can uncover fraudulent activities. Separation of duties is put into place to ensure that one entity cannot carry out a critical task alone.

6. **C.** There are several examples of separation of duties, this is just one of them. It is important that a system is set up for proper code manipulation to take place when necessary, instead of allowing a programmer to make changes arbitrarily. These types of changes should go through a change control process and should have more entities involved instead of just one programmer.

7. **A.** There should be controls in place to make sure that the data that is inputted into a system and the results that are generated are in the proper format and have expected values. Improper data being put into an application or system could cause bad output and security issues, such as buffer overflows.

8. **C.** Users should only be able to access the resources they need to fulfill the duties of their positions. They also should only have the level of permissions and rights for those resources that is required to carry out the exact operations they need for their jobs and no more. This second concept is more granular than the first, but they have a symbiotic relationship.

9. **A.** Documentation is very important for data processing and networked environments. This task often gets pushed to the back burner or is totally ignored. If things are not properly documented, employees will forget what actually took place with each device. If the environment needs to be rebuilt, for example, it may be done incorrectly if the procedure was poorly or improperly documented. And when new changes need to be implemented, the current infrastructure may not be totally understood. Continually documenting when virus signatures are updated would be an overkill. The other answers contain events that certainly require documentation.

10. **D.** One cannot properly erase data that is held on a CD-ROM. If the data is sensitive and you need to ensure that no one has access to it, the media should be physically destroyed.

11. **D.** This is not a great question, but could be something you run into on the exam. Let's look at the answers. Different SSL versions are usually not a concern because the two communicating systems will negotiate and agree upon the necessary version. There is no security violation issue here. SSL works at the transport layer; thus will not be affected by what the user does, as stated in answer B. SSL protects against network tapping and wiretapping. Answer D talks about the network segments the company does not own. This is the best answer out of the four, but a company would use SSL to protect data that is traversing through other's equipment. If the data is very sensitive and has to travel outside of the company's network and SSL does not provide the necessary level of protection, a VPN connection may be set up.

12. **C.** Simple Mail Transfer Protocol (SMTP) is the protocol used to allow clients to send e-mail messages to each other. It allows different mail servers to exchange messages.

13. **C.** Spammers will identify the mail servers on the Internet that have relaying enabled and are "wide open," meaning the server will forward any e-mail messages it receives. These servers are put on a blacklist and the servers are used by many different spammers to hide the true origin of the spam messages.

14. **D.** The other three answers provide reasons why fax servers would be used instead of individual fax machines: ease of use, provides more protection, and supplies can be cheaper.

15. **C.** This is the best answer for this question. The other components could provide different levels of protection, but a fax encryptor (which is a data link encryptor) provides a higher level of protection across the board because everything is encrypted. Even if a user does not choose to encrypt something, it will be encrypted anyway before it is sent out the fax server.

16. **C.** This is a product that wraps the different services that are available on a system. What this means is that if a remote user makes a request to access a service, this product will intercept this request and make a determination whether this request is valid and legal before allowing the interaction to take place.

17. **D.** A sniffer is a device or software component that puts the NIC in promiscuous mode, meaning the NIC will pick up all frames it "sees" instead of just the frames addressed to that individual computer. The sniffer then shows the output to the user. It can have capture and filtering capabilities.

18. **D.** The first three are attacks that can directly affect security operations, but known plaintext attack is an attack against cryptography used in the environment, not a direct attack on operations.

19. **B.** For auditing purposes the procedure should capture user ID, time of event, type of event, and source workstation. User ID allows individuals to be accountable for their actions.

20. **C.** Dual control requires that two or more entities work together to complete a task. An example is key recovery. If a key needs to be recovered, and it requires two or more people to authenticate to a system, the act of them coming together and carrying out these activities is known as dual control. This reduces the possibility of fraud.

21. **A.** The last three tasks fall under the job functions of an individual or department that is responsible for controlling access to media. Compressing and decompressing data does not.

22. **A.** Clipping levels are thresholds of acceptable user errors. If the threshold is exceeded, it should be logged and the administrator should decide if malicious activities are taking place or if the user needs more training.

23. **C.** The reason to have tape library management is to have a centralized and a standard way of protecting how media is stored, accessed, and destroyed.

24. **D.** A degausser is a device that generates a magnetic field (coercive magnetic force) that changes the orientation of the bits held on the media (reducing magnetic flux density to zero).

25. **A.** If the operations personnel is limited from what they can access, they would need to participate in collusion with someone who actually has access to the resource. This is a very painful question in the way that it is written, but very close to the way many CISSP exam questions are formatted.

Security Policies

Security policies provide the foundation for an organization's security infrastructure. A *security policy* is a document or set of documents that conveys the management's intentions and decision on how security will play a role within the organization. High-level and typically not technical in nature, security policies are put into place to protect the organization's assets, ensuring that mechanisms are established to protect the assets' confidentiality, availability, and integrity. Policies can also reduce legal liability by following the due care concept.

A security policy should identify critical and important business resources, activities, and operations. Roles within the organization need to be defined, and the type of access each role or group requires for these critical pieces of the organization should be outlined. Then management should decide what degree of access each role or group is allowed and also the type of security controls that should be put into place to ensure that these directives are followed and enforced.

Types of Security Policies

In smaller organizations, it may be possible to have one security policy that covers all necessary subjects. Most organizations, however, are diverse enough to require one general policy and then establish smaller policies that are more specific in nature and support the more general policy. The reason for specialized policies is that there may be specific issues that the management feels need to be addressed in order to have no confusion on the management's security requirements. These specialized policies also provide the company with a stronger legal standing if the policies ever come into question. Some of these can include e-mail usage, remote access, Internet usage, information protection, and extranet and partnership relationships.

There are specific questions that need to be asked and answered when it comes to writing issue- or functionality-oriented policies. The following sections cover some of the questions that should be addressed.

Information Protection Policy

This policy is drafted, implemented, and enforced to identify critical business information and to indicate how the information should be properly protected. The policy should provide high-level guidelines for mid-management, the IT staff, and all employees, which outline how to access and handle various types of information.

The following questions should be asked when developing the policy and answered within the policy:

- What information is critical to business operations?
- What classifications will be used to properly identify the sensitivity level of each type of information?
- How will this information be marked, labeled, and properly destroyed at the end of its life?
- Who requires access to this information and to what extent?
- How will this information be stored and transmitted?
- What type of authorization is required?
- What type of protection should be in place to ensure that the previous issues are enforced?
- What needs to take place for noncompliance activities?
- Who is responsible for enforcing all the issues decided upon within this policy?

Remote Access Policy

This policy outlines and defines what type of remote access will be used within the organization and what is and what is not acceptable as far as remote access is concerned.

The following questions should be asked when developing the policy and answered within the policy:

- Why is remote access required?
- How many and what type of users require remote access?
- What type of remote access should be used in the organization (dial-up, frame relay, Telnet, ATM, and so on)?
- What type of resources and information should remote users have access to?
- What protection mechanisms should be in place to ensure that authorized users can only access the resources authorized?
- What protection mechanisms should be in place to ensure that unauthorized users cannot gain access to the network?
- What type of authorization is required?
- What needs to take place for noncompliance activities?
- Who is responsible for enforcing all the issues decided upon within this policy?

Extranet and Business Partner Policy

If the organization has a connection to another organization's network via an extranet, direct channel, virtual private network (VPN), or any other method, each aspect of this connection should be reviewed and properly planned out prior to implementing it.

The following questions should be asked when developing the policy and answered within the policy:

- What other companies does the organization need to have access to and why?
- How should this connection take place (VPN, extranet, dedicated link, and so on)?
- What resources and information should the other organization(s) have access to?
- What mechanisms should be in place to ensure that these resources are available to them?
- What type of authorization is required?
- Should each organization involved have a security policy for this type of business interaction?
- What measures should be in place to protect the infrastructure from malicious activity pertaining to this type of connection?
- How should the reporting of problems take place?
- What needs to take place for noncompliance activities?
- Who is responsible for enforcing all the issues decided upon within this policy?

Policy Samples

Once these questions have been asked and answered, an actual policy should be drafted. The type of policy and structure and the level of language and formality may be different for different types of organizations.

Information Protection Policy

The following document outlines guidelines for the acceptance, storage, processing, and transmission of information by ABC, Inc. employees. The purpose of this policy is to ensure that information is protected, handled, and transmitted in a secure and appropriate manner. Information should not be modified or disclosed to unauthorized individuals.

In the following text, "users" refers to ABC, Inc. employees and contractors using ABC, Inc. computer systems, resources, and facilities. "Third party" refers to any individual or company not employed by ABC, Inc.

1. Unauthorized modification, transmitting, or other dissemination of proprietary, sensitive, or confidential information of the company is strictly prohibited. Unauthorized dissemination of this information may result in suspension, termination, or result in a substantial civil liability as well as severe criminal penalties under the Economic Espionage Act of 1996.

2. Sensitive and proprietary information should be safely stored and protected while on file servers, workstations, and during any type of transmission. The information should be encrypted and authorized access should be enforced.

3. Any third party must sign a nondisclosure agreement document before entering or touring a facility and before receiving or discussing confidential or proprietary information.

4. Sensitive and proprietary information must be encrypted and digitally signed before it is transmitted across public networks.

5. Any documents, files, attachments, or applications received from outside of ABC, Inc. must be scanned for viruses to protect currently held information.

6. Sensitive and proprietary information should only be accessible to authorized individuals and strict access control, auditing, and monitoring should be in place.

7. The security officer is responsible for ensuring that this policy is properly enforced.

Remote Access Policy

The following document outlines guidelines for individuals to access ABC, Inc.'s computing systems and facility remotely from outside the facility. This includes, but is not limited to, any computer workstation, computer server, device, resources, and network provided by ABC, Inc. The purpose of this document is to ensure that all employees and outside individuals access ABC, Inc. in a secure, predictable, and controlled manner.

In the following text, "users" refers to ABC, Inc. employees and contractors using ABC, Inc. computer systems, resources, and facilities. "Third party" refers to any individual or company not employed by ABC, Inc.

1. Users requiring remote access to ABC, Inc.'s network or resources must be explicitly approved by a department manager and security officer.

2. Any third party that requires access to ABC, Inc.'s network or resources must obtain written approval by management and the security officer. This connection type should be temporary in nature, require strict authentication, and be closely monitored.

3. Users requiring remote access to ABC, Inc.'s network or resources must be adequately authorized via control measures, and a callback method should be implemented for each and every requested connection into the facility.

4. Users requiring remote access to ABC, Inc.'s network or resources can access the network via dial-up Internet service provider (ISP) accounts, Integrated Services Digital Network (ISDN), and cable modems.

5. Users connecting to ABC, Inc.'s facility using always-on broadband Internet connections, as in cable modems, must install antivirus scanning software on their home and mobile computers.

6. Remote access into ABC, Inc.'s facility should be properly audited and monitored for suspicious activity and unauthorized actions.

7. Unauthorized use of remote access privileges by third parties or users may result in the denial of future remote access permissions, suspension, termination, or criminal prosecution.

8. The security officer is responsible for ensuring that this policy is properly enforced.

Writing Security Policies

This section showed only two sample security policies, but there are several types that an organization may require. Developing general and specific policies is important for an organization to cover all of its bases and to ensure there is no confusion on the management's or employees' position when it comes to knowing what is expected.

How the policy is written will be determined on the type of policy, type of organization, and the culture of the organization. If the policy is inconsistent with the culture of the company and with other business policies, there is a greater chance of widespread noncompliance activity taking place. The policy should be realistic and express explicit support by the management. The policy should also be developed in conjunction with compliance-monitoring procedures and disciplinary actions for noncompliance activities to ensure congruency and a synergistic relationship among the different pieces of the security program.

When developing any policy, the following questions should be asked and answered to make sure that no issue was missed and that the policy is as far-reaching as necessary:

- What exactly is being protected?
- Does the policy fit the organization's business needs?
- Does it relate to the activities that actually take place within the organization?
- Does the policy fit the organization's culture?
- Does the policy state what must be done and what happens if these things are not carried out?
- Is the policy enforceable?
- Who is responsible for enforcement of the policy?
- Who developed, approved, and authorized the policy and the items within the policy?
- What deviations to the policy are allowed and how are they handled?
- Who is responsible for updating and maintaining the policy?
- To whom does the policy apply and are there any limitations within the policy?
- What are the ramifications of noncompliance and who is responsible for monitoring and reporting these activities?
- When does the policy take effect?
- How is the policy communicated to each employee?
- How often should the policy be reviewed and updated?
- Is the policy properly supported by all appropriate senior management?

References

Information Security Policies:
www.information-security-policies-and-standards.com

SANS Security Policy Project: **www.sans.org/resources/policies/**

British Standard 7799

The British Standard 7799 is an internationally recognized set of recommendations for developing security policies and conducting auditing. The standard provides comprehensive guidance on many of the issues related to information security. Many organizations use British Standard 7799 as a baseline to start from when developing their policies and indeed their information security programs.

The standards are broken down into ten sections that cover each aspect of an organization's security program. Each section deals with how a specific topic should be incorporated into a security policy and how activities should be properly audited to ensure compliance.

Section Overview

The following list gives a quick overview of each section within the standard:

- **Business Continuity Planning**   Identify critical business resources and develop plans and activities to countermeasure any significant disruption or interruption to them. These disruptions can be small in nature or large natural disasters.

- **System Access Control**   Identify resources that require access control and implement access control mechanisms. These mechanisms should prevent unauthorized access to information and computer systems. Unauthorized access and activity should be detected and dealt with properly. Access control is also an important part of remote access to an organization's assets.

- **System Development and Maintenance**   Confidentiality, integrity, and authenticity of information should be protected. Prevention of modification, misuse, corruption, or destruction of user data should be put into place. IT activities and procedures should be carried out in a secure manner. The security of application software and data should also be maintained.

- **Physical and Environmental Security**   Unauthorized access to a business facility and premises should be prevented to reduce the potential damage and compromise of information and assets, as well as prevent an interruption to business activities.

- **Compliance** Compliance of outlined directives in the organization's security policy and standards should be ensured. Breaches of any criminal or civil law (statutory, regulatory, contractual obligations, and so on) should be avoided.

- **Personnel Security** Users should be aware of potential threats and know how to properly support the organization's security policy. Possible risks to personnel, resources, and the facility should be reduced. Plans should be in place to reduce damage from security incidents.

- **Security Organization** Information security should be maintained within the organization. If the responsibility of managing information processing has been outsourced to another organization, the actual information should still be protected by the organization that is responsible for it.

- **Computer and Network Management** The information processing and communication resources should be protected and their integrity and availability maintained. The infrastructure should be protected and safeguarded against possible threats. Damage to assets and business activities should be prevented. The risk of system failures should also be minimized.

- **Asset Classification and Control** Information and resources should be assigned proper classifications, and each classification should have appropriate protection components in place and maintained.

- **Security Policy** Management direction should be supplied through the security policy, which will be the foundation for the organization's security program.

References

Resources for Security Risk Analysis: **www.securityauditor.net**

ISO/IEC 17799:2000 FAQ: **csrc.nist.gov/publications/secpubs/otherpubs/reviso-faq.pdf**

Who's Who?

Acronyms for companies and organizations are often used in literature without an explaination of who these organizations are and what their function in the world is. This section covers many of the organizations that have been discussed in this book.

NSA

The *National Security Agency* (NSA) is the agency officially responsible for security within the U.S. government. The agency was created in 1952 by President Harry Truman under the Department of Defense (DoD). Only recently has NSA been publicly discussed; for a majority of its life, most U.S. citizens did not know what the NSA was.

The NSA deals with signal intelligence, meaning that it listens to foreign communications that are deemed important and pertinent to U.S. security. The agency has extremely sophisticated and complex hardware, devices, and software to capture signals, decrypt them, and decode their meaning. NSA also conducts in-depth research in cryptology to increase their ability to decrypt other encrypted communication and to develop secure algorithms to protect U.S. military and government communication mechanisms.

NSA is also usually in support of and a catalyst for restricting any type of encryption products that may be sold outside of the United States. NSA does not want potentially threatening countries to acquire encryption mechanisms that would make its job of cracking encryption any harder. So many of the export laws that prohibit certain types of encryption software being sold outside of the United States have a direct correlation to the NSA's directives and requirements.

James Bamford wrote two books about the NSA: *The Puzzle Palace* (Penguin Books USA Inc., 1983) and *Body of Secrets* (Anchor Books, 2002).

References

National Security Agency: **www.nsa.gov**

National Security Agency information: **www.fas.org/irp/nsa**

NIST

The *National Institute of Standards and Technology* (NIST) is a division of the U.S. Department of Commerce. This organization was called the National Bureau of Standards (NBS) until 1988. It issues standards and guidelines to be adopted by U.S. computer system developers and vendors. NIST's core purpose is to promote open standards and interoperability with the hopes of spurring more developments within computer-based industries. The official standards that NIST produces and publishes are called *Federal Information Processing Standards* (FIPS).

In 1987 Congress passed the Computer Security Act, which authorized NIST to be responsible for defining standards to protect and ensure the security of information that is sensitive but unclassified within government agencies. NIST is responsible for sensitive but unclassified information, and NSA is responsible for classified information.

NIST's *Computer Systems Laboratory* (CSL) is responsible for developing technical, management, physical, and administrative standards and guidelines for cost-effective security used to keep the government agencies' sensitive information protected. It is required to work with other government agencies, including the NSA, to ensure the necessary level of protection for government agencies' computer systems and the programs, materials, testing, and reports pertaining to those systems. The NSA is required to provide NIST with technical guidelines dealing with personal identification, telecommunication security, and trusted technologies.

NIST's CSL provides the following:

- Develops computer security standards and works closely with accredited standards committees such as IEEE, ANSI, and ISO to develop and support these standards. The published standards are called FIPS PUBs. (Rainbow Series is an example.)
- Conducts research and publishes results on many security problems and solutions.
- Works with the NSA to ensure that solutions meet DoD security standards for protecting classified and intelligence information.
- Develops test methods to properly test security mechanisms.

U.S. government agencies that employ cryptography must use software that follows NIST standards. Many of the encryption standards mandated by NIST were developed by NSA. The public has been a bit suspicious of this relationship when it comes to developing and approving specific encryption algorithms, especially when they are not up for public review. The fear of the government inserting backdoors into algorithms unknown to the public raises many Big Brother issues and has caused outcries of these issues in the past.

Reference

National Institute of Standards and Technology: **www.nist.gov**

NCSC

The *National Computer Security Center* (NCSC) was established in 1981 within NSA to help support and drive NSA's DoD computer security responsibilities. The NCSC's responsibility was to provide a centralized agency that dealt with the evaluation process of computer security systems and products, provide technical support for government and industry groups doing computer security research and development, conduct and sponsor research in the computer and network security technology sector, develop and provide verification and analysis tools, provide computer security training, and disseminate information to other federal government agencies and to the computing industry. It also published the Rainbow Series of computing security standards.

The lines dividing NIST, NSA, and NCSC have not always been clear because they have overlapping responsibilities and throughout their histories, their responsibilities and missions expanded further into each other's territories. Basically, NSA protects classified military and intelligence information using computer security mechanisms and techniques, and NIST develops standards and computer security training programs. Evaluations of security systems were performed by NCSC through the Trusted Product Evaluation Program (TPEP), which is a part of NSA.

Vendors would request that their products go through the TPEP of an evaluation targeting a particular level of trust rating. These evaluations used the Trusted Computer System Evaluation Criteria (TCSEC) to assess the product and determine if it met the necessary requirements for the requested rating. The results were published in the Evaluated Products List (EPL) in Information Systems Security Products and Services Catalogs.

After the realization that TCSEC did not meet the requirements of all organizations and their security needs, the Common Criteria was developed and accepted. The TPEP was replaced by the *Trusted Technology Assessment Program* (TTAP). TTAP is a program developed and supported by NSA and NIST that performs trusted product evaluations. The evaluations are based on the Common Criteria instead of the TCSEC.

Reference

Commercial Product Evaluations: **www.radium.ncsc.mil/tpep**

ISO

The *International Organization for Standardization* (ISO) was established in 1947 and is an international organization made up of many national standards organizations. ISO's *Open System Interconnection* (OSI) model provides a conceptual model for explaining how data communication takes place. The OSI model promotes open networking environments that enable multivendor computer systems that follow this model to communicate using internationally accepted protocols.

The ISO is a worldwide federation with representatives from more than 100 countries. It is a nongovernmental organization with a mission to develop worldwide standards and promote international exchange of services and goods and to further develop cooperation of intellectual, technological, and scientific concepts between countries all around the world.

Reference

International Organization for Standardization: **www.iso.ch**

ANSI

The *American National Standards Institute* (ANSI) is an organization that defines coding standards and signaling schemes in the United States and represents the United States in the ISO and the International Telecommunication Union (ITU). The organization does not develop standards, but facilitates their development by bringing qualified groups together and providing them with guiding principles.

ANSI had a large part in the development of the ISO and has an active role in governing it today. ANSI promotes and advocates U.S. policies internationally within different regional standards organizations. The ANSI promotes U.S. standards by presenting them to ISOs. The organizations can choose to adopt the standards fully or extract specific parts of the standards to adopt for their regions.

Some of the well-known ANSI standards include C++, SQL, EDI, SONET, FDDI, and ANSI x9 security standards.

Reference

American National Standards Institute: **www.ansi.org**

IEEE

The *Institute of Electrical and Electronic Engineers* (IEEE) is a nonprofit organization that develops standards, submits them for ANSI approval, and forwards drafts to the ISO. This technical association is based in the United States and develops different types of standards, including security standards. The IEEE is made up of a number of committees, or working groups, that work in specific technical areas like communications, nuclear engineering, aerospace electronics, telecommunications, security, and much more. Their local area network/metropolitan area network (LAN/MAN) standards are known as the IEEE 802 standards. IEEE has a technical committee that works strictly with security and privacy issues.

References

IEEE: **www.ieee.org**

IEEE Catalog and Store: **shop.ieee.org**

IEEE Technical Committee on Security and Privacy: **www.ieee-security.org**

Gramm-Leach-Bliley Act

The Gramm-Leach-Bliley act was signed into United States law by former President Bill Clinton on November 12, 1999. The act applies to all national banks and federal branches of foreign banks that are subject to the supervision of the Federal Reserve System, Office of Thrift Supervision (OTS), Comptroller of the Currency (OCC), or Federal Deposit Insurance Corporation (FDIC). The act's main goal is to protect individual private information. Subsidiaries need to implement their own security program or be part of a program that covers the main financial institution and its subsidiaries.

The act requires a financial institution to develop privacy notices that must be given to each of its customers. The privacy notice gives the customer the option of prohibiting the bank from sharing his/her information with any nonaffiliated third-party organization. The act also requires each financial institution to have a comprehensive information security program in place.

The act has several components, and the one that is directly related to information security is Title V, section 502, referred to as "Obligations with Respect to Disclosures of Personal Information." This section mandates financial institutions to implement "administrative, technical, and physical safeguards" for their customers' personal information. The safeguards have three main objectives:

- Provide the necessary level of protection to ensure confidentiality of customer records and information
- Protect information from threats
- Protect against unauthorized access that would result in substantial harm or inconvenience to the customer

The act basically forces financial institutions to have security programs that they really should have had in the first place. A good security program only helps the institution and its customers, but now that it is federally mandated, developing and maintaining the security program will have a new benefit—keeping out of trouble with the Feds.

Security Program Components

The act states that customer "nonpublic personally identifiable information," which is financial information that is not available publicly, needs to be protected. Public information is the customer's name, address, and phone number. Nonpublic information is the customer's bank account information, balances, loan data, and overdraft information.

Responsibility

The board of directors is responsible for approving the security policy and the security program that the financial institution develops. They must also oversee its implementation and maintenance to ensure that it is kept up to date and accurate. The board of directors will often assign some of this responsibility to the appropriate committee. Management must provide a written report of the information security program to the board of directors and appropriate appointed committees.

Risk Management

The risks and threats that can affect the confidentiality of customers' information must be assessed by each financial institution. Potential threats have to be identified and countermeasures should be put into place to ensure that customer information cannot be accessed in an unauthorized method. This includes controlling access, safeguarding the data to protect it while it is being transmitted, and physically protecting the data within the facility. The monitoring of activities involved with the use of customer information, auditing, incident handling, and disaster recovery all have to be addressed, and proper procedures should be developed to ensure that customers' information is protected under all perceivable situations.

Training

The act requires all employees to be properly trained in security issues by attending a security awareness class. This helps to protect customer information and also strengthens the overall security within the organization.

Test Security Measures

Financial institutions must test their security procedures and controls regularly to ensure their effectiveness. The institution has some flexibility on how often to test these measures, mainly because some environments are more complex than others and therefore require more regular testing.

Service Provider

The financial institutions are responsible for their customer information even if it is held at a service provider's facility. It is the responsibility of the financial institution to determine and ensure that their service provider has the necessary security controls implemented. This requires due diligence on the institution's part because they will need to properly select and monitor the service provider they employ.

Disclosing Procedures

Financial institutions must disclose their security policies and practices, which indicates how they protect their customers' data.

Responding to Incidents

The act requires that all intrusions be reported on the interagency Suspicious Activity Report, which is the form used to report credit card fraud, counterfeit money, money laundering, and other suspicious activities.

Summary

The Gramm-Leach-Bliley act provides general requirements for how customer information should be protected and emphasizes the importance of privacy. There are not many specifics, however, and the act does not delve much into the security of the institution as a whole. Although this is an important and useful step in protecting consumers' private information, many security professionals see this as only a first step. There are many security issues that pertain to financial institutions and how they protect bank accounts, transfer funds, deal with internal and external threats, and how they audit, log, and monitor activity. These issues only get more complex when financial institutions offer their customers online banking services and eventually allow their customers to access accounts via wireless mobile devices.

References

U.S. Senate on Gramm-Leach-Bliley: **www.senate.gov/~banking/conf**

Federal Trade Commission on Gramm-Leach-Bliley: **www.ftc.gov/ privacy/glbact**

Compliance Headquarters: **www.complianceheadquarters.com**

Various Networking Components

There are different flavors, characteristics, and standards underneath the Ethernet umbrella. This appendix describes these different components.

Ethernet

Ethernet is defined by the following characteristics:

- Has shared media—all devices must take turns using the same media and detect collisions.
- Uses broadcast and collision domains.
- Uses carrier sense multiple access collision detection access (CSMA/CD) method.
- Supports full-duplex on twisted-pair implementations.
- Can use coaxial or twisted-pair media.

There are a number of Ethernet IEEE 802.3 adaptations.

Ethernet 10 Mbps

- 10Base-2—ThinNet:
  - Coaxial cable—RG-58 A/U
  - Maximum cable segment of 185 meters
  - Baseband transmission
- 10Base-5—ThickNet:
  - Coaxial cable
  - Maximum cable segment of 500 meters
  - Baseband transmission

- 10Base-T:
  - Twisted-pair cable, Category 3, 4, or 5
  - Maximum cable segment of 100 meters
  - RJ-45 jacks
- 10Base-FL:
  - Fiber-optic cable backbones
  - Up to four kilometers of transmission
  - Approved for cross-connects between campus buildings

Fast Ethernet 100 Mbps—IEEE 802.3u

- 100Base-T4:
  - Fast Ethernet over four pairs of Category 3, 4, or 5 unshielded twisted-pair (UTP) wires
  - Maximum distance of 100 meters between hub and computer
- 100Base-TX:
  - Fast Ethernet over two pairs of Category 5 UTP or Category 1 STP
  - Maximum distance of 100 meters between hub and computer
- 100Base-FX:
  - Fast Ethernet over fiber-optic cable
  - Cable runs of up to two kilometers

Gigabit Ethernet 1000 Mbps

- 1000Base-LX:
  - Fiber-optic cable
  - Long-wavelength laser transmissions
  - Up to 550 meters over multimode fiber-optic cable
  - Up to 3,000 meters over single-mode fiber-optic cable
- 1000Base-SX:
  - Fiber-optic cable
  - Short-wavelength laser transmission
  - Works over multimode fiber-optic cable
- 1000Base-CX:
  - High-data-rate twisted-pair cable

Type	Max Length	Bandwidth	Install	Interference	Cost
UTP	100 meters	10–100 Mbps	Easy	High	Cheapest
STP	100 meters	16–100 Mbps	Moderate	Moderate	Moderate
10Base2	185 meters	10 Mbps	Easy	Moderate	Cheap
10Base5	500 meters	10 Mbps	Hard	Low	Expensive
Fiber	2–100 km	100 Mbps–10 Gbps	Very Hard	None	Most expensive

Table E-1   Cable Characteristics

- Used to connect devices over a short distance
- Maximum distance of 25 meters
- 1000Base-T:
    - Four-pair Category 5 cable
    - Maximum distance of 100 meters per station to switch or 205 meters end to end

Fast Ethernet does use CSMA/CD and earlier Ethernet frame formats. Many implementations have subnets that work at 10 and 100 Mbps. The connecting hub must be autosensing to be able to properly negotiate between these different speeds.

Because Fast Ethernet provides much higher transmission speeds, the collision domains must be smaller to ensure an acceptable level of contention and collisions.

Table E-1 outlines the characteristics of different cables and Table E-2 indicates where different twisted-pair cables can be used.

Type	Standard Rating	Description
Type 1	STP	Two-pair 22 AWG wires with outer braided shield; connects computers and MAUs
Type 2	Voice/data grade	Shielded cable; two-pair 22 AWG wires or data and four pair 26 WG for voice
Type 3	Voice grade	Four UTP 22 or 24 AWG wires
Type 4	Undefined	
Type 5	Fiber-optic	Two multimode optical fibers
Type 6	Data patch	Two 26 AWG wires with dual foil and braided shield
Type 7	Undefined	
Type 8	Carpet cable	Two STP 26 AWG; used to string wire under carpets because of its flat jacket
Type 9	Plenum	Teflon-coated two STP AWG 22 pair with foil and braided shielding

Table E-2   Cable Types

Ethernet Frames

Frame formats dictate the type of fields in a frame and the sequence of these fields. This controls how data is packaged into a frame and transmitted over a network.

- **Preamble** This field contains the bit pattern 10101010, which indicates the beginning of a frame.

- **Start frame delimiter (SFD)** This frame contains the bit pattern 10101011, which indicates the actual start of the frame itself.

- **Length of data field (LEN)** This frame indicates how long the data portion is within the frame.

- **Cyclic redundancy check (CRC)** The sender and receiver perform an algorithm that results in a CRC value. If the receiver calculates a different value than what was in the CRC value, the frame is considered corrupt.

Wireless Technologies

Although the 802.11 wireless LAN technology and standard is relatively new, it had a rocky start and has already gone through different versions. The newer IEEE 802.11i standard has been developed to address many of the security issues in the first version released. This appendix covers this standard and how the corresponding technology outlined in the standard works.

The New Wireless Standard

The first wireless LAN standard, IEEE 802.11, has a tremendous amount of security flaws. These are found within the core standard itself, as well as in different implementations of this technology. To address these issues, a new IEEE Task Group has been developed to improve upon the standard and close the holes that the current wireless implementations are faced with. The deficiencies within the original 802.11 standard include no user authentication, no mutual authentication between the wireless device and access point, and a flawed encryption protocol. The encryption protocol allows for specific bits to be modified without the receiver recognizing it, and the different encryption components (key and initialization vectors) do not provide enough randomness to the encryption process. This lack of randomness allows for encrypted wireless traffic to be easily broken with free downloadable tools available on different Web sites.

The use of Extensible Authentication Protocol (EAP) and 802.1X to enforce user authentication and mutual authentication has been integrated into the new WLAN standard. To detect modifications of bits during transmission, Message Integrity Code (MIC) was also integrated. And Temporal Key Integrity Protocol (TKIP) generates random values that are used in the encryption process, which makes it much harder for an attacker to break. To allow for an even higher level of encryption protection, the standard also includes the new Advanced Encryption Standard (AES) to be used in new WLAN implementations. This section will look at these different components and their relationships to one another.

As of this writing the full 802.11i standard is expected to be released in September 2003, but many vendors have already integrated the components in the proposed standard into their new products. The Wi-Fi Alliance certifies 802.11 products and has announced that it will start certifying products based on the core components of the 802.11i standard, which the Alliance collectively calls Wireless Protected Access

(WPA). Basically, the WPA is the specifications that are used for their product certification process.

What Is Wrong with the Current Implementations?

The types of attacks that can be carried out on the current wireless devices and networks are numerous and unnerving. Current implementations are vulnerable to this long laundry list of attacks if they use products that are based purely on the original 802.11 standard. Wireless traffic can be easily sniffed, data can be modified during transmission without the receiver being notified, rogue access points can be erected (that users can authenticate to and communicate with, not knowing it is a malicious entity), and encrypted wireless traffic can be decrypted quickly and easily. Unfortunately, these vulnerabilities usually provide doorways to the actual wired network where the more destructive attacks can begin.

Many vendors who produce WLAN products have developed their own security techniques and technologies to overcome the 802.11 security flaws and issues, but this usually amounts to just wrapping Band-Aids around the crux of the problem, which is a poorly constructed and implemented standard and technology. When vendors are forced to develop their own solutions, there are always many interoperability issues that customers have to deal with.

The 802.11i standard employs two different approaches that provide much more security and protection than the protocol used in the original 802.11 standard, Wired Equivalent Privacy (WEP). This enhancement of security and protection is accomplished through specific protocols, technologies, and algorithms. The first protocol is TKIP, and it is backwards-compatible for the many WLAN products and networks currently implemented in networks everywhere. The TKIP protocol actually works with WEP by feeding it keying material, which is data to be used for generating new dynamic keys, as shown in Figure F-1. WEP uses the RC4 encryption algorithm, and the current implementation of the algorithm provides very little protection. More complexity is added to the key generation process with the use of TKIP, which makes it much more difficult for attackers to uncover the encryption keys. The IEEE working group provided TKIP so that customers would only need to obtain firmware or software updates instead of purchasing new equipment for this type of protection.

802.11i has another capability of providing encryption protection with the use of the Advanced Encryption Standard (AES) algorithm in counter mode with CBC-MAC (CCM), which is referred to as the CCM protocol (CCMP). AES is a much stronger algorithm than RC4 but requires more processing power. AES is not backwards-compatible with current WLAN products, so customers should only implement this configuration if they have not yet deployed a WLAN in their network.

The algorithms, technologies, and protocols that make up the new wireless standard are complex. It is important to understand each component and how they all work together to provide a higher degree of confidence and protection for our future WLAN environments.

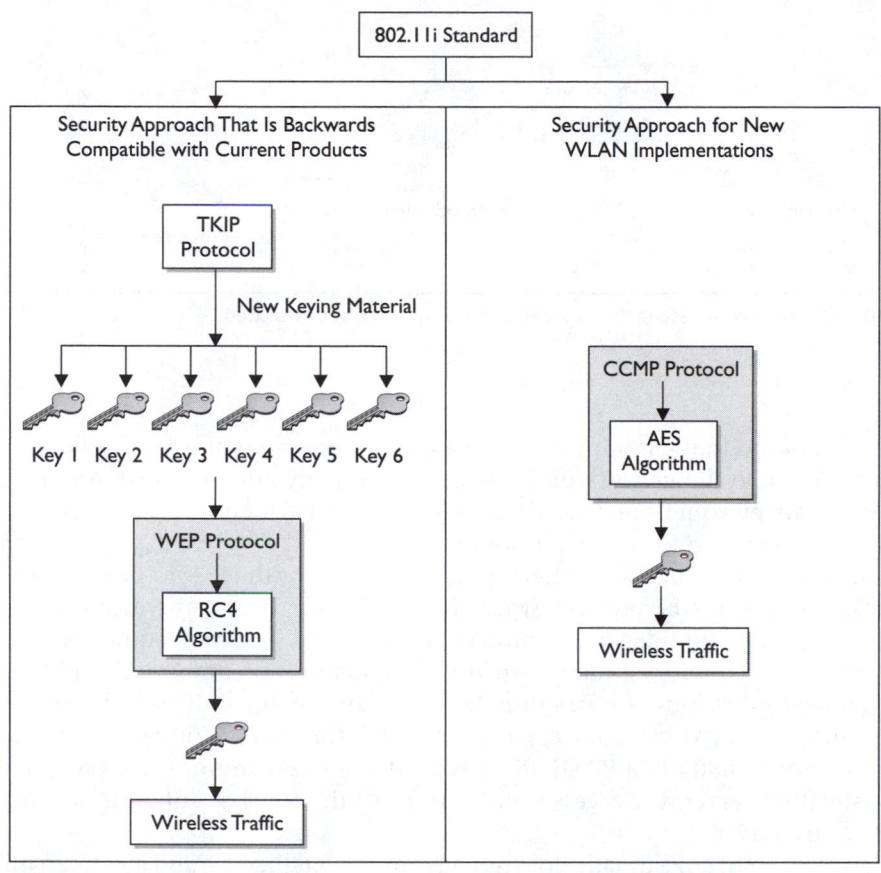

Figure F-1   New keying material is generated by TKIP and passed into the RC4 algorithm.

In this section we will look at the different encryption processes in the 802.11i standard (CCMP and TKIP), and the following sections will cover the other components that make up this standard that are not included in the original 802.11 standard.

802.1X

The 802.11i standard can be understood as three main components in two specific layers. The lower layer contains the improved encryption algorithms (TKIP and CCMP). The layer that resides on top of it contains 802.1X. They work together to provide more layers of protection than the current 802.11 standard.

So what is 802.1X anyway? The 802.1X standard is a port-based network access control that ensures that a user cannot make a full network connection until he is properly authenticated, as shown in Figure F-2. This means that a user cannot access network

Figure F-2   Before accessing the network the user must be authenticated.

resources and no traffic is allowed to pass, other than authentication traffic, from the wireless device to the network until the user is properly authenticated. An analogy is having a chain on your front door, which will allow you to identify a person who knocks before you allow him to enter your house.

By incorporating 802.1X, the new standard allows for the *user* to be authenticated, whereas using only WEP provides *system* authentication. User authentication provides a higher degree of confidence and protection compared to system authentication.

The 802.1X technology actually provides an authentication framework and a method of dynamically distributing encryption keys. The three main entities in this framework are the supplicant (wireless device), the authenticator (access point), and the authentication server (usually a RADIUS server). If the environment does not have an authentication server, the access point can fulfill the roles of authenticator and authentication server.

The access point (AP) usually does not have much intelligence and acts like a middleman by passing frames between the wireless device and the authentication server. This is usually a good approach since this will not require a lot of processing overhead for the AP, and the AP can deal with controlling several connections at once instead of having to authenticate each and every user.

The AP will control all communication and will allow the wireless device to communicate to the authentication server only when all authentication steps are completed successfully. This means that the wireless device cannot send or receive HTTP, DHCP, SMTP, or any other type of traffic until the user is properly authorized. WEP does not provide this type of strict access control; this is just one example of more security being provided by 802.11i.

Another disadvantage of the original 802.11 standard is that mutual authentication is not possible. When using WEP alone, the wireless device can authenticate to the AP, but the AP or authentication server is not required to authenticate to the wireless device. This means that a rogue AP can be set up and capture users' credentials and traffic without the users being aware of this type of attack. 802.11i deals with this issue by using EAP. EAP allows for mutual authentication to take place between the authentication server and wireless device, and provides flexibility in that users can be authenticated by using passwords, tokens, one-time passwords, certificates, smart cards, or Kerberos. This allows wireless users to be authenticated using the current infrastructure's authentication technology that is already in place. The wireless device and authentication server that are 802.11i-compliant have different authentication modules that plug into 802.1X to allow for these different options. So 802.1X provides the framework that allows for the different EAP modules to be added by a network administrator. The two entities agree upon one of these authentication methods (EAP modules) during their initial handshaking process.

The 802.11i standard does not deal with the full protocols stack but addresses only what is taking place at the data link layer of the OSI model. Authentication protocols reside at a higher layer than this, so the 802.11i does not specify specific authentication protocols. The use of EAP, however, allows for different protocols to be used by different vendors. For example, Cisco uses a purely password-based authentication framework called Lightweight Extensible Authentication Protocol (LEAP). Other vendors, including Microsoft, use EAP and Transport Layer Security (EAP-TLS), which carries out authentication through digital certificates. And yet another choice is Protective EAP (PEAP), where only the server uses a digital certificate. These different approaches are illustrated in Figure F-3.

If EAP-TLS is being used the authentication server and wireless device will exchange digital certificates for authentication purposes. If PEAP is being used instead, the user of the wireless device will send the server a password and the server will authenticate to the

Figure F-3   802.11i provides new ways to authenticate.

wireless device with its digital certificate. In both cases, some type of public key infrastructure (PKI) needs to be in place. If a company does not have a PKI currently implemented, it can be an overwhelming and costly task just to secure wireless transmissions.

The steps the server takes to authenticate to the wireless device are basically the same as when a SSL connection is being set up between a Web server and Web browser. Once the wireless device receives and validates the server's digital certificate, it creates a master key, encrypts it with the server's public key, and sends it over to the authentication server. Now the wireless device and authentication server have a master key, which they use to generate individual symmetric session keys. Both entities use these session keys for encryption and decryption purposes, and it is the use of these keys that sets up a secure channel between the two devices.

Companies may choose to use PEAP instead of EAP-TLS because of the hassle of installing and maintaining digital certificates on each and every wireless device. Before you purchase a WLAN product, you should understand the requirements and complications of each method to ensure you know what you are getting yourself into and if it is the right fit for your environment.

As stated earlier, Cisco took a different approach to this authentication game. They implemented LEAP, which is based purely on passwords. This means that no PKI is required and the wireless device and server authenticate to each other by exchanging predetermined passwords.

A large concern with current WLANs is that if individual wireless devices are stolen, they can be easily authenticated to the wired network. 802.11i has added steps to require that the user authenticates to the network instead of just requiring the wireless device to authenticate. By using EAP, the user will need to send some type of credential set that is tied to his identity. When using only WEP, the wireless device authenticates itself by proving that it has a symmetric key that was manually programmed into it. Since the user does not need to authenticate using WEP, a stolen wireless device can allow an attacker easy access to your precious network resources.

Dynamic Keys and the Use of Initialization Vectors

The three core deficiencies with WEP are the use of static encryption keys, the ineffective use of initialization vectors, and the lack of packet integrity assurance. The WEP protocol uses the RC4 algorithm, which is a symmetric cipher. Symmetric means that the sender and receiver must use the exact same key for encryption and decryption purposes. The 802.11 standard does not stipulate how to update these keys through an automated process, so in most environments, the RC4 symmetric keys are never changed out. And usually all of the wireless devices and AP share the exact same key. This is like having everyone in your company use the exact same password. Not a good idea. So that is the first issue—static WEP encryption keys on all devices.

The next flaw is how initialization vectors (IVs) are used. An IV is a numeric seeding value that is used with the symmetric key and RC4 algorithm to provide more randomness to the encryption process. Randomness is extremely important in encryption because any patterns can give the bad guys insight into how the process works, which may allow them to uncover the encryption key that was used. The key and IV value are inserted into the RC4 algorithm to generate a key stream, as shown in Figure F-4. The values (1s and 0s) of the key stream are XORed with the binary values of the individual packets. The result is ciphertext, or encrypted packets.

In most WEP implementations, the same IV values were used over and over again in this process, and since the same symmetric key (or shared secret) is always used, there is no way to provide effective randomness in the key stream that is generated by the algorithm. The appearance of patterns allows attackers to reverse-engineer the process to uncover the original encryption key, which can then be used to decrypt future encrypted traffic.

So now we are onto the third mentioned weakness, which is the integrity assurance issue. WLAN products that use only the 802.11 standard provide a vulnerability that is not always clearly understood. An attacker can actually change data within the wireless packets by flipping specific bits and altering the Integrity Check Value (ICV) so that the receiving end is oblivious to these changes. The ICV works like a CRC function; the sender calculates an ICV value and inserts it into a frame's header. The receiver calculates his own ICV value and compares it with the ICV value that was sent with the frame. If the values are the same, the receiver can be assured that the frame was not modified during transmission. If the ICV values are different, it indicates a modification did indeed take place and the receiver discards the frame. In WEP there are certain circumstances when the receiver could not actually detect when an alteration to the frame took place, thus there is no true integrity assurance.

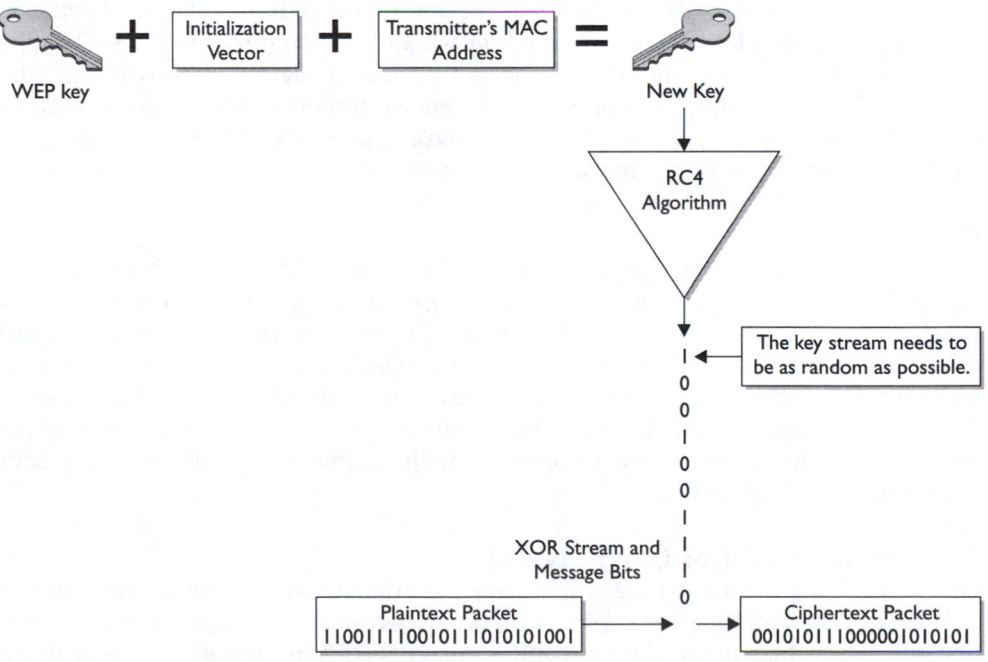

Figure F-4   Several values are used by the RC4 algorithm that are generated by TKIP.

So the problems identified with the 802.11 standard include poor authentication, static WEP keys that can be easily obtained by attackers, IV values that are repetitive and do not provide the necessary degree of randomness, and lack of data integrity. The use of the 802.1X technology in the new 802.11i standard provides access control by restricting network access until full authentication and authorization is completed and a robust authentication framework is supplied that allows for different EAP modules to be plugged in. These two technologies (802.1X and EAP) work together to enforce mutual authentication between the wireless device and authentication server. So what about the static keys, IV value, and integrity issues?

TKIP addresses the deficiencies of WEP pertaining to static WEP keys and inadequate use of IV values. Two very useful and powerful programs, AirSnort and WEPCrack, can be used to easily crack WEP's encryption by taking advantage of these weaknesses and the ineffective use of the key scheduling algorithm within the WEP protocol. If a company is using products that implement only WEP encryption and is not using a third-party encryption solution (as in a VPN), these programs can break their encrypted traffic within minutes to hours. There is no "maybe" pertaining to breaking WEP's encryption; using these tools means it will be broken no matter if 40-bit or 128-bit keys are being used. This is one of the most serious and dangerous vulnerabilities pertaining to the original 802.11 standard.

The use of TKIP provides the ability to rotate encryption keys to help fight against these types of attacks. The protocol increases the length of the IV value and ensures that each and every frame has a different IV value. This IV value is combined with the transmitter's MAC address and the original WEP key, so that even if the WEP key is static the resulting encryption key will be different for each and every frame. (WEP key + IV value + MAC address = new encryption key.) This is illustrated in Figure F-4. So what does that do for us? This brings more randomness to the encryption process, and it is randomness that is necessary to properly thwart cryptanalysis and attacks on cryptosystems. The changing IV values and resulting keys make the resulting key stream less predictable, which makes it much harder for the attacker to reverse-engineer the process and uncover the original key.

TKIP also deals with the integrity issues by using a message integrity check (MIC) instead of an ICV function. If you are familiar with a message authentication code (MAC) function, this is the same thing. A symmetric key is used with a hashing function, which is similar to a CRC function but stronger. The use of MIC instead of ICV ensures that the receiver will be properly alerted if changes to the frame take place during transmission. The sender and receiver calculate their own separate MIC values. If the receiver generates a MIC value that is different than the one sent with the frame, the frame is seen as compromised and it is discarded.

The Answer to All of Our Prayers?

Up to now, if a company required more protection than what was provided in the original 802.11 standard, they had to place a firewall between the access point and the wired network. Also, the wireless devices could have VPN software installed to provide another, stronger, layer of encryption. And as stated earlier, different vendors have come up with their own proprietary security solutions. But hopefully with 802.11i, continual Band-Aids will not need to be applied on top of this wireless technology. Instead, the security will be provided from the core of the technology itself.

So does the use of EAP, 802.1X, AES, and TKIP result in secure and highly trusted WLAN implementations? Maybe, but we need to understand what we are dealing with here. TKIP was created as a quick fix to WEP's overwhelming problems. It does not provide an overhaul for the wireless standard itself because WEP and TKIP are still based on the RC4 algorithm, which is not the best fit for this type of technology. The use of AES is closer to an actual overhaul, but is not backwards-compatible with current 802.11 implementations. In addition, we should understand that using all of these new components and mixing them with the current 802.11 components will add more complexity and steps to the process. Security and complexity do not usually get along. The highest security is usually accomplished with simplistic and elegant solutions to ensure that all of the entry points are clearly understood and protected. These new technologies add more flexibility to how vendors can choose to authenticate users and authentication servers, but that can also bring us interoperability issues because they will not all choose the same methods. This means that if a company buys an AP from company A, then the wireless cards it buys from company B and C may not work seamlessly.

So does that mean that all of this work has been done for naught? No, 802.11i provides much more protection and security than WEP ever did. The working group has had very knowledgeable people involved and some very large and powerful companies aiding in the development of these new solutions. But the customers who purchase these new products need to understand what will be required of them *after* the purchase order is made out. For example, with the use of EAP-TLS, each wireless device would need its own digital certificate. Are your current wireless devices programmed to handle certificates? How will the certificates be properly deployed to all the wireless devices? How will the certificates be maintained? Will the devices and authentication server verify that certificates have not been revoked by periodically checking a certificate revocation list (CRL)? What if a rogue authentication server or AP was erected with a valid digital certificate? The wireless device would just verify this certificate and trust that this server is the entity it is supposed to be communicating with. And if the certificate authority is ever compromised, the whole EAP-TLS infrastructure is compromised, as with any PKI environment.

The original 802.11 standard has received so much bad press and attention that it is very likely that this new working group is working hard to ensure that all of the i's are being dotted and all of the t's are being crossed pertaining to this new release. But time will tell through rounds of testing and real-life implementations. This new improved standard will get us much farther down the security road than we are now, but there are two other things to keep in mind concerning new products being developed and released. First, the vendors need to properly interpret and adhere to the standards to provide the level of assurance and security promised by the standard itself, and second, customers need to have awareness and intelligence about what they are purchasing and implementing into their environments. Many times products and technologies are installed without the company knowing exactly what this newcomer does and how to properly test and secure it. True security is based on education, knowledge, and experience. So the ultimate goal is to have a solid standard that is used to develop a secure product and that the customer is knowledgeable about this new product so that the overall level of protection is actually achieved. If one of these components does not meet its own individual goal, it can bring havoc to the overall objective of efforts.

Today, new WLAN products are already being developed following the stipulations of this new wireless standard; even though it is not completely ratified. Many products will straddle the fence by providing TKIP for backwards-compatibility with current WLAN implementations and AES for companies that are just now thinking about extending their current wired environments with a wireless component. Customers should review the Wi-Fi Alliance's certification findings before buying wireless products, since they have already started assessing systems against the 802.11i proposed standard.

Wireless technologies are fascinating and the capabilities that they provide for individuals and companies are extensive. But these technologies are at an immature state of their evolution, and because of that there are continual changes and new vulnerabilities that can be introduced. Real security is about education and knowledge. Understanding what is being implemented and knowing how new products can open doors to malicious attackers are two of the best protection mechanisms out there.

HIPAA

Many organizations are slowly, and sometimes painfully, learning the business needs for information and network security in their environment. This realization can be driven by the risk of attackers stealing customer credit card numbers, accessing bank account information, defacing Web sites, and/or stealing trade secrets or intellectual property. The time wasted by the IT staff tracking down inside and outside attackers and patching the holes within the infrastructure is also a consideration. However, medical organizations now have additional urgent factors forcing them to take a hard look at the security levels within their business environment. Consequences of inadequate security include increased fines and possible jail time.

Are You HIPAA Compliant?

The *Health Insurance Portability and Accountability Act (HIPAA)*, a recent federal regulation, has been mandated to provide national standards and procedures for the electronic storage, use, and transmission of personal medical information and healthcare data. This regulation provides a framework to ensure security, integrity, and privacy when handling confidential medical information. HIPAA outlines how security should be managed for any facility that creates, accesses, shares, or destroys medical information.

HIPAA also mandates specific Electronic Data Interchange (EDI) standards for transactions such as health plan enrollment, eligibility, premium and claims payments, coordination of benefits, and referrals. This will enforce standardization for how various medical entities communicate with each other by ensuring that the same format is used and understood by everyone involved. Reporting identifiers (IDs) are also mandated. These include provider IDs, payer IDs, patient IDs, and employer IDs. These IDs will be used for all electronic transactions of medical information and provide an organized method for the proper tracking and auditing of medical information activities. This appendix focuses not on the EDI standards, but on the security standards within the HIPAA regulations.

Health records can be used and misused in various scenarios for many reasons. As health records migrate from a paper-based system to an electronic system, they become easier to maintain, access, and transfer, but they also become easier to manipulate. Traditionally, healthcare facilities have lagged behind other businesses in their information and network security mechanisms, architecture, and security enforcement because there was no real business need to expend the energy and money to put these items in place. Now there is.

HIPAA brings steep federal penalties for noncompliance. If medical information is used in a way that violates the privacy standards dictated by HIPAA, even by mistake, there are monetary penalties of $100 per violation up to $25,000 per year, per standard. If protected health information is obtained or disclosed knowingly, the fines can be as much as $50,000 and one year in prison. If the information is obtained or disclosed under false pretenses, the cost can go up to $250,000, and a person could incur up to ten years in prison if there is intent to sell or use the information for commercial advantage, personal gain, or malicious harm. This is serious business.

Oh, How It's Changed

In the past, a patient's medical record consisted of medical information transcribed onto paper bound in a folder. This information was stored in file cabinets and moved or updated manually. Today medical information is stored in databases. It is not only reviewed by the nurse and doctor, but is also reviewed by insurance companies, insurance clearinghouses, group practices, Medicaid agencies, and health practitioners. In addition, this data can be accessed by many types of hospital staff from most computers throughout the hospital, and even by physicians from their portable or home computers. This information usually travels unprotected across the Internet, or other open vulnerable networks, with no real restrictions on who accesses it and what they do with the information once they have it. As the healthcare industry has consolidated medical information electronically, integrated delivery systems have emerged. This means that clinical information can now be shared among multiple hospitals, clinics, insurance companies, and homecare agencies all over the world.

These issues spurred the government to implement new standards that protect private health information from nonconsensual use. These standards give patients the right to access their medical records and the ability to know who else has accessed them. The standards restrict disclosure of this confidential information to the minimum needed for the intended purpose. They also establish new criminal and civil penalties and sanctions for not following the new standards.

What Do I Have to Do?

HIPAA does not spell out specific technology that should be used to provide the necessary security levels, but it provides a broad overview of the necessary architecture and framework it expects to see implemented. The regulation is based on already known and practiced security standards and procedures. If an organization has a good security baseline to start from, these mechanisms may only need to be reviewed, improved, documented, and monitored. If an organization has never considered security, and thus does not have the necessary policies, procedures, or baseline infrastructure in place, a major overhaul of the technology and methods used within the environment may be needed.

HIPAA looks at four major factors affecting an organization's security:

- Administrative procedures
- Physical safeguards
- Technical security services
- Technical security mechanisms

Administrative Procedures:

- Have formal protocols for controlling access to data.
- Certify data systems to evaluate compliance with security standards.
- Develop and maintain chain of trust agreements among regulated entities that will exchange and share health information.
- Use contingency plans to preserve data in the event of an emergency.
- Have formal data processing protocols.
- Have internal security audit procedures.
- Perform authentication and authorization for accessing data, ongoing training, and monitoring of activity by personnel who access medical information.
- Have security configuration management for hardware and software, including the supporting documentation.
- Appoint a security information officer.
- Use formal methods of reporting and responding to security breaches.
- Develop a security management structure that maintains security policy and procedures and provides continual risk assessment capabilities.
- Have proper personnel termination procedures.
- Implement training and security awareness programs.

Physical Safeguards:

- Formally assign the security responsibility to a person or entity.
- Develop access controls to hardware and peripherals.
- Develop disaster and intrusion response and recovery plans.
- Restrict and control physical access to data sites with personal identification verification.
- Maintain maintenance records.
- Enforce a need-to-know basis for access to information and sites.
- Develop and document allowed activities and security configurations at the workstation level.

Technical Security Services:

- Use necessary software controls to provide data integrity, confidentiality, and availability.
- Regulate access to data with a hierarchal system of rights and permissions for personnel.
- Provide data authentication and data integrity.
- Ensure user authentication and access control.

Technical Security Mechanisms:

- Implement necessary security software controls to ensure proper electronic storage and transmission of data.
- Use integrity controls to ensure transmitted or stored data is valid.
- Perform message authentication to ensure that messages were not altered during transmission.
- Use access controls for transmission mechanisms or encryption.
- Use alarms and alerts to signal abnormal communication conditions.
- Maintain audit and log trail information.

Buying a firewall and configuring it is not the first step. A medical organization must understand the factors behind their security challenges. In addition to meeting HIPAA's standards, basic business requirements, objectives, and goals should be fully explored and understood. Real planning is needed to give all management, departments, IT staff, and employees direction on and guidelines for understanding what security means to them and their department.

Establish Security Policies, Procedures, Standards, and Guidelines

Establishing security policies, procedures, standards, and guidelines should be the first task. This provides direction for everyone in the company. A security policy is the overall expression of management's intention on how security should be implemented, maintained, and enforced.

Assess the Security Architecture

Next, the security architecture should be fully examined from a logical and physical point of view. This architecture should be fortified at every front—access points through the firewalls, callback restrictions via modems, virus activity, server configuration, access control mechanisms, virtual private networks (VPNs), encryption, and application security. These processes need to be properly monitored with alerts, alarms, logs, and audit trails of suspicious activity.

Develop a Security Awareness Program

A security awareness program should be developed for the different levels of expertise within the organization. Business contingency plans should also be current, with proper recovery plans in place.

This seems like a lot to review, improve, and monitor. It is, but there's more. In addition to the facility's physical network structure, how people interact with the components in this facility, how data travels throughout this network, management's attitude and activities concerning securing this infrastructure, and the legal and liability issues of security breaches must be considered. This is a lot to take on. These things need to have been accomplished by October 2002 by most facilities, or let the fines begin!

Cultural Issues

Often, implementing the essential security technology mechanisms is easier than getting support personnel to use them correctly. In many organizations, security innovations are met with resistance and opposition. Change is usually hard for people, but when a change restricts actions they previously took for granted, ways of bypassing the changes usually creep in.

For security to be successful, it must be rigorously supported by the highest ranks of management. It must be considered in almost all business decisions. The proper funding must be in place to support it. Different security responsibilities must be assigned to individuals and groups. All employees must understand the meaning of security within their particular organization, the expectations of the organization, and the consequences of noncompliance.

Because a majority of medical facilities have not had restrictions concerning what files can and cannot be accessed, what can be done to the files once they are accessed, whom files can be sent to, and all the necessary overhead that accompanies good security, adjusting the organization's culture may be one of the larger roadblocks to a successful security rollout.

How Do We Implement Our Changes?

This appendix provides only a basic overview of what is required. Each section could easily be a detailed book by itself.

Depending on your expertise and the available time and resources, the most effective first step may be to contact a consultant that specializes in information and network security practices. Outside consultants can provide an objective viewpoint and knowledgeable ideas and solutions not tied to the existing way of doing things. Without this type of perspective, these tasks can be overwhelming.

The next step is to understand the environment, because you can't secure something you don't understand. The network schematic diagram that has been ignored for years needs to be brought out and properly updated. You need to understand how information comes in and goes out of your network, how these entry points provide authentication and authorization, where sensitive information lives, who accesses it, and why. The computers or servers that hold medical information need rigorous scrutiny. What operating system is on these computers? How current are the patches and hot fixes? What access control lists are on these computers, and what users have the right to access the information on these computers? How are these computers physically protected? Who can access these computers remotely and why?

Then you need to review remote users and their abilities. Supporting remote users creates compromising situations for organizations. How are remote users being properly authenticated? How is their activity being tracked? How do you know this isn't an easy doorway for attackers? Do you really need so many remote users? Do they need all the rights and permissions they currently have? How do you provide all the necessary security mechanisms to protect your remote users and your network?

Networks are not islands anymore. What type of access do your employees have to the Internet? How do you know this Internet access is not opening your environment to attacks and security compromises? Are there any backdoors to your network? How do you communicate with other businesses? Is this done securely? Is this monitored and audited properly?

Questions like this can go on and on. It is just as important to ask the right questions as it is to find the right answers. Organizations often don't even know where to begin, much less how to lay out a proper roadmap to accomplish and achieve all the necessary security goals and objectives. This is why the first step can be the most important step.

What Is This All For?

The HIPAA regulation accomplishes several important goals. First, patients have more control over their medical information. They can control whom it is released to; they have the right to see a copy of their health records and the ability to request a correction to their records; and they can give advanced consent for most disclosures of health information, and receive an explanation of their privacy rights and how their confidential information will be used.

Second, the regulation aims to ensure that medical information will be used for health purposes only, with a few exceptions, and not for nonhealth purposes like job promotions or underwriting life insurance products. Medical organizations are now accountable to protect health information against misuse or disclosure. Steep fines and possible jail time back up this accountability.

To comply with the regulations and provide all of these services and this protection, facilities must take a hard look at their current infrastructures and implemented security mechanisms. Most organizations will need to spend a lot of time and money to develop proper plans, security policies, and procedures; implement the necessary security components; and add staff to update, monitor, and audit these new activities.

These steps unquestionably have to take place. The only question is, Are you prepared? If not, do you know how to prepare yourself?

HIPAA Regulation Expectations

The following material provides an overview of what the HIPAA regulations require. Organizations that need to be compliant with the new HIPPA regulations must provide security from several different angles: administrative, physical, and technical. It is important to understand these different categories of security, what falls within them, and what compliancy really means.

Administrative Procedures to Guard Data Integrity, Confidentiality, and Availability

1. **Certification**   Each organization is required to evaluate and certify its computers systems and network designs to verify that the appropriate security has been implemented. This evaluation can be performed internally or by an external accrediting agency.

2. **Chain of trust partner agreement**   If medical data is processed through a third party, all parties involved are required to enter into a chain of trust partner agreement. This means that all parties are bound to a contract promising to protect electronically transmitted data. It is important to have the same level of security for each link of the electronic communication path. The sender and receiver must maintain the integrity and confidentiality of the information while it is in their possession.

3. **Contingency plan**   Organizations must have contingency plans in place to be able to properly respond to and recover from disasters and system emergencies. Periodic backups of data are required. Critical facilities must be available for continuing operations in the event of an emergency. The contingency plan must contain the following:

   - **Applications and data criticality analysis**   Formal assessment of vulnerabilities, risks, sensitivity, and security of its programs and information it receives, stores, transmits, manipulates, and accesses.

   - **A data backup plan**   A documented and routinely updated plan to create and maintain data for a specific period. Exact copies of backup data must be retrievable.

   - **A disaster recovery plan**   Necessary processes that enable an organization to restore any loss of data in the event of a natural disaster, system emergency, or vandalism.

   - **An emergency mode operation plan**   Part of an overall contingency plan that enables an organization to operate in the event of a natural disaster, system emergency, or vandalism.

- **Testing and revision procedures** A documented process of periodic testing of contingency plans to provide training, discover weaknesses, and allow for a revision of the plan as needed.

4. **Formal mechanism for processing records** Documented policies and procedures for the routine and nonroutine receipt, manipulation, storage, dissemination, transmission, and/or disposal of health information.

5. **Information access control** Formal, documented policies and procedures for granting different levels of access to healthcare information that includes all of the following implementation features:

- **Access authorization**

- **Information** Use policies and procedures that establish the rules for granting access.

- **Access establishment**

- **Access modification** Security policies and rules that determine the various types and reasons for modification to an entity's established right of access to a terminal, transaction, program, process, or some other use.

6. **Internal audit** In-house review of the records of system activity (such as logins, file accesses, and security incidents) maintained by an organization.

7. **Personnel security** All personnel who have access to any sensitive information have the required authorities as well as all appropriate clearances. This includes all of the following implementation features:

- **Ensuring supervision of maintenance personnel by an authorized, knowledgeable person** These procedures are documented formal procedures and instructions for the oversight of maintenance personnel when the personnel are near health information pertaining to an individual.

- **Maintaining a record of access authorizations** Ongoing documentation and review of the levels of access granted to a user, program, or procedure accessing health information.

- **Ensuring that operating and maintenance personnel have proper access authorization** Formal documented policies and procedures for determining the access level to be granted to individuals working on, or near, health information.

- **Establishing personnel clearance procedures** A protective measure applied to determine whether an individual's access to sensitive unclassified automated info rmation is permissible.

- **Establishing and maintaining personnel security policies and procedures** Formal documentation of procedures to ensure that all personnel who have access to sensitive information have the required authority as well as appropriate clearances.

- **Ensuring that system users, including maintenance personnel, receive security awareness training**

8. **Security configuration management**   Measures, practices, and develops procedures for the security of information systems that must be coordinated and integrated with each other and with other measures, practices, and procedures of the organization established in order to create a coherent system of security. This includes all of the following implementation features:

  - **Documentation**   Written security plans, rules, procedures, and instructions concerning all components of an entity's security.

  - **Hardware and software installation and maintenance review and testing for security features**   Formal, documented procedures for connecting and loading new equipment and programs, a periodic review of the maintenance occurring on the equipment and programs, and a periodic security testing of the security attributes of that hardware/software.

  - **Inventory**   The formal, documented identification of hardware and software assets.

  - **Security testing**   This process is used to determine that the security features of a system are implemented as designed and that they are adequate for a proposed applications environment. The process includes hands-on functional testing, penetration testing, and verification.

  - **Virus checking**   The act of running a computer program that identifies and disables the following:

    - Another virus computer program, typically hidden, that attaches itself to other programs and has the capability to replicate

    - A code fragment (not an independent program) that reproduces by attaching to another program

    - A code embedded within a program that causes a copy of itself to be inserted in one or more other programs

9. **Security incident procedures**   Formal, documented instructions for reporting security breaches that include all of the following implementation features:

  - **Report procedures**   Documented, formal mechanism employed to document security incidents

  - **Response procedures**   Documented, formal rules or instructions for actions to be taken as a result of the receipt of a security incident report

10. **Security management process**   Creation, administration, and oversight of policies to ensure the prevention, detection, containment, and correction of security breaches involving risk analysis and risk management. This includes the establishment of accountability, management controls (policies and

education), electronic controls, physical security, and penalties for the abuse and misuse of its assets (both physical and electronic), which includes all of the following implementation features:

- **Risk analysis**   A process whereby cost-effective security/control measures may be selected by balancing the costs of various security/control measures against the losses that would be expected if these measures were not in place.

- **Risk management**   Process of assessing risk, taking steps to reduce risk to an acceptable level, and maintaining that level of risk.

- **Sanction policies and procedures**   Statements regarding disciplinary actions that are communicated to all employees, agents, and contractors: for example, a verbal warning, notice of disciplinary action placed in personnel files, removal of system privileges, termination of employment, and contract penalties. They must include employee, agent, and contractor notice of civil or criminal penalties for misuse or misappropriation of health information and must make employees, agents, and contractors aware that violations may result in notification to law enforcement officials and regulatory, accreditation, and licensure organizations.

- **Security policy**   Statement(s) of information values, protection responsibilities, and organization commitment for a system. This is the framework within which an entity establishes the necessary levels of information security to achieve the desired confidentiality goals.

11. **Termination procedures**   Formal, documented instructions, which include appropriate security measures for the ending of an employee's employment or an internal/external user's access. This includes procedures for all of the following implementation features:

- **Changing locks**   A documented procedure for changing combinations of locking mechanisms, both on a recurring basis and when personnel knowledgeable of combinations no longer need-to-know or require access to the protected facility or system.

- **Removal from access lists**   Physical eradication of an entity's access privileges and the removal of a user account(s).

- **Changing access privileges**   Termination or deletion of an individual's access privileges to the information, services, and resources for which he or she currently has clearance, authorization, and need-to-know when such clearance, authorization, and need-to-know no longer exist.

- **Turning in keys, tokens, or cards that provide access**   Formal, documented procedure to ensure that all physical items that give a terminated employee access to a property, building, or equipment are retrieved from that employee, preferably before termination.

12. **Training**   Education concerning the vulnerabilities of the health information in an entity's possession and ways to ensure the protection of that information. This includes all of the following implementation features:

- **Awareness training for all personnel, including management personnel** Security awareness including, but not limited to, password maintenance, incident reporting, viruses, and other forms of malicious software.

- **Periodic security reminders**   Employees, agents, and contractors are made aware of security concerns on an ongoing basis.

- **User education concerning virus protection**   Training relative to user awareness of the potential harm that can be caused by a virus, how to prevent the introduction of a virus to a computer system, and what to do if a virus is detected.

- **User education concerning the importance of monitoring login success or failure and how to report discrepancies**   Training in the user's responsibility to ensure the security of healthcare information.

- **User education about password management**   Type of user training and the rules to be followed in creating and changing passwords, and the need to keep them confidential.

Physical Safeguards to Guard Data Integrity, Confidentiality, and Availability

1. **Assigned security responsibility**   Practices established by management to manage and supervise the execution and use of security measures to protect data and to manage and supervise the conduct of personnel in relation to the protection of data.

2. **Media controls**   Formal, documented policies and procedures that govern the receipt and removal of hardware/software (such as floppy disks and tapes) into and out of a facility. This includes all of the following implementation features:

- **Access control**

- **Accountability**   The property that ensures that the actions of an entity can be traced uniquely to that entity

- **Data backup**   A retrievable, exact copy of information

- **Data storage**   The retention of healthcare information pertaining to an individual in an electronic format

- **Disposal**   Final disposition of electronic data and/or the hardware on which electronic data is stored

3. **Physical access controls**   Formal, documented policies and procedures to be followed to limit physical access to an entity while ensuring that properly

authorized access is allowed. This includes all of the following implementation features:

- **Disaster recovery**   The process enabling an entity to restore any loss of data in the event of fire, vandalism, natural disaster, or system failure.

- **An emergency mode operation**   Access controls in place that enable an entity to continue to operate in the event of a fire, vandalism, natural disaster, or system failure.

- **Equipment control (into and out of site)**   Documented security procedures for bringing hardware and software into and out of a facility and for maintaining a record of that equipment. This includes, but is not limited to, the marking, handling, and disposal of hardware and storage media.

- **A facility security plan**   A plan to safeguard the premises and building (exterior and interior) from unauthorized physical access and to safeguard the equipment therein from unauthorized physical access, tampering, and theft.

- **Procedures for verifying access authorizations before granting physical access**   Formal, documented policies and instructions for validating the access privileges of an entity before granting those privileges.

- **Maintenance records**   Documentation of repairs and modifications to the physical components of a facility, such as the hardware, software, walls, doors, and locks.

- **Need-to-know procedures for personnel access**   A security principle stating that a user should have access only to the data he or she needs to perform a particular function.

- **Procedures to sign in visitors and provide escorts, if appropriate**   Formal, documented procedure governing the reception and hosting of visitors.

- **Testing and revision**   The restriction of program testing and the revision to formally authorized personnel.

4. **Policy and guidelines on workstation use**   Documented instructions/procedures delineating the proper functions to be performed, the manner in which those functions are to be performed, and the physical attributes of the surroundings of a specific computer terminal site or type of site, dependent upon the sensitivity of the information accessed from that site.

- **A secure workstation location**   Physical safeguards to eliminate or minimize the possibility of unauthorized access to information: for example, locating a terminal used to access sensitive information in a locked room and restricting access to that room to authorized personnel, and not placing a terminal used to access patient information in any area of a doctor's office where the screen contents can be viewed from the reception area.

- **Security awareness training**   Security awareness training programs in which all employees, agents, and contractors must participate, including (based on job responsibilities) customized education programs that focus on issues regarding use of health information and responsibilities regarding confidentiality and security.

Technical Security Services to Guard Data Integrity, Confidentiality, and Availability

1. **Access control that includes a procedure for emergency access and the optional use of encryption**   Documented instructions for obtaining necessary information during a crisis. This includes at least one of the following implementation features:

   - **Context-based access**   An access control procedure based on the context of a transaction (as opposed to being based on attributes of the initiator or target).

   - **Role-based access**

   - **User-based access**

2. **Audit controls**   Mechanisms employed to record and examine system activity.

3. **Authorization control**   The mechanism for obtaining consent for the use and disclosure of health information. This includes at least one of the following implementation features:

   - **Role-based access**

   - **User-based access**

4. **Data authentication**   The corroboration that data has not been altered or destroyed in an unauthorized manner. Examples of how data corroboration may be ensured include the use of a checksum, double keying, a message authentication code, or a digital signature.

5. **Entity authentication**   The corroboration that an entity is the one claimed. This includes the following:

   - **Automatic logoff**   A security procedure that causes an electronic session to terminate after a predetermined period of inactivity, such as 15 minutes.

   - **Unique user identifier**   A combination name/number assigned and maintained in security procedures for identifying and tracking individual user identity. This includes at least one of the following implementation features:

     - **Biometric identification**   An identification system that identifies a human from a measurement of a physical feature or repeatable action of the individual (for example, hand geometry, retinal scan, iris scan, fingerprint patterns, facial characteristics, DNA sequence characteristics, voiceprints, and handwritten signature).

     - **Password**

- **Personal identification number (PIN)** A number or code assigned to an individual and used to provide verification of identity.
- **A telephone callback procedure** A method of authenticating the identity of the receiver and sender of information through a series of questions and answers sent back and forth establishing the identity of each.
- **Token**

Technical Security Mechanisms to Guard Against Unauthorized Access to Data That Is Transmitted over a Communications Network

If an entity uses communications or network controls, its security standards for technical security mechanisms must include the following:

- **Integrity controls** A security mechanism employed to ensure the validity of the information being electronically transmitted or stored
- **Message authentication** Ensuring, typically with a message authentication code, that a received message (usually via a network) matches the message sent

These mechanisms use one of the following implementation features:

1. **Access controls** Protection of sensitive communications transmissions over open or private networks so that they cannot be easily intercepted and interpreted by parties other than the intended recipient.

2. **Encryption**

3. **Alarm** In communication systems, any device that can sense an abnormal condition within the system and that can provide, either locally or remotely, a signal indicating the presence of the abnormality. The signal may be in any desired form, ranging from a simple contact closure (or opening) to a time-phased automatic shutdown and restart cycle.

4. **Audit trail** The data collected and potentially used to facilitate a security audit.

5. **Entity authentication** A communications or network mechanism to irrefutably identify authorized users, programs, and processes and to deny access to unauthorized users, programs, and processes.

6. **Event reporting** A network message indicating operational irregularities in physical elements of a network or a response to the occurrence of a significant task, typically the completion of a request for information.

HIPAA Security Requirements Matrix

The following tables describe many of the HIPAA requirements and map them to their corresponding IEEE standards. The column "Identification Steps" lists some example questions an organization can ask itself to see if these necessary items have been addressed or if they are issues that need attention for compliancy purposes.

The tables address the following:

- **Tables G-1 and G-2**   Administrative procedures to guard data integrity, confidentiality, and availability
- **Table G-3**   Physical safeguards to guard data integrity, confidentiality, and availability
- **Tables G-4 and G-5**   Technical security services to guard data integrity, confidentiality, and availability
- **Table G-6**   Electronic signatures

HIPAA Requirement	Description	Applicable IEEE Standard(s)	Implementation Method	Identification Steps
Certification	Each organization is required to evaluate and certify its computer systems and network designs to verify that the appropriate security has been implemented. This evaluation can be performed internally or by an external accrediting agency.	47	Internal or external testing and certification	Check previous and current certifications. Schedule routine certifications. Document procedures. What does the certification cover? What types of tests are carried out? What type of documentation is used to show outcomes of each test? Are there written procedures? Who is responsible for these activities?
Chain of trust partner agreement	If medical data is processed through a third party, all parties involved are required to enter into a chain of trust partner agreement. This means all parties are bound to a contract promising to protect electronically transmitted data. It is important to have the same level of security for each link of the electronic communication path. The sender and receiver must maintain the integrity and confidentiality of the information while it is in their possession.	12 and 47	Signed legal contracts	Identify electronic partners and evaluate data transfer procedures and technology. Review procedural documentation and current contracts. Review the level of security each partner is providing. Who shares medical information? What type of security is used at each partner site? What types of encryption mechanisms are used? Are there any interoperability issues? Are there written procedures? Who is responsible for these activities?
Contingency	Organizations must have contingency plans in place to be able to properly respond to and recover from disasters and system emergencies. Periodic backups of data are required. Critical facilities must be available for continuing operations in the event of an emergency.	17, 47, and 53	Application and data criticality analysis	Review and evaluate current contingency plans, procedures, and documentation. Review critical application and data recoverability procedures. If a disaster happens, how will the data still be available? What steps are taken to ensure continued operations? Has the critical data been identified and mirrored? Are there cold or hot sites available? Are there written procedures? Who is responsible for these activities?

Table G-1 Administrative Procedures to Guard Data Integrity, Confidentiality, and Availability

HIPAA Requirement	Description	Applicable IEEE Standard(s)	Implementation Method	Identification Steps
	Documented and routinely updated plan to create and maintain data for a specific period. Exact copies of backup data must be retrievable.	12, 17, and 47	Data backup	Review and evaluate data backup procedures, schedule timelines, and document procedures. What data is backed up? Where is it backed up to? How often is it backed up? Are there offsite facilities that hold copies? Is there a fireproof safe? Are there written procedures? Who is responsible for these activities?
	Documented process of periodic testing of contingency plans to provide training, discover weaknesses, and allow for revision of plan as needed.	12, 17, and 47	Testing and revision	Review previous contingency testing plans and procedures for updating the plans. Review training activities and supporting documentation. How often is the plan tested? What is done during the test? How is the plan revised? Are there written procedures? Who is responsible for these activities?
	Necessary processes that enable an organization to restore any loss of data in the event of a natural disaster, system emergency, or vandalism.	12, 17, 47, and 53	Disaster recovery plan	Review and evaluate current disaster recovery plans, procedures, and documentation. What steps will be taken to recover from a disaster? When was this plan last updated? Has it been tested? Are there written procedures? Who is responsible for these activities?
	Part of an overall contingency plan that enables an organization to operate in the event of a natural disaster, system emergency, or vandalism.	47 and 53	Emergency mode operations plan	Review and evaluate emergency mode procedures and reaction plans. What happens right after a disaster? What critical functions have to be operational? What is put in place to verify that these functions are operational? Are there written procedures? Who is responsible for these activities?

Table G-1   Administrative Procedures to Guard Data Integrity, Confidentiality, and Availability *(continued)*

HIPAA Requirement	Description	Applicable IEEE Standard(s)	Implementation Method	Identification Steps
Formal mechanism for processing records	Documented policies and procedures for the routine and nonroutine receipt, manipulation, storage, dissemination, transmission, and/or disposal of health information.	12 and 17	Documentation of data policy and procedures	Evaluate current data handling procedures and supporting documentation. How is medical information handled, stored, received, transmitted, and destroyed? Are there written procedures? Who is responsible for these activities?
	The security policies, and the rules established therein, that determine an entity's initial right to access a terminal, transaction, program, or process.	17, 47, and 53	Access establishment	Evaluate current authorization levels and rules implemented to control access to data. Who can access what data? How is this enforced? Are there written procedures? Who is responsible for these activities?
	Security policies and rules that determine the types of and reasons for modification to an entity's established right to access a terminal, transaction, program, process, or some other user.	12, 17, 47, and 53	Access modification	Review the procedures and standards for altering user access levels. Why are access levels changed for users? How is this carried out? Are there written procedures? Who is responsible for these activities?
Internal audit	In-house review of the records of system activity (such as logins, file accesses, and security incidents) maintained by an organization.	12, 17, 43, 44, and 47	Internal audits	Review the previous and current audit documentation and procedures. Are in-house audits carried out? If so, by whom? What is audited? Are there procedures and supporting documentation? How long are the audits kept? Where are they kept and protected? Are there written procedures? Who is responsible for these activities?
Personnel security	All personnel who have access to any sensitive information have the required authorities as well as all appropriate clearances.	17 and 47	Ensure supervision of maintenance personnel by authorized, knowledgeable person	Evaluate authorization and clearance procedures pertaining to accessing information. Who has what access to medical information and why? How is this type of access tracked and enforced? Are there written procedures? Who is responsible for these activities?

Table G-1   Administrative Procedures to Guard Data Integrity, Confidentiality, and Availability *(continued)*

HIPAA Requirement	Description	Applicable IEEE Standard(s)	Implementation Method	Identification Steps
	Ongoing documentation and review of the levels of access granted to a user, program, or procedure accessing health information.	12, 17, and 47	Maintenance of record of access authorizations	Review documentation pertaining to access level evaluation procedures. Is the documentation that explains access authorization updated and maintained? If so, by whom and how often? How does this type of maintenance happen? Are there written procedures? Who is responsible for these activities?
	Formal documented policies and procedures for determining the access level to be granted to individuals working on, or near, health information.	17 and 47	Operating, and in some cases, maintenance personnel who have proper access authorization	Review the access level requirements and updating procedures. Who can have access to medical information? How is this tracked, monitored, and enforced? Are there written procedures? Who is responsible for these activities?
	A protective measure applied to determine that an individual's access to sensitive unclassified automated information is permissible.	17, 47, and 53	Personnel clearance procedure	Review and evaluate current clearance level assignments and procedural activities. Who has what permissions to access and modify medical information? What are the procedures to dictate which users can access different types of information? Are there written procedures? Who is responsible for these activities?
	Ensuring that system users, including maintenance personnel, receive security awareness training.	12, 17, 47, and 53	System users, including maintenance personnel trained in security	Review previous security awareness activities, scheduled events, literature, and documentation. Do all employees receive security awareness training? How often? What is taught in this training? Are there written procedures? Who is responsible for these activities?

Table G-1   Administrative Procedures to Guard Data Integrity, Confidentiality, and Availability *(continued)*

Requirement	Description	Mapped Standard(s)	Implementation	Identification Steps
Security configuration management	Measures, practices, and procedures for the security of information systems that must be coordinated and integrated with each other and with other measures, practices, and procedures of the organization established to create a coherent system of security.	2, 17, 47, and 53	Documentation	Review and evaluate current security configuration management and documentation. When changes are made, how are they implemented? How are they tested? Is this a standard practice? Are there written procedures? Who is responsible for these activities?
	Formal, documented procedures for connecting and loading new equipment and programs, the periodic review of the maintenance occurring on that equipment and programs, and the periodic security testing of the security attributes of that hardware/software.	12, 17, and 47	Hardware/software installation and maintenance review and testing for security features	How are new hardware and software integrated into the environment? Are there specific written procedures? How are they tested? Are security issues readdressed after this type of implementation? Are there written procedures? Who is responsible for these activities?
	The formal, documented identification of hardware and software assets.	12 and 17	Inventory	Is there a list of current hardware and software resources? If so, who maintains it? How often is it updated? Are there written procedures? Who is responsible for these activities?
	Process used to determine that the security features of a system are implemented as designed and that they are adequate for a proposed applications environment; this process includes hands-on functional testing, penetration testing, and verification.	12, 17, and 47	Security testing	Are regular security vulnerability scans performed? Are security features tested? What type of testing is done? How are security mechanism functionalities verified? Are there written procedures? Who is responsible for these activities?

Table G-2   Administrative Procedures to Guard Data Integrity, Confidentiality, and Availability

Requirement	Description	Mapped Standard(s)	Implementation	Identification Steps
	The act of running a computer program that identifies and disables viruses.	12, 17, 47, and 53	Virus checking	Is there antivirus software on each computer? What are the configurations? How often are computers scanned? What happens in case of an infection? How often are the signatures updated? Are there written procedures? Who is responsible for these activities?
Security incident procedures	Documented formal mechanism employed to document security incidents.	12, 17, and 47	Report procedures	Are there written procedures dictating how incidents should be reported? Who is responsible for these reports? Where are they kept? Are there written procedures? Who is responsible for these activities?
	Documented formal rules or instructions for actions to be taken as a result of the receipt of a security incident report.	17 and 47	Response procedures	What happens if there is a security incident? Who is involved? What actions are taken? Are there written procedures? Who is responsible for these activities?
Security process management	Creation, administration, and oversight of policies to ensure the prevention, detection, containment, and correction of security breaches involving risk analysis and risk management. It includes the establishment of accountability, management controls (policies and education), electronic controls, physical security, and penalties for the abuse and misuse of its assets (both physical and electronic).	12, 17, 47, and 53	Risk analysis	Are security risk analyses performed? If so, what is taken into account? How often are they done? Who performs these analyses? Are there written procedures? Who is responsible for these activities?

Table G-2   Administrative Procedures to Guard Data Integrity, Confidentiality, and Availability *(continued)*

Requirement	Description	Mapped Standard(s)	Implementation	Identification Steps
Security process management *(continued)*	Process of assessing risk, taking steps to reduce risk to an acceptable level, and maintaining that level of risk.	17 and 47	Risk management	If a risk analysis is done, what is done with the resulting information? What steps are taken to ensure an acceptable risk level? Who is responsible for risk management? How often is this performed? Are there supporting documents and procedures?
	Statements regarding disciplinary actions that are communicated to all employees, agents, and contractors: for example, verbal warning, notice of disciplinary action placed in personnel files, removal of system privileges, termination of employment, and contract penalties. They must include employee, agent, and contractor notice of civil or criminal penalties for misuse or misappropriation of health information and must make employees, agents, and contractors aware that violations may result in notification to law enforcement officials and regulatory, accreditation, and licensure organizations.	12, 17, 47, and 53	Sanction policy	Do all employees know what actions are expected of them and the consequences of noncompliance? How is this information disseminated? Who is responsible for this policy? Do the employees sign any contracts? What level of protection does this provide? Are there written procedures? Who is responsible for these activities?
	Statement(s) of information values, protection responsibilities, and organization commitment for a system. This is the framework within which an entity establishes the necessary levels of information security to achieve the desired confidentiality goals.	17, 47, and 53	Security policy	Does the organization have an overall security policy? If so, what does it cover? How often is it updated? Are there supporting security policies? Are there written procedures? Who is responsible for these activities?

Table G-2   Administrative Procedures to Guard Data Integrity, Confidentiality, and Availability *(continued)*

Requirement	Description	Mapped Standard(s)	Implementation	Identification Steps
Termination procedures	Formal documented instructions, which include appropriate security measures, for the ending of an employee's employment or an internal/external user's access.	12 and 17	Combination locks changed	What steps are taken when an employee is terminated? Are these procedures documented and enforced? Who is responsible for these activities?
	Physical eradication of an entity's access privileges and removal of user account(s).	12, 17, 47, and 53	Removal from access lists	When an employee is terminated, is her access removed from all network resources? Are the accounts deleted? Who is responsible for these activities?
	Termination or deletion of an individual's access privileges to the information, services, and resources for which he currently has clearance, authorization, and the need-to-know when such clearance, authorization, and need-to-know no longer exist.	12, 17, and 47	Removal of user account(s)	When an employee is terminated, are the corresponding accounts disabled or deleted? Are all privileges and permissions ended properly? Who is responsible for this?
	Formal, documented procedure to ensure all physical items that enable a terminated employee to access a property, building, or equipment are retrieved from that employee, preferably before termination.	12, 17, and 47	Turn in of keys, token, or cards that provide access	When an employee is terminated, are his keys, swipe cards, and physical access mechanisms returned? Are there procedures for these activities? Who is responsible for this?
Training	Education concerning the vulnerabilities of the health information in an entity's possession and ways to ensure the protection of that information.	12, 17, 18, 47, and 53	Awareness training for all personnel (including management)	Is information-handling training performed? If so, how often? What is covered? Who is responsible for these training sessions?

Table G-2 Administrative Procedures to Guard Data Integrity, Confidentiality, and Availability *(continued)*

Requirement	Description	Mapped Standard(s)	Implementation	Identification Steps
Training (continued)	Employees, agents, and contractors are made aware of security concerns on an ongoing basis.	12 and 18	Periodic security reminders	How are employees reminded of security awareness issues? Are there written procedures? Who is responsible for these activities?
	Training in the user's responsibility to ensure the security of healthcare information.	12, 17, and 18	User education about the importance of monitoring login success/failure and how to report discrepancies	How would an employee report identity discrepancies in medical information and how is it handled? Are there procedures for these processes?
	Type of user training in the rules to be followed in creating and changing passwords and the need to keep them confidential.	12, 18, and 47	User education in password management	Do the employees know the password management policy? How is this enforced? Are there written procedures? Who is responsible for these activities?

Table G-2 Administrative Procedures to Guard Data Integrity, Confidentiality, and Availability *(continued)*

Requirement	Description	Mapped Standard(s)	Implementation	Identification Steps
Assigned security responsibility	Practices established by management to manage and supervise the execution and use of security measures to protect data and to manage and supervise the conduct of personnel in relation to the protection of data.	47	Security management and enforcement	How is security monitored? How is it enforced? How are security practices monitored? Who is responsible for these activities?
Media controls	Formal, documented policies and procedures that govern the receipt and removal of hardware/software (such as floppy disks and tapes) into and out of a facility.	17, 47, and 53	Access control	Is hardware and software monitored as it enters and leaves the building? Are there procedures for this? Who is responsible for these activities?
	The property that ensures that the actions of an entity can be traced uniquely to that entity.	17, 18, and 47	Accountability (tracking mechanism)	How are individuals held accountable for their actions? How are users identified? How are actions monitored? How is accountability enforced?
	A retrievable, exact copy of information.	12, 17, 47, and 53	Data backup	Review and evaluate the data backup procedures, schedule timelines, and document procedures. What data is backed up? Where is it backed up to? How often is it backed up? Are there offsite facilities that hold copies? Is there a fireproof safe? Are there written procedures? Who is responsible for these activities?
	The retention of healthcare information pertaining to an individual in an electronic format.	12, 17, and 47	Data storage	How is medical information stored? How is it protected? Is it mirrored and/or backed up? Are there written procedures? Who is responsible for these activities?

Table G-3   Physical Safeguards to Guard Data Integrity, Confidentiality, and Availability

Requirement	Description	Mapped Standard(s)	Implementation	Identification Steps
Media Controls (continued)	Final disposition of electronic data, and/or the hardware on which electronic data is stored.	17, 47, and 53	Disposal	How is data disposed of? Is the information properly destroyed? What are the procedures? Who is responsible for these activities?
Physical access controls (limited access)	Formal, documented policies and procedures to be followed to limit physical access to an entity while ensuring that properly authorized access is allowed.	17	Disaster recovery	What is the process enabling an entity to restore any loss of data in the event of fire, vandalism, natural disaster, or system failure? Are there written procedures? Who is responsible for these activities?
	Access controls in place that enable an entity to continue to operate in the event of fire, vandalism, natural disaster, or system failure.	17	Emergency mode operation	Review and evaluate emergency mode procedures and reaction plans. What happens right after a disaster? Who can access what information right after a disaster? What is put in place to verify that these functions are operational? Are there written procedures? Who is responsible for these activities?
	Documented security procedures for bringing hardware and software into and out of a facility and for maintaining a record of that equipment. This includes, but is not limited to, the marking, handling, and disposal of hardware and storage media.	17 and 47	Equipment control (into and out of site)	Is hardware and software monitored as it enters and leaves the building? Are there procedures for this? Who is responsible for these activities?
	A plan to safeguard the premises and building (exterior and interior) from unauthorized physical access and to safeguard the equipment therein from unauthorized physical access, tampering, and theft.	12, 17, and 47	Facility security plan	What are the security mechanisms in place to protect the facility from undesirable activities? How is the equipment protected? How are these activities monitored? Who is responsible for these activities?

Table G-3   Physical Safeguards to Guard Data Integrity, Confidentiality, and Availability *(continued)*

Requirement	Description	Mapped Standard(s)	Implementation	Identification Steps
	Formal, documented policies and instructions for validating the access privileges of an entity before granting those privileges.	17, 18, and 47	Procedures for verifying access authorizations prior to physical access	What are the facts verified before allowing an entity into the facility? How is this enforced? Are there written procedures? Who is responsible for these activities?
	Documentation of repairs and modifications to the physical components of a facility, such as hardware, software, walls, doors, and locks.	17	Maintenance records	When equipment is repaired, are these activities documented and maintained? Are any modifications to hardware, software, or to the facility tracked? Are there written procedures? Who is responsible for these activities?
	A security principle stating that a user should have access only to the data he or she needs to perform a particular function.	12, 17, 47, and 53	Need-to-know procedures for personnel access	How is it determined who has what access to information? What are the levels of access, and how do the levels correlate their job functionality? How is this enforced? Are there written procedures? Who is responsible for these activities?
	Formal, documented procedure governing the reception and hosting of visitors.	17	Sign-in for visitors and escort, if appropriate	Do visitors have to sign in prior to entering the facility? Are they escorted through any areas? Are there written procedures? Who is responsible for these activities?
	The restriction of program testing and revision to formally authorized personnel.	17 and 47	Testing and revision	When application or hardware testing and revisions need to happen, how is it ensured that the proper people are doing this? Are there written procedures? Who is responsible for these activities?

Table G-3   Physical Safeguards to Guard Data Integrity, Confidentiality, and Availability *(continued)*

Requirement	Description	Mapped Standard(s)	Implementation	Identification Steps
Policy/guideline on workstation use	Documented instructions/procedures delineating the proper functions to be performed, the manner in which those functions are to be performed, and the physical attributes of the surroundings of a specific computer terminal site or type of site, dependent upon the sensitivity of the information accessed from that site.	18	Sensitive information procedures	How are different areas within the environment delineated pertaining to the different information they hold? How are the sensitivity levels determined and enforced? Are there written procedures? Who is responsible for these activities?
Secure workstation location	Physical safeguards to eliminate or minimize the possibility of unauthorized access to information: for example, locating a terminal used to access sensitive information in a locked room and restricting access to that room to authorized personnel and not placing a terminal used to access patient information in any area of a doctor's office where the screen contents can be viewed from the reception area.	17 and 53	Computer placement	Are computers that hold medical information physically protected from unauthorized access? How are they protected? Are there different levels of sensitivity pertaining to information content? Are there written procedures? Who is responsible for these activities?
Security awareness training	Information security awareness training programs in which all employees, agents, and contractors must participate, including, based on job responsibilities, customized education programs that focus on issues regarding use of health information and responsibilities regarding confidentiality and security.	12, 17, and 47		Review previous security awareness activities, scheduled events, literature, and documentation. Do all employees receive security awareness training? How often? What is taught in this training? Are there written procedures? Who is responsible for these activities?

Table G-3   Physical Safeguards to Guard Data Integrity, Confidentiality, and Availability *(continued)*

Requirement	Description	Mapped Standard(s)	Implementation	Identification Steps
Access control	An access control procedure based on the context of a transaction (as opposed to being based on attributes of the initiator or target).	5, 12, 14, 16, 17, 40, and 47	Context-based access	What security mechanisms are in place to provide software access control? How are these monitored and audited? Are there written procedures? Who is responsible for these activities?
	Transforming confidential plaintext into ciphertext to protect it. Also called encipherment. An encryption algorithm combines plaintext with other values called keys, or ciphers, so the data becomes unintelligible. Once encrypted, data can be stored or transmitted over unsecured lines.	1, 6, 12, 14, 17, 21, 22, 23, 24, 26, 28, 29, 30, 31, 36, 47, 49, 53, 54, and 55	Encryption	What encryption mechanisms are in place? Where are they implemented? What data is being encrypted? Are there written procedures? Who is responsible for these activities?
	A procedure for emergency access. Documented instructions for obtaining necessary information during a crisis.	14, 17, and 53	Procedure for emergency access	How is it ensured that necessary entities can access specific information in a crisis? How is this tested? Are there written procedures? Who is responsible for these activities?
	Role-based access control (RBAC) is an alternative to traditional access control models (for example, discretionary or nondiscretionary access control policies) that permits the specification and enforcement of enterprise-specific security policies in a way that maps more naturally to an organization's structure and business activities. With RBAC, rather than attempting to map an organization's security policy to a relatively low-level set of technical controls (typically access control lists), each user is assigned to one or more predefined roles, each of which has been assigned the various privileges needed to perform that role.	14, 16, 17, 40, 41, 47, and 53	Role-based access	Is role-based access control implemented? If so, how is it implemented? What are the definitions of the roles? Are there written procedures? Who is responsible for these activities?

Table G-4 Technical Security Services to Guard Data Integrity, Confidentiality, and Availability

Requirement	Description	Mapped Standard(s)	Implementation	Identification Steps
Access Control (continued)	A security mechanism used to grant users of a system access based upon the identity of the user.	11, 12, 14, 16, 17, 40, 41, 47, and 53	User-based access	Is user-based access control implemented? How is it implemented? How are users identified? Are there written procedures? Who is responsible for these activities?
Audit controls	The mechanisms employed to record and examine system activity.	12, 14, 18, 47, and 53	Audit logs	What activities are audited? How are they audited? Are these audit logs monitored? If so, how often? How long are the audit logs kept? How are they protected? Are there written procedures? Who is responsible for these activities?
Data authentication	The corroboration that data has not been altered or destroyed in an unauthorized manner. Examples of how data corroboration may be ensured include the use of a checksum, double keying, a message authentication code, or digital signatures.	14, 16, 17, 18, 40, and 53	Automatic log off	Is there a security procedure that causes an electronic session to terminate after a predetermined period of inactivity, such as 15 minutes? Are there written procedures? Who is responsible for these activities?
	An identification system that identifies a human from a measurement of a physical feature or repeatable action of the individual (for example, hand geometry, retinal scan, iris scan, fingerprint patterns, facial characteristics, DNA sequence characteristics, voiceprints, and handwritten signature).	14, 16, 18, 40, 47, and 53	Biometrics	Is there any type of biometric access control in place? If so, what type? What is it checking for? How is the biometric system used? Are there written procedures? Who is responsible for these activities?

Table G-4 Technical Security Services to Guard Data Integrity, Confidentiality, and Availability (continued)

Requirement	Description	Mapped Standard(s)	Implementation	Identification Steps
	Confidential authentication information composed of a string of characters.	14, 16, 17, 18, 19, 40, 47, and 53	Password	Are passwords used? Is there password management in place? What are the password requirements? How are they enforced? Are there written procedures? Who is responsible for these activities?
	A number or code assigned to an individual and used to provide verification of identity.	14, 16, 18, 19, 40, and 47	PIN	Are PINs used? Is there PIN management in place? What are the PIN requirements? How are they enforced? Are there written procedures? Who is responsible for these activities?
	Method of authenticating the identity of the receiver and sender of information through a series of questions and answers sent back and forth establishing the identity of each.	14, 17, 18, 47, and 53	Telephone callback	Is a callback function used? Is there callback management in place? What are the callback requirements? How are they enforced? Are there written procedures? Who is responsible for these activities?
	A physical item that's used to provide identity. Typically, this is an electronic device that can be inserted in a door or a computer system to obtain access.	14, 17, 47, 50, and 53	Token	Are tokens used? Is there token management in place? What are the token requirements? How is this enforced? Are there written procedures? Who is responsible for these activities?

Table G-4 Technical Security Services to Guard Data Integrity, Confidentiality, and Availability *(continued)*

Requirement	Description	Mapped Standard(s)	Implementation	Identification Steps
Authorization control	Role-based access control (RBAC) is an alternative to traditional access control models (for example, discretionary or nondiscretionary access control policies) that permits the specification and enforcement of enterprise-specific security policies in a way that maps more naturally to an organization's structure and business activities. With RBAC, rather than attempting to map an organization's security policy to a relatively low-level set of technical controls (typically, access control lists), each user is assigned to one or more predefined roles, each of which has been assigned the various privileges needed to perform that role.	5, 14, 16, 17, 47, and 53	Role-based access	Is role-based access control implemented? How is it implemented? What are the definitions of the roles? Are there written procedures? Who is responsible for these activities?
	A security mechanism used to grant users of a system access based upon the identity of the user.	14, 16, 47, and 53	User-based access	Is user-based access control implemented? How is it implemented? How are users identified? Are there written procedures? Who is responsible for these activities?

Table G-4   Technical Security Services to Guard Data Integrity, Confidentiality, and Availability *(continued)*

Requirement	Description	Mapped Standard(s)	Implementation	Identification Steps
Communications/ network controls		14, 17, 22, 23, 39, 47, 48, and 53	Access controls	What type of access control mechanisms are used for network communication? Are there written procedures? Who is responsible for these activities?
	In communication systems, any device that can sense an abnormal condition within the system and provide, either locally or remotely, a signal indicating the presence of the abnormality. The signal may be in any desired form ranging from a simple contact closure (or opening) to a time-phased automatic shutdown and restart cycle.	14, 17, 18, 35, 36, 37, 38, and 44	Alarm, event reporting, and audit trail	Is data collected and potentially used to facilitate a security audit? What types of alarms are configured? What types of audits are performed? How are events reported? Are there written procedures? Who is responsible for these activities?
	Transforming confidential plaintext into ciphertext to protect it. Also called encipherment. An encryption algorithm combines plaintext with other values called keys, or ciphers, so the data becomes unintelligible. Once encrypted, data can be stored or transmitted over unsecured lines.	1, 6, 12, 14, 17, 21, 22, 23, 24, 26, 27, 28, 29, 30, 31, 47, 49, 52, and 53	Encryption	What encryption mechanisms are in place? Where are they implemented? What data is being encrypted? Are there written procedures? Who is responsible for these activities?
	A communications or network mechanism to irrefutably identify authorized users, programs, and processes and to deny access to unauthorized users, programs, and processes.	12, 14, 17, 18, 20, 22, 23, 31, 32, 33, 34, 51, and 53	Entity authentication	How are users authenticated for network communication? Are there written procedures? Who is responsible for these activities?

Table G-5   Technical Security Services to Guard Data Integrity, Confidentiality, and Availability

Requirement	Description	Mapped Standard(s)	Implementation	Identification Steps
Communications/ network controls (continued)	A security mechanism employed to ensure the validity of the information being electronically transmitted or stored.	14, 15, 17, 18, 22, 23, 45, and 46	Integrity controls	How is data integrity ensured? What technology is in place to monitor data integrity? What data is monitored for integrity? Are there written procedures? Who is responsible for these activities?
	Ensuring, typically with a message authentication code, that a message received (usually via a network) matches the message sent.	14, 15, 17, 18, 22, 23, 25, 45, 46, and 52	Message authentication	Are there message authentication mechanisms in place? Where are they placed? What technology is used? Are there written procedures? Who is responsible for these activities?

Table G-5   Technical Security Services to Guard Data Integrity, Confidentiality, and Availability *(continued)*

Requirement	Description	Mapped Standard(s)	Implementation	Identification Steps
Digital signature. If digital signature is computed by using a private key, the following three implementation features must be implemented: –Message integrity –Nonrepudiation –User authentication Other implementation features are optional.	An electronic signature based upon cryptographic methods of originator. Allows for the authenticity of the sender to be validated and the integrity of the data to be assured.	3, 4, 10, 11, 13, and 20	Ability to add attributes	Are digital signatures used? What algorithm is employed? Attributes are possible capabilities of a digital signature technology: for example, the capability to add a timestamp as part of a digital signature. What attributes are used with these digital signatures? Are there written procedures? Who is responsible for these activities?

Table G-6   Electronic Signatures

Requirement	Description	Mapped Standard(s)	Implementation	Identification Steps
	The attribute that is affixed to an electronic document to bind it to a particular entity. An electronic signature process secures the user authentication (proof of claimed identity, for example, by biometrics such as fingerprints, retinal scans, handwritten signature verification, and so on, tokens, or passwords) at the time the signature is generated. It creates the logical manifestation of signature (including the possibility for multiple parties to sign a document and have the order of application recognized and proven) and supplies additional information such as a timestamp and signature purpose-specific to that user. It also ensures the integrity of the signed document to enable transportability, interoperability, independent verifiability, and continuity of signature capability. Verifying a signature on a document verifies the integrity of the document and associated attributes and verifies the identity of the signer.	3, 4, 11, 13, 14, and 18	Continuity of signature capability	The public verification of a signature will not compromise the signer's ability to apply additional secure signatures at a later date. Can a signer apply a secure signature at a later date? How is this configured? Are there written procedures? Who is responsible for these activities?
	It will be possible to prove the order of application of signatures. This is analogous to the normal business practice of counter-signatures, where one party signs a document that has already been signed by another party.	3, 4, 10, 11, 13, 14, and 18	Countersignature	Are countersignatures allowed? How are the different signatures differentiated? How is this configured? Are there written procedures? Who is responsible for these activities?

Table G-6 Electronic Signatures (*continued*)

Requirement	Description	Mapped Standard(s)	Implementation	Identification Steps
Digital Signatures (continued)	The capability to verify the signature without the cooperation of the signer. Technically, it is accomplished using the public key of the signatory, and it is a property of all digital signatures performed with asymmetric key encryption.	3, 4, 11, 13, and 20	Independent verifiability	How is independent verifiability ensured? What mechanism provides this functionality? How is it configured? Are there written procedures? Who is responsible for these activities?
	The applications used on either side of a communication, among trading partners and/ or among internal components of an entity, and being able to read and correctly interpret the information communicated from one to the other.	3, 4, 7, 8, 9, 13, 14, and 48	Interoperability	What interoperability issues exist among different applications? What interoperability issues exist among different partners? How are these issues dealt with? Are there written procedures? Who is responsible for these activities?
	The assurance of unaltered transmission and the receipt of a message from the sender to the intended recipient.	3, 4, 10, 11, 13, 14, and 18	Message integrity	How is message integrity ensured? What technology and mechanisms are used? How is this configured? Are there written procedures? Who is responsible for these activities?
	It will be possible for multiple parties to sign a document. Multiple signatures are simply appended to the document.	3, 4, 10, 11, 13, and 20	Multiple signatures	Is multiple signature functionality available? What technology and mechanism are used for this? How are they configured? Are there written procedures? Who is responsible for these activities?

Table G-6   Electronic Signatures (continued)

Requirement	Description	Mapped Standard(s)	Implementation	Identification Steps
	Strong and substantial evidence of the identity of the signer of a message and of message integrity, sufficient to prevent a party from successfully denying the origin, submission, or delivery of the message and the integrity of its contents.	2, 3, 4, 10, 11, 13, 14, and 42	Nonrepudiation	Is nonrepudiation functionality available? What technology and mechanism is used for this? How is it configured? Are there written procedures? Who is responsible for these activities?
	A signed document can be transported (over an insecure network) to another system, while maintaining the integrity of the document.	3, 4, 11, 13, 14, and 18	Transportability	How are messages transmitted over an insecure network? How is the message integrity ensured? What technology and mechanism is used for this? How is it configured? Are there written procedures? Who is responsible for these activities?
	The provision of assurance of the claimed identity of an entity.	3, 4, 10, 11, 13, and 20	User authentication	How are users authenticated when using electronic signatures? What technology and mechanism is used for this? How is it configured? Are there written procedures? Who is responsible for these activities?

Table G-6 Electronic Signatures *(continued)*

IEEE Standards

1. ANSI X3.92 Data Encryption Standard

2. ANSI X9.30 Part 1: Public Key Cryptography Using Irreversible Algorithms: Digital Signature Algorithm

3. ANSI X9.30 Part 2: Public Key Cryptography Using Irreversible Algorithms: Secure Hash Algorithm (SHA-1)

4. ANSI X9.31 Reversible Digital Signature Algorithms

5. ANSI X9.45 Enhanced Management Controls Using Digital Signatures and Attribute Certificates

6. ANSI X9.52 Triple DES Modes of Operation

7. ANSI X9.55 Extensions to Public Key Certificates and CRLs

8. ANSI X9.57 Certificate Management

9. ANSI X9.62 Elliptic Curve Digital Signature Algorithm (draft)

10. ANSI X12.58 Security Structures (version 2)

11. ASTM E 1762 Standard Guide for Authentication of Healthcare Information

12. ASTM E 1869 Draft Standard for Confidentiality, Privacy, Access, and Data Security Principles

13. ASTM PS 100-97 Standard Specification for Authentication of Healthcare Information Using Digital Signatures

14. ASTM PS 101-97 Security Framework for Healthcare Information

15. ASTM PS 102-97 Standard Guide for Internet and Intranet Security

16. ASTM PS 103-97 Authentication and Authorization Guideline

17. CEN European Prestandard

18. FDA Electronic Records—Electronic Signatures—Final Rule

19. FIPS PUB 112 Password Usage

20. FIPS PUB 196 Entity Authentication Using Public Key Cryptography

21. FIPS PUB 46-2 Data Encryption Standard

22. IEEE 802.10: Interoperable LAN/MAN Security (SILS), 1992–1996 (multiple parts)

23. IEEE 802.10c: LAN/WAN Security-Key Management

24. IETF ID Combined SSL/PCT Transport Layer Security Protocol

25. IETF ID FTP Authentication Using DSA

26. IETF ID Secure Hypertext Transfer Protocol (S-HTTP)

27. IETF ID SMIME Cert Handling

28. IETF ID SMIME Message Specification

29. IETF RFC 1422 Privacy Enhanced Mail: Part 1: Message Encryption and Authentication Procedures

30. IETF RFC 1424 Privacy Enhanced Mail: Part 2: Certificate-Based Key Management

31. IETF RFC 1423 Privacy Enhanced Mail: Part 3: Algorithms, Modes, and Identifiers

32. ISO/IEC 9798-1: Information Technology—Security Techniques—Entity Authentication Mechanisms—Part 1: General Model

33. ISO/IEC 9798-2: Information Technology—Security Techniques—Entity Authentication Mechanisms—Part 2: Entity Authentication Using Asymmetric Techniques

34. ISO/IEC 9798-2: Information Technology—Security Techniques—Entity Authentication Mechanisms—Part 2: Entity Authentication Using Symmetric Techniques

35. ISO/IEC 10164-4 Information Technology—Open Systems Connection—System Management: Alarm Reporting Function

36. ISO/IEC 10164-5 Information Technology—Open Systems Connection—System Management: Event Report Management Function

37. ISO/IEC 10164-7 Information Technology—Open Systems Connection—System Management: Security Alarm Reporting Function

38. ISO/IEC 10164-8 Information Technology—Open Systems Connection—System Management: Security Audit Trail Function

39. ISO/IEC 10164-9 Information Technology—Open Systems Connection—System Management: Objects and Attributes for Access Control

40. ISO/IEC 10181-2 Information Technology—Security Frameworks in Open Systems—Authentication Framework

41. ISO/IEC 10181-3 Information Technology—Security Frameworks in Open Systems—Access Control Framework

42. ISO/IEC 10181-4 Information Technology—Security Frameworks in Open Systems—Nonrepudiation Framework

43. ISO/IEC 10181-5 Information Technology—Security Frameworks in Open Systems—Confidentiality Framework

44. ISO/IEC 10181-7 Information Technology—Security Frameworks in Open Systems—Security Audit Framework

45. ISO/IEC 10736 Information Technology—Telecommunications and Information Exchange Between Systems—Transport Layer Security Protocol (TLSP)

46. ISO/IEC 11577 Information Technology—Telecommunications and Information Exchange Between Systems—Network Layer Security Protocol (NLSP)

47. NIST Generally Accepted Principles and Practices for Secure Information Technology Systems

48. NIST MISPC Minimum Interoperability Specification for PKI Components Version 1

49. PKCS #7 Cryptographic Message Syntax Standard Version 1.5 or later

50. PKCS #11 Cryptographic Token Interface

51. RFC 1510 Kerberos Authentication Service

52. RFC 2104 HMAC: Keyed-Hashing for Message Authentication

53. For the Record—Protecting Electronic Health Information

54. ANSI X9.42 Management of Symmetric Keys Using Diffie-Hellman

55. ANSI X9.44 Key Transport Using RSA

References

Health Insurance Portability and Accountability Act of 1996: **cms.hhs.gov/ hipaa/**

HIPAA Security Summit Guidelines: **www.wedi.org/public/articles/ HSSGuidelines.doc**

HIPAAviews (security issues in healthcare): **www.hipaadvisory.com/views/**

About the CD-ROM

The CD-ROM that comes with *CISSP Certification All-in-One Exam Guide* includes:

- **Live cryptography video training**   A QuickTime video/audio file with "live" video training on cryptography, presented by Shon Harris. This is a portion of a complete CISSP training product. (For more information on the complete product, please see the ad at the back of the book.) The QuickTime player must be installed on your computer to play this file. It is available from **www.apple.com**. See the following sections for more instructions.

- **Practice questions**   Total Seminars' Total Tester Software with more than 850 practice questions covering all ten CISSP domains. This testing engine features Practice and Final modes of testing.

The CD is set up with an autorun function. If your autorun is not turned on, browse the CD, and double-click the launcher.exe file to access the software menu page. From the software menu page, you can launch the installation wizard (to install the Total Tester) or run the video training QuickTime file.

Running the QuickTime Cryptography Video Sample

Once you have started the launcher.exe file (either through autorun or by double-clicking the file on the CD-ROM), click the "Play CISSP Video Training" link to start the QuickTime file.

Minimum system requirements for the cryptography video sample:

- Windows 98, 800 MHz Pentium II, 24X CD-ROM drive, 64MB RAM, 800 x 600 monitor, millions of colors, QuickTime 5, Microsoft Internet Explorer 5 or Netscape Navigator 4.5, speakers or headphones

- Macintosh OS 9.2.1, 450 MHz G3, 24X CD-ROM drive, 64MB RAM, 800 x 600 monitor, millions of colors, QuickTime 5, Microsoft Internet Explorer 5 or Netscape Navigator 4.5, speakers or headphones

Recommended system requirements for cryptography video sample:

- Windows 2000, 2 GHz Pentium IV, 48X CD-ROM drive, 128MB RAM, 1024 x 768 monitor, millions of colors, QuickTime 6, Microsoft Internet Explorer 5.5 or Netscape Navigator 4.7, speakers or headphones
- Macintosh OS 10.1, 800 MHz G4, 48X CD-ROM drive, 128MB RAM, 1024 x 768 monitor, millions of colors, QuickTime 6, Microsoft Internet Explorer 5.5 or Netscape Navigator 4.7, speakers or headphones

Troubleshooting

This software runs inside of your Internet browser. You must have its preferences set for correct playback of QuickTime movies to view the movie. The QuickTime installer (free download from **www.apple.com/quicktime**) may not change all of your file helpers properly.

After installing QuickTime, if movies take a very long time to load or don't load at all, verify that your browser associates the file type, ".mov" with the QuickTime plugin. To verify this, do the following:

- If using Internet Explorer for Windows, go to Tools | Internet Options | Advanced | Multimedia or Control Panels | QuickTime.
- If using Internet Explorer for Macintosh, go to Preferences | Receiving Files | Helpers.

Technical Support

For technical support of the cryptography video sample, please browse **www.osborne.com** and click the "errata" link. Locate the title of the book for more information.

Installing Total Seminars' Test Software

Click the Install Test Software button on the wizard, and the installation will proceed automatically.

Once you've completed installation, you can open the test program by selecting Start | Programs | Total Seminars and then clicking on the CISSP tests. You can also start the program with the shortcut the installation places on your desktop.

Navigation

The program enables you to take each of the six tests in either Practice or Final mode. An Adaptive mode exam, which uses a large pool of questions, is also included. Begin by selecting a testing mode and specific test from the menu bar.

Practice Mode

In Practice mode, the test includes an assistance window. This gives you access to several features: Hint (helps you figure out the correct answer), Reference (where in the book to learn more), Check (is your selection correct?), and Explanation (a short note explaining the correct answer). This is a good way to study and review: Answer each question, check to see if you answered correctly, review the explanation, and refer to the book for more detailed coverage. At the end of the test, you are graded by topic and can review missed questions.

Final Mode

Final mode enables you to test yourself without the ability to see the correct answers. This is a better way to see how well you understand the material. Upon completion, you receive a final grade by topic, and you can look over the questions you missed.

Minimum System Requirements for Total Seminars' Software

The minimum system requirements for Total Seminars' software include:

- Pentium 200 MHz
- 4X or faster speed CD-ROM
- 16MB of RAM
- 30MB available hard disk space
- 800 x 600 resolution at 256 colors
- Windows 9*x*/2000/XP operating system

Technical Support

For technical support of the Total Tester practice test application, please go to **www.totalsem.com**. For other technical support issues, please go to **www.osborne.com** and click the "errata" link. Locate the title of the book for more information.

A

access   A subject's ability to view, modify, or communicate with an object. Access enables the flow of information between the subject and the object.

access control   Mechanisms, controls, and methods of limiting access to resources only to authorized subjects.

access control list (ACL)   A list of subjects that are authorized to access a particular object. Typically, the types of access are read, write, execute, append, modify, delete, and create.

access control mechanism   Administrative, physical, and technical controls that are designed to detect and prevent unauthorized access to a resource or environment.

access level   The security level dictates the access level, which is determined by the clearance of the subject and the classification or sensitivity of the data.

accountability   A security principle indicating that individuals must be able to be identified and are to be held responsible for their actions.

accreditation   A computer system or network that has received official authorization and approval to process sensitive data in a specific operational environment. There must be a security evaluation of the system's hardware, software, configurations, and controls by technical personnel.

add-on security   Security protection mechanisms that are hardware or software retrofitted to a system to increase that system's protection level.

administrative controls   These controls include the development and publication of policies, standards, procedures, and guidelines, the screening of personnel, security awareness training, the monitoring of system activity, and change control procedures.

AIC triad   The three security principles: availability, integrity, and confidentiality.

annualized loss expectancy (ALE)   A dollar amount that estimates the loss potential from a risk in a span of a year.

single loss expectancy (SLE) × annualized rate of occurrence (ARO) = ALE

annualized rate of occurrence (ARO)   The value that represents the estimated possibility of a specific threat taking place within a one-year time frame.

assurance   A measurement of confidence in the level of protection a specific security control delivers and the degree to which it enforces the security policy.

attack   An attempt to bypass security controls in a system with the mission of using that system or compromising it. A passive attack will listen to data, but not capture and modify it. An active attack modifies data. An attack is usually accomplished by exploiting a current vulnerability.

audit trail   A chronological set of logs and records used to provide evidence of a system's performance or activity that took place on the system. These logs and records can be used to attempt to reconstruct past events and track the activities that took place and possibly detect and identify intruders.

authenticate   To verify the identity of a subject requesting the use of a system and/ or access to network resource. The steps to giving a subject access to an object should be identifying, authenticating, and authorizing.

authorization   Granting access to a subject to an object after the object has been properly identified and authenticated.

automated information system (AIS)   A computer system that is used to process and transmit data. It is a collection of hardware, software, and firmware that work together to accept, compute, communicate, store, process, transmit, and control data-processing functions.

availability   The reliability and timely access to data and resources by authorized individuals.

B

backdoor   Synonymous with **trapdoor**.

backup   Copying and moving data to a medium so that it may be restored if the original data is corrupted or destroyed. A full backup copies all the data from the system to the backup medium. An incremental backup copies only the files that have been modified since the previous backup. A differential backup backs up all files since the last full backup. Backup copies should be kept at an off-site facility. Backups also deal with having redundant hardware to replace failing or failed hardware.

baseline   The minimum level of security necessary throughout an organization.

Bell-LaPadula model   The computer security policy model that the Orange Book used to form and derive its security requirements. When a subject requests to access an object in a system based on the Bell-LaPadula model, the subject's clearance level is compared to the object's classification level to determine if the access requested is allowed. The model uses a formal state transition model that describes its access controls and how they should perform. When the system must transition from one state to another, the security of the system should never be lowered or compromised. *See also* **multilevel secure**, **star property (*-property)**, and **simple security property**.

Biba model   A security model that conforms to a security policy that is more concerned with integrity than confidentiality. The Biba model addresses the integrity of data being threatened when subjects at lower security levels are able to write to objects at higher security levels. If implemented and enforced properly, the Biba model prevents data from any integrity level from flowing to a higher integrity level.

biometrics   When used within computer security, biometrics is used to identify individuals by physiological characteristics. This can be a fingerprint, hand geometry, or pattern in the iris.

browsing   Searching through storage media looking for specific information without necessarily knowing what format the information is in. A browsing attack is one where the attacker looks around a computer system to see what looks interesting or for specific information.

brute force attack   An attack that continually tries different inputs to achieve at a predefined goal, which can be used to obtain logon authentication credentials.

C

callback   A procedure for identifying a system that accessed an environment remotely. In a callback, the host system disconnects the caller and then dials the authorized telephone number of the remote terminal in order to reestablish the connection. This is synonymous with **dial back**.

capability   When a subject has the right to access an object, that subject will have an identifier indicating this right in a system that uses capability-based authorization. A capability indicates the access rights for a specific subject; many times the capability is in the form of a ticket.

category   When mandatory access control (MAC) is implemented, security labels are assigned to every subject and every object. The subject's label is made up of a classification (top secret, secret, and so on) and a category listing what information this subject can actually access. The classification defines the subject's security clearance and the category defines the subject's need-to-know. The classification piece is hierarchical, whereas the category piece is not.

certification   The technical evaluation of the security components and their compliance for the purpose of accreditation. A certification process can use safeguard evaluation, risk analysis, verification, testing, and auditing techniques to assess the appropriateness of a specific system processing a certain level of information within a particular environment. The certification is the testing of the security component or system, and the accreditation is the approval from management of the security component or system.

challenge-response method   A method used to ensure the identity of a subject by sending the subject an unpredictable or random value. If the subject responds with the expected value in return, the subject is authenticated.

channel   A path used to transmit information from one place to another. Many times a channel is referred to as a communication path within a computer system.

ciphertext   Data that has been encrypted and is usually unreadable until it has been converted into plaintext. The unreadable data is also referred to as cipher, cryptotext, and codetext.

Clark-Wilson model   An integrity model that addresses all three integrity goals: prevent unauthorized users from making modifications, prevent authorized users from making improper modifications, and maintain internal and external consistency through auditing.

classification   When mandatory access control (MAC) is implemented, security labels are assigned to every subject and object. The subject's label is made up of a classification (top secret, secret, and so on) and a category listing what information this subject can actually access. The classification level defines the subject's security clearance and the category defines the subject's need-to-know. The classification piece is hierarchical, whereas the category piece is not.

cleartext   *See* plaintext.

closed security environment   An environment in which both of the following conditions hold true: 1) application developers (including maintainers) have sufficient clearances and authorizations to provide an acceptable presumption that they have not introduced malicious logic, and 2) configuration control provides sufficient assurance that applications and the equipment are protected against the introduction of malicious logic prior to and during the operation of system applications.

closed shop   An environment that uses physical controls to protect a facility or department to prevent unauthorized access or entry.

collusion   More than one person would need to work together to cause some type of destruction or fraud; this drastically reduces its probability.

communications security   Controls in place to protect information as it is being transmitted, especially by telecommunication mechanisms.

compartment A class of information that has need-to-know access controls beyond those normally provided for access to confidential, secret, or top secret information. A compartment is the same thing as a category within a security label. Just because a subject has the proper classification, that does not mean it has a need-to-know. The category, or compartment, of the security label enforces the subject's need-to-know.

compartmentalization Isolating the operating system, user programs, and data files from one another within a system to ensure that they do not access each other in an unauthorized and unsecured manner. Breaking down sensitive information into smaller blocks that are isolated to reduce the risk of others figuring out this information and reduce the risk of unauthorized access.

compartmented mode workstation (CMW) A workstation that contains the necessary controls to be able to operate as a trusted computer. The system is trusted to keep data from different classification levels and categories in separate compartments.

compensating controls Controls that are used in place of other controls. For instance, if an environment does not require a high level of security and does not have the necessary access and auditing controls, it can depend on the supervision of employees as a compensating control to the access and auditing controls.

compromise A violation of the security policy of a system such that unauthorized disclosure or modification of sensitive information occurs.

computer fraud Computer-related crimes involving deliberate misrepresentation, modification, or disclosure of data in order to compromise a system or obtain something of value.

COMSEC A government program that deals with communication security techniques to prevent data from being intercepted and/or modified as it is being transmitted.

confidentiality A security principle that works to ensure that information is not disclosed to unauthorized subjects.

configuration management The identification, control, accounting, and documentation of all changes that take place to system hardware, software, firmware, supporting documentation, and test results throughout the life span of the system.

confinement Controlling information in a way so that it is prevented from leaking sensitive data from a program to another program, subject, or object in an unauthorized manner.

contamination Improperly mixing information at different sensitivity and need-to-know levels.

contingency plan A plan put in place before any potential emergencies with the mission of dealing with possible future emergencies. It pertains to training personnel, performing backups, preparing critical facilities, and recovering from an emergency or disaster so that business operations can continue.

control zone   The space within a facility that is used to protect sensitive processing equipment. Controls are in place to protect from physical or technical unauthorized entry or compromise. The zone can also be used to prevent electrical waves carrying sensitive data from leaving the area.

cost/benefit analysis   An assessment that is performed to ensure that the cost of a safeguard does not outweigh the benefit of the safeguard. It does not make good business sense to spend more protecting an asset than the asset is actually worth. All possible safeguards must be evaluated to ensure that the most security-effective and cost-effective choice is made.

> (ALE before implementing safeguard) – (ALE after implementing safeguard) – (annual cost of safeguard) = value of safeguard to the company

countermeasure   A control, method, technique, or procedure that is put into place to prevent a threat agent from exploiting a vulnerability. A countermeasure is put into place to mitigate risk. Also called a **safeguard**.

covert channel   A communication path that enables a process to transmit information in a way that violates the system's security policy.

covert storage channel   A covert channel that involves direct or indirect writing to a storage location by one process and the direct or indirect reading of the storage location by another process. Covert storage channels typically involve a finite resource (for example, sectors on a disk) that is shared by two subjects at different security levels.

covert timing channel   A covert channel in which one process signals information to another by modulating its own use of system resources (for example, CPU time) in such a way that this manipulation affects the real response time observed by the second process.

cryptanalysis   The practice of breaking cryptosystems and algorithms used in encryption and decryption processes.

cryptoalgorithm   A mathematical set of rules that are used to produce a key stream that is combined with plaintext to result in ciphertext or vice versa.

cryptography   The science of secret writing that enables storage and transmission of data in a form that is available only to the intended individuals.

cryptology   The study of cryptography and cryptanalysis.

cryptosystem   The hardware or software implementation of cryptography.

D

data classification Assignments to data that indicate the level of availability, integrity, and confidentiality that is required for each type of information.

data custodian An individual with the responsibility of the maintenance and protection of the data. This role is usually filled by the IT department (usually the network administrator). The duties include performing regular backups of the data, implementing security mechanisms, periodically validating the integrity of the data, restoring data from backup media, and fulfilling the requirements specified in the company's security policy, standards, and guidelines that pertain to information security and data protection.

Data Encryption Standard (DES) A private key, or symmetric key, encryption algorithm that was adopted by the government as a federal standard for protecting sensitive unclassified information.

data flow control Synonymous with **information flow control**.

database shadowing A redundancy mechanism that uses remote journaling and duplicates database sets to multiple servers.

declassification An administrative decision or procedure to remove or reduce the security classification information.

dedicated security mode A system that operates in this mode if all users have the clearance or authorization and need-to-know to all data processed within the system. All users have been given formal access approval for all information on the system and have signed nondisclosure agreements pertaining to this information.

degauss This demagnetizes magnetic media so that a very low residue of magnetic induction is left on the media. It is a process used to effectively erase data from media.

Delphi technique A group decision method used to ensure that each member of a group gives an honest opinion of what he or she thinks the result to a particular risk will be.

denial of service (DoS) Any action, or series of actions, that prevents any part of a system, or its resources, from functioning in accordance with its intended purpose.

dial back Synonymous with **callback**.

dial-up The service whereby a computer terminal can use telephone lines, usually via a modem, to initiate and continue communication with another computer system.

dictionary attack Types of programs that are fed lists (dictionaries) of commonly used words or combinations of characters and apply these values to a logon prompt with the mission of discovering a user's credentials to obtain unauthorized access to a system.

digital signature A tool used to provide the authentication of the sender of a message. It can verify the origin of the message along with the identity of the sender. It is unique for every transaction and created with a private key.

disaster recovery plan A plan developed to help a company recover from a disaster. It is a procedure for emergency response, extended backup operations, and post-disaster recovery when an organization suffers a loss of computer processing capability or resources and physical facilities.

discretionary access control (DAC) An access control model and policy that restricts access to objects based on the identity of the subjects and the groups to which those subjects belong. The data owner has the discretion of allowing or denying other access to the resources it owns.

domain The set of objects that a subject is allowed to access. Within this domain, all subjects and objects share a common security policy, procedures, and rules, and they are managed by the same management system.

dominate Within the mandatory access control (MAC) model, a subject is said to dominate another subject if the first subject's classification is greater than the second's. The first subject must also include at least all the categories of the second subject's categories.

due care Steps taken to show that a company has taken responsibility for the activities that take place within the corporation and has taken the necessary steps to help protect the company, its resources, and employees.

due diligence Continual activities that make sure the protection mechanisms are continually maintained and operational.

E

electronic vaulting The transfer of backup data to an off-site location. This process is primarily a batch process of transmitting data through communications lines to a server at an alternate location.

emanations Electrical and electromagnetic signals emitted from electrical equipment that can transmit through the airwaves. These signals carry information that can be captured and deciphered, which can cause a security breach. These are also called emissions.

embedded system A system that performs or controls a function, either in whole or in part, as an integral element of a larger system or subsystem.

encryption The transformation of plaintext into unreadable ciphertext.

end-to-end encryption A technology that encrypts data at its origin, is transmitted encrypted, and then is decrypted at its destination, versus being decrypted at each and every hop during its travels. Contrast this with **link encryption**.

enticement   Luring an intruder to a system that seems to be vulnerable. Enticement is legal.

entrapment   The deliberate planting of apparent flaws to induce a crime and trick a person into trespassing or performing acts that are deemed illegal. Entrapment is illegal. It is different from **enticement**.

Evaluated Products List (EPL)   A list of equipment, hardware, software, and/ or firmware that have been evaluated and found to meet the necessary requirements of a specific trust level of the Trusted Computer Security Evaluation Criteria (TCSEC) by the National Computer Security Center (NCSC).

executive state   One of several states in which a system can operate, and the only one in which certain privileged instructions can be executed. Such instructions cannot be executed when the system is operating in other (for example, user) states. This is synonymous with **supervisor state**.

exposure   An instance of being exposed to losses from a threat. A weakness or vulnerability can cause an organization to be exposed to possible damages.

exposure factor   The percentage of loss a realized threat could have on a certain asset.

F

failover   A backup operation that automatically switches to a standby system if the primary system fails or is taken offline. It is an important fault tolerant function that provides system availability.

fail-safe   A functionality that ensures that when software or a system fails for any reason, it does not end up in a vulnerable state. After a failure, software might default to no access instead of allowing full control, which would be an example of a fail-safe measure.

firmware   Software instructions that have been written into read-only memory (ROM) or programmable ROM.

formal security policy model   A mathematically precise statement of a security policy. When an operating system is built, it is built upon a predeveloped model that lays out how all activities will take place in each and every situation. This model is expressed mathematically, which is then translated into a programming language. For the model to be secure, it must ensure that the system will not enter an insecure state under any circumstances. This and other requirements are necessary for it to be a secure system and to be acceptable as a basis for trusted computing base (TCB).

formal verification   Using automated tools to aid in the designing and testing of highly trusted systems. The tests are designed to show design verification, consistency between the formal specifications and the formal security policy model, implementation verification, consistency between the formal specifications, and the actual implementation of it.

functional testing   Security testing in which the advertised security mechanisms of the system are tested for their functionality.

G

gateway   A system or device that connects two unlike environments or systems. The gateway is usually required to translate between different types of applications or protocols. The gateway can also filter out unwanted packets.

guidelines   Recommendation actions and operational guides for users, IT staff, operations staff, and others when a specific standard does not apply.

H

handshaking procedure   A dialogue between two entities for the purpose of identifying and authenticating the entities to one another. The dialogue can take place between a user and a computer, a computer and a server, or between two computers. It is an activity that usually takes place within a protocol.

honeypot   A computer set up as a sacrificial lamb on the network in the hope that attackers will attack this system instead of actual production systems.

I

identification   The process that enables one subject to recognize another subject or object. Identification is the first step in the authentication process.

incomplete parameter checking   A system design flaw that results when software does not properly check how data is inputted. The result of this flaw can result in incorrect data-processing results or buffer overflows.

information flow control   A procedure to ensure that information transfers within a system are not made from a higher security level object to an object of a lower security level. *See also* **covert channel**, **simple security property**, and **star property** (***-property**).

information owner   This person is usually a senior executive within the management group of the company. The information owner has final corporate responsibility of data protection and would be the one held liable for any negligence when it comes to protecting the company's information assets. The person who holds this role is responsible for assigning a classification to the information and dictating how the information should be protected.

Information System Security Officer (ISSO)   The person who is responsible for ensuring that security is provided for and implemented throughout the life cycle of a computer system and network from the beginning of the concept development plan through its design, development, operation, maintenance, and secure disposal.

integrity   A security principle that makes sure that information and systems are not modified maliciously or accidentally.

intrusion detection system (IDS)   Software employed to monitor and detect possible attacks and behaviors that vary from the normal and expected activity. The IDS can be network-based, which monitors network traffic, or host-based, which monitors activities of a specific system and protects system files and control mechanisms.

isolation   The containment of subjects and objects in a system in such a way that they are separated from one another as well as from the protection controls of the operating system.

K

kernel   *See* security kernel.

key   In the context of cryptography, a secret value in the form of a sequence of characters used to encrypt and decrypt messages.

keystroke monitoring   A type of auditing that can review or record keystrokes entered by a user during an active session.

L

lattice-based access control   An access control that provides an upper bound and lower bound of access capabilities when sensitivity labels are used.

least privilege   The security principle that requires each subject to be granted the most restrictive set of privileges needed for the performance of authorized tasks. The application of this principle limits the damage that can result from accident, error, or unauthorized use.

life cycle assurance   Confidence that a trusted system is designed, developed, and maintained with formal designs and controls. This includes design specification and verification, implementation, testing, configuration management, and distribution.

link encryption   A type of encryption where the data is encrypted at its origin and decrypted and reencrypted at each hop during its travel to its destination. Each network communication node, or hop, must decrypt it to read its address and routing information. This is different from **end-to-end encryption**.

logic bomb   A malicious program that is triggered by a specific event or condition.

loss potential   The potential losses that can be accrued if a threat agent actually exploits a vulnerability.

M

magnetic remanence   A measure of the magnetic flux density remaining after removal of the applied magnetic force, which is used to erase data. Refers to any data remaining on magnetic storage media.

maintenance hook   Instructions within a program's code that enable the developer or maintainer to enter the program without having to go through the usual access control and authentication processes. They should be removed from the code before being released for production; otherwise, they can cause serious security risks. Also called **trapdoor**.

malware   Malicious software. Code written to perform activities that circumvent the security policy of a system. Examples are viruses, malicious applets, Trojan horses, and worms.

mandatory access control (MAC)   An access policy that restricts subjects' access to objects based on the security level of the subject and the classification of the object. The system enforces the security policy and users cannot share their files with other users.

masquerading   Impersonating another user, usually with the intention of gaining unauthorized access to a system.

message authentication   Making sure that the message sent contains the same information as when it was sent. It ensures that a message was not altered during transmission.

message authentication code (MAC)   A value that is calculated during an encryption process and appended to a message. The receiving system receives the message and performs the same calculations and compares its results to the results appended to the message. If the values are the same, the receiver can be sure that the message was not altered during transmission.

multilevel device   A device that is used in a manner that permits it to simultaneously process data of two or more security levels without the risk of compromise. To accomplish this, sensitivity labels are normally stored on the same physical medium and in the same form (for example, machine-readable or human-readable) as the data being processed.

multilevel secure   A class of systems containing information with different sensitivities that simultaneously permits access by users with different security clearances and needs-to-know, but that prevents users from obtaining access to information for which they lack authorization.

multiuser mode of operation   A mode of operation designed for systems that process sensitive, unclassified information in which users might not have a need-to-know for all information processed in the system. This mode is also for microcomputers that are processing sensitive, unclassified information that cannot meet the requirements of the stand-alone mode of operation.

N

need-to-know   A security principle stating that users should only have access to the information and resources necessary to complete their tasks that fulfill their roles within an organization.

node   A system that is connected to a network.

O

object   A passive entity that contains or receives information. Access to an object potentially implies access to the information that it contains. Examples of objects include the following: records, blocks, pages, segments, files, directories, directory trees, and programs, as well as bits, bytes, words, fields, processors, video displays, keyboards, clocks, printers, and network nodes.

object reuse   The reassignment to a subject of a medium that previously contained information. It can be a security concern because the measures that were taken to erase the information may not have done a thorough job and the information may still be retainable. Therefore, information could be disclosed to unauthorized personnel.

one-time pad   Uses a nonrepeating set of random bits that are combined bitwise XOR with the message to produce ciphertext. A one-time pad is a perfect encryption scheme, because it is unbreakable and each pad is used exactly once.

open security environment   An environment that includes those systems in which at least one of the following conditions holds true: 1) application developers (including maintainers) do not have sufficient clearance or authorization to provide an acceptable presumption that they have not introduced malicious logic, and 2) configuration control does not provide sufficient assurance that applications are protected against the introduction of malicious logic prior to and during the operation of system applications.

operational assurance   A level of confidence of a trusted system's architecture and implementation that enforces the system's security policy. This can include system architecture, covert channel analysis, system integrity, and trusted recovery.

operational goals   Daily goals to be accomplished to ensure the proper operation of an environment.

operator   An individual who supports the operations of computer systems. The individual may monitor the execution of the system, control the flow of jobs, and develop and schedule batch jobs.

Orange Book   The common name for the Trusted Computer Security Evaluation Criteria (TCSEC).

overt channel   A path within a computer system or network that is designed for the authorized transfer of data.

P

partitioned security mode   A mode of operation wherein all personnel have the clearance, but not necessarily the formal access approval and need-to-know for all information contained in the system. This should not be confused with compartmented security mode.

password   A sequence of characters used to prove one's identity. It is used during a logon process and should be highly protected.

penetration   A successful attempt at circumventing security controls and gaining access to a system.

penetration testing   Testing that attempts to circumvent security controls within an environment so that vulnerabilities and weaknesses can be uncovered.

permissions   The type of authorized interactions that a subject can have with an object. Examples include read, write, execute, add, modify, and delete.

personnel security   The procedures that are established to ensure that all personnel who have access to sensitive information have the required authority as well as appropriate clearances. Procedures confirm a person's background and provide assurance of necessary trustworthiness.

physical controls   These controls pertain to controlling individual access into the facility and different departments, locking systems and removing unnecessary floppy or CD-ROM drives, protecting the perimeter of the facility, monitoring for intrusion, and checking environmental controls.

physical security   Controls and procedures put into place to prevent intruders from physically accessing a system or facility. The controls enforce access control and authorized access.

piggyback   Unauthorized access to a system via another user's legitimate connection.

plaintext   In cryptography, the original text before it is encrypted.

playback   Capturing and recording a message and resending the message at a later time in the hope of tricking the receiving system.

privacy   A security principle that protects an individual's information and employs controls to ensure that this information is not disseminated or accessed in an unauthorized manner.

privileged instructions Instructions that are executed by the process of a higher security level within a system. The instructions are usually sent to control mechanisms within the system and can only be executed when the system is operating in an executive state.

procedure Detailed step-by-step actions to achieve a certain task, which are used by users, IT staff, operations staff, security members, and others who may need to install or configure a computer component.

protection ring Supports the integrity and confidentiality requirements of multitasking operating systems and enables the operating system to protect itself from user programs and rogue processes.

protocols A set of rules and formats that enable the proper exchange of information between different systems.

pseudo-flaw An apparent loophole deliberately implanted in an operating system program as a trap for intruders.

public key encryption A type of encryption that uses two mathematically related keys to encrypt and decrypt messages. The private key is known only to the owner, and the public key is available to anyone.

purge The removal of sensitive data from a system, storage device, or peripheral device with storage capacity at the end of a processing period. This action is performed in such a way that there is assurance proportional to the sensitivity of the data that the data cannot be reconstructed.

Q

qualitative risk analysis An analysis that judges an organization's risks to threats, which is based on judgment, intuition, and the experience versus assigning real numbers to this possible risks and their potential loss margins.

quantitative risk analysis A process that attempts to assign real numbers to the costs of countermeasures and the amount of damage that can take place.

R

RADIUS (Remote Authentication Dial-in User Service) A security service that authenticates and authorizes dial-up users and is a centralized access control mechanism.

read An operation that results in the flow of information from an object to a subject and does not give the subject the ability to modify the object or the data within the object.

recovery planning The advance planning and preparations that are necessary to minimize loss and to ensure the availability of the critical information systems of an organization after a disruption in service or a disaster.

reference monitor concept An access-control concept that refers to an abstract machine that mediates all accesses to objects by subjects.

reference-validation mechanism An implementation of the reference monitor concept. A security kernel is a type of reference-validation mechanism.

reliability The assurance of a given system performing its mission adequately for a specified period of time under the expected operating conditions.

remote journaling A method of transmitting data off-site. This takes place as parallel processing of transactions and in real time to provide redundancy and fault tolerance.

repudiation When the sender of a message denies sending the message in the first place or when the receiver denies that the received message was actually received.

residual risk The remaining risk after the security controls have been applied.

threats × vulnerability × asset value = total risk

(threats × vulnerability × asset value) × controls gap = residual risk

risk The likelihood of a threat agent taking advantage of a vulnerability. A risk is the loss potential, or probability, that a threat will exploit a vulnerability.

risk analysis A method of identifying risks and assessing the possible damage that could be caused in order to justify security safeguards.

risk management The process of identifying, assessing, and reducing the risk to an acceptable level and implementing the right mechanisms to maintain that level of risk.

role-based access control (RBAC) This type of model provides access to resources based on the role the user holds within the company or the tasks that user has been assigned.

S

safeguard A software configuration, hardware, or procedure that eliminates a vulnerability or reduces the risk of a threat agent from being able to exploit a vulnerability. Also called a **countermeasure**.

secure configuration management The set of procedures that are appropriate for the process of controlling the life cycle of an application, documenting the necessary change control activities, and ensuring that the changes will not violate the security policy.

secure state A condition in which no subject can access any object in an unauthorized manner.

security evaluation   Assesses the degree of trust that can be placed in systems for the secure handling of sensitive information.

security kernel   The hardware, firmware, and software elements of a trusted computing base (TCB) that implement the reference monitor concept. The kernel must mediate all accesses between subjects and objects, be protected from modification, and be verifiable as correct.

security label   An identifier that represents the security level of an object.

security level   The combination of the classification and the categories listed within a sensitivity label.

security perimeter   An imaginary boundary between the trusted computing base (TCB) and other system mechanisms and functions. It is the distinction between trusted and untrusted processes.

security policy   The set of laws, rules, and practices that regulates how an organization manages, protects, and distributes sensitive information.

security requirements baseline   Minimum requirements necessary for a system to maintain an acceptable level of security.

security testing   Testing all security mechanisms and features within a system to determine the level of protection they provide. Security testing can include penetration testing, formal design and implementation verification, or functional testing.

sensitive information   Information that would cause a negative effect on the data owner if it were lost or compromised.

sensitivity label   A piece of information that represents the security level of an object. Sensitivity labels are used by the TCB as the basis for mandatory access control (MAC) decisions.

separation of duties   A security principle that splits up a task among individuals to ensure that one person cannot complete a risky task by himself.

shoulder surfing   When a person looks over another person's shoulder and watches keystrokes or data as they appear on the screen in order to uncover information in an unauthorized manner.

simple security property   A Bell-LaPadula security model rule that enables a subject to read data within an object if the subject's security level dominates the security level of the object.

single-level security   Pertains to a system that gives access only to users of the same sensitivity level. A single-level device only processes data of a single security level at a time, as opposed to a multilevel device, which can process data at different security levels at one time.

single loss expectancy (SLE)   A dollar amount that is assigned to a single event that represents the company's potential loss amount if a specific threat took place.

$$\text{asset value} \times \text{exposure factor} = \text{SLE}$$

social engineering   The act of tricking another person into telling confidential information by posing as an individual authorized for that information.

spoofing   Presenting false information, usually within packets, to trick other systems and hide the origin of the message. This is usually done by hackers and attackers so they cannot be successfully uncovered.

standards   Rules indicating how hardware and software should be implemented, used, and maintained. They provide a means to ensure that specific technologies, applications, parameters, and procedures are carried out in a uniform way across the organization. They are compulsory.

star property (*-property)   A Bell-LaPadula security model rule that provides a subject write access to an object if the security level of the subject dominates the security level of the object.

strategic goals   Long-term goals that look far into the future. Operational and tactical goals support strategic goals.

subject   An active entity, generally in the form of a person, process, or device, that causes information to flow among objects or that changes the system state.

supervisor state   Synonymous with **executive state**.

system low   The lowest security level supported by a system at a particular time or in a particular environment.

system high   The highest security level supported by a system at a particular time or in a particular environment.

T

TACACS (Terminal Access Controller Access Control System)   A client/server protocol that provides the same type of functionality as RADIUS and is used as a central access control mechanism mainly for remote users.

tactical goals   Midterm goals to accomplish. These may be milestones to accomplish within a project or specific projects to accomplish in a year.

technical controls   These controls include logical access control mechanisms, password and resource management, identification and authentication methods, security devices, and the configuration of the network.

Tempest   The study and control of spurious electronic signals emitted by electrical equipment. Tempest equipment is implemented to prevent intruders from picking up information through the airwaves with listening devices.

threat   Any potential danger to information or systems.

top-down approach   A project that has the initiation, support, and direction come from top management and work its way through middle management and then to staff members.

topology   The physical construction of how nodes are connected to form a network.

total risk   When a safeguard is not implemented, an organization is faced with the total risk of that particular vulnerability.

trapdoor   A hidden entry point into a system or application that is usually triggered by a certain command or keyboard sequence. Software developers and maintainers usually insert them into programming code for easy entry at a later time. This is synonymous with **backdoor**.

Trojan horse   A computer program having an apparently or actually useful function that contains additional hidden, malicious capability to exploit a vulnerability and/or provide unauthorized access into a system. Usually, a user accidentally initializes the Trojan horse.

trusted computer system   A system that has the necessary controls to ensure that the security policy will not be compromised and that can process a range of sensitive or classified information simultaneously.

trusted computing base (TCB)   All of the protection mechanisms within a computer system (software, hardware, and firmware) that are responsible for enforcing a security policy. The TCB is dependent upon its mechanisms and the correct input of the system administrative personnel to properly enforce the security policy.

trusted path   A mechanism within the system that enables the user to communicate directly with the TCB. This mechanism can only be activated by the user or the TCB and not by an untrusted mechanism or process.

trusted recovery   A set of procedures that restores a system and its data in a trusted manner after the system has been disrupted or a system failure has occurred.

U

user   A person or process that is accessing a computer system.

user ID   A unique set of characters or code that is used to identify a specific user to a system.

V

validation   The act of performing tests and evaluations to test a system's security level to see if it complies with security specifications and requirements.

virus   A small application, or string of code, that infects applications. The main function of a virus is to reproduce, and it requires a host application to do this. It can damage data directly or degrade system performance.

vulnerability   A vulnerability characterizes the absence or weakness of a safeguard that could be exploited.

W

wardialing   A long list of phone numbers are inserted into a wardialing program in the hope of finding a modem that can be exploited to gain unauthorized access.

work factor   The estimated time and effort required for an attacker to overcome a security control.

worm   An independent program that can reproduce by copying itself from one system to another. It may damage data directly or degrade system performance by tying up resources.

write   An operation that results in the flow of information from a subject to an object.

INDEX

Numbers

0-10 RAID levels, explanations of, 431
3DES (Triple-DES), overview of, 487–488
10Base-T Ethernet, overview of, 340
10Base2 Ethernet, overview of, 340–341
10Base5 Ethernet, overview of, 340
50-ohm coaxial cabling, use of, 346
75-ohm coaxial cabling, use of, 346
414 Club, purpose of, 609
802.* standards, overview of, 436–439
802.11 and Spread Spectrum, Web address for, 434
802.11 wireless standard
    overview of, 813–822
    problems with, 814–817, 820
802.11i wireless standard
    benefits of, 821
802.11i working group, purpose of, 443
802.1X standard, overview of, 815–818
7799 British Standard, overview of, 235, 799–800

A

A-D
    classes of fires, 277, 281
    security levels in TCSEC, 223–226
A division protection in Orange Book, explanation of, 226
abstraction, explanation of, 210, 705
access control
    categories of, 148–156
    restricting for databases, 666
access control administration
    centralized method of, 144
    Diameter used in, 146
    overview of, 143–147
    RADIUS (Remote Authentication Dial-In User Service), 144–145
TACACS (Terminal Access Controller Access Control System), overview of, 144–146
access control matrix, overview of, 141
access control methods, overview of, 147–156
access control models. *See also* lattice-based access; task-based access
    DAC (discretionary access control), 135–136
    enforcement of, 286
    exam tip for, 156
    MAC (mandatory access control), 136
    overview of, 135, 138
    RBAC (role-based access control), 137–139
    Web address for, 220
access control monitoring, overview of, 168–172
Access Control Policies and Mechanisms, Web address for, 209
access control practices, overview of, 165–168
Access Control Systems and Methodology CBK domain, description of, 4
access control techniques, overview of, 140–143
access controls, 156–164
    coverage by policies, standards, guidelines, and procedures, 83
    establishing for sensitivity classifications, 86
    functionalities of, 156
    mechanisms of, 123–125
    overview of, 107–108
    physical and logical locations used as, 124
    threats to, 172–175
access, explanation of, 107
access points, identifying, 287
access rights, criteria for granting of, 124
access triples, explanation of, 216
accountability
    explanation of, 616
    overview of, 161–164
    role in operational security, 756–757

accountability controls, coverage by policies, standards, guidelines, and procedures, 83

accreditation versus certification, 234–235, 694

ACID (Atomicity, Consistency, Isolation, Durability) test, explanation of, 679–680

ACK (acknowledgment) packets, role in TCP handshakes, 329

ACLs (access control lists)
    dynamics of, 125–126, 142
    role in packet filtering, 372, 374

acoustical-seismic detection systems, features of, 296

active monitoring in Token Ring, explanation of, 343

ActiveX, overview of, 726–727

ad hoc WLANs, explanation of, 441

administrative access controls
    applying to physical security, 284–286
    components of, 148
    coverage by policies, standards, guidelines, and procedures, 83
    examples of, 159–160
    explanation of, 51–52
    overview of, 149–150
    for physical security, 256–257

administrative management, role in operational security, 754–756

administrative/regulatory laws, purpose of, 619

ADO (ActiveX Data Objects), explanation of, 670

advisory policies, explanation of, 81

AES (Advanced Encryption Standard)
    explanation of, 484, 488
    role in 802.11 standard, 814
    Web address for, 491, 509

aggregation in databases, explanation of, 675–676

AH (Authentication Header) protocol, role in IPSec, 527–529

AI (artificial intelligence), use of, 720–721

AIC (availability, integrity, and confidentiality) triad
    example of, 200
    overview of, 54–56
    role in business continuity and disaster recovery, 550–551
    role in cryptosystems, 465

    role in network and resource availability, 429
    role in security models and architectures, 186

ALE (annualized loss expectancy), role in risk analysis, 69–71

algorithms, role in cryptography, 462

alternate power sources, explanation of, 269

ALUs (arithmetic logic units), role in CPUs, 187

amplitude
    role in analog transmission, 332
    of signals, 433

analog signals, explanation of, 351

analog transmission, overview of, 332–333

ANNs (artificial neural networks), overview of, 722–724

ANSI (American National Standards Institute), responsibilities of, 804

answers
    to access control questions, 182–184
    to application and system development questions, 748–751
    to business continuity planning questions, 591–593
    to cryptography questions, 545–547
    to law, investigation, and ethics questions, 653–656
    to operations security questions, 789–792
    to physical security questions, 306–309
    to sample CISSP exam questions, 15
    to security management practices questions, 104–106
    to security models and architectures questions, 250–252
    to telecommunications and networking security questions, 453–455

AntiOnline Computer Security, Web address for, 612

applets
    controlling with browser settings, 725
    explanation of, 724–726

application and system development
    and change control, 698–700
    data types, format, and length considerations, 663
    database management issues, 665–681
    implementation and default issues, 663–665
    role of failure states in, 665

Application and Systems Development Security
CBK domain, description of, 4
application development methodology
and object-oriented concepts, 702–708
overview of, 701–702
application layer
and mail servers, 42
overview of, 316, 323
protecting, 41
and Web server configuration, 42
and Web servers, 42
application-level proxy firewalls, features of,
377–380, 385
application versus environment controls,
661–662
applications and system development, overview
of, 657–658
APs (access points)
role in 802.1X standard, 816
role in WLANs, 441–442
APSTNDP mnemonic, meaning of, 320
ARO (annualized rate of occurrence), role in
risk analysis, 70
ARP (Address Resolution Protocol)
overview of, 356–357
versus RARP, 357
ARP table poisoning, explanation of, 357
Arts top-level DNS domain, meaning of, 393
AS (authentication service), role in KDC, 131
ASICs (application-specific integrated circuits),
role in multilayered switches, 366
ASs (autonomous systems), use in routing
environments, 364–365
assembly language, explanation of, 702
assets and information, value in risk analysis,
63–64
assurance
explanation of, 221
of systems, 229–230
asymmetric cryptography
overview of, 476–480
using with symmetric cryptography,
492–494, 496–497
asymmetric encryption algorithms
ECCs (Elliptic Curve Cryptosystems), 491
El Gamal, 491
RSA (Rivest, Shamir, Adleman), 489

asymmetric services, using with DSL, 419
asynchronous attacks, overview of and
countermeasures for, 239–240
asynchronous token devices, overview of, 120
asynchronous transmission
explanation of, 351
overview of, 333–334
atbash cryptography, explanation of, 458
ATM (Asynchronous Transfer Mode)
characteristics of, 415
combining with IP or frame relay, 414
role in WAN technologies, 410
ATM (Asynchronous Transfer Mode), origins of,
400–401
ATM Forum, Web address for, 415
attack and hack methods. See hack and attack
methods
attack signature-detection tools, purpose of, 163
attackers
identifying, protecting against, and
prosecuting, 612–614
profile of, 29
threats resulting from, 65
vulnerability to, 34
attacks. See also computer fraud
by Chaos Computer Club, 610
chosen-ciphertext attacks, 532–533
chosen-plaintext attacks, 532
ciphertext-only attacks, 531
The Cuckoo's Egg, 608
by Cult of the Dead Cow, 610
DDoS (distributed denial of service)
attacks, 736–737
dictionary attacks, 534–535
DNS DoS attacks, 737–738
DoS (denial-of-service) attacks, 732–733
Fraggle attacks, 734
by Kevin Mitnick, 608
known-plaintext attacks, 531–532
main-in-the middle attacks, 533–534
overview of, 531
by Phone Phreakers, 610–612
replay attacks, 534
Secure DNS attacks, 738–739
side channel attacks, 535–536
smurf attacks, 732–734
SYN floods, 734–736

taking countermeasures against, 41–42
Teardrops attacks, 736
timing attacks, 739
types of, 778–779
attenuation, occurrence of, 339, 349
audit data, protecting, 164
audit information, reviewing, 162–163
audit reductions, explanation of, 163
auditing capabilities, overview of, 161–164
auditing, role in logical access controls, 155–156
auditors, security role of, 91
authentication
    versus authorization, 123
    categories on Google, 164
    diagram of, 120
    explanation of, 110–111
    and identification, 112
    in Kerberos, 130–132
Authentication, Authorization, and Accounting Charter, Web address for, 164
authenticators, using with Kerberos implementations, 131
authoritative name servers, using with DNS, 391
authority, role in business continuity planning, 561
authorization
    access criteria for, 123–125
    versus authentication, 123
    overview of, 123
authorization creep, explanation of, 603
authorization, explanation of, 111
automatic dial-up alarms, overview of, 280
availability, role in AIC triad, 54, 108–109

B

B division protection in Orange Book, explanation of, 225–226
B1 and B2 ratings in Orange Book, explanation of, 202
B2 rating in Red Book, explanation of, 229
B2 ratings versus C1 ratings, 238
back-end tiers, explanation of, 33
Back Orifice tool, Web address for, 778

backdoors
    overview of, 777–779
    overview of and countermeasures for, 238–239
backups
    of hardware, 568–577
    importance of, 559
    performing, 266, 432
    role in physical access controls, 152
    types of, 574
Bank of California, hacker attack on, 23
baseband transmission, explanation of, 334, 351
baselines
    modularity of, 83
    overview of, 81–82
Basic Security Theorem, explanation of, 214
bastion hosts, role in firewall architecture, 381–382
BCP (business continuity planning) controls, coverage by policies, standards, guidelines, and procedures, 83
beaconing in Token Ring, explanation of, 343
beacons, APs (access points) as, 441
behavior-based IDS, overview of, 169
Bell-LaPadula security model
    versus Biba model, 215
    overview of, 212–214, 219
    rules in, 216
best evidence related to computer crimes, explanation of, 631
BIA (business impact analysis)
    performing, 553–558
    Web address for, 566
Biba security model
    overview of, 214–216, 219
    rules in, 216
Bibliofind, hacker attack on, 22
biometric systems, dynamics of, 112–116
birthday attacks, explanation of, 509–510
BISDN (Broadband-ISDN), explanation of, 417
Black Boxes, explanation of, 610–611
blackouts, explanation of, 270
block ciphers, overview of, 480–483
Blowfish, overview of, 489
Blue Boxing, explanation of, 610

Bluetooth wireless technology, access provided by, 438–439

bollards, using, 292–293

boot sector viruses, explanation of, 728

BOOTP (Boot Protocol), purpose of, 357–358

bottom-up approach, explanation of, 59

Brewer and Nash security model, overview of, 218–219

BRI (Basic Rate Interface) ISDN, explanation of, 417–418

bridges
    features of, 359–360
    functionality of, 370
    OSI layer associated with, 361
    versus routers, 360, 363
    Web address for, 361

British Standard 7799, overview of, 235, 799–800

broadband transmission, explanation of, 334, 351

broadband wireless access, explanation of, 438

broadcast LAN transmissions, explanation of, 350–352

broadcast storms, occurrence of, 359

brownouts, explanation of, 270

browser settings, controlling applets with, 725

browsing as hack and attack method, overview of, 774–775

brute force attacks, overview of and countermeasures for, 173–174, 777

buffer overflows
    exploitation of, 663
    functionality of, 188–189
    overview of and countermeasures for, 240

burglar alarms. *See* IDSes (intrusion detection systems)

bus network topology, overview of, 336–338

business continuity planning, 566–567, 630
    developing goals for, 560–562
    developing team for, 562, 564
    enterprise-wide factors related to, 563–565
    interdependencies within, 557–558
    overview of, 550–553
    reasons for, 565
    requirements for, 558–559
    role of documentation in, 577–578
    role of human resources in, 578
    role of testing and drills in, 579–582
    six steps involved in, 565–567

Business Continuity Planning and Disaster Recover Planning CBK domain, description of, 5

business-critical functions, identifying, 566

business requirements, overview of, 61

BXA (Bureau of Export Administration), purpose of, 636

C

C division protection in Orange Book, explanation of, 224–225

C1-C2 ratings in Red Book, explanation of, 229

C2 assurance rating, example of, 81

cable lock, example of, 288–289

cable modems, overview of, 419–420

cabling
    coaxial cable, 346–347
    for Ethernet, 340, 811
    for FDDI, 344
    fiber-optic cabling, 347–348
    fire ratings of, 350
    guidelines for selection of, 350
    overview of, 346
    role in physical access controls, 152–153
    twisted-pair cabling, 346–348

cabling problems
    attenuation, 349
    crosstalk, 349
    noise, 348–349

cache memory, overview of, 189–190

cache poisoning, role in DNS DoS attacks, 738

Caesar Cipher, explanation of, 466–467

callback option, configuring for remote access, 428

Caller ID settings, configuration for remote access, 428

capability tables, role in access control, 141–142

Cap'n Crunch hacker, notoriety of, 611

carrier-sensing and Token-passing access methods, advisory about, 354

CAs (certificate authorities, role in PKI, 497–498

cascading errors, role identifying threats, 66

CASE (Computer-Aided Software Engineering), explanation of, 698, 714–715

catastrophes, explanation of, 568–569

Category 1-7 UTP cable ratings, table of, 348

CBC (Cipher Block Chaining) mode of DES, overview of, 485–486

CBK (Common Body of Knowledge), domains included in, 2–6

CCMP, role in 802.11 standard, 814

CCTVs (closed-circuit TVs), using, 294

ceiling panels, vulnerability of, 260–262

cell suppression, implementing in databases, 677

centralized access control administration, overview of, 144

CER (crossover error rate), role in biometric systems, 113–114

CERT Coordination Center, Web address for, 630

certificates, role in PKI, 498

certification versus accreditation, 234–235, 694

CFB (Cipher Feedback) mode of DES, overview of, 486–487

chain of custody, role in computer forensics, 627–628

change control, overview of, 698–700

change management control, role in security operations and product evaluation, 758–760

channels, role in communication between APs and wireless devices, 442

Chaos Computer Club, attacks by, 610

CHAP (Challenge Handshake Authentication Protocol), overview of, 426–427

checklist tests, role in business continuity planning, 580

checkpoints in databases, explanation of, 675

chemical combustion, suppressing, 282

Chinese Wall security model, overview of, 218

chipping code, role in DSSS, 435

chosen-ciphertext attacks, overview of, 532–533

chosen-plaintext attacks, overview of, 532

CIAO (Critical Infrastructure Assurance Office), purpose of, 27

cipher locks, features of, 288–289

ciphers, types of, 466–468

ciphertext-only attacks, overview of, 531

CIR (committed information rate), role in WAN technologies, 407

circuit-level proxy firewalls
    characteristics of, 385
    features of, 377–380

circuit switching, explanation of, 405–407

circumstantial evidence related to computer crimes, explanation of, 632

CISSP (Certified Information Systems Security Professional)
    requirements for, 1

CISSP exam
    cost of, 3
    day of, 10
    finding testing sites and dates for, 7
    overview of, 2–6
    passing score for, 3
    preparing for, 9–10
    qualifications for, 3
    registering for, 7
    retaking, 3
    sample questions and answers for, 11–15
    scoring of questions in, 2–3
    time allowed for, 9

CISSP.com Web Portal, Web address for, 11

CISSPs (Certified Information Systems Security Professionals)
    annual maintenance fees required of, 8
    becoming, 7
    history of, 6–7
    reasons for becoming certified as, 1–6
    recertification requirements for, 7–8

civil laws, purpose of, 618–619

Clark-Wilson security model, overview of, 216, 219

Classes 1-3 of WTLS, explanations of, 440

classes, grouping objects into, 210

Classical Cryptography, Web address for, 468

classification labels, assigning to subjects in Bell-LaPadula model, 214

clean power, role in electrical power, 269

Cleanroom software development, explanation of, 697

clearance labels, assigning to subjects in Bell-LaPadula model, 214

cleartext, explanation of, 462

client/server model, overview of, 661

Clipper Chip
    explanation of, 461
    key escrow and key recovery used with, 473
    overview of, 470–472

clipping levels, role in security operations and product evaluation, 757–758 closed environment, explanation of, 17

closed versus open systems, 236

clouds, role in frame relay, 408

clustering, overview of, 431–432

CMM (Capability Maturity Model), overview of, 700–701

CMWs (compartmented mode workstations), purpose of, 221

coaxial cable, features of, 346

Code of Ethics, Web addresses for, 597

cognitive passwords, overview of, 118–119

cohesive modules, features of, 711–712

cold sites, placing backups in, 569

collision domains, overview of, 354–355

collision, explanation of, 509

collision-free hashing algorithms, explanation of, 506

collusion, role in personnel controls, 149

COM (Component Object Model), overview of, 716–717

COM top-level DNS domain, meaning of, 392

Commercial Product Evaluations, Web site for, 803

commit statements in databases, explanation of, 674

Common Criteria
    components of, 233
    explanation of, 44
    overview of, 231–234
    Web addresses for information about, 234

compartmented security mode, overview of, 220–221

compiled versus interpreted programs, 703

compression viruses, explanation of, 729

computer architectures
    overview of, 187–199
    threats to, 236–240

computer controls, role in physical access controls, 151

computer-crime examples
    Chaos Computer Club, 610
    The Cuckoo's Egg, 608
    Cult of the Dead Cow, 610
    Kevin Mitnick, 608
    Phone Phreakers, 610–612

computer crimes
    identifying, protecting against, and prosecuting, 612–614
    international cooperation efforts against, 644–645
    investigation of, 625–629
    liability and ramifications of, 614–618
    reporting, 625–627

computer criminals, interviewing and interrogating, 635

Computer Ethics Institute, overview of, 598

computer forensics and collection of evidence, overview of, 627–629

computer fraud. *See also* attacks
    data diddling, 603
    DoS (denial-of-service) attacks, 605
    dumpster diving, 605–606
    emanations capturing, 606
    excessive privileges, 603
    IP spoofing, 604
    password sniffing, 604
    Salami attacks, 602
    social engineering, 607
    wiretapping, 607

Computer Fraud and Abuse Act, purpose of, 641

computer logs, importance in investigating computer crimes, 630

computer operations, coverage by policies, standards, guidelines, and procedures, 83

computer rooms, evaluating physical security of, 262–263

Computer Security Act of 1987, purpose of, 643

Computer Security and Ethics, Web address for, 630

Computer Security Models, Web address for, 220

computer security versus physical security, 254

Computer Underground Digest, Web address for, 612

computers, locking and securing, 288–289

concealment ciphers, overview of, 468

conclusive evidence related to computer crimes, explanation of, 632

confidential classification, definition and examples of, 87

confidentiality
    versus integrity, 215
    role in AIC triad, 55–56, 110
    and TCSEC, 226
configuration management versus change
    control, 698–700
connection-oriented protocols
    versus connectionless protocols, 326–327
    TCP as, 326
Consortiums and Testing Services, Web address
    for, 344
constrained user interfaces, role in access control,
    140–141
construction materials, evaluating for physical
    security, 259–261
content-dependent access control
    overview of, 142–143
    relationship to databases, 677
contention, occurrence in CSMA, 353
contingency planning. See business continuity
    planning
contractors, threats resulting from, 65
control zones, role in logical access controls, 155
controlled access protection in Orange Book,
    explanation of, 224–225
controls for security administration, overview
    of, 51–52
cookies, overview of, 525–526
copper cabling, advantages and disadvantages
    of, 347
copyrights, overview of, 620–622
CORBA (Common Object Request Broker
    Architecture), overview of, 712–714
corroborative evidence related to computer
    crimes, explanation of, 632
cost/benefit comparison
    example of, 74
    role in risk analysis, 62
countermeasures
    determining costs of, 75
    explanation of, 57
    functionality and effectiveness of, 76–77
    selecting for security mechanisms, 74–75
Counterpane Internet Security Inc., Web address
    for, 509
coupling, explanation of, 712

covert channels, overview of and countermeasures
    for, 237–238
CPE (continuing professional education) credits,
    earning, 7–8
CPU modes and protection rings, overview of,
    193–195
CPUs (central processing units)
    accessing memory with, 191
    role in computer architecture, 187–189
crackers and hackers, overview of, 601–608
cramming attacks, explanation of, 779
CRC (cyclic redundancy check) field in Ethernet
    frames, contents of, 812
criminal laws, purpose of, 619
Criteria and Methods of Evaluations of
    Information Systems, Web address for, 230
critical-path analysis, performing for physical
    security, 255
Critical Security Services, AIC (availability,
    integrity, and confidentiality) triad, 56
CRLs (certificate revocation lists), role in PKI, 498
crosstalk, occurrence of, 349
cryptanalysis, explanation of, 461, 463
cryptographic keys, overview of, 121
cryptography
    coverage by policies, standards, guidelines,
        and procedures, 83
    government involvement with, 470–474
    hardware versus software types of, 516–517
    meaning of, 463
    overview of, 457–461
    terminology of, 462–464, 466
    Web addresses for, 480, 486, 491, 500, 516
Cryptography A-Z, Web address for, 514
Cryptography CBK domain, description of, 5
Cryptography Compendium, Web address
    for, 514
The Cryptography Project, Web address for, 514
Cryptography Search Directory, Web address
    for, 509
Cryptography, the Clipper Chip, and the
    Constitution, Web address for, 472
cryptosystems
    explanation of, 462
    goals of, 465
    strength of, 464–465

CSL (Computer Systems Laboratory), purpose of, 802
CSMA/CA (carrier sense multiple access with collision avoidance), use of, 433
CSMA (carrier sense multiple access), overview of, 353
CSU/DSU (Channel Service Unit/Data Service Unit), overview of, 404–405
CTCPEC (Canadian Trusted Computer Product Evaluation Criteria), purpose of, 44
Cult of the Dead Cow, attacks by, 610
cybercrimes. *See* computer crimes
cyberlaw, facets of, 596

D

D division protection in Orange Book, explanation of, 224
DAC (discretionary access control) model
    applying to databases, 677
    managing data owners with, 144
    overview of, 135–136
data backups, role in physical access controls, 152
data classifications
    implementing properly, 86
    overview of, 85–89
    procedures for, 89
data communications protocols, Web address for, 325
data custodians, responsibilities of, 90, 91
data dictionaries, features of, 671
data diddling, overview of, 603
data hiding, explanation of, 210, 704
data link layer in OSI model
    functionality of, 320–321
    and network scanners, 42
    overview of, 320–322, 324
data mining, overview of, 680–681
data modeling, overview of, 709
data origin authentication, role in one-way hashes, 504
data owners, responsibilities of, 90, 91
Data Protection Measures, Web address for, 221
data remanence, explanation of, 761
data structures
    overview of, 711–712
    relationship to TCP/IP, 330–331

data transmission. *See* transmission
data warehousing, overview of, 680–681
database interface languages, overview of, 670
database management
    overview of, 665–666
    software for, 667
    terminology of, 665
database models, overview of, 668–670
database roles, overview of, 36–39. *See also* roles
database security
    example of, 666
    Web address for, 220
database versus operating system security, 677
database views
    overview of, 677
    role in constrained user interfaces, 141
databases
    and aggregation, 675–676
    checkpoints in, 675
    commit statements in, 674
    concurrency problems with, 673
    configuring for disk-shadowing, 574
    entity integrity of, 674
    and inference, 676
    integrity of, 673–675
    referential integrity of, 674
    rollbacks in, 674
    savepoints in, 674–675
    security issues related to, 675–680
    semantic integrity of, 674
    using OLTP with, 678–680
DataFlow Objects, role in IIS servers, 37
datagrams, role in TCP/IP, 330–331
DBMS (database management system), features of, 665
DCE (Data Circuit-Terminating Equipment), role in frame relay, 407–408
DCE (Distributed Computing Environment), overview of, 718–719
DCOM (Distributed Component Object Model), overview of, 716–717
DDE (Dynamic Data Exchange), overview of, 718
DDL (data definition language), role in relational databases, 670–671
DDoS (distributed denial of service) attacks, overview of, 736–737
deadlocks, explanation of, 199

decentralized access administration, overview
of, 146
dedicated links, overview of, 402, 415
dedicated security mode, overview of, 220
Defense Security Service, Web address for, 221
delayed loss, explanation of, 66
Delphi technique, overview of, 73
deluge water sprinklers, overview of, 284
DES (Data Encryption Standard), overview of,
483–487
Designing Switched LAN Internetworks, Web
address for, 367
detection devices, using, 295
Determining MAC Access, Web address for, 137
device versus software security, 658–660
DFS (distributed file service), role in DCE,
718–719
DHCP servers, role in RARP, 357
diagrams, developing for physical security
planning, 255–256
dial-up and RAS, overview of, 416–417
dialog management, role in session layer of OSI
model, 318
Diameter authentication protocol, overview
of, 146
dictionary attacks
explanation of, 604, 777
layer associated with, 40
overview of, 534–535
overview of and countermeasures for, 173
differential backups, explanation of, 574
Diffie-Hellman key exchange, explanation of, 494
digital certificates, role in PKI, 496–497
digital signatures, overview of, 504–506
digital transmission
explanation of, 351
overview of, 332–333
direct evidence related to computer crimes,
explanation of, 632
directory services, overview of, 133–134,
393–394
Disaster Prevention and Recovery Program,
Web address for, 567
disaster recovery planning, 566
overview of, 550–553
phases of, 562–563

requirements for, 558–559
Web address for, 583
disasters, explanation of, 568–569
discretionary protection in Orange Book,
explanation of, 224–225
Discretionary Protection, Web address for, 209
disk-shadowing, configuring databases for, 574
disposal phase of system development, overview
of, 695
distributed access administration, overview
of, 146
distributed data model, explanation of, 668
DMCA (Digital Millennium Copyright Act),
purpose of, 624
DML (data manipulation language), role in
relational databases, 671
DMZs (demilitarized zones)
constructing with firewalls, 372–373, 377
movement of Web servers to, 32–33
use of, 767
DNS (Domain Name Service)
overview of, 390–391
protection offered by, 42
DNS DoS attacks, overview of, 737–738
DNS naming hierarchy, diagram of, 392
documenting processes and procedures,
importance of, 577–578
dogs, using, 294
domains
in CBK, 4–6
overview of, 206–207
doors, evaluating for physical security, 259–260
doorways, protecting from intrusion, 297–298
DoS (denial-of-service) attacks
explanation of, 54
overview of, 605, 732–733, 778
downstream liability, explanation of, 616
DQL (data control language), role in relational
databases, 671
drills and testing, role in business continuity
planning, 579–582
dry pipe water sprinklers, overview of, 283–284
DSL (Digital Subscriber Line)
overview of, 418–419
vulnerability of, 419
DSS (Digital Signature Standard), overview
of, 506

DSSS (direct sequence spread spectrum), overview of, 435

DSU (Data Service Unit) devices, functionality of, 404

DTE (Data Terminal Equipment), role in frame relay, 407–408

dual-homed firewalls
characteristics of, 386
interfaces for, 376–377

due care
demonstrating, 616
explanation of, 85, 614
role in operational security, 754

due diligence
explanation of, 85, 614
role in operational security, 754

dumpster diving, explanation of, 605–606

dynamic access controls, providing with Chinese Wall security model, 218

dynamic keys, using with WEP, 818–820

dynamic packet filtering, role in firewalls, 380–381

dynamic RAM, explanation of, 189

E

e-commerce, ramifications of, 661

e-mail, functionality of, 764–767

e-mail messages, intercepting, 764

e-mail relaying, overview of, 766–767

e-mail security, overview of, 763–764

e-mail standards
MIME (Multipurpose Internet Mail Extension), 517–518
MSP (Message Security Protocol), 519
overview of, 517
PEM (Privacy-Enhanced Mail), 518–519
PGP (Pretty Good Privacy), 519–521
S/MIME (Secure MIME), 518

EAC (electronic access control) tokens, use of, 255

EALs (evaluation assurance levels), assignment of, 231, 233

EAP (Extensible Authentication Protocol), overview of, 427

EAP-TLS, role in 802.1X standard, 817

ECCs (Elliptic Curve Cryptosystems), overview of, 491

ECHO frames, role in ICMP, 358

ECHO REQUEST messages, role in smurf attacks, 732

Economic Espionage Act of 1996, purpose of, 644

EDB (Electronic Code Book) mode of DES, overview of, 485

EDI (Electronic Data Interchange), purpose of, 396

EDU top-level DNS domain, meaning of, 392

education, role in security, 46

EES (Escrowed Encryption Standard), Web address for, 474

EF (exposure factor), role in risk analysis, 69–70

Egghead.com, hacker attack on, 23

EICAR tests, purpose of, 730

EJBs (Enterprise Java Beans), features of, 719

El Gamal, overview of, 491

electrical power
issues associated with, 269–270
preventive measures and good practices for, 272

electrical power supplies, evaluating for physical security, 261

electronic mail gateways, features of, 369

electronic monitoring, role in password management, 117

electronic vaulting, explanation of, 574–575

eMailman, Web address for, 767

emanation security, issues associated with, 166–167

emanations capturing, overview of, 606

emergency response
to disasters, 582–583
and reactions, 285–286

emergency shutoff valves, importance of, 274

emergency system restarts, occurrence of, 762

EMI (electromagnetic interference)
explanation of, 269–270
resistance of coaxial cable to, 346
resistance of fiber-optic cable to, 348

employee safety, enforcing structure for, 92

employees, threats from, 65

emulated services in honeypots, explanation of, 388

encapsulation
   role in OSI model, 314–315, 330
   as variation to tunnels, 421
encryption
   Clipper Chip used for, 470
   link versus end-to-end types of, 514–517
   one-way functions and one-way hashing
      in, 504
   role in logical access controls, 155
   as variation to tunnels, 421
Encryption and Security Tutorial, Web address
   for, 519
encryption-method designs, goal of, 464
encryption methods
   hybrids of, 491–496
   overview of, 474
   symmetric versus asymmetric algorithms,
      474–480
end-to-end versus link encryption, 514–517
end-user environment, stabilizing after
   disasters, 567–568
Enigma machine, history of, 460
Enterasys White Papers, Web address for, 367
enticement versus entrapment, role in honeypot
   systems, 171, 634–635
environment versus application controls, 661–662
environmental issues
   fire prevention, detection, and suppression,
      276–284
   overview of, 273–275
   ventilation, 276
EPLs (Evaluated Product Lists), explanation
   of, 224
EPROM (erasable and programmable read-only
   memory), explanation of, 189
equipment disposal, proper handling of, 624
equipment rooms, evaluating physical security
   of, 262–263
ESP (Encapsulating Security Payload) protocol,
   role in IPSec, 527–529
Ethernet. *See also* Fast Ethernet
   characteristics of, 345
   overview of, 339–342
   versus Token Ring and FDDI, 344
   types of, 809–812
Ethernet frames, overview of, 812
ethical fallacies, examples of, 597

ethical hacking, explanation of, 770
ethics
   Computer Ethics Institute, 598
   and GASSP (Generally Accepted System
      Security Principles), 599–600
   and IAB (Internet Architecture Board),
      598–599
   overview of, 596–597
European Commission proposal on fighting
   cybercrime, explanation of, 645
European Union Principles on Privacy, purpose
   of, 642–643
events, auditing and logging, 161–162
evidence related to computer crimes,
   admissibility in court, 630–633
excessive privileges, overview of, 603
execution domains, explanation of, 207
exigent circumstances, explanation of, 634
expert systems
   overview of, 719–722
   using with IDS, 169
Export Administration Regulations FAQ,
   Web address for, 637
export and import laws, overview of, 636–637
exposures, explanation of, 56–57
external boundary protection mechanisms
   fencing, 292–293
   lighting, 293
   overview of, 292
   surveillance devices, 293–294
extranet and business partner policies, overview
   of, 794–795
extranets, overview of, 395–398

F

F1-F10 ratings in ITSEC, explanations of, 230
facial scan biometric systems, dynamics of, 116
facilities
   evaluating components of, 261–262
   evaluating computer and equipment rooms
      in, 262–263
   physical attributes of, 257–259
facilities management, performing for physical
   security, 255–263
facility access control, role in perimeter security,
   286–289

facility sites, issues related to, 258
fail-safe setting, explanation, 298
fair cryptosystems, explanation of, 473
fake login screen attacks, explanation of, 779
Fast Ethernet, overview of, 341–342, 810. *See also* Ethernet
"Father of Modern Cryptograph," Frederick Friedman as, 460
fax encryptors, explanation of, 769
fax security, overview of, 767–770
fax servers, use of, 768–769
Faximim Fax FAQ, Web address for, 770
FCC (Federal Communications Commission), explanation of, 312
FDDI (Fiber Distributed Data Interface)
    characteristics of, 345
    versus Ethernet and Token Ring, 344
    overview of, 344–345
Federal Privacy Act of 1974, purpose of, 637, 641–642
Federal Sentencing Guidelines
    extension of, 615
    purpose of, 643–644
fencing, using, 292–293
FHSS (frequency hopping spread spectrum)
    versus DSSS, 435–436
    overview of, 434–435
fiber-optic cabling
    features of, 347–348
    origins of, 400
field-powered system sensing cards, features of, 291
fingerprint biometric systems, dynamics of, 114–115
fire detection and suppression, evaluating for physical security, 261
fire detection, types of, 277–280
fire prevention, explanation of, 277
fire suppression, overview of, 281–284
fires
    classes of, 277
    combustion elements associated with, 282
    types of and suppression methods for, 281
firewall architecture
    bastion hosts in, 381–382
    overview of, 381

    screened hosts in, 382
    screened subnets in, 382–384
firewalls
    administering in middle tiers, 36
    comparison of, 385
    disadvantages of, 387
    and dynamic packet filtering, 380
    guidelines for implementation of, 384–387
    and kernel proxies, 380–381
    overview of, 371–372
    and packet filtering, 372–373
    proxy firewalls, 375–380
    and stateful inspection, 373–375
Firm top-level DNS domain, meaning of, 393
fixed-temperature sensors, purpose of, 279
flame-activated fire detectors, overview of, 279
flooring, evaluating for physical security, 260
foreign keys, using with databases, 671–673
foreign nations, effects of information warfare on, 23–25
forensics, overview of, 627–629
forwarding tables, features of, 360–361
fractional T lines, explanation of, 403
Fraggle attacks, overview of, 734
frame relay, 415
    characteristics of, 415
    combining with IP or ATM, 414
    diagram of, 409
    role in WAN technologies, 407–408
frames, role in TCP/IP, 330–331
frequency
    role in analog transmission, 332
    of signals, 433
frequency analysis, vulnerability to, 467
FTP (File Transfer Protocol), port associated with, 329
fuel combustion, suppressing, 282
full backups, explanation of, 574
full-duplex mode of session layer of OSI model, explanation of, 318
full-interruption tests, role in business continuity planning, 581
functional design analysis and planning phase of system development, overview of, 687–688
Fuzzy logic, role in ANNs, 724

G

G8 group, purpose of, 644
gap in the WAP, explanation of, 440
GASSP (Generally Accepted System Security Principles), overview of, 599–600
gateways
    features of, 368–370
    functionality of, 370
Gigabit Ethernet 1000 Mbps, features of, 810
goals, developing for business continuity planning, 562
GOV top-level DNS domain, meaning of, 392
Graham-Denning security models, overview of, 218–219
Gramm-Leach-Bliley Act of 1999
    purpose of, 640–641, 805
    security program components of, 806–807
ground, role in electrical power, 269
groups
    versus roles, 138
    using to assign access control rights, 124
guards and patrol forces, using, 293–294
guidelines
    areas covered by, 83
    modularity of, 83
    overview of, 82
GUIDs (globally unique identifiers), use by DCOM, 718

H

H.323 gateways, overview of, 413–414
hack and attack methods
    backdoors, 777–779
    browsing, 774–775
    overview of, 770–774
    password cracking, 777
    penetration testing, 780–781
    session hijacking, 776–777
    sniffers, 775–776
    superzapping, 774
hacker intrusion, liability of, 618
hackers
    and crackers, 601–608
    profile of, 28

    threats resulting from, 65
    tools available to, 29
hacking
    of American military sites, 24
    and attacking, 28–30
    benefit of, 29–30
    evolution of, 21–23
    explanation of, 770
    international attempts at, 24–25
    Web address for, 175
hacking groups, Web address for, 612
half-duplex mode of session layer of OSI model, explanation of, 318
Halon, advisory about and replacements for, 282–283
hand geometry biometric systems, dynamics of, 115
hand topology biometric systems, dynamics of, 116
handshaking process
    performing in TCP, 326, 329–330
    role of transport layer in, 319
hardware
    backing up, 568–573, 568–573
    providing for physical security, 266–267
hardware segmentation, explanation of, 208
hardware versus software cryptography systems, 516–517
Harrison-Ruzzo-Ullman security model, overview of, 218, 219
hashing algorithms
    output of, 510
    role in message integrity, 506–509
hashing functions
    role in digital signatures, 505
    role in one-way hashes, 502
HAVAL one-way hash function, overview of, 509
HDLC frames, role in X.25 WAN protocol, 409, 415
HDLC (High-level Data Link Control) protocol, overview of, 411
hearsay evidence related to computer crimes, explanation of, 633
heat-activated fire detectors, overview of, 279
heating, ventilation, and air-conditioning, evaluating for physical security, 260
hierarchical data model, explanation of, 668–669

high-level language, explanation of, 702
HIPAA (Health Insurance Portability and
    Accountability Act)
        changes in, 824
        compliance with, 823–824
        implementing changes related to, 827–828
        purpose of, 640
        regulation expectations of, 829–836
        requirements of, 824–827
        security requirements matrix, 837–859
        significance of, 828–829
        Web address for, 862
hiring practices, overview of, 92–94
Homeland Security, purpose of, 27
honeypot systems
        features of, 387–388
        overview of, 170–171
hopping approach of FHSS, explanation of, 434
hops, explanation of, 515
host-based IDS, explanation of, 168
hostnames
        example of, 331
        resolving to IP addresses, 390–391
hot sites, placing backups in, 569–570
hot-swapping disks, purpose of, 430
HSM (Hierarchical Storage Management),
    explanation of, 431, 574–575
HSSI (High-Speed Serial Interface), overview
    of, 411–412, 415
HTML (Hypertext Markup Language), origins
    of, 31
HTTP (Hyper Text Transfer Protocol)
        overview of, 522
        port associated with, 328–329
HTTPS (Hyper Text Transfer Protocol Secure)
    sockets, overview of, 523
hubs, features of, 359
human resources, role in business continuity
    planning, 578
humidity and temperature, regulating, 275
HUNT project, Web address for, 776
HVAC (heating, ventilation, and air-conditioning)
    systems, advisory about, 283
hybrid access administration, overview of,
    146–147

I

I-CASE (integrated computer-aided software
    engineering), explanation of, 715
IAB (Internet Architecture Board), overview of,
    598–600
ICMP (Internet Control Message Protocol)
        overview of, 358
        role in Loki attacks, 237
        role in Smurf attacks, 732
ICV values, role in IPSec, 529
IDEA (International Data Encryption Algorithm),
    overview of, 488
identification
        and authentication, 112
        explanation of, 110–111
IDS sensors, overview of, 169–170
IDSes (intrusion detection systems)
        explanation of, 162
        features of, 296–298
        overview of, 168–170
IEC Online Tutorials, Web address for, 398
IEEE 802.11 wireless standard. See 802.11
    wireless standard
IEEE (Institute of Electrical and Electronic
    Engineers), responsibilities of, 804
IEEE LAN/MAN Standards Committee, Web
    address for, 339
IEEE standards related to HIPAA
        list of, 860–862
        tables of, 838–859
IEEE Standards Working Groups, Web address
    for, 335
IEEE Wireless Standards Zone, Web address
    for, 439
IETF IP Telephony Charter, Web address for, 415
IETF LDAP Revision Charter, Web address
    for, 394
IETF Policy Framework Charter, Web address
    for, 394
IIS (Internet Information Services), vulnerabilities
    of, 37–39
IKE (Internet Key Exchange), using with
    IPSec, 530
illogical processing, role identifying threats, 66
ILOVEYOU virus, damage done by, 613

IMAP (Internet Message Access Protocol)
    overview of, 766
    Web address for, 767
implementation, role in business continuity
    planning, 561
Implementing Complete Mediation, Web
    address for, 206
import and export laws, overview of, 636–637
incident handling
        coverage by policies, standards, guidelines,
            and procedures, 83
        overview of, 629–630
        Web address for, 630
incident response, definition in
    Gramm-Leach-Bliley Act of 1999, 807
incident response policies, developing, 626–627
incremental backups, explanation of, 574
indexes, role in object-oriented design, 707
inference engines, purpose of, 720–721
inference in databases, explanation of, 676
Info top-level DNS domain, meaning of, 393
information
        transporting across borders, 636–637
        unauthorized disclosure of, 165–168
information and assets, value in risk analysis,
    63–64
information classifications
        implementing properly, 86
        overview of, 85–89
        procedures for, 89
information flow security model
        explanation of, 213
        overview of, 217, 219
information hiding, role in OOP, 704
information owners, explanation of, 52
information protection policies
        example of, 795–796
        overview of, 793–794
information security policies, Web address
    for, 797
information warfare
        effect on companies, 25–26
        effect on nations, 23–25
        evolution of hacking, 21–23
        explanation of, 611
        overview of, 21
        significance of`, 27–28

U.S. government's actions against, 26–27
    Web address for, 209
informative policies, explanation of, 81
infrastructure WLANs, explanation of, 441
inheritance, explanation of, 709
input and output controls, role in security
    operations and product evaluation, 763
input/output device management, overview
    of, 198–199
inrush current, role in electrical power, 269
installation/implementation phase of system
    development, overview of, 693–694
insurance, obtaining for security breaches, 26
INT top-level DNS domain, meaning of, 392
integrity
    goals of, 217
    role in AIC triad, 55, 109–110
integrity levels in Biba security model, explanation
    of, 215
intellectual property laws, purpose of, 620, 622
interference
    causes of, 434
    explanation of, 270
internal partitions, evaluating for physical
    security, 261
international espionage, explanation of, 611
Internet
    origins of, 31
    versus Web, 30–31
Internet DNS and domains, overview of, 391–393
Internet Mail Consortium, Web address for, 767
Internet security, 645
        and cookies, 525–526
        and HTTP (Hyper Text Transfer Protocol), 522
        and HTTPS (Hyper Text Transfer Protocol
            Secure) sockets, 523
        and IPSec (Internet Protocol Security),
            527–531
        overview of, 521
        and S-HTTP (Secure Hypertext Transport
            Protocol), 522
        and SET (Secure Electronic Transaction),
            524–525
        and SSH (Secure Shell), 526–527
        and SSL (Secure Sockets Layer), 523–524
        Web address for, 298
internetworks, explanation of, 360

Interpol and Information Technology Crime, Web address for, 645
interpreted versus compiled programs, 703
interpreters, explanation of, 702
Interstar Fax Server, Web address for, 770
intranets, overview of, 395–398
intruders, threats resulting from, 65
intrusion detection, components of, 169
IP addresses, resolving hostnames to, 390–391
IP addressing
    and NAT, 396–397
    overview of, 331
    ranges for, 395–396
    role in ARP, 356
IP (Internet Protocol)
    combining over ATM or frame relay, 414
    dynamics of, 326
    purpose of, 325–326
IP multicast, Web address for, 351
IP spoofing. *See also* spoofing
    layer associated with, 40
    overview of, 604
IPLs (initial program loads), advisory about, 781
IPSec (Internet Protocol Security)
    advantages of using in S/WAN devices, 403–404
    layer associated with, 42
    overview of, 425, 527–531
IPv4 versus IPv6, 331
IPv6, purpose of, 396
iris scan biometric systems, dynamics of, 115
ISACs (Information Sharing and Analysis Centers), purpose of, 27
ISAKMP (Internet Security Association and Key Management Protocol), role in IPSec, 530
(ISC)^2 (International Information Systems Security Certification Consortium)
    establishment of, 6–7
    purpose of, 3
    Web address for, 600
ISDN (Integrated Services Digital Network), overview of, 417–418
ISO (International Organization for Standardization), responsibilities of, 803–804
ISO 17799, explanation of, 235
ISO/IEC 17799:2000 FAQ, Web address for, 800
issue-specific policies, explanation of, 80

IT Security and Crime Prevention Methods, Web address for, 645
ITSEC (Information Technology Security Evaluation Criteria)
    explanation of, 44
    overview of, 229–230
IVs (initialization vectors), using with WEP, 818–820

J

JAD (Joint Analysis Development), explanation of, 697
Java, overview of, 724–726
Java security, overview of, 725–726
JDBC (Java Database Connectivity), explanation of, 670
jittering, explanation of, 413
job rotation
    importance of, 93, 272–273
    role in administrative management, 755
Juggernaut tool, Web address for, 776

K

KDC (Key Distribution Center) in Kerberos
    disadvantages of, 132
    features of, 512
    overview of, 129–130
KDD (Knowledge Discovery in Database), data mining as, 681
Kerberos
    authentication process of, 130–132
    components of, 129–130
    overview of, 129
    weaknesses of, 132
    Web sites related to, 133
Kerckhoff's Principle, explanation of, 470
kernel proxies, role in firewalls, 380–381
Key Escrow Encryption Available, Web address for, 474
key escrow, overview of, 472–473
key exchange, Diffie-Hellman method of, 494
key management, overview of, 511–514
key recovery, explanation of, 473
key rings, role in PGP, 520

keyboard dynamics biometric systems, dynamics of, 116
keys in cryptography
managing, 465
purpose of, 462, 464
keyspaces, role in algorithms, 462–463
keystream generator role in stream ciphers, 482–483
keystroke monitoring, overview of, 163–164
knowledge-based systems, overview of, 168, 719–722
known-plaintext attacks, overview of, 531–532

L

L2F (Layer 2 Forwarding) protocol, overview of, 425
L2TP (Layer 2 Tunneling Protocol), overview of, 424, 425
labeled security protection in Orange Book, Explanation of, 225
labels, assigning to subjects and objects in Bell-LaPadula model, 214
LAN IP addresses and topology, hiding, 41
LAN media access technologies
collision domains, 354
CSMA (carrier sense multiple access), 353
Ethernet, 339–341
overview of, 337–339, 352
polling, 355
table of, 345
token passing, 352–353
Token Ring, 342–343
LAN transmission methods, overview of, 350–351
LANs (local area networks)
versus internetworks, 339
versus WANs, 40–41
Lantronix white papers, Web address for, 335
latency, occurrence in collision domains, 354
lattice-based access, explanation of, 139–140.
See also access control models; task-based access
lattices in Bell-LaPadula model, explanation of, 212–213
Law, Investigation, and Ethics, Web address for, 607

laws
administrative/regulatory laws, 619
civil laws, 618–619
copyrights, 620–622
criminal laws, 619
directives, and regulations, 639–644
intellectual property laws, 620, 622
patents, 621–622
pertaining to software piracy, 623–624
and politics, 44–36
torts, 618–619
trade secrets, 620
trademarks, 621
Laws, Investigations, and Ethics CBK domain, description of, 6
layered approach toward security, overview of, 39–40
layered defense model, implementing physical security in, 254
layering, explanation of, 210
layers, understanding role in environments, 43
layers 7-1 of OSI model, explanations of, 316–322
layers of responsibility
data custodians, 90
data owners, 90
overview of, 89–90
users, 90–91
LEAF (Law Enforcement Access Field) values, role in Clipper Chip, 471
leased lines, overview of, 402, 415
least privilege
overview of, 209
role in administrative management, 755
LEN (length of data) field in Ethernet frames, contents of, 812
life cycle assurance, role in security operations and product evaluation, 757
lighting, using as physical control, 293
line conditioners, using, 271
linear bus topology
cable connections in, 339
explanation of, 336
link versus end-to-end encryption, 514–517
Linux FreeS/WAN Project, Web address for, 404
load balancing, providing with OLTP, 679

load of walls, floors, ceilings, estimating and protecting, 259

local bridges, explanation of, 359

locks

and keys for access control, 287–289

role in preventive access controls, 158

Web address for, 299

log information, protecting, 164

logic bombs, overview of, 730

logical access controls

components of, 148

examples of, 159–160

explanation of, 51–52, 111

overview of, 153–156

for physical security, 257

logon attempts, setting threshold for, 118

logon spoofing, overview of and countermeasures for, 174–175

Loki attacks, explanation of, 237

loss potential of risks, explanation of, 66

losses

deriving for threats, 69

estimating per risks, 68–79

Lucifer project, purpose of, 460–461, 483

M

MAC address, role in ARP, 356

MAC functions, using hashing algorithms with, 502–503

MAC (mandatory access control) model

applying to databases, 677

decision-making process of, 137

overview of, 136

using sensitivity labels with, 136–137

machine language, explanation of, 702

machine versus object code, 724

macro languages, features of, 729

macro viruses, explanation of, 728

magnetic cards, features of, 290

mail servers

layer associated with, 42

use of, 767–768

main-in-the middle attacks, overview of, 533–534

mainframes

history of, 17–18

relationship to servers and workstations, 18–19

maintenance hooks, overview of and counter-measures for, 238–239

malicious software. *See* malware

malware

logic bombs, 730

overview of, 727–728

Trojan horses, 730–731

viruses, 728–730

worms, 730

man-in-the middle attacks, explanation of, 778

management, responsibilities of, 30–31

management training, guidelines for, 94

mandatory vacations, role in administrative management, 756

MANs (metropolitan area networks), overview of, 397–398

mantraps, explanation of, 297

MARS algorithm for AES, development of, 488

masquerading attacks

example of, 357

explanation of, 386

spoofing as, 604

vulnerability of token systems to, 120

MAUs (Multistation Access Units), role in Token Ring, 342

MD2, MD4, and MD5 hash functions, explanations of, 508

MD5 Message-Digest Algorithm, Web address for, 509

MDACs (Microsoft Data Access Components), vulnerability of, 37–39

Media Access Methods, Web address for, 353

media controls, role in security operations and product evaluation, 760–761

meme viruses, explanation of, 729–730

memory

accessing, 191–192

role in computer architecture, 189–193

memory cards, overview of, 121–122

memory mapping, overview of, 190–192

mesh network topology, overview of, 337–338

message integrity

and digital signatures, 504–506

and DSS (Digital Signature Standard), 506

and hashing algorithms, 506–509

and one-way hashes, 501–504
overview of, 501
messages, role in TCP/IP, 330–331
messaging, dynamics of, 705
metadata
role in data mining, 680
role in directory services, 394
metadirectories, role in directory services, 394
methods in computer programs, explanation of, 703
Methods of Transposition, Web address for, 468
MIC (Message Integrity Code), role in wireless technologies, 813
Microsoft's database engine, vulnerability of, 37
mid-management training, guidelines for, 95
middle tiers, explanation and advantages of, 33–35
MIL top-level DNS domain, meaning of, 392
military classifications versus private business, 86–89
military organizations versus private industry, 61
MIME (Multipurpose Internet Mail Extension), overview of, 517–518
minimal protection in Orange Book, explanation of, 224–225
minutiae, role in biometric systems, 114
Mitnick, Kevin, 608, 612
Models of OS Protection, Web address for, 220
modems, functionality of, 332, 334
modulation, role in analog transmission, 332
modules, characteristics of, 712
MOM (motive, opportunity, and means), overview of, 600–601
monoalphabetic substitution cipher, example of, 458
Moore's Law, explanation of, 484
MSP (Message Security Protocol), overview of, 519
MTBF (mean time between failure), role in physical security, 267, 569
MTD (maximum tolerable downtime), estimating, 556
MTTR (mean time to repair), role in physical security, 267, 569
MTUs (maximum transmission units), explanation of, 352
mulitlevel security mode, overview of, 221

multi-homed firewalls, explanation of, 377
multicast LAN transmissions, explanation of, 350–352
multilayered switches, explanation of, 366
multilevel security policies, explanation of, 209
multilevel security systems, Bell-LaPadula model as, 212
multipart viruses, explanation of, 729
multiplexing
example of, 402–403
explanation of, 399–400
multiprocessing, explanation of, 198
multiprogramming, explanation of, 198
multiservice access technologies, overview of, 412–415
multitasking, explanation of, 198
multithreading, explanation of, 198
mutual aids, explanation of, 571

N

NAK timing attacks, explanation of, 739
NAS (network access server) gateway
example of, 369
role in dial-up and RAS, 416
NAT (network address translation)
layer associated with, 41
overview of, 396–397
NCSC (National Computer Security Center), responsibilities of, 803
near-line devices, explanation of, 575
need-to-know principle
explanation of, 125–126
role in administrative management, 755
negligence, proving, 617
NET top-level DNS domain, meaning of, 392
NetStumbler shareware, sniffing for APs with, 442–443
network access, role in logical access controls, 155
network and resource availability, overview of, 429–432
network architecture, role in logical access controls, 153–154
network-based IDS, explanation of, 168
network directory services, explanation of, 133–134

network isolation and segregation, overview of, 388

network layer
and NAT, 41
and network intrusion detection sensor monitors to, 41
and network scanners, 42
overview of, 320–321, 324
relationship of IPSec to, 42
services and ports associated with, 42

network mapping, countermeasures for, 773

network protocols. *See* protocols

Network Safety, Web address for, 397

network scanners, layers associated with, 42

network security
and telecommunications, 312–313
Web address for, 298

network segregation
and isolation, 388
role in logical access controls, 154
role in physical access controls, 151–152

network sniffers
overview of, 171–172
use of, 775

network topologies
bus topology, 336–338
mesh topology, 337–338
overview of, 335–336
ring topology, 336, 338
star topology, 337–338

network traffic, advisory regarding IDS, 169

networking devices
bridges, 359–360
comparison of, 370
firewalls, 371–388
forwarding tables, 360–361
gateways, 368–370
hubs, 359
PBX switches, 370–371
repeaters, 358–359
routers, 361–363
switches, 365–367
VLANs (virtual LANs), 366–369

networking services
and directory services, 393–394
DNS (Domain Name Service), 390–391
Internet DNS and domains, 391–393

NOSes (network operating systems), 389–390
overview of, 388–389

networks
justifications for, 334–335
original connectivity of, 18
security evaluation topics for, 228–229

NICs (network interface cards), input connectors in, 342

NIST (National Institute of Standards and Technology), responsibilities of, 802

no access, defaulting to, 125–126

"no write down" rule in Bell-LaPadula model, explanation of, 213

node authentication, advisory about, 335

noise
explanation of, 269, 348–349
and perturbation, 677
role in electrical power, 271–272

Nom top-level DNS domain, meaning of, 393

nondisasters, explanation of, 568

nondisclosure agreements, purpose of, 93

nondiscretionary access control, overview of, 137–139

noninteference security model, overview of, 217, 219

nonplenum cables, composition of, 350

nonrepudiation, role in cryptosystems, 465

NSA (National Security Agency), responsibilities of, 801

O

OAKLEY protocol, explanation of, 530

object-oriented concepts, overview of, 702–708

object-oriented databases, explanation of, 669–670

object reuse, issues associated with, 166

object versus machine code, 724

objects
accessing with subjects, 216
assigning labels in Bell-LaPadula model, 214
in Bell-LaPadula security model, 213
in Biba security model, 214–215
defining subsets of, 202
grouping into classes, 210
organizing relationships between, 705

reusing, 707
role in access control, 107–108
using references with, 706
obligation, explanation of, 616
OC lines, explanation of, 401
ODBC (Open Database Connectivity), overview
of, 670, 716–717
OFB (Output Feedback) mode of DES, overview
of, 486–487
offsite backup facilities, using, 571
OLE DB (Object Linking and Embedding
Database) explanation of, 670
OLE (object linking and embedding), overview
of, 717–718
OLTP (Online Transaction Processing), using
with databases, 678–680
one-time pads, overview of, 510–511
one-time passwords, overview of, 119
one-way function, role in RSA, 489–490
One-Way Hash FAQ, Web address for, 510
one-way hash functions
attacks against, 509–510
role in message integrity, 501–504
OOA (object-oriented analysis), explanation
of, 708
OOD (object-oriented design), explanation of,
707–708
OOP (object-oriented programming), explanation
of, 702–703
open message format, role in asymmetric
cryptography, 478
open network architectures, explanation of, 314
open systems, explanation of, 316
open versus closed systems, 236
operating systems
versus database security, 677
management of resource requests by, 199
protection mechanisms for, 193
role of input/output management in, 198–199
states of, 196
operation system fingerprinting, explanation
of, 772
operational and maintenance phase of system
development, overview of, 694–695
operational assurance, explanation of, 757
operational goals, role in organizational security
model, 60

operational security
and accountability, 756–757
and administrative management, 754–756
overview of, 754
and product evaluation, 757–763
operations department
deviations from standards in, 781
unscheduled IPLs in, 781
unusual or unexplained occurrences in,
780–781
operations, overview of, 93
Operations Security CBK domain, description
of, 5
opinion evidence related to computer crimes,
explanation of, 632
optical detectors in smoke activated fire
detectors, purpose of, 278–279
Orange Book
areas of, 223
explanation of, 44
lower security level ratings in, 222
overview of, 222–224
problems with, 227
ratings in, 202
ORBs (object request brokers), overview of,
712–714
Order of Concepts for security terminology,
explanation of, 58
ORG top-level DNS domain, meaning of, 392
organizational security policies, explanation of,
79–80
organizational security models. See security
models
OSA (open system communication), authenticating
to APs by means of, 442
OSI (Open System Interconnect) model
application layer in, 316–317
data link layer in, 320–322
development by ISO, 803–804
devices and protocols within, 41
dynamics of, 325
encapsulation in, 314–315
goal of, 314
layers in, 316, 323–324
network layer in, 320–321
overview of, 313–316
physical layer in, 322

presentation layer in, 317
session layer in, 318–319
transport layer in, 319
out-of-band method, role in symmetric
cryptography, 475
overt channels, explanation of, 237
oxygen combustion, suppressing, 282

P

*-property rule in Bell-LaPadula model,
explanation of, 213
packet filtering
advantages and disadvantages of, 372–374
benefits of, 41
characteristics of, 385
versus circuit-level proxies, 378
packet-forwarding, performing with routing
process, 363–365
packet switching, explanation of, 405–407
packets
dynamics of, 327–328
receipt by routers, 362–363
role in TCP/IP, 330–331
PACs (Privileged Attribute Certificates), role
in SESAME, 133
paging, explanation of, 191–192
palm scan biometric systems, dynamics of, 115
PAP (Password Authentication Protocol)
versus CHAP, 426–427
overview of, 424–426
parallel connections, explanation of, 422
parallel tests, role in business continuity
planning, 581
parity bits, purpose of, 501
parity, explanation of, 430
partitioning databases, 677
PASes (Privileged Attribute Servers), role in
SESAME, 133
passive infrared detection systems, features
of, 296
passive system sensing cards, features of, 291
passphrases, overview of, 121
password aging, explanation of, 118
password checkers, overview of, 118
password cracking, overview of, 777
password files, examples of, 534–535

password generators, overview of, 119
password sniffing, overview of, 604
passwords
changing, 273
cognitive passwords, 118–119
managing, 116–118
one-time passwords, 119
overview of, 116
patents, purpose of, 621–622
patrol forces and guards, using, 293–294
pattern matching, explanation of, 720
PBX (Private Branch Exchange) switches,
features of, 370–371, 414
PCCIP (President's Commission on Critical
Infrastructure Protection), purpose of, 26–27
PDDs (Presidential Decision Directives) 62 and
63, purpose of, 27
PEAP versus EAP-TLS, 817–818
peer-to-peer environment, explanation of, 389
PEM (Privacy-Enhanced Mail), overview of,
518–519
penetration testing
explanation of, 770
overview of, 175, 780–781
perimeter security
benefits of, 659
and facility access control, 286–289
overview of, 286
role in physical access controls, 151
Personal Computer Security, Web address
for, 221
personal information, liability of, 617
personnel access controls
examples of, 273
magnetic cards, 290
overview of, 290
role in administrative access controls,
149–150
wireless proximity readers, 290–291
personnel
prescreening, 638–639
responsibilities of, 91–92
PGP (Pretty Good Privacy), overview of,
519–521
Phone Phreakers, attacks by, 610–612
photoelectric devices in smoke activated fire
detectors, purpose of, 278–279

photoelectric or photometric detection systems,
    features of, 295
phreakers
    explanation of, 608
    vulnerability of PBX switches to, 371
physical access, auditing, 298
physical access controls
    components of, 148
    coverage by policies, standards, guidelines,
        and procedures, 83
    dynamics of, 286–287
    examples of, 159
    overview of, 51–52, 151–153
    for physical security, 257
physical layer
    overview of, 322, 324
    and STP, 41
Physical Model of Operations, Web address
    for, 221
physical security, 6
    accomplishing, 254
    applying administrative access controls to,
        284–286
    component selection process for, 265–273
    controls for, 256–257
    countermeasures associated with, 264
    environmental issues related to, 273–275
    explanation of, 20
    overview of, 253–255
    performing backups, 266
    performing facilities management for, 255
    planning for, 255
    power supplies, 268
    providing redundancy hardware for, 266–267
    risks associated with, 264
physical topology, purpose of, 352
PI multicast protocols, class of address used
    with, 351
PIDAS (Perimeter Intrusion Detection and
    Assessment System) fencing, explanation
    of, 292
piggybacking, explanation of, 290
Ping of Death attacks, explanation of, 779
ping utility, ICMP used for, 358
pipes, using with objects, 713
PKI (public key infrastructure), 496–497
    CAs and certificates used with, 497–498

steps involved in, 498–500
    Web address for, 500
plaintext, explanation of, 462
planning horizon, explanation of, 60
planning strategies, selecting for business
    continuity, 566–567
plenum areas, explanation of, 281, 350
point-to-point links, overview of, 402, 415
policies
    areas covered by, 83
    types of, 81–82
policy and procedures, role in administrative
    access controls, 149
politics and laws, overview of, 44–36
polling, overview of, 355
polyalphabetic substitution ciphers, explanation
    of, 458
polyinstantiation, applying to databases, 678
polymorphic viruses, explanation of, 729
polymorphism, overview of, 708–709
POP (Post Office Protocol), overview of, 766
port scanning, explanation of and
    countermeasures for, 772–773
portable fire extinguishers, using, 277–278
ports, numbers assigned to, 327–328
positive drains, purpose of, 274
positive pressurization, explanation of, 276
postmortem review phase of system
    development, overview of, 695–697
power fluctuations, explanations of, 270
power supplies, types of, 268
PPP frames, explanation of, 423–424
PPP (Point-to-Point), overview of, 422–423
PPTP (Point-to-Point Tunneling Protocol),
    overview of, 423–424, 425
preaction water sprinklers, overview of, 283–284
preamble field in Ethernet frames, contents
    of, 812
presentation layer, overview of, 317, 323
preset locks, features of, 288
preventive access controls, overview of,
    157–160
PRI (Primary Rate Interface) ISDN, explanation
    of, 417–418
primary and secondary DNS servers, using, 391
primary keys, using with databases, 671–673
primary power sources, explanation of, 269

primary storage, explanation of, 192

principles, role in Kerberos KDC, 130

Pringles cans, use of, 443

priorities, role in business continuity planning, 561

privacy
of confidential information, 636–637
issues pertaining to, 637–639

private business versus military classifications, 86–89

private classification, definition and examples of, 87

private connections, explanation of, 420

private industry versus military organizations, 61

private keys
in asymmetric cryptography, 476–477
explanation of, 121
role in PGP, 519

privileged mode of rings, explanation of, 193, 196

procedure disclosure, definition in Gramm-Leach-Bliley Act of 1999, 807

procedures
areas covered by, 83
overview of, 82–84

process activity, overview of, 195–198

processes
comparing to phone calls, 197
versus threads, 196

Product Ciphers FAQ, Web address for, 514

product evaluation, role in operational security, 757–763, 803

programmable locks, features of, 288–289

project initiation phase of system development, overview of, 684–685

property, definitions of, 639

proprietary classification, definition and examples of, 87

protection mechanisms
cost effectiveness of, 265
for external boundaries, 292–296

protection profiles in Common Criteria, explanation of, 232–233

protection rings, explanation of, 193–195

protective mechanisms
overview of, 74
selecting countermeasures for, 74–75
vulnerabilities of, 42–43

protocols
advisory about OSI layers associated with, 320
for application layer of OSI model, 316
ARP (Address Resolution Protocol), 356–357
for data link layer of OSI model, 321
explanation of, 313
ICMP (Internet Control Message Protocol), 358
for layers in OSI model, 323–324
for network layer of OSI model, 320
overview of, 355–356
RARP (Reverse Address Resolution Protocol), 357–358
role in logical access controls, 155
for routes, 362
for session layer of OSI model, 318
at transport layer of OSI model, 326
for transport layer of OSI model, 319
Web address for, 325

prototyping software development
explanation of, 698
overview of, 715

proximate causation, explanation of, 617

proximity detection systems, features of, 295

proxy firewalls, features of, 375–380

proxy software, benefits of, 41

prudent person rule, explanation of, 615

pseudo-flaw, explanation of, 728

pseudo-noise sequences, explanation of, 435

PSTN (public-switched telephone network), functionality of, 412, 414

public classification, definition and examples of, 87

public key cryptography, advisory about, 479

public keys
in asymmetric cryptography, 476–477
explanation of, 121

PVCs (permanent virtual circuits), role in WAN technologies, 408

Q

QL (query language), role in relational databases, 671

qualitative risk analysis. *See also* risk analysis
overview of, 72–73
versus quantitative risk analysis, 73–74

quantitative risk analysis. *See also* risk analysis
  overview of, 66–67
  versus qualitative risk analysis, 73–74
questions, 104–106
  about access control, 178–182
  about application and system development,
    744–748
  about cryptography, 540–544
  about law, investigation, and ethics,
    648–653
  about operations security, 784–789
  about physical security, 302–306
  about security management practices,
    99–104
  about security models and architectures,
    245–249
  about telecommunications and networking
    security, 448–452
  for business continuity planning, 586–591
  on sample CISSP exam, 11–15
Quick Tips
  for access control, 176–178
  for application and system development,
    740–744
  for business continuity planning, 584–586
  for cryptography, 536–540
  for law, investigation, and ethics, 646–648
  for operations security, 783–784
  for physical security, 299–302
  for security management practices, 96–99
  for security models and architectures,
    241–245
  for telecommunications and networking
    security, 444–448

R

r-utilities, weaknesses of, 775–776
RA (registration authority), role in PKI,
  497–498
RAB (RAID Advisory Board), classifications
  developed by, 430
race conditions, explanation of, 239
RAD (Rapid Application Development),
  explanation of, 697
RAD University Networking Tutorials, Web
  address for, 409

RADIUS (Remote Authentication Dial-In User
  Service)
    overview of, 144–146
    versus TACACS, 145
RAID (Redundant Array of Inexpensive Disks),
  overview of, 430–431
Rainbow Series, overview of, 227–229
RAM (random access memory), explanation of,
  189, 192
rapid prototyping, using with CASE tools, 715
RARP (Reverse Address Resolution Protocol),
  overview of, 357–358
RAS (Remote Access Service) and dial-up,
  overview of, 416–417
rate-of-rise temperature sensors, purpose of, 279
Rationale Behind the Evaluation Classes, Web
  address for, 206
RBAC (role-based access control), overview of,
  137–139
RC4 encryption algorithm, role in 802.11i
  standard, 814–815
RC5, overview of, 489
RC6 algorithm for AES, development of, 488
RCP function, role in DCE, 718
ready operating state, explanation of, 196
realms in Kerberos, explanation of, 130
Rec top-level DNS domain, meaning of, 393
reciprocal agreements, explanation of, 571–572
recovery and restoration, overview of, 578–579
recovery planning, explanation of, 551
Red Book, overview of, 228–229
Red Boxes, explanation of, 610
redundant sites, purpose of, 572
The Reference Monitor Concept, Web address
  for, 206
reference monitors, overview of, 204–205
references
    "802.11 Alphabet Soup", 439
    802.11 and Spread Spectrum, 434
    Access Control Models, 220
    Access Control Policies and Mechanisms, 209
    AES (Advanced Encryption Standard),
      491, 509
    ANSI (American National Standards
      Institute), 804

AntiOnline Computer Security, 612
ARP (Address Resolution Protocol), 357
asymmetric cryptography, 480
ATM (Asynchronous Transfer Mode), 410, 415
Authentication, Authorization, and Accounting Charter, 164
authentication categories on Google, 164
BIA (business impact analysis), 558, 566
biometric systems, 116
bridges and switches, 361
business continuity planning, 566, 567
Cable Modem Info, 420
CERT Coordination Center, 630
CISSP and SSCP Open Study Guides, 58
CISSP.com, 95
CISSPs (Certified Information Systems Security Professionals), 11
Classical Cryptography, 468
Collision Domains white paper, 355
Commercial Product Evaluations, 803
Common Criteria, 234
computer security, 220, 607, 630
Computer Underground Digest, 612
Consortiums and Testing Services, 344
copyrights, 622
Counterpane Internet Security Inc, 509
Criteria and Methods of Evaluations of Information Systems, 230
cryptography, 461, 472, 480, 486, 491, 509, 514, 516
The Cryptography Project, 514
CSI, 11
CSI Intrusion Detection System Resource, 170
data classifications, 89
data communications protocols, 325
Data Protection Measures, 221
Database Security, 220
Defense Security Service, 221
Designing Switched LAN Internetworks, 367
Determining MAC Access, 137
Disaster Prevention and Recovery Program, 567
disaster recovery planning, 566, 583
Discretionary Protection, 209
DSL (Digital Subscriber Line), 419
EES (Escrowed Encryption Standard), 474
eMailman, 767

Encryption and Security Tutorial, 519
Enterasys White Papers, 367
Ethernet and Fast Ethernet, 342
Export Administration Regulations FAQ, 637
Faximim Fax FAQ, 770
FDDI (Fiber Distributed Data Interface), 344
frame relay, 409
Frame Relay Forum, 415
GASSP (Generally Accepted System Security Principles, 600
Gramm-Leach-Bliley Act of 1999, 807
Guide to Understanding DAC in Trusted Systems, 136
Guide to Wireless LAN Technologies, 434
hacking and hackers, 175
hacking groups, 612
HIPAA (Health Insurance Portability and Accountability Act), 862
honeypot systems, 171
HSSI (High-Speed Serial Interface), 411
IAB (Internet Architecture Board), 600
ICMP (Internet Control Message Protocol), 358
IEC Online Tutorials, 398
IEEE LAN/MAN Standards Committee, 339
IEEE Standards Working Groups, 335, 804
IEEE Wireless Standards Zone, 439
IETF IP Telephony Charter, 415
IETF LDAP Revision Charter, 394
IETF Network Access Server Requirements, 429
IETF Policy Framework Charter, 394
IMAP (Internet Message Access Protocol), 767
Implementing Complete Mediation, 206
incident handling, 630
Information Security Policies, 797
Information Security Policy World, 85
Information Warfare Site, 209
Internet Mail Consortium, 767
Internet/Network Security, 298
Internet Security Recommendations, 645
Interpol and Information Technology Crime, 645
Interstar Fax Server, 770
intranets, 396
Intrusion Detection FAQ, 170
IP multicast, 351
IPSec (Internet Protocol Security), 531

(ISC)² (International Information Systems Security Certification Consortium), 11, 600

ISO (International Organization for Standardization), 804

ISO/IEC 17799:2000 FAQ, 800

IT Security and Crime Prevention Methods, 645

ITSEC (Information Technology Security Evaluation Criteria), 230

Kerberos, 133

Key Escrow Encryption Available, 474

Lantronix white papers, 335

Law, Investigation, and Ethics, 607

Linux FreeS/WAN Project, 404

locks, safes, and security, 299

MAC (mandatory access control) model, 136

MD5 Message-Digest Algorithm, 509

Media Access Methods, 353

Methods of Transposition, 468

Models of OS Protection, 220

NAT (network address translation), 397

NCSA Security Policies and Procedures, 85

Network Intrusion Detection Systems FAQ, 170

Network Operating Systems, 390

Network Safety, 397

NIST Computer Security Resource Center, 58

NIST (National Institute of Standards and Technology), 802

NSA (National Security Agency), 801

One-Way Hash FAQ, 510

Packet Switching Simulation, 407

PAP (Password Authentication Protocol), 427

Personal Computer Security, 221

PGP (Pretty Good Privacy), 520–521

Physical Model of Operations, 221

PKI (public key infrastructure), 500

PPP (Point-to-Point), 427

Product Ciphers FAQ, 514

protocols, 325

RAD University Networking Tutorials, 409

RAID Basics, 431

Rainbow Series, 228

RAM (random access memory), 189

Rationale Behind the Evaluation Classes, 206

The Reference Monitor Concept, 206

Remote Access, 428–429

Risk Associates, 78

Routing Basics, 365

RSA SecurID, 121

S/MIME and OpenPGP, 524

S/MIME Mail Security, 767

SANS Institute, 58

SANS Institute Security Policy Project, 85

SANS Security Policy Project, 797

Secure Electronic Commerce System, 519

security, 612

Security in Open Systems, 164

Security Issues in SQL, 675

Security Issues in WWW, 524

Security Links, 524

Security Policies and Baseline Standards, 85

security risk analysis, 800

Security Strategies for E-Companies, 461

Security Technology Issues, 474

Single Sign-On Deployment Guide, 128

smart cards, 123

social engineering, 607

software life cycles, 698

Spread Spetrum Primer, 434

SSH (Secure Shell), 527

steganography, 469

Strategic Security and Intelligence resources, 78

Symmetric Key Cryptography, 476

T1 lines, 403

token-based authentication, 121

Token Ring, 343

trusted computer systems, 227

Unix/Linux Internals Course and Links, 189

U.S. Bureau of Industry and Security, 637

using with objects, 706

Voice Telephony Over ATM, 415

VoIP Quick Start Guide, 415

WANs (wide area networks), 398

WAP (Wireless Application Protocol), 441

WarDriving.com, 443

Web66 Network Construction Kit, 339

"Wireless Goal: Don't Get Whacked", 441

regulatory policies, explanation of, 81

relational data model, explanation of, 668

relational database components, overview of, 670–671

relay agents, use of, 767

relevant evidence related to computer crimes, explanation of, 633

reliable evidence related to computer crimes, explanation of, 633
remote access
  and cable modems, 419–420
  dial-up and RAS, 416–417
  and DSL (Digital Subscriber Line), 418–419
  guidelines for, 427–429
  and ISDN (Integrated Services Digital Network), 417–418
  overview of, 416
  and tunneling protocols, 421–427
  VPNs (virtual private networks), 420–421
remote access policies
  example of, 796
  overview of, 794
remote access Trojans, explanation of, 731
remote bridges, explanation of, 359
Remote Data Service, vulnerability of, 37
remote journaling, explanation of, 575
repeaters
  features of, 358–359
  functionality of, 370
  OSI layer associated with, 361
replay attacks, overview of, 534
REPLY frames, role in ICMP, 358
residual risk versus total risk, 77–78
resource and network availability, overview of, 429–432
resource isolation, overview of, 208
resource records, role in DNS, 391
responsibility
  designation in Gramm-Leach-Bliley Act of 1999, 806
  explanation of, 616
  layers of, 89–92
  role in business continuity planning, 561, 564
restoration and recovery, overview of, 578–579
retina scan biometric systems, dynamics of, 115
RFI (radio frequency interference), explanation of, 269–270
Rijndael algorithm for AES, development of, 488
ring architecture, determination of, 193–194
ring network topology, overview of, 336, 338
ring wraps, role in FDDI, 345
rings 0-3, diagram of, 194

risk analysis. See also qualitative risk analysis; quantitative risk analysis
  automating, 67–68
  gathering data for, 67
  goals of, 62
  outcome of, 70–71
  overview of, 62–63
  performing, 77–78
  purpose of, 49
  quantitative approach toward, 66–67
  steps involved in, 78
  steps of, 68–71
  terminology of, 70
risk analysis phase of system development, overview of, 685–688
risk analysis teams, building, 63
risk assessment and analysis, performing, 553–558
risk management
  definition in Gramm-Leach-Bliley Act of 1999, 806
  overview of, 61–62
risk management phase of system development, overview of, 685
risks. See also total risk versus residual risk
  estimating losses associated with, 68–69
  explanation of, 56, 61
  handling, 78
  loss potential of, 66
  reducing, assigning, and accepting, 69
  types of, 62
roaming, explanation of, 437
roles. See also database roles
  versus groups, 138
  implementing database security with, 666
  using to assign rights to users, 124
  using with RBAC, 138
rollbacks in databases, explanation of, 674
rolling hot sites, using as facility backups, 573
ROM (read-only memory), explanation of, 189
rotation of duties, role in personnel controls, 150
routers
  versus bridges, 360, 363
  features of, 361–363
  functionality of, 370

OSI layer associated with, 361
role in Internet DNS and domains, 391
routing, overview of, 363–365
RPCs (remote procedure calls), role in
applications and systems development, 664
RSA (Rivest, Shamir, Adleman), overview of,
489–490
RSA SecurID, Web address for, 121
rule-based access control, overview of, 140
rule-based programming, explanation of, 720
rules, role in packet filtering, 372
running key ciphers, overview of, 468
running operating state, explanation of, 196

S

S-HTTP (Secure Hypertext Transport Protocol),
overview of, 522
S/MIME (Secure MIME), overview of, 518, 524,
767
S-RPC (Secure RPC), use of, 775
S/WANs (Secure WANs), overview of, 403–404
safeguards, guidelines for selection of, 76–77
safes, Web address for, 299
safety requirements, adhering to, 265
Salami attacks, overview of, 602
sandboxes, role in Java security, 725
sanitized media, explanation of, 761
SANS Security Policy Project, Web address
for, 797
SANs (storage area networks)
explanation of, 431
using, 575–576
SAs (security associations) in IPSec, explanation
of, 528
savepoints in databases, explanation of,
674–675
SBU (sensitive but unclassified) classification,
definition and examples of, 88
scanning devices, benefits of, 43
schema, role in directory services, 394
screened hosts
characteristics of, 386
role in firewall architecture, 382
screened subnets
characteristics of, 386
role in firewall architecture, 382–385

script kiddies, explanation of, 603
scripting, overview of, 128–129
scytale ciphers, explanation of, 459
SDH (Synchronous Digital Hierarchy), origins
of, 402
SDLC (Synchronous Data Link Control),
overview of, 411–412, 415
secondary evidence related to computer crimes,
explanation of, 631
secondary storage, explanation of, 191
secret classification, definition and examples
of, 87
secret keys
explanation of, 475
management by Kerberos, 130–131
secure and signed format, role in asymmetric
cryptography, 478–479
Secure DNS attacks, overview of, 738–739
Secure Electronic Commerce System, Web
address for, 519
secure message format, role in asymmetric
cryptography, 477
secure state in Bell-LaPadula model, explanation
of, 213
secured areas, characteristics of, 263
security
approaches toward, 658–659
areas of, 20–21, 200
attributes of, 108–109
checklist for, 165
components of, 96
conceptual diagram of, 20
decline in assurance of, 201
environmental demands of, 660–661
fundamental principles of, 53–56
guidelines for, 30, 79
implementing in layers, 156–157
layered approach toward, 39–40
overview of, 219
relationship to software releases, 660
role of education in, 46
versus software functionality, 662–663
taking architectural approach toward,
40–43
terminology of, 56–58
vulnerabilities in, 36
Web addresses for, 299, 612

security administration, supporting controls for, 51–53

security administrators, responsibilities of, 90–91

Security and Freedom through Encryption Act, purpose of, 643

Security Architecture and Models CBK domain, description of, 5

security awareness
overview of, 94–95
training for, 150

security breaches
of infrastructure and code, 38
obtaining insurance for, 26
sources of, 38–39
staying up to date on, 43

security components, relationships between, 57

security controls, services provided by, 159–160

security guards and patrol forces, using, 293–294

Security in Open Systems, Web address for, 164

Security Issues in WWW, Web address for, 524

security kernel, explanation of, 205

security labels, treatment in Orange Book, 225

Security Links, Web address for, 524

security management, 4
example of, 53
overview of, 49–50
responsibilities of, 50–51

security mechanisms
overview of, 74
selecting countermeasures for, 74–75
vulnerabilities of, 42–43

security models
and architectures, 186–187
Bell-LaPadula, 212–214
Biba, 214–216
Brewer and Nash, 218
Chinese Wall, 218
Clark-Wilson, 216
explanation of, 185
Graham-Denning, 218
information flow, 217
noninteference, 217
overview of, 59–61, 210–211
versus security policies, 211

state machines, 211–212
threats to, 236–240

security modes of operation
compartmented security mode, 220–221
dedicated security mode, 220
mulitlevel security mode, 221
overview of, 220
system-high security mode, 220

security perimeters, overview of, 203–204

security policies
advisory about, 186
components of, 83–84
dynamics of, 58–59
examples of, 795–796
explanation of, 149
extranet and business partner policies, 794–795
implementing, 79–80, 84–85
information protection policies, 793–796
overview of, 208–209
remote access policies, 794, 796
versus security models, 211
writing, 797

security principles
AIC triad, 53–56
availability, 108–109
confidentiality, 110
integrity, 109–110

security professionals, security role of, 91

security risk analysis, Web address for, 800

security roles, list of, 91

Security Strategies for E-Companies, Web address for, 461

Security Technology Issues, Web address for, 474

security training, types of, 94–95

security trends, overview of, 17–20

segments, role in TCP/IP, 330–331

self-garbling viruses, explanation of, 729

Sendmail, use of, 765–766

senior managers, security role of, 91

sensitivity classifications
for commercial business, 86
criteria for, 88
examples of, 87
handling requirements for, 86

sensitivity labels, overview of, 136–137

separation of duties
enforcing, 149, 216
example of, 692
explanation of, 92
role in administrative management, 754
serial connections, explanation of, 422
Serpent algorithm for AES, development of, 488
server clusters, explanation of, 431
servers. *See also* Web servers
hacking, 22
relationship to mainframes and
workstations, 18–19
service bureaus, offsite backup facilities as, 570
service providers, definition in
Gramm-Leach-Bliley Act of 1999, 807
SESAME (Secure European System for
Applications in a Multi-vendor Environment),
overview of, 133–134
session hijacking, overview of, 776–777
session keys
decrypting with unit keys, 471
overview of, 494–496
role in Kerberos authentication, 131
session layer in OSI model, overview of,
318–319, 323
SET (Secure Electronic Transaction), overview
of, 524–525
SFD (start frame delimiter) field in Ethernet
frames, contents of, 812
SHA (Secure Hash Algorithm), explanation of,
506, 508
shells, role in constrained user interfaces,
140–141
shift alphabet, explanation of, 466–467
shoulder surfing, explanation of, 55
side channel attacks, overview of, 535–536
signature-based IDS, overview of, 168
signature dynamics biometric systems,
dynamics of, 115
simple security rule in Bell-LaPadula model,
explanation of, 213
simplex mode of session layer of OSI model,
explanation of, 318
simulation tests, role in business continuity
planning, 581
single points of failure, overview of, 429–430

Single Sign-On Deployment Guide, Web address
for, 128
single sign-on methods, examples of, 128–134
single sign-on systems
Kerberos, 129–132
overview of, 126–128
SESAME (Secure European System for
Applications in a Multi-vendor
Environment), 133
SKA (shared key authentication), authenticating
to APs by means of, 442
SKIP (Simple Key for IP) protocol, explanation
of, 530
slamming attacks, explanation of, 779
SLAs (service level agreements), role in physical
security, 267
SLE (single loss expectancy), role in risk
analysis, 69–71
SLIP (Serial Line Internet Protocol), replacement
of, 422
smart cards, overview of, 121–123
SMDS (Switched Multimegabit Data Service)
characteristics of, 415
overview of, 411
smoke activated fire detectors, overview of,
278–279
smoke detectors, placement of, 280
SMTP (Simple Mail Transfer Protocol)
functionality of, 765
port associated with, 328
smurf attacks, overview of, 732–734
sniffers
as hack and attack method, 775–776
overview of, 171–172
SNMP (Simple Network Management
Protocol), port associated with, 329
social engineering, explanation of, 55, 607
SOCKS as circuit-level proxy gateway, features
of, 379–380
software
backing up, 573–577
versus device security, 658–660
illegal use of, 624
software architecture, overview of, 709–710
software backup facilities, choosing, 577
software development, methods of, 697–698.
See also system development

software development phase of system
development, overview of, 691–693

software escrow, overview of, 701

software functionality versus security, 662–663

software life cycles, Web addresses for, 698

software piracy, laws pertaining to, 623–624

software versus hardware cryptography systems,
516–517

SONET rings
MANs as, 398–399
origins of, 400–402

source routing, explanation of, 360–361, 386

SPI (security parameter index) in IPSec,
explanation of, 528

spiral software development, explanation of, 697

spoofing. *See also* IP spoofing
explanation of, 386
at logon, 174–175
as masquerade attack, 604

spread spectrum wireless communications,
overview of, 433–436

SQL security issues, Web address for, 675

SSH (Secure Shell), overview of, 526–527

SSIDs (Service Set IDs), role in WLANs, 442

SSL (Secure Sockets Layer)
layer associated with, 42
OSI layer associated with, 320
overview of, 523–524
vulnerability of, 533

STA (Spanning Tree Algorithm), using with
bridges, 361

staff, training, 95

standards
areas covered by, 83
modularity of, 83
overview of, 80–81

star network topology
cable connections in, 339
overview of, 337–338

state machine model, overview of, 211–214

state transitions, explanation of, 212

stateful filtering
characteristics of, 385
versus stateful inspection, 373

stateful inspection, role in firewalls, 373–375

stateless protocols, HTTP as, 522, 525

static electricity, preventive steps against, 275

static RAM, explanation of, 189

static routing, use of, 364

statistical IDS, overview of, 169

stealth viruses, explanation of, 729

steganography, overview of, 469

stopped operating state, explanation of, 196

storage, types of, 191–192

Store top-level DNS domain, meaning of, 393

STP (shielded twisted pair) cabling
explanation of, 346
layer associated with, 41

strategic goals, role in organizational security
model, 60

stream ciphers, overview of, 481–483

striping, explanation of, 430

strong authentication, explanation of, 112

strong password policies, benefits of, 777

Strong Star Property rule in Bell-LaPadula
model, explanation of, 213

structure, enforcing for employee safety, 92

structured analysis approach, explanation of, 709

structured protection in Orange Book,
Explanation of, 225–226

subjects
accessing objects with, 216
assigning labels in Bell-LaPadula model, 214
in Bell-LaPadula security model, 213
in Biba security model, 214–215
defining subsets of, 202
granting access rights to, 124
role in access control, 107–108, 107–108

SubSeven tool, Web address for, 778

substitution ciphers
example of, 458
overview of, 466–467

sufficient evidence related to computer crimes,
explanation of, 633

supervisor mode of rings, explanation of, 193

supervisory structure, role in administrative
access controls, 150

superzapping, overview of, 774

surges, explanation of, 270

surveillance devices, using, 293–294

surveillance, search, and seizure, overview of,
633–635

SVCs (switched virtual circuits), role in WAN
technologies, 408

switched networks, use of, 366
switches
    features of, 365–367
    functionality of, 370
    Web address for, 361
switching, role in WAN technologies, 405–407
symmetric cryptography, 476
    overview of, 474–476
    using with asymmetric cryptography,
        492–494, 496–497
symmetric keys, role in one-way hashes, 503
symmetric services, using with DSL, 419
symmetric systems
    3DES (Triple-DES), 487–488
    Blowfish, 489
    DES (Data Encryption Standard), 483–487
    IDEA (International Data Encryption
        Algorithm), 488
    RC5, 489
SYN flood attacks, overview of, 734–736
SYN (synchronous) packets, role in TCP
    handshakes, 329
synchronous token devices, overview of, 119–120
synchronous transmission, explanation of,
    333–334, 351
system access, role in logical access controls, 153
system administrators, responsibilities of, 90
system and applications development, overview
    of, 657–658
system architecture, overview of, 200–209
system authentication, role in one-way
    hashes, 504
system cold starts, occurrence of, 762
system controls, role in security operations and
    product evaluation, 761–762
system design specifications phase of system
    development, overview of, 688–691
system development. *See also* software
    development
    disposal phase of, 695
    functional design analysis and planning
        phase of, 687–688
    installation/implementation phase of,
        693–694
    life cycle phases of, 683–697, 696–697
    management of, 682–683

operational and maintenance phase of,
    694–695
overview of, 682
phases of, 696
postmortem review phase of, 695–697
project initiation phase of, 684–685
risk analysis phase of, 685–688
risk management phase of, 685
software development phase of, 691–693
system design specifications phase of,
    688–691
system-high security mode, overview of, 220
system mechanisms, trusting, 201, 203
system reboots, occurrence of, 762
system sensing cards, types of, 291
system-specific policies, explanation of, 80
systems
    assurance of, 229–230
    evaluating trust levels of, 203
    evaluation of, 229–230
    functionality of, 229–230
    providing trust on, 208–209
systems evaluation methods, overview of, 222

T

T-carriers, overview of, 402–403
T1 and T3 lines, origins of, 400–401
TACACS (Terminal Access Controller Access
    Control System)
    overview of, 144–146
    versus RADIUS, 145
tactical goals, role in organizational security
    model, 60
tape vaulting, explanation of, 576–577
task-based access, explanation of, 139. *See also*
    access control models; lattice-based access
TCBs (trusted computing bases)
    components of, 221
    explanation of, 202, 205
    versus security perimeters, 204
TCP/IP model versus OSI model, diagram
    of, 314
TCP/IP (Transmission Control Protocol/Internet
    Protocol)
    and data structures, 330–331
    overview of, 325–331

TCP (Transmission Control Protocol)
as connection-oriented protocol, 326
handshaking process in, 329–330
overview of, 326–329
versus UDP, 327, 329–330
TCP Wrappers, explanation of, 773
TCSE ratings versus ITSEC ratings, 230
TCSEC (Trusted Computer System Evaluation
Criteria)
and confidentiality, 226
explanation of, 44, 222–223
team, developing for business continuity
planning, 562, 564
Teardrop attacks, explanation of, 736, 779
technical access controls. See logical access controls
technical departments, training, 95
technical versus logical access controls, advisory
about, 111
Telecommunications and Network Security CBK
domain, description of, 4
telecommunications
evolution of, 399–402
and network security, 312–313
Telnet, port associated with, 328
temperature and humidity, regulating, 275
temperature combustion, suppressing, 282
Tempest, overview of, 167
Ten Commandments of Computer Ethics, list
of, 598
terminations, specifying procedures for, 93
test security measures, definition in
Gramm-Leach-Bliley Act of 1999, 806
testing
and drills, 579–582
role in administrative access controls, 150
role in business continuity planning,
561, 567
TGS (ticket granting service), role in KDC, 131
ThickNet, overview of, 340
thin clients, overview of, 133
ThinNet, overview of, 340
threads versus processes, 196
threat analysis, performing, 69
threats
assessing probability of, 68
deriving losses for, 69
explanation of, 56

identifying during risk analysis, 65–66
relationship to vulnerabilities, 65
three-tier architectures, explanation of, 33–35
tickets in Kerberos, explanation of, 130
TIM (time-based induction machine), role in
IDS, 169
time-loss curve graph, diagram of, 556
time of day, using as access control, 125
timing attacks, overview of, 739
TKIP (Temporal Key Integrity Protocol), role in
wireless technologies, 813–815, 820
TNI (Trusted Network Interpretation), overview
of, 228–229
TOC/TOU (time-of-check versus time-of-use)
attacks, explanation of, 239–240
token devices, overview of, 119–120
token passing, overview of, 352–354
Token Ring
characteristics of, 345
versus Ethernet and FDDI, 344
overview of, 342–343
top-down approach, overview of, 58–59
top secret classification, definition and
examples of, 87
torts, purpose of, 618–619
total risk versus residual risk, 77–78. See also risks
TPEP (Trusted Products Evaluation Program),
explanation of, 224
trade secrets, overview of, 620
trademarks, purpose of, 621
traffic analysis attacks, explanation of, 779
traffic-flow security, role in encryption, 515
traffic sniffing, layers associated with, 40
training
definition in Gramm-Leach-Bliley Act of
1999, 806
guidelines for, 95
role business continuity planning, 581
transaction redundancy, components of, 575
transaction type restrictions, using as access
controls, 125
transient noise, role in electrical power, 269
translation bridges, explanation of, 359
transmission
analog and digital types of, 332–333
asynchronous and synchronous types of,
333–334

broadband and baseband types of, 334
overview of, 332
terminology of, 351
transparent bridging, explanation of, 360
transponder system sensing cards, features of, 291
transport layer
overview of, 319, 323
and SSL (Secure Sockets Layer), 42
transport mode of IPSec, explanation of, 527
transposition ciphers, overview of, 467
tree bus topology, explanation of, 336
Trojan horses, overview of, 730–731
trust
and assurance, 221–222
providing on systems, 208–209
trust levels versus available resources, diagram
of, 207
trusted applets, explanation of, 726
trusted computer systems, Web addresses for
information about, 227
trusted computing bases, overview of, 202–203
trusted paths, explanation of, 175
trusted recovery, role in security operations and
product evaluation, 762
trusted systems, explanation of, 203
tunnel mode of IPSec, explanation of, 527
tunneling protocols, overview of, 421–427
turnstiles, explanation of, 297
twisted-pair cabling, features of, 346–348
two-factor authentication, explanation of, 112
two-tier architectures, overview of, 33–36
Twofish algorithm for AES, development of, 488
Type I and II errors, generating with biometric
systems, 113

U

UDP ports, availability of, 772
UDP (User Datagram Protocol)
as connectionless-oriented protocol, 326
role in Fraggle attacks, 734
versus TCP, 327, 329–330
unclassified classification, definition and
examples of, 88
unicast LAN transmissions, explanation of,
350–351
unit keys, decrypting session keys with, 471

UPSes (uninterrupted power supplies), using, 268
URLs (Uniform Resource Locators),
components of, 391
U.S. Bureau of Industry and Security, Web
address for, 637
U.S. government, taking actions against
information warfare, 26–27
user mode of rings, explanation of, 193, 196
users
responsibilities of, 90–91
threats resulting from, 65
UTP cable ratings, table of, 348
UTP (unshielded twisted pair) cabling, explanation
of, 346–347
UUIDs (universal unique identifiers), use by
DCE, 718

V

validation versus verification, 691
value of assets and information
assigning during risk analysis, 68
costs involved in, 64–65
determining, 63–64
variance-detection tools, purpose of, 163
ventilation, regulating, 276
verification versus validation, 691
verified protection in Orange Book, explanation
of, 226
virtual circuits, role in WAN technologies,
408–409
virtual machines, diagram of, 197
virtual passwords, explanation of, 121
virtual storage, explanation of, 191–192
viruses
layer associated with, 40
overview of, 728–730
threats resulting from, 65
visual recording devices, using, 294
VLANs (virtual LANs), role in switching
networks, 366–369
voice print biometric systems, dynamics of, 116
Voice Telephony Over ATM, Web address
for, 415
VoIP (Voice over IP)
characteristics of, 415
use of, 412–413

volatile RAM, explanation of, 189

voltage fluctuations, types of, 270

voltage regulators, using, 271

VPN tunneling protocols, overview of, 425

VPNs (virtual private networks)

    overview of, 420–421

    tunneling used with, 421

vulnerabilities

    explanation of, 56

    relationship to threats, 65

vulnerability scanning tools, features of, 773–774

W

waiting operating state, explanation of, 196

walk-through tests, role in business continuity planning, 580

walls, evaluating for physical security, 259, 293

WAN technologies

    ATM (Asynchronous Transfer Mode), 410

    characteristics of, 415

    CSU/DSU (Channel Service Unit/Data Service Unit), 404–405

    frame relay, 407–408

    HDLC (High-level Data Link Control) frames, 411

    HSSI (High-Speed Serial Interface), 411–412

    SDLC (Synchronous Data Link Control), 411–412

    SMDS (Switched Multimegabit Data Service), 411

    switching, 405–407

    virtual circuits, 408–409

    X.25, 409

WANs (wide area networks)

    versus LANs, 40–41, 337–338

    overview of, 398–399

    Web address for, 398

WAP (Wireless Application Protocol)

    overview of, 439–440

    Web addresses for, 441

war driving, overview of, 442–443

wardialing attacks

    brute force attacks used for, 174

    explanation of, 778–779

identifying remote access modems with, 416–417

warm sites, placing backups in, 569–570

water and gas lines, evaluating for physical security, 261

water sprinklers, types of, 283–284

waterfall software development, explanation of, 697

wave-pattern detection systems, features of, 295

WBS (work breakdown structure), role in system development, 690

Web-based activities, vulnerabilities of, 38

"web of trust," role in PGP, 519

Web server configuration, layer associated with, 42

Web servers. *See also* servers

    hacking, 22

    layers associated with, 42

    movement to DMZs, 32–33

Web sites

    "802.11 Alphabet Soup", 439

    802.11 and Spread Spectrum, 434

    Access Control Models, 220

    Access Control Policies and Mechanisms, 209

    AES (Advanced Encryption Standard), 491, 509

    ANSI (American National Standards Institute), 804

    AntiOnline Computer Security, 612

    ARP (Address Resolution Protocol), 357

    ATM (Asynchronous Transfer Mode), 410, 415

    Authentication, Authorization, and Accounting Charter, 164

    authentication categories on Google, 164

    Back Orifice tool, 778

    BIA (business impact analysis), 558, 566

    biometric systems, 116

    bridges and switches, 361

    business continuity planning, 566, 567

    Cable Modem Info, 420

    CERT Coordination Center, 630

    CISSP and SSCP Open Study Guides, 11, 58, 95

    CISSP.com, 95

    CISSP.com Web Portal, 11

    Classical Cryptography, 468

Code of Ethics, 597
Collision Domains white paper, 355
Commercial Product Evaluations, 803
Common Criteria, 234
computer security, 607
Computer Security and Ethics, 630
Computer Security Models, 220
Computer Underground Digest, 612
Counterpane Internet Security Inc., 509
Criteria and Methods of Evaluations of
    Information Systems, 230
cryptography, 461, 472, 480, 491, 500, 509,
    514, 516
CSI, 11
CSI Intrusion Detection System Resource, 170
data classifications, 89
Data Protection Measures, 221
Database Security, 220
Defense Security Service, 221
Designing Switched LAN Internetworks, 367
Disaster Prevention and Recovery
    Program, 567
disaster recovery planning, 566, 583
Discretionary Protection, 209
DSL (Digital Subscriber Line), 419
EES (Escrowed Encryption Standard), 474
eMailman, 767
Encryption and Security Tutorial, 519
Enterasys White Papers, 367
Ethernet and Fast Ethernet, 342
Export Administration Regulations FAQ, 637
Faximim Fax FAQ, 770
FDDI (Fiber Distributed Data Interface), 344
frame relay, 409, 415
GASSP (Generally Accepted System Security
    Principles, 600
Gramm-Leach-Bliley Act of 1999, 807
Guide to Understanding DAC in Trusted
    Systems, 136
Guide to Wireless LAN Technologies, 434
hacking and hackers, 175
hacking groups, 612
HIPAA (Health Insurance Portability and
    Accountability Act), 862
honeypot systems, 171
HSSI (High-Speed Serial Interface), 411
HUNT project, 776

IAB (Internet Architecture Board), 600
ICMP (Internet Control Message
    Protocol), 358
IEC Online Tutorials, 398
IEEE LAN/MAN Standards Committee, 339
IEEE Standards Working Groups, 335, 804
IEEE Wireless Standards Zone, 439
IETF IP Telephony Charter, 415
IETF LDAP Revision Charter, 394
IETF Network Access Server Requirements, 429
IETF Policy Framework Charter, 394
IMAP (Internet Message Access Protocol), 767
incident handling, 630
Information Security Policy World, 85
Information Warfare Site, 209
Internet Mail Consortium, 767
Internet/Network Security, 298
Internet Security Recommendations, 645
Interpol and Information Technology
    Crime, 645
Interstar Fax Server, 770
intranets, 396
Intrusion Detection FAQ, 170
IP multicast, 351
IPSec (Internet Protocol Security), 531
$(ISC)^2$ (International Information Systems
    Security Certification Consortium), 11, 600
ISO (International Organization for
    Standardization), 804
IT Security and Crime Prevention
    Methods, 645
ITSEC (Information Technology Security
    Evaluation Criteria), 230
Juggernaut tool, 776
Key Escrow Encryption Available, 474
Lantronix white papers, 335
Law, Investigation, and Ethics, 607
Linux FreeS/WAN Project, 404
locks, safes, and security, 299
MAC (mandatory access control) model, 136
MD5 Message-Digest Algorithm, 509
Media Access Methods, 353
Methods of Transposition, 468
Models of OS Protection, 220
NAT (network address translation), 397
NCSA Security Policies and Procedures, 85

Network Intrusion Detection Systems FAQ, 170
Network Operating Systems, 390
Network Safety, 397
NIST Computer Security Resource Center, 58
NIST (National Institute of Standards and Technology), 802
NSA (National Security Agency), 801
One-Way Hash FAQ, 510
Packet Switching Simulation, 407
PAP (Password Authentication Protocol), 427
Personal Computer Security, 221
PGP (Pretty Good Privacy), 520–521
Physical Model of Operations, 221
PKI (public key infrastructure), 500
PPP (Point-to-Point), 427
Product Ciphers FAQ, 514
RAD University Networking Tutorials, 409
RAID Basics, 431
Rainbow Series, 228
RAM (random access memory), 189
Rationale Behind the Evaluation Classes, 206
The Reference Monitor Concept, 206
Remote Access, 428–429
Risk Associates, 78
Routing Basics, 365
S/MIME and OpenPGP, 524
S/MIME Mail Security, 767
SANS Institute, 58
SANS Institute Security Policy Project, 85
SANS Security Policy Project, 797
Secure Electronic Commerce System, 519
Security in Open Systems, 164
Security Issues in SQL, 675
Security Issues in WWW, 524
Security Links, 524
Security Policies and Baseline Standards, 85
Security Strategies for E-Companies, 461
Security Technology Issues, 474
SESAME (Secure European System for Applications in a Multi-vendor Environment), 133
"Smart Cards: A Primer", 123
social engineering, 607
software life cycles, 698
Spread Spetrum Primer, 434

SSH (Secure Shell), 527
steganography, 469
Strategic Security and Intelligence resources, 78
SubSeven tool, 778
Symmetric Key Cryptography, 476
T1 lines, 403
token-based authentication, 121
Token Ring, 343
trusted computer systems, 227
Unix/Linux Internals Course and Links, 189
U.S. Bureau of Industry and Security, 637
Voice Telephony Over ATM, 415
VoIP Quick Start Guide, 415
WANs (wide area networks), 398
WAP (Wireless Application Protocol), 441
WarDriving.com, 443
Web66 Network Construction Kit, 339
"Wireless Goal: Don't Get Whacked", 441
Web top-level DNS domain, meaning of, 393
Web versus Internet, 30–31
Web66 Network Construction Kit, Web address for, 339
well-known ports
    explanation of, 328
    role in dynamic packet filtering, 380
WEP (Wired Equivalent Privacy)
    deficiencies of, 818–820
    dynamics of, 814
Western Union, hacker attack on, 23
wet pipe water sprinklers, overview of, 283
white noise, explanation of, 168
windows, evaluating for physical security, 260
WinNuk attacks, explanation of, 779
wireless LAN technologies
    overview of, 813–822
    Web site for, 434
wireless proximity readers, features of, 290–291
wireless standards, overview of, 436–439
wireless technologies and communications, overview of, 432–443
wiretapping, overview of, 607
wiring for Ethernet, overview of, 340
WLAN components, overview of, 441–443
work area separation, role in physical access controls, 151–152

workstations, relationship to mainframes and servers, 18–19
worms, overview of, 730
WPANs (wireless personal area networks), standard related to, 438
WTLS (Wireless Transport Layer Security), functionality of, 440

X

X.25 WAN protocol, overview of, 409, 415
XML (EXtensible Markup Language), explanation of, 670

XOR operations
    role in one-time pads, 510
    role in stream ciphers, 482

Z

zones
    role in DNS servers, 391
    using as alternative to Tempest, 168

INTERNATIONAL CONTACT INFORMATION

AUSTRALIA
McGraw-Hill Book Company Australia Pty. Ltd.
TEL +61-2-9900-1800
FAX +61-2-9878-8881
http://www.mcgraw-hill.com.au
books-it_sydney@mcgraw-hill.com

CANADA
McGraw-Hill Ryerson Ltd.
TEL +905-430-5000
FAX +905-430-5020
http://www.mcgraw-hill.ca

GREECE, MIDDLE EAST, & AFRICA
(Excluding South Africa)
McGraw-Hill Hellas
TEL +30-210-6560-990
TEL +30-210-6560-993
TEL +30-210-6560-994
FAX +30-210-6545-525

MEXICO (Also serving Latin America)
McGraw-Hill Interamericana Editores S.A. de C.V.
TEL +525-117-1583
FAX +525-117-1589
http://www.mcgraw-hill.com.mx
fernando_castellanos@mcgraw-hill.com

SINGAPORE (Serving Asia)
McGraw-Hill Book Company
TEL +65-6863-1580
FAX +65-6862-3354
http://www.mcgraw-hill.com.sg
mghasia@mcgraw-hill.com

SOUTH AFRICA
McGraw-Hill South Africa
TEL +27-11-622-7512
FAX +27-11-622-9045
robyn_swanepoel@mcgraw-hill.com

SPAIN
McGraw-Hill/Interamericana de España, S.A.U.
TEL +34-91-180-3000
FAX +34-91-372-8513
http://www.mcgraw-hill.es
professional@mcgraw-hill.es

UNITED KINGDOM, NORTHERN,
EASTERN, & CENTRAL EUROPE
McGraw-Hill Education Europe
TEL +44-1-628-502500
FAX +44-1-628-770224
http://www.mcgraw-hill.co.uk
computing_europe@mcgraw-hill.com

ALL OTHER INQUIRIES Contact:
McGraw-Hill/Osborne
TEL +1-510-420-7700
FAX +1-510-420-7703
http://www.osborne.com
omg_international@mcgraw-hill.com